(handwritten) Political Culture
- Ideology
- Values
- Symbols

Politics
Seventh Edition
in Canada

(handwritten, left) Structure
- Economic
- external/
- territorial/
- Demographi'

(handwritten, right) Agency
- Historical events
- Actors

Robert J. Jackson   Doreen Jackson

Politics
Seventh Edition
in Canada

Culture, Institutions, Behaviour and Public Policy

PEARSON
Prentice
Hall

Toronto

Library and Archives Canada Cataloguing in Publication

Jackson, Robert J., 1936–
        Politics in Canada : culture, institutions, behaviour and public
policy / Robert J. Jackson, Doreen Jackson. — 7th ed.

Includes index.
ISBN 978-0-13-206938-0

        1. Canada—Politics and government. I. Jackson, Doreen, 1939–
II. Title.

JL65.J32 2009   320.971   C2008-900874-X

ISBN-13: 978-0-13-206938-0
ISBN-10: 0-13-206938-5

Vice President, Editorial Director: Gary Bennett
Sponsoring Editor: Carolin Sweig
Senior Acquisitions Editor: Laura Paterson Forbes
Marketing Manager: Judith Allen
Developmental Editors: Emily Jardeleza, Suzanne Schaan
Production Editors: Joe Zingrone, Kevin Leung
Copy Editor: Joe Zingrone
Proofreaders: Colleen Ste. Marie, Tara Tovell
Production Manager: Peggy Brown
Composition: Debbie Kumpf
Permissions and Photo Research: Natalie Barrington
Art Director: Julia Hall
Cover Design: Anthony Leung
Cover Image: Veer Inc.

Statistics Canada information is used with the permission of Statistics Canada. Users are forbidden to copy the data and redisseminate them, in an original or modified form, for commercial purposes, without permission from Statistics Canada. Information on the availability of the wide range of data from Statistics Canada can be obtained from Statistics Canada's Regional Offices, its World Wide Web site at www.statcan.ca, and its toll-free access number, 1-800-263-1136.

Photo Credits
Page 1, © The Canadian Tourism Commission (CTC) by Jim Cochrane; page 61, © CTC by Mike Pinder; page 69, © Wayne Cuddington, the *Ottawa Citizen*; page 143, © CTC by Bob Anderson; page 162, © Robert Cooper/Library and Archives Canada/PA141503; page 179, © Philippe Landreville, photographer/Supreme Court of Canada Collection; page 240, © Reuters/Shaun Best; page 250, courtesy Saskatchewan Archives Board; page 279, © *Winnipeg Free Press*; page 379, © Corel; page 489, © CP PHOTO/Ryan Remiorz; page 499, © CTC by Pierre St. Jacques; page 532, © Sgt. Frank Hudec, Canadian Forces Combat Camera.

1 2 3 4 5   12 11 10 09 08

Printed and bound in the United States of America.

Brief Contents

Contents

Part II   Culture   61

Part III   Institutions   143

Chapter 5   The Constitution   144

Chapter 10 **Public Administration and Democracy   354**

Part IV   Political Behaviour   379

Chapter 11   Political Parties   380

List of Close-Up Boxes

Preface

This seventh edition of *Politics in Canada* continues to stress the importance of politics in the study of Canadian government with up-to-date examples, issues and research. It provides a general treatment of Canadian federal politics, useful for both introductory and advanced courses. The book purposely avoids the rigidity imposed by the adoption of a single approach or framework for the study of politics, but goes well beyond mere description of governmental institutions and processes. It attempts to provide a coherent and critical understanding of Canadian politics, eschewing the simplicities of myths and the trite application of simplistic and naive approaches.

Students need to acquire skills and then hone them to become critical thinkers and concerned citizens. *Politics in Canada* explains and uses the most sophisticated theories, but also makes sense of the seemingly incoherent events in the day-to-day world. As in earlier editions, the text is clearly and concisely written with little academic jargon.

We aim to offer a novel perspective on politics. The text provides an objective and detached perspective on the relationships among culture, institutions, behaviour and public policy, and a well-rounded view of the entire political process. It discusses the historical development and background of Canadian politics, but concentrates on the contemporary, offering the latest information and perspectives on such vital topics as the persistence of minority governments, the Canadian Constitution; the Stephen Harper cabinet and Parliament; federalism, regionalism, nationalism and the threat of Québec separatism; interest groups; conflict of interest and ethics in politics; electoral change and party developments. We examine issues concerning Native peoples in Canadian society; the growing role of women in public affairs; the negative image of politics and politicians in society; how Parliament and the public service can be reformed; the legacy of high government debts and the economic implications of a strong Canadian currency. We relate these and other issues to NAFTA, placing Canadian government in a global framework. We also examine the interrelationship of domestic, foreign and security policies since the terrorist attacks of September 11, 2001 (9/11), and the ensuing war in Afghanistan. We conclude the book with an examination of international terrorism and Canada's evolution within a North American security framework.

While *Politics in Canada* retains much of its original structure, each section has been thoroughly revised and rewritten to make it as clear, concise and up-to-date as possible. We have incorporated the newest social science research, including books, journal articles, government publications and official government inquiries that highlight various aspects of Canadian history, society, and politics.

Beginning with Chapter 2, each chapter focuses on a Critical Debate theme. This encourages the student to read and study the material presented critically with the specific purpose of forming a coherent, thoughtful and informed argument about a significant, current issue that encompasses the topic presented. At the end of each chapter, two competing arguments, with opposing points of view, are provided in answer to the Critical Debate question. These are sample arguments that students are invited to consider, debate, criticize, expand on, and make their own.

New to the Seventh Edition

Content: We have made revisions throughout the text to reflect changing political issues, events and research. Major new sections have been added on minority governments; recent developments in political parties and the party system; interest groups; the 2006 general election; ethics in Parliament; regionalism; Aboriginal and Québec nationalism; Canadian foreign and security policy since 9/11; and the war in Afghanistan. All new aspects of federalism, including health policy, are analyzed. We use 2006 Census data and material from the 2007 Human Development Index to update all topics.

Close-Up Boxes: New text boxes have been added to highlight topics of current interest and further integrate the four themes of culture, institutions, behaviour and public policy.

Organization

The orientation of this volume is comprehensive, drawing upon a wide variety of concepts, and theories and criticisms of Canadian politics. Each chapter is organized around one or two central concepts, which are discussed in general terms before being applied to the Canadian context and used in a Critical Debate.

There are five parts. The first is introductory; the remainder correspond to the four elements incorporated in the title: culture, institutions, behaviour and public policy.

Part I, the **Introduction**, consists of two chapters. Chapter 1 establishes Canada's place in the world and introduces students to two paramount, current issues: governing with a minority government, and Canadian unity, both of which are dealt with throughout the book. In this chapter, we introduce theories and approaches that are used in the study of politics, analyze some key concepts—*power, state, nation, citizenship, nationalism, regionalism* and *democracy*—and offer a rationale for the organization of the book. We also outline career options for political science graduates. In Chapter 2, we provide historical, economic and contextual background through an examination of the origins and development of the Canadian people and state. The chapter traces the growth and changing nature of the population from the Aboriginals who first inhabited the land to the multi-ethnic, multicultural society of today. Similarly, we trace the development of the Canadian state, both in terms of the physical boundaries of the country and the expansion of the role of government in Canadian society. Here, the text draws attention to the new issues of developments in the North and Artic sovereignty. The Critical Debate asks to what extent constraints or opportunities posed by history, geography, economy and demography have made Canada what it is today.

The two chapters in Part II, **Culture**, provide an intimate portrait of Canadian society. In Chapter 3, we examine Canada's political fabric including the political, ethnic and regional cleavages that define politics in this country. We focus on the different background and aspirations of French Canadians, English-speaking Canadians and Native peoples, stressing the importance to the Canadian political community of overarching, commonly shared values that help preserve the unity of the country. This chapter examines current issues such as immigration, multiculturalism, regionalism and Aboriginal concerns in order to understand Canada's political culture and how it relates to politics in practice. The Critical Debate asks whether there is a distinctive Canadian political culture, and of what it consists. Chapter 4 asks how Canadians acquire the political ideas that underlie their political behaviour. Families and peer groups play a role, as do institutions such as schools, universities, the media and even government. Two very significant cleavages that cut horizontally across Canadian society—gender and class—are also highlighted. The impact of these factors on the political orientation of Canadians and to Canadian unity is described and assessed.

The Critical Debate concerns national identity and the extent to which the government should be involved in promoting it.

Part III, **Institutions**, argues that political institutions reflect both the structure and values of society. It contains six chapters dealing in turn with the constitution, federalism, nationalism and regionalism, the executive, Parliament and bureaucracy. This section has been considerably revised and refocused, with new material on minority governments, civil liberties, political ethics, Aboriginals, regionalism and an enhanced discussion of the key concepts and mechanisms of federalism.

Chapter 5 examines the country's constitutional development and controversies concerning constitutional change. It also discusses the court system and assesses the growing role of the courts in the political process. It highlights the controversial issue of civil liberties in an age of "global terrorism." The Critical Debate concerns constitutional amendments and whether they are necessary and possible. In Chapter 6, we examine past and present developments in Canadian politics and invite informed discussion about whether Canada's federal system is balanced and fair. New fiscal arrangements between the federal government and the provinces and territories are assessed. Chapter 7 looks at various concepts of nationalism and regionalism, and then focuses on nationalism in Québec, Aboriginal nationalism and Western Canadian regionalism. In Chapter 8, we consider the Conservative minority government that took office in 2006, including the executive—the inner circle comprising the prime minister, Stephen Harper, his ministry, cabinet and the central coordinating agencies—that forms the nexus of political power in Canada. In this chapter, the Critical Debate invites your assessment of prime ministerial power. Chapter 9 focuses on Parliament and includes revised discussions of the committee system and Senate reform. The Critical Debate asks what aspects of parliamentary reform are necessary or desirable. Chapter 10 details recent changes in government organization, the public service, and the 2007 federal budget. The Critical Debate concerns controversial viewpoints on bureaucratic power. Does the Canadian bureaucracy have too much power? Are major reforms necessary and possible?

Part IV, **Behaviour**, demonstrates how both culture and institutions structure individual and collective action in the political process. Chapters 11, 12 and 13 discuss, respectively, political parties, elections and electoral behaviour, and interest groups. The party system has undergone another realignment with the development of a stronger Conservative Party, which has reunited the fragmented centre-right and right-wing electorate and restored the Conservatives' power as a major party in Parliament. Chapter 11's Critical Debate concerns how well Canadian parties perform their functions. Is their legacy one of unfulfilled promise? Chapter 12 includes a study of the 2006 general election and an up-to-date discussion of electoral reform. The Critical Debate concerns whether Canada should opt for more electoral change or keep the status quo. Chapter 13 deals with the new rules governing interest groups and lobbying. It also considers the growth of movements that share many of the same functions of interest groups, and examines the women's movement in particular. It provides new perspectives on the subject of advocacy. The Critical Debate asks whether lobbying is a necessary evil.

Lastly, in Part V, **Public Policy**, culture, institutions and behaviour are linked together as determinants and components of Canadian public policy and the policy-making process. Chapter 14 deals with domestic public policy and includes approaches to the study of public policy and its instruments, as well as a discussion of current economic problems and policy constraints. The Critical Debate asks whether public policy is rational, comprehensive and justifiable. Chapter 15, on Canada in the world, examines Canada's response to the terrorist events of 9/11. It deals with many new developments in international economics; Canadian foreign, defence and security policy (including Canada–US relations, free trade, NAFTA, national security policies); and peacekeeping. The Critical Debate asks whether Canada has an independent and meaningful foreign policy.

Appendix 1 presents excerpts from Canada's Constitution. In Appendix 2, you will find the Supreme Court of Canada's 1998 ruling on the three questions relating to the unilateral secession of Québec from Canada.

Politics is an honourable and worthy profession. In this book, we give credit where it is due for substantial achievement, but also find many political reforms desirable. Our overall tone is optimistic but concerned about the fundamental ability of the Canadian political process to meet its major challenges—its ability to transcend regional and cultural cleavages and assure the survival of Canada in an age of "assymetrical war" while the country addresses internal issues as well as the war in Afghanistan and the fallout from the US-led battles in Iraq.

Supplements

For Students

Companion Website (www.pearsoned.ca/jackson): Students who visit this online Study Guide will find practice quizzes to check their knowledge of each chapter as well as links to help them with further research on specific topics. The Companion Website also provides access to *Pearson's Research Navigator*[TM] with *ContentSelect*, a database of journal articles and advice on writing papers and citing sources.

This Companion Website includes Grade Tracker functionality. With Grade Tracker, the results from the self-test quizzes are preserved in a grade book. Each time students return to the CW, they can refer to these results, track their progress and measure their improvement. The access code bound into this book is required to sign in at the Grade Tracker website. The access card is also available for purchase alone (ISBN 978-0-13-812842-5).

By distributing a CourseID that allows students to enrol in their class, instructors can take advantage of the Class Manager function to assign marks for participation or for quiz scores. Ask your Pearson sales representative for an Instructor Access Code Card (ISBN 978-0-13-812844-9).

For Instructors

MyTest (www.pearsonmytest.com): Pearson Education Canada's MyTest is a powerful assessment generation program that helps instructors easily create and print quizzes, tests and exams, as well as homework or practice handouts. Questions and tests can all be authored online, allowing instructors maximum flexibility and the ability to efficiently manage assessments at any time and from anywhere. The testbank for *Politics in Canada* includes approximately one thousand questions, including multiple-choice, short answer and essay questions.

Instructor's Resource CD-ROM (ISBN 978-0-13-812752-7): This resource CD includes the following instructor supplements:

- ***Instructor's Manual:*** This manual contains lecture notes, suggested activities and a guide to resource material.

- ***PowerPoint Presentations:*** Key figures and tables from the text are provided in PowerPoint format for classroom use.

- ***Test Item File:*** All the test questions from the Pearson MyTest (see above) are provided in Microsoft Word format.

Most of these instructor supplements are also available for download from a password protected section of Pearson Education Canada's online catalogue (vig.pearsoned.ca). Navigate to your book's catalogue page to view a list of those supplements that are available. See your Pearson sales representative for details and access.

Acknowledgments

The authors are extremely appreciative of the many students, professors and interested readers who have taken the time to comment on aspects of *Politics in Canada* and given support and encouragement. Many friends, scholars and students have contributed, directly and indirectly, to the discussion of ideas and issues the book contains. The very long list must include Michael Atkinson, Nicolas Baxter-Moore, Scott Bennett, Alan Cairns, Barbara Caroll, Terry Caroll, Brian Crowley, Abbie Dann, Piotr Dutkiewicz, John Fakouri, Jean-Pierre Gaboury, Brian Galligan, Janice Gross-Stein, Jack Grove, Ken Hart, Carl Hodge, Kal Holsti, Bill Hull, Tom Joseph, Robert Keaton, Ken Kernaghan, Peyton Lyon, Maureen Mancuso, Roman March, Bill Matheson, Ken McRae, Greg Mahler, Henry Mayo, Allan McDougall, John Meisel, Kim Nossal, Randy Olling, Jeremy Paltiel, Anton Pelinka, David Siegel, Richard Simeon, Michael Stein, Sharon Sutherland, Stewart Sutley, Elliott Tepper, Hugh Thorburn, Martin Westmacott, Patrick Weller and Glen Williams.

Over many years, reviewers of the various editions have diligently ferreted out errors of omission and commission in the preliminary manuscripts. We gratefully acknowledge the insight and detailed knowledge that Keith Brownsey, Donald Blake, Fred Englemann, Nibaldo H. Galleguillos, Rob Huebert, Christian Leuprecht, Peter McCormick, Susan McCorquodale, Mary Beth Montcalm, David E. Smith, Miriam Smith, Elizabeth Smythe, David Stewart, Tracy Summerville, Paul Whyte, Robert Williams, and Nelson Wiseman have brought to our manuscript.

This seventh edition has been enhanced by the wisdom and perceptive comments of Dave Baugh, James Lawson, James Lightbody, Chaldeans Mensah, Grace Skogstad, Tracy Summerville, Michael Temelini and Stephen Tomblin. We thank them for their thoughtful suggestions, corrections and encouragement. We are also grateful to our friends and colleagues at Pearson Canada for bringing the seventh edition of *Politics in Canada* to fruition. They include developmental editor Emily Jardeleza, acquisitions editor Carolin Sweig, marketing coordinator Bethany Jolliffe, production manager Peggy Brown, production editor Kevin Leung and Joe Zingrone, who once more edited a manuscript for us with diligence and humour. At the University of Redlands, Starla Strain provided organization and support in many ways, enabling us to devote time and energy to the project.

We also wish to express our gratitude to two very special people—Velma, a wonderful mother and friend whose enthusiasm for politics is a delight, and Nicole, our extraordinary daughter whose love of government and politics has taken her to a new world of challenges.

Robert J. Jackson and Doreen Jackson
University of Redlands, California,
and Carleton University, Ottawa,
February 2008

A Great Way to Learn and Instruct Online

The Pearson Education Canada Companion Website is easy to navigate and is organized to correspond to the chapters in this textbook. Whether you are a student in the classroom or a distance learner you will discover helpful resources for in-depth study and research that empower you in your quest for greater knowledge and maximize your potential for success in the course.

Companion
Website

[www.pearsoned.ca/jackson]

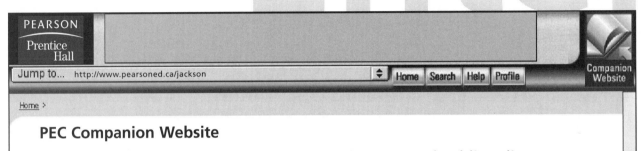

PEARSON
Prentice
Hall

Jump to...   http://www.pearsoned.ca/jackson   Home   Search   Help   Profile

Companion
Website

Home >

PEC Companion Website

Politics in Canada: Culture, Institutions, Behaviour and Public Policy, Seventh Edition, by Jackson and Jackson

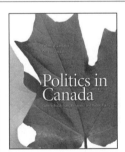

Student Resources

The modules in this section provide students with tools for learning course material. These modules include:

- Multiple-Choice Quizzes
- Short-Answer Questions
- Essay Questions
- Web Destinations

In the quiz modules, students can send answers to the grader and receive instant feedback on their progress through the Results Reporter. Coaching comments and references to the textbook may be available to ensure that students take advantage of all available resources to enhance their learning experience.

Politics
in Canada

Seventh Edition

Part I
Introduction

C anadian politics is an exciting and complex field of study. Political issues, leaders and governments in Canada seem to be in a state of constant effervescence and controversy. Yet, beneath the divisions and apparent turmoil is a framework of laws, procedures, customs and culture that keeps the changes within reasonable limits.

The study of politics requires three major tools. First is an understanding of the approaches available to facilitate the study and an appreciation of their strengths and weaknesses. Second is an understanding of the complexities of basic concepts such as democracy, power, nation, state and even politics itself. Third is a fundamental knowledge of the unique features of Canada—its land, its economy, its people, its historical background, and its form of government and policy-making.

The focus of our study is on how democratic political institutions resolve conflict and work for the betterment of society. For that reason, Chapter 1 of Part I introduces three of the most consuming topics of our time: the federal Conservative minority government elected in 2006, which affects almost every facet of politics; regional fragmentation, in particular Québec nationalism; and the trade-offs caused by the search for both security and freedom in an era of global terrorism. These three core issues form much of Canadian politics today and are discussed in their various aspects throughout this book. The first issue, the federal minority, suggests weakness at the centre of government; the second, regional fragmentation, weakness at the regional level; and the third, global terrorism, weakness at the international level. Chapter 2 analyzes and explains the devel-opment of the Canadian state and how it evolved into the contemporary world.

Chapter 1

Governing Canada

Issues and Challenges

Politics in Canada has vital consequences for the well-being of every person in the country, rich or poor, young or old, male or female, French- or English-speaking. While politics can be untidy, messy and often a subject of derision and scorn, its mere existence constitutes proof of the rule of law, democracy and open governance. It is a vital and difficult subject for students, indeed all citizens, to appreciate and evaluate.

The themes covered in the arenas of politics and governance require the student to have a knowledge of the past as well as a good grasp of today's facts and complex values. Serious study of politics is not for amateurs. Careful attention to language and the nuances of definitions and explanations is necessary for all dialogues or narratives about the subject. It is imperative that you be aware of the most recent information about our political leaders, their election travails and their governments' records. Let's begin, therefore, with the most recent federal government of Stephen Harper.

The January 2006 federal election gave Canadians their second minority government in a row. The Conservative Party took power with only 124 of 308 seats, forming the first non-Liberal government since 1993. When the new session of Parliament opened, Prime Minister Stephen Harper needed to enlist at least 30 opposition votes in the House of Commons to uphold his government. The New Democrats, with 29 MPs, were a single vote short of holding the balance of power. The separatist Bloc Québécois was reduced by 3 seats to 51 and the Liberals formed the Official Opposition with 103 MPs.

Many observers wondered whether such a weak federal government would be able to meet the dual challenge of separatism from Québec and severe regional pressures from Eastern and Western Canada. Would the Conservatives be able to offer continual stable government and coherent public policies in fields such as parliamentary ethics and health care, in addition to a continual reduction in the government debt? Could the new government reconcile the need for both security and civil liberties in an era of "global terrorism"?

In the Québec referendum of October 1995, almost half of the population of Canada's second-largest province indicated they were ready to create a new country. In 2008, even though Jean Charest, a federalist Liberal, is premier of Québec and the federalist Conservatives are in power in Ottawa, the division over the future integrity of Canada remains a fundamental issue facing the country. This ongoing Québec issue is regularly supplemented by regional discord in both the East and West. Atlantic Canadians object to their share of federal revenues, and some westerners have felt so marginalized that they have called for separation from Canada. In January 2006, in part mobilized by the Alberta provincial Conservative government's opposition to federal social policies—particularly heath and hospital care—westerners elected the vast majority of the Conservative candidates who formed the new federal government. People in the West were demanding adjustments in what they considered to be the preponderance of power in Central Canada. Even the newly elected Conservatives faced early regional pressures; some Tory MPs resigned over issues related to equalization payments.

With federalism increasingly under attack and unstable minority governments persisting in Ottawa, it is not easy to anticipate what lies ahead for Canada. Rapid social and economic developments are changing the political culture, behaviour and public policies of the country. International issues of globalization and terrorism are compounding domestic problems. To comprehend and participate in the direction of this change, Canadians must confront some very basic questions: Who are Canadians? Who do they want to be?

Canadians constantly must reassess who they are as a people, what values they wish to uphold and what languages they want to speak. They must decide how they can best organize themselves and what institutions are worthy of their loyalty. These questions can be answered realistically only by maintaining an objective and comparative perspective concerning how Canada works. How does it compare to the rest of the world? How does it compete in the new global order?

The earliest political science texts on Canada focused on the country's march to independence and autonomy. Later volumes concentrated on understanding Canada in the context of new academic developments in political science—concepts, frameworks and theories that came mostly from the United States. Today, the fundamental concern is to understand how Canadians will confront new challenges. The questions are not so much concerned with whether the twenty-first century will belong to Canada but with whether there will indeed continue to *be* a powerful, united Canada in this century.

CLOSE-UP ON
Careers

WHAT CAREER OPTIONS DOES POLITICAL SCIENCE PROVIDE?

Political science comes equipped with its own tool kit of specialized vocabulary, methods, and subject matter. It provides a broad understanding of political systems and political behaviour that makes students a more informed and discriminating members of society. In doing so, political science offers a great many career options. A few students will become so fascinated with, and involved in, political science research that they will choose to stay in the field, teaching at a university or college where they can continue to explore various issues and theoretical concepts. Many other students will find that their courses in political science provide an extremely useful background for careers such as secondary school teaching, journalism, law, business, government, political activism, NGO (non-governmental organization) administration, diplomacy and social work.

The various levels of government in Canada employ millions of Canadians. Government, in fact, is the country's largest employer. Employment possibilities span the various branches of the civil service that deal with a wide range of social concerns. Politicians also employ aides, consultants, and so on. Many other professions also require people who understand how governments work. Political journalists, for example, need political knowledge, exploratory skills, and methods of analysis. Businesses, NGOs, interest groups and social workers need to deal with governments on a regular basis.

So, even for those who do not wish to specialize in political science, undergraduate training in this field provides a useful background for many careers—sometimes directly following a bachelor's degree, and sometimes as a stepping stone to law school, journalism school or some other specialty. But most important, political science or its equivalent is a necessary ingredient of good citizenship. It prepares students to think critically and be active, informed participants in political life. Good citizenship is a responsibility that requires going well beyond simply casting a ballot at election time.

Source: Adapted from Robert J. Jackson and Doreen Jackson, *Introduction to Political Science: Comparative and World Politics*, 5th ed. (Don Mills, ON: Pearson Prentice Hall, 2007).

There have been many turning points in Canadian history, but possibly none were more important than those that occurred in 1867, 1931, 1982, 1992, 1995, 2004, and 2006. In 1867, the new state of Canada was born. In 1931, Canada received independence from Britain. It took another half century, until 1982, before Canadians had the courage and confidence to patriate the Constitution and break the last link with the mother country. Finally, in 1992 a massive constitutional reform proposal, the Charlottetown Accord, which had been fashioned and sold to Canadians by the leaders of Parliament and all ten provinces and territories, was defeated when the people stood defiantly against it in a referendum. In the 1995 referendum on sovereignty, Québeckers came within half a percentage point of dividing the country in two. In 2004 (Liberal) and 2006 (Conservative), weak and somewhat dispirited federal governments were elected to solve the divisions and dilemmas in the country.

These seven historical events, and others like them, such as the 1998 Supreme Court decision on separatism, have had profound effects on the evolution of Canada's culture, institutions and public policy. The 1992 referendum on the Charlottetown Accord marked the end of the politics of the twentieth century. It indicated a shift to a new politics—one that is more open, less elitist and, perhaps, more threatening to the status quo and the institutions of Canada. The 1995 Québec referendum ended the dream that Canada could easily confront the twenty-first century as a harmonious country ready to compete at the global level. And the 2004 and 2006 elections did not make governing easier. They emphasized the geographically and politically fragmented nature of Canada, and produced relatively unstable minority governments.

Today, cleavages of the past continue to divide French and English, Aboriginal and settler, westerner and easterner, man and woman. But these cleavages have been given new direction and emotion in parties and movements and in novel approaches to old problems. What will their legacy be to Canadians in the coming years? In this and subsequent chapters, we shall marshal evidence about what is old and what is new in Canadian politics. We shall, for example, assess arguments about individual versus collective rights and examine movements and parties to determine if Canada is on a new trajectory or if it is simply "old wine in new bottles."

New developments need to be examined in light of the experience of the past as well as the dimmer light of the future. Today, as the last vestiges of a colonial past are disappearing, Canada ranks proudly among the world's states. A brief profile of the country—its political base, people and socio-economic status—reads impressively when examined in a comparative perspective.

Since Confederation, Canada has enjoyed a stable, liberal-democratic government; it is one of the very few countries in the world that has never experienced a civil war or a military coup. This stability has been achieved despite many factors that complicate political decision-making. Its physical size alone is a great barrier to progress. Canada has several thousand square kilometres more area to administer than all of Europe combined. A Canadian driving from St. John's, Newfoundland, to Victoria, British Columbia, covers the same distance as a Spaniard driving from Madrid and traversing at least ten countries to get to Mongolia.

This enormous land mass houses over 32 million people, yet Canada has a population problem. Four-fifths of the territory has never been settled permanently. This results in great regional imbalances in population, from congested urban centres to uninhabited wastelands. Certain areas are being depopulated, while there is an undesirably fast rate of growth in others. Large tracts of precious farmland are being devoured by greedy cities. Today, in this country that was settled originally by farmers, most of the population lives in urban areas that occupy 1 percent of the land. Only one-eighth of the territory is suitable for agriculture; settlement has therefore been confined to a long, thin line along the southern border, linked by the world's longest national highway.

To these problematic demographic and geographic factors must be added the unique ethnic composition of the population. Besides the original Native groups and the two founding French and English populations, over one hundred other ethnic groups make their homes in Canada. The French Canadian people are centred in Québec but are in no sense limited to that province. Large pockets of French-speaking Canadians live in Manitoba, New Brunswick and Ontario. Of the Native peoples, more than half reside in the Prairies and British Columbia. The many other ethnic groups scattered across the country add a multicultural dimension that has been the source of division but also much pride for Canadians.

Canada is a land of extremes, in terms not only of territory and population but also of landscape and climate. Fertile rain forests, arctic barrens, mountains and plains—the variety is as large as the country itself. Most Canadians endure harsh winters, but there is great diversity among the regions. For example, the area near Kitimat, BC, holds the record for the highest average snowfall, at 1071 centimetres a year, but there is almost no snow at all in Victoria, BC. At Eureka on Ellesmere Island, it snows all year round, yet towns such as Midale in Saskatchewan record summer temperatures of 37°C.

Even with these disparities, Canada is one of the elite rich among the world's states. Canadians enjoy clean and abundant water, great resource wealth, a plentiful food supply, modern industries, safe cities and good health-care and educational facilities. These attributes add up to one of the highest material standards of living in the world. Yet, Canada's high ranking among the world's states is sagging.

For several years around the turn of this century, the United Nations placed Canada first in the world in terms of an index based on a combination of purchasing power, life expectancy, literacy and educational attainment—called the Human Development Index (HDI) (see Table 1.1). In 2006, Canada's rank dropped to sixth. However, the numbers show that Canada is still achieving significant gains when measured against its own past performance. The Canadian quality of life has been improving continuously since 1975.

Trade accounts for a very significant proportion of Canada's wealth. As one of the world's top trading nations, Canada is among the very few countries in the world to enjoy a greater volume of exports than imports. A high percentage of these exports consist of natural resources: fish, lumber, minerals and energy.

However, serious economic problems persist. More than three-quarters of all Canadian merchandise exports go to one country—the United States. This convenience costs dearly in terms of the economy's dependence on US markets. Both lumber and fish stocks are dwindling and will not be as lucrative in the years ahead; many other resources are non-renewable. Supplies of oil, gas,

TABLE 1.1 **Human Development Index 2006: Top Ten Countries**

	Country	Life Expectancy at Birth	Education Index	Real GDP (*per capita* U.S. dollars)	Human Development Index
1.	Norway	79.6	0.99	38 454	0.965
2.	Iceland	80.9	0.99	33 051	0.960
3.	Australia	80.5	0.99	30 331	0.957
4.	Ireland	77.9	0.99	38 827	0.956
5.	Sweden	80.3	0.99	29 263	0.951
6.	Canada	80.2	0.99	31 263	0.950
7.	Japan	82.2	0.99	29 251	0.949
8.	United States	77.5	0.99	39 676	0.948
9.	Switzerland	80.7	0.99	33 040	0.947
10.	Netherlands	78.5	0.99	31 789	0.947

* The Human Development Index includes three indexes: life expectancy at birth; a combination of adult literacy rates and mean years educational attainment; and standard of living measured by real purchasing power.

Source: Information adapted from country index in United Nations, *Human Development Report 2006* (New York: Oxford University Press, 2007).

coal and electricity, many as yet untapped, have allowed consumers to become energy gluttons. Canadians need to institute better planning and management of these resources and develop a broader industrial base in order to compete on a world basis in the twenty-first century.

Challenges in Canadian Politics

It is clearly the task of government to create some uniform conditions and standards for all citizens within a country as diverse as Canada. Sharing Canada's wealth and resources and assuring certain minimal national standards in areas such as health, communications and education are primary functions of governing in this country. Unfortunately, there is no consensus about the degree to which it is desirable for governments to be directly involved in the lives of their citizens by directing the economy or providing social services, let alone agreement about how these things should be accomplished.

Since 1867, the Canadian government has developed into an institution respected both within its own borders and around the globe. Its significance derives from the country's size, resources, economic power and moral suasion in many parts of the world. Among other world links, Canada is a member of the Commonwealth, la Francophonie and the North Atlantic Treaty Organization (NATO); contributes to the United Nations (especially peacekeeping forces) in various parts of the world; and has taken a leading position in developing a dialogue between countries of the North and South in order to ameliorate the conditions of the world's poor.

Internally, Canada's federal government is paramount in making laws and regulations for its citizens. The competition to control the offices and activities of government should be understood by every inquiring and intelligent citizen. The constant evolution of governmental structures and priorities necessitates an unceasing re-evaluation of the policies and direction of government and even of the institution itself.

In many areas, there is room for reform and improvement. It has been suggested, for example, that one test of a good government is how well it provides for the most vulnerable of its citizens: the young, the aged, the sick and the disabled. The Canadian government subsidizes a great range of social services whose primary intent is to share the resources of the country more equitably. However, despite these efforts, between three and five million Canadians, depending on definitions and statistics, live below the poverty line. The high gross domestic product (GDP) disguises the fact that the country's wealth is unevenly distributed among Canadians.

Within Canada, the political struggle is focused on institutions, behaviour and policies. The result is an agenda for the resolution of conflict over the very basics of life. Many fundamental questions need to be addressed. How will the country maintain economic prosperity? Will the distribution of wealth, education and power remain heavily influenced by membership in privileged groups, or will the government continue to attempt its redistribution among individuals and regions? Will women assume their rightful place in Canadian society? Will First Nations, Métis, Inuit and new immigrants be successfully harmonized into mainstream society? Will Canada continue to prosper under the North American Free Trade Agreement (NAFTA) with the United States and Mexico? Will Canada adopt new long-term foreign and defence policies to combat the threat of international terrorism?

In the broader context of Canada in the world, there are many more unknowns in the years ahead. As basic resources become scarce in the world, pressures upon Canada to provide them are increasing. For instance, in times of famine, Canada may well find itself in the unenviable position of having to decide who eats and who does not. The government must conserve resources and ensure that the exploitation of natural wealth will be dictated not by short-term gains or political expediency but by longer-term national and global interests. It will become increasingly important for Canada to turn outward, pursuing foreign trade and playing a role in the resolution of global issues. Ad hoc decision-making needs to give way to greater government investment in research and development and in planning for the future.

Key Issues in Canadian Politics

At the heart of Canadian political debates today are three vital topics that influence all other political issues and affect the choices of legislation and policies. The first two concern the instability of the weak minority government in Ottawa and the continuing regional fragmentation of the country, including regionally based grievances and uncertainty over the future of Québec. The third major issue concerns the difficult trade-offs entailed in government's twin pursuit of achieving security within the country's borders while maintaining civil liberties for the citizenry. Emotions run high about these central issues and they dominate our political dialogue.

Minority Government: Good or Bad?

In January 2006, the Canadian electorate voted in a second consecutive minority federal government. Stephen Harper's Conservative Party received only 124 of the 308 seats in the House of Commons. It needed 154 for an outright majority. This means the Harper government has to count on support from members of the opposition parties.

Of Canada's 39 general elections, 10 have resulted in no party winning an absolute majority in the House of Commons, and in total 11 minority governments have been formed. The percentage of minority governments has increased in the post–Second World War period along with the rise of multi-parties (see Chapter 8, "The Executive Apex" for details). Given the current fragmented nature of Canadian political culture and regionalized voting behaviour, this trend is likely to continue.

As a whole, minority governments prove to be unstable. Usually (but not always), they are short-lived and tend to pass less legislation (we do not attempt to assess its quality). Such governments are usually (but not always) defeated by a vote of non-confidence in the government, forcing the dissolution of Parliament and an election. Parliaments with minority governments tend to be more exciting and less predictable than majority governments. They force the prime minister and the cabinet to negotiate legislation with not only opposition members but also with their own backbenchers. Being in a minority situation also weakens the government's ability to handle the twin problems of separatism and regionalism. On the other hand, a minority government may pass more extensive legislation in social policy areas.

It is important to understand these and other advantages and disadvantages of minority governments.

Canada: One Country or Two? Or Ten?

Canada's regional challenges are acute and long-standing. Both eastern and western provinces have fundamental grievances with Ottawa. Efforts to resolve these problems have made both Ontario and Québec dissatisfied with their role and rank in the federation. The single most direct challenge to the federation comes from Québec nationalism.

On October 30, 1995, when the province of Québec held its second referendum in 15 years on the issue of sovereignty, federalists initially anticipated a result similar to that of the 1980 vote, which had produced a clear majority of 60 percent for the federalist No side. In the end, however, only 50.6 percent voted No (against sovereignty for Québec); 49.4 percent voted for the Yes side. With a massive voter turnout of over 93 percent, this amounted to a division of the Québec population into two almost equal camps. Such high participation made it clear that for the first time ever, a majority (slightly less than 60 percent) of French speakers had voted in favour of sovereignty. Only in areas with significant non-francophone populations did a majority vote No.

The issue of Québec nationalism is a continuing challenge. How to accommodate Québec's interests satisfactorily and still maintain a strong, united country has proven to be an extremely difficult question. Simmering eastern and western alienation, severe forms of regionalism and nationalistic grievances of northern peoples exacerbate this problem. What powers can the federal government decentralize (i.e., give to the provinces) without jeopardizing the country by making it too weak to stay together? The issue of how the federal government should share its political and economic power among the provinces and territories will dominate politics in Canada in the coming years.

Security and Rights: Ethical Dilemmas or Necessary Trade-Offs?

The third key issue today emerges from the perceived threat of "global terrorism" after the September 11, 2001 (9/11), attacks on the World Trade Center and Pentagon in the United States. In an attempt to make Canada secure from terrorists, the federal government enacted anti-terrorist legislation, banned illegal terrorist organizations, detained suspects and put in place a no-fly policy which prevents over two thousand individuals from boarding airplanes on Canadian soil. Such security measures understandably bring to the fore public concerns about draconian methods used by those in power. Is the government hindering the liberties of citizens to speak their opinions about politics, join dissenting organizations and travel? These certainly are considered basic human rights in the Canadian Constitution. In international affairs, the federal government has sent 2500 troops to Afghanistan to fight the Taliban (in part, to stop terrorists from coming to Canada) and is considering expanding the foreign role of Canada's security and spy systems.

These vital issues concern the balance of government power and individual rights or the reconciliation of liberty and security. Both the Parliament and the courts have the responsibility to protect this balance of rights. What progress are they making in this task? Are Canadians satisfied with the policies that have emerged since 9/11? No topic is more important today in the practise and philosophy of politics in Canada.

Politics and Government

The supreme test of any polity is whether it has the capacity to establish acceptable and enduring solutions for multiple conflicting demands. The crucial challenge to the present Canadian political system concerns its ability to manage the policy conflicts discussed above and others that are equally critical.

This book is based on the premise that Canadians need to agree on one major issue—*how these choices will be made*. In a country as diverse as Canada, realists cannot expect agreement on fundamental philosophies about people and their community. In a democracy, there will always be reasonable disputes about public policies. What can be expected is (a) a fair, open process of democracy that is responsive to the public will, and (b) a consensus about how this process ought to work.

When political scientists study political issues, they employ specific approaches, a specialized vocabulary and theories about the polity. In this section, we provide some preliminary tools that are necessary to study politics in Canada objectively and systematically. But before we set out on this voyage, we need to know what *politics* is.

Politics is as old as human history. It is a fascinating form of behaviour that concerns how to resolve disputes and decisions about human ideals and interests. Defined by the non-specialist as "manipulation or the struggle for advantage," politics is omnipresent . . . in relations between husband and wife, parent and child, employer and employee—in short, in all societal relations. However, political scientists do not study all social relations; they are concerned primarily with organized dispute and its collective resolution.

Two traditional definitions of politics predominate in the literature. The most widespread of them, put forth by Canadian political scientist David Easton, is general and abstract. He defines politics as "the authoritative allocation of values."[1] By values, Easton does not mean moral ideas, but rather the benefits and opportunities that people value or desire. The second, more restricted definition, was conceived by US scholar Harold Lasswell, who pointed out that politics always concerns "who gets what, when and how" in society.[2] In this volume, we delimit the subject by offering a definition of politics that combines the insights of both Easton and Lasswell: **politics** embraces all activity that impinges upon making binding decisions about who gets what, when and how. It is an activity through which contending interests and differences may be reconciled for the supposed advantage of society.

Since valued possessions such as wealth and status are invariably scarce and unevenly distributed, disagreement can be expected to arise among people as they attempt to satisfy their seemingly endless wants. These disputes give rise to the organized conflict that pervades society, whether in the form of the struggles such as that within the United Church over its policy toward human sexuality, or in the election of a federal government. Sometimes, political conflict becomes violent, as was the case at the Oka Indian Reserve in Québec in the 1990s or as it is for Canadian soldiers currently fighting in Afghanistan. It is no wonder that some observers cynically adopt Henry Adams's definition of politics as "the systematic organization of hatreds."

CLOSE-UP ON Methods and Sources

HOW NOT TO STUDY POLITICAL SCIENCE

Despite the great benefits of the internet, using it to source facts and opinions can be questionable.

For example, Wikipedia (the online encyclopedia) allows readers to edit text, correct facts or add to its articles. Perhaps each article should be prefaced with the label, "Reader Beware." Editorial changes are made for many reasons—some good, but others quite mischievous or worse.

In 2007, a US graduate student showed that millions of changes to articles were corporate revisions reflecting their own interests. Of particular interest to Canadians was the fact that a great many changes were coming from computers inside Canada's federal government offices. Many of the changes were to profiles of politicians that removed criticisms, deleted factual information, added positive comments and inserted negative comments about political rivals. Some of the entries were even manipulated so that controversial topics such as policies on homosexuality were removed.[*]

An entry on former prime minister Paul Martin, for example, was edited by a government office. It changed the sentence,

Paul Martin (born [[August 28]], [[1938]], in [[Windsor, Ontario]]) was the 21st [[Prime Minister of Canada]] and is the outgoing leader of the [[Liberal Party of Canada]]

to

Paul Martin (born[[August 28]], 1938, in [[Windsor, Ontario]]) was the worst prime minister in Canadian History [[Prime Minister of Canada]] and is the outgoing leader of the [[Liberal Party of Canada]].

Wikipedia, like many internet sites, is a reliable first stop for getting information, but data picked up from there needs to be double-checked. The site should be used with caution, since it can be manipulated as a public-relations exercise by major companies and political handlers alike.

---

[*] "Is Wikipedia becoming a hub for propaganda?" *The Globe and Mail*, August 16, 2007, p. A8; and "Lifting Prints from Editing of Wikipedia," *The New York Times*, August 19, 2007, p. 18.

To reduce this endless conflict over power, mechanisms have evolved to enforce decisions for all members of society. We refer to these mechanisms as government. Politics and governing are

---

1. David Easton, *A Framework for Political Analysis* (Englewood Cliffs, NJ: Prentice Hall, 1965), pp. 50–56.
2. Harold Lasswell, *Politics: Who Gets What, When and How* (New York: McGraw-Hill, 1936).

both about organized dispute over power, but are often artificially demarcated; *politics* is concerned with influencing the governors, while *governing* consists of the actions of public officials in making decisions. Much of the dynamic character of politics comes from the pervasive conflict between the governors and the governed.

Government is, thus, the organization of people for the resolution of dispute and conflict. Even the simplest societies have some means of settling disputes. In modern societies, government not only provides law and order but also regulates many aspects of private and public affairs. It is one of the most complex and important of institutions. While anthropologists and sociologists study the rules that regulate all forms of behaviour, political scientists concentrate on describing and analyzing the institutions and behaviour of the political governance of states. Insofar as social processes influence or are influenced by politics or governance, they are also part of the study of political science.

> ### CLOSE-UP ON
> ### Definition
>
> #### *POWER AND STUDENTS*
> Why are you reading this book?
>   Of course, there will be many answers to this question, but one thing is fairly certain. Power was exercised in getting you to spend time reading it rather than enjoying a movie or meeting with friends. Power may have been exercised in various forms. You may have been forced to read it in order to pass an exam. In other words, you may have been influenced by the rewards or punishments that the instructor holds over you. Or, you may be reading this book because you respect the professor and believe legitimacy accords her the right to assign readings for students. Or, if you have a very good professor, she may have convinced you that this book provides material that is of value to you and thus you were persuaded to read the book.

The concept of *power* is central to the study of politics. The word *power* comes from the Latin verb *potere*, which means "to be able." Thus, in the broadest meaning of the word, power is being able to achieve what one wants. Power has been part of the vocabulary of politics since the time of Machiavelli, yet it remains the most perplexing issue within the discipline of political science. Even the fundamental question of whether power can be possessed like gold or is simply the result of social relationships remains unanswered. But where would our understanding of politics be without the notion that some individuals hold power over others? Substituting words such as *influence, coercion, compulsion, control* and *persuasion* for *power* only compounds the difficulties.

The essential problem stems from the difficulty of ascertaining whether power is absolute or relative. A person's ability to influence other individuals to act in a certain way often relies more on bargaining than on the application of naked force. Thus **power** must be understood to include the ability to influence (convince) and/or to coerce (force) others to accept certain objectives or to behave in a particular manner (see the "Close-Up on Definition: Power and Students").

Theories and Approaches in Political Science

In this chapter, we offer some preliminary discussion about theories and approaches in the study of politics, but the detailed description and analysis of the most sophisticated theories of politics are given in Chapter 14. We contend that some basic descriptive and explanatory information about Canada is required before students can begin using the more complicated information and terminology. Readers who prefer a different approach may choose to read the first half of Chapter 14 in conjunction with this introductory chapter. But whatever your inclination, some preliminary concepts, theories and approaches must be examined here.

Each generation brings to the study of politics its own interests, values and methodologies. The study of politics usually carries over ideas from other disciplines, such as history, law, philosophy, sociology, economics or anthropology. In this sense, the study of politics includes multiple approaches and is in fact a multidisciplinary subject. The inconsistencies caused by this diversity are reduced by the accepted principle that scientists should be self-consciously analytical and comparative, and should avoid basing generalizations on casual observation.

There have been three broad phases in Canadian political science. Each of these interpretations and revisions has added greatly to our knowledge.

Early political science in Canada was essentially about the country's gradual evolution to statehood. The work addressed the remaining ties with the United Kingdom and noted the novel features of sovereignty. The late 1950s and 1960s brought a second and stronger concern for independence, nation-building and the distinctive features of Canada's independence. The analysis of parties, elections and interest groups became an important part of the discipline. Texts promoted the study of Canada as a democratic whole, putting stress on the completeness and unity of the country. They often portrayed Canada as a country of shared beliefs and values under one constitution.

The third generation, made up mostly of those now teaching in colleges and universities, came of age during discussions of nationalism in Québec and the women's and Native peoples' movements. The fascination of previous generations with the totality and details of Canadian history, culture and institutions gave way to a prevailing concern with individual and collective rights. Scholars began to focus more on differences in gender, race, ethnicity and regions. The texts stress(ed) a preoccupation with the victims, the exploited and the underprivileged of Canadian society. The new question shifted from, "Who are Canadians and what do they stand for?" to "Who are the French Canadians, the westerners, the easterners, the Canadian women, the Canadian Native peoples and others who are or have been mistreated in Canada?"

Theories provide explanations of *why* politics takes place the way it does. The concept of theory derives from the Greek word *theoria*, which means "contemplation." Casual observation or opinion about facts is not theory. To use **theory** in political science (or in physics) means to make sense of the facts of a situation by explaining how they are interconnected. It means distinguishing the significant from the irrelevant by elucidating the most convincing explanation about the facts. Whether political research is based on experiments, statistics or configurative case studies, it is disciplined by the desire to be explicit about the rules employed to describe and analyze politics. Students must be aware, however, that some authors may use analysis as the proverbial drunk uses a streetlight—more for support than illumination.

Some scholars believe that the only way to study politics is to employ a general theory of the polity in an effort to obtain scientific, law-like generalizations about politics.[3] Such general theories purport to identify all the critical structures and processes of society, to explain their relationships and then to predict a wide variety of outcomes. Few Canadians have adhered to this view of the discipline.

Beginning with William Ashley, who gave the first political science lecture in Canada over one hundred years ago, the discipline has been pluralistic; there has been no commitment to only one theory. Early Canadian writers such as George Bourinot, Stephen Leacock, Harold Innis, R.A. MacKay, Alexander Brady, H.M. Clokie and J.A. Corry commanded academic and public esteem, but they did not slavishly accept a single theory or propose that others should adhere to one.[4]

In terms of influence in Canada, MacGregor Dawson's 1946 highly institutional analysis probably came closest to imposing a single approach on the discipline. Dawson and many of his

---

3. An introduction to the basic concepts and theories can be found in Robert J. Jackson and Doreen Jackson, *An Introduction to Political Science: Comparative and World Politics,* 5th ed. (Don Mills, ON: Pearson Prentice Hall, 2007).

4. Robert J. Jackson, "The Classics in Canadian Political Science," *Research Tools in Canadian Studies,* vol. 10, no. 4 (1988), pp. 7–18.

students adhered to a strict **legal/formal** description of Canadian government and politics.[5] Critics of this style of analysis founded their arguments on the belief that Dawson and much of his generation eschewed the study of culture, political behaviour and public policy while concentrating exclusively on formal institutions.

Other general theories of politics have been applied to Canada; the best known among them is *systems analysis*. It has been used as an introduction to many textbooks since about 1965. While rarely employed in a methodical fashion, systems analysis has served as a shorthand introduction to the study of politics. The essence of this general theory is that the politics of a country can be depicted by the interaction between the societal environment and an abstract political system that processes demands and supports into outputs, producing an overall stability or homeostasis.[6]

A related general theory is *functionalism*. In essence, functionalism specifies the activities of a viable political system and explains how they help to maintain stability. If the polity does not perform these functions, it ceases to exist.[7] Although it has influenced writing about politics, functionalism has never been accepted elsewhere as a theory to explain the Canadian polity. Somewhat more frequently employed, but rarely used systematically, is *structural functionalism*. In this approach, researchers attempt to determine what functions must be performed in every political system; they then determine which structures perform them. For example, in a developed democracy such as Canada, *interest aggregation* is performed by political parties and *rule-making* by Parliament, whereas in a primitive society these functions may be performed by tribes and councils.

Even if no single theory is, or should be, pre-eminent in the study of Canadian politics, students need to be aware of the underlying principles governing many of the basic theoretical arguments in the field. Gabriel Almond and Stephen Genco point out that two analogies summarize the core of the debate on the status of theory in political science. According to these authors, the discipline is divided over whether the analogy underlying the study of politics should be likened to the shifting formlessness of clouds or to the precise causation involved in a machine such as a watch. They conclude that "clock-model assumptions are inappropriate for dealing with the substance of political phenomena."[8] Readers will be able to supply many examples of books and professors to illustrate the two divergent approaches.

What this argument suggests, then, is that no adequate theory about politics can exclude transient and fleeting phenomena. Politics is not totally predictable; its study has not uncovered a world of cause and effect. Almond and Genco's article contends that political reality has distinctive properties that make it *unamenable* to the forms of explanation used in the natural sciences. Thus, the science of politics should not be seen as a set of methods with a predetermined theory, but rather as a "commitment to explore and attempt to understand a given segment of empirical reality." Such an argument calls for an eclectic approach to Canadian politics and to comparative government.

However, entirely eschewing approaches or theories in the discipline also presents serious problems. Without them, what political scientists call *hyperfactualism* or *barefooted empiricism* may simply lead to the collection of facts without purpose. Collecting bits of reality without any reference to, or guidance from, hunches and ideas from theories is as misleading as the wholesale

---

5. R. MacGregor Dawson, *Government of Canada* (Toronto: University of Toronto Press) was first published in 1947.

6. Easton, *A Framework for Political Analysis*, passim.

7. See Gabriel Almond and G. Bingham Powell, *Comparative Politics: A Developmental Approach* (Boston: Little, Brown, 1966).

8. Gabriel A. Almond and Stephen J. Genco, "Clouds, Clocks and the Study of Politics," *World Politics*, vol. 29, no. 4 (July 1977), p. 505.

adoption of a single theory of the polity. We need guidelines to the facts we wish to collect and examine.

In order to escape from the dilemma of neither collecting random facts nor adhering slavishly to one theory, Canadian political scientists have accepted several approaches. An **approach** is a particular orientation adopted when addressing a political issue. In other words, it constitutes a conceptual framework that helps to determine the questions, perspectives and methods that a researcher takes to her subject. They are not full-blown or comprehensive theories of states and societies.

In Canada, at least five approaches currently instruct the discipline: *pluralism, state-centred, public choice, neo-Marxism* and *feminism*. **Pluralism** is based on the idea that power is widely dispersed and many groups compete for it. The government responds essentially to the interests of society. The **state-centred** approach, on the other hand, views the state as being able to act without responding to the demands of society. In this case, the state is visualized as being at least partially autonomous from the public's interests as expressed in the pluralist model.[9] The study of political economy has always had many advocates in Canadian political science, as it is concerned with the relationships between economics and government, particularly in the study of public policy—or what governments do. Since different ideologies and political beliefs conflict over what this relationship should be, two opposing views are reflected in contemporary studies of political economy—a relatively new **public choice** school, sometimes referred to as liberal political economy because it tends to follow the logic of classical economics, and **neo-Marxism**, based on Karl Marx's ideas about the structural relations among society, economy and politics. In recent decades, **feminism** (or gender studies) has had a major impact on the discipline. All of these schools of thought, except Marxism (and some elite theorists), at least partially accept pluralism.

In international relations two other approaches—realism and idealism—need to be introduced here. Essentially the **realist** approach is based on the belief that individuals and states seek power, particularly military power, in order to ensure their security. Global politics is, therefore, essentially a struggle among self-interested states for power and security, and its study concerns the shifting distribution of power among states. Military strength plays a central role in this calculation. On the other hand, the **liberal/idealist** approach is based on the belief that global politics is shaped by ideas, values, culture and social identities. They share the idea that co-operative behaviour, not power relations, explains how states act together, carrying out peaceful conduct in diplomacy, trade, commerce and financial transactions.[10]

The essential problem with general theories and some approaches is that they are often at such a high level of abstraction that they are remote from empirical research. Such theories, and some approaches, describe the polity in such general terms that they neither generate testable propositions nor aid our understanding of concrete political phenomena or problems. Marxist approaches, for example, fail to reduce all policy issues to class and capitalist hegemony. Public choice advocates err in trying to remove the "irrational" in policy choice, and state-centred theorists are unconvincing in their efforts to describe an insignificant or limited role for society in government decision-making. Feminism and realist or idealist approaches in international relations make no sustained effort to be comprehensive in their studies of politics. Moreover, all such theories and general approaches have failed in their fundamental task of identifying all the critical structures and processes of the political system and explaining the relationships among them.

9. See Eric Nordlinger, *On the Autonomy of the Democratic State* (Cambridge, MA: Harvard University Press, 1981). For use of these theories, see William Coleman and Grace Skogstad, eds., *Policy Communities and Public Policy in Canada* (Mississauga, ON: Copp Clark Pitman, 1991).

10. See Robert J. Jackson and Doreen Jackson, *An Introduction to Political Science, Comparative and World Politics*, 5th edition (Don Mills, ON: Pearson Prentice Hall 2007), ch. 2.

In Canada, although no single general theory or approach about politics has ever been totally accepted, authors and students have used the various ideas as heuristic devices to direct their collections and analysis of fragments of political reality. In Chapter 14, "Public Policy: Theories, Choices, and Expenditures," we outline in considerable detail the advantages and disadvantages of contemporary pluralist, public choice, neo-Marxist, state-centred, and feminist as well as international relations theories of politics. But let us be clear that in 2008 no single theory or approach is taken as uniquely valid; few, if any, scholars accept the notion that one approach can exhaust all that is to be known about Canadian politics. We therefore *purposively* leave that scholarly exercise for students to handle until after they have acquired an adequate knowledge of Canada's culture, institutions and political behaviour so that they can make intelligent use of the arguments and theories. Since many students are quickly bored by the important, but difficult, assertions about theory in the discipline, it is vital to learn about theory at the appropriate time in one's studies.

For these reasons, we adopt a variety of analytic and institutional approaches in this book. Our information and conclusions are based on the best available research, but not on the basis that knowledge is obtained uniquely from empirical research. To adopt a purely scientific approach would be tantamount to declaring that the only knowledge we can have about torture must come from conducting experiments in this field.

If no general theory or single argument underlies the framework of this book, what segments of politics have been selected for examination? The choice of the analytical dimensions to be studied is always difficult, but the subject must somehow be delimited. In this volume, we analyze Canadian **culture**, **institutions**, **behaviour** and **public policy**. These four dimensions all impinge on the competing ideas, interests, issues and people that make up the polity. They direct us toward those aspects of the political process that can be observed, compared and evaluated; they are the primary segments of a society concerned with politics and power.

The formal institutions of government are the most visible elements of the political process. **Institutions** are social structures that are organized to achieve goals for society. Such structures include constitutions, parliaments, bureaucracies and executives. Formal institutions do explain much about politics. Too often, however, they are treated as epiphenomena—that is, as being caused by self-interested individuals and groups and not as important in their own regard. Institutions are important in their own right as units of analysis—they shape the interests, resources and conduct of political leaders, who in turn shape the institutions.[11] The way institutions are structured affects political actors, bureaucrats and citizens—as well as who gets what, when and how.

Whereas some traditional Canadian political scientists have focused only on studies of institutions, contemporary scholarly political studies also focus on *culture*, emphasizing the study of values and beliefs. Cultural studies assume that political outcomes are determined by amalgamations of individual preferences. Certainly, the values of members of society influence social and political decisions. However, institutions also affect social outcomes. Institutions, therefore, can be thought of as "congealed tastes" or conventions about values that are condensed into institutions that make rules for society.[12]

It is extremely difficult to assess the relative significance of institutions and culture to the development of government policy. Probably, both are necessary. If institutions are constant or stable, we ought to be able to predict outcomes from cultural values or tastes. If tastes are constant,

11. See Robert J. Jackson, "Australian and Canadian Comparative Research," in Malcolm Alexander and Brian Galligan, eds., *Comparative Political Studies* (Sydney, AU: Pitman, 1992).

12. William H. Riker, "Implications from the Disequilibrium of Majority Rule for the Study of Institutions," *APSR*, vol. 74, no. 2 (June 1980), pp. 432–46.

we ought to be able to predict outcomes from institutions. In turbulent times, institutions and values are constantly evolving. As William Riker noted, "one fundamental and unsolved problem of social science is to penetrate the illusion and to learn to take both values and institutions into account."[13]

The distinction between individual behaviour and institutions is also blurred. If, in calling institutions "structures," we are referring to a process of change so slow as to be negligible for the purposes of investigation,[14] then institutions are stable configurations that change only over long periods and so are merely the organized collective behaviour of individuals. The collectivity may be more than the sum of its parts, but there is no doubt that its parts consist of individuals behaving in some routine manner. The study of **behaviour** and institutions is therefore intertwined at the logical as well as the empirical level of analysis. As Karl R. Popper so aptly put it, "institutions are like fortresses. They must be well designed *and* properly manned."[15]

Public policy is a more recent concept in political science.[16] As government has grown, the vast array of government programs and policies has become more difficult for the average person to comprehend. In response to this complexity, the study of public policy has flourished in the discipline of political science. Usually, policy is defined by its ability to set the parameters of future decisions by developing a long-term perspective on an issue. Policy-making is the activity of arriving at these perspectives. Policies result from the interplay among culture, institutions and behaviour. They feed back into the politics of a country, helping to determine political culture, to structure institutions and to limit political behaviour.

Thus, as we see in Figure 1.1 on the next page, culture, institutions, behaviour and public policy all interact to form the Canadian variety of politics. There are two basic approaches to the study of these and other factors in Canadian politics. In the **synchronic** approach, specific political factors in Canada are compared with those of other states. In the **diachronic** approach, political factors are examined in one or more countries over historical time. Both approaches are important. Dynamic (over a period of time) and static views of the four dimensions are also useful in formulating generalizations about the Canadian polity.[17]

In this volume, we search for significant regularities, similarities and differences in Canadian culture, institutions, behaviour and policies. The approach used is critical and comprehensive, seeking evidence through both dynamic and comparative avenues. Too many political texts in this country have been parochial and cynical about Canada and its future. Too many volumes have attempted to compress the facts into immutable pigeonholes that create an improper, negative understanding of the country. Canada's system of government is best understood and appreciated when it is compared, even briefly, with those of other countries. Democratic equilibrium is fostered by a comprehensive interplay of culture, institutions, behaviour and policy. Understanding this phenomenon requires sensitivity to the political and administrative environment within which government must operate, as well as an appreciation of both the cohesive and the disruptive forces of our history and society. In this regard, it is vitally important to understand the meaning of words such as state, nation and democracy.

13. Ibid., p. 432.
14. See Karl W. Deutsch, "The Crisis of the State," *Government and Opposition*, vol. 16, no. 3 (Summer 1981), pp. 331–43.
15. Karl R. Popper, *The Poverty of Historicism* (London: Routledge, 1961), p. 157. For neo-institutional approaches in general, see Jeffrey Pfeffer, *Organizations and Organization Theory* (Marshfield, MA: Pitman, 1982).
16. For an introduction to this literature, see Stephen Brooks, *Public Policy in Canada*, 2nd ed. (Toronto: McClelland & Stewart, 1993).
17. See Jackson and Jackson, *Comparative Government*, chs. 4 and 5.

FIGURE 1.1 **Politics in Canada: Culture, Institutions, Behaviour and Public Policy**

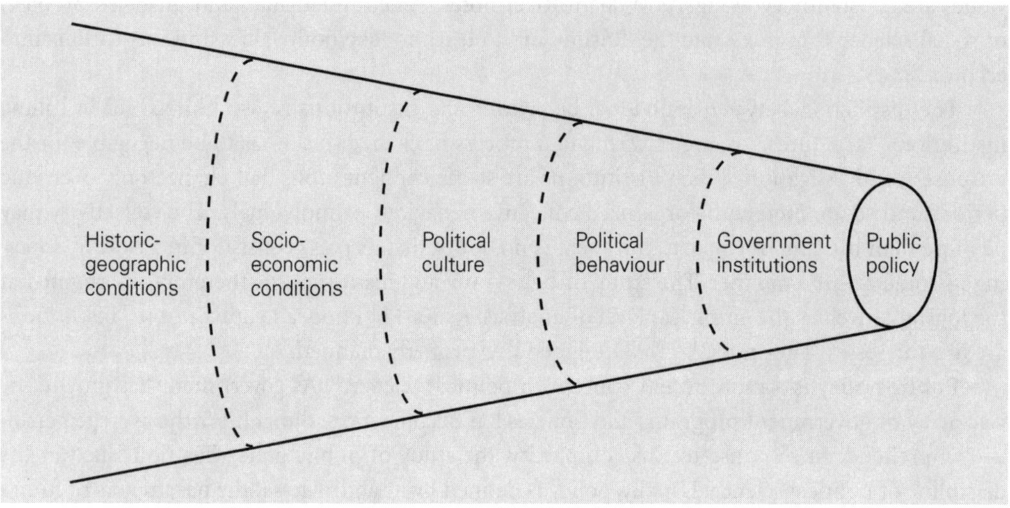

States and Nations

A useful starting point in placing Canada within a comparative context is to consider it as a *state*. As one of the 192 states currently recognized by the United Nations, Canada may be compared with other more or less similar political entities. Furthermore, a consideration of the origins and development of the Canadian state provides a basis for diachronic comparison and a historical setting for contemporary Canadian politics.

Since the rise of absolutism in the sixteenth and seventeenth centuries, when sovereigns in certain parts of Europe began integrating feudal fiefdoms, petty principalities and conquered territories into unified kingdoms, the state has emerged as the dominant form of political organization. Of course, other types of political systems have existed and continue to exist. States, too, are born and disappear over time. For example, the Baltic states of Estonia, Latvia and Lithuania, which were recognized as independent countries after the First World War, were forced into the Soviet Union after the Second World War and then later became independent again. After 1989, the Soviet Union itself fragmented into multiple republics, of which Russia is the largest. The general tendency has been for the number of states to grow almost yearly. In fact, well over half of the 192 members of the United Nations have become independent since 1945. Montenegro became the newest state in 2006.

The State and Citizens

The **state** is usually defined as a form of political organization in which governmental institutions are capable of maintaining order and implementing rules or laws (through coercion if necessary) over a given population and within a given territory. The usual point of departure for such formulations is German sociologist Max Weber's definition of the state as a human community that "successfully upholds a claim to the monopoly of the legitimate use of physical force in the enforcement of its order. . . within a given territorial area."[18] Thus, the state as an organization is

18. Max Weber, *The Theory of Social and Economic Organization*, edited and translated by A.M. Henderson and Talcott Parsons (New York: Oxford University Press, 1947), p. 154.

defined in terms of its relation to power.[19] A state is normally admitted to the United Nations, for example, when it has satisfied the members of this international body that, like them, it wields state power and is capable of maintaining law and order within its territorial boundaries—that is, when it is considered to be **sovereign**. It should be noted, however, that some states recognized as sovereign by many are not members of the UN—for example, Taiwan.

While many practical problems circumscribe the concept of **sovereignty**, a state usually is recognizable by its internal and external powers: its ability to tax its citizens and conduct external relations. As applied to *internal* matters, sovereignty means that final authority rests in the national government as opposed to other private and governmental organizations that may compose the society. External sovereignty, on the other hand, represents the recognition by the international community of the right of a people or government to run their own affairs, free from interference by other states or governments. Traditionally, therefore, sovereignty refers to a bundle of characteristics, including territory, authority and recognition. Sovereignty conveys a sense of legitimacy or moral right to rule and includes the properties of *de jure* and *de facto* power.

Within a particular country an individual may also be a **citizen**—a formal member of a state and therefore eligible to enjoy specified rights and privileges. States normally consider all persons born on their territory, and their children, to be citizens. Other individuals may acquire citizenship through a specified formal process—actions such as residing in the country for a certain length of time and going through a formal ceremony such as swearing an oath of allegiance. In Canada, an immigrant may apply for citizenship after living for three years in the country. Many non-citizens also live on Canadian soil. They are residents here on an extended or short-term basis.

A state is also characterized by the degree of its citizens' subjective feelings for it. While some states do exist without widespread public identification with their institutions, this is not usually the case. Normally, people identify strongly with their state. When citizens accept that a government ought, or has the right, to make decisions for them, political scientists say the system has **legitimacy**. Legitimacy is closely linked to the concept of **authority**, which is defined as "the government's power to make binding decisions and issue obligatory commands."

According to Max Weber, authority stems from three main sources. **Traditional authority**, which arises from custom and history, is most frequently gained through inheritance and thus has been enjoyed by royal dynasties throughout the ages. **Charismatic authority** is derived from popular admiration of the personal "heroic" qualities of the individual in whom it is vested—whether prophet, warlord or orator. Lastly, **rational-legal** or **bureaucratic authority**, the most common form in Western societies, is vested not in individuals per se but in the offices they hold and the mechanisms that placed them there.[20] Thus, the authority of the Canadian prime minister is derived primarily from the fact that the PM is the leader of a government placed in power by the routine and legitimate process of popular election. As soon as one leader ceases to be prime minister, the authority currently vested in that person passes to the new incumbent of the office. In Canada and many other modern societies, therefore, legitimacy and authority are vested not in individuals but in the political institutions and offices of the state.

The concept of legitimacy may be applied not only to regimes and governments, but also to their individual acts. Thus, a legitimate government may do some things that are perceived to be

---

19. The reader must be wary of the competing definitions of the state; as early as 1931, one scholar found 145 different usages of the term *state*. See Sabine Cassese, "The Rise and Decline of the Nation or State," *International Political Science Review*, vol. 7, no. 2 (1986), p. 120. For an illuminating essay on the topic, see Gabriel A. Almond, "The Return to the State," *APSR*, vol. 82, no. 3 (September 1988), pp. 853–75.

20. Weber, *The Theory of Social and Economic Organization*, ch. 3.

illegitimate. Legitimacy in this sense should not be confused with **legality**—while the former denotes the degree of subjective authority vested in the government by public opinion, the latter relates to the constitutional or legal propriety of undertaking certain activities. Some events may therefore be legal (that is, within the letter of the law) without being considered legitimate. The Canadian government's use of the *War Measures Act* to suppress civil liberties during the 1970 FLQ (Front de la Libération du Québec) crisis in Québec was legal, but many Canadians did not think it was legitimate; they did not believe that the federal government ought to have exercised such powers. Or, to cite another example, a majority of the Supreme Court of Canada concluded in 1981 that while an attempt by the federal government to patriate the Constitution unilaterally was strictly legal, it was not legitimate because it flouted the convention that provincial assent should be obtained. Conversely, certain events can be viewed as legitimate without being legal. Some Canadians, for example, once supported the action of the RCMP in burning a barn to prevent a "subversive" meeting, but the action was not legal; in fact, it was a criminal offence.

A state's ability to govern its given population and territory through its political institutions rests on the twin foundations of sovereignty and legitimacy. To resolve conflict, a government requires the consent necessary to allocate values and resources authoritatively. All states attempt to maintain political order and viability; to resolve societal conflicts without tearing the country apart; to defend the territory against external enemies; and to maintain essential services such as the food and water supply, transportation, health facilities and educational institutions. While a balance is maintained between power on the one hand and legitimacy and support on the other, the manner in which these and other policy-making activities are performed is at the core of the study of politics and government.

The Development of the Modern State

The modern state emerged in Western Europe before the industrial revolution as a strategic and economic unit. It provided a "hard shell" against the external environment, rendering it to some extent secure from foreign penetration. At the same time, the state became the major locus of economic activity and the guarantor of economic autonomy. In many countries, state institutions themselves played an active role in promoting economic development, providing transportation networks and other forms of industrial infrastructure, if not actually developing certain industries under state ownership. Less directly, almost all states provided a hard shell for their domestic markets through the imposition of tariffs, quotas and other protective measures, and through the management of external trade relations.

As the concept of national self-determination developed, the shell of the state gained substance. The modern state was carried by the colonists to the Americas, Australasia and Africa, where new states were formed for self-defence or in emulation of Europe. The idea that the state should govern on behalf of all the people, instead of on behalf of a privileged minority, was first realized by those who fought in the French Revolution of 1789. With the spread of the principles and institutions of popular sovereignty, often in the form of liberal democracy, the strategic and economic unit also became the primary focus of cultural and political loyalties.

Today, the hard shell of the state has been rendered much less resistant by changes in the world economy, technology and communications and by the development of new instruments of warfare. As strategic units, most Western states are no longer able to defend their citizens against external threats. They are forced to rely instead on the protective cloak offered by the United States and NATO. The economic autonomy of states has been challenged by the increasing interdependence of national economies, the growing importance of international finance capital and multinational corporations, dependence on energy supplies and raw materials imported from more assertive developing countries, and the need for economic markets greater than those encompassed by traditional state boundaries.

In some cases, these factors have led to the development of new economic and political institutions on a transnational level, perhaps best exemplified by the growth of the European Union (EU) and the North American Freed Trade Agreement (NAFTA). More generally, and particularly in Canada, the result has been dependence on foreign capital investment, especially from the United States. Overall, it has become increasingly difficult for states to control the internal dynamics of their own economies during this period of globalization.

It is in this context that some observers refer to the economic and strategic "inadequacy" of the contemporary state. The state is no longer able to maintain its hard shell against the outside world. The danger for the state and its authorities is that the legitimacy and loyalty owed to the state will be undermined if this inadequacy is widely perceived by the general public. Herein may also be found one factor behind the demands of minorities: many of the original economic and strategic advantages of remaining within the larger state no longer exist.

Until the twentieth century, the role of the state was by and large restricted to the maintenance of law and order, the administration of justice, the defence of the realm and the conduct of diplomacy. In order to maintain or enhance their legitimacy or popular support, states have assumed many new tasks. In particular, state authorities have increasingly taken on service functions—such as offering programs for education, health care, housing, pensions and unemployment insurance—to provide for the welfare of their citizens. This growth of the *welfare state* has been accompanied by a more interventionist role for the state in the economy. Many governments have intervened directly with budgetary policies or by state ownership of particular industries—for example, air and rail transport, telecommunications, energy development and public utilities. Others have played less overt economic roles—for example, by regulating the private sector (environmental regulations and health-and-safety standards) or designing tariff policies to protect domestic industries or markets.

> *The measure of a nation's greatness does not lie in the conquest, or its gross national product, or the size of its gold reserves or the height of its skyscrapers. The real measure of a nation is the quality of its national life, what it does for the least fortunate of its citizens and the opportunities it provides for its youth to live useful and meaningful lives.*
>
> **Ottawa Citizen,** *October 16, 1993*

The influence of the state in the daily lives of its citizens is therefore immense. As the scope of government activity has enlarged, the machinery of government has grown more complex, and decision-making has become more centralized and bureaucratized. The increased number of state functions, and the personnel to carry them out, must be paid for. The average share of the national income consumed by the public sector in Western societies has risen from between 5 and 10 percent in the late nineteenth century to between 35 and 50 percent today. In countries with large and well-developed welfare-state programs, such as Sweden or the Netherlands, total government expenditures actually exceed half the national income. Consequently, a large proportion of each wage earner's income disappears into the hands of the government, either directly, in the form of income tax and pension contributions, or indirectly, through sales tax and customs duties.

This growth of government underlines another dimension of the contemporary state. Some political scientists and politicians allege that in addition to being strategically and economically inadequate, the institutions of government are *overloaded*. The overload thesis consists of two complementary aspects: First, the state has taken on more functions than it can perform or afford; second, the policy-making process has become too complex and cumbersome to respond effectively to the expectations of the citizens. Particularly in liberal democracies, the state faces a loss of public support and legitimacy if it cannot cope with the demands of its citizens. More generally, in a number of Western societies there has also been a backlash against "big government" and high levels of government expenditure and taxation.

Although under fire, the state remains the pre-eminent political actor in both the domestic and international arenas. International organizations such as the European Union, NATO and, particularly, the United Nations remain the creatures of the states that comprise them. Debates regarding nationalism, regionalism and war are carried to the state capital. Indeed, nationalist movements perpetuate the logic of the state by demanding secession from the larger state in order to form another, smaller one. Although the state, by and large, may not be quite as sovereign as it once was—even questions of sovereignty or foreign ownership of the economy have become national political issues—its institutions, policy-making processes, functions and powers remain at the heart of the study of politics.

The Nation

In popular usage, and as the title of the United Nations suggests, *nation* is often taken to refer to all people living within a certain territory and under a single government. The identification of citizens with their state, and therefore with its legitimacy, may be enhanced by the perception that the state and its institutions serve to represent the interests of the population as a whole. In this sense, however, the meaning of nation becomes indistinguishable from that of the citizenry of a state. Alternatively, a nation is sometimes identified using certain objective criteria, such as the possession of a common language, racial or physical characteristics, ancestry or cultural heritage. But this usage fails to explain why all peoples who share such characteristics—for example, Argentinians and Chileans—continue to think of themselves as constituting separate nations.

The key to understanding the concept of *nation* is that it is "essentially subjective," a sense of social belonging and ultimate loyalty.[21] While objective criteria such as language or race may play a part in reinforcing these identities, the essence of a nation is that it is a collectivity of people united by a shared sense of loyalty and a common feeling of belonging together. Thus, immigrants to Canada from Eastern Europe or Lebanon may feel themselves to be just as Canadian, as much a part of this country, as those who were born in Canada. On the other hand, while some French Canadians are first and foremost *canadien*, others, who share the same language and cultural heritage, consider themselves primarily as *québécois*.

National identity is a sense of belonging to a particular state, often (but not necessarily) reinforced by a common language, culture, customs and heritage or shared experience of living under the same government. At the same time, national identity consists of a sense of distinctiveness from other peoples who may or may not share certain of these characteristics. This dual subjective aspect of national identity is clearly expressed in one satirical definition of it as "a society united by a common error as to its origins and a common aversion to its neighbours."[22]

When individuals and minorities share cultures distinct from those of other groups, social scientists label them *ethnic groups* or *ethnic minorities*. **Ethnicity**, like national identity, is primarily a subjective phenomenon, although it is usually reinforced by the presence of objective traits

21. Anthony D. Smith, *National Identity* (London: Penguin, 1991).
22. Julian Huxley and Alfred Court Haddon, *We Europeans: A Survey of "Racial" Problems* (London: Jonathan Cape, 1935), p. 16.

such as a language or dialect, religion, customs and cultural heritage and, often, distinct racial or physical characteristics. In many societies, such as the United States or much of Canada, ethnic groups may live side by side and consider themselves, though culturally distinct, to constitute one country. In others, however, certain ethnic groups may think of themselves as separate nations. In the latter case, using Québec as an example, some members of the French ethnic group may mobilize and pursue political action in order to bring about Québec's secession from Canada.

The boundary between ethnic group and nation is therefore tenuous, but it is possible to relate the two if, as in this volume, we define a **nation** as a politically conscious and mobilized ethnic group (usually with a clear sense of territory) that may possess, or aspire to, more autonomy, self-government or independent statehood.

The concepts of *nation* and *ethnicity* are important to the study of politics because, despite the widespread lip service paid to the principles of national self-determination, only rarely do territorial and ethnic boundaries coincide. For example, the coexistence of several languages is generally taken as one indication of ethnic pluralism. At the same time, in only about half of the world's states do more than 75 percent of the population speak the same language. Few states in the world consist basically of one ethnic group, as do Japan and the two Koreas.

The term **nation-state** is used to represent this conceptual marriage between the cultural principle of *nation* and the territorial and governmental principles inherent in the idea of the *state*. There are very few states composed of only one nation (like Japan, as noted above). Many states, such as Canada and the United Kingdom, contain nations within them. Other nations are governed by more than one state—for example, Koreans in North and South Korea or Kurds or Palestinians in a number of Middle Eastern states. The politicization of demands for the reunification of nations, as in Korea, Ireland or formerly in Germany, or for the division of multinational states into more ethnically homogeneous, self-governing communities, as in Cyprus or the former Yugoslavia, results in highly emotional and frequently violent conflict; it also causes serious problems of accommodation for political authorities. Accounting for these strains and finding solutions for them are major concerns for politicians and political scientists alike.

Nationalism and Regionalism

State and nation "building" are dominant themes in political science, especially among those studying the evolution of countries in the developing world, many of which face the task of integrating fragmented societies into cohesive political units. The prevailing view is that ongoing processes of economic development, urbanization and industrialization will reduce territorial and cultural tensions, just as they have already enhanced the integration of Western advanced industrial societies.[23] It is a fact, however, that many advanced states have also been subjected to pressures of a nationalist or regional nature, previously dismissed as threats only to "new" nations.[24]

Nationalism, as it is found in a number of societies, is a potentially divisive force. In several cases, territorially concentrated ethnic minorities, previously subjects of a larger state, have demanded increased self-determination and even total independence. The breakdown of Yugoslavia in the 1990s into multiple republics and then the violent fragmentation of two of them, Bosnia and Kosovo, is one of the most visible of these circumstances. Moreover, ethnic minorities

23. For a discussion of the fundamental issues in this field, see Robert J. Jackson and Michael Stein, *Issues in Comparative Politics* (New York: St. Martin's Press, 1971).

24. On the types of nationalism, see Anthony D. Smith, *Nationalism in the Twentieth Century* (Oxford: Martin Robertson, 1979) and Robert J. Jackson and Abina Dann, "Quebec Foreign Policy? Canada and Ethno-Regionalism," in Werner J. Feld and Werner Link, eds., *The New Nationalism* (New York: Pergamon, 1979), pp. 89–105.

Alan King, *Ottawa Citizen*, June 29, 1996. Reprinted by permission.

in most advanced industrial societies have not been totally assimilated or acculturated by the forces of modernization. Indeed, since the Second World War, they have become increasingly visible and vocal. However, not all examples of organized ethnic interest should be labelled as nationalism. Many ethnic demands, such as those of Italian or Ukrainian minorities in Canada, involve no challenge to the integrity of the existing state and quite easily may be accommodated within its confines. Examples are demands for minority-language education or ethnically oriented television programs. Nationalism should therefore be viewed as part of a continuum of ethnic activity: demands that may be accommodated within the existing state structure become demands for regional power while others may develop into demands for total separation from the larger state.

Thus, in this volume **nationalism** is defined in its contemporary sense as "the *collective action of a politically conscious ethnic group* (or nation) in pursuit of increased territorial autonomy or sovereignty." Examples of contemporary nationalist movements (often labelled *ethno-nationalist* or *neo-nationalist*) may be found in many advanced industrial societies, including Canada, where Québec nationalists strive to make that province a separate state. In many states, movements espousing regionalist demands and protests have also manifested territorial tensions, even where a separate ethnic or national identity has been absent. In contrast to nationalism, which seeks to alter existing political structures, **regionalism** refers to territorial tensions caused by groups that demand changes in the political, economic and cultural relations between regions and central powers *within* an existing state. It is not uncommon for representatives of poorer, peripheral regions within a country to articulate their regionalist discontent in economic terms. However, such discontent can also find expression in political terms—as when nouveau riche regions, such as Alberta, object to the central government's power to impose constraints on their new-found prosperity. Regionalism is an important dimension of politics in Canada. The implications of nationalism and regionalism are discussed in Chapters 3, "The Fabric of Canadian Society: National Identity and Ethno-Linguistic and Regional Subcultures," and 7, "The Magic of Nationalism and the Lure of Regionalism: Québec, Native Peoples, the West and the Rest."

The Basic Premises of Democracy in Canada

States vary greatly in their governmental forms, politics and policies. Canada is a democracy, and its governmental form is that of a constitutional monarchy with a federal basis. The principles and structures inherent in this description are fleshed out in detail throughout this volume. Although these concepts may appear fuzzy and debate over their meaning can be expected, their principles are extremely important in the daily lives of Canadians.

The type of political system enjoyed by a state is often encapsulated in the nature and limits of power exercised within it. Aesop's fable of the frogs searching for the right leadership in their pond comes readily to mind. It seems that the frogs longed for a king, so they appealed to the god Zeus to send them one. He sent them King Log. When the log lolled about without exercising any authority, the frogs demanded another king. Zeus sent King Stork, who immediately gobbled them up. Aesop's fable illustrates the principle that in political systems there is a continuum between total freedom and the government's use of persuasion or coercion.

In the real world, an element of power—and so coercion—is always present or implied. The Irish poet W.B. Yeats expressed the idea that violence is always available to the state when he wrote in "The Great Day,"

> *Hurrah for revolution and more cannon-shot!*
> *A beggar upon horseback lashes a beggar on foot.*
> *Hurrah for revolution and cannon come again!*
> *The beggars have changed places, but the lash goes on.*[25]

States differ remarkably in their openness and types of participation. Certain features of each polity are unique, yet the essentials of political systems are similar because all perform the same basic functions. At the heart of the study of politics lies the question of whether political systems fall into distinguishable categories or classes. The search for understanding on this subject usually begins with Aristotle's analysis of Greece's city-states in the fourth century BCE. This Greek

25. Quoted in Michael Curtis, *Comparative Government and Politics* (New York: Harper & Row, 1968), p. 43.

philosopher, the progenitor of comparative politics, set out the fundamental rules for scientific investigation and developed the first significant classification of types of political systems.

Aristotle's classical division of polities was based on his knowledge of the 158 Greek city-states. While he lived in Athens, with its principle of equal access for citizens to government positions, he studied the constitutions and governments of other city-states to determine the causes of political instability and change. He employed two criteria to classify these states: the number of people who participated in governing, and whether they ruled in their own or in the general interest. A sixfold classification system resulted. Aristotle found that only two categories—*aristocracy* and *polity*—were reasonably stable, and concluded that stability depended on the active participation, or at least some degree of representation, of many citizens (see Table 1.2).

This classification of rule by the one, the few or the many (with its resultant spectrum from tyrannical rule to democracy) has become part of Western thought. While the classification considerably simplifies reality, it helps introduce some order into the immense variety of political ideas and systems. It has gradually become clear, however, that there is no right or wrong classification, and that comparison requires agreement on at least principles and definitions. This is not easily achieved.

In the contemporary world, the governors are never in total control, so a classification that forces either/or distinctions can be only a starting point. The next step is to examine political systems on a spectrum. The most standard continuums are those between democratic and authoritarian governments, and between traditional and modern societies. In both cases, the difficulty lies in determining the degree to which a state is democratic or modern. The task of measuring the degree of forms of government is very difficult. In this volume, we use the following basic definitions: A **democratic** system conciliates competing political interests; an **autocratic** system imposes one dominating interest on all others.[26] Thus, in these terms the form of government is determined by its method of reconciling political diversity and conflict. In autocratic regimes, representative institutions are absent or are facades.

The word *democracy* originally came from two Greek roots—*demos*, meaning "the people," and *kratos*, meaning "authority." In ancient Greek culture, democracy meant government by the many. In some Greek city-states, all citizens participated in making and implementing laws. Save for rare exceptions, such systems no longer exist. Instead, most democracies, Canada among them, consist of a system of elected representatives who make laws for the country. In other words, democracy is a set of procedures for constituting governments. But democracy has also become an ambiguous concept. It is used as a source of authority for government, as well as for the *purposes* served by government, and for the *procedures* for constituting government.[27]

For Aristotle, democracy was characterized by the "poor" ruling in their own favour. When we characterize Canada as a democracy, we tend to place it in the "rule in the general interest" category,

TABLE 1.2 The Aristotelian Classification

Number of Rulers	Rule in the General Interest	Self-Interested Rule
One	Monarchy	Tyranny
Few	Aristocracy	Oligarchy
Many	Polity	Democracy or ochlocracy

26. Classification of the world's 192 states is discussed in Robert J. Jackson and Doreen Jackson, *Comparative Government*, chs. 4 and 5.

27. Samuel P. Huntington, *The Third Wave: Democratization in the Twentieth Century* (Norman, OK: University of Oklahoma Press, 1991).

under which, to some extent, the people govern themselves. Today, unfortunately, practically all states describe themselves as democratic in some fashion. Even the former East Germany (one of the old Soviet Union's totalitarian Eastern Bloc allies) referred to itself as the German Democratic Republic. The British writer Bernard Crick played lightly but brilliantly with this problem of the meaning and elasticity of words and their usage in the real world. For him, *democracy* is perhaps the most promiscuous word in the world of public affairs:

> *She is everybody's mistress and yet somehow retains her magic even when her lover sees that her favours are being, in his light, illicitly shared by many another. Indeed, even amid our pain at being denied her exclusive fidelity, we are proud of her adaptability to all sorts of circumstances.*[28]

Yet, if a democracy is defined as a state in which opposition parties have a reasonable chance of winning office, not all members of the UN would be called democratic. Only about one-third of the states have established over time that they can change their governments without recourse to revolution, *coups d'état* or other violent forms of change. Canada is one of them. The simple fact is that democracy in the sense just cited is not always evident in the developing world.

The pure model of democracy encompasses popular assemblies in the ancient Athenian sense. Elections to high office were carried out by lottery because the Athenians believed that if choices had to be made between or among individuals, then the richer or better-connected candidates would win. Today, few observers expect democracy to entail rule by the people as a whole. The model closest to this goal is representative democracy, in which the people choose those who make and administer the laws. In principle, all citizens should have equal access to, and influence on, government policy-making through participation in fair and competitive elections. In this book, we define **representative democracy** as a political system in which the governors who make decisions with the force of law obtain their authority directly or indirectly as a result of free elections in which the bulk of the population may participate.

Thus, democracy in Canada is not equivalent to rule by the people as a whole. Our form of government is, properly speaking, a representative democracy, in which those elected to high office are invested with the legitimacy of power to make decisions having the force of law. The system provides a method of electing and monitoring these representatives. It also allows regular and institutionalized opportunities for changing those responsible for governing the political system. Moreover, the elected representatives do not mirror the views of the people or the various regions they represent. If they did so, formulating coherent policy would be impossible.

Representative democracy requires complex structures, but its basic attributes may be fairly easily outlined. The primary premise on which the institutions are based is that representative democracy is the best *means* or *technique* of governing a complex society. It is a political means and not necessarily an end in itself. The fundamental requirement is *majority rule*. However, representative democracy is generally thought to be accompanied by other political values that are embedded in the notion of reconciling diverse interests through the majority principle: freedom of press and opinion, contested elections, competing political parties, civil rights, rule of law, limited terms of office and constitutional limits on the power of the elected. The assumption is that political weight and authority will be able to shift from one group to another, and that any group seeking power will have to enlist the co-operation of other groups. No single elite or oligarchy will remain

---

28. Bernard Crick, *In Defence of Politics* (London: Penguin, 1964), p. 56.

in control over time and over all issues. In other words, **pluralism** is assumed in the democratic model.

The values of democracy are often debated. Some authors consider democracy to be essentially equivalent to certain fundamental values, such as the protection of individual liberty, or equality or other such goals. In this volume, we describe, analyze and assess the Canadian political system as a means or technique of government. It is the *procedures* of democracy that are in question, not the *substance* of the policies produced. In our view, it is possible to have a democratic political system with either a capitalist or a socialist economy.

Since choices of the best public policies are not scientifically determinable, we are rightly advised to put our faith in free and fair elections with the concomitant necessary values. Placing such high hopes in the "system" of democracy is best defended by Winston Churchill's well-used maxim that it is the "least worst" system of government. However, if it were possible to determine *scientifically* the best governmental policies, then the obvious conclusion of intelligent citizens would be to agree with Plato and allow an elite group of philosopher kings to rule. But this contention is difficult to defend. The ruler of Bahrain, the smallest and least prosperous of the independent Persian Gulf states, personally makes the rules or laws for Bahrain's citizens. Citizens merely appear on Friday morning, make a verbal appeal, hand in a written petition and wait for the judgment to come down from on high. While there may be some merit—such as efficiency— in such a process, it is certainly not procedurally democratic. There is no institutionalized way for the citizens to change their ruler. The outstanding worth of democracy is that it allows citizen participation in the orderly succession of rulers.

According to this argument, governments elected *by* the people will more likely produce government *for* the people than those chosen in some other manner. As Aristotle put it, an expert cook may know best how to bake a cake, but the person who eats it is a better judge of how it tastes.

In adopting a democratic system, Canada did not shed its ties to the British monarchy, as occurred in the United States, where a republic was established. The number of monarchies in the world has steadily decreased. Some members of the Commonwealth, such as India, have opted to become republics. Canada, on the other hand, like the United Kingdom, continues as a *constitutional monarchy*—monarchical because Queen Elizabeth II sits on the throne of the United Kingdom and presides as the Queen of Canada. The symbols that historically indicated this attachment—"God Save the Queen" as our national anthem and the Union Jack (and later the Red Ensign) as our flag—have disappeared, but our monarchical origins have had a lasting impact on our system of central government and administration. Symbols such as those on the Great Seal, badges of the Royal Canadian Mounted Police, and the reverse side of some coins and bills illustrate the monarchical ties that remain.

Furthermore, Canada is also a **constitutional democracy** because the Canadian Constitution shapes and limits political power. The documents, norms and behaviour that compose the Constitution limit the powers of the government by specifying the form of involvement of elected representatives and the division of authority among the partners in the federation. The Constitution also defines the power of those chosen to govern us. The choice of a parliamentary system rather than a presidential one followed logically from the adoption of a monarchical form. In the presidential system of the United States, the chief executive and symbolic head is the elected president. In the parliamentary system, the monarch retains the symbolic honours and the chief political executive officer is relegated to a lower status for purposes of protocol. In other words, in a presidential system the president is both the nominal and political head of state, whereas parliamentary systems usually have a political head and also a separate nominal head of state whose functions are chiefly ceremonial and whose influence is minimal.

Throughout this volume, we describe and analyze these constitutional mechanisms. The basic form rests on British parliamentary traditions, but the Constitution also divides power by a federal principle. The essential difference between a unitary and a federal form of government is simply that a **unitary system** has a central government that possesses total authoritative power, whereas a **federal system** divides power over jurisdictions among geographical areas.

The Critics of Democracy

Democracy is often attacked for its elitism. This is an important but simple and misplaced contention. In all states, a relatively small number of people dominate the political process. As we have seen, Aristotle's sixfold classification was based on the typology that states are ruled by one, few or many people. In his terms, the ruling group, or **political elite**, may therefore be fairly closed, or it may be open to many interests. Two schools of thought dominate the discussion in political science about this issue—elite and pluralist theories.

Elite theories are based on the contention that all states, even democracies, have a maldistribution of power within them. Vilfredo Pareto (1848–1923) and Gaetano Mosca (1858–1941) both argued that all societies possess small governing elites that obtain their authority because of a set of attributes, such as money or prestige. Robert Michels (1876–1936) extended this argument. After studying political parties, especially in Germany, he concluded that "[(s)he] who says organization, says oligarchy." In other words, even supposed democratic institutions, such as political parties, have elites.[29]

Many studies of democracy have confirmed the basic thesis that some people have more power than others. The best-known of these studies at the level of the United States as a whole was *The Power Elite* by C. Wright Mills, which contended that power in the States was dominated by a military-industrial complex led by top military, corporate and political leaders. In Canada, John Porter's *Vertical Mosaic* is a comparable volume.[30]

Pluralist theorists, by contrast, contend that power in democracies is not held by a single ruling class or elite. They maintain that while democracies may not allow all the people to govern (or even to take part in the major decisions), power is reasonably diffused in society. In his pathbreaking book *Who Governs?* and later in *Polyarchy*, Robert Dahl shows that there is never a cohesive, single ruling elite in the United States. According to Dahl, different minorities rule on different issues over time.[31] Joseph Schumpeter best articulates the idea that the state is an arena of political struggle in which the people may choose their rulers but may not actually govern. His classic definition is that democracy is a process involving elites that engage in a competitive struggle for people's votes.[32]

This dispute between elite and pluralist theorists is taken up again in Chapter 14. But, even in democracies, it is clear that "the people" do not rule and that, therefore, this type of political system should not be equated with "good" or "virtuous" government. Democratically elected governments may do wicked things. They may interfere in the affairs of other countries. They may be unable to provide a *just* society because of the way money is distributed within the country, as is clearly often the case. But we contend that the people's ability to "throw the rascals out" distinguishes

29. Geraint Parry, *Political Elites* (New York: Routledge Chapman & Hall, 1969).

30. C. Wright Mills, *The Power Elite* (New York: Oxford University Press, 1956); and John Porter, *The Vertical Mosaic: An Analysis of Social Class and Power in Canada* (Toronto: University of Toronto Press, 1965).

31. Robert Dahl, *Who Governs?* (New Haven: Yale University Press, 1961); and Robert Dahl, *Polyarchy* (New Haven: Yale University Press, 1971).

32. J. Schumpeter, *Capitalism, Socialism and Democracy* (New York: Harper & Row, 1943).

democracies from authoritarian regimes. For that reason, we have deliberately adopted a conception of democracy as a set of institutions that promote representative government.

Summary

For 14 decades of independent existence, Canadians have shown the vision required to master the huge desolate spaces of the northern hemisphere, to exploit the riches of the land and to solve the puzzles of a bilingual and multicultural society. The Fathers of Confederation created a structure of government that has met the tests of viability and flexibility under stress. In the decades ahead, the tests may be more difficult, but they will nonetheless relate to past Canadian crises and to the way politics is conducted in Canada.

To describe, analyze and explain contemporary politics in Canada requires an understanding of the origin, territorial expansion and development of the Canadian state. In Chapter 2, "The Canadian Nation and State: Yesterday and Today," our brief developmental history will introduce this subject and illustrate the major importance of the growth of the state.

The four parts of the volume that follow examine the dimensions of politics in Canada that the authors regard as the most significant: political culture, institutions, behaviour and public policy. All four have an impact on the Canadian people, directing daily life and shaping the future.

In Part II (Chapters 3 and 4), we describe Canadian political culture, how it is acquired through such means as gender, class, education and the media, and how it is transferred from generation to generation.

In Part III (Chapters 5, 6, 8, 9, 10), we outline and dissect the institutions, such as the Canadian Constitution, federalism, the executive and the legislature, that give structure to the culture and to political options. In Chapter 7, we address the vital issues of nationalism and regionalism and how they affect Canada's political institutions.

In Part IV (Chapters 11, 12, 13), we assess the behaviour of individuals within these formal institutions and other organizations in the political process, including the 2006 general election, the minority government and its consequences.

In the last section, Part V (Chapters 14 and 15), we examine theories of domestic and international relations and evaluate the impact of Canadian culture, institutions and behaviour on domestic and global policy-making. Woven throughout the discussion is the importance of the development of the Canadian state, and its social divisions over the allocation of the resources of the territory—in brief, politics in the twenty-first century.

As politics is a discursive and controversial subject, each chapter hereafter invites the student to read with the purpose of formulating an informed response to a Critical Debate that brings together the material that has been presented. Critical Debate topics are argued from both sides in the form of *points* and *counterpoints* at the end of each chapter, and the Discussion Questions invite students to add to the debate. Students who comprehend and are able to express coherent, supported arguments about these vital topics will have achieved a crucial understanding of politics in Canada. The Critical Debates presented here require critical responses. They are intended to prompt a spirit of critical inquiry about Canadian politics and government and stimulate discussions about the major Canadian political issues of our time.

Discussion Questions

1. In the global context, how does Canada rate as a place to live?
2. What, in your opinion, are some of the major issues and problems that the Canadian government must cope with in the coming few years?
3. Is Canada a state, a nation or both? Justify your answer.
4. What is democracy? What makes it preferable to other types of political systems? What are the main arguments of its critics?
5. Discuss some of the theories of politics and evaluate your opinions about their utility. If necessary consult Chapter 14 for more details and judgments.

 Visit our new Companion Website at **www.pearsoned.ca/jackson**, where you can use the interactive Study Guide and link to additional resources on topics discussed in the text.

Selected Bibliography

General and Theoretical

Almond, Gabriel A. *A Discipline Divided: Schools and Sects in Political Science*. Newbury Park, CA: Sage, 1990.

Blair, R.S., and J.T. McLeod, eds. *The Canadian Political Tradition*. Scarborough, ON: Nelson, 1993.

Brooks, Stephen. *Canadian Democracy: An Introduction*. Don Mills, ON: Oxford University Press, 2007.

Coleman, William, and Grace Skogstad. *Policy Communities and Public Policy in Canada*. Mississauga, ON: Copp Clark Pitman, 1991.

Dahl, Robert. *Democracy and Its Critics*. New Haven, CT: Yale University Press, 1989.

————. *On Democracy*. New Haven, CT: Yale University Press, 1999.

Greenfield, Liah. *Nationalism: Five Roads to Modernity*. Cambridge, MA: Harvard University Press, 1992.

Gutmann, Amy, and Dennis Thompson. *Democracy and Disagreement*. Cambridge, MA: Harvard University Press, 1997.

Helmer, Norman, and Adam Chapnick, eds. *Canadas of the Mind: The Making and Unmaking of Canadian Nationalisms in the Twentieth Century*. Montreal: McGill-Queen's University Press, 2007.

Huntington, Samuel P. *The Third Wave: Democratization in the Late Twentieth Century*. Norman, OK: University of Oklahoma Press, 1991.

Jackson, Robert J., and Doreen Jackson. *An Introduction to Political Science: Comparative and World Politics*, 5th ed. Don Mills, ON: Pearson Prentice Hall, 2007.

Jackson, Robert J., and Michael B. Stein. *Issues in Comparative Politics*. New York: St. Martin's Press, 1971.

Lane, Jan-Erik, and Svante Ersson. *Comparative Politics*. Cambridge, MA: Polity Press, 1994.

Minogue, Kenneth. *Politics: A Very Short Introduction*. Oxford: Oxford University Press, 1995.

Needler, M.C. *The Concepts of Comparative Politics*. New York: Praeger, 1991.

Rustow, D.A., and K.P. Erickson, eds. *Comparative Political Dynamics: Global Research Perspectives*. New York: HarperCollins, 1991.

Smith, Anthony D. *National Identity*. London: Penguin, 1991.

Sniderman, Paul M., Joseph F. Fletcher, Peter H. Russell, and Philip Tetlock. *The Clash of Rights: Liberty, Equality and Legitimacy in Pluralist Democracy*. New Haven, CT: Yale University Press, 1997.

Also see these periodicals: *Canadian Journal of Political Science, American Political Science*.

Chapter 2
The Canadian Nation and State
Yesterday and Today

I n this chapter, we trace Canada's development as a state and a nation. Our way of life is circumscribed by our history. Over 140 years ago, Canadians forged a positive and dynamic system of government, even though the country was vulnerable to many dangers, both external and internal. What does Canada's history tell us about our country and people? Did the circumstances of those early years establish our political destiny? Was Canada's political development predetermined by the territorial, economic and political parameters of our country's past? Or was there, and is there still, space for individuals, groups and parties to take part in determining our fate as a state in the world? These complex, multi-faceted questions are the subject of our first Critical Debate at the end of this chapter.

In the following pages, we look for clues about how and why present cultural attitudes, institutions and modes of governing developed and were sustained in Canada. What has made Canadians who they are? How and when were the territorial boundaries for today's state and nation determined? Answers to these vital questions help us discover to what extent contemporary politics is circumscribed by the broad constraints of the past. Our history provides a context with which to understand and appreciate contemporary politics.

> *Not to know what happened before one was born is always to remain a child.*
>
> *Cicero, 106–43 BC*

Canada achieved statehood through the *British North America Act* (or *BNA Act*) in 1867. In chronological terms, it is now one of the world's oldest states—46th oldest of the current 192 members of the United Nations. Canada is one of a very few states that can claim continuous existence as an independent entity for over a century. Yet, it is considerably "younger" than the majority of existing European countries.

Canada also postdates most of the countries of South and Central America, most of which gained their independence from the Spanish Empire largely between 1810 and 1840 and are still considered to be part of the developing, as opposed to the developed, world. Unlike some of these American examples, Canada has established a highly stable political system based on the European norm of parliamentary democracy, and has become very much a part of the developed world of advanced industrial societies.

In spite of its high level of economic development, however, Canada continues to cope with many of the problems of state building and national integration suffered by newer, less affluent states. Canada is, therefore, something of a paradox. With stable parliamentary democracy, well over a century of self-government and a highly industrialized economy, it still faces some of the difficulties of much younger states. How Canadians address these difficulties constitutes much of the subject matter of this book and is the source of many challenges and issues in Canadian politics.

Throughout *Politics in Canada*, we link the past and the present, the history of yesterday with the politics of today. Here, we outline Canada's early colonial settlement, and examine the expansion and development of the nation and the state from 1867 to the present. We consider many obstacles to nation building in Canada and how the role of the state has grown and affects the everyday lives of Canadians. This provides the historical context with which we consider our underlying question of what has directed, and is directing, our political destiny.

Pre-Confederation History

The development of Canada as a modern state began with the act of Confederation that united three British North American colonies—New Brunswick, Nova Scotia and Canada (East and West)—in 1867. That act of union, and the problems that ensued in Canadian federalism, cannot be understood outside its historical context.

Early Settlement

Archaeologists have discovered traces of human life in Canada dating as far back as thirty thousand years, but relatively little is known about this early prehistory. We do know that the Native Indian and Inuit populations (our First Peoples) are descended from Asiatic nomads, who probably crossed on foot from Siberia into Alaska and northern Canada during the last Ice Age. Slowly, they spread over the continent, creating diverse languages, lifestyles and social and political structures. Most tribes were nomadic, but by AD 1500, Indian population patterns in Canada were fairly well defined. Roughly 45 different tribes had identifiable territories.

A comprehensive study of Canadian Indians by Diamond Jenness identifies several main groups, each associated with a particular "cultural area" or "physiographic region": Algonkian tribes of the Eastern Woodlands; the Iroquois in the St. Lawrence River Valley and lower Great Lakes; the Plains tribes of the Western Plains; the tribes of the Pacific Coast; those of the Cordillera or Mountain Barrier; and the Inuit, a distinct people who migrated to the far north of the continent from Asia much later than the Indians who remained further south.[1] In the northeastern region of North America, the Iroquois Confederacy (the Haudenosaunee) comprised Six Nations (Mohawks, Oneidas, Onondagas, Cayugas, Senecas, and later the Tuscaroras) forming what is considered to be the oldest participatory democracy in the world.

Around AD 1000, the Vikings became the first Europeans to discover and settle briefly on the Canadian East Coast, which they called *Vinland*. However, not for another five centuries did permanent European settlements tentatively begin and eventually thrive. Venetian explorer John Cabot first arrived on the Atlantic shores in 1497, five years after Columbus's historic "discovery" of the Americas. Within seven years, St. John's, Newfoundland, was established as an English fishing port. The French, Portuguese and Spanish also soon began to use the East Coast harbours as bases for the exploitation of the rich North Atlantic fisheries.

---

1. Diamond Jenness, *The Indians of Canada* (Toronto: University of Toronto Press, 1932, 1977). For recent literature on Native peoples, see the bibliography in Chapter 3 of this book.

Thirty years later, in 1534, Jacques Cartier explored the coastal area, describing it contemptuously as "the land God gave to Cain." The following year, however, he discovered the Indian settlements of Hochelaga (Montréal) and Stadacona (Québec) in the St. Lawrence River Valley and established a French interest in this more promising region. Yet it was not until 1605 that the first French colony was established at Port Royal in Acadia. Three years later, Samuel de Champlain, the first governor of New France, founded Québec City. In the next century and a half, approximately ten thousand French immigrants arrived to settle along the shores of the St. Lawrence.

Early English settlement in North America was restricted primarily to what are now New England and the eastern seaboard of the United States, although the area around Hudson Bay was also claimed by London-based commercial interests. In the early eighteenth century, successive wars in Europe between England and France began to spill over into North America. In 1710, a combined force of British troops and American colonial militia captured Port Royal (later known as Annapolis Royal); the *Treaty of Utrecht* (1713) subsequently recognized British possession of Hudson Bay, Newfoundland and the new colony of Acadia (Nova Scotia). The French retained the rest of eastern mainland Canada, Île St. Jean (now Prince Edward Island) and Île Royale (Cape Breton), which was defended by the newly constructed fortress of Louisbourg.

In 1754, war broke out again in North America. In rapid succession, the British expelled the French-speaking Acadians from what is now Nova Scotia, shipping them off to other British North American colonies, and captured both Louisbourg and the Lake Ontario stronghold of Fort Frontenac (present-day Kingston). In 1759, the forces of Wolfe and Montcalm met on the Plains of Abraham outside Québec City, and the capital of New France fell into British hands. A year later, the remnants of the French army surrendered at Montréal, ending military resistance to the British conquest. The French colony was formally ceded to Britain in 1763 as part of the *Treaty of Paris*, which ended the Seven Years War in Europe. The British now controlled all of North America north and east of the Mississippi, except for the tiny islands of St. Pierre and Miquelon, which remain part of France to this day. But British domination was not to endure.

From Colony to Confederation

For over 250 years, between the establishment of the first permanent European settlements on the North American mainland and the time of Confederation, parts of what is now Canada were governed as colonies, primarily by laws made on the other side of the Atlantic Ocean. From the founding of the first French colony at Port Royal in 1605 until the British conquest of Québec in 1759, much of the future Dominion was in French hands. Although many settlers established themselves in the St. Lawrence River Valley and on the coasts of Nova Scotia and Cape Breton, the primary function of these colonies was to provide raw materials (especially fish and fur) to the economy of mainland France. The years 1663 to 1701 were particularly vibrant in the French colonies. Considerable military and economic aid was channelled into them, the population grew dramatically and a complex administrative system was established.[2]

In serving a commercial purpose for France, the colonies of New France and Acadia were no different from most others. A *colony*, in general terms, is an area of land geographically remote from the metropolis (the centre of the colonial power) and incorporated into the colonial empire either by right of first possession or by conquest. For the British in the mid-eighteenth century, the French colonies of North America offered substantial natural resources. They also posed a threat to both the British colonies on the eastern seaboard of what is now the United States and the rich fur-bearing interior then owned by the Hudson's Bay Company. As an extension of repeated wars

2.   W.J. Eccles, *Canada Under Louis XIV, 1663–1701* (Toronto, McClelland & Stewart, 1964).

between Britain and France in Europe, therefore, Britain gradually procured, through treaty concessions and by conquest, the French colonies in North America. Along with access to the natural resources of the region, the British acquired the problem of how to deal with the French-speaking population that had settled there—a problem that grew in complexity as the number of British merchants and English-speaking immigrants to the colonies increased.

The American Revolution

In 1776, the southern colonies of British North America revolted against the British Crown in order to found the United States of America. Forty thousand Empire Loyalists—American colonists loyal to the Crown—sought refuge in the remaining British colonies, particularly in the Maritimes (where their influx resulted in the creation of the colony of New Brunswick in 1784) and in what is now Ontario.

The boundaries between the newly sovereign United States and the British colonies were gradually settled over the next century. The *Treaty of Paris* had established an approximate southern border for the new British acquisition of Québec between the Atlantic Ocean and the western tip of Lake of the Woods (now the Ontario–Manitoba border). Large parts of this border were subsequently adjusted by *Jay's Treaty* in 1794 and the *Webster-Ashburton Treaty* of 1842. The *Rush-Bagot Treaty* of 1817 clarified the boundary through the Great Lakes. In 1818, the *Treaty of London* fixed the westward border along the 49th parallel to the Rockies and paved the way for western settlement. The final step, to the Pacific Ocean around the southern tip of Vancouver Island, was determined by the *Oregon Treaty* of 1846. Two remaining treaties settled smaller land disputes: in 1872, the San Juan Islands were ceded to the United States, and the boundary between Alaska and British Columbia was finally agreed upon in 1903. British dominion over the Arctic Islands had passed to Canada in 1880.

These boundary agreements were all achieved without violence. The War of 1812–14, the single major hostile outbreak between the United States and Canada, was mostly an affirmation of US sovereignty against what was seen as British interference. The United States resented the British seizure of neutral US ships on the suspicion that they were trading with the French, with whom Britain was once again at war. As well, Americans accused British traders of arming and inciting a potential Indian rebellion in the US Midwest. Despite incursions by each side into the territory of the other, the *Treaty of Ghent* of 1814 left the pre-war boundaries intact. If the war achieved anything on the Canadian side, it was to lay the base for a future Canadian nationalism, as well as for the periodic upsurges of anti-Americanism that still come to the fore within Canadian political culture today.

Founding Nations and the Origins of Government in Canada

Relations between the British Crown and the Aboriginal population in British North America were, in the early colonial years, straightforward and accommodating. Before 1867, Aboriginals were seen as valuable allies who helped extend the fur trade to the Pacific, and in doing so helped define the boundary between Canada and the United States.[3] Later, they were allies in the struggle against threats of American incursion. The *Royal Proclamation of 1763* recognized Native land rights and described a rough Proclamation Line that divided hunting grounds from land that could be settled by Europeans. The Crown retained title to the land mass of Canada but recognized the right of Native peoples to use and occupy the land. The Proclamation did not, however, state the exact eastern or western extent of the reserved lands. It was a vague document that belied the harsh treatment Natives would later receive.

3. Randall White, *Voice of Region* (Toronto: Dundurn Press, 1990), p. 16 and ch. 2.

As settlements grew and pushed farther westward, the Crown undertook separate treaty negotiations with tribes that occupied different sections of land, striking bargains concerning land use. In 1830, Indian settlement on reserves commenced under government trusteeship, and efforts began to integrate Aboriginal peoples into non-Aboriginal society. Meanwhile, contact with Europeans was disrupting traditional Indian and Inuit ways of life, exposing them to European technology, religion, disease and death. Before Europeans arrived, there were roughly one million Native people in what is now Canada. By Confederation, only about 140 000 remained.

Among the Europeans, the cessation of hostilities with the United States allowed the British colonial administrators in Canada to return to the long-term problem of relations between the two European founding nations of British North America.[4] The intention of the British government in 1763 had been to promote immigration by English-speaking Protestant settlers and to assimilate the French-speaking Roman Catholic population as rapidly as possible. However, in the first few years, only about two hundred English families, mostly merchants, settled in the new colony. For this reason, neither of the first two British governors was prepared to establish the representative assembly in the new colony as promised in the *Royal Proclamation of 1763*. Such a body would have represented only the 600 English settlers and not the 90 000 French who, as Roman Catholics, were excluded from the franchise under British law at that time.

With the failure of the assimilation strategy and the growing realization that French Canadian loyalty might prove vital as the southern colonies became increasingly restive, Governor Carleton persuaded the British government to revise its policy toward Québec. The *Québec Act of 1774* withdrew the provision for an assembly, placing full authority in the hands of the governor and an appointed advisory council consisting of both English and French speakers. French culture was to be preserved. Neither language was specifically guaranteed, but Roman Catholics were allowed freedom of worship and the right to hold civil office. The Catholic Church was given official sanction, and both French civil law and the seigneurial landholding system were retained.

The French population warmly approved the *Québec Act*. Many English Canadians, on the other hand, resented it. The break in the tradition of representative government was anathema to many English-speaking colonists, who felt unjustly deprived of their right to a representative assembly and British civil law—rights to which they had grown accustomed. The English merchants were slightly mollified by the expansion of the colony's boundaries to encompass the rich fur-trading area between the Ohio and Mississippi Rivers—but most of that gain was soon lost under the *Treaty of Versailles*, which finally settled the American War of Independence in 1783.

Partly in response to demands from the Empire Loyalists who had settled in what is now Ontario, the British next attempted to satisfy both ethnic communities with the *Constitutional Act of 1791*. This Act maintained the commitment to the French culture established by the *Québec Act*, but within a new political context. The old colony of Québec was divided in two: Upper Canada, west of the Ottawa River, which was predominantly English-speaking; and Lower Canada, which was predominantly French. The right of representative government was now granted to each group, and, whereas French civil law and seigneurial landholding were retained in Lower Canada, English common law and freehold land tenure were established in Upper Canada. Thus, English Canadians outside Montréal were placated and the French Canadians were largely protected from absorption and conflict.

---

4. These are the people present from early settlement to 1867. It should be noted that the Western provinces were later settled largely by immigrants who were not of French, English or Aboriginal extraction. In this larger sense, Canada had many founding nations, including Ukrainians, Germans and a host of other ethnic groups, all of which often are included under the English-speaking umbrella.

This promising new arrangement deteriorated in only a few years. The appointed members of the governors' legislative councils often abused their privileged positions in order to enhance their personal wealth and power, and paid scant attention to the elected members of the assemblies. Political and social agitation began against Upper Canada's *Family Compact* and Lower Canada's *Château Clique*. Finally, open rebellion under the leadership of William Lyon Mackenzie in Upper Canada and Louis-Joseph Papineau in Lower Canada forced Britain to re-evaluate its policies once again.

In 1838, Lord Durham was dispatched to recommend a course of action. In Lower Canada, he found all the problems of the other British colonies, plus an ethnic war. Britain's approach, he decided, had been wrong; the colony of Canada should have remained united so that the French population gradually would have been assimilated. His recommendations included reverting to the pre-1791 union and granting responsible government.

The British government did not accept Durham's philosophy wholeheartedly; instead, it took a middle course. The *Union Act of 1840* re-established the two Canadas as one political unit (although each was to retain its own legal system), with English as the sole official language of record. Although Durham had recommended representation by population, the two former colonies were each granted 42 members in the new joint assembly. Canada West (formerly Upper Canada), with its lesser numbers, gladly accepted this equality of representation. Not surprisingly, however, a decade later, after rapid immigration had elevated its population to majority status, Canada West declared the allocation grossly unfair. Durham's other major recommendation, that the government be made responsible to the elected assembly, was not implemented in 1840, though it became effective in practice some eight years later. Also in 1848, the two languages were declared officially equal.

Perhaps because of the half-hearted adoption of Durham's recommendations, or because of the separation of the two Canadas fifty years earlier, relations between the two founding nations did not unfold as Durham had predicted. Repeated attempts to find a workable solution to the ethnic problem failed. From about 1849, government cabinets in the reunited colony included representatives from both ethnic groups. Rather than a single prime minister at the head of government, there were two party leaders, one from each group, as well as separate attorneys general to mirror the dual legal system. Some legislation applied to one or both; sometimes dual legislation was enacted. For a number of years, the capital of the colony even alternated between Toronto and Québec City, until Queen Victoria settled the problem by deciding on the (then) backwoods logging outpost of Bytown (now Ottawa).

The theory of co-operation was excellent, but the practice impossible. Soon, Montréal merchants in Canada East were openly supporting union with the United States, while George Brown's Reformers in Canada West demanded *rep by pop* (representation by population) and, eventually, a federal solution to the colony's governmental problems. Ethnic and religious antagonisms were exacerbated to such an extent that it became impossible for any government to retain the confidence of the assembly. By 1857, the government had reached an impasse. In their search for a compromise, French and English leaders came to embrace the goal of British North American unity.

Constitutional Compromise: The Grand Design

In decisive ways, Canadian Confederation was a response to events in the United States. In the mid-1860s, British–US relations were at a new low, and the Canadian colonies were isolated and vulnerable to attack. The US Civil War was drawing to a close and the army of the northern states would soon be available to attack Canada. Westward migration in the United States had become a threat to the political vacuum west of the colony of Canada. Furthermore, Britain had neither the resources nor the desire to protect these colonies from US aggression.

In 1864, therefore, after having discouraged for several years the efforts by those few Canadians who wished to have the issue of a federal union of British North America taken seriously (notably Macdonald, Cartier, Galt, Tupper, Tilley, Brown and McGee), the British government suddenly deemed it propitious to encourage Canadian unity and independence. It was recognized that if British North America were united it would be more economically viable and easier to defend and, as a self-governing dominion, more responsible for the costs of its own defence. New Brunswick and Canada, which shared long boundaries with the United States, supported a union, but Nova Scotia, which had no US border, was less easily persuaded.

The September 1864 Charlottetown Conference, instigated by the Nova Scotia premier, Dr. Charles Tupper, was originally called to discuss the prospects for Maritime union. The Canadians invited themselves and mischievously had the agenda changed to deal with their proposals for a larger entity. From the beginning, the Québec and Maritime leaders were adamant that the new arrangements should be federal in order to prevent Canada West from dominating the future dominion by virtue of its population. Despite his centrist tendencies, John A. Macdonald was willing to accept federalism rather than delay or thwart the project on this point. Thus, Charlottetown concluded with a basic agreement that the new larger union would be a federal arrangement and that another meeting would be held.[5]

The Québec Conference followed in October 1864 and, within 3 weeks, the leaders produced the 72 resolutions that provided the basis for Confederation. They concluded that "the sanction of the Imperial and Local Parliaments shall be sought for the Union of the Provinces on the principles adopted by the Conference."[6] The legislature of Canada debated and adopted the 72 resolutions by a 3-to-1 majority (with most of the "nays" coming from Canada East). But Canada was the only colony to approve the project formally. The government of New Brunswick called a general election and was soundly defeated. Premier Tupper, fearing similar unpopularity in Nova Scotia, avoided an assembly vote on the resolutions by introducing a motion to approve Maritime union. Prince Edward Island and Newfoundland rejected any association with the conference or its proposals. The Canadian group persevered, however, and took the results of the Québec Conference to London, where, this time, they received a sympathetic audience.

Although the colonies were by then internally self-governing, Britain retained direct influence over their policies through its colonial governors. Britain refused to consider Nova Scotia's stated preference for a Maritime union, and the governors of the Maritime colonies were instructed to sway their respective political executives in favour of the proposed wider confederation. By 1866, the legislatures of both Nova Scotia and New Brunswick (the latter now under threat of invasion from the United States by the Fenians)[7] had reconsidered their earlier dismissal of the Québec Resolutions and sought a renewal of consultations toward a union with Canada East and Canada West.

In December 1866, delegates from the three participating colonies incorporated the essence of the Québec Resolutions into an act of confederation at the Westminster Palace Conference in London. The *British North America Act* (*BNA Act*) was given royal assent on March 29, 1867, and came into effect three months later on July 1, 1867, without the colonies having any further opportunity to discuss or approve it.

5. See Figure 6.1 on page 196 in Chapter 6, "Contested Federalism," for further explanation of federal government, unitary government and confederation.

6. Quoted in R. MacGregor Dawson, *The Government of Canada*, 5th ed., revised by Norman Ward (Toronto: University of Toronto Press, 1970), p. 32.

7. The Fenian Brotherhood, an organization of Irish Americans, sought to pursue the cause of Irish independence by provoking war between Britain and the United States.

The *BNA Act* brought into formal existence the Dominion of Canada. In light of the continuing tensions between the English and French camps, it is somewhat ironic that their combined leadership provided the direct impetus for Confederation. The French Canadian leaders at that time supported the federal union, although there was some fear that the addition of the largely English-speaking Maritimes would further exaggerate the minority status of French Canadians within Canada. However, it was Nova Scotia, not French Canada, that welcomed Dominion Day in 1867 by draping the streets in black.

It should be noted that the Canadian people did not directly approve Confederation. There was no referendum or election to determine public sentiment, nor was the omission deemed significant at the time. Confederation grew out of the gentlemanly agreement of a few men united by a noble ideal regarding the type of political system most appropriate to achieving their common goals. In the final analysis, it was a series of external circumstances that eventually allowed the Fathers of Confederation to proceed on the path to statehood. Had these men not acted when they did, it is questionable whether the Canadian state ever would have existed. The Canadian colonies almost certainly would have been annexed or absorbed by the United States by the turn of the century. As one historian observed, "perhaps the most striking thing about Canada is that it is not part of the United States."[8]

The union of 1867 provided immediate solutions to three major problems facing the former colonies and the British government. The reorganization of the internal government of the United Provinces of Canada (by the creation of the separate provinces of Ontario and Québec) provided relief from the political impasse there. The threat of US invasion was allayed once Nova Scotia and, particularly, New Brunswick joined Canada and arrangements had been made to connect the provinces by rail. Lastly, the provisions made in the *British North America Act* to bring other territories into the union laid the basis for a "Dominion from sea to sea."

These tentative steps toward the development of a Canadian state were merely the beginning of a long and sometimes arduous process of territorial consolidation, national integration and state building.

The Land and the People

The concept of a country or state embodies four interrelated ideas:

- a clearly defined area or territory;
- a set of state (or political) institutions that governs the territory and maintains both internal and external sovereignty;
- a given population that is subject to the state; and
- a sense of common identity (*nationhood*) among that population.

The Dominion of Canada, founded by the *BNA Act* in 1867, was considerably smaller—in both area and population—than it is today. Consequently, before we examine the problems encountered by the new dominion in developing a sense of nationhood and attaining sovereign status, we need to understand the territorial and population expansion of Canada.

The Expansion of Territory and Borders

The territorial borders formulated at Confederation were gradually expanded and filled in over the succeeding years. In 1670, England's King Charles II had granted all the lands that drained into Hudson Bay to a company of that name. Eventually the company sold it to the Canadian government

---

8. J.B. Brebner, *Canada: A Modern History* (Ann Arbor: University of Michigan Press, 1960), p. ix.

for $300 000. In 1870, both Rupert's Land and the North-Western Territory were formally annexed to the Dominion (see Figure 2.1). In the same year, the Red River Colony (under the new name of Manitoba) became the first additional province in the union, although it was much smaller than it is today. Lured by the promise of permanent railway communications with Eastern Canada, British Columbia was admitted by imperial order-in-council in 1871. Two years later, the previously uninterested Prince Edward Island also decided to join the union.

The next major jurisdictional change occurred in 1905, when Alberta and Saskatchewan were carved out of a large portion of the Northwest Territories and granted provincial status. Seven years later, Manitoba, Ontario and Québec were allowed to annex more land from the territories to assume, more or less, their current forms. The tenth and final province, Newfoundland (now

FIGURE 2.1 Canada's Boundary Changes

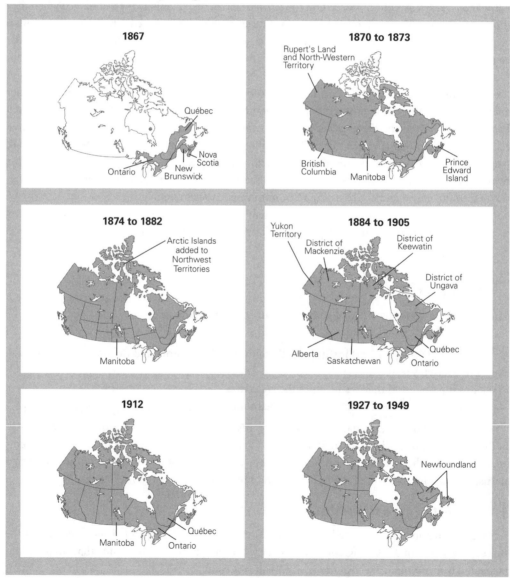

Source: Adapted from the Department of the Secretary of State of Canada, *Symbols of Nationhood* (Ottawa: Supply and Services, 1991), p. 16. Reproduced by authority of the Minister responsible for Statistics Canada, 1993.

officially Newfoundland and Labrador), entered the federation in 1949, 82 years after the original invitation and even then only after it held 2 referendums to decide its future.[9]

The rest of the land within the boundaries of the Canadian state, the Northwest Territories and the Yukon Territory (created out of a western strip of the Northwest Territories in 1898) remained under federal jurisdiction. In 1990, an agreement on the largest land claim in Canadian history gave about 18 000 Inuit ownership of an area about half the size of Alberta. As part of the bargain, they relinquished title to roughly 80 percent of their ancestral land claim. In return, they received the promise of self-government, a cash settlement of more than $1 billion over 14 years and title to 35 000 square kilometres of land in the eastern Arctic.

Shortly after, a political accord made provisions to divide the Northwest Territories and create a new territory, Nunavut (meaning "our land" in Inuktitut). This was accomplished in April 1999 (see Figure 2.2). In 2008, the Nunavut government achieved full political powers along the lines of the Northwest Territories legislature in Yellowknife. Inuit constitute about 85 percent of the new territory's population, so they have attained virtual self-government. However, now less than half the population of the Northwest Territories (which previously had a 61 percent Native majority) consists of Native peoples (Dene, Métis and Inuit).

Canada's external boundaries have therefore changed very little since shortly after Confederation. Except for the 1949 addition of Newfoundland, all of Canada's current territory was formally part of the Dominion by 1882. Since then, the territorial development of the Canadian state has been primarily a process of internal adjustment. However, this process is not

FIGURE 2.2 **Map of Nunavut: Canada's Newest Territory**

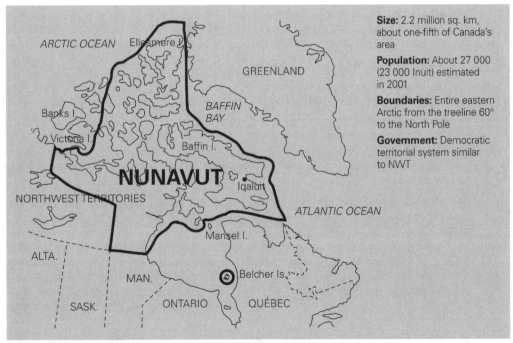

Nunavut—the new territory carved from the Northwest Territories in 1999. The division created three northern territories: Yukon Territory, Northwest Territories and Nunavut. The area of Nunavut is twice the size of British Columbia, but its entire population would fill less than half of Vancouver's 60 000-seat BC Place.

9. See Henry B. Mayo, "Newfoundland's Entry into the Dominion," *CJEPS*, vol. 15, no. 4 (November 1949), pp. 505–22.

necessarily complete. Internally, for example, there is a lingering boundary dispute between Québec and Labrador. Québec has never accepted the 1927 decision of Britain's Judicial Committee of the Privy Council (JCPC) that gave more than 260 000 square kilometres of Labrador to Newfoundland. Externally, maritime boundaries have taken on new importance in recent years, with ownership of potentially huge reserves of offshore oil and natural gas at stake.

Some significant changes occurred regarding maritime boundaries in the 1970s. Following incidents with a US oil tanker early in that decade, Canada extended its territorial waters from 3 miles to 12 miles—so that waters within 12 miles attained the legal status of land (except for the right of innocent passage for foreign ships). In 1970, the *Arctic Waters Pollution Prevention Act* unilaterally gave Canada the right to create environmental regulations in Arctic waters in a zone within 100 miles from the nearest Canadian land (but did not provide sovereign control). Then in 1977, Canada declared a 200-mile Exclusive Economic Zone, including an exclusive fishing zone.

CLOSE-UP ON
Boundary Disputes

CANADA'S NORTHERN SOVEREIGNTY IN DOUBT?

Canada's borders are not as secure as one might think. Canada currently has four border disputes in the North, and they are escalating as the warming climate makes Arctic waters more navigable and natural resources more accessible. There is considerable prestige and resource wealth at stake. A US survey estimated that the Arctic seabed accounts for up to a quarter of the world's undiscovered oil and gas.*

In 2004, the federal government launched a five-year plan to march soldiers through all of its uninhabited Arctic territory, and enhance satellite surveillance in order to exert Canadian sovereignty over it. In 2007, Prime Minister Stephen Harper earmarked $3.1 billion for six to eight patrol ships capable of operating in ice up to a metre thick. The government also announced plans to have a deep water port on the north end of Baffin Island to base and service the ships and an army training centre in the region for the army and the Canadian Rangers—the latter being part-time reservists (largely Inuit) who provide a small military presence by conducting patrols in northern areas.

The four boundary disputes are as follows:

1. Canada and Denmark both claim Hans Island, a tiny, barren island in the Arctic between Canada's Ellesmere Island and Greenland. It is only a kilometre wide and 3 kilometres long. Danish frigates can navigate the ice to get there; Canadian frigates can't.

2. Canada and the United States disagree over the maritime boundary between the Yukon and Alaska, a potentially rich resource area.

3. Canada is engaged in a dispute with the United States, Japan and the European Community over the status of the Northwest Passage. Canada considers it to be part of its internal water system, while the others say it is an international strait open to all.

4. Canada, Denmark and Russia all have overlapping claims in the polar region. The Danes hope to prove that the Lomonosov Ridge, an underwater mountain range, attaches the Danish territory of Greenland to the North Pole. Russian scientists claim to have discovered a ridge from the Russian continental shelf underwater for 1500 kilometres past the North Pole and Ellesmere Island. But, since Canada has not yet mapped its Arctic and continental shelves, it can't be sure whose claims are correct. Canadian efforts to do so are ongoing, so that the government may lay claim under international treaty to submarine territory.

As of early 2008, before the new bases are operational, Canada's northern force consists of occasional army patrols, a joint-service task force of 150 soldiers and civilians that flies surveillance missions and coordinates ground patrols in the North and the Canadian Rangers.

The Globe and Mail, Friday, August 3, 2007, p. A12.

These rights have been sanctioned by The United Nations Convention on the Law of the Sea (UNCLOS), although the boundaries are contested where overlapping claims exist. UNCLOS had 155 signators as of July 2007 (including Canada, but not the US). The treaty establishes navigational rules and sets out countries' rights to minerals and fish 200 nautical miles off their coastlines. It also allows states to claim territory based on the undersea extent of their continental shelves.

In the North, Canada has four ongoing international territorial disputes (see the "Close-Up on Boundary Disputes: Canada's Northern Sovereignty in Doubt?"). Five countries—Canada, Denmark, Norway, Russia and the United States—all have claims to Arctic Ocean frontage.

Population Growth

At the time of Confederation, the population of the member provinces totalled approximately 3.5 million people. The number of Canadians has steadily increased to 31.6 million as recorded in the 2006 Census. As the size of the population has grown, so, too, has its ethnic diversity. Today, Canada is generally regarded as a multi-ethnic or multicultural society, a view given formal recognition in the *Constitution Act* of 1982 (see Chapter 5).

Even when referring to the time of Confederation, it would be a misleading oversimplification to see Canada's population purely in terms of the two founding European nations or, as John Porter labelled them, "the charter groups."[10] For one thing, the English-speaking segment was by no means homogeneous, consisting as it did of immigrants from England, Scotland and Ireland, the descendants of the Empire Loyalists and many subsequent settlers from the United States who had migrated north in search of farmland or employment offered by the economic expansion of Canada West.

Second, as the Census of 1871 illustrates, although members of the two charter groups constituted over 90 percent of Canada's population at that time, representatives of other ethnic groups had already arrived or had been previously established in the new dominion. In addition to the Native peoples, both Indian and Inuit (roughly 0.7 percent of the total population), there were nearly 30 000 Dutch (0.9 percent), over 200 000 Germans (5.8 percent) and a smattering of other ethnic minorities, including some African Americans and First Nations allies (chiefly in Nova Scotia and southwestern Ontario), who had arrived with the Loyalist influx.

Since Confederation, the population of Canada has grown rapidly through a combination of natural increase (the excess of births over deaths in any given period); a generally high rate of immigration; and, to a lesser degree, the incorporation of new territory (for instance, approximately 360 000 people were added to Canada's population by the accession of Newfoundland in 1949).

Immigration patterns over the past century (see Figure 2.3 on the next page) have made Canada a truly multicultural society. In 1871, 61 percent of the population was of British origin, and 31 percent French. In the 2001 Census, only 14 percent of Canadians who claimed a single ethnic heritage said they were of British origin, and 6 percent said French. Apart from these two large groups, the census also categorized over two hundred smaller ethnic groups. Until about forty years ago, most immigrants came from Europe, but now a larger number come from Asia than from any other location.

Furthermore, Canada is a "nation of many tongues." Although the 2001 Census showed that roughly 82 percent of Canadians claimed English or French as the language first learned in the home, the remaining 18 percent cited over 100 other languages. The integration of this multicultural and multilingual population into a Canadian society that seeks to have a common sense of national identity and political community has posed additional challenges for the development of the state.

---

10. John Porter, *The Vertical Mosaic: An Analysis of Social Class and Power in Canada* (Toronto: University of Toronto Press, 1965), p. 60 ff.

FIGURE 2.3 **Immigrants as a Percentage of Total Population, 1901–2001**

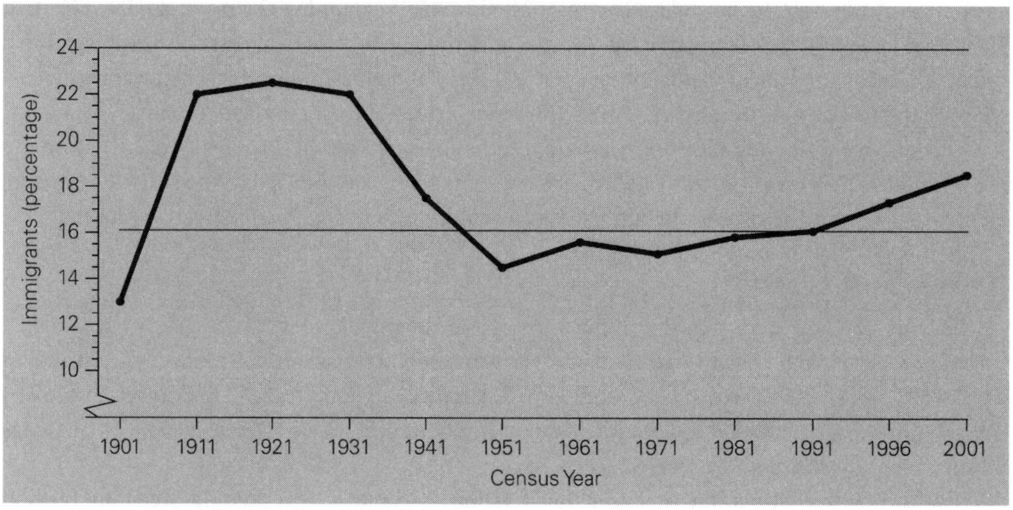

Source: Reproduced from Statistics Canada, *The Daily*, Catalogue 11-001, December 8, 1992, and updated with census data from 2001.

Demographic Trends

The 2006 Census showed that Canada's population grew by 5.4 percent in the five years since the preceding Census. Roughly two-thirds of the country's population growth now comes from immigration; one-third comes from the natural increase of births over deaths. The vast majority of the population growth took place in metropolitan areas, two-thirds of it in Alberta and Ontario, and nearly all of the remaining third was in British Columbia and Québec. Growth rates higher than the national average were concentrated in southern Ontario, Québec, British Columbia and the Calgary–Edmonton corridor in Alberta. More than four-fifths of Canadians now live in urban centres. The rural population increased by 1 percent in 2001–2006, with rural areas close to urban centres growing much more than remote ones (see Table 2.1).

The population, therefore, is extremely concentrated and highly urban—more than 80 percent of Canadians, nearly 25 million people, lived in urban centres in 2006. The urbanization rate has been rising since 1931. It is concentrated in three ways: more than 90 percent live in a 320-kilometre strip along the Canada–United States border; about 60 percent live in Central Canada in Ontario and Québec (see Figure 2.4); and over three-quarters live in metropolitan areas. In 2006, Canada had six metropolitan areas with more than one million inhabitants—Toronto, Montréal, Vancouver, Ottawa-Gatineau, Calgary and Edmonton.

CLOSE-UP ON Demographics

SHOULD THE CITIZENSHIP OATH BE REVISED?

Canadian citizenship was created in 1947. Before that, Canadians were subjects of the United Kingdom's monarch, and immigrants took an oath of allegiance to the British Crown in order to become citizens. After 1947, the oath was adapted to include, "…and that I will faithfully observe the laws of Canada and fulfill my duties as a Canadian citizen."

The current oath came into effect in 1977 as part of the *Citizenship Act:*

I swear (or affirm) that I will be faithful and bear true allegiance to Her Majesty Queen Elizabeth the Second, Queen of Canada, Her Heirs and Successors, and that I will faithfully observe the laws of Canada and fulfill my duties as a Canadian citizen.

Jean Chrétien's government attempted to change the citizenship oath by eliminating the reference to the Queen and her heirs and successors. It passed through second reading in the House of Commons but then was dropped from the Order Paper.

Should the oath of allegiance be revised or left as it is?

TABLE 2.1 **Population Growth in Canada by Region Type, 2001 to 2006**

Regions	2001	2006	Growth (in percentage)
Metropolitan areas (CMA) and mid-size urban centres (CA)	24 084 698	25 631 557	6.4
Total of rural regions and small towns	5 922 396	5 981 340	1.0
Rural regions close to urban centres	1 289 265	1 350 098	4.7
Remote rural regions	4 578 298	4 571 530	−0.1
Territories	54 833	59 712	8.9
Canada	30 007 094	31 612 897	5.4

Source: Adapted from Statistics Canada, censuses population, 2001 and 2006. Accessed April 17, 2007, from www12.statcan.ca/english/census06/analysis/popdwell/tables/table8.htm.

Three basic variables affect demography: fertility, mortality and immigration. As in other developed countries, Canadian fertility rates began to decline in 1961 after the baby boom of the late 1940s and 1950s. In 2006, the average number of births per Canadian woman was 1.5, well below the 2.1 children per woman needed to sustain the country's population. By way of comparison, in 1956 the average number of births per woman was four. High fertility rates correlate with several different variables: women who marry young, remain married, live in rural areas, are not well educated and work in the home. Given current social patterns, these variables indicate that low fertility rates will continue in the near future. For example, the average age of marriage in 2001 was 29 compared to 25 in 1956.

Mortality rates have also changed dramatically. The average life expectancy at Confederation was about 45; in 2006, it was closer to 80. Women live roughly 5 years longer than men (82.5 and 77.7 years, on average, respectively). Life expectancy for women is still increasing, but men are living longer, closing the gap. The lowest life expectancy correlates with a few specific groups: unskilled and blue-collar workers, the unmarried and Native Indians. The population is aging, however, which means the annual number of deaths is increasing.

Immigrants play a vital role in Canada's development. Population projections show that, if current trends continue, net immigration could become the only source of population growth by

FIGURE 2.4 **Population Distribution in Canada, 1956 and 2006**

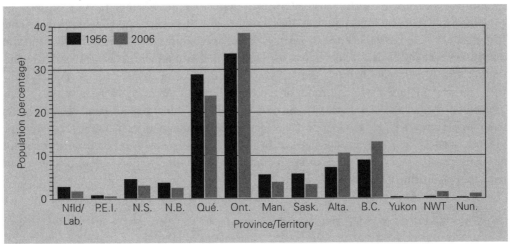

Source: Adapted from Statistics Canada, http://www12.statcan.ca/English/census06/analysis/popdwell/tables/table1.htm.

about 2030. Canada has one of the largest proportions of foreign-born residents of any country in the world. Recent immigrants are more educated and urbanized when they arrive than previous immigrants were; when they settle in Canada, they settle in cities; and they are producing fewer children than earlier waves of immigrants. If fertility rates remain at 1.5 children per woman and mortality and immigration continue at today's annual rate of 240 000, the population will not decline in the next 50 years and can be projected to be at 43 million by the year 2056.

Internal migration, too, plays an important role in Canada's demography. Canada has a very mobile population, enabling swift population changes in response to challenging economic circumstances, although a small minority of the population does most of the migrating. Emigration has also been a significant factor in recent years. During the 1990s, almost half a million Canadians left the country as part of a *brain drain* to higher-paying jobs in the United States and elsewhere.

In overall composition, Canada's population is now middle-aged and getting older rapidly. In 1881,

> ## CLOSE-UP ON
> ## Demographics
>
> ### STRATEGIES TO DEAL WITH A SHRINKING POPULATION
>
> Without immigrants, Canada's population would be shrinking. The government has some options, but all have implications for Canadians. Which of the following strategies would you advise them to try?
>
> - do nothing; let the population shrink
> - keep increasing immigration
> - launch a massive public-relations campaign to convince women to have more babies
> - provide bigger baby bonuses
> - give free daycare
> - allow generous parental leaves
> - keep people in the work force longer
>
> Do you have a different idea?
>
> Of all the provinces, Québec has the most generous parental-leave package, and it also has an inexpensive daycare program. Births in that province increased in 2006 for the first time in many years.

the median age was 20; by 2006, it was 39.5, an all-time high.[11] This trend is due mainly to the low birth rate and greater longevity. The number of Canadians aged 65 and older in 2006 was 17.7 percent, a rise of 1.5 percent from 1996. But only 13.7 percent of the population is aged 14 or under, a drop of 2.8 percent since 1996. The percentage of the population in the age bracket of 15–64 is 68.6 percent, and the fastest-growing group within that population is the oldest, the 55 to 64 year olds. This means that fewer and fewer workers are supporting more and more elderly people. If this continues, in the near future we can expect labour shortages, higher wages, lower unemployment, rising health-care costs and other social and employment adjustments as more people leave the work force than enter it (see Figure 2.5).

For a more complete picture of the Canadian population, these demographic facts must be combined with social stratification data. This is discussed in detail in Chapter 4, but here we note that social class can be characterized by such variables as economic circumstances, education and occupation. Canadians as a whole have experienced an absolute increase in real wealth in this century, and, as we saw in Chapter 1, they are also very well off compared to citizens of other countries. This rosy picture masks a plethora of problems, however. An aging population causes new problems of inequalities of opportunity and distribution of wealth in Canada (see Figure 2.6).[12] As older people retire, a bigger economic burden falls on the remaining workers. By 2041, almost one in four Canadians will be of pensionable age. In anticipation of problems, the federal government has made changes to the old-age security program and issued dire warnings about future benefit reductions and rising health-care costs.

---

11. Median age is the point where exactly one-half of the population is older and the other half is younger.

12. See David Fort, "Awakening the Intergenerational Equity Debate in Canada," *Journal of Canadian Studies*, Spring 2005. Available online at http://findarticles.com/p/articles/mi_qa3683.

FIGURE 2.5 **The Senior Boom and the Baby Bust: Canada's Population Trends Over 65 and Under 15**

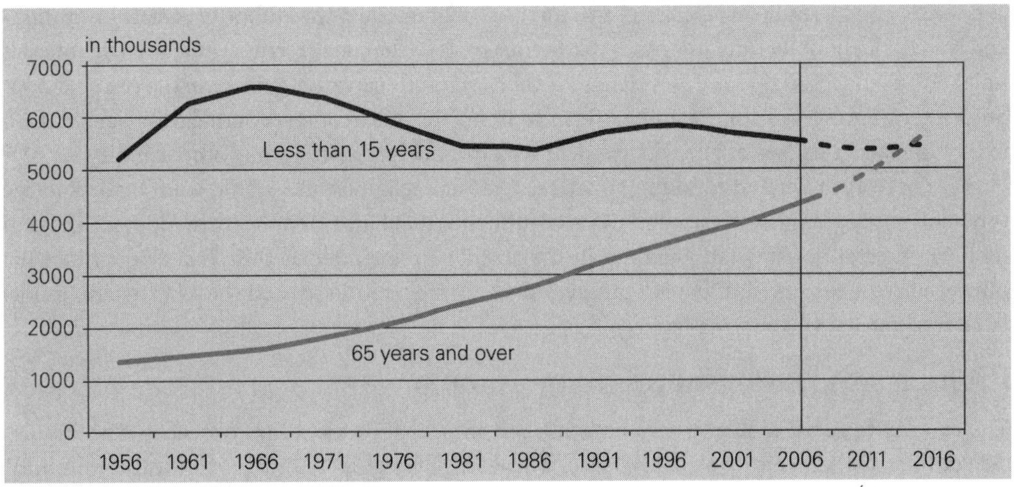

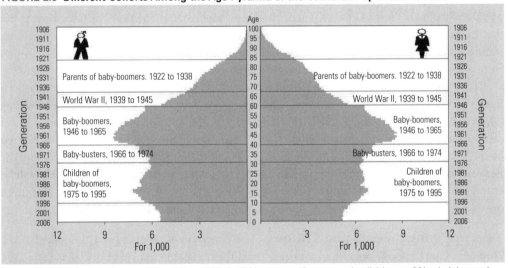

Source: Statistics Canada, censuses of population, 1956 to 2006; and Alain Bélanger, Laurent Martel and Éric Caron-Malenfant. 2005. *Population Projections for Canada, Provinces and Territories 2005–2031*, Statistics Canada Catalogue no. 91-520, scenario 3. Available at www12.statcan.ca/english/census06/analysis/agesex/charts/chart1.htm.

FIGURE 2.6 **Different Cohorts Among the Age Pyramid of the Canadian Population in 2006**

Source: Statistics Canada, Census of Population, 2006. Available at www12.statcan.ca/english/census06/analysis/agesex/charts/chart7.htm.

Developing a Canadian National Identity

Most analysts agree that two factors—successful national integration and a clearly defined and legitimate role for the state—are prerequisites for the emergence of stable political systems.[13] In ideal terms, the development of a sense of national identity among the inhabitants of a territorial state increases the sense of loyalty and legitimacy accruing to that state. The state thus replaces region, church or ethnic group as the primary focus of citizen allegiance, reducing the number and intensity of potential sources of conflict within the population.

13. For example, Gabriel Almond and G. Bingham Powell, *Comparative Politics: A Developmental Approach* (Boston: Little, Brown, 1966). For more recent literature extending this idea to multiculturalism and the state, see Will Kymlicka and Wayne Norman, eds., *Citizenship in Diverse Societies* (New York: Oxford University Press, 2000).

The establishment of the second factor—called *state building*—similarly involves integration and consolidation. Again, in ideal terms, the imposition of the supreme authority of state institutions and laws throughout the land integrates the various parts of the state's territory into a single cohesive unit and guarantees its domestic sovereignty—that is, its authority over and above the rival claims of other internal sources of political influence. In addition, the state requires external sovereignty, which frees it to manage its own affairs, independent of constraints imposed by any other country.

We have already referred to the historical, regional, religious and ethnic conflicts and to the problems of geographic diversity and external influence that hampered the formation of a sense of national integration and state building in Canada. The remainder of this chapter examines the impact of these factors on Canada's progress since Confederation toward the *ideal-typical* model of an integrated and sovereign modern state.

Problems of Nation Building in Canada

The concept of national identity is rather like a coin in that it, too, bears two sides. The "heads" side of the national identity coin consists of a sense of belonging to a single political community, while the "tails" side represents a sense of distinctiveness from all other peoples. In different countries and different periods, one side or the other will predominate. It sometimes seems that in Canada there is a distinct bias in favour of tails.

On one side of the coin, the emergence of a Canadian identity has largely involved a process of differentiation from the United Kingdom and the United States. The need for Canadians to cut the colonial ties that bound them to the United Kingdom in the nineteenth and early twentieth centuries has more recently transformed into the problem of establishing a Canadian identity and culture that is distinct from that of the United States.

The other side of the coin, the development of a sense of belonging together, has been hindered by several obstacles: the historic conflict between English-speaking and French-speaking Canadians; the definition of a satisfactory relationship with Native peoples; the integration of minority ethnic groups into the community; and the pervasive effects of regionalism, exacerbated by the federal nature of the political system, the uneven distribution of economic activity and the peculiar configuration of settlement in Canada. Many aspects of each of these problems will be examined in greater detail in other parts of the book (notably, Chapters 3, 4, 6 and 7), but an overview linking the various obstacles to nation building in Canada is provided here.

External Impediments and Politics   The American Revolution and the influx of the Empire Loyalists into the northern colonies marked the initial differentiation of Canada from the United States, based on loyalty to the British Crown and Empire. The identification with Britain was further strengthened by the successful defence of Canada in the War of 1812 and by massive immigration from Britain in the next few decades.

Canadian Confederation was "largely a response to the American presence; as a defence strategy, as imitation, and as a general alternative."[14] Faced with a potentially expansionist United States, the Fathers of Confederation were motivated by "the fear of slow death by absorption and a quick one by annexation [that] hung over Canadian constitutional debates."[15] The British, for their part, were increasingly unwilling to devote resources to the defence of their North American

---

14. John H. Redekop, "Continentalism: The Key to Canadian Politics," in Redekop, ed., *Approaches to Canadian Politics*, 2nd ed. (Scarborough, ON: Prentice Hall, 1983), p. 35.

15. Janet Morchain, *Sharing a Continent* (Toronto: McGraw-Hill Ryerson, 1973), p. 108.

colonies and were happy to give them self-government. Indeed, for many Canadians of British stock, the new Canadian nationality created at Confederation did not negate continued loyalty to the British Empire—a dual allegiance remained widespread, although dwindling, among English Canadians up to the First World War.

After 1920, this duality gradually declined in favour of a more exclusive identification with Canada. Growing national consciousness was bolstered by the adoption of specifically Canadian national symbols such as the Maple Leaf flag to replace the Red Ensign, the substitution of "O Canada" for "God Save the Queen" as Canada's national anthem and the patriation of the Constitution. A degree of imperial and monarchical sentiment lives on, partly because of reinforcement by continued immigration from the United Kingdom and by the activities of organizations such as the Imperial Order of the Daughters of the Empire and the Monarchist League, and partly because remnants of the Tory and Empire Loyalist traditions remain as components of Canadian political culture. A movement to depose the Queen as head of state and to make Canada a republic has never taken hold here as it has in Australia. But these elements aside, the separation of Canadian national identity from British influence is complete.

For many Canadians, there is a more pressing need today to assert Canada's distinctness from the United States. Concern is directed toward the economic and cultural penetration of Canada by its much larger neighbour. Economic relations, including Canada's trade dependence on the United States, US ownership of much of Canadian industry and natural resources, and the impact of economic interdependence promoted by the North American Free Trade Agreement (NAFTA) are among the major foreign policy issues examined in detail in Chapter 15. But just as important for many Canadians, and more pertinent to the present discussion, is the issue of cultural independence from the United States.

It is, of course, difficult to separate the economic from the cultural dimensions of Canada–US relations, since the concern for cultural independence seems to mirror economic realities. Since the Second World War, the United States has been responsible for well over 70 percent of foreign investment in Canada—in some quarters, this has been viewed as a major cultural threat. Concern over assimilation into the United States, or continental North American culture, waxes and wanes. The proximity of most Canadians to the border with the United States, the existence of a shared language, the relative size of the two populations and the penetration of Canadian society by US mass media are all viewed as potential threats to the emergence or maintenance of a distinct Canadian identity. A determination to resist total cultural assimilation remains a fundamental component of the Canadian national identity.

Internal Impediments and Politics There are several *internal* impediments to nation building in Canada, all of which have been present in different degrees since 1867.

Charter Groups First, harsh conflicts between French and English Canadians have surfaced on numerous occasions since Confederation. The execution of Louis Riel, the conscription crises of 1917 and 1944, the October Crisis of 1970, the exclusion of Québec from the constitutional settlement of 1982 and the failure to resolve the constitutional dilemma with either the Meech Lake Accord or Charlottetown Accord are among the low points in relations between the two charter groups (for details, see Chapters 5, 6 and 7). No satisfactory long-term *modus vivendi* has ever been apparent between the founding nations. Today, the Parti Québécois and the Bloc Québécois officially espouse separation from the Canadian state and the foundation of an independent, sovereign state of Québec. As of the Québec election in 2007, all three of the major political parties in the province favoured "autonomy" in various guises.

Non-Charter Groups A second impediment concerns the integration of non-charter ethnic groups into Canadian society. To a degree, government policies and popular support for multiculturalism have allowed ethnic minorities to preserve their own cultural identities and heritage while becoming part of Canada's social tapestry. The general pattern has been for immigrants to concur with the norms of their host society and for the host society to accept them. However, both institutionalized (governmental) discrimination and public racism, even racial violence, have surfaced at various periods of Canadian history.

Perhaps the most disruptive impact of minority ethnic groups on nation building in Canada has occurred with respect to the French–English relationship. The fact that, until recently, the majority of new immigrants have tended to learn English rather than French as their first official language, even in Montréal, has augmented the minority status of French-speaking Canadians in Canada and exacerbated relations between the two charter groups (see Chapters 3 and 7).

Native Peoples A third impediment to nation building concerns Canada's Native peoples. For a long time, they were deliberately excluded from the nation-building process. The expansion of the Canadian colonies and state in the nineteenth century brought Native and European groups into direct competition for possession of land. Following the conquest of Québec, the British authorities made repeated attempts to accommodate the interests of the French-speaking population, but they demonstrated little regard for the rights and customs of Canada's Native peoples. Successive colonial and, later, dominion administrations deprived the Indians of their land (by fair means or foul) as part of the process of opening up Western Canada for settlement and railway construction,

Nation-state building requires political co-operation.

Rodewalt illustration, originally published in *Policy Options*.

herding them onto reserves and subjecting them to the draconian, paternalistic measures of the nineteenth-century Indian acts (see Chapter 3).

Although some of the more discriminatory provisions of the legislation pertaining to Native people have since been relaxed—for example, after 1960 Indians on reserves were at last allowed to vote in federal elections—status Indians still occupy a dependent, quasi-colonial position vis-à-vis the federal government. Non-status Indians and Métis who attempt integration into mainstream society usually find themselves among the poor and underprivileged sections of the Canadian population, and are often subjected to discrimination and racial stereotyping.

Because of their geographical isolation, the Inuit were largely bypassed in the process of nation building and modernization until roughly five decades ago. Like status Indians, the Inuit, until 1950, were explicitly excluded from the federal franchise. Even then, many Inuit living in the high Arctic could not actually exercise their right to vote until 1963, following the creation of a new parliamentary riding covering the entire Northwest Territories. From 1953 to 1962, there was a constituency of Mackenzie River, which excluded the territorial districts of Keewatin and Franklin. From 1963 to 1979, the Northwest Territories riding covered all three districts. After the 1979 general election, the NWT was represented by two members of Parliament, one for Western Arctic and one for Nunatsiaq. In addition, in 1975 the NWT and Yukon were finally given representation in the Senate—one senator each. Finally, in 1999, when Nunavut and its new government were inaugurated, the new territory was represented in the federal Parliament by one MP (the former Nunatsiaq representative) and one senator (like the other territories).

During the past five decades, the Inuit have been forced into coexistence with an advanced industrial society within the Canadian state. Their traditional lifestyle has been encroached upon by attempts to develop Arctic energy and other mineral resources and by the construction of radar stations and other military installations. Many Inuit, like the other Native groups, are resentful of the disruption of their customary mode of life by modernization and economic development.

For Native organizations such as the Inuit Tapirisat of Canada or the Dene Nation, minority status and the lack of institutionalized channels have made it difficult to compete within the established mechanisms of federal–provincial negotiation. It is perhaps not surprising that some Native groups feel themselves to be non-participants in the Canadian state, and actively oppose further modernization and development.

Regionalism Fourth in this examination of the impediments to nation building in Canada is regionalism. Regionalism is not a new phenomenon in Canada. Even in pre-Confederation days there was little contact among the colonies of British North America. The events leading up to the establishment of the Dominion of Canada suggest profound regional differences in attitudes toward the founding of the state. Today, well into the second century of Confederation, many of those differences and local interests continue to exist.

The persistence of regionalism within the Canadian state can be ascribed to such factors, as the sheer size of the country, the different historical backgrounds of the provinces as well as their populations, and the uneven development of economic activity across Canada. The regions have separate economic interests to advance and protect. Thus, there are several economic bases for regional conflict: oil-producing versus oil-consuming regions, agricultural versus industrial areas and resource-rich versus poorer provinces, among others.

Another factor that promotes regionalism in Canada is the country's peculiar pattern of settlement, with about 90 percent of the population clustered within a strip 320 kilometres wide, extending

16. Richard Simeon, "Regionalism and Canadian Political Institutions," in J.P. Meekison, ed., *Canadian Federalism: Myth or Reality*, 3rd ed. (Toronto: Methuen, 1977), pp. 301–2.

along the US border. One result is that, unlike in many other Western societies, there is no single centre of population concentration to serve as a cultural and economic core. Nor is there a dominant city in Canada. Rather, Canada has a *polycephalic* city network, with several regional centres (Halifax, Montréal, Toronto, Winnipeg, Calgary, Vancouver, etc.) as the political, economic, social and cultural nexuses for the populations clustered around them. Instead of possessing a single metropolis dominating and easing the integration of the peripheries of the state (such as Paris and London), Canada consists of a series of core–periphery (or city–hinterland) relationships that divide the country into more or less self-contained regions and communication networks.

Even within Central Canada (Ontario and Québec), which is sometimes portrayed as the centre in relation to the peripheries of east and west, no dominant city emerges. Ottawa is the political capital of Canada, but little else; Toronto is the economic and cultural centre of Ontario, as well as a provincial capital; Montréal is the economic core of Québec and the cultural centre for French Canadians; Québec City, instead of Ottawa, is increasingly viewed as the political capital by Québec nationalists. Clearly, none of these can claim to dominate Central Canada, let alone the whole country.

The federal system of government compounds the effect of this core–periphery network. The fact that regional interests are primarily articulated by provincial governments in competition with each other and with the federal government is chiefly responsible for the frequent equation of *regions* with *provinces* in Canada. But provincial governments exaggerate differences between regions and understate intra-regional variations. Richard Simeon, for one, has argued that the provincial governments have a "vested interest in maintaining and strengthening the salience of the regional dimension"; each one, therefore, "is motivated to accentuate the degree of internal unity, and to exaggerate the extent of difference with Ottawa."[16] Thus, while Canada's federal system was intended to reflect and take into account the diversity among the original provinces, it has perpetuated, institutionalized and exacerbated regional differences and conflicts among the members of the Canadian federation.

A final factor contributing to the persistence of *regional particularism* in Canada is the relatively weak, nationally oriented mass media. Where the media focus is on local news about political and social issues, there is little opportunity for the consumer to acquire knowledge about other parts of the country or to learn what people elsewhere think about his own region. Despite their best efforts, the Canadian mass media have provided only a minimum integrative force (see Chapter 4).

We conclude that a number of factors combine to ensure the persistence of regionally based attitudes and interests in Canada: the sheer size of the country, historical patterns of ethnic settlement, variations in economic activity and wealth, uneven population distribution and the polycephalic city network, the institutionalization of regional differences by the federal system and the vested interests of provincial governments, and the lack of information and awareness of the regions of Canada about one another and about national affairs. The results are that Canadians often do not share a strong sense of belonging together, and regional or provincial interests frequently take precedence over those of the state.

Nation Building and Contemporary Politics

Canadians today, on the whole, accept the diversity of their country. Increasing cultural and religious heterogeneity has brought some clashes and soul searching about what constitutes "reasonable accommodations" by mainstream societies in recent years. However, issues are being resolved peacefully, and in courts where necessary (see Chapter 3). The willingness to accept diversity may well be one of the distinguishing marks of the Canadian national identity—a contrast to the pressures toward conformity that characterize many other national cultures, in particular the United States. However, potential dangers lie in store for the Canadian state when latent cleavages become politicized.

Some of the most vitriolic debates among Canadian politicians, including the long, drawn-out and bitter wrangling over the Constitution, reflect the persistence of divisions among regions and between the two founding nations. Concern about anglophone oppression—real, perceived or reconstructed—fuels the nationalist aspirations of the groups that wish to lead Québec out of Confederation. Based on a sense of physical and political marginality, similar resentment against "the centre" or "the East" underlies potential problems in the West. A combination of regional economic disparities, perceived historical grievances and (in some cases) physical remoteness often exacerbates tensions among the provinces and with the federal government.

Relations between the various levels of government and Native populations also reflect what might be called "the unfinished nation-building process" of contemporary politics. The relative isolation of most indigenous groups, whether on reserves or in the Far North, is gradually being ameliorated by the expansion of state activity and by the ongoing process of economic development. Native people have increasingly been drawn into the mainstream of economic and political life. As they have become more politicized, they have introduced new political issues that governments need to address. Pressures for, and conflict over, self-government and the settlement of Native land claims are likely to continue throughout this century.

In a country as large and diverse as Canada, it may be unrealistic to expect the process of nation building to eradicate all differences or disparities. As we argue in Chapter 3, certain over-arching values and attitudes shared by all Canadians have developed that counterbalance the potentially disintegrative effects of ethnic and regional differences. But the historic rivalries remain. In Chapters 6 and 7, we discuss in detail the continued impact of these divisions upon the contemporary politics of Canadian federalism. Perhaps, when all is said and done, one of the fascinations of Canadian politics is that the country has survived for as long as it has, despite the persistence of strains and conflicts left unresolved in the nation-building process.

The Development of the Canadian State

Although the boundaries of the Dominion of Canada were defined early in its history, the acquisition of sovereignty over the territory they enclosed was a somewhat slower process. We saw in Chapter 1 that sovereignty is defined in terms of power, both external and internal. A state is considered *sovereign* when final authority rests in the national government so that internally it is able to tax and coerce its citizens, and externally it can conduct relations with the international community free from outside interference by other states and governments.

The major task initially was to establish external sovereignty. This process was naturally linked to Canada's gradual acquisition of independence from Britain. In fact, the goal of external sovereignty existed even before Confederation, as the elected assemblies of the British North American colonies strove for responsible self-government within the context of Britain's colonial administration. Progress was slow. In the early years, these assemblies were dominated by their respective governors and their appointed executive and legislative councils.

By the time Lord Durham recommended the political union of Upper and Lower Canada under "responsible government" in his 1838 report, the governors' powers were under strenuous attack. Although the British government implemented the first of Lord Durham's recommendations, the *Act of Union*, the second, responsible government, was initially ignored. The first governor of the new united colony of Canada, Lord Sydenham, combined his gubernatorial duties with those of prime minister and leader of his own party of adherents, appealing directly to the population to provide his followers with a majority in assembly elections. This practice was followed by other colonial governors and eventually proved to be counterproductive, since elections confirmed that power resided, in part at least, in the people, and not solely in the Crown. *Representative government* thus arrived slowly with the acceptance that the legislative branch must be representative of the citizenry.

In 1846, a change in the British government produced an administration more sympathetic to responsible government in the colonies, and newly appointed governors of Canada and Nova Scotia were instructed in 1847 to select their councils from the leaders of the majority factions or parties in their respective assemblies. Within a year, non-confidence motions that passed in the popular assemblies resulted in changes of ministries in united Canada, Nova Scotia and New Brunswick.

In this fashion, the principle of **responsible government**, whereby the governor retained his advisors only as long as they were collectively able to retain majority support in the assembly, became established in British North America. The next stage in the development of representative and responsible self-government occurred over the next decade with the effective separation of the political executive (cabinet) from the formal executive (the governor). Governors increasingly absented themselves from the deliberations of their political advisors, while acting on their recommendations.

Thus, even before Confederation, the Canadian colonies had achieved a moderate degree of self-government by developing responsible government and parliamentary democracy. But their assemblies and governments were not sovereign; there were constraints upon their autonomy and on the supremacy of their parliamentary institutions. When the British North American colonies were each granted assemblies in the eighteenth century, they were given the power to legislate on local matters, subject to two conditions: first, that they did not attempt to enact laws having effect outside their territorial boundaries; and second, that their laws did not contravene the established laws of England.

Obstacles to the outright independence of governmental institutions continued, even after the creation of the new dominion in 1867. First, legislative competence within Canada was divided between two different levels of government, federal and provincial. This in itself did not directly affect the external sovereignty of the Canadian state, but it did have an indirect impact: neither the federal division of powers nor any other provisions of the *BNA Act* could be amended by any Canadian legislature, only by the British Parliament. Moreover, the creation of separate fields of legislative competence had important and restrictive consequences for internal state building.

Second, certain matters were withheld from all levels of government in Canada. In particular, legislation having extraterritorial effect (such as laws pertaining to copyright or merchant shipping) was reserved exclusively for the British Parliament. Similarly, the Canadian government was not regarded as an independent actor in the world of international relations. Canada was effectively an appendage of Britain when it came to the conduct of diplomatic affairs, which remained the exclusive preserve of the British government.

Third, even within the legal competence of Canadian federal or provincial legislatures, parliamentary supremacy could be overridden by the powers of reservation given to the governor general and the lieutenant-governors (as representatives of the Crown in Canada) and by the powers of disallowance retained by the British government.

These factors and others (for example, the retention until 1949 of the Judicial Committee of the Privy Council in the United Kingdom as the highest court of appeal, a device that permitted substantial outside meddling in Canada's internal affairs) combined to maintain Canada in a quasi-colonial relationship with Britain long after Confederation.

External Sovereignty and Its Constraints

In the twentieth century, however, two major periods of constitutional change, some fifty years apart, secured Canada's de facto and de jure independence from the United Kingdom.

The first series of events involved the Imperial Conferences of 1926 and 1930, culminating in the 1931 *Statute of Westminster*. At the Imperial Conference of 1930, the disallowance and reservation powers of the British government and the governor general were declared constitutionally obsolete. They had, in any case, long ceased to be of much practical relevance. The *Statute of Westminster* paved the way for the dominions to emerge as independent foreign-policy actors by stating that a dominion parliament had full power to make laws having extraterritorial operation.[17] A further provision of the Statute laid down that the British Parliament no longer had the right to legislate for any dominion except at the request of the dominion concerned—for example, by way of a petition to amend the *BNA Act*.

These changes highlight the role of the *Statute of Westminster* as the watershed between the effective ending of colonial status for Canada and its emergence as a more or less independent state. According to the historian A.R.M. Lower,

> the Statute of Westminster came as close as was practicable without
> revolutionary scissors to legislating the independence of the "Dominions." There
> is good ground for holding December 11, 1931, as Canada's Independence Day,
> for on that day she became a sovereign state.[18]

Further colonial remnants were removed in 1949. That year, the Supreme Court replaced the British Judicial Committee of the Privy Council as Canada's highest court of appeal. In addition, the *British North America Act* (No. 2) of 1949 permitted the Parliament of Canada to amend certain portions of the Act without recourse to Westminster. However, in order to achieve fundamental constitutional reforms, it was still necessary for the Canadian government to go cap in hand to Westminster to ask for amending legislation from the British Parliament. While Westminster was traditionally willing to accede to any such requests from Canada, the necessity remained a limitation to Canada's self-determination.

Thus, one of the dominant political issues of the 1970s was Prime Minister Pierre Trudeau's crusade to patriate the Canadian Constitution—a quest that finally came to fruition with the passage of the *Canada Act* by the British Parliament in 1982. The Act gave effect to Canada's request for Britain to consent to the *Constitution Act, 1982*. At last, Canada, like other sovereign states, had its own Constitution and was able to determine its internal political structure without reference to external authorities. In formal terms at least, it was the year 1982, over half a century after the *Statute of Westminster* and 115 years from Confederation, that marked the final stage in Canada's evolution from colony to sovereign state.

This final, formal severance of ties with the United Kingdom did not mean, however, that Canadian governments could do just as they pleased. In the modern era, increasing interdependence among states and their economies has severely constrained the capacity of governments to act independently of all external pressures. This is especially the case for countries that have a high degree of economic integration with larger, more powerful neighbours.

17. It should be remarked that, a few years earlier, Canada had already negotiated and signed its first treaty with the United States, the *Halibut Treaty* of 1923, after the king of England gave specific permission to do so.

18. Arthur R.M. Lower, *Colony to Nation: A History of Canada*, 4th ed., revised (Don Mills, ON: Longman Canada, 1964), p. 489.

While Canada is a genuinely sovereign state in international law, the nature of its relationship with the United States imposes limits upon government policy-making. Canada's defence policy is conducted within the context of the NATO alliance, in which the United States is the most powerful player—a position it uses to attempt to sway the policies of its partners. Canadian fiscal and budgetary policies are heavily influenced by US interest rates and by capital flows between the two countries. Energy and industrial policies have to take into account US ownership of Canadian branch plants and US investment in Canadian resources. The success of Canadian environmental policy depends partly, for example, upon the extent to which the White House and Congress can be persuaded to impose their own controls on the emission of industrial pollutants. As well, large international corporations have acquired more economic power than most governments. Thus, contemporary issues of external sovereignty now revolve not around Canadian–British relations, but Canadian–US ones (examined more closely in Chapter 15).

Internal State Building

In contrast to the drawn-out process of Canada's acquisition of external sovereignty, the initial stages of internal state building were quite rapid. After the political unification of the original provinces in 1867 and the subsequent expansion of Canada's territory, it was imperative to integrate this vast area into a governable political entity. The three major components of this integration process were the imposition of law and order over the entire territory, the development of means of transportation and communication, and the creation of a viable national economy.

Law and Order   As we have noted, one of the key characteristics of a modern, sovereign state is the government's ability to ensure that its laws are obeyed and, where necessary, to utilize its monopoly of the legitimate use of physical force in order to maintain its authority. Since 1867, Canadian governments have not been averse to using large-scale coercion when deemed necessary. On at least four occasions—the Riel Rebellions of 1869–71 and 1885, the Winnipeg General Strike of 1919 and the 1970 October Crisis—large numbers of police and troops were mobilized to crush perceived or actual uprisings against the Canadian state.

One year after Confederation, the federal government created the Dominion Police to enforce laws in Central and Eastern Canada. The major symbol of central authority in Western Canada in the late nineteenth century was the red coat of the Mountie. Four years after the annexation of lands from the Hudson's Bay Company in 1869, the North-West Mounted Police force (later combined with the Dominion Police to become the Royal Canadian Mounted Police, or RCMP) was created to impose a uniform code of law on the territories. The Mounties were responsible for keeping the peace in all federally administered lands from the US border to the Arctic and between Hudson Bay and the Rocky Mountains. The RCMP still maintains a federal presence throughout Canada. In addition to its tasks of enforcing federal laws everywhere and acting as the sole police force in the territories, the force is under contract to perform police functions in every province except Ontario and Québec and in a vast number of municipalities.

Transportation   The second component of internal state building in the new Dominion of Canada was the improvement of transportation and communications links among its provinces and regions for security purposes, for economic reasons and for the movement of people, mail and other sources of information. In the second half of the nineteenth century, the most efficient form

---

19. *British North America Act*, section 145—repealed in 1893 after the government had fulfilled its duty.

of transport for all such purposes was the railway. Thus, one of the conditions under which New Brunswick and Nova Scotia were willing to join Confederation was that a railway be built to link Halifax and the Saint John valley to the St. Lawrence. The construction of this "Inter-colonial Railway" was enshrined in the original *BNA Act* as one of the duties of the federal government.[19]

Transportation became even more of a challenge as the dominion spread from sea to sea. The building of a transcontinental railway consequently became one of the most important political issues and objectives of Canada's first twenty years. Through a mixture of government intervention and private enterprise, Canada's railway system slowly took shape, highlighted by the completion of the transcontinental Canadian Pacific Railway when the famous "last spike" was driven in 1885.[20]

A Viable National Economy   Railway construction was also very much a part of the third aspect of state building. The so-called National Policy, first publicized by John A. Macdonald in the general election campaign of 1878, became the basis for Canada's economic development for the next fifty years. The **National Policy** consisted of three interrelated objectives: the development of a comprehensive railway system; the opening up of Western Canada by encouraging immigration, settlement and agriculture on the prairies; and national economic development by protecting Canadian industries through an external tariff.

In order to realize the dream of a dominion stretching *a mare usque ad mare*, and also to forestall US expansion into Western Canada, people needed to settle the vast, open plains between Manitoba (at that time little more than the area around Winnipeg) and British Columbia. The government therefore opened the door to immigrants, largely from central and Eastern Europe, and gave them land grants and financial aid to help them become established on the prairies. The railways were vital to such settlement, particularly for the transportation of wheat and other prairie products to markets in the East and for export abroad.

At the same time, the Macdonald government attempted to develop other sectors of the Canadian economy. Canada required secondary or manufacturing industries to provide jobs for its non-agricultural labour force. But such emerging industries required protection from more advanced foreign competition. Inter-provincial tariffs had already been removed to aid the free flow of raw materials and goods within Canada. Now, as the third plank of the National Policy, the government imposed an external tariff designed to reduce the flow of imports (especially certain manufactured products) into the country. The tariff did aid indigenous economic development in certain industries. As well, in combination with the new railways, it increased the volume of east–west trade within Canada at the expense of north–south trade with the United States.

The National Policy was an explicit attempt by Canadian governments of the late nineteenth century to enhance the economic and political integration of the dominion. To a certain extent, it was as important for its symbolic contribution to nationalism and independence as for its contribution to Canada's economic development; in fact, its economic impact has often come under critical re-evaluation by historians and political scientists.[21] But the National Policy is also noteworthy in that it represented the first major incursion of the state into economic life in post-Confederation Canada.

20. See Pierre Berton's popular histories *The National Dream: The Great Railway, 1871–1881* and *The Last Spike: The Great Railway, 1881–1885* (Toronto: McClelland & Stewart, 1970 and 1971).

21. For an overview of the critiques of the National Policy, see Michael Bliss, "'Rich by Nature, Poor by Policy': The State and Economic Life in Canada," in R.K. Carty and W.P. Ward, eds., *Entering the Eighties: Canada in Crisis* (Toronto: Oxford University Press, 1980); and Wallace Clement and Glen Williams, eds., *The New Canadian Political Economy* (Kingston and Montréal: McGill-Queen's University Press, 1989).

The Growth of the State

One important trait of the modern state has been its inexorably expanding significance in the lives of its citizens. Whether this phenomenon is referred to as the growth of the state, the growing sphere of government or the enlargement of the public sector, it is common to all countries, particularly the industrial societies of the Western World. In the second half of the nineteenth century, when the Canadian state began to take shape, the role of government was much more limited than today, and included no major welfare programs.

By contrast, contemporary states, including Canada, offer free primary and secondary education and subsidize university and college education; provide massive medical care, unemployment and old-age pension programs; and are involved in a wide variety of other social welfare policies. In addition, the state has become increasingly important in the economic sphere: as an owner and entrepreneur in resource development, transportation and other nationalized industries; as a regulator of both the public and the private sector; and as a manager of the national economy, through economic and regional planning, intervention in the capital and credit markets, budgetary policy and its own spending decisions. Consequently, in some Western societies, total government expenditure per annum well exceeds 50 percent of the total national income.

This last point raises the question of how the growth of the state can be measured in real terms. As the state has expanded its activities, so has government expenditure grown. Of course, even if a government continues to perform exactly the same functions over time, expenditure in money terms will increase as the cost of goods, labour and services purchased by the government also grows. Therefore, when an attempt is made to measure the growth of government (and the growth of the state) in real terms, it is usually expressed as a proportion of the country's gross national product (GNP), its gross domestic product (GDP) or some other indicator of national income, expenditure or product.

As well, the growth of the role of the state can be measured in terms of the increase in governmental activities: the number of new government programs, new laws and regulations, and new statutes establishing new public corporations or nationalized industries. A third way of expressing the growth of the state is in terms of the actual size of government—that is, either the number of governmental organizations or the percentage of the labour force employed by the state. These government activities and employees must be paid for; the state must have revenues in order to meet its expenditures. Thus, a final indicator of the growing role of the state is the size of government revenues, especially those accruing from the taxation of individual and corporate citizens.

The Extent of the State in Canada

Internal state building in Canada has been more complex than in many other states because of the federal nature of the political system. Rather than a simple one-to-one relationship between unitary state and society, Canadian state building has consisted of a trilateral relationship among society, provincial governments and federal institutions. Competition between the particularistic objectives of province building and the centralizing bias of federal state building has aggravated existing regional conflicts and the broader context of federal–provincial relations. Despite these complexities, political institutions have assumed an increasingly activist role in Canadian society and the economy.

The initial thrust of state intervention in Canada was primarily economic. As the example of the National Policy indicates, the role of the state was originally conceived as one of indirect intervention (through taxes, land grants and so on) to provide the infrastructure and other conditions conducive to private sector economic development. In the twentieth century, however, the state intervened more directly in the economy, especially through public ownership of Crown corporations. The federal government takeover of Canadian National Railways in 1917 was followed in the 1930s by the establishment of the Canadian Radio Broadcasting Commission (now the CBC), the Bank of Canada and Trans-Canada Airlines (later Air Canada); later examples include Atomic Energy of Canada Limited (1952), Telesat Canada (1969) and Petro-Canada (1976). Moves by the federal government since the mid-1980s to reduce its role have, however, altered this original pattern to some extent (see Chapter 14).

While Canadian state institutions have a long history of intervention in the economic sector, the development of social policies leading to the current welfare state system occurred relatively late. This tardiness has been attributed to many factors: the delayed nature of Canada's industrial revolution; the weakness and late emergence of the working class as an organized political force, and the strength of the wealthier business community in restricting the role of the state to merely promoting and protecting white collar interests. It is not surprising that many innovations in social policy were initiated by provincial governments in the Prairies, where frontier isolation created a somewhat collectivist culture.

Although some programs had been introduced earlier (for example, workers' compensation in almost every province by 1920 or the federal government's old-age pension legislation of 1927), it was not really until the period between 1930 and 1945 that the Canadian welfare state began to take shape. The combined impact of the Depression and the Second World War created a climate more conducive to social intervention by both federal and provincial governments. At first, the federal government provided a series of temporary relief measures to alleviate poverty in the Depression, but more permanent legislation followed, especially in the fields of unemployment insurance (1940) and family allowances (1944).

Since the Second World War, both federal and provincial governments have introduced many programs into the welfare state system, including health-care plans and hospital insurance, the Canada and Québec Pension Plans, housing policies, grants for higher education and guaranteed income supplements, among others. As a percentage of national income, total government spending at all levels on welfare state policies (health, education and social welfare) approximately tripled from the end of the Second World War until the 1990s. But from a state-building perspective, it may be argued that it was in the decade preceding 1945 that the major shift in perception of the role of government occurred, allowing Canada to join the ranks of other welfare societies. At that time, Canadians began to view poverty less as a sign of individual weakness, and more as a social problem whose alleviation could be beneficial to the rest of society and that therefore could be regarded as a responsibility of the Canadian state.

Once governmental responsibility for social welfare functions was accepted, the last major step in the state-building process was accomplished. Since that time, the role of the state (or government, or the public sector) in Canadian society has continued to expand, with minor reversals. Whether the size of the state is measured by the proportion of national income spent by governments, the number of laws and regulations or the number of public servants, twenty-first-century Canada differs greatly from the nineteenth-century laissez-faire state.

Critical Debate
Constraints or Opportunities?

What does Canada's history tell us about our country and people? Did the circumstances of those early years establish our political destiny? For example, was Canada's political development predetermined or constrained by the territorial, economic and political parameters of our country's past? Or was there, and are there still, opportunities for individuals, groups and parties to matter in determining our fate as a state in the world?

Point

The history of Canada's territorial, social and economic circumstances did circumscribe and determine how and when Canada would develop politically. It influenced and constrained political life, and the historical development of the Canadian state and its people. The historical determinants, both external and internal, continue to have a profound impact on Canadian politics.

Externally, the main influences have always come from the United Kingdom and the United States. The country's roots are primarily British, and the political aspirations of Canadians have never varied far from the British models of representative and responsible government. Coming of age as a state, however, required slowly severing colonial bonds with the UK. The United States was always a powerful neighbour on the continent. The threat implied by its presence encouraged Confederation, and Canadians are still defining themselves by their relationship with this southern giant. In other words, Canadians in the early years defined themselves primarily in terms of how they differed from Britain. Gradually, the interest in Britain has been replaced by concerns about the United States.

Internally, geography and demography have created issues that always will be present in Canadian politics. The country was, from the outset, composed of both French and English. It developed as a nation of immigrants, ensuring that certain political issues flowing from that reality would always be present.

The territorial outline of the country was largely settled by the time of Confederation. It is an expansive, northern territory with a harsh climate that restricts population to a relatively narrow band along the US border. The outlying provinces are far from the government in the centre, with unique regional circumstances that can be divisive. Sheer distance, plus the historical decision to preserve the Québécois as a distinct minority in Canada, necessitated a federal system of government. They also ensured that the distinctive concerns of the provinces and regions would always cause strains with a central government that would have to focus on the needs of the country as a whole.

Economic disparities between the regions and provinces ensure that finances will always be a key area of political dispute. Jurisdictional arguments, especially over ownership and control of natural resources, exacerbate federal–provincial tensions. Attempts to reduce regional economic disparities are frequently declaimed as unfair by the "have" provinces and inadequate by the "have-nots." The politicization of Native movements is a new phase in a long-standing historical issue in regional and ethnic politics in Canada.

Many of the major issues and conflicts emerging from the processes of nation building and state building in Canada have been only partially resolved. Consequently, some of the most contentious subjects of debate in the political arena today have their origins in the strains and antipathies created by the evolution of the state. Furthermore, these same strains often hamper the reconciliation of other, apparently unrelated disputes among actors in the Canadian political system.

Even the final settlement of Canada's sovereign status vis-à-vis the United Kingdom served to exacerbate tensions. The proclamation of Canada's new Constitution on April 17, 1982, caused political controversy and acrimony in parts of the country. Thousands of Québécois joined René Lévesque at a Montréal demonstration to protest Québec's exclusion from the constitutional accord between the federal government and the nine other provinces. Later, in October 1995, a Québec referendum on independence came within about half a percentage point of permanently dividing the country. In the same vein, Aboriginal organizations, whose demands for the entrenchment of Native rights in the 1982 Constitution had not been fulfilled, also boycotted the patriation ceremonies and declared that any Indians celebrating the event were committing treason against their nation.

Clearly, many of the major issues in contemporary Canadian politics have their source in the origins, expansion and development of the state over the past three hundred years. Furthermore, the attitudes, myths and grievances that evolved from the nation-and state-building experiences profoundly affect the approach of contending sides to other, less directly related issues.

Counterpoint

History is not destiny. There is considerable room for individuals, parties and groups to influence political change. Canadian history is marked by a number of turning points in which individuals and groups have made profound decisions that directed the course of political development and influenced who and what Canadians are today.

French–English relations provide a good example of a long-standing policy concern that has seen many turning points because of remarkable leadership (or the lack of it) by individuals and groups. The British, with an assimilation strategy, tackled the issue in 1763. It failed. In 1774, Governor Carleton persuaded the British government to change its policy and preserve the French culture. Shortly after the British devised the *Constitutional Act of 1791*, again in an attempt to satisfy both communities, political and social agitation and finally open rebellion erupted. The rebellions were led by William Lyon Mackenzie in Upper Canada and Louis-Joseph Papineau in Lower Canada, and forced Britain to re-evaluate its policies. Lord Durham decided in 1838 that assimilation would indeed have been better, but his recommendations were only half-heartedly adopted, and, as we know, events reached an impasse in about 1857.

Confederation itself is an example of a few Canadians (Macdonald, Cartier, Galt, Tupper, Tilley, Brown and McGee) having the perspicacity and tenaciousness to bring about the federal union of British North America. If they had not persevered, the colonies would almost certainly have been annexed or absorbed by the United States. As one historian observed, "perhaps the most striking thing about Canada is that it is not part of the United States."[22]

Often, there are choices to be made and it takes firm, coordinated leadership to make things happen. Throughout Canada's history, strong leaders and political parties have made vital policy decisions that have changed the course of history. Sir John A. Macdonald's National Policy; Lester Pearson's support for medicare, welfare programs and peacekeeping; Pierre Trudeau's patriation of the Constitution from Britain; and Brian Mulroney's free trade policy with the United States are all good examples.

Canadian politics is much more than the product of territorial, social and economic forces of the country's historical past. When we examine Canadian culture, institutions, behaviour and public policy, we can find many examples where events and policies have been altered by the foresight and determination of individuals. We can also find events and policies that have been altered by unfortunate incidents of stupidity or sloth.

22. J.B. Brebner, *Canada: A Modern History* (Ann Arbor, MI: University of Michigan Press, 1960), p. ix.

Discussion Questions

1. What is your stand on the Critical Debate above, and what can you add to it?
2. Can you find in pre-Confederation history the roots of political problems that remain unresolved in Canada today?
3. In what ways has the ethnic composition of the Canadian population changed since Confederation?
4. What is sovereignty? What are the main historical steps since Confederation that have made Canada a sovereign country?
5. How and why did the Canadian state grow in the twentieth century? Is the trend continuing today?
6. Trace the origins of representative and responsible government in Canada.
7. What are the benefits and costs of nation building?

Visit our new Companion Website at **www.pearsoned.ca/jackson**, where you can use the interactive Study Guide and link to additional resources on topics discussed in the text.

Selected Bibliography

Ajenstat, Janet, *The Canadian Founding: John Locke and Parliament*, Montréal: McGill-Queen's University Press, 2007.

Clement, Wallace, ed., *Understanding Canada: Building on the New Canadian Political Economy*. Montréal: McGill-Queen's University Press, 1997.

—————. and Leah F. Vosko, eds., *Changing Canada: Political Economy as Transformation*. Montréal: McGill-Queen's University Press, 2003.

Conrad, Margaret, and Alvin Finkel. *History of the Canadian Peoples*, Vol. II, 3rd ed. Don Mills, ON: Pearson Education Canada, 2002.

Dickason, Olive Patricia, *A Concise History of Canada's First Nations* (adapted by Moira Jean Calder). Don Mills, ON: Oxford University Press, 2006.

Gibbins, Roger. *Conflict and Unity: An Introduction to Canadian Political Life*. Scarborough, ON: Nelson Publishing, 1994.

Kaplan, William, ed. *Belonging: The Meaning and Future of Canadian Citizenship*. Montréal: McGill-Queen's University Press, 1993.

Ray, Arthur J. *I Have Lived Here Since the World Began: An Illustrated History of Canada's Native Peoples*. Toronto: Lester Publishing, 1996.

Part II
Culture

Politics does not take place in a vacuum. Government and politics exist within the context of culture and society, where they are nourished by ideas, people and events, and shaped by various accidents of history, geography, and even of climate and natural resources. Governments reflect the political ideas and interests of the people they serve. The internal cleavages and conflicts that exist in society—about how we should live and what is fair and unfair—are played out on the public stage of politics and government.

Part II of *Politics in Canada* focuses on the cultural environment of government and politics. Canadian society is like a tapestry composed of three interwoven strands. The primary strand consists of the shared ideas and aspirations that help draw Canadians together and provide an overarching national identity. Two major secondary strands highlight the colours and patterns of this social fabric: the country's ethno-linguistic groups and several distinctive regions with unique identities. Together, these three interwoven strands of society provide a richly layered tapestry that comprises the Canadian political culture.

Canadians acquire political ideas, values and beliefs from many sources. The ethno-linguistic, class and gender groups into which they are born and in which they live provide some parameters for this learning. Institutions such as the educational system, the media and government all play a role. Yet, even taken together, these socialization mechanisms have been limited in their ability to shape citizens who have a strong national identity.

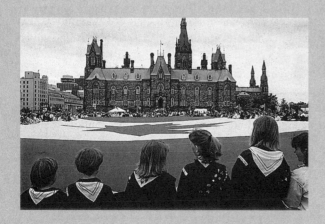

Chapter 3

The Fabric of Canadian Society

National Identity and Ethno-Linguistic and Regional Subcultures

Certain myths about Canada and Canadians are common in other countries, some based on reality, some not. These include conceptions of Canadians as a solid, stolid, northern, reliable, prosperous, tough, unsexy people blessed with good government and policies and one of the world's greatest police forces. At home, Canadians often characterize themselves as modest, hard-working and tolerant peacekeepers who distrust personal achievement among their peers. Potential Canadian heroes are regularly cut down to size. The story is told of a Nova Scotia fisherman who observed some lobsters, several of which appeared to be trying to climb out of a pail. "These are definitely Canadian lobsters," he concluded. "Whenever one tries to crawl out, the rest try to pull it down."

In this chapter, we look beyond such impressionistic generalizations to learn in a systematic way who Canadians are and what motivates them to act politically. We examine the attitudes and values that Canadians hold about themselves, their country and their system of government, all of which in turn affect their political behaviour.

It is possible to conceive of the political culture of Canada as a colourful tapestry, composed of different strands or elements. Here, we examine the overarching strand of Canada's political culture, and then, in order to achieve a more meaningful view of the whole, focus on ethno-linguistic and regional subcultures. When these basic units are interwoven and viewed together as a whole, the unique design of the Canadian tapestry becomes visible.

In your own experience, is there is a distinctive Canadian political culture? If so, of what does it consist? Does it have an impact on political institutions, political behaviour and public policy in a way that might help us understand politics in Canada? Develop your ideas about this topic as you read through the chapter, and apply them to the Critical Debate at the end. But first, let us clarify the concept of political culture.

What Is Political Culture?

Political culture is one of the most controversial concepts in political science. The term was first used in political science in the United States and only later applied in Canada.[1] It has been defined in a multitude of ways.

We use the term **political culture** in this book to refer to the broad patterns of individual values and attitudes toward political objects. These may be concrete objects such as government institutions or national symbols such as the flag, but they may also be intangibles such as power. In the latter case, it is important to understand how Canadians perceive the distribution of power

---

1. The concept was introduced by Gabriel Almond in "Comparative Political Systems," in Gabriel Almond, *Political Development* (Boston: Little, Brown, 1970). For a concise history of the term *political culture* and its application to the Canadian situation, see David Bell and Lorne Tepperman, *The Roots of Disunity*, 2nd ed. (Don Mills, ON: Oxford University Press, 1991), ch. 1.

between themselves and government, and what institutions or positions they view as the greatest sources of political power. Students of political culture, therefore, attempt to determine the degree of citizens' knowledge and awareness of the political system, as well as the attitudes they hold about politics and political objects.

Political culture is just a small part of the general culture of a society, but it serves many purposes: It draws individuals together; supports judgment and action; helps to constitute the character and personality of a community; differentiates one community from another; and encourages its members to seek common objectives. What citizens know and feel about their political system affects the number and kinds of demands they make on the system and also their responses to laws and political leadership. Political culture renders the government's decision-making processes acceptable by demarcating the boundaries within which the government can and cannot legitimately act.

Citizens of all countries develop perceptions and expectations about what their political system can and should do for them, and what obligations they have in return. This process provides the value structure within which political decisions are made. It delineates the accepted parameters of government and individual political activity, and enables organizations and institutions to function coherently.

Understanding the relationship between political culture and the political system assists in identifying and appreciating how political change can be effected. The extent to which values and beliefs are shared greatly affects the degree of national cohesion and stability in a country. Deep cleavages over such issues as language or economics obstruct the sharing of values and beliefs and contribute to political instability. Knowledge about the political attitudes of individual citizens helps to predict their political actions both inside the democratic system, through such means as voting, and outside the electoral process, through demonstrations, strikes and even violence. Citizens' beliefs and values are scrutinized to determine their effect on voting behaviour and other forms of political participation or non-participation.[2]

As we shall see, social scientists have studied Canadian political culture in two main ways. Some have employed empirical methodology, using surveys and questionnaires to learn about mass attitudes and behaviour. Others have carried out research on the historical development of political ideas. Although they cannot be compared directly, and each has shortcomings, both methods contribute to an understanding of the Canadian political system.

Three Strands of Canadian Political Culture

For the sake of simplicity, in this chapter the subject of political culture is divided into three sections that correspond to the three strands of which it is composed.

The first section is devoted to the values and attitudes common to *all* citizens of the state—here, we search out the roots of Canadian heritage. We also attempt to determine whether there is a common ideology behind Canadian political thought and, if so, what its origins may be. With this broad level of interpretation, we also consider what characteristics distinguish Canadian citizens from those of other countries. The pan-Canadian attitudes and values that form this strand reveal the framework of Canadian political culture—and indicate the extent of Canadian national identity, the glue that keeps our society together.

In the second section, we examine the most important subcultures created by *ethnic* and *linguistic* cleavages in the country. The focus here is on three distinct groups: (1) the French Canadian community, whose cultural and linguistic differences are reinforced by historical, geographical and economic circumstances; (2) the broad range of ethnic and visible minorities who constitute the "English-speaking" sector, as it is generally called because of the official bilingual status of the country; and (3) the Aboriginal peoples.

In the third section, we explore *regional subcultures* in Canada. People of different origins and interests settled in areas that offered greatly varied resources and potential for industrial development. The values and beliefs Canadians hold about their political system today are conditioned by the historical, geographic and economic characteristics of the region in which they live. Canada's federal system of government has reinforced and perpetuated these regional subcultures. In this section, we consider how distinctive the regions are, and what evidence exists that there are several geographically based political cultures in Canada.

Because political values and beliefs are far from uniform across the state, some scholars argue that there is no such thing as a Canadian political culture, but rather that there are several cultures based on ethnic or regional divisions. We argue that regional and ethnic political subcultures do exist, but are tied together by the overarching values of a national culture. We examine the three strands of Canadian political culture under three headings: nation-state political culture, ethnolinguistic political culture and regional political culture.

Nation-State Political Culture

Nation-state political culture encompasses the values and attitudes that pertain to the *entire* Canadian political system and are expressed in common symbols such as flags and anthems. These include traditions of democracy, personal freedom and civil liberties, respect for the law and the coexistence of heterogeneous communities that underlie the political system. Deep historical roots anchor these political ideas.

These facets of the Canadian identity are rounded out by a picture of Canadians as inhabitants of a huge, diverse country with a harsh northern climate, a federal system of government and a parliamentary system adopted from the United Kingdom with some modifications inspired by the United States. Canada has evolved from a country of Aboriginal peoples and two European nations to one that includes people of widely diverse origins. The values of that heritage are expressed in official policies of bilingualism and multiculturalism.

Ideology and Political Culture

There are a few classic arguments about which traditional values form the base of Canada's political system. Before we consider them, it is important to clarify the confusion that sometimes arises between the terms *political culture* and *ideology*. Both refer to political attitudes, values and beliefs, but ideologies are more coherent and explicit. As used in this book, ideology is narrower in scope than political culture. **Ideology** refers to an explicit doctrinal structure, providing a particular diagnosis of the ills of society, plus an accompanying "action program" for implementing the prescribed solutions. Ideologies have provided the inspiration and reasoning for many social reforms. They have also provided the justification for revolutions and wars. They provide a central motivating force in politics by introducing such grand ideas as freedom, justice, equality, the good life—big questions that engender political struggle and conflict. Political culture, on the other hand, refers to vaguer, more implicit orientations, whether or not they embrace any explicit, formal ideology.

In Canadian society, we can identify three major ideologies—socialism, conservatism and liberalism. Liberalism and conservatism originated in Europe in the nineteenth century as philosophers and thinkers struggled to create logical and consistent patterns of thought about how to restructure the medieval social and political order that new developments were rendering obsolete.

Liberalism became the ideology of the rising commercial class, while *conservatism* justified the positions of the aristocracy and Church. Both ideologies spawned political parties. Liberal thought became dominant in the Western World in the latter part of the nineteenth century, and for that reason some view the nineteenth century as the century of liberalism. *Socialism* developed slightly later in response to more fundamental changes in society. The technological advances of the industrial revolution had brought the growth of a large urban working class that existed in wretched conditions. Socialists sought to ameliorate the lot of these workers. By the beginning of the twentieth century, the ideological and party battlefield was a three-way contest as socialist ideology produced socialist, labour and communist parties in Europe.

There are several competing interpretations of the origin of political thought in Canada. Louis Hartz's work is a source of many ideas concerning the traditional attitudes and values that underlie Canadian political culture.[3] It was published in 1953, before the popularization of the concept of political culture. Consequently, the word *ideology* is used not as an action-oriented system of ideas, but as a relatively vague set of attitudes that form the foundation of political culture. Had the systematic discussion of political culture begun a decade earlier, Hartz and other authors might have substituted *political culture* for *ideology*. As it is, much of the literature that followed Hartz, and that is discussed here, uses the latter term in the sense of a set of general principles about politics.

The thesis put forward by Hartz, and later expanded by Kenneth McRae,[4] is that North America, like other societies founded by European settlement, is a *fragment society*. According to Hartz, the New World societies based their political cultures on single European ideologies brought as "cultural baggage" during colonization. Immigrants to the new land did not represent all elements of the society that they had left, only some of them. Institutions and myths set up and passed on by the founding peoples perpetuated those beliefs and values.

McRae argues that, because it has two founding nations, Canada is a classic instance of a *two-fragment* society. The settlers in New France represented one fragment, the feudal strain from France. As a result, a kind of "feudal catholicism" dominated rival ideologies there, and excluded others through expulsion or assimilation. The second fragment, found in English Canada, was very similar to its liberal US counterpart. English-speaking immigrants were predominantly liberal. In pre-revolutionary United States, the liberalism of the philosopher John Locke became the prevailing ideology. The beliefs for which Locke was the primary spokesman were based on the importance of the individual, free enterprise and the right of the individual to pursue personal interests without government interference. Loyalists who flooded into Canada at the time of the American Revolution brought these liberal values with them—along with strong anti-American, pro-British sentiments.

The differences that developed between English Canada and the United States were subtle and minor, according to Hartz and McRae. In both cases, liberal ideology had "congealed" before socialism developed in Europe; therefore, socialism did not take hold in North America. Liberal thought, with its belief in maximizing individual freedom and satisfaction of private desires, is widely diffused and dominant in the political culture of English North Americans. However, Hartz, McRae and others argue, Canadian thought is more conservative and collectivist than that of the United States. For instance, Canadians feel strongly that the state is responsible for its citizens and is obligated to provide for their collective well-being. Citizens of the US, on the other hand, believe in non-interference by the government and the primacy of individual liberties.

---

3. Louis Hartz, *The Liberal Tradition in America* (New York: Harcourt Brace & World, 1953).

4. Louis Hartz, ed., *The Founding of New Societies* (New York: Harcourt Brace & World, 1964). See McRae's analysis in "The Structure of Canadian History" in Chapter 7. See also Kenneth D. McRae, "Louis Hartz's Concept of the Fragment Society and Its Applications to Canada," *Canadian Studies/ Études canadiennes*, vol. 5 (1978), pp. 17–30.

Later, George Grant, writing on this matter, lamented the widespread diffusion of liberal thought in Canada. He warned that the triumph of liberalism over conservatism and socialism in Canadian society represents the defeat of Canadian nationalism because it brings total conformity with the ideological structure of the United States.[5] Others have argued that Canadian anglophones have never been able to accept liberal ideology totally, because it was the natural culture of the Americans. They see the tension between adhering to the British connection and fostering antipathy toward US culture as the origin of a serious identity crisis for Canadians.[6]

Hartz's fragment theory of political culture considers the culture of founding groups as a kind of "genetic code," one that does not determine, but rather imposes boundaries on, later cultural developments. This approach offers the advantage of historical depth, since political thought is viewed as a phenomenon that develops over time, rather than being static. A drawback is that it fails to explain how fragment cultures survive, how they are transmitted to new immigrants and new generations. Why, for example, did new immigrant groups not establish new, competing cultures? This question is considered in the next chapter.

Part of the Hartz and McRae thesis has been challenged by Gad Horowitz, who maintains that the respective heritages of Canada and the United States are very different because Canadian liberalism had not "congealed" before British and European immigrants arrived in Canada in the late nineteenth and early twentieth centuries, bringing with them newer ideas from the old societies.[7] For Horowitz, the fact that a socialist movement grew illustrates that, unlike the United States, Canada has had an enduring, though small, socialist fragment. Thus, political thought in Canada was not totally buried beneath an unqualified liberalism. Even among the English-speaking group, Horowitz maintains, there is no single dominant ideology.

In another study, Roger Gibbins and Neil Nevitte find that Americans display "far greater attitudinal coherence, and stronger ideological linkages among sets of attitudes," than do English-speaking Canadians. Québec francophones diverge even more from Americans in that they demonstrate the "virtual absence of an ideological right." The authors maintain that the political culture of the United States "is more ideologically structured than that found in English Canada, and even more so than that found in francophone Québec."[8]

Other authors, such as Seymour Martin Lipset, conversely have stressed the conservative inheritance of the Canadian political culture.[9] He concluded that Canadian values are generally conservative, closer to those of Europeans than Americans. Lipset credits Canada–US differences to very different "formative events" in the history of the two countries. He noted that Canada became independent through evolution; the United States, through revolution. Canada had a relatively civilized westward expansion, not a "wild west." Religious traditions, too, differed: Canada was settled predominantly by Anglicans and Roman Catholics rather than by Calvinists and fundamentalists. Many of Lipset's conclusions about Canadian values have been challenged by other scholars, such as Neil Nevitte (see the "Close-Up on Culture: Value Changes").

5. George Grant, *Lament for a Nation: The Defeat of Canadian Nationalism* (Toronto: McClelland & Stewart, 1965).

6. Bell and Tepperman, *The Roots of Disunity*, ch. 3.

7. Horowitz, "Conservatism, Liberalism and Socialism in Canada: An Interpretation," *CJEPS*, vol. 32, no. 2 (May 1966), pp. 143-71. See also Horowitz, "Notes on 'Conservatism, Liberalism and Socialism in Canada'" *CJEPS*, vol. 11, no. 2 (June 1978), pp. 383–99.

8. Roger Gibbins and Neil Nevitte, "Canadian Political Ideology: A Comparative Analysis," *JPS*, vol. 18, no. 3 (September 1985), pp. 577–98.

9. Seymour Martin Lipset, "Revolution and Counterrevolution: Canada and the United States," in O. Kruhlak et al., eds., *The Canadian Political Process: A Reader* (Toronto: Holt, Rinehart and Winston, 1970), pp. 13–38.

Colin Campbell and William Christian have added to the debate by rejecting the view that the Canadian ideological system congealed in the way suggested by either McRae or Horowitz.[10] They maintain that the Loyalists introduced strains of <u>Tory</u> thought into English Canada. More liberally inclined immigrants went to the United States, while more conservative individuals chose to move to Canada and remain under the British Crown. Of course, French Canada was even further removed from the liberalism of John Locke. "Many of the immigrants to New France had left France at a time when liberal ideas were virtually non-existent, and hence they brought with them to the new land an attitude to the state and to the society which was more tory/feudal than liberal."[11] As for Canadian socialism, Campbell and Christian contend that it was indigenous, a natural product of the Great Depression.

In yet another approach to the topic, Gordon Stewart traces the roots of Canada's political culture to the historical circumstances of its colonial political system. Stewart builds on the work of Hartz and McRae by assessing the "workings of politics" during the colonial period. He concludes that the impact of the 1790–1850 formative period was so powerful that "it created a distinctive and enduring pattern of Canadian politics."[12] Stewart argues persuasively that characteristics of the Canadian political culture, such as patronage, influence, active government and intense localism, were imported and firmly established during the colonial period and "went from strength to strength" after Confederation in 1867.

These various interpretations suggest that Canadian political culture, unlike its US counterpart, was open to both conservative and socialist thought. Canadian political culture has a European flavour, placing a high value on tradition, order, historical continuity and group interests rather than individual interests. But Canadian liberalism is, as David Bell and Lorne Tepperman aptly phrase it,

CLOSE-UP ON Culture

VALUE CHANGES

A study by Neil Nevitte challenges some of Seymour Martin Lipset's contentions about Canadian values. Nevitte found that in recent years there have been significant value changes on a whole range of issues. Canadians, he says, have become less preoccupied with accumulating material goods and more concerned with what has come to be termed "post-materialism" values. An increasingly large proportion of the Canadian population has been born since the traumas of the Second World War and the Depression. As a consequence, Nevitte maintains, they are more concerned with "self-actualization" and less with acquiring material goods.

Politically, Nevitte says, post-materialists tend to think of themselves as "new left," a concept that refers to concern for the environment, tolerance of alternative lifestyles (e.g., same-sex marriage) and veering away from traditional Church-inspired notions of moral standards. They are also less concerned with traditional notions of authority. As Canadians have become better educated and more cosmopolitan, Nevitte says, they have also become more difficult to govern. While they are politically motivated, their attachment to traditional political parties and to hierarchical institutions has declined. Canadians are, therefore, less deferential than they used to be.

Another new study by two US and two Canadian academics concludes that the difference in values between Americans and Canadians today is not as acute as generally assumed. They find Canadians to be more left-leaning than Americans on gay rights and affirmative action, and also in their belief that governments should ensure jobs and a decent living standard. Apart from these areas, they say, differences are not marked.

Are your observations in accord with these new value studies?

Sources: Neil Nevitte, *The Decline of Deference* (Peterborough, ON: Broadview Press, 1996); and Paul M. Sniderman et al., *The Clash of Rights: Liberty, Equality and Legitimacy in Pluralist Democracy* (New Haven, CT: Yale University Press, 1997).

the ideology of the dominant class; it has the full force of the state, Church, media and educational system behind it: it has been trained into all of us.[13]

10. William Christian and Colin Campbell, *Political Parties and Ideologies in Canada: Liberals, Conservatives, Socialists, Nationalists*, 2nd ed. (Whitby, ON: McGraw-Hill Ryerson, 1983).

11. Ibid., pp. 227–28.

12. Gordon T. Stewart, *The Origins of Canadian Politics: A Comparative Approach* (Vancouver: University of British Columbia Press, 1986), p. 92.

13. Bell and Tepperman, *The Roots of Disunity*, p. 232. Also see David Bell, "Political Culture in Canada," in Michael Whittington and Glenn Williams, eds. *Canadian Politics in the 21st Century*, 6th ed., Toronto: Thompson Nelson, 2004.

We agree. It is our contention that liberal values, based on belief in a capitalist society, a market economy and the right to private property, dominate in Canada, although not to the exclusion of other perspectives.

Overarching Values

The political values of a country form the broad base of its political system. Though generally taken for granted and not necessarily explicitly articulated, **values** are deeply held ideas that set the parameters of acceptable behaviour and underlie citizens' attitudes toward specific political objects, providing guidelines to define what is right or wrong and what is or is not valuable or acceptable in society. In Canada, these values include certain democratic rights and, as we have seen, liberal values with strains of conservative and socialist thought. The implicit values of Canadians, as formalized in the Charter, are rooted in the Western political tradition and the Judeo-Christian religious tradition, and are reflected in political symbols such as national emblems or institutions. Many are enshrined in the country's Constitution. In April 1982, the *Canadian Charter of Rights and Freedoms* became the first comprehensive statement of the fundamental values of Canadians to be entrenched in the Constitution (see Chapter 5). The preamble sets out the premise that "Canada is founded upon principles that recognize the supremacy of God and the Rule of Law." The Charter then proceeds to guarantee the fundamental rights of Canada's "free and democratic society."

Democracy, as we discussed in Chapter 1, is such an ambiguous concept that it has become a cliché to claim it as a basic value. All types of political systems espouse it. However, in Canada, democratic rights are outlined in the *Charter of Rights and Freedoms.* One is the individual right to *fundamental freedoms.* These include (1) freedom of conscience and religion; (2) freedom of belief and expression, including freedom of the press and freedom of association; (3) freedom of peaceful assembly; and (4) freedom of association.

Another democratic right is *equality* before and under the law, without discrimination. In the political sphere, equality presumes associated values such as *universal suffrage* and elections contested by competing political parties that give voters alternatives from which to choose.

Another associated value is acceptance of the *rule of law,* with civil rights for all citizens. Still another implicit value of representative democracy is *majority rule.* In Canada, by convention, governments are based on an ability to retain a majority of votes in the House of Commons, and members of Parliament are elected in a system that gives credence to the majority principle but that, in fact, allows members to be elected by a plurality.

It also is deemed necessary to protect *minority rights* in Canada, so a few specific *collective* rights are also protected in the Constitution. These include French and English minority-language rights in the federal and Québec legislatures and courts, and Roman Catholic and Protestant minority education rights. Basic collective rights are generally considered inviolable, beyond even the right of the majority to change.

Comparing Canada to the United States also can help to identify Canadian values. Lipset's study found Canadians to be more aware of class, elitist, law abiding, statist and collectivity-oriented than Americans.[14] He traced many of these differences to British values that remained strong in Canada long after they were abruptly curtailed in the United States by the American Revolution. Beyond Lipset's reasoning, it can be said that Canada encourages ethnic minorities to preserve their culture. Multiculturalism is a reflection of the ideal of tolerance that, although not always lived up to, is

14. Seymour Martin Lipset, *Continental Divide* (New York: Routledge, 1990), p. 8. See also David Thomas, ed., *Canada and the United States: Differences that Count* (Peterborough, ON: Broadview Press, 2000).

highly valued by Canadians (more on that below). Compromise, too, is highly valued. This is evident in the workings of the federal system of government itself, which seeks to accommodate diverse regional interests. It can also be seen in the international reputation Canada has earned as a peacekeeper under the United Nations' auspices.

Canadian values and characteristics are changing over time, however—often in line with those of other industrialized states. In a comparative context, Neil Nevitte concludes that today Canadians have a greater sense of material well-being than do Americans. As well, contrary to Lipset's earlier study, he finds them to be less deferential than Americans—more willing to engage in boycotts and other forms of low-level political protest. In some economic values, such as orientation toward economic competition, free enterprise and workplace participation, Canadians and Americans are, he says, close. However, on levels of political interest, as well as permissiveness, absence of restrictions on euthanasia, homosexuality or abortion, Canadian orientations are more like those in Europe.[15]

Overarching Symbols

CANAD = KANATA

The political values of a country may be symbolized by such objects as flags, anthems, leaders, national holidays and historical heroes that help enforce respect for and emotional attachment to political institutions and can be a focal point for national unity. Symbols can take on many meanings. It is notable that the Inukshuk, a lifelike figure of stone traditionally erected by the Inuit to mark territory for various purposes, was adopted as a symbol of the 2010 Winter Olympics in Vancouver. This figure is taking on meanings such as co-operation, leadership, safe journey, friendship, welcome and multiculturalism, and is appearing ever more widely as a Canadian symbol.

The name *Canada* itself symbolizes the Aboriginal heritage of the country. *Kanata*, the Huron-Iroquois word for "village" or "settlement," became *Canada* and by 1547 was used on maps to designate everything north of the St. Lawrence River. The first use of *Canada* as an official name was in 1791, when the Province of Québec was divided into the colonies of Upper and Lower Canada. In 1841, the two Canadas were reunited as the Province of Canada. At Confederation, the new country assumed the official title the Dominion of Canada.[16]

Canada's passage from colony to nation is clearly reflected in the country's changing national symbols. In the early stages, they manifested a dual allegiance to Britain and Canada, but over time began to reflect national pride and unity with fewer and fewer references to Britain.

The evolution of the Canadian flag is perhaps the best illustration. At Confederation in 1867, Canada was granted permission to fly the Red Ensign, the flag of the British Merchant Navy. Attempts to replace it with a uniquely Canadian flag began as early as 1925 but did not succeed until four decades later. The transition was difficult. There were bitter debates, both in and out of Parliament, concerning not only the choice of a replacement but also the question of whether

15. Neil Nevitte, *The Decline of Deference* (Peterborough, ON: Broadview Press, 1996).
16. The Secretary of State, *Symbols of Nationhood* (Ottawa: Supply and Services, 1991), p. 5.

Canada should jettison the Red Ensign that represented its historical attachment to Britain. In the end, of course, a flag was selected that featured a red maple leaf, a distinctively Canadian symbol that had been adopted separately by both English and French Canadians well before Confederation, and that has deep historical roots in heraldic arms, regimental colours and literary publications.[17] The present flag was flown for the first time on February 15, 1965, and today many Canadians would not leave the country without a tiny facsimile on their lapels or knapsacks.

A similar evolution occurred in the acquisition of a Canadian coat of arms. Following the First World War, representation was made to the Crown for a coat of arms that was uniquely Canadian. For years, a controversy simmered over whether Canada should be symbolized by living green leaves or dead red ones. (Sir Robert Borden, then prime minister, thought green far more appropriate.) The dispute was not settled until 1957, when it was agreed that three red leaves would adorn the base of the shield and a lion would proudly display a fourth.

Another progression to a specifically Canadian symbol occurred in the choice of the national anthem. The English version of Alexander Muir's "The Maple Leaf Forever" was quite unacceptable to French Canadians for the good reason that it referred to the French defeat at Québec. At Confederation, therefore, "God Save the Queen" became the unofficial anthem. After being played in many different versions over the years, on July 1, 1980, "O Canada," based on music written by Calixa Lavallée a century earlier, was finally proclaimed Canada's national anthem. The many English versions have resulted from often-intense disagreement over the wording. Rather than inspiring loyalty and devotion, phrases that include "native land," "sons' command," "true North" and "God" tend to give rise to resentment among immigrants, women, westerners, easterners and atheists. And, of course, there are also royalists who still prefer "God Save the Queen." The French version of "O Canada," with lyrics that resemble the English only in that they refer to the same country, also contains some controversial wording.

It is important that a symbol of unity cause as little friction as possible, and Canadian efforts to compromise were evident at the formal adoption ceremony for the new anthem. There had been hot debate in 1980 over whether the choir should sing first in English or in French. What was later called a "typically Canadian" solution was found: the choir was divided in two and sang both versions simultaneously.

Minor conflicts and reminders of the British heritage have emerged from time to time with regard to other symbols. One concerns the country's official name, the Dominion of Canada. For most of our history, the first of July—Canada's national holiday—was known as Dominion Day. Although the word *dominion* had been chosen explicitly by the Fathers of Confederation to mean sovereignty from sea to sea, many Canadians came to feel that it smacked of colonial dependence. With some trepidation because of the controversy the topic engendered, in November 1982 the Canadian Parliament finally changed the title of the holiday to Canada Day—in spite of the country's official name.

In 2007, for the first time a Victoria Cross medal (VC) was produced in Canada and presented to a Canadian by Queen Elizabeth at the 90th anniversary of the Battle of Vimy Ridge. The medal had not been awarded to a Canadian since 1945 because of a controversy about whether an award of British origin should be given in Canada. Although Canada had assumed the responsibility for the decoration in 1993, the 2007 production, selection and award of the honour completed the formal reinstatement of the VC in Canada.

---

17. Strome Galloway, "Why the Maple Leaf Is Our National Emblem," *Canadian Geographic* (June 1982). Red and white are the official colours of Canada, appointed by George V in 1921.

In many countries, the Constitution provides a concrete focus for pride and unity. This has only recently been the case in Canada. As with the other symbols we have discussed, the process of moving away from British ties and establishing a unique, Canadian symbol was not easy. The 1867 *British North America Act*, Canada's written constitution, was passed by the British Parliament. It was increasingly embarrassing to Canadians in the twentieth century as a national symbol, both because it could not be amended without British approval and because it contained no formal guarantee of human rights. In the spring of 1982, Canada revised and patriated the Constitution. Like the US Constitution, the new document has provided a common focus of pride for Canadians, although the fact that it was patriated without the approval of Québec is still contentious (see Chapter 5).

Two other predominant political symbols deserving of mention here, although they are discussed extensively in Chapters 5 and 8, are the monarch and her representative, the governor general. Canada is a constitutional monarchy, and the role of Her Majesty Queen Elizabeth II as sovereign of Canada and head of state is ceremonial. As sovereign, she personifies the nation, and for many she is a symbol of allegiance, unity and authority. Federal and provincial legislators, cabinet ministers, public servants, military and police personnel and new citizens all swear allegiance to the Queen (not the flag or Constitution). Laws are promulgated and elections are called in the Queen's name. She is custodian of the democratic powers vested in the Crown.

Historian W.L. Morton pointed out that allegiance to a monarch alleviates pressures for uniformity: "Anyone … can be a subject of the Queen and a citizen of Canada without in any way ceasing to be himself."[18] The monarchy, in this sense, is well adapted to the bilingual, multicultural and regional character of Canada.

Yet, the appropriateness of the English monarchy as a symbol for some English and many French Canadians has often been questioned. An overtly hostile reception for the Queen during a royal visit to Québec in 1964, for example, prompted officials of the Québec government to disassociate themselves and their constituents from the monarchy. It is evident that the ability of the monarchy to serve as a unifying symbol for Canada's two founding cultural groups is limited.

The role of governor general has evolved considerably from its British origins. The Queen's representative to Canada was originally selected in Britain. However, since 1936, the governor general has been appointed only after consultation with the Canadian cabinet, which means, in effect, that the prime minister makes the choice. The appointment of the first Canadian, Vincent Massey, came in 1952. This transition to a Canadian governor general nominated in Canada may have increased the potential of the position to become a unifying symbol for Canadians.

Myths surrounding defining moments or events may create emotional bonds that endure and come to mean much more than historical facts alone might warrant. For example, much has been made of "the last spike" since the completion of the Trans-Canada Railway, which became the fulfillment of a national dream.[19] Or, the Battle of Vimy Ridge, a heroic but minor battle in the First World War that is celebrated in Walter Allward's magnificent memorial erected at Hill 62 in Belgium—a national monument that transcends regional fractures.[20]

Finally, we must allude briefly to historical heroes as symbols of national pride and unity. Gradual evolution to nationhood, as opposed to dramatic revolution, does not produce charismatic hero material. And independence on the instalment plan has no glamour as a national event.

18. Quoted in ibid.
19. Pierre Burton, *The Last Spike: The Great Railway 1881–1885*. Toronto: McClelland & Stewart, 1971.
20. Geoffrey Hayes, Andrew Iarocci and Mike Bechthold, eds. *Vimy Ridge: A Canadian Reassessment*. Waterloo, ON: Laurier Centre for Military Strategic and Disarmament Studies and Wilfrid Laurier University Press, 2007.

To compound the difficulties, French and English Canadians each tend to cultivate their own heroes, based on different interpretations of history. In fact, heroes in one community often gained reputations by resisting or defeating their counterparts in other parts of the country. The dearth of common national heroes and events to rally around has undoubtedly encouraged substitutions from south of the border, a problem discussed more fully in the following chapter. F.R. Scott aptly described this situation in a satirical poem entitled "National Identity"[21]:

The Canadian Centenary Council
Meeting in Le Reine Elizabeth
To seek those symbols
Which will explain ourselves to ourselves
Evoke unlimited responses
And prove that something called Canada
Really exists in the hearts of all
Handed out to every delegate
At the start of the proceedings
A portfolio of documents
On the cover of which appeared
In gold letters
not
A Mare Usque Ad Mare
not
E Pluribus Unum
not
Dieu et Mon Droit
but
Courtesy of Coca-Cola Limited.

Political Attitudes

Overarching values set the general parameters of political behaviour in Canada. Specific attitudes toward political objects are more differentiated than basic values and are more fleeting, but they may be more immediate determinants of political behaviour. Three types of attitudes can be distinguished: cognitive, affective and evaluative. *Cognitive attitudes* reflect the degree of knowledge, accurate or otherwise, that citizens have about political objects. *Affective attitudes* reflect the degree of citizens' attachment to, or rejection of, the political objects that surround them: How do Canadians feel about their country, their government or the political symbols we have discussed? *Evaluative attitudes* reflect the moral judgments made by individuals about the "goodness" or "badness" of political objects. These three types of attitudes are interrelated and often difficult to distinguish in practice.

Attitudes toward specific political issues of the day, as opposed to more permanent political objects, are ephemeral. Issues change and so do people, but institutions and symbols remain. Such transient attitudes are sometimes defined as public opinion, and although they can be important in determining short-term behaviour, they are less helpful in understanding the overall political culture of a country. An Angus Reid poll published in 1996, for example, indicated that Canadians perceived jobs, national unity, economy, deficit and health care, in that order, to be the most important issues facing the country at that time (see Figure 3.1). These perceptions can change

21.   From *The Collected Poems of F.R. Scott*, John Newlove, ed., 1981. Used by permission of The Canadian Publishers, McClelland & Stewart Ltd., Toronto.

FIGURE 3.1 **Measurements of Trust, 2003**

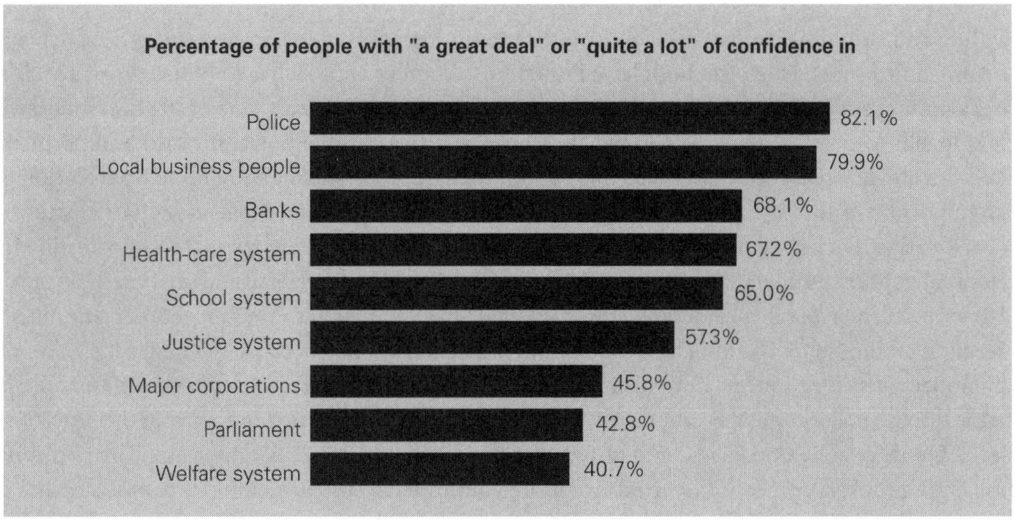

Percentage of people with "a great deal" or "quite a lot" of confidence in

Police	82.1%
Local business people	79.9%
Banks	68.1%
Health-care system	67.2%
School system	65.0%
Justice system	57.3%
Major corporations	45.8%
Parliament	42.8%
Welfare system	40.7%

Source: Survey by Statistics Canada as reported in *The Globe and Mail*, July 7, 2004, p. A3. Reprinted with permission.

dramatically over time. In the 2004 federal election, for example, the major issue was considered by many to be health care; in the 2006 election, it was political corruption.

With respect to cognitive attitudes, Canadians appear to possess the basic information necessary to allow them to operate effectively at both provincial and federal levels of government. They also demonstrate a high degree of feeling for both their country and their province of residence.[22]

Despite these positive attitudes, however, there are disquieting findings about the nature of some specific affective attitudes toward objects in the Canadian political system. Declining respect for and confidence in government institutions and politicians have been shown in many studies over the years. The Citizen's Forum on Canada's Future (the Spicer Commission) and the Royal Commission on Electoral Reform and Party Financing both witnessed an outpouring of criticism stating that Canada lacked responsible leadership, current leaders were not trustworthy, Canada lacked strong leaders and so on.[23] A Statistics Canada survey in 2003 indicated confidence in Parliament was only about half that for police or local business people (see Figure 3.1).

Such attitudes can fluctuate wildly over relatively short periods and are not uniform across the population; however, they have been persistent in recent years, and are of particular concern because they permeate the youth of the country. At least some of this negative emotion can be related to the state of the economy, political scandals and unpopular policies. Cynical attitudes do not, of course, preclude diffuse support for the government in Canada or necessarily hamper political participation at either level of government. Neither do they indicate a rejection of government authority. Despite their skepticism, individual Canadians are quite willing to comply with basic political laws, and major political groups rarely offer unconditional resistance to government legislation. Acts of Parliament are automatically considered legitimate and are carried out voluntarily by citizens without the need for the use of coercive security forces. Crimes against the state are rare, even when laws are unpopular.

22. For a study of the *sources* of political knowledge, both factual and conceptual, see Ronald D. Lambert et al., "The Social Sources of Political Knowledge," *CJPS*, vol. 21, no. 2 (June 1988).

23. Citizen's Forum on Canada's Future, *Report to the People and Government of Canada* (Ottawa, Supply and Services, 1991); and Royal Commission on Electoral Reform and Party Financing, *Reforming Electoral Democracy*, vol. 1 (Ottawa: Supply and Services, 1992).

Behaviour: Participation and Efficacy

Values and attitudes are often difficult to ascertain. Impressionistic studies and survey research are helpful, but, as we have noted, both have limitations. Another approach is to induce from people's behaviour the attitudes and values that make them act in a certain way. One of the best inductive methods is to examine the extent to which people *participate* in the political world around them and then to generalize from this behaviour about their culture. The individual's self-perception is an important factor here because self-esteem can affect the degree and intensity of participation.

Relative to most democratic countries, Canadians traditionally participated very readily in electoral politics—until recently, roughly 75 percent voted regularly in federal and provincial elections. However, turnout sank considerably lower in 2000, 2004 and 2006 to the mid-60-percent range. Election studies show that much of the decline in participation is because the new generation of potential voters is not turning out to cast a ballot (see Chapter 12 on elections). French Canadians are less active politically at the national level than English Canadians, but more active at the provincial level. On the whole, Canadians tend to feel that their individual vote is important. Their reasons for feeling they should vote are mixed. Some are committed to the principles of democracy and a feeling of civic duty; others feel it important to render judgment on a government or certain politicians, perhaps seeking to punish parties or politicians by voting them out of office.

Apart from the act of voting, however, overall feelings of political efficacy are low. As a result, Canadians are said to have a *quasi-participant* political culture. Canadians are not confident that they can understand and affect the political process. In general, they express feelings of distrust, cynicism and powerlessness in the face of government domination by powerful interests. But Canadians are not alone in harbouring these sentiments. Comparative analysis of responses to similar questions raised in surveys undertaken in Canada and the United States indicates that, on most items, Canadians have as high a sense of efficacy as Americans, and similar levels of trust in government.

Active participation in politics beyond casting a ballot is low in Canada.[24] Only 4 or 5 percent of the electorate participate regularly in political parties or hold elected office at either the federal or provincial level. Unless the level of interest is artificially high because of colourful personalities or issues, Canadians retain a vague spectator interest in politics and rarely show strong ideological commitment. Political protest, even peaceful demonstration, is undertaken by only a very small percentage of Canadians (see Figures 3.2 and 3.3). Moreover, political participation aside from voting is very *uneven* across different groups in Canadian society. The higher an individual's social status, the more likely she is to participate politically. The most active participants tend to be wealthy, well-educated, male, middle-aged Protestant members of the English "charter group." Historically, women have participated less than men.[25] Lower socio-economic and less well-educated groups participate only infrequently. As we have noted, however, recent research by Nevitte indicates that Canadians are becoming more willing to participate in boycotts and other low-level forms of protest. Participation in parties and elections is discussed further in Chapters 11 and 12.

Although there is a drastic drop in political participation when voting is excluded, it must be noted that only 25 to 30 percent of Canadians confine their participation exclusively to casting a ballot. About 60 percent of the public participate in at least one political activity in addition to voting. Although Canadians are less active politically than would befit the democratic ideal, they

---

24. See William Mishler and Harold D. Clarke, "Political Participation in Canada," in Michael S. Whittington and Glen Williams, eds., *Canadian Politics in the 1990s*, 4th ed. (Scarborough, ON: Nelson, 1995).

25. The absolute number of women voters is higher than that of male voters, but comparatively few women seek political and governmental power. See Chapters 4 and 12.

FIGURE 3.2 **Number and Type of Organizations Canadians Are Involved In, 2003**

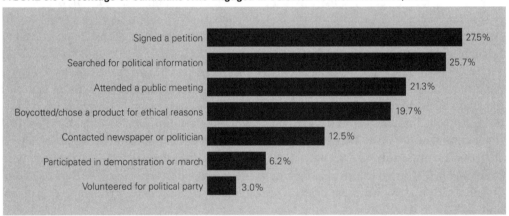

Number of organizations

None	37.9%
One	25.3%
Two	16.7%
Three or more	18.9%

Types of organizations

Sports or recreation	28.7%
Union or professional	24.9%
Cultural, educational or hobby	17.7%
Religious-affiliated	16.7%
School, community etc.	16.5%
Service club or fraternal organization	7.9%
Political party or group	4.7%
Other type	5.6%

Source: Survey by Statistics Canada as reported in *The Globe and Mail*, July 7, 2004, p. A3. Reprinted with permission.

FIGURE 3.3 **Percentage of Canadians Who Engaged in Selected Political Activities, 2003**

Signed a petition	27.5%
Searched for political information	25.7%
Attended a public meeting	21.3%
Boycotted/chose a product for ethical reasons	19.7%
Contacted newspaper or politician	12.5%
Participated in demonstration or march	6.2%
Volunteered for political party	3.0%

Source: Survey by Statistics Canada as reported in *The Globe and Mail*, July 7, 2004, p. A3. Reprinted with permission.

are considerably closer to that goal than citizens of many of the world's states. Unfortunately, the least influential in society—the poor, the young and the old, for example—participate the least in the political process, and exhibit the least political efficacy.

National Identity

The overarching values, symbols, attitudes and behaviour discussed above form the basis of Canadian national identity. A strong national identity subsumes and tempers the aspirations of ethno-linguistic and regional groups within the country. Canadians do have warm feelings about their country. In a 2003 survey by Statistics Canada, 85 percent of the 25 000 people consulted said they had a very strong or somewhat strong sense of belonging to Canada. Even in Québec, 74 percent of respondents said they felt a strong sense of attachment to their country.[26] In spite of this, for reasons that we explore below, national identity is relatively weak.

26. The Statistics Canada survey from 2003 was reported in *The Globe and Mail*, July 7, 2004, A3.

There are several components of a strong **national identity**:

- emotional attachment to the geographic territory;
- common culture with shared values and aspirations that generate pride in traditions and customs and create a sense of familiarity and belonging;
- common past with heroes and myths; and
- special kinship through a common language (bilingual or multilingual countries such as Belgium, Canada and Switzerland are rare; most have one official language).

The next sections examine the ethno-linguistic and regional components of Canada's political culture with a view to what they consist of and how they do or do not contribute to a strong national identity.

Ethno-Linguistic Cleavages and Political Culture

There are many political subcultures that do not share all of the values and attitudes discussed above. Among the most significant of these are ethnic groups. As we noted in Chapter 1, **ethnicity** is primarily a subjective phenomenon, although it is usually reinforced by different customs, language, religion, dialect and cultural heritage, and sometimes distinct racial or physical characteristics. Language can be particularly significant in defining an ethnic group. **Ethnic origin** refers to the ethnic or cultural group(s) to which an individual's ancestors belonged; it pertains to the ancestral roots or origins of the population and not to place of birth, citizenship or nationality. Ethnically, of course, there is no such thing as a Canadian race.

In Canada, cultural pluralism has also been encouraged by the size of the country, its sparse population and, particularly, the federal system of government. If an original decision had been made to engulf minorities in a unitary rather than a federal system of government, cultural diversity might not have been sustained, and perhaps ethnic groups would not have the political significance they do today. That pluralism, which is a significant, vibrant and humane cultural characteristic of Canada, also creates serious ethno-linguistic cleavages. By **cleavages** we mean major and persistent differences among groups—differences that are politically relevant. Ethno-linguistic cleavages are significant in terms of political debate and controversy, and even national unity.

There are three major ethno-linguistic cleavages in Canada that profoundly affect the country's political culture. The first, between the two founding European nations, French and English, is based on the conception of Canada as a bicultural, bilingual state. The second important division pits the interests of these two founding groups against more recent and varied ethnic groups to arrive in Canada, and is based on the conception of Canada as a multicultural country. The third cleavage concerns the country's original inhabitants, the Native peoples, who today are struggling for recognition and self-government. We consider each in turn.

Before we begin, however, let us recall the changing ethnic composition of Canadian society. Ethnicity as defined in the Canadian census refers to the ethnic or cultural group(s) to which an individual's ancestors belonged. The concept is fluid and complex. There are more than one hundred ethnic groups in Canada and the relative size of the groups has changed considerably over time. The 1996 Census found that for the first time in history less than half of Canada's total immigrant population came from European countries, and, as we shall see, this trend is continuing. The largest ethnic groups are still people with British or French backgrounds, but their percentages are dropping. More indicative than self-ascribed ethnicity to determine the size of the French population is mother tongue—see below.

The French–English Cleavage

The primary cleavage in Canadian politics is between the French- and English-speaking populations and is based on the different histories, cultures and languages of the two groups. The 2006 Census enumerated 6.9 million Canadians who claimed French as a mother tongue—22.1 percent of Canadians.[27] Nearly 86 percent of them were concentrated in the province of Québec. Francophones, particularly in Québec, have distinct characteristics based on their common ethnolinguistic and historical background. English-speaking Canadians, in comparison, encompass multiple linguistic groups with many different ethnic and religious backgrounds. More than 17.5 million Canadians reported English as their mother tongue—58 percent of all Canadians. The remaining 18 percent of the population are allophones—that is, they claim a mother tongue other than English or French. While francophones are relatively culturally homogeneous and united in their cultural goals, the rest of Canada—grouped as English-speaking Canadians—are often unable to speak with one voice as a *cultural nation*.

The cleavage dividing French and English developed very early in Canadian history. We have discussed Hartz and McRae's concept of New France as a fragment founded by bearers of a French feudal tradition. From 1663, when it came under royal control, the political development of the colony was dominated by French-style absolutism. When the British conquest ended French rule, most merchants and officials returned to France, and the forces of modernization and change departed with them. The culture of New France was preserved by a few remaining institutions: the Catholic Church, the French language and civil law, and the feudal landholding system.

Historical events therefore produced a political subculture very different from its English Canadian counterpart. The most visible differences are found in language, a civil law code unique to Québec, and traditions, myths and heroes based on early Québec history. Less tangible, but real nonetheless, is a fear of assimilation that permeates politics because of francophone minority status.

In direct contrast to the encapsulated and preserved feudal fragment in New France, Canadian anglophone society was open to outside influences. An extremely high percentage of the early inhabitants of the northern British colonies were Loyalists who fled the American Revolution; indeed, their numbers—30 000 to 60 000—submerged the fewer than 15 000 English colonists already in Canada. The Loyalists brought with them attitudes still prevalent today in English Canadian society: some aspects of the liberal US tradition, but also anti-American sentiments and a corresponding loyalty to the British Crown. Some authors have termed this bond with Britain a colonial mentality, "an artificial loyalty to the Crown that grew ever more strained as new Canadians without British origins poured into the population."[28] Arguably, the net effect was to delay the development of a unified and coherent national identity.

French and English Canadians often get into emotional tangles because of different, and often confused, definitions of the word *nation*. To French Canadians, the word tends to mean "people" or "society." To English Canadians, it generally means "nation-state, the combined people of a country." Léon Dion's description of this difference is tripartite: francophones see Canada as two distinct societies or nations, one French-speaking and the other English-speaking; these two

27. *Mother tongue* is defined as "the first language a person learned at home in childhood and still understood at the time of the census." The Constitution of Canada mandates a federal responsibility for the census and statistics (section 91.6). A full census is carried out every ten years; a shorter version of the census is carried out five years after each full census. In the partial census, all receive a questionnaire and one in five gets a longer list of questions. The data used in this chapter comes from various census tracts updated to 2006 when available. Data can be found online at www.statcan.ca, but also in various press releases, newspaper reports, provincial, federal, legislative and departmental documents.

28. Bell and Tepperman, *The Roots of Disunity*, 1st ed., p. 63.

societies are qualitatively equal in every way; and the Canadian Constitution should accordingly give special status to francophones within federal political institutions and also to the province of Québec.[29] Thus, while it is thought that many anglophones view Canada as one nation, with an enclave of French Canadians in Québec, francophones begin with the dualistic conception of a political system composed of "Québec and the rest of the country." This conception of Québec as a separate nation can be traced throughout the history of the province.

In 1867, the Fathers of Confederation created what has been called a *political nation*, giving Canada every power a political nation needed to thrive. George-Étienne Cartier negotiated for Québec and gave his strong support to this vision. But he also saw it as the responsibility of the provinces to preserve what he called *cultural nations*—cultures imported from England, Ireland, Scotland and pre-revolutionary France. After Cartier's death, however, his Québec critics claimed that Confederation was really a "compact" between French and English nations. This myth flourished, nourishing the notion of "two founding nations" that provided French Canadians with a collective claim to equality rather than minority status within Canada. The word *compact* also implied a right to secede from the bargain. This compact myth continues to be expounded by Québec's political leaders.

> Canada is *"not a real country."*
>
> **Lucien Bouchard, former premier of Québec**

Whether Canada is one nation or two, or more, is obviously a matter of definition. In the first chapter, we defined a nation as a politically conscious and mobilized ethnic group (usually with a clear sense of territory) that may possess or aspire to autonomy, self-government or independent statehood. Canadians are politically conscious and have a clear sense of territory, but they are not one ethnic group, so they do not fit our definition of a nation. Canada is a state rather than a nation. Québec francophones constitute a nation according to this definition, but their territory includes many people who do not fit that designation. And many more Canadian francophones live outside the province. Their designation as a nation according to our definition is also tenuous. The question of whether or not Québec is a nation has become something of a political minefield because recognition of Québec as a nation implies to French Canadian sovereignists their right to separate from Canada. In 2006, the federal Parliament passed a resolution that the Québécois are a nation within a united Canada (see Chapter 7 on nationalism).

Several historical crises marked the breakdown of goodwill between English- and French-speaking people in Canada, stimulating frustration and eventually separatist movements. Although Canadians outside Québec give them relatively cursory recognition, some French Canadians dwell upon these events and find in them the emotional justification for the need to defend themselves as a distinct cultural minority in Canada. They include the Manitoba schools question (1885–96), conscription issues during both world wars (1917, 1942) and the rejection of the Meech Lake Constitutional Accord (1990). These events and the growth of nationalism in Québec are discussed more fully in Chapters 5, 6 and 7.

French Canadians: A Cultural Nation The 2001 Census shows that francophones are increasingly concentrated in Québec, but other significant groupings reside in Ontario and New Brunswick. Over the years, French Canadian culture has developed and thrived.

29. Léon Dion, *Québec: The Unfinished Revolution* (Montréal: McGill-Queen's University Press, 1976), p. 180.

Until the 1960s, the Roman Catholic Church was usually successful at directing and fostering attitudes of withdrawal and non-participation among French Canadians in Québec. They were concerned mainly with *la survivance*, cultural preservation that necessitated resistance to change and withdrawal from external influences that would alter the composition of francophone society. French Canadians were content to resist change, rather than control it. They neither participated as a group in the political affairs of the country nor even exploited to any degree the control that they, the majority, could have wielded within their own provincial jurisdiction.

The situation began to change in the early 1960s, when the election of the Jean Lesage government on a *maîtres chez nous* platform revealed a change in the character and aspirations of French Canadian society—the beginning of the Quiet Revolution. The influence of the Catholic Church had declined dramatically. Québec francophones had come to believe that if they were to maintain their identity they had to take control of their own destiny. Because of these factors, Québec politics changed from a defensive, conservative nationalism to a modern politics of liberalism, socialism and even more radical thought.

The Quiet Revolution soon became a challenge to Canadian federalism (see Chapters 6 and 7). The Royal Commission on Bilingualism and Biculturalism confirmed that the constitutional state of affairs established in 1867, and never before seriously questioned, was being rejected by francophone Québeckers. The strategy of *la survivance* had been replaced by *l'épanouissement*—in this case, a desire to develop French Canadian culture to its full extent and participate actively in fulfilling francophone aspirations.[30] Thus, until the Quiet Revolution, the needs and aspirations of both communities and governments were relatively congruent; since then, they have often diverged or conflicted.

During the 1960s, the federal Liberal government responded to the Quiet Revolution by declaring Canadian federal institutions to be officially bilingual. It increased the number of bilingual civil servants in the government and improved government services in both languages. As early as 1973, many public service positions were designated bilingual, a process that continues to this day.

The rise in Québec national consciousness directed and channelled economic, social and political change in that province. The provincial government became the focus of political modernization, assuming a much greater role in the economy and society than ever before. Traditional socio-economic patterns gradually shifted as the anglophone business elite left the province in great numbers and francophones began to occupy an ever-larger proportion of the economic middle class in Québec. A prolific and dynamic francophone business elite eventually moved beyond Québec into other Canadian and international markets. Francophones soon controlled a greater portion of the province's economic base and held more senior management positions than ever before.

French-speaking Canadians, particularly in areas where they are more concentrated, do share a distinct history, language and culture. That does not prevent many of them from feeling they are Canadian. Acadian author Antonine Maillet made this clear in an interview when she was awarded the prestigious Prix Goncourt for French literature. She was asked how she regarded herself—as Acadian, French, French Canadian, French Acadian, Canadian or some other. She replied that she considered herself to be *all* of them in different proportions. Like Antonine Maillet, Canadians have *layered* cultures. Belonging to an ethnic group, whether French or any other, need not detract from a sense of being Canadian.[31]

---

30. For a more detailed discussion of Québec's Quiet Revolution, see Kenneth McRoberts, *Misconceiving Canada: The Struggle for National Unity* (Don Mills, ON: Oxford University Press, 1997).

31. See Antonine Maillet, "Canada: What's That?" *Queen's Quarterly*, vol. 99, no. 3 (Fall 1992), pp. 642–50.

Nationalist Attitudes of French Canadians Attitudinal surveys of French Canadians have, for practical reasons, generally been confined to citizens of Québec. What attitudes do francophones hold about their province, country and federal and provincial governments? In Québec, where political and ethnic boundaries more or less coincide, people often hold political attitudes that are distinct from those of other regions or provinces. But research on Québec attitudes is replete with controversy. The results seem to shift because of particular events and the manner and type of questions asked in the surveys. The more questions are posed in terms of the outright separation of Québec from Canada, the fewer positive responses are given. The more they imply a "renewed" Canada, a "reformed" constitution or the like, the more positive the responses are. In other words, response pattern is significantly determined by the nuances in the questions.

Public opinion polls in Québec have shown considerable ambiguity concerning French Canadian desires for federalism, sovereignty and independence. To illustrate the point, a cartoon run in *l'Actualité* in 1992, summarizing the divided and indecisive results of polls, showed a puzzled young boy saying, "It's like having to choose between chocolate and ice cream for life … it's very hard when you like them both!"[32] The intensity and forms of loyalty among French Canadians have changed over time. Between surveys done in 1970 and 1977, for example, the group's self-identification increased substantially from French Canadian, in which identification was with all French in Canada, to Québécois, limited to the francophone population in the province of Québec. This was accompanied by increased support for sovereignty-association. A 1992 study, however, concluded that in spite of the growth of support for sovereignty-association in recent years, Québécois still preferred federalism:

> *From 1977 to 1991, many studies have measured both support for sovereignty-association and support for some form of renewed federalism, and they have in all instances found greater support for the latter.*[33]

A majority of Québec francophones have long demonstrated a preference for remaining in Canada. But polls indicate that they want to stay only if their culture and language can be protected. This implies the need for special powers for Québec, a privilege that raises objections and hostility in other provinces. Following the failure of Québec's 1995 referendum and the responses of the federal government, separatist agitation greatly diminished.

Surveys that measure the relative attachment of francophone Québeckers to Canada and Québec do indicate a tie to Québec that is somewhat or much stronger than their attachment to Canada. A Statistics Canada survey in 2003 indicated that 74 percent of Québeckers felt a strong tie to Canada, while 82 percent felt a strong sense of attachment to their province.[34] This supported Maurice Pinard's conclusion that in ethnically segmented societies, because of the segmentation, people tend to develop a system of dual loyalties. His surveys show that if there is a system of dual loyalties, loyalty to Québec often seems much stronger than loyalty to Canada.

English-Speaking Canadians: The Rest of Canada

While French Canadians enjoy cultural unity, English-speaking Canadians are a cultural mix. In fact, 43.3 percent of Canadians claimed an ethnic background other than Canadian, French or

---

32. "Mon père m'a dit que c'est un peu comme s'il fallait choisir entre le chocolat et la crème glacé pour la vie … c'est très difficile quand on aime les deux!" *L'Actualité* (July 1992), p. 20.

33. Maurice Pinard, "The Dramatic Re-emergence of the Quebec Independence Movement," *Journal of International Affairs,* vol. 45 (Winter 1992), pp. 471–97.

34. *The Globe and Mail,* July 7, 2004, A3.

British in the 2001 Census. They reported more than two hundred mother tongue languages in 2006. Anglophones often find their values and interests challenged by the newer groups, and newcomers often feel threatened and discriminated against as well as resentful of what they view as francophones' sense of entitlement to extra privileges. There is evidence, however, that Canadian identity increases with successive generations in Canada, so that time gradually weakens these negative feelings.[35]

> *There is no real Ontario culture.*
>
> **Diane Lemieux, former Québec cabinet minister**
>
> *Quebec's culture is more distinctive, but Ontario's is more diverse.*
>
> **Journalist Sandra Martin**[36]

Ethnic groups in Canada are unevenly mixed throughout the population. In 2001, 94 percent of immigrants who had arrived during the 1990s were living in metropolitan areas. Nearly three-quarters of them lived in Toronto, Vancouver and Montréal. Whereas Toronto and Vancouver attract a disproportionate number of newcomers, the amount of immigration to Montréal is in line with its population share within Canada.

World history shows that many states can successfully accommodate vast ethnic differences, but they do so in different ways. The United States is often viewed as a "melting pot" because it was built through shared experiences and commitment to similar political ideals and values. Canada, on the other hand, is more comparable to a "fruitcake" because the Canadian approach has been to encourage different cultures to exist side by side in harmony and tolerance—not to "boil them down" in one melting pot. In other words, the Canadian model has been *integrative* or *pluralist*, as opposed to *assimilationist*. That approach was established in the Constitution (see Chapter 5) and continued with policies such as official bilingualism, multiculturalism, constitutional guarantees for Aboriginal rights and equality provisions in the 1982 *Charter of Rights and Freedoms*.

When non-English- or non-French-speaking immigrants (allophones) choose Canada, they usually learn to speak English or French, and the process of *cultural layering* that Antonine Maillet spoke of begins. As the flow of immigrants to Canada increases and the ethnic composition of the country changes, there is a growing challenge to maintain the balance between national loyalty and respect for diversity. The importance of this challenge cannot be overstated.

Immigration: Patterns and Policies Immigration is a shared jurisdiction between the federal and provincial governments. Accordingly, both levels of government consult annually about desired numbers of immigrants and settlement measures. Because of its special concerns, a *Canada–Québec Accord* gives Québec the unique responsibility for the selection of immigrants coming to that province.

Since Confederation, immigrants have come to Canada in several large waves, the first three of which were related to depressed economic and/or postwar conditions in Europe. The first wave, between 1896 and 1914, was composed mostly of British labourers, Eastern European peasants and US farmers. A second, smaller wave in the mid-1920s brought mostly Central and Eastern Europeans to clear marginal land and increase settlements, particularly in the West. Many were refugees and most were very poor. Immigration ceased almost completely during the Depression in the 1930s. The third wave did not begin until after the Second World War—it lasted until 1960.

---

35. See *Ethnic Diversity Survey, Portrait of a Multicultural Society*, 2002. Statistics Canada, 89-593-XIE, available on Statistics Canada's website, www.statcan.ca.

36. Quotes from *The Globe and Mail*, March 10, 2001.

Predominantly European in origin, it included a significantly larger number of better-educated professionals than the earlier waves.

The Canadian *Bill of Rights* of 1960 dramatically changed Canada's immigration policy. For the first time, a federal statute in Canada barred discrimination on the grounds of race, national origin, colour, religion or gender. In 1962, changes in federal immigration regulations shifted the main source of immigrants from those with British or French origins to Asians. Immigration levels rose again in the mid-1960s in a fourth wave and has remained well above 100 000 for most of the period until today. In the 1960s, Canada also introduced a points system that favoured highly skilled foreigners by assigning points for education and work experience and accepting those who earn high scores. In 1992, the pinnacle of the fourth wave, Canada accepted 253 000 immigrants and refugees. In 1995, a new ten-year immigration plan took effect and increasing numbers of immigrants were selected on the basis of their skills and capacity to "settle in" and contribute quickly to the Canadian society and the economy.[37] Throughout the 1990s, Canada accepted annually under 1 percent of the population, roughly 235 000 immigrants a year, including a small percentage of refugees and asylum seekers. This increased to about 240 000 a year from 2001 to 2006. Of the 1.8 million immigrants who arrived between 1991 and 2001, 58 percent came from Asia and the Middle East, and 20 percent from Europe. Nearly two-thirds of Canada's population growth comes from immigrants.

Overall, this immigration has created a multi-ethnic population and provided the fuel for economic growth in Canada. Between 2001 and 2006, immigrants added more than 1.6 million Canadians (see Figure 3.4), and this was responsible for raising Canada's population growth rate from 4.0 percent to 5.4 percent. From 2001 to 2006 Canada had the highest population growth of the G8 countries, due to immigration (see Figure 3.5).

FIGURE 3.4 Annual Numbers of Immigrants Admitted to Canada, 1901–2006

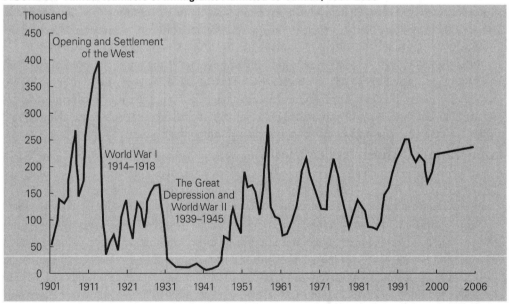

Sources: Adapted from Citizenship and Immigration Canada, http://www.cic.gc.ca/english/pub/facts2002/immigration/immigration_1.html; and Statistics Canada, 2006 Census: *Portrait of the Canadian Population in 2006*, http://12.statcan.ca/english/census06/analysis/popdwell/NatlPortrait1.cfm.

37. Applicants need to earn 67 points on a 100-point test that gives points for education, work experience, command of languages, and being between 21 and 49 years old. As of 2007, there is a backlog of more than 800 000 applications and waits of 4 years or more.

FIGURE 3.5 **Population Growth in G8 Countries from 2001 to 2008**

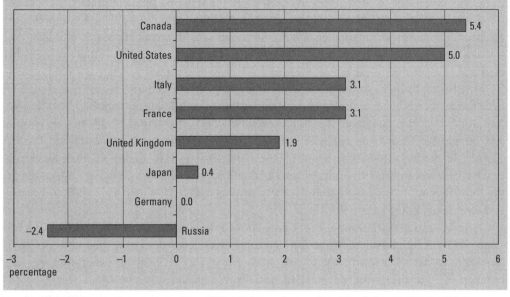

Sources: Statistics Canada, Census of population, 2006, US Census Bureau—Population Estimates, Program Istituto Nazionale di Statistica, Institut National des Statistiques et des Etudes Economiques, United Kingdom National Statistics, Statistics Bureau of Japan, Federal Statistical Office of Germany and Federal State Statistics Service of Russia.

Multiculturalism: Solution or Problem? Over the years, the reception and accommodation of newcomers to Canada have changed considerably. The initial tendency was toward assimilation. Later, however, during the high immigration period of the later 1940s and the 1950s (a period of economic recovery marked by a rising tide of Canadian nationalism), cultural pluralism, more commonly known as multiculturalism, gained popularity. **Multiculturalism** postulates that within the context of Canadian citizenship and economic and political integration, ethnic customs and cultures should be valued, preserved and shared. As noted above, it is an *integrative* approach, as opposed to an *assimilationist* one. The basic assumption of this policy is that confidence in one's own cultural foundations helps to break down prejudice and discrimination between ethnic groups.

There were many reasons for the growth of liberal views toward ethnic groups. Economic prosperity had eased cultural conflicts, and the new wave of immigrants (many of whom were educated or professional Europeans) helped to break down the rigid correlation between class and ethnicity. Britain was declining as a world power and therefore provided a less attractive model; at the same time, rising Canadian nationalism required a new self-image to distinguish Canada from the US melting pot. Perhaps the most immediate reasons for the advance of pluralist ideas at this time were the dramatic changes brought about by the Quiet Revolution in Québec. Many ethnic groups found the dualist image conveyed by the recommendations of the Royal Commission on Bilingualism and Biculturalism offensive and sought official assurance that their own aspirations and interests would not be overlooked.[38]

In the early 1970s, the federal government and the provincial governments of Ontario, Manitoba, Saskatchewan and Alberta formally adopted a policy of multiculturalism. In 1971, the

38. *Report of the Royal Commission on Bilingualism and Biculturalism*, Book 4 (Ottawa: Queen's Printer, 1970). In fact, it was in response to ethnic groups' pressures that the Royal Commission produced this volume dealing with the role of "other ethnic groups" in Canada.

federal government defined Canada as being *multicultural within a bilingual English–French frame-work*, and established a cabinet position of minister of state for multiculturalism. Services on which ethnic groups could draw were steadily increased throughout the 1970s. A comprehensive *Multiculturalism Act* was passed in 1988, and a separate department, Multiculturalism and Citizenship Canada, was established in 1991, later to become part of the portfolio of Canadian Heritage.

Apart from financial issues, multiculturalism creates a tension between duality and plurality in Canadian society. A commitment to multiculturalism makes it difficult to discriminate between "ethnic" and "official" languages in geographical areas where other-ethnic groups are concentrated and outnumber French- or English-speaking minority populations. In Toronto and Western Canada, in particular, where large other-ethnic populations exist under an English-language umbrella, there is pressure to make French equal only to other minority languages. According to the 2001 Census, 61 percent of immigrants who arrived in the 1990s used a non-official language as their primary home language.

Only in Australia is the proportion of population born outside the country higher than it is in Canada: 22 percent of Australia's population in 2001 was foreign-born compared to 18 percent in Canada.[39] To date, Canadian society has proven remarkably resilient in accommodating large numbers of newcomers with relatively little social stress. However, it is vital that adequate infra-structures such as language, culture and citizenship training are available to help immigrants adapt and integrate. This is particularly urgent, since the pattern of immigrant sources has changed dramatically over the last few decades, with increasing numbers coming from developing countries, especially ones in Asia and the Middle East.

Racism As of 2001, almost four million Canadians were members of visible minority groups—nearly 14 percent of the total population (see Figure 3.6). The *Employment Equity Act* defines visible minorities as "persons other than Aboriginal peoples, who are non-Caucasian in race or non-white in colour." Their number is growing much faster than the total population: it grew 25 percent between 1996 and 2001, while the total population grew by only 4 percent. In 2001,

FIGURE 3.6 Percentage of Visible Minorities, Canada, 1981–2001

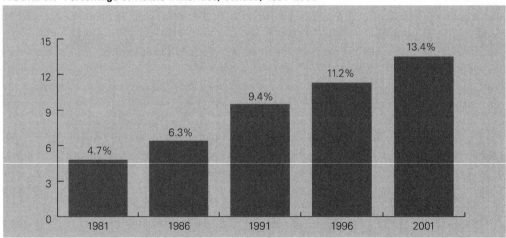

Source: From the Statistics Canada publication, *Canada's Ethnocultural Portrait: The Changing Mosaic, 2001 Census,* Catalogue 96F0030, January 21, 2003, http://www12.statcan.ca/english/census01/Products/Analytic/companion/etoimm/charts/canada/vismin.cfm.

39. Statistics Canada, 2001 Census: www12.statcan.ca/english/census01/products. Accessed July 5, 2004.

Chinese constituted the largest visible minority group, surpassing one million for the first time. Along with South Asians and blacks, they accounted for two-thirds of the visible minority population in Canada.

More than half of Canada's visible minorities live in Ontario and British Columbia. In 2001, they formed 36.9 percent of Vancouver's total population, 36.8 percent of Toronto's and 13.6 percent of Montréal's. Vancouver's visible minority population is almost entirely Asian.[40]

In spite of Canada's integrative and pluralist model, ethnic cleavages persist. Ethnic visible minorities tend to integrate less easily into Canadian society than do white European immigrants. In part this is because they struggle against racist attitudes in the population. *Racial discrimination* is the imposition of handicaps, barriers and different treatment on individuals because of their race. It is fed by prejudice and negative stereotypes. It creates a vicious cycle in which mainstream society is fearful and suspicious and the minority group is withdrawn and defensive. Often, minority groups become concentrated in specific neighbourhoods or geographical areas, and this tends to reinforce their social and ethnic differences.

Unintentional *institutional* discrimination known as *systemic discrimination* creates an additional hurdle for visible minorities, manifesting itself in high levels of unemployment and exclusion from certain sectors of the economy. The worst incidents of racial bigotry in Canadian history include the Chinese head tax imposed to prevent Chinese immigrants from coming to Canada after the completion of the Canadian Pacific Railway, the internment of Japanese Canadians during the Second World War, and the often-shabby treatment of Native peoples. Racist ideologies are condemned, but still persist.[41]

On the other hand, there is evidence that such incidents are more the exception than the rule. In 2002, a government survey on ethnic diversity asked people whether they had been discriminated against or treated unfairly in Canada in the past five years because of their ethnicity, culture, race, skin colour, language, accent or religion. Ninety-three percent said they had never, or rarely, experienced discrimination or unfair treatment for these reasons. Only 5 percent of visible minorities said they had been discriminated against or treated unfairly sometimes or often.[42]

Over the years, systemic discrimination has been studied and addressed by public policy solutions. The problem has not, however, improved. It is clear that attitudinal changes need to be continually addressed to foster awareness, understanding and tolerance—particularly since Canadians must anticipate an even greater racial mix in the population in the years to come. If recent immigration trends continue, projections show that by 2016, visible minorities will account for one-fifth of Canada's population.

Ethnicity and Political Culture   Cultural groupings within a state—**subcultures**—can be disruptive to the dominant political culture if group ties are stronger than loyalty to the country. Does ethnic diversity in Canada fragment the overall political culture and make the country less cohesive? Certainly, Canada has experienced several ethnic crises in which group loyalties conflicted strongly with larger community loyalty, although these were confined to the two founding groups. In these extreme situations, doubts were raised about the efficacy of the federal system of government to meet the needs of an ethnically diverse country and even about whether the country should stay united. However, it would be pessimistic to regard such crises as the norm.

40. Statistics Canada, 2001 Census, "Canada's Ethnocultural Portrait: The Changing Mosaic."

41. See Jean Leonard Elliot and Augie Fleras, *Unequal Relations: An Introduction to Race and Ethnic Dynamics in Canada* (Scarborough, ON: Prentice Hall, 1992). As of February 2006, individuals who paid Chinese Head Tax can apply for symbolic *ex gratia* payments of $20 000.

42. From www.statcan.ca/Daily/English/030929/d030929a.htm. Accessed July 5, 2004.

One can draw optimistic conclusions about the multi-ethnic nature of Canadian society from research by David Elkins that reinforces the suggestion of the Bilingualism and Biculturalism Commission that multiculturalism strengthens Canadian unity. Elkins concluded that ignorance of one's own and other nations is associated with parochial, localist sentiments, while knowledge about and appreciation of other nations is an enriching experience that encourages individuals to feel warmer toward their own country.[43] He also found that native-born Canadians are more provincially oriented than immigrants, and that the longer immigrants are in the country, the more provincially oriented they become. Another counterintuitive finding about immigrants to Canada is that they are on average slightly more positive in their political attitudes than native-born Canadians.

Cartoon by Steve Nease. Used with permission.

As well as having warmer feelings toward the whole country than do native-born Canadians who remain in one region, immigrants and internal migrants adopt norms and patterns of behaviour characteristic of the province in which they settle. This assimilation to provincial values and attitudes appears to be a function of both length of residence and type of background. Relatively recent or first-generation immigrant minorities tend to be concerned primarily with problems of adjustment to their new circumstances, whereas well-established minorities are less concerned with the persistence of their ethnicity than with increasing their collective economic and political strength. When language, religious affiliation and adherence to custom are used as criteria, ethnic identity is not static, but changes steadily from one generation to the next as individuals adapt to Canadian circumstances. The 2001 Census, for example, showed that 11 percent of those with a first language other than English or French were able to speak *both* official languages—2 percent more than those whose first language was English.

Today, except in Québec, minority groups are most valued where they are most concentrated. The 2001 Census results showed Ontario to be by far the largest centre for nearly all ethnic groups, followed by British Columbia and Alberta. Low acceptance of minority groups by Québec respondents reflects the tendency of some French Canadians to regard other cultures and languages as a potential threat. Any acceptance of other-ethnic claims, it is argued, undermines the concept of dualism for the country and reduces the French claim to that of the largest of the minority cultures. When Donald Blake examined the attitudes and voting behaviours of white, majority Canadians faced with concentrations of visible minorities in their communities, he found that

---

43. David Elkins, "The Sense of Place," in David J. Elkins and Richard Simeon, eds., *Small Worlds* (Toronto: Methuen, 1980), pp. 1–30.

positive attitudes toward visible minorities increased as neighbourhood socio-economic status went up.[44]

Bilingualism and multiculturalism are uniquely Canadian responses to uniquely Canadian circumstances. To date, research supports the positive effect of the cultural mosaic and indicates that multiculturalism is not to be feared, but encouraged (see Figure 3.7). Ethnic cultures erode over time: studies of language, religion and customs as indicators of ethnic strength all support this view. Given this erosion, it is sometimes argued that multiculturalism is a form of assimilation. On the other hand, there is no doubt that to encourage immigrants to remain in a cultural ghetto, emphasizing their differences from mainstream Canadian culture, delays their integration into Canadian society and thereby fragments national cohesiveness.

In many ways, the term *multicultural* is misleading: multi-ethnic may describe the Canadian reality more accurately. Whether or not one views multiculturalism as a viable government policy depends on how it is defined. Jean Burnet commented that

> *multiculturalism within a bilingual framework can work, if it is interpreted as is intended—that is, as encouraging those members of ethnic groups who want to do so to maintain a proud sense of the contribution of their own group to Canadian society.*[45]

In this way, the policy becomes something very Canadian: a voluntary, minor differentiation among peoples who are equal participants in society. Cultures cannot be preserved in their entirety; immigrants do adapt to the language and customs of the majority, but in doing so they add a richness, variety and depth to the cultural tapestry. The formal adoption of bilingual and multicultural policies enshrines ethnic tolerance among the other important values of Canadian government but it does not necessarily mean that such tolerance is realized in society.

FIGURE 3.7 Attitudes about Cultural Diversity in Canada, 2004

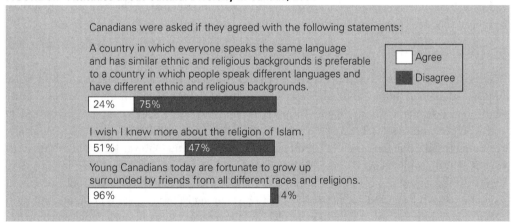

Canadians were asked if they agreed with the following statements:

A country in which everyone speaks the same language and has similar ethnic and religious backgrounds is preferable to a country in which people speak different languages and have different ethnic and religious backgrounds.
24% / 75%

□ Agree
■ Disagree

I wish I knew more about the religion of Islam.
51% / 47%

Young Canadians today are fortunate to grow up surrounded by friends from all different races and religions.
96% / 4%

Source: Survey by the Centre for Research and Information on Canada, reported in *The Globe and Mail* July 1, 2004. Reprinted with permission.

44. See Donald E. Blake, "Environmental Determinants of Racial Attitudes among White Canadians," *CJPS, 36*:3, July/August 2003.

45. Jean Burnet, "The Policy of Multiculturalism within a Bilingual Framework: An Interpretation," in A. Wolfgang, *The Education of Immigrant Students: Issues and Answers* (Toronto: Ontario Institute for Studies in Education, 1975). See also Ronald Beiner and Wayne Norman, eds., *Canadian Political Philosophy: Contemporary Reflections* (Don Mills, ON: Oxford University Press, 2000), especially Part 3 on multiculturalism and identity.

> *There cannot be one cultural policy for Canadians of British and French origin, another for the original peoples and yet a third for all others. For although there are two official languages, there is no official culture, nor does any ethnic group take precedence over any other. ... A policy of multiculturalism within a bilingual framework commends itself to the government as the most suitable means of assuring the cultural freedom of Canadians.*
>
> **Prime Minister Pierre Trudeau in Parliament, October 8, 1971**

Multiculturalism is a work in progress—the more multicultural Canadian society becomes, the more accommodations will be required to guard peace, harmony and democracy. This became evident after the terrorist attacks of September 11, 2001, against targets in the United States raised awareness, and even fear, about many cultural and religious minority groups throughout North America. The issue of how much accommodation should be made for cultural groups became an electoral issue in Québec in 2007. See the "Close-Up on Culture: Modern Issues and Challenges for Multiculturalism."

A recent study by Robert Putnam, an expert on civil society and democracy, concludes that diversity has a negative impact on community and social cohesion. This, he says, is because it diminishes our "social capital," meaning our networks of friendship, neighbourhood and trust. He found that people living in very diverse communities tend to withdraw from community activities and distrust their neighbours. They are less likely to believe in welfare or social funding if it does not apply to them.[46] Since the children of immigrants are particularly resistant to psychological integration into their new countries, Putnam's findings could have serious implications for Canada over the next two generations. Will Kymlicka argues that the success of multiculturalism in Canada can be measured in two ways: by finding whether Canadians are making progress in breaking down group inequalities (political, economic and cultural) and whether they are protecting the rights of individuals in groups (e.g., women and gays and lesbians).[47] This will become a more significant issue for Canadians in coming years.

Native Peoples: Indians, Métis and Inuit

A second ethno-linguistic division lies between Canada's Native peoples—status and non-status Indians, Métis and Inuit—and other Canadians. In 2001, nearly one million people claimed Aboriginal ancestry, of whom roughly 73 percent were North American Indians, 23 percent Métis and 4 percent Inuit (see Table 3.1).[48] Each group is distinctive. In 2001, the three largest groups according to language were Cree (80 000); Inuktitut (29 700); and Ojibway (23 500), but there are over 50 Aboriginal languages. These Native peoples are spread through every province and territory, with the largest population in Ontario and the largest percentage of the populations in the territories, Manitoba and Saskatchewan. The birth rate among Native peoples is declining, but more slowly than it is in the rest of Canada's population. Aboriginal women have 2.5 children compared to 1.5 across the entire population.

46. Robert D. Putnam, "E Pluribus Unum, Diversity and Community in the Twenty-First Century," *Scandinavian Political Studies*, Vol. 30, Issue 2, June 2007, pp. 137–174.

47. Report on the 2007 Couchiching Institute on Public Affairs, *The Globe and Mail*, August 13, 2007, p. A4.

48. Statistics Canada, 2001 Census data: www.12.statcan.ca/english/census01/products/highlights. Accessed May 7, 2004.

CLOSE-UP ON

MODERN ISSUES AND CHALLENGES FOR MULTICULTURALISM

As Canada has become more multicultural, cultural clashes between new visible minorities and the norms and rules of mainstream Canadian culture have become more frequent. Courts have increasingly been called on to resolve difficult issues. But legal decisions cannot provide the entire answer because what is needed is to find a balance between individual rights, beliefs and values and collective interests. Rights and freedoms are not absolute, but must exist in equilibrium with collective societal interests.

In the second half of the twentieth century, religion in the public sphere in Canada was relatively discreet, with only minimal physical or visual presence in workplaces and public schools. That has changed recently as the numbers of Canadians belonging to new minority religions have increased. Visual symbols such as turbans, veils and headscarves as affirmation of religious identity are common, and at least one group has requested that sharia law be instituted to resolve certain family disputes in Ontario.

Such novel realities played an important role in Québec during the 2007 provincial election campaign. The government faced public outcries and even death threats over issues related to whether or not Muslim women could vote without lifting their veils to identify themselves.

The issue spilled over into the federal arena as well. Elections Canada did not require women to take off their veils during three federal by-elections in September 2007, claiming that electoral law did not require visual identification if the voters in question provided two pieces of identity. The Harper government was not satisfied with this and introduced Bill C6 in October 2007—a bill that would force individuals to show their faces at the polls in the future. The bill is currently lodged in committee and may or may not pass.

Québeckers, like all Canadians, are struggling to decide what "reasonable accommodations" they should make for religious minorities. An 11-year-old girl from Ontario was forbidden to play soccer in Québec while wearing her hijab. In another case, when a Sikh teenager was granted permission by a Québec lower court to wear his kirpan (a small ceremonial dagger, a symbol of his faith) to school, protest was so heated that the youth needed police protection to go to class. In 2006, after four years of legal argument, the Supreme Court of Canada upheld the lower court ruling. The case became an issue in the 2007 election campaign when l'Action démocratique du Québec (ADQ) leader Mario Dumont declared the decision was an assault on Québec's values.

In yet another case, a sugar shack—*une cabane à sucre*—served traditional pea soup, but without ham, for Muslim visitors, and also allowed them to use the building for prayers. The event raised a heated debate across the province over how far their relatively homogeneous society should be required to change its traditions in order to accommodate foreign cultures and religions. A Commission was set up to study the issue. Dumont and his ADQ party again portrayed the incident as an insult to Québec traditions. Some argue that, given the ADQ's rise in popular vote in the 2007 Québec election, a great many people may agree with Dumont.

In the examples of the Sikh teenager and the *cabane à sucre*, what do you think would have been "reasonable accommodation"? Is Canada achieving an appropriate equilibrium between collective societal interests and individual rights that will allow people to live together in peace? Can both secular and religious values be accommodated at the same time?

TABLE 3.1 Aboriginal Identity Population, Canada, 2001

*Aboriginal Population	North American Indian	Métis	Inuit
976 305	608 850	292 305	45 070

* 20 percent sample data. Includes multiple Aboriginal responses and Aboriginal responses not included elsewhere.

Source: Statistics Canada 2001 Census data. Data is presented in two online reports: *Canada's Ethnocultural Portrait: The Changing Mosaic*, and *Aboriginal Peoples of Canada: A Demographic Profile*, both available at Statistics Canada's website, www.statcan.ca.

The term *Indian* was legally defined in the first *Indian Act* in 1876. Since then, anyone whose name appears on the band list of any Indian community in Canada, or on a central registry list, is considered to be Indian. There are about six hundred bands or **First Nations**, a significant number of whom live on reserves. There are status and non-status Indians. The concept of *status Indian* was adopted in order to determine who had rights to Indian land. Status Indians may be registered members of a band that "took treaty" with the Crown, surrendering land rights for specific bene-fits, or registered individuals who did not. Since they are registered, both types of status Indians receive benefits and privileges from the federal government. Many status Indians live on reserves, but more than half live in urban centres. The highest number is in the Greater Toronto Area, but Aboriginal people form a higher percentage of the city populations in smaller cities such as Winnipeg, Regina and Saskatoon.

Non-status Indians are individuals of Indian ancestry and cultural affiliation who actively or passively have given up their status rights but not their Indian identity. Métis, for example, are descendants of unions between whites (Europeans) and Indians. They retain their Indian identity but do not enjoy special status under federal policy. The exact size of the Métis population is not known, but they represent roughly 40 percent of the total Aboriginal non-reserve population. Apart from a few settlements in Alberta and Manitoba, Métis and non-status Indians do not have reserves. Most live in urban areas. The largest Métis populations are in Winnipeg and Edmonton. The rest are thinly scattered across the country and do not benefit from the special provisions for reserves and services under the *Indian Act*. In 1985, Parliament provided a procedure to restore Indian status to those who had lost it.

Inuit in Canada are scattered throughout the Arctic in eight distinct communities. Their population of just over 56 000 is young and growing quickly; it increased by 12 percent between 1996 and 2001. Inuit have never been subject to the *Indian Act* and were largely ignored by govern-ment until 1939, when they officially became a federal responsibility. Since that time, they have been classified as "Indians" for the purposes of the Constitution. At various times, the government has tried to relocate them into permanent settlements, but the results were disastrous, breaking their traditional lifestyles and leaving them dependent on the state.

Today's Aboriginal issues are rooted deep in the past. While nineteenth-century British authorities made extensive efforts to accommodate the French minority, they demonstrated little concern for the rights of the First Nations who, at the time, were self-sufficient and self-governing. Indian territory was set aside and could not be purchased or settled without the agreement of the Crown and the Aboriginal peoples. When European settlers needed land, land cession agreements were made in which the Aboriginals received payments and reserves for their exclusive use. Today, there are just over 2300 reserves, and about 60 percent of status Indians live on them.

At Confederation, the federal Parliament was assigned legislative jurisdiction over Natives and the land reserved for them.[49] Shortly thereafter, Parliament passed legislation in the form of the *Indian Act* that represented a clear policy of assimilation of Aboriginal peoples. When the govern-ment wanted to proceed with its trans-Canada railway, it signed treaties with Aboriginals where the railway needed to pass—in Ontario, the Prairies and British Columbia. These treaties served to extinguish Aboriginal rights and replace them with treaty rights. Natives surrendered land titles for reserves and other relatively minor benefits. The deals invariably favoured the government; it got the land it wanted, but gave small, barren reserves and little else in exchange. Essentially, Indians

---

49. *BNA Act*, 91:24. For background, see J.R. Miller, *Skyscrapers Hide the Heavens: A History of Indian–White Relations in Canada* (Toronto: University of Toronto Press, 1989).

on reserves were to be protected temporarily until they learned European methods of farming. They would then be qualified to relinquish their Indian status. Reserve privileges were considered a kind of probationary period of Canadian citizenship. Métis were not covered by these treaties, or by the *Indian Act*. As we saw in Chapter 2, led by Louis Riel, the Métis rebelled when settlers became a majority in their territory in Manitoba and Saskatchewan, but their protest was crushed.

The *Indian Act* of 1876 was amended frequently, but always with the aim of suppressing Native traditions and extending government control over status Indians on reserves. It remains an essentially nineteenth-century statute that reflects early biases and intentions. Although it has been widely condemned as paternalistic, the *Indian Act* was intended to protect Native people within Canadian society and to provide a broad range of social programs. All First Nations people receive the same benefits as other Canadians, such as child allowances and pensions, and status Indians also have a right to a wide variety of other benefits in the field of education, health care and housing. In fact, however, Native peoples have been left dependent on governments.

In 1969, when an initiative of the Trudeau government—the White Paper on Indians—called for the complete integration of the Indian population into Canadian society, it spurred the development of an Aboriginal movement in Canada. Over the next decade, Aboriginals organized and began to fight back. The Assembly of First Nations was formed to speak for status Indians. The Native Council of Canada speaks for non-status Indians; the Métis National Council and the Inuit Tapirisat organize and communicate their respective constituents' concerns.

On the government side, the Department of Indian and Northern Affairs Canada (INAC) has primary responsibility for meeting the federal government's constitutional, treaty, political and legal responsibilities to Aboriginals. Its role is to settle and implement land claims, negotiate self-government agreements and advance political evolution while managing natural resources and protecting the environment.

Relative Deprivation   The traditional ways of life of Canada's Aboriginals have been eroded over the years and their economic well-being seriously threatened. As a whole, compared with other citizens, Canada's Native peoples are economically deprived. Many are plagued by alcoholism and depression as they strive to cope with the loss of their traditional lifestyle. Métis and non-status Indians usually find themselves among the underprivileged of Canadian society and are subject to similar racial stereotyping and prejudice. The Inuit, because of their location in Nunavut, the Northwest Territories (NWT), northern Québec and Labrador, largely have been bypassed in the economic and political modernization of Canada.

> *We cannot escape the fact that we have built a great liberal democracy in part through the dispossession of Aboriginal peoples and the imposition of our cultural norms.*
>
> **The Royal Commission on Aboriginal Peoples, 1996**

Past treatment of Native peoples is shameful for Canadians. The condition of status Indians who live on reserves today is indicative of the problem. In modern times, this population has grown substantially, largely because of reductions in infant mortality rates and high rates of fertility. Approximately 40 percent are between the ages of 15 and 35, compared to 35 percent of the total Canadian population.

Despite (some would say because of) government assistance, Indians on reserves generally live in abysmal social conditions. While all non-Native municipalities in Canada meet basic standards, one in five Indian reserves has water and sewage systems comparable to the worst developing countries.[50] As well, the rate of tuberculosis is 43 times higher than among non-Aboriginals born in this country. Some of the best-off reserves are among the Cree in Québec, where settlements with governments have enabled them to evolve into increasingly suburban societies while still preserving important parts of their culture.

During the post–Second World War period, Indian migration to cities increased dramatically due to poor conditions on the reserves. However, even there, the migrants suffered from conditions they had hoped to escape—high unemployment and economic deprivation. Off reserves, the prison incarceration rate of Aboriginals is five to six times higher than the national average. Natives are more than three times as likely as non-Natives to die a violent death before age 65 and about twice as likely to die of any cause before 65.

Redressing Grievances: Land Claims and Self-Government

While they are divided on many other issues, Native peoples are united in a quest for settlement of their land claims and recognition of their "inherent right of self-government."

Land Claims Land claims are an urgent, ongoing problem. **Comprehensive settlements** determine land and money settlements, clarify Native hunting, fishing and trapping rights and clarify future economic development of disputed land. In some areas, treaties have not been signed; in others, they were but were blatantly unfair or not respected. In recent years, governments have sped up attempts to negotiate comprehensive and specific land-claims agreements. These are intended by governments to replace undefined Aboriginal rights with defined rights in an agreement or treaty. Where treaties exist, courts are forcing governments to live up to former treaty obligations and are providing compensation where it is due. (See Chapter 7 for detailed information on land claims.)

Aboriginal Self-Government Aboriginal self-government is another broad, contentious and ongoing issue. Attempts to achieve constitutional recognition for Aboriginal self-government failed with the collapse of the Charlottetown Accord (see Chapter 5), and the Supreme Court has never ruled whether there is an Aboriginal right to self-government. In fact, there is no agreement about what self-government means. For some, it means a level of government much like a municipality. Others believe the First Nations should constitute a third order of government. According to some Native leaders, such rights should not even be defined in documents such as the Constitution because they are "inherent rights."

Under self-government, as conceived by recent governments, First Nations would remain subject to almost all federal and provincial laws and their powers would be only slightly greater than those of Canadian villages, towns or cities. However, Native leaders maintain they cannot accept any imposition on the inherent right of their people to govern themselves. They argue that no Canadian government is in a position to grant a right that predates it and that has no source in any imperial, colonial or dominion authority. They consider that their right to govern themselves is a pre-existing, continuing, natural right given to them by the Great Creator. It cannot be given or taken away by any government. They reason that they have never given up their right to self-government, and it has never been extinguished by any legislation (because such power could not exist). The courts and international law affirm that Aboriginal rights may be extinguished only by treaty or conquest, or by an explicit act of the Parliament of Canada.

---

50. From a draft report by Health Canada and Indian Affairs, in the *Ottawa Citizen*, May 3, 1995.

> *We've made enough mistakes for them. It's time for them to make their own mistakes.*
>
> **Jean Chrétien, former prime minister**

In spite of these differences, however, the federal and several provincial and territorial govern-ments are negotiating agreements with First Nations peoples concerning how they will relate to other governments in Canada within the existing constitutional framework. Many limited self-government arrangements already exist that give bands powers equal to or greater than those of a municipal government, allowing Native reserves to organize their land and allocate their resources. Public opinion polls indicate strong support for Native self-government, although it appears that neither the Canadian public nor Native groups themselves have a clear idea of what exactly is meant by the term or what it will cost. (Aboriginal self-government is discussed in Chapter 7.)

Other Vital Issues There are several other areas where conflicts and controversies have arisen and continue to arise between Native peoples and other Canadians. Most have to do with special regu-lations for Native peoples, such as the right to hunt and fish where and when other Canadians cannot,[51] or the issue of tax exemption for status Indians. Since 1995, status Indians have been required to pay income tax on employment income earned off reserve. Historically, when assimi-lation was the official government policy, Indian babies were often removed from their homes and adopted by non-Aboriginals. Until the 1970s, Indian children were forced to leave home and attend residential schools, often far from their homes. These homes were often badly run and physically and emotionally abusive. Other issues include the right to have gambling casinos on reserves, and cigarette and other types of smuggling through Indian reserves on the Canada–US border. Occasionally, development has gone ahead on disputed land, causing violent confrontations. Such an example took place in Oka, Québec, in 1990 when a dispute over land led to an armed confrontation between Mohawks and Québec's provincial police—a police officer was killed. More recently, confrontation over development on disputed land in Caledonia, near Hamilton, Ontario, has been an ongoing dispute in 2007–08 (see Chapter 7).

Another issue that brings First Nations peoples into conflict with other Canadians concerns Aboriginal justice. Disproportionate numbers of Aboriginals are incarcerated in Canadian jails. Attempts are being made to rectify this situation. In 1995, the federal government amended the *Criminal Code of Canada* to read, "All available sanctions other than imprisonment that are reasonable in the circumstances should be considered for all offenders." The amendment calls for leniency in sentencing Aboriginals who transgress Canadian laws, and allows them to be dealt with in more appropriate ways. As well, more Aboriginal police are being recruited. And some provinces are allowing Aboriginals to police their own reserves and have their own justices of the peace and correctional services.

In late 1996, the Royal Commission on Aboriginal Peoples recommended that the relationship between Aboriginals and non-Aboriginals in Canada should "be restructured fundamentally." Some of its specific recommendations proposed radical changes such as a new third level of government. The Liberal government adapted the Royal Commission's recommendations into four basic principles: renewing the partnerships; strengthening Aboriginal governance; developing a new fiscal relationship; and supporting strong communities, people and economies. Progress to

---

51. A controversial Supreme Court ruling on Aboriginal fishing rights in the Maritime provinces in 1999 (in *R. v. Marshall*) led to violent protests by non-Native fishers. The Court was forced to clarify its position in a second ruling stating that Native fishing rights were not absolute and could be regulated by the federal government.

provide fairness and equity in the relationship between Aboriginals and other Canadians was stagnant for decades, but since the 1970s, aspects of life have slowly improved for some Native peoples.

Regional Cleavages and Political Culture

There is widespread acceptance in the theoretical literature of comparative politics of the thesis that strong regional interests are incompatible with mature statehood, and that state building involves a gradual reduction of conflict between regional and national interests. While this contention is not without severe critics, it remains one of the primary hypotheses about the growth and development of states and their legitimacy.[52] In this section, we address the question that links culture and regionalism: how strong is regionalism in Canada, and is it increasing or decreasing? Other aspects of regionalism are discussed in Chapters 2, 5, 6 and 7. The strong effect of regionalism on electoral results is discussed in Chapter 12.

Impressive factual data exist about distinct regional forms of social behaviour in Canada. Some researchers have argued that Canada has not merely one or even two political cultures, but several that are regionally based. In light of the distinctions we made earlier, these are not *cultures* per se but, rather, important subcultures within the overarching Canadian political culture. The establishment of a federal form of government created a structural guarantee that some form of regionalism would flourish in Canada; indeed, it was chosen partly because it would allow regional diversity.

Numerous factors promote and sustain this constitutionalized regionalism. People of varying historical, cultural and linguistic backgrounds settled in different parts of the country. Geographical and economic disparities among the regions fostered distinct viewpoints, loyalties and attitudes toward national political problems. Regional economic disparities based on natural resources, manufacturing centres, climate and proximity to markets created "have" and "have not" provinces. People living in the various regions of Canada feel the impact of these differences in terms of average disposable income, unemployment rates and poverty levels. Distinct political cultures and ways of life arise based on different circumstances and needs. The institutions and policies of the provincial governments reflect differences in the values and attitudes of their citizens.

The term **regionalism** implies a socio-psychological dimension in that the population displays an emotional identification with or attachment to a given territory. There is also a political dimension, in that specific interests—cultural, economic and political—can be defined and articulated for a particular area. There is general agreement that regions are more than purely scientific artifacts, but many different opinions surface about exactly what they are, how many there are or what their boundaries might be.

Some researchers hold that the boundaries of each of the ten provinces demarcate regions with separate political cultures. Others maintain that there are three, four or five regions. In the following pages, we have adopted a popular conception of Canadian regional boundaries wherein six regions are identified: the Atlantic provinces (Newfoundland and Labrador, Nova Scotia, New Brunswick and Prince Edward Island); Québec; Ontario; the Prairies (Manitoba, Saskatchewan and Alberta); British Columbia; and the North (Yukon, Northwest Territories and Nunavut) (see Table 3.2). However, basing regions on provincial boundaries (or groups of provinces) is largely a convenience, and significant variations in cultural patterns certainly occur within and across these borders.

---

52. See Raymond Breton, "Regionalism in Canada," in David Cameron, ed., *Regionalism and Supranationalism* (Montréal: Institute for Research on Public Policy, 1981) and Donald Savoie "All Things Canadian Are Now Regional," *Journal of Canadian Studies*, (Spring 2000). Available online at http://findarticles.com/p/articles/mi_qa3683.

TABLE 3.2 **Percentage Distribution of Canadian Population by Province and Region, 2006**

Province	%	Region	%
Newfoundland and Labrador	1.6	Atlantic Provinces	7.2
Prince Edward Island	0.4	Québec	23.9
Nova Scotia	2.9	Ontario	38.5
New Brunswick	2.3	Prairie Provinces	17.1
Québec	23.9	British Columbia	13.0
Ontario	38.5	Northland	0.3
Manitoba	3.6		100
Saskatchewan	3.1		
Alberta	10.4		
British Columbia	13.0		
Yukon Territory	0.1		
Northwest Territory	0.1		
Nunavut	0.1		
	100		

Source: Data adapted from Statistics Canada 2006. Census data available at www.statcan.ca.

Six Regional Profiles

Four main categories of regional differences lead researchers to expect cultural diversity: physical factors (such as climate, terrain and land quality); demographic factors (including ethnic and religious composition, and urbanization); economic development (including natural resources and type of economy); and services that affect the quality of life (such as transportation, health and welfare). Figure 3.8 shows population growth of the provinces and territories from 1996 to 2006.

FIGURE 3.8 **Population Growth of Provinces and Territories, 1996 to 2001 and 2001 to 2006**

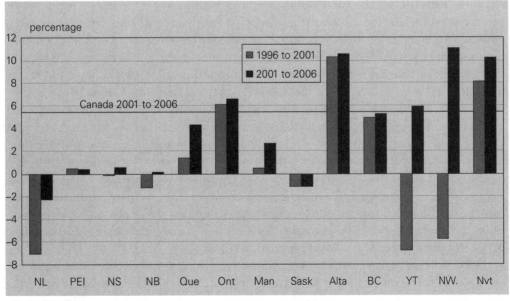

Sources: Statistics Canada, censuses of population, 1996, 2001 and 2006. Available at www12.statcan.ca/english/census06/analysis/popdwell/charts/chart4.htm.

TABLE 3.3 Median Family Income in Constant (2000) Dollars for All Census Families,[1] for Canada, Provinces and Territories, 2001*

Name	Median Family Income ($)		% Change
	2000	1990[2]	
Canada	$55 016	$54 560	0.8%
Newfoundland and Labrador	$41 214	$42 792	−3.7%
Prince Edward Island	$46 543	$45 606	2.1%
Nova Scotia	$46 523	$47 442	−1.9%
New Brunswick	$45 558	$45 194	0.8%
Quebec	$50 242	$49 891	0.7%
Ontario	$61 024	$60 853	0.3%
Manitoba	$50 934	$49 462	3.0%
Saskatchewan	$49 264	$46 889	5.1%
Alberta	$60 142	$56 140	7.1%
British Columbia	$54 840	$56 146	−2.3%
Yukon Territory	$63 490	$64 504	−1.6%
Northwest Territories	$69 046	$69 850	−1.2%
Nunavut	$39 424	$42 005	−6.1%

[1]Includes all families not identified separately.

[2]Median family incomes for 1990 are in 2000 constant dollars.

*20 percent sample data

Source: From the Statistics Canada publication, *Income of Canadian Families, 2001 Census*, Catalogue 96F0030, May 13, 2003, www12.statcan.ca/english/census01/products/analytic/companion/inc/provs.cfm. Accessed August 7, 2004.

Table 3.3 indicates in concrete terms the comparative economic position of families across the country. The following brief profiles of Canada's six regions illustrate some of these important differences.

Atlantic Provinces The four Atlantic provinces in 2006 made up roughly 7 percent of the population of Canada. The inhabitants are largely of British and Irish ancestry, with pockets of Acadian French centred in New Brunswick. The majority are Protestant, but Roman Catholics constitute the largest single denomination. The formal educational level in the region is relatively low, and the people are relatively poor. The Atlantic provinces usually have the highest unemployment levels in Canada (see the "Close-Up on Culture: Atlantic Canada in Comparative Perspective"). Most people reside in rural areas and small towns. Economically, the major contribution comes through the declining fisheries, and more than half of Canada's total are located here. However, in August 2007, Newfoundland and Labrador signed an agreement with industry partners to develop Hebron-Ben Nevis, the fourth oil field set to be developed offshore of Newfoundland. If provincial projections are correct the province will earn about $16 billion from Hebron over a 25-year period. The Atlantic provinces are seriously deficient in secondary industries and contribute less than the other regions to the national wealth in proportion to the population. Both internal and external communications are relatively inadequate. Federal transfer payments make up 30 to 50 percent of provincial revenues.

A low birth rate combined with low immigration and a tendency toward outward migration have often meant a net loss of inhabitants for the region as a percentage of the country's total population and a higher median age than for Canada as a whole. The region recorded a serious population decline between 1996 and 2001, but in the next five years it remained stable. Prince Edward Island is Canada's least populous province. Its growth stayed relatively stable at 0.4 percent between 2001 and 2006. Nova Scotia is the most populous Atlantic province. In the same period, it grew marginally at 0.6 percent. In New Brunswick, the population remained virtually unchanged in spite of increased international immigration. Newfoundland and Labrador lost 1.5 percent of its population in the intercensus period. Its fertility rate was lowest in the country.

Québec The province is the bastion of French language and culture, and is largely Roman Catholic. Since the Quiet Revolution, it has become an increasingly secular society. Eighty percent of Québec residents claimed French as their first language at the time of the 2006 Census; 8 percent claimed English; and 12 percent another.[53] The province's population growth was 4.3 percent from 2001 to 2006, three times higher than the previous five years but still below the national average of 5.4 percent. The growth was due largely to international migration and less out-migration to other provinces than previously. Québec's percentage of Canada's population in 2006 was down to 23.9 from 28.9 percent in 1966. Half of Québec's population (3.6 million) in 2006 lived in the Montréal metropolitan area—the second largest metropolitan area in the country after Toronto. Economically, Québec and neighbouring Ontario are the most industrialized regions, making major contributions to agriculture, mining, forestry, electric power, manufacturing and construction. Québec, like the rest of Canada, has a rapidly growing urban population that is located in a few major cities. Also like much of the rest of Canada, Québec is becoming more pluralist, but there is a visible minority presence only in Montréal—the rest of the province, including Québec City, is homogeneous.

Ontario Canada's most populous province, Ontario holds over 38 percent of the total population. Although still predominantly of British stock, Ontarians include large groups of French, Italian and German, in that order, and many other ethnic groups in smaller numbers. In 2001, over half of the Canadian population with non-official first languages resided in Ontario. They represented about 24 percent of the provincial population. Roman Catholic and Protestant denominations dominate, but many other religious groups are also represented. In fact, southern Ontario is one of the most religiously diverse regions in the world.

As noted above, Ontario, along with Québec, forms the industrial heartland of Canada. However, employment in manufacturing has been falling since 1990 and factory jobs and exports are currently being hurt by the rising Canadian dollar.

The number of Ontario residents regularly increases at a rate above the national average (an increase of 6.6 percent from 2001 to 2006, or 1.6 million people, half of Canada's population growth in that period). Much of the growth is due to immigration—more than 600 000 immigrants settled in the province in those five years. Two-thirds of Ontarians live in the Greater Golden Horseshoe region extending along Lake Ontario, and they make up one-quarter of all Canadians. The Greater Toronto Area (GTA) now houses over five million people.

CLOSE-UP ON Culture

ATLANTIC CANADA IN COMPARATIVE PERSPECTIVE

The Atlantic region is commonly regarded by Canadians as a collection of four have-not provinces. This idea should, however, be kept in perspective. Together, Nova Scotia, New Brunswick, Newfoundland and Labrador, and Prince Edward Island do have incomes lower than in other parts of the country but they are not poor by other standards. According to one study comparing the data of the Atlantic region with that of the 1996 United Nations Human Development Index, "Atlantic Canada's performance ... is roughly one percent ahead of the U.S. and Japan, but as much as three to four percent ahead of Italy." If the region had been categorized as a country in 1996, Atlantic Canada would have ranked as the second-best place in the world to live.

Source: *Ottawa Citizen*, June 10, 1996.

---

53. See Table 7.1 on page 229 in this book.

Prairie Provinces The three Prairie provinces—Manitoba, Saskatchewan and Alberta—are ethnically diverse and still reflect the influence of the European peasants who flocked to settle the prairie farmlands in the late nineteenth and early twentieth centuries. The first European settlers in the region were Scottish crofters in the Red River valley in Manitoba. Today, the largest single group in the Prairie region is still of British origin, but there are exceptionally high numbers of people of German and Ukrainian descent, a large percentage of Natives, as well as many citizens of Polish, Dutch and Scandinavian origin. No single religion dominates. Economically dependent on natural resources, the Prairie provinces make outstanding

Aislin, *The Gazette* (Montreal). Reprinted with permission.

contributions in agriculture, particularly wheat and cattle, as well as mining and oil and gas production. New techniques are allowing the tar sands of Alberta to be turned into oil at decreasing cost, so that Canada now has the world's second-largest oil reserves (behind only Saudi Arabia). Canada has about 180 billion barrels of proven oil reserves, but about 95 percent are in the tar sands.[54] Development of the Alberta oil fields has dramatically increased the prosperity and prestige of that province in recent years, making it Canada's richest province. It has no provincial sales tax and its economy is growing well above the national average. As of 2004, it became the first province to be debt free. As of 2008, Alberta's economic boom is still strong, but in Saskatchewan and Manitoba, cuts in farm subsidies, shrinking agricultural profit margins, mad cow disease and drought have caused a decline in farming and caused a population drain to larger Canadian cities and the United States.

Since the Second World War, the agrarian nature of the Prairie region has been changing and an increasing percentage of the population is urban (although Saskatchewan is still one of the least urbanized Canadian provinces). This region is home to 17.1 percent of Canadians. Alberta is the most urban of the Prairie provinces, and the most attractive for immigrants because of plentiful job opportunities in the oil and gas industries. There has been a significant increase in net migration in the region because of Alberta's prosperity during the past decade. Between 2001 and 2006, Alberta grew by 10.6 percent. It was the fastest-growing province in the period, and its share of the country's total population was over 10 percent for the first time. Manitoba barely grew faster than the previous intercensus period at 2.6 percent. Saskatchewan's population shrank through migration to other provinces, but the province's fertility rate was above the national average at 1.9 percent. Albertan's average age, at 35, was the youngest in the country as reported in the 2001 Census; however, Manitoba is the only province where the population is more youthful in rural and remote areas than in urban areas. Alberta was the fastest-growing province from 2001 to 2006—its share of the country's total population was 10 percent for the first time.

54. *The Economist*, December 3, 2005, p. 9.

British Columbia Cut off from the rest of the country by the Rocky Mountains, British Columbia has roughly 13 percent of the total Canadian population. Immigrants in the early years were primarily British, but today the ethnic composition is diverse because of high immigration and internal migration. Vancouver's population passed the two million mark in 2006. It has the highest proportion of visible minorities of all Canadian cities—about 37 percent, and they are almost entirely Asians. Religious affiliation is also diverse; however, the United and Anglican churches make up the majority. Economically prosperous, British Columbia makes major contributions through fisheries and forestry and, to some extent, through manufacturing and construction. Despite relying on primary resource industries, the region is relatively urban, with a number of heavily populated centres. Its population increase from 2001 to 2006 was 5.3 percent, close to the Canadian average of 5.4 percent. That growth was due to immigration, as fertility rates in BC were below the national average at 1.4 children per woman.

Northwest Territories, Yukon and Nunavut Canada's largest region, the vast northland of the Northwest Territories, the Yukon Territory and Nunavut (which became Canada's newest and largest territory in 1999), comprises 39 percent of the country's total land mass. However, the thinly scattered population, which includes the Indian Dene Nation, several Inuit peoples and Métis, and a small white population, constitutes a mere 0.3 percent of the Canadian population, in spite of rapid growth in percentage terms since 1971. The population living in the three territories surpassed 100 000 for the first time in 2006. Natural increase is the reason for high growth rates in NWT and Nunavut (11 and 10.2 percent respectively) as there is little international migration or migration from the provinces. In Yukon, the increase was largely due to migration from provinces.

To date in this region, only the Yukon Territory has full control of its onshore natural resources. The economy of the Yukon has grown rapidly over recent decades largely because of demand for certain minerals, but the economies of the Northwest Territories and Nunavut remain precarious. All three still depend on federal subsidies, which make up 60 percent of budget revenues in the Yukon and Northwest Territories and more than 80 percent in Nunavut. There are currently in the range of 130 companies exploring in Nunavut, looking for uranium, gold, diamonds, silver, zinc, nickel, copper, iron ore and sapphires. It already has its first successful diamond mine. Aboriginal groups in the Arctic, as in the south, benefit from special federal programs; most do not pay taxes, but the Inuit do. The territorial populations are more concerned about issues like the environment, development and defence as they work toward financial independence and see the effects of climate change on their traditional life. Developments increasingly are encouraged to respect local culture and safeguard the environment as well as to generate jobs for the local population.

Communications in the entire region are tenuous and, as we have seen, living conditions are difficult. Nunavut is Canada's largest jurisdiction—with one-fifth of the country's land mass, it spans three time zones. The creation of the territory resulted from the first agreement to give Native people powers of self-government equivalent to those of a province. Only in this territory do Natives outnumber non-Native inhabitants. Nunavut also has the youngest population in the country—the median age is just 22.1 years, 15.5 years younger than the national median of 37.6. Median ages in the NWT and Yukon, at 30.1 and 36.1 respectively, are also lower than the national average.

As we can see, major differences in historical development, ethnic and demographic make-up, and economic structure are evident in the six regions of Canada. However, since provincial governments provide the only institutional focus through which regions can mobilize, it is questionable whether particular groups of provinces can ever be as effective politically as individual provinces. Indeed, it is not even clear that they want to be.

Regional Alienation: Distance and Division

Canada faces persistent demands from alienated regions, especially the western provinces. Western discontent reflects the region's unique history and population mix. Canada developed around the concept of two founding peoples, but, as we have seen, this was never the West's vision of the country. In this region, people do not tend to state their interests in terms of the early history of Central and Eastern Canada. Largely because of the above-mentioned fruitcake mix of cultures and a relatively small francophone population, their political vision tends to be based more on economic development than cultural interests.

> *We in Atlantic Canada have not yet made the decision to develop as a region. We are four separate, competitive, jealous and parochial provinces.*
>
> **Former premier of Prince Edward Island, Alex Campbell**

Regionalism and its impact are discussed at length in Chapters 6 and 7. Here, it is important to note, however, that regional economic disparities and the manner they are dealt with are distinguishing features of Canadian politics. Since Confederation, the belief that the rich provinces and regions should help the poorer ones has been a fundamental part of Canadian political culture. Sharing through redistribution is built into the political system and is viewed by Canadians as the "just" way to cope with differences in wealth.

Disputes over formulas and provincial jostling for a fair share of the economic pie take place within this basic redistribution framework. One study commissioned by the Task Force on Canadian Unity in 1978 concluded that attachment to either region or province does not threaten national integration.[55] It has even been suggested that regional discontent may be more a fabrication of elites than a strong feeling of the mass public because the local political elite often benefit when they exacerbate differences while the federal government is listening. Provincial premiers play on regional sentiments when they want to strike tough financial bargains with the federal government.[56]

Regional Political Cultures

Richard Simeon and David Elkins are among those who argue that Canada embraces several regional political subcultures within the Canadian state.[57] They concluded that

> *there are indeed differences between the provinces which may be called cultural, which are rooted in the matrix of historical and sociological factors unique to each province.*[58]

It is interesting to speculate on the possible sources of the cultural variations among the provinces. Some of the factors outlined in the regional profiles above are undoubtedly significant. Levels of industrialization and economic development are extremely low in the Maritime

55. Relevant findings from the Atlantic Provinces Study conducted for the Task Force on Canadian Unity can be found in Gibbins, *Regionalism*, pp. 179–80.

56. See Robert J. Lawson, "Understanding Alienation in Western Canada: Is 'Western Alienation' the Problem? Is Senate Reform the Cure?" *Journal of Canadian Studies*, Spring, 2005. Available online at *http://findarticles.com/p/articles/mi_qa3683*.

57. Richard Simeon and David J. Elkins, "Regional Political Cultures in Canada," *CJPS*, vol. 7, no. 3 (September 1974), pp. 397–437. The revised version of this article is "Provincial Political Cultures in Canada," in *Small Worlds*, pp. 31–76

58. Ibid., p. 68.

provinces, and high in Ontario and British Columbia. Emigration from the Maritime area has often been high, while immigration to that region remains low. The fragility of the economy and the consistent historical inability of Maritime governments to solve the problem likely engender lack of political trust and feelings of inability to change the situation. As well, the peculiar pattern of settlement along the US border and the polycephalic city network that we discussed in Chapter 2 help perpetuate regionally based interests and attitudes.

Although it has become widely accepted among Canadian political scientists that regionalism is an important facet of Canadian life, the salient spatial boundaries of the regions have not been determined. Nor has the theoretical explanation of their persistence been satisfactorily developed. Some argue that it is wrong to conclude that Canadian politics is largely regional, because there has been no thorough study of class structure, or of the socio-economic issues dividing political right and left branches of public opinion. After analyzing a national sample survey, one study, for example, concluded that Canadian politics is regional only if political views are narrowly defined as attitudes toward electoral politics and governmental institutions.[59] Other researchers have shown that regional variations in opinions are neither strong nor consistent on topics that have no readily apparent territorial connotations, and that Canadians over the past thirty years have grown closer in their responses to important public policy issues, regardless of region.[60]

It is worth keeping in mind that one of the most salient characteristics of Canadians is not that they live in different regions, but that 80 percent of them are urban. In the 2006 Census, Canada had six metropolitan areas with more than 1 million people: Toronto, Montreal, Vancouver, Ottawa-Gatineau and, for the first time, Calgary and Edmonton. These six centres alone had a total of 13.6 million people, 45 percent of the country's population. Urban growth has been steady since 1901 (see Figure 3.9).

Regional cleavages, like ethnic divisions, are not necessarily detrimental; they can be healthy, and non-threatening to national cohesiveness. One study shows that although regional loyalty is often high

FIGURE 3.9 Canadian Urban Population Growth, 1901 to 2006

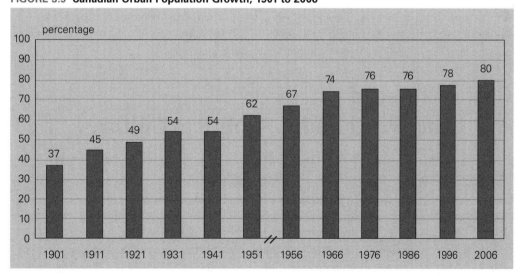

Sources: Statistics Canada, censuses of population, 1996, 2001 and 2006. Available at www12.statcan.ca/english/census06/analysis/popdwell/charts/chart5.htm.

59. M. Ornstein et al., "Region, Class and Political Culture in Canada," *CJPS,* vol. 8, no. 2 (June 1980), p. 267.

60. Roger Gibbins, *Regionalism,* p. 184; and Simeon and Blake, "Regional Preferences," p. 100.

in Canada, it is not held at the expense of national loyalty. In fact, feelings toward province and nation are strongly correlated—positive feelings toward the province are usually accompanied by positive feelings for the country. In addition, the more knowledgeable Canadians are about their country, and the more sensitive they are to regionalism, the more they favour the federal government over their provincial governments. Canadian nationalists not only tend to be well informed about Canada, they are also a cosmopolitan people who feel warmly about other countries.[61]

In conclusion, then, it is a mistake to exaggerate the divisive effect of regional differences in Canada. Not enough is known about whether territorial identities are compatible with strong national identification. But it is clear that strong regional identities alone do not prove that national identification is weakened or threatened. Western regional demands are not nationalistic; in fact, they usually do not call for separation. Western regional leaders restrict their demands to changes in the economic and political arrangements between the region and the federal government.

There is enough evidence to indicate that multiple ethnic loyalties need not be feared—they make Canada richer as a country. However, when strong regional loyalties are linked to general perceptions of injustice, regionalism may become a potent political force. The federal government must be sensitive enough to relieve tensions on these occasions. David Elkins expressed the matter this way:

> Multiple loyalties can have ... a civilizing result, since they encourage us to reject absolute choices and teach us to give assent and express dissent in graduated and qualified terms.[62]

Three major political developments during the 1980s and '90s have dramatically affected the direction of the Canadian political culture in recent years: the *Charter of Rights and Freedoms* has shifted Canada toward a more individualist focus and away from the country's communitarian, collectivist roots; the Free Trade Agreement (FTA) with the United States is having a *homogenizing* effect on Canadian culture by opening the borders further between the two countries; and the North American Free Trade Agreement (NAFTA) with the United States and Mexico is having similar repercussions. However, despite these developments, Canadians in all regions are quite similar in their expectations and preferences with respect to most areas of public policy. They want provincial or regional equity in government services and programs.

Critical Debate
A Distinctive Canadian Political Culture?

Is there a distinctive Canadian political culture? If so, of what does it consist? Does it have any impact on political institutions, political behaviour and public policy?

Point

*There is **no** single Canadian political culture. Political culture in this country is badly fragmented. These disjointed and fractious cultures continuously pressure and attempt to influence political institutions, behaviour and public policy.*

---

61. David Elkins, "The Sense of Place," in *Small Worlds*, pp. 23 and 25.
62. Ibid., p. 26.

Canada is not a single cultural unit, and never has been. Governments have tried to impose unity through flags, anthems, rituals and laws, but these have never been enough to meld the population into a single national unit. Because of its history, geography, immigration patterns and federal system of government, it is divided into many overlapping regional and ethnic camps, each narrowly interested in its own selfish concerns and self-advancement. When they have to choose, these bickering groups rarely put Canadian interests above parochial concerns. One often has the impression that if a better offer came along, any of them might leave the fold.

Regionalism is rampant. Ontario is a dominating, populous, self-centred bully; Québec is continually blackmailing the country, trying to get more than its fair share; the Maritime provinces are always looking for a handout; the Prairies are preoccupied with being out of the political loop and therefore not getting their proper piece of the pie; Alberta is unwilling to share its resources; located far from the centre and cut off by the Rocky Mountains, British Columbia would rather build its ties with the United States; the North is a financial drain preoccupied with the interests of Native peoples.

The federal system of government tries to accommodate the various regions and ethno-linguistic groupings, but ethno-linguistic cleavages are too great. It is often in the political interests of the provincial or federal political elites to frame issues so that their own interests and ambitions are accommodated. Bilingual policies that are demanded by French Canadians are resented in areas where French speakers are in a minority or are non-existent. Native peoples demand huge land settlements and compensation to redress past wrongs. Immigrants cling to multiculturalism policies because they don't want to feel like second-class citizens.

One might well ask, "Will the real Canadians please stand up?"

| Counterpoint

Yes, there is a distinctive political culture. It consists of overarching values that spring from the ideologies brought by our founding peoples. Canada's colourful political culture, buttressed by regional and ethno-linguistic groupings, constitutes the personality of the country. It guides Canadians' expectations and the demands they make on their leaders and institutions. It governs their responses to laws and leadership.

Canadians have a rich variety of perceptions and knowledge about their country, their provinces and their regions. The very nature of the country, with its geographical, historical, economic and demographic differences, dictates that this will be so. This diversity itself is the heart of the distinctive Canadian political culture.

Canadians did not create an ideologically based nation. Ideological diversity resulted naturally from a combination of such factors as a strong US influence, a high rate of population turnover and significant regional, economic and ethnic differences. Canadians also suffered a prolonged condition of colonial mentality that delayed the development of national symbols and pride. When the Constitution was brought home from Britain in 1982, Canada finally matured legally. Perhaps political and cultural maturity will follow.

It is difficult to measure something as elusive as a sense of political community. Regional and ethnic cultures do exist, but the models of governing that Canada inherited from the United Kingdom and the United States have fostered certain types of values, attitudes and behaviour toward the political system and government-related activities. The collective heritage of beliefs, opinions and preferences shared by Canadians is greater than the rhetoric of provincial autonomy and regional and ethno-linguistic cleavages would lead one to believe.

The federal structure and the party system exaggerate differences that exist among Canadians. In a successful federal system, citizens should feel positively about both federal and provincial levels of government. Canadians do. Those who feel strongly about their province also tend to feel strongly about their country. The two are not mutually exclusive; rather, they are strongly correlated.

The Earl of Balfour wrote in 1927 in his introduction to Walter Bagehot's book on the British constitution that "our whole political machinery presupposes a people so fundamentally at one that they can safely afford to bicker: and so sure of their own moderation that they are not dangerously disturbed by the never-ending din of political conflict."[63] It is not clear exactly what the British people were "fundamentally at one" about, nor is it clear today for Canadians, but the cohesion in the Canadian political culture has been strong enough to permit division and conflict without the eruption of widespread and continual violence. Politicians and government officials can rely on deep-seated attitudes to maintain the authority of government in Canada.

There is a distinctive Canadian political culture. Within the country, provincial political cultures are strong, and provide an assimilative framework for immigrants and internal migrants. However, this should not be seen as subverting the whole. The provinces also have many features in common. There is unity in diversity, just as the very different strands of which it is composed determine the strength and beauty of a tapestry.

Discussion Questions

1. What is your position on the Critical Debate, and what can you add to it?
2. Which concept or concepts do you believe more adequately represent the overall Canadian political culture—*melting pot, bicultural, multicultural, regional,* or *tapestry*?
3. Can the French and English concepts of *nation* be reconciled? Is Canada one nation or two? Or more?
4. Is multiculturalism a disruptive or integrative force in Canadian society?
5. What are the main grievances of Canada's Aboriginal peoples and what should be done to redress them? Is the federal government taking appropriate steps?

Visit our new Companion Website at **www.pearsoned.ca/jackson**, where you can use the interactive Study Guide and link to additional resources on topics discussed in the text.

Selected Bibliography
Political Culture—General

Behiels, Michael D., and Marcel Martel, eds. *Nation, Ideas, Identities: Essays in Honour of Ramsay Cook.* Don Mills, ON: Oxford University Press, 2000.

Beiner, Ronald, and Wayne Norman, eds. *Canadian Political Philosophy: Contemporary Reflections.* Don Mills, ON: Oxford University Press, 2000.

Bell, David V.J. *The Roots of Disunity: A Study of Canadian Political Culture.* Don Mills, ON: Oxford University Press, 1992.

Byers, Michael. *Intent for a Nation: What is Canada For?* Vancouver: UBC Press, 2007.

Campbell, Colin, and William Christian. *Parties, Leaders and Ideology in Canada.* Whitby, ON: McGraw-Hill Ryerson, 1996.

Cohen, Andrew. *The Unfinished Canadian: The People We Are.* Toronto: McClelland & Stewart, 2007.

Grant, George. *Lament for a Nation: The Defeat of Canadian Nationalism.* Ottawa: Carleton University Press, 1997.

63. Introduction by the Earl of Balfour to Walter Bagehot, *The English Constitution* (London: World's Classics Edition, 1955), p. xxiv.

Iacobucci, Frank. *Uneasy Partners: Multiculturalism and Rights in Canada.* Waterloo, ON: Wilfrid Laurier University Press, 2007.

MacGregor, Roy. *Canadians: A Portrait of the Country and Its People.* Toronto: Viking, 2007.

Mackey, Eva. *The House of Difference: Cultural Politics and National Identity in Canada.* London, Routledge, 1999.

Nevitte, Neil, ed. *Value Change and Governance in Canada.* Toronto: University of Toronto Press, 2002.

Stewart, Ian. *Roasting Chestnuts: The Mythology of Maritime Political Culture.* Vancouver: UBC Press, 1994.

Webber, Jeremy H.A. *Reimagining Canada: Language, Culture, Community and the Canadian Constitution.* Montréal: McGill-Queen's University Press, 1994.

Wiseman, Nelson. *In Search of Canadian Political Culture.* Vancouver: UBC Press, 2007.

Ethnic Relations/Multiculturalism

Bissoondath, Neil. *Selling Illusions: The Cult of Multiculturalism in Canada.* Toronto: Penguin, 1995.

Driedger, Leo. *Multi-Ethnic Canada: Identities and Inequalities.* Ottawa: Renouf, 1996.

Edwards, John, ed. *Language in Canada.* Cambridge, UK: Cambridge University Press, 1998.

Kelly, Ninette, and Michael Trebilcock. *The Making of the Mosaic.* Toronto: University of Toronto Press, 1998.

Silver, A.I. *The French-Canadian Idea of Confederation, 1864–1900,* 2nd ed. Toronto: University of Toronto Press, 1997.

Stein, Janice Gross, et al. *Uneasy Partners: Multiculturalism and Rights in Canada.* Waterloo, ON: Wilfrid Laurier University Press, 2007.

Troper, Harold, and M. Weinfeld, eds. *Ethnicity, Politics and Public Policy: Case Studies in Canadian Diversity.* Toronto: University of Toronto Press, 1999.

Wsevolod, W. Isajiw. *Understanding Diversity: Ethnicity and Race in the Canadian Context.* Scarborough, ON: Thompson, 1999.

Regionalism (See also Chapters 6 and 7)

Bercuson, David J., and Barry Cooper. *Deconfederation.* Toronto: Key Porter, 1992.

French Canada (See also Chapter 7)

Behiels, Michael D. *Canada's Francophone Minority Communities.* Montréal: McGill-Queen's University Press, 2004.

Young, Brian, and John A. Dickinson. *A Short History of Quebec.* Mississauga, ON: Copp Clark Pitman, 1988.

Native Peoples (See also Chapter 7)

De Pasquale, Paul W., ed., *Natives and Settlers Then and Now: Historical Issues and Current Perspectives in Treaties and Land Claims in Canada.* Edmonton: University of Alberta Press, 2006.

Micklem, Patrick, et al. *Aboriginal Self-Government: Legal and Constitutional Issues.* Ottawa: Canada Communication Group—Publishing for the Royal Commission on Aboriginal Peoples, 1995.

Smith, Melvin H. *Our Home or Native Land? What Governments' Aboriginal Policy is Doing to Canada.* Victoria, BC: Crown Western, 1995.

Trigger, Bruce G., and Wilcomb E. Washburn, eds. *The Cambridge History of the Native Peoples of the Americas.* Cambridge, UK: Cambridge University Press, 1996.

Chapter 4

Social and Political Context and Cleavages

Education, Media, Government, Gender and Class

Since Confederation in 1867, strands of national, ethno-linguistic and regional cultures in Canada have become layered and intertwined, creating the political culture of a relatively prosperous and peaceful country. However, differences among these three cultural strands have created tensions in the body politic, contributing to societal cleavages and providing a sometimes difficult environment for politics in Canada. How is this political culture maintained over generations of Canadians? What institutions and processes contribute to what Canadians think and feel about their country, their government and politics in general? What other social cleavages influence the political culture?

Not all Canadians have equal chances to succeed in life. They have different personal characteristics, abilities and health, and are born into different social and economic circumstances. Factors such as gender, education and socio-economic class help to shape an individual's ideas and orientation to politics. A woman from a poor, rural family with little education has experiences, opportunities and self-expectations that are vastly different from those of a man raised in a wealthy, urban, well-educated, professional family. As they go through life, these two individuals will experience unique treatment from parents, peers, teachers and employers. What is expected of them and what kinds of opportunities will be open to them differ greatly.

The chance circumstances into which one is born, then, help to shape an individual's general political culture. Gender assignment and socio-economic class, in particular, provide and also deny opportunities and experiences. Based on these factors, individuals may be inclined to take particular stands on issues, orient themselves on such abstract constructs as a left–right political spectrum and decide how, and even whether, they wish to participate in the political process. It is therefore important to understand how institutions and social groupings help to determine who and what we are as Canadians.

In this chapter, we examine some of the major ways that Canadians acquire political ideas and orientations about their country and its government and politics. We begin by looking briefly at the general process of socialization by which values and attitudes are learned, particularly at how the process occurs in families and peer groups. We then focus on the controversial roles played by three institutions—the educational system, media and government—in transmitting ideas and contributing to political orientations in Canada. In 2004, during Paul Martin's brief and turbulent tenure as prime minister, the issue of government advertising became particularly contentious because of the previous Chrétien government's botched attempt to strengthen national unity following the 1995 Québec referendum.

In the last section, we look at gender and socio-economic class, two social divisions that help to define who and what we are in society, and in doing so, condition political orientations. Combined with the ethno-linguistic and regional cleavages we discussed in the last chapter, gender and class round out the picture of how Canadians are divided in their political quest for who gets what, when and how.

Throughout, we invite you to formulate your ideas about the Critical Debate at the end of the chapter: "Should Canada Do More to Build a Strong National Identity?" In the Critical Debate, we ask if socializing agents adequately prepare Canadians to understand and participate in the construction of a strong, united country, and whether the federal government does enough or too much in this regard.

Acquiring Political Orientations

Acquiring political ideas and orientations is a lifelong process. Political culture is learned and transmitted at both the individual and community levels through **political socialization**. Children experience casual, informal learning of values and attitudes from family and peers, and more direct learning in schools. As they mature, other more explicit agents of political socialization and such factors as socio-economic class become influential. While political socialization is a continuous, lifelong process, some stages may be more important than others.

Development of the political self begins in childhood. By 5 or 6 years of age, children in Western societies acquire emotional attachments, which are nearly always positive, to the political community to which they belong. Symbols of the political community such as flags and anthems generally are regarded positively. Children identify with a gender group, social and economic class, and an ethnic or racial group, although again with little or no factual knowledge. Laws are regarded as absolute and unchanging; authority is perceived in people. such as police officers, firefighters or teachers, rather than in abstract terms, such as politics or responsible government. Political attitudes and beliefs learned at this time are less likely to change than those learned later, which involve more concrete information. This is important for the development and maintenance of the country's political culture, as it allows a high degree of continuity about basic values to be taken for granted in the political system.

Between the ages of 7 and 13, children increasingly relate to more abstract political symbols. They develop the capacity to see political leaders more critically, and their factual knowledge increases. Ages 11 to 13 may be the most significant in terms of the ability to reason and grasp abstractions. This stage is followed by a gradual increase in political involvement in the remaining adolescent years. Of course, political learning continues during adulthood, but although adults may alter their ideas and orientations toward specific government policies and develop evaluations of political parties and leaders, they are less likely than adolescents to change broad cultural attitudes and beliefs about ideological goals or conceptions of the legitimate means of such endeavours as selecting political leaders.[1]

Although an individual's political attitudes are formed early and tend to persist, they are retained to different degrees. If, for example, socialization is inconsistent, attitudes may be weakly held. The more diverse the agents of political socialization to which an individual is exposed, the greater the likelihood that contradictory messages will be received and changes or discontinuities in attitudes will occur. Some forms of socialization are indirect in that they are not overtly political. Others are relatively direct in that they transmit explicit political orientations.

Families and Peer Groups

Families are primary socializing agents They are generally important in determining the *extent* and *direction* of political learning, but the political learning that takes place within them is likely to be sporadic and incomplete. Attitudes and beliefs learned in childhood, such as love of country, tend to be intensely held and lasting. Families influence children in three main ways: 1) They provide

---

1. Richard E. Dawson, Kenneth Prewitt and Karen S. Dawson, *Political Socialization*, 2nd ed. (Boston: Little, Brown, 1977), ch. 5.

role models and sometimes even direct teaching about politics. Children from families that are active in partisan politics are more likely to be politically active when they grow up. 2) Families instill social attitudes and personality traits that influence how children will later react to the political world. 3) Finally, families provide social and economic surroundings, determine the social class of children as well as their educational values and first language, and, often, even direct what other socialization agents will affect the child—as wryly noted in verse:

> They f— you up, your mum and dad.
> They may not mean to, but they do.
> They fill you with the faults they had
> And add some extra, just for you.
>
> *Philip Larkin, excerpt from "This Be the Verse"*

Since families help to perpetuate traditional values, attitudes and behaviour, they are generally considered to be beneficial in countries that are trying to maintain the status quo, but as a hindrance in those trying to alter the political culture or instigate radical changes in society. In Canada, the fact that families are shrinking in size, breaking apart more readily and are increasingly headed by a single parent may hinder their effectiveness as a socializing agent.

Peer groups are another primary agent of socialization. Friends, sports teams and clubs of all sorts comprise this amorphous group that takes on increasing significance as a child reaches the age of 13 or 14, and continues to be influential throughout adulthood. Political socialization by peers, like that by the family, is haphazard because it is not usually the primary aim of the relationship. Peer groups often assume relatively greater importance in complex urban settings that are normally more impersonal and less family oriented than in rural societies. Peers use means such as persuasion, ostracism and ridicule to pressure individuals to conform to group norms and attitudes.

Peer-group and family socialization can be given much credit for the persistence of minority groups in Canada. Mennonite communities, for example, attempt to limit close personal relationships to group members so that traditional values will be reinforced.

Education and Political Orientations

The Canadian educational system, pressured from without by foreign cultural influences and fragmented from within by regional and ethnic interests, strives in an ad hoc and diffused way to impart to students an awareness of a common heritage and to instill national pride. Lack of centralized control and cultural pressures from the United States make this goal difficult, if not impossible, to achieve. Canadians often act less as "Canadians" than as self-interested groups of regions/provinces, ethnic affiliations or special interests that undermine national pride and unity.

The educational system influences political culture in many ways. It is a major source of information about politics and how the political system works. It teaches the basic skills that people need in order to participate and take leadership roles in society. Together with occupation and income, education is a principal determinant of social status. It helps to increase political awareness, expand opportunities and develop students' political skills necessary for effective participation. It teaches immigrant children one or both official languages and provides them with basic citizenship training. Post-secondary education has almost become a necessity for holding high public office. Education is the primary means by which people achieve upward mobility and escape from poverty. A university education does not guarantee financial success, but it certainly

FIGURE 4.1 Employment Growth by Level of Educational Attainment, 1990–2003

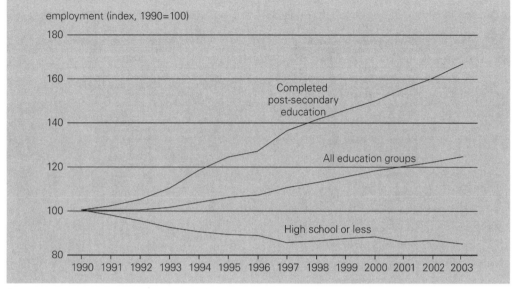

Source: Adapted from Statistics Canada Labour Force Survey. Published in *The Budget Plan*, 2004, (Ottawa: Public Works, 2004) p. 108. Reprinted by permission of Public Works and Government Services Canada.

improves the odds (see Figure 4.1). Increasing proficiency in literacy and numeracy "significantly improves the probability of being employed, the number of hours worked, and income."[2]

Today, free and compulsory primary and secondary education is provided to all Canadian children. However, significant inequalities in opportunities persist for reasons such as financial resources, family interest or variation in quality of schools in different municipalities.

At 8 percent of gross domestic product (GDP), Canada's expenditure on education is among the highest of the industrialized countries of the Organisation for Economic Co-operation and Development (OECD). Canadians have more education than ever before and are staying in school longer. They are among the most highly educated in the world and perform well on international tests. Forty-one percent of Canadians aged 25–64 had post-secondary education in 2001; over 20 percent had a university degree. Canada ranked highest in post-secondary education attainment among the OECD countries but dropped to fifth in the proportion of those with university education specifically (see Figure 4.2 on the next page). Gender bias in educational institutions has greatly diminished—women accounted for much of the increase in university graduates from 1971 to 1996, and are now over 50 percent at the undergraduate level.

In the next sections, we briefly survey the decentralized organizational structure of education in Canada. Then we focus on curriculum and subject content in Canadian schools to illustrate briefly how they strengthen regional and ethnic cultures at the expense of Canadian national identity.

Organizational Structure   The educational system in Canada is poorly equipped to build a strong Canadian identity (see the "Close-Up on Culture: Lack of Civic Knowledge in Canada?").[3] The fact that responsibility for education is largely provincial and extends downward to the municipal level

2. See Statistics Canada, "Literacy and employability," *Perspectives on Labour and Income*, March 2007, vol. 8 no. 3. Available online at www.statcan.ca/bsolc/english/bsolc?catno=75-001-X20071039605.

3. For a discussion of the relation between education and values in Canada, see Peter C. Emberly and Waller R. Newell, *Bankrupt Education: The Demise of Liberal Education in Canada* (Toronto: University of Toronto Press, 1994).

FIGURE 4.2 **International Ranking of Post-Secondary Education Attainment (Percent of Population Aged 25–64)**

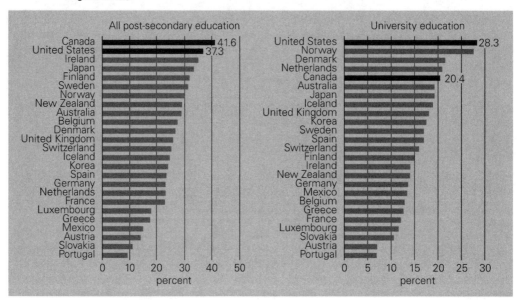

Source: *Education at a Glance*, Copyright OECD, 2003.

CLOSE-UP ON Culture

LACK OF CIVIC KNOWLEDGE IN CANADA?

A survey conducted by the Angus Reid Group in 1997 indicated that a large number of Canadians lack the civic knowledge required to understand and participate in the country's public life. Forty-five percent of respondents failed to answer correctly at least 12 of 20 basic questions on Canadian history, culture, government institutions and laws. In other words, the survey indicated that nearly one in two Canadians would fail the citizenship exam given to immigrants.

The following results were found in conducting the survey:

- Ninety-five percent of Canadians knew the title of the national anthem, but only 63 percent knew the first two lines. (Québec residents did the best on this question.)
- Only 8 percent correctly named the Queen as Canada's head of state; 57 percent believed the prime minister fills this role.
- Less than one-third were able to name the Charter of Rights and Freedoms as the part of the Constitution that protects Canadians' civil rights.
- Thirty-six percent could not place the date of Confederation anywhere in the nineteenth century.

If a Canadian citizen does not know such basics as what Confederation signified in Canadian history, or who the head of state is, or what the *Charter of Rights and Freedoms* is, what does that tell us about socialization in Canada? What does it tell us about politics in Canada? What, if anything, should be done about this situation?

Source: *The Globe and Mail*, October 11, 1997.

makes it difficult to establish uniform standards and provide equitable funding across the country. The constitutional division of powers also makes it impossible to ensure that nationwide interests are put ahead of parochial, provincial interests in terms of curriculum or subject content—or indeed, even considered at all.

In 1867, the Fathers of Confederation (in Section 93 of the *British North America Act*) placed education "exclusively" under the control of each province, recognizing the differences that existed at the time. However, the Constitution also granted Protestant and Roman Catholic minority rights and privileges in relation to education, and the federal government maintained direct control over the education of Native peoples.

At Confederation, the few degree-granting institutions that existed in Canada were largely supported and controlled by religious groups for the primary purpose of training clergy. Shortly thereafter, English-language institutions began to offer practical and scientific studies under secular control, while the French-language sector continued to emphasize classical studies under clerical control. As demands for university education escalated after the Second World War, coming to a head in the 1960s when baby-boom children graduated from high school in record numbers, provincial governments increasingly became involved in planning university development, and religious sponsorship and control diminished.

During the 1950s, the federal government inaugurated a system of grants in which funds for education were distributed to the provinces according to their population size. The provinces in turn distributed the funds to the universities based on full-time enrolment figures. In this manner, the universities became heavily dependent on public support.

The fact that the provinces retain the constitutional authority for education, while the federal government bears approximately half of the financial responsibility for post-secondary education, has obviously hindered the development of a cohesive, national educational system. To make matters worse, since federal financial transfers to the provinces for post-secondary education are based on population, not on the number of students enrolled, the current system of university finance penalizes provinces for attracting students from outside their boundaries. Provinces fund their own universities directly and do not pay for students who choose to study in another Canadian province.

Curriculum and Subject Content   The educational curriculum is potentially a major instrument of political socialization. However, in Canadian schools instruction is diffuse and ad hoc. Across Canada generally, some attempts are made to have children understand and relate emotionally to their country. In Ontario, for example, the Ministry of Education dictates that national symbols are to be regularly brought to children's attention and the proper reverence for them encouraged. As well, an important aim of many of the subjects taught is to impart an awareness of a common heritage and to build national pride. The general assumption is that learning the history, geography, literature and language of one's country helps create citizens with positive attitudes and beliefs about their state. Consider how effective the teaching of Canadian history and literature is in this regard.

Canada's educational institutions are particularly pressured from the United States. For example, textbook markets are so much larger and more lucrative south of the border that it is financially advantageous for Canadians to adopt US texts rather than use Canadian-written and -published material. The relative lack of Canadian content in textbooks is a source of ongoing concern. Several attempts have been made to regulate this situation in English Canada, where the problem is most acute. In Ontario, for example, a primary or secondary school book now must be written by Canadian authors and manufactured in Canada to be approved as a text; and every province has a "Canada first" policy, meaning that if a Canadian text is available, it must be given priority. Similarly, Canadian immigration regulations include Canadian-first hiring policies, which require that before hiring a non-Canadian, employers must demonstrate that there is no qualified Canadian available. This applies particularly to university professors and heads of cultural institutions.

History and Literature   Curriculum and subject material are not standardized, but are left to provincial jurisdictions. Students in different provinces therefore often learn quite different material and from quite different points of view. In the 1970s, the Royal Commission on

Bilingualism and Biculturalism revealed the extent to which textbooks expounded various myths and historical memories—and also focused on the differences between English and French texts in this regard.[4] In light of the Royal Commission's findings, many school textbooks were revised to eliminate blatant biases. Glaring stereotypes, such as the portrayal of Canada's Native peoples as "savages," "heathens" and "fiends" were also removed. However, differences remain to this day. The Québec nationalist interpretation of historical events has become standard in that province's textbooks, and that nationalist perspective is the accepted filter used to analyze political issues. Students across the country continue to learn the nature and glory of the established order through a combination of facts and myths, yet Canada's two European founding nations do not share a common national mythology.

Conflicting interpretations of Canadian history are regionally, as well as ethnically, motivated. Leading historians from Central and Western Canada have developed contrasting theses. For example, Donald Creighton saw Canada as an extension of Ontario. His *Laurentian thesis* holds that Canada developed around the extension of the trade routes, that the crucial drive behind Confederation was the commercial development of the St. Lawrence, and that the annexation of the West was an extension of this drive.[5] W.L. Morton's Western interpretation, on the other hand, is that Creighton does not take account of regional experience and history, but instead distorts local history and confirms "the feeling that union with Canada had been carried out against local sentiment and local interest."[6]

Morton contends that the study of Canadian history has been limited to the history of the economic and commercial development of Upper and Lower Canada, with little regard for the vigour of regional sentiment. For Morton, the Prairie provinces, unlike British Columbia or the Maritimes, had no option but to join Canada, as the colony of a colony, and have never existed outside that subordinate position. According to Barry Cooper, the result of this emphasis on commercial development and economic exploitation of the West by the Loyalist heartland has led to a split between political allegiance and local identity. "That split appeared and still appears, as a sense of sectional or regional injustice."[7] Often, political movements or minor political parties, such as Social Credit, United Farmers of Alberta or Reform, have turned such regional grievances against Ottawa and promoted a Western sense of identity.

Divisions within the Canadian political culture are revealed not only in historical interpretations but also in the works of novelists and poets. These works become instruments of political socialization; they mirror and reinforce attitudes about such issues as national unity and regional identity, as the following examples illustrate. Literary critic Northrop Frye wrote that the literature of one's own country could provide the cultivated reader with "an understanding of that country which nothing else can give him."[8] He found in Canadian literature signs of a closely knit, beleaguered society held together by unquestionable morals and authority—what he termed a *garrison mentality*.

Margaret Atwood expanded this theme, basing her conclusions on a survey of both English and French Canadian literature. The aim of garrison life is survival, and survival, she claimed, is

4. See Marcel Trudel and Geneviève Jain, *Canadian History Textbooks: A Comparative Study*, Studies of the Royal Commission on Bilingualism and Biculturalism, no. 5 (Ottawa: Queen's Printer, 1970), ch. 4.

5. Donald G. Creighton, *The Commercial Empire of the St. Lawrence, 1760–1850* (Boston: Houghton Mifflin, 1958).

6. W.L. Morton, "Canadian History and Historians," in A.B. McKillop, ed., *Contexts of Canada's Past: Selected Essays of W.L. Morton* (Toronto: Macmillan, 1980), pp. 33–34.

7. Barry Cooper, "Western Political Consciousness," in Stephen Brooks, ed., *Political Thought in Canada* (Toronto: Irwin Publishing, 1984), p. 228.

8. Northrop Frye, *The Bush Garden: Essays on Canadian Imagination* (Toronto: Anansi, 1971), p. 183.

"the central theme for Canada."[9] Literary critic Dennis Duffy further concluded that the strong garrison will of Central Canada was reinforced by political strength. The Canadian identity, he argued, has been restricted to the Loyalist heartland and does not extend to the Maritimes or the West.[10] Such literary analyses correspond to historians' emphasis on the importance of Central Canada and may, as Cooper speculates, help to explain Western political consciousness. If national unity is a symbol expressing "Canadian" identity, and that identity is limited to the Loyalist heartland, then westerners distrust national unity "as the manifestation of the garrison will."[11]

The tradition of the *political novel* is weak in English-speaking Canada. Hugh MacLennan's *Two Solitudes* is one of the very few works of English fiction to explore the French–English dynamic in Canada.[12] As an English Canadian (and long-time Montréal resident), MacLennan struggled to understand the different historical and cultural realities of the French and English in Canada, and suggested in his novel that hope *did* exist for understanding and tolerance between the two large linguistic groups. He maintained that as long as the fate of a person or nation is still in doubt, the person or nation is alive and real. It is only of the dead that no questions are asked. The issue MacLennan wrote about in 1945 is still relevant today.

Literature and theatre in Québec are flourishing, but they exist in isolation from English-speaking Canada. Artistic works are often highly political and supportive of Québec nationalism. In 1993, for example, Marcel Dubé's 1965 play *Les beaux dimanches* was revived. This popular, classic text of Québec nationalism contains long speeches about the historical humiliation of the Québec people and the negative aspects of federalism, set in the context of an appealing story of sexual infidelity and moral aimlessness. Dubé's highly political message is that independence can lead francophone Québeckers out of their "misery."

Today, as the Canadian ethnic tapestry has become increasingly complex, one could perhaps speak more accurately of Canada's three, ten or even more solitudes. Ethnic and regional interpretations of Canadian history are encouraged and often subsidized by the state. They exhibit subtle differences that contribute to or reflect political divisiveness at the expense of national unity.

Education of the country's First Nations populations presents unique problems. Their education is the responsibility of the federal government, and is administered by the Department of Indian and Northern Affairs. From its earliest days, the traditional, tacit goal of the government was to provide Native children with the knowledge and skills of mainstream Canadian culture and encourage them to identify with common values. This goal has shifted in more recent years to celebrate Native ethnic culture and pride. Some argue that in the former system Native students learned neither Canadian nor ethnic pride, but instead became alienated and disillusioned and that this contributed to high dropout rates at school and related social and economic problems.

As in other facets of educational socialization, the task is to establish an appropriate balance— to celebrate the ethnic differences and contributions that Native peoples make, while at the same time ensuring that they are not isolated, and that they learn to share and help develop the values of a strong and united Canada.

> *Some countries you love. Some countries you hate. Canada is a country you worry about.*
>
> **Robertson Davies, novelist**

9. Margaret Atwood, *Survival: A Thematic Guide to Canadian Literature* (Toronto: Anansi, 1972), p. 32.

10. Dennis Duffy, *Gardens, Covenants, Exiles: Loyalism in the Literature of Upper Canada/Ontario* (Toronto: University of Toronto Press, 1982), pp. 131–32.

11. Cooper, "Western Political Consciousness," p. 235.

12. Hugh MacLennan, *Two Solitudes* (Toronto: Collins, 1945).

The Media and Political Orientations

Mass communications constitute an increasingly important socializing agent both within and across borders, breaking down the barriers of distance.[13] Media can integrate or fragment the political culture of a country. They have the potential to reach vast audiences and manipulate subject content either to reinforce or to challenge the norms of society. One of the ways they do this is by acting as gatekeepers, selecting which facts, beliefs and perspectives will be covered and how they will be presented. In doing so, they help to shape the values of society and influence the political process. At their best, the media offer citizens a broad range of information and erudite commentary, and provide a voice for governments and opposition parties alike. At their worst, the media offer a distorted selection of facts and unbalanced, biased viewpoints.

The most significant political role of the media is in setting the agenda for public discussion and debate—that is, in helping to determine which issues people think and talk about. They also conjure up positive or negative views of the country and its institutions and help legitimize issues and actors. They build and destroy the public images of political figures by issuing labels (both good and bad) and via selective reporting and commentary. Investigative journalism, in particular, exposes corrosive issues and invites strong public reactions.

In Canada, there is little scientific evidence concerning the direct impact of the mass media's agenda-setting on national cohesion. However, it is generally accepted that the extent to which the media provide common images and a cross-regional flow of information, as well as the way in which they present regional and ethno-linguistic conflict, has a significant bearing on national unity. Because of Canada's federal structure, there is always a danger that the communications system will be either too strongly centralized or too fragmented. Centrally controlled media may produce hostility and alienation rather than assimilation to a national culture.

The publicly owned Canadian Broadcasting Corporation (CBC), CBC Newsworld and the French-language Radio-Canada; the privately owned English-language CTV, with NewsNet and its French subsidiary, TVA, and CanWest Global Communications provide national television service from coast to coast. *The Globe and Mail* and the *National Post*, both English-language newspapers, also contribute greatly to developing the national political agenda in Canada. Two other newspapers, the *Toronto Star* and Montréal's *Le Devoir*, help to set the agenda for national and public affairs, although they are regionally based.

These limited Canadian media sources face many restraints on their attempts to set the agenda for public debate. The obstacles include editorial policy, technological limitations and financial constraints—including the need to attract the large middle class and therefore obtain substantial advertising money. Their relationship with politicians is highly complex. It is particularly intense during elections, where every aspect of the campaign involves the media—as we discus in Chapter 12.

How do the media affect national unity, and what do Canadians think about politics? We focus here on four main problems: the lack of truly nationwide communications in Canada where all regions contribute significantly to the information flow; US influence; regional divisions; and ethnic cleavages. First, however, we briefly consider the history of communications networks in Canada.

Media Origins and Government Policy To build a strong national identity, it is important that citizens from various provinces and regions exchange ideas and information among themselves more than with external groups. In this respect, it is unfortunate that Canada shares the North American continent with the most powerful country in the world, a country that not only

13. Arthur Siegel, *Politics and the Media in Canada*, 2nd ed. (Whitby, ON: McGraw-Hill Ryerson, 1996), especially pp. 82–83. Also, see David Murray, Joel Schwartz and Robert Lichter, *It Ain't Necessarily So: How Media Remake Our Picture of Reality* (New York: Penguin, 2002).

is English-speaking but also extends along the most densely populated border of almost every Canadian province. The history of media development in Canada is to a great extent the record of a struggle by the Canadian government to counter influences of foreign penetration and bind the country together by better internal communications. Challenges to Canadian sovereignty have often come from US cultural influences in the form of movies, books and other print forms and television.[14]

North–south communications between the proximate English groups in Canada and the United States flow naturally, while internal communications among French and English regions as well as among the widely separated provinces of English Canada are artificial and need to be protected and nourished. Since the early 1840s, the development of modern communications systems has facilitated the natural north–south links and increased the threat of cultural domination from the south. East–west links, in contrast, have always been a challenge to maintain.

Canadian radio services, and later television, were also established in direct response to US infiltration of the Canadian market. Radio began with private initiatives and carried a high percentage of US programs. The government established the CBC in 1932 to provide radio services that would carry more Canadian content; CBC Radio operated separate English and French stations and co-operated with affiliated private stations. The same motivation brought CBC Television in 1952. In 1977, the CBC began to televise proceedings in the House of Commons on a second channel. Finally, in 1989 it set up an English-language all-news television channel, CBC Newsworld.

From newspapers to radio and television channels, through cable and pay television, and, finally, to satellite transmission, the common concern has been how best to protect Canadian cultural sovereignty from massive US media penetration. One secretary of state for communications warned that Canada would be "an occupied land, culturally" unless the government took action against the spread of US media—and urged the adoption of a national cultural policy similar to its National Energy Program.[15] However, steps to achieve such a policy have been slow and uncertain.

Several federal commissions, from the Aird Report in 1929 to the Davey Report on the mass media in 1970, studied and directed the course of broadcasting in Canada. In late 1982, the Applebaum-Hébert Report added a new dimension to discussions of cultural policy in Canada by advocating a federal system of arm's-length funding for all cultural agencies. It was followed in 1986 by the comprehensive report of a federal Task Force on Broadcasting Policy. These early reports set the agenda for discussions of federal cultural policy to the present day.

Broadcast Media: Television and Radio

Canada's broadcasting system is a mixed public and private system with more than six hundred private radio and television stations; a national public broadcaster; many community, campus, Aboriginal, English, French and third-language services; and a range of foreign offerings. The 1991 *Broadcasting Act* authorizes the system, as part of its mandate to

- safeguard, enrich and strengthen the cultural, political, social and economic fabric of Canada;
- be effectively owned and controlled by Canadians;
- operate primarily in English and French; and
- include a national public broadcaster, a single regulator and a single system.

14. Franklyn Griffiths, *Strong and Free: Canada and the New Sovereignty* (Toronto: Stoddart, 1996).

15. *Toronto Star*, November 29, 1981. For a useful account of government policy in the cultural industry field, see Stephen Brooks, *Public Policy in Canada: An Introduction* (Toronto: McClelland & Stewart, 1989), ch. 10.

Canadians spend an average of 21.1 hours a week watching television. There is at least one television set in 97 percent of Canadian households; 84 percent of adults, 87 percent of teens and 90 percent of children watch it every day.[16] Television is a primary source of information for most Canadians, and the chief means of communication between political leaders and the general public. It is a powerful medium. As TV audiences have grown, broadcast journalists have increasingly filtered the relationship between politicians and Canadian citizens. Television has placed demands on political leaders, and they in turn have learned ways to maximize their exposure and get the message they want conveyed to the public.

Consider some of the ways politicians are affected by television. Physical attributes and speaking style can jeopardize an individual's chances for political success. Much personal charm is often lost in the electronic transmission, as are intelligence and persuasive arguments. As David Taras notes,

> *Television by nature coarsens and distorts reality. Virtually all mannerisms are exaggerated: imperfect chins look more imperfect, a hand seems to shake more than it actually does, sudden movements give someone a frenetic look.*[17]

Consequently, politicians have to learn techniques to become more "mediagenic." Their mode of speech must be lively rather than slow and deliberate, but not too fast or staccato. Complex ideas need to be compressed into seven- or ten-second clips; they have no time for deep or thoughtful arguments.

Considering how influential television is, it is not surprising that there are major concerns in Canadian politics about how much the government should regulate its content. The primary question driving this issue has been, How real is the danger of assimilation into the US cultural milieu? Over 80 percent of Canadians have direct access to stateside television channels. All of Canada's national broadcasters show a preponderance of US programs—and surveys show that Canadians overwhelmingly prefer them to Canadian alternatives.[18] Former CBC president A.W. Johnson expressed deep concern about US influence:

> *The plain truth is that most of our kids know more about the Alamo than they know about Batoche or Chrysler's Farm. They know more about Davey Crockett than they do about Louis Riel.*[19]

Halting the drain of CBC television audiences who prefer to watch popular US programs has been a major problem for the public broadcaster. Many years after Johnson made his remark about US television's influence on Canadian children, then newly appointed president of the CBC Robert Rabinovich raised eyebrows when he candidly expressed to CBC Radio's *As It Happens* a sentiment felt by many Canadians:

> *My favourite TV show is* Law and Order.

Over the years, the federal government has attempted to increase the quantity and quality of Canadian programming in order to counter the threat of US cultural domination. First, as we have seen, CBC Radio and Television were created to be unifying forces and Canadian content was made

16. Lambert et al., "The Sources of Political Knowledge," p. 103.

17. David Taras, *The Newsmakers: The Media's Influence on Canadian Politics* (Scarborough, ON: Nelson, 1990), p. 122.

18. Ronald R. Manzer, *Canada: A Socio-Political Report* (Whitby, ON: McGraw-Hill Ryerson, 1974), p. 110.

19. A.W. Johnson, *Broadcast Priorities for the 1980s*, CBC Corporate Statement to the CRTC, 1978, p. 3.

part of their mandate. Second, the Board of Broadcast Governors and the Canadian Radio-television Commission (now **the Canadian Radio-television and Telecommunications Commission [CRTC]** were established to regulate both the CBC and all private broadcasting in Canada. The CRTC was given the goal of safeguarding, enriching and strengthening the cultural, political, social and economic fabric of Canada by regulating the content and standards of Canadian programming. It was given responsibility to set and enforce complicated Canadian-content guidelines for all licensed broadcasters and to determine the percentage of Canadian content and the time frame within which such programming must appear for both television and radio. The CRTC reports to the Parliament of Canada through the minister of Canadian Heritage (responsible for the *Broadcasting Act*) and works with Industry Canada, which is responsible for the *Telecommunications Act*.

The *Broadcasting Act* states that the Canadian broadcasting system should, through its programming, serve the needs and interests and reflect the circumstances of Canadians, including the multicultural and multiracial nature of Canadian society. To promote a "national conversation," therefore, the CRTC regulates which channels broadcast distributors offer and gives priority to Canadian signals to protect the small Canadian market.

The nationalistic recommendations of the CRTC are often highly controversial and politically unpopular. For example, the federal cabinet has often rejected its proposals for tougher Canadian-content rules because they would be strongly opposed by large sections of the public. Ministers argue that stiff regulation of programming and scheduling might mean loss of audience and advertising revenue, and, more recently, that an interventionist approach is obsolete given the advent of international satellite television, DVDs and the internet. The CRTC's steep requirements that there must be a domestic channel for every foreign one carried by a licensed Canadian satellite company, and that only CRTC-approved non-Canadian channels can be made available to customers caused substantial delays in bringing digital satellite to Canadian consumers.

The CRTC allows the prime minister special access to the broadcast media. Of course, the prime minister can ask for time on CBC television and radio at any time, but through an instruction from cabinet, the CRTC can invoke section 18(2) of the *Broadcasting Act* and demand access to all stations. Such an invocation constitutes a directive to all licencees to broadcast any program deemed to be "of urgent importance to Canadians generally."

The extent to which the CBC, under the watchful eye of the CRTC, has been successful in its mission as a public service is open to debate. It does ensure that some of the major people involved in broadcasting in Canada are Canadians. However, the subjects, values and ideas conveyed are often "Americanized" to increase their appeal to a broader North American audience and, therefore, make them more profitable. Canadians have shown a predilection for domestic news and public affairs programs, but even these rely heavily on US sources. This means that US foreign reports tend to displace not only Canadian reports, but even Canadian domestic news.

In 2002, Canadian programming accounted for 39 percent of our television viewing time. Francophones watch significantly more Canadian television than anglophones—for francophones, it accounted for 69 percent; for anglophones, 29 percent. And, while francophones spent 36.8 percent of their viewing time watching Canadian news, public affairs programs and documentaries, for anglophones, the corresponding proportion was only 15.8 percent. Anglophones watched far more foreign programming than francophones generally (see Table 4.1).[20] English-speaking Canadians also increasingly prefer getting their news from Canadian sources, but their public affairs programming from the US—especially programs like *60 Minutes*.

20. Statistics Canada, *The Daily*, December 2, 2002, Television viewing, p. 3

TABLE 4.1 **Percentage Distribution of Television Viewing Time, Francophone and Anglophone, 2001**

Type of Program	All Television Stations					
	Canadian Programs		Foreign Programs		Total	
	% Francophone	% Anglophone	% Francophone	% Anglophone	% Francophone	% Anglophone
News, Public Affairs and Documentary	36.8	15.8	2.6	10.4	39.4	26.1
Other	31.7	12.9	28.9	61.0	60.6	74
Total	68.5	28.6	31.5	71.4	100	100

Source: *The Daily*, Dec. 2, 2002. Adapted from information available at www.statcan.ca/Daily/English/021202/d021202a.htm. Accessed July 5, 2004.

Since the media help to set the agenda for public discussion and debate, it is not surprising that a society dependent on another country for its view of the world will absorb some of its norms. Clearly, the public's reliance on US media has a bearing on the fragility of the Canadian national identity. Restricting US cultural penetration, however, presents a serious dilemma. If Canadians believe in a free press and a free flow of information, then they should leave the borders open to all communications without restriction. An author once described the Canadian solution to the dilemma this way: we "follow a classical liberal ideology and let the media directors, advertisers and people choose the media and the media content they wish."[21] This situation reinforces US influence and weakens Canadian identity.

Financing is another ongoing problem for the CBC in carrying out its mandate concerning Canadian programming. The Mother Corp, as it is sometimes known, has been underfunded since 1953, and this has hampered effective planning in the face of severe competition from a rapidly expanding private television broadcasting system, both here and in the United States. Despite election promises to support the CBC, budget cuts by the federal Liberal government in the 1990s were particularly severe, causing staff and programming cuts and closure of some regional stations. The CBC absorbed more than $300 million in budget cuts from 1993 to 1999.

The economic dilemma for all Canadian broadcasters is that profitability rests largely on the use of imported programs. The United States exports expensively made programs for which costs are amortized in its large domestic market. Canadian networks can then purchase these products for a fraction of their cost. Private broadcasters try to provide programming with the highest possible appeal at the lowest cost and therefore want to import US-made shows. This pits them against the CRTC, whose role is to enforce minimum Canadian-content levels.

The CBC has to cope with these economic problems while carrying out its two conflicting mandates. It is required to promote a national identity and culture and, at the same time, cater to regional, ethnic and other minority interests. Establishing an appropriate balance has proven difficult. Broadcasting does a great deal to develop regional identities and particularistic concerns but is less successful at reinforcing national values and promoting national unity.

In particular, the media in Canada have difficulty bridging the country's ethnic cleavage. In the early years, rather than providing a powerful unifying link for the whole country, television broadcasting achieved the opposite. In Québec, where the full range of programming was local, the

21. Frederick Elkin, "Communications Media and Identity Formation in Canada," in B.D. Singer, ed., *Communications in Canadian Society* (Toronto: Copp Clark, 1975), p. 232.

identity that was reinforced was not Canada's but Québec's. Television helped shape and preserve the distinctiveness that led to Québec nationalism. Montréal sociologist Maurice Pinard commented

> *The Québec nation was born with television... I mean by that the Québec nation, as opposed to the French-Canadian people, which is something else altogether.*[22]

Despite the growing availability of English-language television stations, 87.5 percent of francophone viewers watch French-language stations.[23]

Even entertainment shows separate the two language communities. In the 1960s and 1970s, French Canadian entertainers such as Pauline Julien and Robert Charlebois were at the forefront of the independence movement. Their role was so prominent that former Parti Québécois leader Jacques Parizeau quipped that the Quiet Revolution was brought about by "three or four ministers, 20 civil servants and 50 chansonniers."[24] Today, many Québec artists like Céline Dion do not publicly endorse the separatist crusade and are building careers in the US market in English, but programming in Québec continues to be distinctively francophone.

English Canadian television programs also tend to restrict their focus to their own language group. They frequently feature Americans but only rarely francophone Canadians. Different agendas in the French and English media are often evident in political biases. For example, while English CTV is generally judged to be neutral and the CBC to be establishment-oriented in political leanings, Radio-Canada is considered more partisan, often leaning to the left and the Parti Québécois. A good example was the four-part series titled *The History of Nationalism in Québec*, broadcast on Radio-Canada in 1992. French-speaking Québeckers were presented as oppressed victims persecuted by *les Anglais* for more than two hundred years. All the social and economic problems of French Canada were depicted as the fault of *les Anglais*. It was nationalist mythology presented on television as fact.

Québec nationalism has even had an impact on the structure of the CBC. The president of the CBC is a political appointee, often with no previous background in broadcasting. The president presides over the CBC board—which is also appointed by the federal government. The controversial appointment system reflects the fact that, since 1968, prime ministers have been concerned with what they perceive as a separatist threat at Radio-Canada, so they want to determine who holds these key positions.

Communication issues have also often generated considerable friction between federal authorities and other ethno-cultural groups. Native audiences, for example, were slow to get services, although by 1993 all communities of five hundred or more people had, or were in the process of getting, radio and television services. This progress has assured more community control of northern broadcasting, but decisions about policy and funding are still made in Ottawa. As with northern education policy, efforts are being made to develop and fund programs that are relevant to northern communities and to Native people in particular. Similar efforts are being made to provide programming in foreign languages for large other-ethnic communities. But the problem remains how to balance the need to foster national unity while at the same time celebrating differences.

Technological change is making regulatory control of Canadian content much more difficult. In 1994, DirecTV offered Canadian viewers 150 television channels of entertainment and information

22. Quoted by Daniel Drolet in "TV Shapes Quebec's Distinctiveness," *Ottawa Citizen*, February 3, 1991.
23. Rhéal Séguin, "Use of French Rising in Québec," *The Globe and Mail*, June 19, 1991.
24. Peter Maser, "The Muting of the Strident Indépendantistes among the Artistic Community," *Ottawa Citizen*, June 20, 1992.

in the first direct broadcast satellite service backed by a major US company. It was the first serious threat to Canadian broadcasting from private satellite television operators. Since the CRTC had no legal jurisdiction over what the satellite carries, but the service did, in effect, contribute to the Canadian broadcasting system, the service was not legalized. Many frustrated Canadians purchased illegal US "grey market" satellite systems from DirecTV anyway. After years of systems failures and content controversies, Canadians eventually wound up with two digital satellite companies of their own, thus enabling the CRTC to exercise its mandate concerning programming. In 2004, the CRTC approved the addition of nine new non-Canadian, third-language satellite services to accommodate Canada's increasingly diverse population. The new services allowed consumers to receive programs principally in Spanish, Arabic, German or Romanian, and included access to the controversial Arabic-language news and public affairs programs of Al Jazeera.

As of 2008, the two licensed satellite providers were Star Choice and Bell ExpressVu. In April 2007, Telesat Canada, a world pioneer in satellite communications and systems management, launched the Anik F3 satellite, with the aim of providing broadcasting and telecommunications capacity and business communications throughout North America. At least 75 percent of Canadian homes now subscribe to cable television, for which television signals are received from large satellite dishes and then transmitted. The penetration rate for satellite-transmitted broadcasting is therefore growing substantially. If you add the worldwide reach of internet access to the mix as a source of both information and entertainment, it is clear that Canadians cannot be confined to using domestic media outlets. They can order the information and entertainment they want when they want it. They are able to put together their own newscasts and choose areas that interest them. Governments have little control. Eventually, networks, if they exist at all, will be transformed and broadcast executives will lose their power to decide what transmissions individuals receive.[25]

Print Media: Newspapers

The print media, unlike the broadcast media, regulate themselves through a press council and are free of direct regulation by government. They have a more restricted but also more attentive public than television has. As of 2008, there were 102 daily English- and French-language newspapers across the country (see Table 4.3 on page 123). Only about half of all Canadians read newspapers, but they tend to be among the best educated.[26] Data also show that "the most politically attentive individuals regard newspapers as the single most important source of political information."[27] Reading newspapers and magazines appears to be more "instructive" in terms of both factual and conceptual knowledge than is viewing television. Newspaper headlines, in particular, influence what the public perceives to be the most important problems facing the country.[28] This is signifi-cant in view of the fact that television is growing as the preferred source of political information among Canadians, and that fewer young people are reading newspapers.

The Globe and Mail is read by nearly three-quarters of the country's top decision-makers, and more than 90 percent of media executives read it regularly for ideas and trends. Since it became available on a nationwide, day-of-issue basis in the early 1980s, the *Globe* has gained considerable strength as a national newspaper. It is Toronto-based and, although it does carry national and international material, it is strongly biased toward central Canada and basically views the periphery

25. See Richard Collins, *Culture, Communication and National Identity: The Case of Canadian Television* (Toronto: University of Toronto Press, 1990).

26. Statistics Canada, *Canada: A Portrait* (Ottawa: Ministry of Industry, 2002), p. 114.

27. Lambert et al., "The Sources of Political Knowledge," pp. 373–74.

28. Fletcher, *The Newspaper and Public Affairs*, p. 17.

and the whole country from a central perspective. The *Toronto Star*, Canada's largest independent daily, can be considered national only by virtue of a few widely syndicated articles. The *National Post*, launched as a national newspaper in 1998 and also based in Toronto, has become more significant across the country. In the francophone community, *Le Devoir* is comparable to *The Globe and Mail*. Canadian Press (CP) (a co-operative news agency, owned and operated by Canadian dailies, that provides information to more than one hundred media outlets) and a few national magazines must also be included as part of the national scene.

These national networks are supplemented by a wide range of regional and local daily newspapers that are primarily community-oriented. They, too, depend on centre-oriented agencies such as CP for national and international news, reinforcing the influence of the central establishment on content and values. The steadily improving quality of CP and increased regional coverage by *The Globe and Mail* in tandem with the internet have contributed to a better cross-regional flow of information, as has the development of major newspaper chains at the expense of independent dailies.

Given the importance of newspapers in setting the national agenda, *control* is an important issue, and ownership restrictions have been designed to protect Canadian culture. While newspapers must be Canadian-owned, there are no rules about concentration of media ownership. Canada's two major royal commissions into the media—the Davey and Kent commissions in 1970 and 1981 respectively—had both recommended that safeguards be introduced to prevent concentration of ownership, but their views were largely ignored, and by the mid-1990s the consolidation of Canadian media companies had accelerated, gaining momentum by 2000. Within Canada, media concentration has been fluid and has often been a source of controversy. In 1992, for example, three major chains, Thomson, Southam and Hollinger, dominated the market in Canada, controlling over 64 percent of all dailies. Ninety dailies out of 108 belonged to the chains. By 1996, Conrad Black had added Southam to his Hollinger enterprise and controlled 58 newspapers with roughly 43 percent of Canadian newspaper circulation. Four years later, in 2000, a debt-ridden Black suddenly retreated from the newspaper scene and CanWest Global Communications, run by the Asper family took over a huge chunk of Hollinger Inc. That deal made CanWest Global, already the second-largest private national TV network, the country's biggest owner of newspapers at that time, with more than 200 publications, including 14 major dailies, numerous internet sites and a 50 percent share in Hollinger's *National Post* newspaper.

By 2003, sales and mergers put most of Canada's news media, including newspapers and broadcast stations, in all of the major cities in the hands of two media giants: CanWest Global and Bell Globemedia. In December 2005, Bell Canada Enterprises (BCE) sold most of its stake in Bell Globemedia, with the Thompson family (based in Toronto) becoming the major shareholder. In New Brunswick, the Irving family currently owns nearly all the daily newspapers, a number of weeklies and several radio stations.

This kind of domination by a few owners poses serious questions about lack of competition, diminishing diversity and possible conflict of interest. Both Black and the Asper family, for example, were notorious for heavy-handed imposition of their ideological perspectives on the newspapers they controlled—from editorials to cartoons. Individuals were fired, reputedly for producing editorials or cartoons that conflicted with company policy. The arguments against media concentration that had been aired during the Davey and Kent Commissions gained momentum, and, in 2003, a House of Commons committee on Canadian heritage released a range of proposals to curb concentration of ownership and improve media content. Then a Senate committee began hearings into media concentration—it reported in June 2006.

Advocates claimed convergence would lead to cost savings, increased advertising revenues and greater efficiencies, both necessary for newspapers in many Canadian communities to survive.

(In fact, convergence failed to bring in revenues for Bell Globemedia and for CanWest.) Critics argued that too much news now came through "one pipeline," that the quality of journalism had gone down as a result of convergence and that editorial independence was constantly being threatened. They pointed out that freelance writers were losing because media companies tend to buy articles and reuse them throughout their chains, in all media forms, at bargain-basement prices. Cost-cutting by media conglomerates has also led to the closing of some Canadian news bureaus (see Table 4.2).

> *Most democratic societies recognize the need to ensure the printed word and visual image should not be monopolized. If diversity of opinion lies at the heart of democracy, then surely no one person or company can be permitted to dominate what Canadians see, hear and read.*
>
> **Campaign for Press and Broadcasting Freedom, Canada**
>
> *There is no role for governments in regulating the news media. And that's what freedom of the press is all about.*
>
> **Anne Kothawala, president and chief executive of the Canadian Newspaper Association**

The June 2006 Senate report made forty recommendations, including several about concentration of ownership, but the controversy continues and the report is not binding—it is up to the government to decide whether to act.

Although it would appear to be in the national interest to maintain a diversity of news sources, research has been unable to prove that chain ownership affects the quality of newspaper news or editorial coverage. However, the issue points out the need for vigilance and for high-quality professional journalism. As Kent maintained, journalists always endure conflicting pressures, and when matters become too complex, only the most diligent cope by becoming more sophisticated and professional. As the possibilities for manipulation of the press by industry increase, the need for sophisticated investigative journalism is even greater. However, the reality seems to be that journalism has become *less* serious—much of it has become a kind of "infotainment."

Ownership of newspapers is constantly changing, and is currently a lesser issue than it has often been in the past. With 99 dailies in Canada, there are 15 different ownership groups (see Table 4.3). The largest ownership group is Quebecor/Sun Media/Osprey Media, which owns 37 newspapers. CanWest Global is second largest with a total of 13 newspapers, including the *National Post*, in various provinces.

TABLE 4.2 Canadian Foreign News Bureaus, November 2005

Organization		Foreign BureausLocations
CanWest	2	Washington and London
CBC	12	Bangkok, Beijing, Dakar, Jerusalem, London, Mexico City, Moscow, New York, Paris, Rio de Janeiro, Shanghai, Washington
CTV	9	Beijing, Jerusalem, Kampala, London, Los Angeles, Moscow, New Delhi, New York, Washington
The Globe and Mail	7	Beijing, Jerusalem, Johannesburg, London, Moscow, New York, Washington
La Presse	3	London, Paris, Washington
TorStar	6	Delhi, Hong Kong, Israel, London, Mexico, Washington

Source: *Final Report on the Canadian News Media*, vol. 1, Standing Senate Committee on Transport and Communications: www.parl.gc.ca/39/1/parlbus/commbus/senate/Com-e/tran/e/repfinjun06vol1-e.htm#_ftn9. Accessed December 13, 2007.

TABLE 4.3 **Chain Ownership of Canadian Daily Newspapers, March 2008**

Ownership Group	Number of Dailies	Examples
Glacier Ventures International Corp.	9	*Cranbrook Daily Townsman; The Citizen*
Quebecor/Sun Media/Osprey Media	37	*The Barrie Examiner; The Kingston Whig Standard; North Bay Nugget; Le Journal de Montréal; The London Free Press; Calgary Sun*
Brunswick News	3	*The Daily Gleaner*, Fredericton
FP Canadian Newspapers	2	*Winnipeg Free Press*
Transcontinental Inc.	11	*The Daily News*, Halifax; *The Telegram*, St. John's
CanWest Global Communications	13	*Calgary Herald; National Post; Ottawa Citizen; The Vancouver Sun*
Halifax Herald Ltd.	1	*The Chronicle-Herald*, Halifax
Power Corp of Canada	7	*La Presse*, Montréal; *La Tribune*, Sherbrooke
CTV Globemedia Inc.	1	*The Globe and Mail*
Black Press	1	*Red Deer Advocate*
Continental Newspapers Canada Ltd.	3	*Penticton Herald; The Chronicle Journal*, Thunder Bay
Glacier Canadian Ventures/ Alta Newspaper Group LP	3	*The Record*, Sherbrooke; *Lethbridge Herald*
Torstar Corp.	4	*The Hamilton Spectator; Toronto Star*
Sing Tao Newspapers (Canada 1988 Limited)	1	*Sing Tao Newspapers*
Independents	4	*Le Devoir*, Montreal; *Flin Flon Reminder*

Source: Data from the Canadian Newspaper Association. Information available online at www.can-acj.ca/Client/cna/cna.nsf/web/FactsOwnership. Accessed March 14, 2008.

News and Editorials   News presentation and editorial comment have a considerable impact on the political agenda in Canada. We have seen that economics constitutes a powerful factor in US influence on all Canadian media. The effects of economics are particularly evident in news reporting. The relative cost of "made-in-Canada" news-gathering is prohibitive, so Canadian outlets rely heavily on US agencies and wire services. This is particularly true in international news, but Canadian news is also distorted by the amount of coverage accorded to US domestic news. Topics of interest in the United States automatically become of interest to Canadians.

Another barrier to developing a national political agenda in Canada is the fact that the two founding nations live in separate media worlds that reinforce their linguistic and cultural differences. Newspapers serving anglophone and francophone communities normally focus on different headlines and stories; each often views even Canadian national events from quite different perspectives. Overall, there is a degree of stereotyping and insularity that fosters misunderstandings.

Editorials and news presentation do reflect community norms and generally support the status quo, tending to reinforce the prevailing institutional and cultural patterns of authority and orientation. This "middle of the road" tendency has been explained by three factors. First, since they must compete for advertising revenue, the media attempt to maximize their audience or readership by such methods as packaging news as entertainment and conforming to existing community values. Second, advertisers wield indirect influence on the content and direction of news and programming.

For example, editors or station managers would hesitate, and probably decline, to run a story that was adverse to the interests of a generous sponsor. Third, as the 1970 Special Senate Committee on the Mass Media suggested, many newspapers may be unwilling to challenge the existing power structure in their community because of "lassitude, sloppiness, smugness and too chummy a relationship."[29]

In the past twenty years or so, there also has been a trend toward "judgmental" journalism that stresses opinion over facts. The resulting, predominantly negative, tone of political coverage encourages a lack of respect for politicians, civil servants, government agencies and Parliament. For example, in 1992, a two-hour television program, *The Betrayal of Democracy* (PBS), examined the role of television and the press in the breakdown of the democratic process and the alienation of the body politic from decision-making. The thesis of the television special was that, wherever possible, government intentionally excludes citizens from the political process.

'Having decreed that only violence will successfully attract their attention, the media then denounces violence.'

Paul Gilligan, *Ottawa Citizen.*

> *It reduces democracy to a charade in which power is exercised for the benefit of assorted corporate elites ... and the elected officials who rely on them for the funds to remain in office.*[30]

Television news plays a major role in this charade. It limits the amount of air time devoted to political figures to about five seconds per appearance, reducing political discourse to meaningless slogans and simple-minded catch phrases. Too often, Canadian journalists treat public affairs as theatre and gossip, stressing personalities over social issues, style over substance. However, it may not be entirely their fault. As one study noted,

> *the vast majority of viewers/listeners/readers want all things on their information menu to be black or white, true or false, good or bad—preferably seasoned with a pinch of sensationalism and intimate personal detail of the famous, and served on a platter of conventional belief.*

Government Information and Political Orientations

The federal government plays a major role in shaping and reinforcing political culture. It informs, educates or propagandizes in order to increase public support and loyalty to the state. It takes on responsibilities for protecting Canadian heritage, even to the point of trying to protect Canada's

29. Special Senate Committee on Mass Media, *The Uncertain Mirror*, vol. 1 of the Report of the Special Senate Committee on Mass Media (Ottawa: Information Canada, 1970), p. 87.
30. Quoted by John Haslett Cuff in "Media and Democracy's Decay," *The Globe and Mail*, April 15, 1992.

cultural industries from trade challenges from the United States (see Chapter 15). For maximum impact, governments time their political announcements and broadcasts for peak (or minimal) exposure, advertise their policy positions, televise parliamentary debates and record statements in *Hansard*. Public servants answer questions and distribute information, including government booklets. Government ceremonies such as the Speech from the Throne are celebrated to instill respect and a sense of historical continuity.

It is the responsibility of the Department of Canadian Heritage and its portfolio partners and agencies to help Canadians overcome differences and distances and to understand and appreciate the values shared by all Canadians. It is a very wide mandate that covers subjects such as citizenship and identity, diversity and multiculturalism, women, sport and youth. Canadian Heritage sponsors a wide variety of events celebrating Canada—such as ceremonies for Canada Day, projects to promote multiculturalism and racial harmony, initiatives to honour Canadian heroes, booklets to promote symbols of Canada, winter games, francophonie celebrations and so on. It also contributes to international events connecting Canadians to the world.

Such government communications with Canadians have increased dramatically in recent years. One reason has been the perceived need to refurbish the image of Parliament and federal institutions; another has been the need to promote national unity and combat the centrifugal forces of separatism and regionalism. These concerns date back to the late 1960s when protest movements and vocal separatists started reinforcing the growing cynicism and hostility of Canadians toward the federal government and its work. Since then the federal government has asked questions about why it does not reap adequate credit for its work and its programs. Is the problem a breakdown of communications between the government and its citizens?

Early Government Information Services

In 1969, the federal government set up the Task Force on Government Information to address these and other problems of government information. Its report ushered in a controversial era in government information programming. Modern Canadian governments have all advertised to inform the public about such topics as new laws and regulations; in fact, each government department has a budget for such purposes. However, as a result of the 1969 report, a new agency, Information Canada, was set up to provide a direct information service for selling and distributing government pamphlets and providing other information across the country. It included a small "federalism" section, the aim of which was "a defence in depth of Confederation."

Information Canada was immediately attacked as a partisan party propaganda device by both the media and the opposition parties. It was disbanded in 1976. However, a year after its demise, other efforts were instigated to help government departments advertise their services. The government, in a word, went into the marketing business—to sell itself.

Promoting Canada: Government Advertising

The greatest criticism of government information services is that they can be viewed, justifiably or not, as a vehicle for publicizing the programs, policies and views of the governing party—as a partisan political instrument. As well, there are two ongoing controversies about government advertising. One is the use of advocacy advertising techniques; the other concerns financing. Both issues are volatile. In 2004, disclosure of scandals concerning the Chrétien regime's handling of political advertising helped reduce Paul Martin's government to a minority situation in his first election as leader, and contributed to the Liberals' loss to the Conservatives a year and a half later (see the "Close-Up on Behaviour: The Auditor General versus the Government").

In essence, **advocacy advertising** means selling ideas as if they are products or services. It is used by governments to sustain or change public attitudes concerning the fundamental values that underlie social and political institutions. Because advocacy advertising allows governments to inform Canadians without the intermediary interpretation of the press, government representatives tend to view it as a means to build national unity. Government advertisements, therefore, are designed to underscore what the federal government sees as basic national values and to promote understanding of national goals. For instance, ads extolling the virtues of Canada's multicultural society have carried logos such as "Growing Together" and "We Have a Lot to Offer Each Other."

This type of service becomes controversial when advertisements extol clearly partisan policy positions. One of the best examples was Liberal government advertising concerning the patriation of the Constitution. In October 1980, the Trudeau government awarded contracts (without competition) to three advertising agencies that had done work for the Liberal Party in the previous election campaign. The advertisements they generated were designed to convince Canadians that the Constitution should be rewritten and patriated despite the differing opinions of provincial premiers and political parties. This aggressive approach, the government declared, was necessary for informing the public on a matter of national interest.

However, many commentators felt that this powerful sales effort weakened Parliament and democracy in Canada by undermining the traditional relations among MPs, the electorate and the government. One widely criticized television commercial featured Canada geese as the backdrop for a constitutional message. A federal member of Parliament complained at the time that, "I'll never be able to look at Canada geese or a beaver in quite the same way again. I'll see them as Liberals in disguise."[31] There is little doubt, however, that the advertising campaign contributed to ensuring that the federal message was heard in all provinces. Given the regionalization of the press, which often allows provincial premiers and opponents of the federal government to monopolize news coverage, federal government advertising may arguably have been necessary for redressing any distortions in the information received by the public.

This scenario was repeated in 1992 by the Mulroney government. Canada's 125th birthday celebrations coincided with the Progressive Conservative government's efforts to "sell" the Charlottetown Accord to the public. Efforts to make Canadians feel good about themselves and their country were expensive, and "just happened" to appear to be trying to make them feel good

CLOSE-UP ON Behaviour

THE AUDITOR GENERAL VERSUS THE GOVERNMENT

In February 2004, Auditor General Sheila Fraser created a media frenzy when she reported that she had discovered a web of fake invoices, double-billing and fictitious public works ministry contracts funnelling large commissions, from 1997 to 2001, to several Québec public-relations companies aligned with the federal Liberals. The scandal ended the brief honeymoon of Paul Martin's government, causing the Liberals' approval rating to drop from 48 percent to 39 percent almost overnight. Martin staffers blamed Jean Chrétien's camp for the scandal, saying the former prime minister had created the culture that allowed such largesse to happen. Martin immediately called a judicial inquiry and said that even as minister of finance he had not known about the advertising program.

The scandal was largely about $250 million that had been poured into the province of Québec after the 1995 referendum there had nearly caused the breakup of the country. Of that amount, $100 million for an advertising program was supposedly intended to raise the profile of the federal government in Québec in order to counter separatist forces. However, the auditor general could not trace where the money actually went. She found that most of the payments were merely large commissions to public-relations firms to do nothing more than transfer money from one government agency to another. The firms, coincidentally, had given the Liberal Party large financial donations in recent years.

Was it justifiable for the government to spend money in Québec this way given the extremely threatening climate of the post-referendum period?

31. Quoted in Frances Phillips, "And Critics Have a Go at Ottawa," *Financial Post*, May 13, 1982.

about the PC party as well. The Department of the Secretary of State was responsible for promoting the birthday celebrations and, as political commentator Hugh Winsor noted,

this relatively minor department is merely a convenient umbrella for the cabinet's propaganda thrust, and the shots are being called in the Federal–Provincial Relations Office and [Senator Lowell] Murray's committee.[32]

"Warm tummy, feel good" advertising filled the media in 1992 as the government spent $21 million on a year-long federal advertising campaign, awarding the most lucrative advertising contracts in Canadian history (without competitive bids) to companies with close political ties to the Mulroney government.[33] The ads reflected the government's twin themes of unity and prosperity. One controversial ad consisted of a song about pride in one's country, sung by a young Mila Mulroney look-alike over a montage of wheat fields, Rockies, fishing harbours and totem poles. The syrupy lyrics had been composed for the PC party and, arguably, created a partisan "add-on" for the Tories. The primary goal of the campaign was to make viewers more receptive when Ottawa tried to sell them a constitutional package later in the year.

When the referendum on the Charlottetown Accord was called for October 28, 1992, it, too, was packaged and sold by the government. The Yes supporters included the leadership of all three major federal parties and almost all of their provincial counterparts, 191 local or community-based non-partisan organizations, prominent Canadians recruited as voluntary national chairs, and the leadership of the Native, labour, corporate, university, media and cultural elites. The Yes side also had state-of-the-art technology, and polling contracts were handed out freely (largely to Tory agencies); a bureaucrat from the Federal–Provincial Relations Office (FPRO) remarked confidentially, "there is no budget here. The sky is the limit."[34]

The No side, in contrast, had a tiny one-room office, no government funding and no logistical support. Confident in its superior structure, organization and financing, the Yes side dismissed its opponents as malcontents and "enemies of Canada." Instead of an informative campaign that countered the objections of its opponents, the government waged a campaign based on emotion, spending its public resources completely on one side of the referendum question. It failed.

A few years later, after the very close 1995 Québec referendum, the federal government was anxious to counter separatist "myths" about the failure of federalism. It took out full-page newspaper advertisements to counter claims that Québec was putting more money into the federation than it was getting out; it sent brochures to every Québec household asserting that Prime Minister Jean Chrétien had lived up to his referendum promise to recognize the distinctiveness of Québec; the heritage minister conducted a flag-giveaway campaign. The strategy culminated with the creation of a new federal agency—the Canadian Information Office with a budget of nearly $120 million in 1997—dedicated to fostering patriotism and promoting the benefits of federalism. Its pro-federalist programs included a subsidy for a television series about Québec hockey hero Maurice Richard, a postage stamp design competition and more.

Unfortunately for the federal government, the 2004 report by the auditor general revealed that millions of dollars from the budget had been misspent or gone missing in the rush to promote Canada (see the accompanying "Close-Up on Behaviour: The Auditor General Versus the Government"). Prime Minister Paul Martin appointed Justice John Gomery to head a commission

---

32. See Hugh Winsor, "Bidding to Quicken Patriotic Heartbeat," *The Globe and Mail,* May 28, 1992.
33. Mark Kennedy and Chris Cobb, "Ad Contracts Given without Bids," *Ottawa Citizen,* February 6, 1993.
34. Quoted in Brooke Jeffrey, *Strange Bedfellows, Trying Times* (Toronto: Key Porter, 1993) pp. 117–18. Elections Canada revealed that the Yes forces spent 13 times more money than the No forces.

to investigate and report on what became known as the sponsorship scandal (a.k.a. AdScam). Its first report was delivered in late 2005; the final report in February 2006. Despite the fact that Paul Martin was not directly implicated, it had dramatic electoral repercussions for the Liberal Party, as Stephen Harper's Conservatives ousted the Liberals from power in the January 2006 federal election.

The question of government advertising promises to be a hot topic in the years ahead. The federal government has a responsibility to inform Canadians about its policies and programs and yet refrain from using its resources to disseminate partisan political propaganda. Divisions in Canada's political culture can be alleviated to a degree by ensuring that all citizens are exposed to views that represent the country's interests, not just those of a particular region, province or ethnic group. It is the responsibility of the opposition parties to ensure that the government does not abuse this right, and to date, with significant help from those such as the auditor general, they have shown a marked ability to detect and publicize infractions. When the sponsorship scandal began to emerge, the government instituted tighter controls on federal advertising practices, but it was too late to curb the political damage to the Martin government (see the "Close-Up on Behaviour: New Federal Advertising Practices").

CLOSE-UP ON Behaviour

NEW FEDERAL ADVERTISING PRACTICES

In April 2003, Scott Brison, minister of public works and government services, announced that an extensive overhaul of the government's advertising process was underway. A moratorium on all advertising went into effect in March 2004 and ended after the election campaign in June.

New advertising initiatives must now comply with . . . measures that are more stringent than for any other procurement process. Agencies will be selected from a pre-approved list established through competitive processes, subcontracting will be regulated, and departments and agencies wishing to conduct an advertising campaign must justify the purpose and value, follow rules in selecting an advertising agency, and document their activities to support expenditures.*

In 2006, the Conservative government, as part of the *Federal Accountability Act*, legislated that an open, fair and transparent bidding process would be required for advertising activities.

---

* Scott Brison, quoted in *The Globe and Mail*, July 31, 2004, B5.

Gender, Class and Political Orientations

In the last chapter, we discussed Canada's ethno-linguistic and regional subcultures and the resultant cleavages that divide Canadians into separate groups, creating different "layers" of political culture. There are two other cleavages based on differences in class and gender that cut relatively evenly across all of Canadian society. Surrounding each of these cleavages are many groups and organizations that make unique demands on governments and society. Some are highly organized to achieve their ends; others have little or no cohesiveness. Some have considerable power and influence; others have very little.

In the next sections, we examine how differences over gender and class in Canada affect how individuals think and behave politically.

Gender Stratification and Inequality

In Canada, women make up slightly more than half the population. Throughout history, discrimination against women has been enforced by social customs and laws. As the bearers of children, endowed with less obvious physical strength than men, women have been assigned, and have generally accepted, primary responsibility for children and the family. Until relatively recently, even in developed countries, women were barred from such societal participation as owning property, holding public office, voting and even attaining higher education (see the "Close-Up on Women and Education: A Pioneer of the Women's Movement"). In recent decades, however, women's roles in society have undergone massive changes, particularly in industrialized countries.

In 1991, the United Nations released the first major statistical portrait and analysis of the situation of women, providing evidence to back up claims of relative deprivation. The UN continues to monitor and update statistics about the achievement of women around the world in its *Human Development Report.*[35] This report provides the best comparative information to date on the condition of women.

Around the world, both households and governments have spent fewer resources to educate and train girls than boys, reducing the potential social, economic and political contributions of women to society and leaving them at a disadvantage in making major life decisions. However, the UN studies also show that in much of the world today this has changed or is changing. Primary education has been accepted as a fundamental goal by all countries, and enrolment of girls in primary and secondary schools is now comparable to that of boys in most countries. At the university and college levels, female enrolment is also increasing. And in the developed regions, western Asia, some countries of southern Africa and Latin America and the Caribbean, enrolment of the sexes is now nearly equal. In Canada, women receive over half of all B.A.'s, almost half of all M.A.'s, and about 32 percent of all Ph.D.'s (see Figure 4.3 on the next page).

Increased education has brought more of the world's women into political life. Routes to power in government decision-making are traditionally through political candidacy and the civil service. In most countries, women have been more successful in local than national elections. Statistics on women in bureaucratic careers are not generally available, but one pattern is clear: significant percentages of women work at the lower echelons, but their representation dwindles rapidly as pay and status increase.

Although the status of the world's women has improved dramatically in the past century, there is still a long way to go before gender equality will be reached socially and politically. The UN's 1995 *Human Development Report* said that on every continent women work longer hours, earn less money and are more likely to live in poverty than men. The report estimated that 70 percent of the world's poor are women. In 2003, 12 percent of Canadian women lived in poverty—nearly 2 million women. As well, 38 percent of lone-parent families headed by women were poor; 31 percent of single, widowed or divorced women over 16 were poor.[36] There is a need to end occupational segregation and wage discrimination everywhere, and to recognize women's unpaid work as economically productive. Many women in Canada have fewer job opportunities and lower earnings than men; more live in poverty. Political scientists may debate the underlying causes of gender inequality but there is no doubt about its existence.

CLOSE-UP ON Behaviour

WOMEN AND EDUCATION: A PIONEER OF THE WOMEN'S MOVEMENT

In Britain in the late nineteenth and early twentieth centuries, an early feminist, Eleanor Sidgwick, fought for the right of women to have access to university education. She maintained that there are two gifts, one moral and one intellectual, that it is the special privilege of a university to bestow.

The moral gift is "the sense of membership of a worthy community, with a high and noble function in which every member can take part, and at the same time not so vast in extent as to reduce the individual to insignificance." The intellectual gift is the "habit of reasonable self-dependence," which higher education promotes in three ways: it encourages labour, care and precision of thought in arriving at sound conclusions; it teaches a sense of the limits of one's own knowledge and its relation to other areas of learning; and it provides encounters with teachers who think for themselves and advance as well as impart knowledge.

In its time, this was a profoundly subversive argument, as it maintained that intellectual processes were not determined by gender. Today, of course, Canadian women take full advantage of equal access to higher education.

Source: Gillian Sutherland, "The Education of Women in Cambridge," in Richard Mason, ed., *Cambridge Minds* (Cambridge, UK: Cambridge University Press, 1994), p. 42.

---

35. *The World's Women 1970–1990: Trends and Statistics* (New York: United Nations, 1991); and United Nations, *Human Development Report*, updated yearly (New York: Oxford University Press).

36. *Women in Canada 2005: A Gender-Based Statistical Report*, Statistics Canada, 2006, p. 144.

FIGURE 4.3 **Percentage of Women and Men Aged 15 and Over with a University Degree, 1971 to 2001**

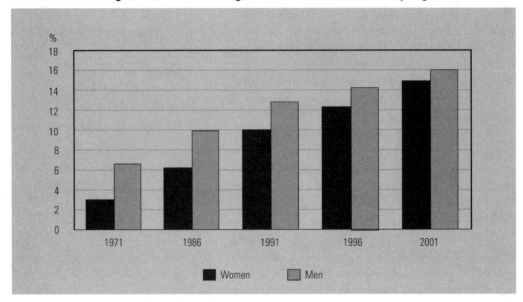

Source: Statistics Canada, Censuses of Canada. Catalogue no. 89-503-XIE.

Gender Theory

Gender theory explanations about the causes of gender inequality have gained credibility as a subdiscipline in most of the social sciences.[37] The fundamental point on which all feminists agree is that orthodox theories about politics tend to ignore gender and harbour unconscious assumptions about the role of women. Like ethnicity cleavages, gender cleavages are generated by prejudice and also by systemic discrimination. The issue is not new. In the nineteenth century, John Stuart Mill argued that the subjugation of women is a selfish, egotistical conspiracy by men who want to keep women as a free source of domestic labour.[38] It is, he said, in men's interest to preserve a male-dominated society, so they claim that the subjugation of women is natural, even divinely ordained. Karl Marx and Frederick Engels held that the subjugation of women is based on economic reasons. According to them, it serves the interests of the capitalist class because the female homeworker is unpaid, and this keeps the working class without resources. The traditional family is part of the scheme to ensure the subordination of women, keeping them dependent on their wage-earning husbands.[39]

Feminists believe in removing barriers to the full equality of men and women. Early Canadian feminists such as Agnes Macphail, Canada's first woman elected to Parliament, believed that women's inequality was based on their lack of political and legal rights. Over time, those battles were fought and won; women received the right to vote federally in 1918, and gained legal equality rights in the *Charter of Rights and Freedoms* in 1982.

37. See, for example, Michèle Barrett and Anne Phillips, *Destabilizing Theory: Contemporary Feminist Debates* (Stanford, CA: Stanford University Press, 1992); and Sandra Lipsitz Bem, *The Lenses of Gender* (New Haven, CT: Yale University Press, 1993).

38. John Stuart Mill, *The Subjection of Women* (London: Dent, 1970). First published in 1869.

39. *Women and Communism: Writings of Marx, Engels, Lenin and Stalin* (Westport, CT: Greenwood Press, 1973); and Canada Year Book 1999, p. 192.

People call me a feminist whenever I express sentiments that differentiate me from a doormat or a prostitute.

Rebecca West, writer

In the nineteenth century, the belief that women inherit physical attributes that determine their personality (such as emotional, intuitive, nurturing and passive traits) was accepted even by the first wave of feminists who won political rights for women. Today, second- and third-wave feminists argue that gender role differences are not inherent but learned. They point out that learning patterns have discouraged females from participating fully in public life. Gender roles learned in childhood through family, school and other social contacts are carried through to the workplace and other adult social settings. Roles learned in childhood shape the aspirations of children, and this, in turn, helps to provide continuity in society. By the same token, however, clinging to past roles can also make attitudinal change slow and stressful.

Feminists have targeted society's attitudes toward traditional gender roles and stereotypes and brought new issues into the country's political agenda. They have made specific attempts to change the heavily gender-specific socialization of boys and girls. Books that contain traditional stereotypes of adventurous, mischievous boys and docile little girls have been superseded by stories containing less narrowly defined roles; many toys have become more saleable to boys and girls alike; girls are encouraged to study mathematics and science and aspire to careers other than teacher, nurse or secretary; boys are encouraged to be more sensitive and share household chores. Changes have not been restricted to childhood socialization: gender biases are routinely detected and gender-neutral terms promoted. In short, the issue of gender has become highly politicized.

Canadian Women Today The role of women has changed dramatically over the years. In 1901, only 13 percent of Canadian women worked outside the home. In 2004, over 77 percent of women aged 25–44 were part of the paid workforce; 28 percent of employed women worked part-time and 7 percent were self-employed. Women in Alberta were most likely to be employed, but those in Ontario, the other Western provinces and Prince Edward Island also were more likely than those in Québec and the remaining Atlantic provinces to work outside the home.[40] Most of that change occurred since the 1950s as improved household technology and contraceptives enabled women to make more choices concerning their lives. Women have entered the workforce often for economic reasons but also in cognizance of the argument that they cannot be dependent and equal at the same time. However, even when employed full-time, women are still largely responsible for looking after their homes and families.

In some respects, the role of women has been slow to change. Significant differences still exist between the economic and social conditions of men and women in Canadian society. Women are disproportionately represented among the poorest in Canadian society. They make up the majority of lone parents, and single mothers are among the most economically disadvantaged in the country. As well, single persons over age 65 have the lowest incomes of any group over 24 years of age, and women comprise about 71 percent of this category. Since the Canada/Québec Pension Plans (CPP and QPP) are based on earnings, lower women's earnings are reflected in lower benefit plans in retirement.

---

40. Statistics Canada, *Women in Canada: A Gender-Based Statistical Report,* 5th ed. (Ottawa: Ministry of Industry, 2006) Statistics Canada Table 5.2, Catalogue 89-503-XIE, p.119. See also Kathleen A. Lahey, "Women and Employment: Removing Fiscal Barriers to Women's Labour Force Participation," *Status of Women, Canada,* publication # 03-S-007, 2007.

Women are also poorly represented in upper-level political and occupational hierarchies. However, they are increasingly entering political life through non-governmental organizations (NGOs), women's movements and associations. They also are becoming more active in the politics of their local communities in such areas as discrimination, poverty, health and environmental issues, violence against women and peace movements.

There have been many firsts for women in recent times (see Table 4.4). However, despite these breakthroughs and the fact that there is no *formal* barrier to their full and equal participation, women are still less active than men in politics. They vote and join some activities, such as political campaigns, as frequently as men, but as a group they participate significantly less in more active or demanding roles (see Chapter 11 for more on this). Women made up a mere 20.9 percent of members of Parliament elected in 2006 (and only 24.5 percent of candidates from the five major parties that ran). On the other hand, the fact that they are graduating from universities in record numbers has allowed women to move into areas such as law and commerce, where they are now represented in numbers relatively equal to men. In medical and health-related fields, 65 percent of managers are now women. However, women account for only about one in five employed in professional positions in the natural sciences, mathematics and engineering.

As they have participated more in the workforce, women have brought new issues to the government's policy agenda: affirmative action; legal equality rights; equal access to opportunities; pay equity; abortion rights; and child care.[41] Pay equity and sexual harassment policies have contributed to a more egalitarian workplace for women. In 2003, women's earnings were only 71 percent of men's. In some cases, such as for single women and those who are under age 25, women now earn approximately the same as men. Status of Women Canada is the federal government agency (within Canadian Heritage) that promotes gender equity and the full participation of Canadian women in the social, cultural and political life of the country. It focuses on economic well-being, systemic violence against women and human rights issues and is headed by the minister of heritage and the status of women.

In November 2006, Stephen Harper's government removed the word *equality* from Status of Women Canada's mandate, cut 43 percent of its operating budget and announced that 12 of its 16 regional offices would be closed. It also imposed a ban on all federally funded advocacy for women's equality. As a result, several equality-seeking groups such as the Canadian Research Institute on the Advancement of Women are currently being forced to cut back on their activities or to close altogether.[42]

There appears to be a growing awareness and acceptance among both men and women of the need to address and solve gender-related problems. Some scholars, however, have expressed a thoughtful note of caution. The late Christopher Lasch, for example, feared that, far from having civilized corporate capitalism, the feminist movement had been corrupted by capitalism and had adopted mercantile habits of thought as its own. He questioned whether the prospect of upward mobility alone could confer meaning in the lives of women—any more than it could in the lives of men.[43]

---

41. For a standard overview, see Sandra Burt, "Looking Backward and Thinking Ahead: Toward a Gendered Analysis of Canadian Politics," in Michael S. Whittington and Glen Williams, eds., *Canadian Politics in the 21st Century,* 4th ed. (Scarborough, ON: Nelson, 2000), pp. 176–90. More progressive views about both the composition and even the definition of gender-related issues would include topics such as what constitutes a family and who should receive government benefits.

42. National Union of Public and General Employees, January 28, 2007. Accessed from www.nupge.ca/news_2007/n28ia07a.htm.

43. Christopher Lasch, *Women and the Common Life* (New York: W.W. Norton, 1996).

TABLE 4.4 Significant Dates in Attainment of Legal and Political Equality for Women in Canada

1916	Manitoba, followed by Saskatchewan and Alberta, gives vote to women in provincial elections
1917	British Columbia and Ontario give vote to women
1917	Women serving in Armed Forces and women with male relatives in uniform are allowed to vote in federal elections
1918	Nova Scotia gives vote to women
1918	Women are given franchise in federal elections
1919	New Brunswick approves women's suffrage
1919	Women gain the right to stand in federal elections
1921	Agnes Macphail is the first woman elected to Parliament
1922	Prince Edward Island approves women's suffrage
1925	Newfoundland approves women's suffrage
1928	Supreme Court rules women are not "persons" and cannot be appointed to Senate
1929	British Privy Council overturns Supreme Court decision
1930	Cairine Wilson is first woman appointed to the Senate
1940	Québec gives vote to women (the last province to do so)
1947	Married women are restricted from holding federal public service jobs
1955	Restrictions on married women in federal public service jobs are removed
1957	Ellen Fairclough is sworn in as first female federal cabinet minister
1967	Royal Commission on Status of Women is established
1971	*Canada Labour Code* is amended to allow women 17 weeks of maternity leave
1973	Supreme Court upholds section of *Indian Act* depriving Aboriginal women of their rights
1973	Supreme Court denies Irene Murdoch right to share in family property
1977	*Canadian Human Rights Act* is passed, forbidding discrimination on basis of sex
1981	Canada ratifies UN Convention on the elimination of all forms of discrimination against women
1982	Bertha Wilson becomes first woman appointed to the Supreme Court of Canada
1983	Affirmative-action programs are made mandatory in the federal public service
1984	Twenty-eight women are elected to Parliament, six appointed to cabinet
1984	Jeanne Sauvé becomes Canada's first female governor general
1985	Section 15 of *Charter of Rights and Freedoms* comes into effect; employment equity legislation is passed
1989	*Indian Act* is amended to remove discrimination against Aboriginal women
1989	Audrey McLaughlin becomes first woman to lead a significant political party (the NDP)
1991	Rita Johnston serves briefly as BC premier after Bill Vander Zalm resigns, becoming Canada's first female premier
1993	Catherine Callbeck is first woman elected premier (PEI)
1993	Kim Campbell serves briefly as Canada's first woman prime minister
1999	Beverley McLachlin is first woman appointed as chief justice of the Supreme Court
2004	General election: 65 women are elected to Parliament—the largest number ever
2006	Sixty-four women are elected to Parliament

We examine further the role of women in Canadian government in Chapters 8, 9 and 10. The role of women in political parties and elections is discussed in Chapters 11 and 12, while we focus on the women's movement in Chapter 13. Gender theory is compared to other political science theories in Chapter 14.

Class Stratification and Inequality

Differences in socio-economic class represent another cleavage in society that helps define political ideas and orientations. Economic inequalities are responsible for profound differences in health, education and quality of life. Upward movement between classes is possible but can be extremely difficult, and the gap between the richest and poorest Canadians is growing.

Defining *class* is controversial and problematical. **Class** refers to a rank or order in society determined by such characteristics as education, occupation and income. These characteristics provide "objective" indicators that sometimes are different from "subjective" or self-assigned rankings. Depending on which types of indicators are used, different class lines can be detected in the Canadian population.

Class was an important component of Karl Marx's thought. Using economic criteria, he divided capitalist societies into the **bourgeoisie** (the economic elite), a small **petite bourgeoisie** (small business people, farmers, self-employed professionals), a **new middle class** (civil servants, teachers, salaried professionals) and the **proletariat** (workers). Marx expected the proletariat eventually to revolt against exploitation by the bourgeoisie, and create a new and egalitarian, classless society. History has not unfolded this way. In Canada, as elsewhere, the "new middle class" has grown, the elite "bourgeoisie" has become more powerful and internationally based, and the "proletariat" is too weak, fragmented and dependent on state subsidies to be able to revolt. However the 2001 Census figures showed that Canadian society is becoming increasingly polarized economically. The richest 10 percent of the population increased their income by over 14 percent in a decade while the bottom 10 percent increased their income by less than 1 percent, and median family incomes stagnated. Incomes of the 20 percent immediately below the mean actually fell.

Class divisions based on wealth and income are evident in Canada. In 1999, the richest 10 percent of families accounted for 53 percent of the total wealth, while the poorest 10 percent had a negative net worth—their debts were greater than their assets.[44] At the top of the economic scale, a tiny elite, or *upper class*, of roughly 2 to 3 percent of the population holds the top positions in business, industry, professions and the bureaucracy. The extensive holdings of a very few individuals and families in real estate, natural resources, communications and various commercial enterprises, including large corporations, set them apart from other Canadians.[45] They include some of the wealthiest families in the world—for example, the Irving family (which owns much of the New Brunswick economy); the estate of Ken Thomson (whose assets have included the Hudson's Bay Company, Zellers and numerous publishing houses); the extended Bronfman family (assets include Seagram's, London Life, Brascan and Noranda, to name a few); and the Weston family (assets include Loblaws food enterprises and Holt Renfrew). Many of these wealthy Canadians also head international firms. Usually, they have inherited significant wealth. Less wealthy, but still with multi-million-dollar incomes, are corporate chief executive officers (CEOs)—Gerald Schwartz of Onex Corporation, for example, earned over $49 million in 2001.[46] Together, these individuals control many of the large corporations operating in Canada; as well, some sit on the boards of directors of major Canadian banks while others are executives of foreign-owned firms.

In the 1960s and '70s, Anglo-Saxon Protestants monopolized this wealthy stratum of Canadians, but the makeup of Canada's wealthy has been changing. Several large corporate families in Canada

---

44. Statistics Canada, *Canada: A Portrait* (Ottawa: Department of Industry, 2002), p. 131.
45. Each year the *Financial Post* lists the wealthiest individuals and corporations in Canada.
46. "The Globe Survey of Compensation," *The Globe and Mail*, April 23, 2002, p. B6.

today are Jewish or French Canadian, or of other ethnic backgrounds. What they have in common is their desire to keep governments from interfering in their business ventures. It is in their interest to keep taxes low; prevent wealth taxes; gain tax shelters, tax loopholes and write-offs; keep government regulations minimal and so on. Many maintain close ties with whatever political party controls the government. The Senate, particularly the Banking Committee, serves as a "lobby within" the government for big business.[47]

The vast majority of Canadians today are part of the huge *middle class*—over 80 percent of the population—that is sandwiched between the tiny economic elite and about 16 percent of the population who are relatively economically deprived. The shape of the economic hierarchy, therefore, is less like a pyramid and more like a bulging onion. Income, occupation and lifestyle subdivide the members of the middle stratum into upper-middle and lower-middle class. The upper-middle tier is generally well educated and financially secure. It does not function as a single unit but has a variety of economic interests and political demands. Many are self-employed, or employers.

Also in the middle class are those who generally work for someone else. They tend to earn less than the upper tier. They include civil servants, teachers, nurses, social workers and others who work in the public sector. Often, they belong to unions. Both groups are well educated with above-average incomes. They pay a significant amount of tax to governments but they have no umbrella lobby group to work for their collective class interests.

At the bottom of the middle class, or in a class of its own, is the working class. This group is generally considered to consist of those who do manual as opposed to intellectual work. As a group, this class is less educated and generally earns less money than others in the middle class. Although many of them are unionized, and therefore earn higher wages, changes in the Canadian economy in the 1980s and '90s dramatically increased unemployment in this group. The proportion of blue-collar jobs in the work force increased only marginally, while unskilled and labourers' jobs in fishing, mining, agriculture and other primary resources declined sharply. Job losses, combined with inflation and increased taxation, make these individuals particularly vulnerable to dropping into the lowest stratum of economically deprived Canadians. Increasingly, this group is working part-time in poorly paid, non-unionized jobs. Many rely on employment insurance (EI) between jobs.

Within the large middle economic tier, Canadians of Anglo-Saxon origin appear to have no particular advantage over other groups. Jews, Asians, Dutch and Italians, for example, do equally well or better in terms of average income, percentage of white-collar jobs and percentage with some university education. One ethnic group, however, ranks consistently low in socio-economic stratification characteristics—Native people, many of whom live in extreme poverty.

There is no internationally accepted definition of poverty—not even of what it is or how it is to be measured. The *poor* in Canada are generally considered to be those who exist below the **low-income cut-off (LICO)**, a theoretical criterion set by Statistics Canada to indicate those who are substantially worse off than the average (and who therefore might not be "poor" by other standards). The LICO is calculated in such a way that any individual or family that spends more than 20 percent over the average on the necessities of life—food, clothing and shelter—is considered to be living in poverty. In dollar terms, Statistics Canada defines this line according to family type and location—for example, as an annual income below $26 049 for a family of four in a city of 100 000 to 5 000 000. These individuals rely on state benefits such as employment insurance and welfare to exist. In 2000, about 13 percent of families lived at or below that line. The lowest proportion of poor families lived in Prince Edward Island and Alberta; the highest percentage was in Newfoundland and Labrador.[48]

---

47. See Linda McQuaig, *Behind Closed Doors* (Toronto: Penguin, 1987).

Poverty figures include those who spend about 55 percent or more of their income on food, shelter and clothing. Financial planners agree that families or individuals should not spend more than 30 percent of their income on housing, but that is becoming increasingly difficult in urban Canada. Nearly 45 percent of renters in British Columbia, Nova Scotia, and Newfoundland and Labrador paid more than one-third of their income on housing.

Those economically worse off in Canadian society are most likely to be one-parent families, more than 60 percent of which are headed by females; the young, of whom more than a million live in poverty; the single elderly, who are mostly widows; and Native people. As we have seen, this group also tends to be the least educated. Poverty creates a trap that restricts choices in life; it also often makes people more vulnerable to violence and abuse. The implications for children are particularly severe. Nearly 18 percent of Canada's children—among the most vulnerable in our society—live in poverty. Aboriginal children and immigrant children are particularly badly off, as are children in the provinces of British Columbia and Newfoundland and Labrador (see Figures 4.4 and 4.5).

Poverty is strongly linked to poor health, low achievement in school, delinquency, frequent criminal behaviour and higher-than-average infant mortality. It also means fewer educational opportunities; higher mortality rates; more physical and mental illness; more substandard and hazardous working conditions; higher crime rates (poverty is the best predictor of delinquency); and higher suicide and divorce rates. Government programs like the GST (goods and services tax) credit, the Canada Child Tax Benefit and employment insurance help reduce the rate of child and family poverty (see Figure 4.6 as well as Figure 4.7 on page 138).

Because the poor have little or no voice, the federal government set up the National Council of Welfare (NCW) in 1969 as an advisory group on behalf of welfare clients. The Canadian Council on Social Development (CCSD) is a non-profit social policy organization that does research on

FIGURE 4.4 Child Poverty Among Selected Social Groups, 2001

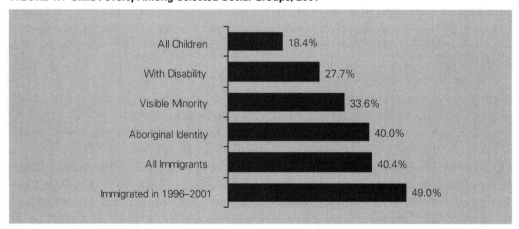

Source: Statistics Canada's *Canada Census 2001. In Campaign 2000: 2006 Report Card on Child and Family Poverty in Canada:* www.campaign2000.ca/rc/rc06/06_C2000NationalReportCard.pdf. Accessed May 23, 2007.

48. Poverty data is from the Urban Poverty Project 2007, Canadian Council on Social Development (www.ccsd.ca/media/2007/pr_com_profiles.htm). In Canada, anyone who falls below this "poverty line"—Statistics Canada's LICO—is defined as poor. However, the LICO is a relative measure, closely tied to the average income and consumption patterns of the average Canadian. As such, some claim it tells more about how well off the typical Canadian is than it does about the condition of the truly poor. Furthermore, the line itself is disputed. Christopher Sarlo, for example, in *Poverty in Canada*, noted that half of the households headed by someone 65 years of age or older were considered poor, but almost half of them owned a home, 90 percent mortgage-free. Christopher Sarlo, *Poverty in Canada* (Vancouver: Fraser Institute, 1992). Updated November 2006.

FIGURE 4.5 **Child Poverty in Canada and the Provinces, 2004**

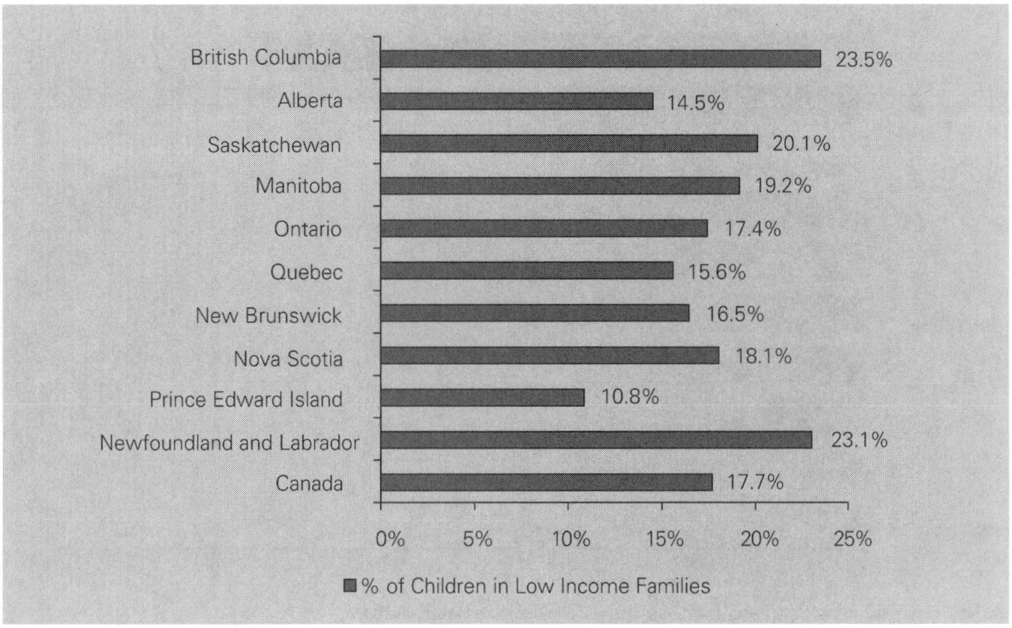

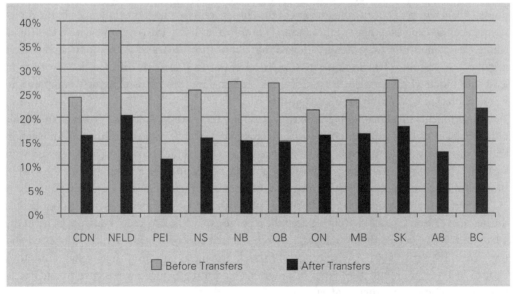

Source: CCSD using Statistics Canada's Survey of Labour and Income Dynamics (SLID) masterfile, 2004. In *Campaign 2000: 2006 Report Card on Child and Family Poverty in Canada*: www.campaign2000.ca/rc/rc06/06_C2000NationalReportCard.pdf. Accessed May 23, 2007.

FIGURE 4.6 **Impact of Income Transfers on Family Poverty, Canada and Provinces, 2004**

Source: CCSD using Statistics Canada's SLID Masterfile, 2004. In *Campaign 2000: 2006 Report Card on Child and Family Poverty in Canada*: www.campaign2000.ca/rc/rc06/06_C2000NationalReportCard.pdf. Accessed May 23, 2007.

issues such as poverty. And the National Anti-Poverty Organization (NAPO), formed in 1971, serves to unite several hundred local and provincial poverty groups. Canadians do not have equal chances to prosper. The educational system and social programs currently in place are not adequate to break the cycle of poverty for the least fortunate. The odds of leading a secure, healthy life decline as one moves down the social scale.

FIGURE 4.7 Distribution of Average Canadian Family Income by Decile, 2001 Census

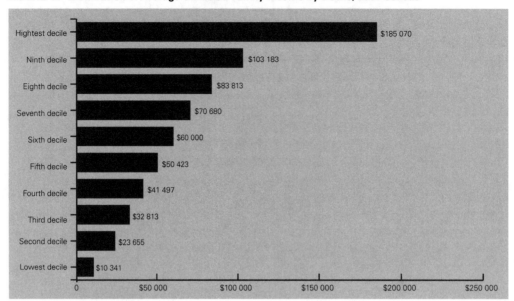

Source: Courtesy of the Canadian Council on Social Development. Data available at
www.ccsd.ca/pr/2003/censusincome.htm.

The inequalities of opportunity and distribution of wealth in Canada have significant implications for politics. Some writers have concluded that the economic elite is also a dominant political force, that the political and economic elite are linked together and share a "confraternity of
power."[49] There is no doubt that members of the elite exercise considerable influence in the direction of economic development of the country. On the other hand, the economic elite is far from a
ruling class. One study, for example, showed that about three-quarters of the political elite have
middle-class origins.[50] This indicates that political power in Canada is diffused downward to at
least the middle class. As well, the political decision-making process is extremely complex and
virtually precludes control by one small group.

Governments must maintain popular support, and this puts considerable power in the hands
of the majority of the people through voting, membership in political parties, running for election
and so on. Unfortunately, members of the lowest socio-economic stratum are preoccupied with
survival. They express low feelings of personal political power and efficacy, and participate least in
the political system. We discuss the importance of class in voting behaviour in Chapter 12.

Income disparity is significantly affected by public policy. Government benefits to poor people
during the 1970s in Canada slightly reduced the income gap, while neo-conservative policies in the
1980s and '90s increased the overall gap between the rich and poor. This trend was arrested and
reversed in the early 2000s. A wide range of federal, provincial and municipal welfare initiatives
exist to help the poor, but these types of programs tend to be reduced when governments at all
levels attempt to balance their budgets.

---

49. The ideological elite is described in John Porter's *The Vertical Mosaic: An Analysis of Social Class and
    Power in Canada* (Toronto: University of Toronto Press, 1965), p. 460, and later elaborated on by Wallace
    Clement in *Canadian Corporate Elite* (Toronto: McClelland & Stewart, 1975).

50. Dennis Olsen, "The State Elites," in Leo Panitch, ed., *The Canadian State* (Toronto: University of Toronto
    Press, 1977).

Critical Debate
Should Canada Do More to Build a Strong National Identity?

Do socializing agents adequately prepare Canadians to understand and participate in the construction of a strong, united country, and does the federal government currently do enough or too much in this regard?

Point

Many factors condition the political ideas and orientations of Canadians. Informal socializing agents, such as the family and peer groups, and more formal institutions, such as the educational system, the media and even government, help determine the factual knowledge, attitudes and values Canadians have about politics, politicians and government. Other factors, such as gender and socio-economic class, define the environment in which a person lives, determining life chances and also shaping political attitudes and values. However, no socializing agents are very effective in building a strong Canadian political culture. Therefore, governments need to be more proactive in promoting values such as tolerance and unity and not wait idly by while ethnic and regional forces pull the country apart.

Political socialization in Canada is too haphazard. Early socialization through families and peer groups is casual and informal. Socialization by education and the media is fragmented with little state direction. Education is under provincial, not federal, jurisdiction, and the mass media, including radio, television and the press, all act independently to varying degrees.

There are many powerful obstacles to building a strong Canadian political culture. Both the media and the education system reflect and reinforce regional, linguistic and ethnic cleavages. French- and English-language media in Canada reinforce the linguistic and cultural isolation of the two official language groups. Educational institutions harden provincial, regional and French–English differences, and US influence is pervasive in Canada.

In view of these obstacles to building strong, common political orientations, the federal government needs to speak more directly to Canadians through such means as advocacy advertising in order to inform them and thereby influence their values and beliefs. It needs to strengthen communications, facilitate access to government and improve the circular flow of information between government institutions and the public. Such methods, although often controversial, are necessary to bring the federal government closer to the people.

Over the past three decades, the federal government has tried to combat divisive forces in Canada's political culture through such means as regulating Canadian content in the broadcasting media, supporting gender equality in the workplace and emphasizing the need for different sectors of society to work together to reduce child poverty. Such actions are to be applauded. The federal government alone speaks for all Canadians. It needs to be proactive in finding ways to promote Canadian unity and tolerance if Canada is to build a strong national political culture.

Counterpoint

Obstacles to nation-building are part of the normal constraints of a democratic federal political system. It is true that such obstacles are particularly numerous in Canada because of its bilingual and multicultural character and because it is located next to a superpower. However, in liberal democratic societies, individual freedoms ought to be respected. The state should not assume direct control of the agents of socialization.

Few Canadians would want totally centralized government socialization in order to instill a stronger national culture—if it did move in that direction we would have an authoritarian government. Efforts by the federal government to impose ideas from the centre would be severely resisted. Regional subcultures are already strongly embedded and based on different interpretations of Canadian history, literature, mythology and ethnicity, often reinforced by different media and political leaders in a federal system.

Canadian political culture, initiated and reinforced as it is by the socialization process described in this chapter, contains at least the minimal level of national identity required to legitimize the Constitution and the democratic political process. Canadians expect to live in a liberal society free of government control and indoctrination. They value the assumptions and processes of parliamentary democracy and expect the political system to manage the tensions caused by the various societal cleavages—and to do so democratically.

The federal government is doing enough, and should stay out of the advocacy advertising business. For the party in power, it is just too tempting to use public funds to disseminate free propaganda for its own purposes while claiming that it is for the good of the country.

Discussion Questions

1. What is your stand on the Critical Debate, and what can you add to it?
2. Can you detect ways that family, peers, educational institutions and the media have politically socialized you? Describe the process and the effect it may have had on you personally.
3. Can you recall a recent instance of government advertising? In your opinion, was it justified? In what circumstances is it acceptable or unacceptable?
4. How do class and gender influence politics in Canada? Urbanization? (Revisit Chapters 2 and 3.)
5. In what ways have the social and political orientations of women changed since the Second World War? What major challenges have been met with respect to political equality for women, and what are some problems that still exist?
6. Try the practice citizenship test on the internet at www.cic.gc.ca/english/resources/publications/look/look-22.asp. Are the questions fair?

Visit our new Companion Website at **www.pearsoned.ca/jackson**, where you can use the interactive Study Guide and link to additional resources on topics discussed in the text.

Selected Bibliography

Education

Emberly, Peter C. *Values, Education and Technology: The Ideology of Dispossession.* Toronto: University of Toronto Press, 1995.

Horn, Michael. *Academic Freedom in English Canada: A History.* Toronto: University of Toronto Press, 1999.

Strum, Philippa, and David Biette, eds. *Education and Immigrant Integration in the United States and Canada.* Washington, DC: Woodrow Wilson International Center for Scholars, Migration Policy Institute, 2005.

Media

Beaty, Bart, and Rebecca Sullivan, *Canadian Television Today.* Calgary: University of Calgary Press, 2006.

Corner, John, and Dick Pels, eds., *Media and the Restyling of Politics.* London, UK: Sage, 2003.

Lorimer, Roland, and Mike Gasher. *Mass Communications in Canada*, 4th ed. Don Mills, ON: Oxford University Press, 2001.

Nesbitt-Larking, Paul. *Politics, Society and the Media: Canadian Perspectives*, 2nd ed. Peterborough, ON: Broadview Press, 2007.

Siegel, Arthur. *Politics and the Media in Canada*, 2nd ed. Whitby, ON: McGraw-Hill Ryerson, 1996.

McKie, Craig, and Benjamin Singer. *Communications in Canadian Society*, 5th ed. Scarborough, ON: Thompson Educational Publishing, 2001.

Taras, David. *Power and Betrayal in the Canadian Media*. Peterborough, ON: Broadview Press, 1999.

——————, Marie Bakardjieva, and Frits Pannekoek, *How Canadians Communicate II: Media, Globalization and Identity*. Calgary: University of Calgary Press, 2007.

Women/Gender

Ascott, Jane, and Linda Trimble, eds. *In the Presence of Women: Representation in Canadian Governments*. Toronto: Harcourt Brace, 1997.

Evans, Patricia M., and Gerda R. Wekerle, eds. *Women and the Canadian Welfare State*. Toronto: University of Toronto Press, 1997.

Gingras, F.P., ed. *Gender and Politics in Contemporary Canada*. Don Mills, ON: Oxford University Press, 1995.

MacIvor, Heather. *Women and Politics in Canada*. Peterborough, ON: Broadview Press, 1996.

Class

Battle, Ken. *Minimum Wages in Canada: A Statistical Portrait with Policy Implications*. Ottawa: Caledon Institute of Social Policy, 2003.

Ismael, Shereen. *Child Poverty and the Canadian Welfare State: From Entitlement to Charity*. Calgary: University of Alberta Press, 2006.

Part III
Institutions

In this part of the book, we examine how the institutions of the Canadian political system are based upon, and reflect, the essential characteristics of Canadian political culture and social cleavages. Political institutions reflect the structure and values of society. They establish the process through which public policy is created, implemented, enforced and changed. They also limit the ability of those in government to exercise political power.

Canada's Constitution and its many laws and procedures embody the aspirations of Canadians and guide political activity. Many paradigms are used to study these relationships. With the help of the courts, the federal constitutional structure also shapes the priorities of contemporary politics and should protect civil liberties in an age of global terrorism. The economic issues of federalism concern how resources are collected and distributed among Canadians in different provinces and regions. The political issues involve, above all, nationalism and regionalism; indeed, in some years, Québec nationalism has assumed such significance that it dwarfed all other political issues, shaking the very foundations of the country.

The formal and political executive — the governor general, prime minister, ministry and cabinet — provide leadership (or lack of it) in creating and applying society's laws. Parliament is another vital player in the political process. It gives the executive the power to govern while providing checks on government authority. The bureaucracy, which consists of oft-maligned public servants, forms the permanent administration that carries out the plans of its transient political masters. Together, these core institutions form the nexus of political power in Canada. The underlying question in Part III of *Politics in Canada* is, "Do institutions matter?"

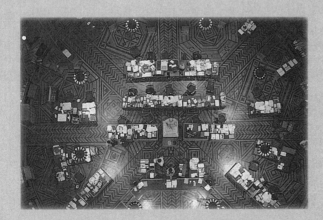

Chapter 5

The Constitution

Legal Foundations, Failed Reforms, Civil Liberties and the Courts

The establishment of stability and order is a persistent goal of all societies. One way to achieve this end is to create a set of laws and principles that embody the aspirations of the society and, at the same time, provide guidelines for political activity. Although it may take an infinite variety of forms, such a set of rules and procedures is commonly referred to as a constitution.

Some societies rely on a single, written document that provides both a statement of principles and a detailed explication of the relative authority and jurisdiction of the various actors in the political process. In other societies, values and political traditions are so firmly rooted in the political culture that no attempt to codify them is considered necessary. The true test of the significance of a constitution, be it written or unwritten, is the nature of its relationship to the society that produced it. Some constitutions are nothing but a set of lofty platitudes that are rarely observed, while others play an integral role in political affairs.

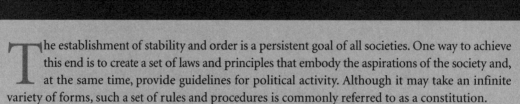

No civilization ... would ever have been possible without a framework of stability, to provide the wherein for the flux of change. Foremost among the stabilizing factors, more enduring than customs, manners and traditions, are the legal systems that regulate our life in the world and our daily affairs with each other.

Hannah Arendt

In this chapter, we explore the meaning of the term *constitution*, and trace the evolution of the Canadian Constitution since 1867. Efforts to patriate the Constitution and develop an amendment procedure acceptable to all the provinces have created enormous controversy in the past half-century. Although the British Parliament passed the 1982 *Canada Act* that brought the Constitution home, arguments over the nature of the Canadian Constitution remain a lively political pastime. The defeat of the Meech Lake and Charlottetown Accords and the 1995 Québec referendum on separation did not end constitutional wrangling, nor did the controversial 1998 Supreme Court ruling stating that the federal government would be obligated to enter into sovereignty negotiations with Québec after a referendum vote showing a clear majority in favour of separation.

In the penultimate sections of this chapter, we discuss the courts and judicial interpretations of the *Charter of Rights and Freedoms*, as these topics are part of the ongoing development of the Constitution. The search for a balance between security and civil liberties forms an important part of this deliberation. The role of judges in interpreting the Constitution, particularly the Charter, is vital.

The Critical Debate to consider while you are reading the chapter is whether there is a substantial need to make major, innovative amendments to the Canadian Constitution and, if so, whether such changes are possible given current restrictions.

Law and the Constitution

Early societies tended to be dominated by individuals who sought to establish traditions and informal rules to govern their people. Today, the tendency is for basic rules to be formalized into what is commonly referred to as a constitution. The origin of this concept can be traced to Greek and Roman times. Further democratic constitutional development flourished during the eighteenth and nineteenth centuries, and since then it has become practically universal for political power to be organized by some form of constitution.[1]

In every political system, there is a need to have guidelines for government action—a supreme law or constitution of the state that defines and limits political power. Thus, the fundamental aspect of a **constitution** is that it states the governing principles of a society. In modern times, the word is used both empirically and normatively: to depict the organization of government, and to devise contraints on its action.

Constitutionalism means that everyone, including the government, is subject to the rules of the constitution. It depicts the government as the servant of society, not its master. The government may exercise authority and even use coercion, but it must do so according to the rules set out in the constitution, and it must abide by judicial interpretations of its actions.

Although constitutions are products of historical development, they also tend to reflect current conditions. By absorbing contemporary elements, constitutions are able to help shape the future by incorporating the norms of political life. As well, constitutional authorities in most countries insist on the need to incorporate **individual rights** into the supreme law as well as to set the parameters for government action. Therefore, the vast majority of contemporary written constitutions contain a discussion of natural rights and the goals of universal liberty, peace and prosperity. The French *Declaration of the Rights of Man and Citizens* and the US Constitution, with its *Bill of Rights*, include statements supporting the principle of the natural rights of *individuals*. Even the constitutions of the most repressive regimes are likely to refer to these objectives.

Many constitutions also acknowledge **collective** or **group rights**. In Canada, such "rights" were accorded to the ethno-religious-linguistic francophone group of Québec and some historical communities along the eastern seaboard by the *British North America Act of 1867*. Both *individual* and *group* rights are found in today's *Charter of Rights and Freedoms*. Of course, the fact that such rights are incorporated into a constitution is no guarantee of their actualization. In situations of real or perceived emergency, such claims may carry little weight in even the most liberal of societies.

The Rule of Law

Above all else, a constitution embodies the rule of law. In addition to setting out a commitment to certain general goals, a constitution is intended to provide a guarantee of impartiality and fairness. The authority of the state is to be exercised rationally and without malice, with all citizens being protected from the abuse of power. The **rule of law** means that a citizen, no matter what her transgression, cannot be denied the due process of law. It therefore regularizes the relationship between citizens and their government. No individual or institution is above the law, no one is exempted from it and all are equal before it. No government or administrative official has any power beyond that awarded by law. Whether or not it is formally included, the rule of law is a fundamental principle without which any constitution, written or unwritten, would be meaningless.

Courts are the guardians of the rule of law, and as such should be beyond partisan influence. The principle of the independence of the judiciary is firmly established, with a history of nearly three hundred years. It can be traced to the English *Act of Settlement* of 1700 that resulted from the English Revolution of 1688, and provided that judges could be removed only if both Houses of Parliament formally asked the Crown for their removal. Following these British traditions, Canadian judges

---

1. For details about different types of constitutions, see Robert J. Jackson and Doreen Jackson, *An Introduction to Political Science: Comparative and World Politics*, 5th ed., (Don Mills, ON: Pearson Prentice Hall, 2007).

remain free to deliver decisions against the interests of influential individuals, institutions or governments without fear of recrimination.

In Canada today, judges of the highest courts (the Supreme Court of Canada and the Federal Court of Canada) and also the most important provincial trial courts (the highest courts of the provinces, as well as the provincial courts of appeal) are removable only by an address to the governor general by both Houses of Parliament. Such an address would take place only after a formal investigation by the Criminal Judicial Council, including all the chief justices in Canada. No higher-court judge has ever been removed in this fashion. As a further precaution against undue influence on judges, the Canadian Constitution provides that almost all courts are established by the provincial legislatures, but that all judges from county courts upward (except courts of probate in Nova Scotia and New Brunswick) are appointed by the federal government. This tradition of the independence of the judiciary is particularly important in constitutional development because courts interpret the written Constitution and, therefore, define the limits of federal and provincial power as well as apply the *Charter of Rights and Freedoms.*

Aside from the Constitution, the two main sources of law in Canada are *statutory* enactments—legislation passed by the Parliament of Canada and the provincial legislatures—and case law developed by the courts, also known as **common law** or unenacted law. Common law is based upon the rule of precedent, **stare decisis**. That is, the judiciary is bound by previous decisions in deciding current cases. This has resulted in the development of a body of case law that provides guidelines for judges in rendering decisions. As new problems are brought before the courts, judges refer to previous decisions that are deemed relevant, and apply the deciding arguments when making their own judgments. If there is no appropriate precedent, judges rely on common sense and reason. Existing principles are thereby broadened and the body of case law is expanded. *Judicial interpretation* is, thus, an important source of our law.

The relationship between these two major sources of law is defined by the doctrine of **parliamentary supremacy**, a basic premise of parliamentary democracy, which dictates that all 11 legislatures have the authority, in theory, to repeal or modify any legal principle that applies to their jurisdiction. This power is not absolute, however. While Canada's Constitution grants legislative authority to the 11 legislatures, the legislative competence of each is specifically limited to certain classes of matters. The Supreme Court's ability to declare an act **ultra vires** (beyond a legislature's jurisdiction) on the basis of Canada's federal division of power is an important qualification. The *entrenchment* of individual and group rights in Canada's *Charter of Rights and Freedoms* also limits the extent of parliamentary supremacy by placing a body of rights beyond the reach of any legislature. **Entrenchment** means that the provisions are embedded in the Constitution so that they are protected and can be changed only by formal amendment procedures.

As well as stating fundamental principles, written constitutions describe the organization of government. Some are remarkably complicated documents outlining the entire government structure and the relative powers and limitations of the various institutions in the political process. There seems to be a general belief that the greater the detail in explicating these relationships, the less the likelihood of the abuse of power. At a minimum, most written constitutions outline the powers and duties of the executive, the legislature, the judiciary and, sometimes, other institutions such as the bureaucracy or the military. However, in modern, complex societies it is not easy to assign one specific function to any one of these bodies since they all perform multifunctional tasks. The courts, for example, adjudicate the law, but, as we will see, in their accumulated judgments they also legislate.

However restrictive the legal restraints are on the exercise of power, nearly all constitutions contain provisions for enhanced executive power in emergency situations. War, civil unrest or natural disaster may require a government to act in a way that, under normal conditions, would be illegal.

The real test of a constitution is whether, after such a crisis, there is a speedy return to compliance with constitutional strictures. The use of the *War Measures Act* to suppress civil rights in Québec in 1970 by the federal Liberal government of Pierre Trudeau was a worrisome example of how constitutions allow governments to handle crises, but the subsequent return to normal procedures after the perceived crisis was a vindication of the viability of Canada's constitutional democracy.

We need not search far to find examples in other countries where constitutional restraints on the exercise of power have been easily subverted by exaggerated crises. Once a group obtains a power base in society, either inside the institutional structure or outside it, the potential always exists to manipulate the provisions of the constitution or even suspend it entirely. As we have said, a written constitution is no guarantee that fundamental principles will be upheld. Unless it is congruent with the prevailing political culture and norms about justice, it stands little chance of having a lasting effect.

We mentioned earlier that some countries possess what are referred to as **unwritten constitutions**. This is not a contradiction in terms; rather, it indicates that certain fundamental principles may be so firmly entrenched in the political process of the state that no formal document outlining them is considered necessary. The Constitution of the United Kingdom is perhaps the best-known example. In this case documents such as the *Magna Carta* of 1215, the *Habeas Corpus Act* of 1679 and the *Reform Bill* of 1832 exist, but they do not make up *the* constitution. Despite these and other documents and legal precedents, the real core of Britain's unwritten constitution is the set of values and norms embedded in the political culture: the rights of freedom of speech and assembly and the right of the opposition to participate in the political process, among others. The existence of an unwritten constitution provides certain advantages for a state. It makes it possible, for instance, to adapt more readily to change without the constraints required by a formal constitutional amendment process.

The Origin and Evolution of the Canadian Constitution

In this section, we examine the evolution of the Canadian Constitution from the period before the 1867 *British North America Act* (now renamed the *Constitution Act, 1867*) to the passing of the *Canada Act* in 1982.[2] While many Canadians assume that until 1982 the *BNA Act* was the entire Canadian Constitution, this assertion should be qualified. The Canadian Constitution has always been a *hybrid* of the written and unwritten types. Important elements of Canada's unwritten Constitution evolved in Britain for many decades before Confederation. As British colonists emigrated to Canada, they brought with them basic constitutional principles such as the rule of law and the right of parliamentary opposition. The *BNA Act*, with its provision that Canada was to have a form of government "similar in principle to that of the United Kingdom," intended not only that certain institutional arrangements with respect to the formal executive were to be reproduced, but also that the British parliamentary system, with all its embedded values, was to be transplanted.

Important elements of the Canadian Constitution were therefore already implicitly in place when the Fathers of Confederation met at Charlottetown in 1864. As Ronald I. Cheffins phrased it, "a literal reading of the Act itself is not only of little value in understanding the realities of political life, but is in fact dangerously misleading."[3] Even vital procedural matters bearing on the governing of the country go unmentioned in the *BNA Act*: for example, the executive roles of the

---

2. Two copies of the original *BNA Act*, to which Queen Victoria gave royal assent on March 29, 1867, can be seen in London, England—one in the Victoria Tower of Westminster Palace and the other in the Public Records Office. Reproductions are in the National Archives of Canada.

3. Ronald I. Cheffins, *The Constitutional Process in Canada* (Toronto: McGraw-Hill Ryerson, 1969), p. 9.

prime minister and cabinet are not mentioned specifically. Constitutional rules that are accepted practice or tradition without being enshrined in the written constitution are called **conventions**. Canada would not be able to govern itself without conventions, such as the concept of **responsible government**, which requires the government to resign when it is defeated in Parliament over a major issue. Moreover, many issues that preoccupy governments today were not covered in the 1867 document. Over time, all levels of government have found ways to expand their responsibilities without increasing their constitutional authority.

The *British North America Act*

Simply put, the *British North America Act* sets out the basic terms of federalism and sketches the machinery of government based on the British model. The Act was the product of lengthy, complex negotiations between the political leaders, as they had differing expectations of what federalism would mean for their respective regions. They all made efforts to obtain concessions and guarantees that would protect matters of vital local concern. For example, French Canadians sought protection for their culture and language as the price for joining the union, while Nova Scotians were concerned about economic concessions and subsidies. Agreement on the organization and structure of the Senate proved particularly difficult to achieve.

The *BNA Act* lacks the stirring rhetoric of the US Constitution, and whatever commitment it has to the fundamental rights of individuals is merely implied; in fact, the statute is as significant for what it does not say as for what it does say. Designed to enable the provinces to join in a political union, the *BNA Act* was not intended to establish a truly independent state, as it provided that the formal authority of Canada was to continue to be vested in the British monarch and that the Act itself could be amended only by the British Parliament.

The established provinces continued to adhere to their colonial constitutions, and the provinces added after Confederation received their constitutions from the federal government. In English-speaking provinces, the heritage from the United Kingdom included the common law tradition. However, since Confederation did not change existing law, Québec continued to have a system of civil law based on French traditions such as the *Code Napoléon*. According to the *BNA Act*, criminal law was to be a federal responsibility and similar throughout the land. However, general principles such as liberty and the rule of law were considered protected by common law and hence were not included.

The *BNA Act* is reasonably detailed with respect to the machinery of formal executive power and on matters concerning the **division of powers** between the federal and provincial governments. Over time the Act has become less clear-cut on the latter matters as jurisdictional issues have become more complicated.[4] The intent of the authors was, therefore, to create a strong central government. The federal government was given responsibility for the important matters of trade and commerce, defence and foreign affairs. Jurisdiction over education, welfare and other matters perceived to be of lesser and only local interest in 1867 was left to the provinces. As we see in the next chapter, the responsibilities of the provinces became relatively more important over time and, when early legal disputes did ensue between the two levels of government, the British Law Lords often sided with the provinces. At times, therefore, the *BNA Act* was very restrictive and often created an impasse in federal–provincial relations.

We have said that the *BNA Act* did not contain a procedure for amendment except by the passage of a bill in the British Parliament. Over time, this role of the British Parliament was restricted. In 1931, the *Statute of Westminster* curtailed the British Parliament's ability to legislate

---

4. See Garth Stevenson, *Unfulfilled Union: Canadian Federalism and National Unity*, 4th ed. (Montréal: McGill-Queen's University Press, 2004).

for Canada except at the request of the Canadian government. In 1949, Louis St. Laurent's government secured an amendment to the *BNA Act* that widened the scope of the Canadian Parliament's authority to undertake amendments: it was empowered to amend the Canadian Constitution on its own except when it affected provincial interests, the five-year term of Parliament, and the language and educational rights of minorities. Despite these changes, however, the *BNA Act* remained an Act of the British Parliament, a fact that raised the ire of Canadian nationalists. It was not until 1982 that the *Canada Act* was passed, severing this link between Canada and the United Kingdom. In total, the *BNA Act* has been amended only 18 times.

Although the *BNA Act* was the centrepiece of Canada's written Constitution, there were other relevant documents. Besides the various amendments to the *BNA Act* and the *Statute of Westminster*, the Canadian Constitution before 1982 could be said to include the *Royal Proclamation of 1763*, the *Colonial Laws Validity Act* of 1865, the various acts admitting new provinces to the federal union, the Letters Patent, concerning the office of the governor general, and a whole range of common-law precedents and orders-in-council.

Whether a constitution originates as a single, written document or as a cluster of laws and agreements, major changes to it occur through judicial interpretation. There is always a need for a court to resolve disputes over jurisdictional authority, especially in a federal system. For most of Canadian history, the court of final appeal was the **Judicial Committee of the Privy Council (JCPC)**—the superior court of the United Kingdom. As we noted, the JCPC tended to define federal authority as narrowly, and provincial authority as widely, as possible.

The emergency powers of the federal government, expressed in the clause, "Peace, Order and good Government" granted extensive residual power to the federal government, but they were interpreted by the JCPC in a way that virtually nullified the centralizing intentions of the authors of the *BNA Act*.[5] These rulings of the JCPC on the law of Canadian federalism were the source of considerable controversy, as many felt that the "law lords" were too far removed from the political realities of Canada to render appropriate decisions.

The reign of the JCPC as the court of last appeal ended in 1949. In that year, the **Supreme Court of Canada** became the final arbiter of *constitutional review*, the highest court for civil, criminal and constitutional cases. Until 1982, however, the Supreme Court was limited by the nature of the parliamentary system and the absence of an entrenched bill of rights. It was concerned mainly with jurisdictional disputes, and did not take the activist role for which the US Supreme Court is widely known. Moreover, the provinces became reticent to take jurisdictional matters to the Supreme Court because of an alleged pro-centralist bias, and such disputes have increasingly had to be resolved outside the judicial process through the mechanism of federal–provincial conferences.

This is not to argue that the Supreme Court is irrelevant on federal issues. On the contrary, there have been very important decisions by the Court on matters such as offshore oil and mineral rights and resource taxation, not to mention its rulings on the federal government's plan of unilateral patriation of the Constitution. Since 1982, the Court has also taken a renewed interest in cases involving civil rights and liberties that can have an influence on federalism. A discussion of the Court's interpretations concerning the *Charter of Rights and Freedoms* is found in the sections below on the evolution of the Charter.

The second important determinant of power between federal and provincial governments rests on the financial strength of the two jurisdictions. The *BNA Act* conferred on the federal government the ability to raise money by any system of taxation, while at the same time it gave responsibility for most areas of growing expenditure to the provinces. From the beginning, provincial authorities

---

5. See Peter J.T. O'Hearn, *Peace, Order and Good Government* (Toronto: Macmillan, 1964).

were restricted to collecting revenue through direct taxes or the sale of natural resources. (Direct taxes must be paid by the individual or firm assessed, but indirect taxes may be passed along to other persons or institutions.)

Thus, it appeared from strict interpretation of the 1867 Act that the provinces could not levy a sales tax (indirect) on commodities that would be passed along to consumers. However, by the ingenious device of making vendors tax collectors for the provincial governments, the rules of the *BNA Act* were evaded and the provinces were able to employ both types of taxation. Today, even such ploys as this are considered insufficient to alleviate provincial budgetary needs.

In summary, the *British North America Act* was an attempt to graft a federal system of government onto a British heritage of representative and responsible cabinet government. The Fathers of Confederation, as Janet Ajzenstat concluded, went to the bargaining table with quite different philosophical positions on human nature and government.[6] They also had to take into account two dissimilar linguistic groups, a federal system and complex financing regulations. The result is a perplexing division of jurisdictions between the two levels of government, federal and provincial. And, although the Crown, government and Parliament are the central governmental institutions, they are not totally powerful in Canada, as they are in the United Kingdom.

There are, then, three fundamental cornerstones of the Canadian system of government, all of which are enshrined in the Constitution. They are *democratic responsible government*, the *rule of law* and *federalism*. In Chapters 6 and 7, we define and analyze the details of federalism and nationalism, and, in Chapter 8, we examine the formal executive, which is bound by principles of responsible government. Here, we discuss the Constitution and, briefly, the basic federal bargain, both of which constitute key elements in Canada's political system. Then we outline the court system and analyze recent constitutional developments.

The Constitutional Bargain: Federal, Provincial and Municipal

The need for a "federal bargain" that would apportion powers between the central and the regional governments was obvious in the nineteenth century. Georges-Étienne Cartier and other French Canadian leaders demanded an element of isolation from central government authority as part of the bargain. No matter what type of system was adopted, some independence had to be granted to the local entities. John A. Macdonald, meanwhile, preferred a unitary to a federal form of government.[7] The federal principle was therefore accepted as a necessary compromise and as a protection for provinces and language groups. Since then, for better or worse, the federal dimension has pervaded the history and development of Canada.

The ten provincial constitutions follow the federal pattern. In each of the provinces, the Queen is represented by a lieutenant-governor appointed by governor-in-council on the advice of the prime minister. The lieutenant-governor acts on the advice and with the assistance of her ministry or executive council, which is responsible to the legislature, and resigns office under circumstances similar to those for the federal government. Provincial legislatures are elected for a maximum of five years and, unlike the federal Parliament, which has two houses, today they are all unicameral.

6. Janet Ajzenstat, *The Political Thought of Lord Durham* (Montréal and Kingston: McGill-Queen's University Press, 1988); and "The Constitutionalism of Etienne Parent and Joseph Howe," in Janet Ajzenstat, ed., *Canadian Constitutionalism: 1791–1991* (Ottawa: Canadian Study of Parliament Group, 1992).

7. P.B. Waite, *The Life and Times of Confederation, 1864–1867* (Toronto: University of Toronto Press, 1962). See Chapter 6 of this text for further explanation of the terms *federal government, unitary government* and *confederation*.

The three northern territories remain under the constitutional authority of the federal government. Several federal statutes—the *Yukon Act, Northwest Territories Act, Government Organization Act, Federal Interpretation Act* and *Nunavut Act*—provide their legal structures, and the Charter also provides a degree of independent legitimacy in sections 3 and 30 by referring to the legislative assemblies of the territories. In political terms, the first two territories have been given fully elected assemblies, responsible executives (called councils), and a form of delegated responsibility for most matters under provincial jurisdiction. The commissioners, who are appointed by the minister of Indian and northern affairs, act as quasi–lieutenant-governors under the authority of the minister. Nunavut, the new territory carved out of the Northwest Territories, gained official status only on April 1, 1999, but now has the same form of government.

As well as being subject to the laws of the federal and provincial governments, Canadians are regulated by local governments. Whether designated as city, town, village or township, these authorities are created by the provinces to provide such services as transportation, public health, garbage disposal, recreation, firefighting and police work. Local school boards are usually empowered to administer education at the primary and secondary levels.

Today, federalism is central to the way Canadians think about their politics. The winning entry in a contest for Canadian jokes was a Canadian version of the ancient elephant joke: Of three students, the American wrote his essay on "The President and Elephants," the French student discussed "Sex and the Elephant," while the Canadian's topic was "Elephants: A Federal or Provincial Responsibility?"

The Federal–Provincial Division of Powers

The Fathers of Confederation regarded the US Civil War as an example of what could happen to a country if the central government did not have strong powers; they referred to this when they assigned the flexible or **residual clause** to the federal government. **Section 91** of the Constitution states,

---

It shall be lawful for the Queen, by and with the Advice and Consent of the Senate and the House of Commons, to make Laws for the Peace, Order, and good Government of Canada, in relation to all matters not coming within the Classes of Subjects by this Act assigned exclusively to the Legislatures of the Provinces.

In other words, this clause gives the federal government jurisdiction over areas not listed specifically as provincial spheres of power. In addition to granting this sweeping authority, **section 91** specifies 29 items as belonging exclusively to the federal government, among them trade, commerce, banking, credit, currency, taxation, navigation, citizenship and defence.

Section 92, on the other hand, delineates 16 specific areas of provincial jurisdiction, including direct taxation, hospitals, prisons, property and civil rights. These latter subjects, although of only limited and local concern in 1867, were later to become much more important than the Fathers of Confederation could have foreseen in their era of more or less laissez-faire government. *Section 93* says that education comes under provincial jurisdiction, but circumscribes that power by special rules setting up denominational schools in Ontario and Québec.

Section 95 establishes **concurrent** or shared federal and provincial powers in regard to agriculture and immigration. The federal Parliament, however, is paramount in these two fields. In other words, if there's a conflict between federal and provincial laws over agriculture or immigration, the federal law prevails in the courts. Students can read the details of these federal–provincial powers at the back of this book in Appendix 1, "A Consolidation of the Constitution Acts, 1867 to 1982."

Despite these rules, the constitutional status of the provinces appeared relatively insignificant in early Canadian history. The Constitution provided such disproportionate power to the national government that some experts have even referred to the period as one of *quasi-federalism*—that is, one whose appearance is federal (i.e., with divided jurisdictions), but whose reality is unitary (i.e., with only one level of government) because little significant power rests in the subunits.

This assertion is based on constitutional powers. First, the central government could **disallow** provincial legislation even when the *BNA Act* assigned the subject matter of the legislation to the provinces. This rarely used power was to be employed in extreme circumstances. For instance, during the Depression years of the 1930s, it was used to stop several acts of William Aberhart's Social Credit government in Alberta. In disallowing Aberhart's proposal to print money, for example, the federal government argued that such an action would destroy the banking system. Although disallowance was used 112 times after Confederation, it has not been used since 1943.

The second and third major powers were those of veto and reservation. At one time, the lieutenant-governors may have had the power to employ the royal prerogative to **veto** (block) legislation. Since they did not exercise it, however, it atrophied as a power. On the other hand, the constitutional ability of lieutenant-governors to **reserve**, or hold back, provincial legislation for federal approval has been used quite often: some seventy bills have been reserved since 1867.[8]

The most recent case occurred in 1961, when the lieutenant-governor of Saskatchewan, Frank Bastedo, without first consulting the federal government, reserved provincial legislation that he believed was of doubtful validity. The Department of Justice in Ottawa quickly decided that the bill was within provincial jurisdiction, so the lieutenant-governor was asked to give his assent to the bill. It seems unlikely that such extreme power will be wielded again in Canada, except perhaps in a circumstance as grave as the secession of a province from the federal union. Moreover, while the federal government may have the legal authority to block any provincial legislation initiating secession, a "technical" solution of this type would not be satisfactory. If a provincial movement toward secession were clearly supported by a popular mandate, legal devices alone could not prevent it.

Problems over the Division of Powers

While the *BNA Act* was a centralist document, it is important to note that the meanings of many key words in the Act have changed over time. Leaving aside for the moment the matter of how judicial interpretation has changed the document, it is clear that certain terms were not defined precisely and others took on new meanings over time. As well, the Fathers of Confederation could not have predicted how certain matters would develop.

Over time, omissions in the *BNA Act* created a void that both federal and provincial authorities sought to fill to their own advantage. For example, section 109 gave control over natural resources to the provinces—but did this control include offshore resources and the taxation of these resources? Section 93 gave power over education to the provinces, but today it is a matter for debate whether education, as a provincial responsibility, encompasses cultural matters, broadcasting, occupational training and research.

The conflict over division of powers is well illustrated by the case of natural resources. Although the *BNA Act* assigned the ability to make laws concerning resources to the provinces, it gave the federal government a major voice in the sale of resources by its control of interprovincial and international trade. Thus, the provinces "control" the oil because it is under the ground, the oil wells are "owned" by private or public companies, and the Parliament of Canada "exercises" some authority over oil through taxation and jurisdictional powers.

6.　R. MacGregor Dawson, *The Government of Canada*, 5th ed., revised by Norman Ward (Toronto: University of Toronto Press, 1970), pp. 213–17.

It could be different. Through use of the **declaratory power** (*BNA Act* s. 92.10(c)), the federal government can assume jurisdiction over any "work" that is for the benefit of Canada as a whole. For example, in the 1920s Parliament declared that every grain elevator was under federal control, but it did not assume ownership. Federal control over uranium exploration is a more recent example. The provinces have always contested the use of this declaratory power, but the courts have continually backed the federal authorities' right to employ it.

Technological breakthroughs permitting the exploitation of offshore resources have also resulted in hot disputes. In 1967, the Supreme Court ruled in an advisory opinion that Ottawa, not British Columbia, owned the resources off the West Coast. In 1977, the federal government proposed temporary arrangements with three Maritime provinces that would have given Ottawa 25 percent and the provinces 75 percent of their offshore resources. Newfoundland never accepted this bargain, and Nova Scotia quickly backed out after a provincial election.

In 1979, the Progressive Conservative government of Joe Clark offered to give complete control of offshore resources to the provinces; however, the return of the Liberals in 1980 left the situation in limbo. Disputants on both sides of the East Coast question finally applied to the courts for settlement: Newfoundland to the provincial Court of Appeal, Ottawa to the Supreme Court of Canada. After a long-running battle, the courts awarded ownership of offshore resources along the East Coast to the federal government, but the battles have continued.

It is clear that the Constitution has been inadequate in plainly demarcating all jurisdictions. As Garth Stevenson has pointed out, there are now very few areas of policy that are handled by only one level of government:

> *The only exclusively federal areas appear to be military defence, veterans' affairs, the post office and monetary policy. The only exclusively provincial areas appear to be municipal institutions, elementary and secondary education and some areas of law related to property and other non-criminal matters.*[9]

In all other areas, there is either tacit or explicit agreement by the two major levels of government to engage in activities in the same fields. Sometimes this is harmonious, as for example when the federal government allows the provinces to regulate interprovincial highway transportation. In other areas, such as international trade, employee training, communications, language and culture, the two levels are in constant conflict. Perhaps the most significant new issue concerns natural resources. The federal government can sign an agreement like the *Kyoto Accord* but still have difficulty implementing it because of the constitutional role of the provincial governments in the environmental field.

Another aspect of the division of powers that continues to cause controversy concerns joint responsibilities. Section 95 of the Constitution declared joint or **concurrent jurisdiction**—power shared between the Parliament of Canada and the provincial legislatures—in the areas of agriculture and immigration. Moreover, de facto concurrent powers have arisen in some other fields because of the federal government's control of **spending power**.

While the federal government may have little or no jurisdiction over a particular matter such as education, consumer protection or the environment, this does not prohibit Ottawa from spending money in these areas. The provinces have had great difficulty saying no to such largesse. Moreover, although not mentioned in the Constitution, scientific research, recreational activities, tourism and protection of the environment all are handled as if they are areas of concurrent jurisdiction.

9. Garth Stevenson, "Federalism and Intergovernmental Relations," in M.S. Whittington and G. Williams, eds., *Canadian Politics in the 1980s*, 2nd ed. (Toronto: Methuen, 1984), p. 378.

".. MY NAME IS BOB, AND I'M AN ASYMMETRICAL FEDERALIST".."

Reproduced with permission; Gable, *The Globe and Mail*.

Another issue in Canadian government stems from **asymmetrical federalism**—or the principle that some provinces are treated constitutionally differently than others. From 1867 onward, there has been a degree of asymmetry in the system. The *British North America Act* gave Québec special constitutional status in the use of the French language, denominational schools and the *Code Civile*. The ferry service between Prince Edward Island and the mainland was specifically mentioned in the *BNA Act* as something to be subsidized. Today, Québec collects its own income tax, while all the other provinces have theirs collected by Ottawa. Alberta, Ontario and Québec are the only provinces to collect their own corporation taxes. And, to end this list of some of the many asymmetrical situations, eight provinces (but not Ontario and Québec) have contracts with the RCMP to carry out provincial policing duties.

Conflicts over jurisdictional boundaries are to be expected in federal systems. Canada certainly has been no exception to this rule. Successive court decisions by the JCPC of the United Kingdom and, later, the Supreme Court of Canada have cleared up some, but by no means all, questions about jurisdiction in various policy fields. The precise lines of authority remain blurred in many areas. Dissent has arisen mainly over the fact that matters that have grown in significance over the years, such as property and civil rights, are within the provincial sphere, while the "Peace, Order and good Government" (a.k.a. POGG) clause in section 91 gives competing authority to the federal government in the same fields in the case of an emergency. Due to changes in the nature of social and economic policy, this federal power has increasingly conflicted with the specific powers accorded the provinces.

In such disputes, court decisions have varied from restrictive interpretations that left the federal government with very little authority except in the gravest emergencies (e.g., *Local Prohibition*, 1896; *Hodge v. The Queen*, 1883; *Board of Commerce*, 1992; and *Toronto Electric Commissioners v. Snider*, 1925) to granting the federal government such wide scope that specific powers that appeared to fall exclusively in the provincial field were undermined (e.g., *Canada Temperance Act*, 1878, and *Russell v. the Queen*, 1882).

Even such major events as the Great Depression were not considered significant enough to offset clearly and permanently the arguments that, first, social legislation was under provincial jurisdiction because of the property and civil rights clause and, second, Canada's federal Parliament was restricted to those fields in its specific jurisdiction (*Snider*, 1925). Thus, even in the face of this supreme test of government authority, the federal government could do no more than supply funds to the provinces for fighting the effects of the Depression. It could not act itself. Therefore, Prime Minister R.B. Bennett's legislation for social insurance, marketing schemes and minimum wages was struck down by the JCPC in 1937—an action that undermined the federal government's ability to provide any relief in the crisis.[10]

This constitutional position was short-lived. During the Second World War, a surge of nationalism made it possible to circumvent restrictive interpretations of the *BNA Act*. The federal government assumed almost unlimited powers, and the JCPC, apparently sensing the national mood, shifted its position. The result was the 1946 *Canadian Temperance Federation* judgment, which declared that laws going beyond local interests could be the concern of the federal authorities.

A 1949 amendment to the *Supreme Court Act* gave the power of final arbitration over jurisdictional authority to the Supreme Court. The JCPC's authority was terminated. Since then, the federal government has been able to refer either its own legislation or that of a province to the Supreme Court, while a provincial government can refer either its own or federal legislation to the superior court of that province, from which the case may proceed to the Supreme Court on appeal. Since the federal government appoints not only Supreme Court justices but also all judges to provincial superior and county courts, it exercises great power in this field.

The belief that a wholly Canadian court would be more inclined to take into account Canadian reality and adopt a broader interpretation of federal powers has been borne out by history. Since the ascendancy of the Supreme Court of Canada, the federal government has obtained authority over radio, telecommunications and nuclear energy. A classic example of the centralist orientation of the Court was indicated by the 1952 *Johannesson* case, in which the Court upset earlier judgments by proclaiming that since aeronautics was of "national importance" it belonged to the federal authority.

In the 1975 *Anti-Inflation* case, the Supreme Court interpreted the federal division of powers in Canada in a similar way. It ruled that the federal government could impose pay restraints on Canadians if a national emergency existed. The JCPC had limited the use of the federal government's authority to emergencies such as war, pestilence and famine, but Canada's Supreme Court now added economic factors to the list. It thus greatly broadened the interpretation of the POGG clause. The Court did not approve the federal government's contention that controlling inflation concerned all of Canada, ruling only that Parliament could enact legislation in the field of economic regulation during an emergency. Since the *Anti-Inflation* case, the pro–central government tendency of the Supreme Court has been shown in such cases as *General Motors v. City National Leasing* (1989), which culminated in a robust reading of federal authority in the fields of trade and commerce.[11]

Rhetoric and Reality over Constitutional Amendment

Changing a constitution is an amazingly complex process.[12] In political science terminology, a **rigid constitution** is one that is difficult to amend, whereas a **flexible constitution** can be more easily

---

10. See Mallory, *Social Credit and Federal Power in Canada*, p. 51.

11. *General Motors v. City National Leasing* (1989) 1 S.C.R. 641.

12. See R.D. Olling and M.W. Westmacott, *Perspectives on Canadian Federalism* (Scarborough, ON: Prentice Hall, 1988).

adapted to changing circumstances. Though arguments may be articulated both for and against the use of either type of amending formula, it is clear that all constitutions must provide *some* means to adapt themselves to new circumstances (see the "Close-Up on Institutions: Constitution-Speak—Some Jargon You Need to Know"). It is clear that the Canadian Constitution has become more "rigid" since its patriation in 1982 along with some federal laws passed in the intervening time.

Changing the Canadian "federal bargain" struck in 1867 has been extremely difficult. The 1931 *Statute of Westminster* declared that the Parliament of the United Kingdom could no longer legislate for Canada except at the latter's request. At the time of its passage, the British government attempted to persuade Canada to accept a specific amending formula and to cut the last tie with the United Kingdom. Unfortunately, Canadian politicians could not agree on how such a mechanism would work. The British Parliament, therefore, remained responsible for constitutional amendment in Canada. On several occasions after that date, the Constitution was amended in the UK after a request from Canada. Provincial compliance was obtained, for example, in the 1940 amendment that gave the federal Parliament jurisdiction over unemployment insurance; the 1951 amendment that gave Parliament shared power over old-age pensions; and the 1960 amendment dealing with the retirement of judges. On the other hand, no provincial agreement needed to be sought, nor was it, when the modes of representation in the Senate (1915) and the House (1946, 1952 and 1974) were amended.

In view of the practices adopted on these occasions, it is clear that a constitutional convention had developed with regard to the amendment of the *BNA Act*. The British Parliament accepted each of the 18 amendments that emanated from a joint address of both houses of the Canadian Parliament. For those amendments that affected the federal balance, the provinces were always consulted and agreed to the proposals. But no substantial amendment was ever made at the request of any province or group of provinces, since the British Parliament accepted as legitimate only communications that arrived by way of the federal Parliament.

Despite this rigidity on fundamental issues, however, many minor aspects of the Constitution were eligible to be changed without the passage of British legislation. From the beginning, for example, the provinces were allowed to amend their own constitutions in all spheres except those concerning the powers of the lieutenant-governor. Moreover, with the passage of the *BNA Act*

CLOSE-UP ON Institutions

CONSTITUTION-SPEAK—SOME JARGON YOU NEED TO KNOW

Amending Formula: The rules for changing the Constitution. The debate over the amending process is essentially over whose voices should be needed to make a change in the law—the provinces, the regions or the people themselves.

Asymmetry: Different provinces with different powers. Essentially, Québec wants powers that not all other provinces want. Should Canada accommodate more differences among the provinces, or would that violate the idea of equality?

Bipolar Federation: A Canadian federation of two units—Québec and the Rest of Canada.

Common Market: Five to ten constituent units with a minimal federal government.

Concurrency: Refers to powers that are exercised by both the federal government and the provinces.

Concurrency with Provincial Paramountcy: Both levels of government act together, but the provinces have the final say if federal and provincial governments disagree.

Confederation of Regions: A loose confederation of four or five regions.

Executive Federalism: Decision-making by the prime minister, the ten premiers and their governments—pejoratively called bargaining behind closed doors.

Residual Power: The federal government has the ultimate power to deal with matters of national concern to safeguard "Peace, Order and good Government."

Seven and 50: Not a cocktail mix. Stands for seven provinces with more than 50 percent of the national population—the requirement for most constitutional changes. Other important changes require unanimous consent.

Suspensive Veto: Resolution dies if the House of Commons votes against a proposed constitutional amendment. However, if resolution passes in the Commons but the Senate votes against it, the amendment is merely delayed for six months. Then the Commons votes on it again and, if it passes, the constitutional amendment proceeds without Senate approval.

Triple-E Senate: Equal, elected and effective—an elected Senate that has an equal number of seats for each province and that would be as effective as the House of Commons.

(No. 2) in 1949, the federal Parliament was empowered to amend the Constitution, except with regard to provincial powers, rights and privileges; the rights of minorities with respect to schools and language protection; the extension of the life of Parliament beyond five years; and the necessity to call at least one session of Parliament per year. These were extensive exceptions, however, as they prevented Ottawa from amending anything that touched on the nature and division of federal–provincial responsibilities, the fundamental cornerstone of the Canadian political system.

Moreover, an institution, such as the Senate or the Supreme Court, may be considered to be either purely in the federal sphere or to belong to the provinces as well. The Senate has a regional basis to its representation and the Supreme Court is the final arbiter of federal–provincial disputes. Such institutions could not be reformed constitutionally without substantial provincial agreement.

From 1931 until 1981, strenuous efforts were made to cut the remaining ties to Britain. Bringing the Constitution home (or *patriation*) involved two seemingly insoluble conundrums: How much provincial participation should there be before a decision is made to patriate the Constitution? What type of amendment process should ensue? Only when Canadian leaders came to an agreement on these two matters would they be able to amend the Constitution without recourse to Britain. The question in Canada had never been *whether* the country should have its own constitution, but *what* that constitution should be.

Although efforts to find an acceptable constitutional agreement started in the 1930s, only in the 1960s did coherent discussions take place between the federal government and all of the provinces. Two of the resulting proposals almost succeeded: the Fulton-Favreau formula of 1964 and the Victoria Charter of 1971. The former was significant in Canadian constitutional development because it was the first mechanism that ever received the unanimous support of all ten provincial premiers.

The 1964 Fulton-Favreau formula proposed drawing up a set of amending mechanisms that would have changed depending on the issue at stake. Parliament would have been able to amend the Constitution subject to approval of the provinces, with the rules for this approval varying issue by issue. Matters such as the powers of the provinces, the use of French and English, and the number of senators in the Senate, for example, would have been amended only if all the provinces agreed with Parliament. Changes in education, on the other hand, could have been made with the consent of all the provinces except Newfoundland.

Still other portions of the Constitution would have been changed only if Parliament could obtain the agreement of two-thirds of the provinces, representing at least 50 percent of the population of Canada. The reality behind this last requirement was that either Ontario or Québec would have had to concur with all changes in this domain. Furthermore, Parliament acting alone could have changed those aspects of the Constitution directly related to the functions of the federal government. For a time, it appeared that the Fulton-Favreau formula might gain acceptance and thus form the basis for the patriation of the *BNA Act*. However, misgivings in Québec prevented its adoption.

In 1971, another federal–provincial conference came to a tentative agreement on an amending formula. Unlike the Fulton-Favreau formula, the Victoria Charter would not have required the unanimous consent of the provinces for any amendment. Instead, all changes would have required the agreement of Parliament and a majority of the provinces, including all provinces with over 25 percent of Canada's population, at least two Atlantic provinces and two Western provinces with 50 percent of the population of the West. As with the Fulton-Favreau formula, it seemed for a time that the Victoria Charter might gain acceptance, but it, too, failed to receive the support of Québec.

In each of these cases, the essential stumbling block to finding an amendment formula was always Québec's desire to be treated as a province unlike the others ("*une province pas comme les autres*"). To many Québeckers, the idea that federalism refers to a process involving ten equal provinces and the federal government working as one state is unacceptable. They argue that Canada is a union of two "founding peoples," not ten "equal provinces." As we saw in Chapter 3, this is based on the view that the Canadian Constitution is a *compact* between two cultural groups or between English and French provinces.[13]

By extension, some Québeckers argue that Québec would be best able to protect its own interests if it were a state. From this standpoint they develop one of two possible strategies. Some accept the federal system, but want a *special status* for Québec, in which cultural fields such as education and communications would be left totally to Québec and the federal government would not intervene in matters such as language policy. In practice, all premiers of Québec since Maurice Duplessis have taken this stand as their minimum position. Even the non-separatist premiers Lesage, Johnson and Bourassa argued that Canada consists of "two nations"—and current premier Jean Charest agrees.[14]

The second strategy advocated by some Québécois is separation from Canada. The rise to power of the Parti Québécois in November 1976 made this strategy a possibility. Lévesque, Parizeau, Bouchard and Landry all argued that it was impossible for Québec francophones to protect their language and culture within the federal system and that separate status was essential.

The history and detailed development of this option are discussed in Chapter 7; however, a word on the right of constituent provinces to secede from their state may be useful here. As a general rule, such a right does not exist in any of the established federal states—Canada, the United States, Australia, Germany or Switzerland. On one occasion, in 1935, the state of Western Australia attempted to secede from Australia and actually passed a referendum to this effect, 136 653 votes to 70 706. The Parliament of the United Kingdom, however, would not allow the case to go forward as British legislation and the proposal died.

Patriation of Canada's Constitution

The long and at times bitter debate over constitutional patriation ended in 1982 with the passage of the *Canada Act* by the British Parliament. While patriation of the Canadian Constitution was primarily symbolic in that it did not represent any major changes in federal–provincial jurisdictions or the structure of central government, the inclusion of an entrenched *Charter of Rights and Freedoms* and an amending formula has had profound significance.

The catalyst for what became the final round of the constitutional negotiations leading to patriation was the 1980 Québec referendum on sovereignty-association. In May 1980, Premier René Lévesque's Parti Québécois *indépendantiste* government sought authority to negotiate sovereign political status for Québec with continued economic association with Canada.[15] During the provincial referendum campaign, opponents of this proposal—including the federal Liberal Party—pledged that Canada would begin a process of "renewal" and constitutional change to address the concerns of Québec citizens if they said no to the referendum question. Ultimately, Québec voters rejected Lévesque's plan by a convincing margin, 60 to 40 percent. Patriation of the Constitution was thereby given new momentum, with Prime Minister Pierre Trudeau and the federal Liberals exhorting Canadians to renew federalism in order to reciprocate Québec's gesture of confidence.

---

13. See Ramsay Cook, *Provincial Autonomy, Minority Rights and the Compact Theory, 1867–1921*, Study no. 4, Royal Commission on Bilingualism and Biculturalism (Ottawa: Queen's Printer, 1969).

14. See Edward McWhinney, *Canada and the Constitution, 1979–1982* (Toronto: University of Toronto Press, 1982).

15. See Québec's White Paper on sovereignty-association, *Québec–Canada: A New Deal* (Québec: Gouvernement du Québec, 1979).

The concept of *renewed federalism*, while vague, allowed Trudeau to renew his efforts for patriation. The federal government and the provinces conducted a series of meetings culminating in September 1980 in Ottawa. However, government leaders made no progress on the agenda items, which included patriation, an amending formula, a *Charter of Rights and Freedoms*, the principle of equalization, reform of the Senate and the Supreme Court, and redistribution of powers between the two levels of government. Faced with an intransigent group of provincial premiers, Trudeau decided that the federal government would proceed "unilaterally."

Trudeau's controversial *unilateral patriation package* proposed an entrenched charter of rights as well as equalization and amendment formulas. Of the ten provincial governments, however, only New Brunswick and Ontario supported the federal government. The federal government justified its action on the premise that, as the representative of all Canadians, it legitimately spoke for the interests of all citizens. A special Joint Committee of the Senate and the House of Commons was formed to review the government's resolution. After prolonged debate and more than seventy substantial changes, the government's resolution was adopted. The federal Progressive Conservative Party opposed the government's unilateral action. The New Democratic Party (NDP), however, supported the package after it won amendments guaranteeing provincial ownership of natural resources.

The Roles of Britain and the Supreme Court

The 1949 amendment to the *BNA Act* had made it clear that the federal Parliament alone could amend only those provisions that were already under federal jurisdiction. The procedure for other constitutional changes required a joint address from the House and Senate to the British Parliament. While Britain had always acted automatically on receiving such an address, its role in this particular crisis was uncertain. Canada had seldom made requests affecting the division of powers without first obtaining provincial consent, and British parliamentarians were faced with a dilemma, since either accepting or rejecting the Canadian federal government's unilateral request for patriation would leave many Canadians unhappy. Trudeau's remark that British MPs should "hold their noses" and pass the request made their task no easier.

Politicians in the UK hoped to escape the dilemma by telling their Canadian counterparts that, given strong provincial opposition, Westminster would be reluctant to pass the request without a ruling by Canada's Supreme Court on the legality of unilateral patriation. Meanwhile, six of the provinces had brought the question of unilateral patriation before the Supreme Court.

The Court's ruling, delivered September 28, 1981, offered both sides a measure of support. By a vote of seven to two, the judges ruled that the federal government could "legally" and "unilaterally" submit the constitutional resolution to the British Parliament. However, by a six-to-three vote, the Court ruled that a constitutional convention requiring provincial consent also existed, and that the process embarked upon by Ottawa "offended the federal principle." The Court left vague the extent of provincial consent required by this convention, and further noted that conventions are not enforceable by law. Federal justice minister Jean Chrétien agreed, arguing that it is not up to the courts but rather to politicians to decide what political conventions should be.

The patriation package was thus tossed back into the political arena. As a result, another First Ministers Conference was held in November. The federal government was adamant that a patriation package should include a charter of rights and an amending formula similar to that offered at the Victoria Conference in 1971. It proposed that constitutional change should require the consent of Parliament and a majority of legislatures in Canada's four major regions: two in Atlantic Canada, Québec, Ontario and two in the West. The veto power of the two largest provinces would thereby be guaranteed. Almost all the provinces opposed this formula.

Earlier in 1981, those premiers (including René Lévesque) who were against the federal plans had argued for a patriation package of their own. They had proposed that constitutional change should require the consent of Parliament and seven provinces representing at least 50 percent of the population. This proposal would have allowed a province to "opt out" of any amendment that took away existing provincial rights or powers, and would further have entitled any such province to fiscal compensation. Acceptance of this plan by Québec became the basis for later federal efforts to discredit the argument that traditionally Québec had a constitutional veto.

The Gang of Eight, as the opposing provincial premiers were dubbed, was also against many clauses in the proposed Charter of Rights. The eight premiers feared that the Charter would give new powers to federally appointed judges and reduce provincial authority. Their other concerns included the prospect of expensive and time-consuming redrafting of provincial legislation to comply with the new charter, the hint of importation of US jurisprudence in the language of the legal rights section and the direct recourse to the courts that the charter would grant to individuals.

Federal–Provincial Constitutional Agreement

The November 1981 federal–provincial conference ended in agreement between the federal government and nine out of the ten provinces. Québec was the exception and never did agree to patriation. The major compromise among those who did sign the agreement was over the inclusion of a **notwithstanding clause** that allowed Parliament or a provincial legislature to override most Charter provisions by declaring that they were doing so when passing legislation. A **sunset clause**, requiring renewal of this exemption every five years, was also included. In the absence of such a renewal, the Charter's provisions would take precedence.

Those who favoured inclusion of the notwithstanding clause argued that it provides an important democratic check, maintaining the pre-eminence of the legislatures in the event of an "awkward" court ruling. The idea of using notwithstanding clauses is of long duration in Canada. It was found in the *Canadian Bill of Rights* passed by the federal Parliament in 1960, as well as in the provincial bills of rights passed by Alberta, Québec, Saskatchewan and Ontario. The federal government used it during the 1970 October Crisis in Québec.

Critics of the notwithstanding provision argued that it circumvents the very purpose of an entrenched charter, which is to give the courts the authority to protect fundamental individual freedoms in the event that legislatures and governments fail to do so. According to one constitutional expert, "if legislatures are given the power to cancel … judicial authority they are most likely to use it when there is a failure of restraint."[16]

Other compromises concerning the Charter were also necessary to obtain provincial agreement to patriation. The case of Native peoples provides a pertinent example. Recognition of their treaty rights was originally excluded from the Charter at the insistence of those provinces that were concerned that Native land claims might reduce provincial control over natural resources. It was only after intense lobbying by Native groups that recognition of these rights for First Nations peoples was later restored. In section 25, Native people were guaranteed that the Charter could not be construed "so as to abrogate from any aboriginal, treaty or other rights or freedoms that pertain to the aboriginal peoples of Canada." For greater assurance, section 35 specified that "treaty rights" were defined as "rights that now exist by way of land-claim agreements or may be so acquired."

Another important lobbying effort ensured the restoration of the rights of an overlooked majority group: women. Section 28 of the Charter—which simply stated, "notwithstanding anything in this Charter, the rights and freedoms referred to in it are guaranteed equally to male

16. Noel Lyon, *The Globe and Mail*, November 17, 1981.

and female persons"—was excluded by one of the early agreements. In response to this, the Ad Hoc Committee of Canadian Women on the Constitution was formed, and in just three weeks it successfully lobbied all ten provincial premiers to reverse their stand on the issue. Equality of men and women was thus placed outside the reach of the notwithstanding clause.

A further major compromise leading to the success of the November 1981 conference concerned the amending formula. Instead of the federal Liberal proposition, the formula preferred by the provincial Gang of Eight was adopted. It called for future jurisdictional amendments to be made by a joint resolution of both the Senate and the House of Commons, as well as by a resolution of the legislative assemblies of at least two-thirds of the provinces, representing at least 50 percent of the population of Canada.[17] In addition, it granted dissenting provinces the right to opt out of all amendments that affected their status and powers.

While federal–provincial agreement on a patriation package removed much of the hesitancy of British politicians to grant the federal government's request for patriation, Native groups continued to press their opposition in the British courts, arguing that the British Crown was still responsible for them. The British courts rejected this claim, however, finding that while no government should derogate the Aboriginal rights guaranteed in treaties signed with the British and Canadian governments, responsibility for Native groups had long since passed from the Crown in Britain to the Crown in Canada.

The British Parliament was presented with the revised Canada Bill in mid-February of 1982. Despite Québec's objections, the bill was speedily passed by large majorities at every stage. On March 29, the Queen gave royal assent to the *Canada Act*, 115 years to the day after the *BNA Act* had received assent. In Ottawa, on April 17, 1982, the Queen proclaimed the *Constitution Act, 1982*, completing the patriation process (see the "Close-Up on Institutions: Canada's Constitutional Highlights" on page 163).

The New Canadian Constitution

As part of the final patriation package, there were several changes to the Constitution, none of which affects the main structure of government or specifically alters the division of powers between Parliament and the provincial legislatures. In other words, the main institutions from the *BNA Act* that we discussed earlier remained in place. However, the impact of the changes has been immense and they are noted below and in the next section on the Charter.[18]

Change I: There are now five legal formulas for amending the *Constitution Act*. The *first formula* concerns amendments that require *unanimous consent* (section 41). These deal with amendments to the office of the Queen, the governor general and the lieutenant-governors; the right of a province to at least as many seats in the House of Commons as it has in the Senate; the use of the English and French languages (except amendments applying only to a single province); the composition of the Supreme Court of Canada; and amendments to the amending formulas themselves. Amendments in these areas must be passed by the Senate and the House of Commons (or by the Commons alone if the Senate has not approved the proposal within 180 days after the Commons has done so) and by the legislature of every province. This means that every province has a veto over these types of amendments.

17. The latest general census would be referred to for such information. While the Senate may delay constitutional change, it does not possess an absolute veto. After 180 days, an amendment may be concluded without its agreement.
18. These amendments are concisely summarized in James Ross Hurley, *Amending Canada's Constitution* (Ottawa: Supply and Services, 1996).

The *second formula* concerns amendments under the *general procedure* (section 38). They include amendments that

- take away any rights, powers or privileges of provincial governments or legislatures;
- deal with the proportionate representation of the provinces in the House of Commons;
- deal with the powers of the Senate, the method of selecting senators and their residence qualifications;
- concern the constitutional position of the Supreme Court of Canada (not including its composition, which is covered under the first formula above);
- concern the extension of existing provinces into the territories; and
- concern the *Charter of Rights and Freedoms.*

Amendments in these areas must be passed by the Senate and the House of Commons (or by the Commons alone if the Senate delays more than 180 days), and by the legislatures of two-thirds of the provinces with at least half the total population (excluding the territories). This means that any four less-populous provinces or Ontario and Québec together could veto any amendments in this category, and that either Ontario or Québec would be needed as one of the seven provinces to pass any amendment.

The *third formula* deals with matters that apply to *one or several, but not all, provinces* (section 43). Amendments in these cases must be passed by the Senate and the House of Commons and by the legislature or legislatures of the particular province or provinces concerned. This includes changes in provincial boundaries or changes relating to the use of the English or French language in any province or provinces.

The *fourth formula* concerns *changes in the executive government* of Canada or changes in the Senate and House of Commons that are not covered by the first two formulas. Such amendments can be made by an ordinary act of the Parliament of Canada (section 44). The *fifth formula* concerns amendments that can be made by *individual provincial* legislatures alone (section 45). In the original *BNA Act, 1867* (section 92), with the exception of the office of the lieutenant-governor, provinces could amend their own constitutions. Section 92 (1) was repealed and this amendment clause moved to section 45, which places the provinces in a position equivalent to that of the federal government.

Change II: The first three amending formulas *entrench* specific parts of the written Constitution. This means that neither Parliament alone nor any provincial legislature has the power to affect them. All changes must be made according to the particular formula that applies. Procedural requirements are also set out (section 39) that establish maximum and minimum times within which constitutional amendments must be passed.

Change III: The provinces obtained *wider powers over their natural resources* than they had before. Each province now controls the export within Canada of the primary production from its mines, oil wells, gas wells, forests and electric power plants, provided it does not discriminate against other parts of the country in prices or supplies. The federal government can legislate on

CLOSE-UP ON
Institutions

CANADA'S CONSTITUTIONAL HIGHLIGHTS

A: Actual Constitutional Decisions

1867	*British North America Act* (now the *Constitution Act, 1867*) is enacted
1931	*Statute of Westminster.* Britain can no longer legislate for Canada except at the request of the Canadian government
1949	An amendment to the *BNA Act* widens the scope of the Canadian Parliament's authority to undertake further amendments
1949	Supreme Court of Canada becomes final court of appeal
1961	Diefenbaker's *Bill of Rights* is enacted
1964	Fulton-Favreau formula is rejected by Québec
1971	Victoria Charter is rejected by Québec
1980	Québec referendum on sovereignty-association is defeated
1981	Supreme Court rules Trudeau's constitutional resolution is valid but violates political convention
1981	First ministers make three significant changes to resolution; package is rejected by Québec
1981	Constitutional resolution is passed by Parliament
1982	*Canada Act* passed by British House of Commons and patriated; the *Charter of Rights and Freedoms* and an amendment formula become part of the Canadian Constitution; Québec does not sign
1984–2008	Nine minor changes to Constitution

B: Constitutional Developments and Proposals (see also Chapters 6 and 7)

1990	Meech Lake Accord fails
1991	Spicer Royal Commission reports
1992	Dobbie-Beaudoin Joint House and Senate Committee report is published followed by constitutional conferences
1992	Charlottetown Accord is signed by federal and provincial leaders; it is later in the year massively rejected by voters in a general referendum
1995	Québec referendum on independence is very narrowly defeated
1995–96	Parliament passes legislation 1) containing a distinct society clause for Québec; 2) allowing Québec, Ontario, British Columbia and any two Maritime or Prairie provinces to veto any further constitutional change; and 3) committing the federal government to refrain from using its spending power to create new shared-cost programs without the consent of the majority of provinces
1997	Calgary Declaration—an attempt by nine premiers to restart constitutional negotiations with Québec
1998	Supreme Court answers three questions about Québec separatism
1999	Federal Parliament passes the *Clarity Act* and Québec responds with its own legislation
2003	Election of federalist Jean Charest as premier of Québec
2006	House of Commons passes resolution stating that Québeckers form a nation within a united Canada

these matters, however, and, in case of conflict, the federal law will prevail. The provinces can levy indirect taxes on their mines, oil wells, gas wells, forests and electric power plants and primary production from these sources. Such taxes must be the same whether or not the products are exported to other parts of the country.

Change IV: Provisions were included concerning *Native peoples.* First, the Charter is not to be construed so as "to abrogate or derogate from any aboriginal, treaty or other rights or freedoms that pertain to the aboriginal peoples of Canada" (section 25). Second, the existing Aboriginal and treaty rights of the Native peoples of Canada are recognized and affirmed (this includes Indian, Inuit and Métis peoples).

Change V: Section 36 (1) on *equalization and regional disparities* declares that the federal government and Parliament and the provincial governments and legislatures "are committed to promoting equal opportunities for the well-being of Canadians, furthering economic development to reduce disparities in opportunities; and providing essential public services of reasonable quality to all Canadians." In section 36 (2), the federal government and Parliament "are committed to the principle of making equalization payments to ensure that provincial governments have sufficient revenues to provide reasonably comparable levels of public services and reasonably comparable levels of taxation."

Change VI: Official English and French versions of the Constitution are equally authoritative.

Change VII: The 1982 *Constitution Act* includes a *Charter of Rights and Freedoms*. (The very important addition of the Charter is discussed in considerable detail below.)

Change VIII: The Charter is to be interpreted "in a manner consistent with the preservation and enhancement of the multicultural heritage of Canada" (section 27).

The constitutional amendment system that is now in place is quite rigid, so that the chances of further change to the Constitution by amendment are minimal (see the "Close-Up on Institutions: Constitutional Negotiations—A Unique Canadian Style?"). Despite constant efforts and even a national referendum, there have been only nine minor amendments to the Constitution since 1982 (not including electoral redistribution changes):

- In 1984, the Constitution was amended to provide for consultation with the Aboriginal peoples of Canada before any amendment is made with respect to their rights.
- In 1987, an amendment dealt with the entrenchment of the denominational school rights of the Pentecostal Association in Newfoundland.
- In 1993, the New Brunswick legislature and the federal Parliament used section 43 to make New Brunswick a bilingual province.
- In 1994, an amendment changed the Constitution so that the federal government could be relieved of the obligation of providing steamboat services for Prince Edward Island upon the completion of the bridge joining the island to the mainland.
- In 1997, fifth and sixth amendments changed the educational rights in Newfoundland and ended the province's constitutionally established church-run school system.
- After the 1997 general election, the federal Parliament passed a seventh constitutional amendment that changed Québec's religion-based educational system to one based on French and English school boards.
- In 1999, the federal Parliament gave representation in the House and Senate to the new territory of Nunavut in its eighth amendment.
- In 2001, Ottawa and St. John's agreed to change the name of Newfoundland to Newfoundland and Labrador in its ninth amendment.

The right to amend the Constitution is finally in Canadian hands, but those hands are fairly firmly tied except on very minor issues that concern only one province. For a discussion of recent political compromises about future amendments, see Chapter 7. However, despite all the earnest

CLOSE-UP ON Institutions

CONSTITUTIONAL NEGOTIATIONS— A UNIQUE CANADIAN STYLE?

Section 49 of the 1982 Constitution necessitated that a First Ministers Conference be held within fifteen years to review the new amendment provisions — i.e., by April 17, 1997. The issue, put on the agenda by Prime Minister Jean Chrétien at a first ministers meeting in June 1996, ended in a farce. The premier of Saskatchewan, Roy Romanow, argued that the necessity to meet had already been satisfied during the Charlottetown negotiations in 1992. Quebec premier Lucien Bouchard quickly left the room, saying that he was "under a strict political and legal obligation not to hear anything about the question of section 49 discussion—even about the relevancy of discussing it." A few other premiers joined Bouchard in the washroom. Meanwhile, back in the meeting room, the majority of their colleagues quickly agreed that the constitutional necessity to review the amendment provisions had already been met. After the meeting, the first ministers were not certain whether they needed a legal judgment on the matter.

Source: Adapted from the *Ottawa Citizen*, June 22, 1996.

talk and serious proposals about how the Constitution should be amended, no substantive changes have taken place.

The *Charter of Rights and Freedoms*

At the time Canada became an independent country in 1867, civil liberties in Britain were protected by traditions, customs and political culture. Civil liberties were, if you wish, ingrained in the values and beliefs of politicians and the people. Canada, too, relied on the traditional rights provided by British common law and, after 1960, on a statute—the *Canadian Bill of Rights*—which listed the fundamental freedoms that existed in Canada. The Bill of Rights was never **entrenched** in the Constitution so that it could be amended by the passage of ordinary legislation. Despite these safeguards, many Canadians believed that there was a need for a constitutionalized charter of rights and freedoms that would restrict the actions of governments. Why?

The answer is that despite the rule of law and British traditions, Canada's record of ensuring the protection of its citizens' rights was not without blemish. The most celebrated example was the **Québec Padlock Law** of 1937, legislation enacted by the Québec government banning the propagation of "Communism and Bolshevism." That law would have allowed Premier Maurice Duplessis to padlock any premises allegedly used for such purposes and to move arbitrarily against other groups opposed to his regime. Also, in Alberta in 1938, the provincial legislature enacted the Press Bill, which allowed the government to force newspapers to reveal the sources of unfavourable comment. A third example occurred in 1953, when Québec restrained the freedom of religion of Jehovah's Witnesses by restricting their right to hand out pamphlets without permission.

Although the courts subsequently overturned these three pieces of legislation, the rationale cited by the judges in their decisions strengthened the argument for the entrenchment of basic rights in the Constitution. The courts based their rulings *not* on the fact that the legislation represented a violation of fundamental rights, but rather on the contention that provincial governments did not have the right to restrict civil liberties because of the constitutional division of powers. In all these cases, the courts declared the actions **ultra vires**—i.e., not within provincial jurisdiction.

Another notable example of a violation of basic rights in Canada's history was the federal government's internment of Japanese Canadians during the Second World War. Under the *War Measures Act*, thousands of people were uprooted from their communities and placed in camps for the duration of the war—for "security" reasons. Decades later, in 1970, Prime Minister Trudeau again invoked the *War Measures Act*, this time in response to the terrorist activities of the Front de la Libération du Québec (FLQ). This action suspended civil liberties and allowed the government to arbitrarily detain hundreds of suspects. Both of these cases indicated that violations of basic democratic rights could not be prevented without written constitutional guarantees—hence, a charter was necessary.

The 1982 Charter is a significant improvement on the *Canadian Bill of Rights* because it applies to the federal and provincial governments equally and because, unlike ordinary legislation, it is entrenched in the Constitution, and therefore can be altered *only* through the constitutional amendment process. It consists of a short *preamble*—"Whereas Canada is founded upon principles that recognize the supremacy of God and the rule of law"—followed by 34 sections. The first section *defines the limits* of Canadians' rights and freedoms, stipulating that they are "subject only to such reasonable limits prescribed by law as can be demonstrably justified in a free and democratic society."

The Charter protects *fundamental freedoms*, including those of conscience and religion, of thought, belief, opinion and expression, and of peaceful assembly and association. The basic democratic rights named in the document include the right of every citizen to vote; a five-year limit on the terms of federal and provincial legislatures, except in time of real or apprehended war, invasion or insurrection; and the requirement for legislatures to meet at least once every 12 months.

The Charter also protects *mobility rights*—i.e., the right of Canadian citizens to enter, remain in and leave Canada, and to move to and work in any province. These rights are limited, however, by recognition of provincial residency requirements as a qualification for the receipt of social services. Affirmative-action programs, whose purpose is to ameliorate the conditions of a socially or economically disadvantaged people, are also allowed if the rate of employment in that province falls below the national employment rate.

Legal rights such as the traditional right to life, liberty and security are listed, along with new legal rights provisions. For example, unreasonable search or seizure and arbitrary detention or imprisonment are prohibited. A detained individual is guaranteed the right to be informed promptly of the reasons for detention, to have counsel without delay and to be instructed of that right, as well as to have the validity of the detention determined and to be released if detention is not justified. Individuals charged with an offence have the right to be informed without delay of the specific offence and to be tried within a reasonable time. They have a right against self-incrimination and are to be considered innocent until proven guilty by an impartial and public hearing. Individuals are not to be deprived of bail without just cause, and are permitted trial by jury where the maximum punishment for the offence is imprisonment for five years or more, except in the case of a military offence tried before a military tribunal. They are not to be punished for an action that was not illegal at the time of commission. If acquitted, an individual may not be tried for the same offence again or, if found guilty and punished, may not be tried or punished again. Finally, if the punishment for the offence has changed between the commission of the crime and the time of the sentencing, the individual is subject to the lesser punishment.

Individuals are also protected against cruel and unusual treatment or punishment. Witnesses who testify in any proceedings have the right not to have any incriminating evidence they might give used against them in any other proceedings, except in prosecution for perjury. Evidence obtained in a manner that infringes upon an individual's rights and freedoms shall be excluded if its admission would "bring the administration of justice into disrepute."

The Charter further provides *equality rights* guaranteeing that every individual is equal before and under the law without discrimination, particularly without discrimination based on race, national or ethnic origin, colour, religion, sex, age, or mental or physical disability. However, affirmative-action programs aimed at improving the conditions of groups discriminated against are allowed.

The importance of *linguistic rights* is acknowledged in the Charter. English and French are recognized as Canada's official languages and have equal status in all institutions of Parliament and the federal government. Both languages are also recognized in the province of New Brunswick. Thus, in Parliament and New Brunswick's legislature, both languages may be used in debates and other proceedings. Parliamentary statutes and records, as well as proceedings of the courts, are published in both languages. Individuals have the right to communicate with any head or central office of Parliament or the Government of Canada in either official language, and the same right applies when persons communicate with other government offices if there is significant demand.

Under the Charter, all citizens of Canada who received their primary education in Canada in either French or English have the right to have their children educated in the same language even if it is the minority language of the province in which they reside. This right, however, applies only "where numbers warrant"—i.e., where the number of children requires the provision of public funds for minority-language instruction. Minority-language education rights are also guaranteed to the children of Canadian citizens whose first language learned and understood is that of the English or French linguistic minority of the province in which they reside, whether or not the parents were able to receive their primary education in that language. This latter guarantee is not applicable to Québec until it is approved by the Québec National Assembly—and to date it has not been.

The Charter includes a variety of other *specific rights*. The rights of Native peoples are not to be diminished by the Charter's provisions; for example, the provision that guarantees language education rights in French and English may not be interpreted to deprive the Native people of James Bay of their right to educate their children in Cree. More broadly, the Charter may not be used to deprive anyone of existing rights and freedoms, and its interpretation must recognize Canada's multicultural heritage. The Charter's provisions are to be applied equally to males and females—this absolute guarantee of gender equality was put in the Constitution as section 28 only after considerable lobbying by women's groups.

The rights in this impressive list, however, are not all inviolable. Many readers will recall that the 1982 Constitution was patriated only through a series of political compromises. The leaders agreed to *allow restrictions on citizens' rights* in two general ways. First, the Charter begins with an overarching exception when it claims that the rights and freedoms are guaranteed, "subject only to such reasonable limits presented by law as can be demonstrably justified in a free and democratic society." This means that the courts are allowed to decide whether a piece of federal or provincial legislation that restricts freedoms is valid according to *their* definition of "reasonable limits." The Supreme Court, for example, has allowed the Ontario legislature to impose censorship on films as long as the criteria used are prescribed by law.[19] Second, section 33 allows a province or Parliament to enact laws overriding certain Charter provisions. They can pass legislation *notwithstanding* the Charter on fundamental freedoms, legal and equality rights by means of a notwithstanding clause. They cannot, however, use this device on democratic, language or mobility rights. A **notwithstanding** procedure becomes inoperative after five years and must be repassed if it is to remain valid.

We examine some significant Charter cases later in the chapter, following a survey of courts in Canada.

Impasse with Québec and Renewed Constitutional Talks

Despite the fact that the major proponents of the new Constitution were from Québec—including Prime Minister Trudeau, one-third of his cabinet and almost all of the 75 MPs from Québec—that province's political leaders opposed the 1982 constitutional reform with every defence possible except revolution. Premier René Lévesque criticized the Constitution's failure to recognize "in any tangible way" the character and needs of Québec as a distinct national society. The document, Lévesque alleged, treated Québec as merely another province of Canada. He argued that Québec's cultural security was threatened by the restriction of its exclusive rights in linguistic matters. As will be shown in Chapter 7, the Charter's guarantee of access to English-speaking schools conflicted with Québec's Bill 101, which restricted admission to English schools in that province. Finally, he disliked the amending formula's removal of what Québec considered its traditional veto over constitutional changes. While the Constitution gave Québec and the other provinces financial compensation in the important areas of education and culture, Lévesque charged correctly that the amending formula did not guarantee financial compensation for provinces that chose to opt out of other programs set up by constitutional amendment.

Québec's attack on the new Constitution did not stop with the election of Pierre-Marc Johnson as leader of the Parti Québécois in 1984 or with the death of Lévesque in 1987 (see Chapter 7). But when Robert Bourassa led the Liberals to victory over Johnson in the 1985 election, the tone of Québec–Ottawa relations changed. Bourassa believed that he could strike a deal with the newly elected Progressive Conservative prime minister, Brian Mulroney—and he was right.

19. *Ontario Film and Video Appreciation Society v. Ontario Board of Censors* (1984), 45 O.L.R. (2d)80.

The Failed 1987 Constitutional Accord (Meech Lake and Langevin)

The new 1984 federal PC government conducted months of bargaining to design amendments that would secure Québec's political assent to the new Constitution. In April 1987, Prime Minister Mulroney and the ten premiers reached unanimous agreement on a draft of what was called the Meech Lake Accord. The final text for the constitutional amendment was agreed to after an all-night bargaining session in June in the Langevin Block on Parliament Hill and is known as the Langevin Amendment to the Meech Lake Accord (we refer to the entire package simply as the Meech Lake Accord).

Québec Liberal premier Robert Bourassa had five conditions going into the bargaining session of April 1987 at Meech Lake: a formal voice for Québec in Supreme Court appointments; a say on immigration policy; limits to federal spending powers in areas of provincial jurisdiction; a veto on constitutional amendments affecting the province; and recognition of Québec as a "distinct" society. While it was generally agreed that Québec should be granted "renewed federalism," the nine other premiers also made demands and virtually all were accommodated. Therein lay the crux of criticism of the accord—that to achieve an agreement, the prime minister gave away powers that were necessary to maintain a strong federal government.

Political agreement on the Meech Lake Accord was billed as a historic breakthrough. There were seven main areas of change: distinct society, the Supreme Court, spending powers, veto power, immigration, the Senate and the amending formula. When the euphoria subsided, however, serious flaws in the accord made it the subject of national dissension and concern. None of the federal political parties was willing to risk the political consequences of voting against the accord in the House of Commons, although the Liberals submitted eight amendments and the NDP, two. None of these changes was accepted, but Liberal leader John Turner and NDP leader Ed Broadbent demanded party discipline in voting in favour of their respective resolutions. Parliament passed the Meech Lake Accord with little dissent. But as Meech's amendments called for major constitutional revisions, they required the approval of Parliament and all ten provincial legislatures.

The Meech Lake Accord, though hotly discussed in 1987, was not a significant issue in the 1988 general election. It was overshadowed by the issue of free trade. All three major political parties agreed that the benefit of winning Premier Bourassa's support for a revised Constitution was greater than the problems inherent in the ambiguities of the accord. No party wanted to risk the wrath of Québec voters by endangering the agreement, although the Liberals did present a series of amendments that they promised to implement as soon as the accord became law.

In the final analysis, the Meech Lake Accord was defeated because it required unanimity from the provinces, and two (Manitoba and Newfoundland) failed to pass the necessary resolution before the ratification deadline of June 23, 1990. When the proposals did not obtain unanimity, the whole package died and constitutional matters became even more complicated. Canada did not expire with the Meech Lake Accord, as Mulroney had threatened. Life went on. However, the Québec independence issue—dormant since the 1980 referendum—was given a new burst of respectability. Predictably, Premier Bourassa announced he would not attend any future federal–provincial conferences, and the Québec National Assembly passed Bill 150, which required a referendum on sovereignty to be put to the people of Québec by October 26, 1992.

A New Constitutional Approach

Following the death of the Meech Lake Accord, there was an appropriate period of political mourning followed by numerous government-sponsored conferences, symposiums, federal–provincial meetings and even a royal commission. Having insisted that it was Meech or death, Prime Minister Mulroney

Reproduced with permission of Dennis Pritchard.

needed time to resuscitate the corpse. Unfortunately, the federal government ignored the report of then PC cabinet minister Jean Charest's parliamentary committee providing detailed proposals to amend the Meech Lake Accord while leaving its substance intact. That sober report had received all-party and unanimous agreement in the House of Commons, but it was left shelved and forgotten.[20]

The Meech Lake failure had not killed Canada, but it had ended unity within the PC Party. When the accord died on June 23, 1990, Mulroney's minister of the environment, Lucien Bouchard, left the federal cabinet and formed the *indépendantiste* Bloc Québécois with a band of dissident Québec nationalists who already held seats in the House of Commons. The Québec government, meanwhile, continued to be bound by Bill 150, which called for a provincial referendum on sovereignty by October 26, 1992. The National Assembly set up the Commission on the Political and Constitutional Future of Québec (known as Bélanger-Campeau). Québec's most divisive input into the constitutional debate came on January 28, 1991, from the Liberal Party's Allaire Report, *A Quebec Free to Choose*, a document that proposed drastic decentralization of the country. According to the report, Québec would "exercise exclusive discretionary and total authority in most fields of activity," and 22 domains would be in the exclusive power of Québec.

The strong decentralizing thrust of the Allaire Report was unacceptable to most Canadians because it would have greatly weakened the country. However, it was intended to keep pressure on the federal government and set a strong negotiation position for Québec—and *that* it accomplished. The Allaire proposals cried out for asymmetry with different statuses for different provinces or regions within the country depending on their special needs. As mentioned earlier, Canada already has some asymmetry in such areas as agriculture, immigration and the environment. But this did not mean that further asymmetry would be acceptable.

20. For a history of the negotiations and events leading up to the Charlottetown Accord, see Robert J. Jackson and Doreen Jackson, *Politics in Canada*, 3rd ed. (Scarborough, ON: Prentice Hall, 1994), pp. 216–23. For a comparative analysis, see Michael B. Stein, "Improving the Process of Constitutional Reform in Canada," *CJPS*, vol. 30, no. 2 (June 1997), pp. 307–38.

The "Pearson Building" Proposals By the spring of 1992, it was time for Brian Mulroney to begin a countdown. Both the federal government and the provinces were under pressure from the date of Québec's looming referendum. On July 7, 1992, the federal government, nine provinces, two territorial governments and Native leaders came to a new tentative agreement. Its proposals would have given greater power to the provinces and weakened federal authority. Québec representatives, of course, had neither attended the meetings nor agreed to the proposals they produced.

Characterized by those present at that decisive meeting in the Lester B. Pearson Building as a constitutional breakthrough, the proposals would have amended the Constitution in multiple respects. Québec would have received everything mentioned in the Meech Lake Accord, including a veto over future constitutional amendments and recognition as a "distinct society," in return for satisfying Alberta's desire for a Triple-E Senate. Aboriginals, too, would have had their wishes granted, with a form of self-government. News commentary tended to concentrate on whether the agreement would "fly" with all the provinces and "sell" in Québec. An "agreement at any price" was necessary to save Canada. It was the "do or die" atmosphere of Meech all over again.

The Failed 1992 Charlottetown Accord

The Pearson Building agreement drew Québec's Premier Bourassa back to the bargaining table on August 4, 1992, along with the prime minister, the other premiers, and the leaders of the territories and the Aboriginal communities. The result was the complex and controversial constitutional deal known as the Charlottetown Accord, agreed to on August 28, 1992. It consisted of an agreement on principles—not a legal text—about what changes should be made to the Constitution and on how to put the tentative principles to Canadians in a countrywide referendum. All contemporary constitutional issues stem from this foundation.

Meech Plus: The Response to Québec

The Meech Lake proposals had consisted of five parts—distinct society status and a veto for Québec, immigration powers, restrictions on federal spending and appointments to the Supreme Court—each of which responded to an earlier demand by the government of Québec. The same demands were addressed by the Charlottetown Accord, but that accord went much further. It included proposals to add a definition for *distinct society* to the Constitution in a new clause that would ensure that "Quebec constitutes within Canada a distinct society, which includes a French-speaking majority, a unique culture and a civil law tradition." As well, the proposals affirmed the role of the legislature and government of Québec "to preserve and promote the distinct society of Québec."

In other areas, the Charlottetown proposals slightly softened the Meech Lake Accord. Under Meech, Québec was to receive a fixed share of immigrants to Canada. Under Charlottetown, Ottawa would only have been committed to negotiate agreements with the provinces, a policy that was already the practice. And, if the federal government spent money in a *new* Canada-wide shared-cost program in a field of exclusive provincial jurisdiction, as in Meech, a province would have been able to claim compensation if it had a program that was "compatible with the national objectives." On Supreme Court appointments, there was no change from Meech. The current practice of appointing three Supreme Court judges from Québec would have been constitutionalized, only now Ottawa would have been required to select all judges from lists supplied by the provinces.

The main difference between the Meech Lake Accord and the Charlottetown proposals was over the constitutional veto. Charlottetown would have given all provinces a veto over future constitutional changes to the country's major political institutions. On the surface, this looked as though it met Québec's earlier demands, but in fact it fell far short. The veto would have applied only *after* the Charlottetown changes were made part of the Constitution, in particular those concerning reform of the federal institutions.

Clearly, most of the offers that were made to Québec in Meech Lake were included in Charlottetown, but some were watered down. The deal, therefore, was bound to find opposition both inside *and* outside Québec. It called for major innovation in the way Canada is governed. It included a Canada clause, a new division of powers, new Native self-government clauses, a social and economic union, and institutional changes in the House of Commons and Senate.

The Canada Clause   A *Canada clause* was to be included in the Constitution to express fundamental Canadian values. That clause was extremely important, as it would have been **justiciable**—that is, the courts would have been able to use the Canada clause to guide *all* interpretations of the *entire* Constitution. As an interpretative provision, it would have been binding on the courts in every constitutional case.

Eight "fundamental values" were expressed in the Canada clause. They included values related to democracy, Aboriginal rights, the distinct society of Québec, linguistic duality, racial and ethnic equality, individual and collective human rights, the equality of female and male persons and the equality of the provinces.

On scrutiny, the Canada clause revealed errors in consistency and fairness. It proposed a hierarchy of fundamental Canadian values. While "Canadians and their governments" would have been committed to the development of minority-language communities, only "Canadians" were committed to racial and ethnic equality, individual and collective human rights, the equality of female and male persons and the equality of the provinces. The implication was clear: governments would have been committed to take action—and presumably to spend money—to defend some groups, but not others.

Moreover, some Canadian groups were left out of the Canada clause altogether. Whereas the *Charter of Rights and Freedoms* stipulates equality for people who are physically or mentally disabled, and asserts that individuals should not be discriminated against by age, the proposed Canada clause overlooked these values altogether. Thus, the clause provided a hierarchy in which some groups would be protected by government; other groups would be protected only by Canadians; and still other groups such as the disabled, seniors and children would not be mentioned at all.

Division of Powers   The 1992 Charlottetown proposals called for the constitutional decentralization of many federal powers. Job training and culture were to be given to the provinces congruent with their present authority in the field of education. In job training, the federal government's power would have been narrowed to exclusive jurisdiction for unemployment insurance and involvement in the establishment of national objectives for labour market development. As well, the federal government would have been excluded from a meaningful role in retraining workers for the new global economy. Culture, too, would have been divided artificially between two levels of government. The provinces would have had exclusive jurisdiction over culture "within the provinces," and the federal government would have retained powers over existing national cultural institutions, including the grants and contributions delivered by those institutions. If these proposals had been constitutionalized, the designation of culture as an area of exclusive provincial jurisdiction would have led to endless constitutional wrangling in the Supreme Court. As well, the Charlottetown Accord called for the federal government to withdraw from several areas, including forestry, mining, housing, recreation, tourism, and municipal and urban affairs.

At best, in all of these decentralizing proposals, policies on which Canadians have grown to depend might have remained intact. At worst, some important policies might have been discontinued. This wide spectrum of possibility proved that the federal government still did not have a handle on viable constitutional change.

Native Self-Government   The demands of Native peoples were not addressed by the Meech Lake proposal and, in the final analysis, this omission contributed to its demise. Charlottetown's Canada clause declared that Aboriginals "have the right to promote their languages, cultures and traditions and to ensure the integrity of their societies, and that their governments constitute one of *three orders* of government in Canada." The proposals also included an expanded definition of Aboriginals, a political accord for the Métis and treaty rights to be affirmed in the Constitution.

Even among staunch supporters of the Aboriginal cause, there was considerable controversy over these undefined rights. The most direct attack on the concept of Aboriginal rights came from a Québec government report that described the proposal as "unquestionably the most profound change to the political structure of Canada since 1867."[21] The report declared that a self-government clause would "threaten Québec's territorial integrity and weaken provincial powers," and without Québec's approval would probably be unconstitutional "because creating a new order of government requires the unanimous consent of all the partners to Confederation." Furthermore, the Québec report argued that such an agreement would violate the Charter, which calls for all Canadians to be treated equally under the law. It judged that approval of Aboriginal self-government would be exorbitantly expensive, and that territorial disputes and land claims would have a much stronger legal basis.

Elsewhere, the main complaint was that too many small governments might emerge if Native self-government were placed in the Constitution. Worries were also expressed that band and tribal councils would want to negotiate their own laws to govern schools, justice systems, child-welfare agencies and other community organizations. Critics asked if self-government could mean up to six hundred tiny governments. If so, would this constitute a new form of segregation? Would the *Criminal Code* apply to Native peoples? Would educational standards or environmental regulations apply?

Even among those who favoured self-government for Native peoples, there was a concern that the participants in the negotiations did not fully understand the implications of the changes for such issues as jurisdictions, lands, resources, human rights, and economic and financial considerations. Many Aboriginals knew that their rights could be protected in ways other than constitutional amendment. They have received self-government in negotiated treaties in northern Québec, the Yukon, British Columbia, Nunavut and elsewhere. It is clear that Indians, Inuit and Métis also have rights by virtue of their ancestors' occupancy and use of Canada before European colonization. They can also legitimately claim that *inherent* rights exist in section 35 of the *Constitution Act, 1982*, which states simply that "[t]he existing aboriginal and treaty rights of the aboriginal peoples are hereby recognized and affirmed." For greater clarity and certainty, clause 35(3) affirms that "treaty rights" include "land claims agreements" now and in the future.

Social and Economic Union   If the Charlottetown agreement had been passed, the country would have enjoyed a "social and economic union." The agreement set out objectives for the social union on such topics as providing "a health care system which is comprehensive, universal, portable, publicly administered and accessible," "high quality primary and secondary education to all individuals resident in Canada" and "reasonable access to post-secondary education." Laudable as these goals are, they are merely slogans and platitudes. Even the first ministers realized this when they concluded in the agreement that citizens could not rely on these statements in the courts. They were—as they agreed—"not justiciable." They might also have pointed out that a non-enforceable social charter is no substitute for real legislative capacity to set national standards.

The Charlottetown agreement committed governments to free trade within Canada. Among other clauses, it called for "the free movement of persons, goods, services and capital," "full employment" and a "reasonable standard of living." These clauses (which were to be placed in the

21. *The Globe and Mail*, July 23, 1992.

Constitution) could not have been taken before the courts. Canadians were asked to trust the rhetoric of political leaders. Even Michael Wilson, the government's trade minister, attacked the Pearson Building proposals for providing too many exceptions—enough to outweigh any good done by the provision of an economic union. The final Charlottetown agreement was even worse than Wilson imagined. It did not *commit* the 11 governments to anything at all regarding social and economic union, nor did it allow the courts to make decisions on the basis of the clauses in this section.

Proposed Institutional Changes

Charlottetown called for a drastic overhaul of federal institutions. The changes can be summarized briefly as follows:

House of Commons   If the proposals had been accepted, the membership of the House of Commons would have been increased to 337. As well, Québec would have been guaranteed no fewer than 25 percent of the seats in the House of Commons in perpetuity.

Senate   Had Charlottetown gone through, these changes would have been effected:

1. The Senate was to be elected either by the people of a province or territory or by a legislative assembly.
2. It was to total 62 senators, composed of 6 senators from each province and 1 senator from each territory.
3. It would not be able to force the resignation of a government.
4. The Senate would have had some authority over legislation:
   i)   It would have been able to delay revenue and expenditure bills for thirty days by a suspensive veto. After that period, the House of Commons would have been able to act on its own. But fundamental policy changes to the tax system (such as the goods and services tax and the National Energy Program) were to be excluded from this section and handled as ordinary legislation.
   ii) It would have had veto power over all legislation on natural resources.
   iii) It would have been able, by a majority vote, to trigger a joint sitting with the House of Commons on all ordinary legislation. The joint sitting would have ultimate authority over this referred legislation.
   iv) On matters that materially affect the French language or culture, a double majority of anglophone and francophone senators would have been required.
5. The Senate would have had to ratify the appointment of the governor of the Bank of Canada and other key federal appointments.

Institutional Complexity and Inadequacy

Critics listed ten ways that these proposed institutional arrangements were inadequate:

1. It would increasingly be regarded as unfair to give Québec 25 percent of the seats in the House of Commons in perpetuity. In 1992, Québec had 25.3 percent of the population. Demographers predicted it would drop below 25 percent by the end of the decade (it did so by 1997) and down to 23.5 percent by 2011. In contrast, Ontario, British Columbia and Alberta are all predicted to grow substantially (and they have).
2. Equal provincial representation in the Senate would be a source of constant irritation. Ontario, with a population of ten million, would have been awarded six senators—the same number as Prince Edward Island, which is the size of Nepean, a suburb of Ottawa. The distortion was too great.
3. National standards should be maintained in federal institutions. With these new proposals, Canada would have had senatorial elections in some places and nominations in others. It would not have been seen as an improvement to allow the Québec National Assembly rather than federal prime ministers to appoint senators.

4. Since there were to be simultaneous elections for the House and Senate, appointed senators from Québec or elsewhere made no sense. After a general election that swept one party into power in Ottawa, the Québec National Assembly could have appointed senators who did not reflect that change. The electoral results would count everywhere but Québec—or wherever senators were appointed.

5. There would have been too many ways for the Senate to tie up the government and prevent it from acting. Fifty percent of the Senate (representing at minimum only 13.2 percent of the Canadian population) would have been able to block all taxation on natural resources and force all ordinary legislation to a joint sitting with the House of Commons.

6. The Senate's power to send all ordinary legislation, including such major issues as the goods and services tax, to a joint sitting with the House was faulty. Government business would have been disrupted and responsible government diminished.

7. The double majority of anglophone and francophone senators required to pass language and cultural legislation might have proven troublesome. A double majority meant that as few as three Québécois senators would be able to block all the remaining senators from action. A majority of English senators could have blocked something Québec wanted in this field.

8. The Senate was to have a controlling veto over higher government appointments. The House of Commons, the major democratic institution, would only have been able to scrutinize appointments. Why? Could it have been so that a tiny proportion of the public representing the smallest five provinces could prevent appointments that the government, the majority of the members of the House of Commons and most of the people wanted?

9. If the Senate delayed the legislation of a minority government, the situation would have been destabilizing for responsible government. When there was a divided House, a joint sitting would not have been controlled by MPs. The combination of House and Senate could have blocked legislation and forced the formation of a new government, a new cabinet coalition or a general election. As well, politicians often block one bill in order to prevent a totally different one from getting through. Senators would have been able to block appointments, taxation on resources, and language and culture bills, and force ordinary legislation to a joint sitting until they got compromises on other matters of which they disapproved.

10. The costs of Parliament would have been much too high given the size of the Canadian population. Taxpayers would have picked up extensive new bills. A House of Commons with 337 seats would have made it more than three-quarters the size of the US House of Representatives (435) with one-tenth the population. As well, members cost more than senators and elected senators would cost more than appointed senators. The costs of paying for the new Parliament would have been too great.

The proposed Rubik's cube of institutions would work effectively *only* when the following *two conditions* prevailed: First, Canada would need a majority, not a minority, government. On this point, one should remember that since the Second World War, many governments have been in a minority situation. Second, there would have to be a federalist government in Québec. Without these two conditions in place, the constitutional arrangements would further weaken government and fracture the federal system. If there were a separatist government in Québec, the federal government would be handicapped when dealing with it.

The Charlottetown Senate: A Fatal Attraction?

Prime Minister Mulroney was cornered by the proponents of a Triple-E Senate. His 1984 and 1988 electoral successes and the composition of his cabinet and caucus were based on a Québec–Alberta alliance. If he opted for what Québec wanted—namely Meech Lake Plus—he would lose support in the West, particularly in Alberta, unless he also appeased westerners with a form of Triple-E. For that reason, he accepted the Charlottetown proposals for the Senate—a combination of deals. If the Triple-E Senate could have been devised to strengthen national institutions, it might have been acceptable—but, alas, the politicians wanted to develop a Triple-E Senate that would have strengthened the role of the provincial premiers in the system and weaken the federal government.

The main problem with the existing Senate is that it lacks legitimacy because those serving are made senators by political appointment. The Charlottetown agreement pretended to remedy this. In fact, it would have made it worse. The Senate would have consisted of a hodgepodge of elected and appointed members because the rules could be different for each province. Québec, for example, said that it would appoint its six senators by a vote in the National Assembly, while, elsewhere, senators would have been elected directly by the people. In Québec, ordinary citizens would not even have to be consulted. Such a senate would have no more legitimacy, and perhaps less, than the current upper house.

The 1992 Constitutional Referendum

On August 28, 1992, the prime minister, the ten premiers, first ministers of the two northern territories and leaders of the major Native communities agreed on the constitutional text discussed above. More significantly, they agreed to put the Charlottetown package of proposals to the people in a referendum on October 26, 1992. All three federal party leaders also agreed to the Charlottetown Accord and to the referendum. The opponents of the accord appeared weak and disunited. Jacques Parizeau, leader of the Parti Québécois, and Lucien Bouchard, leader of the Bloc Québécois, were opposed. Preston Manning was the most outspoken leader outside of Québec to criticize the referendum proposal, although he was joined by Liberals such as Sharon Carstairs in Manitoba. But the real leader of the No side proved once again to be the former prime minister, Pierre Trudeau, who attacked the constitutional deal with fervour and logic.

As the third national referendum in Canadian history (for the constitutional campaign, politics and earlier referendums, see Chapter 12), it proved a divisive, corrosive event. In the final analysis, six provinces decisively voted against the deal and only Newfoundland, Prince Edward Island and New Brunswick voted strongly for it. Ontario very narrowly supported the deal, while Yukon voted against and the Northwest Territories voted for the deal. At the national level 72 percent of the Canadian electorate cast their votes and defeated the proposal 54.4 percent to 44.6 percent. The Charlottetown proposal was dead.

The defeat of the Charlottetown Accord can be explained as the result of a combination of beliefs. Some Québeckers did not believe that the accord gave them enough powers; many English Canadians thought it gave Québec too much; there was a general disillusionment and distrust of political leaders throughout the country; and the deal was too complex and cumbersome for a constitutional amendment. At any rate, the unexpected defeat led federal and provincial politicians to one conclusion: it was time for a moratorium on constitutional discussions. With a federal election due before the end of 1993 and a Québec provincial election in 1994, the leaders returned to "politics as usual."

The Liberal government also relegated constitutional reform to the back burner when it came to power in 1993. Prime Minister Jean Chrétien took the stance that many arrangements between the federal government and the provinces could be dealt with through administrative arrangements outside the Constitution. This, for example, has been the case to an extent with some changes in the relationship between the federal government and Native peoples. Some First Nations have achieved much of what they had wanted from the Charlottetown Accord without a constitutional amendment; others have not. Alas, such doctrines about the administrative devolution of power have not been accepted throughout the country and major problems in federal–provincial relations continue to dominate much debate in Canadian politics, in particular over Québec's future adherence to the Constitution.

In the next two chapters, we examine contested federalism, separatism in Québec, the 1995 Québec referendum, the federal responses to Québec separation and the serious regional challenges to Canada. Here, we spotlight the constitutional issues that relate to civil liberties in an age of global terrorism and study the court system, especially the Supreme Court, as an interpreter of the constitution and Canadian rights and freedoms.

Civil Liberties in a Time of Terrorism

The events of September 11, 2001 (9/11) and the consequent US "war on terrorism" made it imperative for Canadian leaders to consider the level of security at home. Terrorists use unconventional methods to attack vulnerable targets in free and open societies, creating a siege mentality—leading to paranoia about unusual and suspicious behaviour and promoting a culture of fear. The dilemma for democrats is that their society may respond by turning against itself, destroying the freedom and openness it admires. As governments pursue more and more security for citizens at home, civil liberties are, to an ever larger degree, reduced. What moral balance is appropriate? The issue comes down to whether democratic states can subdue virulent terrorism without surrendering the freedoms of their own country. What costs are acceptable in this struggle?

In Canada, terrorism has always been handled as a criminal matter, not as something under the purview of international relations. That has changed. Before 9/11, the main issue involved immigrants and security. The most pertinent example concerned the process by which non-Canadians could be tried and deported as dangerous to the country.

The national **security certificate** process, which emanates from the *Immigration and Refugee Protection Act*, is used to jail non-Canadians (foreign nationals or permanent residents) thought to be a threat to national security and then, if necessary, deport them to a foreign country. The process has been used for several decades and about two dozen foreign nationals were named as dangerous to Canada before 9/11—several more have been named since then. Under the program, two cabinet ministers sign a certificate labelling a non-Canadian citizen a threat to national security. The government then attempts to show a judge that it acted reasonably in so labelling the individual as dangerous. A first hearing is held in secret—the named person is not present and has no lawyer present. At that stage, the judge cross-examines the state's witnesses. In the second hearing, the case is opened up to allow the presence of the defendant, but still the counsel is not allowed to act. It has often been argued that this system is unfair because the judge may ask questions of the government witnesses, but is not really equipped to do a proper cross-examination. The system has also been criticized by civil libertarians because it contravenes the *Charter of Rights and Freedoms* and allows the possibility of the security service sending named individuals to countries where they could be tortured.

On February 23, 2007, the Supreme Court unanimously suspended for a year those provisions of the *Immigration and Refugee Protection Act* that prevent a fair hearing and said that a new law must be written that complies with the Charter. In other words, the Court concluded that in the search for a balance between security and rights, the Constitution could not be considered "a suicide pact," but, nevertheless, that the law must not undermine Canadian individual and collective rights. Secret hearings violate those rights—named individuals should be allowed to know the case against them and be able to mount a proper defence. The federal government announced in 2007 that it would replace the security certificate process, and legislation was passed. Special counsels with security clearance can now be appointed to act on behalf of the accused. The situation remains murky, however, as it is not clear whether a defendant's lawyer can act as a special counsel.

Recently, many changes have been made to Canadian laws and procedures in the security field. After the events of 9/11, the Canadian government declared that it needed to pass an *Anti-Terrorism Act* that would allow officials to identify, prosecute, convict and punish terrorist groups. It needed new definitions and stronger investigative tools for security agencies. The *Criminal Code* was therefore amended to include two new anti-terrorist conventions of the United Nations—suppression of terrorist financing and also terrorist bombings—as well as new definitions and procedures for handling terrorists. Bill C36 was introduced and passed to accomplish these tasks. It applies to both citizens and non-citizens and for this reason is quite different than the above-mentioned security certificate program.

In the *Anti-Terrorism Act*, terrorist activity is defined as action inside or outside Canada that is

> *an offence under one of the ten UN anti-terrorist conventions and protocols…*
> *[or] taken or threatened for political, religious or ideological purposes and*
> *threatens the public or national security by killing, seriously harming or*
> *endangering a person, causing substantial property damage that is likely to*
> *seriously harm people or by interfering or disrupting an essential service,*
> *facility or system.*

The legislation forced people who had information relevant to an investigation to appear before a judge and supply that information (i.e., investigative hearings); made it possible for people who had committed no crimes to be arrested (i.e., preventative arrest) and allowed information to be kept secret from accused individuals. Clearly, the overall effect of the Act entailed an assault on individual rights and liberties. For that reason, Parliament insisted that the legislation include a sunset clause of three years.[22]

On March 1, 2007, the federal government's *Anti-terrorism Act* came back to Parliament and was stripped of two of its clauses—those on extraordinary investigative hearings that compelled testimony and those on preventative arrest that allowed security services to detain terror suspects without charges being placed. Despite government arguments in defence of the clauses, they were killed by the opposition parties in a vote of 159–124. Since then, the government has said it would like to renew these two sections of the law. To date, this has not been done.

One major and dramatic case of alleged terrorism in Canada has come to the fore since 9/11. Eighteen suspected terrorists were rounded up in southern Ontario for allegedly participating in a terrorist training camp and other related activities between March 2005 and June 2006. The charges alleged these individuals had plotted to storm Parliament, behead MPs and blow up several landmarks using truck bombs. The evidence presented at the preliminary hearings remains under a publication ban because the formal trials have not yet begun. The 18 accused are Canadian-born Muslims, including four youths who have already been released by the court. These trials will likely not conclude for some time.

As of June 18, 2007, a Canadian no-fly list has been put into effect. A list of some two thousand people "reasonably suspected" by the Canadian Border Services Agency, the RCMP and CSIS has been created—these are people believed to be a threat to the safety of commercial aircraft, passengers or crew. They include the names of suspected terrorists or those linked to known terrorist groups as well as individuals convicted of serious crimes. While citizens may appeal having their names on the list, they have no legally enforceable right of appeal to have their names excluded no right to a hearing, no right to receive written reasons for their names being placed on the list, and no right to compensation for any damages caused to them or their businesses. Canada's federal and provincial privacy commissioners have expressed serious concerns about the

22. Details can be found on the Department of Justice website: www.justice.gc.ca.

policy and suggested it may contravene Canada's Charter. They have asked that it be suspended pending a thorough review.

Before the existence of a formal no-fly list, there was an informal government list of suspected terrorists. The best-known example of the list being used involved the case of Maher Arar. A Canadian and an Ottawa software engineer, Mr. Arar was detained in 2002 during a stopover at New York's JFK Airport and sent by US security agents to Syria. In Syria, he was held without charge, and was abused and tortured until 2005. Later, he was exonerated of all charges by a Canadian judicial inquiry headed by Justice Dennis O'Connor. In a 1600-page indictment of the authorities involved in Arar's case, Justice O'Connor concluded, "I am able to say categorically that there is no evidence that Mr. Arar has committed any offence or that his activities constitute a threat to Canadian security." The judge recommended a complete overhaul of the civilian review process for the RCMP because the Mounties' anti-terrorism squads had erroneously put an Islamic extremist label on Arar. Eventually, it was disclosed that both the RCMP and CSIS had worked with the CIA on the case and these outfits endorsed the use of torture on him. The deputy head of CSIS wrote, "I think the US would like to get Arar to Jordan where they can have their way with him."[23]

Should Parliament pass a law providing guidelines for the construction of such lists and should it insist on an oversight body of parliamentarians for all Canadian security institutions, including the RCMP? See Chapters 9 and 15 for discussions of particular issues concerning terrorists, security institutions and the parliamentary bodies expected to handle them.

The Structure and Role of the Courts

The Canadian *judiciary* rules in disputes about the Constitution and the law. Whether it is **civil law** (regulating disputes between two or more private parties) or **criminal law** (regulating crimes such as theft or murder), the judges deliberate in courts. The basic, unitary structure of the judiciary or court system in Canada is that of a pyramid with a very wide base and a narrow tip—the Supreme Court of Canada—at the apex. Immediately below the Supreme Court of Canada in the judicial pyramid are the provincial superior courts.

Each province has a superior trial court of general jurisdiction (sometimes called the Superior Court or Supreme Court or the Court of the Queen's Bench) that is charged with administering all laws in force in Canada, whether enacted by Parliament, provincial legislatures or municipalities. Since 1987, they all have an appeal court as well. Some also have county or district courts of both civil and criminal jurisdiction.

Article 96 of the Constitution stipulates that appointment to these superior district and county courts is made by the governor general, but, in practice, these appointments are made by the federal cabinet. In other words, while each province determines how many judges it will need in the federal courts, Ottawa determines who will be appointed and how they will be paid. All provinces have courts staffed by judges appointed by the province to deal with lesser criminal and other cases. These provincial courts include magistrates' courts, family courts and juvenile courts. The appeal divisions of the provincial supreme or superior courts hear appeals from the lower courts and from certain provincial administrative tribunals.

The Supreme Court of Canada was established in 1875 by the *Dominion Act* as a general court of appeal for Canada. As we have seen, however, it was not the *final* court of appeal; that function was performed in Britain by the Judicial Committee of the Privy Council until 1949. Today, nine judges serve on the Supreme Court, three of whom must come from the civil law tradition, meaning—for

23. *The Globe and Mail*, August 10, 2007. For more details, see *Commission of Inquiry into the Actions of Canadian Officials in Relations to Maher Arar* (www.ararcommisssion.ca/eng/26.htm).

practical purposes—from Québec. All are appointed by the **governor-in-council**[24]—the formal executive authority of the governor general applied upon the advice and consultation of the cabinet—and do not have to retire until age 75. In 1999, Prime Minister Chrétien appointed Beverley McLachlin to succeed Antonio Lamer as chief justice of the Court (see Table 5.1). As of 2008, a majority of the judges sitting were appointed by Prime Minister Chrétien.

In 2004, Prime Minister Paul Martin appointed two new judges, Louise Charron and Rosalie Silberman Abella, to the Supreme Court bench after a superficial parliamentary hearing. Members of Parliament had no chance to question the future judges or to analyze a list of other potential judges. But in 2006, when Prime Minister Stephen Harper appointed his first Supreme Court judge, Marshall Rothstein, he allowed members of all four political parties to question the nominee before an ad hoc committee. Although the questions were not difficult, there is now a precedent that judges should be called before a public nomination hearing in the House of Commons when they are appointed by the prime minister.

The Right Honourable Chief Justice of Canada, Beverley McLachlin, P.C.

Copyright Philippe Landreville, photographer: Supreme Court of Canada Collection

As it is the highest court in the land, the Supreme Court of Canada's decisions are binding on all other Canadian courts (see Figure 5.1 on the next page). The Supreme Court deals primarily with cases that have already been appealed at least once the Court the lower courts. In these

TABLE 5.1 Supreme Court Judges, 2008

Judge	Year Appointed	Province of Birth	Appointing Prime Minister
Chief Justice Beverley McLachlin	1999	Alberta	Mulroney*
Mr. Justice Michel Bastarache	1997	New Brunswick	Chrétien
Mr. Justice William Ian Corneil Binnie	1998	Ontario	Chrétien
Mr. Justice Louis LeBel	1999	Québec	Chrétien
Madam Justice Marie Deschamps	2002	Québec	Chrétien
Mr. Justice Morris J. Fish	2003	Québec	Chrétien
Madam Justice Louise Charron	2004	Ontario	Martin
Madam Justice Rosalie Silberman Abella	2004	Ontario	Martin
Mr. Justice Marshall Rothstein	2006	Manitoba	Harper

*McLachlin was first appointed to the Supreme Court by Brian Mulroney in 1989, and was made chief justice by Jean Chrétien in 1999.

24. *Governor-in-council* is the formal or legal name under which cabinet makes decisions. For a complete explanation, see Chapter 8, "The Executive Apex: Governor General, Prime Minister and Cabinet."

FIGURE 5.1 The Basic Canadian Court System

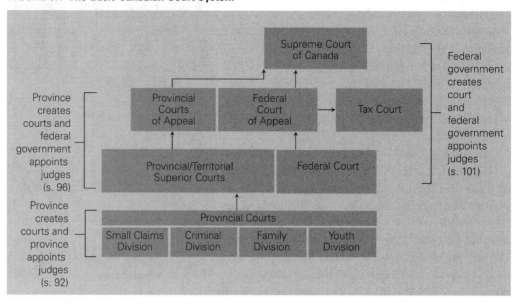

situations, the Court is appealed to in order to render "an authoritative settlement of a question of law of importance to the whole nation."[25] On rare but important occasions, Canada's highest court also deals with questions referred to it directly by the federal government.

Canada's Supreme Court does not agree to hear all appeals. The significance of its work lies in the fact that it can be highly selective, concentrating its efforts on questions that are of fundamental importance to Canadian society and then shaping the direction of the law by applying general rules to the specific circumstances at hand. One should remember as well that, as a general court of appeal, the Supreme Court has a right of final say in all areas of law for the country. This combination of selectivity and breadth gives it an extremely powerful role. Since the 1982 adoption of the *Charter of Rights and Freedoms*, the Supreme Court has also greatly increased its competence to adjudicate in cases involving civil liberties. It has become the final arbiter of the division of power between governments and the line between the powers of both levels of government and the rights and freedoms of citizens.

Below the Supreme Court of Canada but separate from the provincial courts is the **Federal Court of Canada**, which was established by Parliament in 1971. The Federal Court, which has both a trial and an appeal division, settles claims by or against the federal government on matters relating to maritime, copyright, patent and trademark law and federal taxation statutes. It also has a supervisory jurisdiction related to decisions of tribunals and inferior bodies established by federal law. There are a few other specialized federal courts, such as the Tax Court of Canada, whose decisions are subject to review by the Federal Court. Decisions of the Federal Court of Appeal can be appealed to the Supreme Court when the matter in controversy exceeds a set amount of money. Otherwise, an appeal to the Supreme Court requires either the volition of the Supreme Court itself or the agreement of the Federal Court of Appeal. If the dispute is interprovincial or federal–provincial in nature, the route of appeal to the Supreme Court is automatically open.

25. Peter H. Russell, "The Jurisdiction of the Supreme Court of Canada: Present Policies and a Programme for Reform," *Osgoode Law Journal* (1969), p. 29.

In recent years, there have been some new approaches in the judicial system to satisfy the needs of Canada's multicultural community. In 1999, a new kind of court was created as the **Nunavut Court of Justice** in the North. It combines the power of a superior trial court and territorial court, so the same judge can hear all cases that arise in the territory. Most of the communities are small and isolated—the judge travels to them from Iqaluit "on circuit." **Sentencing circles** originated in the Yukon Territorial Court in the 1990s and they are now used in many parts of the country in cases involving Aboriginal offenders and victims. Although not part of the court in a technical sense, the circles (consisting of members of the community, such as elders, the offenders in question, victims and their families, and court officials) meet to discuss the offence and its causes. They try to work out ways to reintegrate the offender in the community and may propose unique sentencing options that might include, for example, restitution to the victim, community service or counselling rather than prison time.

Compared to other countries with a federal system of government, Canada's judicial system is one of the most integrated in the world. The Canadian Constitution provides for an *integrated system* because it requires federally appointed judges for provincial superior and intermediate courts. Canada is the only federation to have this element of judicial integration. As well, Parliament established the Supreme Court as a general court of appeal rather than one that is limited to federal law and constitutional law. Another integrating feature of the judicial system is that Parliament has exclusive jurisdiction in the area of criminal law, even though provincial legislatures have powers to establish courts of criminal jurisdiction. This means that provincially established courts administer federal law. However, over time, the unitary nature of the judicial system has become slightly more federal, with the proliferation of both provincial and federal courts that are established and staffed by their respective levels of government.

The Fathers of Confederation did not establish the Supreme Court of Canada in the Constitution, but left Parliament to propose and establish it through legislation. In the early years of its history, the Court was a subordinate, secondary institution. Until 1949, Canadians had access only to the British Judicial Committee of the Privy Council (JCPC), the Supreme Court of the United Kingdom. Not until appeal to that body was abolished did Canada's Supreme Court assume leadership of the Canadian judicial system. In 1974, its jurisdiction was changed, allowing it to control its own agenda. Finally, the patriation of the Constitution in 1982, with its *Charter of Rights and Freedoms*, heralded a new and expanded role for all courts in Canada, especially the Supreme Court.

In a 1981 hallmark decision, the Supreme Court judges ruled in the *Patriation Reference* case that Pierre Trudeau's government could legally patriate and amend the Constitution unilaterally, but warned that to do so would violate an established "constitutional convention." This ruling on a question of constitutional convention was unique in that it reached beyond the law into the realm of politics. It amounted to a legal green light combined with a political red light. Under the circumstances, Trudeau chose to return to the constitutional bargaining table with the provincial premiers and seek an acceptable compromise before proceeding with patriation.

The *Constitution Act, 1982* greatly increased the political importance of the Supreme Court of Canada. Under the *Charter of Rights and Freedoms*, the Supreme Court can overrule legislation and executive acts of government not only on the grounds that they violate the federal division of powers, but also when they are thought to violate the fundamental rights and freedoms of citizens. Increasingly, judges are perceived less as fulfilling an essentially technical and non-political role and more as promoting change in public policy. As Canadians become more conscious of this enhanced judicial power, they will undoubtedly want to scrutinize more closely the impartiality claims of judges.[26]

26. For an excellent summary, see Andrew D. Heard, "The Charter in the Supreme Court of Canada: The Importance of Which Judges Hear an Appeal," *CJPS*, vol. 24, no. 2 (June 1991), pp. 289–307.

The appointment procedure may become the object of public debate. Since the Supreme Court was not established by the Constitution, but by federal legislation, there is no mention in the Constitution either of its composition or the method by which judges are appointed. The only mention of the Supreme Court in the *Constitution Act* concerns the amending formula, which requires the agreement of Parliament and all of the provincial legislatures for any change in the composition of the Supreme Court, and the agreement of Parliament and two-thirds of the provinces representing 50 percent of the population for any other constitutional change of the Court. Current reform proposals for the Court, therefore, centre on establishing it in the Constitution so that it will not have to depend on federal legislation for its existence and so that its composition or method of appointment cannot be easily changed.

There is also pressure to reform the process of appointing Supreme Court judges. It has been proposed, for example, that potential government appointees always be confirmed by parliamentary hearings or that the prime minister choose nominees from a shortlist drawn up by a nominating committee with wide representation.[27] The above-mentioned 2006 parliamentary vetting of Justice Marshall Rothstein is the first indication that the process may become more open and debated in the future.

Charter Cases and the Constitution

Charter cases involve complex issues ranging from Sunday closings of stores to missile testing to abortion. The role of the Supreme Court in such controversial issues is vital in the policy-making process. In 1987, on the fifth anniversary of the Charter, Supreme Court judge Gérard La Forest commented that he found working with the Charter almost overwhelming at times because of the abstract principles and lack of familiar paths:

> *What is liberty? What should the limits be to it? We all know what we think ourselves. But when it comes to defining liberty, each and every state restriction exists in a proper context. There is no way to escape these problems.... When you are dealing with the Charter, you really don't know what path to choose. This is all new. We are still groping—and I think it's healthy to grope.*[28]

The early court cases were important for the development of "Charter politics." The first Charter decision of the Supreme Court was *Law Society of Upper Canada v. Skapinker* in May 1984. It involved the claim that Ontario legislation making Canadian citizenship a condition for practising law violated section 6, the mobility rights section, of the Charter. The Court declared that the Ontario law was not designed to impede movement across provincial borders and therefore did not thwart the mobility guarantee in the Constitution.

The next four cases concerning Charter claims—the *Protestant School Boards, Southam, Singh* and *Big M Drug Mart*—were all upheld by the Supreme Court. These decisions went beyond a traditional legalistic approach. The interpretations were based on broad historical and philosophical considerations. In *Southam*, for example, Chief Justice Dickson

> *traced the right to security from unreasonable searches back to the common law concept of trespass and its application by English judges in the eighteenth century to make an Englishman's home his castle. He then followed the*

27. Jacob S. Ziegel, "Merit Selection and Democratization of Appointments to the Supreme Court of Canada," *Choices: Courts and Legislatures*, vol. 5, no. 2 (June 1999), pp. 3–19.

28. Quoted in Kirk Makin, "Charter's Mandate Gives Judges Role of Wary Surgeons," *The Globe and Mail*, April 14, 1987.

evolution of this private property interest into a wider concern with personal privacy as a fundamental value of a liberal society.[29]

Many of the Court's other early Charter decisions were more restrained. In *Operation Dismantle*, for example, a coalition of unions and peace groups tried to use the Charter to overturn the decision of the Canadian government to allow testing of US cruise missiles in Canada. They claimed that the agreement increased the likelihood of Canada getting involved in a nuclear war, and that this threatened to deprive Canadians of their right to life, liberty and security of the person under section 7 of the Charter. The Federal Court of Appeal concluded that the courts could review executive actions and cabinet decisions; however, it upheld the government's authority to make decisions on matters of defence and national security. Four of the five Federal Court judges declared that the coalition had failed to prove that the decision to test the missiles was a break with principles of fundamental justice. The decision of the Supreme Court against the coalition was based on the contention that this issue was not a proper question to bring before the courts because "even with the best available evidence, judges could do no more than speculate about the consequences of cruise missile testing."[30] The Court indicated that Charter claims should be rejected when they involve "complex determinations about future behaviour which cannot be satisfactorily assessed through the judicial process."[31] According to one of the most persuasive arguments of the Court, the Charter's guarantees are not, and cannot be, absolute. "We must all die, and many are, at one time or another in their lives, imprisoned or made insecure."[32]

The first cracks in judicial unanimity appeared in the Supreme Court's decision involving section 8 of the Charter (on search and seizure)—the *Therens* case—in which the judges ruled by seven to two that Breathalyzer evidence obtained from someone who had not been advised of her right to counsel could not be used against her in court. Since this event, there have been enough dissenting opinions in other cases to lead some experts to say that it is tentatively possible to assess the judges, or groups of judges, in terms of their *liberal, activist* or *conservative* tendencies. As ideological differences between the judges become more apparent, we can expect the choice of Supreme Court justices to become more politicized, as is the case in the United States. Governments will want to choose judges of their own political persuasion in order to ensure that their legislative programs survive future court challenges. The process of appointing judges will inevitably become more controversial.

The majority of Charter cases have arisen concerning the legal rights clause of the Constitution. About two-thirds of the cases heard since 1982 have been on legal rights.[33] These judgments have significantly affected the conduct of police officers and the administration of justice. The *Therens* case, discussed above, threw out improperly obtained Breathalyzer evidence. In *Clarkson v. The Queen 1986*, the Court overruled a murder conviction because the accused was too drunk to have understood her right to counsel. In *Manninen 1987*, a robbery conviction was overturned because the accused had not been allowed to telephone his attorney.

Such legal rights issues can become highly political. In *Seaboyer 1991*, the Court ruled that a portion of the rape shield law violated the right to a full answer and defence when it prevented a

---

29. Peter H. Russell, *The Judiciary in Canada*, p. 360. For a detailed study of Charter cases and the Constitution, see Michael Mandel, *The Charter of Rights and the Legalization of Politics in Canada* (Toronto: Wall and Thompson, 1989); and Rainer Knopff and F.L. Morton, *Charter Politics* (Scarborough, ON: Nelson, 1992).

30. Russell, *The Judiciary in Canada*, p. 360.

31. Ibid.

32. *Operation Dismantle v. The Queen*, [1985] S.C.R. 651.

33. James B. Kelly, *Governing with the Charter* (Vancouver: UBC Press, 2005), p. 107.

person accused of sexual assault from cross-examining his alleged victim about her past sexual activity. Assailed by feminist groups, Parliament amended the law to give the trial judge discretion in such cases. Once again, this case illustrates the political nature of Supreme Court judgments and their impact on both interest groups and politicians.

Some of the best-known public policy issues involve Charter decisions by the Supreme Court on fundamental freedoms. The Court threw out the *Lord's Day Act* as an infringement on people who did not accept the Christian Sabbath.[34] On the other hand, the same Court upheld an Ontario act preventing Sunday shopping as long as it was based on a secular rather than religious foundation.[35] Other court cases concerning fundamental freedoms included those on language legislation, pornography, freedom of the press, street prostitution and the right to die.

Equality Rights Cases

The Charter's equality provisions took effect in 1985.[36] Legal equality, including protection from discrimination, is the starting point for any move toward greater equality of opportunity. In the past decade and a half, women's groups have organized effectively to have the courts examine issues such as child care, harassment and violence. Common-law and gay and lesbian rights activists have also made effective cases. The Supreme Court rulings have indicated that while the Constitution explicitly promises equality to every *individual*, it is also meant to apply to disadvantaged *groups* such as women and minorities. Critics ask why Canada prohibits discrimination only on the basis of sex, national or ethnic origin, race, age, colour, religion or disability, when other characteristics such as character and ability are also acquired by chance.

In 1989, the first equality case involved a white, Oxford-educated, male US citizen, Mark Andrews, who argued that he had been discriminated against when British Columbia's law society would not let him become a lawyer because he was not a Canadian citizen. He won his case. The Supreme Court argued that equality rights protections in section 15 of the Charter were intended to protect the disadvantaged. It also ruled that Mark Andrews was a member of a disadvantaged group (non-citizens) and as such was the victim of illegal discrimination. The Court went on to say that equality does not mean sameness; sometimes, groups need to be treated differently. Based on this argument, the Court later ruled in a different case that female guards were allowed to see male prison inmates while they were using the toilet, but male guards could not do the same with female inmates.[37]

> **CLOSE-UP ON**
> **Institutions**
>
> ### THE SUPREME COURT AND SEX: PRIVACY AND THE PRESUMPTION OF INNOCENCE
>
> In 1997, Parliament amended the *Criminal Code* to outline the conditions under which a court could disclose medical, counselling or therapeutic records held by the Crown or a third party relating to a complainant in a sexual assault case. There were many challenges to this law by defence lawyers who argued that unless they had access to these records, their clients' right to a fair and full defence would be thwarted.
>
> Two principles clash here: the accused's right to a fair trial and the complainant's right to privacy. In November 1999, the Court ruled by a vote of seven to one that the rape shield law was constitutional. This means that judges continue to have the power to block defendants from obtaining such records. The sole dissenting judge, Chief Justice Antonio Lamer, said that the onus should be on the Crown to explain why such disclosure would be unwarranted.
>
> Should the law privilege the privacy of the alleged sexual assault victim over the rights of the accused to a fair trial? Or, is this law reasonable? Should the courts be allowed to make the final decision in such cases?

---

34. *R. v. Big M Drug Mart Ltd.* (1985), 1 S.C.R. 295.
35. *R. v. Edwards Books and Art Ltd.* (1986), 2 S.C.R. 713.
36. The courts were immediately flooded with serious but also quite imaginative cases such as one in British Columbia where a chicken owner argued against pet discrimination, saying a local bylaw was unfair because it prohibited fowl within city boundaries. The bylaw was upheld.
37. *The Globe and Mail*, April 17, 1995.

The Mark Andrews decision was a precedent for women and minorities—as subsequent decisions in this field stem from the Andrews case. The following decisions reflect how the equality section has been interpreted.

In May 1995, the Supreme Court announced three significant decisions concerning the equality rights section of the Charter. In all three cases, the question concerned what constituted discrimination. The first decision was scrutinized by supporters of women's rights; the two others particularly concerned those who supported gay and common-law couples. In essence, the Court was being asked to lead social change, or to give official recognition to changes that had taken place.

In the first case, *The Queen v. Suzanne Thibaudeau*, a divorced woman in Québec argued that the fact that she (and not her former husband) had to pay tax on support payments for their two children meant that she was being discriminated against. The Court disagreed five to two. It found that there was no discrimination—the government had already taken this kind of situation into account in taxing divorced parents—and that "the tax burden of the couple is reduced and this has the result of increasing the available resources that can be used for the benefit of the children."[38] The decision created a dilemma for the federal government: If the government retained the system that taxed the recipients of child support, it would face continued agitation from lobbyists claiming it was unfair to women. If it changed the rules to shift the tax to the parent making the support payment, it would anger others. It decided to legislate in favour of the parent to whom child support was paid.

The second case, 1994's *The Queen v. Egan*, concerned a gay couple from British Columbia. James Egan, a pensioner, applied for a spousal pension for his male partner (the law at the time allowed spouses of some pensioners to receive an allowance). Mr. Egan's request was turned down, and he appealed to the Supreme Court on the basis that he had been discriminated against because of the definition of *spouse* in the *Old Age Security Act*. Again, the Court disagreed, even though it unanimously found that gays and lesbians are covered by the equality provisions of the Charter and cannot be discriminated against on the grounds of sexual orientation. The Court's argument was that Parliament had set up spousal pensions to benefit aged, needy married couples and that marriage is by nature heterosexual. Marriage is "fundamental to the stability and well-being of the family," the Court stated in its decision, so the government was not discriminating in this case, but making a political choice. Under section 1, the Constitution stipulates that governments may violate constitutional rights when it is "reasonable" to do so in a free and democratic society.

The judges were badly split in the Egan case (five to four). Two of the dissenting judges even wrote, "This distinction amounts to clear denial of equal benefit of the law." One group of judges stressed the traditional family structure and opposed extending to gay couples government benefits that were originally designed for the traditional family. Four other judges took a broader view of the contemporary family. They said that legislatures should treat different family structures, including gay and lesbian couples, roughly the same. The "swing vote" was that of John Sopinka, who agreed that discrimination existed in this case but said he was willing to defer to Parliament on the matter. He added that "equating same-sex couples with heterosexual couples . . . is still generally regarded as a novel concept."[39] In other words, despite its negative conclusion, the Court agreed that sexual orientation was analogous to the enumerated categories deserving of equal rights protections in the Charter.

Lesbian and gay activists saw the Court's recognition of sexual orientation as a basis of discrimination as a *victory* for gay rights, even though the specific case had been lost. The decision

38. *The Globe and Mail*, May 26, 1995.
39. Ibid.

had been only one vote away from a win and there was speculation that in future cases, Sopinka might be swayed or a new judge might change the composition and orientation of the Court. The ruling put pressure on the federal government to move faster on gay rights legislation if it wanted to avoid a spate of lawsuits. In 1996, the federal Parliament amended the human rights legislation to add "sexual orientation" to it.

The third case, *John Miron et al. v. Richard Trudel et al.* (1995), proved a clear victory for John Miron and Jocelyn Vallière, a common-law Ontario couple with two children. Mr. Miron had been injured in a car accident as a passenger travelling with an uninsured driver. Miron would have been covered under provincial law by Ms. Vallière's insurance policy, but only if they were married. The Court decided five to four that the provincial policy constituted unjustifiable discrimination by the Ontario government against common-law couples because it required insurance companies to provide benefits to married couples. The ruling went on to argue that common-law couples were a historically disadvantaged group entitled to constitutional protection. This decision meant that federal and provincial governments have had to examine a wide array of laws to ensure that they comply with the ruling.

In the next set of major Charter equality cases, in 1997, the Supreme Court came closer to establishing the importance or effect of equality rights in the Charter. In *Eaton v. Bryant*, the Court ruled that an Ontario school could place a child in a special education class as long as the child did not suffer adverse effects. In *Eldridge v. British Columbia*, the Court drew the same distinction when it ruled that the British Columbia Medical Services Commission violated the Charter when it failed to provide sign-language interpreters, causing a child to suffer adverse effects. According to the Court, equal access to medical treatment requires the provision of sign-language interpreters in hospitals. And lastly, in *Benner v. Canada*, the Court ruled that the *Citizenship Act* violated equality rights when it made a distinction between males and females in concluding that, before being granted citizenship, a man required a security check if his mother was a Canadian citizen but not if his father was.

The equality case that provoked the most publicity and political controversy involved the *Vriend* decision of April 1998. In that case, the Supreme Court concluded that gays and lesbians should be granted the same protection of their sexual orientation under section 15(1) as other people under the Alberta *Individual Rights Protection Act* (IRPA). The decision was remarkable because it was based on a ruling that "a legislative 'omission' bears judicial disapproval on the same basis as the legislature's positive acts."[40] In other words, the Court ruled not on what was *in* the Act but on what had been *omitted* from it. The Court ruled, in effect, that sexual orientation had to be "read into" the IRPA. This decision is often taken as evidence of a new dynamic interaction between the branches of government. In fact, after the decision, all provincial human rights rules were amended to include sexual orientation as part of their equal rights codes.

On the political front, the Progressive Conservative premier of Alberta, Ralph Klein, hinted that he might invoke the notwithstanding clause to overrule the Supreme Court's judgment on this subject, but he backed off when the expected public approval did not emerge. While social conservatives tried to force the premier to nullify the Court ruling on gays and lesbians, Klein demurred, declaring, "It's like that train. You can't stop it; you have to deal with it."[41] To put it another way, politicians have to put up with Supreme Court rulings whether they like them or not.

Drawing a line between acceptable and unacceptable forms of discrimination is, according to a former Supreme Court justice, one of the most difficult tasks under the Charter: "We are talking

---

40. Frederick Vaughan, "Judicial Politics in Canada: Patterns and Trends," *Choices: Courts and Legislatures,* vol. 5, no. 1 (June 1999), p. 15.

41. *Maclean's*, March 29, 1999.

about inserting equality into life which is not equal."[42] There are several problems. The Court could require citizens to show that an instance of alleged discrimination is unfair, or it could require governments to justify differing forms of treatment. Prohibitive costs and poor public financing for test cases may make litigants reluctant to challenge governments in court for alleged discrimination. Another issue is deciding how to prove discrimination. Mr. Justice Lamer asked, "What the courts will want is up in the air. Will we need statistical evidence? How will we get at the records we need?"[43] Furthermore, can the courts determine what constitutes equality without giving Parliament an opportunity to respond legislatively? In 1988, for example, the Federal Court decided that a section of the *Unemployment Insurance Act* discriminated sexually against natural fathers because it denied them paternity leave benefits. Eventually, the federal government agreed and extended the benefits to fathers. Clearly, this type of ruling affects the balance of power between Parliament and the courts.

Although equality rights have become a fast-growing area of Charter litigation, it is still too early to determine how far the Supreme Court will expand rights for women, the disabled and others. But there is a "consistent trend towards a liberal judicial philosophy," according to Professor Frederick Vaughan, an astute commentator on judicial trends in Canada.

The controversial issue of same-sex marriage reached its zenith at the beginning of the twenty-first century. On June 10, 2003, the Ontario Court of Appeal ruled in *Halpern v. Canada* that the opposite-gender requirement for marriage is unconstitutional and directed that marriage in the province of Ontario be open to same-sex couples. Similar decisions by the British Columbia Court of Appeal and the Québec Superior Court also effectively allowed same-sex couples to marry. After the high courts of six provinces and one territory ruled that the traditional definition of marriage as a union between a man and woman was discriminatory and perhaps unconstitutional, the prime minister announced that Ottawa would not appeal the decisions and that the federal government would draft legislation to legally recognize the union of same-sex couples, while recognizing the freedom of churches and religious organizations not to perform marriages against their beliefs. In September 2003, the House of Commons rejected 137–132 an opposition motion reaffirming the traditional definition of marriage. Prime Minister Chrétien requested a ruling from the Supreme Court as to whether traditional marriage laws were discriminatory and violated the *Charter of Rights and Freedoms*. In December 2004, the Supreme Court gave the go-ahead to the federal government to introduce legislation redefining marriage across the country to include same-sex couples. It stopped short, however, of defining traditional marriage as unconstitutional. It also ruled that the federal government had exclusive authority over the definition of marriage.

Later, in 2005, in spite of the Liberals' tenuous minority government situation, Prime Minister Paul Martin promised to press ahead with the legislation. Opposition lobbies, including the Canadian Conference of Catholic Bishops, vowed to fight any legislation in favour of equal marriage, while gay rights groups expressed their great enthusiasm for legislation that would make Canada the third country after Belgium and the Netherlands to permit gays and lesbians to marry. In June 2005, Parliament voted to extend marriage rights to gay and lesbian couples throughout Canada.

The controversy that began with the introduction of the *Charter of Rights and Freedoms* continues (see Table 5.2 on the next page for significant Court decisions). Both supporting and opposing factions can point to disappointing judgments and unfulfilled expectations. However, a definitive verdict on the value of the Charter will not be clear until much more time has passed. The issue of the power of the courts vis-à-vis legislatures is still open for future problems and decisions.

---

42. Mr. Justice Lamer, quoted in *The Globe and Mail*, April 14, 1987.
43. Ibid.

TABLE 5.2 **Ten Decisive Decisions by the Courts on Charter Cases***

1984	Skapinker: Ontario law did not violate "mobility rights."
1985	Singh: Provided refugees the right to a full and oral hearing because of "fundamental justice."
1985	Big M Drug Mart: Struck down the *Lord's Day Act* on Sunday shopping as a violation of "freedom of religion."
1986	Oakes: Established guidelines for interpreting the "reasonable limits" clause.
1988	Morgentaler: Outlawed *Criminal Code* restrictions on abortion employing the "security of the person" clause.
1990	Keegstra: Determined that "freedom of expression" does not apply to disseminating hate literature.
1992	Butler: Limited "freedom of expression" in relation to pornography.
1993	Rodriguez: Concluded that "security of the person" does not include right to assisted suicide.
1995	Egan: Determined that "equality rights" included sexual orientation.
2003	Halpern: Ontario Court of Appeal ruled that same-sex marriage was legal and constitutional.
2004	Reference: Supreme Court ruled that federal legislation redefining marriage to include same-sex couples would be constitutional.

*For a complete list of Charter cases, see http://scc./lexum.umontreal.ca.

Politics and the Supreme Court

R.I. Cheffins and P.A. Johnson argue that the importance of the Charter for Canada's constitutional future is that it is "centralizing, legalizing and Americanizing."[44] By "centralizing," they mean that it provides a common national standard for the protection of civil liberties and engenders national debates that transcend federal–provincial or regional differences. By "legalizing," they mean that policy issues are now handled in a more legalistic manner. And by "Americanizing," they are referring to Canada's political system becoming more like that of the United States. Another commentator has summed up the legalizing and politicizing effect of the Charter this way: it tends "to judicialize politics and to politicize the judiciary."[45]

Clearly, the nine justices of the Supreme Court of Canada play a very powerful political role today. They can overturn legislation that, according to their judgment, conflicts with rights guaranteed in the *Charter of Rights and Freedoms*, and they can have a major say on social policy matters such as marriage, union rights and abortion that used to be in the exclusive domain of politicians. This power has been particularly evident in cases concerning legal rights. In January 1988, for example, the Supreme Court declared that the federal abortion law did not conform to the Charter and struck it down, leaving Canada with no legislation in this field of social policy. In the famous *R. v. Morgentaler* case, a majority of the Supreme Court judges ruled that the law restricting access to therapeutic abortions violated the security of the person of the woman and constituted a "profound interference with a woman's body."[46] Despite parliamentary efforts to regain control of abortion policy (the first attempt was defeated in the House of Commons and

44. R.I. Cheffins and P.A. Johnson, *The Revised Canadian Constitution: Politics as Law* (Toronto: McGraw-Hill Ryerson, 1986), pp. 148–49.

45. Peter H. Russell, "The Political Purposes of the Canadian Charter of Rights and Freedoms," *The Canadian Bar Review, 61*, 1983, p. 51.

46. *R. v. Morgentaler* (1988), 1 S.C.R. 30.

the second was defeated in a tied vote in the Senate), the Supreme Court's judgment remains in place with little likelihood of successful legislation. In 1991, the Supreme Court reaffirmed the position that an unborn child (a fetus) is not a person.

Critics of the Charter insist that it inhibits rather than fosters progressive social change. They maintain that by framing the agenda for debate, the courts can limit social reform. The rights protected under the Charter are, they claim, a reflection of middle-class preoccupations; no basic entitlement is included for a decent level of education, housing, nutrition or health care. However, section 36 of the Charter does enshrine the commitment of both federal and provincial governments to provide "essential public services of reasonable quality to all Canadians." And, although it does not protect present social and economic arrangements, the Charter identifies and protects the political and legal rights essential to those who promote social change.

The Charter's detractors also contend that it confers too much power on lawyers and judges, enabling judges, who are not elected, to strike down measures enacted by the majority. One Charter supporter, Robert Sharpe, answers these criticisms by pointing out that we cannot equate democracy with "the raw will of the majority":

> *A true democracy is surely one in which the exercise of power by the many is conditional on the respect for the rights of the few.*[47]

It is unfortunate, but true, that the majority at times overlooks minority rights. The Charter assigns courts the responsibility to ensure that the claims of minorities and those without influence are considered. Ultimately, of course, elected officials have the final say, because the Charter provides that equality rights are subject to the legislative override provision (the notwithstanding clause) that can be used if legislatures disagree fundamentally with the courts.

Section 24(2) of the Charter declares that a court shall exclude from the proceedings evidence that was obtained in a manner that infringed upon or denied any guaranteed right or freedom. Canadian judges are proving willing to dismiss illegally obtained evidence because it might "bring the administration of justice into disrepute," but these new exclusions are making law enforcement more difficult. Until 1982, illegally obtained evidence was accepted in the courts; today, it is not.

One further area of apprehension concerning the Charter lies in the realm of political culture. Some scholars see the Charter as promoting a shift of values toward those of the United States. They maintain that the long-standing, collectivist values that emphasize tradition, order and historical continuity (as discussed in Chapter 3) are becoming more closely aligned with US values that stress individual interests above those of the collectivity. This reflects the emphasis the Charter puts on individual versus group interests. As Cheffins and Johnson put it, the Charter "will bring an essentially counter-revolutionary, non-rationalist communitarian society into direct collision with individual-focused legal rights based upon Charter arguments." Doing so, they maintain, will accelerate the Americanization of Canada.[48]

However, the Charter also has a clearly positive side. Judges have taken the stand that citizens should be allowed to ask courts to declare laws unconstitutional when there is a potential infringement of their rights; they do not have to wait until their rights are actually violated. In response to this, many laws that threatened to deprive individuals of basic rights have been struck down. Former Supreme Court Justice Lamer commented that as a result, governments have been more careful since 1982 in drafting laws.[49] This was evident in 1986, when a parliamentary subcommittee presented

47. Quoted in the *Toronto Star*, April 11, 1987.
48. *The Revised Canadian Constitution*, p. 152.
49. Quoted in *The Globe and Mail*, April 14, 1987.

85 recommendations for making federal law conform to the Charter. Part of that list, including discrimination against gays and lesbians in the federal jurisdiction, was acted upon quickly and outlawed.

We conclude that Canadian judicial tradition will continue to influence the conduct of judges when they assess Charter implications, especially in issues of equality. While the opportunity for a more active, interventionist and, some might argue, more creative role for the judiciary now exists, this will not bring about sudden change. There will be a gradual but constant evolution in the power of the Supreme Court. Clearly, the Charter and Supreme Court judgments based on it have become an important Canadian symbol and a significant part of the policy process, a balance to both executive and legislative power.

Critical Debate
Constitutional Revision: Necessary and Possible?

Is there a substantial need to make major, innovative amendments to the Canadian Constitution? Are such changes both necessary and possible?

⌐ Point

Yes, it is time to radically change the Constitution to enhance its efficiency, increase its fairness and reduce the "democratic deficit" that has evolved since 1867.

That Canada does "not work" is patently clear. Québec leaders are constantly arguing that they want to separate from Canada; provincial premiers from coast to coast believe that the fiscal system is unfair; and all leaders, including Prime Minister Stephen Harper, think that social programs, in particular the *Canada Health Act*, need to be reformed. The *Charter of Rights and Freedoms* has allowed judges to become our political masters, determining public policy in the most crucial fields and reducing our MPs to mere eunuchs.

Pierre Trudeau's patriation of the Constitution without Québec's approval has left a gap in the democratic legitimacy of the Constitution. The failure to pass the constitutional amendments of the Meech Lake and Charlottetown agreements despite their nearly unanimous approval from political leaders in Ottawa and the provincial capitals has left Canada with only piecemeal reforms to the federal system. The amendment formula is now so rigid that it, too, needs to be changed. The fact that Parliament has had to legislate to ensure that all regions are in agreement with future constitutional amendments and that Ottawa alone recognized Québec as a distinct society is proof that more needs to be done.

The distribution of powers between the provinces and federal government is now outdated. Ad hoc adjustments have given Canada an asymmetrical federalism in which some provinces have programs paid for by Ottawa while others do not. Ottawa uses its extra-constitutional spending powers to bend the provinces to its will and ensure that provincial leaders cannot bear in mind local conditions when they make public policy.

The consequences of an unreformed constitution are overly complex federal–provincial arrangements, disgruntled provincial politicians and dissatisfied citizens. We should change the legislative system by electing a Senate, reducing the courts' ability to use the Charter to overrule legislative intent, getting rid of the federal spending power and constitutionalizing the main principles of Meech Lake and Charlottetown.

Let's get on with it. Where there is a will, there is a way.

Counterpoint

There is no need to amend the Constitution significantly and no possibility that it could be accomplished. The Constitution has worked well since 1867 and continues to do so. There will always be strains and arguments over the distribution of power in a large federal state like Canada.

Many people do not fully understand that the Canadian Constitution is not a single document providing clear direction to the political process. As in most democratic countries, it is both a product of the political system and a significant factor in shaping it. The Canadian Constitution includes both written and unwritten dimensions. Among the unwritten elements are the British parliamentary heritage and the democratic norms and values inculcated in Canadian political culture. The written dimensions of the Canadian Constitution include the well-known *British North America Act* of 1867 (now the *Constitution Act, 1867*) and the *Canada Act of 1982*, as well as a number of other acts and documents. The *Constitution Act* has been altered or expanded numerous times since 1867 by formal amendments and legal interpretations by the Judicial Committee of the Privy Council and the Supreme Court of Canada. It has proven remarkably flexible when necessary.

Since the patriation of the *Canada Act, 1982*, with its new amending formula and *Charter of Rights and Freedoms*, the role of the courts in the political process has increased considerably. The new Charter is even more comprehensive than the *Bill of Rights* in the United States, and it has strengthened the position of the judicial branch of government in Canada. The Charter ensures that legislators who enact laws must be prepared to justify any inequality of burdens those laws may impose. By doing so, it allows an avenue for minorities and other previously unempowered groups to participate more effectively in the law-making process. This new feature in the Constitution will greatly increase litigation, but should also enhance the democratic quality of government and provide arbitration by a forum that is less vulnerable to the influence of powerful majorities than is the political arena. Court decisions have already begun to alter subtly the makeup of the country by reducing situations where laws vary from province to province.

The 1992 Charlottetown Accord was designed to accommodate provincial interests in Confederation. Its defeat has prevented Canada from becoming more decentralized by constitutional means. But challenges to the viability of the state continue unabated. We have patriated the Constitution only to find ourselves mired in constitutional deadlock. Even if we admitted that we need to change the Constitution it is very unlikely to be accomplished. The amendment procedures may well prove too rigid to resolve the deficiencies that are already glaringly evident in the country. The constitutional dilemma of how to solve regional aspirations as well as Québec's precise demands while retaining a powerful federal government is probably the most vital political challenge facing Canadians.

There is no agreement, however, on how to amend the Constitution to resolve these issues. Canadians are divided, and will continue to be, on what changes are acceptable. Those that satisfy some desires for reform alienate others. As Niccolo Machiavelli (1469–1527) warned in *The Prince*, there is nothing more difficult to arrange, more doubtful of success and more dangerous to carry through than initiating changes in a state's constitution.

Discussion Questions

1. Where do you stand on the Critical Debate? What can you add to it?
2. What were the two basic obstacles to the 1982 patriation of the Constitution, and what compromises were reached to try to solve them? Why did Québec not agree with the compromises?
3. What were the main additions to the Constitution when it was patriated in 1982? Why was it patriated without Québec's approval?
4. Describe and evaluate the current formulas for amending the Constitution.
5. How has the *Charter of Rights and Freedoms* affected equality and other rights in Canada? Has the Charter protected civil liberties in an era of global terrorism? Has the Charter given too much power to the Supreme Court and weakened the executive and legislative branches of government?

Visit our new Companion Website at **www.pearsoned.ca/jackson**, where you can use the interactive Study Guide and link to additional resources on topics discussed in the text.

Selected Bibliography

Ajzenstat, Janet, ed. *Canadian Constitutionalism: 1791–1991*. Ottawa: Canadian Study of Parliament Group, 1992.

Bakan, Joel, and David Schneiderman. *Social Justice and the Constitution*. Don Mills, ON: Oxford University Press, 1992.

Behiels, M. *The Meech Lake Primer: Conflicting Views on the 1987 Constitutional Accord*. Ottawa: University of Ottawa Press, 1989.

Conklin, William. *Images of a Constitution*. Toronto: University of Toronto Press, 1993.

Cook, Curtis, ed. *Constitutional Predicament*. Montréal: McGill-Queen's University Press, 1994.

Greene, Ian. *The Courts*. Vancouver: UBC Press, 2005.

Heard, Andrew. *Canadian Constitutional Conventions*. Don Mills, ON: Oxford University Press, 1991.

Hogg, Peter. *Constitutional Law of Canada*, 4th ed. Toronto: Carswell, 1997.

Jackson, Robert J., and Doreen Jackson. *Stand Up for Canada: Leadership and the Canadian Crisis*. Scarborough, ON: Prentice Hall, 1992.

Kelly, James B., *Governing With the Charter*. Vancouver: UBC Press, 2005.

Lenihan, Donald, Gordon Robertson, and Roger Tassé. *Canada: Reclaiming the Middle Ground*. Montréal: Institute for Research on Public Policy, 1994.

Manfredi, C., 2nd ed. *Judicial Power and the Charter: Canada and the Paradox of Liberal Constitutionalism*. Don Mills, ON: Oxford University Press, 2001.

Martin, R. *The Most Dangerous Branch: How the Supreme Court of Canada Has Undermined Our Law and Our Democracy*. Montréal: McGill-Queen's Press, 2003.

Milne, David. *The Canadian Constitution*. Toronto: Lorimer, 1991.

Monahan, Patrick J. *Meech Lake: The Inside Story*. Toronto: University of Toronto Press, 1991.

Morton, F.L., and R. Knopff, eds. *The Charter Revolution and the Court Party*. Peterborough, ON: Broadview Press, 2000.

Reesor, B. *The Canadian Constitution in Historical Perspective*. Scarborough, ON: Prentice Hall, 1992.

Russell, Peter H. *Constitutional Odyssey*. Toronto: University of Toronto Press, 1991.

Sartori, Giovanni. *Comparative Constitutional Engineering*. New York: New York University Press, 1995.

Smith, Jennifer. *Federalism*. Vancouver: UBC Press, 2004.

Watts, Ronald L., and Douglas M. Brown, eds. *Options for a New Canada*. Toronto: University of Toronto Press, 1991.

Weaver, R. Kent. *The Collapse of Canada?* Washington: Brookings Institution, 1992.

Whitaker, R. *A Sovereign Idea*. Montréal: McGill-Queen's University Press, 1992.

The Courts

Gall, Gerald L. *The Canadian Legal System*, 3rd ed. Toronto: Carswell, 1990.

Green, Ian. *The Charter of Rights*. Toronto: Lorimer, 1989.

Knopff, Rainer, and F.L. Morton. *Charter Politics*. Scarborough, ON: Nelson, 1992.

Mandel, Michael. *The Charter of Rights and the Legalization of Politics in Canada*, rev. ed. Toronto: Wall and Thompson, 1994.

Manfredi, Christopher P. *Judicial Power and the Charter: Canada and the Paradox of Liberal Constitutionalism*. Toronto: McClelland & Stewart, 1993.

McCormick, P. *Canada's Courts*. Toronto: Lorimer, 1994.

McCormick, P., and I. Greene. *Judges and Judging*. Toronto: Lorimer, 1990.

Morton, F.L. *Law, Politics and the Judicial Process in Canada*, 3rd ed. Calgary: University of Calgary Press, 2002.

——————, *Morgentaler v. Borowski: Abortion, the Charter and the Courts*. Toronto: McClelland & Stewart, 1992.

Sharpe, Robert J., Katherine Swinton, and Kent Roach. *The Charter of Rights and Freedoms*, 2nd ed. Toronto: Irwin Law, 2002.

Yates, Richard, and Ruth Yates. *Canada's Legal Environment*. Scarborough, ON: Prentice Hall, 1993.

Chapter 6

Contested Federalism

Division of Powers and Finances

In this chapter, we explore the meaning of federalism and its importance in Canada. One conclusion is obvious. Rather than being a fixed, immutable institutional structure, Canadian federalism has changed dramatically over the years. It is not a simple, static division of powers, but a process whereby the two levels of government adapt and change in order to reduce tensions within the political environment. Although the Canadian federal structure has proven remarkably resilient, during the past few decades powerful pressures have emerged that threaten to overwhelm the system. The ultimate outcome of what is often referred to as the "crisis of Canadian federalism" is by no means certain. Whether these forces will result in a truncated Canada or serve to strengthen the federal system will depend on a number of factors, including leadership, economic prosperity and political circumstances.

Developments in federalism reach into the lives of all Canadians. The threat of Québec separation, the sense of grievance in eastern and western provinces, the controversies over language and educational rights for minorities, the disputes over resource control—these and many others are manifestations of conflicts over the authority and jurisdiction of the federal system. The vast array of social services and programs available to Canadian citizens today is the outgrowth of federal–provincial interaction. While certain programs may be supported by only one level of government, the majority of them require the financial co-operation of both Ottawa and the provinces. The procedures that lead to the interaction of the federal and provincial governments in these activities reveal much about Canadian politics. On the other hand, the federal system complicates the handling of many issues—for example, economic planning, and control of inflation, job creation, pollution, safety and women's rights.

In Chapter 5, we outlined the constitutional provisions that formally define the relationship between the federal and provincial governments. However, the conduct of politics within Canada's federal structure is also affected by the dynamic social and economic realities of the country. Therefore, more is required to comprehend Canadian federalism than a discussion of the legal division of powers and jurisdictional niceties. We need to understand the complex financial relations among governments as well as the political challenges that often pose a threat to the country.

We focus here on financial relations; the next chapter deals with the political challenges of nationalism and regionalism. The Critical Debate here asks if Canada's federal system allocates powers and finances in a balanced and fair way. Given federal–provincial divisions and disputes, can the country act comprehensively to solve its major problems, particularly in fields such as health care?

What Is Federalism?

To a large extent, federalism has replaced empire as a means of governing diverse peoples living on large land masses. Two dozen of the world's states are federal, including most of the large ones.

However, it is also apparent that there are approximately eight times as many unitary as federal states, and that, even within the systems labelled *federal*, the term means quite different things to different people.[1] There is little similarity in the federal aspects of countries such as the United States, Australia and Canada compared with Argentina, Brazil, Mexico, Nigeria, the Federated States of Micronesia and the United Arab Emirates. Moreover, some historically federal countries have imploded—the USSR has been dismantled, Czechoslovakia has divided and the component parts of the former Yugoslavia have formed several new countries.

Simply put, federalism refers to a division of jurisdiction and authority between at least two levels of government. It is usually characterized by the existence of one central government and two or more regional governments governing simultaneously over the same territory and people. Therefore, **federalism** can be defined as a government that is divided between a central and regional governments in such a way that each level of government oversees certain areas of the nation's affairs, on which it makes final decisions.

This definition implies that each level of government has more or less complete authority over some specific spheres of activity, while on a few other matters there may be a degree of concurrent jurisdiction. There is certainly no single, ideal way to divide this authority. What is important is that each level has a degree of autonomy. In the federal form, the various levels of government obtain their respective powers from the country's constitution, not from each other. Citizens are legally bound to obey the laws of more than one level of government, and each level may interact directly with citizens.

The history of the concept of federalism has been traced back to the fusion of ancient Israelite tribes. In North America, its first occurrence has been ascribed to the Five Nations of the Iroquois Indians. Its modern meaning, however, is best dated to the eighteenth century. During that period, the United States Constitution provided a system of government that has been emulated ever since. The two main parts of the theory of US federalism was the idea of distribution of government power on a geographical basis, and the philosophy that unity and diversity can coexist.

Concepts of Federalism

There are many varieties of federalism. Some systems have a federal constitutional structure, but political and social forms that reduce the significance of the bargain between the central and regional governments. An example has been Mexico, where, historically, the quasi-one-party system linked the political forces together in such a way as to produce a state very similar to those that are unitary. On the other hand, some unitary states are highly decentralized—as much or more than many federal states. Britain, for example, is unitary but has been decentralizing more over time. In summary, federal states may be centralized or decentralized—and so may unitary systems.

While considering the continuum of federalism, it is important to note its polar ends: the unitary and confederation forms of government. As its name implies, **unitary government** is characterized by one level of political authority. In this form, the central government grants and amends the powers of local or provincial authorities. The archetype of this form may well be France, where virtually all significant final decisions about political life are made in Paris. On the other hand, except in Canada and Switzerland, **confederation** refers to a loose alliance of sovereign states that band together for very narrow reasons. The United States in the period of the Articles of Confederation, 1781–1787, is a good example of this form. Admittedly, there may be a fine line between certain decentralized federalisms and confederal states. Perhaps the only way to differentiate

---

1. Robert J. Jackson and Doreen Jackson, *An Introduction to Political Science: Comparative and World Politics* (Don Mills, ON: Pearson Prentice Hall, 2007).

between the two types is to ascertain whether the various regional units are completely, as opposed to partially, sovereign.

A useful continuum measures federalisms from *centralized federalism*, in which the central government dominates or encroaches on the sub-units, to what may be referred to as *decentralized federalism*, in which the sub-unit governments dominate (see Figure 6.1). For a variety of reasons, most federal states today are of the centralized variety. The requirements of national security, the welfare state and, in general, the growing complexity of society are all factors conducive to a centralization of power at the national level. There are, however, states in which the various regional sub-units retain significant powers. Furthermore, there are countries in which it is possible to discern pendulum swings along the continuum over a period of decades. Although centralized federalism is the more common form today, there is nothing intrinsically superior or inferior about the arrangement.

Many scholars dislike the apparent formalism in these legal, political and territorial definitions of federalism. Economists and some political scientists even speak of a *federal society*, one in which economic, religious, racial or historical diversities are territorially grouped. Some, for example, believe that certain societies are intrinsically federal because they are pluralist, and that federalism is simply the institutional outcome of the forces that exist in these societies. The inherent difficulty with such definitions is that they concern more than federal unions and could just as well apply to any state composed of more than one ethnic group. Other scholars believe that non-territorial federalism can exist. They cite examples such as Estonia in 1925 or Cyprus in 1960. In these instances, legal jurisdiction over cultural and educational affairs was accorded to groups wherever they lived, and was not based on a geographic division of the state.

Federalism and Separatism

Why is federalism adopted? What are its advantages? On these questions there is much disagreement among scholars. Some argue that federalism is synonymous with liberty, that it is a protection for minority rights. Others believe it is chosen essentially to achieve unification without the loss of separate identities by the units. On the other hand, many have argued that quite a few of the so-called altruistic objectives often attributed to federalism are inaccurate and perhaps misleading.[2] Britain, one of the world's most liberal democracies, is a unitary state, while a number of non-democratic countries have adopted, at least on paper, the federal form. In short, federalism may be good, bad or indifferent, depending on other circumstances.

FIGURE 6.1 Continuum of the Degree of Centralization of Authority

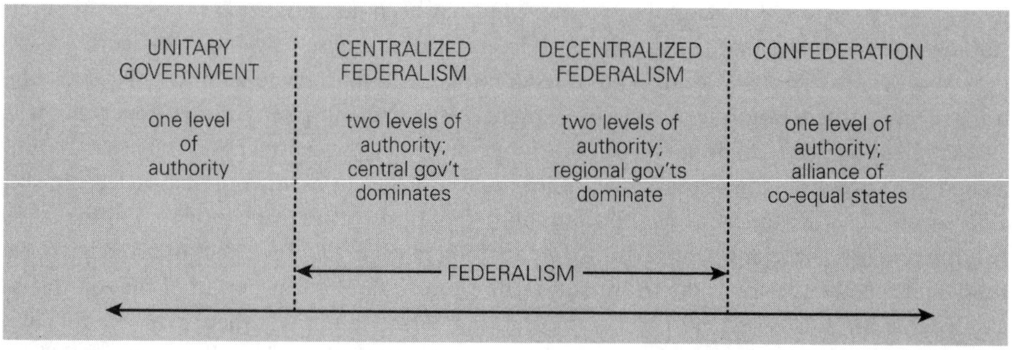

UNITARY GOVERNMENT	CENTRALIZED FEDERALISM	DECENTRALIZED FEDERALISM	CONFEDERATION
one level of authority	two levels of authority; central gov't dominates	two levels of authority; regional gov'ts dominate	one level of authority; alliance of co-equal states

FEDERALISM

Source: Adapted from concepts proposed by William H. Riker in *Federalism: Origin, Operation, Significance* (Boston: Little, Brown, 1964).

2. For an excellent critique of meaning and measures of federalism, see Jonathan Rodden, "Comparative Federalism and Decentralization," *Comparative Politics, 36*, 4 (July 2004), pp. 481–500.

Whatever the ultimate purpose of federalism, it is characteristically adopted because the leaders of the constituent units believe that they have something to gain that they could not achieve independently. The most often-cited motivations underlying federal unions are the desire for military security and economic or political expansion. A large geographic unit with a degree of coordination of resources provides a more effective defensive unit than a collection of smaller, independent states. And such a unified entity stands a good chance of being able to expand economically and politically. The possibility for state aggrandizement, rather than lofty idealism, seems to be a more accurate assessment of the motivations for federalism.

While the various sub-units may perceive gains from a federal union, they must also take certain drawbacks into consideration. In order to realize their objectives, the sub-units are obliged to give up some privileges and powers to the central government. Before doing this, they may seek certain guarantees and safeguards to enable them to maintain at least a modicum of separate authority. These guarantees are usually in the form of a written constitution that clearly divides political authority and jurisdiction and spells out certain limitations and restrictions on the new government.

A constitution is, therefore, often referred to as the "umpire" of federalism, serving to protect as well as limit. Whether the constitution is a single, written document or an unwritten collection of statutes and understandings, what is important is that the *federal principle* be enshrined in a way that recognizes the diversity of the country and at the same time provides a check on arbitrary rule by the central government. The component units are usually given equal or disproportionately strong representation at the centre. This is often achieved by having two legislative chambers—one based on population, the other on recognition of regionalism. And the importance of constitutions to federal systems is demonstrated by the continuing controversies over how they may be amended or altered.

Many apparently stable federal constitutional systems have endured stresses and strains and, on occasion, have failed. Ronald Watts has found four common conditions of failure: regional divergences of political demands, weak communications along with a diminution of the original impetus for union, and external influences.[3] All these conditions are present in Canada to some degree; in fact, they are present to some extent in *all* federations—both those that have failed and those that have succeeded. Examples of peaceful secessions include very loose confederations such as Malaysia (Singapore was virtually expelled) and the tenuous arrangements of Syria–Egypt and Senegal–Mali. Three former Eastern Bloc countries (the Soviet Union (USSR), Czechoslovakia and Yugoslavia) fell apart when the glue of communism was removed. The other cases of federal division involved violence. The lesson is clear: rancour and civil war have been the usual means by which federal states have divided.

Thus far, we have described federalism in terms of constitutions that divide the authority of the central and sub-unit governments and balance regional interests. Nonetheless, readers must not take too legalistic an approach and overlook the fact that federalism is fundamentally based on a sociological reality.[4] Were it not for societal diversity, federalism would not be as prevalent in the world as it is today. While federal states may be formed for essentially narrow, pragmatic reasons, this political arrangement is ultimately a recognition that the various sub-units are different and that their special qualities should be preserved and protected.

---

3. R.L. Watts, "Survival or Disintegration," in Richard Simeon, ed., *Must Canada Fail?* (Montréal: McGill-Queen's University Press, 1977), pp. 42–60.

4. See Michael Stein, "Federal Political Systems and Federal Societies," in Meekison, ed., *Canadian Federalism: Myth or Reality*, pp. 30–42.

The Trajectory of Canadian Federalism

The Origins of Federalism

As noted in Chapter 2, the motivations for establishing a federal union in Canada in the 1860s were mixed. Both military security and economic expansion were central themes in the speeches and political programs of the contemporary leaders. Foremost among this handful of politicians was John A. Macdonald, who played the leading role in establishing the federal union in 1867 by placating the objections of the smaller Maritime provinces and holding forth the prospect of a glorious national destiny.[5] By the 1860s, Macdonald, among others, was keenly aware of the need for greater military security. The victory of the northern states in the US Civil War had sent a shiver up the spines of Canadian leaders. British interests in Canada had made no secret of their support for the American Confederacy and, after Appomattox, there was expectation in some corners that Canada might be annexed as part of the spoils of war. Raids by fanatical Fenians across the border into Canada added more urgency to plans for some type of national unification. The British, for their part, were tired of the burden of defending their colonies in North America and were not averse to the prospect of turning over to Canadians the responsibility for their own defence.

At the same time, Macdonald recognized the great potential of the unsettled western territories for the development of a transcontinental nation. The possibility of economic development and expansion was, therefore, another significant motivating factor in establishing federalism. He thought that a political union would not only improve internal trade between the Maritime provinces and Upper and Lower Canada, but also help in the drive to settle the Prairies and the far west before the United States moved into the vacuum.

Each of the British colonies in North America saw certain specific advantages for itself in the new enterprise. The leaders from Upper Canada, a growing and prosperous area, looked forward to further economic expansion and development. Those from Lower Canada, while uneasy about their English Canadian neighbours, were willing to accept a federal union if their language and culture could be protected by law. The sparsely populated Maritime colonies of Nova Scotia and New Brunswick were perhaps the most reluctant, but at the same time they, too, were attracted by economic advantages—namely, the building of a transcontinental railway and various subsidies from the future federal government. The Charlottetown and Québec Conferences, discussed in Chapter 2, culminated a long process of negotiation resulting in the Dominion of Canada.

The Early Evolution of Federalism

While the 1867 *BNA Act* authorized the establishment of a type of government in Canada "similar in principle to that of the United Kingdom," the resulting form of government necessarily differed in that jurisdiction and authority were divided between the central government and the provinces. We have seen that the architects of the federal system sought to establish a strong central government, mindful as they were of the threat posed by the movement for states' rights in the American union to the south, which had led to the bloody Civil War of 1861–65. Even a cursory reading of the *BNA Act* confirms the impression that the central government was meant to be predominant. Reversing the US example, it was the federal government in Canada that was to be the beneficiary of the residual "Peace, Order, and good Government" (POGG) clause. The limited jurisdiction of

---

5. See Donald Creighton, *John A. Macdonald: The Young Politician* (Toronto: Macmillan, 1952), *John A. Macdonald: The Old Chieftain* (Toronto: Macmillan, 1955), and *The Road to Confederation: The Emergence of Canada, 1863–1867* (Toronto: Macmillan, 1964); Peter Waite, *The Life and Times of Confederation, 1864–1867* (Toronto: University of Toronto Press, 1967); and Richard J. Gwyn, *John A: The Man Who Made Us, Volume One, 1815–1867* (Toronto: Random House, 2007).

the provinces was meant to underscore their subordinate position in the federation. While reference is often made to the "Confederation Agreement," it is clear that the authors did not intend that Canada be a confederation in a genuine political sense, but rather a centralized federation.

In a summary article, Howard Cody traced the evolution of federal–provincial interaction in Canada since 1867.[6] While his argument lacks a rigorous definition of *interaction*, his précis does provide an instructive history of federal–provincial relations. Cody identifies at least four eras, and suggests that there have been several pendulum swings between centralization and decentralization (see Figure 6.2 on page 202). While Canada clearly began as a centralized federation, during the latter part of the nineteenth century the relative power of the provinces grew, due to a series of judgments by the Judicial Committee of the Privy Council (JCPC) in the United Kingdom. We have noted earlier in this text that in jurisdictional disputes referred to the JCPC, there was a consistent pattern of interpretation favouring provincial rights. Forceful provincial leaders such as Sir Oliver Mowat and Honoré Mercier had the effect of eroding the original dominance of the central government to the point that the *BNA Act* was interpreted by the JCPC as an international treaty rather than as the founding document of a country. This period of decentralized federalism, lasting into the early twentieth century, has been roundly condemned by Garth Stevenson:

> *This peculiar situation, which even the Australians had the foresight largely to avoid, had the effect that for almost a century the most influential concepts of Canadian federalism were largely defined by outsiders, men who had no practical knowledge of Canada, or of federalism, and who were not even required to live in the society that to a large degree was shaped by their opinions.*[7]

According to this historical summary, the pendulum began to swing back toward a centralization of authority with the introduction of what became known as *conditional grants*. Under the *BNA Act*, the provinces assumed jurisdiction over such matters as education and social welfare, which originally required very little expenditure. As the demand for social services grew in the twentieth century, the provinces found themselves starved for funds. The provisions of the Act made it virtually impossible for them to raise the revenues needed to meet public needs. To help them escape from this impasse, the central government in Ottawa offered the provinces grants "on the condition" that the money be spent in a specified manner. The provinces resented this intrusion but had no choice. The hardships of the Depression further deepened the dependency of the provinces on the federal government. In addition, the need to prepare Canada for war in 1914 and again in 1939 naturally tended to centralize power in Ottawa. Except perhaps in Québec, where there was considerable opposition to the two world wars and especially to the policy of conscription, the national government became a focus of patriotism and loyalty for most Canadians.

The dominance of Ottawa can be said to have continued until the late 1950s, when another pendulum shift occurred. New ideas about decentralization had begun to circulate as early as 1937, with the recommendations of the Royal Commission on Dominion–Provincial Relations, perhaps better known as the Rowell-Sirois Commission. This commission was charged with investigating the reasons for the near-bankruptcy of the provinces and recommending ways to revitalize the federation. While its suggestions could not be implemented until after the Second World War, the Rowell-Sirois Commission came out strongly against the conditional grants procedure. In addition,

6. Howard Cody, "The Evolution of Federal–Provincial Relations in Canada: Some Reflections," *American Review of Canadian Studies*, vol. 7, no. 1 (Spring 1977), pp. 55–83.

7. Garth Stevenson, *Unfulfilled Union: Canadian Federalism and National Unity*, 4th ed., (Montréal: McGill Queen's University Press, 2004).

it recommended that Ottawa take over such expensive responsibilities as unemployment insurance and pensions, and generally seek to equalize the financial resources of the provinces.

As the provinces began to obtain relief from their heavy financial burdens through new fiscal mechanisms, important changes were also occurring in postwar society. Beginning in the 1960s and with increasing momentum through the decade, Québec underwent the Quiet Revolution, in which traditional French Catholic values and occupational patterns were transformed. A new, confident French Canadian elite, epitomized by the government of Jean Lesage, led the assault on Ottawa's "paternalism." Ottawa countered with an expansion of what were referred to as *conditional grants* or *shared-cost* programs, which nonetheless tended to be regarded as distorting provincial spending priorities and therefore still engendered antagonism. In the spirit of Mowat and Mercier, Québec politicians insisted on the right to exercise their independence by "opting out" of certain programs so that they could go their own way—only now with federal funding. Ottawa had no coherent or effective response with which to meet this challenge. Québec's agitation in the 1960s for *special status* only served to give the other provinces new ideas.

The long-standing sense of grievance in the Western provinces against Ottawa also began to erupt during this period. Buoyed by their enormous resource revenues, the provinces of Alberta and British Columbia in particular sought greater political clout within the federation to match their recently acquired wealth. While they were not sympathetic to the cultural and linguistic aspirations of the Québécois, the Western provinces shared with them a degree of antipathy toward the perceived paternalism of the federal government in Ottawa as well as its perceived favouritism toward Central Canada.

Modern Federal–Provincial Mechanisms and Conflict Resolution

The historical interplay of federal–provincial relations has brought into being numerous institutions for coordinating policies and resolving disputes between the federal and provincial governments. As we pointed out in the previous chapter, both levels of government manage most fields of public policy and many fields are jointly financed. Both areas necessitate considerable federal–provincial interaction.

In the early days of Confederation, there was not much need for formal federal–provincial consultation, and what meetings did occur were of an ad hoc nature, convened to discuss specific problems. However, increased financial power expanded the fields of influence of both levels of government. Commitment to economic policies aimed at full employment, economic growth and trade liberalization, as well as to a wide range of social policies, resulted in a dramatic increase in intergovernmental relations. Effective intergovernmental consultation thus became a basic requirement for the maintenance of Canadian federalism. Such open lines of communication are perhaps indicated by the widespread establishment of departments or offices whose sole purpose is dealing with federal–provincial issues.

Intergovernmental relations immediately after the Second World War were characterized by constant, reasonably harmonious exchanges of ideas, financial decisions and policies. This period has been labelled one of *co-operative federalism*, albeit with a decided federal predominance. Economic times were good as a result of the postwar boom, and federal–provincial relations were primarily concerned with social programs that did not necessarily involve regional conflict.[8] As a

8. Timothy B. Woolstencroft, *Organizing Intergovernmental Relations*, Institute Discussion Paper No. 12 (Kingston, ON: Institute of Intergovernmental Relations, 1982), p. 12.

rule, bureaucrats from both levels of government dominated intergovernmental relations, often resolving problems before they reached the political agenda.

The 1960s and 1970s, however, were characterized by less co-operation and more confrontation. Economic downturns and the ascendancy of provincialism (concern for the jurisdictional integrity of the provinces) changed the conduct of relations between levels of government. The term coined to describe this new relationship was *executive federalism.*

The clearest sign of the change from co-operative to executive federalism was the shift of intergovernmental talks from among public servants behind closed doors to among politicians, often in the full glare of publicity. The most public institution in intergovernmental relations today is the *First Ministers Conference,* at which the leaders of the eleven governments and three territories meet to hammer out deals, in recent years under the scrutiny of television cameras.

Some of the most important of these meetings lately have been named *Constitutional Conferences.* In recent years, the necessity to hold First Ministers Conferences has even found a place in the Constitution itself. For example, the 1982 constitutional patriation required two substantive meetings of the leaders to deal explicitly with the rights of Canada's Aboriginal peoples. And, if the Meech Lake Accord had been ratified (see Chapter 5), two annual meetings would have been forced upon the First Ministers thereafter.

While Ottawa may have thought that it could placate opposition through such conferences, the meetings also provide an instrument for the expression of provincial discontent and resistance. Certainly, the conferences have increasingly become political forums in which each premier appeals not to the other heads of government, but directly to his own electorate. Richard Simeon has argued that intergovernmental bargaining has become more like the *diplomatic* relations *between* states than the usual politics *within* a single state.[9] Responsible only to the people who elect them, provincial leaders today are well organized and prepared to take on the federal government through their counter-proposals and independent programs. Moreover, a new practice has developed: the provincial premiers often meet in advance of First Ministers Conferences and approach the final bargaining table as a unified group opposed to the federal government. Thus, Ottawa is no longer able to overwhelm its partners in the federation.

There is little question that the era of executive federalism has been one of decentralization characterized by intergovernmental conflict. D.V. Smiley, for example, argues that the rise of intergovernmental specialists has made federal–provincial conflicts more intractable, perhaps to the point of being irreconcilable.[10] Representatives of each level of government, guarding their positions, promote their own narrow interests exclusively, thereby impeding compromise.

Yet, this argument confuses the process of intergovernmental relations with the causes of conflict. Intergovernmental specialists have also facilitated co-operation and compromise between governments. Intergovernmental interactions promote consultation between governments and thus contribute to the effectiveness and harmony of intergovernmental co-operation. As well, the concern for jurisdictional integrity has not totally displaced the ability of government officials to resolve conflicts as, for instance, in the oil-pricing agreements of 1973–74, the Alberta–Ottawa energy agreement of 1979, the constitutional agreement of 1982, the Meech Lake Accord of 1987 and the Charlottetown agreement of 1992. Intergovernmental interaction provides a means of communication between governments, encouraging an awareness of the views of their respective cabinets and bureaucracies—a necessary precondition to achieving compromise.

9. Richard Simeon, *Federal–Provincial Diplomacy: The Making of Recent Policy in Canada* (Toronto: University of Toronto Press, 1972).

10. D.V. Smiley, "An Outsider's Observations of Federal–Provincial Relations among Consenting Adults," in Simeon, ed., *Confrontation and Collaboration,* pp. 109–11.

The constitutional details described in Chapter 5 and this general review of the evolution of federalism reveal the basic patterns of political interaction. Figure 6.2 portrays the pendulum swings that we have been describing, and illustrates some developments in federal–provincial interaction. While some specific dates are given, changes of this nature take place very gradually, and we have simply used some specific event or individual to mark a turning point when, in fact, the transformation may have been building for some time.

Despite the imprecision with respect to time in Figure 6.2, it is important that federalism be perceived as something other than a static phenomenon. Of utmost concern today is the fact that the pendulum has been moving toward decentralization with such swiftness that it has threatened to overwhelm the Canadian federal system. While change is to be expected as the normal course of events in any federation, such pressures threaten Canadian unity with a new intensity. With the first election of the Parti Québécois as the government of Québec in 1976, Canada entered a new period of *contested federalism*. The development of a fractured party system more recently has also weakened the federal government (see Chapter 11).

Contested Federalism and Decentralization

Canadian scholars have advanced at least five models of federalism. These models, known by the terms *quasi-federalism* or *compact*, *classical*, *co-operative* and *diplomatic federalism*, may be used to help

FIGURE 6.2 The Evolution of Canadian Federalism from 1867 to 2008, Indicating Swings of Centralization and Decentralization

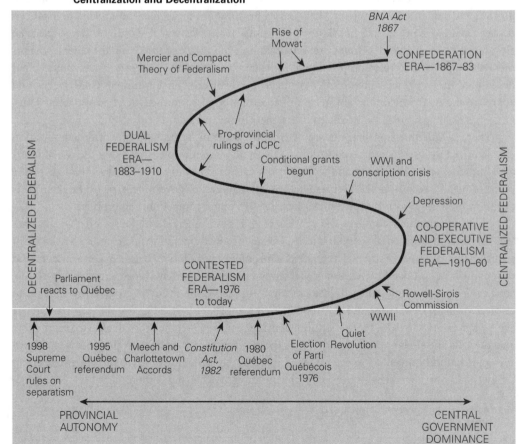

Source: Based on an idea from Howard Cody, "The Evolution of Federal–Provincial Relations in Canada," *American Review of Canadian Studies*, vol. 7, no. 1 (1977), pp. 55–83.

explain various aspects of federal–provincial relations in Canada. While they are often put forward as if they refer to the evolution of federalism, they more adequately depict which relationships between the federal and provincial governments predominate at any one time. Moreover, there are many other ways to depict the state of federalism. In fact, since the 1976 rise of the Parti Québécois in Québec, *contested federalism* better describes Canadian reality than any of the other somewhat dated terms above.

The evolution of Canadian federalism has led to considerable entanglement between federal and provincial programs. Besides the obvious overlap due to concurrent provincial and federal responsibilities in agriculture and immigration, there are, for example, departments of health, the environment, natural resources, fisheries and transport at both levels of government. There are several hundred bilateral and multilateral programs or agreements between Ottawa and the provinces. The result of this evolution in duplication is that more than half of federal programs at least partially overlap with those of the provinces.

Despite this situation, however, Canada has not been evolving toward a centralized federation as claimed by some critics of the government in Ottawa. Canada remains one of the most decentralized federations in the world. The trend, if any, has been toward *more* decentralization. The provinces have *increased* their power in recent decades. There are numerous examples. In the 1950s, the federal government collected almost three times as much tax revenue as the provinces. Today it collects only slightly more than the provinces. The number of federal employees as a ratio of the country's labour force has actually dropped by almost half since the early 1950s.

Notwithstanding these trends, 1993's incoming federal Liberal government accepted the argument for more decentralization. Pummelled by Québécois separatist forces and neo-conservative decentralizers in some provincial capitals and the West's newly formed Reform party, Jean Chrétien's Liberals began dismantling some federal programs. They withdrew from certain areas of provincial jurisdiction, including labour market training, social housing, mining, forestry and recreation. They reduced the payments for health and social programming and at the same time set up a new fiscal structure for transferring money to the provinces—called the *Canada Health and Social Transfer* (see "Health and Social Programs" below).

Yet, manoeuvres such as those made by the Chrétien government of the 1990s do not satisfy the advocates of radical decentralization. Québec *separatists* want the complete dismantlement of Canada. Even Québec *federalists* want massive decentralization and control over practically all federal jurisdictions. Premiers from English Canada also talk about the need to give the provinces many more powers. Following the initiative of Jean Charest, as a Liberal but nationalist premier of Québec, the provinces have set up a new interprovincial Council of the Federation (including the ten provincial premiers and the three territorial leaders) in an attempt to provide provincial solidarity when approaching the federal government. Under Charest's leadership, Québec has recently been pushing for an as yet undefined "Charter of open federalism."

The Canadian federation has reached a new stage at which the balance required between solidarity and autonomy of the union is in danger. The era of contested federalism is truly with us. Between the "sirens for separation" and the "foghorns for enhanced provincial powers," there are few who stand up for the tremendous benefits of Canada's federal system of government. The regionally fragmented results of the 2004 and 2006 national elections and the resultant minority governments have exacerbated the problem.

Financing Federalism

Since Confederation, money and ways of obtaining and spending it have made up a crucial aspect of federal–provincial interaction in Canada. While some conflicts revolve around highly symbolic issues (e.g., nationalism), others are overtly mundane—such as the central issue of money. Funding issues affect the very basics of Canadian life, from health and welfare to education and poverty.

Four general economic problems lie at the root of federal–provincial financial arguments; all four are interwoven with political sensitivities and historical exigencies.[11] In this section, we examine these problems, tracing the conflict they have engendered from 1867 to the current era.

The first and most obvious problem of federal–provincial financial relations is that there has always been a *fundamental incongruence* between jurisdictional responsibilities and sources of revenue at the two levels of government. As noted above, at the birth of the union, the central government acquired the most significant revenue sources and agreed to pay some limited subsidies and annual grants to support the obligations of the provinces. The intention was to create a highly centralized federal system. The Constitution entitled the federal government to raise money "by any mode or system of taxation" (*BNA Act*, 91.3), while the provinces were limited to direct taxation (*BNA Act*, 92.2). As provincial expenditures grew rapidly, the provinces found it necessary to acquire more revenues. This became a constant source of tension and political conflict.

The second problem can be traced to the fact that the provinces have differed widely in their fiscal capacities. In the early years, a relatively prosperous province such as Ontario or even Québec was fortunate in having a strong tax base in the form of a concentration of corporate activities and personal fortunes, and, therefore, had the ability to raise adequate funds to provide social services. Poorer and relatively depressed provinces, such as those in the Maritimes, were plagued with an inability to obtain sufficient tax revenue; increasing the rate of provincial taxation would only lower individual incomes and undermine economic growth. While in every federation, some regions are better off than others, in Canada, the discrepancies have been extraordinarily sharp. Over time, the ability to obtain high tax revenues has shifted from province to province—for example, from Ontario to Alberta during periods of high energy prices. But the problem of lower revenues persists for the poorer provinces.

The third problem has resulted from the joint occupancy of tax fields. As we mentioned above, the *Constitution Act of 1867* gave the provinces control only over *direct taxation*, while the federal government was granted a blanket authorization to tax in *any* manner. **Direct taxation** refers to individual income tax, corporate income tax and succession duties, among others. The federal government could levy **indirect taxation** through customs and excise duties, but could also institute its own direct taxation in competition with the provinces. Moreover, the provinces eventually managed to obtain the right to collect indirect taxes as well. Thereafter, both the provinces and the

---

11.   J.C. Strick, *Canadian Public Finance*, 2nd ed. (Toronto: Holt Rinehart and Winston, 1978) pp. 100–1.

federal government began to levy taxes on the same sources. The competition for revenue sources became one of the most contentious aspects of federal–provincial fiscal relations.

The fourth problem relates to the implementation of fiscal policy. In an age of modern economics, with its long-term budgetary manipulation of the economy, the possibility exists that without close co-operation between federal and provincial taxation and spending policies, the overall economy will not be effectively controlled. If, for example, the federal government were seeking to cut taxes to stimulate the economy, while at the same time the provinces were deciding to increase taxation, the impact of the federal initiative would be negated. Without a degree of co-operation, there is a significant danger that federal and provincial policies could work at cross-purposes. Today, a degree of coordination and consultation between the federal government and the provinces exists, but certainly not all difficulties of this type have been resolved (see the "Close-Up on Institutions: Québec's Objection to Ottawa's Spending Power").

Bearing in mind these four problems, we survey the historical evolution of federal–provincial financial relations in Canada.

CLOSE-UP ON Institutions

QUÉBEC'S OBJECTION TO OTTAWA'S SPENDING POWER

Québec insists on protecting education and health as areas of exclusive provincial jurisdiction, as defined in the Constitution. The federal government, however, has a mandate to finance projects it feels are of high priority for the country as a whole. It wants to ensure that all Canadians share funds set aside for areas of research and development, even though they might concern the fields of health and education, which are provincial jurisdictions.

In the February 1997 federal budget, the Chrétien government announced that it would set up the Innovation Foundation. This new foundation would give out $8 million to be invested in the research of hospitals, universities and colleges in order to help stem the brain drain of highly qualified researchers to the United States. The Québec government announced that if any universities and hospitals in the province accepted money from the Innovation Foundation, the Québec government would simply subtract the same amount of money from what the province would otherwise have given them.

Was Québec's stand legitimate? Was it wise politically?

A Brief History of Fiscal Federalism

In 1867, the federal government took over existing provincial debts and agreed to pay per capita subsidies and annual grants to the provinces to support their activities. However, the provinces did not acquire enough revenue from direct taxation to cover their rapidly escalating obligations. The federal subsidies promised in 1867 were helpful, but never sufficed to meet growing needs. Federal subsidies continued to decline as a proportion of provincial revenue—from 58 percent in 1874 to 8 percent in 1929. As well, as time went on, economic disparities between the provinces widened.

The First World War period was characterized by strong economic regulation by Ottawa. Increased military expenditures required the imposition of additional taxes to cover the federal debt, which exceeded $2 billion at the end of the war. The federal government also soon took up direct taxation in the form of personal and corporate income taxes to meet its own obligations.[12]

As we have seen, the early twentieth century saw an important development in federal–provincial fiscal relations: the use of *conditional grants*—sometimes called *grants-in-aid* or *shared-cost grants*. The federal government was willing to provide funds to the provinces for specific programs on condition that the money was spent in accordance with federal standards. These grants closed the provincial budgetary gap somewhat but did little to redress the fundamental problem of unequal fiscal capacity. The money was typically offered on a take-it-or-leave-it basis and, while tempting for most provinces to accept, it could disrupt budgetary planning and priorities. Perhaps more significantly, the provinces grew increasingly annoyed at the paternalistic way in which the grants were set up and administered.

---

12. J.C. Strick, *Canadian Public Finance*, p.102.

Before 1930, then, the provinces were already straining under various new obligations. The Great Depression had a devastating impact on their fragile finances. Their tax base was eroded, yet the demand for services, especially in the welfare field, had increased dramatically. Federal conditional grants were stepped up but were insufficient and led to a certain amount of heavy-handed federal intervention. The 1930s became known as the "decade of the tax jungle." Uncoordinated joint occupancy of tax fields, duplication of administrative bureaucracy and high regressive taxation (sales taxes) all served to exacerbate the effects of the Depression. While other countries were able to launch coordinated assaults on economic stagnation, Canada was caught in a serious bind. The Depression revealed that the division of federal–provincial fiscal jurisdictions was inadequate for the twentieth century; some major restructuring would be necessary if the country were to survive as a coherent federal system.

As we noted earlier, the Royal Commission on Dominion–Provincial Relations (the Rowell-Sirois Commission) was established in 1937 to study the issue. Experts were given a sweeping mandate to examine the problems of the federal system and to offer recommendations that would bring about a degree of congruence between obligations and revenue sources. When the commission presented its recommendations in 1940, it suggested that the federal government assume responsibility for personal and corporate income tax collection, the accumulated debt of the provinces and the support of the unemployed through a social security program.[13] In addition, the commission recommended a system of national adjustment grants to subsidize the poorer provinces so that the level of social services could be standardized across the country. The latter proposal ran into immediate opposition, especially from wealthier provinces that did not wish to support their poorer compatriots. The outbreak of the Second World War diverted everyone's attention from the issue. Finally, as R.M. Burns concluded, patriotism "accomplished what financial reasoning could not."[14]

The wartime period of relative economic prosperity eased the burden of the provinces. Citing the emergency, the federal government usurped the income tax and succession duty fields for itself. In return, the provinces were given compensatory payments. Thus began a complicated series of tax-rental and tax-sharing agreements.[15] The federal government took over, in effect, virtually all provincial sources of revenue from direct taxation in exchange for a payment of "rent." It is clear from this why the federal government in the war years and in the postwar decade was in a position of considerable dominance over the provinces.

By the end of the Second World War, the federal government was spending approximately three-quarters of the money spent by all governments in Canada. It had built up an impressive bureaucratic infrastructure and was intent on implementing its vision of Canada's future. As the war emergency ended, the government in Ottawa began to assume responsibility for the problems of postwar reconstruction. At this time, a new attitude toward the role of government in society also appeared. The concept of the balanced budget was replaced by Keynesian economic theory: the federal government committed itself to maintaining a high and stable level of economic growth and employment throughout the country. To do so, it had to adjust federal tax rates and levels of expenditure. It was able to obtain provincial agreement for an extension of the tax-rental arrangement until at least 1952.[16] The pre-eminence of the federal government did not begin to erode until the end of the 1950s, as the various tax-rental agreements between it and the provinces

---

13. Moore, Perry and Beach, *The Financing of Canadian Federation* (Toronto: Canadian Tax Foundation, 1996), pp. 11–13.

14. R.M. Burns, "Recent Developments in Federal–Provincial Fiscal Relations in Canada," *National Tax Journal*, vol. 15, no. 3 (September 1962), p. 228.

15. See Stevenson, *Unfulfilled Union*; and Strick, *Canadian Public Finance*, pp. 106–12.

16. Strick, *Canadian Public Finance*, p. 107.

began to engender opposition. Québec, for its part, began to resent both this arrangement and the conditional-grants scheme.

As the 1960s approached, the lack of correlation between revenue sources and expenditure responsibilities was accentuated. The welfare state entered the "big money" era. The provinces again began to feel the financial pinch of education and health care, while the federal government was virtually left out of these important jurisdictional areas. Increased provincial responsibilities were matched by the increasing competence and aggressiveness of provincial bureaucrats. The federal government seemed to be losing its grip on the economy as the country experienced a recession and slow economic growth. Sensing weakness, the provinces began to claim more responsibility for their own economies and questioned the feasibility of a national economic policy.

The most obvious indication of provincial self-assertion was in the area of tax-sharing. Tax-sharing was a continuation of the tax-rental program; however, instead of per capita grants, the provinces were to get a fixed percentage of three standard taxes: personal income taxes, corporate tax and federal succession duties. Tax-sharing protected provincial autonomy to some extent and was supplemented by an unconditional grant. Despite this apparent liberalization of federal policy, Ontario and Québec objected to the arrangement and the federal government introduced a tax-abatement system for the two provinces. This meant that the federal government moved out of the tax field to a considerable degree so that the provinces could levy their own taxes. This agreement encouraged agitation by all the provinces for a better deal.

During the 1960s, the abatement system was gradually extended to all provinces. Ottawa thus partially withdrew from the personal and corporate income tax field. Although the federal government continued to collect the tax (and return part of it to the provinces), as long as the provincial tax base remained the same as the federal tax base, the provinces had more room for increasing their taxes. In other words, the provincial portion could vary considerably. In 1966, the tax arrangements were opened up for periodic review, with the provinces asking for even more tax room and federal money. At that time, the government in Ottawa was in no mood to compromise and the arrangement was extended virtually unchanged. By 1972, however, the abatement system was practically at an end. The federal government introduced a guarantee program to prevent provincial loss of revenues resulting from a rationalization of their tax base with that of the federal government.

Today, Ottawa still collects income taxes (at rates set individually by the provinces on residents' income) for all the provinces except Québec. With the exception of Ontario, Québec and Alberta, all provinces also have tax-collection arrangements with the federal government for corporate income taxes.

Basic Concepts of Fiscal Federalism

Arrangements for the transfer of funds from the federal government to the provinces have evolved over the years from relatively simple grants to complex financial arrangements. To understand these arrangements, it is necessary to understand some basic concepts, including conditional grants, unconditional grants and spending power.

Conditional Grants, Unconditional Grants and Spending Power   As we have said, **conditional grants** are funds given by the federal government to provincial governments on the condition that they are spent in a certain way. In Canada, such grants have been considered essential because of the unequal distribution of financial resources across the country. The first conditional grants in Canada were paid out for agricultural instruction in 1912. Larger-scale grants were offered in 1927 to help the provinces finance old-age pensions. These grants also helped to alleviate the financial problems of the 1930s. After the Second World War, increased spending on health and welfare necessitated another major expansion in the field of conditional grants.

The federal government was able to act in these fields, which are under provincial jurisdiction, because of its spending power. **Spending power** refers to the federal government's blanket authority to spend money for any purpose in any field, even if it has no legal jurisdiction over the area. In most conditional-grants programs, Ottawa offered to pay half the costs of a specific program, with the provinces paying the rest. These were shared-cost programs, or so-called "50-cent dollar" programs, in which Ottawa paid 50 percent of costs. They were an attractive proposition for some provinces. Provincial leaders might sometimes have preferred to spend the money on other programs, but there was no way to shift the conditional resources unless Ottawa agreed.

In 1964, as a result of criticism of these programs, the federal government began to allow any province that did not want to be involved in a joint-cost venture to receive an equivalent sum of money, either by way of a federal tax withdrawal or in another form. Only Québec took Ottawa up on this offer, highlighting its claim to "special status" within Confederation. Québec's "different" status was also confirmed by the development of its own hospital and old-age pension schemes.

As the financial health of the provinces improved, it was inevitable that they would seek a revision of these fiscal arrangements. In 1977, led by Québec, and to some extent Alberta and Ontario, the provinces won the struggle to end the restrictive conditional-grants system. Ottawa increasingly offered **unconditional grants**—money that the provinces could spend in any way they wished since the money was not designated for any specific policy field. This shift from conditional to unconditional grants can be considered an example of the decentralization of the federal system during the period.

Figure 6.3 highlights the correlation between conditional and unconditional grants, and constitutional centralization and decentralization.

Key Mechanisms

Over the years, various mechanisms have been put in place to implement conditional and unconditional grants. They include equalization grants and established program funding.

Equalization Grants We have seen how the differing fiscal capacities of the provinces have posed a continuing problem in federal–provincial relations since Confederation. In 1867, the

FIGURE 6.3 Degree of Centralization as Affected by the Federal–Provincial Financial Transfers and the Distribution of Power

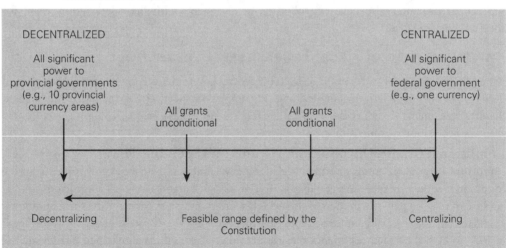

Source: Adapted from Thomas J. Courchene, "The New Fiscal Arrangements and the Economics of Federalism," in *Options: Proceedings of the Conference on the Future of the Canadian Federation* (Toronto: University of Toronto Press, 1977), p. 315.

FIGURE 6.4 **Federal and Provincial-Territorial Revenues (Public Accounts Basis)**

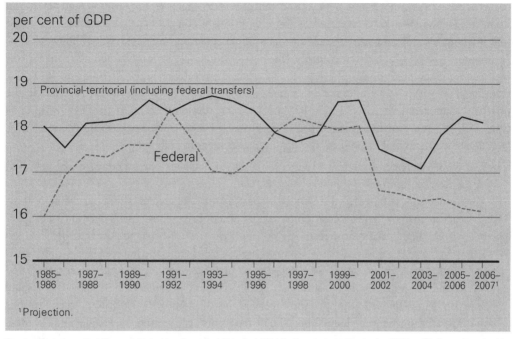

Source: Department of Finance, Federal and provincial-territorial Public Accounts and budgets, 2007, p. 50. Reproduced with the permission of the Minister of Public Works and Government Services, 2008.

financial gap between richer and poorer provinces was already wide; it has been growing ever since. A primary objective of fiscal policy since the Second World War has been to narrow this gap and provide a degree of economic stability. The main mechanism for accomplishing this has been, and continues to be, the provision of equalization payments to the provinces. **Equalization payments** are unconditional transfer payments to the provinces from the federal government calculated according to the ability of each province to raise revenue. The payments enable less affluent provinces to provide an average level of public services to their residents without resorting to excessive levels of taxation. (See Figure 6.4 for amounts of provincial/territorial funding, including equalization payments.) Since 1957, they have been calculated to bring provinces up to a national average based on a number of provincial revenue sources.

The ultimate objective of equalization policy is to establish a national standard for social services and strengthen federalism by meeting the needs of the less affluent elements in the union. However, the federal government has not been able to convey a sense of the urgency of this endeavour. In terms of per capita provincial government expenditures, equalization payments have proven successful, but they have not brought the have-not provinces up to the level of the wealthier ones. The provinces may be relatively equal in terms of providing government services, but interprovincial and interregional disparities remain, despite the presence of equalization payments.

Apart from the equalization program, federal transfers to all but the two poorest provinces are basically paid by taxpayers to the province in which they reside. They do not distribute income across provincial borders. The equalization program is, therefore, vital to achieve *horizontal equity* (the reduction of disparities between provinces in the treatment of persons in similar economic circumstances) as well as *vertical equity* (the reduction of inequalities in real income among individuals). It is not surprising, then, that the concept of equalization was enshrined in the Canadian Constitution of 1982 with the unanimous consent of all governments.

The continued debate and rancour over the equalization system reached a new level in the fall of 2004. The federal government promised the provinces that the equalization and territorial financing formula would be increased by more than $33 billion over the next ten years, but also that it would set up an advisory panel to propose a new plan on how these funds should be allocated among the provinces and territories. The plan, entitled *Achieving a National Purpose: Putting Equalization Back on Track* was put in place with the Conservative budgets of 2006 and 2007. The traditional principles remain the same as equalization payments: payments are unconditional (the province may spend the money any way it chooses); they are made to the less prosperous provinces; and as a province's fiscal capacity improves, the equalization payments decline.

The new system and its political ramifications included the following:

1. The fiscal capacity of all ten provinces is used to calculate the standard to be achieved throughout the country.
2. The number of tax bases from which the indicators are determined is reduced from 33 to 5.
3. A fiscal cap ensures that equalization payments do not bring a province's overall fiscal capacity to a level higher than those receiving no payments from the federal government.
4. Fifty percent of the revenues from resources are excluded from the figures. This was designed to respect the Offshore Accords that were signed between the federal government and Newfoundland and Labrador and Nova Scotia in 2005 and provide for payments to offset any reductions in equalization that would otherwise be affected by their offshore revenues. This did not satisfy those who claimed that the prime minister promised to exclude all oil and gas revenues from the calculation. The governments of both provinces officially complained that Ottawa reneged on its promise; a Tory federal backbencher from Nova Scotia voted against the budget and was ejected from caucus.

Under this program, only three provinces, Alberta, Ontario and British Columbia, received no funds in 2007–08, while the other seven provinces received equalization funds (see Figure 6.5).

FIGURE 6.5 Equalization Payments in 2007–08

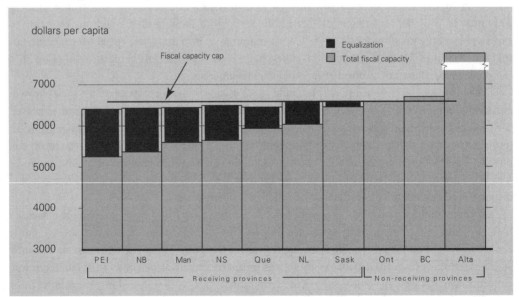

Source: Department of Finance, Budget 2007, p. 55. Reproduced with the permission of the Minister of Public Works and Government Services, 2008.

TABLE 6.1 **Territorial Formula Financing Program for Canada's Three Territories**

	Northwest Territories	Yukon	Nunavut	Total
	(millions of dollars)			
2006–07 legislated payments	753	514	839	2106
2007–08 guaranteed minimum allocation	778	537	865	2180
2007–08 renewed TFF	788	540	893	2221

Source: Adapted from the Department of Finance, Budget 2007, p. 20.

Under the new system the three northern territories are handled differently than the ten provinces. Their special challenges include small communities (often widely distributed), extreme population increases, and very high costs of public services such as hospitals, schools social services and infrastructure. The Territorial Formula Financing (TFF) makes up over two-thirds of government revenues in the Yukon and Northwest Territories and more than three-quarters of the revenue of Nunavut. Under this new TFF, over $2 billion was allocated to the three territories in 2007 (see Table 6.1).

Established Program Financing Conditional grants, like equalization transfers, have changed over time. The first significant, comprehensive innovation came in 1977. In that year, the federal program offered the provinces a hybrid **block grant** (a grant of one large sum of money from Ottawa to the provinces to be spent in certain policy fields) earmarked for health and post-secondary education.[17] This block grant program, called **Established Program Financing** (EPF), had both a conditional and an unconditional aspect. The federal monies had to be spent in the general fields of health and education as outlined, but within these broad parameters the provinces were largely free to make their own policy choices.

For the years 1977 to 1982, EPF provided two types of funding for provincial expenditures on health care and post-secondary education—a tax transfer of personal and corporate income tax points and a cash transfer.[18] While the federal government interpreted EPF as giving autonomy to the provinces, the legislation also placed some of the most expensive areas of social services squarely in the laps of the provincial governments. From the provinces' point of view, the federal government, which got them into these expensive fields in the first place, simply wished to prepare to disengage itself when costs began to rise.

In spite of the move to block funding in the EPF, the federal government was able to determine how some of the funds were used. In 1984, for example, the *Canada Health Act* declared that the health transfer would be reduced for any province that allowed doctors to extra bill or employ user fees.

After the major changes of 1977, the next round of negotiations over the renewal of federal–provincial fiscal arrangements came in 1982. The atmosphere of the negotiations was strained. The federal government sought to correct what it perceived as two fundamental problems.[19] First, there was a growing fiscal imbalance between the federal and provincial governments. While the federal government's deficit was increasing, there was an overall surplus in provincial revenues.

17. David B. Perry, "The Federal–Provincial Fiscal Arrangement Introduced in 1977," *Canadian Tax Journal*, vol. 25, no. 4 (July/August, 1977), pp. 429–40.

18. Tax points or tax transfers consist of a reduction in federal taxes and an equivalent increase in provincial taxes.

19. Allan J. MacEachen, Deputy Prime Minister and Minister of Finance, *Federal–Provincial Fiscal Arrangements in the Eighties: A Submission to the Parliamentary Task Force on the Federal–Provincial Fiscal Arrangements* (Ottawa: Supply and Services, April 23, 1981), pp. 8–11.

Second, the federal government wanted to maintain what it called a proper *political balance*. Ottawa argued that its contributions to provincial government services were not sufficiently visible and that this both hindered proper government accountability for taxes and expenditures, and deprived the federal government of recognition for the assistance it did provide. Thus, the federal government sought to cut back the level of transfers to the provinces.

The provinces, on the other hand, generally favoured maintenance of the status quo. They argued that the federal deficit was not due to federal transfers to the provinces but, rather, to federal policies of indexation, tax expenditures, the subsidization of oil and gas prices, and interest rate policies. The provinces also noted that the overall provincial revenue surplus was the result of the resource wealth of a few provinces and did not reflect the overall fiscal capacity of all the provinces. The have-not provinces were especially concerned with the future of the equalization program. The wealthier provinces, for their part, sought to protect the money they already received from the EPF block grants.

Fiscal Arrangements in Flux In spite of opposition, Ottawa remained determined to reduce its transfers to the provinces. In 1982, after months of inconclusive bargaining, the federal government enacted a new set of fiscal arrangements. The EPF formula was amended so that the provincial entitlement was determined for a base year with escalation indicators applied for economic and population growth. From this aggregate number, the federal government subtracted the amount of revenue generated by the tax points given to the provinces and then paid out the remainder as a cash grant. In the succeeding years, the federal government reduced the escalation factor and thus limited the total EPF entitlement of the provinces. This action had the effect of transferring an increasing share of the burden of these programs to the provinces. As Allan M. Maslove summarized the situation,

> *Given that the tax points transfer continues to generate more revenue from year to year, the residual cash transfer is diminishing and is projected to approach zero in the not too distant future.*[20]

In 1982, changes were also made in the calculation of equalization payments. The federal government proposed Ontario as the standard for determining eligibility for equalization payments, thereby ensuring the province's continued exclusion from receiving such grants. However, the poorer provinces (and Ontario) objected to having their level of receipts contingent upon Ontario's economic performance, especially in light of that province's economic stagnation during those years. Ottawa therefore dropped the so-called "Ontario standard," replacing it with a formula based on the average revenue of five provinces.

For the 1988–93 period, transfers from the federal to the provincial and territorial governments remained mostly in Established Program Financing, the equalization program and the **Canada Assistance Program (CAP)**, a program by which the federal government finances welfare and other provincial social services. The CAP was a shared-cost program established in 1966. Under its terms, the federal government paid 50 percent of provincial and municipal programs in welfare, day care, child-welfare services and homemakers' assistance. The only restriction on federal funding for the CAP was that the provincial social assistance programs had to be based on "need." Programs could vary widely across the country. (See Table 6.2 as a reference for current federal–provincial financing arrangements.)

---

20. Allan M. Maslove, "Reconstructing Federal Fiscalism," in Frances Abele, *How Ottawa Spends, 1992–93* (Ottawa: Carleton University Press, 1992), pp. 57–77.

TABLE 6.2 **Basic Federal–Provincial Financing in Canada, 2008**

	Unconditional	Conditional	New conditional block (began 2004)
Grants			
Programs	Equalization	Canada Assistance Plan (CAP) (Welfare funding)	Canada Health Transfer (CHT) (funding for heath) Canada Social Transfer (CST) (funding for education, social, etc.)
Funding Mechanisms	Based on revenue sources	Proportion of actual expenditures	Each a combination of cash and tax point room

The New Systems During Contested Federalism

Health and Social Programs, 1996–2005   In 1995, federal finance minister Paul Martin announced that a major shift in the block funding of provincial transfers would take effect in 1996–97. The Established Program Financing and the Canada Assistance Program would be folded into a new block-grant system called the Canada Health and Social Transfer (CHST). The federal Liberals defended the new CHST on the ground that it would simultaneously eliminate federal authority over provincial spending and reduce overall costs. However, at the same time, the federal government maintained that it would continue to apply its laws in the Canada Health Act and the CAP rules concerning residency requirements.

This new federal approach was established on the principle that its transfers would not be based on provincial costs. It reduced the total federal funds for social programs by some $7 billion. This reduction was approved by those who advocate more decentralization and censured by those who feared it would lead to a reduction in national standards in the fields of health, education and welfare. However, as soon as the federal deficit reached zero in 1997, the finance minister announced that he would put a floor on CHST transfer reductions. While the premiers applauded the minister for this decision, they asked for even more money from the federal coffers. Ottawa said that it would find more money if there could be a deal on such topics as internal trade and mobility for all Canadians along with a new agreement on the Canadian social union.

The result was another compromise, a framework for consultation and modifying social programs that concerned both the federal government and the provinces. While of limited legal significance, *A Framework to Improve the Social Union for Canadians* was accepted by nine premiers and the federal government on February 4, 1999. Only Québec declined to sign it. With the signing of the document, Ottawa agreed to collaborate with the provinces over any future Canada-wide initiatives in fields such as health care, post-secondary education and social assistance. Ottawa also agreed to provide one year's notice of any future funding changes, and promised to consult the provinces on any direct payments to individuals. Most important, once Ottawa and any six provinces agree on objectives, new programs in fields such as home care or pharmacare can be set up by the federal government as long as each province can work out the details of its own program. If a province already has a program in place that meets the objectives of the policy, it will still receive the federal funds. In other words, the federal government, in effect, allowed provincial constraints on its spending power and in return received provincial acceptance for its willingness to compromise and undertake consultation.[21]

This agreement was applauded by Saskatchewan premier Roy Romanow as "80 per cent of the solution to Canadian unity" and by Ontario premier Mike Harris as capping a "tremendous day."[22] But Québec premier Lucien Bouchard would not sign the agreement, under which, he claimed, "six provinces and the federal government could trigger a new program, define national objectives, devise a framework for accountability, and then Québec, to get compensation for its part of the program, would have to abide by the national objectives."[23] Premier Bouchard asked that Québec be compensated without having to give any commitment to national objectives. It was classic Canadian federalism.

Minister of Finance Paul Martin summarized the government's position:

> *Provinces will now be able to design more innovative social programs that respond to the needs of people today rather than to inflexible rules. However, flexibility does not mean a free-for-all.*[24]

Despite this justification, however, there is little doubt that the Liberal government had decided to loosen its control over provincial transfers in order to reduce the pressure on its finances while also placating nationalist tendencies in Québec (see Figure 6.6). In light of the massive debt and the continuing separatist challenge in Québec, the Liberal government decided to decentralize the country to the largest degree possible without amending the Constitution: one major step was to change the method of distributing federal transfers to the provinces.

Health as *the* Priority, 2004– The twenty-first century has witnessed an explosion in health-care costs. An aging population, new technologies and new demands have driven the costs to new heights. With such large sums of money involved, and the public's desire for even more health-care money, it is not surprising that to a very large extent federal–provincial relations have become heath-care relations. Infectious disease breakouts, such as of severe acute respiratory syndrome (SARS) and avian flu, have only compounded the problem.

CLOSE-UP ON Institutions

FUNDING FOR COLLEGES AND UNIVERSITIES

As of 2004, the federal government began to grant funds to the provinces as part of the Canadian Social Transfer. It continued operating the Millennium Scholarship Fund of up to $3 billion, with money going to students on the basis of both merit and need. The federal government also increased funding for university research with such programs as the Canada Foundation for Innovation, the Canada Research Chairs and the Canadian Institutes of Health Research.

Is this use of federal money in post-secondary education justified, or should it be left to the provinces to decide how to allocate funds in this area? What kind of transfer of money to students would you and your fellow students prefer?

---

21. Jennifer Smith, "Informal Constitutional Development: Change By Other Means," in Herman Bakvis and Grace Skogstad, eds., *Canadian Federalism: Performance, Effectiveness, and Legitimacy* (Don Mills, ON: Oxford University Press, 2002), pp. 50 ff.

22. *MacLean's*, February 15, 1999.

23. Ibid.

24. *Ottawa Citizen*, February 28, 1995.

FIGURE 6.6 **Basic Federal Financing for "Richer" and "Poorer" Provinces before 1996 and Today**

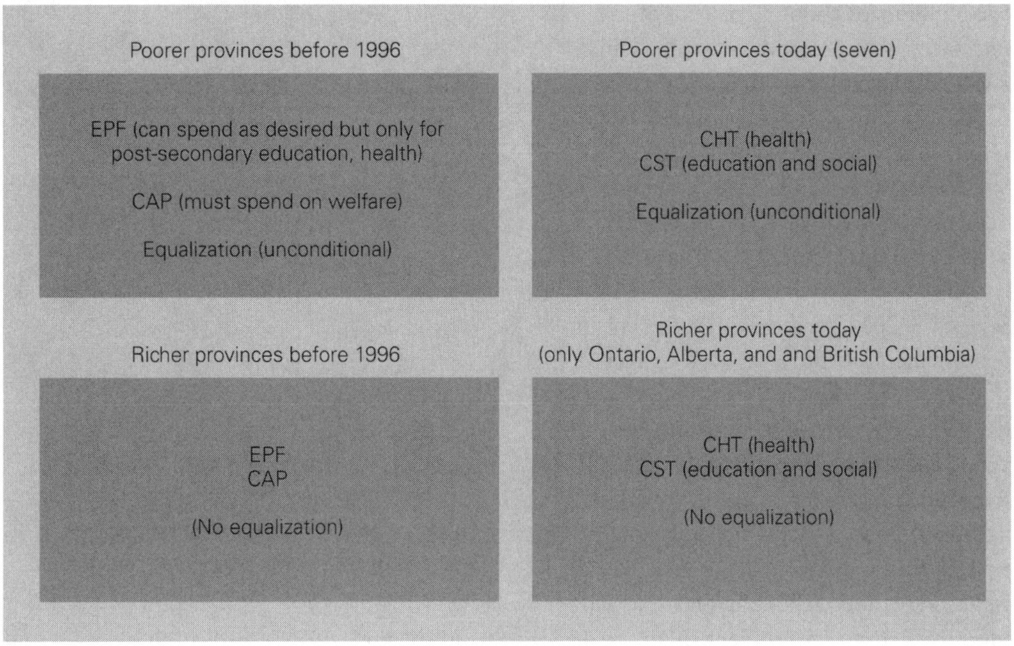

Poorer provinces before 1996

EPF (can spend as desired but only for post-secondary education, health)

CAP (must spend on welfare)

Equalization (unconditional)

Poorer provinces today (seven)

CHT (health)
CST (education and social)

Equalization (unconditional)

Richer provinces before 1996

EPF
CAP

(No equalization)

Richer provinces today
(only Ontario, Alberta, and and British Columbia)

CHT (health)
CST (education and social)

(No equalization)

Source: Department of Finance, Budget 2007, p. 55.

It was the constant squabbling between the federal and provincial governments over heath-care costs and rules that led to the federal Parliament passing the *Canada Health Act* in 1984. The *Canada Health Act* is at the heart of provincial complaints today. It penalizes provinces that do not meet the five conditions in the Act, including accessibility, comprehensiveness, portability, proper administration and universality. Despite the fact that much of the discussion is only public posturing, the provinces maintain that the federal government does not give them enough money for the increased costs of health care and have begun to experiment with forms of private health care. Some provinces have allowed private, for-profit clinics to perform surgical procedures and private health clinics have charged *facility fees*.

> *Physicians of the utmost fame,*
> *Were called at once; but when they came,*
> *They answered, as they took their fees,*
> *"There is no cure for this disease."*
>
> *Hilaire Belloc in* Cautionary Tales

In response to provincial pressures and public clamour for action, the federal government set up a Commission on the Future of Health Care in Canada headed by Roy Romanow, and the Senate completed a major research project on the topic headed by Michael Kirby.[25] Both reports called for an infusion of more federal cash into the programs and for more accountability. Both reports opposed the privatization of health care in the country.

In an effort to end the long-festering issue of health-care funding, the 2003 First Ministers Conference reached an accord on Health Care Renewal. That agreement saw the federal government contribute $34.8 billion for health over the next five years, and a further $2 billion was added in

25. Gerard W. Boychuk, "The Federal Role in Health Care Reform: Legacy or Limbo," in G. Bruce Doern, ed., *How Ottawa Spends 2003–2004*, pp. 89–104 (Toronto: Oxford, 2003).

2004, making the federal contribution $36.8 billion, or about 40 percent of the total of health-care costs in the country. In 2004, the federal government divided the CHST into two parts—the **Canada Health Transfer** (CHT) and the **Canada Social Transfer** (CST)—thus separating health-care costs from those of other social programs.

The policy debate continues. In September 2004, the federal government, ten provinces and three territories agreed to a new ten-year plan to sustain the health-care system. The first ministers agreed to a set of principles including such items as universality, accessibility and portability, but added the notion of jurisdictional flexibility. The primary issues continued to be the amount of

Charest returns from the health-care summit with his loot. Aislin, *The Gazette* (Montreal). Reprinted with permission.

funds the federal government should make available to the provinces; privatization; primary and home care; long waiting times; and prescription drugs. The provinces and territories insisted that there be a significant increase in the amount of money available, and the federal government countered that there had to be commitment to its demands as well.

As part of this new ten-year plan, the federal government agreed to provide an extra $18 billion over the next 6 years in the field of health care and guaranteed a 6 percent annual increase after that until 2015. Not all commentators were pleased with the results. Senator Michael Kirby, for example, said that "what it does is put the patient—the health care system—on life support, but it does not put it on the road to full recovery."[26]

The federal government's demands for national targets on waiting times and an increase in home care were partially met. The first ministers could not agree on a national data collection system, but each jurisdiction agreed to establish comparable indicators and benchmarks for medically accepted wait times, starting with cancer and heart treatments, diagnostic imaging procedures, joint replacements and sight restoration. The ministers also agreed to increase the amount of funds for short-term acute home care, short-term acute community mental health home care and end-of-life care. Lastly, the ministers agreed to establish a task force to report on a national pharmaceutical strategy.

In order to bring Québec on side for the new health care arrangement, the federal government agreed to a side deal with Premier Jean Charest. The written agreement—entitled, "Asymmetrical Federalism that Respects Québec's Jurisdiction"—exempted Québec from some of the promises made by other provinces.[27] Québec promised to reform its own home care services in its own way. It agreed to set its own benchmarks for waiting times, and establish indicators that would be comparable with the other provinces.

This was not the first time that Québec had been allowed to make a special deal with the federal government. For many years, Québec has had a separate pension plan and has been allowed to opt out of some federal–provincial social programs. But this agreement's explicit assertion of

26. *The New York Times*, September 17, 2004.

27. See http://pm.ca/grfx/docs/QuebecENG.pdf.

the principle of "asymmetrical federalism" was unique, and gave a more explicit legitimacy to the practice. Then federal intergovernmental affairs minister, Lucienne Robillard, declared that other provinces could come to a one-to-one agreement with the federal government in the future, and that this offer was not limited to Québec.

Are we at the beginning of a new era in federalism? Is such an explicit acknowledgement of asymmetrical federalism and its flexibility the sign of a new co-operative federal government, the result of a weak minority government in Ottawa, the recognition of past practice or the caving of the federal government to provincial demands? All of these assertions have been made by politicians and commentators since the ten-year health agreement was signed.

Health and Social Programs, 2006– Stephen Harper's government continued the basic framework for the CHT and CST transfer, but made some changes to provide more transparency and predictability in the process. The CST was extended to 2013–14, putting it in line with the long-term plan for equalization, territorial funding and the CHT. The amount of funds given for the various components of CST—namely post-secondary education, social programs and support for children—was segregated to improve transparency. In 2007–08, education received $2.4 billion, social programs got $6.2 billion and support for children was given $850 million. Moreover, as the CHT had already received a commitment of 5 percent annual growth until 2013–14, the CST was given a 3 percent growth assurance until the same date.

As Table 6.3 shows, the funding for all of the federal–provincial programs is now in place until 2014. This indicates an immense federal commitment to provincial/territorial expenditures. In

TABLE 6.3 Total Federal Funding to Provinces and Territories, Budget 2007

	2005–2006	2006–2007	2007–2008	2008–2009	2009–2010	2010–2011	2011–2012	2012–2013	2013–2014
				(millions of dollars)					
Equalization and Territorial Formula Financing									
Equalization	10 900	11 282	12 768	*12 918*	Formula Driven ⟶				
Territorial Formula Financing	2000	2106	2221	*2285*	Formula Driven ⟶				
Total	**12 900**	**13 388**	**14 989**	***15 203***					
Other Support									
Canada Health Transfer	19 000	20 140	21 348	22 629	23 987	25 426	26 952	28 569	30 283
Canada Social Transfer	8 225	8 500	9 737	10 537	10 853	11 179	11 514	11 859	12 215
Labour market training				500	500	500	500	500	500
Infrastructure[1]	3197	3114	4335	4653	5442	5597	5669	5698	5680
Canada ecoTrust for Clean Air and Climate Change[2]			506	506	506				
Total	**30 422**	**31 754**	**35 927**	**38 826**	**41 288**	**42 702**	**44 635**	**46 626**	**48 678**

[1] Includes $33 billion for the long-term plan for infrastructure as well as $4 billion from sunsetting infrastructure initiatives.

[2] Canada ecoTrust for Clean Air and Climate Change notionally allocated over three years.

Source: Adapted from Department of Finance, Budget 2007, p. 39. Reproduced with the permission of the Minister of Public Works and Government Services, 2008.

2008–09, the commitment is for $39 billion of federal tax dollars to be transferred to the provinces and territories. Despite the usual amount of obvious politicking and grandstanding, which included federal efforts to shore up support for Jean Charest in the 2007 Québec provincial election, Ottawa's overall approach to federal–provincial fiscal relations seems reasonable.

Critical Debate
Canada's Federal System, Balanced and Fair?

Does Canada's federal system allocate powers and finances in a balanced and fair way? Given federal–provincial divisions and disputes, can the country act comprehensively to solve its major problems, particularly in fields such as health care and post-secondary education?

⎮ Point

No, it does not. The whole arrangement is mysterious and difficult to understand. In a democracy there needs to be a high degree of openness and transparency. The system is overloaded with overlapping jurisdictions and programs and is unfair to some provinces and territories.

The federal government is much too powerful. By its control of the spending power, it insists on getting its way with provincial premiers who are forced to go along in order to obtain adequate funds for their programs. The system requires the premiers to be beggars at the federal table or to scream like children to the press for not being reasonably treated by the prime minister.

The equalization program is a sham. Even Québec is treated as a "poor" province and gets money from the federal purse. Despite some improvements by the current Conservative government, the funds from conditional programs like the Canada Health Transfer and Social Transfer are still too little to cover the fields of health care and education, and there is no guarantee that Ottawa will not reduce its commitment even further when the economy dips. It did last time. In order to reduce waiting times to see doctors and improve the technology of hospitals, the provinces and territories are being forced to take evasive action in semi-privatizing their health systems.

The rules set by Ottawa in the conditional programs are much too inflexible to run a large and modern country. Decisions are best when they are set by the people affected by them—in other words, by the provinces themselves.

Depending on the political forces of the day, the degree of centralization and decentralization between federal government and provincial/territorial authorities changes. There is no long-term coherence between the requirements of provincial leaders and the fiscal resources made available to them. The amount of funds that they get should be set permanently by the Constitution, as in Germany, not left dependent on the goodwill of the federal government.

Recent problems in waiting times for doctors, inadequate equipment for procedures such as MRIs and slow and poor emergency handling in the SARS and avian flu cases illustrate the need to get a better grip on health-care policy in the future. Funding for post-secondary education is inadequate. These issues cannot and will not be solved under the current federal system of financing.

⎮ Counterpoint

Yes, it is. Rather than being an esoteric topic, federalism is simply a means of dividing political authority. There is nothing intrinsically good or bad about this constitutional arrangement, but in Canada it works fairly well.

It is true that a review of the history of federalism in Canada reveals pendulum swings of centralization and decentralization. These shifts were due to judicial interpretations of the Constitution as well as to the impact of particular individuals and historical events. The best-known Father of Confederation, Conservative Prime Minister Sir John A. Macdonald, thought of federalism as a means for subordinating provincial governments in the political system. His argument has been called a "quasi-federalist" position. Others have interpreted federalism as an agreement or "compact" between the English and French.

Sometimes, federalism has been described as a clear-cut or "classical" division of powers between the federal and provincial governments. However, over time, the original financial and legislative powers have had to be changed—on occasion radically and for the better. Adjustments to harsh economic reality (such as the Great Depression and two World Wars) and societal concerns forced the constitutional system to move from a strict separation of powers to a more "co-operative" system. Some authors have even characterized the federal system as one of federal–provincial "diplomacy" rather than "co-operation" to indicate how the process has evolved and how much the provinces have been asserting their power in the state. In recent years, unfortunately, we have moved to a period of *contested federalism* that has frustrated many Canadians, but this can be overcome with co-operative leadership from Ottawa and the provincial and territorial capitals.

The federal dimension provides advantages to Canada. It helps create similar living standards across the country, providing relatively similar health, education and social policies to all Canadian citizens. It redistributes funds from richer to poorer provinces in order to provide horizontal equality across the country. It decentralizes some decision-making and allows a degree of cultural and linguistic autonomy. But it may give too much clout to either the federal or the provincial governments. In the former case, there can be an erosion of provincial prerogatives, as when the federal government is required to aid the provinces in new, but essentially localized, matters. On the other hand, too much provincial control may make it difficult to handle countrywide problems.

Despite a few difficult periods, federalism in Canada has proven remarkably resilient and adaptable. A degree of movement along the centralization–decentralization continuum is to be expected and is not in itself a matter for much concern. However, Québec and, to some extent the West, continue for quite different reasons to seek changes in the present relationship. The possibility that Québec may eventually break away from the federal union is not to be dismissed. Neither should feelings of alienation in Western or Atlantic Canada be ignored. The problem, as suggested, is not so much with federalism as it is with the deep cleavages and divisions in our society.

In the search for a creative compromise, politicians will have to enunciate and examine Canada's fundamental problems. Any redefinition of federal arrangements must rest between national and provincial aspirations. Reconciliation must be built on recognition that Canada has two linguistic groups and several cultures that are often in conflict, as well as heterogeneous socio-economic regions. The first fact demands constitutional and institutional guarantees; the second, a proper division of the public purse and power. While provincial distinctiveness is the fundamental reason for all federal systems, a sense of positive consensus among the different regional groups is also imperative if Canadian unity is to endure.

Discussion Questions

1. What is your stand on the Critical Debate and what can you add to it?
2. Describe the basic federal–provincial distribution of powers in the Constitution and assess how court interpretations of it have changed from Confederation to today in terms of centralization and decentralization.

3. What are the key mechanisms for redistributing federal tax dollars to the provinces? How were they changed in 1996, 2004 and 2007?

4. Compare the concept of *contested federalism* to the idea of "rebalancing" the Constitution that is often debated by both federal and provincial politicians.

5. Did the Liberal governments of Jean Chrétien and Paul Martin loosen their control over spending power in order to meet the challenge of a massive federal debt or to placate Québec separatists? How has Stephen Harper changed the central government's approach to federalism?

Visit our new Companion Website at **www.pearsoned.ca/jackson**, where you can use the interactive Study Guide and link to additional resources on topics discussed in the text.

Selected Bibliography

Bakvis, Herman, and Grace Skogstad, eds. *Canadian Federalism: Performance, Effectiveness and Legitimacy*, 2nd ed. Don Mills, ON: Oxford University Press, 2008.

Bothwell, Robert. *Canada and Quebec: One Country, Two Histories*, rev. ed. Vancouver: UBC Press, 1998.

Burgess, Michael. *Comparative Federalism: Theory and Practice*. London: Routledge, 2006.

Gillespie, W. Irwin. *Tax, Borrow and Spend: Financing Federal Spending in Canada*. Ottawa: Carleton University Press, 1991.

Howlett, Michael, and David Laycock. *The Puzzles of Power*. Mississauga, ON: Copp Clark Pitman, 1994.

Hueglin, Thomas O., and Alan Fenna. *Comparative Federalism: A Systematic Enquiry*. Peterborough, ON: Broadview Press, 2006.

Lazar, Harvey, ed. *Canada: The State of the Federation 1997: Non-Constitutional Renewal*. Kingston: Institute of Intergovernmental Relations, 1998.

McBride, Stephen. *Paradigm Shift: Globalization and the Canadian State*. Halifax: Fernwood, 2001.

Murphy, Michael, ed. *Quebec and Canada in the New Century: New Dynamics, New Opportunities*. Montréal: McGill-Queen's University Press, 2007. (Part of a series entitled, "Canada: The State of the Federation, 2005.")

Peach, Ian, ed. *Constructing Tomorrow's Federalism: New Perspectives on Canadian Governance*. Winnipeg, MB: University of Manitoba Press, 2007.

Rocher, François, and Miriam Smith, eds. *New Trends in Canadian Federalism*. Peterborough, ON: Broadview Press, 1994.

Simeon, Richard. *Political Science and Federalism: Seven Decades of Scholarly Engagement*. Kingston: Institute of Intergovernmental Relations, 2002.

Stevenson, Garth. *Federalism in Canada*. Toronto: McClelland & Stewart, 1990.

——————. *Unfulfilled Union: Canadian Federalism and National Unity*, 4th ed. Montréal: McGill-Queen's University Press, 2004.

Swinton, Katherine. *The Supreme Court and Canadian Federalism*. Toronto: Carswell, 1990.

Tomblin, Stephen G. *Ottawa and the Outer Provinces: The Challenge of Regional Integration in Canada*. Toronto: Lorimer, 1995.

Vipond, Robert C. *Liberty and Community: Canadian Federalism and the Failure of the Constitution*. Albany, NY: State University of New York Press, 1991.

Watts, Ronald L. *The Spending Power in Federal Systems: A Comparative Study*. Montréal: McGill-Queen's University Press, 1999.

Westmacott, Martin, and Hugh Mellon, eds. *Challenges to Canadian Federalism*. Scarborough, ON: Prentice Hall, 1998.

Chapter 7

The Magic of Nationalism and the Lure of Regionalism

Québec, Native Peoples, the West and the Rest

We have seen how questions about the authority and jurisdictions of the federal and provincial governments regularly give rise to political conflict in Canada. The most divisive of these issues have been over nationalism and regionalism. The Canadian federal structure has been remarkably resilient in meeting its various challenges since Confederation in 1867, but powerful pressures concerning the rights and privileges of certain groups have always had considerable influence on the political agenda.

Since the 1960s, Québec nationalists have developed strategies to achieve separation from, or sovereignty-association with, Canada, creating the most serious challenge that the country has ever endured. Their challenge culminated in 1995 with a claim that federalism was obsolete and incompatible with the aspirations of their society, creating a "crisis of Canadian federalism" that nearly destroyed the country. Meanwhile, Native peoples, who had previously been in large measures without organization and leadership, consolidated their various groupings, aired their grievances and successfully pressured governments about their concerns, particularly their claims for land and self-government.

Other pressures, often economic in nature, have regularly arisen because of strong regional dissatisfactions in Western Canada in particular, but also in the Atlantic region. In the 1980s, for example, both regions fought against federal control of local resources, the West because of oil and natural gas, the Atlantic provinces because of offshore petroleum. In both regions, the grievances tend to centre on perceived federal injustices and inadequate governmental responses to local concerns, as when the Atlantic provinces complained that the federal government did little to protect Atlantic fish stocks from foreign overfishing, or when Western grain farmers fought federal freight rates. Occasionally the conflicts are between regions, as with the clash between Québec and Newfoundland over the Churchill Falls hydroelectric project in Labrador. These regional pressures have never threatened the imminent destruction of the country as Québec separatism did in 1995, but they have been unrelenting and constitute a serious, ongoing challenge to federalism in Canada.

This chapter therefore has three parts. Following a general discussion and definition of the concept of nationalism, the first part examines nationalism in Québec. It focuses on the development of the separatist movement, including the 1995 referendum, the Supreme Court judgment on separatism, the resultant federal and provincial legislation and the repercussions for Canada–Québec relations today. The language of separatism has changed over time, but the concept is very much alive. The second part of this chapter is concerned with the background and contemporary significance of what is sometimes referred to as *Native nationalism*. It examines the grievances and the political issues involved in settling Native land claims and demands for self-government. The third section begins with a discussion and a definition of *regionalism* and then considers its political ramifications in Western Canada.

The Critical Debate that threads through this chapter concerns both nationalism and regionalism and the challenges each presents to the federal status quo. Are separatism and regionalism justifiable positions in Canada? What should the federal response be to these vital, divisive issues?

What is Nationalism?

Nations, National Identity and Nationalism

Recall that internal and external impediments to state-building in Canada were discussed in Chapter 2. The theme was pursued further in Chapters 3 and 4 when we examined the strengths and weaknesses in Canada's political culture—the overarching values, symbols, attitudes and behaviour that form the basis of the Canadian state. We also considered the ethno-linguistic and regional subcultures that are part of the overall Canadian culture and saw how the government promotes Canadian identity in various ways in an attempt to build strong feelings that help subsume and temper the aspirations of regional and ethno-linguistic groups within the country. Most Canadians have warm feelings about their country—they are proud of a great many of its features, and they like to identify themselves as Canadians. However, Canadian national identity has not been strong enough to subsume and temper the aspirations of Québec nationalists, some Native peoples and disgruntled regionalists.

The term **national identity** tends to be associated with states. As a state, Canada has a degree of national identity, although, as we have seen, it is somewhat fragile. Recall that there are several components of a strong national identity: emotional attachment to the geographic territory; a common past with heroes and myths; special kinship through a common language; a unique culture with shared values; and a common literature and history that generates pride in traditions and customs, and creates a sense of familiarity and belonging.

It is important now to distinguish the concept of *nation* from that of *state*. The two are not used synonymously in political science. As we learned in Chapter 3, English-speaking Canadians commonly use the word *nation* loosely to mean the same thing as *country*, while francophone Québeckers see Canada as two distinct societies or nations. Recall from Chapter 1 that we define a **nation** as a politically conscious and mobilized ethnic group (usually with a clear sense of territory) that *may* possess or aspire to autonomy, self-government or independent statehood. According to this definition, Canada is a state, but it is not a single nation. A **state** is a form of political organization in which governmental institutions are capable of maintaining order and implementing rules or laws over a given population and within a given territory.

When a nation acts within a state to achieve separatist aspirations, we refer to this behaviour as nationalism. Thus, **nationalism** is defined as the collective action of a politically conscious ethnic group (or nation) in pursuit of increased territorial autonomy or sovereignty. In common usage, the word *nationalism* is generally used to mean "love of country." In this sense, Canada as a whole may exhibit aspects of nationalism, particularly when it is under threat. However, to distinguish and clarify the phenomenon, in this section we follow the scholarly tradition of using nationalism to refer to the collective action of ethnic groups in search of a new state.

Disputes about nationalism abound. Some see it as anti-colonialism, and believe it is fundamentally different in established states than in developing countries. Others contend that nationalism can appear only in modern, developed political systems and that it is a product of modernity that arrived with the industrial revolution in Europe.

Although there is an ethnic component to nationalism, clearly not all ethnic interest groups or nations are nationalistic. Many ethnic demands, such as those for minority-language education or ethnically oriented television programs, involve no challenge to the integrity of the existing state. Most authors, however, contend that nationalism is closely associated with ethnicity. Some even see it as the political manifestation of ethnicity.[1]

Theorists attempt to determine the causes of nationalism and, on occasion, its consequences. There are myriad theories about this topic. We conclude from the literature that several factors are generally thought to give rise to nationalism. Clearly, ethnicity alone is not nationalism and regionalism is not nationalism—although the two may coincide. Nationalist movements encompass at least the following features:

- common ethnicity
- common grievance or threat
- common territory
- leadership
- great emotional intensity
- common goal (usually for a separate state)

Québec can be said to have nationalism because the separatist movement there embodies all six of these factors. The term is less accurate for Native peoples. It can be argued that although the various First Nations have strong emotional attachments to traditional territories they tend to be fragmented and dispersed, lacking territorial affinity and common objectives. Almost without exception they wish to remain Canadians with the full protections of the Canadian Constitution and as a group they do not seek to gain the status of an independent state. However, they do share a common Aboriginal identity, and some groups, like the Inuit and the Cree, do have common territory. Part of their grievance against the state is that they want (or have wanted) their territorial claims resolved. Native peoples may also have common goals of self-government. In this latter sense they, too, can be considered to constitute a nationalist movement.

Regionalism, on the other hand, is not nationalism, because while people in a region may have some cultural affinity as a subculture, and share some grievances against the state, they do not have the underpinning of ethnicity that provides the enduring emotional intensity needed for nationalism.

Nationalism has appeared in diverse forms in many different states over the centuries. It has been used to justify economic expansionism, protectionism and imperialism. As an ideology it has been employed to espouse the supremacy of particular nations or peoples; it has justified quests for emancipation from colonial rule; and it has been an integrative force in newly independent multiracial or tribal societies in the developing world.[2] It has also been savagely attacked.

> *[Nationalism is] an infantile sickness . . . the measles of the human race.*
>
> *Albert Einstein*

Nationalism can be a divisive force. Territorially concentrated ethnic minorities that are the subjects of a larger state sometimes seek increased self-determination, or even total independence.

---

1. There are many interpretations of nationalism. See A.D. Smith, *Theories of Nationalism* (Oxford, UK: Oxford University Press, 1994); A.D. Smith, *Ethnicity and Nationalism* (Leiden, the Netherlands: Brill, 1992); the classic by Hans Kohn, *The Idea of Nationalism: A Study of Its Origins and Background* (New York: Macmillan, 1944); and Liah Greenfeld, *Five Roads to Modernity* (Cambridge, MA: Harvard University Press, 1992).

2. On the types of nationalism, see Anthony D. Smith, *Nationalism in the Twentieth Century* (Oxford, UK: Martin Robertson, 1979). On the "new" nationalism, see Michael Ignatieff, *Blood and Belonging: Journeys into the New Nationalism* (Toronto: Viking, 1993).

The breakdown of the former Yugoslavia into multiple republics and the subsequent violent fragmentation of two of them, Bosnia and Kosovo, is an example of divisive nationalism.

There are examples of contemporary nationalist movements in many advanced industrial societies: among the Scots and Welsh in the United Kingdom; the Bretons and Corsicans in France; the Flemings and Walloons in Belgium; and, of course, the Québécois in Canada. In each case, ethnic minorities have reduced any previous commitment they may have had to the larger state and acted collectively to develop political parties, nationalist and cultural organizations, and sometimes even terrorist groups in order to pursue fundamental changes in the territorial boundaries and sovereignty of the state.

Ethnic nationalist groups in Canada, especially in Québec, have pursued varying degrees of autonomy, up to and including independent statehood. In particular, they have utilized the mechanisms of federalism to challenge the federal status quo. Throughout Canadian history, provincial government power has been used to press ethnic nationalist and regionalist demands on Ottawa.

> *If every ethnic, religious or linguistic group claimed statehood, there would be no limit to fragmentation; and peace, security and well-being for all would become even more difficult to achieve.*
>
> **Boutros Boutros-Ghali, former secretary-general of the United Nations**

Nationalism in Québec

Roots of Nationalism: Early French–English Conflicts

After Confederation, the English minority within Québec dominated urban, political and economic life. By then, the French were a minority in Canada. Most francophones were in Québec, but there were pockets of French-speaking people in Ontario and what were to become the Maritimes and the West.

The Manitoba Schools Question and Louis Riel   French–English conflicts erupted periodically after Confederation, mainly over linguistic and education rights. One of the first disputes was in Manitoba. With its large French-speaking community, Manitoba was created in 1870 on the same basis as Québec, with rights to Roman Catholic schools and bilingual education. By 1885, however, French-speaking Métis in the West were being swamped by English-speaking settlers. To protest land losses, they rallied around Métis leader Louis Riel, who had returned from exile in the United States to lead a rebellion against the government.

English Canadians saw Riel as a traitor or a madman and sent troops to quell the disturbance. Riel was defeated and executed. French Canadians grieved for Riel as a patriot who died in the struggle to preserve the "Frenchness" of his people. Manitoba's ethnic groups were thus polarized, and the stage was set for the restriction of French-language rights there. Only five years after the Riel Rebellion, the government of Manitoba established a completely non-sectarian educational system in which Roman Catholic schools no longer received provincial aid and French could no longer be used in the secondary schools. Francophones were outraged.

Two decisions of the British Judicial Committee of the Privy Council (JCPC) upheld the validity of the Manitoba law, but affirmed the power of the federal government to restore school privileges. This unique situation posed a problem for French Canadians inasmuch as it divided them over whether to support their provincial politicians (who were against the principle of federal veto power) or their church (who wanted Roman Catholic schools in Manitoba). Québeckers wanted the legislation removed, but to defeat it they had to support a "federal disallowance" of provincial legislation, even though they were against the principle of federal veto power.

The faltering federal Conservative government introduced remedial legislation in 1896, but then withdrew it under pressure. A bizarre general election ensued in which *Manitoba* francophones supported the Roman Catholic Church and the federal Conservative party in demanding federal disallowance of the Manitoba law, while *Québec* francophones supported the Liberal party, which argued for provincial autonomy and opposed the federal use of the disallowance power. Ironically, the Liberals were also supported by anti-French, anti-Catholic forces. The Liberals won in 1896, and thus Québec francophones were instrumental in blocking legislation that would have protected French Canadian interests in Manitoba.

The Erosion of French-Language Rights outside Québec   We noted in Chapter 5 that the Confederation arrangement allowed all provinces to legislate in the field of education. It also gave constitutional protection to both the English and French language in the federal Parliament and the legislature of Québec. In the other provinces, however, there was no such protection. The practice until the 1940s was for English-speaking Canadians, wherever they were in the majority, to deprive French-speaking minorities of public school facilities in their native language and to refuse them the use of their language in government institutions. Even within the federal government, where the *BNA Act* had affirmed the right of both groups to communicate in their own languages in debates, records, journals and courts, most government employees were unilingual English.

In 1935, French Canadian historian Abbé Lionel Groulx published the following historical summary of French-language and school rights (or lack of rights) *outside* Québec:

- 1864, Nova Scotia: French-speaking Catholic Acadians are forbidden to have French schools
- New Brunswick: Catholic schools are closed and teaching of French (and in French) is forbidden in public schools
- Prince Edward Island: Catholic and French schools are outlawed
- Manitoba: Separate (Catholic) schools are outlawed and teaching of French (and in French) is forbidden at the secondary level
- Northwest Territories (including what is now Alberta and Saskatchewan): Teaching in French is outlawed in public schools and Catholic schools are prohibited
- Alberta and Saskatchewan: The regulations of 1892 (Northwest Territories) are confirmed
- Ontario: By regulation (Regulation No. 17), French is outlawed in Ontario schools
- Manitoba: Teaching French is forbidden at all levels
- Saskatchewan: Teaching French is prohibited even outside school hours[3]

Abbé Groulx argued that each of these rulings deprived French Canadians of their basic human rights. In combination they formed the history of the loss of French rights outside of Québec. The result was the eventual abandonment by francophone Québeckers of French Canadians outside their province, and the gradual assertion of Québec nationalism.

Conscription   Ethnic division appeared in another guise in the conscription crises of both the First and Second World Wars. The 1917 federal election was fought on the conscription issue. The governing Conservatives united with English-speaking Liberals to run Union candidates in the election. They won, but they captured only three seats in Québec. The election divided the country along ethnic and linguistic lines; every riding in which French was the majority language voted against the Unionist government and its policy of conscription. Fortunately, the war ended before conscription could be enacted and, therefore, the crisis between English and French subsided.

However, the repercussions for the Conservative Party, which was the dominant partner in the Unionist government and had argued strongly for conscription, were severe. In the first post-war

---

3. André Bernard, *What Does Quebec Want?* (Toronto: Lorimer, 1978), p. 27, taken from Abbé Lionel Groulx, *L'enseignement français au Canada* (Montréal: Granger Frères, 1935).

election, in 1921, the Conservatives lost *all* their Québec seats to the Liberals. Provincially, as well, the Conservatives were severely defeated. Except for the Diefenbaker sweep in 1958, the Conservative party did not regain the confidence of French Canadians until the Mulroney victory of 1984.

In 1942, during the Second World War, the conscription issue arose again and this time the federal government called a *referendum*. The campaign was bitter. French-speaking Québec voted against conscription by a huge majority, while English-speaking Canada was overwhelmingly in favour. Overall, 65 percent of Canadians favoured conscription (see Chapter 12). Prime Minister Mackenzie King postponed the imposition of conscription, and the delay minimized the crisis because, once again, the war ended before conscripts were sent into battle. However, the humiliating helplessness of the French in the face of an English-majority decision on a topic of life or death was fuel for Québec nationalism.

Modern Nationalism in Québec

After Confederation, two strains of nationalism developed in Québec. The first, advanced by Abbé Lionel Groulx, called for a rural vision of Catholic and anti-materialist values, and, on occasion, led to proposals for an inward-looking, corporatist and authoritarian solution to the Québec situation. The second, led by Henri Bourassa, politician and editor of *Le Devoir*, called for a pan-Canadian vision and an equal partnership between English and French Canada. For Bourassa, the Canadian dilemma could be resolved by building a bicultural and bilingual state.

The inward-looking strain of Québec nationalism was characterized by the Union Nationale governments of Maurice Duplessis, 1936–39 and 1944–60. The rural-based Union Nationale espoused old-style nationalism buttressed by patronage and intimidation. It was successful until the 1949 Asbestos strike, which lasted four months and allied the US-owned asbestos company and the Duplessis government against the workers, who were supported to a large extent by Québec's developing intelligentsia. In the late 1950s and 1960s a fundamental change became apparent in the aspirations of Québec francophones. What began as a "Quiet Revolution" eventually became an outright challenge to Canadian federalism and the very existence of the Canadian state. Québec changed dramatically. The era saw widespread rejection of both clerical influence and Duplessis manipulation. Values changed dramatically from rural to urban and from religious to secular. Industrialization and urbanization eroded Union Nationale support.

The new, outward-looking strain of nationalism was typified by the Québec Liberal Party, which Jean Lesage led to victory in 1960. Lesage's Liberals reversed the philosophy of previous governments in Québec. As well as preserving the *patrimoine* (the language, religion and culture of a traditional Québec), they also defended *la nation* in terms of the economy and social structure of the province. The new government dramatically increased the role of government in society; it secularized the school system, nationalized hydroelectricity and reformed the civil service.

Led by a new middle class, French Canadian nationalism gave way to Québec nationalism. Nationalists were appalled that the use of the French language was on the decline in Canada and that Québec's share of the Canadian population was dropping. The *épanouissement*, or flowering, of Québec-based nationalism was encapsulated in the 1960 political phrase *maîtres chez nous* (masters in our own house). A state-centred nationalism complemented and to some extent replaced the traditional nationalism.

Québec's new challenge to Canada came in many guises—judicial, social and political. Objections ranged from attacks on specific centralizing mechanisms, such as the constitutional power of disallowance, to general claims that the *BNA Act* did not define a true federal system. Some Québec francophones thought the federal union lacked the free consent of the contracting parties—in other words, it did not provide a basis for the right of self-determination. Others were federalists who objected to what they perceived as economic injustice (including Léon Dion, current federal Liberal leader Stéphane Dion's father, who was a respected but frustrated federalist and Québec nationalist).

Québec increased political pressure on the federal government throughout the 1960s. Some French Canadians took up separatism for Québec as their goal, maintaining that only with their own government could they fulfill the aspirations of their community. Their slogan, *Vive le Québec libre*, gained international credibility following a supportive declaration by visiting French president Charles de Gaulle in 1967. Nationalists criticized the use of English in the private sector, in banks and the federal public service as well as the economic domination of anglophones.

The Front de la Libération du Québec (FLQ) represented the most extreme separatists. The group initiated terrorist activities, which culminated in the October Crisis of 1970, in which a British diplomat was kidnapped and the Québec minister of labour, Pierre Laporte, was kidnapped and murdered. The *War Measures Act* was invoked by the federal government to deal with the events—the first and only time that the Act has been invoked in peacetime. The basic freedoms of many Canadians, mostly French-speaking, were infringed upon. Hundreds of Québeckers were arrested. When the crisis atmosphere faded, many Canadians were uncertain as to whether such large-scale repression had been warranted.[4]

As Québec nationalism grew in the 1960s and 1970s, Québec intellectuals became increasingly divided. Pierre Elliott Trudeau and his friends Jean Marchand and Gérard Pelletier entered federal politics, where they offered the vision of a bicultural and bilingual federal state, but with no special status for Québec. Later, as prime minister, Trudeau became the major spokesman for Henri Bourassa–style nationalism.

Separatist Parties in Québec   There have been four "successful" nationalist parties in Québec, not counting the current Action démocratique du Québec (ADQ), which is "autonomist." The first, the Parti Patriote, led by Louis-Joseph Papineau, was elected with a large majority in the early nineteenth century. In an attempt to win parliamentary control over government expenditures and other concessions, the party instigated an armed rebellion in 1836–37. The British quelled it.

The second nationalist party, the Parti Nationale led by Honoré Mercier, was elected in 1886 but defeated in 1892 because of financial problems, corruption and lack of support for constitutional change. In 1936, the Union Nationale, led by Maurice Duplessis, came into office and remained relatively strong until 1960. Finally, René Lévesque formed the Parti Québécois (PQ) in 1968, bringing nationalists together under a new umbrella organization.

After two electoral defeats, the Parti Québécois softened its stance from outright independence to **sovereignty-association**—political independence but with economic association, to reassure those who were apprehensive about the economic consequences of separation. The party also promoted its vision of a Québec in which no taxes would be paid to Ottawa and citizens would be subject to no federal law. During the 1976 election, Lévesque proposed two referendums: one on the right to negotiate sovereignty-association, and a second for Québeckers to ratify the eventual results of the negotiations. This approach worked.[5] The PQ became the fourth nationalist party to gain control of the government in Québec. The party's demand for separation (which had negative connotations) changed to sovereignty (which had positive connotations).

In 1994, a young Québécois, Mario Dumont, was elected to the Québec National Assembly as founder of a new party, the Action démocratique du Québec (ADQ). The party was initially

---

4. See Denis Smith, *Bleeding Hearts . . . Bleeding Country: Canada and the Québec Crisis* (Edmonton: Hurtig, 1971).

5. For a summary, see William Coleman, *The Independence Movement in Québec 1945–1980* (Toronto: University of Toronto Press, 1984).

sovereignist, but in the 2007 Québec election, Dumont called instead for a politically and financially autonomous Québec within Canada. His party came second in the election, ahead of the PQ. Although Dumont says he is no longer a sovereignist, it is not clear how the new term *autonomist* means anything different. A dictionary definition of *autonomist* is "possessed of autonomy, self-governing, independent." This is difficult indeed to distinguish from the goals of outright sovereignists or separatists. The confusion grows, as all the other Québec parties have followed suit and now call themselves autonomist.

As language policy is one of the most controversial social policies in Canada and the focus of considerable ethnic nationalism in Québec, any discussion of the development of Québec nationalism must include an overview of the language issues.

Language Issues   Canada's Confederation arrangement was essentially a bargain between the French and English in British North America to create one strong political unit that would protect the rights and assist the advancement of two culturally diverse peoples. On this basis, linguistic duality was embedded in the *British North America Act* of 1867. Linguistic duality has had both positive and negative repercussions. For decades it has evoked divisive social and political tensions between French- and English-speaking Canadians. At the same time, however, it has been one of Canada's most distinctive constitutional traits and, for many, has enriched the experience of being Canadian.

The legal basis for language regulation in Canada is found in three jurisdictions: (a) the Constitution; (b) federal law; and (c) provincial law.

a) The Constitution establishes the framework for rules about language usage and development. In 1867, the *BNA Act* specified that the federal Parliament and the Québec National Assembly were to function in French and English. Much later, in 1982, the *Charter of Rights and Freedoms* enshrined English and French as the two official languages of Canada for matters pertaining to federal institutions. Minority-language rights were enshrined in section 23 of the Charter, which stipulates that citizens of Canada whose first language is that of the French or English minority of the province in which they reside, or who have received their instruction in one of these languages in Canada, have the right to have their children educated in that language wherever numbers warrant. To amend the minority-language guarantees in the Constitution, all ten provinces and the federal Parliament must agree.[6]

b) Within the parameters established by the Constitution, the federal government creates language policies within its jurisdiction. In 1963, the federal Liberal government declared Canadian federal institutions to be officially bilingual. This was accomplished in the *Official Languages Act of 1969*. Updated and amended in 1988, it has two parts: it regulates bilingualism in federal organizations and federally regulated institutions such as banks and airlines; and it provides a framework for promoting the two official languages. For example, it gives Canadians the right to be served by federal institutions in the official language of their choice where "significant demand" exists; it allows federal employees the right to work in the official language of their choice; and it requires an equitable distribution of English and French Canadians in the public service.

c) Provincial assemblies, too, can pass legislation on language policies. As we have seen, historically such legislation has often been restrictive and controversial. In Québec, the provincial government maintains an Office de la Langue Française, which enforces the *Charte de la Langue Française*. This Charter makes French the official language of the province and the normal language of communications, business and the workplace generally.

---

6. Governments cannot use the notwithstanding clause to deny these Charter guarantees. In early 1993, Parliament and the New Brunswick legislature passed a constitutional amendment guaranteeing equal status for New Brunswick's French- and English-language communities. (See Chapter 5 of this text.)

TABLE 7.1 Percentage Population of Québec by First Language, 1971–2006

	First Language			
	Anglophone	**Francophone**	**Allophone**	
	%	**%**	**%**	**Total**
1971	13.1	80.7	6.2	100
1981	10.9	82.5	6.6	100
1991	9.2	82.0	8.8	100
1996	8.8	81.5	9.7	100
2001	8.3	81.4	10.3	100
2006	8.2	79.6	12.2	100

Note: Over the years, the formulas for determining mother tongue had varied based on single and multiple responses, but data is approximately comparable.

Source: Statistics Canada census data, various years.

The 1982 *Charter of Rights and Freedoms* expanded the basis for legal challenges by aggrieved minorities on constitutional grounds. Since it came into effect, many cases have been brought to the Supreme Court to challenge provincial governments and force them to accommodate language minorities in their laws and schools.

Because language is such a vital part of French culture, language policy permeates politics in Québec. The widespread fear that French language and culture are in decline in Canada, or may soon be, is used by Québec sovereignists to rally support. Québec's fertility rate is lower than that for Canada as a whole, which, as noted, is not adequate to sustain the current population level. Québec, therefore, sees a need to attract, hold and integrate immigrants into the French culture and language (see Table 7.1).

Canada's francophone population is increasingly concentrated in Québec. The percentage of Canadians with French as their first language began to drop in 1951. At that time, the French-language group accounted for 29 percent of the total population, compared to only about 22.1 percent by 2006. About 85 percent of Canada's French-speaking population lives in Québec.

The 2006 Census describes the situation of the francophone population in Canada:

- The proportion of francophones in Québec has changed little over the century. In 1900, 83 percent of the province's population spoke French; in 2006, 79.6 percent declared French as their mother tongue, and 81.8 said they spoke French at home.
- The English-speaking community in Québec dropped from 24 percent at the time of Confederation to 16 percent in 1970, and then to 8.2 percent in 2006. For the first time in 3 decades, it increased by nearly 3 percent between 2001 and 2006. There are more allophones (people whose first language is neither French nor English) in Québec than anglophones—12.2 percent. Table 7.1 shows the percentage of English, French and allophone residents in Québec at the time of the last six censuses.
- The English in Québec are learning more French than previously and so are new immigrants to the province. Québec's requirement for immigrant children to go to French schools has increased the assimilation rate of these children into French.
- In most other provinces, however, the proportion of francophones continues to decline because of the high rate of assimilation. For Canada, including Québec, mother tongue percentages are English, 57.8; French, 22.1 and other, 20.1 (see Table 7.2).

A 1999 study by the Québec Conseil Supérieur de la Langue Française concluded that the French language was entering a period of slow but steady decline in Canada. Higher Asian immigration

TABLE 7.2 **Mother Tongue in Québec and All of Canada (percentages), 2006 Census**

	Mother Tongue		
	English	French	Other
Québec	8.2	79.6	12.2
Canada	57.8	22.1	20.1

Source: 2006 Census: *The Evolving Linguistic Portrait,* available at http://12.statcan.ca/english/census06/analysis/language/highlights.cfm.

and growing numbers of allophones in Québec indicated that Chinese would soon be spoken more than French in English-speaking Canada and French would continue its slow decline in Québec.[7] Its forecast was sound. Since Québec's population is growing more slowly than the national average, its demographic weight within Canada (mother tongue) is likely to decline below its 22.1 percent in 2006. Given these trends, Canadians should expect Québec francophones to continue or even to increase their struggle to preserve the pre-eminence of the French language and culture within their province.

Language Law in Québec In the 1960s, motivated by the demographic concerns described above, Québec authorities began to assert and protect the province's distinctive character (see Table 7.3). A spiral of restrictive language laws began with an attempt to force immigrants to have their children educated in French. The result has been a roller coaster of laws and appeals accompanied by raging debates about "language police" and such topics as whether fast food outlets should be called "Kentucky Fried Chicken" or "Poulet Frit Kentucky."

In 1977, the new Parti Québécois government introduced Bill 101 as the *Charter of the French Language in Québec*. It was much stronger in its promotion of French than the previous Bill 22 had been, and it circumscribed the use of English. For example, it restricted access to English schools. Regardless of where a child came from—even from another province within Canada—he or she had to be educated in French unless one of the parents had been educated in an English school *in* Québec. The law also made French the language of commerce and business. Any company with more than fifty employees was instructed to conduct all internal business in French. Furthermore, English, or even bilingual, commercial signs were made illegal by 1981. Towns, rivers and mountains that bore English names were to be renamed in French.

After the federal government patriated the Constitution in 1982 without Québec's approval, the angry provincial government passed Bill 62 to ensure that Québeckers' fundamental freedoms and legal and equality rights would be subject only to the provincial charter of human rights, not to its new federal counterpart. The Québec government stated that it would append a new clause to each Québec law stating that all legislation would operate "notwithstanding" the provisions of the new *Charter of Rights and Freedoms*. The notwithstanding clause allows infringing legislation relative to some rights in the Charter but not minority language rights. To bypass this obstacle, Québec relied on section 1 of the Constitution, which states that the federal Charter guarantees the liberties it sets out "subject only to such reasonable limits prescribed by law as can be demonstrably justified in a free and democratic society."

The Québec government hoped to prove in court that Bill 101's provisions could be justified on these grounds. However, in 1985 the Supreme Court ruled that the section of Bill 101 limiting eligibility to attend English-language schools to children who had at least one parent who had received primary education in English in Québec was "incompatible" with the constitutional guarantees set out in the Charter.

7. Conclusion of a study by the Conseil de la language française, *The Globe and Mail,* October 28, 1999.

TABLE 7.3 **Language Policy in Québec, 1968–2008**

1968	Catholic school board of St. Léonard attempts to coerce allophone children to attend French-language schools
1969	Québec's Union Nationale government responds: Bill 63 allows parents in Québec to educate children in language of choice
1970	Union Nationale defeated by Robert Bourassa's Liberal party
1974	Bill 22 replaces Bill 63; French is given primacy in the workplace, but linguistic dualism is preserved in several areas; children of immigrants must be enrolled in French schools, except children who demonstrate sufficient knowledge of English
1977	Bill 101, *Charter of the French Language*, declares French the official language of Québec, promotes French much more than Bill 22 and restricts use of English; it further restricts access to English schools and takes measures to make French the language of commerce and business in Québec
1982	*Charter of Rights and Freedoms* is passed with the *Canada Act, 1982*
1982	Bill 62 comes into effect; a new clause is to be appended to each Québec law stating it will operate "notwithstanding" the provision of the federal Constitution
1984	Bill 57 is incorporated into the *Charter of the French Language*, providing guarantees for the survival of English institutions and modifying certain language requirements for businesses
1985	Supreme Court rejects Québec's 1982 argument over Bill 101 and declares sections are incompatible with the *Canadian Charter of Rights and Freedoms*
1987	Québec Court of Appeal rules that banning languages other than French on commercial signs violates freedom of expression as provided by the Québec and Canadian charters of rights
1988	Supreme Court invalidates section 58 of Bill 101 requiring French-only commercial signs in Québec
1988	Premier Robert Bourassa invokes the notwithstanding clause from section 33 of the *Canadian Charter of Rights and Freedoms* in order to pass Bill 178
1988	Bill 178 is passed in the National Assembly—continues ban on languages other than French on outdoor signs, and allows English and other languages on indoor signs if French is predominant
1993	Bill 178 is up for renewal (the five-year limit having expired on the use of the notwithstanding clause to override the Supreme Court judgment on the language of signs) but, in June, the National Assembly passes Bill 86, which replaces parts of Bill 101 and all of Bill 178. Since Bill 86 is in line with the Charter and Supreme Court decisions, it does not require the notwithstanding clause. It restores bilingual signs
1996	The Parti Québécois government introduces policy papers indicating it intends to pass more invasive, detailed legislation to increase use of the French language in Québec
1999	A Québec lower court strikes down a section of Québec's language law requiring that French be predominant on commercial signs
2000	Québec Superior Court overturns the 1999 lower court decision
2005	Supreme Court rules that limiting access to English schools does not violate the *Charter of Rights and Freedoms*
2008	Court battles continue over which children are eligible to attend English private schools in the province

In the mid-1980s, following several court challenges, francophone attitudes toward enforcement of Bill 101 began to soften. The Québec government passed Bill 57, modifying certain requirements for bilingualism and relaxing rules for internal and inter-institutional communications. These special arrangements were meant to encourage businesses to stay in Montréal. However, in December 1988, the Supreme Court ruled that section 58 of Bill 101, concerning sign laws, violated both the Canadian and Québec guarantees of freedom of expression. The sign law was ruled invalid.[8] Nationalists as well as sovereignists were enraged and feared a massive unravelling of the Québec language charter.

Almost immediately, Robert Bourassa, then Québec's Liberal premier, invoked the notwithstanding clause of the Charter, which allows the federal Parliament or any provincial legislature to pass legislation infringing on individual rights. (An automatic "sunset clause" causes the legislation to lapse after five years unless it is re-passed in the legislature concerned.) In 1988, using the notwithstanding clause to make it constitutionally valid, Québec's National Assembly passed Bill 178, a controversial sign law that expanded on Bill 101. Bill 178 banned languages other than French on *outdoor* signs but allowed languages other than French on *indoor* signs, providing that French was predominant. Predictably, language wars in Québec escalated with ridiculous debates over the size, colour and placement of letters on signs. Self-appointed "language police" reported offenders.[9]

Before December 1993, when the five-year limit on the invocation of the notwithstanding clause concerning Bill 178 was to expire, a new and less controversial law was put in place. The National Assembly passed Bill 86, replacing all of Bill 178 and parts of Bill 101. It modified somewhat but did not change the essentials of the original bills—for example, slightly easing but still restricting access to English-speaking schools, and changing the sign law so that French was required to appear predominantly along with any other languages. Bill 86 was in keeping with the spirit of the earlier Supreme Court ruling and did not require the notwithstanding clause to be used again. This legislation helped to defuse the volatile language issue in Québec, at least in the short run.

Today, a majority of Canada's French-speaking population appears to support the current language policies, but the small anglophone population resents the restrictions on access to English-language schooling, claiming that it is "strangling" their community. Language remains an emotive tool for nationalist platforms.

Bilingualism: Arguments For and Against   Language policy in Canada is highly politicized. It has become a magnet for intolerance, often based on misinformation and misunderstanding. A few facts should help dispel some myths.

Bilingualism in Canada does not mean that all Canadians must speak both French and English. Rather, it means that Canadians have the right to communicate with their federal government and federally regulated institutions in the official language of their choice and also to have their children educated in that language, wherever numbers warrant. The policy is based on the belief that a bilingual government will increase sensitivity, tolerance and respect between the two language communities.

By these criteria, official bilingualism has had mixed results. On the one hand, immersion programs in schools have produced more bilingual Canadians. The 2006 Census indicated that bilingualism had progressed across the country since 1961. In Québec, 68.9 percent of anglophones reported knowing both English and French. A total of 7.4 percent of Canadians outside the province

8. The Supreme Court presented two judgments. One was a challenge to section 58 of Bill 101 by five businesses that questioned the rule that commercial sign laws in Québec had to be in French only. The second was the case of Allan Singer dealing with the legality of English-only signs. In the first case, the Supreme Court declared that the sign law was a violation of freedom of expression and stated that a ban on other languages was not needed to defend the French language. In the second case, the Court ruled that the province was entitled to pass a law requiring the predominant display of the French language.

9. In April 1993, the United Nations Human Rights Commission found that Bill 178 contravened the International Covenant on Civil and Political Rights, which Canada had signed. It stated that any limitation on an individual's right to express ideas freely, including advertising, violates the principle of freedom of expression, and argued that francophone rights are not threatened by the ability of others to advertise in a language other than French.

made the same claim. New Brunswick, the only officially bilingual province, had the highest bilingualism rate among anglophones outside Québec at 16 percent. Over 42 percent of francophones reported being bilingual. On the other hand, the assimilation of francophones outside Québec has continued.

In English-speaking Canada, particularly since Québec decided to make French pre-eminent, demands have arisen to end official bilingualism. The desire to revert to unilingualism, however, is often merely a superficial response to separatists (who do not speak for all francophones). Often, too, it is based on people's frustration with thinking that they always see job postings requiring that applicants be bilingual. In fact, very few government jobs require the holder to be bilingual. Across the four Western provinces, where the complaints are often strongest, only about 3 percent of federal government jobs are designated bilingual. Francophones represent just over 2 percent of the population there, so the match is appropriate.

In difficult economic times, it is not surprising to hear claims that official bilingualism is a punitive and expensive failure that deprives anglophones of jobs and impoverishes Canadians as a whole. Such claims are highly exaggerated. In fact, the federal government spends only about one-third of 1 percent of the total federal budget to provide federal services in both official languages. The cost to the federal government of providing services in both official languages has been calculated at $13 a year for each Canadian, or 3.5 cents a day.[10] This is hardly an outrageous amount to pay in order to treat fellow Canadians with dignity and respect. The issue of language and culture underlies the political issues that came to a head in two Québec referendums, in 1980 and 1995.

Escalation of Nationalism

In 1980 and again in 1995, Québec governments held referendums with the intent to take Québec out of Canada and form an independent country. This history is very complex, as the two events were entwined with other constitutional issues and partisan politics.

The Québec Referendum, 1980   In May 1980, the Parti Québécois government of René Lévesque called a referendum on sovereignty-association. The vote required Québec residents to choose between *Oui*—for the Québec government to negotiate sovereignty-association—and *Non*—for it not to negotiate. This extremely mild resolution was defeated by almost six out of ten votes. The *Non* forces achieved such strong support at least partially because Prime Minister Trudeau promised "renewed federalism" to alleviate Québec's concerns.

During the ensuing 1981 Québec election, Levesque and the PQ promised to call another sovereignty referendum in the future. They formed a new government with 80 of 122 seats in the National Assembly.

Repercussions of Constitutional Patriation, the Failed Meech Lake and Charlottetown Accords   As we read in Chapter 5, René Lévesque refused to sign the 1982 constitutional amendment package to patriate the Constitution from the United Kingdom. When the federal government and the other nine provinces went ahead without Québec's approval, they handed the separatists an emotional weapon. The country, Lévesque said, had separated from Québec. Although Prime Minister Trudeau and a high proportion of the federal cabinet were from Québec, and public opinion in Québec at the time favoured patriation, the PQ claimed that it alone spoke for the province, and it boycotted federal–provincial meetings.

After the Progressive Conservatives under Brian Mulroney won the 1984 federal election, Lévesque ended the boycott and the PQ officially became a moderate nationalist party. However,

10. Office of the Commissioner of Official Languages, *Official Languages: Some Basic Facts* (Ottawa: Supply and Services, 1992), p. 16.

before the next provincial election, Lévesque resigned and soon after died—the party developed major internal splits. In 1985, the PQ was badly defeated by Robert Bourassa's Liberals.

Immediately upon taking office, Premier Bourassa began to espouse policies that blended federalism and Québec nationalism. In 1985, he successfully demanded that five conditions be included in the Meech Lake Constitutional Accord (see Chapter 5); and in 1988, as we have seen, he employed the notwithstanding clause of the new Constitution to prevent the use of English signs for business purposes in the province.

When the Meech Lake Accord failed in May 1990, several Québec members of the Liberal and Conservative federal caucuses, led by Lucien Bouchard (former minister of environment in Prime Minister Mulroney's cabinet), left their parties to form a separatist group in the House of Commons—the Bloc Québécois. The federal government continued its efforts to build a constitutional agreement that would bring Québec "on board." This eventually resulted in the Charlottetown Accord, which was put before the Canadian people for approval in a referendum in October 1992. Québec massively rejected the proposal, and Québec nationalists resumed their call for separation.

The Bloc made significant progress under Lucien Bouchard. In the 1993 general election, it won 54 seats, and became Her Majesty's Loyal Opposition in the House of Commons. The Bloc's next stated goal was to join the Parti Québécois in a campaign to separate Québec from Canada. This became more probable when the PQ under Jacques Parizeau won the 1994 provincial election and promised a referendum on sovereignty by the end of 1995.

The Québec Referendum, 1995   The general election of October 1993 and the Québec election of September 1994 set the stage for a dramatic separatist offensive and a clash of Québec and Canadian nationalists.

Strategy and Tactics: The PQ and the Bloc   In 1994, Jacques Parizeau announced that a referendum on sovereignty would be held in Québec within a year. A draft bill on sovereignty was unveiled, and the vote was planned for the next spring.

Polls indicated that a consistent majority of Québeckers opposed outright separation, but that that support would rise if an association with Canada were adopted as part of the plan. The PQ formed a temporary alliance with the Bloc Québécois and the Action démocratique du Québec (ADQ), and on June 12, 1995, the three party leaders asked Québeckers to support independence for Québec *along with political* and economic association with Canada if the Yes side won the referendum. The plan was that Québec would first declare independence and then negotiate with Canada for one year over an economic and political association; in other words, after a Yes vote, the Québec National Assembly would proclaim sovereignty and then offer a new set of institutions to Canada.

If negotiations with Canada succeeded, they said, a treaty would be put in place to provide for a customs union; a monetary policy; citizenship; and the mobility of people, capital and services. If negotiations failed, Québec would become an independent country anyway, while maintaining the Canadian currency and passport.[11]

The thrust of this deal was put into question form for the Québec population to vote on in a referendum on October 30, 1995. The question was highly criticized for being ambiguous and

---

11. Parizeau set in motion two studies to determine how easy the transition of sovereignty would be. One was secret, and it reported that to avoid "absolutely enormous costs" as Canada's national economy disintegrated, Québec would have to agree to a Canada–Québec customs union with common external tariffs. So, for all its sovereignty, Québec still would not be able to send its own representatives to global trade talks at GATT or WTO. See Paul Wells's "To the Brink and Back," commenting on the biography of Jacques Parizeau by Pierre Duchesne, *Le Regent*, in *Maclean's*, April 26, 2004, p. 64.

misleading (see "Close-Up on Institutions: The Québec Referendum Question, October 30, 1995"). It required those who supported the sovereignist option to vote Yes, and those who did not support it to vote No.[12]

Lucien Bouchard led the campaign. His speeches emphasized perceived historical "humiliations" of French-speaking Canadians, the definition of French-speaking Québeckers as a "people" and the need for Québeckers as a people to negotiate "equal to equal" with Canadians, not just as a province like the others.

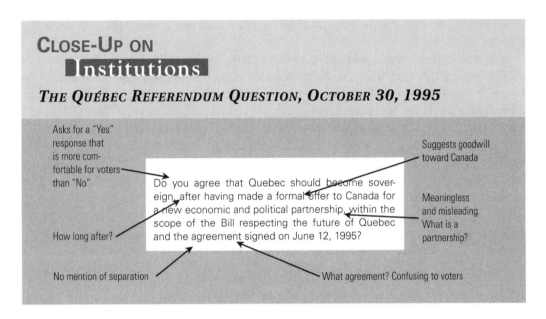

CLOSE-UP ON
Institutions
THE QUÉBEC REFERENDUM QUESTION, OCTOBER 30, 1995

Asks for a "Yes" response that is more comfortable for voters than "No"

Suggests goodwill toward Canada

Do you agree that Quebec should become sovereign, after having made a formal offer to Canada for a new economic and political partnership, within the scope of the Bill respecting the future of Quebec and the agreement signed on June 12, 1995?

Meaningless and misleading. What is a partnership?

How long after?

No mention of separation

What agreement? Confusing to voters

Strategy and Tactics: The Federal Government   Provincial Liberal leader Daniel Johnson appointed Michel Bélanger as president of the organization for the No side, and the federal government appointed Québec minister Lucienne Robillard to speak for the federal cabinet. The opposition attacked the referendum question as vague and misleading. No matter what the spin doctors tried to call it, they argued, the issue was about the separation of Québec from Canada. Prime Minister Jean Chrétien put it bluntly the day after the PQ plan was announced: "It's a mirage. It is still a proposition for separation, but they don't have the guts to say they are separatists." Chrétien declared at home and abroad that Québec would never leave Canada. He said separatists have

> *a contempt for democracy . . . the way of those who count on tricks and turnaround. . . . There is now a very cynical and very transparent attempt to confuse Québeckers, to mislead them, to suggest that you can separate from Canada and still be Canadian.*[13]

He adopted the strategy of lying low and letting the provincial leader direct the No forces. Daniel Johnson for the Québec Liberals took a cool, unemotional approach that appealed to reason.

---

12. According to Jacques Parizeau's biographer, the question initially included the word *country*—"Do you agree that Quebec should become a sovereign country . . ."—but when their private polls showed the Yes vote would rise if they removed *country*, it was taken out. Pierre Duchesne, quoted in *Maclean's*, April 26, 2004, p. 64.

13. *The Globe and Mail*, May 4, 1995.

Initial polls favoured the No forces but, once Bouchard took the lead for the separatist forces, the polls started to reverse. The dollar plunged. With just over a week to go, Chrétien suddenly cancelled other obligations and addressed a federalist rally in Verdun. The next night, sensing how close the referendum would be, he addressed the country on television pleading for Canadian unity and suggesting that the federal government would promote acceptance of Québec as a distinct society and provide a limited veto for Québec.

Canadians responded to the threatened breakup of their country with an unprecedented outpouring of emotion. Citizens from outside Québec came by the thousands to a massive rally in downtown Montréal, and more rallies and vigils were held in every province the weekend before the vote.

Meanwhile, the Cree and the Inuit in northern Québec (whose large territorial claims can be seen in Figure 7.1) held their own separate referendums. Both groups voted massively against the sovereignist proposal, and their leaders expressed a desire to remain in Canada no matter what the outcome of the October 30 referendum.

The Outcome and the Aftermath   In a massive voter turnout of over 93 percent, Québeckers voted very narrowly, 50.6 percent to 49.4 percent, to reject the sovereignty proposal. The Yes side had made major gains in the vast, mainly francophone regions that stretch from Îles de la Madeleine in the east to Abitibi in the northwest of Québec. Voters produced margins of 50 percent to 70 percent for the Yes side in many areas that had voted No in 1980. (Figure 7.2 shows the growth in, and waning of, support for separatism in Québec in elections and referendums from 1966 to 2007.) All regions of the province except Montréal, the Eastern Townships and the Outaouais voted Yes. Even Jean Chrétien's riding of St. Maurice voted Yes.

FIGURE 7.1 Map Showing Aboriginal Territorial Claims in Northern Québec

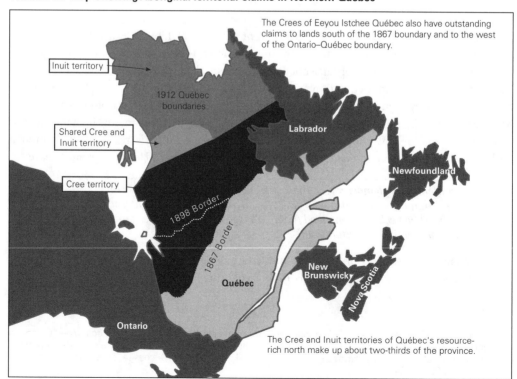

Source: Grand Council of the Crees of Québec.

Roughly 80 percent of Québec's anglophones and allophones live in Montréal and its suburbs where, together, they form about one-third of the population. This numerical strength clearly acted as a powerful counterweight to the francophone vote of the area, which was roughly evenly split. Outside Montréal, with the exception of a handful of ridings along the Ontario boundary and the US border, the anglophone population constitutes less than 2 or 3 percent of the population. In these areas, the Yes side won easily.

The close finish encouraged Premier Parizeau to adopt a confrontational tone. He said that separatists had not really lost the referendum because more than 60 percent of francophones had voted for independence. He spoke of the "temptation for revenge" and singled out and insulted many people in Québec and the rest of Canada.[14] His outburst sullied the idea of ethnic nationalism in Québec and encouraged the sovereignty movement to become more inclusive.

> *It's true that we have been beaten, but by what? Essentially, by money and ethnic votes.*
>
> **Jacques Parizeau, former premier of Québec**

The polarization of the Yes and No votes was clearly along ethnic lines, but other forces also seem to have been at play. The division, for example, was typified by urban–rural splits, in which recession-ridden rural areas felt deprived of what they perceived as the political power, economic clout and good life that adhere to big cities such as Montréal.

Leaders for the Yes forces vowed that another referendum would be held in the near future. Within days of the referendum, however, Jacques Parizeau resigned as premier and was replaced by Lucien Bouchard, who gave up his seat in the House of Commons.

Some Issues from the Referendum Campaign   The campaign raised several controversial issues that could have been problematic in the event of a successful referendum for the Yes side. As we shall see, several of them were clarified by the federal government after the referendum, but some remain unsolved.

FIGURE 7.2 **Support for Separatism in Québec, as Expressed in Key Provincial Elections and Referendums**

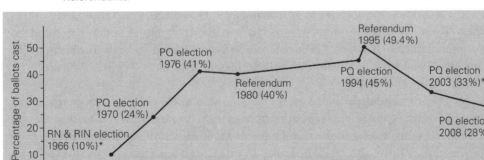

*Ralliement Nationale (RN) and Ralliement pour l'Indépendance Nationale (RIN) and Parti Québécois (PQ) percentage votes.

** The anti-separatist Liberal Party led by Jean Charest won the 2003 election with a majority, and was re-elected in 2007 with a minority.

14. *The Globe and Mail*, October 31, 1995.

- *The dollar.* Could an independent Québec keep using the Canadian dollar? There are no precedents where large countries have taken such an option, although some small, dependent countries do use the US dollar. Currency comprises more than "banknotes"; it is a system of payments, compensation and settlement. In the event of separation there would be a sudden exodus of business and investment capital from Québec so that it would be forced to choose between severely decreased credit and recession or the establishment of a new currency.[15]

- *Passports.* The Canadian government and Parliament decide who can have a passport. The question of dual citizenship remains unresolved.

- *Debt.* Since the country's debt is in Canada's name, Canada would remain liable for all of it. Without Québec, Canada could collect only about three-quarters of its former revenue, however. Negotiations about Québec's share of the national debt would be required.

- *Majority vote.* How big a majority would a province need to achieve in order to separate? Would 50 percent plus one be large enough? (In 1999, Prime Minister Chrétien declared unequivocally that 50 percent plus 1 would not be enough. See the Supreme Court judgment in Appendix 2.)

- *Negotiators.* With whom would leaders of a sovereign Québec negotiate? Could a federal prime minister elected in Québec negotiate for the rest of Canada in the event of a Québec vote for independence? Prime Minister Chrétien said he could not do so.

- *Economic repercussions.* What exactly would be the economic repercussions of separation? The majority opinion of economists appears to be that uncertainty and the high debt load would lead to a flight of capital. Constitutional lawyer Patrick Monahan concluded, "The economic dislocation in parts of the country would be far greater than that experienced in the Great Depression of the 1930s."[16]

- *Constitutional status of a UDI.* What would come of the fact that a Québec separation by a *unilateral declaration of independence* (UDI) would clearly be unconstitutional? Would other Canadians have the right to contest it? Until terms with Canada were worked out, the federal government would have no choice but to object to the Québec action in the courts.

- *Use of force.* Would Canadians use force to defend the country against a Québec UDI? They would probably not need to. Rather, the new self-declared state of Québec would have to enforce its unconstitutional claims by coercing those Québeckers who did not agree with them. The new Québec government would have to pass laws, control its citizenship and monitor immigration. It would need a new court system backed up by its own army, police and prison system. States cannot exist without these structures, or they become mere colonies of another state.

- *Other groups' independence.* In the event of a UDI, what would prevent other groups or "nations" within Québec from separating from the new country? Aboriginal claims are strong, and would receive international support. Montréal and the western part of the province near Ottawa also would be certain to vote against separation. Would they be legally entitled to separate from a new Québec?

15. See Stéphane Dion, "The Dynamic of Secessions: Scenarios after a Pro-Separatist Vote in a Québec Referendum," *CJPS*, vol. 27, no. 3 (September 1995), pp. 533–51. The January 1993 example of the breakup of the former Czechoslovakia is instructive on this point. At the beginning, both new countries tried to share the same currency, but a flight of capital from Slovakia after the split forced the Slovaks to create their own, devalued currency.

16. Patrick J. Monahan, "Cooler Heads Shall Prevail: Assessing the Costs and Consequences of Québec Separation," *C.D. Howe Institute Commentary*, no. 65 (January 1995).

- *Tension and violence.* If a UDI were accepted, this breach of the rule of law could lead to nightmare scenarios of ethnic tension and violence.[17] The Canadian territory would be divided and truncated. The state would, in fact, have to be reinvented, raising the fundamental question of whether Canadians in the remaining provinces would want to continue sharing citizenship under a common constitution.

Two Underlying Issues: the Right to Self-Determination, and Borders   The issue of Québec independence raises questions about the right of people to self-determination and statehood. International law is instructive but not conclusive on this point. Two principles clash, in fact, as international law seems to recognize both the right to self-determination and also the inviolability of borders. In the final analysis, what actually settles questions of this nature is the political action of other states in recognizing a new country or in defending the original country's territory.

The first question is the principle of self-determination. In international law, the right of self-determination extends only to those situations in which people a) are experiencing foreign or alien domination, or b) are subject to discriminatory regimes. Neither of these situations applies in Québec, where citizens have democratic rights as part of Canada.

> *In international law, Québec cannot separate from Canada without Canada's consent.*
>
> **Jean Chrétien, former prime minister**

Recognition of new states has often been accorded without the parent country's consent, however. For example, when Canada recognized Ukraine in December 1991, it went against the so-called principle of consent. Canada rushed to recognize Ukraine before there was any consideration of Russian consent. Canadian leaders did not even wait for other countries in the United Nations to make a declaration. On the other hand, in the cases of Slovenia, Croatia, Serbia, Montenegro and Kosovo, the Canadian government waited to see what decision other states would take before recognizing these two new states.

The second question concerns borders. If Québec did unilaterally declare independence, what territory could it claim? Using the same logic as employed above, it could claim only the territory and people over whom it could maintain effective control. If two rival governments contest a territory, political, and not legal, justifications finally resolve the issue. Borders must be adjusted to conform to the reality of who has the power and legitimacy.

Aboriginal peoples would have the legal justification and power to stay within Canada even if there were a Yes vote in a referendum. The Constitution makes it clear in section 91(24) that "Indians and their lands" come under the federal authority, and section 35(1) protects Aboriginal rights and treaties, which were made with Canada and not Québec. Moreover, at a minimum, the federal government would have a moral duty to help those Canadians who did not wish to stay in Québec—including Aboriginals and, for example, some Montréalers and Canadians in the western part of Québec.

Is the Constitution Merely a Red Herring?   During the referendum, some individuals argued that legal issues would be irrelevant "red herrings" if Québec seceded unilaterally. This argument has serious implications.

Since secession would destroy or alter fundamental institutions in Canada such as the monarchy, governor general and lieutenant-governors, a change of such magnitude would require the most

---

17. For a comparative study of peaceful successions, see Robert A. Young, "How Do Peaceful Successions Happen?" *CJPS*, vol. 27, no. 4 (December 1994), pp. 773–92.

rigid constitutional amendment rule (i.e., the unanimous consent of all the provinces of Canada plus a majority of members of both houses of Parliament). Neither federal nor provincial politicians alone have authority to agree to a unilateral declaration of independence.

It is clear, therefore, that a unilateral declaration of independence by Québec would be unconstitutional. Since the Canadian Constitution provides no rules about the right of a province to secede from Canada, the courts would be called upon by the federal government or by private interests to contest the validity of the referendum and/or any UDI decision. Yet, the federal government and the courts have no justification or legal obligation to pay any attention to a UDI. Thus, constitutionally speaking, in the event of a UDI, political legitimacy and power would remain with the federal government.

> *The Prime Minister has a Constitution to abide by and there is no mechanism in the Constitution that permits the separation of any part of the Canadian territory.*
>
> **Jean Chrétien, former prime minister**

Without the legal guidance of a constitution there would be chaos if a Québec government chose a UDI. When there is no legal framework, politicians become dictators and the political system becomes authoritarian. If Québec were to vote Yes in a future referendum, the federal government would be required to adhere to the Constitution. Without adherence to the Constitution there would be no authoritative body to deal with Québec, or no process of law or system of deliberation for the future of Québec. Whose law would apply to Canadians in Québec who wanted to retain their status and pay taxes to Ottawa? What courts would determine the status of the Crees and Inuit who did not want to belong to a new state of Québec?

Lucien Bouchard and Jean Chrétien, 1995. Two solitudes.

"The will of the people" is important. But how can democracy be actualized? What constitutes a fair and just process? Answers to these questions cannot be determined outside the Constitution. To say that this legal issue is irrelevant or a red herring is tantamount to saying that a small majority in one province alone could effectively deprive thirty million citizens of their country.

Referendum Fallout:
Federal Strategy and Non-constitutional Reform

On October 24, 1995, six days before the Québec referendum, a desperate Jean Chrétien promised Québeckers that he was open to change, including constitutional amendment, and would fight for the concept of a "distinct society" for Québec. Under his tutelage, the government's response was formulated in two plans, called Plan A and Plan B.

Plan A   Plan A was essentially a reconciliation effort—to sell a majority of Québeckers on the success of Canada and the benefits of staying in the federal union. In a sense, this plan began with the giant No rally in Montréal on October 27, 1995, which led to the following.

1) an *overhaul of the cabinet,* in which two star candidates from Québec, Stéphane Dion and Pierre Pettigrew, were approached and brought into cabinet as minister for intergovernmental affairs and minister for international co-operation respectively.

2) steps to meet the *distinct society* and *veto* promises. Within weeks of the referendum, one "resolution" was passed in the House of Commons, recognizing Québec as a distinct society and another one concerning the veto.

   The result of these proposals was a step-by-step process of non-constitutional reform. Parliament had to pass a motion on the distinct society of Québec because the provinces would not allow any distinct society concessions to be entrenched in the Constitution. (See the "Close-Up on Institutions: Parliament's Distinct Society Motion" on the next page.) The resolution proclaims the distinct character of Québec's unique culture, the civil law tradition and the French-speaking majority in the province. The House of Commons and Senate claim that they will "undertake to be guided by this reality."

   Québec was also given a form of veto over future constitutional changes. A statutory (but not constitutional) veto was approved by Parliament. It affirmed that any constitutional change approved by Parliament would require consent from Ontario, Québec and British Columbia, as well as two of the four Atlantic provinces and two of the Prairie provinces. In effect, Parliament agreed to bind itself to the demands of the stronger provinces, in particular Québec.[18] (Alberta and British Columbia are required by their own laws to put all constitutional proposals to a provincial referendum.)

3) *decentralization* measures to show that the government was flexible concerning Québec's desires. The prime minister created a new committee to recommend decentralization measures. That committee's report formed the basis of the Throne Speech in February 1996. The speech contained many mini-measures to show that Canada was on the side of fundamental change in the federation. It emphasized devolving powers to the provinces in areas such as forestry, mining, recreation, tourism and social housing. A third non-constitutionalized reform came from the government's commitment that it would not use its spending power to encroach further into areas of provincial jurisdiction (such as a national daycare program) without the consent of a majority of the provinces. The government also promised that any new program would be designed so that non-participating provinces could be compensated.

18. Andrew Heard and Tim Schwartz, "The Regional Veto Formula and Its Effects on Canada's Constitutional Amendment Process," *CJPS*, vol. 30, no. 2 (June 1997), pp. 339–58.

At the First Ministers Conference in June, an agreement on labour market training was reached in which $2 billion was handed over to the provinces—at least a quarter of which went to Québec. The decentralization of labour market training was significant, as it had been a symbol of federal intransigence in Québec—proof, according to separatists, that federalism could not work.

4) a campaign to *extol the virtues of being a Canadian*. Other initiatives were undertaken, such as free distribution of flags and the setting up of a Unity Information Office (UIO). These plans were intended to counter the negative image of Canada that the separatists had propagated during the referendum. The UIO claimed that separatist leaders had distorted history and continually used emotive words such as "conquered," "rejected," "hoodwinked" and "betrayed" to describe relations with the rest of Canada. It was partly money distributed under this initiative that caused a furor in 2003 when the attorney general found much of the money unaccounted for (see Chapters 4 and 8).

CLOSE-UP ON
Institutions

PARLIAMENT'S DISTINCT SOCIETY MOTION

Whereas the people of Québec have expressed the desire for recognition of Québec's distinct society,

1) the House of Commons recognizes that Québec is a distinct society within Canada;
2) the House recognizes that Québec's distinct society includes its French-speaking majority, unique culture and civil law tradition;
3) the House undertakes to be guided by this reality; and
4) the House encourages all components of the legislative and executive branches of government to take note of this recognition and be guided in their conduct accordingly.

Plan B Dubbed "tough love" by some, Plan B was meant to clarify rational, logical terms for secession—without using harsh federal threats about the risks of partition.

The first step in Plan B occurred in April 1996, when the federal government intervened in a court challenge. Specifically, the federal intervention countered Québec's claim that the Constitution and courts would be irrelevant if Québeckers voted for separation. The federal government wanted to "clarify" that the Constitution would still apply after a Yes vote. Prime Minister Chrétien also reiterated that Québec would never be able to leave Canada unilaterally—even if a majority of Québeckers voted Yes in the next referendum. The law must be respected, he said. The rest of Canada would have to approve the terms of separation through a constitutional amendment.[19]

In order to buttress Prime Minister Chrétien's position, in September 1996 the federal government sought a ruling from the Supreme Court of Canada on three specific questions, hoping to establish that a unilateral declaration of independence by Québec would be illegal. Despite objections from Québec, the Court ruled unanimously that there was no constitutional bar to such an advisory role and that the questions were justiciable. However, the Court's conclusions in 1998 were woolly and controversial, based more on its broad understanding of Canadian democracy than on a strict reading of the constitutional text and documents. The Court based its interpretation on the "underlying principles" of the Constitution, including principles of federalism, democracy, constitutionalism, the rule of law and respect for minorities. Clearly aiming for a political compromise, it concluded as follows:

Question 1: *Under the Constitution of Canada, can the National Assembly, legislature or government of Québec effect the secession of Québec from Canada unilaterally?*

Ruling: "The Constitution vouchsafes order and stability, and accordingly secession of a province 'under the Constitution' could not be achieved without principled negotiation with other participants in Confederation within the existing constitutional framework."

19. *Ottawa Citizen*, May 15, 1996.

And more directly: "The democratic vote, by however strong a majority, would have no legal effect on its own and could not push aside the principles of federalism and the rule of law, the rights of individuals and minorities, or the operation of democracy in the other provinces or in Canada as a whole. Democratic rights under the Constitution cannot be divorced from constitutional obligations."

Clearly, the Court concluded that a regular constitutional amendment would be required in order for separation from Canada to be constitutionally valid. But the Court did not stand with this strong statement alone. It added, "nor, however, can the reverse proposition be accepted: the continued existence and operation of the constitutional order could not be indifferent to a clear expression of a clear majority of Québeckers that they no longer wish to remain in Canada."

The Court judgment then went on to virtually demand that "negotiations" take place if there is a "demonstrated majority support for Québec secession."

Question 2: *Does international law give the National Assembly, legislature or government of Québec the right to effect the secession of Québec from Canada unilaterally? In this regard, is there a right to self-determination under international law that would give the National Assembly, legislature or government of Québec the right to effect the secession of Québec from Canada unilaterally?*

Ruling: "[I]n the circumstances, the 'National Assembly, the legislature or the government of Quebec' do not enjoy a right at international law to effect the secession of Quebec from Canada unilaterally."

Question 3: *In the event of a conflict between domestic and international law on the right of the National Assembly, legislature or government of Québec to effect the secession of Québec from Canada unilaterally, which would take precedence in Canada?*

Ruling: In view of the answers to Questions 1 and 2, the Court ruled that this third question did not need to be answered.

Because this Supreme Court decision may play a major role if there ever is a majority vote for separation in Québec, the complete text of answers and summary is included in Appendix 2.

The immediate political fallout from the judgment was controversial. The federal minister of intergovernmental affairs, Stéphane Dion, seized on the *clear question* and *clear majority* clause in the text. He proffered that any referendum question with the word *partnership* in it would be invalid and that a referendum would need a greater than 50-plus-1 majority to be acceptable to the federal government.

On the other hand, separatists latched on to the crucial Supreme Court ruling that negotiations would necessarily have to follow a positive vote on separation in Québec. The idea that the federal government and the provinces would have to negotiate after a positive provincial referendum encouraged separatists to believe that their demands were legitimate and reasonable.

The Supreme Court decision did help to dampen emotional ire in Québec. However some federalists were concerned that if Québec should vote to separate, one or all of the provinces or the federal government might object to negotiating with the secessionists. The separatists could claim legitimately that the Court had backed their demands for negotiations. The objection was that the Court's judgment in forcing negotiations appeared to be reaching beyond its mandate. Nothing in the Constitution says that those opposed to the separation of Québec are required to negotiate secession. What appears to be a hasty and ill-considered decision by the Court may one day do more harm than good for the unity of Canada.

In response to the ongoing charge that the federal government had not been proactive enough about Québec separatism, the Chrétien government tabled and passed Bill C20 in December 1999. This legislation, the **_Clarity Act_**, sets out the rules by which the government and Parliament of Canada would react to any future separatist referendum. It concludes that the federal government will not enter into any negotiations over separation with a province unless the House of Commons determines that 1) the referendum question is "clear" and 2) a "clear" expression of will has been obtained by a "clear" majority of the population. The goal is to ensure that everyone agrees in advance on what constitutes a clear referendum question.

Few states make such direct provisions concerning their own destruction, but the Liberal government defended the need to clarify precisely how the federal government and Parliament would handle another referendum in Québec. Predictably, this legislation drew vitriolic comments from the Bloc Québécois in Ottawa, and the Parti Québécois government immediately tabled a competing bill in the National Assembly (Bill 99), claiming that only the Québec people can decide on the legal status of their province and that a 50-percent-plus-1 vote would be considered enough for a referendum victory.

Despite the posturing, neither bill is constitutionalized, and both can be changed by any future legislature. In 2004, Jean Lapierre, Paul Martin's Québec lieutenant (and a founder of the Bloc Québecois) referred to this when he called the *Clarity Act*

useless . . . because it wouldn't change anything. If there was a will in Québec, a clear will to separate, they would not be able to stop a will like that by trying to have tricks.[20]

However, the constitutional amendment process remains intact; the secession of a province from Canada would require resolutions to be passed in the federal Parliament and all ten legislative assemblies. There is no easy route to political change around this high obstacle. In 1997, nine premiers and two territorial leaders met in an effort to reactivate discussions on Canadian unity with the goal of bringing Québec back to the table. In what became known as the Calgary Declaration, they produced a framework for constitutional discussions that stressed the equality of the provinces, as well as guidelines for public consultations.[21] However despite the development of a framework for negotiations their initiative did not proceed. Table 7.4 summarizes some important highlights in Canada–Québec relations from 1976 to 2008.

Québec Nationalism Post-1995

Shortly after the referendum, Lucien Bouchard replaced Jacques Parizeau as leader of the PQ and premier of Québec. By then, however, Québeckers were more concerned with issues such as the economy, health care and taxes than with separation. In 2001, Bouchard left politics, to be replaced as premier and head of the PQ by Bernard Landry. The next provincial election, in 2003, brought the Liberals back to power in Québec, this time led by Jean Charest. It was the first time since the 1960s that a Québec election was not dominated by debates over Québec's relationship with the rest of Canada. In 2005, André Boisclair was chosen leader of the Parti Québécois and, in early 2007, led the party to a humiliating third-place finish in the provincial election. The Liberals clung to power with a minority government, and l'Action démocratique du Québec (ADQ), led by Mario Dumont, came second. Boisclair quickly resigned and was replaced by Pauline Marois.

Québec sovereignty, deprived of charismatic leadership and emotive issues or perceived injustices, for the time at least, fell dormant and off the political agenda. Québec's relations with the rest of Canada normalized, as though the combination of referendum fatigue, the *Clarity Act* and the trauma of almost losing a country left little taste for more knife-to-the-throat bargaining. This does not mean, however, that nationalism is dead in Québec.

20. *The Globe and Mail*, February, 2004.

21. See the product of the premiers' meeting in Calgary, September 14, 1997, at www.scics.gc.ca/cinfo/ 85006504_e.html.

TABLE 7.4 **Canada–Québec Relational Highlights, 1976–2008**

1976	Pierre Trudeau puts forward constitutional proposals concerning patriation and an amending formula based on the 1971 *Victoria Charter*; discussions with provinces begin
	Parti Québécois wins the Québec election; René Lévesque is premier
1978	Trudeau introduces Bill C60, providing for patriation
1980	Liberals win federal election
	Québec sovereignty referendum fails
1981	PQ wins Québec election
	Supreme Court rules that federal unilateral action is legal but not conventional
	Agreement is reached between the federal government and nine provinces; Québec does not sign
1982	Québec Court of Appeal rejects Québec government's claim of veto power over constitutional change
	Constitution is patriated with a revised amending formula and a charter of rights
1984	Trudeau announces intention to resign
	Conservatives win federal election; Brian Mulroney becomes prime minister
1985	Québec Liberal party wins provincial election; Robert Bourassa becomes premier
1987	Meech Lake Accord is signed by all first ministers—must be ratified by the federal Parliament and all provincial legislatures within three years
	Québec is the first province to ratify Meech
1988	Conservatives win federal election
1989	Clyde Wells becomes premier of Newfoundland
	Meech Lake dies—Newfoundland and Manitoba do not ratify before the deadline
1991	Allaire Report recommends Québec powers increase
	Mulroney unveils a new set of proposals
1992	Ottawa and nine provinces reach consensus about constitutional reform; Québec does not participate
	Bourassa joins discussions
	Charlottetown Accord is announced
	Mulroney announces referendum on Charlottetown
	Charlottetown referendum results in a 55 percent to 45 percent rejection
1993	Brian Mulroney resigns as prime minister
	Liberals win the federal election; Jean Chrétien becomes prime minister
	Parti Québécois wins Québec election; Jacques Parizeau becomes premier
1995	Referendum in Québec on sovereignty fails narrowly; Bouchard replaces Parizeau as premier of Québec
1996	Parliament passes legislation allowing Québec, Ontario, British Columbia and any two Maritime or Prairie provinces to veto any further constitutional change
	Federal government refers three questions about Québec separatism to Supreme Court
1998	Jean Charest becomes leader of Liberal Party of Québec
	Bouchard's Parti Québécois is victorious in provincial election
	Supreme Court rules on questions concerning separation of Québec
1999	Federal Parliament passes the *Clarity Act* and Québec responds with its own legislation
2003	Liberal party wins Québec election
2005	André Boisclair elected leader of the Parti Québécois
2006	House of Commons passes a resolution saying that the Québécois form "a nation within a united Canada"
2007	Parti Québécois drops to third-party status in a Québec election with only 28 percent of the vote. Jean Charest's Liberal government is reduced to a minority with the Action démocratique du Québec (ADQ) coming in second place
	Boisclair resigns as PQ leader and is replaced by Pauline Marois

> *If I had a dollar for every time that sovereignty was declared dead, I'd be rich!*
>
> **Michael C. Auger, *columnist*, Le Journal de Montréal**

The call for formal constitutional recognition of Québec as a "nation" remains a trigger for conflict. This was clear in September 2006, when Liberal leadership candidate Michael Ignatieff reopened the controversial and divisive issue upon releasing a campaign manifesto calling for "ratification of a new Constitution" that would recognize Québec as a nation. The Bloc Québécois took the opportunity to ask the House of Commons to recognize Québec as a nation. Prime Minister Harper responded,

> *Do the Québécois form a nation within Canada? The answer is yes. Do the Québécois form an independent nation? The answer is no and it will always be no.*[22]

However, the exchange precipitated the prime minister to move a resolution in the House of Commons that

> *The Québécois form a nation within a united Canada.*

Most Liberals, including Stéphane Dion, supported the resolution. It was not a constitutional change, nor was it a prelude to one. Supporters argued that the resolution clarified the situation because it did not say that *Québec* is a nation, which would have implications of statehood, but rather that the "*Québécois* are a nation within a united Canada." They maintained the resolution would clarify the issue and prevent federalists from being backed into a corner by separatists' demands. Opponents of the resolution feared that the move would "bolster the separatists' argument that they are not being recognized and strengthen their resolve to form an independent society."[23]

Québec's Major Grievances

Shared grievances are a vital ingredient of nationalism. According to former Québec premier Bernard Landry, Québeckers are victims of discrimination in that they do not get their fair share of federal spending. This argument, however, was challenged by Stéphane Dion, the current federal Liberal leader and former minister of intergovernmental affairs in Jean Chrétien's Liberal government. Using 1998 data, Dion concluded[24]

- ✓ Québeckers received 24.2 percent of total federal spending. Since Québec's population is 24.2 percent of the Canadian population, the redistribution is eminently fair. Obviously, Québec does not get 24.2 percent of every item in the federal budget, but it does get that much overall. It is a favourite ploy of premiers to point at one particular item that is lower and complain that they are not getting their fair share.
- ✓ Québec contributed 20.6 percent of federal revenues. Its contribution to Canada's GDP is 21.8 percent. "This shows that Québec is contributing in accordance with the size of its economy and receiving in accordance with the size of its population."

---

22. *Maclean's*, December 11, 2006, p. 23.
23. CTV news report, "Quebec Nationhood: A Loaded History," November 22, 2006. Accessed April 9, 2007, at www.ctv.ca/servlet/ArticleNews/story/CTVNews/20061122/quebec_nation_061122/2.
24. Stéphane Dion, "Tell the truth, Bernard," *The Globe and Mail*, March 15, 2001.

✓ Québec is slightly less wealthy than the average Canadian province. On a per capita basis, the four Atlantic provinces, Manitoba, Saskatchewan and the three territories obtain a greater proportion of transfer payments than Québec does, but only Ontario and Alberta are considered "rich" provinces in the equalization formula.

✓ Québeckers receive 21.2 percent of federal research and development spending. This cannot be considered lower than its population share because the number includes spending undertaken in the National Capital region. Québec's share of federal R&D spending outside the National Capital Region is 26.8 percent.

✓ Québec suppliers receive federal spending on goods and services roughly equivalent to the size of Québec's economy within Canada.

✓ Québec business subsidies are 16.5 percent of total spending. However, this category is only 2.6 percent of the federal budget. Part goes to Western farmers who do not have marketing boards. "Most Quebec farmers are helped by marketing board quotas, and this kind of assistance does not appear in the federal budget."

✓ The proportion of federal public servants in Canada that works in Québec is 23.1 percent. The number would be higher, but the Québec government assumes some responsibilities that most other provinces leave to the federal government (like policing).

> *Québec is neither the spoiled child nor the victim of the federation. It receives its fair share of federal spending as a province somewhat less wealthy than the Canadian average.*
>
> *Stéphane Dion*

In summary, Québec leadership was, and remains, divided in its vision for the province. *Separatists* favour outright statehood for Québec; *sovereignists* favour a greater degree of independence for Québec, but do not necessarily define sovereignty as an absolute break from Canada; *devolution sovereignists* favour an extreme decentralization of Canada in which very few powers would be left to the central government; and *federalists* favour the continued existence of Québec within Canada. The proportion of the Québec population in each camp varies.

After the 1995 referendum, discussion and overt support for the separatist and sovereignist options faded for nearly a decade. However, in the 2004 and 2006 general elections, the Bloc Québécois received considerably more support than the Liberals, encouraging provincial PQ leaders to speculate publicly on another referendum. When leader Bernard Landry quit in 2005 he was replaced by André Boisclair. Under Boisclair's leadership in the 2007 Québec provincial election, the Parti Québécois dropped to third-party status, losing its second-place status to the conservative

Aislin, *The Gazette* (Montreal), April 10, 2007. Reprinted with permission.

Action Democratique (ADQ) even though the Liberal government of Jean Charest was reduced to a minority. Boisclair was replaced as leader by Pauline Marois. In the fall of 2007, about 45 percent of Québeckers told pollsters they would still vote Yes in another referendum. Relations between Québec City and Ottawa in 2008 are good, in large part because Stephen Harper's minority Conservative government needs to gain more seats in Québec if it is to win a majority government.

ADQ leader Mario Dumont won votes with a new vocabulary—he abandoned the terms *separatist, sovereignist* and *devolution sovereignist* in favour of *autonomist*. He and his party want more autonomy for Québec. It is not clear what the difference is, if any, between an autonomous Québec and an independent one. Another word game has begun in la belle province.

Nationalistic Grievances and Aspirations of Canada's Native Peoples

Native peoples exhibit some aspects of modern nationalism. Indians (First Nations), including status and non-status Indians, Métis and Inuit, form distinctive groups, but they are all descendants of Canada's first inhabitants. They also have in common a long, shared history with non-Natives and their governments. For many decades, this relationship was fraught with injustices related to land and a lack of respect for Aboriginal values and traditional way of life. Today, issues emanating from that relationship form the basis of many grievances and goals that can be interpreted as contributing to Aboriginal nationalism.

In spite of recent consciousness raising about these issues, and considerable efforts by governments to resolve them, Aboriginals as a group remain among the poorest of Canadians. In Chapter 3, we discussed many of the social and cultural issues that regularly arise as Aboriginals come into conflict with other Canadians in their struggle to maintain their traditional ways in a changing environment and improve the social and economic conditions of their communities. The most significant issues concern land claims and self-government, which underlie and contribute to the serious socio-economic problems of many Aboriginal communities. To understand them, it is necessary to know the history of these people.

We noted that section 91 (24) of the *Constitution Act, 1867* gives the federal government exclusive jurisdiction over First Nations and lands reserved for them. Today, however, many non-status Indians, Métis and Inuit are also subject to provincial laws. Aboriginal grievances therefore are directed against both federal and provincial governments. They begin with the fact that they are unable to negotiate as equals.

Politically, Native peoples still occupy a dependent, semi-colonial position in regard to the federal and provincial governments. Proposals to end Indian status and repeal the *Indian Act* have been called for by Natives struggling for greater recognition of their traditional rights, settlement of their land claims and the power to manage their own affairs. Former grand chief of the Assembly of First Nations Georges Erasmus put the case this way: "we want to have a relationship with this country that is nation to nation" as expressed in the "two-row wampum" analogy of the Mohawks:

> *The two-row wampum is an agreement whereby two nations coexist and travel the River of Life in peace and friendship. . . . Legally, it means that each of the two nations retains its own respective laws and jurisdiction. Neither of the two nations can apply or impose its laws over the other.*[25]

---

25. As recorded in documents sent to Québec premier Robert Bourassa, August 20, 1990.

Aboriginal people have different values from mainstream Canadians because of their unique history in a hunting-and-gathering economy. The values of these diverse groups of people tend to be collectivist, based on an organic concept of community where individuals are seen as a specialized part of the whole society. Decision-making is generally consensual, not majoritarian. Traditional leadership tends to be diffuse, with different leaders in different areas of specialization. Today, as we see below, these values are being incorporated into new government organizations in the North, and also in First Nations self-government agreements.

The Royal Commission on Aboriginal peoples reported recommendations in 1996. Essentially, it concluded that more than 150 years of colonial and Canadian governments' policy direction has been wrong.[26] The Chrétien government responded, recognizing publicly the mistakes and injustices that had been committed against Aboriginals in the past. As recognition of their commitment to change, the government introduced a new plan with four objectives:

- renewing partnerships;
- strengthening Native governance;
- developing a new fiscal relationship; and
- establishing programs to help support Native communities and economies.

This was followed with a five-year plan called Aboriginal Human Resources Development Strategy, focusing particularly on improving the job prospects of Aboriginal peoples.

In Chapter 3, we described the Native peoples, their history, culture and heritage. In Chapter 5, we outlined recent constitutional developments that addressed their concerns. Here, we focus on the main factors that contribute to expressions of nationalism among Aboriginals. They emanate essentially from the issue of Aboriginal rights.

Aboriginal Rights

Aboriginal rights are based on Native peoples' occupancy and use of North America before Europeans arrived. They are the rights they had before their contact with non-Native settlers. Traditional Aboriginal societies were based primarily on hunting and gathering and, to a minor extent, on agriculture. This relationship to the land therefore defines Aboriginal culture and economy. Aboriginals consider that land was put here by the Creator for the use of *all* people and, therefore, belongs to everyone living today and to the unborn to come.

The British Proclamation of 1763 recognized the rights of the First Nations and provided that they could not be taken away without due process—i.e., a negotiated treaty. These obligations were passed on to Canada through the BNA Act (the *Constitution Act, 1867*), section 91 (24). Section 35

CLOSE-UP ON
Nationalism

RECOGNIZING LOUIS RIEL

Canada's Métis have long sought recognition by the government for their Aboriginal heritage. They won recognition of their constitutional rights in 1993 when the Supreme Court ruled that Métis people can claim Aboriginal rights to hunt for food out of season without licences if they can prove their heritage, just as status Indians can.

More than a decade later, Prime Minister Paul Martin offered the Métis another kind of recognition. He said his government would review the century-old treason case of the revered former Métis leader, Louis Riel. Riel led the Red River Rebellion in 1869 and was captured and hanged for treason after he led the 1885 North-West Rebellion. Martin was proposing to honour the Métis hero by officially recognizing Louis Riel's contribution, not just to the Métis, but to Canada as a whole.

Clement Chartier, president of the Métis National Council dismissed the overture, however: "We're not interested in seeking a pardon or exoneration for Mr. Riel. What we are interested in is seeing the government redress those things that Mr. Riel stood for and died for, in particular, the substantive rights of the Métis nation. . . . Mr. Riel, to us, is a hero and a martyr. It's not going to really change any of that if he is pardoned or exonerated."*

* Quoted in *The Globe and Mail*, August 4, 2004, A3.

---

26. Canada, *Report of the Royal Commission on Aboriginal Peoples*, 5 vols. (Ottawa: Canada Communications Group Publishing, 1997).

of the *Constitution Act, 1982* states that "the existing aboriginal and treaty rights of the aboriginal peoples are hereby recognized and affirmed." Clause 35 (3) affirms that "treaty rights" include "land claims agreements" now and in the future.

The Canadian Constitution therefore recognizes Aboriginal and treaty rights, and the *Charter of Rights and Freedoms* protects them in that Aboriginal or treaty rights cannot be abrogated by anything in the Charter (section 25). These rights are recognized and even protected, but without specifying exactly what they are. It is generally agreed, however, that they include rights to hunt and fish, harvest food and have access to and occupancy of land to conduct these activities. Court decisions have never been able to define Aboriginal rights adequately. However, they have ruled that where previous treaty or land-claims agreements are not in place surrendering such rights, governments are bound by the Constitution to protect or compensate Aboriginals before they can sell the land or grant interest in it to third parties.

Louis Riel

The recognition and affirmation in the Constitution of the existing treaty rights of all Canadian Aboriginal peoples was the beginning of a new stage in Aboriginal-state relations as the federal government actively addressed Aboriginal grievances. Conferences were held from 1983 to 1987 in an attempt to go even further and constitutionalize self-government rights through an amendment to the new *Constitution Act*. Several provinces opposed the idea, however, and when these talks failed, the government's efforts at constitutional reform moved on to the Meech Lake Accord. But neither Aboriginals nor their issues were included in the meetings or the final accord. Because of the lack of recognition for their concerns, Native MPP Elijah Harper blocked approval of Meech by Manitoba's legislature. Since unanimity was required for it to become law, the constitutional reform package failed.

Next came the Charlottetown Accord. This time, Native peoples and their concerns were included in the deliberations, and the final proposal went a considerable way toward satisfying their demands. Among a host of other proposals concerning the promotion of Aboriginal languages, cultures and traditions, the final draft stated that Native peoples should form a "third level" of government in the country. But the Charlottetown Accord, which included a massive number of proposed changes in other areas as well, failed when the package was defeated in a national referendum.

Native peoples continued their struggle to redress their grievances and unmet aspirations. In particular, they still wanted (and want) the right to self-government constitutionalized. Many provinces were against Aboriginal self-government, but the most direct attack on the concept of Aboriginal rights came from a Québec government report that concluded that a self-government clause would threaten Québec's territory and weaken provincial powers.

Considerable progress has been made toward reaching an understanding and agreement about what Aboriginal rights actually entail. In particular, they include rights associated with the occupancy and use of lands. Courts have recognized that Canada's Aboriginals have title to lands not explicitly surrendered to the Crown in the past, through treaties or land claims. This ruling clarified that neither federal nor provincial governments can sell or grant interests in public lands to individuals or corporations if they have not been explicitly surrendered to the Crown through treaties or land claims. There is also a vague, general consensus that Aboriginal peoples should be able to enjoy certain rights of self-government (seen for example in native policing on reservations), but this is such a complicated area that courts have not ruled whether it, like territorial rights, is in fact an Aboriginal right.

Land Claims and Other Land Issues

Section 35 (3) of the *Constitution Act, 1982* clarifies that "treaty rights" include rights that now exist by way of land claims agreements or may be so acquired. This means that land claims agreements are constitutionalized and cannot be changed at will by governments.

Significant disputes remain over issues of land. Over the years, numerous treaties were signed giving North American Aboriginals reserves in exchange for land. Many of them were so blatantly unfair to the Indians that they have been challenged in the courts. In cases where reserves are inadequate for the economic development and resource needs of their communities, it is recognized that a secure and expanded land base is required in order for them to become economically self-sufficient. The alternative would be for them to remain dependent on governments.

Where treaties were never signed, Aboriginal peoples were left with no land rights. The Métis were particularly dispossessed in this regard. As a result, Aboriginal title, or the claim to land based on traditional occupancy, had to be tested in the courts. In the 1973 Calder case, the Supreme Court recognized this idea of Aboriginal title.[27] Soon after, the federal government announced that it would negotiate Aboriginal title even when no treaties existed. This offer later expanded to include claims against *unjust* treaties.

As a result, there are two kinds of land claims in process today: **comprehensive claims** dealing with cases of Aboriginal title not covered by treaty or other legal means, and **specific claims** dealing with challenges to existing treaties.

Despite the federal government's constitutional authority over Native peoples, *provincial* governments are in control of public lands, and this complicates negotiations. In the North, where the federal government has legal jurisdiction of the land, claims have moved relatively quickly. By 1993, Canada's entire North above the sixtieth parallel was covered by final agreements or agreements in principle about land claims. In Yukon, several First Nations bands have signed self-government and final land claims agreements with the federal and territorial governments. The territory of Nunavut is inhabited almost solely by Inuit, and has full government institutions equal to other territories or provinces.

Further south, progress is complicated by provincial jurisdiction, natural resource companies and non-Aboriginal settlements on disputed land. Claims have moved slowly. The main settlements to date have been in Québec and British Columbia. The 1975 *James Bay and Northern Québec Agreement* among the Cree, Inuit and Québec government was the first. It allowed for the flooding of many hundreds of square kilometres of hunting lands in exchange for a package that included $232.5 million, guaranteed incomes for Cree hunters and subsidized housing. Vast herds of caribou and ancestral gravesites were flooded.

A second settlement between the Cree and the Québec government, in 2002, was the first agreement in Canadian history to recognize the full autonomy of an Aboriginal people as a "native nation." The agreement opened a vast territory to mining and hydroelectric development in return for substantial powers for the Crees to help manage mining, forestry and energy development, as well as a large cash settlement. Another settlement success was the Nisga'a treaty in British Columbia in 1999, which gave the Nisga'a of northern BC $253 million over 15 years, along with 2019 square kilometres of land, resource rights and powers of self-government.

27. *Calder v. Attorney General of B.C.,* [1973] S.C.R. 313.

Other progress concerning land claims has been made in the courts. In recent years, the Supreme Court clarified aspects of land claim settlements, fishing rights and Métis rights. In 1997, for example, it ordered that oral history evidence be admissible in certain court cases. It also clarified that a group must establish its exclusive occupation of the land in question at the time the Crown asserted sovereignty (see the "Close-Up on Institutions: Some Significant Developments in Aboriginal Affairs, 1996–2008"). In 2002, the Supreme Court ruled that if Aboriginals can prove that their forebears honestly believed they had reserve lands set aside for them, but in fact did not receive them, they still might have a legal case for their claim.

About half of the more than six hundred status First Nations bands of Canada have not ceded their traditional territories by treaty with the Canadian government. They include the Natives of most of British Columbia, Québec, the Northwest Territories and large parts of Yukon. They claim outstanding Aboriginal rights over, and title to, their traditional lands, and have asserted historic rights to roughly half the country. In British Columbia, for example, overlapping claims by bands have claimed 110 percent of the provincial land mass.[28] Fifty claims are under negotiation in BC alone. The current comprehensive land-claims process is notoriously complicated and slow; only a few claims can be in negotiation at any one time, and each case can take as many as twenty years to settle. At this rate, claims will still be heard for decades to come. In 2002, to help speed up the process of specific claims, a new claims commission was set up with the power to grant awards of up to $7 million.

Meanwhile, as cases drag on for years, confrontation between Natives and other Canadians are sometimes severe. In early 2006, for example, a land dispute developed between Henco Industries and Six Nations Natives over a 40-hectare tract of land in Caledonia, near Hamilton, Ontario. A group of Native protesters seized an unfinished housing development, saying the land had been taken from them by the Crown two hundred years ago. Violent clashes between First Nations members and local residents erupted as the protesters blocked roads and rail lines. The federal government was forced to become involved and about a year later gave the Ontario government over $26 million to help cover the massive costs related to the dispute. Negotiations between the Six Nations members and the federal government are still ongoing as of early 2008.

There are other complications to territorial claims. One is that Québec's Indians do not want to remain part of that province if it decides to separate from Canada. The Assembly of First Nations' report on the Charlottetown constitutional proposal stated,

> *If Québec has the right to separate from Canada, First Nations have the right to make their own decisions. And if that means separation from Québec, so be it.*

In June 2007, Prime Minister Stephen Harper announced his intention to overhaul the land-claims process and have a new impartial Specific Claims Tribunal speed up the processing of the massive backlog of more than eight hundred cases. Since current claims take 13 or more years to resolve treaty issues that go back more than a century, few people would not agree that everything that can be done to speed up the process should be done. Unless that happens, First Nations protests such as the day of protest organized across the country by the Assembly of First Nations in June 2007 can be expected to continue. Since the proposed commission will have the authority only to deal with certain specific claims and award compensation but not declare ownership or title of lands, it remains to be seen whether delays for the resolution of valid claims will change. Native leaders are particularly

---

28. The government has stated that it will cede no more than 5 percent of the total BC land mass to settle all claims, and that no privately owned land will be included. Most Crown land will also be protected. This figure was chosen because Indians make up roughly 5 percent of the BC population. *The Globe and Mail*, May 29, 1995.

anxious to resolve ownership issues so that they will be able to control their own resources and have a chance to improve their immense social problems. They see that Aboriginal groups in the North—in Nunavut and the Northwest Territories and the Yukon—have negotiated 21 land claims since 1975, a process that has given them more control over development in a vast stretch of territory.

Self-Government

In Chapter 3, we learned that when European settlers arrived in North America with their political institutions, Indians became "wards of the state" rather than enfranchised citizens. Over time, this relationship evolved and Indians gained the right to vote and participate in Canadian political life, as well as receive the same rights as other Canadian citizens. However, Aboriginal peoples want more. They argue that under section 35 of the *Constitution Act of 1982*, they have the right to govern themselves according to their own traditional values and methods. They want federal and provincial governments to recognize that this is an *inherent right*, and to negotiate self-government agreements based on that recognition.[29]

Advocates of Native self-government, as outlined vaguely in the Charlottetown Accord, said there was no cause for worry on either theoretical or practical grounds. On the theoretical side, the deal stated that a law passed by a government of Aboriginal peoples "may not be inconsistent with those laws which are essential to the preservation of peace, order and good government in Canada." But this did not eliminate the fears of opponents to self-government, because the text also specified that "this agreement would not extend the legislative authority of Parliament or the legislatures of the provinces." On practical grounds, Charlottetown did clarify some aspects of Native self-government as outlined in the accord, and the proposals circumscribed the power of Aboriginal

29. Michael Whittington, "Aboriginal Self-Government in Canada" in Michael Whittington and Glen Williams, eds., *Canadian Politics in the 21st Century* (Toronto: Nelson, 2000), p. 109. Also see John H. Hylton, *Aboriginal Self-Government in Canada: Current Trends and Issues*, (Saskatoon, SK: Purich Publishing Ltd. 1999); and Frances Abele and Michael J. Prince, "Four Pathways to Aboriginal Self-Government in Canada," *The American Review of Canadian Studies*, vol. 26, no. 4, Winter 2006, p. 268 ff.

CLOSE-UP ON
Institutions

SOME SIGNIFICANT DEVELOPMENTS IN ABORIGINAL AFFAIRS, 1996–2008

Since 1996, a combination of events and court rulings has strengthened the hand of Aboriginal peoples regarding land claims and other rights. The major developments include

1996: The *Report of the Royal Commission on Aboriginal Peoples* is released.

1997: The Supreme Court of Canada overturns a decision by a British Columbia court in ruling that Aboriginal oral histories are a valid basis for land claims. It also confirms that Native lands cannot be sold, except to the Crown. These lands are communally owned with exclusive right of use by the Native communities concerned.

1998: The federal minister of Indian affairs responds to the 1996 Royal Commission with a Statement of Reconciliation, apologizing for the residential school system and allocating $600 million for Native initiatives.

1998: British Columbia, Ottawa and Native leaders initial the Nisga'a land claim, giving the Nisga'a $253 million over fifteen years and more than two thousand square kilometres of land, resource rights and powers of self-government. The deal was approved by the House of Commons after an arduous debate in late 1999.

1999: The Supreme Court of Canada rules that a 1760 treaty gives the Mi'kmaq year-round fishing rights. The Court later clarifies the decision by claiming that the federal government still has a role to play in issues relating to fishing regulations in the area.

1999: The Federal Court of Appeal rules that the National Energy Board did not adequately deal with Native concerns when it granted a private company rights to build a $1.7 billion Sable Island natural gas pipeline.

1999: Nisga'a land claim is approved by the House of Commons.

2002: Agreement is made between Cree and the Québec government: *Ross River Dena Council Band v. Canada*, June 20, 2002. Aboriginals who can prove their forbears believed reserve lands had been agreed upon (not verified in an order-in-council) may have a legal case against the government.

2003: Supreme Court rules in *R. v. Powley* that the Métis people are a distinct Aboriginal group with a constitutional right to hunt for food.

2005: *Labrador Inuit Land Claim Agreement* is signed, the first to be formalized in Newfoundland and Labrador.

2007: Lheidli Tenneh First Nations in Northern BC narrowly rejects a land claim settlement.

groups to act precipitously by calling for an orderly transition negotiated "in good faith." However, such a process would have been extremely drawn out and slow to implement. Moreover, some provinces could still have opted out of the agreement, and there was no guarantee of how much federal or provincial funding would have been available to pay for self-government.

Since the failure of the Charlottetown Accord, the problem has been that although the federal government agrees with constitutionalizing self-government in principle, it has been unwilling to reopen constitutional negotiations to confirm it. As well, several provinces remain strongly opposed to recognizing such an inherent right in the Constitution, since it would require reopening a whole new and divisive bargaining session. To create a new order of government for Aboriginals would require the unanimous consent of all the partners to Confederation, and provincial leaders argue essentially that it would be too expensive, and that if it were allowed it would give a much stronger legal basis for even more land claims.

> ## CLOSE-UP ON
> ### Claims Initiatives
>
> ### CANADA'S SPECIFIC CLAIMS ACTION POLICY, 2008: KEY INITIATIVES
>
> - Create a new tribunal staffed with impartial judges who make final decisions on claims when negotiations fail
> - Arrange for more transparent financial compensation through dedicated funding for settlements in the amount of $250 million a year for ten years
> - Speed up processing of small claims and improve flexibility in the handling of large claims
> - Refocus the existing Indian Specific Claims Commission to concentrate on dispute resolution
>
> Source: Accessed at www.pm.gc.ca/eng/media.asp?id=1695 on June 12, 2007.

As a result, the federal government, and some provincial governments, have moved piecemeal to negotiate self-government agreements with Aboriginal people who have expressed such a desire. The negotiations do not affect any claims to an Aboriginal inherent right to self-government.

The *Indian Act* has long provided for limited local government on reserves through band councils. However, their jurisdictions are very narrow, and many communities want them to be much wider. Essentially, groups advocating self-government want control over areas such as the use of their land, community development, economic development, education, policing and so on. They have no interest in broader concerns such as foreign affairs, defence or banking. However, many of the areas targeted for self-government, like health care and education, are under provincial or territorial jurisdiction. Agreements must be reached about funding and sharing of interests not only with the federal government but also with provincial and municipal governments.

Once some self-government agreements were achieved, the concern became how they would be protected once put in place. Statutes are unsatisfactory because they could be changed at any time by the legislature that passed them. The only real way to protect the agreements would be to conclude section 35 treaties, as is done with land claims, so that they would have constitutional protection and could be amended only if both or all parties to the agreement give their consent. Since this can be achieved as a policy issue, it does not require constitutional change. Jean Chrétien's government took the stand that the principle of inherent right to Aboriginal self-government was already present in section 35 of the 1982 *Constitution Act*. It therefore proceeded to allow some aspects of self-government agreements to become section 35 treaties.

Nunavut was created through an agreement among the Tungavik Federation of Nunavut (TFN), the federal government and the government of the Northwest Territories to establish the new territory through federal legislation. It came into existence in 1999. The newest territory's inhabitants are roughly 85 percent Inuit. Nunavut's agreement is not technically a self-government pact, though, because it is similar in form and legal status to the agreements for the other two territories, and all residents of the territory have equal political rights regardless of ethnicity. However, the Inuit are confident of maintaining a majority, so it amounts to self-government.

First Nations self-government agreements in Yukon were the first to be ratified through the same process as the final agreements for land claims of a section 35 treaty.[30] This process has become a model for the negotiation of self-government and comprehensive claims to come, a precedent for later agreements. The Nisga'a and Labrador Inuit Association (LIA) agreements that followed were built on, and added to, the Yukon model. Meanwhile, new agreements are being protected as section 35 treaties, and others are being redone to achieve protection.

These model agreements resolved some important and very complicated problems concerning Aboriginal constitutions—issues of citizenship, areas of jurisdiction, intergovernmental relations and financing, to name a few. They allowed the new governments a wide range of legislative powers, but also allowed them to assume their responsibilities at their own volition when they were ready to do so. Very few Aboriginal governments are in a position to finance themselves with their own revenue sources, and the major cost implied in this new level of government is, and will continue to be, an ongoing issue. Many federal and provincial politicians are still wary of the unforeseen implications of self-government agreements. Some provincial governments are so cautious that they refuse to allow negotiated self-government agreements to obtain section 35 treaty status.

Most progress has been made on the community-based aspects of self-government. Aboriginal people now control 80 percent of their program funding from DIAND (the Department of Indian Affairs and Northern Development), and Aboriginal authorities increasingly deliver services such as police, education and child welfare. In 1999, the *First Nations Land Management Act* was passed. However, its successor, the *First Nations Government Act*, died in committee. It was intended to reform and modernize the First Nations governance systems, but First Nations peoples were divided about its content.

In August of 2007, however, the governments in Ottawa and Québec signed an agreement-in-principle with the Inuit of Québec. The agreement is remarkable in that, if passed through the Québec National Assembly and the House of Commons, a giant, mineral-rich region covering one-third of Québec above the 55th parallel (that once formed part of Rupert's Land) is slated to become a self-governing region with its own elected assembly by 2009. The self-governing region, to be called **Nunavik**, will represent 14 Inuit communities and a public service responsible for services such as education and health, and will be the first self-government agreement that is not based on ethnicity. Both Ottawa and Québec City will retain all legal powers in the region.

When Paul Martin became prime minister in late 2003, he made Aboriginal issues a priority. He established a cabinet committee on Aboriginal affairs, which he chaired, and set up a new Aboriginal affairs secretariat within the Privy Council. The Conservative government, elected in January 2006, recognizes the obligation of the federal government to improve the living conditions of Aboriginal Canadians, but it has

Courtesy of Patrick Corrigan.

different priorities. The 2007 budget cancelled the **Kelowna Accord**, an agreement reached by the previous Liberal government, the provincial and territorial governments and Native groups to increase funding on various Aboriginal programs by $800 million in the fiscal year 2006–07 and by $5.1 billion over the following five years. Instead, the 2007 budget decreased the funding for Aboriginal programs to $150 million in 2006–07 and $300 million in 2007–08. The Conservative government has, however, recognized that the *Indian Act* should be replaced by a modern legislative framework that will provide for the devolution of legal and democratic responsibility to First Nations to manage "their own affairs within the overall constitutional framework of the Canadian state."[31]

What Is Regionalism?

Regionalism has much in common with nationalism. It, too, appears across a wide spectrum, ranging from distinct but quiescent subcultures to separatist demands. But regionalism is only a distant relative of nationalism. In contrast to nationalism, which entails radical alteration of existing political structures, **regionalism** refers to territorial tensions brought about by groups that "demand a change in the political, economic and cultural relations between regions and central powers *within* the existing state."[32] Regionalist discontent is usually expressed in economic terms. It is found in peripheral and poorer regions of countries. However, regional discontent can also find expression in political terms, particularly when prosperous regions find themselves forced by the federal government to share their wealth with other provinces.

In the short term, because regionalism does not directly challenge territorial sovereignty, it appears to present less of a threat to the existing state structure than does nationalism. Regionalism does not have the underpinning of ethnicity that provides the strong emotional intensity needed for nationalism, even though its proponents may have common grievances, common territory, leadership and some common goals. In the long term, however, persistent indifference to regionalist demands by central authorities may result in a serious loss of legitimacy for the state in certain parts of the country. Moreover, in extreme circumstances such indifference could also provide the basis for the development of a separatist movement. This does not mean that regionalism isn't important politically or that outbursts of nationalist assertions will be avoided. It does mean, however, that nationalist movements do not develop based solely on regionalism.

Because regionalism does not take a nationalist form, but is nevertheless such a fundamental part of how Canada is governed, we describe its various political manifestations in appropriate places throughout the book. Regional political subcultures are discussed in Chapter 3. Major historical manifestations of regionalism have appeared in the guise of demands for power and economic resources to be transferred from Ottawa to the regions. These are discussed in Chapter 5 when they involve constitutional changes. The ongoing demands and controversies surrounding the distribution of federal–provincial powers and funding, and the arguments for centralized and decentralized government to accommodate regional demands are found in Chapters 5 and 6. The impact of regionalism and specific regional demands on government institutions are covered in Chapters 8 and 9. Chapters 11 and 12 discuss the manifestation of regionalism in political parties and elections.

Here, we do not want to reiterate these discussions, but rather to touch on some of the highlights in order to clarify the parallelism between the political forces of nationalism and regionalism, consider the causes of Western regionalism in particular and stress the importance of the topic.

31. See www.conservative.ca/EN/2692/41651. Accessed April 10, 2007.

32. Riccardo Petrella, "Nationalist and Regionalist Movements in Western Europe," in C. Foster, ed., *Nations without a State* (New York: Praeger, 1980), p. 10 (emphasis added). See also Janine Brodie, "Regions and Regionalism," in James P. Bickerton and Alain G. Gagnon, eds., *Canadian Politics* (Peterborough, ON: Broadview Press, 1994), pp. 409–25.

At the very least, regionalist protests add to the flow of demands that must be considered by policy-makers. Because most Canadian political parties, including government parties, to some extent have regional concentrations of support, regionalism has become an important, perhaps even the dominant, dimension of political life in this country.

If the greatest modern challenge to federalism is the threat of Québec separatism, the next in significance is undoubtedly the manifestation of alienation in some of the regions. All of the non-central provinces have some grievances against Central Canada and its governments in Ottawa, Toronto and Québec City. The litany includes complaints about official bilingualism, monetary policy, tariff policy, spending decisions and the treatment of fisheries and resource industries. The Atlantic provinces have always been characterized by a fierce pride and independence, but these qualities have been mitigated by a need for federal financial assistance. Their regional concerns over equalization payments are discussed in Chapters 6 and 14. Perhaps the most long-standing grievance in the area is over the hydroelectric development of Churchill Falls in Labrador, in which the federal government did not support Newfoundland. In 1967, Newfoundland wanted to develop the hydroelectric potential of this section of the upper Churchill River to sell to US markets. However, Québec refused to let Newfoundland transmit the power through its province. The federal government had the power to impose a corridor through Québec, but did not because it feared that if it did it would fuel Québec separatism. Consequently, Newfoundland was forced to sign an agreement that was highly in Québec's financial favour. That agreement will not expire for almost another 35 years and is hurting the financial ability of Newfoundland and Labrador to fund further power development.

In this section, we focus on the West, where alienation comprises economic discontent, antipathy—toward French Canada in particular—and demands for a stronger Western role in the federation.

Alienation: Views from the West

As we saw in Chapter 3, regional alienation is a major component of Western Canada's political subculture.[33] Throughout the West's history, there has been a strong belief that the resource-rich Prairie provinces have been exploited by federal government policies representing Central Canadian interests. This belief is based on the perceived economic and political domination of the rest of the country, especially by Montréal and the tiny but populous Golden Horseshoe area of southern Ontario. Westerners regularly note that until the election of the Conservatives in January 2006, Canada had spent the previous 36 years under prime ministers from or representing Québec, and just 15 months under PMs from the West.

> *We have always had a sense of economic exploitation. This notion has marked all political parties in the West. The cartoon that has captured these sentiments is one of a large cow standing on a map of Canada munching grass in Alberta and Saskatchewan, with milk pouring from a bulging udder into the large bucket in Ontario.*
>
> **Harry Strom, former Alberta premier**

The main thrust of Western discontent, however, hinges on a feeling of marginalization and alienation from the centres of economic and political power rather than on a simple desire for

---

33. On the concept of Western alienation, see Roger Gibbins, *Prairie Politics and Society* (Toronto: Butterworths, 1980); and Larry Pratt and Garth Stevenson, eds., *Western Separatism* (Edmonton: Hurtig, 1981).

separation from those centres, and may "reflect frustration at the lack of national integration as much as it does resistance to integration."[34]

Since the early days of Canada, perennial disagreements have arisen over federal freight-rate and tariff policies, which were blamed both for making the West a captive market for higher-priced manufactured goods from Central Canada and for increasing the cost of exporting products from the West. Westerners argue that such policies have allowed the East to remain the industrial heartland of Canada, while the West carries a disproportionate share of the costs.

Largely because of a mix of cultures and a relatively small francophone population in the West, political vision in the Prairies is based more on economic development than on cultural interests. Recent regionalist sympathies in the West have grown out of the period of economic prosperity in the 1970s and early 1980s. The scarcity and high cost of non-renewable energy in the form of oil and gas spurred Western economic development. Once one of the weak partners of the federal union, the West began to acquire enormous economic power through its sale of natural resources. As this economic wealth was exploited, migration to the West increased, and the region found itself capable of challenging what it considered the intolerable domination of Central Canada.

Regional Frustration, 1970–2008

Modern economic issues dividing Western and Central Canada continue to be interpreted within the context of alienation. Since the 1970s, regional criticism of the political and economic dominance of Central Canada has been expressed in a desire for constitutional reform. The Western provincial governments, for example, refused to compromise over patriation of the Constitution in 1982 until the federal government reduced its power, especially on economic issues. In other words, the jurisdictional issue of whether the provinces or the federal government should control resource development spilled over into the constitutional arena.

Western alienation in the early 1980s resulted in the formation of various groups and political parties dedicated to separating of the Western provinces from Canada. The separatist agitation was ignited by the re-election of the federal Liberals under Pierre Trudeau in 1980. This election effectively disenfranchised Western Canada politically, as the Liberals captured no seats west of Manitoba, but still managed to carry a majority. Subsequently, the Liberal government initiated two aggressive federal policies: unilateral patriation of the Constitution despite provincial objections; and implementation of the National Energy Program, which many westerners perceived as an attempt to rob them of their resource wealth.

The two leading separatist groups that combated the federal government in that period were the Western Canada Federation (West-Fed) and the Western Canada Concept (WCC). Frustrated by their lack of political power within the federal government, westerners also felt powerless against other "centralist" policies, including bilingualism, metrication and immigration.

Yet, the popularity of Western separatism dissipated as quickly as it had risen. As one observer noted, "the spontaneity of the separatist movement was both the most important reason for its success and its greatest handicap in developing into a solid, permanent political movement."[35] While the movement provided an outlet for the expression of frustration, there was little agreement among the groups, let alone within them, on strategy. Internal dissension assured that minor electoral successes were short-lived.

---

34. Gibbins, *Regionalism*, p. 181. See also J.F. Conway, *The West: The History of a Region in Confederation* (Toronto: Lorimer, 1983).

35. Denise Harrington, "Who Are the Separatists?" in Pratt and Stevenson, eds., *Western Separatism*, p. 24.

The acute sentiments of Western alienation that characterized the early 1980s declined when high oil prices, which had spurred the National Energy Program, dropped shortly after the Progressive Conservatives under Brian Mulroney won the 1984 general election in a landslide. The West supported Mulroney, and, with his victory, the Western regionalists expected to obtain strong and effective representation in government. To some extent, these expectations were justified: Mulroney dismantled the National Energy Program and the Trudeau marketing restrictions on the sale of oil and natural gas.

However, in October 1986, the Mulroney government awarded a valuable maintenance contract for the armed force's CF-18 fighter jets to a Montréal company instead of one in Winnipeg. Westerners were outraged. The Meech Lake initiative also infuriated them. For many, the feeling that the political system was stacked against the West simmered. They felt that the small elite running the federal Progressive Conservative party excluded them. After having supported Brian Mulroney, they turned on him as a symbol of Québec values, including special status for Québec, government largesse and opposition to capital punishment.

Westerners wanted a more democratic political process that included referendums, free votes and greater accountability of both their party and their government. Their dissent was given voice by Preston Manning, son of the former Social Credit premier of Alberta. In the 1988 general election, Manning headed the newly established Reform Party, and conducted a credible campaign for Western interests. Its demands for free trade and Senate reform found a ready audience among "small-c" conservative voters. The party named 72 candidates, and while it did not win any seats, it did garner 15 percent of the votes in Alberta and affected PC and NDP results throughout the West.

Reform won 51 seats in the next general election in 1993, mainly in Alberta and British Columbia. Given the collapse of the PCs, Reform had an opportunity to develop a strong party and take the PCs' place. Instead, Preston Manning chose to accentuate "Western" concerns in the 1997 election. His party won 60 seats (all from the West) and he became leader of the Official Opposition in the House of Commons.

The Reform Party continued to play on Western alienation. It called for changes to the Senate in order to reduce the power of Central Canada, and for populist devices such as referendums, recalls and initiatives to reduce the power of the House of Commons. But the centrepiece of Reform policy was the explicit demand for a reduction in taxation and government expenditures. The party also stood against bilingualism, declaring that attempts by the federal government to "politicize and institutionalize and constitutionalize English–French relations on a national basis . . . have led again, as they have in the past, not to unity but to crisis."[36]

> *Reform is founded on the belief of many Canadians that our political process needs fundamental reform, that our Parliament is too partisan, too undemocratic and too unaccountable. To remedy this we have proposed serious changes . . . to bring Canadians directly into decision-making on the most critical issues in society, issues such as abortion, capital punishment and constitutional reform.*
>
> **Preston Manning**

To broaden Reform's base, Manning tried to join forces with the Progressive Conservatives, but, failing in that, he founded the Canadian Alliance party to succeed Reform. He promptly lost the party leadership. In 2000, the Canadian Alliance peaked at 66 MPs, but support outside the

---

36. Robert J. Jackson and Doreen Jackson, *Stand Up for Canada: Leadership and the Canadian Political Crisis* (Scarborough, ON: Prentice Hall, 1992), p. 198.

West still did not materialize. The realization that it would never advance beyond being a regional political rump motivated the amalgamation with the PCs in 2003 to form the Conservative Party of Canada (see Chapter 11).

Under the leadership of Stephen Harper, the new Conservative Party became the Official Opposition in 2004 and formed a minority government in 2006. It has strengthened its relationship with Québec and pursued policies that are hard to differentiate from the preceding Liberal government. Its conservative base in the West is silent as the prospect of a Conservative majority government is on the horizon. The party will eventually need to consolidate common ground that accommodates both the right-wing Western values of Reform and also those of the so-called *red Tories* from the former PCs, who value more moderate, inclusive policies, and are conciliatory toward Québec.

In the recent past, when the political right has won power federally it has been because there was a pragmatic union of the party on the right of centre with decentralist westerners and left-of-centre nationalist Québeckers who are also decentralists. It happened under John Diefenbaker in 1958 and again under Brian Mulroney in 1984. A majority Conservative government now might at least temporarily redress the attitude of many westerners that they put more into the federation than they receive in benefits. However, the potential for continued challenges remains—perhaps awaiting only a major confrontation with the federal government over the future of Québec within the federation, or perhaps another confrontation over energy.

The underlying problem of regional alienation continues to be easy to state, but not resolve. The combined population of Ontario and Québec considerably exceeds 50 percent of the entire country and this gives them a large majority of the members of the House of Commons. Because of this, the outer regions often believe that the federal parliamentary system represents only Central Canada and, therefore, to an extent, is itself merely a regional government. Yet if democracy prevails—that is, the rule that votes should count relatively equally—the most populous provinces and regions will always have a majority.

Many solutions to alienation have been proposed over the years by westerners: switch political parties, abolish parties, create new parties, reform the electoral process, decentralize more powers to the provinces, achieve Senate reform, abolish party discipline and so on. All of these proposals are discussed in coming chapters. Some of the demands are obviously based on genuine grievances. Others are mere posturing as the premiers of provinces unify to present a chorus of complaints to the central government to win financial concessions. Few premiers have anything useful to say about the country beyond their provincial borders. As one commentator put it,

> *The premiers ask not what they can do for their country; they ask what their country can do for them.*[37]

The premiers, like municipal politicians, tend to show a remarkable obliviousness toward what might be best for all Canadians, not just those they specifically represent. As mayor of Calgary in the 1980s, for example, Ralph Klein blamed "eastern bums and scums" for coming to Alberta and straining the city's social services. As premier, Klein's views were equally outspoken.

Meanwhile, in theory at least, the federal government continues to be the one government voice that speaks for Canadians as a whole. It continues the principle of redistribution—collecting tax money from Canadians and redistributing it according to established formulas based on need, so that the prosperity of one region or province will be shared with others that are demonstrably less fortunate. This enables all Canadians to have the possibility to receive similar access to education, health

---

37. Andrew Cohen, "Ten little men short of ideas," *The Globe and Mail*, July 15, 2003.

care and other benefits. Federal governments also are extremely respectful of regions in the assignment of cabinet portfolios, so that regions do get cabinet representation even when they have not supported the government. Federal–provincial conferences are held regularly in attempts to make accommodations and reach understandings, although they are often occasions for the provincial premiers to "gang up" on the federal government to demand more money and powers.

There are several issues that have been contentious in the past few years. In 2004, then Alberta premier Ralph Klein spoke of "the things that seem to irk Western Canadians." Topping the list, he said, was health care and bovine spongiform encephalopathy (BSE—known as mad cow disease). The health-care issue has been contentious since the 1990s, when Alberta's PC government privatized and deregulated services such as car licensing, liquor retailing and electricity distribution, and flirted with doing the same thing with aspects of health care. The idea of privatizing health care dismayed Canadians, who hold that the *Canada Health Act* represents a core Canadian value (see Chapter 6). The concern over BSE was that a US ban on live cattle was still in place 14 months after BSE was discovered in Alberta. The ban caused severe economic trauma to Canadian cattle farmers, most of whom are from the West. Although the ban was lifted the following year, the perception that the federal government did not act effectively to get it lifted quickly created considerable ill will.

The list of what irks westerners would undoubtedly include other policy irritants initiated by former Liberal governments in Ottawa, such as the gun registry—a federal program to register guns that was unpopular with Western gun owners in the first place, and then ran massively over budget; the Wheat Board—a governmental regulating body for marketing Western grain that is so resented by some farmers that they would rather to go to jail than pay fines for breaking the rules; and the *Kyoto Accord*—many Westerners claim that the implementation would disrupt the economy and cause serious losses to companies connected to the oil industry (supporters argue that the adjustment would be short and would benefit the economy as a whole).

Then, of course, there are structural irritants that are perceived to impede Western influence: the appointed Senate, and public policy made by unelected judges in the Supreme Court. These complaints are capped by the basic dislike Albertans have for equalization payments and financial transfers to "have-not" provinces. Since Alberta is a "have" province, Albertans see their money flowing to Québec and "Liberal" Atlantic Canada. Compounding this is Western distaste for the electoral finance law enacted in 2004 that financially rewards parties for votes won in elections. From a Western viewpoint, the law provides an unmerited financial bonanza for the separatist Bloc Québécois (the BQ received considerably less money before the revised electoral financing rules were brought in).

The 2006 election has done a lot to diminish the frustration westerners experienced after the 2004 federal vote. It satisfied their ongoing complaints that prime ministers come mostly from Québec; that Ontario and Québec decide the outcome of elections; and that votes cast after the polls close in Québec and Ontario carry little or no weight. In 2004, for example, three quarters of Western ridings had voted Conservative, but the Liberals still won a minority government. The depth of feeling was evident in renewed calls for building a "firewall" around Alberta "to limit the extent to which an aggressive and hostile federal government can encroach upon legitimate provincial jurisdiction" (a call later rejected by former premier Ralph Klein):

> *If we cannot achieve more Western influence within Ottawa (the purpose of Senate reform),*
> *let's pursue reasonable policies to reduce Ottawa's influence in the West: Withdraw from the*
> *Canada Pension Plan and create our own provincial pension plans; collect our own income*
> *taxes; cancel our contracts with the RCMP, and create our own provincial police forces; take*
> *control of our health-delivery systems; and use the notwithstanding clause when nine, non-*

> *elected judges in Ottawa try to impose their notion of good public policy on our democratically elected governments.*
>
> **Ted Morton, professor and Alberta MLA**[38]

Since the minority win by the Conservative Party in 2006, calls for Western separation and regional alienation have basically ceased. The West is in. In 2008, it is Ontarians who feel hard done by because of a declining manufacturing economy and a highly valued Canadian dollar.

It is important to keep in mind that in spite of fringe-group separatists and the posturing of the premiers, regional disparities and the manner they are dealt with are distinguishing features of Canadian politics. The belief that the rich provinces and regions should help the poorer ones has been a fundamental part of the Canadian political culture. The idea of sharing through redistribution is built into the political system and is viewed by most Canadians as the just way to cope with differences in wealth. We can expect this idea to continue to permeate politics in Canada.

Critical Debate
Nationalism and Regionalism: Uniters or Dividers?

Are nationalism and regionalism justifiable positions in Canada, or are they simply divisive? What should the federal government do about these vital and controversial issues?

| Point

Separatism is the extreme expression of nationalism. It is not a justifiable position in Canada. Neither are expressions of virulent regionalism that divide the country and diminish the prosperity and security of Canadians as a whole. The federal government should maintain a hard line on these issues, preserving a strong central authority that can even out economic and social disparities among provinces and regions. A minority of Canadians must not be allowed to tyrannize the majority with threats and intimidation.

In the cases of both French Canadians and Native peoples, historical injustices have been committed by the governing authorities of Canada, whether by design, neglect or ignorance. However, virtually all of those injustices have been, or are in the process of being, corrected.

Canada has a long and internationally respected history of democracy. There are recognized and legal ways to bring issues before our government and settle disagreements in courts. In the province of Québec, where ethnic and regional boundaries largely overlap, citizens are treated fairly within the federation. Canada's prime ministers have been from Québec for more than two-thirds of the sixty years that have passed since the end of the Second World War, although Québeckers comprise roughly a quarter of the population. Many governors general, ministers of finance, ministers of foreign affairs and other top leaders have come from that province. Québec has constitutional rights that guarantee its representation in the House of Commons and Senate regardless of whether

38. F.L. (Ted) Morton, "The firewall's looking good again," *The Globe and Mail*, July 2, 2004. Stephen Harper was one of six signators of the original "firewall" letter published in the *National Post* as an open letter to Premier Ralph Klein on January 24, 2001. Available on the web at www.cbc.ca/canadavotes/leaders parties/leaders/pdf/firewall.pdf. Accessed September 9, 2007.

there is a decline in population. Francophones are able to communicate with the federal government in their own language, and many government positions are designated bilingual.

Most of the financial grievances touted by Québec nationalist leaders are inaccurate and intended to stir up emotional support for separatism. Separatist leaders have a vested interest in division and therefore appeal to historical injustices and ethnic insecurities. Their continual threat of separatist referendums is a drain on the time, finances and emotions of other Canadians.

As for the nationalist aspirations of Canada's Native peoples, they largely concern land claims and self-government. Tremendous progress has been made in both areas since the 1970s and continues today, largely due to the effective organization and leadership of the various Native groupings themselves. When it proved politically impossible to amend the Constitution to accommodate Native self-government aspirations, the impasse was broken by going forward with agreements and making them section 35 agreements so that they were, in effect, constitutionalized without having to get formal changes to the Constitution. Other serious problems on reserves are being addressed by political actions. By working within the system, Native peoples have won many of their demands and considerable respect from other Canadians.

Unlike nationalism, regionalism is an expression of alienation that results from factors such as history, geography, immigration patterns and natural resources that cannot for the most part be changed. Because of such differences and disparities, each of Canada's provinces and regions has its own particular grievances and demands. It is up to the federal government to do the difficult job of balancing the needs of the various regions while working for the good of all Canadians.

In the past couple of decades, westerners have perceived that their interests have not been met in Ottawa. But since the bulk of the population of Canada resides in Central Canada, it is not realistic to expect that the West will get its way on issues without convincing at least Ontario or Québec to agree to its concerns and demands. The basic philosophy of federalism is one of sharing, of redistributing wealth so that all Canadians enjoy a common standard of living. In our democracy, groups that want to change major policies have to support pan-Canadian political parties that can attract enough voters to form the government. In order to accomplish this, they must work with a majority of Canadians and several provinces.

A degree of regionalism and nationalism is inevitable in Canada. Compromises can and should be made to accommodate regional and nationalist interests but, in the end, such interests must not be allowed to override those of the majority. Canadian democracy works, and works well.

Counterpoint

Neither separatism nor regionalism exists without some reason, and therefore both are eminently justifiable positions. They are indications that the voices of particular groups are not being heard and that their interests are not being accommodated. In our democracy, they provide a mechanism for the relief of social pressures. Canada has a strong enough national identity to withstand such issues.

Regions and provinces must be able to counter the strong centralizing tendencies and preferences of the federal government. They have a democratic right to voice their opinions, needs, preferences and dreams, and to try to address them through the political system. The federal government needs to listen much better to what the regionalists and nationalists are saying, and should be more willing to compromise and not act so rigidly about guarding its powers. It is an unfortunate fact of life that minority demands often must be made long and strong before they are recognized and responded to. In the years after Confederation, both francophones and Native peoples suffered from government policies of assimilation. Without strong voices, they would be much worse off today than they are.

During the past four decades, powerful nationalist pressures in Québec created serious challenges to the federal political system. Two referendums, one in 1980 and another in 1995, asked Québeckers if they wanted to separate from Canada. Canadians outside Québec stood by helplessly, not knowing whether the country would disintegrate. The 1995 referendum was so close that the government found it necessary to clarify what would happen in the event of yet another such occurrence. The Supreme Court issued its 1998 decisions on the constitutionality of secession efforts, and both the federal and Québec legislatures responded with their own policies. The federal government also attempted to rebalance the federal financial equilibrium by decentralizing in targeted areas. These actions would not have been taken without the very strong pressures brought to bear by the Québec separatist movement.

Similarly, the nationalist aspirations of Canada's Native peoples are based on common historical grievances. Since Native peoples are not a cohesive group sharing the same goals, and because they are scattered across Canada's entire land mass, and since their cultural history is so different from other Canadians, it took a very long time for Natives to achieve the respect that they deserve. They needed leadership and organization, and with it they have learned to work within the framework of democratic government. It is this willingness that has earned them respect and enabled them to make such progress toward their goals.

Western regionalism, too, is based on grievances. But the grievances are not ethnically based, and for the most part are not separatist-oriented, but rather result from a frustrated expression of disillusionment. The regional differences of geography, resources and population persist, and must be asserted. Only the continued expression of dissatisfaction will convince other Canadians that some political accommodations are necessary. Some form of enhanced regional representation, whether through Senate reform or electoral change, should result from these regional pressures. Dissatisfaction in the West brought massive political change to Ottawa in some of the last general elections, with the arrival of the Reform and Canadian Alliance parties—and since 2003, we've had a reunited right with the formation of the Conservative Party of Canada.

The concerns of Québec and the West must be balanced by the federal government, and in a way that will leave Canada strong and united. Similarly, the concerns of Native peoples must be recognized and settled.

It is still not clear whether Canadian federalism will be able to meet the challenge of Québec separatism while still attending to the concerns of other regions. The West in particular, located far from the political centre in Ottawa, showed its own unique concerns when it abandoned its traditional support for the Progressive Conservatives and New Democrats and voted for a new protest party. The result brought a new dynamic to Parliament, with the Reform/Alliance parties and currently the new Conservatives (who joined forces with the old Tories). The West-supported Conservatives were strong enough in 2004 to win 99 seats and form the Official Opposition in the House. In 2006, this new configuration of Canadian politics allowed for the election of a leader from the West as prime minister of Canada. Although Stephen Harper did not achieve the majority government he and the Conservatives wanted, they may be able to do it next time.

Discussion Questions

1. What is your position on the Critical Debate, and what can you add to justify it?
2. Is the French language threatened in Québec? Why or why not?
3. Is there such a thing as Aboriginal nationalism? Why or why not?

4. Do you approve of how the federal governments of Chrétien, Martin and Harper have responded to Québec since the 1995 referendum?

5. How is regionalism in Western Canada similar and dissimilar to Québec separatism? Will the election of Stephen Harper as prime minister of a majority government change the situation?

 Visit our new Companion Website at **www.pearsoned.ca/jackson,** where you can use the interactive Study Guide and link to additional resources on topics discussed in the text.

Selected Bibliography
Nationalism and Québec Nationalism

Beheils, M., ed. *Quebec Since 1945: Selected Readings.* Toronto: Copp Clark Pitman, 2000.

Bothwell, Robert. *Canada and Quebec: One Country, Two Histories*, rev. ed. Vancouver: University of British Columbia Press, 1998.

Carens, Joseph H., ed. *Is Quebec Nationalism Just? Perspectives from English Canada.* Montréal: McGill-Queen's University Press, 1995.

Côté, Marcel and David Johnson. *If Quebec Goes: The Real Cost of Separation.* Toronto: Stoddart, 1995.

Gagnon, Alain, and Rafaele Iacovino. *Federalism, Citizenship and Quebec: Debating Multinationalism.* Toronto: University of Toronto Press, 2007.

Gibbins, Roger and Guy Laforest, eds. *Beyond the Impasse: Toward Reconciliation.* Montréal: Institute for Research on Public Policy, 1998.

Gibson, Gordon. *Plan B: The Future of the Rest of Canada.* Vancouver: Fraser Institute, 1994.

Hillmer, Norman and Adam Chapnick, eds. *Canadas of the Mind: The Making and Unmaking of the Canadian Nationalisms in the Twentieth Century.* Montréal: McGill-Queen's University Press, 2007.

Ignatieff, Michael. *Blood and Belonging: Journeys into the New Nationalism.* Toronto: Viking, 1993.

Johnston, Richard, et al. *The Challenge of Direct Democracy: The 1992 Canadian Referendum.* Montréal: McGill-Queen's University Press, 1996.

Keating, Michael. *Nations against the State: The New Politics of Nationalism in Quebec, Catalonia and Scotland.* New York: St. Martin's Press, 1996.

Kenerman, Gerald. *Multicultural Nationalism.* Vancouver: UBC Press, 2005.

MacMillan, C. Michael. *The Practice of Language Rights in Canada.* Toronto: University of Toronto Press, 1998.

McRoberts, Ken. *Beyond Quebec: Taking Stock of Canada.* Montréal: McGill-Queen's University Press, 1995.

——————. *Misconceiving Canada: The Struggle for National Unity.* Toronto: Oxford University Press, 1997.

Monahan, Patrick J., and Michael J. Bryant, *Coming to Terms with Plan B: Ten Principles Governing Secession* (Toronto: C.D. Howe Institute, 1996).

Shugarman, David. *Misconceiving Canada: The Struggle for National Unity.* Toronto: Oxford University Press, 1997.

Smith, Anthony D. *National Identity.* Las Vegas: University of Nevada Press, 1991.

Taylor, Charles. *Reconciling the Solitudes: Essays on Canadian Federalism and Nationalism.* Guy Laforest, ed. Montréal: McGill-Queen's University Press, 1993.

Trent, John E., Robert Young and Guy Lachapelle, eds. *Quebec–Canada: What Is the Path Ahead?* (Ottawa: University of Ottawa Press, 1997.

Young, Robert A. *The Struggle for Quebec.* Montréal: McGill-Queen's University Press, 1999.

Regionalism

Braid, Don, and Sydney Sharpe. *Breakup: Why the West Feels Left Out of Canada.* Toronto: Key Porter Books, 1990.

Gibbins, Roger, and Loleen Berdahl. *Western Visions, Western Futures.* Peterborough, ON: Broadview Press, 2003.

Tomblin, Stephen G. *Ottawa and the Outer Provinces.* Halifax: Lorimer, 1995.

Tomblin, Stephen G., and Charles Colgan, eds., *Regionalism in a Global Society: Persistence and Change in Atlantic Canada and New England.* Peterborough, ON: Broadview Press, 2004.

Native Peoples

Alfred, Gerald, *Heeding the Voices of our Ancestors: Kahnawake Mohawk Politics and the Rise of Native Nationalism.* Don Mills, ON: Oxford University Press, 1995.

Asch, Michael, ed. *Aboriginal and Treaty Rights in Canada: Essays on Law, Equality and Respect for Difference.* Vancouver: UBC Press, 1997.

Frideres, James S. *Aboriginal Peoples in Canada: Contemporary Conflicts*, 6th ed. Don Mills, ON: Prentice Hall, 2002.

Guibernau, M.G., and Hutchinson, J., eds., *Understanding Nationalism.* Cambridge, UK: Polity Press, 2001.

McKee, Christopher. *Treaty Talks in British Columbia: Negotiating a Mutually Beneficial Future*, 2nd ed. Vancouver: UBC Press, 2000.

Scott, Colin H., ed. *Aboriginal Autonomy and Development in Northern Quebec and Labrador.* Vancouver: UBC Press, 2001.

(See also the Selected Bibliographies in Chapters 2, 3 and 6.)

Chapter 8
The Executive Apex
Governor General, Prime Minister and Cabinet

In Canada, there are three separate branches of governmental institutions: the executive, the legislature and the judiciary. Here, we describe and explain the nature of *executive* power, both ceremonial and political. In many respects, this power is comparable to a Shakespearean drama: there is a world of difference between appearance and reality. This is particularly the case in parliamentary minority situations, as the 2004 Liberal government of Paul Martin and the 2006 Conservative government of Stephen Harper illustrate very well.

The nature of political power and its exercise is an exceedingly complex and fascinating phenomenon. The analysis of leaders and their policies has always been a favourite pursuit of political scientists and pundits. Perennial debates and studies consider who really exercises power, what the machinery of leadership is and whether power is shifting in some fashion. It is complicated because, as we saw in Chapter 1, political power is an abstract commodity, changing in response to the dynamic political and social environment in which a variety of issues, problems and personalities come and go. Political power is, in a manner of speaking, like a complex mathematical equation in which there are a few constant values and many indeterminate ones.

In contemporary states, the task of applying the rules of society is concentrated in a core **executive**. This broad term is used to depict the institutions, personnel and behaviour of governmental power. Generally, there are two kinds of rules in a society—constitutional laws, or the basic rules of the game, and less fundamental laws, such as policies and resolutions. Both types of rules are implemented by the executive, which, in performing this function, plays a vital role in the political system.

Canada's constitutional heritage from Britain includes a *formal* executive, the Crown and the governor general, and also a *political* executive concerned primarily with the realities of power in contemporary Canadian politics. We begin this chapter by examining the formal executive, including the heritage of parliamentary government and its effects on executive power. Next, we outline the role of the prime minister and the structure of cabinet decision-making. The cases of majority and minority governments are carefully dissected. These analyses are followed by an examination of the administrative agencies that support the executive by providing specialized research, advice and assistance in policy formation and implementation. Studies of ethics, conflict of interest and patronage fill out this section.

The Critical Debate for this chapter concerns power. Does the prime minister exercise too much power? Does Canada really have a presidential government in disguise? How does the prime minister's power change depending on whether there is a minority or majority government?

The Formal Executive: Crown, Monarchy and Governor General

The *Constitution Act, 1867* (formerly the *BNA Act*), sets out in general terms the powers and prerogatives of formal authority in Canada. Section 9 declares that the "Executive Government and Authority of and over Canada . . . is vested in the Queen." This principle is fleshed out in the

formal Exec
Crown + governor general

Letters Patent and must be understood in the light of the traditional *royal prerogative* (see below).[1] While there is no question that the powers of the formal executive are largely ceremonial, it would be incorrect to dismiss them as trivial and meaningless. There have been situations in which the formal executive has proven a very important element in the political process itself.

Pomp and Circumstance: Crown and Monarch

Following British tradition, the ornate parts of the Constitution place supreme authority of the Canadian state in the sovereign. Government functions are carried out in the name of the *Crown*. In Britain, the Crown has been defined as "the sum total of governmental powers synonymous with the Executive."[2] In Canada, the term **Crown** refers to the composite symbol of the institutions of the state. The Crown may be involved in court proceedings.[3] It also assumes a variety of other duties and responsibilities—for example, government property may be held in the name of the Crown.

The Crown retains some rights from the feudal period, but most of its present authority comes from constitutional and statute law. Its few remaining *prerogative powers* can be traced to the period of authoritarian rule in Great Britain when the Crown possessed wide discretionary authority. With the rise of Parliament and the gradual movement toward popular sovereignty, the authority of the Crown eroded to a very few **reserve powers**. Although Parliament and the political executive still govern in the name of the Crown, there is little question that the power of the monarch is severely limited. Even the ability of the monarch to stay on the throne is no longer a right. In the cases of both James II and Edward VIII in Britain, it was clear that they could not retain their crowns unless the ministers and Parliament were prepared to accept them.

The reigning monarch, currently Queen Elizabeth II, is the personal embodiment of the Crown. The contemporary functions of the monarch are largely ceremonial and non-partisan. The monarch reigns, but does not govern. As British constitutionalist Walter Bagehot put it, the monarch's functions are mainly of the "dignified," not the "efficient," type.[4] By this, Bagehot meant that the monarch does not actually govern the country but, rather, carries out myriad ceremonial responsibilities that generate mass support for government, while the ministers carry out the "efficient" procedures that operate the machinery of government.

Although the monarchy is of necessity personified in an individual, one should separate individual peculiarities and institutional strengths. Individuals come and go, but the Crown is permanent. It provides history, tradition and an institutional framework that can promote political stability as long as the institution is regarded as legitimate by a large majority of the people. The ancient flummery surrounding the monarch induces respect for authority from many people and is part of what has been called "the living dead of the constitution."

The Governor General and Lieutenant-Governors

Since the monarch was not based permanently in Canada, a representative known as the governor general was originally appointed by the British government as dictated by the *Constitution Act, 1867*. As Canada evolved out of colonialism toward autonomy, the nature of this executive link was modified. The Imperial Conference of 1926 sought to make the governor general a representative of the Crown, *not* of the British government. In 1947, new **Letters Patent**—the instruments that the sovereign makes applicable to each governor general through a commission of appointment—

---

1. See Andrew Heard, *Canadian Constitutional Conventions* (Toronto: Oxford University Press, 1991).
2. E.C.S. Wade and A.W. Bradley, *Constitutional Law*, 8th ed. (London: Longman, 1970), pp. 171ff., 678ff.
3. Since the passage of the *Crown Liability Act* of 1952, the Crown can be sued like any other litigant.
4. Walter Bagehot, *The English Constitution* (London: World's Classics, 1928).

completed the process by allowing the governor general the power to exercise the powers of the sovereign. However, the monarchical link was never ended. The Queen continues to be Canada's monarch: she makes royal tours to Canada and acts as the symbolic head of the Commonwealth, of which Canada is a member.

As the Queen's representative, the governor general is appointed by Her Majesty on the recommendation of the Canadian prime minister and the cabinet. In 1952, the office was further Canadianized by the appointment of Vincent Massey, the first Canadian to hold the position (see Table 8.1). It has since become customary to alternate the position between English- and French-speaking Canadians. The appointment of Edward Schreyer in 1979 added a new dimension to this trend, since he was an English-speaking Canadian from neither charter group. The next appointee, in 1984, Jeanne Sauvé, a French Canadian, became the first woman to hold this high office. Governors general have often been selected from outside the partisan political sphere, mainly from the diplomatic or military establishment, but many have been politicians. In 1994, Prime Minister Chrétien appointed the Liberal Senate speaker, Roméo LeBlanc, an Acadian, as governor general, and in 1999 he chose Adrienne Clarkson, a bilingual journalist who was the first member of a visible minority to be chosen as head of state. In 2005, Michaëlle Jean, a Québec journalist, took over as head of state.

The governor general, in performing the Queen's "dignified" roles in Canada, provides little practical input into the political process. The tenure of office is usually five years, but the officially recognized term is six years, which has on occasion been extended to seven. In the event of the death, incapacity, removal or absence of the governor general, the chief justice of the Supreme Court, Canada's leading judge, acts as the administrator and may carry out all duties of the office.

The functions of the governor general as head of state provide the official monarchical structure of the Canadian government on an everyday basis. First, many purely ceremonial functions such as conferring Order of Canada awards or reviewing troops are carried out by the appointee. Second, the governor general also acts as a symbol of the state. After studying loyalty in many political regimes, theorists have found that individuals may be socialized into acceptance of authority through their attachment to august figures such as the governor general.

The governor general is bound to act on almost every piece of advice given by his ministers. Nevertheless, certain functions are the governor general's alone. The most important of these stem from the **prerogative powers** left to the monarch—powers that have not been bypassed by constitutional or statute law. The Letters Patent provide the governor general with all the powers of the Queen "in respect of summoning, proroguing or dissolving the Parliament of Canada." Clearly, the most significant power is the duty to appoint a prime minister. In order to exercise this

TABLE 8.1 Canadian Governors General, 1952–2008

	Year Appointed
Vincent Massey	1952
Georges Vanier	1959
Roland Michener	1967
Jules Léger	1974
Edward Schreyer	1979
Jeanne Sauvé	1984
Ramon Hnatyshyn	1990
Roméo LeBlanc	1994
Adrienne Clarkson	1999
Michaëlle Jean	2005

prerogative power, the governor general must have a reasonably free hand to make decisions based on the circumstances and precedents.[5]

On two occasions in the 1890s, the governor general had to help find someone to be prime minister because the Conservative Party had no clear successor to the outgoing leader.[6] In cases where there is a leader of a party who can command a clear majority of the seats in the House of Commons, the governor general has nothing to do but select the obvious candidate. Today, if there were no obvious leader after a prime minister died in office, for example, the cabinet and/or caucus would undoubtedly name an interim leader pending a leadership convention, and the governor general would name this person prime minister.

A major issue remains. If there were no majority for any leader in the House of Commons, the governor general might have to use his discretion in selecting the prime minister. In 28 of the 39 elections since Confederation, one of the two major parties obtained an absolute majority of the seats in the House, so the governor general was not required to exercise personal discretion. However, when election results are confused or produce no majority, the governor general could be forced to exercise the prerogative in an independent manner. Such discretionary power would always be subject to controversy, and in every case but one

> ### CLOSE-UP ON
> ### Institutions
>
> ### KING–BYNG AND DISSOLUTION, 1926
>
> Governor General Lord Byng declined King's request for dissolution and an election. Instead, he called on Conservative leader Arthur Meighen to form a new administration. The governor general was cognizant of two special factors: the House was in the process of discussing a censure motion against the minority Liberal government, and the Conservatives held the largest number of seats in the House.[*] It was theoretically possible that the Progressive party, which held the balance of power in the House, could have supported a Tory minority government.
>
> As it turned out, however, the Progressives would not give their continued support to the new Conservative government and within three days the government fell. Meighen, in turn, had to ask the governor general for dissolution of Parliament. In the election that ensued, the Liberals charged that the governor general had favoured the Conservatives and that the British were again interfering in Canada. The electoral victory of the Liberals demonstrated that, although the governor general may possess some constitutional powers about the dissolution of Parliament, the people are the final arbiters of whether the action is appropriate.
>
> _____
>
> [*] The results of the previous election in 1925 were Conservatives, 116; Liberals, 101; Progressives, 24; and others, 4 seats.

(discussed below) the governor general has chosen as prime minister the leader of the party that received the *largest* number of seats in the House of Commons—even if the party did not obtain a *majority* of the seats.

For purposes of discussion, the dissolution of Parliament is too often separated from the appointment of the prime minister. But the two are logically related. It is generally agreed that only a prime minister can ask for and obtain dissolution of Parliament; however, a governor general once refused such a request. This incident was the famous King–Byng case in 1926 (see the "Close-Up on Institutions: King–Byng and Dissolution"). The precedent is now fairly firm that governors general should follow the advice of their prime ministers on the dissolution of Parliament. In December 1979, Progressive Conservative PM Joe Clark, who headed a minority government, was defeated on the budget. Although, theoretically, the Liberals could have been asked to try to form a government, the governor general consulted Mr. Clark and dissolved Parliament without discussing the matter with any of the opposition parties.

Can a governor general dismiss a government? It has always been assumed that this would prove impossible when one party controls a majority in the House. However, the Australian

---

5. For a thorough study of the precedents see Andrew Heard, *Canadian Constitutional Precedents* (Toronto: Oxford University Press, 1991).

6. J.T. Saywell, "The Crown and the Politicians," *Canadian Historical Review* (December 1956), pp. 309–37. John A. Macdonald (1891) and John Thompson (1894) both died in office without obvious successors in place.

Canberra Case upset the certainty of this contention. While the Australian constitutional structure differs from that of Canada in many respects (especially in the fact that the upper house is an elected body), it has generally been assumed that the governors general of both countries were unable to dissolve Parliament. In the November 1975 Canberra case, however, the Australian Senate continually held up supply bills from the lower house, creating a financial crisis. The Liberal and Country parties controlled the Senate, while the lower house was controlled by the prime minister, Gough Whitlam, and his Labor Party. The governor general wanted to dissolve both houses. Whitlam refused, and the governor general dismissed him. The governor general asked the leader of the opposition to form a government on the condition that he would immediately request dissolution. In the bitter election campaign that followed, the Liberal–Country coalition was elected. In other words, the governor general's recommendation was electorally upheld.

The effect of this precedent is difficult to determine, since nothing equivalent has occurred in Canada. In view of the changing nature of the Commonwealth and the weakening bonds between the members, constitutional precedents are likely to prove more and more inconsequential over time. It is fairly safe to say that no governor general in Canada will follow the Australian example, but the matter is not entirely settled.

Perhaps more important than formal constitutional power is the governor general's opportunity to advise prime ministers. The governor general meets regularly with the prime minister to discuss general points, personnel or appointments, and on such occasions prime ministers have been known to solicit advice on policy matters. In other words, the governor general has a degree of access that is denied to most individuals. Sir Wilfrid Laurier confided, "The Canadian Governor General long ago ceased to determine policy, but he is by no means, or need not be, the mere figurehead of the public image. He has the privilege of advising his advisers, and if he is a man of sense and experience, his advice is often taken."[7] Or as former governor general Adrienne Clarkson, put it when she was asked a sensitive question, "If I have a view on that, I will communicate it to the prime minister, to whom I have a direct conduit."[8]

The monarch has a representative in each province as well as in Ottawa. A **lieutenant-governor** appointed by the governor-in-council on the advice of the prime minister (often chosen from a provincial list) represents the monarch in each province. The lieutenant-governor acts on the advice, and with the assistance, of his ministry or executive council at the provincial level of government, which is responsible to the legislature, and resigns office under circumstances similar to those for the federal government. It is unclear whether a lieutenant-governor can today delay or kill a bill by refusing to sign it. (See the discussion of reservation and disallowance in Chapter 5.)

The Political Executive

Apart from the ceremonial functions of government discussed above, the main task of the executive is providing leadership. The determination of which bodies constitute the executive is complex, as there is no accepted view of how government should be organized. As a result, *executive leadership* may refer to formal roles, individuals, types of activities or the results of such activities. The executive leaders discussed here have been selected on the basis of their formal roles. They include the prime minister, the ministry—including the cabinet—and their immediate staff.

The central feature of any survey of Canada's political heritage must be the pervasive impact of the British model of parliamentary government. Although other aspects of Canadian life have been

---

7. O.D. Skelton, *Life and Letters of Sir Wilfrid Laurier*, vol. II, David L. Farr, ed. (Ottawa: Carleton University, 1965), p. 86n. Originally published in Toronto, 1921.

8. *The Globe and Mail*, September 9, 1999.

strongly influenced by the United States, the parliamentary form of government is firmly entrenched and has proven remarkably resistant to change. The Constitution established a type of government based on the British example, with the exception that there was to be a federal division of legislative powers in recognition of the diversity of the country. Canada was to be governed by a parliamentary system with British historical traditions and procedures, and by a constitutional monarch represented by an appointed governor general.

Although the Constitution makes it clear that the governor general is the country's formal executive, the powers and prerogatives of the position are in fact severely limited. As we have seen, only in extraordinary situations has a governor general attempted to interfere directly in the political process. Executive power, although carried out in the name of the governor general, resides elsewhere in the political structure.

The Constitution also established the Queen's **Privy Council** for Canada. This body was created to assist and advise the governor general. The members of this largely ceremonial body are nominated by the prime minister and appointed for life. As it includes current and former ministers of the Crown, as well as a few other politically prominent individuals, it cannot function as a decision-making body.[9] In reality, a committee of the Privy Council, known as the **cabinet**, comprising current ministers of the Crown, constitutes the real executive power in Canada. The authority of the prime minister and the ministers rests not on the written Constitution but on convention. As members of the Privy Council, the ministers have the right to the titles *honourable* and *privy councillor* for life, while the prime minister is designated as *right honourable* for life.

The term **governor-in-council** refers to the formal executive authority of the governor general carried out upon the advice and consultation of this committee of the Privy Council, today known as the cabinet. The decisions rendered by cabinet on specific matters carrying legal force are referred to as **orders-in-council**. Technically speaking, a cabinet directive is an agreement arrived at in Council with the governor general absent. However, the governor general is obliged by convention to grant formal approval to virtually any cabinet decision or bill approved by Parliament. Thus, while Canada does have a monarchical form of government embodied in the governor general, and certain legal procedures emanate from this fact, the real executive power belongs to the cabinet. Its power, in turn, comes from maintaining at least a plurality of supporters in the House of Commons.

We have described the largely ceremonial role of the formal executive in the parliamentary system. There are other, equally significant features of the monarchical form of government that impinge upon the operations and powers of the political executive in Canada. Perhaps most significant is the fact that, as in the British parliamentary system, the executive and legislative powers are combined. Today, Canadians vote for 308 members of the House of Commons; the prime minister and almost all members of the cabinet emerge from this body of representatives. Earlier in Canadian history, during the 1890s, both Sir John Abbott and Sir Mackenzie Bowell sat in the Senate when each was appointed prime minister, but convention now demands that the prime minister be a member of the House of Commons either before or shortly after investiture.

The prime minister and his personally selected cabinet constitute the government; they formulate policy and direct administrative operations as long as the House of Commons supports them. When they no longer receive such support, they are replaced or Parliament is dissolved and elections are called. The crucial point is that both the prime minister and the cabinet ministers are simultaneously members of the legislature and the executive. Canada, therefore, has **parliamentary government**. In contrast, the presidential form of government in the United States provides a clear separation of

---

9. For example, all provincial premiers were made privy councillors in 1967 to celebrate Canada's Centennial.

executive and legislative powers. The US Constitution is based on the premise that a concentration of power is undesirable and that law-making and implementation should be separated by preventing the overlap of key personnel. The presidential–congressional system of *checks and balances* creates an atmosphere of public political bargaining not found in Canada. In the United States, the executive must rely on Congress to authorize funds to implement policy, and the Senate must confirm presidential appointments to cabinet, the diplomatic service, federal courts and other boards and commissions.

Also in contrast to the Canadian Constitution, the US chief executive is elected independently by voters, and tenure in office in no way depends on the fate of the legislative program. The executive can frustrate Congress because, for instance, Congress relies on the president to implement its policies, and the executive often controls the information needed to formulate effective policies in Congress. On the other hand, the US legislature can and often does reject executive proposals, an exceedingly rare event in Canada, where a major rejection could cause the government to fall and a new election to take place.

Both houses of the US Congress share fully in legislative activity, and there is often rivalry between them. Unlike their Canadian counterparts, national parties in the United States have little power as organizations over the representatives or senators they may help to elect. Once in office, US politicians have greater latitude on issues and are much more independent than Canadian MPs, who belong to disciplined, tightly controlled parties. Figure 8.1 illustrates the fusion of power in the Canadian system—where the prime minister is both the leader of the largest party in the legislature and the leader of the administration—and compares it to the US presidential system. Anyone familiar with the parliamentary system and the relatively smooth flow of operations resulting

FIGURE 8.1 Parliamentary and Presidential Government

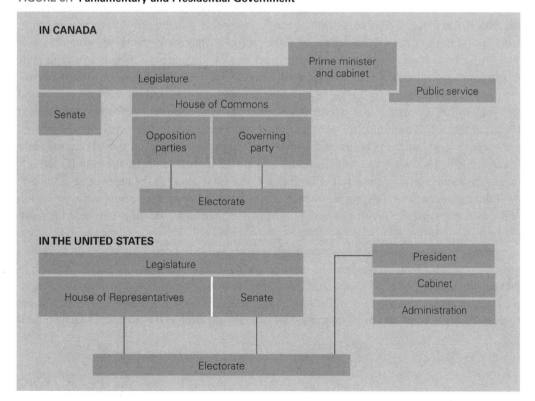

from the fusion of executive and legislative powers may wonder how the US system, with its built-in conflict and rivalry, can possibly work effectively.

Whereas in the United States an individual cannot hold a post in Congress and an executive position at the same time, precisely the opposite is true in Canada. All members of cabinet, including the prime minister, must be elected to the House of Commons or at least appointed to the Senate. What is perhaps most important to remember in considering the implications of different types of governmental structures is that the principle of fusion of powers creates, at least theoretically, a form of government that is more coherent and responsive to the will of the people. Assuming a parliamentary majority backs it, the Canadian political executive can be assured of legislative support on most of the bills and programs it wishes to enact. It will, of course, be held accountable at the next election, but during the interim it is relatively free to pursue its goals.

The Powers of the Prime Minister

The prime minister is unquestionably the central figure in Canadian politics. As we have suggested, the pre-eminence of the prime minister and the cabinet has evolved more from tradition than from any specific part of the Constitution or statute. The basis of the prime minister's power and authority is leadership of the party that commands at least a plurality, and normally a majority, of the seats in the House of Commons. The prime minister is, above all else, an elected member of Parliament who has been chosen national leader of the party at a leadership convention. As leader of the party that has been victorious at the polls, the prime minister can claim that the "right" to govern is based on a popular mandate. The link with the people gives the prime minister enormous legitimacy and authorizes the pursuit of his programs and policies under the cloak of popular support until the next election. As leader of the party and the holder of this mandate, the prime minister can command obedience and support from cabinet ministers and backbenchers alike.

The prime minister and cabinet together control the making and signing of treaties and the conduct of international relations, including the declaration of war and peace, as these are prerogative powers of the Crown. Another major source of the prime minister's power is control over appointments. The prime minister selects the members of the **ministry** (whether in cabinet or not) from the membership of the parliamentary caucus. In 1993, Prime Minister Chrétien inaugurated this new ministry system based on a similar one in Britain. In both his first and second governments, Paul Martin in 2003 and 2004 employed the same ministry system. In 2006, Stephen Harper appointed 25 ministers (full members of cabinet) and 6 secretaries of state (with a reduced ministerial salary). Since the 1970s, each minister has been sent a so-called **ministerial mandate letter** which explains what the prime minister expects the minister to accomplish in his department. These letters may be the result of centralized decision-making in the Privy Council Office[10] *or* of discussions between the prospective minister and the prime minister about what they think needs to be done in a given portfolio. In other words, they may be dictatorial in nature or the result of personal compromises.

Selecting a cabinet may be the most difficult task for a prime minister. In fact, once, in signing a visitor's book, Sir John A. Macdonald entered his occupation as "Cabinet-Maker."[11] A number of factors may influence the prime minister's selection of ministers. Most importantly, there is an obvious advantage in appointing ministers who reflect the regional and ethnic diversity of the country. A persistent effort is made to have at least one minister from every province and a significant

---

10. Luc Bernier, et al. *Executive Styles in Canada* (Toronto: University of Toronto Press, 2005).

11. Cited in R.M. Punnett, *The Prime Minister in Canadian Government and Politics* (Toronto: Macmillan, 1977), p. 56.

representative from the largest ethnic and religious groups in the country. This practice is frustrated, of course, when the party does not hold any seats in a particular province or has not attracted any candidates from a specific ethnic or religious group. After nominating Michael Fortier as a senator in 2006, Prime Minister Stephen Harper appointed him as minister of public works—this was done so that Harper could bolster the representation of Québec in his newly formed cabinet.

Courtesy of Patrick Corrigan.

Another factor in the selection process is that posts may be used as a reward for favours or services rendered to the prime minister or the party. Conversely, positions may be withheld as a punishment for some misdemeanour. On occasion, a talented but troublesome member or a rival for the party leadership may be included in the ministry in order to silence his opposition to the leader. The prime minister may also appoint a particular member on the basis of that person's ability and popular appeal. It is evident that the PM must have a certain number of energetic and effective ministers to run the key portfolios of the government, because there could be political repercussions if ministers were perceived as bumbling, lazy or incompetent. On the other hand, the prime minister cannot afford to be constantly upstaged and overshadowed by cunning ministers.

The prime minister, in consultation with other ministers, is also responsible for appointing parliamentary secretaries. The first two parliamentary secretaries were appointed by order-in-council in 1916, and thereafter their numbers slowly increased until proper legislative recognition was given them with the 1959 *Parliamentary Secretaries Act*. That Act, as amended in 1971, provides for the appointment of the same number of parliamentary secretaries as there are ministers. **Parliamentary secretaries** are appointed by the prime minister to aid ministers in their duties, but have no statutory authority. As one parliamentary secretary put it, "there's no rule; it depends entirely on the minister you are dealing with. Some are given considerable responsibility, others very little. It depends on the understanding between the two people concerned."[12] Usually, parliamentary secretaries have at least the approval of their minister before being appointed, but even this is not always the case. The prime minister may make an appointment without any consultation whatsoever.

In 2004, Prime Minister Martin appointed 28 parliamentary secretaries and informed them that they would have special responsibilities in a minority government—they were to form a "two-way link between ministers and parliamentarians from all political parties." Perhaps more significant in the long run was that, for the first time, parliamentary secretaries were sworn in as privy councillors so they could see cabinet documents and attend cabinet meetings. In 2006, Prime Minister Harper appointed 26 parliamentary assistants.

12. Quoted in Claude Majeau, "The Job of a Parliamentary Secretary," *Parliamentary Government*, vol. 4, no. 3 (1983), p. 3.

> *Now that the Cabinet's gone to dinner,*
> *The Secretary stays and gets thinner and thinner,*
> *Racking his brains to record and report,*
> *What he thinks that they think they ought to have thought.*
>
> *Anonymous*

The prime minister, in addition to choosing the members of the executive, also makes a great many other crucial appointments: senators, judges and the senior staff of the public service. Through these selections, the PM makes his influence felt throughout the governmental structure. Legally, the prime minister's appointments are mere recommendations of appointment, forwarded to the governor general for formal approval. However, despite the governor general's apparent power of discretion, a modern prime minister's appointees are never rejected. In fact, as we have seen, the prime minister chooses the governor general. In all, there are well over two hundred of these positions for a prime minister to fill.

Historically, the prime minister had the sole right to advise the governor general to dissolve Parliament. This power has recently been reduced, although the prime minister still has considerable flexibility in determining the date of federal elections by his control over the legislative agenda and relations with the opposition parties. But, as of 2006, unless the government is defeated by a vote in the House of Commons, Parliament automatically lasts for a fixed term of four years. Until this new law came into being, Parliament was normally dissolved only when the prime minister believed that the party had a good chance of victory at the polls. The power of dissolution could be used to impose solidarity on cabinet or caucus. It was a potent weapon, helping to maintain the stability of the cabinet system.

Today, the prime minister has little flexibility in this regard. He can attempt to control proceedings in the Commons, but if his government is defeated, he must ask the governor general for dissolution and an election. If he is not defeated, then Bill C16, an amendment to the *Canada Election Act*, triggers the fixed election date. In this case, an election is held on the third Monday in October in the fourth calendar year following the last general election.

A final major basis of the prime minister's pre-eminence is his power to control the organization of government. Nearly every PM has plans for a new organizational structure to streamline or modernize the government. Cabinet structure can be modified, portfolios limited or amalgamated, bureaucratic agencies abolished, Crown corporations created and royal commissions appointed— all on the initiative of the prime minister. However, while the power to make these changes certainly exists, the prime minister must be mindful that unwarranted or unnecessary modifications may generate significant opposition. The prime minister's power to initiate organizational changes extends across the entire government, but there is a tendency to focus on the various executive coordinating agencies that fall directly under his jurisdiction. Each prime minister can, therefore, be expected to make some changes in the Prime Minister's Office (PMO) and the Privy Council Office (PCO) to reflect his own interests or special needs.

The office of prime minister in Canada today is very strong. Whether the current status of that office is beneficial for the country and its political process is a matter that will continue to be debated for years to come. Without taking sides, we can consider what has given rise to the controversy about executive leadership. While Canada's total population has risen gradually, the demand for services of all kinds has grown exponentially. To meet these needs, the government has developed large departments and bureaucracies. Faced with a cumbersome and ever-expanding government sector, prime ministers introduced aspects of systematic planning to replace the somewhat haphazard, ad hoc policy-making of previous administrations. While pushing for the reform of House procedural rules to streamline the legislative process, the government simultaneously expanded the size and functions of the central coordinating agencies, especially the PMO and PCO.

> *When you're in government . . . the choices you make are not between . . . strawberries and cream or crème caramel for dessert. You have to sometimes choose between cod liver oil or cough syrup.*
>
> **Bob Rae, former Ontario premier**

The takeover of exceptional policy-making authority by the prime minister and central executive agencies is resented by ministers, middle and upper echelons of the civil service and members of Parliament, and distrusted by the press and opposition parties. Journalistic reports often abound of the existence of a coterie of insiders who, from outside the bounds of parliamentary control, are able to manipulate the levers of power in Ottawa. While the descriptions of flagrant abuse of power may be overstated,[13] the potential for its occurrence has been very real indeed. The power of the prime minister and the executive staff has become enormous and pervasive. Once elected, a prime minister can shape the direction and content of policy, and, except in extraordinary situations, can count on dominating the political process until deciding to call an election.

The political resources of the prime minister, then, are undeniably potent and broad. But the power of the prime minister is not exercised in isolation. The prime minister and his colleagues must take care to guide the cabinet and caucus toward policies that avoid hostile reactions from Parliament and the public. As well, the prime minister must secure the loyalty of followers or risk being voted out of office. As summarized in *The Canadian Legislative System,*

> *The Prime Minister's influence stems from an ability to command the maximum possible amount of information about the political environment and to use this resource in persuading political actors to follow his policy initiatives. Administrative secrecy and collective ministerial responsibility permit the executive to acquire requisite political knowledge without revealing conflicts or divisions that may occur within its ranks. However, the ability to conceal the process of decision-making at this level in government has sustained the erroneous idea that the executive works in isolation from parliamentary influence and has contributed significantly to the impression that the government acts independently of public opinion.[14]*

At certain times, the prime minister can act independently; at others, he is forced to rely on party colleagues. Malcolm Punnett provides a succinct criticism of the thesis of prime ministerial government. After a detailed examination of the governing style of Canada's prime ministers, he concluded that the argument for prime ministerial government is not justified "because of the fundamental distinction that exists between the seeming concentration of power in the hands of the prime minister of the day and the realities of his position."[15] The prime minister is constrained in the choice of ministers by the difficulties of holding a cabinet together; of directing a complex government machine; and of securing agreements to proposals from the cabinet, backbench and often other parties.

13. Walter Stewart, *Shrug: Trudeau in Power* (Toronto: New Press, 1971).
14. Robert J. Jackson and Michael Atkinson, *The Canadian Legislative System,* (Toronto: Macmillan, 1980), p. 56.
15. Punnett, *The Prime Minister,* p. 157.

There are four basic models of executive government in the political science literature:[16]

1. *prime ministerial*, in which decisions are taken by the prime minister acting alone;
2. *ministerial*, in which decisions are taken by individual ministers in their own spheres of interest;
3. *cabinet*, in which cabinet under the direction of the prime minister makes decisions;
4. *inner-group*, in which decisions are made by a subgroup of cabinet along with the prime minister.

Considering the constraints listed above, it is our view that the first model does not apply to Canada. No Canadian prime minister can really act alone, and all these models fail to take ministers and bureaucrats into account. Of course, some prime ministers have tried to take more than their share of decision-making responsibility. R.B. Bennett simultaneously held the posts of prime minister, minister of finance and external affairs, and is said to have acted independently of his cabinet colleagues. A favourite joke was often told about him in the 1930s:

Visitor to Ottawa: "Who is that man coming toward us?"
Ottawa resident: "Mr. R.B. Bennett, the new Prime Minister."
Visitor to Ottawa: "Why is he talking to himself?"
Ottawa resident: "He is holding a cabinet meeting."[17]

However, even Bennett had to avoid coalitions of conflicting interests and often ran into difficulty.

Prime ministers obtain much of their strength from holding their team together. This must be done with conciliation, tact and only rarely force. Most prime ministers bring particular skills to bear on this responsibility. For example, Pearson and Martin were, and Harper is, a conventional CEO type of leader; King was a master electioneer. Mulroney and Chrétien combined both talents. The skills required for the job are so varied that no prime minister can be said to have possessed all of them. What all prime ministers must demonstrate is the ability to coordinate their colleagues and, hence, policy. The primary ingredient of this ability is anticipation of the actions of all the major actors in the political system. Recent prime ministers have accomplished this by relying on a small coterie of ministers to help them come to compromises and conclusions. Prime Ministers Trudeau, Mulroney, Martin, and Harper employed a Priorities and Planning Committee of Cabinet to obtain information and enhance consensus. Clark constructed an inner cabinet to accomplish the same end. On this evidence, the usual pattern for PMs could be described as one where they set up an informal partial cabinet to help run the government. This is a far cry from the arrangement suggested by those who contend that Canada now has prime ministerial government.

The prime minister chairs the cabinet and is the pivotal figure in the cabinet committee system. Despite Stephen Harper's reputation as a very centralized and controlling decision-maker, no leader, including Prime Minister Harper, can possibly deal with the multifarious matters needing attention and therefore must delegate authority and responsibility to cabinet members. Before turning to a consideration of the operations of the cabinet and its methods of arriving at policy decisions, we shall briefly examine the history and approaches of Canada's prime ministers.

Prime Ministers in Practice

Canada has had 22 prime ministers since Confederation—9 Liberal and 13 Conservative/Progressive Conservative. All but Kim Campbell, who was prime minister for a few months in 1993, have been male. Joe Clark, at the age of 39, was the youngest in Canadian history. The selections of Kim Campbell, Jean Chrétien, Paul Martin and Stephen Harper continued the tradition of highly educated party leaders; every appointment since the First World War has gone to a university

16. Ibid., p. 86.
17. Earnest Watkins, *R.B. Bennett: A Biography* (London: Secker and Warburg, 1963) p. 167.

graduate. With regard to area of residence in adult life, there have been three Maritimers as prime ministers, seven Québeckers, six Ontarians and six westerners (see Table 8.2 on page 280). Stephen Harper was born in Ontario but educated and elected in Alberta. Three provinces—Prince Edward Island, Newfoundland and Labrador, and New Brunswick—have never had a prime minister elected in one of their federal constituencies. Kim Campbell was the second prime minister from British Columbia. John Turner, the first, became a British Columbia member of Parliament shortly before he lost the 1984 election and was replaced as prime minister.

Lester B. Pearson

The regional pattern of electoral support for parties in Canada is illustrated by the fact that all nine Liberal prime ministers have come from Ontario or Québec (John Turner's BC credentials notwithstanding), whereas the Conservatives have come from various parts of the country. On the other hand, the Liberals have balanced Canada's religious and ethnic diversity better than the Conservatives in their choice of prime ministers. Of the 22 prime ministers, 8 have been Roman Catholic and 14 Protestant; the Liberals have had 6 Roman Catholics and 3 Protestants. Moreover, since the 1880s, Liberal Party leaders (not prime ministers) have often been drawn alternately from English Canada (Blake, 1880; King, 1919; Pearson, 1958; Turner, 1984) and French Canada (Laurier, 1887; St. Laurent, 1948; Trudeau, 1968; Chrétien, 1993).

In this regard, the case of Paul Martin is interesting. He was raised and educated in Ontario but made his home and constituency in Québec. If we accept Martin as being from English Canada, then the December 2006 selection of Québecker Stéphane Dion continues the tradition.

For decades, Tory prime ministers tended to have much more parliamentary experience than their Liberal counterparts. Until Clark, Mulroney and Campbell, all Conservative prime ministers had ten years' or more legislative experience at the federal or provincial level before their appointments. Stephen Harper had roughly eight years of experience as an MP before becoming prime minister. Experience in cabinet before becoming prime minister, however, has been minimal for both parties; all but four had only two years' experience or less. Sir Charles Tupper had the most experience in federal and provincial cabinets, but he lasted only two months as prime minister. Pierre Trudeau, by contrast, with no provincial experience and only one year of cabinet experience, survived 11 years in his first period as prime minister and after an electoral defeat was re-elected to another majority mandate. Neither Brian Mulroney nor Stephen Harper had had any cabinet experience when they became prime minister.

CLOSE-UP ON THE Executive

THE BEST PRIME MINISTER IN FIFTY YEARS: LESTER B. PEARSON

In June 2003, Lester B. Pearson was voted the best Canadian prime minister of the past fifty years by a panel of history and public policy experts. The vote was arranged by the journal *Policy Options*. Among Pearson's most notable achievements for Canada were

- a new flag
- a leadership role in establishing the Royal Commission on Bilingualism and Biculturalism
- increased Old Age Security
- the advent of medicare
- groundwork for the free-trade agreement with the Canada–US Auto Pact

Pearson accomplished all this in two minority governments—after he had won a Nobel Peace Prize for a highly regarded peacekeeping initiative.

Who would you have chosen as the best prime minister?

Source: Adapted from *Policy Options*, June/July 2003.

TABLE 8.2 **The Prime Ministers of Canada**

Prime Minister	Party	Tenure	Birthplace	Adult Residence	Age as PM	Occupation
Sir John A. Macdonald	Lib.-Con.	July 1, 1867–Nov. 5, 1873	Britain	Ontario	52–76	Law
Alexander Mackenzie	Lib.	Nov. 5, 1873–Oct. 9, 1878	Britain	Ontario	51–56	Journalist/Stonemason
Sir John A. Macdonald	Con.	Oct. 9, 1878–June 6, 1891				
Sir John Abbott	Con.	June 15, 1891–Nov. 24, 1892	Québec	Québec	70	Law/Lecturer
Sir John Thompson	Con.	Nov. 25, 1892–Dec. 13, 1894	Nova Scotia	Nova Scotia	48–50	Law/Lecturer
Sir Mackenzie Bowell	Con.	Dec. 13, 1894–Apr. 27, 1896	Britain	Ontario	70–72	Journalist
Sir Charles Tupper	Con.	Apr. 27, 1896–July 8, 1896	Nova Scotia	Nova Scotia	74	Doctor
Sir Wilfrid Laurier	Lib.	July 9, 1896–Oct. 6, 1911	Québec	Québec	54–69	Law
Sir Robert Borden	Con.	Oct. 7, 1911–July 10, 1920	Nova Scotia	Nova Scotia	57–65	Law
Arthur Meighen	Con.	July 10, 1920–Dec. 29, 1921	Ontario	Manitoba	46–52	Law/Business
W.L. Mackenzie King	Lib.	Dec. 29, 1921–June 28, 1926	Ontario	Ontario	47–73	Civil Service
Arthur Meighen	Con.	June 28, 1926–Sept. 25, 1926				
W.L. Mackenzie King	Lib.	Sept. 25, 1926–Aug. 7, 1930				
R.B. Bennett	Con.	Aug. 7, 1930–Oct. 23, 1935	New Brunswick	Alberta	60–65	Law/Business
W.L. Mackenzie King	Lib.	Oct. 23, 1935–Nov. 15, 1948				
Louis St. Laurent	Lib.	Nov. 15, 1948–June 21, 1957	Québec	Québec	66–75	Law
John Diefenbaker	Con.	June 21, 1957–Apr. 22, 1963	Ontario	Saskatchewan	51–67	Law
Lester B. Pearson	Lib.	Apr. 22, 1963–Apr. 20, 1968	Ontario	Ontario	65–70	Civil Service
Pierre Elliott Trudeau	Lib.	Apr. 20, 1968–June 4, 1979	Québec	Québec	48–65	Law/Lecturer
Joseph Clark	Con.	June 4, 1979–Mar. 3, 1980	Alberta	Alberta	39–41	Journalist
Pierre Elliott Trudeau	Lib.	Mar. 3, 1980–June 30, 1984				
John Turner	Lib.	June 30, 1984–Sept. 17, 1984	Britain	Ontario	55	Law
Brian Mulroney	Con.	Sept. 17, 1984–June 25, 1993	Québec	Québec	45–54	Law/Business
Kim Campbell	Con.	June 25, 1993–Nov. 4, 1993	British Columbia	British Columbia	46	Law
Jean Chrétien	Lib.	Nov. 4, 1993–Dec. 12, 2003	Québec	Québec	59–69	Law
Paul Martin, Jr.	Lib.	Dec. 12 2003–Feb. 6, 2006	Ontario	Québec	65–67	Law
Stephen Harper	Con.	Feb. 6, 2006–	Ontario	Alberta	46–	Economist

The durability of Canadian prime ministers varies enormously. Unlike US presidents, who by law can serve only two terms, Canadian prime ministers retain power as long as the public and House of Commons support them. Some prime ministers in Canada have lasted longer than those in almost all Anglo-American and continental European countries.

The 22 Canadian prime ministers can be divided into 3 broad groups on the basis of their tenure in office. The shortest careers were those of Meighen, Thompson, Abbott, Bowell, Tupper, Clark, Turner and Campbell, who all served for less than 2 years (the shortest periods were held by Sir Charles Tupper, 69 days; John Turner, 80 days; and Kim Campbell, 133 days). Seven prime ministers stayed in office for 5 to 11 years: Borden, St. Laurent, Mackenzie, Bennett, Diefenbaker, Pearson, Mulroney and Chrétien. Four have towered above the rest: King, 22 years; Macdonald, 20 years; Trudeau, over 15½ years; and Laurier, 15 years. Laurier's fifteen consecutive years in office were the longest continuous term enjoyed by any prime minister; Trudeau's 15½-year term was broken in the middle by an electoral loss. These four individuals held the office of prime minister for over half of Canada's history since Confederation: 72 out of 141 years, as of 2008.

How have prime ministers' terms ended? Few have retired entirely by their own choice; their careers usually ended in a general election defeat. Abbott, Borden, King, Pearson, Trudeau and Mulroney retired at their own discretion. Twelve lost their positions through defeat in a general election; one (Mackenzie Bowell) because of a cabinet revolt, two (Macdonald and King) through defeats in Parliament. Only Macdonald, King, Meighen and Trudeau managed to stay on as leader and win another general election after their party was defeated in a previous election. Macdonald and Thompson died in office. Jean Chrétien was forced out by party pressures and conceded the Liberal Party leadership to Paul Martin on December 12, 2003, who in turn served a relatively short, two-year stint as a minority PM before being defeated in the January 2006 general election.

Getting rid of a prime minister, even via the electoral route, is extremely difficult. The statistics show that prime ministers were defeated in roughly one-third of all elections, whereas in more than two-thirds they were returned to the House of Commons, albeit more than half the time with a reduced mandate. Jean Chrétien's 1997 victory followed the usual pattern. Brian Mulroney chose to stand down in June 1993 rather than go into an election with a high level of personal unpopularity. His replacement, Kim Campbell, lost the general election of 1993 in a disastrous fashion. And Paul Martin's forces drove Jean Chrétien out of office in 2003 (see Chapter 11).

The Ministry and Cabinet

We have said that the prime minister determines which individuals serve as ministers and secretaries of state, and also the extent of their duties. In some parliamentary countries, such as Australia and New Zealand, particular caucuses select the ministers, and the prime minister merely assigns the portfolios. In Canada, however, the prime minister has a free hand, although traditionally most members of the ministry are selected from the House of Commons and, more rarely, the Senate.

In selecting future colleagues for the front bench, the prime minister takes into consideration a number of factors, one of them cabinet size. Until 1993, all members of the ministry were in cabinet—there were no ministers outside of it—so with the appointment of each new minister, the size of cabinet grew. Over time, the size of cabinets gradually increased. By the end of the Trudeau era in 1984, the cabinet included 37 ministers. John Turner's appointments temporarily reduced this number, but the situation was immediately reversed when Brian Mulroney became prime minister. He named the largest number in Canadian history to cabinet—40 ministers. Paul Martin had only slightly fewer at 39, but Stephen Harper reduced cabinet size by a third.

When Jean Chrétien became head of government in November 1993, he adopted a new system for central government administration. As we have seen, Chrétien appointed two types of ministers—some politicians were appointed to full cabinet and a smaller number were made ministers of state. Like full ministers, the ministers of state were sworn to the Privy Council and bound by the rules of collective responsibility. But they were allowed to attend meetings of cabinet only on request and were given a lower salary and fewer staffers than full cabinet ministers. In Paul Martin's second government, there were 30 full ministers, 8 ministers of state and the prime minister, comprising an overall ministry of 39. Stephen Harper appointed only 25 ministers and 6 ministers of state with smaller duties and salaries.

Needless to say, nearly all cabinet ministers are chosen from the House of Commons, although in some historical periods a number have been appointed from the Senate, particularly when the governing party lacked elected representatives from a particular region—as the PCs did from Québec in 1979 and the Liberals did from the West in 1980–84. In 1997, for example, after the Liberals lost all their seats in Nova Scotia, Senator Alasdair Graham from Nova Scotia was appointed as government leader in the Upper House and joined the Chrétien cabinet as Nova Scotia's sole representative. Stephen Harper, as mentioned, appointed Michael Fortier from Québec to the Senate and to his cabinet in 2006 in order to boost his Québec caucus.

The composition of the ministry and cabinet also depends on how many seats the government controls in the House of Commons. Most elections have produced *majority governments*, based on the support of only one party in the House of Commons. Only twice have *coalition* cabinets been formed from more than one party. On other occasions, the government had to persist with less than a majority of the members of Parliament. Such *minority governments* have proved quite unstable and have tended to pass less legislation than governments based on single-party, majority control of the House (for details, see below). On such occasions, prime ministers have to construct their cabinet carefully to ensure a majority of members will support it.

Cabinet positions are all doled out to members of the prime minister's own party in Parliament or the Senate. There have been few exceptions. General Andrew McNaughton was defence minister in 1944–45 without holding a position in either house. After being defeated twice at the polls, he gave up the post. On the other hand, Lester Pearson was appointed secretary of state for external affairs in 1948, then stood for election in a by-election and won. As noted earlier, the prime minister's choice of ministers is limited by certain considerations, foremost among them regional, ethnic and religious representation. Regional representation is generally, but not necessarily, the most important factor. There is usually a cabinet member from each province (with the frequent exception of Prince Edward Island) and from the largest cities, with the most populous urban regions receiving extra members.

The correspondence between distribution of cabinet ministers and provincial population has been relatively constant since Confederation. As a general rule, Ontario has had more members in cabinet than any other province, with Québec second. However, in recent years this principle has varied somewhat. Because of his landslide victory in Ontario and slim results from his own province, Jean Chrétien initially chose 12 full ministers from Ontario and only 7 from Québec for his 1997 ministry. In 2004, Paul Martin chose 16 from Ontario, 8 from Québec and 8 from the West (see Table 8.3). The composition of Stephen Harper's first cabinet was novel and very interesting. He broke the traditional regional composition by including 12 ministers from the West, 10 from Ontario, 6 from Québec, and only 3 from the Maritimes.

Ethnicity is also significant. According to Malcom Punnett, 28 percent of the total number of cabinet ministers serving between 1867 and 1965 were French Canadians, a figure that was remarkably close to the French Canadian percentage of the population.[18] Prime ministers also attempt to appoint a chief lieutenant from the opposite official-language group. The most successful alliance, for example, may have been between Macdonald and Cartier. Brian Mulroney, a Québecker, appointed his first chief lieutenant from Yukon. Jean Chrétien, a francophone, appointed Herb Gray from Ontario as his deputy prime minister, while Paul Martin chose an Albertan as his deputy. Joe Clark also found it

18. Malcolm Punnett, *The Prime Minister*, passim.

TABLE 8.3 **The 2004 Liberal and 2006 Conservative Ministers by Region and Gender**

A. Region	2004 Ministry Membership	2006 Conservative Ministry Membership
Québec	8	6
Ontario	16	10
West	8	12
East	6	3
North	1	0
B. Gender		
Male	30	24
Female	9	7

Ministry includes the prime minister, ministers and secretaries of state at initial inauguration and does not include individual ministerial shuffles.

necessary to appoint three French-speaking members of the Senate to his cabinet to balance his weak support in Québec. As we have seen, Stephen Harper added Michael Fortier to the Senate and put him into the cabinet in order to obtain a powerful minister to handle Québec issues.

Nearly all of Canada's minority groups, as well as one majority group—women—have been consistently unrepresented or under-represented in cabinet. No significant room has been made in cabinet for Native peoples, for workers and unskilled labourers, or for the poor, all of whose interests have been consistently under-represented. Other, smaller ethnic groups have usually been under-represented in cabinet. Over-represented are those with higher education and high social status occupations. The most over-represented group is lawyers, who have held approximately half the positions in cabinet since Confederation; they are an elite, extremely well-educated, financially successful group representing less than one percent of the population. Historically, about one-fifth of cabinet members have been business people, less than one-tenth have been farmers, and fewer still have come from the public sector.

The composition of the 2006 Harper ministry followed these principles closely. With the exception of Prince Edward Island, every province received one or more ministers, and the membership was reasonably representative of the provinces on a basis proportional to their population, with the exception of Québec. The new government members in 2006 were highly educated and professionally trained; they still did not form a social or economic cross-section of Canadians. Business (slightly up to 30 percent) and law (slightly down to 26 percent) continued to be the leading employment background areas of ministers. There were few farmers (only 4 percent) and, as usual, labourers and the poor were not represented at all. Women were still in a minority position and their numbers comprised 7 in a ministry of 31. The Tories had given Canada its first female prime minister, Kim Campbell, and Jean Chrétien countered in 1993 by appointing Sheila Copps as the first

Reproduced with permission. Gable, *The Globe and Mail.*

female deputy prime minister. In 1997, Herb Gray replaced Copps. Paul Martin later made Anne McLellan his deputy PM.[19] In a much smaller ministry, Stephen Harper did not appoint a deputy prime minister. He did, however, adjust his cabinet composition in 2007 to account for the dismissal of his defence minister over problems with the handling of the war against the Taliban in Afghanistan.

Coalition and Minority Governments

Constitutionally, the governor general accepts the incumbent prime minister's choice of whom to appoint as the incoming prime minister. If, in an election, the incumbent PM's party wins the largest number of seats or nearly the same as the second-place party, there is a very high probability that the prime minister will stay on. If soundly beaten, however, the prime minister will ask the governor general to call on the leader of the Opposition to form a government. Of Canada's 39 general elections, 10 have resulted in no party winning an absolute majority in the House of Commons, and the percentage of minority governments has increased in the post–Second World War period with the rise of the multi-party system.

If no party has a majority of members of the House of Commons, a cabinet based on a minority of members will be set up. Such a government is called a **minority government.** In other words, a minority government is one that emerges from an election that accords it less than a majority of members of the House of Commons. As we have seen, a **majority government**, by contrast, is one based on the governing party having a majority of the MPs in the House.

In many other democratic countries, particularly in Europe, multi-party legislatures with no single party controlling a majority of members of the legislature usually have **coalition governments**, with the administration formed by more than one party. States such as Austria, Switzerland and the Netherlands have continual coalition governments and still manage a high degree of government coherence in law-making because of long established norms and practices that enable coalitions to hold together despite party pressures.

Coalition governments have *not* been the norm in Canada. Only once in Canadian history has a coalition been constructed from more than one party, and this was during the First World War. At other times—11 times since Confederation (8 times since 1945)—the government has had to persist with less than a majority of MPs. A confusion of numbers comes from the fact that there were two different minority governments in the 1926 Parliament. On average, these minority governments were usually (but not always) short-lived and tended to pass less legislation (we do not attempt to assess the quality of the bills). Most of these governments were defeated by a vote of non-confidence in the government, forcing a dissolution and election.

Coalition Governments

Since 1867, there has been only one coalition federal government in Canada, although the first prime minister, Sir John A. Macdonald, did achieve Confederation based on a government with a combination of Liberals and Conservatives.

1917–20 In an attempt to confront anti-conscription forces in the country, Sir Robert Borden put together a Unionist government consisting of his Conservative Party, pro-conscription Liberals and other notables to fight the 1917 election. He and his coalition were successful, electing members to 65 percent of the seats in the House of Commons. When Borden resigned in 1920, however, the coalition fell apart. The Conservatives took the blame in Québec for the conscription measures and the Liberals were elected to a minority government in 1921. This coalition experiment has not been repeated.

19. For comparison of the Chrétien and Martin governing styles see "The Chrétien Legacy," *Policy Options* (November 2002), pp.6-43; and "Paul Martin's Legacy," *Policy Options* (October 2002), pp. 6–18.

Minority Governments

1921–25 A Liberal minority government, led by William Lyon Mackenzie King, obtained support of the Progressives by accepting pro-Prairie farm legislation such as lowering freight rates and tariffs. With the support of the Progressives, King managed to last several years. The nature of this House as a minority government is in question, as the Liberals did have by far the largest number of seats of any party: 117 seats to the Progressives' 64, the Conservatives' 50, Labour's 3 and a single independent.

1925 Two minority governments, one Liberal and one Conservative, were set up in a relatively short period. In the election, 116 Conservatives, 101 Liberals and 28 others were elected. Despite winning fewer seats than the Conservatives, Liberal prime minister Mackenzie King refused to resign. He relied on the support of the Progressive party and held on to office for a few months by setting up a liaison committee between a cabinet committee and the executive of the Progressive Party. Moreover, T.A. Crerar, a leading Progressive MP, eventually crossed the floor and joined the Liberals as a minister.

Later, facing certain defeat in the House, King left office when Governor General Lord Byng would not allow dissolution and an election. The Conservatives under Arthur Meighen formed a government, but it was defeated only a few days later. This time, the governor general allowed dissolution, and an election followed in 1926. King and his Liberals won enough seats to form a majority government. This issue, known as the King–Byng Affair, is often cited by constitutional lawyers to illustrate the governor general's power to prevent the calling of an early election, but also to show that the people can overturn a governor general's decision if it flies in the face of his politically elected leaders.

1957–58 John Diefenbaker won a minority government in 1957, with his PCs winning 112 seats to the Liberals' 107, Social Credit's 19, the CCF's 25 and 2 independents. Diefenbaker's is the only minority government that did not fall via a vote of no confidence. His popularity rose greatly throughout the period and he called an election in 1958 and won a large majority, even in Québec.

1962–63 Diefenbaker formed a second Progressive Conservative minority government in 1962. The PCs received only 116 seats, while the Liberals had 100, Social Credit, 30, and the NDP, 19. This meant the government could survive as long as it obtained the support of one of the two minor parties. Diefenbaker delayed calling the House for as long as possible and then introduced uncontroversial legislation exclusively. Finally, both opposition parties joined the Liberals to defeat Diefenbaker on his opposition to nuclear weapons as part of a continental defence shield. They forced a no-confidence vote and an election ensued, putting the Liberals in office.

1963–65 A Liberal minority, headed by Lester B. Pearson, relied on the support of the NDP. Pearson allowed the adoption of many ideas from the NDP, including legislation on pensions and foreign ownership.

1965–68 In a second Liberal minority, again headed by Pearson, the Liberals once more relied on the support of the NDP. They were very close to a majority and had to obtain only a few opposition votes to survive. Again, legislation was affected by NDP viewpoints.

1972–74 Pierre Elliott Trudeau and the Liberals were reduced to a minority situation in 1972 after their astonishing victory in 1968. The results gave 109 seats to the Liberals, 107 to the PCs, 31 to the New Democrats and 15 to the Créditistes. Despite the reduction of Liberal seats and the popularity of the leader of the PCs, Robert Stanfield, Trudeau stayed in office. He played parliamentary politics with the NDP; the Liberal overtures were spearheaded by Allan J. MacEachen and his parliamentary secretary, John Reid. In 1974, Trudeau's Liberals once again formed a majority government.

1979–80 In May of 1979, Joe Clark's PCs ousted Trudeau and won a minority government. Clark said he would govern as if he had a majority. He relied on Liberal, NDP and Créditiste help on various measures. But his fiscal policy proved unpopular and he was defeated on legislation in the House, apparently by a mistaken view of how many votes he could muster.

2004–06 Paul Martin's Liberals were elected with a minority government. Even with the theoretical help of the NDP, the two parties had only 154 seats, one seat shy of an implicit coalition majority. The Martin government tumbled in a vote of no confidence, leading to the 2006 winter election.

2006– Stephen Harper carried the Conservatives to a victory in January 2006, but the win did not deliver the majority the Tories had wanted. The opposition was split three ways with the Liberals as the Official Opposition and the Bloc Québécois and NDP coming in third and fourth respectively. Party defections and constant bargaining and compromises characterized the House during the period. The Liberal-dominated Senate made policy-making particularly complex for the Conservative government.

Analysis: Problems or Advantages of Minority Governments

The actual number of seats usually, but not always, determines which party forms the government (see Table 8.4). Leaders with fewer seats in the House than other parties have managed to stay in power—witness King in 1925 (the Liberals had 101 seats and 40 percent of the vote while the Conservatives had 116 seats and 46 percent of the vote). Minor parties have had more influence on policy than their support in the country warranted. In order to remain in office, both Pearson and Trudeau had to make major concessions to the NDP. To date, Stephen Harper has been able to astutely play one opposition party off against another. However, the frustrations over calculations and concessions to the other parties are immense. Harper not only has to deal with the House opposition parties but also with a Senate dominated by the Liberals.

An early election is almost certain in the case of a minority government, but it is also empirically proven that opposition parties in the House tend to do electorally "worse"—i.e., their number of seats tends to go down after they have served in a minority Parliament. Elsewhere, we have demonstrated that the number of bills introduced and passed, and even the total pages of legislation passed have proven to be much lower during minority governments. In other words, it takes longer to pass legislation.

TABLE 8.4 **Minority Governments: Party Composition of the House of Commons**

Party	Liberal	Conservative	Progressive	Labour	Social Credit	CCF/NDP	Créditiste	Bloc	Ind.
1921	117	50	64	3	—	—	—	—	1
1925*	101	116	24	2	—	—	—	—	2
1926	116	91	13	3	11	9	—	—	2
1957	107	112	—	—	19	25	—	—	2
1962	100	116	—	—	30	19	—	—	—
1963	129	95	—	—	24	17	—	—	—
1965	131	97	—	—	5	21	9	—	2
1972	109	107	—	—	—	31	15	—	—
1979	114	136	—	—	—	26	6	—	—
2004	135	99	—	—	—	19	—	54	1
2006	103	124	—	—	—	29	—	51	1

* Two minority governments were formed following this election—first Liberal, then Conservative.

Parliament is a more exciting and less predictable place during minority governments. Historically, social policy has been dramatically changed in such situations. Minority governments under both Pearson and Trudeau passed important social legislation. With the support of the NDP, they passed the Canada Pension Plan, the Canada Assistance Plan, the Guaranteed Supplement for seniors and medicare. Would the Liberals have passed these measures without the prodding of the NDP? What changes have the opposition parties brought to Stephen Harper's election manifesto?

A minority situation also affects the type of tactics used by leaders of all parties. Prime ministers must keep both their own backbenchers and opposition parties contented. Their tactics may include reducing the length of sessions, avoiding controversial legislation to postpone the date of defeat, making deals and compromises with other parties and setting up a liaison system with opposition parties and soliciting their views. The government attempts to play off one minor party against another by supporting policies that one of the parties does not like. In other words, the prime minister uses a "divide and rule" strategy. On occasion, prime ministers have also given out patronage, contracts and employment to members of the opposition parties.

Opposition parties, too, have some new tactical issues to face during a minority Parliament. They must appear responsible and not be seen to be opposing the government *just* for partisan reasons. On the other hand, they cannot be seen to be pandering to the government. They know that the lack of an overall majority allows the prime minister some leverage because he can claim that the opposition parties are undermining good and strong government. But, clearly, governing without a majority is extremely difficult.

Cabinets and Political Power

In theory, the Canadian system of government is premised on both *collective* and *individual ministerial responsibility*. Cabinet solidarity, or **collective ministerial responsibility**, allows ministers to be frank in private but requires them to support the government in public. As a group, ministers are supposed to be held accountable to Parliament for their government's actions. They may speak about policy only after it has been agreed to in private by their colleagues. The convention of collective responsibility is so pervasive that ministers are expected to support each other even *before* the issue has been discussed in cabinet. Ministers act collectively in cabinet to develop policy, approve draft legislation, manage the country's finances and adopt orders-in-council. Cabinet deliberations are held in secret, individual opinions are not publicly voiced, and ministers are not supposed to speak or act except in the name of the entire cabinet.

The personal responsibility of each minister is referred to as **individual ministerial responsibility**. Ministers receive confidential advice from the public service, make important decisions and then are held accountable for these decisions in Parliament and the country. In other words, in theory at least, there is a trade-off: public servants forgo public praise in order to avoid public blame, while ministers accept both credit and criticism.

Public policy derives from a multitude of sources, but it is the individual minister who puts the final stamp of approval on departmental initiatives. Politicians cannot hope to duplicate the expertise that derives from administration or the information that comes from permanent contact with interest groups. And yet only a minister may carry forward departmental requests to the cabinet. This relationship between minister and department places approval or disapproval upon the appropriate and responsible political official. While ministers may delegate authority to their officials, they remain at the apex for appeals of administrative decisions and must be involved in the initiation and defence of new policies. The complexity of a minister's task can be illustrated by the example of the minister for industry, trade and commerce. In one year, the department took 4700 decisions—

the minister kept control of only 190 of them, but these constituted well over half the department's expenditures.[20]

In practice, however, it is nearly impossible to adhere to these constitutional doctrines at all times. Where is the line to be drawn between ministerial and departmental responsibility? Ministers do not even know most of the details of decisions that are carried out in their names. They cannot be held responsible for every departmental activity, and, increasingly, ministers have been voicing this problem openly. One even claimed he could not be held accountable for the "shabby research" conducted by his department. The main check on ministerial responsibilities, therefore, is not the minister's will or the public servants' activities, but the free and open debate that takes place in Parliament and society about ministers' actions. The minister is judged in the department, in cabinet, Parliament, before the media and on the hustings.

The prime minister and cabinet are assisted in their tasks by the central agencies discussed in the next section of this chapter. Individual ministers are supported by their departments and by their political appointees. The personnel budget for each minister's office is used to employ an executive assistant, special assistants, a private secretary and other support personnel. The importance and even the titles of these officials may change with governments. Political aides are part of what has been called the "para-political bureaucracy."[21] About five hundred staffers are employed in ministers' offices, hired by ministers on an individual basis to perform largely partisan tasks. Their employment is not subject to the regulations of the public service (and hence are called *exempt staff*) and, until recently under provisions of the 1967 *Public Service Employment Act*, they were given high priority for permanent positions in the administration after three years of consecutive political service. The 2006 *Federal Accountability Act* eliminates this priority right to public service positions after political staffers cease to be employed by a minister.

The importance of these staffs varies greatly. Depending on the ministers' views and confidence, they may be engaged in any number of personal concerns. Liaison work with the department, constituency, party and Parliament is perhaps the most important. Their partisan work for the ministers is clearly significant. If they are competent, they strengthen both the minister and the party in power. Their work on policy is generally underdeveloped because, with few exceptions, they do not have the necessary competence or experience in the field to which they are assigned. Their most important policy work is in their "gatekeeping" functions: determining who gets an appointment with the minister and what documents, papers and letters the minister reads.

Policy-Making in Central Government

In recent years, prime ministers have made many major alterations in the internal organization of government. In the 1963 Pearson government, full cabinet was the major vehicle for cabinet decision-making: it reviewed almost every decision taken in committee. After Pierre Trudeau came to office in 1968, cabinet and committee meetings were scheduled on a more regular basis and *committees* became much more powerful. The 1979 Clark, 1980 Trudeau and 1984 Mulroney cabinets decentralized decision-making even further with the introduction of the Policy and Expenditure Management System (PEMS—see below). Committees were empowered to make final decisions on many policy and financial issues. In 1989, Brian Mulroney dismantled PEMS and announced a major structural rearrangement of cabinet and its committees as well as the process for cabinet deliberation.

20. Ian Clark, "A 'Back to Basics' Look at the Government Decision-Making Process," unpublished paper, November 4, 1983, p. 13.

21. Blair Williams, "The Para-Political Bureaucracy in Ottawa," in Harold D. Clarke et al., eds., *Parliament, Policy and Representation* (Toronto: Methuen, 1980), p. 218.

As we have seen, in 1993 and 1997, Jean Chrétien changed the governmental system by adding the ministry to cabinet. At the end of 1999, the federal cabinet consisted of 28 members, including the prime minister, out of a ministry of 37. In the second Chrétien term, cabinet as a whole continued to be the main steering organization. Cabinet was divided into only four committees—Economic Union, Social Union, Special Committee of Council and Treasury Board—each with the power to bring forward recommendations to cabinet. Initially, unlike other recent prime ministers, Jean Chrétien reverted to the secretive practice of neither publicly naming the members of these committees nor specifying their functions. While *The Canada Gazette* for two decades had named all members of cabinet committees, the 1993 Liberal government reduced the transparency at the very core of democratic government. After much criticism, however, the Chrétien government once again made this information public.

Paul Martin's 2004 government retained the distinction between ministry and cabinet begun by Chrétien. Martin appointed 39 members to the ministry: 31 cabinet ministers and 8 ministers of state. But the PM set up a brand new system of committees. He eliminated the Priorities and Planning Committee, giving its functions to the whole cabinet, and set up 8 cabinet committees, reinstating the role of an operations committee used by Brian Mulroney.

The 2006 Harper system went back to some earlier formulations (see Figure 8.2). Priorities and Planning became the major committee. Chaired by the PM, it included the chairs of other committees and some political heavyweights. It provided strategic direction on priorities and expenditure management, and also ratified committee recommendations. The **Operations Committee** controls the day-to-day co-ordination of government priorities for the cabinet. It looks after issues management, legislation, house planning and communications. **Social Affairs** integrates policy development in health

FIGURE 8.2 **The Ministry and Cabinet in the 2006 Conservative Government**

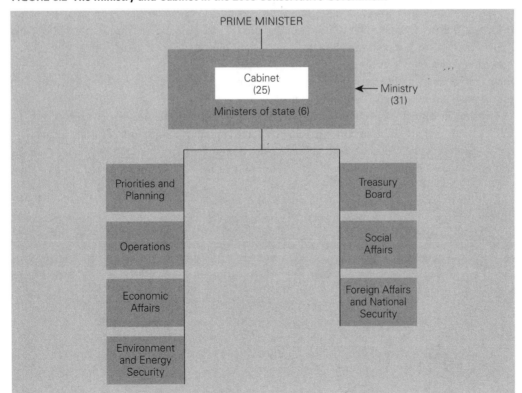

care, justice, Aboriginal, training and skills development, culture and immigration. **Economic Affairs** considers economics, international trade, natural resources, fisheries, agriculture and regional development topics. **Foreign Affairs and National Security** handles foreign issues, defence and national security. **Environment and Energy Security** considers environmental and energy policies.

Finally, the **Treasury Board Committee** is the only committee of cabinet named in the Constitution. Chaired by the president of the Treasury Board, it has legal responsibility for the authorization of expenditures and is the committee that allocates resources within the government. It is the only committee that does not position itself into a circle for policy deliberations, but sits like a jury, facing any petitioners and acting as a tribunal.

Ministers are expected to bring substantial policies to their cabinet colleagues for resolution. The formal process for cabinet approval of a document is illustrated in Figure 8.3. The minister's memorandum is forwarded to the Privy Council Office, which distributes it to the cabinet members. The memorandum is then discussed by the appropriate cabinet committee and forwarded to cabinet for final determination. As Figure 8.3 indicates, the Privy Council Office briefs both the chairs of committees and the prime minister. The prime minister is also briefed by the Prime Minister's Office. This series of actions completes the process and cabinet gives final approval or disapproval in a record of decision. Of course, private conversations about government policies, whether over the telephone, via email or in person, add immeasurable complexity to the pattern of cabinet business.

The **memorandum to cabinet** (**MC**) is the formal document used by a minister to put his views to cabinet. Each memorandum is numbered and awarded a security classification. The MC consists of an *advocacy* document followed by a detailed *analysis* section. The ministerial recommendation is formulated to convince his colleagues of the appropriate course of action, while the analysis is devised as background notes and may be made public under the *Freedom of Information Act*. Ministers may also bring issues directly to the cabinet table.

All ministers are allowed to place major policy and legislative proposals on cabinet's list of priority problems. Cabinet cohesiveness is maintained by encouraging each minister to believe that he will succeed in persuading colleagues to accept some of these proposals. If serious cabinet dissent emerges over a minister's ideas, that minister will be asked to reconsider and resubmit them. Each is made to feel part of a team that values one another's proposals. The participants are united for their own survival—and they know it!

Orders-in-council are issued by cabinet to carry out government rule-making and administration. In most cases, they are authorized by provisions contained in statutes. Some orders, however, fall under the royal prerogative. Upon passage, all orders-in-council are published in *The Canada Gazette*. Until recently, their numbers increased yearly. For example, in 1982, 4379 were passed, ranging from

FIGURE 8.3 **The Formal Cabinet Policy Process, 2008**

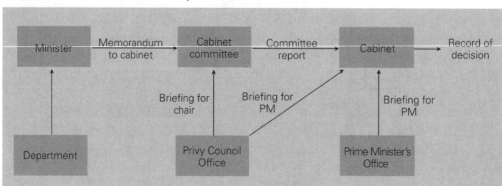

trivial to urgent. By 1988, however, the number had dropped to 3223. This was not due to a reduction in cabinet activities, but rather to a new process in which more than one appointment was made in the same order. Approximately a quarter of the orders consisted of regulations for administering the country; the next greatest number and the most visible, however, were those for appointments. By convention, the prime minister recommends roughly a hundred deputy head positions on his own authority. The other two thousand full-time order-in-council positions involve the prime minister and/or other ministerial decisions.

How successful a cabinet is depends to a large extent on its management of several critical factors, including taxation, expenditures and the legislative program. By controlling these, as well as the machinery of government and senior personnel, the government is able to effect major decisions. Through strategic planning, the government attempts to employ all these resources to accomplish its goals. In theory, the government places all the goals and issues into a hierarchy of interests, but in practice this rarely works. For one thing, long-term policy goals often have to give way to short-term administrative matters. For another, issues change over time, and the government must be prepared to adjust its targets. Finally, ultimate determination occurs within the ephemeral world of politics, where politicians come and go, change their opinions and are themselves divided over policies. A slight change in personnel can affect the distribution of power that first established the priority. Nevertheless, the idea of strategic planning comes from the desire to achieve comprehensive, non-urgent policy-making to help counter the piecemeal policies emanating from individual departments. The central coordinating agencies aid the government in these various tasks.

The Central Coordinating Agencies

In response to the large scope of the government's role in Canadian society and to the corresponding need for effective policy formation and implementation, new executive agencies have been created or expanded. Some of these central coordinating agencies have a special responsibility to support the prime minister, cabinet and ministry. Some have little legal authority, but are organized under the prime minister's prerogative for the machinery of government. While their stated purpose is to streamline the governmental process, the executive agencies have often received considerable public attention and have drawn accusations that Canada is being run by a cabal of "superbureaucrats" who are powers unto themselves. The closed nature of these agencies makes them a target for criticism. To a considerable extent, they also have become recruiting grounds for senior positions throughout the public service.

The centralization of power in the hands of the prime minister and these coordinating agencies appears indisputable. This development has probably been inevitable, given the range of demands for government action in Canada. We discuss briefly the duties and responsibilities of the four most important executive agencies: the Prime Minister's Office; the Privy Council Office, including the Intergovernmental Office; the Treasury Board; and the Department of Finance. The first two report directly to the prime minister; the other two have their own ministers.

The Prime Minister's Office

Of the various executive support agencies, the Prime Minister's Office (PMO) is the most overtly political and partisan. The upper echelon of the PMO is composed of personal appointees of the prime minister and sometimes includes those referred to as "Ottawa's best and brightest." It is the largest and most important of the exempt staffs, and only very rarely are public servants employed in this central agency. While the PMO lacks the statutory authority of the other executive agencies, its importance is based on the style and personality of the prime minister.

Sometimes, on the advice of ministers and other advisors, the PMO drafts the Speech from the Throne. Perhaps its most crucial task, however, is to act as a monitoring agency, tracing political developments and their implications for the prime minister and his career. (For an outline of the traditional structure of the PMO, see Figure 8.4.) An official explained the PMO's role as follows:

> *We are just a valve at the junction of the bureaucratic and the political. We add a little of the political ingredient when it appears that it has been overlooked. For instance, if I know that an official in PCO is working on a briefing note to the PM on an issue which I am responsible for, I'll go to him and express the political point of view—I guess we are sort of a Distant Early Warning System for things that are going to cause trouble politically.*[22]

The Prime Minister's Office has grown immensely over the years. The office has usually had a budget of over $6 million per annum. The importance of the PMO is determined solely by the prime minister's personality and needs. For some first ministers, it has become perhaps the most important part of the governmental policy-making apparatus.

In concert with the Privy Council Office, the PMO provides the prime minister with a range of technical and political advice that may not otherwise be available. The emphasis of the PMO is on the development of practical policy suggestions relevant to the political fortunes of the prime minister and his party. In addition, the PMO does considerable public relations work. It gathers surveys on the popularity of the prime minister and specific policy initiatives, and helps with preparing press conferences and dealing with the media generally. As a rule, officials in the PMO know and accept the marketing maxim, "It's the sizzle, not the steak, that sells." Other related responsibilities include answering the prime minister's mail, coordinating the daily appointment schedule and searching for candidates for riding nominations and awards.

FIGURE 8.4 The Prime Minister's Office (Basic Form)

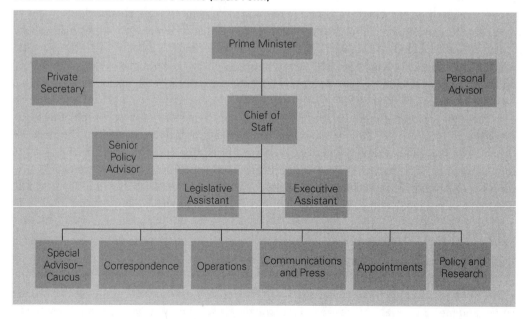

22. Cited in Colin Campbell and George J. Szablowski, *The Superbureaucrats: Structure and Behaviour in Central Agencies* (Toronto: Macmillan, 1979), p. 66.

The organization and structure of the PMO remain the prerogative of the prime minister. Throughout Canada's early history, the office was a small, relatively insignificant body. However, under Pierre Trudeau, it achieved unprecedented importance. In 1968, Trudeau appointed Marc Lalonde, who had been with the Pearson government, to the position of principal secretary. In 1984, Brian Mulroney went even further. He increased the staff to approximately two hundred employees and put many of his friends in the PMO. He appointed his law school friend, Bernard Roy, as his chief of staff. Later, the position was held by Derek Burney, a career public servant; Norman Spector, from the Federal–Provincial Relations Office; Stanley Hartt, an old friend; and the staunchest Tory of them all, Hugh Segal.

The extent of the power and influence of the chief of staff position depends in large measure on the ability of the individual and the amount of authority the prime minister is willing to delegate. In 1993, Prime Minister Chrétien appointed Jean Pelletier, former mayor of Québec City and a defeated Liberal candidate, as his first chief of staff, and Eddie Goldenberg, a lifelong friend, as senior policy advisor. In 2004, Paul Martin appointed long-time Liberal Francis Fox as his senior advisor for a few months, eventually replacing him with Hélène Chalifour as principal secretary. To date, Prime Minister Harper has not appointed a principal secretary, but his chief of staff, Ian Brodie, has established a reputation as his policy co-ordinator.

The PMO has achieved considerable importance and is likely to continue to be extremely influential in policy-making at the political apex. With its large budget and staff, the PMO is crucial to the government of the day. The senior people on staff act as the prime minister's personal advisors and help to sort out cabinet and party conflicts.

The Privy Council Office

The Queen's Privy Council for Canada was established by the Constitution to advise the governor general. It is a ceremonial body composed mostly of current and former ministers of the Crown. The cabinet, as we have seen, is a committee of the Privy Council. The main organization supporting the cabinet and prime minister is the **Privy Council Office** (**PCO**). The top position in the PCO is held by the **clerk of the Privy Council**. This position, which has existed since 1867, is mentioned in the Constitution. It was combined with the function of **secretary to the cabinet** in 1940.

The PCO is the prime minister's department and cabinet's secretariat. It supports the prime minister, ministers who are in the PM's portfolio (in 2007, this included the president of the Queen's Privy Council, the minister for intergovernmental affairs, the leader of the government in the House of Commons and minister for democratic reform, and the leader of the government in the Senate), and cabinet as a whole. It performs many of the same functions as the PMO (such as providing notes and/or giving oral briefings for ministers) but is staffed by career bureaucrats seconded from various government departments. It is responsible for developing and coordinating overall government policy. Although the prime minister, on the advice of the clerk, appoints the top echelon of PCO staff, there is little emphasis on partisan politics. There have been some exceptions, however—for example, in his first term in office, Brian Mulroney appointed his friend and political advisor Dalton Camp as a senior policy advisor in the PCO. Under all recent prime ministers, the PCO, like the PMO, has flourished in size and scope of responsibility, but it has rarely had political appointees on its staff.

The Privy Council Office possesses an impressive research capability and acts as the "eyes and ears" of the cabinet in coordinating the numerous governmental departments and agencies. With a staff of about five hundred officers and support personnel, the PCO is divided into several principal units. While the structures and powers of these units change with the styles of different prime ministers, the PCO tends to include plans, operations, intergovernmental affairs, machinery of government, foreign affairs, senior personnel and security and intelligence units (for its structure in 2008, see Figure 8.5). Each of these divisions has its own staff and is responsible for advising the prime minister, the plenary cabinet and the various cabinet committees on matters of national policy. To achieve this, the PCO employs a wide range of talent—from clerical staff and legal counsel to technical and scientific experts.

The clerk of the Privy Council also heads Canada's civil service. The role and stature of the clerk of the Privy Council, like those of the officers of the PMO, depend to a great extent on his rapport with the prime minister. Any PM would likely consider the clerk to be a crucial appointment, since this individual is in charge of coordinating cabinet activities. The clerk's staff sets agendas, takes the minutes of cabinet meetings and conveys cabinet decisions to the bureaucracy. Kevin G. Lynch currently holds the position and he is supported directly by an array of senior public servants.

The relationship between cabinet ministers and officers of the PCO is usually cordial and constructive. Although the staff of the Privy Council may be expert on specific matters of policy, in the end it is the elected ministers, whatever their knowledge or qualifications, who must make the decisions. In principle, the PCO exists to advise and suggest alternatives in an objective and dispassionate manner, since the weight of public responsibility is not on its shoulders. Officials know, however, that they must develop answers that will be acceptable to their political masters. Most of them learn quickly that this characteristic is more important than being outspoken and speaking their mind.

The PCO has a difficult task to perform within the Canadian government. It must be able to offer expert advice to the prime minister on the widest possible range of problems and policies. Given such expectations, it is not surprising that the PCO is considered one of the most prestigious agencies of the government.

Issues of concern to the federal government and the provinces are periodically negotiated and adjusted through the mechanism of federal–provincial conferences. As we discussed in Chapters 6 and 7, federalism has recently been characterized by a strong challenge to Ottawa's power, particularly from the richer Western provinces and Québec. Within the Privy Council Office, a new central agency—the **Federal–Provincial Relations Office** (**FPRO**)—was established in 1974 and was designated a separate department under the prime minister in 1975. Until 1993, it functioned independently of the PCO while reporting directly to the prime minister. As part of the 1993 restructuring, the FPRO was subsumed once again by the PCO. The name of the FPRO has recently been changed to **Intergovernmental Affairs Secretariat** to indicate that it is responsible for issues concerning Aboriginals and territorial governments as well as the provinces. It continues to conduct research and analysis to help coordinate Ottawa's interaction with the provinces and to anticipate provincial reactions.

In 2004, the federal government indicated its concern for international crises and terrorism by appointing a new national security advisor to the prime minister inside the PCO. This office continues in 2008 with an associate deputy of cabinet responsible for intelligence, threat assessment integration and intra-agency co-operation.

The Treasury Board

The third central coordinating agency is the Treasury Board, which, as we have noted, is constitutionally a committee of the Privy Council—i.e., of cabinet. In 1966, following recommendations of the Glassco Royal Commission on Government Organization, the staff of the Treasury Board was removed from the jurisdiction of the Department of Finance and elevated to the legal status of a separate government department. A cabinet minister, designated the president of the Treasury Board, heads the board and its secretariat. The Treasury Board itself includes other cabinet ministers, one of whom is usually

FIGURE 8.5 **Basic Privy Council Office Structure in the Harper Government, 2008**

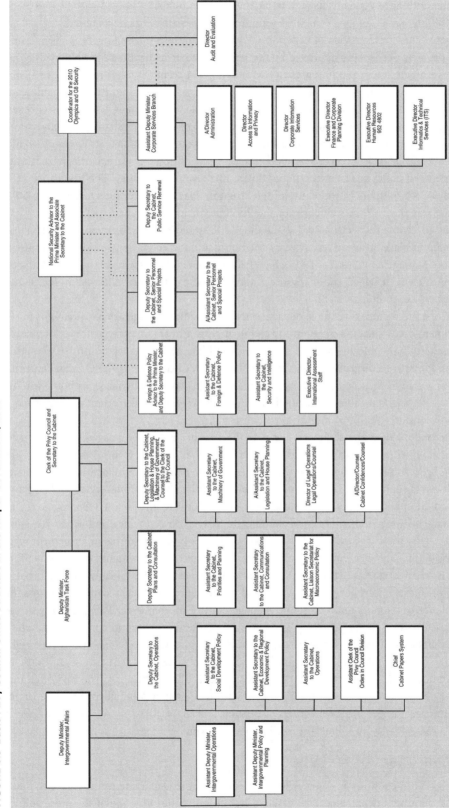

Source: PCO Organization Chart, www.pco-bcp.gc.ca. Reproduced with the permission of the Minister of Public Works and Government Services Canada, and courtesy of the Privy Council Office.

the minister of finance. Aided by its secretariat, the Treasury Board is charged with two broad areas of responsibility: review of government expenditures and personnel management.

Responsibility for the review of expenditures means that the annual budgets of all government departments are screened and approved by this agency. The Treasury Board monitors all requests for money, evaluates them and provides an overall budget in keeping with the priorities and objectives expressed by the prime minister and cabinet. There is continuous consultation and negotiation between the Treasury Board and representatives of each department, who are usually senior bureaucrats and the minister. Each department attempts to maximize its share of the government's budget, and it is up to the Treasury Board to assess these requests and make its recommendations.

The task of the Treasury Board would be exceedingly difficult, if not chaotic, were it not for improvements in policy-making techniques during the past four decades. The first major reform came in the 1960s with the introduction of the Program, Planning and Budgetary System (PPBS). The second was the 1979 introduction of the Public Expenditure Management System (PEMS). Despite the government's decision to disband the PEMS system in 1989, its financial control procedures remain in place. In more recent years, the board and its secretariat, working under the new Expenditure Management System (EMS), have been delegated the responsibility for advising cabinet on the efficient management of resources. It reviews the *departmental business plans* required under the new expenditure system.

In theory, these procedures force departments to frame their budgetary requirements in terms of government goals and objectives and in the format of a business plan. Whether the Treasury Board has been fully able to meet its heavy responsibility in budgetary control is a matter of contention for various disgruntled department heads and, of course, for the Official Opposition. In fairness, it should be noted that its task is complex. It is continually faced with pressure from both within and without cabinet. Inevitably, no matter how worthwhile certain programs may be, there is only a finite amount of money to pay for them.

The second major responsibility entrusted to the Treasury Board is management of civil service personnel. In 1967, the Treasury Board replaced the Public Service Commission as the official employer of government personnel; it is thus the responsible party in any collective bargaining negotiations. It exerts control over salaries and job classifications across the civil service, and its purpose is to expand the application of the merit principle. What motivates the Treasury Board above all else is a desire to encourage the effective utilization of human resources. A new Public Service Human Resources Agency was legislated in 2003 to put in place a new human resources management regime.

To assist the cabinet members of the Treasury Board, there is a highly qualified staff—the **Treasury Board Secretariat (TBS)**. The **secretary to the Treasury Board** heads the secretariat, and in 2003 a distinct comptroller general was added in the government. The **comptroller general** is responsible for developing and enforcing financial control mechanisms. This person has deputy head status reporting to the secretary and helps select the departmental comptrollers, who are required to approve all future spending proposals. Among the TBS staff are some of the brightest and most efficient members of the public service. Its economists, statisticians and efficiency experts conduct much of the preliminary analysis of departmental budgets. The TBS often makes preliminary budgetary adjustments and other decisions that may be challenged by department heads or ministers at the formal meetings of the board itself. Needless to say, the specialized staff of the TBS can also play an important role in policy-making.

The Department of Finance

The fourth central coordinating agency of the executive is the Department of Finance. While it is a regular government department, by virtue of its subject matter it is one of the most politically sensitive. Created in 1967 out of the financial bodies that predated Confederation, its authority is assigned under the *Financial Administration Act*. Finance shares some of the general concerns of the Treasury Board, but its chief preoccupation is analyzing taxation policy and the impact of government activity on the economy. That is, the department is concerned with monitoring Canada's economic prospects and predicting the probable level of tax revenues available to the government. Finance also engages in long-range economic forecasting and suggests ways to maximize the performance of the economy.

The Department of Finance provides most of the information that reaches the cabinet on the performance of the economy. It is on the basis of these facts that cabinet committees weigh and sift through various programs and proposals to establish priorities. The department's predictions and analyses assist other policy-makers in their attempts to achieve maximum use of available resources. Public servants employed by Finance concentrate on analyzing four areas that make up the department's statutory authority: taxation policy, economic development and government finance, fiscal policy and economic analysis, and international trade and finance.

Taxation policy is handled by individual units within the department. Specialists analyze existing tax measures from the perspective of the business community. A personal income tax unit examines proposals relating to personal taxation, and deferred income plans such as retirement savings plans, trusts and partnerships. Other tax units attempt to determine the effects of taxation on the distribution of income, on the long-term growth of the economy and on the behaviour of individuals and corporations. Finally, the Department of Finance maintains an international tax policy unit that negotiates tax treaties with foreign countries and examines the effects of foreign taxation on the Canadian economy.

With respect to the second responsibility, economic development, Finance seeks to devise policies and strategies that encourage the overall growth of the Canadian economy. For instance, policy analysts study plans to foster the development of Canada's natural resources and to promote industrial growth in such diverse fields as communications, transportation, nuclear energy and manufacturing. The Department of Finance is also involved in providing government loans to promote economic development and in negotiating financial guarantees to Crown corporations.

The third responsibility of Finance is fiscal policy and economic analysis. The department monitors all indicators of the overall economic conditions of the country and prepares forecasts used in the development of the annual government budget. This involves establishing the annual fiscal framework and maintaining a close link with the Treasury Board Secretariat.

The fourth concern of the Department of Finance is international trade. It investigates and reports on proposals concerning the Canadian customs tariff and its relation to the General Agreement on Tariffs and Trade (GATT) and various bilateral trade agreements such as the Canada–United States Free Trade Agreement (FTA) and the North American Free Trade Agreement (NAFTA). Recommendations on international trade policy, particularly imports, are formulated. The department maintains a liaison with international financial organizations and, of course, seeks to promote export development. The international finance section is also concerned with the balance of payments and foreign exchange matters.

The Department of Finance maintains a relatively high profile among government departments. Its minister is more than a spokesman for economic decisions made by the cabinet. While the minister of finance must carry out cabinet's directives, other ministers become involved so late in the budget-planning process that, in effect, the finance minister has the dominant voice. It is the minister who presents the government's budget to Parliament and is inevitably the object of criticism or praise by the press and the opposition parties.

Government Ethics: Honesty and Corruption

Canadians expect a high degree of integrity from their public leaders. Over the years, a complicated, tortuous and confusing imbroglio of laws, rules and regulations and codes have been written in an attempt to ensure the ethical conduct of politicians and public servants. On the whole, these regulations have emerged haphazardly and as the result of specific scandals and crises. Until very recently, there has been very little desire on the part of federal politicians to write new, more coherent sets of guidelines or laws.

In this section, we examine the main types of behaviour that create ethical problems for politicians, and the rules that are in place to prevent infractions. We review the major cases of alleged government impropriety since 1995, including the ethics regime of Jean Chrétien's Liberal government. We conclude with a discussion of the most recent ethics legislation by Stephen Harper's government.

Conflicts of Interest

One issue that haunts members of the cabinet as well as other politicians is conflict of interest. A **conflict of interest** is a situation in which a prime minister, minister, member of Parliament or public servant has knowledge of a private, personal economic interest sufficient to influence the exercise of public duties and responsibilities.[23] Even if the conflict is not illegal, it may create suspicions that the decisions or actions of such individuals are not impartial.

Public attitudes about which situations constitute conflict of interest for ministers have changed considerably over the years; behaviour that was considered normal a few decades ago now engenders cynicism, suspicion and moral condemnation. Until the 1960s, MPs routinely carried on with their private businesses after they became ministers, and conflict-of-interest queries were raised only when their ministerial decisions clearly produced private advantage. In those years, politics was still a part-time, rather poorly paid occupation, and ministers and prime ministers openly and frequently engaged in potentially conflicting activities; they sat on boards of directors, carried on legal practices and accepted private trust funds. It is even said that C.D. Howe, a respected Liberal minister, routinely checked his stock listings before going to cabinet to make important economic decisions for the country.

After several mini-scandals in the Pearson government, public tolerance of such practices began to wane. In 1972, Prime Minister Trudeau issued formal guidelines for cabinet ministers. Like Pearson, he chose to rely on guidelines rather than legislation to handle the problem.[24] A registry of ministers' financial holdings was to be kept, and they could choose one of three options:

1. divest themselves of their financial holdings;

2. place their financial holdings in a blind trust (which meant, in theory, that ministers could not know what their holdings were and therefore would not be able to act on privileged information); or

3. place them in a frozen trust (meaning that ministers could know what their assets were but would not be able to change them).[25]

23. This is essentially the definition used by Justice William Parker in his 1987 report on the conflicts of interest of former cabinet minister Sinclair Stevens. See *Commission of Inquiry into the Facts and Allegations of Conflict of Interest Concerning the Honourable Sinclair M. Stevens* (Toronto: The Commission, 1987), p. 294.

24. Pierre Trudeau, *Statement on Conflict of Interest*, House of Commons, July 18, 1973.

25. See Robert J. Jackson and Michael Atkinson, *The Canadian Legislative System* (Toronto: Macmillan, 1980), pp. 209–10.

These guidelines provided ambiguous instructions for federal ministers about how to arrange their personal affairs to avoid the possibility of conflict of interest. Possible disclosure of conflict situations was considered to be a sufficient deterrent, since it would cause political embarrassment and negative publicity to the extent that a cabinet minister might feel it necessary to resign in order to protect the government's integrity. However, the guidelines did not provide sufficient sanctions to deter potential conflicts, nor did they establish appropriate mechanisms to determine whether such violations were taking place.

At that time, ordinary MPs and senators were not subject to specific rules outside those contained in the *Criminal Code*, covering topics such as bribery; the *Parliament Act*; and the rules of the House and Senate, which prohibited specific forms of behaviour. Reformers tried, to little avail, to make the rules more specific. In 1973, Liberal cabinet minister Allan MacEachen tabled a Green Paper entitled, *Members of Parliament and Conflict of Interest*, which called for legislation that would apply to all politicians.[26] The Green Paper defined conflict of interest as a "situation in which a Member of Parliament has a personal or private pecuniary interest sufficient to influence, or appear to influence, the exercise of his public duties and responsibilities."[27] Opposition to this legislation was severe in both houses and no legislation could be passed. On the first attempt to pass legislation based on the Green Paper, the Senate blocked the proposal; on the second attempt, Parliament was dissolved in 1979 before the bill reached second reading.

Prime Minister Joe Clark made the guidelines for ministers more stringent in 1979 by extending them to the immediate families of ministers. Blind trusts became mandatory, and for two years after leaving cabinet ex-ministers could not serve on boards of directors of corporations with which they had dealt as ministers; they could not act on behalf of such people or corporations, or act as lobbyists. For one year, they could not accept jobs with companies with which they had dealt, nor could they act as consultants for them. These guidelines were maintained from the Clark government through to the beginning of the Mulroney government in 1984.

In 1984, the federal government set up a Task Force on Conflict of Interest (which produced the *Sharp-Starr Report*). It concluded that there was a need to improve regulations. The task force proposed appointing two ethics officers: a commissioner and a counsellor. The *ethics commissioner* would function as a police officer responsible for seeking out and investigating potential conflicts of interest, whereas the *ethics counsellor* would inform ministers what the law and ethics code demanded of them so that they could obey it. No specific action was taken on the report, however.

In 1985, Prime Minister Mulroney abolished the old ethics code and introduced a new set of conflict-of-interest guidelines for cabinet ministers and civil servants. Like the earlier version, it

CLOSE-UP ON Institutions

MORALITY IN PARLIAMENT

Professors Ian Greene and David P. Shugarman believe that the ethics of politicians affect the public:

> Leaders who are considered self-interested and untrustworthy create a malaise in government circles that tempts public servants to behave unethically to protect themselves. And these factors combine to erode the public's trust in government as a whole. Conversely, if those at the top are perceived as fair and honest, then these values tend to permeate the entire society.*

Is there empirical evidence to support this contention? Do you agree with the principles stated in this quotation?

* Ian Greene and David P. Shugarman, *Honest Politics* (Toronto: Lorimer, 1997), p. 213.

26. For a more detailed examination, see Robert J. Jackson, "Honesty and Corruption in Canadian Federal Government and Politics," in Jenny Fleming and Ian Holland, eds., *Motivating Ministers to Morality* (London: Ashgate, 2001).

27. Privy Council Office, Canada. *Members of Parliament and Conflict of Interest*, MacEachen Green Paper (Ottawa: Information Canada, 1973).

stopped short of full, mandatory disclosure in order to strike a balance between protecting the public interest and protecting the private affairs of ministers. The restrictions on business dealings of immediate family members, for example, were dropped. It did, however, state explicitly that ministers should not hire their own immediate relatives (or other ministers' relatives) for government jobs.

The ambiguity and lack of enforcement provisions in the new ethics guidelines led to a major conflict-of-interest case in 1986–87, when cabinet minister Sinclair Stevens was faced with a series of conflict allegations. A key charge against Stevens was that his wife had obtained a $2.6 million loan from a consultant to a company that had received grants from Stevens's government department. Stevens had ostensibly placed his business holdings in a blind trust; however, the trust was considerably less than "blind" because of his connections with several individuals, including his wife (who remained an officer of the company) and his secretary, who could have provided Stevens with information about the affairs of his blind trust. The Parker Commission, which investigated the case, concluded that Stevens had violated the conflict code 14 times. In 2004, a federal court judge overturned the 17-year-old public inquiry report that had found Stevens guilty. Justice John O'Keefe exonerated Stevens on the grounds that Justice Parker had drafted his own definition of conflict of interest. The term wasn't defined in the codes of conduct that applied to the period Stevens was minister.

Concerned that Canadians were indeed losing confidence in the integrity of politicians and politics in general, and also that his government had an extremely poor image in this regard, Mulroney decided that guidelines were no longer sufficient and introduced conflict-of-interest *legislation* in early 1988. The bill attempted to force enough disclosure to keep government leaders honest, yet not infringe on their private lives so much that highly qualified individuals would be deterred from entering politics. However, Bill C114 died on the Order Paper when the 1988 general election was called. In the last days of the Mulroney government in 1993, another, more stringent, bill was introduced, but it, too, died on the Order Paper when the 34th Parliament was dissolved.

When he came to office late in 1993, Prime Minister Jean Chrétien took a radically different approach to conflict of interest. Arguing that "integrity in government is not simply a matter of rules and regulations—it is also a matter of personal standards and conduct,"[28] he hired former cabinet minister Mitchell Sharp for one dollar a year as a special advisor on integrity of government.

In June 1994, the prime minister unveiled yet another ethics package about the conflict-of-interest code and lobbying rules. Public officials (ministers, secretaries of state, parliamentary secretaries and senior public servants) were instructed to disclose their assets and outside activities confidentially to a newly appointed ethics counsellor, who was made responsible for both conflict-of-interest and lobbying rules. Problems still existed, however, because the ethics counsellor was not accountable to Parliament, only to the prime minister. As well, despite various allegations of wrongdoing and the consequent resignation of two ministers, the government would not agree that codes of conduct should be legislated or that regular MPs should even be covered by a code.

Nevertheless, as they do today, the *Criminal Code*, the *Parliament of Canada Act*, and Standing Orders of the House of Commons and Rules of the Senate continued to apply to any minister, MP or senator involved in fraud, influence peddling or breach of trust. The *Criminal Code* makes certain practices, such as bribery, illegal; the *Parliament of Canada Act* forbids MPs from having government contracts; and the Standing Orders of House of Commons and Senate rules ban certain behaviour and require certain disclosures—such as the necessity to make public a financial interest when speaking or voting in Parliament. But much of the unethical conduct that has taken place has not been illegal or even against parliamentary rules. Most of the conflict of interest, patronage, and gains have been about broad unethical behaviour not covered by the rules (see our discussion below).

28. Press release from the Office of the Prime Minister, November 4, 1993, p. 3.

Patronage and Pork-Barrelling

Closely linked to conflict of interest is a little-studied field—the world of political patronage and its relative, pork-barrelling. **Patronage**, in the broad sense, concerns the awarding of contracts, employment and other material benefits to individuals or groups on the basis of partisan support rather than according to merit. It means granting jobs and contracts for political reasons. It can include illegal practices such as vote buying, "treating" (paying for votes with liquor) and other forms of bribery. **Pork-barrelling**, on the other hand, extends favours to whole regions or communities as an inducement for support. Patronage and pork-barrelling usually break no laws but often raise serious questions about ethical conduct.

Some regard patronage and its less attractive cousin as essential parts of politics, providing the oil that makes the system run smoothly and the glue that keeps the major parties together and the political system stable. For others, patronage and pork-barrelling are immoral activities that impede honest, efficient government services. All would agree, however, that they are enduring features of the Canadian political system. It is in the shadowy world where interest-group behaviour, patronage and pork-barrelling meet, and where secret negotiations lead to connections between influence and favours, that corruption adds its cynical, malodorous quality to Canadian politics.

Patronage has been an important part of the Canadian political culture since the pre-1867 colonial period.[29] The notion that only party supporters have the right to government positions and favours was imported from Britain and has become a distinctive feature of Canadian politics, although it has been modified over time. Patronage traditionally provided an inducement for loyalty and for mobilizing participation. Moreover, the early history of patronage in Canada reflects the struggle to shift control over the distribution of political favours from the monarch and government in Britain to the prime minister and cabinet in Canada—in effect, to "patriate" the power of patronage.

Four distinct stages have been noted in the development of patronage in Canada.[30] In the colonial years, the British governors dispensed patronage, using it to maintain deference and loyalty in the colonists. With the advent of responsible government, the privilege of dispensing patronage shifted to the elected representative. In the second stage, after Confederation, patronage was used first by Sir John A. Macdonald and later by Sir Wilfrid Laurier to help build national parties that would unite a widely scattered population. These prime ministers used material benefits openly and freely to recruit party members and maintain an active party organization. The third stage of patronage development began about the time of the First World War, when Mackenzie King began his long career as prime minister. Patronage and pork-barrelling remained an important part of party management, but during this period the civil service became separate from the party in power, dramatically changing the close relationship that had previously existed between the government and the public service. The final stage of patronage development began in the 1960s as technological and cultural changes contributed to public intolerance of some of the traditional inducements to loyalty and participation.

Modern prime ministers endeavour to find more acceptable inducements to loyalty and discipline, such as the strength of their personality and popular policies. They use the media—television in particular—to appeal directly to citizens. However strong these direct appeals have become, they have not yet supplanted patronage. It is no surprise that opposition parties seem to have more trouble than governing parties in maintaining internal party cohesion; the government holds all the patronage and pork-barrelling resources in its own hands and is often able to secure loyalty from those who either receive favours or expect to.

29. Gordon T. Stewart, *The Origins of Canadian Parties* (Vancouver: UBC Press, 1986).
30. Jeffrey Simpson, *Spoils of Power: The Politics of Patronage* (Toronto: Collins, 1988), p. 6.

Several aspects of patronage have contributed to its sullied reputation. It plays to human weaknesses, encouraging unethical behaviour by individuals, institutions and groups in society. It also has an inflationary aspect: one reward creates a demand for more, and the demand always exceeds supply. The use of patronage to bind together religious, French–English or regional interests is no longer sufficiently broad; it must now extend to women, youth, Natives and those of various ethnic groups.[31]

Recent prime ministers have been plagued with the problem of dispensing patronage without compromising their public position.[32] Joe Clark incurred the wrath of party rank and file when he delayed too long in filling patronage positions. He lost his chance to dispense rewards when his minority government was defeated in 1979. John Turner lost the 1984 election when he declared he "had no option" but to honour the "orgy" of appointments demanded by departing Prime Minister Trudeau. Despite the fact that Brian Mulroney had made a major issue out of patronage in his successful 1984 election campaign, calling the actions of Turner and Trudeau "scandalous," "vulgar" and "unacceptable," he proceeded to fill patronage positions and award government business to party and personal friends. He also saw his own popularity, and that of his party, fall to record lows after patronage binges during his two terms in government.

In 1993, the new Chrétien government promised to increase integrity in government and decrease patronage appointments. The country waited in vain for the concrete results of these assertions, as almost all of the government appointments in the Chrétien era went to well-known Liberals—former governor general Roméo LeBlanc the most prominent among them.

The Chrétien Regime: Laws, Rules and Institutions

Ministers, Parliamentary Secretaries and Senior Officials Jean Chrétien's new code covered all members of cabinet, parliamentary secretaries, members of the ministers' staffs and over 1200 senior officials in the federal public service. The spouses and dependants of ministers were also covered, as they had to disclose their activities, but they were not required to follow the rules of the code in regard to disclosure.

Section 3(1) of the code declared that "public office holders shall act with honesty and uphold the highest ethical standards so that public confidence and trust in the integrity, objectivity and impartiality of government are conserved and enhanced." It listed in section 3(5) the principles and compliance measures that were intended to prevent "real, potential or apparent conflicts of interest." Also, public employees were required to provide a report to the ethics counsellor tabulating their assets, liabilities and outside activities. The counsellor reviewed the list and told the public official appointees what to do to be in accordance with the code. Ministers were prohibited from engaging in a profession, actively managing or operating a business or serving as a corporate director. Moreover, they could not hold office in a union or professional association or act as a paid consultant.

Appointees' assets were also listed and monitored. Exempt assets, such as homes, vacation properties, bank accounts and fixed income investments, as well as mutual funds were not further controlled. "Declarable" assets had to be made public, but the office holder could continue to handle them. They included ownership of family or local businesses, farms under commercial operation and rental properties. "Controllable" assets were those such as publicly traded securities, including shares in a stock market, which could be affected directly or indirectly by government action. Office holders were required to divest themselves of all these types of controlled instruments.

31. Ibid., p. 15. Patronage is discussed further in Chapter 11.

32. John Sawatsky, *The Insiders: Government, Business and the Lobbyists* (Toronto: McClelland & Stewart, 1987), chs. 17–19.

Office holders could use one of three strategies: They could 1) sell the assets; 2) put them in a blind trust (i.e., they could not obtain information on the composition of their assets as they would be managed at arm's length); or 3) in certain cases they could create a "blind management" agreement—for example, if an MP owned a private company that might do business with the government. In the latter case, the office holder was prevented from making any decision on the management of his assets.

Only one position, that of **ethics counsellor**, was formally created, not two, as earlier envisioned. On June 16, 1994, Howard Wilson was appointed Prime Minister Chrétien's ethics counsellor. He reported directly to the prime minister only. It was his duty to uphold the code of conduct for public office holders. Wilson also had the responsibility of enforcing a law—the *Lobbyists Registration Act*. However, although it was unlegislated, his most important responsibility was to probe the ethical conduct of cabinet ministers whenever requested to do so by the prime minister. Mitchell Sharp (who co-wrote the earlier *Sharp-Starr Report* in 1984) was employed on the prime minister's exempt staff as an ethics advisor.

When he and the Liberals came to power, Prime Minister–elect Chrétien asked Mitchell Sharp to interview prospective cabinet ministers in order to identify anything in their records that might embarrass the new government. Sharp interviewed each candidate for cabinet, asking them whether they and their spouses could live with conflict-of-interest guidelines, and whether they had skeletons in their closet, tax arrears or personal problems. This procedure kept two individuals out of cabinet, and caused a few others to request a change of portfolio to avoid potential conflicts.

CLOSE-UP ON Institutions

THE 2003 CONFLICT OF INTEREST AND POST-EMPLOYMENT CODE FOR PUBLIC OFFICE HOLDERS

CABINET MEMBERS, SECRETARIES OF STATE, PARLIAMENTARY SECRETARIES, MINISTERIAL STAFFS AND FULL-TIME GOVERNOR-IN-COUNCIL POSITIONS

The major provisions were

- the requirement to disclose all assets and liabilities to the ethics counsellor, including the assets and liabilities of spouses and dependent children;
- the requirement to disclose all business interests and either sell or put into trust those interests whose value could be affected by government decisions or policy;
- the requirement to disclose all significant outside activities during the previous two years, including charity work and trusteeships;
- the requirement not to retain or accept directorships or offices in a financial or commercial operation, hold a union or professional position, practice a profession, operate a business or serve as a paid consultant;
- the requirement that for a period of one year (two years for cabinet ministers) after leaving office, they cannot lobby their former departments or work for any people or entities they dealt with in the year before they left their respective offices.

In addition to the public code, Prime Minister Chrétien, with the advice of Howard Wilson and Mitchell Sharp, also declared that ministers could not communicate with government tribunals except under very specific circumstances. The ethics counsellor summarized this rule as such: "Ministers shall not intervene, or appear to intervene, on behalf of any person or entity, with federal quasi-judicial tribunals on any matter before them that requires a decision in their quasi-judicial capacity, unless otherwise authorized by law."[33] The rule did not restrict backbench MPs in their dealings with administrative tribunals, but it did hold ministers to a higher standard of accountability. At issue was finding the right balance between ensuring ministers could not use their positions to unduly influence tribunals and giving them enough freedom to help their constituents.

---

33. Howard Wilson, "Principles Respecting Government Contacts with Judicial and Quasi-Judicial Bodies." Notes for Speech to the 15th Annual Administrative Law Seminar, (Ottawa 1998); "Ethics and Government: the Canadian Case," in *Australia and Parliamentary Orthodoxy* (Canberra: Department of the Senate, 1999).

Members of Parliament and Senators   As we have seen above, at this time there was no specific legislation or even code of conduct for regular MPs in the field of conflict of interest. Attempts at reform always met with obstacles; although several bills were introduced on the topic, none was passed. A joint committee of the two houses in the 36th Parliament concluded that there should be a code for both senators and MPs, but a bill was never produced, as senators and MPs behind the scenes said they would not approve the legislation.

The *Criminal Code* and House and Senate rules continued to apply but, alas, there was still no ethics code. The rules that did apply were therefore not codified or coherent, and were often contradictory. Loopholes existed in many fields. Free foreign travel was unregulated, although MPs (but not senators) had to declare trips. Fees for speaking and consulting required no declaration, and relations with lobbyists were uncontrolled. In other words, there was no systematic transparency. Under the standing orders, MPs had to declare any private interests in any matter before the House, but there was no annual registry as in the United Kingdom or Australia to publicize this material.[34]

Evaluations of the Chrétien Ethics Regime
There were four significant problem areas in the Chrétien rules:

1. *Minimal Consultation with Opposition Leaders:* The Liberal campaign platform in 1993 (known as the Red Book) stated that opposition leaders would participate in the development of the ethical guidelines governing cabinet ministers. This was not done.
2. *Ad Hoc Nature of Rules:* The rules were malleable enough so that subsequent prime ministers could change them at will. The rules were not regularized in the form of regulations or laws approved by Parliament.
3. *Lack of Independent Investigative Powers:* The ethics counsellor was responsible for investigating conflict-of-interest allegations against anyone the prime minister asked him to investigate. The counsellor then reported his findings directly to the prime minister. There was nothing to compel the ethics counsellor to investigate conflict-of-interest allegations raised in the media or by the House of Commons. Howard Wilson did not seek out and investigate possible conflicts of interest, but merely advised those who asked him what the law was, so that they could obey it. There was no way he could legitimately investigate the prime minister.
4. *Lack of Accountability and Openness:* The Liberals promised that the "ethics counsellor . . . would report directly to Parliament." However, Wilson was not accountable to Parliament—he reported, personally and privately, to the prime minister.

Critics of the ethics counsellor raised an important issue: why should the ethics counsellor not report to Parliament as well? If the counsellor reported to Parliament, it was argued, the office would gain a degree of independence that traditional cabinet appointees lack. Moreover, what would have happened if the prime minister had been embroiled in conflict of interest himself?

Just how effective the two newly created offices (ethics counsellor and ethics advisor) were in regulating levels of honesty in public life is difficult to assess, as the officials carried out their activities in secret. Mitchell Sharp's interviews produced some notable successes. Two potential ministers withdrew their names for cabinet appointments in 1994 when they were told of the conditions in the prime minister's code. Both MPs, however, joined the cabinet at a later date. No potential ministers were prevented from joining the cabinet in later Chrétien administrations.

Did these new offices and guidelines mean that the government and its ministers really acted more ethically? The Liberal government and ethics counsellor's office said definitely yes; however, the

the U.K. Register of Member's Interests requires the detailing of private interests, holdings, investments, gifts received, trips taken and other sources of income. See Maureen Mancuso, *The Ethical World of British MPs* (Kingston: McGill–Queen's Press, 1995).

opposition parties said definitely no. Chrétien's team and the ethics counsellor stressed what they call "integrity," while opposition members and some reformers put more emphasis on "compliance" and enforcement.

Ethics Investigations, 1993–2006

Well-publicized allegations against Liberal cabinet ministers after the Chrétien code was put into effect include the following cases.[35] They clearly indicated the need for new rules.

- 1995: Michel Dupuy, heritage minister, wrote to the Canadian Radio-television and Telecommunications Corporation (CRTC) in support of a constituent's application for a radio license in Montreal. Despite the fact that the rules about ministers contacting quasi-judicial bodies were somewhat vague, Dupuy did break the prime minister's code. The PM defended Dupuy, but later dropped him from cabinet. The guidelines for ministers writing to tribunals were also tightened.
- 1995: When critics asked Prime Minister Chrétien to instruct the ethics counsellor to examine an alleged improper relationship between Liberal senator Pierre DeBané and Canada Post president George Clermont, the prime minister replied that it was not up to the government to impose ethical standards on MPs and senators, but up to Parliament.
- 1996: Defence minister David Collenette was accused of interfering with a quasi-judicial body after he wrote to the Immigration Board on behalf of a constituent. Collenette clearly had violated the rules. Howard Wilson concluded that Collenette had indeed broken the cabinet rules. Collenette resigned but later returned to cabinet in another portfolio. (Collenette was a close personal friend of the prime minister.)
- 1996: Like Collenette, former immigration minister Sergio Marchi was questioned for writing a letter to the Immigration Board. Marchi wrote about a board decision involving a killer who successfully appealed his deportation order. Wilson declared that the letter was not an attempt to intervene and did not violate any cabinet guidelines.
- 1996: Youth minister Ethel Blondin-Andrew was found to have used government credit cards to pay for her Hawaii vacation and a fur coat. She claimed that she paid the government back. Wilson concluded that there was no wrongdoing.
- 1998: Finance Minister Paul Martin was accused of a conflict of interest over changes to the *Income Tax Act* that benefited shipping companies. Opposition parties alleged that the changes could benefit Martin's company, Canada Steamship Lines Ltd., but Wilson said Martin was unaware of the changes because a junior minister had handled the issue in government and this cleared Martin of any conflict.
- 1998: Former transport minister Doug Young was accused of a conflict when, after being defeated in the previous election, he obtained a share in a toll highway company that received federal funding when he was transport minister. Wilson found that there was no conflict.
- 1998: The Andy Scott Affair. Solicitor General Andy Scott's conversation about an Asia-Pacific Economic Cooperation Conference inquiry was overheard on an airplane and subsequently reported in the media. Mitchell Sharp admitted in one news article that he had discussed the solicitor general's conduct with the prime minister, but Wilson was not consulted. When a reporter asked Wilson whether the prime minister had instructed him to investigate Scott, Wilson replied, "No."

35. For greater detail on these and other cases as well as the ethic counsellor's action, see Robert J. Jackson, "Honesty and Corruption."

- 2000: Jane Stewart, minister for human resources, was held responsible for the "job-creation scandal" in which grants and contribution programs such as the Canada Jobs Fund were shown to have been mismanaged by over $1 billion. The department approved the majority of applications even though crucial information was missing, and then failed to follow up on most of them. The auditor general concluded that there had been widespread deficiencies in the process and this allegation launched a series of other allegations about political interference. The case raised the issue of whether a minister who provides benefits to his constituents is engaging in ethical misconduct or simply following democratic practices. Just what is ethical misconduct in such a case? Wilson maintained this issue did not come under the guidelines' jurisdiction.

- 2000–01: During the 2000 election campaign, Jean Chrétien was accused of phoning the head of the Business Development Bank of Canada on behalf of a constituent. Chrétien asked him to help secure a mortgage of $615 000 for the owner of the Auberge Grand-Mère, a hotel in the PM's hometown of Shawinigan. Howard Wilson was asked to investigate and did so. He concluded that this action did not constitute ethical misconduct under the rules, as the prime minister was acting like any other MP in supporting members of his riding. However, the facts in this case are murky, and Chrétien's behaviour continued to be questioned. The so-called Shawinigate scandal was one of the major causes of Chrétien's downfall as Liberal leader and prime minister.
- 2002–06: After the separatists' near success in the 1995 Québec referendum, the federal government began a series of actions to encourage future Québec support for Canada. It aimed to spread money throughout Québec to demonstrate Ottawa's largesse in competition with the separatists. In what became known in the press as AdScam, questionable decisions and sloppy administration led the auditor general, Sheila Fraser, to find that the sponsorship program was administered outside normal Treasury Board and Public Works guidelines. She concluded that over $100 000 had been misappropriated and given to a handful of Liberal-friendly advertising firms. Fraser concluded that the department "broke every rule in the book." The Crown corporations Via Rail, Canada Post, the Old Port of Montréal and the Business Development Bank (BDB) were all implicated.

There was much political fallout from AdScam: an RCMP investigation, Commons committee hearings and a judicial inquiry ensued to determine if there was any wrongdoing or criminal activity. Among the casualties was former public works minister Alfonso Gagliano, who, as former minister responsible for Québec, took much of the political blame and was eventually retired from his position as ambassador to Denmark. Officials in the Department of Public Works were also censured by the House committee, but they fought back. Chuck Guité, a former public servant who was given wide powers to distribute the funds in Québec, denied any wrongdoing and said that Québec separatism forced him to act. "When you're at war, you drop . . . the rules."[36] Among other events, Michel Vennat was fired as head of the BDB, André Ouellet was dismissed as head of Canada Post and Jean Pelletier was fired as head of Via Rail (Pelletier later sued the government for wrongful dismissal and in 2007 he won remuneration for lost wages and damage to his reputation).

The **Gomery Commission**, formally the **Commission of Inquiry Into the Sponsorship Program and Advertising Activities,** headed by retired Justice John Gomery was established to follow up on the Auditor General Fraser's report on allegations of corruption related to the AdScam. The final report of February 1, 2006, cleared outgoing prime minister Paul Martin of wrongdoing, but named several businessmen as being involved in scandals and implicated Jean Chrétien and his senior staff in the affair. The report also made suggestions about the need to reform federal government institutions.

36. *The Globe and Mail*, April 3, 2004.

There is no doubt that Paul Martin paid the biggest political price for the sponsorship scandal. Martin had been minister of finance when the AdScam infractions began. Later, as prime minister, he was forced to declare that he had known nothing about the scandal until it became public in 2002 and that the Liberal Party was "not corrupt." The allegations of corruption helped to turn public opinion against Martin's Liberals. This resulted in a minority government for Martin after the 2004 election and the Liberals' eventual loss of the 2006 election (see Chapter 12).

Several other allegations of conflict of interest were made during the 2002–06 period, but the ethics commissioner dismissed all of them as baseless.[37]

From Martin's Incrementalism to Harper's Comprehensive Reforms

As part of Paul Martin's effort to differentiate his new December 2003 government from the previous regimes of Jean Chrétien, he immediately declared, "The core principles of the new government will be transparency, accountability, financial responsibility and ethical conduct." Martin updated the conflict-of-interest and post-employment code for public office holders and named a new ethics commissioner responsible for policing it. The code covers ministers, ministers of state, parliamentary secretaries, members of ministerial staff and all order-in-council appointees. Martin did not rescind the old code (discussed above), but he added new rules reducing the possibility of the improper use of government aircraft; requiring all gifts worth more than $1000 to be put into the government inventory; stating that the ethics commissioner must approve before public office holders accept any gifts, hospitality or benefits; and requiring public disclosure of liabilities. The prime minister would also be required to make a public statement to the commissioner about his own compliance with the rules.

In 2004, Parliament formally established the position of the **ethics commissioner** and also a *Senate ethics officer*. The new, independent commissioner reports directly to the House of Commons (i.e., not the PM) and has the authority to review the actions of *all* members of Parliament, including ministers and the prime minister.

As well, just before the 2004 election was called, new conflict-of-interest rules were added to the Standing Orders. Essentially, the 25th *Report of the Standing Committee on Procedure and House Affairs* was added to the Orders and made applicable to MPs at the beginning of the next session of Parliament. These rules require the disclosure of major assets, liabilities and outside income of MPs, their spouses and dependent children. Disclosures must be made to the commissioner within sixty days of the resumption of Parliament. In particular, all funds received from the government must be noted. This information is to be kept confidential by the commissioner, but he is required to prepare a public summary of the most important details of the disclosure materials.[38]

During the federal election campaign of November 2005–January 2006, Stephen Harper unveiled a new 52-point ethics package. After the Conservatives won their 2006 minority government, one of their first acts was to change the rules for ethics in government. A comprehensive *Federal Accountability Act* (Bill C2) was passed and granted royal assent on December 12, 2006. This omnibus bill includes new rules for donations to political parties; a five-year lobbying ban on former ministers, their aides and senior public servants; amendments to the *Lobbyists Registration Act*; and enhancements to the power of the auditor general. It also created a new parliamentary budget officer, whose mandate is to provide objective economic and financial analysis to Parliament.

---

37. *Annual Report of the Ethics Commissioner*, June 2006 found at Commiwww.parl.gc.ca/oec-bce.
38. For details see Report 25, Standing Committee on Procedure, April 27, 2003.

The *Accountability Act* also created a conflict-of-interest law, which came into effect on July 9, 2007. This was the first comprehensive law governing the ethical conduct of office holders. It allows for the appointment of a new commissioner of conflict of interest and ethics. The legislation includes the *Conflict of Interest and Post-Employment Code for Public Office Holders* mentioned above. The new rules also prevent public office holders and MPs from holding personal trusts and private interests from which they could derive personal benefit. From now on, public office holders are required either to sell all of their assets in an arm's length transaction or place them in a fully blind trust.

The new commissioner took responsibility for the *Accountability Act* and also for the *Conflict of Interest Code for Members of the House of Commons*, which had been adopted by the House on June 11, 2007, and incorporated earlier rules from the Standing Orders. With a budget of just over $5 million for 2007–08, the commissioner has the power to initiate formal investigations, hold politicians responsible for their actions and even fine violators. The prime minister is now prevented from overruling the commissioner on all aspects of government ethics. The Senate objected to its members being included in some of these provisions—their behaviour continues to be guided by the Senate ethics officer appointed in 2005.

It remains to be seen whether these new rules and ethics officials will end conflict-of-interest infractions in Canadian politics. The long history of conflict, especially in light of recent allegations about former prime minister Brian Mulroney, and the 2008 allegations concerning treatment of the late MP Chuck Cadman, makes one cautious, even though legislated checks may prove valuable.

Critical Debate
Too Much Prime Ministerial Power?

Does the prime minister exercise too much power? Do we really have presidential government in disguise?

| Point

Yes to both questions. The scope of authority of the Canadian prime minister is analogous to that of the US president. However, because there are some minor checks on prime ministerial power, it should be called prime ministerial power not presidential power.

While the *Constitution Act, 1867,* established a formal executive in the person of the governor general, there is no question that real political power is exercised by the prime minister based on the possession of an electoral mandate. The fusion-of-powers principle, along with other aspects of the British parliamentary tradition such as party discipline and cabinet solidarity, confers upon the political executive the opportunity to carry out its program knowing that it can count on consistent legislative support except during minority governments. The prime minister has extraordinary powers, such as the authority to make cabinet appointments, reorganize the government structure and dissolve Parliament at his or her discretion.

Changes in the rules of House of Commons procedure and the expanding jurisdiction of government have lessened the effectiveness of Parliament in its tasks of scrutiny and deliberation. The House rules permit the government to guide legislation through with a minimum of delay or modification. The opposition parties, lacking adequate research and basic information, may resort to fiery oratory but are rarely able to conduct thorough scrutiny and effective criticism.

Denis Smith has proven that Parliament over time has surrendered its important roles of providing a forum for serious public debate and developing public policy.[39] Smith also argues that the establishment of a presidential-style control of government has been evolving for many years. Recent prime ministers have merely refined and consolidated it. According to Smith, Canada's parliamentary system is devised in such a way that a great deal ultimately depends on the prime minister.

The prime minister appoints ministers and controls their tenure almost entirely. Although cabinet may include some unusually powerful and prestigious figures, in the end, the decisions it reaches depend on the priorities and orientations of the prime minister. Cabinet policy becomes government policy, and backbenchers have little choice but to vote in obedience to the party and prime minister.

This leads to the obvious conclusion that Canada actually has an elected dictator who could lead a corrupt government. Something should be done about it.

Counterpoint

No. We do not have all-powerful prime ministers. The role is not becoming more presidential in character. The prime minister is held in check by many political forces—note how the federal Liberals forced Jean Chrétien out of office in 2003.

Despite journalistic impressions to the contrary, there is no evidence that prime ministers have overstepped their proper authority or that their actions portend grave consequences for responsible government and the parliamentary system. Fortunately for Canada, its prime ministers have thus far been relatively enlightened figures.

However, the centralization of power in the hands of the executive and its specialized agencies is a serious matter. Some will find even the appearance of presidential-style government difficult to accept, but the centralization of power is likely inevitable. An extraordinary apparatus and structure of power has been built up around the prime minister over the years. This is a political reality, although critics should not overlook the obvious constraints and limitations within which the prime minister must operate.

Clearly, there are powers and advantages in the prime minister's position. At the same time, we must not overlook the many limitations on it. Canada does *not* have prime ministerial government, but it is certainly a powerful position. If a prime minister is to remain in office, he or she must maintain the solidarity and loyalty of party colleagues. Even the opposition parties can kick out of office a prime minister who does not hold the support of a majority of members of the House. A minority government can create a very weak prime minister.

Discussion Questions

1. Which side of the Critical Debate do you support? How can you strengthen your case?
2. Where does political power lie in the Canadian system? With the prime minister? With cabinet? With the Queen or her representative, the governor general? With Parliament? With the people of Canada?
3. What are the four central coordinating agencies in Ottawa and what are their functions?
4. Are ethics and conflict-of-interest rules tough enough and clear enough to guarantee responsible government?
5. Is patronage an essential part of the Canadian political system?

39. Denis Smith, "President and Parliament: The Transformation of Parliamentary Government in Canada," in Thomas Hockin, ed., *Apex of Power* (Scarborough, ON: Prentice Hall, 1977), pp. 308–25. For details, see Report 25, Standing Committee on Procedure, April 27, 2003.

Visit our new Companion Website at **www.pearsoned.ca/jackson,** where you can use the interactive Study Guide and link to additional resources on topics discussed in the text.

Selected Bibliography

Bakvis, Herman. *Regional Ministers: Power and Influence in the Canadian Cabinet.* Toronto: University of Toronto Press, 1991.

Bliss, Michael. *Right Honourable Men: The Descent of Canadian Politics from Macdonald to Mulroney.* Toronto: HarperCollins, 1994.

Cameron, Stevie. *On the Take: Crime, Corruption and Greed in the Mulroney Years.* Toronto: Macfarlane, Walter & Ross, 1994.

Campbell, Colin, and M.J. Wyszomirski, eds. *Executive Leadership in Anglo-American Systems.* Pittsburgh, PA: University of Pittsburgh Press, 1991.

Dobbin, Murray. *Paul Martin: CEO For Canada?* Toronto: Lorimer, 2003.

Gray, John. *Paul Martin: The Politics of Ambition.* Toronto: Key Porter Books, 2003.

Greene, Ian, and David P. Shugarman. *Honest Politics.* Toronto: Lorimer, 1997.

Levine, Allan. *Scrum Wars: The Prime Minister and the Media.* Toronto: Dundurn Press, 1993.

Mancuso, Maureen, R. Price, and R. Wagenberg, *Leaders and Leadership in Canada.* Toronto: Oxford University Press, 1994.

Mancuso, Maureen, Michael M. Atkinson, André Blais, Ian Greene, and Neil Nevitte. *A Question of Ethics: Canadians Speak Out* (rev. ed.). Don Mills, ON: Oxford University Press, 2006.

Pal, Leslie A., and David Taras, eds. *Prime Ministers and Premiers: Political Leadership and Public Policy in Canada.* Scarborough, ON: Prentice Hall, 1988.

Savoie, Donald J. *Governing from the Centre: The Concentration of Power in Canadian Politics.* Toronto: University of Toronto Press, 1999.

Simpson, Jeffrey. *The Friendly Dictatorship.* Toronto: McClelland & Stewart, 2001.

Smith, David E. *The Invisible Crown: The First Principle of Canadian Government.* Toronto: University of Toronto Press, 1995.

—————. *The Republican Option in Canada: Past and Present.* Toronto: University of Toronto Press, 1999.

Strom, Kaare. *Minority Government and Majority Rule.* Cambridge, UK: Cambridge University Press, 1990.

Ethics in Government

Fife, Robert, and John Warren. *A Capital Scandal: Politics, Patronage and Payoffs—Why Parliament Must Be Reformed.* Toronto: Key Porter Books, 1991.

Gibbons, Kenneth, and Donald Rowat, eds. *Political Corruption in Canada.* Toronto: McClelland & Stewart, 1976.

Greene, Ian, and David Shugarman. *Honest Politics: Seeking Integrity in Canadian Political Life.* Toronto: Lorimer, 1997.

Hoy, Claire. *Friends in High Places: Politics and Patronage in the Mulroney Government.* Toronto: Key Porter Books, 1987.

Hyde, Anthony. *Promises, Promises: Breaking Faith in Canadian Politics.* Toronto: Viking, 1997.

Kernaghan, Kenneth, ed. *Do Unto Others: Ethics in Government and Business.* Toronto: Institute of Public Administration of Canada, 1991.

————— and John W. Langford. *The Responsible Public Servant.* Halifax: Institute for Research on Public Policy, 1990.

Langford, John W., and Allan Tupper, eds. *Corruption, Character and Conduct: Essays on Canadian Government Ethics.* Toronto: Oxford University Press, 1994, pp. 67–89.

Lemieux, Vincent. *Le patronage politique: Une étude comparative.* Québec City: Les Presses de l'Université Laval, 1977.

Mancuso, Maureen, Michael M. Atkinson, André Blais, Ian Greene, and Neil Nevitte. *A Question of Ethics: Canadians Speak Out* (rev. ed.). Don Mills, ON: Oxford University Press, 2006.

Privy Council Office, Canada. *Members of Parliament and Conflict of Interest.* [MacEachen Green Paper] (Ottawa: Information Canada, 1973).

Simpson, Jeffrey. *Spoils of Power: The Politics of Patronage.* Toronto: Collins, 1988.

Chapter 9

Legislative Politics

Symbolism or Power?

In a parliamentary democracy, the federal legislature, or Parliament, should be one of the most important institutions in the political life of the country. However, in Canada a certain degree of dissatisfaction exists among academic and media observers, much of the general public and even parliamentarians themselves about the role of Parliament. There is perennial debate on the subject of parliamentary reform. At times, dissatisfaction with Parliament verges on outright cynicism. But the reality is that Canadian democracy could not function without it.

In this system, the political executive receives its power to govern from the legislature. The government needs the approval of Parliament to legitimate its policies and activities, particularly for the expenditure of public funds. The prime minister and cabinet are also accountable to Parliament, and may continue to govern only as long as they retain the *confidence* of Parliament or, more correctly in the case of Canada, at least the tacit support of a majority of the House of Commons. Thus, while Parliament gives the executive the authority to govern, it also serves as a check on the absolute or irresponsible use of government power. Parliament provides an arena for debate in which the major political issues of the day may be aired—and subsequently relayed to the public by the mass media. As such, it is a public forum for opposition parties to criticize the government of the day and to demonstrate why they, not the governing party, should be returned with a majority of seats at the next general election.

Last, but not least, Parliament serves important functions on behalf of Canadian citizens. In the theory of **parliamentary democracy**, Parliament is the "repository of popular sovereignty": in making laws and ensuring the responsibility of government, Parliament exercises power on behalf of the general public, power vested in it by the electoral process. It is not possible in a country the size of Canada for all citizens to participate directly in the legislative process. Instead, Canada is a **representative democracy** in which, from time to time, voters choose certain individuals (members of Parliament) to represent their interests in making national policies. On a more practical level, a significant part of the role of parliamentarians is catering to the needs of their constituents. Members of Parliament and their staff spend much of their time taking up the problems of citizens with ministers, public servants or representatives of government agencies. All Canadians, especially those with no well-organized business lobby or trade union to represent them, need Parliament.

Thus, Parliament is indeed an important institution in Canadian political life. The ongoing debates about parliamentary reform reflect its significance. But it is not always easy to determine whether the importance of Parliament is derived from its *power* to enact legislation, hold the government accountable and control the public purse strings, or from its perceived *symbolic role* as the repository of popular sovereignty, an arena for political debate and the legitimizer of the actions of government and, perhaps, of the entire policy process.

Like other legislatures, the Parliament of Canada is a multifunctional institution. It plays several roles important to the political process. Accordingly, its members have a multitude of tasks to perform—as senators and MPs, as members of cabinet and the opposition, as members of party caucuses and parliamentary committees, and as individual representatives of their constituents. There is a constant tension, visible in many of the reform debates, among the various roles of Parliament and among the tasks that members are expected to carry out.

In this chapter, we examine how these tensions are reconciled through the process of *legislative politics*. We look at several aspects of this reconciliation, but we commence our examination by defining what a legislature is. Then, in the sections that follow, we consider the role of legislatures with particular reference to the concepts of the *power* and *symbolism* of parliaments and to the various meanings that may be attached to the term *legislative politics.*

The Critical Debate in this chapter concerns the vital question of parliamentary reform, particularly the cases for and against an elected Senate. Does Parliament need major reform? For example, does the House and its committees need to be made more effective in controlling the executive? Should the Senate be elected to enhance its credibility? Marshal your arguments!

What Is a Legislature?

Legislatures are among the most pervasive of political institutions. In 2008, almost all of the more than 192 independent states in the United Nations had some kind of parliamentary chamber; many of these also had legislative assemblies at the subnational level, such as the provincial assemblies in Canada. The very ubiquity of the institution makes the definition of the word *legislature* and the specification of its functions difficult. It was once common, if not entirely correct, to base such a definition on the characteristics of the British Parliament. However, easy conceptualization has been hindered by the proliferation, particularly in the developing world, of institutions that call themselves "legislatures" or "parliaments" but that have methods of recruitment, powers and relations to other political structures that are widely divergent from those of traditional models.

Some authors avoid this matter of definition altogether—taking for granted that their readers already know what a legislature is. Another strategy is to present a checklist of characteristics that, taken together, are both necessary and sufficient to distinguish legislatures from other political institutions. Thus, the late Nelson Polsby argued that a

> *mélange of characteristics—officiality, a claim of legitimacy based on links with the people, multi-memberedness, formal equality, collective decision-making, deliberativeness—typifies and distinguishes legislatures in a wide variety of settings.*[1]

While Polsby's approach is primarily structural, an alternative is the functional perspective that defines legislatures in terms of the tasks or purposes they serve, in the political system. According to this idea, legislatures perform a multitude of functions in addition to the "legislative" or "law-making" role, functions that vary from country to country and even over time within the same political system. The role of the Congress of People's Deputies in China, for example, is very different from that of Congress in the United States, and the functions of the British Parliament today have changed considerably since its so-called "Golden Age" over a century ago. The fact that many of the functions attributed to legislatures are also performed by *other* political institutions adds to the terminological confusion.

---

1. Nelson Polsby, "Legislatures," in F. Greenstein and N. Polsby, eds., *Handbook of Political Science*, vol. 5 (Reading, MA: Addison-Wesley, 1975), p. 260.

In a comparative study of legislatures, Michael Mezey offers a perception of the concept in which both structural and functional elements are combined:

> *I think of a legislature as a predominantly elected body of people that acts collegially and that has at least the formal but not necessarily the exclusive power to enact laws binding on all members of a specific geopolitical entity.*[2]

This constitutes a valid definition, but there is one major problem with it in the Canadian context. In applying this definition individually to each chamber or "house" of bicameral parliaments, Mezey excludes the Canadian Senate from consideration as a legislature, since its members are appointed rather than "predominantly elected." As well, he does not tell the reader just what a senate is. If it is not a legislature or at least a part of one, what is it? Of course, there would be no problem in the Canadian case if the definition were applied to the whole Parliament (i.e., the Senate and the House of Commons), since it is "predominantly elected." The application of this definition may, therefore, be broadened to cover bicameral parliaments if both chambers collectively are considered to constitute the legislature, as long as the lower house (or, in parliamentary systems, the house to which the government is officially responsible) is predominantly elected. With the addition of this proviso, the simplicity and clarity of this conceptualization make it a suitable working definition for this chapter.

The Roles of Legislatures

A frequent source of confusion in the study of parliamentary institutions is the notion that "legislatures must legislate." Given the similarity between the two words and the mythology surrounding the role of legislatures, this assumption is not surprising. But it may lead to unfulfilled expectations of what legislatures ought to do and to overly simplistic criticisms of parliamentary institutions. For this reason, at least one author uses *parliament* as a generic term for national legislative assemblies in preference to *legislature* because the latter is "too restrictively an implied definition of what these bodies do."[3] On the other hand, most legislatures do spend a substantial portion of their time in consideration and passage of legislation. For instance, approximately one-third of all oral debates in the Canadian House of Commons are devoted to discussion of government legislation, as are between one-quarter and one-half of all Commons committee meetings.[4] The essential point is that a distinction must be drawn between the legislative function—the task of initiating, formulating and enacting bills or statutes—and the legislature as an institution. The legislative function is complex, involving various other actors in the process of devising and drafting bills even before the legislature considers the bills and decides whether they are to become part of the law of the land. As institutions, legislatures are multifunctional, and the passage of legislation is but one of a number of roles they perform.

A bewildering array of legislative functions now appears in the literature. More than a century has passed since the English constitutionalist Walter Bagehot described the major roles of the British House of Commons as *elective, expressive, teaching, informing* and *legislative.*[5] Given the reputation of the British legislature as "the mother of parliaments," it is perhaps not surprising that

---

2. Michael L. Mezey, *Comparative Legislatures* (Durham, NC: Duke University Press, 1979), p. 6.
3. David M. Olson, *The Legislative Process: A Comparative Perspective* (New York: Harper & Row, 1980), p. 11.
4. See Thomas A. Hockin, "Adversary Politics and Some Functions of the Canadian House of Commons," in R. Schultz et al., eds., *The Canadian Political Process*, 3rd ed. (Toronto: Holt, Rinehart and Winston, 1979), p. 318.
5. Walter Bagehot, *The English Constitution*, 1st ed., 1867 (London: Fontana/Collins, 1963), pp. 150–54.

many subsequent classifications have been based loosely upon Bagehot's classic formulation, although his categories have often been relabelled with more current terminology or jargon. In fact, after the Second World War, as political scientists increasingly oriented their research to non-Western societies, it became apparent that some legislatures had no real power to make laws, to constitute or remove governments, or to articulate the grievances of the population. New functions had to be added to the list to describe the roles of what were little more than "rubber stamp" assemblies. As a result, attention was drawn to the more symbolic functions of parliaments, such as *legitimation* of the regime and *integration* of the political community.

The relative importance of the activities of legislatures varies from country to country and, over time, within individual systems. As a consequence of erroneous preconceptions of what legislatures *ought* to do, this change in the relative salience of different functions has led some commentators to lament the "decline of legislatures." Here, *decline* refers to the diminishing power of the more established parliaments of Western Europe and the original members of the British Commonwealth. Particular attention is given to the dominance of cabinet and the bureaucracy in the legislative process. Much of the blame for this situation has been placed on the growing volume and increasingly technical nature of legislation in the modern state, and on the lack of resources available to parliamentarians for coping with this complexity, or on the adverse effect of the emergence of cohesive, disciplined political parties upon the role of individual parliamentarians.

This supposed decline in the powers of parliaments is considered undesirable, especially when parliaments' present roles are compared with the so-called "Golden Age of Parliament" in Britain. Admittedly, there was a time when much legislation was either initiated or introduced by private members, when the volume of parliamentary business was sufficiently meagre to allow members to spend long hours in debate and displays of grandiose rhetoric, when legislators were virtually independent and formed ad hoc majorities according to each issue, and when governments were frequently removed and replaced by Parliament without resorting to general elections. But this situation existed only in a few countries for a short period during the mid-nineteenth century. Although a dominant executive has historically been the norm in Britain, many of the myths that currently surround legislatures originated in this brief and rather exceptional interlude. Not unnaturally, some of these idealistic views also entered the mythology of Canadian parliamentary democracy.

Although the activities of legislatures have changed over time in response to alterations in the political and socio-economic environment, the decline of some functions has been matched by an enhancement of others. To talk of the "strength" or "weakness" of a legislature is difficult. The concept of power is extremely complex, particularly as it relates to the legislative process. If a given parliament accepts the vast majority of the legislation placed before it by the government, it is not possible to be sure whether this demonstrates that the legislature is weak vis-à-vis the executive, or strong for forcing the government to introduce only those measures that have a high probability of success.

Similarly, *power* and *symbolism* are often posed as dichotomous concepts: either a legislature is powerful or its weakness makes it primarily symbolic. While this may be partly true in the short term, it may also be argued that, in the long term, only a powerful or effective legislature will have sufficient efficacy to perform a symbolic role in maintaining the legitimacy of the policy process and its outputs. All too often, the power of a legislature is equated with the extent of its involvement in the legislative process, especially with the initiation of legislation or the frequency with which it rejects government policies. But legislatures have multiple functions, and many of their activities other than law-making reflect their importance in the political system and contribute to their public image and symbolic capabilities. Thus, power and symbolism, rather than constituting polar opposites, are parallel concepts that may be applied to the many activities undertaken by legislatures.

Legislative Politics

As the title of this chapter suggests, legislative behaviour in the Parliament of Canada is highly political. But what is meant by the term **legislative politics**? Perhaps the closest analogy we can draw is to the concept of politics as it appears in the popular phrase "office politics"—that is, interaction and competition. There is constant politicking in the life of a legislature—whether in the form of opposition parties seeking to influence or change the policy of the government, or of the legislature as a whole seeking greater opportunities for effective participation in the decision-making process, or of members of the same party vying for advancement within the legislative or government hierarchy.

Nonetheless, all members of the legislature are bound together by their participation in the institution and by codes of ethics and behaviour that are often incomprehensible to the outsider. Political foes on the floor of the House may be friends outside the chamber, while colleagues from the same party may be fiercely antagonistic. Similarly, members from polar extremes of the political spectrum may join forces in defence of the sovereignty of Parliament while waging a fierce war of rhetoric and competing ideologies.

The Legislative Process in Parliament

The *Constitution Act, 1867* established the Parliament of Canada as a bicameral legislature consisting of an appointed upper house, the Senate, and a popularly elected lower house, the House of Commons. Indeed, the Constitution also says the Queen is part of the Parliament of Canada. The monarch plays a formal role in the legislative process through her representative, the governor general, inasmuch as all bills must receive royal assent before becoming part of Canadian law.

In strictly legal terms, the two chambers of the Parliament of Canada have equal legislative powers in that all bills must be passed in their entirety by both houses in order to receive royal assent, and neither chamber has the power to override the veto or the amendments of the other. However, the Senate rarely employs its amendment powers or vetoes bills; it usually backs down when there is dissension between the two chambers. As a result, many commentators view the Senate as the junior partner in the parliamentary process and often virtually ignore the upper house in analyzing the Canadian legislature. The fact remains, however, that both chambers must pass all bills before they become law. The free trade gambit of 1988, when the Liberal-dominated Senate forced a general election by refusing to pass the required legislation, is the most important recent example of senatorial power.

The Parliamentary Life Cycle

The Senate and the House of Commons may meet as legislative bodies only during a parliamentary session. **Parliaments** are labelled by consecutive numbers that change after each general election. For example, the 308 MPs returned to the House by the 2006 federal election collectively constituted the 39th Parliament. In each Parliament, there may be one or more *sessions*, depending upon the wishes of the government of the day and its ability to manage its legislative program, and upon the length of the Parliament—that is, how much time elapses between general elections.

Each parliamentary session begins with the governor general's summoning the MPs and senators to Parliament at the request of the prime minister. Members of both houses come together in the Senate chamber, amid great pomp and ceremony, to hear the governor general deliver the **Speech from the Throne**, outlining the government's proposed legislative program for the forthcoming session. The speech echoes promises made during the federal election campaign—tempered today by the federal Conservatives' minority situation. After the speech, MPs return as usual to their chamber to commence business. In the Commons, the debate on the Throne Speech usually occupies the first few days of the session; afterward, the normal timetable of the House comes into effect. A break taken by the House within a session is called an **adjournment**.

Another ceremonial occasion, known as the **prorogation of Parliament**, brings a session to a close. The governor general again acts upon the advice of the prime minister to prorogue Parliament; therefore, the length of a session is often determined by the government's ability to tidy up the loose ends in its legislative program. Any legislation that has not successfully completed all the stages of the process automatically dies when Parliament is prorogued: if the government is still committed to it, the bill must go through the entire process again in the next session. Sometimes, governments introduce bills close to the end of a session to test parliamentary and public reactions before redrafting them for introduction in the next session.

At one time, each session of Parliament lasted a year or less, but sessions have generally become longer in recent years. Thus, in one outstanding example, the first session of the 32nd Parliament lasted an unprecedented three years and eight months. Also in the past, MPs and senators used to enjoy a break between sessions, in addition to their vacations from Ottawa when Parliament was adjourned or in recess. Today, prorogation of one session is often followed immediately by the summoning of the next. Finally, there must be a proclamation by the governor general announcing the dissolution of the House of Commons. **Dissolution** brings the Parliament to an end and, in its wake, a general election.[6]

Fixed Election Dates

A new approach to parliamentary reform has been to change the rules for determining the date of a general election. In early 2006, the Conservative government introduced Bill C16, legislation to amend the *Canada Election Act*, to bring in fixed election dates for MPs. The bill received royal assent on May 2, 2007. It provides, subject to an earlier dissolution of Parliament, that a general election must be held on the third Monday in October in the fourth calendar year following polling day for the last general election, with the first one scheduled for Monday October 19, 2009. The bill neatly avoids the need for a constitutional amendment by beginning with a subsection stating that nothing in the bill affects the powers of the governor general, including the power of parliamentary dissolution.

Types of Bills

It is necessary to distinguish between the various types of legislation, since the nature of a bill helps determine its route through Parliament. Parliamentary procedure distinguishes among bills on constitutional and legal grounds on three major levels (see Figure 9.1). First, legislation can be divided into **private** and **public bills**. Private bills are those that confer special powers or rights upon specific individuals, groups or corporations, rather than upon society as a whole. They are sometimes utilized to incorporate companies or certain religious and charitable organizations and, until 1964, were required for granting divorces to residents of Québec and Newfoundland. These bills constitute an extremely small proportion of total legislative activity.

Public bills seek to change the law concerning the public as a whole, and are divided into two types: **government bills**, those introduced by the cabinet as government policy; and **private members' bills**, those introduced by individual members of Parliament. In the nineteenth century, when the business of government was relatively limited, private members' bills were an important component

---

6. In theory, the governor general retains some discretionary power in the matter of dissolution; see Chapter 5.

FIGURE 9.1 **The Types of Bills**

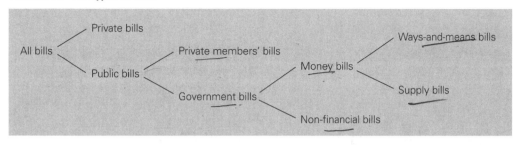

of legislative activity. Today, with a restricted number of specific slots in the parliamentary timetable, few even come to a vote, and it is quite unusual for Parliament to pass even one private member's bill during a session.

Government bills are further divided into **financial (money)** and **non-financial bills**. Under the Constitution, money bills, which authorize taxation and appropriations (or expenditures), must be introduced first into the House of Commons, and then only by a minister of the Crown, by *Royal Recommendation*. These special provisions relate to the traditional right of Parliament to demand that the Crown hear grievances from the people before **granting supply**—that is, before approving the funds necessary to conduct the Crown's affairs. The consideration of financial measures is therefore intended to be a time when the cabinet accounts for its management of the economy and (usually but not always) survives an opposition motion to the effect that the government has failed in its responsibilities. Taxation measures are introduced as **ways-and-means bills** and have become known sarcastically as the "ways and means of getting the public's money."

Before we leave the subject of the types of legislation, we should comment on **delegated** or **subordinate legislation**. This type of legislation refers to the power to make decisions—called "regulations" or "statutory instruments"—that have the force of law. Such legislative power is delegated by Parliament under various statutes to the **governor-in-council** (the cabinet), to ministers of individual government departments and to a number of agencies and boards. For example, the *Fisheries Act* allows the passage of subordinate legislation on issues such as fishing seasons, numbers and types of fish that may be caught, and the dates for opening and closing the fishing season. Such subordinate legislation takes the form of "regulations" and in principle is approved by cabinet, but is scrutinized by Parliament only *after* it is announced in *The Canada Gazette*.

Today, the Joint Committee on Scrutiny of Regulations (composed of MPs and senators) may examine a regulation and even recommend that it be rescinded. Unless the government receives a vote of the House of Commons against the Joint Committee's recommendation, the regulation is automatically repealed.

The Stages of Legislation

The vast majority of bills passed by the Canadian Parliament are government bills. Although government legislation may be introduced first in the Senate (an increasingly rare occurrence), money bills are constitutionally prohibited from this route. Figure 9.2 on the next page illustrates the major stages in the passage of a typical government bill originating in the lower house.

Once the pre-parliamentary processes of policy formulation are over, the minister responsible for the legislation asks the House for leave to introduce the bill. This motion is not debatable. A short description of the aims of the bill may be given. Acceptance of the *first reading* motion "that this bill be read a first time and be printed" is a matter of course and no vote takes place. It allows

FIGURE 9.2 **How a Government Bill Becomes Law**

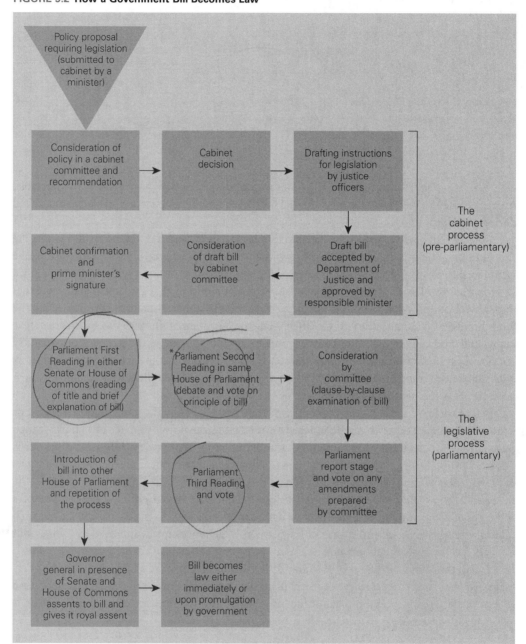

* Since 1994, bills have been referred to a committee *before* second reading.

the bill to be printed, numbered (with a "C" prefix if it originates in the House of Commons, "S" if in the Senate) and distributed to MPs. Numbers C1 to C200 are reserved for government bills, C201 to C1000 for private members' public bills and C1001 on for private members' private bills. The bill is now on the **Order Paper**, the schedule of pending parliamentary business.

The *second reading* motion, usually proposed by the sponsoring minister, permits debate on the principle of the bill; no amendments are accepted by the speaker. The debate is monopolized by the government and opposition front benches. Normally, the opposition attempts to prove that the legislation is inadequate, while the government defends the overall content and principles of the proposed legislation. Since 1994, as an alternative, bills have been permitted to proceed to the committee stage before second reading.

After second reading, unless otherwise ordered, a bill must be sent directly to a House of Commons committee. This is the *committee stage*. (For money bills and certain other legislation upon which the House agrees, the Committee Stage is undertaken by the Committee of the Whole, the whole chamber sitting in committee chaired by the deputy speaker.) At this stage, the bill undergoes detailed clause-by-clause consideration. Amendments may be moved by both government and opposition members. The amended bill is then voted on as a whole.

Except in the case of bills examined by the Committee of the Whole, which go straight to *third reading*, the recommendations of the appropriate committee are presented to the House at the *report stage*. Debate is allowed on both the principle and the details of the bill; amendments proposed by the committee are voted on and further amendments may be introduced. Sometimes, the opposition reintroduces amendments defeated in committee or the government seeks to reinstate original clauses altered by the committee. At the conclusion of the debate, a vote is taken on the whole bill, including amendments. Unless unanimously agreed otherwise by the House, third reading commences after the report stage with the motion "that the bill be now read a third time and passed." Debate is not unknown at this point, but usually takes place only at the insistence of the opposition. A final vote is then taken on the bill.

When the bill has successfully negotiated the various debates, amendments, attempted hoists and **divisions** (formal votes) in the House of Commons, it has to begin the whole process again in the Senate. However, the upper house usually provides a smoother path than the lower chamber. First and second readings are over quickly. At the Committee Stage, the Senate does its major legislative work, as it rarely uses its powers to amend the substance of a bill. The Senate is not allowed to increase taxation or spending. As in the House of Commons, the bill as amended in committee is reported back to the Senate for debate, possible further amendment and acceptance. After the final consideration of the bill by the Senate and the third reading vote, it is reported to the House of Commons whether the Senate has rejected, amended or passed the bill.

If the bill is *defeated* by the Senate (which is extremely unusual), it is lost and must pass through the entire process again, from the start. A bill passed by the Commons but *amended* by the Senate returns to the lower house for consideration of the amendments. Since such changes are more often to the wording or to a minor detail of the bill (rather than its substance), they are often accepted by the responsible minister. Once this has happened, or if the bill is passed intact by the Senate, it is ready for **royal assent**. In this final stage of the process, the governor general, sitting in the Senate before the assembled members of both houses, puts the final seal of approval on the bill. The bill thereby becomes an act of Parliament of Canada and is henceforth law unless a requirement for formal government **proclamation** is contained within it.

Money bills follow the same general process as other government legislation, but are unique for four reasons. First, as noted above, they must originate in the House of Commons. Second, ways-and-means bills are not considered in legislative committees in the Commons but by the Committee of the Whole. Third, there are political limitations upon the Senate's ability to amend such bills. Fourth, money bills tend to have a longer gestation period than other bills, because they are not themselves the only, or even the most important, basis for debate. In the case of tax bills, much debate centres on the budget speech delivered by the minister of finance, which outlines the government's economic policy and summarizes the changes that will subsequently appear in tax legislation. With **supply** or **appropriation bills**—those that authorize the spending of public money by government departments

Richard Row Illustration, Toronto.

and other agencies—the key debates occur during the consideration of departmental estimates by standing committees. Once the estimates are examined, appropriation bills are always passed quickly to give legislative effect to the government's spending proposals.

The entire legislative process is thus complex and variable. The amount of time taken by a bill to pass and its likelihood of success depend upon a number of factors: the importance or controversial nature of the given bill and also of other legislation under consideration at the same time; the partisan composition of the two chambers and the presence or absence of a government majority; the willingness of the government to impose, and of Parliament to accept, procedural devices to shorten debate and speed passage of the bill; and lastly, the mood of the House at a particular moment. Despite the apparent dominance of governments over the legislative process, the whole procedure is much like an obstacle course to the minister introducing a piece of contentious legislation.

The House of Commons

It is not unreasonable to suggest that, when most Canadians talk about *Parliament*, they really mean the *House of Commons*. After all, when people vote for a member of Parliament, they are electing a member of the House of Commons, not a senator. And when they write to their MP, they expect their representative to take action on their behalf. Moreover, media attention is focused mainly on the House of Commons, because it is the chamber to which the government is responsible, and because the more newsworthy and dramatic confrontations in Canadian legislative politics usually occur there.

The job of an MP is multifunctional. In theory at least, members of the Commons are constituency representatives, caucus members, orators, lawmakers and watchdogs over the government and bureaucracy. Most of the time, however, MPs are bound by party discipline and show little initiative outside of caucus.

In 2007, 242 men and 63 women were sitting in the House of Commons (three seats were vacant). Their average age was 52 years. They obtained a salary of $150 800 of taxable income and an office budget that averaged $258 100 (see Table 9.1 on the next page). Members of Parliament usually hire four full-time assistants in their Ottawa offices, and at least one more to manage inquiries at

Reproduced with permission of Dennis Pritchard.

TABLE 9.1 **Salaries and Benefits for Parliament and Government, 2008**

I Members of Parliament	
Salary	$150 800
Pensions (members pay 10% of annual salary)	75% of average of best six years' service (at the rate of 5% per year with minimum of six years' service)
Member's Office Budget	average of $258 100
Travel	64 return trips between Ottawa and constituency
Telephone, mail, equipment and supplies	Paid and basically unlimited
II Senators	
Salary	$116 000
III Officers of Government or Parliament (in addition to the above)	
Prime minister	$150 800
Leader of Official Opposition, speaker and all ministers	$72 200
Secretary of state	$54 100
Parliamentary secretaries	$15 200
Other officials (leaders, deputy speakers, party whips, chairs)	$5500–$72 000

their constituency office. Still, for most members, these resources have barely kept pace with the growth of constituency business in the form of correspondence, telephone calls, emails and personal contacts over recent years. Indeed, while most MPs are adequately staffed for their role as constituency representative, they are not "over-serviced" with respect to either their legislative functions or active participation in the committee system.

Some recent reforms and innovations have enhanced the ability of individual MPs to perform their parliamentary tasks. The new standing committees enable individual members to have more input into policy formulation. Reduction of the maximum length of speeches in the House allows more members to take part in debates, and the possibility of a ten-minute rebuttal/debate after each speech has provided more interest and flexibility. But, by and large, effective participation in debate or in the scrutiny of government legislation and estimates is hampered by lack of information, resources and policy expertise. The development of a heightened role for the backbencher in the legislative process requires more than procedural reform of the House of Commons.

Of course, there are exceptions—members who carve out a particular area of specialization or who adopt some issue as their own may become very important in the process. The attitude of members themselves, and their relations with their constituents, also encourages concentration on representational activities. The electorate is becoming more demanding. With the ever-increasing volume of government legislation and the seemingly omnipresent role of the government, there is significant pressure from constituents for MPs to act as intermediaries on their behalf in disputes with departments and other central agencies. Such "ombudsman" work usually involves simple, concrete problems readily solved by a telephone call to a department or a brief negotiation with a minister. Policy-making, on the other hand, requires abstract, generalized conceptualization of an issue and a long-term commitment to pursue a particular solution. In terms of results for effort expended, the role of ombudsman may be more rewarding than that of lawmaker for the majority of members.

Conflict and Compromise

The tone of legislative politics in the House of Commons is profoundly affected by two key factors inherited from the British political tradition: first, an adversarial system of party politics, with a clear dichotomy between government and opposition; second, a code of rules and procedures governing the behaviour of members that counteracts, to some extent, any potential hostility arising from the partisan nature of the House.

The adversarial pattern of relations between government and opposition is clearly reflected in, and perhaps reinforced by, the physical layout of the House. In many legislative chambers, such as the US House of Representatives or the German *Bundestag*, all elected members sit in a semicircle facing the speaker of the House. However, the seating plan of the Canadian House of Commons follows the British model, forcing government and opposition to face one another across the floor of the House with the government to the speaker's right and the opposition parties to the left. The leaders of the two major parties confront each other like old-time gunfighters, each surrounded by her immediate lieutenants and backed by the rest of the supporters. This face-to-face confrontation, separated only by the open floor of the House, clearly demarcates the government from the opposition and reinforces the sense of political identity and party cohesion on both sides of the Commons.

In the central area of the chamber, between the two main rivals, sit the officials of the House. Most conspicuous among them is the **speaker,** who, under the Constitution, "shall preside at all meetings of the House of Commons." The speaker is officially an impartial arbiter elected by the whole House and is not permitted to vote in the House (votes are cast when a "division" is called). An exception to this rule is for casting the deciding vote in the event of a tie, when convention dictates that the speaker support the government of the day.

The prime minister used to nominate the speaker; however, the position became increasingly non-partisan over time. After 1963, the leader of the Opposition seconded the prime minister's nomination and, in 1979, Liberal James Jerome became the first speaker to serve under two different parties when Prime Minister Joe Clark nominated him to continue the same role he had under the previous Liberal government. Discussions about how to reform the process for selecting a speaker were carried on for several years until both the Lefebvre and McGrath parliamentary reform committees recommended that the speaker be elected by secret ballot. Eventually, the government agreed with this proposal and new Standing Orders to that effect were passed. On September 30, 1986, for the first time, the speaker was elected by a secret ballot of all members of the House. It took the members 12 hours and 11 ballots to elect John Fraser from among the 39 candidates. In January 1994, Gilbert Parent became the second elected speaker after six rounds of voting that included a tie on the fifth ballot. In 2004 and 2006, in both minority Parliaments, Peter Milliken was re-elected as speaker.

The speaker is in charge of the administration of the House of Commons. This includes overseeing the staffing of the House with secretaries, clerks and so on. As well, the speaker shares responsibility with the Board of Internal Economy (a body composed of the speaker, two members of the Privy Council, the leader of the Official Opposition and four other members—two from the government caucus and two from the opposition benches) for the economic management of the House, and manages the annual estimates of the cost of running the House of Commons. In the political function of chairing the House, the speaker is aided by a deputy speaker, also elected by fellow MPs at the beginning of each Parliament. The speaker also is assisted by two chief permanent employees of the Commons, the clerk of the House and the administrator. The clerk is responsible for ensuring that relevant documents are printed and circulated, and advises the speaker on the day's parliamentary business. The administrator deals with financial and management issues.

The leader of each party in the House designates an MP as manager of party conduct in the House—known as the party's **House leader.** The government House leader is also a member of cabinet, responsible for obtaining agreement among parties in setting the timetable for the House. The House leader has the authority to negotiate the timetable and lists of speakers.

In addition to these individuals, there is a professional staff to manage the day-to-day activities of the House. The staff includes translators; transcribers, who record verbatim the House of Commons debates in a publication called *Hansard*; secretaries; security personnel; maintenance staff; and staff for the library of Parliament.

In keeping with the Westminster model of the United Kingdom, the speaker is simultaneously an ordinary member of the House of Commons and an impartial arbiter removed from the political struggle by the conventions and traditions that bind the office. In the midst of the potential chaos and conflict engendered by the partisan nature of the House, the speaker is responsible for enforcing the rules designed to permit its orderly functioning. The speaker must therefore be a skilled parliamentarian, well versed not only in the formal rules contained in the Standing Orders of the House but also in unwritten conventions established by past practice.

Certain rules are explicitly designed to reduce the temperature of party politics in the legislature by limiting the direct personal interaction of the members. Verbal confrontations during debate are somewhat constrained by the requirements that no member may speak officially without recognition by the speaker, to whom all statements must be addressed. Thus, members do not speak to one another directly. Neither may they speak *of* one another directly, inasmuch as individuals are referred to not by name but through more impersonal titles, such as "the prime minister," "the leader of the Opposition" or "the honourable member for constituency X."

If all else fails and the debate becomes heated, the dignity of individual members and of the House as a whole is protected by the proscription of certain terms deemed to constitute *unparliamentary language.* It is not permitted, for example, to use expressions that cast doubt on the legitimacy of a member's birth nor to allege that a speech has been inspired by intoxicating substances. One of the most common infringements of the rule is the suggestion that another member is "lying" to the House. For example, in March 1993, New Democrat MP Dave Barrett was suspended from the Commons for a day after refusing to withdraw an accusation that the government was telling "lies."

The rules of unparliamentary language often have the effect of testing the verbal ingenuity of members in order to convey the sense of a particular epithet without the use of forbidden terms. There may also be other ways of getting one's point across without breaching the rules. Former Conservative MP Gordon Aiken reports the clever and entirely legitimate device employed by one member who became exasperated by criticism from the other side of the House:

> *"Mr. Speaker," he asked, properly addressing the Chair, "would it be out of order if I called the honourable Member a son-of-a-bitch?" The Speaker nodded his head. "I thought so," said Clancy, resuming his seat.*[7]

Also among the conflict-regulating devices in the House of Commons are the Standing Orders, the procedures and regulations adopted by members for their internal self-government, and the rules of debate. Perhaps most important among the latter is the principle that once recognized by the speaker, every MP has the right to speak for a certain length of time without interruption, as long as the speech remains relevant to the motion before the House. The speaker must ensure that members from both sides of the House get a fair hearing, but it is not unknown for the opposition parties to

---

7. Gordon Aiken, *The Backbencher* (Toronto: McClelland & Stewart, 1974), p. 66.

complain that the speaker is favouring the government side. The rules also protect certain persons (particularly the royal family, the governor general and the Senate) from explicit attacks in the Commons.[8]

Once a member has the floor, the member's colleagues or opponents are not always capable of containing themselves; thus, some expressions of support and disagreement are, within certain bounds, sanctioned by the speaker. Outbursts of laughter and cheering or antagonistic remarks are accepted as part of the debate; the euphemistic reporting in *Hansard* of "hear-hear!" or "oh, oh!" may disguise a multitude of sins.

All of these formal devices help to maintain peace and reduce conflict emanating from the partisan composition of the House. Other effective mitigating factors are the sense of corporate identity shared by members of the Commons and the extent to which MPs from both sides of the House interact in informal situations outside the chamber, often forging friendships across party lines. Amid the rhetoric, the struggle is, after all, "often carried on more in the spirit of a game than a war."[9]

The Business of the House

Once the currents of conflict and compromise within the House of Commons are appreciated, the way in which the House works can perhaps best be understood with reference to the detailed business in the House.[10] Not all parliamentary weeks and days, however, are precisely the same. Daily sittings and endings differ from day to day. Some activities, such as private members' business, occur in different time slots and the whole week's agenda can be disrupted by major events such as debates on the Speech from the Throne and budget deliberations. The timetable of the House of Commons reflects a compromise among the competing demands of the various groups within it. On the basis of practical usage rather than procedural formality, the business of the House may be arranged into five broad categories: routine business, urgent business, government business, private members' business and opposition business.

The *routine business* of the House usually begins after the daily Question Period and consumes 15 to 20 minutes. The speaker works through a list of routine proceedings, not all of which arise on any particular day: announcements and the raising of questions of privilege; the presentation of reports from interparliamentary delegations and committees; the tabling of documents and government papers for the notice of members; statements by ministers regarding government policy; the introduction and first reading of Commons bills and the first reading of public bills originating in the Senate; government notices of motions to be introduced later in the Orders of the Day; and other motions, particularly those requesting concurrence in committee reports and those pertaining to special arrangements for the sittings and proceedings of the House.

Next, the speaker calls on the parliamentary secretary to the government house leader to notify the House regarding government responses to **questions on the Order Paper** (written questions which, after a minimum 48 hours' notice, are usually answered in print in the day's *Debates*) and, on occasion, to reply to requests from members for the tabling of government papers in the House. The Commons is then ready to proceed with what the government regards as the main business, the **Orders of the Day**—the ongoing debate on government legislation.

---

8. Through precedent established by past speakers, this protection has been extended to the judiciary, lieutenant-governors and others of "high official station."

9. R.M. Dawson, *The Government of Canada* (Toronto: University of Toronto Press, 1967), p. 356.

10. For a succinct summary of procedural rules and timetables, see House of Commons, Précis of Procedure (Ottawa: House of Commons, various editions).

The **Standing Orders**, or rules of the House, permit any member to move "under SO 52 that this House does now adjourn" in order to discuss "a specific and important matter requiring urgent consideration." This motion could, at one time, exhaust considerable time in the House. Today, the speaker rules immediately upon the validity of the request. A rule in the affirmative gives the member leave to introduce the adjournment motion later that day. The Standing Order concerned is primarily utilized by the opposition to introduce debate on an issue that is not on the government Order Paper or to criticize the government.

The other procedure classified as *urgent business* is the opportunity for MPs to make statements lasting sixty seconds to the House under Standing Order 31, immediately preceding Question Period. Standing Order 31 permits members to make only a very brief statement to the House, allowing them to make a point or gain the desired media exposure without going through the pretense of formulating a motion. It is an excellent example of sensible and pragmatic innovation in House rules to satisfy the needs of individual members while adhering to the formal proceedings of the Commons.

The bulk of the time of plenary sessions of the Commons is consumed by the Orders of the Day, during which the House deals with the public business placed before it. The greater part of this period is devoted to *government business* in the form of the Throne Speech debate, motions dealing with the passage of bills and the referral of legislation, estimates and investigatory tasks to standing and special committees. **Orders** are the prime means by which the House of Commons formulates instructions in response to motions. They serve to guide the speaker and other members and direct the officers of the House to pursue particular courses of action. Some orders, for example **Standing Orders**, are general and more or less permanent, applying mainly to the procedures of the House. Others are more particular: for example, that a bill must "now be read a second time" or that it must be sent to committee. In the long run, of course, these latter cases result in a change in public policy through new laws.

Some motions result not in orders but in **resolutions**, which is a source of confusion for observers of Parliament. From time to time, the House makes a resolution on a particular issue on which the government subsequently takes no action. With the exception of *constitutional resolutions*, resolutions are *not binding*; they are simply expressions of the *opinion* of the Commons, as opposed to orders, which are expressions of its *will*. While orders reflect the power of the Commons to impose its will on others, resolutions are primarily symbolic outputs of "Parliament as rhetoric," although they may often be influential in legitimating policies for which the government wants a public expression of support from the House.

Not all of the business conducted during the working week is instigated by the government. *Private members' business* is listed under four categories: requests for tabling papers and documents; private members' bills; private members' motions; and, occasionally, private bills. Since 1986, **private members' motions and bills** have been handled under new procedures. Today, all of them are placed in a lottery or draw. The first thirty items chosen are placed in an "order of precedence," and the Standing Committee on Procedure and House Affairs selects up to five motions and five bills to be voted on automatically. This means that the old system, in which almost every private member's motion or bill was debated and then "talked out," has been replaced by a compulsory vote on at least ten items after as many as five hours of debate. Under the new rules, therefore, more private members' bills are assured a guaranteed vote.

On certain sitting days during the year, government motions do not dominate the Orders of the Day. At the start of the session, the House is permitted six days to debate the *Address in Reply* to the Speech from the Throne; since the Throne Speech contains only vague policy outlines, rules of relevancy are relaxed and debate takes a very general course. A further four days are allocated for the Budget Debate—officially, to discuss the finance minister's proposals, but effectively, again, to articulate broad criticism of the government's record. As well, after the abolition of the old Committee of Supply in 1968, the opposition parties were compensated by the allocation of twenty *Supply* (or *Opposition*) *Days*, spread unevenly over the three supply periods of the session, on which opposition motions could be debated. Today, such debates rarely focus specifically on government expenditures, although that was the original intent. Instead, Opposition Days provide time for individual opposition parties to attack the government, to propose alternative policies and to introduce motions of non-confidence in the government. There are, however, both practical and political limitations on the ability of the opposition parties to effect radical criticism of government activities or produce startlingly different policy proposals.

Far more effective as an instrument for the opposition—primarily because of the amount of media attention devoted to it and because no notice of content is required—is the **Oral Question Period**.[11] This is invariably the high point of the sitting day in the Commons. In theory, it provides an opportunity for any member who can catch the speaker's eye to ask a question of the prime minister or a member of cabinet—in fact, the speaker calls almost all members according to lists supplied by the party whips. Although, technically, questions should be for the purpose of eliciting information and be "concise, factual and free of opinion and argument which might lead to debate,"[12] Question Period in reality provides a forum for the opposition parties to embarrass the government, criticize its policies and force discussion on issues of the day, frequently based on media stories, leaks by disaffected public servants and complaints from the public.

As a mechanism for surveillance and accountability of the government, Question Period has many advantages, but it is not perfect. Although the speaker permits supplementary questions, no formal debate is allowed, and ministers can often manoeuvre to avoid the main substance of a question. The time limit of 45 minutes each day is often too short for the number of questions that members wish to raise, yet government backbenchers use up some of the period to ask questions of "minor" constituency interest or to feed "friendly" queries to their own front bench. Finally, the division of the opposition into two or more parties frequently results in a lack of structure or continuity to the proceedings.

To surmount this problem, each party caucus orchestrates its efforts at Question Period in order to provide a more effective attack on specific government ministers. To this end, the opposition parties have a "tactics" meeting each day during parliamentary sessions. At these meetings, they analyze press clippings, determine the order of the questions and practise their political stances. Despite problems, well-directed opposition tactics can make the daily Question Period an important occasion for calling the executive to account for its actions, for effective participation by backbenchers and for the public to see responsible government at work. Considerable effort goes into ensuring that the right "clip" will appear on the television evening news.

Occasionally during Question Period, a member who is dissatisfied with the response from a minister will shout "tonight" across the floor of the chamber. This refers to what is commonly known as "The Late Show," more formally the *daily adjournment debate*, which takes place four days a week at 6:30 p.m. Unless the House has agreed to sit beyond the normal hour of adjournment for some special purpose, the speaker proposes on these days "that this House do now adjourn," then recognizes in turn a maximum of three members who have made it known that they

---

11. The first oral question was asked within three weeks of the first session of the first Parliament in 1867. For a complete history, see W.F. Dawson, *Procedure in the Canadian House of Commons* (Toronto: University of Toronto Press, 1962); and Francis J. Schiller, *The Evolution of Oral Question Period* (unpublished thesis, Carleton University, September 1992).

12. Ruling given by Speaker of the House Roland Michener, cited in *House of Commons Debates*, February 26, 1959, p. 1393.

wish to speak. Members usually take up unresolved issues from the Oral Question Period; they are permitted to speak for up to seven minutes, addressing their point to a minister or parliamentary secretary.

Under contemporary rules, the House has a four-and-a-half-day working week that may be increased by evening sittings for emergency debates or long series of divisions continuing after the normal hours of adjournment. The House is by no means full most of this time; in fact, it is usually crowded only for Question Period, for important divisions on major items of government legislation and for non-confidence motions. Since October 1977, the public has been able to see empty spaces in the chamber on televised House proceedings, despite occasional attempts by members to arrange themselves around and behind whoever is on camera.

But the average viewer may not be aware that attendance at plenary sessions of the House of Commons is only a part of the total workload of MPs. Apart from their role as members of the House, MPs serve on parliamentary committees, are members of parliamentary parties or caucuses, and have large caseloads of constituency duties to perform. An analysis of procedure and legislative politics in the chamber of the House of Commons is, therefore, only a part of the story of how Parliament works; the next three sections provide a more complete picture by discussing the role of committees, party competition and individual members in the life of the House.

MPs in Groups: The Committee System

Much of the significant work of members of Parliament takes place not in plenary sessions but in committees. In 1986, the House of Commons adopted a new committee system that has been slightly amended over time.[13] There are now four basic kinds of committees.

First is the **Committee of the Whole**, in which the entire complement of MPs sits in the chamber in one large committee under the chair of the deputy speaker or the deputy chair of committees, and uses committee rules rather than House procedures to govern its activities. At one time, the majority of bills were considered by the Committee of the Whole rather than being sent to smaller, more specialized standing committees, but enormous pressures on the timetable of the House and the workload of MPs have resulted in much more limited use of this procedure. Today, the use of the Committee of the Whole is largely reserved for money bills or, on very rare occasions, to expedite the passage of other legislation.

The second type of committee consists of the relatively permanent House standing committees (see Table 9.2). **Standing committees** are set up for the life of a Parliament. Their composition of 7 to 15 members is proportional to party standings in the House. In principle, they elect their own chairs, but the government and opposition House leaders control the selection. These committees are empowered by the Standing Orders to study and report on all matters relating to the department or departments that are assigned to them. In particular, they are to report on program and policy objectives and effectiveness; immediate, medium-term and long-term expenditure plans; the relative success of the department(s); and all other matters of mandate, management, organization and operation. These responsibilities are usually carried out by studying the particular department's annual report and estimates. Standing committees may also handle the committee stage of legislation, and this has once again become the standard practice. A minority parliament presents difficult issues concerning membership and especially the chairs of such committees.

13. An assessment of these basic reforms is found in Robert J. Jackson, "Executive Legislative Relations in Canada," in Robert J. Jackson et al., eds., *Contemporary Canadian Politics* (Scarborough, ON: Prentice Hall, 1984), pp. 111–24.

TABLE 9.2 **House of Commons Committees, 2008**

A. House Standing Committees
Aboriginal Affairs and Northern Development
Access to Information, Privacy and Ethics
Agriculture and Agri-Food
Canadian Heritage
Citizenship and Immigration
Environment and Sustainable Development
Finance
Fisheries and Oceans
Foreign Affairs and International Development
Government Operations and Estimates
Health
Human Resources
Industry, Science and Technology
Justice and Human Rights
National Defence
Natural Resources
Official Languages
Procedure and House Affairs
Public Accounts
Public Safety and National Security
Status of Women
Transport
Veterans Affairs
B. Joint Committees with the Senate
Library of Parliament
Scrutiny of Regulations

In 2004, there was talk of setting up a new "Committee of Parliamentarians" or a security oversight committee for national security whose members would be given security clearance in order to have access to certain documents. An interim committee was set up to advise the government. It recommended such a committee and the Liberal government introduced Bill C81 to accomplish this task, but it died on the Order Paper when the January 2006 election was called. Discussions continue on the topic and it was proposed again in the committee's recent report on the *Anti-terrorism Act*. As of 2008, the government had not responded to the report and the Standing Committee on Public Safety and National Security remains without the ability to do the job it should be doing in scrutinizing issues in national security.

The standing committees are empowered to form subcommittees and to "send for persons, papers and records" to aid in their deliberations. Moreover, according to Standing Orders 10 and 102, all individuals appointed by order-in-council are scrutinized by the committees and may be called before their members after their appointments have been published in *The Canada Gazette*. This includes all deputy ministers, heads of Crown corporations, ambassadors and others appointed to high government positions (excluding judges). In 1994, the Finance Committee was assigned a new responsibility to participate in pre-budget discussions. It now begins to study the government's financial policies in early September and reports by the end of December—before the annual budget is delivered.

Third, the two **joint standing committees** are composed of members of both the House of Commons and the Senate. The role of the Standing Joint Committee on Scrutiny of Regulations is significant as this committee is empowered to scrutinize all delegated legislation by departments, agencies, boards or other authorities. The second joint standing committee is the Library of Parliament Committee, which monitors the work of the library and research branches.

The fourth type of committee, the **legislative committees**, may receive bills for examination after second reading. The duty of each committee is limited to an examination of its bill, and witnesses are called only on "purely technical" matters. The number of legislative committees depends on the amount of legislation before the House; sometimes there are very few committees, at other times a large number. After the committee reports back to the House on its bill, the committee is dissolved. The parties appoint members of legislative committees, and their numbers, up to thirty, are proportionate to party standings in the House. The chairs, however, are *not* appointed from within the committee membership. Instead, at the beginning of each session, the speaker appoints at least ten members to chair legislative committees. Together with the chairs of the Committee of the Whole, they constitute the Panel of Chairmen. The speaker then selects which of them will chair each new legislative committee as bills are presented to the House.

Committee Recruitment, Composition and Staffing

The *Committee of Selection*, more commonly known as the *Striking Committee*, allocates membership in the standing and legislative committees. Today, the Committee on Procedure and House Affairs acts as the Striking Committee. The composition of each committee is roughly proportional to the partisan party representation in the Commons as a whole—although a majority government always claims more than 50 percent of the members and the Official Opposition is usually over-represented compared with minor parties. Individual MPs are appointed to committees on the basis of their chief whip's recommendations, although these often reflect the personal preferences of the member and are usually in accordance with membership in party caucus committees. Recent procedural changes, in addition to reducing the number of MPs on each committee, permit only pre-selected alternate members to substitute for absentees.

The chair and vice-chair of standing committees are elected at the start of each session by the committee members and, since 1968, have almost all been members of the governing party. By standing order, however, the opposition provides the chair of the Public Accounts Committee, Access to Information, Privacy and Ethics, Government Operations and Estimates, and the Standing Committee on the Status of Women. Where there is more than one candidate for the chair, the vote is held by secret ballot. Given the preponderance of government members filling these offices, committee chairs are frequently placed in an ambiguous position by conflicting expectations about their roles: while their responsibility for presiding over committee meetings requires them to be as impartial as the House speaker, their selection by the government majority results in pressure to serve the interests of the government in pursuance of its policy goals. In a minority parliament, the choice of which party obtains the chairmanship of a committee becomes extremely partisan.

Committee deliberations are expedited by the work of several parliamentary organizations. The staff of the Committees and Private Legislation Branch of the Commons provides procedural and administrative support. Research assistance comes from the Research Branch of the Library and outside consultants. The Board of Internal Economy has sometimes allocated funds to standing committees. The leadership of the committees may use this money to retain the services of experts and professional, technical and clerical staff. The significance of this fund should not be exaggerated, however.

Some commentators have insisted that Canadian committees should have the high level of staffing and research resources enjoyed by congressional committees in the United States, but such an increase would be unlikely, in itself, to enhance the influence of committees in the legislative process:

> *Until committees are given an independent capacity to influence public policy,*
> *it is unlikely that the addition of even the most competent of research assistants*
> *will do more than contribute to the frustrations of MPs and researchers alike.*[14]

As this quotation suggests, there have long been doubts among both politicians and academic observers as to whether the committee system in the House of Commons is effectively fulfilling its major functions. Despite recent innovations, many misgivings persist.

The Committee System at Work: An Evaluation

Committees in the House of Commons now have three principal areas of operation: detailed consideration of legislation after a bill has passed second reading in the House; scrutiny of the financial aspects of government and bureaucracy; and investigation of reports, policy proposals and other items.

Consideration of Legislation The Committee Stage of the legislative process is designed to provide an opportunity for the clause-by-clause examination of the details of each bill by a small group of relatively specialized MPs in legislative committees. Amendments to bills may be proposed in committees and, if accepted, subsequently will be recommended for adoption by the whole House at the report stage. Sometimes, the opposition members of a committee try to investigate the general policy behind a bill, especially since they have an opportunity—denied them during debates in the House—to question public servants and other witnesses. However, amendments of principle or major policy differences introduced by the opposition during majority governments have little hope of adoption in committee, especially if party divisions have been reinforced by heated debate at the second reading. Hence, such amendments are usually presented solely for propaganda purposes.

Finally, many amendments constitute genuine attempts to improve the bill—either by proposing substantive changes to its provisions or by altering technical details, wording or the administration of the legislation. Amendments may also be introduced by the government itself to correct problems that have become apparent at the committee stage, or in response to interest-group pressure or to provincial government or departmental concerns. Thus, although some observers have suggested that the number of amendments accepted at this stage may indicate the influence of the committees, the sources of amendments are so many and varied that the measure is at best imprecise.

Once adopted by committee, the fate of amendments in the House usually depends upon the minister's willingness to accept them at the report stage. The government is more likely to agree to amendments when they are supported by influential groups or by provincial governments, are technical rather than substantive in content and relate to bills of a minor or relatively non-partisan nature. Some notable amendments to government legislation have been achieved, but in general the committees do not provide a significant increase in the ability of the opposition parties to influence the executive's legislative program. Usually, a government exerts very tight control over

---

14. R.J. Jackson and M.M. Atkinson, *The Canadian Legislative System: Politicians and Policy-Making* (Toronto: Macmillan, 1980).

what amendments will be accepted within the committees, and many successful amendments originate from the government itself. Of course, in a minority situation the government cannot control the committees in the manner it does in majority parliaments.

Scrutiny of Public Expenditure The second main function of the committee system is the scrutiny of public expenditure. It is performed through two mechanisms: first, detailed examination of the main estimates (proposals to spend money) of individual departments by the appropriate standing committees each spring;[15] second, investigation of the government's spending practices by the Standing Committee on Public Accounts.

The **estimates** represent the government's projected spending patterns for the forthcoming financial year. They are approved by the Treasury Board and tabled in Parliament each February in the so-called *Blue Book*. Before 1968, the main estimates were considered in the Committee of Supply (i.e., the whole House), wherein the supply motion gave the opposition a chance to criticize the government's policies and management of the nation's finances. Since 1968, the supply procedure has been replaced by the introduction of Supply or Opposition Days and the referral of estimates to the newly established standing committees. Today, main estimates are referred to committees on March 1st and must be reported back by May 31st. If a committee has not reported by that date, the Standing Orders provide that the estimates "shall be deemed to have been reported."

Theoretically, the opportunity for parliamentary scrutiny of government policy is best afforded by consideration of departmental estimates. Since the government cannot spend money for any purposes not specifically approved by Parliament and since the estimates procedure allows MPs to investigate the aims of public expenditure, the process should permit the committees to scrutinize and influence the direction of government policy. However, this opportunity is by and large not realized to its full potential. Since *only* ministers of the Crown can propose public spending, no committee member can recommend an increase in funding for any program—committees can only accept, reduce or reject outright the proposed amounts. Thus, in reality and for political reasons, members avoid cutting estimates and only do so on rare occasions. The opportunity to influence financial planning is further limited by infrequent ministerial attendance at committee sessions, and by the considerable information gap that exists between MPs and the departmental officials defending their proposed expenditures.

Then there is the attitude of MPs themselves. To many committee members, the estimates procedure is a boring, routine task, devoid of publicity and offering little political mileage. Hence, many meetings are conducted in the absence of a quorum, and it is not unusual for committees to approve votes at the outset of the meeting—when a quorum is present—and then proceed to question witnesses on the dollars that have just been approved. Those members who do participate are most likely to use the estimates process to relay constituents' complaints to departmental bureaucrats or to gain information that may be of use in their constituencies or in embarrassing the government at some future time. Even where there does exist "that rare bird, 'the economy hawk,' who swoops down on the plentiful bait of departmental spending" attacks are saved for the minor items, "like trips and potted plants, that indicate waste and extravagance."[16]

In general, therefore, it is clear that MPs show little commitment to reducing public expenditure or to increasing the efficiency of government departments—however much lip-service they may pay to these aims. Such goals are hampered by the fact that each committee considers the estimates of only one government department at a time, with few opportunities for comparing spending patterns

15. Supplementary estimates, which detail additional funds required to meet unforeseen circumstances or to compensate for inflation, are tabled later in the financial year.

16. Paul Thomas, "Parliament and the Purse Strings," in H.D. Clarke et al., eds., *Parliament, Policy and Representation* (Toronto: Methuen, 1980), pp. 166–67.

among departments or evaluating the total projected expenditure. One change in the publication style has helped: the estimates are now accompanied by an overall government fiscal plan.

Despite its many weaknesses as a mechanism for parliamentary surveillance of government, the current estimates procedure does have some redeeming qualities. Its very existence leads government departments to take extra care in preparing estimates and to eliminate potential excesses before they are spotted by MPs. It also provides an opportunity for members to meet bureaucrats face-to-face and carry out representative functions on behalf of their constituents. As well, committee debate provides an additional forum for the opposition to criticize government policies and program priorities implicit in the projected spending patterns. But, overall, the standing committees, in their estimates function, are incapable of exercising adequate control over government finance or substantially influencing the content of government policy.

The second mechanism for overseeing public expenditure is the post-audit function of the Standing Committee on Public Accounts. This committee is somewhat unusual in that, since 1967, it has always been chaired by a member of the opposition. As well, it receives expert assistance from the **auditor general**, an independent officer of Parliament. The committee's examination of the annual Public Accounts has often resulted in criticisms of government efficiency and recommendations for improvements in spending practices. Its activities concerning the Québec sponsorship scandal—the so-called AdScam—are discussed in Chapter 8.

Investigations   Part of the conventional wisdom concerning committees is that, as small groups, they permit MPs to interact in a manner rather different from their behaviour in the House. In particular, a less formal environment and a relative absence of publicity in committees should permit the development of a less partisan atmosphere and enhance corporate identity. This ought to facilitate objective criticism of government policies and increase the opportunity for meaningful participation by members. It is in the performance of their investigative function that Canadian standing committees most often live up to that conventional wisdom by displaying non-partisanship, group cohesion and autonomy from party and government control. A good example of such activities was in the Standing Committee on Finance in 1987. Combining the new reforms with good leadership and expertise, the committee produced excellent investigations of the government's White Paper on tax reform, the near collapse of the Canadian Commercial Bank, the Green Paper on financial services, credit card rates and the designation of Vancouver and Montréal as international banking centres.[17]

Investigations may take place at three stages in the policy process. A committee may hear evidence from interested parties and formulate recommendations to help the government establish priorities on an issue for which no policy has yet been formulated. Alternatively, a committee may be utilized to establish reactions to a particular set of policy proposals, usually contained in a government White or Green Paper.[18] Or, a committee may evaluate the strengths and weaknesses of existing policies and their administration, especially in an extension of its role as estimates scrutineer. Committee reports can elicit considerable partisan controversy (see the "Close-Up on Institutions: To Leak or Not to Leak" on the next page). In most policy areas, investigatory tasks are referred to the appropriate standing committee, but certain complex or contentious issues sometimes require the establishment of an ad hoc or special committee.[19]

17. See Robert J. O'Brien, "The Financial Committee Carves out a Role," *Parliamentary Government*, vol. 8, no. 1 (1988), pp. 3–10.

18. A White Paper is intended to state relatively firm government policy. A Green Paper is a government document with suggested policy options. In Canada, this distinction is not held rigidly; on rare occasions, the government has even published papers with other colours, thus further distorting the distinction.

19. Robert J. Jackson, "The Unreformed Canadian House of Commons," *Les Cahiers de Droit*, vol. 26, no. 1 (March 1985), pp. 161–73.

Committees: Problems and Reforms

Certain problems experienced by the House of Commons committee system since its inception in the late 1960s have been resolved by a number of reforms. First, a reduction in the number of members of each committee has permitted individual MPs to become more specialized. Second, smaller committees have operated more efficiently than their larger predecessors and reduced partisan conflict to some extent. Third, the reforms also introduced the practice of drawing up a list of alternate members for each committee. Now, when committee members are unable to attend a meeting, only designated alternates may substitute for them. Previously, any member of the House could substitute in committee hearings, usually to maintain the government's majority when votes were held. Today, alternate members are kept informed of the business before the committee, so they at least know which piece of legislation they are voting on. But these lists keep growing in size and reduce the idea of small, specialized committees.

An unresolved criticism of the system relates to the lack of autonomy of Commons committees. Committees cannot operate unless their activities are specified in the Standing Orders or unless they receive a reference from the House instructing them to pursue a particular topic. Standing committees have authority to study the mandate, management and operations of their own departments. The House of Commons may limit the number of referrals to a given committee, or it may so overburden it with work that there is insufficient time for detailed consideration of any item.

This lack of autonomy is further complicated by the fact that committees do not enjoy a consistent workload throughout the year. At the beginning of a session, the workload is generally light. The major bills in the government's program usually reach the legislative committees in the spring, just when members of the standing committees are supposed to be carefully scrutinizing the spending proposals in the main estimates. The expenditure scrutiny function is therefore undermined, as some of the most experienced members have little time for deliberation. Reports on the estimates are often brief and hastily written, and some committees never do report to the House.

Another traditional problem faced by committees has been the fate of their final reports. Prior to 1982, there was no guarantee that a report would ever get a hearing in the House or provoke any government reaction. Under the new House rules, at the request of a committee the government must table a comprehensive response to its report within 150 days. However, it is still too easy for the government to ignore committee proposals and criticisms. The Communications and Culture Committee was simply told that its 1987 report was rejected—all one hundred recommendations were to be reconsidered—and that the job of the committee was to recommend policy, not legislation. However, even if, under the new rules, it is not obliged to adopt recommendations put forward by committees, the government does have to explain its reaction to Parliament.

The procedural reforms of the 1990s, which originated in the Lefebvre and McGrath reports, have thus gone some way toward resolving the problems experienced by committees. But problems do remain. First, in order to function effectively, committees require more professional research

CLOSE-UP ON Institutions

TO LEAK OR NOT TO LEAK

The leaking or disclosing of government and parliamentary papers before their publication is an age-old tradition in Canada. It provides much of the excitement of politics, in particular for the press.

In 1999, House of Commons Speaker Gilbert Parent attempted to do something about these leaks. The question of leaking parliamentary committee reports before they were tabled in the House was sent to the Procedure and House Affairs Committee, which concluded that "between September 1997 to the end of December 1998—at least 19 committee reports out of 50 have been leaked in whole or in part. This represents 38 percent of substantive reports."*

The controversial issue reached the level of farce when the report of the committee investigating leaks was itself leaked to the press before it was tabled.

Should Parliament or the government do something to prevent in camera discussions or conclusions from being disclosed prior to their being made public? On the other hand, is it a democratic right to leak documents with which one does not agree?

*Procedure and House Affairs Committee, February 1999.

staff, expanded budgets for financial autonomy and more generalized references in the Standing Orders to reduce government control over referrals and committee workloads. Second, partisanship continues to dominate committee activities. The House has very few members who are so secure of re-election and independent of party finances that they can ignore the directives of their leader or the party whip. Since only about a quarter of MPs are very active in committees, there are also many operational difficulties—overlapping memberships, scheduling conflicts and other practical irritants such as lack of adequate staff and even meeting rooms.

But the area of committee work most in need of reform may well be the expenditure scrutiny function. A paper prepared for the Special Committee on Procedure by MPs Ron Huntington and Claude-André Lachance made specific proposals (not subsequently adopted) for increasing financial accountability, as did the *Final Report* of the Lambert Royal Commission in 1979.[20] We have already mentioned proposals for the establishment of a General Estimates Committee that would develop an overview of total government spending. Perhaps reform needs to go even further and establish a National Finance Committee, similar to that proposed by the Lambert Commission. Such a committee would analyze both revenues and expenditures in order to bridge the gap between standing committees' consideration of individual departmental estimates, the debate in the whole House on the finance minister's economic review and taxation proposals in the budget.[21] There is also need for a separate committee to review the finances of Crown corporations.

Lastly, Canada has little or no parliamentary scrutiny of legislation that could affect our rights and freedoms. Despite their lack of an equivalent constitutional guarantee of rights and freedoms, Australia, Britain and New Zealand all have parliamentary committees to ensure that legislation is in line with human rights. Canada does not. Moreover, at the time of writing, the Standing Committee on Public Safety and National Security remains without the ability to do the job it should be doing: scrutinizing details of issues in national security.

MPs in Parties: Government and Opposition

In contrast to the nineteenth century, it is now rare to find independent members in the House of Commons. Today, almost all MPs belong to a political party, which has a profound effect on legislative politics in both houses. The government relies on its backbenchers to remain loyal in order to secure passage of its legislative proposals and even to stay in office. The opposition parties, as well, rally their troops to present a coherent attack on the government. This process often requires individual members to compromise their short-term interests for the unity of their party.

The role of the independent MP is tenuous indeed. From 1940 to 1993, 31 MPs ran for re-election in the next general election after parliamentary sittings during which they crossed the floor. Only 12 of these were successful, and three ran under their original party banner. These figures show that although an MP may think she is acting in the constituents' interests when breaking party ranks, the electorate does not reward such behaviour at the polls. This finding is in direct contrast to the idea that the people want MPs to be "free" to vote according to conscience.[22] The election of former Liberal, but later independent, John Nunziata in 1997 is an example of the exception to the rule, but he tried it again in the next election and failed in that second attempt.

---

20. *House of Commons Special Committee on Procedure*, Seventh Report (Ottawa: Queen's Printer, 1982); Royal Commission on Financial Management and Accountability (Lambert Commission), *Final Report* (Ottawa: Ministry of Supply and Services, 1979), especially ch. 22.

21. Lambert Commission, *Final Report*, ch. 21; and Jackson, "The Unreformed Canadian House of Commons," p. 11.

22. See Robert J. Jackson and Paul Conlin, "The Imperative of Party Discipline in the Canadian Political System," in Mark Charlton and Paul Barker, eds., *Contemporary Political Issues*, 2nd ed. (Scarborough, ON: Nelson, 1994). For parallels with Britain, see Robert J. Jackson, *Rebels and Whips* (London: Macmillan, 1968).

The 36th and 37th Parliaments are more confusing to analyze because of the realignment of conservative forces with the final amalgamation of Reform, Alliance and PC parties into one party. In each of 2004 and 2006, only one independent was elected (see Chapters 11 and 12). The importance of party is clearly demonstrated in the minority government periods. Any and all deviations from the party line are quickly noticed and reprimanded

Political parties have a profound effect on legislative politics in both chambers and their committees. The government relies on cohesion among its backbenchers to keep it in office and to secure the passage of its legislative proposals. Effective opposition likewise depends on the ability of minority party leaders to mobilize their MPs in specific directions. In both cases, individual members often have to compromise their own short-term interests and aims so that party goals may be achieved.

Intra-Party Relations: Rebels and Whips

Some observers argue that cohesion is imposed upon MPs through party discipline—that backbenchers, especially on the government side, are forced to adhere to the directives laid down by party leaders. Others portray cohesion as the product of a commonality of views, the result of consensus arrived at through regular meetings of the party caucus. Certainly, party leaders, especially of the governing party, have a number of sanctions and rewards at their disposal to ensure or at least encourage backbenchers to toe the party line.

On the negative side, individual members who consistently oppose the party leadership or fail to vote with their colleagues on important issues may be coerced in a number of ways, culminating in the threat of expulsion from the party. Without the official backing of the party, a rebellious MP would have to contest the next election as an independent candidate with little probability of success. They may lose their positions on parliamentary committees, as several Liberals did when they rebelled against their government's gun control legislation in June 1995. Even Warren Allmand, one of the party's most senior MPs, lost his position as chair of the Commons Justice Committee for voting against his party on another occasion.

More sizable revolts within the governing party may be met with the threat of dissolution of Parliament. Given the high turnover of seats at every general election, this may quell dissent, especially among those backbenchers who represent marginal constituencies. But the dissolution of Parliament on these grounds is a double-edged sword, since it constitutes a public admission of division within the government party and the possible defeat of the prime minister in a general election.

While these negative sanctions are the "sticks" in the enforcement of party discipline, party leaders also have a number of "carrots" available. The prime minister has a large patronage fund that may be used to reward loyal, well-behaved members: promotion to cabinet minister, parliamentary secretary or committee chair; appointment to the Senate; and numerous positions in public corporations and Crown agencies. Some of these perks are also potentially available to the leadership of the major opposition parties, but the government has considerably more of them at its disposal.

Party discipline implies a *conflict approach* to the maintenance of party unity, that there are inherent divisions between leaders and backbenchers that can be overcome only through coercion. On the other hand, it may be argued equally that party cohesion is based primarily on the existence of consensus (rather than conflict) among MPs in each parliamentary party.[23] According to the latter view, party unity is based on a *value consensus*, a commonality of opinions on major issues shared by members of the same political movement and reinforced by regular meetings of

---

23. The consensus view of party cohesion is emphasized by Allan Kornberg, "Caucus and Cohesion in Canadian Parliamentary Politics," *APSR*, vol. 60, no. 1 (March 1966), pp. 83–92.

the party caucus. Another view is that unity may be based on the deference of backbenchers toward party leaders—a willingness to accept the decisions of those who derive their legitimacy from selection by national conventions and who, in this era of personality politics, may be perceived as largely responsible for the electoral success of the party. It may also be argued that peer-group pressure from fellow party members serves to reinforce party solidarity.

In all parties, the **House leader**, a member appointed by the party leader to manage party conduct in the House of Commons, is assisted by other MPs—a **chief whip** and assistant whips—who help to maintain party cohesion and manage parliamentary activities. The number of whips depends on the size of caucus, but their role is invariable. They keep in close touch with the members, informing them of their duties in the House and in committees. While the whips can make use of some minor rewards and punishments, caucus cohesion is maintained more by party and leader loyalty than by the whips' ability to sanction members. The **party caucus** is a uniquely Canadian institution. Every Wednesday morning while Parliament is in session, all members of the House of Commons (together with any senators who wish to attend) meet in their respective party groups. Caucus meetings are held in private, away from the press and public. In the opposition parties, unlike on the government side, there is relatively little distinction in status between leaders and backbenchers; consequently, all MPs feel equally entitled to air their point of view, and debate is often quite heated. However, in both opposition and government caucuses there are very few formal votes and the party leader normally sums up the caucus consensus.

In the governing party, the prevailing attitude is that the primary task of government backbenchers is to support the executive and its legislative program, and since members are often consulted only after policies have already been decided by cabinet, the major function of the government caucus is to enforce party discipline and ensure cabinet has control of the policy process. Thus, there is "little doubt that the government caucus is of greater utility to the ministry than to the members, and that it is in effect the chief instrument of government control of the House of Commons."[24] However, governments do *not* act in the face of clear caucus opposition. In 1996, Finance Minister Paul Martin, for example, gave in to caucus demands that he not amend the *Bank Act* to permit banks to sell insurance, and Human Resources Minister Doug Young was forced by caucus to add amendments to an unemployment scheme that would have reduced the amount of money for seasonal workers. In the 37th Parliament, the Liberal government was often bested by its own backbenchers when they supported Paul Martin rather than the prime minister, Jean Chrétien. The most significant event took place in November 2002, when Martin's forces joined the Canadian Alliance to pass a motion 174–87, against government advice, to have committee chairs elected in a secret ballot.[25]

Upon becoming prime minister in December 2003, Paul Martin inaugurated some reforms and promised other far-reaching ideas. The system for controlling backbench votes was changed. Votes are classified as three-, two- or one-line. *Three-line votes* are for votes of confidence in the government and for a limited number of other fundamental bills of importance to the government. All government party members are expected to support these votes. *Two-line votes* are for votes on which the government has taken a stand but on which private members, unlike ministers and parliamentary secretaries, are free to vote in any way they choose. *One-line votes* are "free votes" in that all party members, including ministers, are free to vote as they please.

The short-lived 2003 government of Paul Martin also promised an action plan on democratic reform. The plan envisaged private members with more freedom to voice their constituents' views

24. Mark MacGuigan, "Backbenchers, The New Committee System, and the Caucus," in Paul Fox, ed., *Politics: Canada*, 4th ed. (Toronto: McGraw-Hill Ryerson, 1977), pp. 436–37.

25. *The Globe and Mail*, November, 6, 2002.

on free votes, continued election of House committee chairs, a commitment to send more bills to committees before second reading, a greater role for committees in reviewing heads of Crown corporations and agencies, and deputy ministers having their appointments monitored by committees. The government promised to consult the Standing Committee on Justice on how to seek prior parliamentary review of Supreme Court judges; how to strengthen the ability of ministers' offices to relate to Parliament; and how to set up an all-party committee to examine management of the House and reforms. Before any significant changes took place, however, the government was defeated. The 2006 Harper government also promised parliamentary reform. In 2007, the minister for democratic reform commissioned papers, public opinion surveys and public consultations across the country on both Senate and House reform.

Inter-Party Relations

Although the relationship between government and opposition is basically confrontational, both sides of the House have developed behavioural norms to make Parliament work. Opposition members recognize the government's responsibility to govern, and sometimes lend their support to that end; simultaneously, they retain the right to criticize government policy. The government, in turn, recognizes the opposition's right to criticize, but denies it the right to obstruct. The debates on the budget and the Throne Speech, and the allocation of Supply Days, on which the opposition parties may choose the topics for debate, constitute formal recognition of the right to criticize the government's record in general terms. The rules of debate, the committee system and the Question Period permit criticism of individual items of policy or administration. Less formally, while the governing party has final control over the timetable of the House, both government and opposition recognize the value of agreements between respective House leaders or party whips concerning the disposal of parliamentary time in order to foster a spirit of co-operation.

Occasionally, however, co-operation breaks down. This usually takes place when the government, confronted with what it views as obstruction by the opposition, attempts to push through a bill with what the opposition regards as unseemly haste. When this occurs, both sides have various procedural weapons at their disposal. The government may resort to **closure** (SO 57), an unpopular measure whereby all outstanding discussion and divisions on a particular stage of a bill must be completed within the next sitting day instead of being adjourned from one day to the next, as unfinished business usually is. Closure is a device to which governments turn with the greatest reluctance because of its procedural complexity and political ramifications.[26] As one author has commented, notice of closure

> *resembles so much a death sentence and a public execution that ministers shrink from using it; and when they do, the opposition, regardless of their true sentiments, feels obliged to lament the end of a thousand years of freedom and democracy.*[27]

A less drastic alternative to closure as a means of limiting debate lies in a pre-arranged *allocation of time* to a particular bill or its various stages under SO 78. Here, a balance of power is maintained between government and opposition by rules that become more complex procedurally as they require less inter-party co-operation.

26. On the origins and historical and use of *closure*, see W.F. Dawson, *Procedure in the Canadian House of Commons*, pp. 121–30.

27. J.B. Stewart, *The Canadian House of Commons: Procedure and Reform* (Montréal: McGill-Queen's University Press, 1977).

In the 32nd Parliament, for example, the opposition found dramatic weapons to confront an uncooperative government. In March and April 1981, the Progressive Conservatives tied up the business of the House of Commons with a collective *filibuster*—an endless series of *points of order* and *questions of privilege*—in order to prevent further discussion of the resolution on patriation of the Constitution until after it had been ruled upon by the Supreme Court. For two weeks in March 1982, the division bells that call MPs to vote were left ringing on Parliament Hill as the Opposition boycotted the House in protest against the Liberals' omnibus bill on energy security. In both cases, the government was forced to compromise its original proposals in order to get the House back to work. The McGrath reforms prohibited the future use of a *bell-ringing filibuster*. Now, by Standing Orders, the bells can ring only for 15 minutes, unless it is on a non-debatable motion, in which case 30 minutes is required. The whips may request that a vote be delayed for a day, but during the deferral the bells may not ring and the House continues its normal business.

In the 34th Parliament, the PC government's use of closure and time allocation took on a new and harsh quality. From 1913, when closure was first used, until the 1984 election, the device was employed only 19 times. During the 33rd Parliament, it was used only twice between 1984 and 1988. But from 1988 until mid-April 1993, it was employed 15 times—almost as many times as in the whole history of closure since 1913. To top it off, time allocation was used 25 times in the 34th Parliament (up to mid-April 1993), much more than in earlier Parliaments. These "gag" rules were nearly always imposed over fairly controversial items such as the free trade legislation, the goods and services tax (GST) and the *Drug Patent Act*, revealing the partisan nature of their use. This process changed drastically when the consecutive Liberal and Conservative minority governments were elected in 2004 and 2006.

The parliamentary system enhances adversarial politics, as it is the function of the opposition to criticize. This responsibility becomes significant when there is a minority government, as the opposition parties must constantly decide whether they will try to defeat the government. Politics *among* the opposition parties can become as important as those *with* the government. Tactics and political manoeuvring may eventually lead to both government and public distaste.

The parliamentary system also creates a dilemma for the government in that it is its job to get bills passed, and yet it must allow the opposition time to criticize. In any case, the parliamentary rules are so weighted in favour of the government that the cabinet generally gets it way. Before the opening of the 35th Parliament, Reform Party MPs predicted that MPs would no longer engage in destructive bickering; instead, the new Parliament would be a model of dignity and decorum. Reform leader Preston Manning vowed there would be none of the old "whimpering and snivelling" from the Official Opposition.[28] Initially, this was the case; the Liberals, Reform and Bloc functioned as three solitudes. Then, fewer than nine weeks into the session, the atmosphere in the House resumed its usual pattern of exchanging insults and accusations. Speaker Gilbert Parent begged MPs to refrain from "going back and forth with insults."[29] It was not long before the Liberals began using time allocation to cut off debate.

In their adversarial relationship with the government, opposition parties are disadvantaged by the former's control over the parliamentary timetable and access to departmental information. But the opposition does have sanctions to prevent what it sees as abuse of the parliamentary process. Even the complaint that opposition parties lack the research facilities to compete with the government's monopoly on bureaucratic information has been partly blunted by the provision of public funding for partisan activity by caucus research groups.

28. *The Globe and Mail*, March 19, 1994.
29. Ibid.

Indeed, many of the difficulties encountered by the opposition in formulating effective criticism of government policy have less to do with House of Commons procedures or research facilities than with standard problems that also afflict parliamentary oppositions in other Western democracies.[30] One is that the Official Opposition in Parliament often has trouble being heard above the hubbub coming from other political actors. Major interest groups and private research institutes frequently offer articulate and well-publicized criticisms of government policy, and, in a federal context such as Canada,

> *there is little doubt that the clashes between the provinces and the federal government . . . detract attention from the federal parliamentary opposition on some of the most important issues in Canadian politics.*[31]

Sometimes, too, it may be difficult for the opposition parties to offer clear-cut alternatives to government policy. Some issues do not lend themselves to a confrontational style of politics since they cut across party lines. This is especially true of moral issues such as abortion, AIDS, capital punishment, same-sex marriage or euthanasia. On other social and economic policy issues, the development of an ideological consensus that supports the mixed economy and the welfare state tends to preclude the presentation of radical policy alternatives by a "loyal" opposition.

Oppositions have increasingly had to be content with criticizing the specifics of government policy and its administration (rather than developing comprehensive alternatives) and with presenting themselves as an alternative source of leadership and government personnel. In this regard, the opposition parties have been greatly aided by the introduction of television cameras into the House of Commons. Broadcasting Question Period and major debates not only provides a wider audience for their criticisms of the government, but also gives nationwide exposure to the leaders of the opposition parties and their teams. Direct communication with the electorate via television may in fact have greatly improved parliamentary oppositions' ability to present themselves as viable alternatives.

House of Commons: Symbolism or Power?

> *The reform of parliamentary procedure should be an ongoing process. Parliament is in a constant state of evolution, and if its practices are to be effective, they must be adapted when necessary to meet the changing needs of Parliament and reflect the changing conditions of society and the nation.*[32]

As this passage from a report by a Special Committee on Standing Orders and Procedures illustrates, members of the House of Commons are perfectly aware of the necessity to reform the roles, procedures and customs of the chamber in order to maintain Parliament as a central institution in Canadian society. Yet possibly the most enigmatic feature of parliamentary democracies is that ordinary members know that they possess almost limitless authority to change the structures of their legislatures but nevertheless persist in ignoring this power.[33]

Periodically, Canadian MPs undertake systematic reforms of the way in which they conduct their activities. After a wave of reforms in the late 1960s, notable among them the establishment of

---

30. For an extended discussion, see Robert J. Jackson, "Models of Legislative Reform: Diagnosis and Prescription," *Le Contrôle de l'Administration et la Réforme parlementaire, Collection Bilans et Perspectives*, no. 4 (Ste-Foy, QC: École nationale d'administration publique, 1984), p. 4.

31. Jackson and Atkinson, *Canadian Legislative System*, p. 119.

32. House of Commons Special Committee on Standing Orders and Procedures, Third Report (Ottawa: 1982), p. 5.

33. Jackson, "Models of Legislative Reform," p. 4.

the modern system of committees, more than a decade elapsed until the next round of innovation and experimentation. In the early 1980s, the Lefebvre and McGrath reform committees ushered in major innovations in the election of the speaker, private members' business, committee structure, scheduling and other items of importance. As we mentioned above, Stephen Harper's government has also proposed major changes to the way the House and Senate are elected and do business.

Consequently, a voluminous body of literature exists on proposals for House of Commons reform.[34] It is not our intention to add to it here, although we have drawn attention to areas in which reform may be desirable, and have made some specific proposals. It may even be argued that little that is new or innovative can be added to the catalogues of recommendations. What may be more useful is to provide some criteria for evaluating existing and future reform proposals.

First, it should be emphasized that one cannot turn back the clock to the "Golden Age of Parliament" of the mid-nineteenth century. We cannot ignore all the other changes that have taken place. There has been a remarkable growth of the public sector and state intervention. Constituents today expect more of both their governments and their members of Parliament, and there are more of them to bring problems to each MP. Traditional federal government responsibilities have become increasingly technical in nature, placing additional burdens on parliamentarians. The mass media has created direct channels of communication between government and the general public that have altered the representative, intermediary functions of MPs. Such trends cannot be reversed. Nor, in the absence of substantial realignment of the perceptions of Canadian citizens about the role of government in society, can the scope of federal government activities be significantly reduced. Realistic proposals for reform of the House of Commons must therefore be formulated within this context.

The objectives of parliamentary reform may be grouped under the two broad headings of *power* and *symbolism*, the central themes of this chapter. Some reforms are oriented toward increasing the power of Parliament—strengthening the Commons vis-à-vis other institutions and increasing its ability to control, criticize and hold government accountable for its actions. Other proposals are primarily symbolic in nature inasmuch as they seek to enhance the image of the House of Commons as a key institution in the democratic process. As we noted earlier, these two categories are not necessarily mutually exclusive, since a Parliament that is perceived as weak and ineffective will not be able to sustain, in the long run, the degree of legitimacy necessary to fulfill its symbolic functions. However, the concepts of power and symbolism do serve as useful organizing devices.

When it comes to a reform measure designed to increase the power of the House of Commons, the probability of success depends upon various implicit norms and constraints that result from the realities of legislative politics in the chamber. First, governments will not accept organizational or procedural changes unless they are assured that changes favourable to the government will also be adopted. Thus, reform packages must be designed to maintain a balance between the competing needs of government and opposition. If, for example, the opposition is to gain increased opportunities for surveillance and criticism of the administration, the government must be guaranteed certain concessions with regard to limiting debate. Political reality dictates that the government will simply deploy its majority in the House to defeat "unbalanced" reform proposals.

We may be sure that governments will continue to deploy their forces cohesively on matters affecting their interests. Proposals that seek to enhance the influence of backbenchers by advocating, for example, that "leaders of both government and opposition parties recognize and adopt in practice a less stringent approach to the question of party discipline and the rules governing confidence,"[35]

---

34. Among the many comprehensive "reform designs," the reader may wish to consult the discussion in both editions of Jackson and Atkinson, *The Canadian Legislative System*.

35. T. d'Aquino, G.B. Doern and C. Blair, *Parliamentary Democracy in Canada* (Toronto: Methuen, 1983), p. 30.

are politically naive and based on misleading comparisons with the United States, where members of Congress are deemed to be more powerful because they work in a state of partisan anarchy.

Finally, with respect to measures to enhance the power of the House of Commons, it must be emphasized that it is much easier to alter procedures and institutions than to change the attitudes and behaviour of politicians. Many reformers criticize the lack of opportunities for ordinary members to participate in the policy process or to control government spending effectively. They do not acknowledge that many MPs fail to take advantage of the opportunities that already exist—either because they choose not to, or because pressures of work and competing commitments prevent them from doing so. Thus, members do not take the scrutiny of government estimates very seriously, because much of it is boring, routine work. More committees or more powers for committees will not help; rather, there must be some perceived reward for effective participation, such as exposure to constituents through the televising of committee hearings.

Reforms designed to increase the power of Parliament vis-à-vis other actors, such as the government and the bureaucracy, may have a beneficial effect on the symbolic functions of the House of Commons in legitimating government policies and many other aspects of the political system. But other reforms might also raise the level of esteem in which it is held by the Canadian public. Thus, although the members of recent parliaments and the governments they sustain may be reasonably representative of Canadian voters across the country, electoral reform might further assure the integrative capacity of the House as a representative institution.[36] Increased travel by committees and countrywide consultation would bring Parliament closer to the people. So, too, would a more dynamic presentation of the televised House proceedings—for example, letting Parliamentary Channel cameras do more than merely focus on one talking head at a time, or, following the popular precedent set with the Special Committee on the Constitution, allowing cameras more consistently into committee meetings, where so much of the House's work is done.

As reformers seek to strengthen the House of Commons, all too often the other potential strengths of the House—as a representative institution, as a symbol of societal integration, as a link between government and citizens—are neglected. Changes related to both power *and* symbolic innovations should be advocated.

The Senate

Canada is one of the minority of countries in the world with a bicameral legislature—that is, with a second chamber or upper house in addition to the (usually) popularly elected lower house. Second chambers have been adopted or retained for a number of purposes, among them their ability to provide, at the national level, representation of the constituent parts of a federal system and representation of a particular class (or estate) to act as a conservative restraint upon the potentially unbridled progressivism of the lower house (making it "the chamber of sober second thought"). But the essential case for an upper house has always been that the formulation of legislation and policy issues ought to receive a second consideration, and possibly be rejected, or delayed, by a chamber different from the first in character and composition.[37]

While the notion of the second chamber as a provider of sober second thought is almost universal, the other functions of upper houses can often be related to their mode of selection. In federal systems, all of which give their subnational territorial units some representation in the national legislature, membership in the upper house is determined in different ways. Sometimes, the

---

36. See the discussion of the impact of the electoral system on the House of Commons in Chapter 12.

37. Robert J. Jackson and Doreen Jackson, *An Introduction to Political Science: Comparative and World Politics* (Don Mills, ON: Pearson Prentice Hall, 2003), chs. 12 and 13.

public elects members directly, as in the United States and Australia. Sometimes, members are delegates from the state governments or legislatures, as in Germany. Elsewhere, members are appointed as representatives of various economic, occupational or cultural associations, as in the Portuguese Corporative Chamber before 1975. In still other countries (notably Belgium, Italy and Japan), the upper house is popularly elected, but is designed to give rise to a chamber with a political complexion different from that of the lower house. Finally, the historically conservative and upper-class tone of the British House of Lords has been modified by the appointment of life peers and by more recent reforms that have dramatically reduced the number of hereditary peers from the upper house.

Recruitment and Formal Roles

Canada's Senate appears, at first glance, to fit none of these models. It is the only legislative chamber in the Western World whose members are all appointed. Senators receive their positions from the governor general at the behest of the government of the day. Thus, Canadian senators cannot claim to represent directly, or to be delegates of, any electorate, any subordinate level of government or any specific interests within society.

Although Canada is unique in appointing its senators, as in most other countries there is a regional basis to the system. Since April 1999, the membership of the Senate has been fixed at 105, with 24 each from 4 main regions—Ontario, Québec, the West (6 from each of the 4 provinces west of Ontario) and the Maritimes (10 each from New Brunswick and Nova Scotia, four from Prince Edward Island)—together with 6 from Newfoundland and Labrador, and 1 each from Yukon, Nunavut and the Northwest Territories. There is also a provision in the Constitution for the appointment of an additional 4 or 8 senators (drawn equally from the 4 main regions) to allow for breaking a deadlock within the Senate and the Commons. After the 1988 federal election, Tory PM Brian Mulroney used this procedure to prevent the Liberal-dominated upper house from blocking his government's GST legislation. For the first and only time in Canadian history, 8 additional senators were appointed—temporarily increasing the number.

A senator nominally "represents" the province from which she was appointed and, unlike a member of the House of Commons, must reside and own property in that province. Thus there is a regional or provincial underpinning to the composition of the Senate, and the Fathers of Confederation did perceive the second chamber as a "federal" institution. According to Sir John A. Macdonald,

---

> *In order to protect local interests and to prevent sectional jealousies, it was found requisite that the great divisions into which British North America is separated should be represented in the Upper House on the principle of equality.*[38]

Most federal systems give their constituent states equal representation in the upper house or at least some modified form of representation by population. Although the "great divisions" of Canada are equally represented in the Senate, there are obvious inequities in representation among provinces. The least populated areas get the same number of seats as the most populous.

The unique appointment process means that Canadian senators cannot be held accountable or responsible to the provinces and regions they were originally intended to represent. Instead, the representation of provincial or regional interests in the federal policy-making process has become increasingly institutionalized in the form of federal–provincial conferences and in the regional composition of the cabinet.

---

38. *Parliamentary Debates on Confederation of the British North American Provinces,* Québec City, 1865 (Ottawa: Supply and Services, 1951), p. 29.

If the Canadian Senate does not fill the role of guardian of regional or provincial interests in the federal system, neither does it necessarily seem designed to provide a more mature or conservative restraint upon the youthful enthusiasm of the House of Commons. Constitutionally, senators must be at least 30 years of age, but this is considerably younger than almost all new MPs who win election to the lower house. And although the Constitution determines that senators must own property exceeding $4000 in value—a sum that in the mid-nineteenth century limited potential membership to a fairly narrow and privileged minority—this figure has not been revised since 1867. Thus, the constitutional requirements for membership in the Senate are no longer of great relevance to its composition or perceived role within the legislative process.

Today, the Liberals have a majority in the Senate with 62 members. In 2006, the average age of a senator was just over 65. Senators were originally appointed for life, but since 1965, newly appointed members have had to retire at age 75. One observer noted, with a touch of black humour, that this formal change has had little practical relevance:

> Senators, on the average, die at the age of 74. . . . Therefore, the introduction of a compulsory retiring age at 75 would by no means seriously affect the existing situation in the Senate; it would rather formalize a practice already present.[39]

One potential advantage of the appointment process is that it can be used to give recognition to economic, ethnic and religious groups that are under-represented in the House of Commons. Thus, members of organized labour have been appointed, as have farmers—although not nearly as many as their numbers in the population would warrant. The Protestant minority in Québec and English-speaking Catholics elsewhere have also tended to be over-represented in the Senate to compensate for their relative lack of seats in the Commons.[40]

As of today, women remain underrepresented in the Senate. The first woman senator, Cairine Wilson, was appointed in 1930, after a long constitutional wrangle that was resolved by a decision from the Judicial Committee of the Privy Council that women were equally "persons" under the relevant sections of the *BNA Act* and therefore were eligible for appointment to the Senate.[41] The fact that, in 2007, only 32 senators were women demonstrates that Senate appointments have not been systematically used as a means of redressing inequities of representation in the House of Commons. Rather, appointments of women as well as leading figures from minority groups have been symbolic, "a token of recognition of their relative importance in the social and political system of the country."[42] At the same time, there were seven senators of Inuit, Métis and First Nations origin. Often, such appointments have been motivated by purely partisan interests in an attempt to win electoral support from specific groups.

This last point underlines the true nature of the system used in naming senators. Although, in formal terms, "qualified persons" are "summoned" to the Senate by the governor general, in practice, as with other such appointments, the real power of selection rests with the prime minister. The fact is, therefore, that the basis of appointment to the Senate is unashamedly partisan. Senatorships have invariably been regarded as the choicest plums in the patronage basket and they have been used continually as rewards for faithful party service. There have been few more blatant examples of this in recent decades than Pierre Trudeau's appointments as he retired and Brian Mulroney's nominations of former ministers, MPs, fundraisers and employees.

39. Kunz, *The Modern Senate of Canada*, p. 71.

40. Robert A. Mackay, *The Unreformed Senate of Canada*, rev. ed. (Toronto: McClelland & Stewart, 1963), pp. 148–49.

41. On the question of women in previous Senates and the development of minority group representation in the upper house, see Kunz, *The Modern Senate of Canada*, pp. 46–56.

42. Kunz, *The Modern Senate of Canada*, p. 46.

It must be acknowledged that the partisan nature of Senate appointments may have some positive value for the political system. It does allow cabinet ministers and other long-serving party members to be "promoted" to secure, well-paid Senate seats rather than being "relegated" to the backbenches. In this way, the prime minister can reshuffle the cabinet and introduce new blood without appearing to demote colleagues. It also sometimes occurs that a party candidate regarded as potential ministerial material fails to win or retain a seat in the House of Commons. The Senate provides two alternative strategies for a prime minister wishing to include such an individual in the government. One is to elevate to the Senate a member of the caucus who holds a safe seat. This allows a promising candidate to be "parachuted" into that vacant seat at the ensuing election. The other is to appoint the potential minister directly to the Senate and allow her to hold the portfolio from that vantage point.

Although this "renewal" function tends to give rise to a Senate composed mainly of semi-retired party faithfuls, the upper house is far from being a geriatric retreat. The number of appointments of relatively young senators has increased in recent years, and some members have played important roles within their national party organizations. Senators are, for example, in an ideal position to direct election campaigns, since they are close to the centres of power in Ottawa but do not have to seek personal re-election.

From the foregoing discussion, it may appear that the Senate fulfills only imperfectly many of the formal roles normally ascribed to second chambers. It is neither manifestly a representative of provincial rights nor of minority groups; neither is it a straightforward champion of a particular class nor a sanctuary for aging politicians. Therefore, to ascertain the place of the upper house within the Canadian legislative process, we need to consider the actual work done by the Senate and senators' own perceptions of their task.

Organization and Rules

The Senate has two senior officers: the government House leader and the speaker. The *government House leader* is appointed by the prime minister to represent and speak for senators in cabinet and, conversely, to be the voice of the cabinet in the Senate. Only rarely are there senators in cabinet other than the government House leader. The **speaker of the Senate**, unlike the elected House speaker, is appointed by the governor general on the recommendation of the prime minister for the term of the Parliament. The duties of this position are similar to those of the speaker of the House of Commons.

As of 2008, senators earn $125 800. Their other perks include offices, secretarial help, mailing privileges, free telephone service and so on. Although it is rare for a senator to be fired, it is possible for one of several reasons: if the senator fails to attend two consecutive parliamentary sessions, loses Canadian citizenship, ceases to meet the residence and property qualifications, is adjudged bankrupt or is convicted of a criminal offence. No one can hold a seat in the Senate and the House of Commons at the same time. Like MPs, senators are bound by conflict-of-interest rules, although these are not as stringent as for cabinet ministers (see Chapter 8).

Many senators hold positions with private companies, are connected to other people who have holdings in corporations, or are with law firms that represent clients who do business with the government. For this reason they have been called the "lobby from within" and have reaped considerable public condemnation for informal conflicts of interest. Former Liberal senator Michael Kirby, for example, was a member of the Senate banking committee for many years, but he regularly did market research for private business during the same period. This situation is an ongoing problem because there are no appropriate legal guidelines to regulate senators' behaviour.

Legislative Politics in the Senate

Many observers have challenged the status of the Senate as an independent and non-partisan counterweight to the Commons. According to this view, senators are admitted to the Red Chamber because of partisan appointments; as such, they are vulnerable to external pressures and vested interests. F.A. Kunz posits a contrary view. While admitting that "it would be rather naive to expect a person who is summoned to the Senate at the (average) age of fifty-eight to forget his entire political background,"[43] he argues that strongly held partisan convictions are counterbalanced by the process of socialization into the norms of the upper chamber that a new senator undergoes.

Certainly, the career backgrounds of senators show them to be highly political.[44] However, there is also strong evidence that, once institutionalized into the norms and values of the upper house, senators often forgo overt displays of partisan attachment in favour of other roles. Many perceive themselves to be independent statespersons placing their expertise and experience at the service of the country as a whole rather than serving particular party interests. The higher incidence of cross-voting (voting across party lines) in the upper house on important issues of government legislation would suggest that partisanship is lower in the Senate than in the House of Commons. In 2007, the party composition of the Senate was 62 Liberals, 26 Conservatives, 4 independents, 1 NDP and the remaining spots were vacant.

Usually, the Senate does not reject government legislation. Despite the fact that the Canadian upper house is one of the few second chambers to retain a full set of legislative teeth, it has mostly failed to make use of them. On the few occasions when the upper house has thrown caution to the wind and blocked government initiatives, it has been threatened with dire consequences. Most senators are fully aware of the erosion of senatorial powers and, in some cases, the abolition of second chambers elsewhere. Moreover, the self-perceived role of elders would appear to forbid the obstruction of legislation passed by a House of Commons mandated by popular will. Instead, one of the most important legislative functions performed by the Senate consists of the detailed scrutiny of bills with a view to removing ambiguities of interpretation in the original wording and amending technical items that fall within the particular expertise of individual members.

On occasion, however, the Senate has acted decisively to reject government legislation. As early as 1875, the Senate blocked the construction of an Esquimalt–Nanaimo railway. Then, in 1913, it defeated the Borden Naval Bill and in 1926 it terminated Mackenzie King's old-age pension legislation. More recently, during the tenures of Brian Mulroney and Jean Chrétien, there were constant clashes between the House and Senate. The Liberal-dominated Senate interfered with or delayed a borrowing bill, the drug patent bill, and copyright, immigration and income tax legislation. The Senate tried to amend the Meech Lake Accord, unemployment insurance payments and the goods and services tax; it succeeded in rejecting an abortion bill when a free vote was called, the first senatorial veto in three decades. In the 35th Parliament, the PCs initially held a majority of seats in the Senate even though they had only two MPs in the House. With the help of a Liberal senator, they stopped the passage of Bill C22, the cancellation of the Pearson Airport development legislation, and delayed many other bills. In the 37th and 38th Parliaments, the Liberals had a clear majority of senators and government legislation passed smoothly through the upper house.

The most important instance of the Senate blocking the elected House was the decision of Liberal senators, at the request of John Turner, to prevent the passage of free trade legislation. When the trade bill reached second reading, the Grit senators abstained and allowed the bill to go

43. Ibid., pp. 113–15.

44. Colin Campbell, *The Canadian Senate: A Lobby from Within* (Toronto: Macmillan, 1978), p. 53 and Appendix 2 of this text.

to the Foreign Affairs Committee. In a deliberate provocation of the Progressive Conservative government, the Liberal-dominated committee set up an extensive program of hearings. The government was forced to go to the people on November 20, 1988, an election for which the Senate had helped to set the date and the agenda—a clearly partisan act.

Prior to the 1984 general election, it appeared that the Senate was developing a new role in the legislative process—that of a supplier of ministers. Ministers in the Senate ensured regional and linguistic balance in the cabinet to parties that were denied House of Commons representation from major regions of the country. In 1979, Prime Minister Clark, with only two Progressive Conservative MPs elected in Québec, recruited three ministers from the Senate to bolster francophone representation in his cabinet. Similarly, in 1980, with no Liberal MPs from the three Western provinces, Prime Minister Trudeau included three Western senators in his government. Although opposition MPs criticized the appointments on the grounds that these ministers held no popular mandate, they did provide the Senate with an enhanced opportunity to oversee the work of government and to participate more fully in legislative–executive relations. In the 34th Parliament, with a majority of Conservative MPs elected from all parts of the country, Prime Minister Mulroney had little need of senators to build his cabinet. However, Senator Lowell Murray played an important role in the PC cabinet, as did Senator Joyce Fairbairn in Jean Chrétien's first Liberal cabinet during the 35th Parliament and Alasdair Graham in the 36th Parliament.[45] Prime Minister Harper appointed Michael Fortier from Québec to the Senate so he could use him as a cabinet member and as his Québec lieutenant.

Senate: Symbolism or Power?

Like the House of Commons, the Senate continues to be the subject of ongoing debate on parliamentary reform. As Henri Bourassa claimed half a century ago, such debate is something that "comes periodically like other forms of epidemics and current fevers."[46] However, in the last two decades, a qualitative shift in the motivation for reform has occurred. With reference again to the central concepts of this chapter, it might be said that the objectives have changed from altering somewhat the symbolism of the Senate to radically restructuring its power in the Constitution. In the past, demands for restrictions on the power of the upper house came, not surprisingly, from governments confronted by a "hostile" Senate. Mackenzie King in 1927, John Diefenbaker in 1962 and Brian Mulroney in 1988 sought—or threatened—Senate reform after an opposition majority in the second chamber had blocked government legislation. It is also unsurprising that proposals designed to enhance the effective functioning of the upper house have often come from within the Senate itself.

Some critics of the role of the Senate have not contented themselves with proposing minor reforms or even reduced powers. The Progressive Party of the 1920s, the CCF and its descendant, the NDP, have all advocated nothing less than abolition of the second chamber, arguing that an unelected body has no place in the legislative process of a democratic society. But total abolition of the upper house is not only constitutionally difficult; it is also politically impractical. When Canada's Constitution was patriated in 1982, the Senate's powers were left virtually intact with one important exception: the Senate, acting alone, can now block legislation on Senate reform for only 180 days, after which a constitutional amendment regarding the Senate can be made without its approval.

45. For a comparison of recent comments on the House, see Jennifer Smith, "The Canadian House of Commons at the Millennium," *Canadian Public Administration, 42*, 4 (December 1999), pp. 398–421; and Jonathan Malloy, "The House of Commons Under the Chrétien Government," in *How Ottawa Spends: 2003–2004* (Don Mills, ON: Oxford University Press, 2003), pp.59–71.

46. *House of Commons Debates*, 1926, p. 648.

Historically, demands for Senate abolition and attempts at reforming the upper house have sprung from dissatisfaction with the role and powers of the Senate as the second chamber in the parliamentary system. More recent proposals—from the draft for a new Canadian Constitution through the various constitutional discussions of the late 1970s, the Alberta success in "electing" a senator in 1989, to the provisions in the Meech Lake and Charlottetown Accords—were predicated upon the assumption that the upper house could be reshaped into an institution designed to correct perceived deficiencies elsewhere in the political system. As federal–provincial and regional tensions became more acute, reform of the Senate was viewed as a panacea for all manner of perceived ills afflicting Canadian society.

The many reform designs produced a variety of schemes for a more equitable geographical distribution of seats in the upper house, usually to the potential benefit of Western Canada.[47] They ranged from allowing some provincial input into the existing appointment system,[48] to joint selection by the federal Parliament and the provincial legislatures in a proposed "House of the Federation," to having an upper house consisting of delegates chosen by and representing provincial governments in a so-called "House of the Provinces" modelled after the German *Bundesrat* (upper house). The *Bundesrat* model, first discussed by academics in the 1960s, was subsequently endorsed by some provincial governments and other public bodies.

The January 1984 report of the Special Joint Committee on Senate Reform recommended that senators be directly elected by the citizens of Canada in order to give the Senate legitimacy.[49] It also proposed amendments to the traditional powers of the Senate. In particular, it suggested that the present absolute veto be replaced by a suspensory veto of up to 120 days, so that legislation passed by the House of Commons could be delayed but not rejected outright. The report argued that, while this may represent a diminution of the formal powers of the upper house, senators might be willing to exercise lesser powers in exchange for playing a more effective role in the legislative process.

In the 1990s, a Western initiative for a new "Triple-E" Senate became prominent among the reform proposals. The desire for a Senate that would be *elected*, *effective* and *equal* for all provinces received the support of the Western provinces. They favoured the idea of an equal number of senators from each province, regardless of its size or population. In the early deliberations, larger provinces tended to support the idea of a "Double-E" Senate, one that would be *elected* and *effective* in its functioning but whose membership would be based on some principle of representation by population.

CLOSE-UP ON Institutions

FAIRNESS OR SCANDAL IN THE SENATE?

In early 1998, Senator Andrew Thompson became the first member of the upper house to be suspended from his duties. Senator Thompson had missed almost all Senate meetings for several years, maintaining that he was very ill and had to stay in Mexico for medical reasons. In the wake of media disclosures that brought negative publicity about the upper house, the Senate formally required Thompson to explain his absences. When he failed to do so, the Senate found Thompson in contempt. It suspended him even though he had never violated any senatorial rules or those of the Constitution. He had not, as alleged, missed two consecutive sessions of Parliament and he had always filed medical certificates in his absences.

Was the Senate justified in suspending the senator when he had not "technically" broken any law or rule?

---

47. See Canada West Foundation, *Regional Representation: The Canadian Partnership* (Calgary: Canada West Foundation, 1981).

48. The 1969 White Paper and the 1972 Special Committee Report proposed that the provinces would submit short-lists of nominees from which the prime minister would choose one-half of the future appointees.

49. Special Joint Committee of the Senate and of the House of Commons on Senate Reform, Report (Ottawa: Queen's Printer, 1984). For the detailed views of one of the authors on Senate reform, see Robert J. Jackson, "Remarks to the Special Joint Committee of the Senate and of the House of Commons on Senate Reform," June 23, 1983.

During the 1987 impasse over constitutional reform, Prime Minister Mulroney made a political commitment that until there was a comprehensive constitutional change concerning the Senate, he would nominate senators only from lists supplied to him from provincial governments. This commitment was given in order to obtain a consensus over the Meech Lake Accord. The practice had no constitutional authority, however, and quickly evaporated after Meech died. Stan Waters from Alberta was the only *elected* senator to be appointed under these rules. In 2007, Prime Minister Harper appointed Bert Brown as senator from Alberta using the same logic.

In 1992, federal and provincial leaders and their assemblies agreed upon the constitutional package known as the Charlottetown Accord. It proposed a modified Triple-E Senate. Under the Charlottetown Accord, there would have been 62 senators—6 from each province and 1 from each territory. Except in Québec, where the National Assembly would have appointed them, senators would have been elected directly by the people. The details of this proposal and the story of its defeat in the October 1992 referendum are discussed in Chapter 5. Suffice it to say that the defeat of the Charlottetown Accord left Canada with the same method of appointing senators and the same senatorial powers it had before the accord.

And so the debate continues.[50] While the internal organization and procedures of the Senate have evolved over the last three decades, and one minor adjustment has been made to Senate tenure, the objectives of Senate reform have changed, perhaps rendering the task more difficult. However, as long as federal–provincial wrangling over the Constitution continues, and until an accepted means of amendment can be found, the Senate will maintain its role as a usually cooperative, sometimes cantankerous, but invariably dignified part of the legislative process.

Senate Reform Proposals in the 39th Parliament

Early in its mandate, the Harper minority government announced that it was "pursuing comprehensive Senate reform" and that "pending the pursuit of a constitutional amendment under subsection 38(1) of the *Constitution Act, 1982* for direct election to the Senate" it wanted to create a method to ascertain the preferences of electors on appointments to the Senate and to reduce the tenure of senators. In other words, frustration with the rigidity of the Constitution led the Conservative government to propose Bill C43, which never got past first reading in the House of Commons and Bill S4, which was held up in a Senate committee.

Bill C43 has had no significant debate in Parliament. In essence, the bill would allow the electors of each province to be consulted with respect to their preferences for the appointment of senators. At the time of a general election, the government would be able to order a consultation with the public in relation to the appointment of senators by the prime minister. The bill also specifies the mechanism (chief electoral officer) and method of voting and counting of votes (preferential system which takes into account first and subsequent preferences) of these public consultations.

The second of these bills would limit the tenure of new senators to eight years. There is some dispute among scholars over the constitutionality of this proposed legislation, but we agree with the majority of members of the Special Senate Committee on Senate Reform that Parliament can "proceed to amend the *Constitution Act, 1867*, acting under the authority of section 44 of the *Constitution Act, 1982*, without resorting to the complex amending formula in section 38(1) of the Act." Presumably, the prime minister may consult or take advice from whomever he wishes before making an appointment to the Senate. He already does consult widely. And he may also choose *not* to consult anyone.

---

50. See Robert J. Jackson, "Reforming an Unreformed and Unreformable Senate," remarks to the Senate and staff, March 29, 1993, and published by the Senate.

The Constitution says only that the governor general will summon to the Senate those named by the government, subject to minor qualifications (section 24). The constitutional issues concern whether the Supreme Court can or should have a say about this consultative process. In a 1980 judgment by the Supreme Court of Canada in the upper house reference case, the court ruled that alterations to the Senate that would affect the "fundamental features, or essential characteristics" given to the Senate as a means of ensuring regional and provincial representation in the federal legislative process could not be made by Parliament alone. But this case does not provide a good precedent, as it was bypassed by the constitutional patriation of 1982. And at any rate, Bill C43 does not affect the regional representation issue since the government would still be required to follow the traditional rule for choosing which areas of the country that the senators come from and how many come from each region.

Do these two bills meet the major objectives for reform of the Senate? On the whole, they would appear to meet the criterion of increased legitimacy, as they would increase democratic participation and accountability. Legislative effectiveness would appear to remain undiminished, but one could argue that more legitimate senators (i.e., chosen by consultation) would have more weight in the legislative process than those remaining from earlier methods of selection. As the number of senators for each province could not be adjusted, the criterion of enhancing regional and provincial influence would not be enhanced. There are arguments for re-assigning the number of senators inside the federation generally, but it would require a constitutional amendment. At a minimum, the current regional representation would not be weakened by this formula. There may be a minor issue about the actual number of years that a senator could sit, but fewer than eight is probably too short. Nine or twelve years might be a reasonable compromise.

This proposal may move the country further along the road to democratic reform. The delusion that the Senate cannot be reformed without a constitutional amendment has been broken and there is some possibility that Canada could lose its reputation as the only federal system in the world with a wholly appointed upper house with no public consultation in its selection.

It is time to reform the Senate *within* the present constitutional framework and many reform proposals are possible—from narrow procedural changes, such as having the Senate use regionalized committees to discuss legislation, to the government's wider proposal to allow public consultations before the prime minister chooses senators. The major drawback of Bill C43 is that, if it passes, it will be a piece of ordinary legislation (not "constitutionalized") and therefore could easily be amended or repealed in the future.

Critical Debate
Should There Be Parliamentary Reform?

Does Parliament need major reform? Does the House need to be made more effective in controlling the executive? Should the Senate be elected to enhance its credibility?

Point

Not only is reform needed, but a reformed House of Commons and an elected Senate are absolute necessities. They are also favoured by the vast majority of Canadians.

For MPs to be effective, party discipline needs to be reduced. Individual MPs should play a more active role in policy-making and in controlling the executive. By reducing party discipline, members would be able to pay more attention to their own views and those of their constituents. There is no need to "whip" votes that do not affect confidence in the government. There is no requirement for party discipline in committees.

Major procedural reform is also needed. By rules in the standing orders, the speaker of the House is now elected by secret ballot. Similarly, the chairs of committees should be selected by their own members. Committees should be able to determine their own priorities and have the proper resources available to fund their research and activities. Private members' business is laughable. Such bills rarely get anywhere. The procedure should be changed to allow committees to determine which bills in their jurisdiction will come to a vote.

As for the upper house, either the Triple-E Senate—equal, elected and effective—or some version of a Double-E would be preferable to what we have now. The upper house has no legitimacy and is based on nineteenth-century ideas of class and aristocracy. The prime minister approaches senatorial appointments as mere acts of patronage.

Between the two, the Triple-E Senate would be the preferable option, as it would give every province an equal number of seats. However, since a Double-E Senate might not require a constitutional amendment it might prove more achievable. As an elected body, the new Senate would have a high degree of legitimacy, act as a check on single-party government and provide increased power for the regions in the federation. The election of senators would also reduce the number of patronage appointments in Ottawa and would be a boon to Canadian democracy.

If a national election formula cannot be agreed upon, the prime minister should let it be known that he will appoint senators only when they're nominated by a premier. In 1989, Alberta held a "senatorial election" when a vacancy opened during the period in which Prime Minister Mulroney said he would appoint senators from provincial lists. A Reform Party candidate, Stan Waters, won the election and Mulroney felt duty-bound to appoint him. Alberta has held several more such elections since and created a list of "senators in waiting," including political scientist Ted Morton. Of them, only Bert Brown has made it to the Senate, and that was by a Harper appointment in 2007.

There are many models for Senate reform. Australia, the United States and Germany all have upper houses that are elected and their systems of government work better than Canada's system does to promote regional interests in their federations. Let's get on with it!

Counterpoint

Parliament does not need major reform. There is a lot of nonsense argued on this topic. Reform designs must maintain a delicate balance of power. Proposals that threaten to upset this balance are effectively doomed to fail.

Demands that Parliament be made more powerful must take into account the fact that the Canadian legislative apparatus performs different roles. In the United States, members of Congress are perceived to be more influential because they are relatively independent of party ties, but Congress does not have the same importance in sustaining the political executive in office and legitimizing its policies. Hence, any attempt to reduce the level of discipline in the Canadian House of Commons must be accompanied by a careful reconsideration of the concept of responsible government, which is based on the assumption of cohesive party behaviour.

Similarly, the US Congress is perceived to be influential in part because much of its work is carried out by powerful Senate and House committees. The Canadian House of Commons could grant increased powers and delegate heavier workloads to committees, but only at the ris' reducing the current importance of plenary sessions to the House both as a forum for debate a as a place where the business of government and opposition is *seen* to be done.

Party discipline is not something that can be determined from the outside. If members want to be free of their party whips, they can be. Nothing compels them to accept the views of their leaders or whips. They *choose* to obey. And it is better that they do so, because it is preferable to have them follow the dictates of their parties than to follow the whims or pressures of outside interests, such as lobbyists.

As for the procedures of the House, some tinkering is possible but it will not really have much effect on strengthening the role of backbenchers. The fact is, we have a responsible cabinet system of government with a strong prime minister, and that is the kind of leadership Canadians want and need.

The same delicate balance between power and symbolism must also be maintained in attempts to reform the upper house. Admittedly, the Senate as currently constituted possesses more formal power than legitimacy in the eyes of most Canadians. But many proposed reform designs would tilt the balance too far the other way.

Some supporters of Triple-E point to the example of the United States to illustrate what a good idea it is. But the Canadian and US political systems are very different, and no single feature transferred from one to the other will work the same way in its new surroundings. In particular, the US system includes a strong president whose powers can be used to overcome the divisions caused by a deadlock between the House and Senate. This is simply not the case in Canada. We do not have an elected president to promote unity for the country and effectiveness for government. Deadlock and delay would paralyze government in this country if Senate powers were equal to those of the House. How could a do-nothing government solve regional alienation? Moreover, there is no reliable evidence that the US political system delivers peace, order or good government any better than the Canadian system already does.

Other Triple-E supporters argue that Australia may be an even better model than the United States for Canada to follow, because it has a relatively similar system of government. This is true. But even here one should be extremely cautious. The reality is that the Australian Triple-E Senate has done little to ameliorate regional tensions and has sometimes exacerbated them. Even with reform, Australian party politics still rules the day, and party discipline in the upper chamber ensures that senators only rarely vote against measures supported by their own party in the lower chamber. In effect, this means that Australian senators are *not* more effective advocates for the regions they represent than are the members of the lower house.

In Canada, citizens know who to credit or blame for different policies and outcomes, and ideally can support the incumbent party or choose among other competing visions or platforms at election time. If the proposed elected Canadian Senate blocked legislation regularly, what would happen to the idea of responsible government? How could the government be held responsible to the people when the proposals that the House initiates are ultimately turned down by the Senate? Clearly, the two concepts of responsible government and regional representation are in irremediable conflict. If we decide that regional representation should dominate, then we should jettison responsible government, separate the executive and legislative branches, adopt the US congressional system and elect a president. The problem for the Senate is simple: if it does little, it is accused of being a "rubber stamp"; but if it acts decisively, it is reprimanded for blocking "the will of the people." Calls for Senate reform have been made since as far back as 1893. It is time to reform the Senate *within* the current constitutional framework.

Discussion Questions

1. Which side of the Critical Debate do you agree with? Are you for an elected Senate? What can you add to the discussion?
2. What is the value of Parliament? Of mechanisms such as Question Period in the House?
3. Is the procedure of passing a bill into law too cumbersome and time-consuming? What measures do government and opposition parties use to speed up or delay passage of bills?
4. Is strict party discipline a necessary part of the Canadian parliamentary system?
5. Should the Senate be abolished or reformed? Explain. Given Canada's procedures for constitutional amendment, do you think constitutional change is likely to be achieved? Do the two recent legislative proposals of Stephen Harper's Conservative government solve the problem?

Visit our new Companion Website at **www.pearsoned.ca/jackson**, where you can use the interactive Study Guide and link to additional resources on topics discussed in the text.

Selected Bibliography

Brooks, Stephen. *Canadian Democracy.* Toronto: McClelland & Stewart, 1992.

Docherty, David C. *Legislatures.* Vancouver: UBC Press, 2004.

Eagles, Munroe, et al. *The Almanac of Canadian Politics.* Peterborough, ON: Broadview Press, 1991.

Fleming, Robert. *Canadian Legislatures 1992.* Agincourt, ON: Global Press, 1992.

Franks, C.E.S. *The Parliament of Canada.* Toronto: University of Toronto Press, 1987.

Fraser, John A. *The House of Commons at Work.* Montréal: Les Editions de la Chenaliere, 1993.

House of Commons. *Précis of Procedure.* Ottawa: House of Commons, revised periodically.

————————. *Standing Orders of the House of Commons.* Revised periodically.

Jackson, Robert J., and Michael M. Atkinson. *The Canadian Legislative System,* 2nd ed. Toronto: Macmillan, 1980.

Joyal, Serge, ed. *Protecting Canadian Democracy: The Senate You Never Knew.* Montréal and Kingston: McGill-Queen's University Press, 2003.

Lijphart, A., ed. *Parliamentary versus Presidential Government.* Oxford, UK: Oxford University Press, 1992.

Mancuso, Maureen, et al. *A Question of Ethics: Canadians Speak Out.* Toronto: Oxford University Press, 1998.

Seidle, F. Leslie, ed. *Rethinking Government: Reform or Reinvention?* Ottawa: Renouf, 1993.

Smith, David E. *The Canadian Senate in Bicameral Perspective.* Toronto: University of Toronto Press, 2003.

————————. *The People's House of Commons: Theories of Democracy in Contention.* Toronto: University of Toronto Press, 2007.

Sproule-Jones, Mark. *Governments at Work.* Toronto: University of Toronto Press, 1993.

Weaver, R. Kent, and Bert A. Rockman, eds. *Do Institutions Matter: Government Capabilities in the United States and Abroad.* Washington, DC: The Brookings Institution, 1993.

White, Randall. *Voice of Region: The Long Journey to Senate Reform in Canada.* Toronto: Dundurn Press, 1990.

Chapter 10

Public Administration and Democracy

Public Servants, Budgets and Accountability

In Canada, as in other democratic societies, a distinction is made between transient politicians and the permanent administrators who carry out the goals and purposes of their political masters. Constitutionally, the elected executive of the federal government is responsible for formulating policies. The administrative process of implementing those policies is entrusted to permanent state officials employed by the departments, agencies and public corporations that constitute the federal bureaucracy.

In the modern state, however, the traditional dichotomy of *politics* and *administration* is not as clear as it once appeared. First, the vastly expanded scope and complexity of contemporary public policy have rendered politicians increasingly dependent upon permanent administrators for information, advice and execution of government policy. Furthermore, as we noted in Chapter 9, Parliament has delegated to the bureaucracy substantial decision-making autonomy in many areas of technical policy-making in the fields of regulation and administrative procedure. Fears have consequently been expressed about this increasingly "political" role of the bureaucracy and a perceived lack of bureaucratic accountability in many areas of government policy-making.

At the same time, expansion of the responsibilities and activities of the Canadian government has effected a commensurate growth in the size and scope of public administration. The sheer size and complexity of the bureaucratic leviathan give cause for concern. Its administrative secrecy, the apparent impenetrability of its processes and its lack of open accountability have been cited as threats to responsible, democratic government.

The Critical Debate for this chapter concerns controversial viewpoints on bureaucratic power. Does the Canadian public service have too much power? Are major reforms necessary and possible?

What Is Bureaucracy?

For centuries, political rulers have relied on permanent officials to carry out the routine tasks of administering government policies. From tax collectors and magistrates of ancient times to modern government departments, public administration is as old and ubiquitous as government itself. *Bureaucracy*, on the other hand, is a relatively new and more limited phenomenon. The term originated as a satirical combination of the French *bureau* ("desk") and the Greek *kratein* ("to rule"), on the analogy of *democracy* and *aristocracy*. In popular parlance, it has come to signify depersonalization, inefficiency and inflexibility. But, while anyone who has encountered bureaucratic "red tape" may consider such characterizations to be appropriate, these organizations are central to the effective management of modern life.

Similarly, bureaucrats, who carry out the functions of bureaucracies, are regularly characterized as overpaid, underworked, inefficient and self-serving. Witness this quip by the honourable member from Kicking Horse Pass (alias Dave Broadfoot, formerly of the Royal Canadian Air Farce):

Q: How many civil servants does it take to screw in a lightbulb?
A: One, but he's been promoted three levels by the time it's all screwed up.[1]

Yet, Canadians turn to public servants to solve society's toughest problems. Politicians routinely run for office on promises of reducing bureaucracy, then discover that they cannot do without its officials.

The Concept of Bureaucracy

The term **bureaucracy** may be applied to complex organizational forms in a variety of contexts—business corporations, churches and political structures, such as party organizations, among others. But the term is most clearly and often identified in people's minds with the administrative machinery of government. The size of contemporary states and the innumerable governmental responsibilities entailed in the management of modern societies necessitate complex structures that can *routinize* the administrative decision-making process.

The starting point for most studies of bureaucracy is the *ideal-typical* bureaucratic organization formalized by the German social scientist Max Weber and characterized by

- the specialization of official duties;
- the hierarchical organization of authority;
- operations governed by a consistent application of abstract rules to particular cases;
- impersonal detachment toward subordinates and clients;
- employment based on merit and protection from arbitrary dismissal; and
- maximization of technical and organizational efficiency.[2]

Many characteristics of bureaucracy developed as a consequence of the emergence of democratic forms of government. As the idea of alternation of power between competing parties became accepted under the doctrines of parliamentary democracy and representative government, it became necessary to separate the bureaucracy from the political executive. The bureaucracy thus was enabled to maximize rational administration free from political concerns, and individual public servants were protected from arbitrary dismissal on political grounds as long as they maintained partisan neutrality.

The development of liberal democracy also saw demands for the substitution of *merit* for patronage as the primary method of recruitment to government service and promotion within it. Appointments to administrative office were once made on the basis of family and old-school networks, or as a reward for political services rendered. Democratization of the public service ended that practice and brought a merit system involving open competition.

Finally, certain characteristics of bureaucracy identified by Weber enhance administrative efficiency by routinizing the decision-making process. They are also democratic inasmuch as they protect individuals from arbitrary decisions and ensure that all clients are treated equally. Where there may once have been one law for the rich and another for the poor, operations of the ideal-type bureaucracy apply the same rules to all citizens.

Thus, a neutral, professional public service based on the organizational principles of modern bureaucracy has emerged alongside, and partly as a consequence of, the development of liberal democracy. Yet, there is a fundamental contradiction in the coexistence of bureaucracy and democracy in a society such as Canada.

---

1. From the Royal Canadian Air Farce recording, *Air Farce Live* (CBC Enterprises, 1983).
2. See Max Weber, *The Theory of Social and Economic Organization*, ed. and trans. by A.M. Henderson and Talcott Parsons (Glencoe: Free Press, 1947).

Bureaucracy versus Democracy

Bureaucratic and democratic structures are, in part, founded on different organizing principles: bureaucracy is based primarily on a clearly defined hierarchy of authority established in the interests of efficiency; democracy is based on the principle of fundamental political equality that permits majority rule while respecting minority rights and freedom of dissent. But democratic values also demand that social goals be implemented by the most effective means available so that the "will of the majority" may prevail. Effective methods are more likely to be governed by the dictates of bureaucracy than by those of democracy. Since bureaucratic efficiency is aided by the routinization of decision-making, the quest for effective implementation may result in uniform standards that reflect the will of the majority but neglect minority interest. In a country such as Canada, where minority ethnic, linguistic and regional interests are particularly sensitive, the result may be the exacerbation of potential conflicts and a loss of legitimacy for both the bureaucracy and the entire policy-making process.

This problem has become particularly acute in the modern era, since many areas of government policy are now so complex that the means of implementing public policies are often as important to their outcomes as the choice of goals. Therefore, it is becoming increasingly difficult to maintain the distinction between administrative and political processes.

We have pointed out that, in Canada, ultimate decision-making power in many fields resides constitutionally with the federal government; the bureaucracy is designated as the neutral, professional administrator of policy. But in practice it is difficult to separate the political and administrative dimensions of government action. While not political per se, the bureaucracy does influence the actual formation of public policy in a number of ways.

First, cabinet ministers who are formally responsible for defining public policies only rarely enjoy sufficient tenure to acquire a high degree of expertise in the affairs of their respective ministries. Not only does government occasionally change hands at general elections, but also there are periodic cabinet shuffles in which ministers are moved from one department to another and hence from one policy area to another. It takes time for a minister to come to grips with a new role every time he is shifted. The average departmental tenure of Canadian cabinet ministers is very short, and a federal minister typically must spend a good chunk of that time learning the workings of the department before he can initiate any new policies.

In contrast, the permanence of public servants allows them to develop expertise and practical knowledge on which politicians can draw when formulating policies. Consequently, if "knowledge is power," as Max Weber maintained, then the bureaucracy in a complex, technical society may have great political power. It may screen the data furnished to its political masters, and such filtered information may be fundamental to the direction of government policy.

The relative permanence and access to information enjoyed by bureaucrats may influence the policy process in a number of other ways as well. Bureaucratic tenure permits public servants to develop a more long-term view of policy formulation than is possible for most politicians who must be more responsive to short-term shifts in public opinion. Also, administrative personnel who have close links to "client" interest groups may be in a better position than politicians to identify specific public needs.

Furthermore, the bureaucracy may constitute an *interest group* in its own right.[3] Policy proposals generated within the bureaucracy may influence the government's choice among competing alternatives. All government departments contain a policy analysis unit that monitors and evaluates the impact of ongoing policies. Here again, bureaucrats may be in a better position than politicians

---

3. See the discussion in Chapter 14 on public policy theory.

to recommend the fine-tuning of, or wholesale changes to, existing policies. Finally, even after the government has made a political choice, a degree of discretion must be left to public servants with regard to the implementation of the policy.

> *Empires fall, ministries pass away but bureaux remain.*
>
> *Duc d'Audiffret-Pasquier*

In short, the bureaucracy has numerous opportunities to influence the policy-making process in Canada. But why should the bureaucracy be viewed as a threat to democracy? Critics make several arguments.

First, they allege that the bureaucracy is unrepresentative of the general public and therefore is insensitive to the requirements of citizens. Minority groups and interests that are not adequately represented within the bureaucracy may be neglected.

A second argument is that the bureaucracy is steered by a narrow and cohesive elite that seeks to impose its own vision on society. This argument is sometimes linked to *elite* or *class* theories of politics, which posit that the elitist family and educational backgrounds of bureaucrats render them sympathetic to the interests of friends, relatives and former business colleagues and the upper class.

Third, the growth of the state (the rise in public expenditures and tax increases) is attributed to the expansionary tendencies of public administrators and the empire-building of individual bureaucrats. Supporters of this argument aver that new government programs serve the interests of administrators rather than those of the general public. Furthermore, they demand that measures be initiated to increase transparency, accountability and bureaucratic efficiency.

Fourth, arguments about the lack of financial accountability are often extended to more general criticisms of the lack of popular, parliamentary or governmental control over the bureaucracy. Politicians may be held accountable by the ballot box: if they have not adequately served the needs of the public, then they may be removed at the next election. However, there are no such mechanisms by which permanent public servants may be held accountable.

In later sections of this chapter, we examine various aspects of the bureaucracy and the administrative process in Canada in relation to these arguments. But first, it should be noted that most critics of bureaucracy tend to view it as an undifferentiated, monolithic monster. Nothing could be further from the truth. The Canadian administrative apparatus is a complex hierarchy of different types of government departments, public corporations, agencies and other bodies that serve a wide range of functions. The next section provides a brief guide to the major structures of the administrative apparatus and their respective roles and responsibilities.

Organization of the Federal Bureaucracy

The federal bureaucracy is organized from a mass of workers at its base up to a tiny elite at its pinnacle. The two formal structures of government with which Canadians most frequently come into direct contact are government departments and Crown corporations (or public enterprises). Few citizens escape encounters—some pleasant, some less so—with institutions such as the Department of National Revenue, which collects taxes and customs duties. Other employees of the bureaucracy may embarrass us by searching our luggage for contraband or bombs at the airport. Most Canadians deal with Crown corporations every day: for example, by watching CBC television or by spending money printed by the Royal Canadian Mint.[4]

4. Departmental and other government institutions are constantly changing their structures and names. For the latest nomenclature, see www.psagency-agencefc.gc.ca.

But departmental officials and public enterprises that interact directly with the public are merely the most visible tip of the administrative iceberg. Three basic organizational forms are found in the Canadian federal bureaucracy: departments, public agencies such as Crown corporations and advisory bodies. Government departments are largely responsible for the administration of programs serving the public (e.g., Human Resources) or for providing services to the government itself (e.g., Public Works and Government Services). Crown corporations include public enterprises (e.g., VIA Rail Canada) and regulatory commissions (e.g., the Atomic Energy Control Board). Advisory bodies consist of royal commissions, government and departmental task forces, and a range of advisory councils that collectively provide alternative sources of research and advice for the political executive.

Because of their special role in the policy-making process, and their often-exaggerated elite status, it is possible to classify **central agencies** (introduced in Chapter 8) as a fourth type of bureaucratic organization. With the exception of the Prime Minister's Office (PMO), these agencies are staffed almost exclusively by career public servants. They are all formally headed by a cabinet minister and in all structural and legal respects take the departmental form of organization.

Federal Government Departments

Government departments are administrative units of a government, each of which is headed by a cabinet minister. They are largely responsible for the administration of a range of programs serving the public. While the minister is politically responsible for the activities of the department and for formulating general policy, the administrative and managerial head of each department or ministry is the **deputy minister** (**DM**)—its senior public servant. Departments, on the whole, obtain their staff from the Public Service Commission (although today, much of this authority is delegated to departmental heads) and their funding through the standard appropriation acts of Parliament.

The deputy minister is at the apex of a pyramidal structure of authority and organizational agencies. Two or more **assistant deputy ministers** (**ADM**s), heading branches or bureaus, report directly to the DM. Below the ADMs are directorates or branches, each headed by a director-general or director. These directorates are in turn composed of divisions, headed by directors or divisional chiefs; the divisions are further broken down into sections, offices and units. The exact titles of departmental sub-units and their respective senior officials vary from department to department.

The number of senior officials and the range of sub-units and employees for which they are responsible differ according to the type of department. *Line departments* or *operational departments* generally consist of a large number of sub-units and employ a large staff to deal with the general public. Agriculture and Agri-Food, and Fisheries and Oceans, for instance, each employ several thousand people across the country. *Administrative-coordinative departments,* such as the Department of National Revenue, also tend to be large, complex structures. However, *policy-coordinative departments,* such as Justice, Foreign Affairs and International Trade, tend to be much smaller—in part because they have few, if any, program- or service-delivery functions.

Each new government may change the organization of departments, but such changes require legislation and may be slow to develop. After the September 11, 2001 (9/11) terrorist attacks in the United States, a new Department of Public Safety and Emergency Preparedness was created, which gave the new minister wider control than the former solicitor general had possessed. The department, now called Public Safety Canada, currently includes the RCMP, the Canadian Security Intelligence Service (CSIS), Corrections, Parole Board and Canadian Borders Services. The Department of Foreign Affairs and International Trade (DFAIT) was split into two departments—Foreign Affairs (FAC) and International Trade (ITCan) and then recombined again (see Table 10.1).

TABLE 10.1 **Departmental and Agency Structure of the Public Service, 2008**

Departments
Agriculture and Agri-Food
Canadian Heritage
Citizenship and Immigration
Environment
Fisheries and Oceans
Foreign Affairs and International Trade
Health
Human Resources and Social Development
Indian Affairs and Northern Development
Industry
Justice
National Defence
National Revenue
Natural Resources
Public Safety
Public Works and Government Services
Transport
Veterans Affairs
Western Economic Diversification
Central Agencies
Finance
Privy Council Office
Treasury Board Secretariat

Government Agencies

The second basic organizational form in the federal bureaucracy is the agency. **Agencies** include a wide variety of non-departmental organizations, including Crown corporations, regulatory agencies, administrative tribunals and some advisory bodies (discussed separately). The rationale for distinguishing advisory bodies from agencies is that advisory bodies are primarily involved in formulating policy, while agencies are charged directly with attaining government policy objectives—through administration, public ownership, regulation of the private sector and so on.

Depending upon the definition employed, there are approximately four hundred federal agencies. A number of characteristics distinguish agencies from government departments. For example, agencies are not directly responsible to a minister but usually report to Parliament through a designated minister. The degree of supervision and accountability of agencies varies, but is much less than is the case with departments. The Public Service Commission, Treasury Board and departments set the rules and recruit the personnel of departments, but not of agencies. Departments have deputy ministers as administrative heads, while agencies vary widely in the nature of their management. They usually have boards of directors, led by chairs, commissioners or directors.

Crown Corporations

A **Crown corporation** is a semi-autonomous government agency organized in the corporate form to perform a task or group of related tasks in the national interest. The *Financial Administration Act* (FAA) sets out the financial relationship between different types of Crown corporations and the federal government. It classifies Crown corporations according to their main functions and degree of financial autonomy.

The variety of Crown corporations is immense. The Bank of Canada regulates the money supply, the Royal Canadian Mint prints money, and the Canada Mortgage and Housing Corporation (CMHC) guarantees housing loans. The best-known transportation Crown corporation is VIA Rail. Atomic Energy of Canada, Business Development Bank, Export Development, Farm Credit and the Federal Development Investment Corporation are among those that foster economic development. Canada Post and the Canadian Broadcasting Corporation aid national integration.

In recent years, the government has privatized many Crown corporations. Corporations that can operate in a competitive business environment have been the first to go. Among those no longer with the government are the well-known Air Canada, Canada Ports Corporation, El Dorado Nuclear, Northern Transportation Company, Polymer Corporation, Teleglobe Canada and Petro-Canada (see Chapter 14).

Regulatory Agencies

Among other functions, regulatory agencies may be required by government to influence private or corporate behaviour with respect to prices and tariffs, supply, market entry and conditions of service, product content, and methods of production. Furthermore, some agencies have developed quasi-legislative powers that permit them to formulate general rules applicable to all cases under consideration; an example is the Canadian-content regulations applied by the Canadian Radio-television and Telecommunications Commission (CRTC). Most agencies also enjoy investigative powers, allowing them to undertake research and pursue inquiries within their field of competence.

Independent regulatory agencies receive their major powers from enabling legislation that also sets out the agency's objectives. Commission members are appointed by the governor-in-council (or cabinet), usually for terms of five to ten years. On the whole, the chair and members of the commission are patronage appointments. Most agencies are subject to ministerial directives, but ministers usually are unwilling to infringe upon the traditional arm's-length relationship. Regulatory bodies are required to submit their budgets to the Treasury Board for review (and usually, also, to the auditor general), and present annual reports, through the responsible minister, to Parliament.

A list of important regulatory agencies includes the Immigration and Appeal Board, the Canadian Labour Relations Board, the CRTC, the National Parole Board and many others.

Reproduced by permission, John Beutel, cartoonist for Crown Corp/Private Enterprise.

Advisory Bodies

Federal departments and Crown agencies are designed to deal primarily with implementing and administering government policies. **Advisory bodies**, on the other hand, are federal organizations whose activities are closely related to the formulation of public policies. They include royal commissions, government and departmental task forces and advisory councils.

Royal commissions and task forces are widely employed by the executive as sources of public policy advice. There have been about two hundred of them since Confederation. They are generally set up by the government to investigate an area of critical public concern and to recommend a suitable course of action. Typical issues have included the economy (the Macdonald Royal Commission on the Economic Union and Development Prospects for Canada), cultural policy (the Applebaum-Hébert Federal Cultural Policy Review Committee), Native peoples (the Royal Commission on Aboriginal Issues) and human reproduction (the Royal Commission on Reproductive Technologies). Perhaps the most discussed report in recent years was the 2002 Commission on the Future of Health Care in Canada, headed by Roy Romanow. Its report, entitled *Building on Value*, is discussed in Chapter 6. More politically contentious have been the commissions of inquiry into the Québec sponsorship scandal (the Gomery Commission) and Air India Flight 182.

Such bodies attempt to facilitate wide public understanding of serious national problems and at the same time to provide an informed basis for future policy-making by the government. They generally solicit outside views through public hearings, to which individuals, groups and organizations submit briefs. They also initiate programs of directed and commissioned research. Most of the time, they have no direct policy impact, although they contribute to the debate about issues. Government inquiries can be very expensive.

Semi-Independent Agencies

In addition to privatization, governments have tried to introduce other "business efficiency" practices into the system. One organizational device has been to create semi-independent agencies *inside* the public service. Two examples suffice to explain this organizational form. First, listed under departmental and ministerial authority, but given considerable independence, are operational institutions such as the RCMP, the Canadian Security Intelligence Service (CSIS), Statistics Canada, the Public Service Commission, Elections Canada and the National Archives.

Second, special operating agencies (SOAs) have also been set up to promote arm's-length relationships between departments and special units *inside* the departments. These SOAs are accountable to the department's deputy minister, but because they operate on a cost-recovery basis, they function independently and almost on a commercial basis. The best-known example is the Passport Office, part of the Department of Foreign Affairs and International Trade, which receives its funds by charging the public directly for passports and visas.

Principles and Linkages: Ministers and Mandarins

The chief organizing principle of the public service is **departmentalization**, whereby, at least in theory, every major administrative function in the federal government is allocated to a single department. Two reasons may be cited for a clear apportionment of duties among government departments or agencies: it avoids financial waste and administrative confusion; and it helps to clarify lines of accountability for administrative actions, and thus strengthens another principle of bureaucratic organization in Canada—ministerial responsibility and accountability.

The allocation of duties to government departments may be based on one or more of the following criteria: common purpose, clientele, territory or place, expertise and process. Thus, for example, the Department of Veterans Affairs caters to a specific clientele. So, too, in part does the Department of Indian Affairs and Northern Development, although that ministry's traditional responsibility for overseeing the administration of government in the Yukon, Northwest

Territories and Nunavut has also been based on the criterion of *place*. The Department of Public Works and Government Services is organized according to the use of common facilities—*process*—in acting as a publishing house for much of the federal government.

In many cases, however, these organizational criteria and the activities of individual departments do not correspond. Consequently, different organizational criteria force some departments to pursue internally contradictory goals. In the case of the Department of Indian Affairs and Northern Development, it was argued that the function of protecting and enhancing the interest and way of life of Native peoples in the North is irreconcilable with the objective of promoting northern resource development, and therefore the name was changed to Indian and Northern Affairs from Indian Affairs and Northern Development.

The processes of policy-making and conflict resolution within and among government departments and agencies are often referred to as *bureaucratic politics*. This term is usually associated with the work of Graham Allison, who argued that the conventional model of foreign policy decision-making, the *rational actor model*, did not adequately explain the actions of policy-makers

> ### CLOSE-UP ON
> ### Institutions
>
> #### DEPARTMENTAL NAMES REFLECT VALUES AND BIASES
>
> The names of federal departments often reflect the values and biases of the government. This is particularly evident in the department dealing with immigration. Since Confederation, it has been called
>
> Canadian Immigration and Quarantine Services—1867–92
> Immigration Branch, Department of the Interior —1892–1917
> Department of Immigration and Colonization—1917–36
> Immigration Branch, Department of Mines and Resources—1936–50
> Department of Citizenship and Immigration—1950–66
> Department of Manpower and Immigration—1966–77
> Canada Employment and Immigration Commission —1977–93
> Immigration divided between Department of Public Security and the Department of Human Resources—1993
> Department of Citizenship and Immigration —1993 to present

in the 1962 Cuban Missile Crisis. The rational-actor model suggests that government is effectively a unitary, monolithic actor, with a single set of goals or objectives, which selects from a range of alternatives the policy that best serves its perception of the national interest. Allison contended instead that the policy decisions made during the Cuban Missile Crisis might be better explained by the *bureaucratic politics model*, which assumes that government consists of a variety of individuals, groups and agencies pursuing divergent interests and policy goals and competing to have their respective values and objectives supported in the final policy outcome.[5]

Clearly, the Canadian federal bureaucracy is far from being a homogeneous, monolithic entity. The diversity of structural forms found in departments and agencies, the different philosophies of policy-making and administration that develop in each organization, the periodic conflicts that arise between agencies with regard to policy objectives, jurisdictions and modes of implementation—all suggest that the Canadian bureaucracy is highly pluralistic.

On the other hand, Ottawa is not in a state of anarchy. Inter-agency competition and bureaucratic infighting are not always destructive. Disputes between agencies or departments are constrained by parameters established by cabinet on the range of possible policy alternatives that may be considered on a particular issue. It might even be argued that bureaucratic politics has its advantages. The greater the degree of competition between agencies, the more information and alternative choices cabinet has at its disposal for making policy decisions, and the greater the extent of political control over the policy-making process.

But what control does cabinet have over the administrative process to ensure that policies, once made, are actually implemented? The second major principle of government organization in

---

5. Graham T. Allison, *Essence of Decision: Explaining the Cuban Missile Crisis* (Boston: Little, Brown, 1971).

Canada—and the primary link between the bureaucracy and cabinet, Parliament and the people—is the doctrine of **ministerial responsibility**. The prime minister appoints members of the cabinet to assume responsibility for particular ministries or portfolios and their associated departments, commissions, boards and corporations. Ministers are constitutionally responsible for all the operations of their departments. Thus, legally, it is ministers who are assigned the powers and duties held by their departments.

Departmental officials, on the other hand, are given scant attention in the law and are responsible exclusively to their ministers, not to Parliament. They are supposed to be non-partisan, objective and anonymous—shielded from the glare of public attention and from the partisan political arena of Parliament by their minister—in order to safeguard their neutrality and ensure their ability to serve faithfully whichever government is in power. In the event of a serious error in the formulation or administration of policy within a department, convention dictates that the minister, rather than officials, be held responsible to Parliament; if the minister cannot account for failures to the satisfaction of Parliament, then *convention* dictates that the minister should resign.

Experience has shown, however, that there are severe limitations to the actual realization of the doctrine of ministerial responsibility.[6] The individual responsibility of ministers for the operations of their departments is often sacrificed in favour of another principle or responsibility—the **collective responsibility** of the cabinet to Parliament. Unless political expediency dictates otherwise, as long as a minister retains the confidence and support of the prime minister, that minister is extremely unlikely to be asked to resign. Another problem stems from the fact that ministers cannot be held personally responsible for administrative matters that occurred before their current appointments. Thus, when questions are raised in the House of Commons about wrongdoings, the new minister takes refuge behind this convention, saying that the events took place prior to his appointment; furthermore, former ministers sitting in the House cannot be called to account for the activities of a department for which they are no longer the minister.

Perhaps it is reasonable that ministers not be held responsible to the point of resignation for the administrative errors of public servants. The relative impermanence of cabinet ministers and their multifunctional roles make it impossible for ministers to involve themselves extensively in the management of their departments. Ministers are expected to direct their attention to policy matters rather than to the details of departmental administration. For this reason, one observer argues, it is "unrealistic to expect a minister to accept personal responsibility for all the acts of his departmental officials. Why should a minister 'carry the can' when he has little or no knowledge of its contents?"[7]

If the minister is the link between bureaucracy and cabinet for the purposes of formal political accountability, the **deputy minister** (DM) is equally crucial to effective administration and the coordination and direction of policy implementation. Certain financial and managerial responsibilities are laid down by the *Financial Administration Act* and the *Public Service Modernization and Employment Acts*, or are delegated to the DM by the Treasury Board and the Public Service Commission. Otherwise, the DM possesses only as much power as the minister chooses to delegate. In fact, the *Interpretation Act* indicates that ministers may delegate any and all of their powers under the law to their deputies, except for the power to make regulations and, of course, their parliamentary duties. Exactly how much a minister chooses to delegate is a personal decision.

---

6. Sharon Sutherland, "Responsible Government and Ministerial Responsibility," *CJPS*, vol. 24, no. 1 (March 1991), pp. 91–120, and "The Al-Mashat Affair: Administrative Responsibility in Parliamentary Institutions," *Canadian Public Administration* (Winter 1991), pp. 573–603.

7. Kenneth Kernaghan, "Power, Parliament and Public Servants in Canada: Ministerial Responsibility Re-examined," in H.D. Clarke et al., eds., *Parliament, Policy and Representation* (Toronto: Methuen, 1980), p. 128.

The function of the deputy minister, outside the administrative responsibilities of managing the department, is to act as the minister's chief source of non-partisan advice on public policy. The problem for the DM is how to initiate policy proposals and studies without appearing to undermine the ultimate policy-making responsibility of the minister. In their policy-advisory roles, deputies must strike a delicate balance between political sensitivity and bureaucratic objectivity—especially when they are led by their experience and expertise to disagree with policies put forward by the minister. In such cases, the DM may stress privately the potential difficulties of implementing the policy.

Deputy ministers are appointed by the governor-in-council on the recommendation of the prime minister. Their office is held "during pleasure," which means that they can be dismissed or transferred at any time without assigned cause and that they are not protected by the provisions of the *Public Service Employment Act*. This insecurity of tenure naturally creates further ambiguity about the role of the deputy minister. Deputies who advise against "damn silly decisions" risk being viewed as obstacles to the government in pursuit of its partisan political objectives and, consequently, often get relieved of their positions. On the other hand, deputies who are perceived as successful in administering certain government policies may become identified with programs unpopular with the opposition parties and risk losing their jobs when the reins of government change hands.

The fragmentation of the bureaucracy into many departments and agencies in the interests of efficiency impedes policy coordination somewhat. At the same time, the principle of departmentalization underlies the doctrine of ministerial responsibility that, ideally, should enhance the democratic process by providing a line of accountability to Parliament and the people. Between the cabinet and the great mass of the bureaucracy, the deputy ministers and other senior officials play key pivotal roles. They not only advise their respective ministers on how best to serve the interests of the people and attempt to ensure the efficient management and functioning of their own departments, but they also play an important part in the coordination of policy advice and effective policy implementation throughout the bureaucracy as a whole.

The Public Service

While public administration refers to the structures and principles of organization in the administrative arm of government, the **public service** is the collective term for the personnel employed in those structures. Like other political institutions, the public service has undergone profound changes since Confederation. It has evolved from a loosely organized, patronage-based service, in which most people were recruited on the basis of political connections, to a modern, professionalized bureaucracy appointed on the principle of merit; what was once a predominantly anglophone and almost exclusively male preserve has become an equal opportunity employer that attempts to reflect Canada's ethnic and linguistic diversity and that has introduced affirmative-action programs to promote the participation of women, indigenous peoples, visible minorities and disabled persons.

The hierarchical structure fosters a chain of responsibility within the bureaucracy. Within each department, a descending order of command is evident, with each employee responsible to a superior. This chain of command, which ultimately begins with a government minister, protects against the arbitrary assumption of power by individuals within the bureaucracy. Bureaucratic "red tape" in the guise of standard forms and triplicate copies is in fact a necessary part of the process of horizontal and vertical communication among employees and departments. Given the immense number of people involved and the diversity of their duties, it is easy to appreciate why the bureaucracy's primary goal of efficiency is sometimes difficult to achieve.

Basic Principles of the Public Service

Since 1867, the federal public service has gone through many major transitions. At Confederation, appointment to the civil service was based exclusively on political patronage. The *Civil Service Act* of 1908 began to replace patronage with the merit principle. The **merit principle** is actually based on two interrelated ideas: first, that all Canadian citizens should have a fair opportunity to be hired in the public service and, second, that selection must be based *exclusively* on merit, or fitness to do the job. The Act also created the Civil Service Commission (CSC) to enforce the merit principle in the recruitment and promotion of government employees. The 1918 *Civil Service Act* extended the method of appointment by competitive examination to the entire service and re-emphasized the role of the CSC in enforcing implementation of the merit principle.

The *Civil Service Act of* 1961 gave the Treasury Board sole responsibility for pay determination and administrative organization. In 1967, two acts were passed that affected the role of the CSC and permitted it to become a more specialized staffing body. The *Public Service Staff Relations Act* created a collective-bargaining regime in the public service with the power to enter into collective agreements in the name of the government. Responsibility for classification, pay determination and most conditions of employment rested with the Treasury Board. The *Public Service Employment Act* gave the renamed Public Service Commission (PSC) ultimate responsibility for all elements of the hiring process and staff training (see Figure 10.1). Today, the PSC reports to Parliament, not to the executive, a status that permits it independence in investigating complaints and hearing appeals against the government.

According to the **merit principle**, all appointments to, and promotions within, the public service should be based on ability to do the job, in the interest of creating a qualified and efficient public service. But the role of the Public Service Commission in implementing government directives to promote participation by under-represented groups has threatened to compromise its application of the merit principle. This is not a new issue in public service staffing. Both the 1918 and the 1961 *Civil Service Acts* entrenched absolute hiring preference for war veterans. Then, following the passage of the *Official Languages Act* of 1969 (which required the provision of minority-language services in areas where numbers warranted), the designation of many public service positions as bilingual brought accusations of "reverse discrimination."

The *Public Service Employment Act* forbids discrimination in hiring or promotion on the basis of "race, national or ethnic origin, colour, religion, age, sex, marital status, disability, or conviction for an offence for which a pardon has been granted." However, certain groups have remained persistently under-represented in the public service. To address this, the PSC in 1983 introduced a service-wide affirmative-action program. Affirmative action should not automatically be equated with quota systems or reverse discrimination. Much of the affirmative-action program is oriented toward education, training and career counselling, rather than providing special treatment in hiring or promotion. The PSC insists that the affirmative-action program implemented in 1983

FIGURE 10.1 New Public Service Staffing Accountability Chain

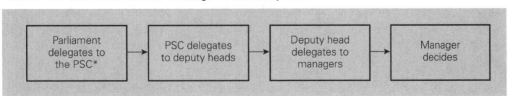

Parliament delegates to the PSC* → PSC delegates to deputy heads → Deputy head delegates to managers → Manager decides

*PSC = Public Service Commission.

does not conflict with merit, which requires that only qualified persons be appointed. The fact that the PSC justifies its programs in such terms reveals its sensitivity to potential criticisms that affirmative action might undermine the merit system.

In 1989, the government set up *Public Service 2000* in an attempt to reorganize the public service to make it more service-oriented and reduce morale problems caused by fiscal restraint. This new set of proposals to streamline public service practices was incorporated into the *Public Service Reform Act, 1992*, which constituted the first major amendments to staffing legislation in 25 years. It provided for more flexible staffing arrangements and mandated the PSC to initiate employment-equity programs while retaining the merit principle.

The reform of human resources management in the public service continued with the four pieces of legislation that constitute the *Public Service Modernization Act* (PSMA), passed in 2003. This Act, put fully in place in 2005, leaves the PSC as a guardian of the merit principle but allows much more delegation of hiring to deputy heads. In theory, these changes will increase the ability of departments and agencies to hire diversely but still keep the merit principle in place. The lead agency in human resources is the Public Service Agency. Training, language education and the new Canada School of Public Service are now administered by this agency.[8]

Profile of the Public Service

The federal government is a major employer in Canada. It employs over 400 000 people, who are spread throughout the country and who work in the public service, military, Crown corporations, agencies, enterprises and the Royal Canadian Mounted Police. An even wider conception of the public service would include workers in Parliament, the courts and political staffs. In the discussion of the characteristics of public servants that follows, we refer only to those employed under the auspices of the Public Service Commission or the narrowly defined "core" public service. In 2006, this core workforce totalled 380 700 public servants.[9]

Entrance into the public service is open and carries no restrictions on age, race, sex, religion, colour, national or ethnic origin, marital status or disability. Recruitment is carried out across Canada on the basis of merit. Qualifications are determined through an entrance exam, the results of which determine the applicant's capabilities and job placement. Historically, the Public Service Commission sponsored recruitment programs, but since the inception of the 2003 *Modernization Act*, departments have had considerably more flexibility in hiring. Since the *Public Service Reform Act*, the PSC has continued to base its employment practices on merit, but it may initiate employment-equity plans to right historical imbalances for designated groups, which include women, Aboriginals, people with disabilities and visible minorities.

Competition and appeal procedures ensure that virtually every employee can elevate his status. When a position is created or becomes vacant, it is advertised. Depending upon the job, the competition is "open" (available to candidates from both within and without the public service) or "closed" (available only to those already in the public sector). Once a suitable candidate has been selected, the appeal procedure allows complaints and criticisms against the appointment to be formally voiced and a board is convened to consider the appeal. In combination with the competition process, this provides an assurance of unbiased hiring and promotion practices.

---

8. Public Service Commission, Annual Report 2005–06 (Ottawa: PSC, 2006).

9. See *The Daily*, March 5, 2007, assessed at www.statcan.ca. Unless otherwise acknowledged, figures relating to public service employees are drawn from the annual reports of the Public Service Commission or the Treasury Board Secretariat.

To some extent, the bureaucracy is expected to be representative of the society it serves. Yet, factors such as region, religion, ethnicity, social class, education, gender and language render Canada a highly heterogeneous society, a situation that might hinder egalitarian representation. In the next section, we outline and assess the composition of the public service in order to illuminate the contemporary patterns of employment found in the bureaucracy.

Language Distribution Some commentators consider the early failure to acknowledge the French fact in Canada to be the most damning indictment of the recruitment methods of the public service. However, it is important to recognize the key role "bilingualization" has played in the public service. Prior to 1918, patronage appointments made by French-speaking cabinet ministers assured at least adequate francophone representation. But with the rationalization of the bureaucracy on the basis of merit, no procedure evolved to replace the patronage system's assurance of adequate representation based on language. The majority of the public service tended to define *merit* and *efficiency* in accordance with its own cultural and educational values; the result was that it was unfavourable to francophones.

Thus, while in 1918, 22 percent of government employees were French-speaking, by 1936, only 20 percent were,[10] and, by 1945, the figure was a mere 12 percent. In 1965, 5 percent of senior executives appointed by the Public Service Commission were French, while 16.5 percent of political appointees to the bureaucracy were francophones.

Many factors combined during these years to reduce the levels of francophone recruitment in the federal bureaucracy. The public service became less attractive to French Canadians because no provisions were made to ensure service to French Canadians who approached the government. Nor were francophones' bilingual skills included in an assessment of their qualifications. Francophones were also hindered by the merit system's examinations and interviews, which reflected the patterns of thought and cultural style of English-speaking Canada. The competitions also emphasized the technical and commercial skills taught in the English educational system, placing French Canadians, with their classical education, at a disadvantage. It is sometimes argued that it is because of this "unsuitable" education that French Canada did not produce the type of administrator who could be useful in the public service.

It was only in the 1960s, after the *Glassco Report* and the *Bilingualism and Biculturalism Report*, that there was widespread recognition of the need to increase francophone representation in the federal government. A tendency developed to "parachute" French speakers into top-level political appointments in the bureaucracy. By finally assuming responsibility for language training in the late 1960s, the Public Service Commission found itself at the centre of one of the most significant transformations ever attempted in the bureaucracy. The PSC was directed to aid the government in achieving full and equal participation of anglophones and francophones in the public service while preserving the merit principle in recruitment and promotion.

Progress is slowly being made toward this goal. The percentage of francophone employees in the public service has increased, so that now participation is more comparable to their distribution in the national population: by 2003, francophone numbers had increased to 31 percent of all public servants. However, closer examination of the distribution of anglophones and francophones within the public service shows that French-speaking Canadians are still relatively disadvantaged. Francophones are somewhat under-represented in the management category of employment, and

---

10. J. E. Hodgetts et al., *The Biography of an Institution* (Montréal: McGill-Queen's University Press, 1972), p. 473.

somewhat over-represented in the administrative support group. Thus, while there remains room for improvement, especially at higher salary levels and ranks, the federal public service has gradually become more representative of the official language composition of the Canadian population. By 2005–06, 24.5 percent of all new positions were labelled "bilingual imperative."[11]

Women and Equity-Designated Groups   If the federal government is to be congratulated for creating a public service more representative of Canada's two main language communities, it has little reason for complacency with regard to its representation of gender and equity-designated groups in Canadian society. They have long faced both institutional and attitudinal barriers to advancement, which are only slowly being broken down by more sensitive recruitment, training and affirmative-action programs. Success is still not complete.[12]

Discrimination against women in the bureaucracy was officially endorsed in varying degrees until 1967. In direct contradiction of the merit principle, anti-female prejudice was built into the very fabric of civil service legislation and personnel practice. As early as 1908, the Civil Service Commission admitted that "there are women who have as good executive ability as men, and who might, on the *mere* ground of personal qualifications, fill the higher positions in the service.[13]

In order to "protect the merit principle from itself," deputy heads were instructed to segregate occupational categories into male and female groups, with women being limited to the lowest clerical levels. Since inequality of opportunity thus became a foregone conclusion, and women were not given access to middle-level positions, the issue of equal pay for equal work could not arise. As

Reproduced with the permission of Dennis Pritchard.

11. PSC, Annual Report 2005–06, p. 52.
12. See Senate Standing Committee on Human Rights, *Employment Equity in the Federal Public Service—Not There Yet* (Ottawa, Senate, 2007).
13. Hodgetts et al., *The Biography of an Institution*, p. 485 (emphasis in original).

Kathleen Archibald points out, this occupational sex-typing of jobs was later used as "evidence" to prove that women were not capable of filling higher executive positions.[14] In the 1918 *Civil Service Act*, gender was mentioned as a "limiting" factor on an individual's qualifications, and in 1921 formal restrictions were placed on employing married women.

Over the next five decades, the concentration of women in the lower white-collar ranks provided the CSC with a cheap labour supply. During the Second World War, however, it became the patriotic duty of women to fill "male" jobs, so that while in 1938, only 17 percent of public service appointees were female, by 1943, this figure had risen to 65 percent. With the enforcement of the "veterans' preference" in 1946, the proportion of female employees was halved, and restrictions were once again placed on employing married women.

In 1955, when one-third of all Canadian working women were married, the CSC finally lifted restrictions on their appointment. The 1950s also witnessed the appointment of the first female civil service commissioner, Ruth Addison. But it was only with the promulgation of the 1967 *Public Service Employment Act* that *sex* was added to *race, national origin, colour* and *creed* as grounds upon which an individual could not be discriminated against.

The federal administration's position on sex discrimination may be altered legally, but the actual situation of women in the bureaucracy is little improved. While women have constituted an increasingly larger percentage of public servants over time, they are still under-represented in the highest-paid groups in the public service. Effective segregation by occupational category still occurs. As of 2006, women constituted 54 percent of all public servants. Nevertheless, a very large majority of the administrative support category recruitments are still women, and they tend to be concentrated in traditional job ghettos within administrative support, clerks jobs, secretarial work, stenography and typing. In the executive group category, on the other hand, while their numbers have certainly increased, women are still seriously under-represented in proportion to their total employment in the public service.

The question of fairness for other historically deprived groups in Canada is a hot topic. Following the *Public Service Reform Act, 1992*, the PSC inaugurated several new programs to improve the recruitment of Aboriginal people, persons with disabilities and members of other minority groups. There has been some improvement. In the executive group—i.e., senior management—the numbers are still small, but at lower levels, there has been more rapid progress. Table 10.2 shows the representation of women, Aboriginal peoples, persons with disabilities and visible minorities in the federal public service in 2005–06. Overall, the composition reflects the workplace availability of three of the groups, but not that of visible minorities.

TABLE 10.2 Representation of Designated Groups in the Federal Public Service in 2005–06

Group	Workplace availability	Representation March 31, 2005
Women	52.2%	53.5%
Aboriginal peoples	2.5%	4.2%
Persons with disabilities	3.6%	5.8%
Members of visible minorities	10.4%	8.1%

Source: Adapted from PSC, *Annual Report*, 2005–06, p. 96.

14. Kathleen Archibald, *Sex and the Public Service: A Report to the Public Service Commission of Canada* (Ottawa: Queen's Printer, 1970), pp. 18–23.

In summary, the Canadian public service has, over the last half century, become more representative of the society it serves. There has been an increased sensitivity to the under-representation of disadvantaged groups in the bureaucracy. At the same time, more readily accessible university education has helped to enhance opportunities for the appointment and advancement of individuals from middle- and lower-class backgrounds.

Bureaucrats and Budgets: Deficits, Debts and Surpluses

If the general public has a single, dominant image of the federal bureaucracy, it is perhaps that of a rather large *drain* down which their hard-earned tax dollars are poured. In one sense, this view is not entirely inaccurate. No government can govern without spending money. But, since most of the money expended by government finds its way back into the Canadian economy, boosting the demand for goods and services, the drain might be as accurately described as a *well* that in many periods of Canadian history has helped to irrigate the economy, providing a stimulus to economic growth.

Nevertheless, the government is also responsible to Parliament and to the Canadian taxpayer for ensuring that there is not too much seepage from the well. Consequently, a major focus of political and administrative reform over the past quarter century has involved the search for greater control and increased efficiency in government spending. During this period, the federal government has gone through several different expenditure–budgetary systems. In the sections that follow, we briefly examine the overall economy and budgetary process and discuss the efficacy of some of the techniques introduced to control and monitor public spending.

The budget and its tax proposals are released only after lengthy preparation. Preliminary discussions are held in the Department of Finance to fix an approximate level of expenditures for the fiscal year and an estimate of revenues expected to be realized from existing tax rates. From these two estimates—expenditure and revenue—emerges a surplus or a deficit. In recent years, the government has had no deficits, but has had to issue securities to finance its debt. The accounts for 2007–08 show that the government raised $236.7 billion in revenue but had $199.6 billion in program expenditures and paid $33.8 billion in debt-servicing charges on its $469.3 billion debt.

Public Sector Economics

To understand the financial situation, one must understand two terms: *debt* and *deficit*. The **deficit** is the amount by which government spending exceeds revenues in one year. The **debt** is the accumulation of deficits over the years. Every year for about three decades before 1998, the Canadian federal government spent more than it took in. That is, it ran a deficit each year. Deficits, added together, represent the debt. As of 2007–08, the national debt was roughly $469.3 billion. High debts require higher taxes because governments must pay interest on the debt.

During the past three decades, the need, obviously, was to balance the annual government budget and start paying off the debt. But this was extremely difficult because the debt was so large that the required yearly interest payments took up a huge percentage of the budget. This left an ever-smaller amount of money each year to cover *other* costs. The federal government was struggling just to balance the books and achieve a zero deficit. It finally did so to great fanfare in 1998. The economy grew and, since the government accounts were balanced, it became possible to begin paying off the debt or to use the surplus for other purposes, such as reducing taxes or increasing spending. These

> ## CLOSE-UP ON
> ## ▌Institutions
>
> ### KEY FINANCIAL TERMS
> **Deficit:** *The annual amount by which government spending exceeds revenues.*
> **Debt:** *The accumulation of annual deficits less surpluses since Confederation.*

are emotional and political issues of great importance to the country. Should surpluses be used to pay off the debt or should they be used to improve services in fields such as health and education?

To compound the problem, a significant percentage of the country's debt is held outside Canada. This means that Canada is always vulnerable to foreign influence. For example, if foreign investors become dissatisfied or fearful that their investment may not produce adequate returns, they can simply withdraw their money and force interest rates up in Canada. This was made clear during the 1995 Québec referendum campaign, when there were indications that, in the event of a successful Yes vote, foreign investors would have sold off their holdings in Canada. This would have caused a substantial drop in the value of the Canadian dollar and forced higher interest rates.

In Canada, the declining economy of the early 1990s brought anger and disappointment. It was clear that the country had been living beyond its means and that changes had to be made. Deciding who would take the brunt of the cuts, however, involved difficult choices. There was, among all the political parties, a noticeable movement away from traditional liberal values to more conservative ways of thinking, as the idea of governments running deficits became less and less palatable. This pattern was reflected particularly in the right-wing PC governments led by Ralph Klein in Alberta. At the federal level, then-finance minister Paul Martin, Jr., also took a more business-friendly position in his quest to cut government debt. Social programs that had been built up in more prosperous times were cut. Governments downsized, drastically reducing the number of public servants and government programs. Proponents argued that governments had grown too big, that many of their functions needed to be eliminated or given over to private enterprise. Social programs, they maintained, were often superficial responses to underlying problems and did not solve anything. Opponents argued that this approach amounted to solving the debt crisis on the backs of the poor. They argued that social services should be maintained and businesses should share the burden more fairly.

Governments have four options for cutting a deficit: decreasing expenditures, increasing taxes, lowering interest rates (to reduce payments on the public debt) and boosting economic growth. All governments hope for the last two outcomes, but, alas, finance ministers have little control in these areas due to Canada's dependence on foreign capital and the country's position in the global economy. The choice, then, is essentially between cutting expenditures and raising taxes.

If Canada is indebted, why do many people around the world persistently conclude that Canada is one of the best countries in which to live? And that, compared to many other countries, it is rich? It is partly because, in terms of the market value of all final goods and services produced in a specific period—its **gross domestic product** (GDP)—Canada does very well. However, when we look at the debt as a percentage of the GDP, we see that the debt increased in percentage throughout the 1980s, plateaued for a few years, increased again in the 1990s, and has now gone down. In 2007–08, it was 31.4 percent. This is a manageable, economically sustainable debt level.

Budgetary Processes

Canada's federal government spends a large amount of taxpayers' money. The federal main estimates (proposed expenditures) for 2007–08 totalled $199.6 billion.[15] As a percentage of GDP in that fiscal year, interest payments on the public debt consumed 2.3 percent. The Canadian budget, or management of the overall revenue and expenditures on an annual basis, entails two separate processes. This runs contrary to the budgetary practices of some political systems (which, unlike Canada, are not British parliamentary in origin) and to those of private businesses, where budgets present detailed targets for *both* spending and revenues.

The minister of finance receives an analysis of the economic situation and outlook from departmental officials. These are supplemented by information from the governor of the Bank of

---

15. Government of Canada, *Budget Plan*, March 2007.

Canada on the general economic outlook, conditions in the money markets, monetary policy and the market's capacity to absorb government bonds. Analysis of this information indicates the budget surplus or deficit and, in the latter event, the size of deficit that can be financed if necessary. All of this information contributes to the government's fiscal strategy.

In matters of taxation, departmental officials advise the finance minister of tax loopholes that may be closed, tax reform proposals made by external sources and possible changes to the customs tariff. From these discussions, a general pattern of taxation policy emerges. Costs of tax reduction and revenues from tax increases are totalled and compared with the estimates and the desired fiscal stance. The road is then clear to begin drafting the Budget Speech. At this point, the finance minister begins consulting various groups. Pre-budget conferences are held across the country. Historically, finance ministers often sprang the budget on the cabinet at the last possible moment before Budget Day. More recently, there has been a tendency to undertake lengthier consultation both outside and inside cabinet.

The actual address and the debate are regulated by the standing orders of the House of Commons. The Budget Speech is often delivered in the evening after the markets have closed. The speech reviews the fiscal plan, the state of the national economy and the financial operations of the government over the past fiscal year, and provides a forecast of spending requirements for the year ahead, taking into account the estimates. At the end of the Budget Speech, the minister tables the ways-and-means motions that become the taxation or excise legislation.

In recent years, particularly before the deficit was cleared from the nation's books, there was considerable debate about the dire state of the federal government's finances. The biggest fear was that Canada might have gotten into a "debt spiral," with the national debt growing faster than the economy. However, a balanced budget was achieved for 2004–05 and has been accomplished each year since then. This meant that there were no further additions to the accumulated net public debt of earlier years. The net debt is forecast to be $469.3 billion or 31.4 percent of Canada's gross domestic product (GDP) in 2007–08 (see Table 10.3). Since taking office in February 2006, the Conservative government has taken a novel approach to the national debt. It promises to dedicate any interest saved from reduction in the debt to the public in the form of a **tax back guarantee**. In 2005–06, the debt was reduced by $13.2 billion and the Conservatives' plan has been to further reduce it in 2006–07 by $9.2 billion and then $3 billion each year after that. The debt reduction translated into a promised $1.1 billion in reduced income taxes for 2007–08 and $1.3 billion for 2008–09.

Of course, not everyone was pleased with the 2007 budget. In particular, the NDP and Liberals complained about the reduction of money for progressive causes. The Conservative government reduced funding for Status of Women Canada by 40 percent and closed 12 of the department's regional offices. It also terminated the Law Reform Commission of Canada.[16]

Who Gets the Loot? The Two Budgetary Processes

There are two separate processes in budget deliberations. The first, the **expenditure budget process**, brings together the estimated spending requirements of all government departments and agencies for the next fiscal year. It takes place under the watchful eye of the Treasury Board, its secretariat and a cabinet committee. These estimates are subsequently submitted to Parliament and its committees for scrutiny and approval by means of supply (appropriations) bills (which grant the government permission to spend public funds). See Table 10.4 on page 374 for an overview of the whole expenditure system (supply process).

---

16. The federal government has also promised to establish a parliamentary budget officer. See the Department of Finance's *Budget 2007,* p. 40.

TABLE 10.3 **Federal Government Budgets for 2007–08 in Billions of Dollars**

Revenue Outlook (where government money comes from)		
	2007–08	**2008–09**
Total budgeting revenues	236.7	243.5
Expenditure Outlook (where government money goes)		
	2007–08	**2008–09**
Program spending	199.6	206.8
Public debt charges	33.4	33.7
Total expenses	233.4	240.5
Planned debt reduction	3.0	3.0
Remaining Surplus	0.3	0.0
Net public debt	469.3	466.3
Net public debt as percent of GDP	31.4	29.7

Note: Totals may differ slightly due to rounding.

Source: Adapted from general tables in *Budget Plan, 2007* (Ottawa, 2007).

The second process, the **revenue process**, concerns the means by which funds are to be raised—by taxation and other measures. It is largely the responsibility of the Departments of Finance and National Revenue. The parliamentary focal point of the revenue process is the Budget Speech delivered by the minister of finance. In line with the language of modern economics, departments are required to produce business plans that link program performance and efficiency to the overall budgetary process. These departmental outlook statements (reports on plans and priorities and departmental performance reports) are circulated to standing committees of the House of Commons for public appraisal (see Table 10.4 on the next page). In 1994, for the first time, the Standing Committee on Finance was involved in the pre-budget consultation process. It continues to review business plans and the overall revenue and expenditure situation in order to advise the minister of finance *before* the budget is delivered.

Democratic Control of the Bureaucracy: *Custodiet ipsos Custodes?*

Bureaucracy, we have said, is an organizational form ideally suited to providing an efficient means of achieving a given objective. In a parliamentary democracy such as Canada's, the selection of policy objectives ought to be the task of the political executive, which in turn is responsible through Parliament to the people. The bureaucracy's role, in theory, should primarily be to implement the goals chosen by politicians in the most efficient and effective way possible. But who guards the guards?

We have seen that in a complex modern society governed by a highly interventionist state, the distinctions between means and ends or administration and politics are not at all clear. Public servants enjoy relative security in their jobs and have immense organizational resources. These advantages give them considerable influence in the policy-making process. Bureaucrats also have discretionary power in many areas of policy implementation, especially where Parliament has delegated regulatory or administrative decision-making authority to government departments, agencies and tribunals. Given these trends, how do politicians keep the power of unelected bureaucrats in check? Of course, cabinet ministers technically control their public servants and Parliament acts as a watchdog, but there are two important ways to curb bureaucratic power: through the reports of the auditor general, and by freedom-of-information legislation.

TABLE 10.4 Supply Process for Main and Supplementary Estimates

	Mar.	Apr.	May	June	Sept.	Oct.	Nov.	Dec.	Jan.	Feb.
Parliament (House of Commons and the Senate)	Standing cttees review S.E.; consider S.E. and interim supply bills	Standing cttees review S.E. and report by May 31		Supply bill debate on M.E. June 30; consider M.E. supply bills		Receives public accounts for previous fiscal year — referred to public accounts cttee	Receives first regular S.E. cttees' review of S.E.	Considers supply bill for first regular S.E. December 10		Receives Budget Speech and M.E.
Governor General	Grants Royal Assent to supply bills; signs warrant to release monies			Grants Royal Assent to supply bills; signs warrant to release monies				Grants Royal Assent to supply bills; signs warrant to release monies		
Treasury Board	President tables S.E. and refers them to cttees; introduces S.E. and interim supply bills			President introduces M.E. supply bill			President tables first regular S.E. and refers them to cttees	President introduces S.E. supply bill		President tables M.E. and refers them to cttees
Treasury Board Secretariat	Informs departments that supply has been approved		Prepares supply bill for M.E.	Informs departments that supply has been approved			Preparation of first regular S.E. and supply bill	Informs departments that supply has been approved	Prepares M.E.	Prepares S.E. and supply bills

Legend: M.E. = Main Estimates
S.E. = Supplementary Estimates
Cttees = Committees

Source: Adapted from the Government of Canada Fiscal Plan, 1991–92 (Ottawa: Supply and Services, 1992). Reproduced by the authority of the Minister responsible for Statistics Canada, 1993.

The Auditor General

The role of the **auditor general** is to provide a critical appraisal of the effectiveness of both public spending and accounting practices—to Parliament and, in particular, to the Public Accounts Committee. The auditor general is directly responsible to Parliament (not the executive), and the auditor's reports on government spending trigger major debates in the House of Commons and the press about government policy-making.

Since 1977, the Office of the Auditor General has had the power to carry out "value-for-money" audits—to assess policy and the substance of spending decisions as well as its annual inspection of the public accounts. It "has become concerned not only with whether federal funds are properly accounted for, but with how they are being managed, at what cost, to what end and with what effectiveness."[17] The growing size and costs of the Auditor General's Office prompted one expert to conclude that the office itself should be subjected to a value-for-money, comprehensive audit.[18]

Parliamentary and administrative reforms to the expenditure budget process have enhanced the potential for democratic control, and the development of multi-year fiscal plans provides a broader, longer-range context for the evaluation of both overall spending plans and individual estimates. Both of these reforms have enhanced the role of the auditor general. The uncovering of AdScam (the Québec sponsorship scandal, as discussed in Chapter 8) was to a large extent the work of the auditor general's staff.

Freedom of Information

In 1983, the federal government took an important step toward providing more open government when it formally promulgated the *Access to Information Act.* With a number of controversial exceptions, Canadian citizens and permanent residents now have the right to examine records that were previously kept secret by federal government institutions. At stake in many cases is the individual's right to know why certain government decisions were taken, and to determine whether these decisions were arrived at fairly or whether mistakes were made. If the government refuses to disclose information on request, an appeal can be made to the information commissioner. The commissioner sends an annual report to Parliament, but John Reid, in his first report in 1999, complained that "not once in 16 years has the designated committee held a hearing to consider the annual report."[19] Ultimate recourse, however, is via the Federal Court of Canada—an expensive procedure, which also raises the undesirable prospect of having the judicial process replace Parliament as the primary mechanism for ensuring bureaucratic accountability.

The *Access to Information Act* is intended to make government more accountable and to reverse people's perception that public servants scheme to hide blunders or alleged corruption from unsuspecting citizens. Still, some observers are skeptical of the value of the Act in its present form. Donald Rowat has argued that some of the exceptions to access "go against the whole spirit of a freedom of information act by absolutely prohibiting certain types of records from being released, thus turning these exemptions into an extension of the Official Secrets Act."[20] Also disturbing is the long list of subjects for which bureaucrats can make discretionary exemptions, thereby limiting "the accountability of the government to Parliament."[21]

---

17. Donald J. Savoie, "Who Is Auditing the Auditor General?" *The Globe and Mail*, August 25, 1995.
18. Ibid.
19. *The Hill Times,* July 26, 1999, p.1.
20. Donald C. Rowat, "The Right of Public Access to Official Documents," in O.P. Dwivedi, ed., *The Administrative State in Canada: Essays in Honour of J.E. Hodgetts* (Toronto: University of Toronto Press, 1982), pp. 185–86.
21. Ibid., p. 187. For a savage report on these activities, see "Spin Control and Freedom of Information" (December 20, 2003).

In the final analysis, public confidence in the *Access to Information Act* depends on how well the mechanics of releasing information work and on whether information that should be released is actually made public. This, in turn, depends upon the extent to which the cabinet and the bureaucracy are willing to comply with the spirit as well as the letter of the new law. The issue of freedom of information will undoubtedly remain on the agenda of public debate as the Act continues to be evaluated.

The Ombudsman and Other Proposals

For many years, there has been a debate about the establishment of a federal **ombudsman**, an independent officer who would be responsible to Parliament for the investigation of citizens' complaints against the bureaucracy. Although the office of the ombudsman might provide an additional mechanism for overall surveillance of the bureaucracy, it should be noted that Canada already has a number of similar specialized officers, including the commissioner of official languages, the privacy commissioner, the information commissioner and the correctional investigator for penitentiary services, who all act as watchdogs over specific aspects of bureaucratic activity. But who *guards* the guardians? The case of George Radwanski is one example of the danger of even these types of appointments. Radwanski was appointed privacy commissioner by Jean Chrétien in 2000, only to resign in 2003 after it was discovered that he had "whitewashed his lavish spending habits."[22]

Other non-parliamentary means of controlling the bureaucracy's role in policy-making have also been proposed. The judicial process, for example, could play a greater role in protecting citizens against arbitrary bureaucratic decisions. But, although there has been an increase in court challenges to bureaucratic decisions since the *Charter of Rights and Freedoms* was implemented, we agree with the conclusion drawn by one opponent of judicial review of the bureaucracy that

> it would be wrong to abandon democratic processes working through Parliament to check bureaucratic power in favour of a more elitist approach based upon courts, lawyers and tribunals as the primary mechanisms for safeguarding the rights of individuals.[23]

Critical Debate
New Despotism?

Does the Canadian bureaucracy have too much power? Are major reforms necessary and possible?

| Point

The bureaucracy does have too much power. Certainly more reforms are needed and they can be made effective and valuable if the appropriate strategies are used.

Many Canadians are rightly suspicious, if not downright cynical, about the federal bureaucracy. In part, this suspicion stems from fear of the unknown or, at least, the inadequately understood. The bureaucracy needs to be made more open and transparent. The number of publicized financial problems and scandals has not decreased over the years, which indicates that much is wrong with the public service.

22. *The Globe and Mail*, June 24, 2003.
23. Paul Thomas, "Courts Can't Be Saviours," *Policy Options*, vol. 5, no. 3 (May/June 1984), p. 27.

Essentially, bureaucracies are always in contradiction to democracy. The rational principle of efficiency is used as an excuse to prevent public servants from bending to the "democratic will." More specifically, the so-called merit principle is used to prevent regions of the country from getting their fair share of appointments; to continue the under-representation of some sections of society, such as the handicapped; and to prevent the less educated and new immigrants are prevented from obtaining their fair share of appointments in the bureaucracy. We should loosen the so-called merit principle to allow the equality rights of Canadians as seen in the *Charter of Rights and Freedoms* to be fully expressed. We need a more representative bureaucracy.

The public service must come under more direct ministerial control. This could be accomplished if ministers took more responsibility for what happens in their departments and if they resigned if there was malfeasance or crime. We can take steps toward more ministerial responsibility by passing laws that require more open government, strengthening the freedom-of-information law and providing protection for "whistle-blowers."

There is also too much waste in the government. Elected politicians in cabinet and the rest of the caucus feel bound to respond to the immediate demands of their constituents and voters in order to secure their re-election. And, since voters and interest groups tend to rush to the defence of threatened programs from which they benefit, reduction of the size of public spending levels is relatively low in the political priorities of public servants. In order to ensure "value for money principles," accounting procedures need to be reformed, the auditor general needs more financial resources, and the controllers' system inside the departments needs to be reformed along the line of good business practices.

The House of Commons should be much more involved in ensuring government accountability. There needs to be a general standing committee to examine the overall relations between estimates and expenditures. The whole supply period could be re-examined along with the rules for financial scrutiny by standing committees and procedures generally. Why should only ministers using royal recommendations be able to make financial proposals—aren't backbenchers elected by the people, too? Is this a democracy or a new form of despotism?

Counterpoint

The bureaucracy does not have too much power. It is not a single monolithic entity whose size and organizational structure automatically present a threat to democratic government.

The bureaucracy is a complex system of competing departments, corporations and agencies established to meet the perceived economic, social and political goals of the public. Contrary to allegations, it is not an elite group, dominated by a single class or ethnic/linguistic group, and thereby unrepresentative of and unresponsive to the public. Concerted efforts have been made over the last few decades to make the bureaucracy more representative, although there is still substantial room for improvement, especially with regard to increasing opportunities for women and Native people.

Nor is there an absence of mechanisms by which control or accountability might be imposed on the bureaucracy by elected institutions. If there is a problem, it may well be described as a *lack of political will* to make use of the control mechanisms that do exist. There are, however, some minor irritants that need adjustment. Government agencies' lack of accountability to Parliament remains a problem. Reports of public enterprises and regulatory agencies are now automatically referred to the appropriate standing committees, but inadequate auditing provisions and difficulties in imposing ministerial responsibility for these semi-autonomous agencies hinder effective parliamentary control in this field.

With these exceptions, however, the mechanisms for parliamentary control of the bureaucracy are largely in place. The key question is whether MPs have the inclination or the time to devote themselves to ensuring bureaucratic accountability. Parliamentarians should treat their surveillance role seriously, but in the absence of a widespread change of attitude in the House of Commons, it seems unlikely that MPs will take full advantage of the opportunities available to them.

Discussion Questions

1. Which side of the Critical Debate do you believe makes the best case? Can you add to the discussion?
2. Are politicians the masters of public servants? Should ministers have to take responsibility for mistakes made by public servants?
3. Describe the mechanisms in place to provide democratic control of the bureaucracy. Does the existence of a federal minority government affect that government's control of the bureaucracy?
4. Distinguish between the deficit and the debt and explain the nature of the financial future Canada faces.
5. What are some major strategies that can be used for cutting the debt? Why is it such a difficult task for governments? What path would you follow if you were finance minister?

Visit our new Companion Website at **www.pearsoned.ca/jackson**, where you can use the interactive Study Guide and link to additional resources on topics discussed in the text.

Selected Bibliography

Albo, Gregory, David Langille and Leo Panitch, eds. *A Different Kind of State? Popular Power and Democratic Administration.* Don Mills, ON: Oxford University Press, 1993.

Blais, A., and S. Dion, eds. *The Budget-Maximizing Bureaucrat: Appraisals and Evidence.* Pittsburgh: University of Pittsburgh Press, 1991.

Brooks, Steven. *Public Policy in Canada: An Introduction,* 3rd ed. Don Mills, ON: Oxford University Press, 1998.

Carleton University, School of Public Administration. *How Ottawa Spends.* Ottawa: Carleton University Press, annual. Edited by different scholars in different years.

Campbell, Robert, Michael Howlett, and Lewslie Pal. *The Real Worlds of Canadian Politics: Cases in Process and Policy,* 4th ed. Peterborough, ON: Broadview Press, 2004.

Dwivedi, O.P., and James Ian Gow. *From Bureaucracy to Public Management: The Administrative Culture of the Government of Canada.* Peterborough, ON: Broadview Press, 1999.

Gillespie, W. Irwin. *Tax, Borrow and Spend: Financing Federal Spending in Canada, 1867–1990.* Ottawa: Carleton University Press, 1991.

Hodgetts, J.E. *Public Management: Emblem of Reform of the Canadian Public Service.* Ottawa: Canadian Centre for Management Development, 1991.

Huddleston, Mark. *The Public Administration Workbook.* New York: Longman, 1992.

Johnson, David. *Thinking Government: Public Sector Management in Canada,* 2nd ed. Peterborough, ON: Broadview Press, 2006.

Kernaghan, Kenneth, and David Siegel. *Public Administration in Canada: A Text,* 4th ed. Scarborough, ON: Nelson, 1999.

——————— and John Langford, *The Responsible Public Servant.* Halifax: Institute of Research on Public Policy, 1990.

McBride, Stephen. *Not Working: State, Unemployment and Neo-Conservatism in Canada.* Toronto: University of Toronto Press, 1992.

Osbaldeston, Gordon F. *Organizing to Govern,* Volumes 1 and 2. Toronto: McGraw-Hill Ryerson, 1992.

Peters, B. Guy. *The Politics of Bureaucracy.* New York: Longman, 1990.

Peters, B. Guy, and Donald J. Savoie, eds., *Taking Stock: Assessing Public Sector Reform.* Montréal: McGill Queen's University Press, 1998.

Savoie, Donald J. *Breaking the Bargain: Public Servants, Ministers and Parliament.* Toronto: University of Toronto Press, 2003.

Part IV
Political Behaviour

Political culture and institutions set the parameters of individual and collective action. Part IV, therefore, examines the political behaviour of individuals and groups as they exercise their democratic rights and influence public policy within these established boundaries.

Political parties are important vehicles of mass participation. Ideally, they should possess the organizational structure and leadership to provide the electorate with viable choices about who will govern them. They are nourished by political ideas that evolved over time as part of Canada's cultural inheritance. Today, liberal, conservative and socialist ideologies contribute to political thought and underpin the many political choices available to Canadians, as do ideas of nationalism, regionalism and neo-conservatism.

Interest groups and social movements also allow collective participation in the political process and seek to influence government. Their relationship with politicians is reciprocal in that each tries to use the other to further its ends. It is up to Parliament to create rules to regulate these groups.

Finally, elections, and to a limited degree, referendums, provide the ultimate opportunity for po-litical activity. Citizens can choose political candidates and, in principle at least, have a voice in the governance of their society. Electoral rules and norms of political behaviour determine how close that choice comes to achieving the democratic ideal.

Chapter 11

Political Parties

Continuity and Transition

Political parties are a vital part of the Canadian political system. They are agents of representative democracy. With few exceptions, local party organizations select candidates who stand for election as members of Parliament. The prime minister is almost invariably the leader of the party that holds the greatest number of elected representatives and is therefore most likely to be able to form a viable government. In short, the party system provides essential organizing and stabilizing functions for government.

In spite of their important role, organized political parties are a relatively recent historical phenomenon. As vehicles of mass participation in politics, they became increasingly significant and formalized as the franchise was extended, providing voters with progressively clearer alternatives. In Canada, Liberal and Conservative party roots extend over a century, while those of the New Democratic Party go back almost half that length of time. In the 1993 general election, two new, regionally based parties—the Reform Party and the Bloc Québécois—burst onto the federal scene, cutting into the traditional bases of support of all three established parties and threatening two of them with extinction. By 2003, Reform's successor, the Canadian Alliance, had united with the foundering Progressive Conservatives to form the new Conservative Party of Canada.

The party system today hovers between continuity and change, fragmented by organization, geography, language and ideology. When parties are unable to represent the country from sea to sea to sea, new parties form to promote specifically regional causes. This provides an outlet for regional frustrations, but it also balkanizes the country and leaves few voices at the centre to stand up for Canada as a whole. Elections of the last fifteen years have fragmented the party system to such a degree that it is currently difficult to achieve a majority government with a strong, united caucus.

In this chapter, we examine the origins and development of Canadian parties and their organization and structure outside of Parliament. We consider the basic functions of parties and invite the reader to ponder the Critical Debate concerning how well Canadian parties perform them. For example, how representative of the Canadian public are they? How democratic are they in formulating party policy? What is the role of the party leader, and is the leadership selection process appropriate? What could parties do better? In other words, is their legacy one of unfulfilled promise? To understand party functions, we begin with a definition and examination of the role of parties, and survey the wide range of party types and party systems that exist as possible alternatives to Canada's.

What Are Political Parties?

Political parties have been defined in a number of ways. Karl Marx, for example, considered them to be a manifestation of class conflict and struggle. Benjamin Disraeli saw them as organized opinion. Perhaps the most useful definition for our purposes is simply that **political parties** are organizations designed to secure the power of the state for their leaders. The goal of political parties is to gain control of the levers of government and thereby realize their policies or programs. People are motivated to join or support political parties by ideas, issues and ideologies such as liberalism, conservatism, socialism and even separatism. In democratic systems, control of government is achieved by open competition in the electoral process. The voluminous literature on political parties provides general, though not unanimous, agreement that parties constitute a crucial link between society and government.[1]

At a practical level, of course, countries have different rules defining what constitutes an officially recognized political party. The *Canada Elections Act* now defines a political party in this country as "an organization one of whose fundamental purposes is to participate in public affairs by endorsing one or more of its members as candidates and supporting their election." Parties have the option of registering with the chief electoral officer, thereby gaining official status under the *Elections Act*.[2] Any political party that runs at least one candidate in a general election or by-election has that option. Registration brings certain obligations and benefits; for example, it allows a party to issue tax receipts for contributions, recover unspent election funds from candidates and have candidate affiliation marked on ballots. To be officially recognized in the House of Commons, a party must have 12 MPs—although the House may allow exceptions. Perhaps the most important aspect of official recognition is that parties are then legal entities, thereby rendering them publicly accountable. They can therefore benefit from the Act, but can also be prosecuted for infractions against it.

Party Functions

Political parties perform several vital tasks or functions in society, including the provision of democratic representation in Parliament; accommodation of society's interests; electoral organization; and government. They are electoral machines that help to organize the electorate by recruiting candidates, organizing campaigns, encouraging partisan attachments, helping individual voters get their names on polling lists and generally stimulating voter participation. They add an important element of stability to the political system by legitimizing the individuals and institutions that form the government. They also provide policy direction, party leaders and cabinet ministers. The governing party serves to fuse the executive and legislative branches of government in Canada, providing the foundation of cabinet government. Within the broad task of organizing the electorate and the government, there are several specific party functions that merit closer analysis.

It is the task of every political party to enlist suitable candidates to stand for election as members of Parliament, with the hope that the best of them will become government ministers and perhaps even prime minister. The ultimate goal of each major party is, of course, to get enough MPs elected to allow it to form a government. To achieve this, each party must select and present candidates and mobilize voters by waging a campaign. The winning party forms the government and decides who occupies the major policy-making posts, the most powerful tools a party can control. It gains control of numerous patronage appointments throughout the government structure, and is able to reward its own supporters while extending its power and influence. Party leaders, therefore, recruit public appointees such as senators and members of Crown agencies; they also help to recruit and elect representatives to the House of Commons.

1. Parties played a major role in Britain for the first time in the eighteenth century. There has been considerable controversy over their desirability, epitomized in the classic works of M.I. Ostrogorski, *Democracy and the Organization of Political Parties*, 2 vols., trans. by Frederick Clarke (New York: Macmillan, 1902); and Robert Michels, *Political Parties: A Sociological Study of Oligarchical Tendencies of Modern Democracy*, trans. by Eden and Cedar Paul (New York: The Free Press, 1966).
2. In 2003, the Supreme Court struck down as unconstitutional a rule that required a party to field a minimum of fifty candidates before it could be officially recognized. This was the outcome of a challenge by Miguel Figueroa, leader of the Communist Party of Canada, which in 1993 was forced to liquidate its assets, pay its debts and give the balance to the chief electoral officer.

A vast number of interests exist in modern, complex societies. Parties *articulate* or express those interests in many ways: they inform public opinion by debating important issues, and they provide a legitimate outlet for dissent and pressure for change. The latter is particularly important for accommodating regional or sectional interests. In fact, parties are often referred to as "gatekeepers" in the political system because they allow certain demands to pass directly to decision-makers while they eliminate or combine others. Political parties also perform the valuable function of bringing together and then simplifying the morass of interests into manageable sets of policy alternatives. By appealing to the many classes, regions, interests and ethnic groups that make up the country, political parties modify conflict and facilitate decisions. This process, known as *aggregation* of interests, is performed by a variety of structures in society, but political parties may be the most important. Parties constantly monitor the electorate for ideas and conduct opinion polls to help them transform public concerns into vote-winning policies. Effective interest aggregation is important for electoral success in Canada.

In stable democracies, political parties normally play a fairly conservative role, reinforcing the established system in order to keep the political process running smoothly. In a parliamentary democracy such as Canada's, which lacks a strong, homogeneous political culture, there is a special need for political parties to play a unifying role as "agencies for the creation of national symbols, experiences, memories, heroes, and villains."[3] The failure of Canadian parties to bind regional cleavages by building strong *national* bases of representation limits their effectiveness. They do, however, inform and educate the public, particularly during elections, by enlisting supporters to participate in the electoral process through volunteer party work as well as voting.

By winning elections, parties form the government and acquire the ability to formulate and present public policy. They provide platforms for election campaigns, but these often don't determine the details of subsequent policy decisions. The cabinet, along with senior civil servants, leads the policy-making function in the legislative process.

Parties offer a useful vehicle for citizens to participate in the political process and provide a training ground for future political leaders. For those who do not aspire to leadership positions, they give social, psychological and, sometimes, economic benefits and the opportunity to participate in party decisions.

Parties play such an important role in our society that it is hard to conceive of democratic government without them. Yet, there is data to suggest that Canadians are increasingly dissatisfied with their political parties and how they perform (see Figure 11.1). In recent decades, tension has often arisen between those who perceive them to be too elitist and want parties to be more responsive vehicles for mass participation, providing opportunities for direct input into public policy, and those who prefer the traditional role of parties as vehicles of accommodation and representation.[4] As you learn more about parties and how the system works, you will be able to decide where you stand on this important issue.

Classifying Parties and Party Systems

Parties

Political parties can be classified in a great number of ways, but particularly by their *type of organization* or by the *type of appeal* they make to the electorate.

---

3. John Meisel, "Recent Changes in Canadian Parties," in Hugh G. Thorburn, ed., *Party Politics in Canada*, 2nd ed. (Scarborough, ON: Prentice Hall, 1967), p. 34.

4. See for example, William Cross, *Political Parties* (Vancouver: UBC Press, 2004), p. 30.

FIGURE 11.1 **Percentage of Canadians Satisfied with Political Parties on a Scale from 1 to 100**

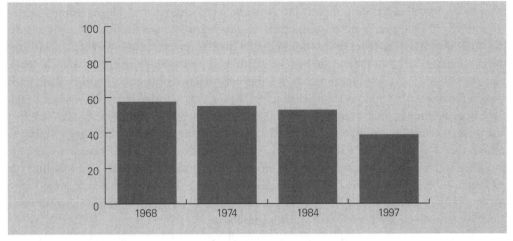

Source: William Cross, *Political Parties* (Vancouver, UBC Press, 2004), p. 4. Data derived from R. Kenneth Carty, William Cross, and Lisa Young, *Rebuilding Canadian Party Politics* (Vancouver, UBC Press, 2000), p. 29.

Classification by Organization Maurice Duverger formulated a widely used, simple scheme that divides political parties into three categories—*mass, cadre* or *devotee*—according to their type of organization.[5] *Mass parties* recruit across class lines to achieve the largest possible membership and then allow that membership a theoretically significant role by functioning democratically. Members have significant power over their executive and the parliamentary wing—including the leader, whom they elect—and a say in policy formulation. The party is financed by membership fees. The theoretical rationale behind mass parties is that a large membership across social class lines helps to counter the power of establishment parties, whose leaders come mainly from the economic, political and social elite of society.

Cadre parties, on the other hand, are highly centralized and recruit only from the politically active elite. They are much less democratic than mass parties, in that an active elite allows the rest of the party to fall dormant until election time. The parliamentary wing of the party selects the leader, who has no formal accountability. Financing is from a relatively narrow base, usually corporations. Today, such parties are often associated with developing nations but are found throughout the developed world as well. *Devotee parties*, Duverger's third type, are built around a charismatic leader; examples would be Germany's Nazi Party under Adolf Hitler or Iraq's Baathists under Saddam Hussein.

Canada's Liberal and Conservative parties began as, and in some respects remain, cadre parties, although over time they have taken on many features of the mass-party model. The NDP began as a mass party but has shifted toward the cadre model, as did Reform/Alliance. Although democratic, the Bloc Québécois under Lucien Bouchard exhibited some features of a devotee party.

Canada's inability to sustain pure mass parties may be explained by Robert Michels's **iron law of oligarchy**, a theory that all large organizations, despite intentions to do otherwise, largely end up in the control of a relatively small group of people at the top.[6] In other words, democracy always gives way to elitism. This has been true of Canadian political parties.

5. The classic discussion of party organization is found in Maurice Duverger, *Political Parties: Their Organization and Activity in the Modern State* (London: Methuen, 1954).
6. Michels, *Political Parties.*

Classification by Appeal Otto Kirchheimer classifies parties on an ideological/non-ideological basis. He distinguishes the *catch-all party* from those with high degrees of ideological commitment.[7] He notes that the mass party and the cadre party became relatively unsuccessful at the polls because they had limited electoral bases (the working class for the mass party and the establishment class for the cadre party) but that they tended to expand their appeal when they sought to include the maximum number of social groups. To do this, they followed two strategies: First, they abandoned strong ideological prescriptions in favour of softer lines and an appeal to moderate voters. Second, the parties promised specific rewards to a wide variety of interest groups, from better marketing assistance to farmers and jobs for students to free trade and better economic conditions for business people. Catch-all parties focus above all on maximizing votes; their platforms become like large vats filled with as many popular ideas and promises as possible. The Republican and Democratic parties in the United States are classic catch-all parties. In Canada, the Liberal and Conservative parties, and increasingly the NDP, are clearly in the catch-all category. They attempt to attract as many voters as possible by making the widest appeal possible.

Another concept is often used to discuss catch-all parties. *Brokerage parties* seek to maintain cohesion across party divisions and maximize their electoral appeal by adopting centrist positions on issues. For decades in Canada, the two major parties were lodged so firmly in the centre of the political spectrum that they were often portrayed as Tweedledum and Tweedledee. They appealed to the same middle-of-the-road electoral supporters, constantly shifting their principles in search of electoral success. This created a flexible, non-ideological *brokerage party system* because the two main parties acted as brokers of ideas, selecting those with the widest appeal and the best chance of attracting electoral support.

George Perlin called the Liberal and Progressive Conservative parties "modified" brokerage parties because there were "some basic differences between them, explained partly by a different internal balance in ideological perspectives and partly by their long-term competitive relationship."[8] The Liberals have been considered centre-left and the Conservatives centre-right, because of a few alleged historical differences such as the Progressive Conservative support of free enterprise and the Liberals' promotion of social legislation and some public ownership. However, they have both displayed remarkable flexibility within this broad range. For example, free trade with the United States historically was a Liberal policy until the PCs took it up in 1985.

Advocates of brokerage theory argue that the many divisions in the country—ethnic, linguistic, geographic, economic and demographic—have forced parties in Canada to occupy the middle of the road in their attempts to win majorities. Brokerage parties do not appeal to specific socio-economic groupings, as they are flexible and opportunistic in order to win elections. By usurping the middle ground, the Liberals and Conservatives have largely restricted radical parties to the sidelines. History and traditional loyalties, rather than the logic or ideology behind party platforms, have been the distinguishing features of Canadian political parties. Divisions such as ethnicity and region have always taken precedence over class.[9]

In contrast to the catch-all party, the *ideological party* adheres strictly to an ideology or consistent set of principles. The NDP fits loosely into this category, as did the former Reform and Canadian Alliance parties. The Bloc Québécois, too, is an ideological party because nationalist ideas underpin its party platform.

7. Otto Kirchheimer, "The Transformation of the Western European Party System," in Joseph LaPalombara and M. Wiener, eds., *Political Parties and Political Development* (Princeton, NJ: Princeton University Press, 1966), pp. 177–200.

8. George Perlin, ed., *Party Democracy in Canada* (Scarborough, ON: Prentice Hall, 1988). See especially articles by Donald Blake, "Division and Cohesion: The Major Parties," pp. 32–53; and Richard Johnston, "The Ideological Structure of Opinion on Policy," pp. 54–70.

9. Richard Johnston et al., *Letting the People Decide* (Montréal: McGill-Queen's University Press, 1992).

Another category here would be *single-issue parties*—parties that limit their policy platform to one issue. An example would be a party that runs for office on a strictly environmental platform, such as the Green Party, which did so at its inception in Canada. The Bloc Québécois is an *anti-system party*—one that does not want to work within the existing political system, but seeks to destroy it and replace it with something else. Since the Bloc seeks to dismantle Canada, it is to that party's advantage to prevent the system of government from working well.

Party Systems

The series of relationships among parties in a political system constitutes the **party system**. Party systems, too, can be classified to assist in making comparisons among states. An example of a classification system devised to distinguish with greater precision among party systems on a worldwide basis is by Joseph LaPalombara and Myron Weiner. Their competitive/non-competitive classification of party systems has since been expanded by others (see Table 11.1).

Competitive systems are classified by the number of parties that compete for, and have access to, legislative power. In the **dominant one-party** system, a single party regularly wins almost every election, even though opposition parties function freely. In the **two-party** system, two major parties dominate; others have only minor political strength. In the **multi-party** system, popular support is divided among several parties so that the largest party must generally form a coalition with one or more other parties to form a government. As indicated in Table 11.1, multi-party systems can be divided further into **multi-party dominant,** in which there are three or more parties, but one of them regularly receives about 40 percent of the vote; or **multi-party loose**, in which there are also three or more parties, but none of them regularly receives 40 percent of the vote. **Non-competitive systems**, in which one party dominates, are classified by other variables, such as how repressive their governments are. A few have been called **mixed and low competitive** because they include elements of the other types. In Mexico before 2000, for example, opposition parties were allowed to exist, but one party dominated to such an extent that the system was almost non-competitive.

Classification systems permit only gross comparisons between states. Not all countries fit neatly into any one category, and a country's classification may change over time. Canada is a prime example. It has a competitive system, but the nature of the system has changed so that Canada does not clearly belong in any of the above categories.

Until the rise of third parties in 1921, the Canadian party system was developing along the lines of a classic two-party system. Since then, particularly after 1961, third parties have fairly

TABLE 11.1 Party Systems Based on Party Competition

Non-Competitive Systems	1. Communist (China)
	2. Authoritarian (Franco's Spain)
Mixed and Low Competitive Systems	1. Low competition (Mexico)
Competitive Systems	1. One-party dominant (Japan until 1993)
	2. Two-party (United States)
	3. Multi-party dominant (three or more parties; one regularly receives about 40% of the vote) (Canada historically)
	4. Multi-party loose (three or more parties; none regularly receives 40% of the vote) (Italy, Canada today)

Source: Adapted from Joseph LaPalombara, *Politics within Nations* (Englewood Cliffs, NJ: Prentice Hall, 1974), ch. 13.

consistently captured about a quarter of the federal vote (see Figure 11.2). Until 1993, the Canadian system, therefore, fell somewhere between the two-party and multi-party systems in the classification scheme set out above. Because of this, the arrangement in Canada was often called a "two-and-a-half party" system. With the election of five parties in 1993, 1997 and 2000, and four in 2004 and 2006, the party system shifted further toward the multi-party end of the spectrum.[10]

The Canadian Party System

From Origins to Two-Party System   It is difficult to pinpoint the date of origin of political parties in Canada. Until shortly after Confederation, Canadian politics was characterized by factionalism. Party structures as we know them today had not yet formed. Often, candidates for elected office did not even commit themselves to a party until they had determined which one would win.

Early parties were loosely organized and even less encumbered by ideology than they are today. In their early years, Upper and Lower Canada, Nova Scotia and Prince Edward Island were all governed by oligarchies. The Family Compact, the Château Clique, the Halifax Compact and the landed proprietors in Prince Edward Island controlled economic and political power in their

FIGURE 11.2 **Tracking Party Fortunes: Percentage of Seats Won by Parties in General Elections, 1945–2006**

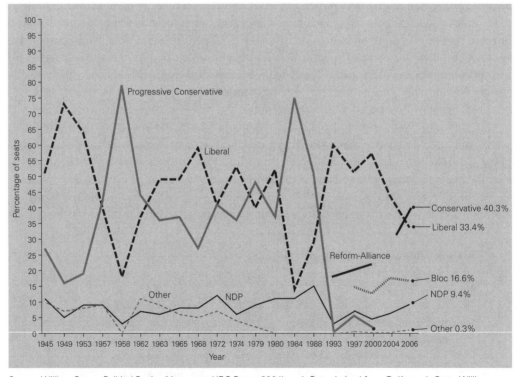

Source: William Cross, *Political Parties* (Vancouver, UBC Press, 2004), p. 4. Data derived from R. Kenneth Carty, William Cross, and Lisa Young, *Rebuilding Canadian Party* Politics (Vancouver, UBC Press, 2000), p. 29.

10. See R.Kenneth Carty, William Cross and Lisa Young, "A New Canadian Party System" in Wjiliam Cross, ed. *Political Parties, Representation and Electoral Democracy in Canada* (Don Mills, ON: Oxford University Press, 2002), pp. 15–36; and "Three Party Systems: An Interpretation of the Development of National Politics," in Hugh G. Thorburn and Alan Whitehorn, eds., *Party Politics in Canada*, 8th ed. (Don Mills, ON: Prentice Hall, 2001).

particular areas. Opposition was fragmented and factional. The prime requisite for the emergence of parties was increased competition for power within the legislature. Nowhere did the factions and interest groups mature into parties until the advent of responsible government. Only when the executive became responsible to the legislature was there a genuine need for political parties to develop. As legislative responsibilities were extended, the franchise expanded; other electoral reforms, such as the secret ballot, were introduced; the pressure for party cohesion increased; and recognizable political parties emerged.

The origin and development of parties were directly influenced by the system of government. Canadian parties developed within the framework of a democratic parliamentary system and, after 1867, a federal constitutional arrangement. They were further influenced by internal factors such as national and industrial development, and external stimuli such as historical precedents and ideological influences from Britain and the United States. Until the 1920s, two major parties, the precursors of today's Liberals and Conservatives, were able to aggregate the various interests, which were not very complex. The economy prospered; regional and rural–urban cleavages were minimal. The parties focused on parochial constituency issues.

Two-and-a-Half-Party System   In 1921, the first minor parties appeared on the political scene and the focus of party politics shifted from constituency to region. In 1921, the Progressives suddenly won 23 percent of the vote, largely in Western Canada. Since that date, there has been at least one minor party represented in Parliament. From 1961 to 1993, the only significant third party was the NDP. From its more radical left-wing origins, the NDP gradually adopted a moderate-left reform position that, at times, has overlapped with centre-left Liberal positions. The middle-of-the-road tendency of all three parties is evident, but the historical relationship among the parties is sufficient to warrant their relative positions on the left–right continuum. Until 1993, the two major parties together consistently won about 75–80 percent of the vote; the NDP, about 15–20 percent.

Canada's modified two-party system began to show signs of shifting toward a multi-party system in the early 1990s. By the run-up to the 1993 general election, the Mulroney (and, during the election campaign, Campbell) Progressive Conservative government was highly unpopular, the Liberals were not regarded as a satisfactory alternative in Québec and parts of Western Canada, and the New Democratic Party remained unable to create a bridge between French- and English-speaking populations. Two new parties, the Reform Party and the Bloc Québécois, filled the breach, sapping the support of the established parties in Québec and the West, particularly that of the PCs and the NDP. Blessed with militants, money and simple messages, the Bloc and Reform attracted roughly 30 percent of the popular vote in the 1993 general election and almost as much or more in the elections of 1997 and 2000.

It could also be argued that, after 1921, the party system generally had the characteristics of a **one-party dominant** system, where one party receives at least 40 percent of the vote.[11] For the first seven decades of the twentieth century, the Liberals dominated. Until 1984, they had fallen below 40 percent of the vote in a federal election only three times: in 1958, 1962 and 1972. They won 18 of the 25 general elections from 1896 to 1984. Until 1984, therefore, the Liberals monopolized bureaucratic and senatorial appointments and all the other advantages of holding power, including the psychological advantages of being perceived as the natural governing party. During that period, the Progressive Conservatives were the main opposition party. From 1984 to 1993, the situation was temporarily reversed and the PCs dominated the party system until their disastrous defeat in 1993. The Liberals returned to power at that time and remained there until the 2006 election of a minority Conservative government.

11. See Thorburn and Whitehorn, eds., *Party Politics in Canada*, 8th ed. (Don Mills, ON: Prentice Hall, 2001).

Toward a Multi-Party System   The 1993 general election dramatically changed the Canadian party system and the next four elections consolidated it. Five parties were elected to Parliament in the first three of these elections, but the Liberals gained the most seats and dominated the multi-party system. In 2004, with four parties elected, the Liberals retained only tenuous control until the Conservatives won a minority government in 2006.

A significant factor shaping the new party system was the growing dissatisfaction in some parts of the electorate that parties were not responsive enough to the concerns of voters, and did not provide enough opportunity for voters to take part in decision making.[12] This was evidenced in a rise of assertiveness and populism in parts of the Canadian electorate, and the parties became more diverse in their ideas and more regionally fragmented in their focus. The changed party system has created or exacerbated some serious problems within it.

Problems in the Canadian Party System: Federal and Regional Characteristics, and Participation

Federal Characteristics   In addition to being competitive, the Canadian party system is both federal and highly regional. While they parallel the federal organization of government, the *provincial* party systems are not identical to their federal counterparts. Federal and provincial parties of the same name often have separate elites, organizations and financial support. Federal and provincial Liberal parties, for example, operate separately in Ontario, Quebec, British Columbia and Alberta, but jointly in the remaining six smaller provinces. A federal party therefore cannot assume ideological congruence or policy support from its provincial counterparts. While the federal Liberal Party and the Québec Liberal Party share neither membership nor ideas, the Bloc and the Parti Québécois share both. Provincial governments generally win support by taking strong stands for provincial concerns against the federal government. For whatever reason, voters do not necessarily support the same parties federally and provincially. As Garth Stevenson speculates,

> *[this] peculiar separation of the party system into federal and provincial layers is perhaps in part a consequence of the intensity of federal–provincial conflict, which makes it difficult for a party affiliated with the federal government to appear as a credible defender of provincial interests.[13]*

The federal structure also encourages the establishment of new parties at the provincial level. Some remain unique to one or to a few provinces and never move into the federal system, while others do enter the federal contest but never come close to power. The Parti Québécois, for example, is an important one-province provincial party. Since 1993, it has thrown its weight behind the Bloc Québécois as the standard-bearer of Québec separatism in the federal Parliament.

Regional Characteristics   Perhaps the most interesting, but also worrisome, feature of the Canadian party system is its strong regional character. In recent years, with the exceptions of 1984 and 1988, general elections increasingly have produced governments with significant regional distortions because the parties were unable to build strong national bases. (See Table 11.2 for an overview of elections from 1867 to 2006.) The distortion was apparent in the percentage of seats the governing party won in each region and also in the regional composition of the government caucus.

---

12. Carty et al, *A New Canadian Party System*, especially pp. 20–21.
13. Garth Stevenson, *Unfulfilled Union: Canadian Federalism and National Unity*, rev. ed. (Toronto: Gage, 1982), p. 182.

TABLE 11.2 **Percentage of Seats in Each Region Won by the Governing Party in Canadian General Elections, 1867–2006**

		% Seats Won by Governing Party in Each Region				
Election	Governing Party	Canada	West	Ontario	Québec	Atlantic
1867	CONSERVATIVE	55.8	–	56.1	69.2	29.4
1872	CONSERVATIVE	51.5	90.0	43.2	58.5	48.6
1874	LIBERAL	64.6	20.0	72.7	50.8	79.1
1878	CONSERVATIVE	66.5	90.0	67.0	69.2	55.8
1882	CONSERVATIVE	66.2	72.7	59.3	73.8	67.4
1887	CONSERVATIVE	57.2	93.3	56.5	50.8	55.8
1891	CONSERVATIVE	57.2	93.3	52.2	46.2	72.1
1896	LIBERAL	54.9	47.1	46.7	75.4	43.6
1900	LIBERAL	62.0	70.6	39.1	87.7	69.2
1904	LIBERAL	65.0	75.0	44.2	83.1	74.3
1908	LIBERAL	60.2	51.4	41.9	81.5	74.3
1911	CONSERVATIVE	60.2	51.4	83.7	41.5	45.7
1917	UNIONIST (CONSERVATIVE)	65.1	96.5	90.2	4.6	67.7
1921	Liberal	49.4	8.8	25.6	100.0	80.6
1925	Liberal	40.4	33.3	13.4	90.8	20.7
1926	LIBERAL	47.3	34.8	28.0	92.3	31.0
1930	CONSERVATIVE	55.9	44.9	72.0	36.9	79.3
1935	LIBERAL	69.8	48.6	68.3	84.6	96.2
1940	LIBERAL	72.7	59.7	67.1	93.8	73.1
1945	LIBERAL	51.0	26.4	41.5	83.1	69.2
1949	LIBERAL	72.5	59.7	67.5	90.4	73.5
1953	LIBERAL	64.2	37.5	58.8	88.0	81.8
1957	Progressive Conservative	42.3	29.2	71.8	12.0	63.6
1958	PROGRESSIVE CONSERVATIVE	78.5	91.7	78.8	66.7	75.8
1962	Progressive Conservative	43.8	68.1	41.1	18.7	54.5
1963	Liberal	48.7	13.9	61.2	62.7	60.6
1965	Liberal	49.4	12.5	60.0	74.7	45.5
1968	LIBERAL	58.7	40.0	72.7	75.7	21.9
1972	Liberal	41.3	10.0	40.9	75.7	31.2
1974	LIBERAL	53.4	18.6	62.5	81.1	40.6
1979	Progressive Conservative	48.2	73.8	60.0	2.7	56.3
1980	LIBERAL	52.1	2.5	54.7	98.7	59.4
1984	PROGRESSIVE CONSERVATIVE	74.8	76.3	70.5	77.3	78.1
1988	PROGRESSIVE CONSERVATIVE	57.3	53.9	46.5	84.0	37.5
1993	LIBERAL	60.9	32.6	99.0	25.3	96.9
1997	LIBERAL	51.5	18.7	98.1	34.7	34.4
2000	LIBERAL	57.1	18.7	97.1	48.0	59.4
2004	Liberal	43.8	15.2	70.7	28.0	68.7
2006	Conservative	40.3	70.6	37.7	13.3	28.1

Legend: Upper-case = majority government
Lower-case = minority government

Note: "West" includes the Northwest Territories, Yukon and Nunavut where applicable.

In the 1980 election, for example, the four Western provinces were virtually excluded from the government caucus, with about 1 percent of the membership. In fact, they have been severely under-represented in virtually all Liberal government caucuses from 1963 onward. From 1921 until 2004, the West was mildly or severely under-represented in all but 4 government caucuses out of 25 (those 4 were Conservative governments). Conversely, Québec was highly over-represented in all Liberal government caucuses from 1921 until 1993. Since then, Québec, too, has been under-represented (see Table 11.3 for a reading from 1945 to present).

Over the twentieth century, the Liberal Party increasingly became the party of Central Canada, winning 85 percent of its seats there in the 1980 election. In 1984, when the Liberals lost their hold on Central Canada, they did poorly in every other province. In 1988, they increased their support in Ontario, the Maritimes and Manitoba, but did poorly again in Québec. Finally, on return to power in 1993, for the first time in many years the Liberal caucus reflected the regional balance of the country. Ironically, its main opposition was from new regionally based parties, the separatist Bloc Québécois and the West-supported Reform Party.

The Progressive Conservative Party, for its part, was traditionally strongest in Ontario, but made a breakthrough in the West with John Diefenbaker's victory in 1957, which was confirmed in a majority government the next year. In 1984, under Brian Mulroney, the PCs won 75 percent of

TABLE 11.3 Regional Composition of Government Caucus and House of Commons, Canadian General Elections, 1945–2006

Election	Governing Party	% Regional Composition of Government Caucus				% Regional Composition of House of Commons			
		West	Ont.	Qué.	Atl.	West.	Ont.	Qué.	Atl.
1945	LIBERAL	15.2	27.2	43.2	14.4	29.4	33.5	26.5	10.6
1949	LIBERAL	22.6	29.5	34.7	13.1	27.5	31.7	27.9	13.0
1953	LIBERAL	15.9	29.4	38.8	15.9	27.2	32.1	28.3	12.5
1957	Progressive Conservative	18.8	54.4	8.0	18.8	27.2	32.1	28.3	12.5
1958	PROGRESSIVE CONSERVATIVE	31.7	32.2	24.0	12.0	27.2	32.1	28.3	12.5
1962	Progressive Conservative	42.2	30.2	12.1	15.5	27.2	32.1	28.3	12.5
1963	Liberal	7.8	40.3	36.4	15.5	27.2	32.1	28.3	12.5
1965	Liberal	6.9	38.9	42.7	11.5	27.2	32.1	28.3	12.5
1968	LIBERAL	18.1	41.3	36.1	4.5	26.5	33.3	28.0	12.1
1972	Liberal	6.4	33.0	51.4	9.2	26.5	33.3	28.0	12.1
1974	LIBERAL	9.2	39.0	42.6	9.2	26.5	33.3	28.0	12.1
1979	Progressive Conservative	43.4	41.9	1.5	13.2	28.4	33.7	26.6	11.3
1980	LIBERAL	1.4	35.4	50.3	12.9	28.4	33.7	26.6	11.3
1984	PROGRESSIVE CONSERVATIVE	28.9	31.8	27.5	11.8	28.9	33.7	26.6	11.3
1988	PROGRESSIVE CONSERVATIVE	28.4	27.2	37.3	7.1	30.2	33.6	25.4	10.8
1993	LIBERAL	16.4	55.4	10.7	17.5	30.2	33.6	25.4	10.8
1997	LIBERAL	11.0	65.2	16.8	7.1	30.2	34.2	24.9	10.6
2000	LIBERAL	9.9	58.1	20.9	11.0	30.2	34.2	24.9	10.6
2004	Liberal	10.4	55.6	15.6	16.3	29.9	34.4	24.4	10.4
2006	Conservative	52.4	32.3	8.1	7.3	29.9	34.4	24.4	10.4

Legend: Upper-case = majority government
Lower-case = minority government

Note: "West" includes the Northwest Territories, Yukon and Nunavut where applicable.

the seats overall: 76 percent in the West, 71 percent in Ontario, 77 percent in Québec and 78 percent in the Atlantic provinces. That electoral breakthrough in Québec finally gave Canada a government with a strong national mandate (see Table 11.2). As Table 11.3 shows, in 1984 and 1988, for the first time since 1958, the percentage regional composition of the Progressive Conservative caucus was extremely close to the percentage regional composition of the House of Commons—just before the party's devastating near-demise in the defeat of 1993.

Severe regional imbalances in the party system make it difficult for the parties to perform many of their important functions. For decades, selection for political patronage positions was distorted by Liberal Party domination of the government, as was recruitment to cabinet. Interest aggregation and articulation by the parties were also distorted when regions were severely over- or under-represented in governments over several decades. When this happened on a regular basis, regional parties flourished as a protest against exclusion. Even the socialization function is distorted when there are regional imbalances, because regional cleavages are exacerbated instead of smoothed over. Different political traditions and social and economic cleavages in the regions tend to encourage viewpoints that are parochial and narrow rather than national, and make Canada difficult to govern.

After the party system fragmented regionally in 1993, it was dominated by the federal Liberals until 2006. In 1997, the Liberals won all but two seats in seat-rich Ontario, but only a handful in Québec, and a few others scattered across the country. Not only was that party confined to narrow geographical regions—so, too, were all the other parties. In 2006, the fragmentation continued when the Conservatives formed a minority government after picking up ten seats in Québec—their largest number since 1988.

Participation   Canadian parties are not highly participatory organizations. Given how important political parties are in our representative democracy one might find it surprising and somewhat worrying that only about 1 or 2 percent of Canadians are estimated to belong to an organized political party between elections. Membership is not restrictive; there is usually a small membership fee, but parties are open to everyone—even non-citizens and those too young to vote. In spite of the fact that parties are easily accessible to people (they merely need to join a local constituency association), very few Canadians belong to them, and those who do spend very little time on party agendas and activities. The newest members appear to be among the least active. Members of the federal Liberal Party are by far the most active.[14] Membership recruitment occurs before leaders are selected and riding candidates are nominated.

Despite their openness to all, parties do not have memberships that are representative of Canadian society. "Party members tend to be well educated, male, old and born in Canada."[15] About 23 percent of Canadians attend university, but more than half of party members have attended. Women are under-represented as regular members and also in decision-making positions. They are best represented in the Liberal and New Democratic parties. Parties have historically had trouble recruiting young members—the average age of party members is 59, with the Liberals having the most representation among younger Canadians. In the country as a whole, about 18 percent of the population is born abroad, but nine of ten party members were born in Canada, and most of them have European ancestry. For decades, the parties have tried to encourage the participation of under-represented groups of Canadians, particularly women, youth and new Canadians. The NDP, for example, provides special committees for women, youth, visible minorities, and lesbians, gays and bisexuals. The Liberal Party has commissions for seniors, women and a young Liberals groups. The Conservative Party, like its predecessors, the PCs and the Alliance, does less in this regard. Only in the

14. Cross, *Political Parties*, chapter 2.

15. On inclusiveness, see Cross, *Political Parties*, especially pp. 20–26.

Liberal Party does membership adequately reflect Canada's linguistic duality, although the Harper government has made progress in this area.

Ideology: The Ideas behind Canadian Political Parties

Recall that **ideology** is an explicit doctrinal structure that provides a particular diagnosis of the ills of society and an "action program" for implementing prescribed solutions for these problems. It is common for ideologies to be associated with particular political parties, structuring their rhetoric and conditioning their policy programs.[16]

Ideological positions are often placed on a left–right spectrum. The concept of left–right stems from politics in France after the Revolution (1789), when different political factions sat in different locations in a semicircular legislative chamber. The most radical elements, who wanted considerable social change and maximum equality, sat on the far left side of the chamber, while the most conservative elements, who wanted no change and maximum inequality, sat on the right. The moderate, middle-of-the-road groups occupied the centre seats. Over time, these groupings became known as the left, centre and right. Gradually, the same labels were applied to groups and ideas outside Parliament, and they were adopted in other countries as a shorthand way to identify and explain various groups or ideas in relation to each other.

The most important modern ideologies are thus often seen as shaded on a spectrum with communism at the extreme left, through social democracy, liberalism and conservatism occupying the centre, to Nazism and fascism on the extreme right (see Figure 11.3).

It is difficult to apply the left–right ideological spectrum precisely in the real world because ideologies are never manifested in a pure form: they vary considerably over time and place. One conservative or liberal regime may be considerably further *left* or *right* than another. Nor do ideologies always proceed neatly on a continuum when one examines specific issues such as freedom of speech or racial equality. An ideology might be relatively extreme with respect to one issue but not another. The left–right notion does, however, prove useful as a general method of categorizing political ideas. We can locate Canadian political parties at the centre of the political spectrum running roughly from social democracy to conservatism.

Within Canadian society, the main ideologies with deep historical roots are conservative, liberal and socialist. Liberalism and conservatism originated in Europe in the nineteenth century, as philosophers and thinkers struggled to create consistent patterns of thought about how to

FIGURE 11.3 The Left–Right Ideological Spectrum

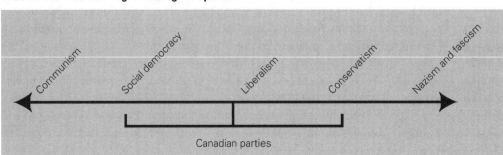

16. This section draws on material from Robert J. Jackson and Doreen Jackson, *An Introduction to Political Science: Comparative and World Politics*, 5th ed. (Don Mills, ON: Pearson Prentice Hall, 2007).

restructure the decaying medieval social and political order. Socialism developed later, but again in response to fundamental changes in economics. By the beginning of the twentieth century, the European political and ideological battlefield was a three-way contest as the socialist ideology added socialist, labour and communist parties to those espousing liberalism and conservatism.

Liberalism

In eighteenth-century Europe, liberalism was the ideology of the rising commercial class that resented the restrictions of the old feudal order on society. The ideas it generated provided guidance in moral, political and economic spheres. Morally, liberalism affirmed basic values including freedom and dignity. Politically, it espoused basic political rights such as the right to representative government. Economically, it was dedicated to the right to private property, free trade and free-enterprise capitalism.

The historical root of *liberal* is the Latin *liber*, meaning "free (man)." The concept of freedom is at the heart of the liberal ideology. Early proponents of liberalism called for freedom (absence of government coercion) in all areas of life: social, political and economic.

John Locke (1632–1704), an English political philosopher, was the most influential of the early thinkers generally referred to as classical liberals. His ideas spread rapidly throughout the Western World. Locke argued that all human beings have the right to life, liberty and property, and that they create government to protect and preserve these basic rights. If the government fails in this task, Locke said, the people have the right to overthrow it.[17] He wrote,

---

Freedom is . . . to have a standing rule to live by, common to everyone of that society and made by the legislative power erected in it.[18]

Civil liberties, or freedoms such as freedom of expression, freedom of speech and freedom to publish and disseminate one's ideas, have been enshrined in the constitutions of most liberal democracies.

Locke and other classical liberals, such as John Stuart Mill and Jean-Jacques Rousseau, wanted governments to maintain law and order, but not infringe on human rights. They wanted to force governments to operate under the strict limits of a constitution. Locke believed that elected legislatures should make decisions for society. His idea of representative government was based on the notion that political authority derives from the people. The elected majority, he said, can make political decisions, but it must respect the natural rights of all citizens.

In one important sense, however, liberalism as it developed in England was quite different from liberalism in France. In England, liberalism was not anti-religious. In France, it was antagonistic to organized religion, and collided with the Roman Catholic Church. The antipathy of the Church toward liberalism was later exported to Québec, where the Church was a very powerful social force for many years and initially prevented liberal ideas from taking root.

Liberalism also had important economic implications for the state. Adam Smith's *The Wealth of Nations* (1793) greatly influenced the development of Western states. It expounded the principle of *laissez-faire*, which essentially means there should be minimum intervention by government in economic affairs. Smith maintained that society, like the physical universe, is governed by natural laws. One such law holds that prices in a free market are determined by supply and demand. Ideally, Smith reasoned, the government would leave the economy to adjust itself through the forces of the free market.

17. John Locke, *Two Treatises on Government*, Peter Laslett, ed. (New York: New American Library, 1965).
18. Locke, "Second Treatise," in *Two Treatises*, ch. 4.

Classical liberalism was deemed harsh to the poor and disadvantaged in society because it opposed redistribution of wealth. At the same time, however, it defended the principle of equality before the law for all individuals. Economic inequality was unavoidable, classical liberals said, but eventually the free-market system would create wealth and raise living standards for everyone.

Modern-day liberalism has abandoned some of the principles of classical liberalism. The new position is often called *reform liberalism* because it expanded or "reformed" the classical approach to the concept of freedom. The initial motivation for this change of philosophy was to relieve the extensive poverty of the new urban working class in Britain.

Reform liberals departed from the classical roots on three essential issues:

1. The idea that government should be left to the propertied class was replaced by democratic principles of mass participation.
2. The concept of freedom was changed to recognize that the state may have to curb some liberties in order to provide a higher standard of living for the least well-off in society.
3. Reform liberals abandoned laissez-faire capitalism to accept the teaching of economist John Maynard Keynes, who argued that reliance on market forces could result in a permanent economic depression, and that this could be avoided by governments adopting appropriate fiscal and monetary measures.

In all, reform liberals reconciled state action with their notion of individual freedom by arguing that economic intervention was necessary to enable individuals to fulfill their potential and to make the market work effectively. They maintained that government must play a regulatory role in protecting society. The governments of Britain, Canada and the United States all followed this modern liberal reasoning after the Second World War.

Contemporary liberal values include respect for individual rights and freedoms, political equality, limited government, rule of law, minimum conditions of life guaranteed by the state, and modified economic freedom. In other words, modern liberalism favours minimal government intervention in the private lives of citizens, but reasonable government intervention in economic affairs. In recent years, however, this philosophy has come under attack from many quarters. In many respects, there has been a return to pre-Keynesian economics. All four parties in the Canadian House of Commons today espouse a kind of nineteenth-century liberalism in stressing the market's role in the regulation of economic life, although now it is in the context of globalization. None of them, however, has completely departed from all aspects of Keynesianism.

Conservatism

The ideology of conservatism justified the positions of the aristocracy and church in the old order of European society. These elements of society resisted the liberal ideology of progressive social change and defended the status quo, seeking to conserve such elements as power, property, status and way of life. *Conservative* comes from the Latin *conservare*, which means "to save or preserve."

English scholar Edmund Burke (1729–97) was the first major figure to define and clarify conservatism. He insisted that society must have a stable order and structure in order for individuals to know their place in the community and live and work within those confines for the good of the whole. Change, he said, must be gradual. Burke believed that being a responsible member of the social whole allowed an individual to achieve greater happiness than could be gained otherwise. Conservatives believed that the social group was more important than individuals and accused liberals of being individualistic and selfish.

Whereas classical liberals were suspicious of state power and wanted to limit it, conservatives believed that state power was necessary to achieve social order. Burke, therefore, opposed extending the right to vote, for example, and defended hereditary aristocracy and the established church. However, Burke also viewed such power as carrying a responsibility to help the weak and less fortunate. In this way, conservatives could argue that their approach was better for the less fortunate of society than was that of the liberals, who believed that everyone, including the poor, should be free to look after themselves. Burke and the early conservatives held basically the same economic views as Adam Smith and the classical liberals.

Like liberalism, conservatism adapted and changed. After the Second World War, conservatives gave qualified acceptance to the notion of the welfare state, but they still sought to preserve traditional moral values and a social structure that would provide leadership. European conservatism was never a strong part of US culture because the United States was founded and populated largely by liberals. However, in the 1930s those who opposed the welfare state philosophy of modern liberalism adopted the conservative label. American conservatism thus stresses individualism, self-reliance and a dislike for state interference, and views the improvement of the human condition as the inevitable outcome of unfettered interaction among self-interested individuals. European conservatism, on the other hand, ranks order and the good of the community above individual freedom. The Canadian Progressive Conservative party espoused both the traditional European and US versions of conservatism at various times in its history. Essentially, the Reform/Alliance parties of the 1990s and 2000s adopted the philosophy of US conservatives. The Conservative Party of Canada that emerged in 2003 represents an eclectic and often contradictory mix of conservative ideas as it attempts to bring its disparate constituency together to solidify its hold on government. By 2007, it had clearly become a brokerage party, moving to the middle of the political spectrum where most votes are found. This may be because minority governments demand compromise, but some disappointed Western conservatives who felt right-wing Reform/Alliance ideas were being shunted aside complained that the prime minister had been "Otta-washed."[19] Other observers argue that the Conservatives will show their true ideological colours only after they win a majority government.

> *You don't win a majority from an ideological position in Canada.*
>
> *Darrell Reid, pollster,* Toronto Star, *July 3, 2007*

Socialism

Within the first few decades of the nineteenth century, the technological advances of the industrial revolution in Europe created a large, urban working class. Socialists sought to improve the lives of these workers by challenging the liberal idea that governments should not be involved in directing the economy of the country. Socialism championed public ownership, a planned economy and state intervention in the market. Workers required help from the state, but classical liberalism held that the economy should be as free of government control as possible.

Initially, there were two versions of socialism: the *utopian* version found in Britain and France, and the *scientific* version of Karl Marx in Germany. The scientific socialists, led by Marx, dominated socialist thought by the end of the century. Within this group, however, a doctrinal split emerged. Those who wanted to work within the framework of parliamentary democracy became known as *democratic socialists*. Those who clung to the Marxist revolutionary prescription came under the label of *communist*. Both groups sought public control of the means of production and an end to the exploitation of labour under capitalism. But communism went much further, promising equalization of material conditions for everyone.

19. *Toronto Star*, "Harper makes a practical shift to the centre," July 3, 2007, p. A16.

Even before the breakdown of communism in the Soviet Union, there were significant changes to socialist thought. In Britain, nationalization of industry was no longer seen as a key component of socialist doctrine. Socialist thinker C.A.R. Crosland maintained that the essence of socialism was instead a set of "moral values" summarized as recognizing the need to

- ameliorate the material poverty and physical squalor produced by capitalism;
- contribute to the social welfare of those in need;
- support equality and the classless society;
- promote fraternity and co-operation; and
- fight the negative effects of capitalism such as mass unemployment.[20]

In 1995, clause 4 of the British Labour Party constitution (which called for nationalizing industries) was deleted—marking a major turning point in the evolution of socialism in political parties and leading to the election of a massive Labour government in 1997. Under the banner of "New Labour," Prime Minister Tony Blair took the Labour Party further to the centre with his "third-way" approach. Aspects of the socialist doctrine and third-way revisionism appear regularly in Canada's New Democratic Party ideology.

Nationalism and Populism

> ### CLOSE-UP ON
> ### Political Behaviour
>
> ### THE BRIEF IDEOLOGICAL SHIFT TO THE RIGHT IN CANADA
>
> In the mid-to-late 1990s, Canada witnessed a profound ideological change in its electorate and also in the political parties that represented it. Right-wing populism appeals to those who feel disadvantaged, and by 1995 Canadians had suffered a decline in real incomes for 8 of the previous 13 years. Many Canadians blamed big, debt-ridden governments for a growing gap between rich and poor. In protest, they joined forces with an unlikely ally—the corporate elite—to demand cuts in social services and lower taxes. Political parties moved to the right to win public support.
>
> Reform was the first party to tap into the ideological shift federally, but the Liberal government also moved to the right very quickly following its 1993 victory. The party that once introduced old-age pensions, universal health care and other social services took up the new mantra of deficit and debt reduction.
>
> By the 2004 election, the deficit and debt were under control and voters were more concerned with how to restore social services that had either been deprived of funds or eliminated. Health care was the major issue, and parties, especially the Liberals and Conservatives, moved back to the central ground.

Liberal values, based on a belief in a capitalist society, a market economy and the right to private property, dominate in Canadian society—however, not to the absolute exclusion of other perspectives. The main parties in the House of Commons from the 1930s until 1993—the Conservative/PC, Liberal and CCF/NDP parties—reflected the broad ideological differences of conservatism, liberalism and socialism but never strayed very far from the opinions of the broader public. The 1993 general election not only destroyed the familiar party system of the House of Commons but also brought in a Québec nationalist party and a populist party from the West—parties with two new ideologies to compete with the standard ideas of the Canadian party system.

In the mid-1990s, parties scrambled to the right on the political spectrum in order to win public support (see "Close-Up on Political Behaviour: The Brief Ideological Shift to the Right in Canada"). The Liberal government in Ottawa moved right very quickly after its 1993 electoral victory, as far or further than the Progressive Conservative government it had replaced, while the New Democratic Party became almost irrelevant. Right-wing populism is an unusual phenomenon in Canada; it appears to be a direct import from the United States. The union of disillusioned voters with the corporate elite was useful for both but was never likely to last because the goals of the two groups are almost diametrically opposed. In effect, they used each other to force governments to downsize.

---

20. C.A.R. Crosland, *The Future of Socialism* (New York: Schocken, 1963), p. 67.

Established Parties: History and Ideas

Parties are not ossified structures. As political institutions that compete for governmental power, they are based on ideologies as well as on the interests and opinions of their members. In order to be successful in elections, party leaders understand that they must appeal to these ideological foundations. But leaders must also try to balance their philosophical principles and the psychology of their membership with those of the mass electorate as they court large numbers of uncommitted voters.

In the following section, we outline the history and fortunes of the four contemporary parties, and also discuss a few minor parties that have had a significant impact on politics over the years.

The Conservative Party: A Party in Evolution

Conservative Party history is long and full of violent upheavals and reversals of fortune. The Conservatives are Canada's oldest party, although they have existed under different names. In the fall of 2003, just in time to confront the Liberals in the 2004 election, the Progressive Conservative and the Canadian Reform Conservative Alliance parties amalgamated to form the new Conservative Party of Canada.

The Progressive Conservative Party   A country's oldest party is often the party of established interests and, in this, Canada is no exception. The privileged elements of Canadian society banded together as early as 1854, under John A. Macdonald. They formed a working coalition of various interests under the label Liberal-Conservative, an alliance that included Eastern commercial interests, conservative French Canadians and Ontario Tories. Their objectives were to bring about Confederation and then work toward a national policy—basically through encouraging national unity and developing the country by promoting a national railway, industry and commerce. Maintenance of the British connection was fundamental, as was the establishment of relatively high trade tariffs.

The party was disliked by farmers in the West because of its empathy for big business, and French Canadians were wary of it because of its strong British connection. Following two major events—the execution of Louis Riel in 1885 and the Conscription Crisis of 1917—Conservative support in Québec disintegrated, and voters in the West also withheld support. The party structure became centralized in Ontario. After the First World War, westerners formed the Progressive Party, which allied itself uneasily with the Liberals.

Another misfortune for the Conservatives was that they were in power during the early years of the Depression. A leadership vacuum compounded their adversities: neither Arthur Meighen nor R.B. Bennett could make inroads into Québec. Then, in the 1940s, the party wooed Progressive support in the West and chose John Bracken, the Liberal-Progressive premier of Manitoba, as its leader, renaming the party the Progressive Conservatives (PCs). George Drew became leader in 1948, but not until John Diefenbaker, another westerner, emerged as leader did Tory fortunes improve. The PCs formed a minority government in 1957, followed by a landslide majority victory the next year.

In 1958, John Diefenbaker's charismatic personality and appeal to diverse Canadian ethnic, economic, religious and regional groups brought his native Prairies into the fold, along with fifty seats from Québec. However, Diefenbaker's capricious leadership in difficult times ultimately alienated French Canada, the large urban centres, business, industry and the intellectual community. Only the West, his gift to the party, remained loyal. Diefenbaker's electoral defeat in 1963 left the Tories divided.

Diefenbaker was removed at a party convention in 1967. The conflict over "the Chief's" leadership and forced removal created factions within the party that plagued the ensuing Stanfield era. The six years of power under Diefenbaker's leadership preceded the PCs' second-longest continuous period as the major opposition party. Diefenbaker's successor, Robert Stanfield, with his honest but plodding image, lost his third and final campaign in 1974 by advocating unpopular wage and price controls. He was replaced by 36-year-old Joe Clark, MP for Rocky Mountain, Alberta, in 1976. This move consolidated Western support, but by then the PCs' other bases of strength had dwindled to the Atlantic provinces and rural and small-town Ontario.

The 1979 election gave the PCs their first hold on power in 16 years, but the prize was snatched away just 8 months later when their minority government was defeated on a budget vote. Prime Minister Clark accepted the vote as a lack of confidence in the government and advised the governor general to dissolve Parliament. That combination of events contributed to a huge Progressive Conservative defeat in the 1980 election. At the next party policy convention, Clark submitted to a routine vote of confidence. Although he won 67 percent of the delegate vote, which was technically more than adequate, he asked the executive to call a leadership convention in 1983 and declared his candidacy. His subsequent defeat by archrival Brian Mulroney was a personal humiliation.

Mulroney, who had run unsuccessfully against Clark in the 1976 leadership convention, was an extremely astute lawyer from Québec who had diligently (some would say cunningly) paved the way to this leadership position over many years.[21] Mulroney met the challenge of building a significant and durable electoral base in Québec. In the 1984 general election, and to a lesser extent in 1988, his PCs won strongly and relatively evenly across the entire country. In the spring of 1993, however, in the wake of constitutional reform failures, scandals and unpopular policies, Mulroney resigned.

In June 1993, Kim Campbell became leader of the party and prime minister. She led the party into a fall campaign that left the PCs in ruins. She lost her own seat and ended up with only two MPs and no official party recognition in the House. Two months later, Campbell resigned and Jean Charest became interim leader. The PCs at least temporarily retained their majority in the Senate and this helped to keep the party alive. Charest was elected leader in 1995 and set about rejuvenating the party organization. In the 1997 election, the number of Tory MPs increased to twenty. Shortly after the election, however, Charest deserted the federal Tories in order to confront the separatist challenge directly as leader of the Liberal Party of Québec.[22]

Meanwhile, the federal PCs selected former prime minister Joe Clark to take over the tattered remnants of their party, an organization deeply in debt and in last place among five parties in the House of Commons. In 2000, the Tories went into the election with a wide but scattered following that made it difficult to win many ridings. They split the vote with the Alliance in several Ontario ridings, and in the end won only 12 seats in the House of Commons. Clark consistently refused to compromise his PC ideals to form a so-called united right, but he stepped down as leader in 2003. The same year, the PC leadership was assumed by Peter MacKay, who summarily backed out of a deal he had made with a leadership rival to keep the PCs as a separate party and negotiated with Stephen Harper and the Canadian Alliance to form a new conservative party.

Historically, the Progressive Conservative Party in Canada was not doctrinaire and never sought ideological purity. The early Conservative Party under John A. Macdonald was dominated by the themes of Canadian nationalism and support for British imperialism with its "innate assumption of

---

21. Patrick Martin, Allan Gregg and George Perlin, *Contenders: The Tory Quest for Power* (Scarborough, ON: Prentice Hall, 1983). Also, see John Sawatsky, *Mulroney: The Politics of Ambition* (Toronto: Macfarlane Walter & Ross, 1991).

22. Despite winning more votes than Bouchard's Parti Québécois in the ensuing 1998 Québec election, Charest's Liberals won only enough seats to form the Opposition. In 2003, however, the Liberals won a massive victory in Québec and Charest became premier. His Liberals won a further minority government in 2007.

moral and racial superiority."[23] Years spent in the political wilderness, pressures from expanding US influence in Canada, and the growing anachronism of British imperialism undermined these Tory traditions. As they entered the 1980s, Progressive Conservatives themselves agreed that their party was "hampered by its public image of being pro–big business and anti-labour, anti-ethnic, anti-women and anti-youth, as well as reactionary on most social issues."[24] This harsh assessment was a formidable burden, and efforts to soften their image, particularly in accommodating women and youth, culminated in the election of their party's first female leader and Canada's first female prime minister in 1993. The party has traditionally been committed to upholding the private enterprise system, but on occasion has let the government intervene in the economy to protect broad collective interests.[25]

Traditionally, the party was less sensitive to francophone interests than were the Liberals, but that changed in 1984 with a leader from Québec. Historically, the party was wary of US influence; it was also pro-British and supportive of agricultural interests. But, again, this changed dramatically under Mulroney, who led the party to a staunch pro–United States position and brought forth both the *Canada–United States Free Trade Agreement* and the *North American Free Trade Agreement*. Mulroney's electoral successes relied heavily on support from both the West and Québec. It was an unlikely union that held together partly because of the desire of both regions for free trade with the United States. In 1993, when those regions deserted the PCs for the Bloc and Reform, the party was crushed by the Chrétien Liberals. Over the next decade, the once-great party of Sir John A. Macdonald was forced to reassess its policies and even its very existence.

The Reform Party/Canadian Reform Conservative Alliance The Reform Party was founded by Preston Manning in late 1987 at the time of the first Mulroney government. Like other Western protest parties, Reform tapped into feelings of economic and political alienation in southern Alberta in particular and the West in general. Its rallying cry was, "The West wants in" (see Chapter 7). It fielded candidates in the 1988 general election and, while it won no seats, Reform captured 15 percent of the popular vote in Alberta. A few months later, it won a by-election in Alberta and sent Deborah Grey to Ottawa as its first MP. In the 1993 general election in which the Progressive Conservatives were reduced to two seats in the House, Reform ran candidates in all provinces except Québec.

The Reform Party benefited from widespread cynicism toward politicians in general and a feeling that the traditional parties had atrophied. Reform appealed particularly to farmers and others who felt outraged and abandoned by the established political parties. The cornerstone of the right-wing Reform policy platform in the 1993 general election was slashing the deficit, which it promised to accomplish in three years. To do this, it vowed to cut programs such as maternity leave and reduce transfer payments for welfare. Job creation was seen primarily as the responsibility of the private sector. Reform espoused the virtues of thrift and self-reliance, cheaper and less intrusive government.

As a populist party, Reform appealed to "plain folks" with "plain talk." Aspects of its platform hearkened back to the defunct Progressive and Social Credit parties. For example, it included support for more democratic input into policies, based on initiative, referendum, recall of MPs, free voting in the Commons and a Triple-E Senate. Economic difficulties and social problems were blamed on scapegoats such as immigrants, bilingualism, multiculturalism, the GST and feminists. The party therefore attracted elements of society that resented immigrants and special status for French-speaking Canadians, among other things.

23. Charles Taylor, *Radical Tories: The Conservative Tradition in Canada* (Toronto: House of Anansi, 1982), p. 211.
24. Ibid., p. 211.
25. See Robert Stanfield, "Conservative Principles and Philosophy," in Paul Fox, ed., *Politics: Canada*, 6th ed. (Toronto: McGraw-Hill Ryerson, 1987), pp. 260–64.

Reform won 52 seats with 19 percent of the popular vote in 1993—not quite enough to become the Official Opposition. It displaced the NDP and PCs to become the strongest voice of Western interests. However, apart from a single seat in Ontario, the party had no representation east of Manitoba.

Once in Parliament, Reformers quickly became identified with the elite politicians they had reviled. They were accused by Liberals of pandering to anti-politician sentiments with their concentration on politicians' pay, pensions and perks. By the end of its first session in Parliament, Reform had not climbed higher than 14 percent in public opinion polls and the leadership was forced to make many changes in the way the party operated in Parliament.[26] Before that period, Reform's organization had allowed no specialization and many areas of government activity were not adequately monitored. These changes complemented a more aggressive Question Period strategy.

By its first convention after the 1993 election, Reform had begun to change from a protest party into one that could assume power in Ottawa. It diluted some of the ideological purity of its policies in favour of approaches the party's parliamentary wing argued would be more defensible and saleable in mainstream politics. At its pre-election 1996 convention, the party's extremist elements were outvoted as the party attempted to project the image of a more moderate, disciplined party ready to extend its reach to Ontario, the Maritimes and even Québec. The party did, however, affirm its stand that family and marriage involves heterosexuals, not gays and lesbians; it called for a referendum on abortion and endorsed the return of capital punishment. Reform also supported equality for all provinces and "special status" for no one, along with twenty decentralizing proposals for a new confederation "and twenty tough realities about secession."

Reform's policies—especially its tough stance against special rights for Québec—captured considerable attention in the 1997 election campaign. Sixty Western MPs were elected. Reform formed the Official Opposition in Parliament and began to assert itself as a national party. Inside Parliament, the leadership developed a more coherent strategy for Question Period and imposed more discipline on caucus members. After only six years in Ottawa, Preston Manning had suspended or expelled six members of caucus.

Manning tried to link the PC and Reform parties, or at least obtain inter-party co-operation, by running joint candidates for the next election to avoid splitting the anti-Liberal vote. However, Joe Clark rejected any such co-operation. When attempts at a merger or co-operation failed, Manning forced the creation of the Canadian Reform Conservative Alliance (more commonly known as the Canadian Alliance), which linked dissident PC/Tory groups with Reform supporters. In the process, however, he lost the leadership of the party to Stockwell Day.

Under its new leadership, the Canadian Alliance was made up primarily of former Reform Party members, disgruntled federal Tories and supporters from a variety of provincial parties, led by Alberta and Ontario Tories. In 2000, the Alliance still failed to make an electoral breakthrough in Ontario (where it won only two seats) or further east (where it won none). Stockwell Day's leadership was severely weakened, and Western discontent with the region's inability to win a strong voice in the new Parliament was high. It was clear that without some sort of unity and balancing of regional interests, the political right had created a scenario of perpetual Liberal Party rule.[27]

The Conservative Party of Canada   Stephen Harper took over the leadership of the Canadian Alliance after Day stepped aside; in 2003, Harper and PC leader Peter MacKay finally merged the PC and Alliance parties into the Conservative Party of Canada. The union was accomplished at a quasi-national convention held at 27 locations across the country. Voting was

---

26. Reform adopted a traditional shadow cabinet system in which individual MPs were given responsibility for questioning and criticizing specific cabinet ministers.

27. The transition period to the Conservative Party of Canada is well documented in Bob Plamondon's *Full Circle: Death and Resurrection in Canadian Conservative Politics* (Toronto: Key Porter, 2006).

Courtesy Patrick Corrigan. Reprinted with permission.

not secret, but by a show of hands, with 90 percent of Tory delegates and 96 percent of Alliance members voting for the union.

Harper was selected leader in March 2004; Peter MacKay of the Progressive Conservatives did not run. The merger was widely depicted as a victory for the Canadian Alliance. It placed the new party in a better position to compete to form a government, which did happen in early 2006 when the Harper-led Tories formed a minority. The Conservatives' challenge is to remain a united front, keep national interests ahead of regional ones and become a nationally based party.

The merger of the two parties marked the end of a forty-year struggle over who would control Canada's conservative voice in Parliament. Since the mid-1960s, when John Diefenbaker was forced out as leader of the PCs, pragmatic moderates had controlled the party. Even though Stephen Harper has taken pains to unite the party, it appears to many former PCs that the moderates have turned the leadership over to those who want a party sitting further right of centre as an alternative to the Liberals. Moderate Tories like Joe Clark say they feel excluded from the party . . . that the merger was more like a takeover:

> *People should take a hard look at how narrow this new party is . . . I think it's a lot narrower than the Progressive Conservative party it pretends to be. I don't see anything like the breadth of view that was in the party I led to office 25 years ago this week. Nothing like the one Mr. Mulroney or Mr. Diefenbaker led to office.*
>
> *Joe Clark, May 21, 2004*

Throughout much of their long history, the Progressive Conservatives were divided over what the party stood for, and they bitterly attacked their leaders when they failed to win elections. It remains to be seen whether the new Conservative Party has resolved these failings. In the 2004 election under Harper, the party held the Liberals to a minority government and came in a credible second, winning 99 seats in the House. In 2006, the minority Liberal government was defeated at the polls and the Conservatives formed their own minority government. Stephen Harper became prime minister with one overriding objective: to win a majority in the next election.

The Liberal Party

The Liberal Party was slower than its Conservative counterpart to develop as a national force. Its predecessors were early reformers who generally advocated a radical transformation of society and wanted to solve major inequities through governmental reform. The opposition to Sir John A. Macdonald's first government consisted of Clear Grits from Ontario, the Parti Rouge from Québec and anti-Confederation Nova Scotia MPs. It was generally considered a more egalitarian grouping than the Conservatives. However, there was no sustained unity among the groups until Wilfrid Laurier became leader in 1887 and transformed them into the national Liberal Party. As Canada's first French Canadian prime minister, Laurier firmly entrenched the Liberal Party in Québec, with assistance from people such as Honoré Mercier and Joseph-Israël Tarte. Laurier still holds the record for the longest continuous term in office as prime minister—from 1896 to 1911.

After Laurier, the Liberal Party endured a decade of discontent that climaxed in bitter division over the Conscription Crisis in Québec. In 1919, the party elected William Lyon Mackenzie King as leader. The Liberals won the 1921 election, and King rebuilt the party into a powerful organization that dominated Canadian federal politics for most of the next six decades. Mackenzie King was prime minister for a record 21 years and 5 months. During his early years in office, King astutely tried to accommodate the agrarian protest from the West by forming an alliance with the Progressives, but that initiative collapsed in later years. Louis St. Laurent, who succeeded King (and was defeated by John Diefenbaker in 1957), his successor, Lester Pearson (party leader from 1958 to 1968; prime minister from 1963 to 1968), and Pierre Trudeau (prime minister from 1968 to 1979 and from 1980 to 1984), who followed Pearson, all more or less successfully accommodated Québec discontent but gradually lost the West.

Trudeau's ascent to the leadership in April 1968 was a dramatic victory by an attractive political neophyte over well-known, experienced Liberal leaders. "Trudeaumania" swept the country and the party won a large majority in the ensuing election. Throughout the 1960s, the Liberal popular vote had increased in the West, and, although the 1968 sweep was not as extensive there as in Ontario and Québec, it represented a Liberal high point. Following that election, the party endured an unrelenting decline in support west of Ontario.

In the wake of accusations of arrogance and insensitivity, the Liberals suffered near-defeat in the 1972 election. However, they won another strong mandate in 1974. Five years later, they received another rebuff at the polls. It was not a crushing defeat—just severe enough to allow the PCs a tenuous minority hold on power. The Liberals' serious problem in 1979 was the fact that half of their MPs were elected from one province: Québec. That November, Trudeau publicly stated his intention to resign as leader, but within weeks the Progressive Conservative government was toppled and a new election called. Trudeau remained leader and the Liberals won a new majority mandate in 1980.

In the spring of 1984, having led his party for over 16 years, Pierre Trudeau resigned. John Turner won the ensuing party leadership convention and called an election within days of his victory. However, Trudeau's bevy of patronage appointments just as he left office had soured the mood of the electorate, and the Liberals won only 28 percent of the popular vote in the 1984 election—the worst result ever for the party in a federal election. Turner stayed on as leader, but his new party caucus was dispirited and fractious. Issues such as the Meech Lake Accord and the Free Trade Agreement with the United States were particularly divisive, and the party went into the 1988 election in debt and divided over both issues and its leadership. The Grits lost again but improved their share of the popular vote to 32 percent and laid the foundation for a future Liberal victory. By 1990, Turner had resigned and Jean Chrétien was elected party leader. He become Canada's twentieth prime minister in November 1993 and led the Liberals to three consecutive election victories.

When the Liberals returned to power in 1993, the need for deficit and debt reduction forced them to abandon policy positions they had supported for generations. In economic policy, trade, human rights, social programs and immigration, the party's conservative, business-friendly element began to dominate. As *The Globe and Mail* put it, "the Liberals . . . spent much of the term cooking from the previous Tory government's recipe book."[28] Prime Minister Chrétien and his team argued that some Liberal values had to be sacrificed for fiscal responsibility. Their policy omissions and reversals included no child-care program, no scrapping of the GST, no withdrawal from NAFTA and continuing high unemployment. By the 1997 general election, however, the financial situation had improved and they had slightly loosened the national purse strings. Their efforts won them another term in office with a small majority.

Jean Chrétien called his third general election for November 2000, only three and a half years into the Liberal government's second mandate. By the fall of 2000, the government's cuts in program spending, a decline in interest rates and a growing economy had provided an unexpected budgetary surplus for three years in a row. Chrétien's electoral instincts were flawless, and he won another majority. However, before finishing his term, he was outmanoeuvred and forced to resign by Paul Martin and his supporters. The Martinites wanted time for the former finance minister to consolidate his leadership before he'd be forced to call the next election. Martin became Liberal leader in late 2003, but—due in large part to the presence of the newly minted and amalgamated Conservative Party—the party won only a minority government in the ensuing 2004 election (see Chapter 12). The government fell roughly a year and a half into its mandate, and, when the party lost the January 2006 election to the Conservatives, it almost immediately began the search for a new leader. The December 2006 leadership convention chose Stéphane Dion.

The philosophical base of the Liberal Party derived originally from British liberalism, but Canadian Liberal leaders have tended to adopt a distinctively pragmatic approach to issues as they arise. Traditional liberal themes such as reform, individual rights, state intervention to enhance the lives of the underprivileged, and national and international conciliation have recurred in various concrete forms in Liberal Party platforms and policies. However, as we have noted, practical politics in Canada tend to be ideologically fuzzy and opportunistic. As one observer put it,

> *certainly there have been sporadic tremors of small "l" liberalism. But whether unemployment insurance or the National Energy Program, the tremors have usually been in isolation, a reflection of an individual minister rather than concerted Government policies.*[29]

After the Second World War, successive Liberal governments gradually expanded their influence in the social and economic spheres. They introduced important social welfare legislation and assumed

---

28. *The Globe and Mail*, editorial, October 28, 1996.
29. John Gray, "Who Will Be the Liberals' New Skipper?" *The Globe and Mail*, January 6, 1982.

more responsibility for directing the Canadian economy, particularly by enforcing wage and price controls in 1975. In the late nineteenth century, when the Liberal Party was generally in opposition in Ottawa and in government in the provinces, it was a staunch defender of provincial rights. When the Liberals held power in Ottawa, however, they espoused strong centralizing policies. In foreign affairs, Liberal policies have been selectively internationalist (see Chapter 15). Internally, bilingualism and a broad commitment to individual and minority rights, both linguistic and legal, were perhaps the most coherently pursued Liberal policies under Trudeau, Turner and Chrétien. Stéphane Dion based his 2006 leadership campaign on the need to protect the environment. He was also closely associated with the *Clarity Act* and the Chrétien government's response to separatism in Québec— policies disliked by many Québeckers.

The New Democratic Party

The roots of the New Democratic Party (NDP) are in the Co-operative Commonwealth Federation (CCF), which held its founding convention in 1933. The original CCF was an assortment of Fabian socialists, Marxists, farmers and labourers under the leadership of J.S. Woodsworth. The party had a predominantly rural backing from the West, and, in its first 28 years, never attracted more than 16 percent of the popular vote. In 1958, the Canadian Labour Congress (CLC) made formal overtures to the party, proposing a broadly based people's movement that would embrace the CCF, the labour movement, farm organizations and professionals. The CCF set up a joint committee with the CLC to create a new party.

In 1961, the CCF was dissolved and the New Democratic Party, with its social democratic platform, was born. The new party retained many CCF leaders, but the participation of organized labour caused difficulties, and tensions between farmers and workers often ran high. The extent to which the party should be influenced by trade unions is still a divisive issue.

Vigorous leadership by Tommy Douglas in the early years, and then by David Lewis and Ed Broadbent, was never enough to overcome the lack of funds and the ideological divisions that kept the NDP as a third party at the federal level. It has never been able to expand its territorial base to Québec except in two by-elections.[30] In 1988, it achieved its best results ever: 43 seats in the House of Commons and 20.2 percent of the popular vote. Despite this good showing, Ed Broadbent resigned and was replaced as leader by Audrey McLaughlin. In 1993, the party was reduced to nine MPs and forced to rethink its purpose and direction. It did not have enough seats to be recognized as an official party in Parliament. It had lost its electoral base in Ontario and the Maritimes and was confined to a handful of MPs scattered throughout the Western provinces. In 1995, the party elected Alexa McDonough, formerly of the Nova Scotia legislature, as leader, and she steered the NDP closer to the political centre with an economic policy of balanced budgets.

In 1997, McDonough led the party back to fourth place in numbers of seats held in the House of Commons, largely because of her appeal in the Maritimes. The party remained in fourth place after the 2000 election, but was reduced to 13 seats from 21. In January 2003, Jack Layton was elected NDP leader. The party won 19 seats in the 2004 election and 29 seats in 2006.

There are several reasons why the NDP has remained a minor party. As a left-leaning party, it has never attracted and consolidated a large base. It has also had no strong position or impact on the country's major French–English cleavage. In the early years, it attracted the votes of discontented westerners. From the 1960s to 1988, the PCs encroached on that base, but in the 1988 election the NDP captured 33 of their 43 seats in the West, mostly in British Columbia and Saskatchewan. They were

30. The NDP has never won a seat in Québec in a general election. The party did win a by-election seat there in 1990, but afterwards was consistently embarrassed by its new Québec MP's independence and nationalist views. The NDP won another by-election seat in 2007.

unable to consolidate these gains, however, as the Reform Party quickly usurped the NDP's traditional protest role and left the New Democrats defending the status quo.

The NDP is considerably stronger at the provincial level than it is federally. In 1999, it formed governments in three provinces—British Columbia, Saskatchewan and Manitoba. Occasionally, the NDP's provincial politics has hurt the federal party. In 1993, NDP premier Bob Rae's tough measures to reduce the Ontario deficit offended many of the NDP's traditional supporters and caused such a deep rift in the national party that in the 1993 general election the federal NDP lost all its seats in Ontario. Federally, the NDP has played a larger role in Canadian politics than its success at the polls would indicate. During the 1972 and 2004 minority governments, for example, tacit support from the NDP was vital to the Liberals, and similarly for the Conservatives in the 2006 minority government.

In general, the NDP platform is based on democratic socialist goals. The NDP is a fairly ideologically based left-wing party. It advocates policies such as government regulation of the economy, including more government control of private enterprise, higher taxes for big business and industry, increased social welfare and protection from US influence. However, the party's leaders have constantly been forced to take on other issues and to compromise the party's strict adherence to social democracy in order to win votes.

The Bloc Québécois

The Bloc Québécois was the first separatist party to sit in Canada's Parliament. Lucien Bouchard founded the Bloc from dissidents working within the federal system. He had come to Ottawa in 1988 as a cabinet minister and friend of Prime Minister Brian Mulroney. But, in May 1990, Bouchard quit cabinet and the Progressive Conservative Party. In resigning, he cast himself as spokesman for a monolithic, humiliated Québec. He said Canada was not even worth attempting to save:

> We must stop trying to fit Québec into the mould of a province like the others. Beyond the legal arguments, there is one argument that is unanswerable. Québeckers do not accept this mould. Their very reality shatters it.[31]

When the Meech Lake Accord died in June 1990, Bouchard set up a legislative group in the House of Commons to work for the dismantling of Canada—following essentially the same path as the provincial Parti Québécois under Jacques Parizeau. A handful of MPs followed him to create the Bloc Québécois, notably Jean Lapierre (who later became Prime Minister Paul Martin's chief lieutenant in Québec).

As we noted in Chapter 7, the Bloc Québécois stated its purpose in a draft manifesto as "solely to promote Québec's profound and legitimate interests and aspirations."[32] In the 1993 general election, the party's limited separatist platform placed the Bloc left of centre on the political spectrum, defending progressive social policies, but also fiscal conservatism, and reconciling the demands of business and labour under the sovereignty banner. The party talked about cutting government waste, job creation and social programs. Its raison d'être, however, was sovereignty. It appealed to uninformed passion—anger, fear and ethnic pride.

The Bloc went into the 1993 election with 8 seats and came out with 54. It won 14 percent of the popular vote in Canada, but 49 percent in Québec, where it ran all of its candidates. It was an impressive win, enough to make a separatist party the Official Opposition in the House of Commons,

31. Quoted in Robert J. Jackson and Doreen Jackson, *Stand Up for Canada: Leadership and the Canadian Political Crisis* (Scarborough, ON: Prentice Hall, 1992), p. 201.

32. Ibid., pp. 201–2.

but it was not the landslide the party had hoped for. Many of the Bloc's votes came from disgruntled federalists, indicating that the party would need to increase its support to win a referendum on sovereignty.

In 1995, when the Québec referendum on separation was narrowly rejected, Québec premier Jacques Parizeau resigned and Bouchard left his position as leader of the Bloc to become provincial leader of the Parti Québécois and premier of Québec. In February 1996, the Bloc establishment elected Michel Gauthier as the new leader. A year later, it replaced him with Gilles Duceppe in a party-wide postal ballot.

The Bloc's 1997 election campaign was poorly managed by Duceppe, and the party tumbled from second to third place. It remained there in 2000, and its proportion of the vote in Québec dropped to 39.9 percent compared to 44 percent for the Liberals. In 2004, after a good campaign, the Bloc regained 54 of Québec's 75 seats. In 2006, it won 51 seats with 42 percent of the vote in Quebec. The party remains a vital force and splits the vote in most ridings, effectively diverting support from the Liberals, who traditionally held the province, and the Conservatives, who made small inroads there in 2006.

Minor and Historical Fringe Parties

There continue to be several minor parties on the fringes of the Canadian party system that never win enough support to gain any influence or credibility. Some are serious, others less so. None has had any lasting significance. In the 2006 election, 16 political parties officially recorded their names with the chief electoral officer and fielded the one or more candidates required to be a registered political party. No candidates from fringe parties won seats in either the 2004 or 2006 elections, but the Green Party, with a full slate of candidates, garnered 4.5 percent of the popular vote, more than the 2 percent threshold required to qualify for funding under new federal party financing legislation.

There are several factors involved in the development of minor parties: ethnicity, regionalism, poor economic conditions, charismatic leadership and ideology. Maurice Pinard theorizes that minor parties arise during a period of one-party dominance when voters are dissatisfied with the traditional party and do not like the existing alternative party.[33] They prefer instead a minor party. At best, minor parties provide flexibility in Canadian politics; at worst, they fragment the country, pitting region against region and creating political instability.

One reason fringe parties have proliferated in recent years is the rise of powerful single-interest lobbies. Some groups that support issues such as English-first or the environment choose to form new parties rather than work through the traditional parties. Generally, fringe parties do not attempt to develop policies on a cross-section of issues, but field candidates on a limited platform or single issue. Two fringe parties of historical significance federally have been Social Credit and the Progressives.

Social Credit   The Social Credit Party originated in the West. It was always a regional party, never more than a third party federally and never a serious threat to the party in power. During the Depression and the agricultural failures of the 1930s, under William Aberhart's leadership, Social Credit advocated the right of the provinces to issue money and credit. In 1935, the party flooded the Alberta legislature with members and sent 15 MPs to Ottawa as well. The party's attempts to institute their radical financial reforms in Alberta were declared unconstitutional by the Supreme Court, but Social Credit persisted as a populist conservative party.

At about the time that Social Credit appeared in Alberta, the party's ideas also took root in Québec. The Québec wing was a failure until the fiery orator Réal Caouette revived it as the Ralliement

---

33. On third parties, see Maurice Pinard, "One Party Dominance and the Rise of Third Parties," *CJPS*, vol. 33, no. 3 (August 1967), pp. 358–73.

des Créditistes. In 1961, the Créditistes joined the national Social Credit Party, but the two groups were never fully integrated. Social Credit collapsed as a federal party in Western Canada in 1968, and many joined the Conservatives. The Social Credit Party won its last seats in Québec in 1979 and dissolved shortly thereafter.[34]

The Progressive Party Also of historical interest is the Progressive Party, which appeared briefly on the national scene in the 1920s and '30s. It consisted of a loose coalition of provincial United Farmers, and was based largely in Manitoba, Saskatchewan and Alberta, with some support in Ontario. The party opposed the National Policy tariff that kept the price of Central Canada's manufactured goods relatively high and drove up the costs of farming. It also opposed discriminatory freight rates that made it cheaper to ship manufactured goods from Central Canada to the West than to ship grain eastward.

The Progressives made a startling appearance in the 1921 election, sending 65 MPs to Ottawa, 15 more than the Conservatives. However, they refused to form the Official Opposition and, with no organization, the party quickly disintegrated as a national movement. Four elections later, it disappeared from the federal scene; its adherents drifted into other parties. In the early 1940s, John Bracken, former Progressive Party leader from Manitoba, became the national leader of the Conservatives and, to take advantage of the potency of the Progressive label in the West, the Conservatives adopted "Progressive" as part of their party's name.

The Green Party The Greens are strongest in British Columbia, where the party has participated in environmental battles for decades. It began as a one-cause party, but by 2004 emerged as a solid, fourth place option outside Québec, with a slate of economic and social policies and candidates in all 308 ridings. It did not win any seats, but, since it won over 3 percent of the vote nationally, it qualified for federal funding of $1.75 for every vote won—over $1 million.

We are now going to be on an equal footing—it changes everything.

Jim Harris, former Green Party leader, 2004

Led by Jim Harris in the 2006 election, the party increased its percentage of the vote. New leader Elizabeth May will be running in Nova Scotia's Central Nova riding against the Tories' Peter MacKay in the next general election.[35]

Party Constitutions, Structure and Organization

We have noted that one outstanding feature of the Canadian party system is its federal nature. The Liberals, Conservatives and NDP have party organizations and run candidates at both levels. Parties at the federal and provincial levels may bear the same name but act quite independently. The Liberals have separate federal and provincial wings in the four largest provinces—Québec, Ontario, Alberta and British Columbia—that are informally linked to varying degrees. The other six provinces and the Yukon have provincial parties that are direct organizational affiliates with the federal liberal party.

34. The best discussion of the Ralliement is in Michael Stein, *The Dynamics of Right-Wing Protest: A Political Analysis of the Social Credit in Quebec* (Toronto: University of Toronto Press, 1973). See accounts of the Social Credit movement in Alberta in C.B. Macpherson, *Democracy in Alberta: The Theory and Practise of a Quasi-Party System* (Toronto: University of Toronto Press, 1953).

35. The Liberals will not run a candidate against May in Central Nova and the Greens are returning the favour by keeping their candidate out of Stéphane Dion's riding. This agreement, when announced, was considered controversial in some quarters.

The Northwest Territories and Nunavut have non-partisan legislatures. The Bloc Québécois exists only in one province, Québec, and is allied with a provincial party of a different name—the Parti Québécois. The NDP is the most integrated party in that individuals who join it at the provincial level are automatically given membership in the national party (except in Québec). It is also integrated financially, save in Québec.

The organizations of the traditional parties are outlined in their constitutions.[36] Essentially, the constitutions formally vest final authority in the *party convention*—including *policy conventions* and *leadership conventions*. The constitutions authorize the appointment of the party executive, the establishment of standing committees and commissions with appointed memberships, and they guarantee regional and bicultural party representation at the executive level. They also indicate the basic philosophical leanings of the parties. Apart from this, the constitutions reveal little about power and influence.

The traditional parties consist of two wings: the parliamentary wing, composed of the party leader and caucus, and a very large, three-tier extra-parliamentary wing. Both are dominated by the party leader, whose role and selection are discussed below.

An executive body and a small permanent office command the apex of the federal parties; a very wide base of constituency associations forms the foundation. Between elections, virtually the whole structure below the apex dissolves, and communication with the party is through the national organization or the parliamentary wing. This is not true of parties in Britain, for example, where the extra-parliamentary party continues to function actively, mobilizing voters and participating in the dialogue between citizen and state. As well, none of the Canadian parties has a permanent office or professional staff that can compare in size or sophistication with those of British parties (although the Conservatives opened a new, technologically advanced building in Ottawa in 2006). The major parties in Canada have had permanent offices only since the mid-1940s. Until their establishment, the entire extra-parliamentary wing of each party was dormant until an election was called, and then it would arise spontaneously to coordinate the campaign.

Figure 11.4 shows the Liberal Party national executive at the heart of the party structure. It elects national officers, establishes party policy and is the party's ultimate decision-making body. The national executive consists of about fifty voting members. Standing committees prepare policy studies in areas including financial management, constitutional and legal affairs, national platform, national campaign and so on. As well, three commissions—the Commission of Young Liberals, the National Women's Liberal Commission and the Aboriginal Peoples' Commission—give these particular groups a voice and formal link in the party to express their special interests. The federal constituency associations are independent organizations of local party activists across the country.

The constituency is the locus of the grassroots organization of each federal party. Constituency executives represent the party in the ridings, recruit local volunteers and raise campaign funds. The constituency level of the party also elects convention delegates and plays a major role in choosing federal candidates. The dedication of members to this basic unit is vital to party fortunes, but it is a relatively weak body within the power structure of the party.

The national office normally sets procedures governing party membership and the selection of delegates to conventions, but formal decisions fall under the jurisdiction of the provincial party organizations. Therefore, rules vary from province to province and even within a province. In spite of large membership bases, there are few active members in any of the parties at this level, and the constituency associations meet infrequently. Parties do not normally contest municipal elections

---

36. The newly formed Conservative Party established an interim joint council to draft its new constitution, establish riding associations and oversee candidate recruitment selection and training. This was ratified at the first convention.

FIGURE 11.4 **Schematic Organization of the Federal Liberal Party: Parliamentary and Extra-Parliamentary**

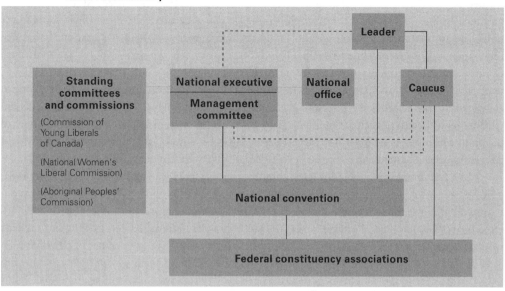

in Canada and therefore cannot draw on the forum of local government for support. As well, there is little congruence between provincial and federal party constituency boundaries. Constituency units are often very large and their members widely scattered. If the party is weak electorally in a particular constituency, funds are inevitably scarce, and it becomes difficult to hold activities and attract new members.

At the upper level of the extra-parliamentary pyramid of each party is the national organization, which unites the provincial associations. The national executive appears in a different form in each party, but it consists essentially of a small elite that conducts party business on behalf of the mass party. It includes a president, vice-president and other officers and several executive committees.

Each of the three national parties has a permanent party headquarters in Ottawa, staffed by a handful of bureaucrats and workers, who are responsible to the party leader as well as executives from the extra-parliamentary organization. The national offices of the traditional parties function as links between the provincial organizations and the elected members of Parliament and act as clearing houses for intra-party communications. Despite its permanent position at the apex of the extra-parliamentary party, the national office is engaged mainly in service and coordinating functions: it organizes conventions, by-elections and general elections and keeps the party alive between elections. The organization of the Bloc Québécois is unique in that, because of its separatist philosophy, it is very closely tied to the provincial Parti Québécois.

It is worth noting the role of women in party organizations. Women did not have the right to vote federally until 1918 (much later in some provincial elections—Québec was the last to grant the franchise to women, in 1940). Nor did they have a representative of their own gender in the federal Parliament until 1921, the first federal election held after the franchise was extended. This first woman MP was Agnes Macphail, who originally sat as a member of the Progressive Party and later joined the CCF.[37]

---

37. Agnes Macphail served as a member of Parliament until she was defeated in 1940 and then moved to provincial politics in her native Ontario. She died in 1954 just before her appointment to the Senate was to be announced.

Until the 1950s, political parties were male preserves despite the individual contributions of women such as Macphail. Women and also youth were gradually acknowledged, but not as full partners. In the Liberal Party, for example, young people were hived off into affiliated organizations: the Young Liberal Federation and the Canadian University Liberal Federation.[38] In 1973, these organizations were replaced by the Liberal Commission (for women) and the National Youth Commission. These organizations are intended to represent and promote the interests of students, youth and women in the party, and to encourage their participation and party activities. A third commission was added later for Native peoples. Eventually, special organizations designed to encourage women to participate in the parties may be abandoned. In the meantime, guarantees of positions on some party executive committees and some assured positions as voting delegates at conventions have helped women to achieve higher visibility within party organizations.

The NDP constitution contains few guarantees with respect to female participation. By 1981, however, the party had an internal affirmative-action program, and two years later approved a requirement for equal representation of men and women on its executive and council. In December 1989, the NDP elected Audrey McLaughlin as its national leader, making her the first woman ever to lead a national party in Canada. Alexa McDonough succeeded her in 1995. Women as electoral candidates and MPs are discussed in Chapters 4, 8, 9 and 12 of this text.

Party Conventions and Leadership Selection

Leadership conventions (or other forms of leadership selection) are convened as necessary to select new leaders, and are generally separate from *party conventions* which are held about every two years to elect party officials, debate policy resolutions and constitutional amendments and raise morale. Both types of gatherings in the traditional parties are large, widely representative gatherings of several thousand delegates, most of whom have already invested considerable time and energy as executive officers for the party or as members of women or youth associations.

Party conventions are representative of a particular party and are therefore far from an exact reflection of society, although they are normally more inclusive of the various age, gender, occupational, ethnic and religious groups than are the party caucuses.[39] Terms such as *democratic* and *representative* are merely part of the rhetoric used by parties and commentators to generate respect and approval for their party conventions, although evolving democratic norms have encouraged parties to make their leadership selection processes more responsive to party members.

Party leadership conventions are particularly important in marshalling enthusiasm to help heal divided parties, especially after difficult periods in opposition. These conventions can have a significant centralizing influence on the Canadian party system.

Setting Party Programs

The issue of extra-parliamentary involvement with policy decisions has been contentious and has evolved over time. By the 1960s, both the Liberal and PC party federations were demanding to be involved in party affairs on a continuing basis. To make the parties more democratic, full-time national directors were hired, national offices were established to operate between elections, conventions gradually became more regular, and women and youth were brought into the main body of the parties.

38. Reginald Whitaker, *The Government Party: Organizing and Financing the Liberal Party of Canada 1930–1958* (Toronto: University of Toronto Press, 1977), pp. 78–79 and 194–95.

39. See J. Lele, G.C. Perlin and H.G. Thorburn, "The National Party Convention," in Thorburn, ed., *Party Politics in Canada*, 5th ed., pp. 89–97.

However, extra-parliamentary parties are still relatively inactive in developing policy options. That remains a function of the parliamentary party based on the reasoning that, in a representative system, cabinet and the parliamentary caucus are best equipped to broker all the various interest into a coherent public policy. Within governing parties, policy-making is increasingly dominated by the prime minister's office. Governing parties are generally less responsive than opposition parties to the more narrow interests of their members because of their wider responsibilities.

There is no permanent, paid body in any of the extra-parliamentary parties that is charged with policy study, and parties commit few resources to ongoing policy study. At the national level, however, parties participate in drafting and passing policy resolutions at biennial national conventions. Before a convention assembles, party associations are invited to send in suggestions for consideration by the convention. In theory, the resolutions presented to the delegates are debated and passed item by item.

Party platforms that are presented at elections generally have contributions from both intra- and extra-parliamentary branches of the parties, but they are generally unsatisfactory. Of necessity, items must be vague enough to carry wide appeal—examples are social reform or improved education—and so end up reading rather like a list of New Year's resolutions. They must also appeal to regional interests, such as Maritime rights, or economic sectors, such as wheat exporters. Party platforms are therefore deliberately vague, broadly based documents of compromise that can be used to unite the party nationally. As the three traditional parties have vied for the middle ground, their policy resolutions have often overlapped.

Even after the platform is drawn up and approved by the national convention, therefore, it is little more than a guide or, as Mackenzie King was fond of stating, a "chart and compass" for the party leader to interpret and follow as deemed opportune when steering the ship of state. The party constitutions give no official status to policy resolutions emanating from the national associations.

Some argue that policy making should be the prerogative of the party elite. A grave shortcoming of the pragmatic policy formulation procedures followed by modern Canadian parties is that parochial concerns often dominate at the expense of a national vision. As Gordon Stewart comments,

from the time that modern party formulation began in the 1840s, Canada's political culture encouraged only the party leader/prime minister and perhaps one or two lieutenants to take long-term national interests into account.[40]

This discourages creative thinking about long-term policy solutions to problems. Stewart goes so far as to call the parties "political dinosaurs"—with great weight and presence but small brains.

The philosophical justification for conventions continues to be that their decisions are representative of the party and thus more democratic than those reached by the parliamentary caucus. The debates give delegates the opportunity to air their views and communicate their policy concerns to the political wing; they also attract free publicity for the parties.

Selecting National Party Leaders

Leadership selection is an internal party matter in Canada. The selection methods have changed dramatically over the years from closed, elite systems to very open, broadly based, more democratic ones. The changes have been huge. Until 1919, leadership selection in Canada followed the British model. Members of the parliamentary caucus and the retiring leader selected the new leader, occasionally with the advice of the governor general, and then presented him to the party. The Liberal

---

40. Gordon T. Stewart, *The Origins of Canadian Politics* (Vancouver: University of British Columbia Press, 1986), p. 100.

Party was the first national political party in Canada to select a leader with the active participation of its extra-parliamentary wing. It happened almost accidentally. The 1919 convention was not intended to be a leadership convention; it was instigated by the leader, Wilfrid Laurier, as a policy convention to help reunite his badly divided party. However, Laurier's sudden death, "combined with the peculiar internal conditions of the parliamentary Liberal party, made the convention appear to be a natural way of selecting the next leader of the Liberal Party."[41] In this way, Mackenzie King became the first party leader selected by a national convention.

The Conservatives chose one more leader—Arthur Meighen—by the caucus method in 1920 before the party felt compelled to follow the democratic precedent set by the Liberals. In 1927, they elected R.B. Bennett at a national convention. The British leadership selection model, whereby party leaders "emerged" after consultations generated by the retiring leader and the party caucus with the parliamentary party, was thus abandoned. Open, more US-style conventions were established, gradually becoming more lavish. Modern leadership conventions are similar to policy conventions in terms of basic organization and participation, and their general rules are common to the main parties, although details vary. (See Table 11.4 for an overview of major-party leaders.)

Only a fraction of party members participated at traditional conventions and therefore in the leadership decision. In the late 1980s and 1990s, therefore, parties began selecting leaders through direct vote by party members. It became the standard method of leadership election at the provincial level, and was adopted federally by the Reform Party and the Bloc Québécois and later by the PCs. However, direct election of leaders by the entire party membership allows wide participation, but little or no opportunity for collective deliberation. The Liberals therefore adopted hybrid methods that combine the widest participation of party members with collective decision making.

The appeal of the convention method is that it gives the impression, justified or not, that the party is "open," "democratic" and "representative" in making its decisions. A drawback is that it was not designed for parliamentary government, but rather for a system with separate legislative and executive offices. It was adapted to Canada's unique federal, parliamentary needs, but not without inevitable contradictions. For example, leadership candidates must support their party in Parliament at the same time as they appeal for delegate support—something very difficult to do when cabinet solidarity is at stake. A legacy of bitter feelings often makes it difficult for the new leader to command the full support of the caucus.

The Liberal Party sends an equal number of delegates from each constituency to its conventions, along with senators, MPs and defeated candidates. A number of delegates-at-large from the provinces also attend, including people who are prominent in party affairs but are not eligible to become delegates in one of the other categories. They also allow *appointed* delegates-at-large and committee members to attend their national conventions, often in the face of vociferous objections that such appointments are elitist and undemocratic. In the Conservative Party as well, ridings are equally represented and categories of ex-officio delegates are designated to participate in conventions.

The NDP's national conventions include broad representation from Parliament, constituencies, youth groups and affiliated organizations such as trade unions and farm groups. The number of delegates from any particular constituency is based on how many members it has. This rewards active associations but does not help the party make inroads into areas where it is weak.

Removing Leaders   Getting rid of an unpopular leader tends to be an awkward and destructive process. Leaders cannot continue in office for long without support of the parliamentary party.

---

41. John C. Courtney, *The Selection of National Party Leaders in Canada* (Hamden, CT: Archon Books, 1997), p. 78.

TABLE 11.4 **Party Leaders: PC, Liberal, NDP, Bloc Québécois, Reform/Alliance and Conservative**

Progressive Conservative Party	Liberal Party	New Democratic Party	Bloc Québécois	Reform Party/ Canadian Alliance	Conservative Party
Sir John A. Macdonald (1854–91)	Alexander Mackenzie (1873–80)	Tommy Douglas (1961–71)	Lucien Bouchard (1991–95)	Preston Manning (1987–2000)	Stephen Harper (2004–)
Sir J.J.C. Abbott (1891–92)	Edward Blake (1880–87)	David Lewis (1971–75)	Michel Gauthier (1996–97)	Stockwell Day (2000–2001)	
Sir John Thompson (1892–94)	Sir Wilfrid Laurier (1887–1919)	Ed Broadbent (1975–89)	Gilles Duceppe (1997–)	Stephen Harper (2001–2003)	
Sir Mackenzie Bowell (1894–96)	Daniel D. McKenzie* (1919)	Audrey McLaughlin (1989–95)			
Sir Charles Tupper (1896–1901)	W.L. Mackenzie King (1919–48)	Alexa McDonough (1995–2003)			
Sir Robert Borden (1901–20)	Louis St. Laurent (1948–58)	Jack Layton (2003–)			
Arthur Meighen (1920–26)	Lester B. Pearson (1958–68)				
Hugh Guthrie* (1926–27)	Pierre E. Trudeau (1968–84)				
R.B. Bennett (1927–38)	John Turner (1984–90)				
R.J. Manion (1938–40)	Jean Chrétien (1990–2003)				
R.B. Hanson* (1940–41)	Paul Martin (2003–2006)				
Arthur Meighen (1941–42)	Bill Graham* (2006)				
John Bracken (1942–48)	Stéphane Dion (2006–)				
George Drew (1948–56)					
John Diefenbaker (1956–67)					
Robert L. Stanfield (1967–76)					
Joe Clark (1976–83)					
Erik Nielsen* (1983)					
Brian Mulroney (1983–93)					
Kim Campbell (1993)					
Jean Charest (1995–98)					
Joe Clark (1998–2003)					
Peter MacKay (2003)					

* Interim leader

Stockwell Day resigned leadership of the Canadian Alliance after a caucus revolt. Jean Chrétien resigned as leader in November 2003 when it became clear that Paul Martin would be able to defeat him because of his superior strength in the constituency delegate selection committees. Neither waited for a **leadership review**, the formal process that allows the party membership to remove an unpopular leader. No Canadian leader has actually ever lost such a vote, but a poorer showing than hoped for has caused leaders to resign, Joe Clark being the best example.

Rules about when a leadership review will be held differ from party to party. Currently, the Liberal constitution states that a

> *resolution calling for a leadership convention shall be placed automatically on the agenda of the convention next following a general election. If such a resolution is duly adopted by a secret ballot the National Executive shall call a leadership convention to take place within one year. . . .*

In practice, Liberal convention delegates have always voted against calling a leadership convention, but the procedure remains a significant reminder that the leader is responsible to the party. In 1992, the Liberals approved giving *all* party members a direct say in reviewing the leader's performance after each election, thereby ending the practice of choosing delegates to vote on the leader's performance at a national convention.

In the Progressive Conservative Party, leadership reviews were first initiated to assess John Diefenbaker's performance in 1967.[42] They later became a regular feature of party conventions. Technically, a Tory leader needed to win only 50 percent of the leadership review vote to continue in office. In 1983, however, Joe Clark resigned as PC leader after he failed to secure more than 67 percent of the voting delegates' support. He then submitted himself as a leadership candidate to consolidate his party support but lost to Brian Mulroney.

The NDP has no leadership review procedure as such, but requires its leader to seek re-election automatically at its biennial national conventions. It opens nominations for the position of leader, but if there is no challenger, no vote is required. In practice, an incumbent has never been defeated.

Recent Leadership Selection   If the leadership review vote requires it, or if the current leader resigns or dies, the parties hold a leadership convention. These are huge events that take several months to organize. Delegates must be chosen, and the manner in which this is done has important consequences for the leadership candidates. Canadian leadership conventions have tended to adopt the festive atmosphere of Republican or Democratic conventions in the US, with flamboyant speeches, entertainment and full national television coverage. There are some important differences, however. Balloting at US conventions is by states rather than individuals, and the votes are announced openly, making the event quite ritualistic and predictable. The US primary system and open delegate selection process tend to produce a winner long before the convention. In Canada, the secret ballot system can lend a degree of suspense that is missing from the US process. In the Liberal selection of Paul Martin in 2003, it was evident well before the convention that he would be the new leader, but the 2006 selection of Stéphane Dion was highly suspenseful. In recent years, the parties have all made changes to make their selection process more open and democratic.

Operating under new rules for the 2003 Liberal leadership convention, all party members in each riding had the opportunity to vote for their preferred candidate and each riding then sent delegates, proportional to the support garnered by each candidate, to the national convention. To

---

42.   John Diefenbaker's leadership was in dispute following his defeat in the 1963 general election, and party president Dalton Camp seized the opportunity to argue for the need to "democratize" the party by assessing the leadership. After a bitter struggle, the Camp faction won and a leadership convention was called in 1967.

participate, one had to be a member of the party by June 20, well ahead of the November election, and the delegates were chosen by September. The delegates were required to vote at the convention according to the mandate they received from their constituency. Paul Martin had over 90 percent of the delegate votes assured by September, so that at the November 2003 convention there was no surprise when he won more than 93 percent of the ballots. By the time of the convention, only one candidate (Sheila Copps) opposed him, and she had already conceded. Martin's forces were accused of gaining control of the party machinery and using it to set membership rules that favoured the frontrunner.[43] The convention had a note of bitterness. As one candidate noted,

> *It's the worst convention I've ever seen. . . . Everybody's angry. This is supposed to be about coming together, family, unity, happy happy. I get here and the big headline is "PURGE!"*[44]

For the 2006 leadership campaign, the party encouraged more candidates to run and democratized the race more. They lowered the entrance fee to $50 000 from $75 000 and capped total spending for any campaign at $3.4 million. For 3 months, 11 candidates aspiring to the leadership sold as many party memberships as possible to anyone who wanted to vote. Other members were recruited by riding officials and on the internet. In the end, roughly 150 000 members were signed up. Only paid members of the party were entitled to elect or be elected as delegates to the leadership convention. New rules controlling the sale of memberships reduced some previous abuses by preventing manipulation of membership forms, eliminating mass purchase of memberships and preventing cash purchases of memberships on behalf of others.

Every party member had the right to vote for her choice of leader, and to choose the delegates who would participate directly in electing the new leader at a convention. Fourteen delegates from each of the 308 federal ridings were chosen to participate at the convention along with MPs, senators, former candidates and party officials.

The delegates were bound on the first ballot to support candidates based on the percentage of votes cast by party members at the riding meeting. After party members had voted for the candidate of their choice at the constituency association, the delegate votes were assigned on a proportional system, so that, for example, if 50 percent of the association members voted for one candidate, half of the 14 delegates would vote for that candidate on the first ballot. The ex-officio members and members from Liberal clubs could vote as they chose. After the first ballot, delegates were free to move to the candidate of their choice. This high degree of fluidity made it impossible to forecast a winner.

At the Montréal convention, eight candidates presented themselves to the delegates. Joe Volpe withdrew even before the first ballot, endorsing Bob Rae. After the first ballot Martha Hall Findlay and Scott Brison dropped out and also endorsed Rae. When Gerard Kennedy withdrew after the second ballot he endorsed Stéphane Dion; Ken Dryden endorsed Rae. When Rae had to withdraw after the third ballot he declined to support a candidate and his supporters split between Dion and Ignatieff (see Table 11.5 on the next page).

Michael Ignatieff had been the frontrunner throughout the campaign, and led on the first ballot. Dion was third on the first ballot, only two votes ahead of Gerard Kennedy. Politicking was intense. When Rae did not throw his support to Ignatieff on the second-last ballot, on the fourth ballot

---

43. The main complaint was that members had to join on or before June 2003 to qualify to vote for delegates to the November convention. By controlling most riding associations, the Martin people could sign up members faster because they had more forms and could slow down the ability of rivals to get the necessary forms. In three of the four largest provinces, Ontario, Alberta and British Columbia, access to membership forms was controlled entirely by Martin supporters.

44. Quoted in "Liberal Red: Bad Blood," *Maclean's,* November 24, 2003.

TABLE 11.5 Leadership Convention Vote, Liberal Party of Canada, December 2006

1st Ballot	Percentage	Votes	2nd Ballot	Percentage	Votes
Michael Ignatieff	29.3	1412		31.6	1481
Bob Rae	20.3	977		24.1	1132
Stéphane Dion	17.8	856		20.8	974
Gerard Kennedy	17.7	854		18.9	884
Ken Dryden	4.9	238		4.7	219
Scott Brison	4.0	192		—	—
Joe Volpe	3.2	156		—	—
Martha Hall Findlay	2.7	130		—	—
3rd Ballot	**Percentage**	**Votes**	**4th Ballot**	**Percentage**	**Votes**
Michael Ignatieff	34.5	1660		45.6	2084
Bob Rae	28.5	1375		—	—
Stéphane Dion	**37.0**	**1782**		**57.4**	**3541**

Source: Parliament of Canada website: www.parl.gc.ca.

the convention delegates chose Stéphane Dion—although he had been the first choice of only 17.8 percent of the voters on the first ballot.

This was the first leadership campaign to be affected by the 2004 election financing rule changes, although the Conservative government's changes of 2006 were not yet in place. The Liberal Party rules set a spending limit of $3.4 million, but the ban on corporate donations meant that none of the candidates were able to raise that much. Winner Stéphane Dion had spent $1.7 million on his campaign; runner-up Michael Ignatieff had spent $2.2 million.

In 2004, for its first leadership selection following its founding, the Conservative Party wanted to hold an election close to the grassroots of the party. Rather than have delegates at a convention choose the leader, party members voted for the leader in their constituencies, while in Toronto, the three leadership candidates made final presentations that were beamed to the ridings. The rules for their leadership selection featured a new point system in which

- a vote was held in each riding;
- each riding was weighted equally;
- each riding was worth one hundred points (i.e., 100 percent);
- in each riding, a preferential ballot (single transferable vote) was used (i.e., when party members ranked their choices in order of preference, if no candidate received more than 50 percent, then the same ballots were counted again). Candidates with the lowest number of first-place choices were dropped and those ballots went to the second choices;
- candidates were assigned points based on their percentage of the vote in the riding (e.g., a candidate winning 29% of the vote got 29 points); and
- to win, a candidate had to obtain a majority of points overall.

Courtesy Patrick Corrigan. Reprinted with permission.

TABLE 11.6 **Leadership Convention Vote, Conservative Party of Canada, March 2004**

1st Ballot	Tony Clement		Stephen Harper		Belinda Stronach	
	vote	%	vote	%	vote	%
	2887	(9.4%)	17 296	(56.2%)	10 613	(34.5%)

The voting results were announced from Toronto (see Table 11.6). Tony Clement won only 9.4 percent of the overall vote and controlled no regions or provinces. Belinda Stronach came first in Atlantic Canada and Québec while Stephen Harper won in British Columbia, the Prairie provinces and Ontario. Harper's 56.2 percent of the vote was enough to win him the leadership outright.

At its leadership convention in 2003, the NDP also opened the vote to all party members. The organizers devised a complex system that combined member and delegate votes. All party members were eligible to vote, ranking leadership candidates in order of preference. Unions and other interest groups were allotted 25 percent of the votes. This guaranteed them a certain degree of influence regardless of how many union members actually participated. Some members voted in advance, over the internet, and did not attend the convention. The result was a small turnout of about 900 and less hoopla than usual. The party used a preferential one member–one vote ballot system for the first time. The winner needed 50 percent plus 1 on the first ballot. If no candidate received 50 percent plus 1, there would be more rounds of voting with the last-place candidate eliminated. Jack Layton won 53 percent on the first ballot, replacing Alexa McDonough.

As for the Bloc Québécois, it was the first party to introduce direct elections for the leader. Leader Lucien Bouchard was acclaimed at a party congress in 1991. Five years later, his successor, Michel Gauthier, was elected by fewer than 160 people, all from Québec, in one of the fastest, smallest and least publicized gatherings to elect an Opposition leader in the postwar era. However, Gilles Duceppe was elected in March 1997 by the entire party membership, using the format of mailed ballots plus a two-day convention.

It is unlikely that parties will abandon conventions because of the media exposure they provide. Nor will they risk returning to earlier models of parliamentary selections that were swift and inexpensive, but smacked of undemocratic elitism.

The Role of the Leader in the Party

The party leader has a pre-eminent role as decision-maker, figurehead and spokesperson of both the parliamentary and extra-parliamentary branches of the party. The image projected by a leader is extremely important because it provides a simple, differentiating feature between the parties, which otherwise often appear very similar to the electorate. A leader with a poor image can ruin the electoral chances of even the most vital party, a circumstance that encourages enormous preoccupation with image-building and the appearance and personality of the leader, often to the detriment of policy issues. The leadership position is prestigious, carrying considerable powers in the parliamentary system. National party leaders ideally are symbols of unity, above sectional interests. The more regionalized the party system becomes, the less easily this ideal can be met.

The prime minister's position at the apex of government, public service and political party was discussed in Chapter 8. Here, it is sufficient to note that the office includes a large support staff and many other perquisites, of which political patronage is foremost. Patronage has, since colonial days, been relatively openly entrenched as a legitimate activity, although it can raise public ire. Prime ministers have used patronage to help build and maintain broad bases necessary for national parties. The prime minister's political patronage powers are second to none. As the top member of the government hierarchy, she has cabinet, government bureaucracy and Senate positions to fill, as well as party appointments.

Opposition leaders, whose capacity for largesse is extremely limited, have a much more difficult time maintaining a united party. Much of the prestige of the leader of the Official Opposition lies in the fact that she is a potential prime minister. But because the job is to lead the offensive against the party in power, opposition leaders are often accused of carping and sometimes even of unpatriotic behaviour for attacking the government.

Party leaders have extensive authority over the extra-parliamentary wing of the party, including the power to approve or disapprove the budget for the activities of the party organization. They also have the right to make key appointments to the national executive and to create ad hoc committees whose authority may supersede that of the officers elected by the national association. For example, the leader makes the appointments to the election campaign committee. Within the parliamentary party, the Opposition leader appoints a *shadow cabinet*, and in many ways enjoys more flexibility than the prime minister does in choosing a cabinet.

The leader of the Official Opposition has special status at official functions and in parliamentary ceremonies and even an international standing with foreign governments, but this position is nevertheless very inferior compared to that of the prime minister. Though her functions are not governed by statute, the role is officially recognized in the procedures of the House of Commons. Canada first officially recognized the existence of the leader of the Opposition in 1905 by granting the occupant of that position a salary equal to that of a cabinet minister.

While the prime minister enjoys the many perquisites of government and the official residences at 24 Sussex Drive and Harrington Lake, the Opposition leader receives, in addition to a salary and expense allowance as a member of Parliament, other perks such as a car allowance and an official residence—Stornoway in Rockcliffe Park. As for facilities on Parliament Hill, the Official Opposition leader, like the prime minister, receives a large staff and offices in the House of Commons. In addition, as a member of Parliament, the Opposition leader is entitled to a suite of offices and a constituency office with a full-time staff in Ottawa and in her riding. In Parliament, the Opposition leader has the right to ask the lead question in Question Period and benefit from the attendant publicity that such prominence entails.

Whether in power or in opposition, the party leader is accountable to the caucus. Without the support of the caucus and the national association, the leader cannot hope for sufficient party unity to achieve electoral victory. The leader's relationship with these two important sectors of the party is complicated because the caucus basically represents federal interests, while the national association tends to be more representative of provincial interests. Placating the two is especially difficult for any opposition party leader who has general responsibility for the conduct of the members of the caucus, but few rewards to offer them. Internecine battles over the leadership reinforce the image of a fragmented party in electoral decline—a problem that beset John Turner before the 1988 election, for example, despite the fact that he'd survived a review in 1986.

Nonetheless, the power of the parliamentary caucus vis-à-vis the leader is limited because regular meetings are held only a half-day each week and even then no votes are taken. The leader simply interprets the general mood in whatever he or she determines is in the party's best interests. This means that there is no recognized independent body within the caucus that can challenge the leader. As we've discussed, getting rid of an unpopular leader who is determined to stay on is a difficult matter that requires at least the threat of a vote of non-confidence at a leadership review.

The superior status of the party leader in the Canadian system is deeply rooted in parliamentary tradition. The leader is the only party member who can claim broadly based legitimacy. Leaders who founded new parties, such as Preston Manning and Lucien Bouchard, were quick to legitimate their position by a vote. Chosen by the national convention but also the voice of the parliamentary caucus, the party leader is the most powerful individual in the creation of party policy. The position is, at least theoretically, a symbol of coherence and cohesion for the party.

Who Are Canada's Party Leaders?

Party leaders tend to exhibit similar characteristics, although these vary somewhat by party. Almost all who enter the fray are white, middle-aged university-educated professionals. Since 1989, when Audrey McLaughlin became leader of the NDP, leadership is no longer strictly a male preserve.

In the past, the typical Conservative or PC leader was a Protestant lawyer from one of the Prairies, Ontario or the Maritimes. Today, that person is expected to be bilingual. Brian Mulroney was the party's first elected leader from Québec, and Jean Charest was the PCs' first francophone leader. Kim Campbell was the party's first leader from British Columbia, and the first woman to lead the party. The typical Liberal leader has been a lawyer, Roman Catholic and bilingual. Except for John Turner (who lived in Ontario but ran for office in British Columbia), the Liberals have always chosen their leaders from Ontario or Québec; normally they have alternated between French- and English-speaking leaders, a tendency that has become a matter of principle for many Liberals.

Prior to the introduction of leadership conventions, leaders of both the Liberal and Progressive Conservative parties were likely to be experienced career parliamentarians at the federal or provincial levels. Since then, previous parliamentary experience has become a less significant criterion. Brian Mulroney was the first leader of either party to win the position with no legislative experience whatsoever. Not until he won a seat in a by-election several months after the convention was Mulroney sworn in as a member of Parliament. Reform leader Preston Manning, too, had never been in Parliament when he became party leader, nor had Stockwell Day for the Alliance and Jack Layton for the NDP (although they had considerable political experience).

Mackenzie King, Pierre Trudeau, Audrey McLaughlin, Alexa McDonough and Michel Gauthier had all been in Parliament less than three years when they were elected leader. Several leaders were relatively unknown even by party activists until shortly before the conventions at which they were chosen. John Turner had been out of politics and disassociated from the Liberal government for years. Lucien Bouchard was first elected to Parliament as a Progressive Conservative in 1988—just two years before he became leader of the Bloc Québécois. It used to appear that a fresh image counted more than the experience of a party veteran, although Jean Chrétien was able to counter the epithet "yesterday's man," and Paul Martin was a minister of finance for many years before becoming leader. Stéphane Dion was brought to the House of Commons by Jean Chrétien shortly after Quebec's 1995 referendum on sovereignty to help the government resolve issues with Québec. Stephen Harper was leader of the Canadian Alliance before it merged with the PCs to become the Conservative Party.

Party Finance

Political parties require funds for three basic purposes: for expensive election campaigns; to maintain a small permanent staff between elections; and to support research and advisory services for the party leader and elected representatives.

Where do these funds come from and who obtains them? In Chapter 9, we discussed how party caucuses receive money for research and for leaders' salaries from the House of Commons. To get such funds, parties must have a minimum of twelve elected members in Parliament. It is difficult for parties to operate effectively or even stay alive without this funding. The Social Credit Party, for example, lost this funding when it dropped to 11 seats in 1974, and it never recovered.

The PCs and NDP faced a similar prospect with their huge electoral losses in 1993, but both managed to bounce back to achieve official status after the 1997 election.

Besides this internal funding, however, parties are actively engaged in seeking funds outside Parliament. Major changes to party funding were initiated in 2004 and 2006. These are discussed in the next chapter on elections.

Critical Debate
Parties: Unfulfilled Promise?

To what extent do Canadian parties fulfill the vital functions required of them, and how could they do better?

Point

An examination of the recent political history of Canada reveals that the traditional parties perform many of their important functions poorly, and because of that, they have caused the party system to fragment to the point where we have seen the growth of regionally based organizations at the federal level.

One important party function is the effective aggregation of demands from society. This role is so poorly performed that there are almost always major distortions in the regional representation of traditional parties in the House of Commons. The new parties that have arisen to fill the vacuum invariably have been even less successful in aggregating interests across the country. Most have attempted to capture votes by presenting a program based on a single ideology or particular principle, or have remained regionally based.

The party system now strongly reflects the decentralized nature of the federal system of government within which it operates. After 1993, the party system fragmented into a multi-party dominant system with the Liberals as the only party able to form a government. But they did not have widespread national representation and were in power largely because of support from Ontario. In 2006, the Conservatives won a minority government but they appear unable to broaden their base sufficiently in Ontario and Québec to win a majority. The Bloc Québécois and NDP are even more regionally based. The Bloc, with its separatist goals, is focused solely on Québec. The NDP is still scattered and has failed to make significant inroads in Québec.

Not one of the parties represents Canadians from all regions. When Québec wants something, it votes as a block for its own regional party. When the West is feeling alienated, it creates its own party to bring its interests to Parliament. Populous Ontario generally determines who will form the government regardless of what the rest of the country wants.

Canadian political parties are also limited in their ability to articulate interests. Party programs, expressed as coordinated and consistent policies, are rare in the Canadian system. Because they attempt to mediate diverse interests, the Liberal and Conservative parties believe they cannot afford the rigidity of firm policy commitments. They discuss issues and develop election campaigns, but elections are a very poor source of policy communication, and often policies are advanced in a random fashion as ad hoc responses to specific problems. Even after winning an election, parties can rarely claim clear policy directives from the electorate, or even that the electorate supports one or all of their policies.

Party organizations are designed primarily to achieve electoral victory for their parties, and their members are concerned with policy-making basically as a means to achieve that goal. Between elections, they hold policy conventions to agree on policies that are generally designed to win electoral support. However, Canadian political parties are not organized very well for policy formulation, and the impact of policy decisions made at conventions on the party leadership is uncertain. In the two major parties, convention policy statements are not binding on the leadership and, although steps are taken to avoid embarrassing contradictions or inconsistencies in party and government policies, such gaffes still happen. Party members en masse do not have much influence over policy formation; senior party bureaucrats and members of the parliamentary party hold much more sway. This is especially true regarding the governing party, because the government caucus, or private meeting of the parliamentary party, has the opportunity to discuss most policy matters before they reach the House of Commons. Decisions tend to be taken by an elite group of actors in and around the leadership of the parliamentary party.

Canadian parties could do a much better job by developing policies to appeal to Canadians in all regions, and by developing more democratic patterns of policy formation.

Counterpoint

Canadian parties perform their functions as well as could be expected in a federal system. It is not the parties, but rather the voters, that need to do a better job.

As far as aggregation of interests or demands from society go, the Liberal and Conservative parties, which have traditionally supplied the managers and decision-makers of Canadian federal politics, bring together coalitions of ethnic and regional interests. This allows a legitimate means of expression to those interests and provides an integrative force in Canadian society. They also educate the electors about the issues and give them choices of policies and leadership. Often, however, the voting public is just too bored, otherwise occupied or too ignorant to listen and make decisions about who to vote for. They prefer sound bites and photo ops to serious discussions about the issues.

The regional fragmentation of the party system is real, and it is serious. But it cannot be blamed on the parties alone. The federal system, population maldistribution and different regional economic interests are perhaps even more to blame. They all promote regionalism. Canadians like to use political parties to protest or to draw attention to their interests. It is perhaps too much to expect two or even three parties to encompass all the diverse and legitimate interests of Canadians from coast to coast to coast. Protest parties provide outlets for pent-up emotions that need to be expressed. They can make the bigger parties listen and take protest issues seriously.

The parties articulate interests well. They are effective "gatekeepers," allowing certain demands, and not others, to reach decision-makers. At the same time, the parties operate openly and freely in society. Changes in funding rules have made parties' finances more transparent so that corporations, unions and special interests have much less chance of influencing policy through the party system.

Clearly, it would be difficult, if not completely chaotic, to try to run a political system without parties to organize, recruit, nominate and get representatives elected. To accomplish this, they do a masterful job of educating the electorate on issues and providing them with opportunities to participate not just through voting, but also through many kinds of party positions—some volunteer, some paid. Parties allow for representation of everyone in society, no matter what ethnicity, religion or gender. And they provide leadership choices.

Our political parties are not perfect, but they are perhaps the best we can expect in this divided country. As Lord Macaulay pointed out in his irreverent analogy,

> *Every political sect . . . has its altars and its deified heroes, its relics and its pilgrimages, its canonized martyrs and confessors, and its legendary miracles.*[45]

Even in this electronic age, political parties still use all the timeless devices of superstition to win converts and maintain their loyalty: conventions are but pilgrimages; heroes and martyrs provide the spiritual glue of the party; relics are the venerated policies and records that provide the proof of vision and ideas of substance. Along with the manipulation, patronage and distortions, however, parties in Canada allow for the orderly election of representatives and leaders to government and are the means by which thousands of Canadians can actively participate and express themselves in the process. In short, parties are a colourful and important part of the democratic process in Canada, and even with their shortcomings it is difficult to conceive of political representation in this country without them.

Discussion Questions

1. What is your stand on the Critical Debate, and what can you add to it?
2. Describe the main factors that fragment Canada's party system.
3. Is there evidence to support the view that the Canadian electorate and political parties have shifted toward right-wing conservative values?
4. Are political parties sufficiently democratic in terms of policy and leadership selection?
5. Could Canadian parties do more to strengthen democracy in Canada?

Visit our new Companion Website at **www.pearsoned.ca/jackson**, where you can use the interactive Study Guide and link to additional resources on topics discussed in the text.

Selected Bibliography

General

Azoulay, Dan. *Canadian Political Parties: Historical Readings.* Toronto: Irwin Publishing, 1999.

Bashevkin, Sylvia B. *Toeing the Lines: Women and Party Politics in English Canada*, 2nd ed. Don Mills, ON: Oxford University Press, 1993.

Campbell, C., and W. Christian. *Parties, Leaders and Ideologies in Canada.* Toronto: McGraw-Hill Ryerson, 1996.

Carty, R. Kenneth, et al. *Rebuilding Canadian Party Politics.* Vancouver: UBC Press, 2000.

Christian, William, and Colin Campbell. *Political Parties and Ideologies in Canada*, 4th ed. Toronto: McGraw-Hill Ryerson, 1995.

Cross, William, *Political Parties*, Vancouver: UBC Press, 2004.

Cross, William, ed. *Political Parties, Representation and Electoral Democracy in Canada.* Don Mills, ON: Oxford University Press, 2002.

Flanagan, Tom. *Harper's Team: Behind the Scenes in the Conservative Rise to Power.* Montréal: McGill-Queen's University Press, 2007.

Gagnon, Alain G., and A. Brian Tanguay. *Canadian Parties in Transition*, 3rd ed. Peterborough, ON: Broadview Press, 2007.

Gibbins, Roger, and Lolelen Youngman. *Mindscapes: Political Ideologies Towards the 21st Century.* Toronto: McGraw-Hill Ryerson, 1996.

45. Quoted by Neil A. McDonald in *The Study of Political Parties* (New York: Random House, 1955), p. 20.

Mancuso, Maureen et al., eds. *Leaders and Leadership in Canada*. Don Mills, ON: Oxford University Press, 1994.

Norris, Pippa, and Joni Lovenduski. *Political Recruitment*. New York: Cambridge University Press, 1994.

Tanguay, Brian, and Alain G. Gagnon, eds. *Canadian Parties in Transition*, 3rd ed. Peterborough, ON: Broadview Press, 2007.

Thorburn, H.G., and Alan Whitehorn, eds. *Party Politics in Canada*, 8th ed. Don Mills, ON: Prentice Hall, 2001.

Ware, Alan. *Political Parties and Party Systems*. Oxford, UK: Oxford University Press, 1996.

Liberal Party

Clarkson, Stephen, and Christina McCall. *Trudeau and Our Times*, Volumes 1 and 2. Toronto: McClelland & Stewart, and Random House. 1990 and 1997.

Greenspon, Edward, and Anthony Wilson-Smith. *Double Vision: The Inside Story of the Liberals in Power*. Toronto: Doubleday, 1996.

Trudeau, Pierre Elliott. *Against the Current: Selected Writings 1939–1996*, Gérard Pelletier, ed. Toronto: McClelland & Stewart, 1996.

Conservative Party

Hébert, Chantal. *French Kiss: Stephen Harper's Blind Date with Quebec*. Toronto: Alfred A. Knopf, 2007.

Plamondon, Bob. *Full Circle: Death and Resurrection in Canadian Conservative Politics*. Toronto: Key Porter, 2006.

Progressive Conservative Party

Campbell, Kim. *Time and Chance: The Political Memoirs of Canada's First Woman Prime Minister*. Toronto: Doubleday, 1996.

Pratte, André. *Charest: His Life and Politics* (trans.). Toronto: Stoddart, 1998.

Smith, Denis. *Rogue Tory: The Life and Legend of John Diefenbaker*. Toronto: Macfarlane Walter & Ross, 1995.

Co-operative Commonwealth Federation/New Democratic Party

Archer, Keith, and Alan Whitehorn. *Political Activists: The NDP in Convention*. Don Mills, ON: Oxford University Press, 1997.

Laxer, James. *In Search of a New Left: Canadian Politics after the Neo-Conservative Assault*. Toronto: Viking/Penguin, 1996.

Whitehorn, Alan. *Canadian Socialism: Essays on the CCF-NDP*. Don Mills, ON: Oxford University Press, 1997.

Reform Party

Dobbs, Frank. *Preston Manning: The Roots of Reform*. Vancouver: Greystone, 1997.

Jeffrey, Brook. *Hard Right Turn*. Toronto: HarperCollins, 1999.

Other Parties

Bouchard, Lucien. *Un nouveau parti pour l'étape décisive*. St. Laurent, QC: Fides, 1993.

Hesketh, Bob. *Major Douglas and Alberta Social Credit*. Toronto: University of Toronto Press, 1997.

Chapter 12
Elections and Political Behaviour
Voting, Public Opinion and the Media

Elections, like parliamentary assemblies, are almost universal. In the past decade, only a handful of the 192 member states of the United Nations have not held a national election to choose either an assembly or a head of state. Elections assume special significance in liberal democracies. They afford citizens the opportunity to choose political representatives from competing candidates and, in principle at least, give people a voice in the governance of their society. The electoral process aggregates various demands in society into a limited number of choices and allows the representation of diverse opinions in the policy-making arena. As a result, the process accords political leaders legitimacy on which to base their rule and their policies. Elections also have a more direct strategic importance, as they decide which parties and leaders achieve power within the political system.

> *The politician who once had to learn how to flatter kings has now to learn how to fascinate, amuse, coax, humbug, frighten or otherwise strike the fancy of the electorate.*
>
> *George Bernard Shaw*

Electoral outcomes are shaped by many factors. Electoral law defines who has the right to participate in the electoral process—parties, candidates and voters. The law may also limit the absolute spending of financial resources by candidates. The type of electoral system is also significant. The method by which voter preferences are translated into representation in political institutions affects the outcome and has a long-term impact on the nature of the party system.

Since the electoral process involves an aggregation of the choices made by each voter—first, whether or not to vote; then, which party and/or candidate to vote for—patterns of individual electoral behaviour clearly determine electoral outcomes. The activities of the mass media and the conduct of election campaigns also influence voter choices.

In this chapter, we examine the mechanics of the Canadian electoral process, including the franchise; the means by which candidates are selected; the legal constraints on election spending; the factors that shape individual electoral behaviour; the role of the media; and a case study of the 2006 general election. First, however, we study elections in comparative terms, considering alternative ways to elect political representatives, and how each affects the formations of governments.

The Critical Debate to consider throughout the discussion is, "What changes, if any, should be made to the Canadian electoral system to make outcomes more democratic? What would be the advantages and disadvantages of reforming the electoral system? Is proportional representation (PR) a system worth considering in Canada?"

Representation and Elections

In large states such as Canada, it is impossible for everyone to be directly involved in the day-to-day policy-making process. In earlier times, when societies consisted mainly of small, more or less autonomous communities, direct democracy was possible; all citizens could participate personally in collective deliberation and decision-making about how they would be governed. To some, this represented the ideal form of democracy. As societies grew larger and more complex, direct democracy was replaced by **representative democracy**, wherein individuals are selected to represent the interests of their fellow citizens in the policy-making process. For the most part, democratic government now means government by representatives of the people, chosen by their peers in elections. Canada is a representative democracy.[1]

Referendums

The major exception to the general rule of indirect representation in modern democracies is the *referendum*. A **referendum**, sometimes known as a **plebiscite** (there is no clear, universally accepted distinction between the two, although in Canada a plebiscite is taken to mean a *non-binding* referendum), is a means by which a policy question can be submitted directly to the electorate for a vote rather than being decided exclusively by elected representatives. A referendum may consist of a single, direct question or statement requiring a simple yes or no vote of the public, or a selection of one alternative from several policy options.

Referendums may be used in various ways. Some are merely *consultative*, providing a kind of official public opinion poll on an issue in order to guide politicians. Others are *binding* in that they force the government to follow the majority decision in the referendum. Still others are essentially *instruments of ratification*, the final seal of approval on a course of action adopted by a law-making institution; this is the case, for example, when proposed constitutional amendments must be ratified by the electorate.

Not all referendums give the electorate a voice in how their country is governed. Especially in non-democratic systems, referendums may be used to give the illusion of popular participation without any meaningful choice. They may be useful in lending an air of legitimacy to decisions already made by the ruling elite. Not surprisingly, the results often provide almost unanimous support for the government's policies.[2]

Where referendums do allow a meaningful choice, however, they can be said to enhance the democratic process. Proponents of referendums argue that they represent a form of direct democracy. Voters are given an opportunity to have a much more direct influence on public decisions than is possible through the election of representatives. Advocates also point out that widespread consultation increases the legitimacy of political decisions. This legitimizing function of referendums is particularly important when it comes to fundamental changes in the political system such as, for example, the ratification of significant constitutional amendments.

Notwithstanding these apparent advantages, referendums are not widely used in most liberal democracies, although there are exceptions such as in Switzerland and Australia. Critics argue that referendums detract from the sovereignty of a legislature by bypassing elected representatives and appealing directly to the voters. Others argue that it is unreasonable to ask relatively uninformed citizens to make decisions, especially on technical or legal matters. Furthermore, it is not feasible to consult citizens on every issue that might be regarded as fundamental.

Another basic criticism of referendums concerns their inflexibility—they usually require a yes or no decision that may oversimplify complex political problems and make subsequent compromise

1. Nadia Urbinati presents a strong argument in favour of representative democracy (as opposed to direct democracy) as the most democratic form of government. See *Representative Democracy: Principles and Genealogy* (Chicago: University of Chicago Press, 2006).

2. David Butler and Austin Ranney, eds., *Referendums around the World* (Washington, DC: American Enterprise Institute for Public Policy Research, 1994).

TABLE 12.1 **Selected Referendums Abroad**

Date	Country and Question
1905	Norway voted to separate from Sweden by 99.95%. Question: "Do you agree with the dissolution of the Union or not?"
1944	Iceland voted to end the union with Denmark by 98.65%. Question: "The Althing resolves to declare that the Danish-Iceland Act of 1918 is terminated."
1990	Lithuania voted to be an independent state by 93.2%. Question: "Are you for the independent and democratic Republic of Lithuania?"
1991	Estonia voted to be independent by 79.6%. Question: "Do you want the restoration of the state sovereignty and independence of the Republic of Estonia?"
1999	Australia voted not to become a republic by 54.4%. Question: A Proposed Law: To alter the Constitution to establish the Commonwealth of Australia as a republic with the Queen and Governor-General being replaced by a President appointed by a two-thirds majority of the members of the Commonwealth Parliament. Do you approve this proposed alteration?"

difficult. As well, there is always the danger that unscrupulous politicians could use a referendum, as Hitler did, to appeal to populist sentiments and gain support for extremist and non-democratic measures. Finally, it is argued that referendums, especially if used frequently, pose a threat to minorities. This would mean that, in a country as diverse as Canada, the uncompromising nature of a referendum is potentially divisive. Majority rule, while a central component of democracy, must be tempered by the protection of minorities, lest it turn into a "tyranny of the majority."

For these reasons, most democracies use referendums with extreme caution and only in specific circumstances. Their most frequent use, perhaps, is associated with the process of constitutional amendment to ratify changes or to decide significant questions of national importance such as sovereignty, secession or autonomy (see Table 12.1). Another common use of referendums is to allow citizens to decide what might be called "moral" issues over which political parties are internally divided. Thus, a number of countries have held national or local referendums on such matters as prohibition, licensing laws and drinking hours, divorce, abortion and nuclear energy. On such sensitive issues, politicians often appear pleased to allow the sovereignty of legislatures to be bypassed and let the citizens decide for themselves.

Referendums in Canada

Only three referendums have been held nationally in Canada, and all of them were consultative.

The first was in 1898, when the federal government was contemplating prohibition of alcohol. Although a small majority voted in favour of prohibition (51 percent), there was a very low turnout (44 percent) and Prime Minister Wilfrid Laurier did not believe that support was strong enough to proceed. It should be noted that the proposal was massively rejected in Laurier's home province of Québec, a fact that undoubtedly influenced his decision.

The second national referendum was called during the Second World War to resolve what is known as the Conscription Crisis of 1942. Prime Minister Mackenzie King proceeded with conscription only after a referendum that asked whether the federal government could overturn its previous pledge *not* to institute a draft. The referendum was supported by 65 percent of the voters. Québec, however, voted heavily against conscription (71 percent), exacerbating poor relations between English and French Canadians. King delayed the implementation of conscription so long that the conscripts were not used in battle.

The third national referendum was on the Charlottetown Accord in 1992. The result was a 54.4 percent popular vote against the accord and 44.6 percent for it. Because of this referendum's significance for contemporary politics, the 1992 referendum is discussed in detail below.

Other levels of government in Canada have also used referendums. At the provincial level, Newfoundland held a referendum on the question of joining Confederation—in fact, it held two. For the first one, in June 1948, Newfoundlanders were given three choices as to their future status. Responsible self-government was supported by 45 percent of the voters, joining Canada by 41 percent, and remaining under the control of a board of commissioners appointed by the British government by 14 percent. Six weeks later, with the choice narrowed to self-government or Confederation, 52 percent voted to join Canada. Newfoundland held another constitutional referendum in 1995 on the issue of reforming the education system. The reforms won 55 percent approval.

The only other province to hold referendums relating to the question of sovereignty was Québec. In May 1980, the Parti Québécois government held a referendum asking the voters of the province for "a mandate to negotiate sovereignty-association" with the rest of Canada. Sixty percent voted No, and the status quo was maintained. In 1995, the Québec government held yet another referendum on independence. This time, the results were so close that barely 1 percent of voters provided the margin of No votes that kept Québec in Canada (see Chapter 7). The threat of a future referendum on this question continues to plague Canadian and Québec politics. During the discussions on constitutional patriation in 1982, Prime Minister Pierre Trudeau suggested that a referendum might be used as a means to ratify amendments on which the federal and provincial governments were unable to agree. Although no such provision was included in the amending formula in the new Constitution, politicians from both Alberta and British Columbia promised they would hold referendums before accepting any future constitutional amendments.

At lower levels of government, referendums have been used for other purposes. In 2005, British Columbia and Prince Edward Island held referendums on whether or not to adopt an alternative voting system (neither won enough support to pass, but the BC government promised another referendum on the topic in 2009). Ontario held a referendum on whether or not to adopt a new voting system in 2007, but the electorate did not support making changes.

Practically every province has had at least one vote on alcohol regulations, and many municipalities have asked their residents to choose between "wet" and "dry"—in other words, to decide whether or not they wanted liquor outlets in their area. In addition, some municipalities have held votes on other issues, sometimes even on matters outside their jurisdiction, such as votes to be "nuclear-free" zones.

The 1992 Referendum   In Chapter 5, we outlined the constitutional issues surrounding the Charlottetown Accord. Prime Minister Brian Mulroney and the ten premiers met in Charlottetown where they gave final agreement to the accord and unanimously decided to hold a national referendum to legitimate the proposal. In the House of Commons, the three party leaders, Brian Mulroney, Audrey McLaughlin and Jean Chrétien, all agreed to defend the accord. They were joined by provincial, territorial and Aboriginal leaders as well as business, labour, and other elites and organizations.

For a time, it appeared that the accord would obtain a majority in every province. However, eventually, three major opposition groups developed. In Québec, the Bloc Québécois and the Parti Québécois argued that Charlottetown was weaker than Meech Lake and did not give enough powers to Québec. In the West, the Reform Party, led by Preston Manning, campaigned against the accord on the basis that it gave too much to Québec and did not assure sufficient protection for the interests of the less populous provinces. Several No committees sprang up at the grassroots level. The most important of these, Canada for all Canadians, argued that the document was incomplete, incoherent

TABLE 12.2 **The 1992 Charlottetown Constitutional Referendum Results by Province**

Province	% Yes	% No
Newfoundland	62.9	36.5
Prince Edward Island	73.6	25.9
Nova Scotia	48.5	51.1
New Brunswick	61.3	38.0
Québec	42.4	55.4
Ontario	49.8	49.6
Manitoba	37.8	61.6
Saskatchewan	44.5	55.2
Alberta	39.7	60.1
British Columbia	31.7	68.0
Northwest Territories	60.6	38.7
Yukon	43.4	56.1

and took away rights already accorded to Canadians under the *Charter of Rights and Freedoms.* Their message was buttressed by former prime minister Pierre Trudeau. Aboriginal people, too, were divided on the accord.

The Yes forces, massively funded by corporations and governments, launched a highly professional campaign based on the election machinery of all three parties and their experts. They campaigned essentially on the basis that a Yes vote was an endorsement of Canada and national unity, obscuring the facts that there was no legal text to the agreement and that it would entail massive reorganization of Canadian government. Their appeal was directed at the emotions of Canadians. They even claimed that the country would fall apart if the Charlottetown plan was not accepted.

Ragtag groupings of No forces battered the details of the deal, proving that approximately one-third of the Canadian Constitution was being amended in just one vote. There was little organization to their attacks, but their lack of cohesion allowed different groups to focus on specific sectors of the country and on particular issues in the agreement. Since the amendments proposed in Charlottetown required the unanimous approval of the legislatures of every province, the No forces attempted to stop the referendum in at least one province. Ethically, no provincial legislative assembly could approve the resolution if its electorate voted No.

In the final analysis, the emotional rhetoric and massive advertising of the Yes forces worked to their disadvantage. Opinion polls showed that many voters used the vote to vent their anger and frustration with the prime minister, premiers and politicians and governments in general. Only in the Maritimes was there a solid Yes vote for the accord. Québec and all of the Western provinces voted strongly against Charlottetown. As Table 12.2 shows, in Ontario, the Yes forces won—but only by a whisker.

The result was a national humiliation for Brian Mulroney, the ten premiers and politicians generally. It set the stage for both the massive defeat of the Progressive Conservative Party in the 1993 general election and the nail-biter 1995 sovereignty referendum in Québec. The constitutional issue was shelved, but the defeat of Charlottetown did not end the need to accommodate a wide range of interests, from Québec nationalism to Aboriginal self-government.

Functions of Elections

The primary function of elections, as opposed to referendums, is to provide a mechanism for selecting individuals to occupy seats in representative institutions. Hence, in Canada, the federal electoral process is the means by which voters throughout the country choose which men and women will represent their interests in the House of Commons.

But in liberal democratic societies such as Canada, elections fulfill an even more important function: they provide orderly succession of government by the peaceful transfer of authority to new rulers. Elections held at regular intervals provide citizens with opportunities to review the record of the government, assess its mandate and replace it with an alternative government in waiting. In certain countries, such as the United States, the political executive (the president) is elected, reconfirmed or replaced by the people directly through the electoral process. In Canada and many other parliamentary democracies, however, the election of constituency representatives to the House of Commons assumes additional significance in that the government is formed by the majority party within the legislature and is subsequently responsible to the legislature for the exercise of executive power until the next election.

Once a government has been elected, directly or indirectly, it may claim a mandate from the voters to rule on their behalf. Thus, the electoral process helps to legitimate the government of the day and also the policies that it has been elected to carry out. Elections also legitimate the entire system of government. When voters turn out in relatively large numbers at the polls, they are expressing confidence in the system by their very participation. It is this function of legitimating the political system that makes elections so common around the world, not just in liberal democracies, but also in communist regimes and other forms of government where no real element of choice is put before the voters. International acceptance can count for at least as much as national legitimation.

In *competitive elections*—those involving more than one party with a chance of forming a government—political parties are forced to aggregate interests in their search for a political majority. Through campaign literature, speeches and personal contacts, candidates attempt to "educate" voters and persuade them to vote the "right" way. But even where there may be only a single slate of candidates, as in the former Soviet Union, the campaigns provide "an immediate and solemn occasion for the transmission of orders, explanations and cues from the government to the population."[3]

Finally, in competitive systems at least, elections provide a forum for airing views not heard in everyday political debate. Widespread media coverage, all-candidates meetings and the distribution of political literature all allow minor parties, interest groups, independent politicians and the occasional "oddball" candidate an opportunity to air their ideas and opinions. To the extent that some people vote for minor parties and independent candidates, elections may be viewed as a kind of safety valve that allows voters to express dissatisfaction with the major parties and support ideas not generally represented in the federal political arena.[4]

Types of Electoral Systems

According to one observer of electoral practices, there are four primary objectives of elections:

1. a legislature reflecting the main trends of opinion within the electorate;
2. a government according to the wishes of the majority of the electorate;
3. the election of representatives whose personal qualities best fit them to govern; and
4. a strong and stable government.[5]

---

3. Guy Hermet, "State Controlled Elections: A Framework," in G. Hermet et al., ed., *Elections without Choice* (London: Macmillan, 1978), pp. 13–14.

4. Andrew J. Milnor, *Elections and Political Stability* (Boston: Little, Brown, 1969).

5. Enid Lakeman, *How Democracies Vote: A Study of Electoral Systems*, 4th rev. ed. (London: Faber and Faber, 1974), p. 28.

There is an ongoing debate in Canada over whether the current electoral system should be changed to provide a more accurate reflection of voter choices. Some electoral systems place a high premium on the concept of *representation*, in that they are designed to ensure that all significant shades of public opinion are represented in parliament. Others are concerned more with achieving majority governments that are usually stronger and more stable than minority or coalition governments.

Several of the provinces have taken the lead in promoting electoral change. In 2005, British Columbia and Prince Edward Island held referendums on whether or not to adopt an alternative voting system for that province, but neither won enough support to pass. A commission in New Brunswick recommended changing to a mixed member proportional system. In 2007, Ontario held a referendum on whether or not to adopt a new mixed member proportional voting system (it did not pass), and the Québec government is studying the issue for its province, although the Parti Québécois strongly opposes the introduction of any proportional representation (PR) system.

Keeping in mind the Canadian situation, and the above four primary goals of elections, we outline here the major types of electoral systems and their effects on party competition and government outcomes. Electoral systems determine how many candidates are elected in each geographical district (usually known as *constituencies* or *ridings*) and how votes are translated into parliamentary seats. Using these criteria, we can identify four basic types of electoral systems: *single-member plurality, single-member majoritarian, multi-member proportional representation* and *mixed systems*. There are many possible variations within each type.

Single-Member Plurality: Disproportional Representation?

The **single-member plurality system** is used primarily in the *Anglo-American* democracies of Canada, the United States and the United Kingdom. It is also used in India, Malaysia and St. Kitts and Nevis. Under this system, one member or representative is elected from each constituency. Each elector has one vote, which is cast by indicating (usually with an *X*) his favourite candidate. The translation of votes into seats is based on the achievement of a plurality—that is, the candidate with the most votes wins. It is important to note that the victorious candidate is not required to gain an absolute majority of votes, but merely to receive more votes than anyone else. For this reason, the system is sometimes labelled as a *simple majority* or *relative majority* (as opposed to an *absolute majority*) system. Following a horse race analogy, this system is popularly known as *first past the post*.

In Canada, all members of the House of Commons are now elected by plurality voting in single-member constituencies. But it is also theoretically possible to conduct elections under the plurality formula in districts that return more than one member. In such systems, the rules are essentially the same, except that the voter has as many votes as there are seats to be filled in the geographical territory. Thus, in a two-member constituency, each voter marks two names, and the two candidates with the most votes are the winners. As recently as the 1965 general election, there were federal constituencies in Canada that returned two members to the House of Commons.[6] However, today, most contemporary national elections that use the plurality formula, including those in Canada, employ single-member constituencies.

Majoritarian, or Absolute Majority Systems

Majoritarian electoral systems based on single-member constituencies are designed to ensure that the winning candidate receives an *absolute* majority of votes cast in the constituency. These formulas are essentially of two types: the alternative vote (AV) and the second ballot.

---

6. See T.H. Qualter, *The Election Process in Canada* (Toronto: McGraw-Hill Ryerson, 1970), pp. 118–23, for a discussion of single-member and multi-member constituencies in Canadian elections.

Under the **alternative-vote system**, used for example in elections to the federal House of Representatives in Australia, voters rank candidates in order of preference. They place *1* beside their favourite candidate, *2* beside their second choice and so on. When the votes are counted, each ballot is assigned to the candidate it ranks first. If a candidate has an absolute majority of votes, that candidate is declared elected. Otherwise, the ballots are recounted. The candidate with the fewest votes is excluded and his supporters' ballots are transferred to the remaining candidates according to the second preferences. This process of excluding candidates and transferring votes continues until one candidate has an absolute majority over all other remaining contenders.

Another variation is the **second-ballot system**, used on occasion in France. In such a system, electors initially opt for a single candidate, but if no one obtains an absolute majority on this first vote, a runoff election is held, usually a week or two later. On this second ballot, candidates who failed to get a specified proportion of the votes the first time around are excluded; only the two leading candidates reappear and, therefore, the elected representative can claim the support of a majority of voters in the constituency.

The second-ballot system has never been used in Canada, but the alternative vote has, although not at the federal level.

Multi-Member Proportional Representation

Multi-member proportional representation systems provide an opportunity to elect two or more members from each constituency. They are designed to ensure that smaller parties, or groups of voters, are represented more fairly than is often the case under single-member plurality or absolute majority formulas. In other words, PR formulas attempt to ensure that parties receive representation in parliament in proportion to their respective shares of the popular vote. PR systems are essentially of two types: party list systems and the single transferable vote (STV) formula.

Party list systems of PR are used extensively in Europe as well as Israel and South Africa. In its simplest form, the **party list system** allows electors in a multi-member constituency to vote *for a party* or a *slate of candidates*, rather than for one or more individuals. Seats are allocated to each party roughly in proportion to its share of the popular vote. Assume, for example, that a constituency sends 10 members to parliament and that 100 000 people turn out to vote. Theoretically, if Party A receives 50 000 votes, Party B 30 000 and Party C 20 000, the resulting seat distribution is 5, 3 and 2 respectively—i.e., each party receives exactly the same percentage of seats as votes. In real life, the percentages of voters are rarely distributed so conveniently, and a number of different procedures exist to allocate seats. But the general effect is that parties receive representation approximately proportional to their popular support.

In party list systems, seats are usually awarded to individual candidates on the basis of their position on the party's slate. Before the election, each party publishes a list of candidates in order of rank. Under normal circumstances, if Party A receives five seats in a hypothetical constituency, the top five names on the party list are declared elected. In some countries, however, the electoral rules permit voters to express preferences for one or more individuals within the party list and, therefore, to effect a change in the rank ordering of candidates. The basic principle of all party list systems is that seats are awarded in the first instance to political parties according to their relative shares of the popular vote; the actual representatives who will occupy those seats are essentially a secondary concern. This is in direct contrast to single-member constituency systems, where the election of individual members is the immediate objective, and the relative strengths of the parties in Parliament is the product of the individual constituency races.

A second variety of proportional representation places greater emphasis on individual candidates than does the party list system. The **single transferable vote system (STV)** is used in the Republic of Ireland and also in Australia for electing the Senate. Representatives are elected from multi-member constituencies, but electors vote for individual candidates rather than for a party list.

With STV, as in the alternative vote system, voters rank candidates in order of preference, and ballot papers are initially assigned to the first-choice candidate. To be elected, a candidate must obtain a specified number of votes, or *quota*. Candidates who receive first-preference votes in excess of the quota are declared elected and their *surplus* votes (those in excess of the quota) are transferred to the remaining candidates according to subsequent preferences. If no candidate receives a quota on the first count, or if seats remain to be filled after all surpluses have been distributed, the least popular candidate is excluded and his votes are transferred. This process continues until all seats have been allocated. Although the STV system need not be used with proportional representation of parties in mind, its effect in countries such as Ireland is very similar to electoral outcomes under other PR formulas.

Unlike the party list form of PR, the STV system has been used in Canada, although again not at the federal level. Several provincial governments are, or have been, to varying degrees, considering a move toward some form of PR to elect their legislatures.

Mixed Systems

Mixed systems or **additional member systems** (**AMS**) represent a combination of plurality and PR formulas. A certain percentage of the seats are filled by plurality voting in single-member constituencies, while the remainder are awarded to parties according to their popular support in order to achieve an approximately proportional representation in the legislature. They are found in the German, Mexican, New Zealand and Venezuelan systems.

In Germany, for example, such a system is used for electing both the federal *Bundestag* (analogous to Canada's House of Commons) and the *Land* (provincial) legislatures. Under the German system, each elector has two votes, one for a constituency candidate and one for a party list. The "first" votes, those for candidates in single-member constituencies, determine half the seats in the *Bundestag*. The "second" votes, cast for a party list, determine the share of total seats each party will obtain. Parties are awarded additional seats if the number of representatives directly elected in the constituencies is lower than their overall proportional entitlement based on their shares of the second votes.

While the German system represents an equal mix of the plurality and PR party list systems, the AMS places emphasis on the plurality formula. Here, the majority of seats in the legislature are still elected in single-member constituencies, but a number of seats are allocated to parties according to their share of the popular vote in order to alleviate the disproportional effects of the plurality system.

The Effects of Electoral Systems

Keeping in mind the Canadian electoral system and what changes might or might not be desirable, we next outline the effects of different electoral systems, keeping in view three main criteria: their impact on representation at the constituency level; the representation of political parties and effects on the party system; and the type of governmental outcome that each system typically produces. These effects are summarized in Table 12.3.

Electoral systems do not completely determine either the nature of party systems or the type of government (majority or minority, single-party or coalition) in any country. Governmental outcomes are largely a function of the balance of party forces; the party system, in turn, is largely shaped by a country's political culture and social structure and by the electoral behaviour of its citizens. However, the electoral system—which translates votes into seats—is a powerful intermediary force, modifying

TABLE 12.3 **Types of Electoral Systems and Their Effects**

Electoral System (Examples)	Constituency Representation	Representation of Parties	Governmental Outcome
Single-member plurality (Canada, US, UK)	– Maintains traditional link between MP and constituents – MPs often elected on a minority of total votes – Discourages multiplication of parties—tendency toward two-party system	– Distortion of votes–seats ratio – Minor parties disadvantaged unless support is regionally concentrated	– Tends to over-represent largest party – Usually single-party majority government – Some alternation of government between two dominant parties
Single-member majoritarian (a) Alternative vote (AV) (Australia House of Reps.)	– Both maintain traditional link between MP and constituents	– Distortion of votes–seats ratio	– Tends to over-represent largest party (parties)
(b) Second ballot (France, historically)	– Representatives party majority usually elected by a majority – Tendency toward multi-party system	– "Wasted vote" thesis does not apply; therefore, small parties survive even if unsuccessful	– Usually single-majority government or stable coalition
Proportional representation (PR) (a) Party list (Netherlands, Switzerland)	– Individual representatives usually owe election more to party than to voters	– Approximate congruence between vote shares and seat allocations	– Coalition governments—may be stable (Sweden) or unstable (Italy, historically)
(b) Single transferable vote (STV) (Rep. of Ireland, Australia Senate)	– Representatives forced to compete for "first preference" votes	– Minor parties usually gain "fair" representation – Easy entry for new parties – Tendency toward multi-party systems	– Alternation of government sometimes
Mixed plurality/PR (Germany, New Zealand)	– Maintains traditional link between MP and constituents – Minor parties usually gain "fair" represen-tation, unless measures are adopted (as in Germany) to prevent representation of "splinter" groups	– Approximate congruence between vote shares and seat allocations	– Reasonably stable coalition government

the competition among parties, distorting or faithfully reproducing the electoral preferences of the voters. Since elections provide the chief mechanism of political participation for most people, the means of translating individual votes into political representation is naturally an important factor in a country's political system.

Which System Best Represents Constituents? One of the advantages claimed for single-member formulas (plurality or majoritarian) is that they maintain the traditional link between the individual MP and the constituents. It is clear what specific individuals the voters chose to represent them and, since the representatives owe their election to the voters rather than to their positions on a party list, it is in their personal interests to represent their constituents if they wish to be re-elected. Furthermore, the representatives' task is made easier because, even in relatively large and populous countries, division into a large number of single-member districts limits the size of the area and the electorate of each constituency. These generalizations apply equally to representatives elected in single-member constituencies under a mixed or additional member system formula.

In party list systems of PR, on the other hand, MPs owe their election (especially their position on the party list) more to their party than to their constituents. Furthermore, constituencies may be too large for individual representatives to maintain contact with all constituents, making it difficult to establish representative responsibility. Thus, members may focus on maintaining their popularity within the party, and hence on their standing on the party list, rather than on representing the interests of their constituents. This is less true with the STV system of PR, especially as it operates in Ireland. There, since each candidate attempts to gain as many first-preference votes as possible, members do have to pay considerable attention to constituency interests.

Which System Gives Fairest Representation? Proportional representation systems are designed to achieve a more or less proportional allocation of seats to parties according to their respective shares of the popular vote. However, the degree of congruence between the percentage of votes and the number of seats won by each party tends to vary from country to country. A key factor here is the number of members returned by each constituency. The Netherlands elects its legislative chamber, the *Tweede Kamer*, by treating the whole country as if it were a single constituency, and achieves an almost perfect correspondence between votes and seats for each party. However, in countries broken into smaller constituencies that return, say, three or four members each, it is more difficult to achieve such congruence; some parties can be persistently over- or under-represented in each constituency and, thus, overall in the legislature.

The proportional allocation of seats according to shares of the popular vote is *least* likely to occur in systems where electoral districts return only one member each—i.e., in single-member plurality and majoritarian systems. Consider the 1979, 1980 and 1984 general elections in Canada, all of which were conducted under single-member plurality voting rules (see Table 12.4). In 1979, Joe Clark's Progressive Conservatives gained more seats than the Liberals and thus formed the government, although they received a smaller share of the popular vote, 36 percent to the Liberals' 40 percent. This outcome was exceptional, and the normal pattern reasserted itself in 1980, with the Liberals getting the most votes and the most seats. In 1984, the PCs returned to power under Brian Mulroney with a massive majority of both votes and seats.

The negative characteristics typically associated with the plurality system include a tendency to favour the two largest parties, with an additional "bonus" of seats for the largest party; and, conversely, a tendency to under-represent third or minor parties, especially those whose support is spread fairly evenly, but thinly, across the country. The Canadian electoral system rewards winners, regardless of the margin of victory. For example, in 1993, it took roughly 31 320 votes to elect a Liberal, but more than 1 000 000 to elect a Progressive Conservative! In 2006, the disparity between seats and percentage votes was considerably less.

TABLE 12.4 **Canadian General Election Results 1979, 1980, and 1984**

| | Shares of Votes and Seats by Party | | | | | | | | |
| | 1979 | | | 1980 | | | 1984 | | |
	% Votes	% Seats	No. of Seats	% Votes	% Seats	No. of Seats	% Votes	% Seats	No. of Seats
LIB	40	40	(114)	44	52	(147)	28	14	(40)
PC	36	48	(136)	33	37	(103)	50	75	(211)
NDP	18	9	(26)	20	11	(32)	19	11	(30)
SC	5	2	(6)	2	0	(0)	0	0	(0)
Other	2	0	(0)	1	0	(0)	3	0	(1)

Note: Percentages may not add up to 100% because of rounding.

Which System Is Most Likely to Produce a Two-Party System?

Because of its tendency to under-represent minor parties, the plurality system is often said to favour the development or maintenance of a two-party system of electoral competition. Maurice Duverger noted two reasons why a single-member plurality system tends to reward the party that comes first with more seats than it deserves, and the second and following parties with fewer seats. First, there is an arithmetical consequence that rewards the party that gets the largest share of the vote with more seats. The exception to this general rule occurs when a minor party has its support strongly concentrated in a particular region, as happens with the Bloc Québécois in Québec. Second, voters who might otherwise support a minor party tend to refrain from voting for it for fear of "wasting" their votes—casting votes that have no effect on the election of individual representatives or on the formation of a government. Thus, Duverger suggested that the association between the plurality electoral formula and the two-party sytem is close to being a "true sociological law."[7] (For seats won by region and party, see Table 12.5 on the next page.)

A further characteristic of the plurality system is that relatively small swings in votes between parties often result in large numbers of seats changing hands. Perhaps the most useful example of this in Canada occurred in the 1935 general election, when Mackenzie King's Liberals swept back into power. Although the Liberals' share of the popular vote increased by less than 1 percent, their number of seats nearly doubled, from 91 to 173. Such amplification of small voting shifts across the country into large-scale changes in seat allocation causes the plurality system to tend to encourage alternation in government between the two dominant parties.

Which Systems Tend to Produce Multiple Parties?

Like the plurality system, the alternative vote and second-ballot formulas both tend to result in severely disproportional allocations of seats, often in favour of the largest parties.

Under PR formulas where all parties receive seats more or less in proportion to their shares of the popular vote, there is also a tendency toward multiple political parties. Some countries attempt to counteract this tendency by imposing a threshold—a certain proportion of votes that small parties must exceed before they are allotted any seats. Germany, for example, makes things more difficult for new or splinter parties by requiring that they must gain at least 5 percent of the popular vote or win seats in three single-member constituencies.

Since PR systems do not give significant bonuses of seats to any party, and are usually associated with multi-party systems, it often happens that no single party is in a position to form a majority

7. Maurice Duverger, *Political Parties: Their Organization and Activity in the Modern State* (London: Methuen, 1954), p. 217.

436 Part IV Political Behaviour

TABLE 12.5 Seats Won in General Elections by Region, 1945–2006

	1945	1949	1953	1956	1958	1962	1963	1965	1968	1972	1974	1979	1980	1984	1988	1993	1997	2000	2004	2006
Atlantic																				
LIB	19	25	27	12	8	14	20	15	7	10	13	12	19	7	20	31	11	9	22	20
PC	6	7	5	21	25	18	13	18	25	22	17	18	13	25	12	1	13	9	–	–
SC	–	–	–	–	–	–	–	–	–	–	–	–	–	–	–	–	–	–	–	–
CCF/NDP	–	1	1	–	–	1	–	–	–	–	1	2	–	–	–	–	8	4	3	3
Reform/A Cons.	–	–	–	–	–	–	–	–	–	–	–	–	–	–	–	–	–	–	7	9
Bloc	–	–	–	–	–	–	–	–	–	–	–	–	–	–	–	–	–	–	–	–
Other	1	1	–	–	–	–	–	–	–	–	1	–	–	–	–	–	–	–	–	–
Total	27	34	33	33	33	33	33	33	32	32	32	32	32	32	32	32	32	32	32	32
Québec																				
LIB	54	66	66	63	25	35	47	56	56	56	60	67	74	17	12	19	26	36	21	13
PC	1	2	4	9	50	14	8	8	4	2	3	2	1	58	63	1	5	1	–	–
SC	–	–	–	–	–	26	20	–	–	15	11	6	–	–	–	–	–	–	–	–
CRED	–	–	–	–	–	–	–	9	14	–	–	–	–	–	–	–	–	–	–	–
CCF/NDP	–	–	–	–	–	–	–	–	–	–	–	–	–	–	–	–	–	–	–	–
Reform/A	–	–	–	–	–	–	–	–	–	–	–	–	–	–	–	–	–	–	–	–
Cons.	–	–	–	–	–	–	–	–	–	–	–	–	–	–	–	–	–	–	–	10
Bloc	–	–	–	–	–	–	–	–	–	–	–	–	–	–	–	54	44	38	54	51
Other	9	5	5	3	–	–	–	2	–	1	–	–	–	–	–	1	–	–	–	1
Total	64	73	75	75	75	75	75	75	74	74	74	75	75	75	75	75	75	75	75	75
Ontario																				
LIB	34	56	50	20	14	43	52	51	64	36	55	32	52	14	43	98	101	100	75	54
PC	48	25	33	61	67	35	27	25	17	40	25	57	38	67	46	–	1	–	–	–
SC	–	–	–	–	–	–	–	–	–	–	–	–	–	–	–	–	–	–	–	–
CCF/NDP	–	1	1	3	3	6	6	9	6	11	8	6	5	13	10	–	–	1	7	12
Reform/A	–	–	–	–	–	–	–	–	–	–	–	–	–	–	–	1	–	2	–	–
Cons.	–	–	–	–	–	–	–	–	–	–	–	–	–	–	–	–	–	–	24	40
Bloc	–	–	–	–	–	–	–	–	–	–	–	–	–	–	–	–	–	–	–	–
Other	–	1	1	1	1	1	–	–	1	1	–	–	–	1	–	–	1	–	–	–
Total	82	83	85	85	85	85	85	85	88	88	88	95	95	95	99	99	103	103	106	106
West*																				
LIB	19	43	27	10	1	7	10	9	2	7	13	3	2	2	8	29	17	17	17	16
PC	11	7	9	21	66	49	47	46	26	43	50	59	51	61	48**	–	1	2	–	–
SC	13	10	15	19	–	4	4	5	–	–	–	–	–	–	–	–	–	–	–	–
CCF/NDP	27	10	21	22	5	12	11	12	16	20	7	18	27	17	33	9	13	8	9	14
Reform/A	–	–	–	–	–	–	–	–	–	–	–	–	–	–	–	51	60	64	–	–
Cons.	–	–	–	–	–	–	–	–	–	–	–	–	–	–	–	–	–	–	68	65
Bloc	–	–	–	–	–	–	–	–	–	–	–	–	–	–	–	–	–	–	–	–
Other	–	–	–	–	–	–	–	–	–	–	–	–	–	–	–	–	–	–	1	–
Total	71	71	72	72	72	72	72	72	70	70	70	80	80	80	89	89	91	91	95	95

* Including the Northwest Territories, Yukon and Nunavut.

** Forty-eight Conservatives were elected, but one died before being sworn in, leaving the official party standing as forty-seven from the West, with one vacant.

Source: Adapted from various editions of the *Canadian Parliamentary Guide* and Elections Canada.

government. In such cases, coalition or minority governments often result. Sometimes such governments can be highly unstable, as in Italy, which has averaged roughly one new government annually since the Second World War. Elsewhere, however, PR formulas may be associated with stable coalitions, as in Austria, Holland or Switzerland. But in these countries special conditions prevail, which, unlike in Canada, propel the governments toward stable coalitions.

Because PR formulas do not exaggerate vote swings to the extent that single-member systems do, alternation of government between major parties or blocs of parties is less frequent in the former. Changes of administration usually result from changes in the alliance strategies of parties in and around the governing coalition, rather than from mass changes in voter allegiance at elections.

Characteristics of Majoritarian AV and Second-Ballot Formulas
Most of the typical characteristics ascribed here to the plurality system are also true of the majoritarian AV and second-ballot formulas. The major exception is that coalition governments are more frequent under the latter two than under the plurality system. Australia has frequently been ruled by coalitions of the Liberal and National parties, but in 2007, Kevin Rudd's Labor Party won a majority government.

How Does the Choice of Electoral System Influence the Formation of Governments?
The electoral system has an impact on the formation of governments. Because the plurality formula favours the development of a two-party system (or at least of one dominant party) and because the largest single party in any election receives a "bonus" of seats, single-member plurality voting is more likely to result in relatively stable single-party governments. Frequently, these governments enjoy majority support in Parliament, although minority governments sometimes occur. This means that cabinets are based on one party, and that fact promotes stable, responsible government. Voters know which party to hold responsible for laws and policies and can either vote for it or vote to "throw the rascals out" at the next opportunity. With a coalition cabinet, on the other hand, voters do not know whom to hold responsible. Nor do they have an opportunity to vote for or against would-be coalitions.

Since PR systems tend to promote multiple parties, multi-party systems may in turn give rise to extremist or narrow-interest parties because they can easily win enough votes to gain some seats. Generally, no party wins a majority of seats, so cabinets are based on fragile coalitions. This promotes cabinet instability and increases the possibility of governmental problems.

To a large extent, *representation* and *governing* are competing and contradictory principles. Yet, democracy requires an acceptance of *both* of these principles. Obviously, in a democracy the people need to be represented in some form or other. Equally, democracy requires a government that can produce coherent policies to be judged by the electorate. It may be impossible to have perfection in both areas at once. Even "perfect" representation of every group in society would have no benefit if it produced fractious, unstable governments based on ever-changing coalitions.

The adoption of PR requires certain conditions in order to achieve stable government. Such conditions are rare. Stable governments elected by versions of PR do exist, but they require conditions such as a relatively small geographical area to administer and a form of coalition spirit found only in what are called *consociational democracies*. The cultural and procedural consensus required to make governments effective in countries with PR has been well documented.[8] The few European countries with PR and stable governments are the exception. New Zealand is often held up as a positive example of PR, but its recent history is a mixed bag, with PR having produced both stable and unstable governments.

---

8. A. Lijphart, *Democracies: Patterns of Majoritarian and Consensus Government* (New Haven, CT: Yale, 1984).

Electoral Change in Canada?

There is considerable discussion about changing Canada's electoral system in the hopes that it could be made fairer. Proponents of change in the provinces and at the federal level point to chronic misrepresentation of voter support in legislatures throughout the country. In the past several federal elections, the second and third parties have received considerably fewer seats than warranted by their popular support. Examine Table 12.6 and you will see, as an example, that in the 2006 election, the Liberals obtained 10 seats more than they would have if the country had had a "pure" proportional system of representation based on one large constituency. The Conservatives received 12 seats more and the Bloc 19 seats more than they would have earned under PR rules. On the other hand, the NDP lost 25 seats because of the current electoral system, and 17 members would have been elected from various other parties if Canada had had "pure" PR. In other words, it would have given Canada a highly fractured party system. If the system had been province-based, the fractionalization would have been even greater.

Advocates who wish to reform the electoral system therefore present electoral systems that combine the advantages and disadvantages of PR and the single-member constituency system.[9] In 2004, the Law Commission of Canada produced a report opting for a *mixed-member proportional* (MMP) electoral system. Such a system provides dual forms of representation—some members are elected in single-member constituencies and others by a proportional representation system. Such mixed member systems are used in New Zealand, Germany and in regional elections in Scotland and Wales. Citizens can vote for the same party or split their tickets—that is, vote for a candidate of one party in the riding and yet choose a member of another party in the proportional representation system. The Law Commission recommended that two-thirds of the members of the House of Commons should be elected in constituencies using the first-past-the-post method, and the remaining one-third should be elected from provincial or territorial party lists. In addition, the commission said one list seat should be allotted to each of the three territories.[10]

The system proposed is unlikely to receive the support of federal parties. It would reduce the chances of majority governments being elected and threaten the integrity of the responsible cabinet system. Canada does not possess many of the components of the few countries that have adopted PR

TABLE 12.6 **How Votes Translated into Seats in the 2006 Election, and How They Would Have Translated in a Pure PR System**

	Popular Vote (%)	Seats Won Under the Current Single-Member Plurality System	Seats That Would Have Been Won Under Pure PR
Liberal	30.2	103	93
Conservative	36.3	124	112
Bloc	10.5	51	32
NDP	17.5	29	54
Green	4.5	0	14
Other	1.0	1	3

Source: Election data available at www.elections.ca/scripts/OVR2006/25/table9.html.

9. See, for example, Daniel Pellerin and Patrick Thomson, "Proportional Representation is Likely to Create More Problems Than it Would Solve: The Single Transferable Vote Offers a Better Choice," *Policy Options*, October 2004, pp. 54–59.

10. Law Commission of Canada, *Voting Counts: Electoral Reform for Canada* (Ottawa: Minister of Public Works, 2004), p. 104.

successfully, so the trade-off of stable government for better representation could have severe repercussions that have not yet been adequately considered. As well, the MMP system raises concerns over the fact that MPs selected from lists compiled by senior party representatives would not be democratically elected and could become appointments to reward party elites. Such appointed MPs would have no local riding to serve and be accountable to.

Public understanding of the processes of electoral reform proposals and particularly of their potential consequences is generally extremely poor. Much public education needs to be done before voters can make a proper decision about what if anything needs to be done and why.

Elections in Canada

The Franchise and the Ridings

Electoral law in Canada has come a long way since Confederation, when electoral rules were patently unjust. The federal **franchise**—the right to vote—was based on provincial laws and was restricted to male property owners. There was flagrant discrimination in favour of the upper classes and the ruling Conservative Party.

The property qualification was doubly discriminatory because citizens were allowed to vote in each area in which they owned property. Instead of having a single election day, voting was staggered so the government could control the timing of elections in each region. Elections were held first in those areas where the government was most popular, moving to areas of lesser support only later. The government benefited from this arrangement, since areas in which government support was not as prevalent were encouraged to fall in line, supporting the likely "winner" in order to gain favours from the future government.

In 1885, balloting was brought under federal jurisdiction, but former restrictions remained and a new one, the disenfranchisement of Asians, was added. In 1917, Canadians of central European descent lost their vote. On the other hand, women, if they were relatives of soldiers, gained the right to vote for the first time, along with Native peoples serving in the Armed Forces, in the expectation that they would support the Union government's call for conscription. The following year *all* women were granted voting rights. Canadians of Asian descent were not granted normal voting privileges until 1948, and the Inuit, disenfranchised in 1934, did not have that right restored until 1950. Religious conscientious objectors, mainly Mennonites, who had been disenfranchised as early as 1920, did not receive voting rights until 1955. Reservation Indians received voter status only in 1960.

In the light of the *Charter of Rights and Freedoms*, which states that every citizen of Canada has the right to vote, the chief electoral officer recommended in 1983 that Parliament reconsider the status of the approximately 80 000 Canadians who continued to be denied that right. Resulting amendments to the *Canada Elections Act* in 1993 removed disqualifications for several groups, including judges, persons who are "restrained of their liberty of movement or deprived of the management of their property by reason of mental disease" and inmates serving sentences of less than two years in a correctional institution. In 2002, the Supreme Court struck down the federal restrictions on voting rights for prisoners serving terms of two years or more, so now *all* prisoners have a constitutional right to vote. Only the chief electoral officer and the assistant chief electoral officer do not have the right to vote. New mechanisms were also established to allow Canadian citizens to vote if they are absent from Canada for fewer than five consecutive years and intend to return to reside in Canada, or if they are temporarily outside of the country or their electoral district.

An interesting confrontation about depriving certain Canadians of their vote occurred while three by-elections were held in Québec in 2007. Prime Minister Stephen Harper wanted Chief Electoral

Officer Marc Mayrand to use his powers to bar Muslim women who wear veils from voting in the by-elections unless they showed their faces. Mayrand refused on the grounds that such a decision concerned fundamental rights protected by the Charter.

Constituency Boundaries

Under federal election law, independent, three-member commissions in each province redraw constituency boundaries once every ten years to ensure that each riding has roughly the same number of voters (see the "Close-Up on Political Behaviour: How Much Is Your Vote Worth?"). The rules for carrying out this re-adjustment of electoral district boundaries are laid out in the *Electoral Boundaries Readjustment Act* (EBRA). Since the 1940s, there have been three fundamental changes to the representation formula and one major change in the boundary readjustment process.[11] In 1985, the *Representation Act* simplified the formula for calculating representation. First, the number of seats for each province is determined (see Figure 12.1). Second, seats are added because of the constitutional rule (the *senatorial floor clause*) guaranteeing that no province shall have fewer members in the House of Commons than it has in the Senate, and the *grandfather clause* guaranteeing that no province shall have fewer seats than it had in 1976 during the 33rd Parliament.[12] Lastly, the seats for the Northwest Territories, Yukon and Nunavut are added. In 2006, this formula determined that the House of Commons would consist of 308 MPs.

A new representation order was proclaimed August 25, 2003, and was in effect for the 2004 and 2006 elections. Based on the 2001 Census figures, the size of the House of Commons increased to 308, and increased the number of seats for Ontario by three, British Columbia by two and Alberta by two. When provincial representation has been determined, electoral boundaries have to be readjusted to take into account population shifts. The redistribution altered boundaries in all provinces, reflecting the shift of population away from the Atlantic provinces and rural areas into big cities. The senatorial floor rule continues to protect the four Atlantic provinces.

In November 2007, the Harper government introduced Bill C22 to change the formula for readjusting seats in the House of Commons among the provinces. The legislation would make

---

CLOSE-UP ON Political Behaviour

HOW MUCH IS YOUR VOTE WORTH?

"One person, one vote" is a basic democratic principle upheld in Canada. However, all votes are not equal. There are huge discrepancies between riding populations, and thus some votes count more than others; small provinces get more seats in Parliament than their population warrants; rural areas elect more representatives than their numbers indicate they should.

Provincial guarantees in the Constitution distort the principle of representation by population. In 1915, the four Atlantic provinces won a constitutionalized "Senate floor" rule: no province can have fewer members of Parliament than it does senators. Based on today's population, Prince Edward Island should have only two MPs, but it gets four; New Brunswick should have nine, not the ten it elects.

The *Representation Act* of 1985 provided more exceptions. No province can have fewer seats in the House of Commons than it had in 1976. That means that Saskatchewan would otherwise have 10 MPs, not 14, as it does now, and Manitoba would have 11 MPs, not 14.

Besides this, constituency populations vary widely. The rule is that constituency populations should not be more than 25 percent larger or smaller than the ideal average—although there can be exceptions. Labrador, for example, with just over 30 000 people, elects one member. So does St. John's West in Newfoundland, with just over 101 000 people. Rural ridings generally have fewer voters than urban ones, so their votes are worth more. Suburban votes are often worth least because of their heavily populated areas.

The faster-growing provinces have 61 percent of the population but 56 percent of the seats. Strict rep by pop would have given them 16 more seats in 2006.*

Should Canada adhere more strictly to rep by pop?

---

* Louis Massicotte, "Electoral Legislation since 1997: Parliament Regains the Initiative," in Jon H. Pammett and Christopher Dornan, eds., *The Canadian Federal Election of 2006* (Toronto: Dundurn, 2006), p. 201.

---

11. R. Kenneth Carty, "The Electoral Boundary Revolution in Canada," *The American Review of Canadian Studies*, vol. 15, no. 3 (1985), pp. 273–87.

12. Québec, for example, is guaranteed at least 75 seats in the House of Commons, giving it one MP for every 96 500 people. In Ontario, Alberta and BC, there is one MP for roughly 106 000 to 108 000 Canadians.

FIGURE 12.1 **Formula for Calculating Representation in the House of Commons**

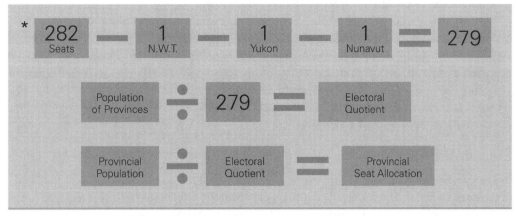

* The calculation starts with the 282 seats that the House of Commons had in 1985. After the calculation of provincial allocations, the total number of seats in 2006 was 308.

Québec's ratio of voters to MPs the new benchmark so that any provinces that are more populous than Québec (to date, just Ontario) would not enjoy the full benefits of seat increases. The controversial proposal is currently under dispute in Ontario, where it is argued that Ontarians will have weaker representation in the federal Parliament than Canadians in other provinces, and also in Québec, where the concern is that British Columbia and Alberta combined would have more seats than Québec.

By-elections

By-elections are held to fill vacancies of legislative seats that occur between general elections. They are held at the discretion of the prime minister, who, within six months of the day the House speaker issues the notification warrant acknowledging the vacancy, may name any voting date. A by-election may be held soon after a vacancy or not at all if the writ for a general election is issued first.

By-elections are limited tools to predict party fortunes in general elections. They tend to be idiosyncratic because of factors such as the small number of seats contested (and therefore the lack of regional representativeness); their inability to alter the government's status (except perhaps in a minority situation); changing political conditions between the time of by-elections and the general election; and the absence of national campaigns by the political parties.[13] A good example of the lack of congruence between by-election and general election results was the Progressive Conservative failure to win a majority government in 1979, although the federal Liberal government had lost 13 of 15 by-elections the previous year.

Nevertheless, by-elections are an important part of the democratic process, providing an outlet for voters to air their frustrations and send the government a message. They also are important in maintaining representation. Canada's election laws are lacking in this regard. Outrageous delays have sometimes occurred between the time seats became vacant and the calling of subsequent by-elections. In 1975, for example, Pierre Trudeau left St. John's West with no representative for 13 months and 10 days.[14] The prime minister will, of course, not be anxious to call a by-election if it is believed the result will be unfavourable. This hesitancy is reinforced by the tendency of governments to lose

13. See Barry J. Kay, "By-elections as Indicators of Canadian Voting," *CJPS*, vol. 14, no. 1 (March 1981), pp. 37–52.

14. This has been the longest vacancy to date.

by-elections. However, most reformers agree that political considerations should not obstruct for very long the basic right of citizens to representation in Parliament.

Usually, a by-election is called because an MP dies or resigns, but occasionally an MP will be asked to resign to allow another individual to win a seat. Prime Minister Chrétien arranged by-elections in 1995 and 1996 to bring strong French-speaking candidates from Québec into his cabinet—Stéphane Dion and Pierre Pettigrew. If the leader of a winning party is defeated in his own constituency, an apparently safe seat is found quickly. When Brian Mulroney became PC leader in 1983, he had not yet been elected to the House, and the member from Central Nova in Nova Scotia resigned to let him contest and win that seat in a by-election.

Electoral Procedure

In 2007, legislation was passed to fix elections dates for the House of Commons every four years in October. The fixed date is a significant change. Previously, prime ministers were required to ask the governor general to dissolve Parliament and call an election at least once every five years, at the prime minister's discretion. This allowed the prime minister to set the date at the most favourable opportunity for the governing party. The fixed date legislation removes this possibility. It will probably mean longer campaigns. Under the previous system, elections were called and over with in less than two months, while fixed dates tend to drag out campaigns, as in the United States, distracting the government from governing in order to concentrate on campaigning. Elections will continue to be held on a Monday, except if the Monday in question is a statutory holiday, in which case it will be held the next day. The next election will be held October 19, 2009, unless Stephen Harper's minority government falls before that date.

The cabinet (officially the governor-in-council) formally instructs the chief electoral officer, an independent official responsible to the House of Commons, to set the election machinery in motion. The chief electoral officer issues the writs of election to the returning officers in all constituencies or ridings, who in turn supervise the collation of voter lists, appoint deputy returning officers for each polling subdivision and receive nominations of candidates.[15] Official election campaigns now last a minimum of 36 days.

The chief electoral officer assumes responsibility for enrolling the voters. The 1997 voter list formed the nucleus of a permanent voter list that is constantly updated from provincial motor vehicle licence bureaus, vital statistics registries, citizenship registries and national revenue records. When a new election is called, electors on the voter list are notified, and any errors or omissions can be rectified. Voting procedure is carefully controlled. Each returning officer designates the locations of the polling stations in his constituency, such as church halls or schools. On election day, the balloting is overseen at each polling station by deputy returning officers and their polling clerks, and two scrutineers are allowed for each candidate. The voter identifies himself to the polling clerk, who has a list of eligible voters for that polling station and gives the voter an official, bilingual ballot that lists in alphabetical order the official candidates and their party affiliations. Candidates not representing a registered party are listed as independents, unless they request the returning officer to show no designation.

There are three days of advance polling for those who are away from their electoral district, and special ballots for residents who reside temporarily outside of Canada. On election day, voters mark their ballot in a private booth and place their own ballot in the ballot box. When the polling booth closes, the deputy returning officer, with the polling clerk and scrutineers, counts the ballots,

---

15. As of 2006, returning officers were no longer appointed by cabinet, but appointed by the chief electoral officer on the basis of merit, for a ten-year term.

seals them in the box and delivers them to the returning officer. An unofficial result is made public shortly after balloting is closed. The official count by the returning officer is not made until the vote from overseas is in. The returning officer automatically requests a recount if the difference between the first and second candidates is less than one one-thousandth of the ballots cast. In the very rare event of a tie vote, a by-election would be held later.

Electoral Irregularities We have noted that Canadians did not benefit from a universal franchise until relatively recently. **Gerrymandering**—deliberate manipulation of boundaries by a governing party for their own benefit—and maldistribution were not brought under control until 1964 with the *Electoral Boundaries Commission Act*.[16]

In the past, fraudulent election irregularities have included multiple voting (ballot stuffing), impersonation, bribery, intimidation and either excluding real names from (false enumeration) or adding fictitious names to (padding) voters lists. None of these actions is an accepted part of the national political culture today, and, if discovered, would damage the popularity and credibility of the candidate involved. Two examples of false enumeration occurred in Toronto in 1957 and 1962, when blocks of names were left off the voter lists. In these instances, court cases led to prosecutions. Most irregularities that occur now are at the municipal or provincial level rather than the federal level. Gifts of money or liquor to voters, for example, have been an accepted part of the Maritime political culture, although the practice is much less common than even a generation ago. In any case, the secret ballot renders such favours almost meaningless today.

One of the most unusual situations in Canadian electoral history occurred in the Ontario riding of York North in the 1988 federal election. The Progressive Conservative candidate was declared the winner on election night. Three days later, a recount awarded the seat to the Liberals. A judicial recount gave the seat back to the PCs before yet another recount returned it to the Liberals, who kept the seat. The exchanges were accompanied by charges of double voting, illegal voting and the exclusion of thousands of eligible votes.[17]

In 2004, missing voting lists delayed voting in Scarborough-Agincourt (Ontario). Thirty-five of 178 polls did not start on time. Several did not open until noon, two-and-a-half hours late. Voter lists were missing from ballot boxes, and without the lists to determine who could vote, no one was allowed to cast a ballot.[18]

The Candidates Virtually any elector can become a candidate.[19] All that is necessary is to file nomination papers with the signatures of one hundred other electors (fifty in larger or remote ridings) and deposit $1000 with a returning officer. The deposit is intended to discourage nuisance candidates, but still allow participation by interested citizens. Local party organizations usually pay the deposit fee for their candidates. It is refundable if minor conditions are met. Candidates may withdraw until three hours after the close of nominations. A prospective candidate need not have the backing of a political party or even reside in the constituency he would like to represent. However, it is extremely difficult for a candidate without party endorsement to be elected in Canada.

Near the time of parliamentary dissolution, party organizations spring to life and rush to choose and legitimate their candidates through the nomination process. Local party organizations generally take the initiative in candidate recruitment, and, although automatic renomination of candidates sometimes occurs, locally controlled delegate conventions are usually held. Local organizations use this opportunity to recruit new members and raise money. The openness of the procedure has some

16. For more on this topic, see John C. Courtney, *Elections* (Vancouver: UBC Press, 2004), ch. 3.
17. *The Globe and Mail*, January 12, 1989.
18. *The Globe and Mail*, June 29, 2004.
19. An elector must be at least 18 years old on election day and hold Canadian citizenship.

problems generally caused by over-zealous recruitment. In some recent elections, for example, many Tories complained that certain ridings had been "captured" by anti-abortionists and some Liberal constituencies were "seized by the mobilization of one ethnic group."[20]

Since 1970, by virtue of the *Canada Elections Act*, all party leaders have had a veto over the choice of their respective party's candidates. However, only in exceptional cases does the national party headquarters or the party leader interfere with local nominations, because interference tends to generate divisive quarrels. Local party associations for the most part retain the main responsibility for candidate recruitment; however, a requirement for candidates to be endorsed by the party leader or a designated representative allows the leader to reject candidates in order to protect "national" party interests.

In February 1992, the Liberal convention gave party leader Jean Chrétien the unique new power of appointing candidates directly without having to go through local riding associations (a practice now commonly called *parachuting*). He used the power in a handful of ridings to parachute in star nominees and to ensure more female candidates. In 2007, Liberal leader Stéphane Dion also invoked the controversial power to place party candidates in ridings on the grounds that it would help him as leader to meet his commitment of running at least one-third female candidates in the next election.[21]

The Campaigns With the announcement of an election, the national headquarters of the largest parties become nerve centres for nation-wide campaigns. All major parties have two focuses during an election campaign: the *national campaign,* the aim of which is electing the party, and 308 separate *constituency campaigns*, which aim to elect individual candidates. National campaigns are dominated by small groups of party elites—political professionals and party insiders. They plan overall strategy, coordinate the meetings and tours of party leaders, issue literature, arrange broadcasts, employ public relations firms, issue news releases and collect public opinion data. They concentrate their efforts in a few key ridings that they identify as critical. All parties have ridings that they have no hope of winning. The central headquarters usually ignore these and use their resources where they are more likely to be effective. That generally means constituency workers in the non-competitive ridings of parties are freer to run their own self-styled campaigns. The more significant the riding is to a party, the less room there is for meaningful grassroots involvement.

Constituency campaigns require committed local volunteers and local candidate supporters. A candidate plans campaign strategy with two goals in mind: retaining traditional party supporters and attracting as many undecided and opponent votes as possible. To achieve these aims, analysis and targeting of the various voting groups in the constituency are essential. Of particular interest to them are swing voters—those who are undecided and might vote for the party. Pollsters identify these groups and canvassers deliver messages determined to be salient for each particular group.

Central parties have adopted sophisticated new technology in recent years and invested considerable time developing advanced voter identification software with which to teach and advise constituency workers. As of 1993, Elections Canada has provided parties with an electronic list of voters' names and addresses riding by riding.[22] Parties have used these lists to create individualized profiles of voters—who has volunteered, who has had contact with the party, who is interested in certain issues, etc., and how to contact them. With this information, parties are able to deliver personalized messages to targeted voters. Phone banks have become increasingly regionalized and centralized. Regional calling centres are set up with "dozens of phone lines, automated calling

20. *The Globe and Mail*, editorial, November 23, 1992.
21. *The Globe and Mail*, August 18, 2007, p. A4.
22. See Cross, *Political Parties*, pp. 119–22.

machines and operators."[23] When central officials identify key ridings, they call into them using automated dialling systems that can reach more than 100 voters in an evening with pre-recorded messages.

William Cross hypothesizes that "the lasting result of these changes is the decline of pan-Canadian election campaigning."[24] He believes that issues are targeted to different regions and constituencies, the country as a whole no longer debates the same topics and different parties focus on different regions of the country. This minimizes national debate and consensus and weakens the unifying nature of national elections. Of course, until the age of mass communications leaders went from province to province changing their message to suit their audience. Today, much of the campaigns are covered on the internet, national radio and television, and through widespread advertising.

In all parties, the leader's role in both the national and constituency campaigns is paramount. The personal charisma and flamboyant campaign style exhibited by Diefenbaker in 1958, Trudeau in 1968, Mulroney in 1984 and, to some extent, Chrétien in 1993 are credited with the large majorities won by their respective parties.

Public Opinion Surveys

The first psephologist (a sociologist who studies election trends), R.B. McCallum, remarked after completing his study of the 1945 general election in Britain that election studies should cease, or they would take all the mystery out of voting and end democracy![25] His ironical advice went unheeded, of course, and survey research now plays a large role in both pre- and post-election analyses in most Western countries.[26]

Recent elections have also witnessed a proliferation of pre-election polls, which are commonly used to predict election outcomes and probe specific issues. Perhaps the most widely known survey organizations are Gallup, Decima, Ipsos Reid, Environics, COMPAS, Ekos, and Léger and Léger, which publish their results in various newspapers. The media compete by offering their own polls. The major television networks conduct national surveys, and local television and broadcasting stations often do their own polls at the town or city level. Many other private surveys are done for various groups by either Canadian or US firms. Large numbers of polls are also commissioned for the private use of political parties.

Canada's immense size and uneven population distribution cause pollsters two major problems: First, it is expensive to sample an adequate number of Canadians to represent the whole population. Second, regions often differ dramatically in their opinions, and are at variance with the national pattern. Whereas in a geographically smaller country like Britain it is usually possible to measure the swing of votes for or against the government as a uniform movement across the country, it is sometimes impossible in Canada because of strong regional differences and the fact that some parties are important in one region while non-existent in others. Historically, Canadian election forecasters have been nervous about predicting the distribution of seats in Parliament from national opinion trends.

The results of election polls have proven remarkably accurate in some years. In 1997, for example, the last Ekos poll indicated the Liberals would win a majority government with 38 percent of the

23. Ibid., p. 121.
24. Ibid., p. 139.
25. R.B. McCallum and A. Readman, *The British General Election of 1974* (Oxford, UK: Macmillan, 1974).
26. See, for example, André Blais, Elisabeth Gidengil, Richard Nadeau, and Neil Nevitte, *Anatomy of a Liberal Victory: Making Sense of the Vote in the 2000 Canadian Election* (Peterborough, ON: Broadview Press), 2002.

popular vote—exactly what they won. On the other hand, they can also be very misleading, as in the 2004 election when virtually all major pollsters published wrong conclusions.

Since 2000, legislation has required media reports on opinion polls to identify the polling organization, the date of the survey, the poll's sponsor, data on the sample, rate of response and margin of error.

The following items serve as a further check on the quality of a poll:

- Is the wording of the question clear? Could the order of the questions affect responses? For example, leading questions are sometimes asked just before a question on voting intentions.
- When was the poll taken? Over what length of time? A poll represents a snapshot of attitudes at a given time, not on the day it is published. The specific day, or even the time of day it was taken, can affect results.
- How many undecideds are there? High numbers can render the results meaningless.
- What is the size of the sample and the sample-error factor? The sample error depends on the sample size. In extrapolating from a few thousand to many million there will always be statistical error. In reputable election polls, the margin is usually between plus or minus 3 percentage points. In Canada, a representative sample of 1500 people, for example, is generally considered to be an accurate reflection of the national opinion within plus or minus 2.5 percentage points, 95 percent of the time.
- What is the percentage of "soft" voters who are only weakly decided and could easily change their positions?
- Is the poll done by a reputable firm? And who paid for the survey?

Even passing all of these checks, as Canada's leading polling agencies invariably do, pollsters can still easily get it wrong when generalizing from opinion polls to national party results.

Media and Voters

The relationship between politicians and journalists is reciprocal: each wants something of the other and affects the other's conduct. During an election campaign, party strategists structure their daily itineraries around the demands of television and, to a lesser extent, radio. For example, the timing and presentations of policy pronouncements can ensure inclusion on network evening newscasts. Policy statements delivered early in the day allow reporters enough time to meet their deadlines. Television crews are provided the best vantage points at campaign rallies and other media events. Appropriate photogenic backgrounds are arranged to highlight the theme of policy pronouncements,

---

CLOSE-UP ON Political Behaviour

POLLING RESTRICTIONS: ARE THEY JUSTIFIED?

In 1993, Parliament amended the *Canada Elections Act* to read,

> No person shall broadcast, publish or disseminate the results of an opinion survey respecting how electors will vote at an election or respecting an election issue that would permit the identification of a political party or candidate from midnight the Friday before polling day until the close of all polling stations.

It did this on the grounds that polls might be wrong or might unduly influence citizens before they vote. But is the influence argument sufficient reason to suspend Canadians' rights to freedom of thought, belief, opinion and expression, including freedom of the press and other means of communication?

Southam Inc. and Thomson Newspapers Co. Ltd. challenged the law in court. In 1996, the Ontario Court of Appeal supported the eve-of-the-election ban on public opinion polls, even though it concluded that "there is no empirical evidence as to the extent of the influence of opinion polls upon the voter, nor can it be said with certainty that the impact of the opinion polls is undue."

In May 1998, by a vote of 5–3, the Supreme Court struck down both the lower court ruling and the law so that opinion polls could be published without restriction before an election. Further legislation in 2000 prohibited the publication of polls on election day.

Has the legislation on polling and advertising reached an appropriate balance?

and advance crews are sent ahead by media outlets to campaign stops to ensure a proper expression of support for their candidate. Candidates can be highly scripted, or shielded from unstructured debate.

The mass media play a crucial role in helping voters choose among parties at election time. There is, therefore, concern about how well they perform this role. Many observers resent the excessive emphasis placed on style rather than substance and complain that Canadian election coverage is conducted as if reporters are covering a horse race or a sporting event. Emphasis tends to be placed on polls, campaign strategies and party prospects in individual ridings in an attempt to determine which party is "winning." Serious analysis of party pronouncements or investigation into areas of voter concern is for the most part ignored. Thus, the voter is provided with scant objective information on which to base a decision. Penetrating the motives of the party campaigns, and thereby focusing on the campaign style of each party, is done at the expense of analyzing campaign issues.

Aislin, *The Gazette* (Montreal). Reprinted with permission.

Emphasis on style also results in *leader fixation*, since campaigns are based around leaders' tours. Polls are used extensively and presented as measures to gauge how the leaders' campaigns are faring. They are used to predict the outcome of the election and to explain it in terms of leader appeal. In this sense, media coverage misrepresents the political system, narrows the focus of public debate and denigrates political leaders and institutions. In recent elections, the media spotlight has almost entirely been on the party leaders rather than on the "team" seeking election. In the many months leading up to the 2006 election, media pundits frequently discussed Stephen Harper in terms of his personality and "likeability." Since becoming Liberal leader in December 2006, Stéphane Dion has often been portrayed as a distracted professor.

We noted earlier that the media are highly political instruments. Television is the most powerful medium of all because of the vast number of voters it can reach. The law strictly governs the media time allotted for parties during election campaigns. According to the *Election Expenses Act*, all broadcasters are required to sell up to a maximum of six-and-one-half hours of prime-time spots to registered political parties at a most-favoured advertising rate. The number of hours is divided among the parties according to a formula based on the number of Commons seats held, the number of candidates each party ran in the previous election and the percentage of the popular vote each party won. Often, only a fraction of the time is actually used because it is so expensive.

Free time is allocated on the same basis as paid advertising; naturally, all of it is used. These time regulations were designed to provide registered political parties with a reasonable opportunity to present themselves directly to the public and help equalize access to the airwaves. However, while this law establishes some equity for the largest federal parties represented in Parliament, it also reinforces the bias against minor and new parties and independent candidates.

Political advertising is also regulated during election campaigns. A controversial amendment to the *Canada Elections Act* in 1993 placed a limit on advertising expenses incurred by non-party organizations (third parties) for the purpose of promoting or opposing a particular registered party or candidate. Such advertising had been used to get around party spending ceilings. The law was challenged and suspended on the basis that it violated freedom of expression under the Charter.[27] However, following a Supreme Court decision these so-called third-party provisions were back in force in time for the 2004 general election. Third parties must not incur election advertising expenses exceeding $168 900 in relation to a general election during a campaign period. Of this, a third party must not spend more than $3378 per electoral district for the promotion or opposition of one or more candidates in that district. The third-party provisions are intended to ensure that spending limits for candidates and parties are not undermined by outside groups.

Parties make extensive media preparations before the election is called (money spent then is not deducted from the party's election spending limits); later, in the midst of a campaign, more commercials may be produced quickly as pollsters target issues of most concern to voters. While there may be something degrading about politicians being packaged and sold like soap flakes, advertising does have positive aspects. Despite evident media distortions, the simplification of issues and the personalization of the political campaigns arouse wide interest and, therefore, probably increase awareness and participation in the democratic political process.

Election Financing

In the early years of the two-party system in Canada, both major parties were financed largely from the same corporate contributors. Provincial and federal parties received allotments from central party funds providing a highly centralized organization of party finance, which had an integrative effect that helped counter the centrifugal forces of the federal system. Party leaders played a key role in collecting and distributing campaign funds because there was no special fundraising structure or permanent party organization.

With the advent of minor parties federally and the increased economic and political strength of the provinces, the centralized nature of party financing began to change. After the Second World War, the concentration on resource and extractive industries, which are under provincial jurisdiction, increased provincial wealth. Large corporations began to seek direct access to provincial governments and to make party contributions at the provincial as well as federal level. Trade union funding was vital to the NDP. Provincial parties in western and central Canada were particularly adept at gathering funds. As the provincial governments and provincial parties increased their wealth and power, they were able to compete more and more successfully with their federal counterparts. Gradually, party financing became decentralized.

Over time, the rising costs of financing general election campaigns raised questions about the degree and fairness of political competitiveness. Does the expense hinder or exclude individuals, groups and parties from active involvement in the election process? The 1974 *Election Expenses Act* represented an important attempt to address such questions. According to its provisions, which were embodied in a series of amendments to the *Canada Elections Act*, the *Broadcasting Act* and the *Income Tax Act*, federal candidates for the first time were required to give a detailed accounting of money received and spent. They were also compelled to observe spending limits, and candidates had to win a minimum percent of the votes to be eligible for subsidies from the national treasury.[28] Overall, the emphasis was on disclosure to keep the system honest—eliminating excesses and maintaining public trust.

---

27. The restriction, supported by the three major parties, is intended to prevent individuals or groups from dominating political discourse during the election campaign.

28. The *Canada Elections Act* has since been amended many times, and in 2000 (through Bill C2) all the changes were consolidated.

The *Election Expenses Act* of 1974 had a profound influence on the fundraising patterns of all Canada's parties. It brought party financing into the open and created a cap for election spending. No longer were parties able to hide the extent of their financial dependence on specific sources. Suspicion that corporations, unions and individuals who contributed might have undue influence on the selection of leaders or the determination of party policies was alleviated to a great degree.

The *Election Expenses Act* was amended in a major way in 2003 by the departing Chrétien government in order to make the process more transparent. These changes shifted the main financing of political parties from private to public funding—from corporate and union donations to the taxpayers. As we saw in the previous chapter, public funds are now paid to the parties based on their performance in the previous election. To receive public funds, parties have to produce detailed financial reports, including a statement on revenue and trust funds. Similarly, they are required to file detailed returns after each election. All individual donations are compensated by generous tax credits. New restrictions on loans to parties, associations and candidates are also being considered.[29]

To keep public funds the main source of party finances the Act also severely capped donations, upending traditional relationships between money and power. Party bagmen whose job was to search out large donations became almost obsolete.

These rules were made even tougher by finance reforms included in the massive *Federal Accountability Act* (C2) passed by the Harper Conservative government in late 2006. Political donations, contributions and gifts are now even more severely limited. They are monitored, and infractions are to be prosecuted under that Act. *No* corporate or union contributions are allowed. Individual contributions of $1000 (indexed to inflation) are allowed annually to each of the following:

- a registered political party,[30]
- the various entities of each registered political party (registered riding associations, nomination contestants or candidates),
- each independent candidate for an election, and
- the leadership contestants in a particular leadership race.

The shift to public funding, which was begun by the Liberals and made even tougher by the Conservatives forces the parties to cultivate more individual donations, something the Conservatives are currently much better at than the Liberals. The PC, Reform and Alliance parties had used direct-mail solicitation and telemarketers for years, and these techniques passed on to the Conservative Party, as did a centralized membership list. The Liberals, on the other hand, traditionally got more than half their donations from corporations, and were late to hire professional fundraisers, emphasize "e-solicitations" and develop a centralized membership list (previously the provinces controlled the lists).[31] The Liberals are therefore currently struggling to adapt. By the end of 2006, 108 890 individuals had donated to the Conservatives, more than four times the number of contributors to the Liberals or NDP. In 2006, the Tories raised $18.6 million compared to

---

29. In May 2007, the government introduced legislation amending the *Canada Elections Act* once again, this time with respect to loans. If passed, there will be restrictions on loans to parties, associations and candidates similar to those on donations. For example, total loans, loans guarantees and contributions by individuals will not be allowed to exceed the annual contribution limit for individuals established in the *Federal Accountability Act* ($1100 in 2007). This will change the nature of leadership race funding. For example, in 2006 Stéphane Dion got loans of $350 000 from one donor in his nearly $1.7 million campaign.

30. Fees paid for a political convention are considered to be contributions to the political party.

31. The Conservatives have built a multi-million-dollar fundraising machine using telemarketing and direct mail frequently tied to party advertising; they run an advertisement and then follow it up with letters targeted to sympathetic voters asking for funds.

$9.8 million for the Liberals.[32] Elections Canada data released in August 2007 showed that the Conservatives continued to dominate in political fundraising.[33] The shift to public funding also removed the influence of unions in the NDP. The NDP will miss union donations, but it has a good grassroots source of funding. The Bloc Québécois never got many corporate donations, so it is doing vastly better now. As well, the new system gives financial incentive for parties to run in every riding and get out all the votes they can. Every vote counts.

In order to prevent outside interference in elections, a 1993 amendment to the *Canada Elections Act* already prohibited contributions to a candidate from sources outside the country.[34] The amendment also set restrictions on third-party election spending. After spending caps had been put in place in 1974, parties and candidates, wealthy third parties—such as associations, corporations or individuals—were sometime used to siphon extra money into a contest to support candidates or parties. After protracted court challenges (one by then Reform Party MP Stephen Harper) the Supreme Court finally ruled in 2004 that the spending limits initiated in 1993 were legal.[35] Currently, therefore, there is a spending limit of $1000 for third parties; groups and persons have to register with the chief electoral officer if they spend $500 on promoting or opposing a party or candidate; groups may not collude to avoid spending limits.

Every registered party also is limited in the amount it can spend for an election. The formula for deciding how much it can spend is based on seventy cents multiplied by the number of names on the preliminary list of electors for electoral districts in which the registered party has endorsed a candidate, or by the number of names on the revised list of electors for those electoral districts, whichever is greater. There is also an inflation adjustment factor. A new allowable electoral expense for a registered party is the cost of election surveys or research during an election period. Spending limits also apply to candidates in an election campaign. The limits vary according to the number of electors in a constituency.[36]

If they comply with requirements concerning the filing of a tax return for election expenses, and if they spend at least 10 percent of an expense ceiling as determined by Elections Canada, public funding is again on tap. Registered parties are reimbursed 50 percent of their total national expenditures. They are also refunded half the costs they incur in the purchase of permitted radio and television advertising time. Individual candidates, too, receive refunds from Elections Canada. Those who garner at least 10 percent of the valid votes cast in their electoral district are refunded their $1000 deposit and reimbursed 50 percent of their election expenses by the receiver-general of Canada.

Electoral Behaviour

Studies of electoral behaviour attempt to describe how and explain why people vote as they do and what impact political events, personalities, issues and other factors have on their decisions.

Voters and Non-Voters　As we have noted, virtually every Canadian 18 years of age and over has the right to vote. However, certain citizens are more apt to exercise their franchise than others. Beginning with the 1993 federal election, voting participation began to decline from about three-

---

32. Funding figures are listed publicly on Elections Canada's website: www.elections.ca.

33. Reported in *The Globe and Mail*, July 6, 2007, p. A6, and August 1, 2007, p. A8.

34. Specifically, contributions are prohibited from any individual who is not a Canadian citizen or permanent resident in Canada.

35. Massicotte, "Electoral Legislation since 1997."

36. The limit is calculated at $2.07 for each of the first 15 000 electors, $1.04 for each of the next 10 000 electors and $0.52 for each elector over 25 000. The formula is subject to certain adjustments and an inflation adjustment factor.

quarters of registered electors. In spite of the fact that measures were taken to make voting easier by such means as allowing mail ballots and early voting, turnout continued to fall. By 2004, it had slid to only 60.5 percent, rising to 65 percent in 2006 (see Table 12.7). Some observers expressed concern that this was an unhealthy sign for Canadian electoral democracy.

> *Elections are the pre-eminent means by which citizens and governments "connect." If the electoral system fails to meet that objective then it contributes to a certain disconnect between citizens and their governments.*
>
> **John C. Courtney** *in* **Elections**

There are several factors involved in whether a person votes or not. Some individuals are more gregarious, and therefore more likely to have a psychological predisposition to participate actively in the electoral process as in other social activities. On the other hand, the poor and the uneducated are much less apt to vote than are individuals in the higher income levels with a college education. The wealthy are more apt to vote because they feel they have much at stake in an election outcome, and highly educated people are more interested and better informed than others. The abstention rate also reflects feelings of efficacy. In general, lower-class citizens have low feelings of efficacy; that is, they don't feel their votes matter, while corporate CEOs, at the other extreme, tend to believe that they can further their interests by electing the right candidate.[37]

> *The returns from voting are usually so low that even small costs [time, energy, etc.] may cause voters to abstain.*
>
> **Anthony Downs,** An Economic Theory of Democracy

Voter turnout in Canada is highest in the middle-aged range; the youngest and the oldest tend to abstain most. Incidental factors such as issues and campaigns may also affect non-voting and so, too, may the level of civic responsibility instilled in some voters through socialization. Research also indicates that voting turnout is higher the more competitive the election.[38]

TABLE 12.7 Voting Turnout in Federal Elections, 1984–2006

Year	Percentage Turnout
1984	75%
1988	75%
1993	69%
1997	67%
2000	62%
2004	61%
2006	65%

Source: www.elections.ca.

37. See Jon H. Pammett and Lawrence LeDuc, "Explaining the Turnout Decline in Canadian Federal Elections: A New Survey of Non-voters" (Ottawa: Elections Canada, 2003).

38. See Lawrence LeDuc and Jon H. Pammett, "Voter Turnout in 2006: More than Just the Weather," in Jon H. Pammett and Christopher Dornan, eds., *The Canadian Federal Election of 2006* (Toronto, Dundurn Press, 2006), p. 314; also, Mark Franklin, *Voter Turnout and the Dynamics of Electoral Competition in Established Democracies Since 1945* (Cambridge, UK: Cambridge University Press), 2004.

Although meaningful generalizations about political participation are difficult to make with precision, it would appear that while socio-economic factors are significant in motivating participation, there is little substantial variation based on ethnicity or regionalism. Interestingly, no significant difference between ethnic groups in terms of their overall index of electoral activity has been found at the federal level. Moreover, levels of participation in the various regions have also been discovered to be roughly similar across the country.

In the 2006 election, held in January in the depths of winter, 65 percent of voters braved the elements and turned out to vote—a higher number in every province than in the previous election. It remains to be seen whether this was a reversal of the former trend.

Electoral Choice   Many factors influence how and why Canadians vote. These can be grouped loosely, as indicated in Figure 12.2, into long-term and short-term factors. Long-term factors contribute to an individual's basic *identification* with a political party. They include socio-economic indicators such as class, religion, gender and ethnicity, urban–rural distinctions and so on. Short-term factors arise from the *specifics* of an election campaign, including issues, leaders, candidates, debates, polls and media coverage. It is possible to visualize voting behaviour as a funnel that has flowing into it long-term factors that endure over time and then short-term factors that have an impact just before the vote emerges at the mouth of the funnel.

Long-term factors begin early in an individual's life, as attitudes toward politics and political parties are acquired through socialization and social group factors. These factors have a bearing on one's political ideas (see Chapter 4), party identification and voting intentions to varying degrees. Long before an election campaign starts, an individual may have acquired a degree of party identification. The *configuration* and *intensity* of social divisions are important factors in whether those divisions affect electoral behaviour. As Martin Harrop and William Miller state,

> *Where cleavages such as class and religion run deep and reinforce each other, so as to give sharply etched sub-cultures, voting choice merely reflects communal loyalties. But where divisions are cross-cutting or simply less intense, voting becomes a genuinely political act, shaped but not dominated by an elector's social identity.*

During the campaign, short-term factors influence the voter, confirming or changing the effect of long-term factors. Two short-term factors in particular are significant: leadership and issues. Changing technology, campaign strategies and media, especially performance on television, have increased the impact of short-term factors on voting in recent years at the expense of long-term factors, including regionalism, religion, urban–rural environment, ethnicity, gender and age.[39] Today, short-term factors can cause significant fluctuation in public opinion. In the following section, we note some of the findings that have emerged in different elections. Some of these variables have more significance in some elections than in others.

CLOSE-UP ON
Voting Behaviours

WHAT SHOULD BE DONE ABOUT LOW VOTER TURNOUT?

Canada's former chief electoral officer, Jean-Pierre Kingsley, was so concerned about declining voter turnout that he suggested two possibilities for improving turnout: compulsory voting and internet voting.

Given that young, non–university educated Canadians in particular tend not to vote, would either of these suggestions be helpful?

Is a higher vote even desirable given the high level of ignorance and unsubstantiated opinion about political policy issues and how government works?

Or are unfounded opinions a small price to pay for democracy? Perhaps people can regard government decisions as legitimate only if they actively participate in the process. What do you think?

---

39. For a more extensive review of the debates about the role of class, region and religion in Canadian voting, and of the concept of party identification, see Elisabeth Gidengil, "Canada Votes: A Quarter Century of Canadian National Election Studies," *CJPS*, vol. 25, no. 2 (June 1992), pp. 219–48.

FIGURE 12.2 **The Funnel of Influence in Voting Behaviour**

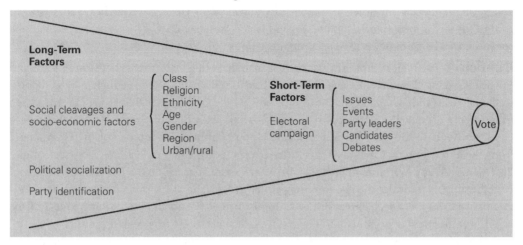

Long-Term Factors in Election Outcomes

Region   People in specific areas of the country have traditionally supported one party over others, and have shifted their allegiance only periodically and in unusual circumstances (see Table 12.5 on page 436).[40] Québec, for example, voted massively Liberal from the days of Laurier until 1984. Aberrations in this pattern did occur, first with the severe defeat of the Liberals by the Progressive Conservatives under Diefenbaker in 1958 and again by Brian Mulroney's PCs in 1984 and 1988. Since 1993, it has been the Bloc Québécois that has routed the Liberals in Québec.

The Prairie provinces and British Columbia voted heavily Progressive Conservative in federal elections from about 1957 until 1993, when they switched their support—largely to the new, populist Reform Party. In 2004 and 2006, they once again voted overwhelmingly, this time for the Conservative Party. British Columbia, Saskatchewan and Manitoba have a history of periodic support for the NDP. In 2006, BC returned ten NDP MPs, Manitoba three, Saskatchewan zero. The Prairie provinces have a tradition of supporting protest parties. In 1997, the West as a whole gave 60 seats out of 91 to the Reform Party. The region gave rise to the Progressives, the CCF, the NDP and the Reform/Alliance parties.

The Atlantic provinces have shifted between the Liberals and Conservatives throughout all of Canadian history. Newfoundland, for example, voted strongly Liberal from 1949 to 1968. That support gradually diminished until 1993, when voters once more gave the Liberals all of their seats. In 2006, Newfoundland and Labrador gave the Liberals four seats, the Conservatives three.

Urban–Rural Environment   Despite its relatively small population and its enormous land mass, Canada has a remarkably large, and growing, urban population. For our purposes, *urban* is defined as habitation in a town or city of at least five thousand people. As we noted in Chapter 1, the Canadian population is overwhelmingly concentrated in urban regions in the provinces of Ontario, Québec and British Columbia. Since 1993 the Liberals have dominated in urban areas. Support for the New Democratic Party also tends to be urban. The Conservatives and the former Reform/Alliance traditionally received a significant amount of rural support. For most of the twentieth century, the Liberal Party was best able to attract a variety of voters by cutting across urban–rural lines. In 2006, the Conservatives were able to form a minority government without winning one seat in Canada's three largest cities: Montréal, Vancouver and Toronto.

40. Region and urban/rural differences are umbrella-type concepts that are difficult to separate from such
     variables as ethnicity, language, religion and class.

The impact of community size on voting is likely to be associated with several other cleavages and voting influences. In order to establish its independent effect, a researcher would have to control for the various historical influences and factors in the political demography of each of the constituencies being examined. This has not been done.

Ethnicity The major ethnic distinction in Canadian voting behaviour is between French- and English-speaking Canadians. French Canadians have traditionally awarded a high level of support to the Liberals (and, of course, the Bloc Québécois) while English-speaking Canadians have been more evenly divided in their support for the Liberals and the Conservatives. The Progressive Conservatives used to attract "disproportionate support" from Canadians of British descent, those from the Protestant monarchies of northern Europe and people of Eastern European origin. Post–Second World War immigrant voters have been more attracted to the Liberals. The ability of the Liberal Party to bridge the two founding ethnic groups and at the same time appeal to immigrant voters was the principal reason for its dominance of Canadian politics during most of the last half of the twentieth century and the first two elections of the twenty-first century.

The 1984 and 1988 elections shattered many of the traditional ethnic patterns of voter support when Québec and the West voted massively for Brian Mulroney and the Progressive Conservative Party. With the rise of the Bloc Québécois in the 1990s, the pattern shifted again with the Tories and Liberals routed from francophone areas in Québec. In the 2004 election, Liberals lost support in Québec where the composition of the ridings was largely francophone, and even in many of its urban English and allophone ridings. It held enough seats, however, to form a minority government—something it could not have done without modest support in Québec. In 2006, the Liberals won only 13 Québec seats and fell from government, while the Conservatives picked up 10 seats there, and gained a minority mandate.

Class Social class has not proven to be a significant determinant of voting behaviour in Canada. However, debate about the importance of class as an indicator of voting preferences continues.[41] Although it may be argued that the results of some opinion polls have shown a degree of class awareness in Canada, there is no evidence to indicate that it has had a significant impact on electoral choice. Historically, only a proportion of working-class voters have supported the NDP, with the Liberal Party tending to attract support from all classes. Moreover, as class orientations are spread relatively evenly across the country, their political impact is effectively nullified by the single-member plurality electoral system. Canada's electoral system and its homogenizing effect, therefore, work against the emergence of class-based politics.

Religion Religion has consistently correlated fairly well with voting behaviour in Canada. Roman Catholics show a strong tendency to vote Liberal, regardless of their ethnicity, region or class. This held true even during the free trade campaign of 1988, when Protestants tended to be pro-PC, Catholics tended to be pro-Liberal and the NDP had no religiously differentiated base. Canadians of "other" or "no" religion were the least partisan politically.[42] Richard Johnston has argued that Catholics are distributed unevenly across the country, and that this allows them to control the electoral agenda where their numbers are relatively large. "Where Catholics are numerous, class or

41. Ronald D. Lambert et al., "Social Class and Voting," in James Curtis et al., eds., *Social Inequality in Canada* (Scarborough, ON: Prentice Hall, 1988); and Keith Archer, *Political Choice and Electoral Consequences* (Montréal: McGill-Queen's University Press, 1990). Also, see Ronald Lambert and James Curtis, "Perceived Party Choice and Class Voting," *CJPS*, vol. 26, no 2 (June 1993), pp. 273–86.

42. See Laurence LeDuc, "The Flexible Canadian Electorate," in H.R. Penniman, *Canada at the Polls*, 1984, pp. 37–54; Richard Johnston, "The Reproduction of the Religious Cleavage in Canadian Elections," *CJPS*, vol. 25, no. 1 (March 1985), pp. 99–113, and the rejoinder by William P. Irving in the same volume, pp. 115–17.

union–non-union differences are suppressed . . . where Catholics are few, class differences, at least in NDP voting, can flourish."[43]

No simple logic is adequate to explain the impact of religious affiliation on voting preference. Religion is often confounded with linguistic and regional patterns. Results of elections since 1984 show that the Liberal Party's hold on its French, Catholic base has been greatly weakened in Québec. The answer is perhaps intertwined with the historical evolution of Canada and its party system. An anti-Catholic sentiment on the part of some Tories during the nineteenth century alienated English Canadian Catholics. As well, French Canadians are overwhelmingly Catholic and, until 1984, tended to vote strongly Liberal. Today, the majority vote for the Bloc Québécois.

Short-Term Factors in Election Outcomes

A useful guide to voting behaviour in any single election is to think of the factors that influence voters as a triangle, with *leaders, issues* and *party identification* each constituting one of its angles. **Party identification** refers to the degree to which citizens identify with a particular party. The degree of party identification indicates the percentage of votes that could theoretically change hands, while leaders and issues, along with leadership debates and specific events, influence voters in the short term, confirming or losing party support.

Voters shift their attention to new problems in each election. For an issue to have an impact on the outcome of an election, it must meet three conditions. First, it must be salient to voters; that is, voters must have an opinion on it and they must consider it relatively important. Second, the issue must be linked with partisan controversy. It will have little impact on election outcomes if all the parties are perceived to have the same position on it. Third, opinion must be strongly skewed in a single direction and not simply reflect the usual degree of attachment to the various political parties.

The perception that issues are an important factor in a voter's choice leads strategists to rely heavily on public opinion surveys. Party planners identify groups that contain possible supporters and strive to mobilize their support through appeals and policies tailored to a winning electoral coalition. The measure of success, of course, is the election result. Although free trade, for example, played a major role in determining voter choice in the 1988 election, it was relatively insignificant in 1993 and hardly mentioned in 1997, 2000, 2004 or 2006.

Modern political leaders tend to embody the party image. This is largely due to television coverage. Leaders put a personal stamp on their parties. John Turner, Pierre Trudeau and Jean Chrétien had very different personal images that adhered to the Liberal Party. The leader plays a central role in determining voter choices. Leadership is an important issue in many campaigns. Inevitably, complex political issues are personalized; personality is often easier for the electorate and the media to evaluate. In 2004, Paul Martin's high personal appeal dipped dramatically after his name was associated with the Québec sponsorship scandal that emanated from Chrétien's government.

It is evident that a number of factors influence voting. The contradictory perceptions and influences weighing on voters' minds as they enter the polling booths are difficult to disentangle. We have identified a number of the leading factors in an attempt to understand electoral choice in a general sense. There is undoubtedly a degree of interaction and reinforcement among the factors that makes the precise independent effect of each difficult to determine. Each campaign is unique in the extent to which leaders, issues and sometimes even party identification are influential.

---

43. Richard Johnston, "The Geography of Class and Religion in Canadian Elections," in Wearing, *The Ballot and Its Message*, p. 128.

Party Identification and Historical Analysis of Electoral Outcomes   It is thought by some that parental party identification is transmitted to children through the socialization process and that the resulting attachment has a long-term effect on voting behaviour, filtering the effects of short-term factors such as party leaders or campaign issues. While in the preceding analysis we discussed "collective" phenomena such as region, class, religion and ethnic identity, the question of party identification directs us to the level of the individual voter. How important is this factor in influencing voting behaviour?

Studies of electoral behaviour indicate that party identification is widespread in Canada but is relatively low in intensity.[44] While there continues to be a small, stable core of loyalists, a significant proportion shifts from one party affiliation to another. The impact of specific issues and the image of the leader are credited with many recent defections from party loyalty. Non-partisans are particularly susceptible to issues, leaders and other short-term factors in the election campaign. Transient and newly eligible voters generally seem to favour the incumbent government.[45]

In Canada, volatility in party identification is tending to increase over time, and this suggests the increasing possibility of large pendulum swings of political support. Michael Stevenson has found that unstable partisanship is at least partially related to ideology. His research indicates that in the 1977–88 period, "the largest bloc of unstable partisans was closest ideologically to the more left-wing stable New Democratic Party partisans, and shifted only between the New Democratic and Liberal Parties." He also found that the smaller bloc of unstable partisans, which moved to the Conservative Party, "was ideologically closest to its more right-wing stable partisans."[46]

André Turcotte found that party was a very important variable in explaining voting behaviour in 2006. The question voters were asked focused on whether party leaders, local candidates or parties as a whole were most important in their decision of whom to support in the election. In that election 53 percent of respondents cited parties as the most important influence on their vote choice, matching 2004 findings. In fact, the party as a whole has proven to be the most important variable for more than one of two Canadians in every election since 1988. Despite some evidence that party identification is declining in significance, the aggregate data on short-term factors in the last six elections up to 2006 appears to contest this argument.

General Election Results, 1867–2006

Since Confederation, Canada has held 39 general elections, which either the Liberals or Conservatives have won.[47] With the exception of the Liberal victory of 1874, the Conservative Party dominated federal politics from 1867 until nearly the turn of the century (1896). However, the Liberal Party has held power for most of the past hundred years. Since 1945, there have been thirteen Liberal governments and seven Conservative (see Table 12.8). The dramatic collapse of the Progressive Conservative Party in the 1993 election left the Liberals with no strong challenger until a newly constituted Conservative Party reduced the Liberals to a minority government in 2004 and then won its own minority mandate in 2006.

44. See LeDuc, "The Flexible Canadian Electorate," pp. 40–41.

45. Alan Frizzell, Jon Pammett and Anthony Westell, *The Canadian General Election of 1988* (Ottawa: Carleton University Press, 1989).

46. Stevenson, "Ideology and Unstable Party Identification in Canada," p. 815.

47. Electoral history is available at the Elections Canada website: www.elections.ca.

TABLE 12.8 **General Election Results, 1878–2006**

Election Year	Gov't Formed	Total Seats	PC Seats	PC % Votes	Lib Seats	Lib % Votes	Con Seats	Con % Votes	CCF/ NDP Seats	CCF/ NDP % Votes	Ref[7] Seats	Ref[7] % Votes	Bloc Seats	Bloc % Votes	Oth Seats	Oth % Votes
1878	Con	206	140	53	65	45	–	–	–	–	–	–	–	–	1	2
1882	Con	211	138	53	73	47	–	–	–	–	–	–	–	–	–	–
1887	Con	215	128	51	87	49	–	–	–	–	–	–	–	–	–	–
1891	Con	215	122	52	91	46	–	–	–	–	–	–	–	–	2	2
1896	Lib	213	88	46	118	45	–	–	–	–	–	–	–	–	7	9
1900	Lib	213	81	47	132	52	–	–	–	–	–	–	–	–	–	1
1904	Lib	214	75	47	139	52	–	–	–	–	–	–	–	–	–	1
1908	Lib	221	85	47	135	51	–	–	–	–	–	–	–	–	1	2
1911	Con	221	134	51	87	48	–	–	–	–	–	–	–	–	–	1
1917	Con[1]	235	153	57	82	40	–	–	–	–	–	–	–	–	–	3
1921	Lib	235	50	30	128	41	–	–	–	–	–	–	–	–	69[2]	29
1925	Lib	245	116	46	99	40	–	–	–	–	–	–	–	–	30[3]	14
1926	Lib	245	91	45	116	46	–	–	–	–	–	–	–	–	20[4]	5
1930	Con	245	137	49	91	45	–	–	–	–	–	–	–	–	17[5]	6
1935	Lib	245	40	30	173	45	–	–	7	9	–	–	–	–	25	16
1940	Lib	245	40	31	181	51	–	–	8	8	–	–	–	–	16	10
1945	Lib	245	67	27	125	41	–	–	28	16	–	–	–	–	24	16
1949	Lib	262	41	30	190	49	–	–	13	13	–	–	–	–	18	8
1953	Lib	265	51	31	170	49	–	–	23	11	–	–	–	–	21	9
1957	Con	265	112	39	105	41	–	–	25	11	–	–	–	–	23	9
1958	Con	265	208	54	48	34	–	–	8	9	–	–	–	–	1	3
1962	Con	265	116	37	100	37	–	–	19	14	–	–	–	–	31	12
1963	Lib	265	95	33	129	42	–	–	17	13	–	–	–	–	24	12
1965	Lib	265	97	32	131	40	–	–	21	18	–	–	–	–	16	10
1968	Lib	264	72	31	155	45	–	–	22	17	–	–	–	–	15	7
1972	Lib	264	107	35	109	38	–	–	31	18	–	–	–	–	16	9
1974	Lib	264	95	35	141	43	–	–	16	15	–	–	–	–	12	6
1979	Con	282	136	36	114	40	–	–	26	18	–	–	–	–	6	7
1980	Lib	282	103	33	147	44	–	–	32	20	–	–	–	–	0	3
1984	Con	282	211	50	40	28	–	–	30	19	–	–	–	–	1	–
1988	Con	295	169[6]	43	83	32	–	–	43	20	–	–	–	–	–	4
1993	Lib	295	2	16	177	41	–	–	9	7	52	19	54	13	1	4
1997	Lib	301	20	19	155	38	–	–	21	11	60	19	44	11	1	2
2000	Lib	301	12	12	172	40	–	–	13	9	66	26	38	11	–	2
2004	Lib	308	–	–	135	37	99	30	19	16	–	–	54	12	1	6
2006	Con	308	–	–	103	30	124	36	29	18	–	–	51	11	1	5

[1] Wartime coalition

[2] Includes 65 Progressives

[3] Includes 24 Progressives

[4] Includes 20 Progressives

[5] Includes 12 Progressives

[6] 169 Conservatives were elected on November 21, 1988, but one died before being officially sworn in, leaving the seat technically vacant.

[7] Includes Alliance

Source: Elections Canada 2006 results available at www.elections.ca.

Case Study of the 2006 General Election

Background   In December 2003, when Paul Martin took over as Liberal leader, Central Canada looked like Liberal nirvana. The Liberals had majority governments in Ontario and Québec as well as nationally, and Paul Martin's new government was at 48 percent in the polls. With a new cabinet and Martin's high personal popularity, the Liberal Party agenda was set for a Throne Speech, a budget and then a quick spring election. But things went very wrong for the Liberals. Only two months after Martin became prime minister, the auditor general released a scathing report on federal funds that had been misspent or unaccounted for in Québec following the 1995 referendum on separatism. The report sparked a national scandal unmatched in recent years (see Chapters 4 and 8 for more about the Québec sponsorship scandal, a.k.a. AdScam). The Liberals plummeted in the polls, especially in Québec, and instead of winning another majority mandate in the June 2004 election, the party was reduced to a minority government—the first minority Parliament in 25 years. The Liberals dropped from 168 to 135 seats, and, at just over 30 percent of the popular vote, it was the party's worst showing since 1984 when Brian Mulroney's PCs ended John Turner's short-lived prime ministership. The Liberals' 20.8 percent share of the popular vote in Québec was their worst result ever. Party coffers were depleted and the sponsorship scandal still loomed large.

The Liberal minority government lasted for 17 months, tenuously clinging to power with NDP support, at one point managing to orchestrate the defection of Conservative Belinda Stronach to the Liberal cabinet in time to win a non-confidence vote. But on November 1, 2005, the first volume of the Gomery Report on the misspent funds in Québec was released. Although Martin was not personally implicated in AdScam, the report outlined an "elaborate kickback scheme" that tarred the party with scandal. The Liberals had promised to call an election within thirty days of the final report, due in February, but they were prepared to be forced to call an election on the issue. In the first week of November, the Martin's government announced massive amounts of spending on up to thirty projects across the country (money that would not count as election spending).

On cue, within days, the opposition parties teamed up against the governing Liberals to pass a motion (171 to 133) saying "that this House has lost confidence in the government," thereby forcing Martin to call a January election. In many ways, it was a surprising and momentous campaign—at 8 weeks, it was the longest in 21 years, significantly longer than the legal minimum of 5 weeks that had become the electoral norm.

The Campaign   The Liberals began the winter campaign optimistically, bolstered by polls indicating that they would win at least another minority government. They had prepared to run on social policy by infusing cash into several areas—health care; post-secondary education; and financial agreements with the provinces concerning daycare spaces. The government had also passed legislation permitting same-sex marriages. Economically, indicators looked good, as there was a large budget surplus and progress was being made in national debt retirement. Unemployment was low, and the party had promised an income tax cut (although the tax relief was largely back loaded to 2010). The party was also confident in the areas of leadership, competence and trust, and national unity issues, primarily because the Gomery Report had not uncovered any new accusations or tied Martin personally to the scandal.

Liberal strategy was to save their policy ammunition until after the holidays and to begin campaigning seriously in early January. They would run a campaign similar to the one they had put together in 2004. Strategists planned to let the Conservatives creep up in the polls; they would then use the fear tactic with the electorate to draw voters back to the "safe" Liberal alternative. The goal was to paint the Conservatives as extremist and scary, much like the US Republicans. In the end, if polling numbers remained close, the party would appeal to NDP supporters to vote Liberal in order to stop Harper.

However, the Liberals underestimated the Conservatives' ability to learn from their mistakes and adapt. The Conservative Party was no longer the brand new amalgamation of two warring parties. It was far more prepared to fight an election. Following the 2004 election, the Conservatives had tried aggressively to improve their appeal among the wider electorate, including in Québec. Stephen Harper moved the party's policy agenda toward the centre and simplified its message. He urged party workers to "remember that staying reasonably close to the median voter is essential for winning elections."[48] Harper tightened his control so that the party spoke with one voice; he also instructed Conservative candidates to call the party's central hotline for assistance whenever the media requested interviews.[49] And, he worked hard on policy development, allocating staff to work on election preparation, culminating in the party's national policy convention in the spring of 2005. Finally, the Conservative campaign focused on targeted groups of voters, and Québec.

The Conservative strategy was to repair the damage done to Harper's image from the previous campaign when the Liberals had claimed that he was ultra–right wing. Now, Harper met that challenge head on by taking the initiative on social policy and values. He attempted to define his image and the issues rather than attack the Liberals on corruption as they'd expected. The promises were not as grand as during the previous election, but they were tailored to the needs and wants of the middle class and young families. Whatever the issue, the Conservative position was designed to be just a little right of the Liberals, enough to be distinct but not extreme. The party paid for better advertising and ran with the slogan, "Stand up for Canada."

Harper began the campaign with an announcement that, if elected, he would commit to holding a free vote in Parliament on the issue of repealing same-sex marriage legislation. If it were defeated, he would not proceed further with the issue. Harper then gave other signals that the party had become more centrist, neutralizing the "scary values" accusation that had plagued the party in 2004.

Instead of coasting, Harper took control of the campaign early by announcing his policy platform bit by bit each day, beginning with a two-stage reduction of the GST/TPS; a promise to reduce health-care wait times; government cheques to parents for $1200 a year for each child under age 6 so that parents could choose their own child-care arrangements; and longer prison sentences for criminals. The Conservatives had an effective spin-doctoring team that followed the leader's tour and got the script they wanted delivered on television.

The NDP and Bloc, meanwhile, also were confident that they would do well in the election. Jack Layton had shown astute leadership for the NDP by winning several positive legislative and budgetary concessions from the Liberals as the price of keeping the minority government in power. Both party leaders focused their energy on attacking the Liberals so they would not lose votes to them as they had in 2004. The Bloc was confident that it would reap the benefit electorally in Québec because of the Gomery Report's negative fallout for the Liberals. Duceppe and his party organizers expected that if they made the scandal the focus of their campaign, the Bloc would dominate federal politics in the province and further the goal of sovereignty for Québec.

The Campaign Trajectory　　Until near the midpoint of the campaign, the Liberals maintained a moderate lead. However, between Christmas and the new year, the Liberals and Conservatives largely reversed their positions in party standings. What caused the shift? Polls indicated that the Conservative Party actually had started to gain strength early in the campaign. This gain was assisted by a specific event in late December. Five days before the non-confidence vote in the House that caused the election,

---

48.　Quoted by Paul Wells, in "The Untold Story: Inside an Epic Battle," *Maclean's*, Feb 6, 2006, p. 19.
49.　Ibid.

the NDP finance critic had asked the RCMP to investigate the government following a sudden jump in value of income trusts. In the last week of December, the RCMP obliged by announcing it was conducting an inquiry into a potential scandal concerning a Liberal leak of financial information before the mini-budget of November 15. Martin's finance minister, Ralph Goodale, was implicated. Liberal denials of wrongdoing fell on deaf ears and the party lost much public trust, just as it was hoping to distance itself from AdScam. There is little doubt that with the prospect of a new scandal, the Conservatives suddenly looked like a better alternative to many swing voters.

According to Jon Pammett and Charles Dornan, the factors in winning elections in Canada are economic policy, social policy, national unity, trust, competence and leadership. The polls show that after the RCMP announcement reduced public trust in the Liberals, the Conservatives managed to pull ahead of the Liberals in all of these key categories.[50] Voter support for the Liberals and Conservatives was virtually tied by December 29.

The Liberal campaign was more negative and disorganized than that of the Conservatives, and the party suffered from the widespread feeling among the electorate that it was "time for a change." Liberal strategists expected that, as in 2004, the Conservatives would make mistakes that the Grits could exploit. Instead, Stephen Harper's team learned from its mistakes and this time the Liberals made gaffes and missteps. The Liberal campaign never took off. It suffered from lack of discipline and much of the time was in disarray. Policies were leaked, and the entire Liberal platform was distributed prematurely. One of the Liberals' negative ads caused embarrassment and had to be quickly withdrawn because it made the unsubstantiated claim that Harper would increase military presence in Canadian cities. Polls indicated that about one-third of electors made up their minds either on the final weekend or even at the ballot box.[51]

Harper was aggressive in announcing appealing social and economic policies to counter the impact of the Liberal budget announcements. He attacked the proposed Liberal national daycare program and offered cash to mothers instead. He rejected tax cuts and offered a popular cut in the GST. When it became clear that Québec was rejecting the Liberals (largely because of the sponsorship scandal), Harper gave voters in that province an alternative other than voting for the Bloc. He promised that, as prime minister, he would be attentive to provincial and especially Québec interests, allowing them to participate in international affairs, particularly in cultural policy. His ability to debate effectively in French boosted his appeal. It appears that some Québec federalists acted on the presumption that a vote for the Conservatives might be more effective in electing an MP than a vote for the discredited Liberals.[52]

The NDP campaigned first against the Liberals, then, as the tide turned, the party adjusted its rhetoric and advertising toward the Conservatives. Jack Layton and his team worked to shift party values so that they would appeal not just to rural Canada but also to the "urban, bohemian creative class of Toronto."[53] They urged voters to think locally about what the NDP could offer, emphasizing ethics, the environment and the unacceptability of private health care.

Media Election coverage, like news reporting generally, is an extremely competitive affair, with national and local newspapers, television, radio and the internet vying for the advertising dollars associated with a large following. In the 2004 election, coverage had degenerated into a seat projection game that left all participants embarrassed by how wrong they were. In 2006, by contrast, coverage

50. Jon H. Pammett and Christopher Dornan, eds., *The Canadian Federal Election of 2006*, (Toronto, Dundurn Press, 2006), ch.1.

51. Ibid., p. 13.

52. Pammett and Dornan, eds., *The Canadian Federal Election of 2006*, p. 16.

53. Paul Wells, "The Untold Story," p. 27.

Reprinted with permission from Torstar Syndication Services.

Preparing the groundwork for the next election.

was generally more restrained. The media tended to focus more on policy announcements and hard news than on opinion, impression, personality and polls. There was much less commentary on AdScam and the Gomery Report than had been widely anticipated at the time of the election call. In fact, the public was generally satisfied with the campaign coverage.[54]

The Conservative organization dealt with the media much more skilfully than it had in 2004, ensuring that its message was accessible and on time for press deadlines. The Liberals, by comparison, were unable to sustain the same easy flow of information to the degree that reporters complained about not receiving news releases or having their telephone calls answered.[55]

Campaign coverage in *The Globe and Mail*, *National Post* and the *Toronto Star* was all relatively similar. Studies showed that supporters of the Liberals and New Democrats tended to read election coverage in *The Globe and Mail*, while Conservative voters followed the campaign in the *National Post*. For leadership debate coverage, viewers on the left of centre tended to watch the CBC, while CTV and Global viewers leaned to the right. Global had more female viewers than male; CBC had more male viewers than female.[56] The media gave the Conservative campaign more positive coverage in 2006 compared to 2004. In Québec, *La Presse* even endorsed Harper, a remarkable and high-profile event.

54. Chris Waddell and Chris Dornan, "The Media and the Campaign," ch. 9, pp. 220–53, in Pammett and Dornan, *The Canadian Federal Election of 2006.*

55. Stephen Clarkson, "How the Big Red Machine became the Little Red Machine," in Pammett and Dornan, p. 51.

56. Pammett and Dornan, p. 246.

Leadership   All four major party leaders were experienced and known to the voters, unlike the 2004 election in which three of the leaders were new. The parties highlighted their leaders during the 2006 campaign, but voters did not really warm up to any of them. Only 23 percent of the electorate indicated that leaders were the most important factor influencing their vote choice. Voters were considerably more influenced by the party as a whole in choosing who to support.[57]

The Liberals went into the election confident of Paul Martin's leadership appeal. However, his public image as a competent financial manager quickly gave way to criticisms of annoying mannerisms, and he often appeared nervous and distracted. He did not clarify what his priorities in government would be if given another mandate, leaving the impression that he had no real vision of what to do with power. Instead, he persisted in stressing that the Liberal vision of government's role was different than Harper's conservative one. Throughout the campaign, his image deteriorated in every region of the country.[58]

Harper, by contrast, came across as less scary than previously and he was able to improve his image and popularity. Conservatives worked hard to let voters see a more personal side of their leader. Liberal attack ads against Harper were less effective this time around than in 2004. The Conservative leader let voters know what his priorities were and, in early January, he listed his party's five governing priorities: passing a federal accountability act, cutting the GST, getting tough on crime, giving parents of small children more cash and cutting health-care wait times. Harper acted more like the leader of a brokerage or pan-Canadian party than he had a decade or so earlier when he worked in the right-wing Reform and Canadian Alliance parties.

> *Over the course of a decade, people's views evolve somewhat and situations change.*
>
> **Stephen Harper in The Globe and Mail, January 16, 2006**

NDP leader Jack Layton emerged from the election as the best-regarded leader in Ontario, and he also improved his image significantly in Québec and Atlantic Canada. The Bloc portrayed its leader as the messenger of negative facts about AdScam, and did not particularly stress Duceppe's leadership capabilities.

Issues   This was not an issue-oriented election. POLLARA (a public opinion and market research firm) post-election surveys showed that only 12 percent of voters listed health care—an important issue in 2000 and 2004—as their most important issue.[59] The Martin Liberals could not separate their image from the alleged botched attempts of the previous Liberal government of Jean Chrétien to promote federalism in Québec. However, even though it was the sponsorship scandal that provoked the motion of non-confidence sparking the election, only 6 percent of voters mentioned it as an important issue. The more general issue of government trust and accountability was perceived by voters as the issue that dominated the campaign, but even it garnered only 14 percent.[60]

Results   Fewer than half of voters knew how they were going to vote when the 2006 election was called. About 26 percent waited until the last days of the campaign to make that decision.[61] The

---

57. André Turcotte, "After Fifty-Six days . . . the Verdict," in Pammett and Doern, *The 2006 Election*, pp. 292–93.

58. Ibid., p. 299.

59. André Turcotte, "After Fifty-Six Days . . . the Verdict," in Pammett and Doern, pp. 286–87.

60. Ibid.

61. Ibid., p. 293.

winning party needed 155 seats to control Parliament. On election day, a turnout of 64.9 percent gave Harper's Conservatives a minority government, with 124 seats out of 308 (see Table 12.9 for a province-by-province breakdown of the results). The election ended 12 consecutive years of Liberal rule and confirmed the new Conservative Party as a serious electoral contender. Electoral politics in Canada is highly regional and volatile, with multi-party contests in many single-member constituencies, and this election was no exception. The turnover of MPs in the House of Commons was high as usual.

The large battlegrounds were Ontario, Québec and British Columbia. After a good campaign, the Conservatives made only modest gains in Atlantic Canada, but broke the Liberal domination of Ontario, winning 40 of the 106 seats there—mainly in rural ridings, with minor gains in the outer suburbs of Toronto. This was a substantial gain of 16 seats for Conservatives in Ontario. In Québec, they picked up 10 seats, their best result in the province since 1988. In the West, it was no surprise that they swept Alberta. They lost five seats in BC, but still won half of British Columbia's 36 seats, 8 of Manitoba's 14 and 12 of Saskatchewan's 14. Western MPs made up roughly half of the new government caucus. However, the Conservatives failed to get a single seat in the three largest urban centres of Toronto, Montréal and Vancouver, which currently hold 48 federal seats. The only provinces to have as many seats as those three cities combined are Ontario and Québec.

NDP voters did not panic and flee to the Liberals as they had in 2004. In British Columbia, Layton made a strong appeal to Liberals to move to the NDP, and they won 10 seats there. The Liberals incurred great losses in their bastion of Ontario—down to 54 of 106 seats—but they still remained the most popular party in the province, the bedrock of the 4 previous Liberal governments. In Québec, the Liberals won only 13 of 106 ridings, but managed to hold most of their Montréal seats. In Alberta, they lost their lone Liberal MP, but in British Columbia, they won 9 seats. The Liberals did almost as well in the Atlantic region as they had done in 2004, but that area has only 32 seats. By focusing on a targeted group of voters, the Conservatives won a minority government. By the end of the campaign, they expanded their base to include more women and francophones.[62]

TABLE 12.9 **Seats Won in the 2006 General Election by Region**

Province	Con	Lib	BQ	NDP	Ind	Total
Alberta	28	0	0	0	0	28
BC	17*	9*	0	10	0	36
Manitoba	8	3	0	3	0	14
New Brunswick	3	6	0	1	0	10
Newfoundland and Labrador	3	4	0	0	0	7
Nova Scotia	3	6	0	2	0	11
Ontario	40	54	0	12	0	106
PEI	10	4	0	0	0	4
Québec	10	13	51	0	1	75
Saskatchewan	12	2	0	0	0	14
Nunavut	0	1	0	0	0	1
NWT	0	0	0	1	0	1
Yukon	0	1	0	0	0	1
National Total	**124**	**103**	**51**	**29**	**1**	**308**

* David Emerson was elected as a Liberal in BC, but changed parties in February 2006 to join the Conservatives. He is counted here as a Liberal.

Source: Adapted from the Elections Canada website (www.electionscanada.ca).

62. Paul Wells, "The Untold Story," p. 35.

The New Democratic Party also did well in Ontario, picking up 12 seats there. It was the party's strongest showing since the 1980s, both in popular support and numbers of seats won, but it was not enough to give the party the balance of power that it had enjoyed in the previous government. The Bloc Québécois, however, was a relative loser. Its share of the Québec vote fell to 42 percent, down 7 points from the 2004 election. It picked up 50 of the province's 75 seats—compared to 54 in the previous election. It appeared that, to a limited extent, citizens in Québec took advantage of being able to vote against the federal government without supporting the separatists.

The Green Party attained serious party status, winning 4.4 percent of the national vote. Its largest base of support was in Alberta, where the Greens won 6.4 percent of the vote. However, since its support to date is not concentrated in any individual ridings, the party has little hope in the current electoral system of gaining any seats unless it makes a quid pro quo deal with the NDP or Liberals (party leaders Stéphane Dion and Elizabeth May have struck such an agreement, but it's limited only to their two respective ridings).

The 2006 election indicated that Canada's party system may be reverting back to the traditional brokerage type model that was interrupted in 1993, with the Conservative Party having moved back into its former pattern of patching together diverse interests and issues at the centre of the political spectrum in order to gain and hold power. As of early 2008, the Conservatives were still in power; they had implemented four of the five chief policies that they set out in the election campaign: a cut in the GST, money for child care, tougher laws against street crime and accountability legislation for politicians and the civil service.

Critical Debate
Electoral Change or Status Quo?

What changes, if any, should be made to the Canadian electoral system to make it more representative of the electorate?

Point

The current first-past-the-post or single member plurality system is easy to understand, but that is about all it has going for it. It distorts representation, aggravates regionalism and too often ends up giving Canadians what is in effect one party rule for years at a time. It should be replaced with a proportional representation system. The situation has improved since election dates were fixed and not left to political opportunism.

The current system is just not fair. In 2004, it gave us a Liberal government based largely on the support of Ontarians. Ontario is labelled as a Liberal province, yet only 45 percent of the province's electorate voted Liberal. With fewer than half of the votes, the Liberals won nearly three-quarters of the province's seats. Skin-of-the-teeth victors take all. A candidate who loses by just one vote loses completely.

In PR electoral systems, each party gets seats in proportion to the percentage of votes they win. That is only fair. Minor parties tend to increase their seat count. If pure PR had been adopted on a province-wide basis, instead of the result in Ontario of Liberals 75, Conservatives 24, NDP 7, it could have been Liberals 47, Conservatives 33, NDP 19, Greens 5, depending on the exact formula. This would have reflected much better the real distribution of votes and enabled Western Canadians to appreciate that Ontarians were not solidly against them, as it appeared.

In Québec, the Bloc Québécois won 54 seats—72 percent of the province's seats. But under PR, they might have taken only 37 seats, the Liberals 25, the Conservatives 7, the NDP 4 and the Greens 2.

If pure PR had been in effect for all of Canada in 2006, instead of Conservatives 124, Liberals 103, BQ 51, NDP 29, Greens 0, we would have had Conservatives 112, Liberals 93, BQ 32, NDP 54, Greens 14 and others 3 (numbers would be adjusted according to statistical rounding). The Conservative minority would have been sensitive to the slightest shift in votes, but the NDP and the Greens would have had considerably more seats. Surely that is closer to what voters intended; a reasonable form of PR would make almost all votes count equally.

It is time to stop giving whatever party is in power a free ride. It never has to negotiate or explain its policies if it has a majority. The current electoral system, by promoting more majority victories, creates smug and self-centred government that indulge in scandalous behaviour and waste taxpayer dollars. Changing to PR could restore Parliament's credibility in the eyes of the electorate.

Turnout almost certainly would not be so low in a PR system. People would be more inclined to vote because they would know that their vote counts, and the two major parties would not take all the seats. Voter apathy weakens the foundations of democracy. The low voter turnout in 2006 (although higher than 2004) illustrated that individuals felt they had little impact on national affairs. PR could help solve this problem.

As for the objections to changing the electoral system, there are many versions of PR. Thresholds can be established to prevent a permanent proliferation of extremely small nuisance parties in Parliament. The Law Commission of Canada placed a proposal for a viable mixed-PR model before Parliament. It should be taken seriously.

Election dates were fixed in order to give all parties an even footing in campaign preparation, and this was a step forward. Being able to choose the date gives the governing party an unfair advantage.

Counterpoint

Canada's electoral system does distort the percentage of votes a party gets when seats are determined. Big parties get more than what might be considered their fair share, and small parties get considerably fewer or even none at all. But that is not bad, as it leads to strong governments. The system should not be changed. Radicals are always trying to fix what is not broken!

Canada needs stable governments to make tough decisions for the good of the country, and our current single-member constituency system provides that. It promotes a two- or two-and-a-half party system, and that is good for Canada overall. Before changing the electoral system, you have to look at how our whole government apparatus works. Changing one part can have a dramatic impact on how other parts function. Under PR, it would be extremely difficult ever to have a majority government in Ottawa. To conclude that fairer representation would give Canadians more stable and better government is wishful thinking.

Many governments in Europe are elected under PR systems. They tend to be multi-party and can be difficult to fine-tune in order to prevent a cycle of minority governments that have to scrounge for alliances to stay in power. PR requires constant negotiation and ad hoc policy planning. For many years, Italy has been the most notorious example of a country that constantly must abide short-lived governments. If Canadians are tired of elections now, they would be bored stiff with even more frequent votes. And citizens would not be pleased about paying for them. Given the current system, people know whom they are voting for. There is no ambiguity about who their individual designated choice is—it is not a confusing list of individuals. It is also clear who is responsible for legislation or policies passed. In a multi-party situation that results in a coalition government, the voter cannot be certain which individuals and/or parties are responsible for legislation and policies. The voter may not be able to hold any individual or party accountable for legislation. As well, in the current system, each elected MP has a constituency to work for and knows many constituents personally. The whole system is user-friendly.

Canada already has strong provincial governments that fight for their regions in forums such as federal–provincial conferences. They join forces to pressure the federal government in groups such as the Forum of the Provinces. Under PR, we effectively would have government by committee, and we all know that committees have many legs, all trying to go in different directions.

Of course, the smaller parties and their supporters think Canada should have PR. Parties like the NDP and the Greens would gain the most from it. The NDP would achieve much higher representation in the House. In 2004, they got 15.7 percent of the vote but only 6.2 percent of the seats. In 2006, they received nearly 18 percent of the vote but only 9.4 percent of the seats. Under full PR, they would have had 54 seats! The NDP would have benefited greatly, but that does not necessarily mean that the country as a whole would do better under PR.

Specialists have often told us that "half a loaf" is all an electoral system can produce. In other words, it is not possible to have 100 percent representation of all our society's groupings and also achieve strong and stable government. If we can't have 100 percent of both (and we can't), it is prudent to opt for better government with good, reasonable representation. After all, there is really no limit to fair representation. What groups should *not* be represented? Dog catchers? University students?

For the most part, Canada has had very competent governments. Majority governments are efficient, particularly when there are many points of view on an issue (and there always are) but a decision must be taken for the good of the whole. There are other ways to tinker with the political system to make it more accountable and transparent. We could, for example, ensure that by-elections must be called within a stated, shorter time frame so that vacant constituencies are not kept for months with no representation. But, we should not change the basic electoral system. And if Canadians do not want to exist in a perpetual state of campaigning, like voters do in the United States, they should pressure to give the choice of a date back to the prime minister. A 36-day campaign is long enough.

Discussion Questions

1. What is your stand on the Critical Debate? What can you add to it?
2. Do you think that Canada should hold more referendums to allow for increased citizen input into decision-making? Why or why not?
3. What factors contributed to Canada ending up with a fragmented party system? What caused the increased regionalization in 2006?
4. Do politicians use the media, or do the media use politicians? Are voters manipulated in the process?

Visit our new Companion Website at **www.pearsoned.ca/jackson**, where you can use the interactive Study Guide and link to additional resources on topics discussed in the text.

Selected Bibliography

Bakvis, H. *Voter Turnout in Canada*. Toronto: Dundurn Press, 1991.

Bell, David V.J., and Frederick K. Fletcher, eds., *Reaching the Voter: Constituency Campaigning in Canada*, vol. 20. Royal Commission on Electoral Reform and Party Financing. Toronto: Dundurn Press, 1991.

Blais, André, et al. *Anatomy of a Liberal Victory: Making Sense of the Vote in the 2000 Canadian Election*. Peterborough, ON: Broadview Press, 2002.

Butler, David, and Austin Ranney, eds. *Referendums around the World*. Washington, DC: American Enterprise Institute for Public Policy Research, 1994.

Butler, Peter M. *Polling and Public Opinion: A Canadian Perspective*. Toronto: University of Toronto Press, 2007.

Canada. *Reforming Electoral Democracy: Final Report*, vol. 1. Royal Commission on Electoral Reform and Party Financing. Ottawa: Supply and Services, 1992.

Caplan, Bryan, *The Myth of the Rational Voter: Why Democracies Choose Bad Policies*. Princeton, NJ: Princeton University Press, 2006.

Courtney, John C. *Elections*. Vancouver: UBC Press, 2004.

Duffy, John. *Fights of Our Lives: Elections, Leadership and the Making of Canada*. Toronto: HarperCollins, 2002.

Elections Canada. Annual Reports of the Chief Electoral Officer. Various years.

Everitt, Joanna, and Brenda O'Neill. *Citizen Politics: Research and Theory in Canadian Political Behaviour*. Don Mills, ON: Oxford University Press, 2002.

Government of Canada. *A History of the Vote in Canada*. Ottawa: Public Works, 1997.

Hébert, Chantal. *French Kiss: Stephen Harper's Blind Date with Quebec*. Toronto: Alfred A. Knopf, 2007.

Johnston, J. Paul, and Harvey Pasis. *Representation and Electoral Systems*. Scarborough, ON: Prentice Hall, 1990.

Johnston, Richard, et al. *Letting the People Decide*. Montréal: McGill-Queen's University Press, 1992.

Lijphart, Arend. *Electoral Systems and Party Systems*. New York: Oxford University Press, 1994.

Milner, Henry. *Civic Literacy: How Informed Citizens Make Democracy Work*. Hanover: University Press of New England, 2002.

Nevitte, N., et al. *Unsteady State: The 1997 Canadian Federal Election*. Don Mills, ON: Oxford University Press, 2000.

Pammett, Jon H., and Christopher Dornan, eds. *The Canadian Federal Election of 2006*. Toronto: Dundurn Press, 2006.

Romanow, Walter I., et al. *Television Advertising in Canadian Elections: The Attack Mode 1993*. Waterloo, ON: Wilfrid Laurier University Press, 1999.

Sayers, Anthony M. *Parties, Candidates and Constituency Campaigns in Canadian Elections*. Vancouver: UBC Press, 1999.

Tremblay, Manon, and Linda Trimble, *Women and Electoral Politics in Canada*, Don Mills, ON: Oxford University Press, 2003.

Chapter 13
Interest Groups and Political Movements
Influencing Public Policy

anadians organize in numerous and sometimes novel ways to influence political decisions. Few individuals wield much political influence on their own; they need to combine with others to have an impact. They may have opinions on a wide variety of subjects and they may desire changes in government policy for either selfish or altruistic reasons. But usually only by joining others can they significantly affect government.

Canadians can join a multitude of groups to enjoy the benefits of collective action or they may hire others to act for them. Practically everyone in Canada belongs to voluntary associations of some sort. Some groups are not politically active; some are set up to fight for a specific issue and disband when it is settled. Others, particularly those representing larger interests, form permanent groups that are engaged in long-term political action. Large or small, permanent or temporary, these groups have the ability to press their needs, principles and demands on other Canadians.

When such groups act in the political arena, without becoming political parties, they are usually called *interest groups*. Interest groups are sometimes accused of having inherently sinister, self-serving intentions—as indicated in terms such as *vested interest, special interest* and *pressure groups*. Because of this, some political scientists prefer to call them *advocacy groups*.[1] Of course, many groups *are* engaged primarily in seeking financial or other benefits for their members, but others want to achieve something that they believe is in the public interest, generally an environmental or social cause such as saving endangered species, global warming or equality rights.

Sometimes, informal networks of groups and individuals form broad collective identities to work for social change. They are based on ideas and altruism and have only loose organizational form. They are neither organized interest groups nor political parties. They are *movements*. Movements are tied to ideologies that seek broad social change on issues such as nationalism, nuclear energy, the women's movement, minorities, the environment, animal rights and nuclear weapons. They often flow across national borders with international links to groups and individuals who share their vision for social and political change, whereas interest groups are more particularistic and normally reside inside national borders. On occasion, both interest groups and movements may transform themselves into political parties, as has been the case with the federal and provincial Green parties in Canada.

The structure and behaviour of interest groups and movements are closely related to the political system in which they operate. In modern democracies, interest groups and social movements voice the social and political demands of their members and defend them in society and in the political forum, playing a mediating function between society and government. In authoritarian or communist countries, where citizens have few legal rights to organize associations, unauthorized interest groups sometimes attempt to influence the government by dramatic demonstrations intended to attract international publicity. This was the circumstance at China's Tiananmen Square in 1989 when students demonstrating for democratic reforms were massacred by the Chinese army. Of course, this can also be the tactic of weak interest groups in democracies that have no other avenues to influence the government.

1. See Lisa Young and Joanna Everitt, *Advocacy Groups*, (Vancouver: UBC Press, 2004), p. 5.

In Canada, interest groups organize legally to petition and cajole the government. They operate in and help to mould the federal political system. Thousands of individuals work in Ottawa representing interest groups. Some interest groups employ experts such as professional lobbyists, public relations firms or highly paid lawyers to promote their agendas. Others occasionally send their local officials or CEOs to argue their cases. Many attempt to attract public attention and garner wider support. What they all have in common is the desire to influence government policy, legislation, regulation or expenditures.

However, for all their importance in the democratic system, there are also problems with interest groups. Who gets to participate in them? Are they just another vehicle for elites to have access to those in political power? Are they able to buy favours at the expense of poorer, less privileged Canadians? Does the public know what different groups are trying to achieve and how they are going about it? Is the government engaged in patronage and pork-barrel activities, giving special favours to some interest groups in return for money or gifts? Are unethical activities such as bribery or blackmail ever involved? Citizens' groups often complain about the influence of big business; business people disparage the persistent pleading of narrowly formed special interest organizations. Some skeptics even harbour the suspicion that interest groups conflict with the basic attributes of democracy because they do not work openly through political parties.

The aim of this chapter is to help the reader understand what interest groups are, what they do, how they do it and what checks are in place to keep the system honest and transparent. Here, we examine the "smoking wars" as a case study of the behaviour of opposing interest groups, and survey the women's movement as an example of a major, multi-faceted social movement. The Critical Debate to consider throughout the discussion asks, "Are interest groups a necessary evil in a democracy?"

What Are Interest Groups?

There are many sociological meanings to the word *group*. If a traveller stops along a highway to ask directions of a farmer, the two are interacting, but they can hardly be said to constitute a group except in the most casual sense. If, however, the traveller belongs to a hiking club that has an organization with a staff and a budget, then its members can be designated as a group. Political scientists are little interested in groups that have no relation to the political system or no organizational element. However, they are very interested in *interest* groups because they are non-governmental associations that aim to affect public policy to further their own interests.

Interest groups are ubiquitous. In order to distinguish interest groups from political parties we define an **interest group** as an organized association that engages in activity relative to governmental decisions and policies but does not seek political power. Our definition is a very wide one that includes many types, from relatively transient and issue-oriented groups to others that are institutionalized, with many general as well as specific interests. Some pursue goals in their own self interest; others work in their view of the public interest.

Paul Pross identifies four prime characteristics of interest groups.[2]

1. They have a formal structure of organization that gives them continuity. Organization is essential to allow them to determine their objectives and strategies for action.
2. They are able to articulate and aggregate interests.
3. They attempt to act within the political system to influence policy outputs.
4. They try to influence power rather than exercise the responsibility of government themselves.

2. A. Paul Pross, "Pressure Groups: Adaptive Instruments of Political Communication," in Pross, ed., *Pressure Group Behaviour in Canadian Politics* (Toronto: McGraw-Hill Ryerson, 1975).

Mobs are not interest groups because they lack organizational structure. Political parties, too, are excluded, although the first three of these criteria apply equally to them. Parties have different goals than interest groups; they seek political power by having their candidates elected to government office, whereas interest groups try to influence political parties and government officials toward certain policies rather than enact these policies themselves. Interest groups can, and often do, try to win the support of all parties.

The similarities between parties and interest groups have led to different opinions about how the two are related. Some analysts, for example, believe that a rise in interest group power has been at least partially responsible for the decline in the role of political parties. In countries where traditionally there are two dominant political parties, the distinction between parties and interest groups is fairly evident. When several small parties compete, minority parties often represent the very narrow interests of one group or geographical area and then the distinction becomes less clear.

Studying Interest Groups: Policy Communities and Networks

Interest groups thrive in **pluralist systems**—that is, in systems that allow a plurality of interests to be pursued by a wide variety of associations. Canada, like other liberal democracies, provides an environment in which most political issues are contested by competing groups. Groups may not get what they want, or have to compromise, but they can often block proposals they are against. The main concern is whether they are able to operate on an equal footing so that the compromise that results is a fair one.

Government–interest group interaction is often studied in light of concepts such as *policy community* and *policy network* that attempt to convey the complex relationships state organizations have with interest groups. Interest groups often band together formally or informally. They become part of a larger **policy community** or **policy network**. Such a grouping includes actors or potential actors, whether inside or outside government, who share a common policy focus and help shape policy outcomes over time.[3] An example might be the close relations between veterans' organizations such as the Royal Canadian Legion and the Department of National Defence. The word *community* implies a closer, more permanent arrangement than *network*, which suggests a looser or more tenuous grouping. Many interest groups are narrow and would be part of only one policy community or network, while others, such as the Canadian Manufacturers Association, are very broad and are part of many.

The underlying idea behind this policy community/network approach to studying interest groups is that public policy is affected by the loose and informal relationship among a large number of specific actors including government agencies, pressure groups, corporations, institutions, media representatives and individuals who are interested in a particular policy field and who attempt to influence it. The concept of *policy community* directs attention away from pure institutional analysis and toward the more amorphous and informal pressures in the policy process. For example, a variety of environmental experts in the private sector spend a lot of time with their equivalents in government departments. The same is basically true in all policy fields. Policy communities can become relatively cohesive and mutually supportive once they achieve recognition and status with a lead government agency.

Clearly, many people are involved in making policy in open and democratic societies. Policy communities are useful in highlighting this, but unfortunately do little to direct one to the source

---

3. William D. Coleman and Grace Skogstad, "Policy Communities and Policy Networks: A Structural Approach," in Coleman and Skogstad, eds., *Policy Communities and Public Policy in Canada* (Toronto: Copp Clark Pitman, 1990), p. 25; also, Susan Phillips with Michael Orsini, *Mapping the Links: Citizen Involvement in Policy Processes.* CPRN Discussion Paper No. F/21. Ottawa: Canadian Policy Research Networks, 1 July, 2002: www.cprn.org.

of policy or its implementation. Moreover, political parties are almost totally omitted from this framework, and that is a serious omission in Canada. While political parties are not the only actors in the policy process, the prime minister and cabinet members (who owe their positions to the success of their party) certainly are powerful figures in the process. (Opposition MPs can also be valuable members of the process, as we shall see.) More research is needed in the area of policy communities to help us understand the role and scope of interest groups.

The most recent notable effort to examine advocacy groups in Canada came as part of a larger "democratic audit process," a research project founded on the notion that Canada suffers from a democratic deficit and malaise. The project uses the language of business administration and accounting—e.g., *audit* and *benchmarks*—to assess the degree of participation, inclusiveness and responsiveness of Canadian democracy across a whole range of institutions and processes.[4] In *Advocacy Groups*, Lisa Young and Joanna Everitt examine selected interest groups to discover who participates in advocacy groups, how they are organized internally, and what determines who prevails in determining Canadian public policy. We shall refer to some of their most important findings in the discussion below.[5]

Analyzing Interest Groups in Canada: Participation, Advantages and Disadvantages

The number and variety of interest groups in Canada is immense—there are tens of thousands, by a conservative estimate. They provide an avenue other than political parties to work with governments to create public policy, and Canadians participate highly in them compared to citizens of other countries. Who participates in interest groups? Young and Everitt found that the majority tend to be "those with higher social status: people with jobs, white skin, university education and higher family incomes."[6] The characteristics are similar to those who participate in political parties, but there are some interesting differences. Interest groups are slightly more inclusive of women than parties are, and youth participate in them more than they do in parties. Interest groups are, however, less inclusive of low-income Canadians than parties are, and university education is a stronger determinant of participation in an interest group than a political party. Ethnic minorities and unemployed Canadians are under-represented to a similar degree in both parties and interest groups.

Interest group participation contributes to Canadian liberal democratic politics in many ways. Such groups provide a major source of mediation between the government and the individual, articulating aggregated opinions and protecting the individual from undue control by the state. They also provide a mechanism for political representation that supplements the electoral process, assisting the political system by marshalling support for issues and providing ideas for public policy. They broaden the scope of issues discussed in election campaigns and, as a whole, are more inclusive of some elements of society than political parties are.

The participation of interest groups can make the political process much more responsive than electoral politics alone to social and economic differences in society.[7] Better resources and

---

4. The complete project includes volumes on elections, political parties, citizens, federalism, advocacy groups, legislatures, cabinets and first ministers, communications technology and the courts. Published by UBC Press in association with the Centre of Canadian Studies at Mount Allison University. Details can be found at www.CanadianDemocraticAudit.ca.

5. Lisa Young and Joanna Everitt, *Advocacy Groups* (Vancouver: UBC Press, 2004).

6. Young and Everitt, pp. 30–33, 43.

7. Adapted from a list by Amitai Etzioni, "Making Interest Groups Work for the Public," *Public Opinion*, vol. 5, no. 4 (August/September 1982), pp. 53–55.

access to decision-makers brings better government responsiveness. Groups sometimes feed the government valuable information, both facts and opinions, that can be used to help formulate policies and test policy proposals. This circular process of communication provides a valuable link between citizens and public policy by helping to keep the government in touch with shifts of opinion in society.

Interest groups also supplement government agencies when bureaucrats delegate administrative responsibilities to certain groups. For example, the Canadian Medical Association (CMA) actually regulates its own professional activity. This largely unpaid service can be an enormous assistance to government bureaucracy—and to the pockets of doctors. As well, professional groups indirectly help the civil service to disseminate information by publishing explanations of government policy in their journals.[8]

But there are many long-standing criticisms of interest groups. Some political scientists argue that whenever collective action takes place, groups with specific economic interests will defeat those representing the general public. The result is inefficient governmental regulation, subsidies and an oligarchic economic organization. Others point out that all groups can't compete on an even footing, so elite segments of society, with their financial and social advantages, are the most effective groups in voicing their demands—and they of course promote the interests of the affluent and powerful against those of the general public. Government funds are often used to assist marginalized or diffuse interests, such as poverty groups, but government support is often volatile. The business community has a privileged relationship with the state compared to other interests and the tax structure favours it over other interest groups. However, there are many examples of citizens' groups successfully challenging business interests. Environmental groups have achieved significant changes in forestry practices in British Columbia, for example.[9] Also, the federal government is not always on the side of big business, as the long-running battle with the wealthy tobacco companies illustrates (see the section below on the "smoking wars"). Similarly, the Liberal government ratified the Kyoto Accord in 2002 against strong protests from the oil and gas industry.[10].

Young and Everitt also point out a problem for interest groups, in that weakly funded groups sometimes suffer inclusion/participation problems that find them overrepresented by older, white, well-educated segments of society. These groups are open to all, but not all choose to, can afford to, or are able to, participate in them. On the other hand, some argue that groups such as women and minorities that have been designated as "special interests" are able to exercise undue influence over policy outcomes to their own advantage.[11]

Yet another criticism of interest groups is that they compete with and bypass representative institutions, undercutting political parties, and thereby weaken representative institutions that are a vital part of democracy. Some observers argue that interest groups weaken Parliament in another way. The *Charter of Rights and Freedoms* protects rights of freedom of speech and assembly but also facilitates interest group litigation. Since the passage of the Charter in 1982, language, gender and ethnic advocacy groups have increasingly pursued legal challenges based on the Constitution in order to have legislation they considered offensive declared unconstitutional. Gender-based organizations, for example, have used the courts to launch attacks on specific public policies such

6. See Evert Lindquist, "Public Managers and Policy Communities: Learning to Meet New Challenges," *Canadian Public Administration*, vol. 35 (Summer 1992), pp. 127–59.

9. See Benjamin Cashore, et al., *In Search of Sustainability: British Columbia Forest Policy in the 1990s* (Vancouver: UBC Press, 2001).

10. Douglas Macdonald, *The Business Campaign to Prevent Kyoto Ratification.* Paper presented to the CPSA, May 31, 2003.

11. Mancur Olson, *The Logic of Collective Action* (New York: Schocken, 1965).

as same-sex marriage. Such litigation allows unelected judges to replace elected representatives as de facto legislators.[12]

Although most groups refrain from illegal and violent tactics, sometimes interest group members who are focused on a single issue lose sight of the bigger picture and try to force their ideas on a reluctant public. In these cases, as has been the case with the pro-life lobby, individuals are harassed, buildings bombed and lives destroyed. Some protests turn violent, and even take on methods of terrorism.

Political scientists usually find such groups to be an inevitable and important part of the political process, but recognize that they must be regulated and as transparent as possible in their dealings with government. Overall, Young and Everitt find that advocacy groups are one of the "healthier elements of Canadian democracy and are satisfied with the relatively recent large proliferation of new groups and how they produce 'something of a counterbalance' to business interests." Governments have generally "achieved a reasonable balance between over- and underresponsiveness to organized interests."[13] The values inherent in their study are explicit: the authors favour more participation, inclusiveness and government responsiveness because they view these as fundamental attributes of democracy. Their conclusions will, of course, be contested by those whose values are based on different premises (such as elite or state-centred theory, discussed in Chapter 13) and who do not agree that increased participation, inclusiveness and responsiveness are necessarily good things in terms of achieving public policy for the good of the whole of society.

Classifying Interest Groups

Two typologies of interest groups have had lasting acceptance in Canadian political science. F.C. Engelmann and M.A. Schwartz divide interest groups into economic and non-economic categories, then subdivide the first into agriculture, labour and business groups.[14] The non-economic category is further subdivided into nine subtypes. Such distinctions, based on the primary basis of affiliation for their members, help to explain the basic differences in origin, activities and goals of the groups.

The economic/non-economic distinction, however, does not convey any significant information about the activities or relative importance of the various groups. In fact, there is a wide disparity in their powers. They range from relatively transient issue-oriented groups to others that are well established and assert a strong influence on political and economic life. They differ in terms of structure, resources, tactics and goals, and while these differences seem to affect the success or failure of groups in reaching their goals, there is very little certainty even to this contention.

Paul Pross addressed this problem in a typology designed to relate the groups to one another and to the policy system at large.[15] Groups are classified as institutionalized, issue-oriented, fledgling or mature; each is then categorized according to its objectives, organizational features and levels of communication with government. Of course, the distinction between the categories is not clear-cut, and any particular group may not conform exactly to this pattern.

Institutionalized groups are relatively well structured and enduring. By Pross's definition, they have five main characteristics: organizational continuity and cohesion; exclusive knowledge of the

12. F.L. Morton and Rainer Knopff, *The Charter Revolution and the Court Party* (Peterborough, ON: Broadview Press, 2000); Gregory Hein, *Interest Group Litigation and Canadian Democracy* (Montréal: Institute for Research in Public Policy, 2000).

13. Lisa Young and Joanna Everitt, *Advocacy Groups*, p. 152.

14. F.C. Engelmann and M.A. Schwartz, *Political Parties and the Canadian Social Structure*, 2nd ed. (Scarborough, ON: Prentice Hall, 1975).

15. Pross, "Pressure Groups," pp. 9–18. See also by the same author, *Group Policy and Public Policy,* 2nd ed. (Don Mills, ON: Oxford University Press, 1992).

appropriate sectors of government and their clients; stable membership; operational objectives that are clear and concrete; and organizational imperatives on which the credibility of the organization is based that generally are more important than any particular objective or specific policy.

At the opposite extreme of institutionalized interest groups are *issue-oriented groups*. Their organizational continuity and cohesion are weak, their knowledge of government poor and their membership fluid. They also have trouble formulating and adhering to long-range objectives, and maintain a low regard for their own organizational mechanisms. What issue-oriented groups lack in size and organization, they make up for in flexibility; they can be excellent vehicles for generating immediate public action on specific issues. They are little affected by fear of disturbing their relationship with government officials. Good examples are some of the early environmental groups and peace organizations in Canada that were very active publicly, but usually short-lived. *Fledgling* and *mature groups* fall between these two extremes.

Canadian Groups: A Catalogue

To familiarize readers with the main groups and lobbies in the political area, we summarize here the activities of some of the largest and most active of them. It is far from an exhaustive list, but it does indicate the multiplicity of groups in Canada. Because of the federal political structure of the country, most of the major interest groups have federated organizations. Both federal and provincial governments, for example, regulate interests in the economic sphere; as a result, most groups representing agriculture, labour and business interests require federated organizations with bureaucracies in Ottawa and the provincial capitals. It should be noted that while the majority of interest groups are privately funded, a number of them are financed in various ways by government.

Business   Business groups are especially active in political persuasion. More than 660 nationally relevant business associations have existed since Confederation, not including 125 farmers' associations.[16] The economic viability of the businesses they represent often directly depends on government policies and contracts. Large organizations such as the Canadian Trucking Association retain offices in the national capital, while others send public relations officers on regular or irregular visits to Ottawa.

The largest business association in the country is the Canadian Chamber of Commerce, which represents some five hundred local chambers and boards of trade. Although its headquarters is in Montréal, its president is frequently in Ottawa representing the business community that funds it. Another powerful organization, the Canadian Council of Chief Executives, represents the executives of 150 of the largest firms in the country.

Business interests in domestic affairs are also defended and promoted by associations representing particular sectors. These include the Canadian Industries Association, which represents manufacturing companies, and the Canadian Nuclear Association, which represents companies and organizations interested in the development of nuclear energy. The interests of manufacturing groups can often be recognized by their names: examples are the Automobile Industries Association of Canada, the Canadian Chemical Producers Association, the Mining Association of Canada, and even the Confectionery Manufacturers' Association of Canada. The petroleum industry is represented by the huge Canadian Petroleum Association, which has member companies involved in the exploration and production of oil and gas, as well as by the far smaller Independent Petroleum Association.

Various financial interests are also well organized. The Canadian Life and Health Insurance Association represents all companies in the insurance business. The Canadian Bankers Association

---

16. William D. Coleman, *Business and Politics: A Study of Collective Action* (Kingston/Montréal: McGill-Queen's University Press, 1988), p. 14.

represents all banks. Small business is centralized as an interest group by the Canadian Federation of Independent Business, which consists of private enterprises.

Business groups often try to influence a government's foreign policy. Probably the most significant of these groups is the Canadian Business and Industry International Advisory Committee (CBIIAC). The CBIIAC is an umbrella organization that includes the Canadian Chamber of Commerce, the Canadian Export Association, the Canadian Import Association and other groups concerned with trade policy. Of course, this means there can be incongruities in the CBIIAC. The Canadian Import Association wants reduction of tariffs and non-tariff barriers, while the Canadian Export Association, representing five hundred corporations, wants to increase access to foreign markets and obtain government assistance and tax concessions.

Agriculture and Fisheries Agriculture has two major organizations. The largest, the Canadian Federation of Agriculture (CFA), enrols about two-thirds of the country's farmers. It is composed of provincial federations of agriculture and many commodity organizations such as the Canadian Pork Council. The CFA makes representations to the federal government, but is somewhat less willing to engage in direct confrontation with the government than is the smaller National Farmers Union.[17] The Fisheries Council of Canada is the largest organization representing fishing interests. It comprises provincial associations of companies in fishing and fish processing.

Labour Labour is a powerful force in Canadian politics. Approximately one out of every three paid workers outside agriculture is a member of a labour union. The major umbrella organization is the Canadian Labour Congress (CLC). It consists of affiliated trade unions. The CLC is a federation of regional organizations with both regional offices and local councils. Representation is geographically dispersed: the Ottawa office deals with issues at the national or international levels, and the regional and local branches focus on issues under provincial jurisdiction.

A second major worker association, the Canadian Federation of Labour, comprises several building trade unions. It differs from the CLC in emphasizing co-operation with the government and in being non-partisan. Québec has its own major labour organization, the Confederation of National Trade Unions, which represents members in a number of Québec labour unions.

Workers are also affiliated with their particular sector of the economy or trade; examples are the Québec Woodworkers Federation and the United Automobile Workers of America. Government employees are represented by organizations such as the Canadian Union of Public Employees (CUPE) and the Canadian Union of Postal Workers (CUPW).

Other Economic Groups Another prominent category of economic interest groups comprises those representing consumers. The Consumers' Association of Canada represents the interests of consumers to government, a function that often brings it into conflict with business and labour.

Professional workers are in a separate category. The Canadian Bar Association, the Canadian Association of Broadcasters and the Canadian Council of Professional Engineers, among others, attempt to secure government policies conducive to their professional interests. Perhaps the best-known group in this category is the powerful Canadian Medical Association (CMA); other prominent organizations in the health field are the Canadian Dental Association and the Canadian Nurses Association.

Non-economic Groups This category is possibly the largest; it is certainly the most diffuse. As we've already indicated, such groups may be transitory or permanent. Religious interests are fostered by the Canadian Council of Churches, the Canadian Conference of Catholic Bishops and the

17. See Riddell-Dixon, *The Domestic Mosaic*, p. 25.

Christian Movement for Peace. Ethnic representation is made by groups such as the Canadian Jewish Congress, the Arab Palestine Association, the Ukrainian National Association and the Canadian Polish Congress. The National Action Committee on the Status of Women (NAC), the largest feminist organization in Canada, represents some six hundred women's organizations; REAL Women and the YWCA also represent some women.

Reproduced with permission, Dennis Pritchard.

Several anti-poverty groups exist in Canada at the national, provincial and local levels. Only one national group has been able to mobilize people actually living in poverty, and the number of participants is not large. Most of these groups could not exist without government support. They are therefore vulnerable to shifts in government policy that cut funding, as has happened in recent years.[18]

Generally weaker and more transitory than the above-named organizations are public interest groups. These issue-oriented groups can pop up any time a corrosive issue arises. Motivated by a mixture of principle and ideology, such groups tend to see themselves as representing the unrepresented or under-represented. Usually, their significance depends on favourable (or unfavourable) media coverage. Think of pro-life and pro-choice groups as examples. Of course, all groups believe they represent the "public interest," but these particular groups specialize in this approach rather than in one based on occupation, nationality, religion, gender or ethnicity. They include such vocal advocates of environmental causes as Friends of the Earth, Greenpeace, Energy Probe, and such peace organizations as Amnesty International and Operation Dismantle.

Lobbying in Canada

Lobbying is the narrow political activity of an interest group that is aimed at securing favourable policy decisions or the appointment of specific government personnel. It takes place at the federal, provincial and municipal levels of government. The term *lobby* comes from the corridor in the British House of Commons where constituents have historically met their MPs to cajole or pressure them about policy legislation. When lobbying takes place behind closed doors, it inevitably raises suspicions about donations to parties or campaigns that may allow access, influence and treatment not available to others. While nothing is more proper in a democratic process than for individuals to attempt to influence their government, it is important to maintain transparency in order to make the process legitimate.

Ottawa and the provincial capitals are full of lobbyists. In Ottawa alone there are well over three hundred trade and professional organizations. These groups, which represent only the tip of a giant iceberg, employ among them several thousand staff. Others hire professional lobbyists to

18. Young and Everitt, pp. 74–86.

improve "public relations" with the government. Individual corporations that cannot afford full-time employees in Ottawa "protect" their interests through their public relations departments and chief executive officers.

Relationships between lobbyists and the government are both antagonistic and accommodating. For example, government regulates business, yet also subsidizes and protects it. Lobbyists are paid to influence the government. Their organizations break down roughly into two groups: those that focus primarily on general government policy, such as the Canadian Council of Chief Executives; and those with a more specific focus, typified by the Pharmaceutical Manufacturers Association of Canada or the Mining Association of Canada. Trade and umbrella groups send scores of lawyers before regulatory tribunals to secure the modification of regulations, while voluntary groups promote their causes with MPs, cabinet ministers and bureaucrats. Yet, the entire scene remains so obscure that a substantial portion of Ottawa's lobbyists describe their occupation simply as "public relations."

Given the complexity of government, lobbying is essential. Lobbyists can offer valuable assistance to government and Parliament by providing facts that are necessary for informed decisions. Governments periodically call lobbyists together for advice or research. They encourage their participation through inquiries, hearings, consultative documents, Green Papers, White Papers and draft bills. They also hire lobbyists of their own to represent Canadian interests in the United States, for example. Lobbyists are useful to governments because their information enables bureaucrats and politicians to develop policies that garner votes.

Since the enactment of the *Lobbyists Registration Act*, the members and organizations of this profession have become well known through publications such as *Lobby Digest* and *Lobby Monitor*. A list of the leading consultant lobby firms would include Government Consultants International, Public Affairs International, William H. Neville and Associates, the Capitol Hill Group and S.A. Murray Consulting. Their major clients include corporations, and these corporations often are clients of more than one firm as they seek to maximize their influence (see Table 13.1). Specialist lobbying firms like these are not the only professional hired guns in the lobbying business. Most law firms in Canada's capitals also lobby—although they prefer to be called consultants or lawyers. Many single individuals, too, such as former MPs, senators and "bagmen" of parties are paid by organizations to work on their behalf.

Since it is so widely practised and performs a valuable function, why then does lobbying have such an unsavoury reputation? A main concern is the close relation of lobbying to **influence-peddling**, in which money is exchanged for favours. Influence-peddling comes under the *Criminal Code* and carries a five-year prison term. But as we have seen, there are other concerns based on the very nature and behaviour of interest groups.

TABLE 13.1 Examples of Consultant Lobbying Firms and their Clients

Firm	Clients
Capital Hill Group	Lockheed Martin; Loews; Canadian Tire
CFN Consultants	Lockheed Martin; Microsoft
Earnscliffe Strategy Group	Petro-Canada; Microsoft; Labatt
Global Public Affairs Inc	BP Canada; Shell Canada
GPC International	Government of Hong Kong; Labatt
Hill & Knowlton Canada Ltd	Motorola; Dow Chemical; Alcan
Sussex Strategy Group	Molson; Ontario Dental Association; Bell Canada

Source: Adapted from the Industry Canada website of lobbyist registrations—available at http://strategis.gc.ca/lobbyist.

Legislation to Control Lobbying

To make lobbying more open and fair, Parliament has established rules to regulate it. An incentive for regulations gained impetus in 1985, when Brian Mulroney's Progressive Conservative government finished its first year in office plagued with scandals and shrouded in rumours of patronage and favouritism. To improve his government's image, Mulroney promised a new code of lobbying conduct. Not surprisingly, the lobbying profession was against any form of regulation.

In January 1987, a parliamentary committee released a unanimous report recommending that registration should be required of paid lobbyists, listing the names of lobbyists, their clients and the issues they represent. Five months later, Bill C82, the *Lobbyists Registration Act*, was tabled. It was a weak bill that did not include many of the more stringent recommendations of the committee. It did not attempt to regulate lobbyists, but simply required registration. Lobby groups were relatively satisfied with the weak measures of the legislation and, in September 1988, the bill was given royal assent. It was proclaimed law in June 1989, when the infrastructure for implementing the bill was in place.

The Act divided lobbyists into two tiers—professional lobbyists and paid lobbyists—and set out different requirements for each.

Tier I included "an individual who, for pay, provides certain types of lobbying services on behalf of a client." These *professional* lobbyists were required to (1) file a new registration for every lobbyist–client relationship; and (2) include in every registration their own name, the name and address of their firm, the names of clients, the names of corporate owners or subsidiaries of the clients, the general area of concern of the lobbying effort and the class of undertaking that the lobbying was intended to influence.

Tier II included those "whose job involves a 'significant' amount of government lobbying for his or her employer"—"in-house" lobbyists employed by corporations, umbrella associations and public interest groups. These lobbyists were required to register within two months of initiating the lobbying activity and every year thereafter. This type of lobbyist needed only to give her name and the name and address of the employer corporation.

Neither group had to provide any financial information. The penalty for non-compliance was a fee of $100 000 and/or a two-year prison sentence.

A provision to review the legislation three years after it came into effect was incorporated into the new Act. The review took place in 1993 and it was evident that reformers wanted major changes while others, particularly lobbyists, wanted to leave the law intact. On the positive side, the *Lobbyists Registration Act* confirmed the legitimacy of lobbying the government in Canada and set up a registry of lobbyists. However, many lobbyists did not register.

During the 1993 general election, the Liberal Party campaigned on the theme of reforming the lobbying business and, shortly after assuming power, Jean Chrétien's new government introduced legislation to make lobbying more transparent. But lobbyists immediately formed their *own* lobbying organization, the Government Relations Institute, to ensure that they would not be adversely affected by new legislation. In particular, they wanted the fees paid to them to remain tax deductible for their clients.

In June 1995, the functions of the *registrar* (who monitors the Registry of Lobbyists) were subsumed in the duties of an **ethics counsellor**. This office submitted an annual report to Parliament about the workings of the *Lobbyist Registration Act* and worked with interested parties to develop a code of conduct for lobbyists. The job of ethics counsellor was to enforce the code after it had been approved by a parliamentary committee. The penalties for non-compliance remained as they were.

Relatively minor amendments to the *Lobbyist Registration Act* were passed in June 1995. As amended, the Act continued to divide lobbyists into two tiers. Tier I included "professional" or "consultant" lobbyists, and Tier II included two defined groups: in-house "corporate" and in-house "organization" lobbyists—employees of corporations or interest group organizations who lobby as a "significant part" of their duties. The amendment also required somewhat more detailed reporting: for example, lobbyists had to identify specifics about what they were lobbying for, and which departments or governmental institutions they lobbied. Contingency fees also had to be disclosed as well as their source and any government funding of the client.

In response to the negative publicity concerning loopholes that allowed lobbying to take place behind closed doors (see the "Close-Up on Behaviour: Plugging Lobbying Loopholes"), further minor amendments to the Act were made in June 2003. Most of the registration obligations that apply to in-house lobbyists for organizations are now also required of in-house lobbyists of corporations. Communications that are simply requests for information are not subject to the Act. But all lobbyists must file a tax return every six months, and if a lobbyist for a corporation or organization has been a public servant, politician or other public office holder, she must disclose the past offices held.

Requiring registration by lobbyists has increased transparency, but there is still need for improvement in this respect at the federal, provincial and municipal levels. Several problems remain:

- Only paid lobbyists have to register—others have *no obligation* to file or disclose information. This provides a gigantic loophole for the use of contingency fees. Essentially, lobbyists who do not receive payment until *after* contacting the officeholder or bureaucrat can avoid disclosing information, because they have not been paid.
- The *definition* of Tier II lobbyists is weak. It includes only someone who devotes a "significant" part of her duties to lobbying. A lobbyist who does not want to register can simply maintain that lobbying is not a "significant" part of her duties.
- Not enough information is required, especially of Tier II lobbyists. Spending *disclosure* might relieve the negative image of lobbyists. As well, the subject categories given are too vague and can be used to mislead rivals or critics.
- Interest groups do not have to file any *information* about their objectives.
- *Enforcement* is inadequate. The ethics counsellor has no power to verify the information submitted by the lobbyists. The RCMP, which enforces the Act, will launch an investigation only when a complaint is raised against an individual. The *Criminal Code*'s statute of limitations on summary offences limits the ability of the RCMP to obtain prosecutions under the Act to a period of six months. By the time a complaint is made, it may be too late to punish the perpetrator.
- *Non-compliance* is a problem. Many lobbyists are reportedly still refusing to register and are getting away with it. A bureaucrat or individual being lobbied is not required to ensure that the lobbyist is registered.
- There is a strong argument that *all* lobbyists should have the same requirements. The two-tier system creates a hierarchy of lobbyists, inferring that some individuals have the potential to be more subversive than others to the policy process.

Close-Up on Political Behaviour

PLUGGING LOBBYING LOOPHOLES

Enforcement problems in the *Lobbying Registration Act* were highlighted in 1999 when Jean Chrétien's government faced criticisms over the so-called Shawinigate affair (named after the Québec riding that Chrétien represented). René Fugère, a friend of then prime minister Chrétien, met civil servants on behalf of a Shawinigan hotel owner. He did not register as a lobbyist. The hotel owner subsequently received a $100 000 government cheque for his business. This incident was investigated by the RCMP in 1999, but no charges were filed against Fugère. He could not be punished for not registering as a lobbyist because the wording of the lobbying legislation was "too vague." In 2001, the ethics counsellor recommended that the *Lobbying Registration Act* should be amended to include the kind of lobbying conducted by Fugère.

Furthermore, one of the main factors behind cynicism about interest groups is that governments spend more money because of lobbying. As we have seen, governments make direct payments to some groups. They also allow corporations to treat lobbying as a business expense, and some types of interest groups are allowed to register as charities and receive tax credits for charitable donations. It can be argued that a more open system would eliminate the source of public discontent. Reformers maintain, therefore, that it is in the public interest for the lobbying registration procedure to provide *access* and *transparency*.

> *Forms of consultation like legislative committees and royal commissions, which are open to a wide range of participation and whose consultation processes are transparent, are of crucial importance, as they provide points of access to the political system for wealthy and poor groups, and for insiders and outsiders.*[19]

Public access should be equitable, not selective or privileged, and the public should have the opportunity to know who is attempting to influence the government. Instead, the legislation provides what one expert calls "little more than a registry of the more professionally minded lobbyists."[20] The public is given the impression that lobbying in Ottawa is controlled, when in fact it is not.[21]

The debate continues. In late 2006, as part of the newly approved *Federal Accountability Act*, the Conservative government amended the *Lobbyists Registration Act* to provide for the appointment of a **commissioner of lobbying** upon approval of Parliament and extended the scope of the commissioner's investigative authority compared with that of the existing registrar of lobbyists.

One can expect that minor amendments will be made to the *Lobbyists Registration Act* in the future, but there will not likely be fundamental changes in the system.

Common Tactics and Strategies

The lobbying strategy chosen by an interest group depends largely on the type of group it is, its resources and the type of issues involved. Some groups concentrate on the pre-parliamentary stages of government, while others prefer buttonholing MPs after the issue is before Parliament (see Figure 13.1). In all cases, the strategies used must include more than an attempt to influence legislators and bureaucrats. Public opinion must be aroused, too. No amount of persuasion of the government will be effective unless public opinion is in agreement with a lobby, or at least not hostile to its demands.

Many lobbyists establish friendly relationships with legislators, bureaucrats, media and other contacts in order to present their cases in informal, friendly ways. This contact generally concerns interests that the MPs already support, and is aimed at convincing them to influence their colleagues. Lobbyists also disseminate literature, present briefs, provide research results, promote letter-writing campaigns, support groups at committee hearings and entertain those they're trying to influence. At the same time, they keep close track of what is happening in Parliament, so that lobbyists and the groups they represent will know when and where to take appropriate action.

Lobbying MPs is probably *least effective* when the policy concerned is already before Parliament in the form of proposed legislation. Policies are made before they reach Parliament, and by the time

---

19. Young and Everitt, p, 102.

20. A. Paul Pross and Iain Steward, "Lobbying, the Voluntary Sector and the Public Purse," in Susan D. Phillips, ed., *How Ottawa Spends*, 1993–94 (Ottawa: Carleton University Press, 1993) p. 121.

21. The number of lobbyists is monitored by the Lobbyists Registration Branch. The numbers are updated regularly; see http://strategis.ic.gc.ca/lobbyist.

FIGURE 13.1 **Basic Model of How Pressure Groups Influence the Government**

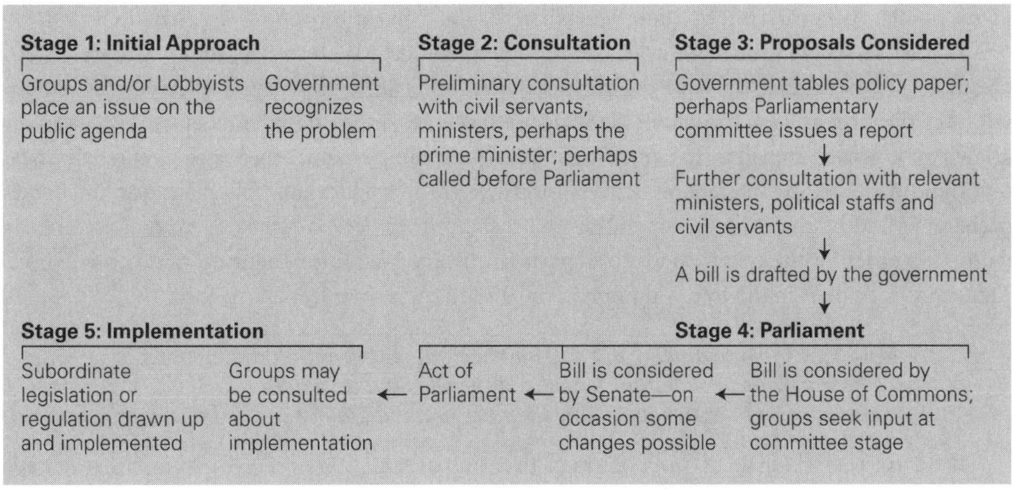

Stage 1: Initial Approach		Stage 2: Consultation	Stage 3: Proposals Considered
Groups and/or Lobbyists place an issue on the public agenda	Government recognizes the problem	Preliminary consultation with civil servants, ministers, perhaps the prime minister; perhaps called before Parliament	Government tables policy paper; perhaps Parliamentary committee issues a report ↓ Further consultation with relevant ministers, political staffs and civil servants ↓ A bill is drafted by the government ↓

Stage 5: Implementation		Stage 4: Parliament		
Subordinate legislation or regulation drawn up and implemented	Groups may be consulted about implementation	Act of ← Parliament ←	Bill is considered by Senate—on occasion some changes possible ←	Bill is considered by the House of Commons; groups seek input at committee stage

they are set in a bill it is difficult for any group to alter them. At this stage, legislation is more apt to be blocked or delayed than changed. The *most effective* form of lobbying, therefore, is probably to target key bureaucrats and ministers while policy is in the gestation stage.

Since public relations campaigns are expensive, groups with large memberships, extensive financial resources and influential connections have major advantages. Direct advertising or program sponsorship is often too expensive for many groups. However, there are other avenues of influence. Poorer interest groups often stage newsworthy events, such as concerts, walkathons or other types of fundraisers, so that information about their group and their activities will be publicized without charge. Some groups employ other tactics to obtain free media coverage. For example, employees might strike against management to force the government to listen to their demands through the media. Picketers affect not only the management of their companies, but also public opinion.

Non-violent demonstrations are yet another means of seeking publicity. It is especially popular with minority and low-income groups. But neither non-violent nor violent protest fits the norms of mutual accommodation between interest groups and policy-makers in Canada. Protest tactics present an ultimatum that precludes negotiation of individual group claims; on the whole, groups that use this strategy are likely to be ignored, discredited or placated with purely symbolic action. Lobbyists who act harshly are often ostracized by government circles.

Access Points: Pre-Parliamentary and Parliamentary

A lobbyist once commented that "our political system is great if the government is doing what you like—otherwise there are never enough access points." To be successful, groups must be flexible

---

CLOSE-UP ON Political Behaviour

USING THE SYSTEM (I)

The following incident illustrates how interest group leaders are able to informally approach and get assistance from cabinet ministers:

A Toronto lobbyist asked an acquaintance, who was a friend of a cabinet minister, to tell the minister over lunch that he wanted to be certain that a particular insurance company would have an opportunity to present a brief at the committee stage of a bill (the *Borrowers and Depositors Protection Act,* 1977). The friend did, and the minister assured him that the company would be heard. It was. *Is this type of intervention legitimate?

---

* Based on a personal interview conducted by the authors.

enough to approach all parts of the legislative process and adapt their tactics to all of the available access points. "We throw out our line everywhere" is the usual approach of successful lobbyists.[22]

Access to the policy process is available through individual MPs by way of the committee system or caucus and the cabinet. But since the bureaucracy is concerned with policy at its earliest formation, it is often the most important focus of lobbying. Such activity at the pre-parliamentary stage has been known to provoke complaints that interest groups bypass ministers and other elected representatives.

In both arenas, the interaction between pressure group leaders and politicians or bureaucrats is characterized by a spirit of co-operation that has been termed an "ethos of mutual accommodation." In order for the system to work, all parties must receive some benefits from the interaction. This ethos is evident in the following remark by an interest group leader:

> *We are concerned to always give full and accurate information to bureaucrats because if we don't create confidence and they depend on advice which is biased toward us—they have a long memory and will hold it against us later.*[23]

If we trace the course of a bill through the pre-parliamentary stages to the parliamentary stages, the relative importance of the various access points becomes clearer. The interaction process can be very complex, and most of it takes place on an informal, confidential basis. The bureaucracy and cabinet are significant access points in the pre-parliamentary stages of a bill. Many political analysts believe that the bureaucracy is the most widely used arena for successful pressure group activity. There is a close relationship between civil servants and pressure groups because civil servants are required to research and evaluate policy proposals for cabinet, to give advice on the public acceptability of these policies and even to help educate and inform the public about them.

The availability of access points varies according to many factors, particularly the pressure group's position within its specified policy community or network. The federal cabinet and lead agency or department form the core of the policy community in their particular policy field. Around the decision-making core are *concentric rings* of other institutions and policy actors such as departments, MPs, provincial governments, interested groups and individuals. The closer they are to the core, the more influential interest groups are. The most influential interest groups tend to have direct, institutionalized access to the policy core. Access to key decision-makers was a main reason the smoking lobby was able to prolong its battle for so long. Egale Canada, the gay and lesbian rights group, is another example of an organization that attributes much of its success to supporters in major government positions.[24]

Successful access to the policy-making process requires knowledge of the institutional and procedural structures of government and the legislative system—such as how a bill originates and what affects its passage. The early stages of a bill's development are particularly important for interest groups because, as we noted in Chapter 9, Parliament passes laws but rarely originates them. Legislation and expenditures are generally approved by the executive as a package. By the time a particular bill reaches Parliament, the government has publicly committed itself to the policies therein, and little can be done to change the details without destroying the delicate compromises on which the "deal" has been constructed.

Another opportunity for pressure groups exists during the drafting and amendment of bills, but this is a difficult stage at which to have much influence. One lobbyist stated his preferences this way: "After a bill is printed it is almost impossible to have a great effect. We prefer the white paper process

22. Based on personal interviews conducted by the authors.

23. Ibid.

24. Young and Everitt, p. 133. Also, Miriam Smith, *Lesbian and Gay Rights in Canada: Social Movements and Equality-Seeking, 1971–1995* (Toronto: University of Toronto Press, 1999).

so that the minister is not married to his bill." Professional lobbyists are particularly critical about the lack of influence in the closed atmosphere around taxation legislation: "Too few people get involved in the final projects. . . . We prefer the American system where there is a greater airing of views on each bill."[25]

Since responsibility for the initiation and control of legislation is in the hands of the government, the cabinet is a natural target for interest group activity. In the pre-parliamentary stages of a bill, a minister is responsible for gathering information from interest groups. This relationship can be exceedingly complex. At the same time, government secrecy requires that the groups not be informed about the government's intentions regarding decisions or policy details. Sometimes the relationships between ministers and interest groups are extremely close—perhaps too close.

Every year, specific groups are invited to present formal briefs to cabinet. This recognition is greatly valued. Apart from publicity and prestige, it gives these groups an opportunity to air their views directly to ministers. Some groups also have excellent relations with Parliament as well. It is important for interest groups to use the access points provided within the political system and establish a framework for mutual consultation. Once a pattern is established, it indicates that the group has obtained recognition as *the* representative for its particular interests. The interaction is a symbol of the compatibility of its goals and tactics with both Canadian political culture and the goals of the government.

Interest groups seek access to individual MPs more for their long-term political influence than because they expect immediate assistance. Since legislation is approved and passed (rather than initiated) in the House of Commons, unless an MP has special information or interest (or is strategically located in a minority government situation) she can be of little direct help to a pressure group. Also, interest group leaders complain that "it is almost impossible to get backbenchers involved in the technical details of bills" and that "there has to be public appeal in order to get backbenchers involved." On the other hand, it is always possible that a friendly MP may bring an issue to the attention of a cabinet minister, become a cabinet minister or, together with enough fellow backbenchers, force desired change in cabinet decisions. In addition, since opposition MPs may, after a future election, gain key positions in the government, even they cannot be ignored. As a rule, however, opposition MPs receive most attention from interest groups during minority governments, when their vote is significant.

An MP may take up the cause of an interest group for various reasons. It may be politically expedient to do so. Or the group may provide information for a well-informed question or speech in the House, which would earn the MP credit and recognition within her party caucus.

Caucus also gives individual MPs an opportunity to express their views directly and privately to ministers. On the government side, an outline of bills that are about to be introduced in the House is presented to the caucus before it is introduced in Parliament. Caucus committee meetings follow in which the MPs can express the interests of groups that have approached them. Caucus continues to debate bills even after they have been introduced in the House, and, on occasion, can even prevent the second reading. If cabinet and interest groups' opinions diverge, it is usual for interest groups to attempt to form a coalition of anti-government forces. It has been noted,

> *Generally, cabinet opinion prevails when the caucus, the provinces, or the relevant interest groups can be attracted to cabinet's side. Cabinet has the least chance of imposing its views where all three of these elements resist its direction.*[26]

---

25. Ibid.
26. Robert J. Jackson and Michael Atkinson, *The Canadian Legislative System*, 2nd ed. (Toronto: Macmillan, 1980), p. 40.

The parliamentary committee system is yet another attractive access point for interest groups because the very purpose of these institutions is to gather information. When legislation is before a House committee, all interests are invited to present briefs. Some scholars have found that committees are the most frequent targets of interest group influence on legislators. In fact, it is not uncommon for interest groups, both in Ottawa and in the provincial capitals, to have their own representatives on legislative committees. The Royal Canadian Legion, for example, is usually well represented on the Committee for Veterans Affairs.

Some interest groups prefer Senate committees over House committees as a lobbying forum. Senate committees tend to handle testimony from corporations less politically than do House of Commons committees. Business people, for example, find dealing with House committees unsatisfactory because the deliberations are unsystematic and partisan.

As we have noted, even after bills have been introduced in the House, a great many devices exist for slowing down their progress. Passage of legislation is at best a very lengthy process, often taking several years, thereby giving interest groups extensive opportunities to lobby and conduct public relations campaigns. And, in many circumstances (such as when a weak government is in power), delaying a bill may be just as effective as killing it.

Political parties constitute a further access point to government decision-making. Interest groups may even attempt to influence the policy resolutions brought forward at party conventions because political parties supply the government leaders, and party decisions may become government policy decisions. However, fearing that such an attachment might close their routes of access to other parties, many groups declare non-partisanship. The Canadian Manufacturers Association is a classic example of a group that has achieved significant success by avoiding identification with a single party. On the other hand, some interests, particularly labour associations, not only openly identify themselves with specific political parties, but also affiliate with them, providing financial and political support. For example, the Canadian Labour Congress first openly identified with, then directly associated with, the CCF/NDP. In 1943, it endorsed the CCF as the political arm of labour in Canada, and in 1961 the joint CLC-CCF Committee founded the NDP, with which it was closely aligned for many years.

Cabinet is closely involved in the policy-making process and is the focus of intense lobbying. It is not, however, a monolithic block, but rather the sum of its ministerial parts. While the whole cabinet is involved in major issues because of the principle of collective responsibility, its committee system forms the nexus of many significant decisions. Moreover, for the lobbyist, access to the committee system involves contact with the relevant minister, often via the ministerial bureaucracy or exempt staff.

Reinforcing the myth of cabinet monopoly is the handy axiom that, while the members of the House of Commons pass legislation, they rarely initiate it. At face value, this statement is true; however, on close examination of the workings of the House, it is revealed to be an oversimplification. Members of Parliament are themselves close friends and allies of ministers. Today, MPs play a more significant role in terms of their increased participation in briefings, committee hearings and new task forces.

Since MPs have a small staff, lobby groups can become a major source of assistance and information. They can brief an MP on the political pros and cons of a particular proposal. This is important to the MPs, who are often much more concerned about public attitudes on legislation than are members of the bureaucracy. Moreover, MPs usually have more time than senior bureaucrats do to see lobbyists. Since cabinet ministers are recruited from the ranks of the government backbench, neither they nor opposition backbenchers can be allowed to feel isolated or ignored.

Even in the short term, the skilful lobbying of backbenchers can have considerable impact on the legislative output of the government. The primary forum for backbench influence is caucus. When a substantial coalition of backbenchers with the support of one or more concerned interest groups opposes the cabinet's position, the likelihood that the government's proposals will be reviewed increases. Further leverage is often available via a three-way alliance of lobbyists, backbenchers and disgruntled provincial governments.

Canadian interest groups also focus directly on the federal bureaucracy. Business groups tend first to approach lower- and middle-level bureaucrats "on the premise that policy becomes more set and less easy to change the higher up it moves and that the lower level bureaucrats rely on business for information."[27] Hence, a reciprocity of dependency exists. Effective lobbying of the public service presupposes, of course, that the lobbyist have a fairly sophisticated understanding of the bureaucratic process and sufficient knowledge about the best timing and point of contact. In the perception of one former lobbyist, the campaign to influence legislative outputs cannot begin too early "because you don't even see the tip of the iceberg until there's a hell of a lot of ice down there."[28]

The effectiveness of focusing on public servants at the pre-parliamentary stage of the process is augmented at later stages. Legislation is often returned to departments for further consideration and for the development of implementation regulations. Thus, the entire process is reopened to groups that seek to block or stall disadvantageous proposals. The complexities of the legislative system and the rough landscape of Canadian politics give some indication of why it is often considered easier to block or slow down proposals than to initiate them.

The increased salience of bureaucracy is common to all advanced industrial societies. There is, however, a tendency to overstress the political significance of the bureaucratic process. This is especially true of journalists, for whom the use of the word *mandarin* or *all-powerful* in reference to senior civil servants carries an aura of omnipotence. Observations abound to the effect that "any lobbyist who is worth either the handsome retainer or the comfortable salary that goes with the title will tell you that the real levers of power in Ottawa lie within the bureaucracy."[29] Those wasting their time with MPs and cabinet ministers, so the reasoning goes, are simply not in the know.

The habit of using language such as "the real levers of power" stems from an inadequate appreciation of the concept of political *power* (see Chapter 1). In this journalistic interpretation, the competition for access to government decision-makers is seen as a zero-sum game. Power is viewed as a kind of football in the lobbyists' free-for-all; if one group has it, other groups do not. The fact is that while certain interests single out specific components of the legislative system for special attention, no successful group fosters the illusion that power has a single address. The most seasoned lobbyists show flexibility, and aim to touch "all the bases." When business groups suspect, for example, that their efforts at the mid-level of bureaucracy are too late or simply insufficient, they send their chief executive officers to engage in discussions with members of cabinet—an activity that is frequently coordinated by large umbrella organizations.

All groups appreciate the importance of closely monitoring developments in Ottawa and making regular contact with government officials. However, no two groups have identical goals or resources, organization or methods. The National Farmers' Union (NFU) does not hesitate to employ confrontational tactics when they are deemed necessary. The larger Canadian Federation of Agriculture (CFA) makes representations to the federal government on matters of macro- and

27. Riddell-Dixon, *The Domestic Mosaic*, p. 7.
28. Quoted in John Gray, "Insiders Go to Mandarins before Minister," *The Globe and Mail*, October 25, 1980.
29. Gray, "Insiders Go to Mandarins before Minister."

micro-agricultural policy, paying special attention to the development of export markets. The NFU places greater emphasis on the economic viability of the family farm and the dignity of the Canadian farmer, but like the CFA it also promotes trade policies that will increase exports and protect domestic producers generally.[30]

The broad membership of the Canadian Business and Industry International Advisory Committee dictates concern with a very wide range of issues. Traditionally, it worked closely with Industry Canada, but departmental reorganization now requires it to give greater attention to Foreign Affairs and International Trade (DFAIT). Other groups feature more exclusive membership and a concomitantly narrower focus, stressing a specific geographic area or a particular sector of the economy. Depending on their styles and resources, some groups consistently stress one link of the legislative process over others.

Regionalism can offer interest groups differing areas of opportunity. David Kwavnick has noted how competition between the Canadian Labour Congress and the Québec-based Confederation of National Trade Unions demonstrates that "rival groups representing the same interest, but having access to different levels of government in a federal system, will attempt to shift power to the level of government to which they enjoy access."[31]

Interest groups exert a long-term, systematic yet flexible effort at as many points of access as possible. Lobbyists are aware that political power is not some finite substance that necessarily ebbs in the legislature as it flows in the bureaucracy. They know that the search for the "real lever of power" is for bare-handed amateurs. Government, like a growing onion, features so many different but similar layers that it is impossible to distinguish which of them really counts. Successful lobbyists have learned that they *all* count—in fact, each layer has meaning only because of its relation to the others.

The relative utility of any one part of the legislative system to lobbyists can and does change over time. This is true even of backbench MPs, who—as we mentioned above—are now considered more suitable targets for lobbying than in the past. Zero-sum journalistic assumptions about the exercise of influence and power can cloud understanding of the subtle relations between administrative and legislative branches of government. Knowledge held by the bureaucrat is not lost to the politician; elected representatives are not overshadowed by civil service technocrats. Few elected representatives or senior public servants would claim to have been the artless victims of manipulative bureaucrats or lobbyists. To paraphrase Duff Roblin, the former senator and Progressive Conservative premier of Manitoba, "I've never had an original idea in my life, but I know one when I see it!" However, MPs can, of course, be manipulated unwittingly (see the "Close-Up on Political Behaviour: Using the System (II)").

CLOSE-UP ON Political Behaviour

USING THE SYSTEM (II)

A high official attached to a certain foreign embassy in Ottawa thought that an issue concerning a certain aspect of his country's relations with Canada should have an airing in the House of Commons. This official contacted an opposition member and armed him with a particularly contentious question with which to confront the government. The member asked the question in the House. The minister of foreign affairs delayed his answer to the next day. He asked his staff to brief him on the substance of the matter so that he could respond. They, of course, sought information from the foreign embassy—information they duly received from the very man who had originally formulated the question and inserted it into the system. The foreign diplomat had, in fact, both set the question and determined the answer.*

Yet, politicians are neither unaware of such manoeuvring nor unappreciative of the perceptions and ideas that filter through this way. Is this appropriate?

* Based on personal interviews conducted by the authors.

30. Riddell-Dixon, *The Domestic Mosaic*, p. 24.

31. David Kwavnick, "Interest Group Demands and the Federal Political System: Two Canadian Case Studies," in Pross, *Pressure Group Behaviour in Canadian Politics*, p. 77.

When substantive legislation is the goal of interest group activity, a sustained campaign is required. It is perhaps in *endurance* that well-financed lobbies have their greatest advantage. The smoking lobby is a prime example.

The "Smoking Wars" of Pro- and Anti-tobacco Groups

Most of the lobbying tactics and strategies described above have been, and continue to be, used by pro- and anti-tobacco legislation lobby groups. Theirs continues to be one of the most sophisticated lobbying campaigns in modern Canadian history. On one side are the tobacco companies; on the other are various health groups such as the Canadian Medical Association (CMA) and the Non-Smokers' Rights Association of Canada. The Government of Canada, in some ways, is the umpire between these two factions.

The "smoking wars" began in earnest in 1987–88 over the government's bill (Bill C51) to ban tobacco advertising and promotion. Despite the fact that roughly 45 000 Canadians die due to smoking or exposure to second-hand smoke every year, regulating the industry was not an easy decision for the government. Over the years, the tobacco industry has had many influential allies; some have been directors of tobacco companies or on their boards, and other allies have been in Parliament itself, in the offices of senior MPs or senators. Tobacco companies have been generous contributors to the coffers of political parties. And governments make huge sums of money from taxes on cigarettes. In the late 1980s, Physicians for a Smoke-Free Canada calculated that the government received $2.2 billion in taxes annually from tobacco sales, $90 million of it from illegal sales to children.[32]

> *Cigarettes provide government with one if its biggest and most reliable sources of revenue: they create tens of thousands of jobs in hard economic times; they present a healthy surplus on the balance of payments; they help the development in Third World countries where tobacco is grown.*
>
> *Peter Taylor,* The Smoke Ring *(1984: xix)*

Despite these facts, the government was determined to ban tobacco advertisements. The well-heeled tobacco manufacturers engaged influential lobbyist William Neville to stop Bill C51 and prevent regulation of their industry. On the other side, health groups banded together to support the bill and counter every tactic Neville and his clients mounted. The campaign quickly went public. In the summer of 1987, the tobacco manufacturers took out full-page advertisements in newspapers. Neville conducted a sophisticated direct-mail campaign to mobilize all those who profit from tobacco and to enlist the support of those who benefit from tobacco company sponsorship. The anti-tobacco campaign retaliated by publishing its own full-page ads attacking the direct-mail campaign, and the Canadian Medical Association had "two physicians in every riding to get in touch with their MP directly and asked all 59 000 physicians in the country to write MPs in support of the bill."[33]

The tactics of industry representatives included giving retailers information kits that included a computer-generated letter of protest to the store owner's MP, followed up by phone calls to encourage the merchants to sign and mail the letters. The Canadian Cancer Society responded with 35 000 black-edged postcards to MPs (one for each tobacco-related death forecast for each MP's riding).

32. Charlotte Gray, "Tobacco Wars," *Canadian Medical Association Journal*, 1997, pp. 237–40.
33. Graham Fraser, "Lobby Fight on Tobacco Legislation Smoulders On," *The Globe and Mail*, December 16, 1987.

Member of Parliament Ronald Stewart spoke out against Bill C51, and the coalition of health groups promptly sent out letters to every household in Stewart's riding, pointing out that he was involved in the wholesale tobacco distribution business. One of the coalition's members commented, "We're trying to be sophisticated enough to use our relatively modest resources to blow the industry's multimillion-dollar campaign out of the water." Neville, on the other hand, claimed that he was merely trying to inform those who would be affected by the legislation.[34]

Besides the sophisticated lobbying techniques in this affair, the contest was unusual in that the tobacco industry did not lobby individual MPs to kill the bill, but only to reduce its priority on the legislative agenda. They knew that to delay legislation could kill a bill as effectively as a defeat. The bill had broad public support, confirmed health benefits and the support of a minister and a majority of MPs, but effective lobbying did delay its passage for a considerable time. Bill C51 did not receive royal assent until June 1988. It didn't take effect until January 1989 as the *Tobacco Products Control Act*, which included rules for advertising and labelling to be phased in over a five-year period.

The tobacco lobby did not give up, but appealed to the Supreme Court of Canada. In September 1995, the Supreme Court ruled in favour of the tobacco lobby. It found that the 1988 *Tobacco Products Control Act* was unconstitutional because Ottawa's nearly total advertising ban violated the industry's right to free speech. Bold, unattributed health warnings, such as "smoking can kill you," were deemed unconstitutional. The decision meant that tobacco companies were free to resume all forms of advertising. The Court justified the decision by declaring that the government had failed to prove that a total ban on advertising was appropriate.

The Supreme Court did preserve Parliament's right to legislate in the matter, however. It said that the federal government must pass a new law if it wanted to continue to restrict tobacco advertising. There was considerable pressure to do so, and in late 1996, the government tabled another bill on smoking. Bill C71 was designed to give Ottawa sweeping powers to regulate the content of tobacco products and to severely limit advertising—including where and in what form tobacco company logos can appear on advertisements for arts and sporting events.

It, too, was challenged by tobacco companies and their allies. First, the right to smoke and to advertise cigarette products were passionately defended by the tobacco industry and its allies. They diverted the argument from health concerns to other issues. They even made survival of the tobacco industry a national-unity issue by arguing that most of Canada's cigarettes are made in Québec and, therefore, impeding the tobacco industry would badly hurt the depressed Montréal economy. Second, it appealed to Canadian nationalism. Tobacco companies for some time had sponsored sports teams and events such as car races and tennis tournaments, and arts events such as the Vancouver International Film Festival and Toronto's jazz festival. Many of these groups had come to depend on tobacco sponsorship and could not find alternative funding. In this particular case, several companies threatened to leave Canada, raising cries (especially in Québec). Third, the industry donated generously to the Liberal Party (some $92 000 in 1994), and also to some individual ministers. Health minister David Dingwall characterized the approach of the tobacco lobby—which included several senators and former high-ranking Liberal and Tory aids—as "tough, vicious and personal."[35]

When Bill C71 reached committee stage in the House, lawyers and lobbyists for the tobacco industry once again claimed that banning advertisements was an infringement of the *Charter of Rights and Freedoms* and was nothing short of trying to reimpose the ban already struck down by the Supreme Court. Critics claimed that in order to justify its new restrictions and its infringement on one of the highest Charter values, the government wanted to prove that these measures would reduce the incidence of smoking among young people.

34. Ibid.
35. *The Globe and Mail*, December 10, 1996.

A new piece of legislation, the *Tobacco Act*, finally was passed in 1997 with key regulations that included restrictions on how tobacco is manufactured, displayed, sold, packaged and promoted. Since December 2000, cigarette packages sold in Canada have had to display information about the product, its emissions and the health hazards associated with it. (The warn-

ings take up 50 percent of the principal display space.) It was a watered-down bill that banned tobacco ads in public places and inside stores, but permitted them in print publications with a "primarily adult readership." Display of brand names at cultural or sports events was limited to 10 percent of the available signage, but sponsorship was permitted. Because of the legislation, it has become more difficult for young people to buy cigarettes. An amendment to the Act was passed by Parliament in 1998 to allow a five-year transitional period leading to a full ban on sponsorship promotions on October 1, 2003, which is now in place.

Industry lobbyists complained that the regulations were unfair. The anti-smoking lobby complained that there was not enough money for enforcement and prevention. While the controls achieved have been significant, about 21 percent of Canadians still smoke. These numbers are down from about 35 percent in 1985, presumably at least partly because of the regulations.[36]

The anti-smoking lobby is winning. Apart from the federal legislation, the lobby is working at provincial and municipal levels of government and has achieved legislation in several provinces and municipalities, restricting smoking in public places and even in cars when children are present. But tobacco companies have kept their products on the market. The tobacco wars have already lasted over twenty years and are certain to continue as new "spitless, smokeless" forms of tobacco use are being researched by various firms.

Lobbying in Canada: Casting the Net Wide

By now it should be apparent that the relatively unregulated practice of lobbying in Canada is enormously complex. There are multiple access points to the legislative process. It is also clear that scenarios of a "virtual monopoly" of cabinet clash with the view of federal bureaucrats as "the" unseen power brokers in Ottawa. Both are misrepresentations of a complicated reality.

The relationship of lobbyists with bureaucrats and politicians in Canada is not one of zero-sum games or sinister cabals. The interaction of interest groups with the political system is at all points permeated by an ethos of mutual accommodation. This process of *elite accommodation* tends to include interest groups, particularly business, with the federal cabinet and the bureaucracy. To some extent, labour is left out of the process. In many industrialized democracies, a social partnership or consensus known as *corporatism* exists instead of Canadian-style accommodation. In the corporatist model, a formal or institutionalized process of consultation among the state, business and labour shapes economic policy for society as a whole. Normally, such a process cannot take place in Canada because no single business groupings or labour association can claim to represent all the significant interests in their respective communities, and even the largest associations are accorded no functional representation in government policy-making.

36. Health Canada, "Research," Canadian Tobacco Use Monitoring Survey, www.hc-sc.gc.ca/hecs-sesc/tobacco/research/ctums/index.html. Accessed November 2003.

Alan King, *Ottawa Citizen*, December 18, 1994. Reprinted by permission.

In Canada, a successful and fruitful relationship with government actors begins with a group's recognition of the complexity of the contemporary democratic state and the opportunities that such complexity offers. A concern to leave no point of contact or influence untried, to cast one's net in as wide an arc as possible, is the cardinal rule of interest group politics. While certain components such as cabinet and the senior bureaucracy may be more significant than others, no facet of the process can be dismissed as unimportant.

The Canadian Senate, for example, is popularly considered to be inconsequential. But, as we have noted, this contention is incorrect from the point of view of the lobbyist. Indeed, one author has called the Senate "a lobby from within," by which he meant that most senators already represented lobbying interests before they were appointed to the upper house.[37] Formally, the Senate can and does make detailed amendments to legislation emanating from the House of Commons. Its committee system is capable of analyzing the impact of legislation on the business community and acting to prevent some government activities.

Finally, it should be stressed that interest group activities do not occur in a vacuum. Casting a wide net also involves the careful and continual nurturing by interest groups of broad public support or opposition to certain policies. The size of the constituency sought will, of course, depend on the nature and substance of the issue. The past record and perceived legitimacy of an interest group affects its ability to harness social support.

Ingredients for Interest Group Success

Perhaps the most fundamental ingredient for the political success of an interest group is that its *values, goals and tactics are compatible* with the country's overall political culture and therefore are perceived as legitimate. Without public support, a group has little chance of receiving government

37. Colin Campbell, *The Canadian Senate: A Lobby from Within* (Toronto: Macmillan, 1978).

recognition. Groups that use the tactic of violent demonstration rather than peaceful negotiation meet rigid resistance in the Canadian system, as do those who approve goals foreign to the Canadian political culture such as, say, state control of family planning or private health care. An *appealing issue* also helps—one that gathers broad public sympathy and increases the size of the group's membership, or at least augments its support. *Good leadership* is also important; a strong, vocal and prestigious leader brings valuable publicity and direction.

A high-status general membership further increases the chance of success, since influential people bring contacts, resources and have easier personal access to bureaucrats and politicians. A permanent organizational structure helps groups act cohesively and minimize internal divisions that weaken them. Sections of society that have common interests but are unorganized, such as homemakers or pensioners, usually have little long-term impact on public policy. Similarly, *large budgets* naturally assist in achieving and maintaining access to policy-makers. Financial resources do not guarantee success, but they certainly increase its possibility. The fact that a large number of interest groups can claim tax deductions and/or other tax advantages because of their organizational status makes them more powerful than less-organized groups.

Often, the key to lobbying success is a *sense of timing*. Clause-by-clause consideration of bills, for example, almost always takes place in one of the several committees of the House of Commons after the bill's second reading. Members of Parliament representing all parties serve on these committees. And, while the government side of each committee is "whipped" to ensure the bill's passage, lobbyists have a chance to secure amendments at this time, either by serving as witnesses or prompting backbench initiatives. *Flexibility* is another important factor in achieving success, since it is often necessary to compromise on one part of a demand in order to achieve another. Successful groups often *join at least temporarily with other groups* to bolster one another's claims. Interest groups must also be flexible enough to make use of all the access points available to them. They therefore need to know where to plug into the policy-making system. An important condition of success consists of knowing where and at what stage access to policy-makers can be achieved. Interest groups tend to be most successful when they can obtain the support of government backbenchers and provincial premiers. Such accommodation makes it difficult for even cabinet to ward off the pressure of interest groups.

Many groups that otherwise would not be able to function receive financial support from government agencies. To receive funding, an interest group must have goals that are compatible with the funding program, and its internal procedures must receive government approval. Most prominent women's organizations in Canada, for example, receive funding from the government, although support has been reduced considerably since 1991. At its height, the National Action Committee on the Status of Women (NAC) received roughly 80 percent of its funding from the federal government. It received money to lobby on a variety of economic and social issues. Receiving that money, initially, was key to the group's early success.[38] Today, anti-poverty groups are better examples of groups that need and get public funds.

What Are Social and Political Movements?

Other kinds of groups that aim to influence governments and change social policy have become influential in many countries and also internationally. These are social and political movements.

---

38. See Leslie A. Pal, *Interests of the State: The Politics of Language, Multiculturalism and Feminism in Canada* (Kingston/Montréal: McGill-Queen's University Press, 1993).

Return for a moment to the four prime characteristics of interest groups. They (1) have an organization; (2) articulate and aggregate interests; (3) act within the political system to influence policy; and (4) seek to influence government rather than exercise government responsibility themselves. Social and political movements share some of these interest group characteristics but they generally have no well-developed formal organization. Rather, they loosely subsume a variety of interest groups that may have different aspirations and agendas, although they share the same broad philosophy. **Social and political** movements are therefore rather fluid expressions of interests or collective identities with a broad, utopian appeal that often flows across state boundaries. Peace movements, environmental movements, women's movements and nationalist movements are examples of broad, unstructured movements that offer a particular vision of how people should live and organize themselves. Social and political movements may include coalitions of many associations and interest groups that support the same general cause. The Canadian environmental movement, for example, is estimated to comprise at least 1800 different organizations.[39]

Such movements bring new issues and problems to public attention outside of the channels of mainstream political parties. Most are broadly based and inclusive, emphasizing citizen participation. They maintain that citizens should have equal opportunity to enjoy the goods and services of society and to participate in the political decision-making process. Movements tend to be relatively inclusive. Environmental groups and women's groups have higher involvement of people from different socio-economic backgrounds than do many other interest groups. There is also higher youth participation in these groups than in political parties. Movements may remain in a loose form as innovators or they may harden into organized cohesive pressure groups, or even become new political parties. Supporters of gays and lesbians, the disabled and animal rights now form specific interest groups.

Some movements have a long history. Nationalist movements, for example, have roots extending back to the seventeenth century. They espouse the belief that certain groups of people represent a "natural" community and should be united under one political system. They stress local identities and loyalties based on ethnicity, language, culture and so on, which may or may not correspond to state boundaries. Sometimes, nationalist movements create a political party, or parties, as in Québec with the Parti Québécois and Bloc Québécois. The same kind of transformation took place in a loose farmers' movement in Alberta at the beginning of the century. In the early 1900s, farmers organized pressure groups to fight for their policy interests in Ottawa. Discouraged with their results in the early 1920s, they entered the political forum as the Progressive Party. In spite of considerable electoral success, they soon withdrew their party status and returned to pressure group activity. What began as a farmers' movement hardened into a pressure group, then a political party and finally reverted back to pressure group activity.

As well as movements with deep historical roots, there are a multitude of modern movements related to what has been called "the new politics." These concern issues such as environmentalism, feminism and other group rights that began to emerge in Western democracies in the 1960s and 1970s.

The environmental movement appeared in Western societies as people became concerned with the deteriorating quality of the environment and the depletion of world resources. Broadly speaking, environmentalists regard economic growth as less important than the protection of "quality of life." They support pollution controls even though these may mean greater expense, hamper industrial development, and limit or decrease material affluence. A great many interest groups come under

---

39. Jeremy Wilson, "Green Lobbies: Pressure Groups and Environmental Policy," in Robert Boardman, ed., *Canadian Environmental Policy: Ecosystems, Politics and Process* (Don Mills, ON: Oxford University Press, 1992).

the umbrella of the environmentalist movement, such as those seeking government regulations on carbon emissions, acid rain, reforestation, preservation of threatened animal species, global warming and so on.

In some countries, the environmental movement has established political parties. In Germany, the Greens have been part of the government coalition as partners in the cabinet. In Canada, the environmental movement includes the Canadian Environmental Network, which contains about two hundred groups as well as small but growing Green parties in several provinces and at the federal level. The federal Green Party garnered enough of the popular vote in the 2004 and 2006 elections to qualify for federal funding.

Ron Inglehart has offered a theory to explain the proliferation of these new movements. He suggests that Western democracies have undergone social, economic and cultural changes that have contributed to a growing politicization of their citizens. At the same time, political behaviour is moving beyond the constraints of traditional organizations such as parties. He says that elite-directed participation is giving way to ad hoc groups concerned with specific issues and policy changes. There are growing numbers of people with strong political skills but without close party ties.[40] Because of this, he predicts more movements and new parties will appear. The established parties, he says, came into being in an era dominated by social class conflict and economic issues, and tend to remain polarized on this basis. But, in recent years, a new axis of polarization has arisen based on cultural and quality-of-life issues. He goes on to say that parties today

> *do not adequately reflect the most burning contemporary issues, and those who have grown up in the postwar era have relatively little motivation to identify with one of the established parties.*[41]

Whether or not Inglehart's explanation for the rise of new movements is valid (and there is considerable evidence against it), there has been a proliferation of new organizations around new issues. The word *movement* has been used to capture these new interests because it implies broad, mass appeal and the notion that there is inevitability for the success of these causes. Recognizing the emotional appeal of movements, parties everywhere have adjusted their platforms to accommodate their demands. In Canada today, the Bloc Québécois espouses nationalist rhetoric, and all three traditional federal parties have adopted policy positions that give credence to the philosophies of environmentalism, feminism and so on. To explore these relations among movements, interest groups and parties and the general appeal of political movements, we assess the women's movement in Canada.

The Women's Movement: A Case Study

The women's movement is one of the most active and widespread movements reaching across national borders today. It has manifested itself on and off since the nineteenth century, seeking rights for women to vote and to hold political positions and appointments for paid employment. The women involved in various parts of the movement share no doctrine per se and, in fact, are often in bitter disagreement about issues and how to achieve their goals. The fundamental point of all feminists, however, is that orthodox theories about politics tended to ignore gender and harboured unconscious assumptions about the role of women in society.

---

40. Ron Inglehart, *Culture Shift in Advanced Industrial Society* (Princeton, NJ; Princeton University Press, 1990), pp. 363–68. For a commentary on Inglehart's ideas, see Thomas M. Trump, "Value Formation and Postmaterialism: Inglehart's Theory of Value Change Reconsidered," *Comparative Political Studies*, vol. 24, no. 3 (October 1991), pp. 365–90.

41. Inglehart, *Culture Shift in Advanced Industrial Society*, p. 363.

Since the 1960s, the movement generally has focused on women's liberation, denouncing traditions of male supremacy in the family and in other political and social structures that assign women an inferior position in society. In short, the various strands of the movement seek for women the same social and political rights enjoyed by men, and share a theoretical assumption that, historically, men have exploited women using gender differences to establish a division of labour. The role of women in society was thereby limited to child-rearing and domestic chores.

To achieve their ends, women's movements have built solid organizational and leadership structures in many countries and also at the international level. At this broad level, the women's movement has no unified ideology, but a neo-Marxist framework has provided some of its ideological basis. Capitalism and its social and political superstructures are often identified as the forces behind the oppression of women. It is argued that since men control the means of production, they have used their position to institutionalize norms and values that keep women in an inferior position.[42] To this end, they identify and expose perceived cultural stereotyping, socialization and distortions of history that have been and continue to be used to ensure male dominance.

To date, the women's movement has generally sought to influence the policies of existing political parties rather than start its own party, although there are women's political parties in a few countries. Since the rise of the modern women's movement, female politicians have become increasingly prominent. Sirimavo Bandaranaike of Sri Lanka was the world's first elected woman prime minister (1960–65, 1970–77, 1994–2000). She was followed by, among many other female leaders, Indira Gandhi in India (1966–77, 1980–84), Golda Meir in Israel (1969–70), Margaret Thatcher in Great Britain (1979–90), the late Benazir Bhutto in Pakistan (1988–90, 1993–96), Kim Campbell in Canada (1993) and currently Angela Merkel in Germany. Although female politicians are particularly well represented in Scandinavia, in most national legislatures their numbers are disproportionately low compared to their share of the population.

In Canada today, many groups advance women's causes.[43] Interestingly, about one hundred women form a core that is active across most of these groups. Susan Phillips's study of 33 national Canadian women's organizations shows that the diverse groups "form an expansive, but loosely coupled, network, that is bound by a collective identity of 'liberalized' feminism."[44]

The 1970 Royal Commission on the Status of Women provided the initial impetus to make gender an important factor in Canadian social and political life. The National Action Committee on the Status of Women (NAC) was established in 1972 to pressure for implementation of the recommendations of the Royal Commission. Initially, about 80 percent of its funding came from the government. NAC has become an umbrella lobbying group for about six hundred local and national member groups representing about three million women.[45]

In its attempt to speak for women, NAC addresses a broad range of issues. In the 1980s, these included free trade, abortion, the GST, child care and the Meech Lake Accord. In the early 1990s, the government's financial difficulties meant a diminishing commitment to the priorities of women.

42. See Robert J. Jackson and Doreen Jackson, *An Introduction to Political Science: Comparative and World Politics*, 5th ed. (Don Mills, ON: Pearson Prentice Hall, 2007).

43. For the history of the women's movement, see M. Janine Brodie and Jill McCalla Vickers, *Canadian Women in Politics: An Overview* (Ottawa: Canadian Research Institute for the Advancement of Women, 1982). See also Susan D. Phillips, "Meaning and Structure in Social Movements: Mapping the Network of Canadian Women's Organizations," *CJPS*, vol. 24, no. 4 (December 1991), pp. 755–82; and Sandra Burt, "The Women's Movement: Working to Transform Public Life," in James P. Bickerton and Alain G. Gagnon, eds., *Canadian Politics* (Peterborugh, ON: Broadview Press, 1994), pp. 209–23.

44. Phillips, "Meaning and Structure in Social Movements," p. 757.

45. For direct funding of advocacy groups, including the women's movement, see Leslie Pal, *Interests of State: The Politics of Language, Multiculturalism and Feminism in Canada* (Montréal, McGill-Queen's University Press, 1993).

NAC interpreted the reduction of its funds as an attempt to "silence" the women's movement. However, the organization continues to be active, especially in rights-related questions. It has continually fought to ensure that (1) equality rights are inviolable; (2) equality rights are clearly articulated in terms relevant to the needs of women; and (3) affirmative action should be more clearly and positively entrenched in the Charter. NAC's funding was cut again by Stephen Harper's Conservative government in 2006, and regional offices were cut. However it continues to operate, largely on the basis of membership fees and donations.

Canadian women do not speak with one voice. REAL Women (Realistic, Equal, Active for Life), formed in 1974, opposes feminist demands, and various anti-abortion groups also attack feminist viewpoints. However, the women's movement in Canada has raised awareness of women's position in society, changed attitudes and introduced many issues into the policy agendas of political parties. It has not tried to create a party itself, but has stayed outside traditional political and interest group organization. Women's groups have extensive ties and interests outside of the women's movement. According to the policy network mapped by Phillips, 29 of 33 national organizations were connected through NAC. REAL Women, the Catholic Women's League and two professional associations were the exceptions.[46]

The women's movement can be credited with improvements in legislation concerning women (such as equal pay for work of equal value, maternity leave, daycare, etc.) as well as with attitudinal changes concerning participation. Details of women's other achievements in Canadian society are discussed in the chapters on political culture, the Constitution, Parliament, political parties, elections and the public service.

Critical Debate
Interest Groups: A Necessary Evil?

Are interest groups a necessary evil?

Point

Interest groups may be necessary, but they certainly are not desirable. They have a notorious reputation for seeking influence behind closed doors to further their own selfish ends regardless of the good of the community. There are many subtle and not-so-subtle ways to influence people in power. The currency may be money, influence, gifts or any number of winks, nods and promises that distort who will be listened to and what decisions will be taken.

There undoubtedly are worthy groups that represent citizens with serious needs. But what assurance is there that the most worthy groups are heard? Deserving groups might be ignored because of lack of funds or prestige, or competition from more powerful groups.

And where is the fine line between information and propaganda in the expert advice offered to lawmakers? An interest group can be expected, even within the realm of mutual accommodation, to give selective information, making its own argument as strong as possible at the expense of its competitor's viewpoint. We know, too, that interest groups are dominated by elites. People with higher social status participate more, and groups tend to be run by the most active and vocal members. What of unorganized interests? Who is to press the urgent claims of pensioners, children or stay-at-home mothers? To be fair, the system should be responsive to those who do not have the resources to sustain mass organization.

46. Phillips, "Meaning and Structure in Social Movements," p. 774.

Representation in the Canadian political system is sought through the electoral process. It is clear that interest groups constitute another legitimate form of political representation. Yet these representatives seek influence on their own initiative and are responsible only to themselves. Some seek the good of the whole, but never to the detriment of their own interests.

Should interest groups play such an important role in making public policy? No. Could the power wielded by interest groups erode political responsibility in a representative democracy? Yes. This problem within the system is aggravated when one political party dominates the government for a long period of time and relationships become ingrained. Then we find more highly placed and experienced bureaucrats leaving the public service to sell their knowledge and contacts through private consulting services. If interest groups are to exist as representative bodies complementary to the elected representatives, steps should be taken to eliminate some of these injustices.

Counterpoint

Interest groups are not a necessary evil. In fact, they are not evil at all, but an important part of the democratic process, allowing another avenue for public participation besides political parties. The relationship between government and interest groups is complex. It is quite likely that if a government were to establish more rigorous rules for lobbying and draw back the veil of obscurity and suspicion, the multifaceted and changing relationship between public and private actors would be acknowledged as normal and healthy.

Interest groups serve the average Canadian well. They are a widely accepted part of the political culture. The interaction between groups and the political system is characterized by an ethos of accommodation or co-operation in which the interaction is deemed mutually worthwhile. Sometimes, terms such as policy community or network are a reasonable depiction of political life. The fact that interest groups are accepted within the political culture means that there is a legitimate channel for complaints and frustrations, an avenue for citizens to articulate and defend viewpoints, so that they do not have to resort to extra-legal behaviour to be heard. Once individuals are part of a legitimized group, they are committed to acting within the system. Interest groups, in this sense, act as a safety valve for individual frustrations by allowing the possibility of joining with others to influence legislation. They thus provide a crucial and culturally acceptable link between citizen and public policy.

Interest groups widen the range of concerns that are taken into account in the legislative process. On the premise that more information can help achieve fairer laws, this is good. Extra representation through interest groups is also good because the constituency form of representation cannot meet all the demands of groups in the political system, and the modern welfare state makes interest group representation a necessary adjunct to government activity. Poor people or children, for example, clearly need groups to speak for their needs and wishes.

Over the years, movements have become a powerful force in changing societal attitudes and influencing governments. They, too, are legitimate and necessary in complex societies. They are amorphous currents of interest that flow easily across borders because of their broad and inclusive philosophies. They often subsume existing interest groups and stimulate new ones; sometimes they stay as movements and sometimes they solidify as political parties. When political parties fragment and represent narrow, regional interests or groups, movements often help to unify people by embracing national and even international issues or points of view. This provides a legal outlet for expression of ideas and organization to help get the attention of governments.

Discussion Questions

1. What is your response to the positions taken in the Critical Debate? What can you add to the debate?
2. Should lobbying be encouraged? More regulated?
3. Is lobbying likely to be more successful in a majority or minority government situation?
4. Is the women's movement a lobby group? Why or why not?
5. Should the government give more money to the National Action Committee on the Status of Women? To REAL Women? To environmental groups such as Pollution Probe or Greenpeace?
6. Choose an interest/advocacy group and research its goals, tactics and strategy. Is it part of a policy network?

Visit our new Companion Website at **www.pearsoned.ca/jackson**, where you can use the interactive Study Guide and link to additional resources on topics discussed in the text.

Selected Bibliography

Interest Groups

Boyce, William, et al. *A Seat at the Table: Persons with Disabilities and Policy Making*. Montréal and Kingston: McGill-Queen's University Press, 2001.

Brooks, Stephen, and Andrew Strich. *Business and Government in Canada*. Scarborough, ON: Prentice Hall, 1991.

Chenier, John A., and Scott R. Duncan, eds. *The Federal Lobbyists, 1999*. Ottawa: ARC Publications, 1999.

Coleman, William, and Grace Skogstad. *Policy Communities and Public Policy in Canada*. Mississauga, ON: Copp Clark Pitman, 1990.

Cunningham, Rod. *Smoke and Mirrors: The Canadian Tobacco War*. Ottawa: IDRC, 1996.

Embuldeniya, Don K. *Exploring the Health, Strength and Impact of Canada's Civil Society*. Toronto: Canadian Centre for Philanthropy, 2001.

Gifford, C.G. *Canada's Fighting Seniors*. Toronto: Lorimer, 1991.

Hein, Gregory. *Interest Group Litigation and Canadian Democracy*. Montréal: Institute for Research in Public Policy, 2000.

Molgat, Anne, and Joan Grant Cummings. "An action that will not be allowed to subside: NAC's first twenty-five years." Accessed July 1, 2003, at www.nac-cca.ca/about/his_e.htm.

Pross, Paul. "Pressure Groups: Talking Chameleons," in M.S. Whittington and G. Williams, eds., *Canadian Politics in the 1990s*. Scarborough, ON: Nelson, 1994.

——————. *Group Politics and Public Policy*, 2nd ed. Don Mills, ON: Oxford University Press, 1992.

Reddick, Andrew. *The Duality of the Public Interest: Networks, Policy and People*. Ottawa: Ph.D. thesis, 2002.

Seidle, Leslie. *Interest Groups and Elections in Canada*. Toronto: Dundurn Press, 1991.

——————. *Equity and Community: The Charter, Interest Advocacy and Representation*. Montréal: Institute for Research on Public Policy, 1993.

Stanbury, William. *Business–Government Relations in Canada*, 2nd ed. Scarborough, ON: Nelson, 1993.

Studlar, Donley T. *Tobacco Control: Comparative Politics in the United States and Canada*. Peterborough, ON: Broadview Press, 2002.

Young, Lisa, and Joanna Everitt, *Advocacy Groups*. Vancouver: UBC Press, 2004.

Movements

Agnew, Vijay. *Resisting Discrimination: Women from Asia, Africa and the Caribbean and the Women's Movement in Canada.* Toronto: University of Toronto Press, 1996.

Boardman, Robert, ed. *Canadian Environmental Policy: Ecosystems, Politics and Process.* Don Mills, ON: Oxford University Press, 1992.

Brodie, Janine. *Politics on the Margin: Restructuring and the Canadian Women's Movement.* Halifax, NS: Fernwood, 1995.

Davies, Miranda. *Women and Violence.* London: Zed Books, 1994.

Schwartz, Mildred A. *Party Movements in the United States and Canada: Strategies of Persistence.* Lanham, MD: Rowman and Littlefield, 2007.

Smith, Miriam. *Group Politics and Social Movements in Canada.* Peterborough, ON: Broadview Press, 2007.

——————. *Lesbian and Gay Rights in Canada: Social Movements and Equality-Seeking.* Toronto: University of Toronto Press, 1999.

Tarrow, Sidney. *Power in Movement: Social Movements, Collective Action and Politics.* Cambridge, UK: Cambridge University Press, 1994.

Vickers, Jill, Christine Appelle, and Pauline Rankin. *Politics As If Women Mattered.* Toronto: University of Toronto Press, 1993.

Part V
Public Policy

Culture, institutions and behaviour come together in the policy-making process. Various theories are employed to describe and explain the political system and its output in terms of domestic and international policy.

A society's political culture shapes the demands made on policy-makers, provides opportunities and imposes constraints on the range of possible responses. Institutions also influence the *process* of policy-making. The room for policy-makers to act is limited by aspects of the Constitution, the federal nature of Canada's political system, the dictates of governmental responsibility and accountability to Parliament, as well as non-institutional factors and, of course, the availability of finances.

Political behaviour, manifested in politics, parties, interest groups and the electoral arena, constitutes the means by which citizens express their demands to policy-makers. The electoral process requires governments to respond to public opinion, influencing the substance and timing of key policy initiatives.

Public policy has both domestic and foreign aspects. To a substantial degree, public policy determines the well-being of a country's citizens as well as their security and influence in the larger world of states.

Policy-making therefore takes place within constraints and choices determined by Canadian culture, institutions and behaviour, and it occurs within a process of international politics and institutions increasingly shaped by the forces of globalization and the war on terror.

Chapter 14

Public Policy

Theories, Choices and Expenditures

In earlier chapters, we examined the role of government in Canada and noted the vast increase in intervention by governments at all levels in most Western industrialized states since the Second World War. State action is more complex than it was formerly and therefore more difficult to understand. The study of public policy stems from the realization that governments play an ever more important role in the social and economic life of the country.

Thus, when governments increase or decrease public spending, or raise taxes or abolish a Crown corporation, we want to know why they have chosen a particular course of action and what has influenced and shaped their decisions. Sometimes, governments fail to act on a particular issue. This, too, is of vital interest to students of public policy. The study of non-decisions helps one understand some of the constraints within which policy-makers operate. The options open to policy-makers are limited by the availability of resources in the physical and economic environments, and also by the cultural, institutional and behavioural patterns examined in earlier chapters.

In this chapter, we demonstrate the nature and extent of linkages between culture, institutions, behaviour and public policy as well as the strengths and weaknesses of theories of pluralism, Marxism and public choice. We also explain state-centred and feminist approaches to the understanding of public policy in light of these four concepts. We discuss the theoretical underpinnings of realism and liberalism/idealism and also offer a prelude to Chapter 15 on international relations. We conclude with a discussion of questions about the relations between public policy and public expenditure in recent governments.

Since making public policy (both domestic and internal) is controversial and politicized, the Critical Debate for this chapter asks, "Is public policy in Canada made in a comprehensive and rational manner? Is it made in an ethical manner? Can it be improved?"

What Is Public Policy?

One of the most common problems in any field of study is securing agreement on the definition and scope of its subject matter. This certainly has been the case in public policy analysis. The word *public* in this context merely points out that the policy in question is initiated and carried out by *public authorities*—those involving the state or government, or the *public sector*—as opposed to policies of *private institutions* such as chartered banks, private-sector corporations or other social organizations. The primary distinguishing feature of *public policy*, therefore, is that it is ultimately backed by the force of law and the coercive sanctions of the state.

The second half of the concept, the word *policy*, is more difficult to delineate. In fact, it may be that no term in political science offers more ambiguity. This ambiguity stems largely from the many contexts in which the term is employed. *Policy* is applied to phenomena ranging from narrow individual decisions (such as building an airport in a particular location) to broad philosophical precepts (such as a vague commitment to a *just society*). However, *policy* as a concept may more usefully be defined as involving a series of more or less related activities, rather than a single decision, since grandiose objectives such as balancing the budget involve changes in a wide range of public policies.

Between these two extremes, *policy* is used somewhat indiscriminately in at least three contexts: to describe the *intentions* of politicians, the *actions* of government or the *impact* of government. These three usages reflect different dimensions of public policy. A policy, whether public or private, is first and foremost a program or course of action pursued in response to a particular problem or issue. But it is also, in most cases, linked to particular goals or objectives (the "intentions" of politicians). Furthermore, the study of public policy is concerned with the effects of policies on society ("the impact of government"), whether such results are the intended or unintended consequences of pursuing certain courses of action.

There is one further dimension of policy that is not revealed by any of the above interpretations of the term. On occasion, a government may decide *not* to take action on a given problem. In this case, "policy" takes the form of inaction or non-intervention rather than a positive series of activities. **Public policy** is, therefore, the broad framework within which decisions are taken and action (or inaction) is pursued by governments in relation to some issue or problem. The study of public policy is "the study of *how*, *why* and to *what effect* different governments pursue particular *courses of action and inaction.*"[1]

This definition raises a further dimension of public policy analysis. How can we divide the total activities of government into more manageable chunks for the purpose of analyzing public policy? A number of classifications of types of public policy may be proposed. The most obvious division is the traditional separation of foreign policy from domestic public policy. **Foreign policy** shapes Canada's place in the international political system and determines Canada's relations with other states and international organizations such as the United Nations and NATO. **Domestic public policy**, on the other hand, is directed toward the internal economic, social and political environment.

As the world becomes more interdependent, it is increasingly difficult to maintain a sharp distinction between domestic and foreign policy. This is especially the case for a country such as Canada whose economy is closely integrated with that of a much larger and more powerful neighbour. But, despite the grey areas created by growing interdependence, there remains a sufficiently clear distinction between domestic and foreign policy, and the respective policy-making processes, to justify the division of these two types of government activity. Therefore, we conform to conventional usage by restricting our discussion of public policy to the domestic activities of government, and we examine foreign policy separately in Chapter 15.

As the umbrella term *foreign policy* covers a number of government activities—ranging from functional areas such as defence, foreign aid and trade policy to policies toward specific regions or countries—so, too, may the domestic activities of government be divided into different policy areas. Again, we find that a much-used dichotomy, social policy and economic policy, serves as a basic organizing device.

Social policy is more easily defined. In general terms, **social policy** encompasses activities oriented toward the education, health and welfare of the population. **Economic policy**, on the other hand, may be applied to two different levels of government activity. From a macro perspective, economic policy refers to the overall management and stabilization of the country's economic environment—that is, to government attempts to control the money supply and interest rates, manage

---

1. Arnold J. Heidenheimer et al., *Comparative Public Policy*, 2nd ed. (New York: St. Martin's Press, 1983), p. 4 (emphasis in original).

government spending and taxation, and foster balanced economic growth, without incurring the "twin evils" of rampant inflation and mass unemployment. Social policy cannot be divorced from economic policy in this broad sense, because public spending on social programs is manipulated to increase or deflate aggregate demand in the economy. Social expenditure is thus one of the tools available to governments in implementing macroeconomic policy. On another level, *economic* policy is also a generic term for a number of sectoral policy frameworks to develop or conserve national resources, promote industrial growth, reduce regional disparities or provide communications and transportation systems. In this sense, economic policy and social policy are more easily distinguished. For a general guide to the overall major policy concerns of Canadian governments, see the "Close-Up on Public Policy: Selected Domestic Policy Activities."

Public Policy and Theories of Policy-Making

The models and approaches used to study public policy may be distinguished from one another by their portrayal of the major actors in the policy process, their assumptions regarding the nature of society and politics, the role of government–state relations, and their evaluation of the interests served by public policy outputs. Each model or approach directs attention to different features of public policy—they are like different lenses through which policy may be observed. They are "as indispensable to political analysis as a map or compass is to a traveller crossing unknown terrain."[2]

There is no universally accepted theory of public policy. Consequently, we outline some of the more frequently used approaches and note some of their respective strengths and weaknesses. To organize our discussion, we have divided the contending theories into two categories: **micro-level** approaches, which focus mainly on the making of individual policy decisions, and **macro-level** approaches, which are more concerned with accounting for broader patterns of public policy as part of the relationship between the state and society.

Micro-Level Approaches to Public Policy Analysis

Micro-level theories of decision-making are intended to explain how individual decisions are taken within a broad framework of public policy. By and large, they concentrate on the study of the selection of the best available means of achieving the goals of governmental action. They assume that governmental priorities and objectives have already been established via the political process, and tend to focus on the choice of *means* to attain those goals via the administrative process.

The most widely known controversy centres on the confrontation between advocates of the *rationalist* and *incrementalist* approaches to decision-making.

The Rational-Comprehensive and Incrementalist Models

The *rational-comprehensive* model can best be described by the elements or stages in the decision-making process. According to this idea, decision-making follows this sequence:

1. The rational decision-maker is presented with a problem that can be distinguished from other problems, or at least compared meaningfully with them.
2. The values, goals and objectives that guide the decision-maker are reviewed and ranked in order of priority.
3. A list of alternative means of achieving these goals is compiled.

---

2. Stephen Brooks, *Public Policy in Canada* (Toronto: McClelland & Stewart, 1989), p. 41.

CLOSE-UP ON

Public Policy

SELECTED DOMESTIC POLICY ACTIVITIES

Domestic public policy

Macroeconomic policy

Social development policies

Monetary policy, fiscal (tax) policy, interest rate policy, prices and incomes policy, balance of payments policy, etc.

Economic development policies

Social policies

Quality-of-life policies

– Education (post-secondary)

– Health care (includes health insurance, health-care facilities, hospitals, etc.)

– Housing

– Income maintenance (pensions, sickness and disability insurance, unemployment insurance, etc.)

– Income redistribution

– Social assistance and welfare

Social development policies for special groups (Native persons, women, veterans, youth, etc.)

– Arts and culture (performing arts, museums, etc.)

– Media (broadcasting and newspapers)

– Environment

– Public health

– Language policy

– Multiculturalism

– Sports and recreation

– Justice and civil liberties

– Police and corrections

– Security

– Industrial and commercial policies (banking, finance, research and development, small business, tourism, sectoral industrial policies, e.g., hi-tech, steel, textiles)

– Resource development policies (agriculture, fisheries, forestry, minerals, energy, etc.)

– Transportation and communication policy (air, rail, road, postal service, telecommunications, etc.)

– Regional development policy (includes northern development)

– Competition policy

– Consumer policy

– Foreign investment policy

– Labour market policy (employment, immigration, occupational training, etc.)

– Labour relations policy

– Science and technology policy

4. The consequences (costs and benefits) that would ensue from each alternative are estimated.

5. Each alternative, and its likely consequences, is then compared with all other alternatives.

6. Finally, the rational decision-maker selects the course of action, and its consequences, that offers maximum attainment of the values, goals or objectives identified in Step 2.[3]

According to the advocates of this model, the end product of the process will be a "rational" decision—that is, one that selects the most effective and efficient means of achieving a given end. Ideally, the rational-comprehensive process may be the way that some decisions *ought* to be made; but does it describe accurately the way in which all, or even most, decisions are made?

Critics maintain that the rationalist model is wrong—it neither describes reality nor represents an ideal to be emulated. First, they argue that very few of the issues confronting governments can be singled out easily for this kind of comprehensive analysis. Second, such a process makes totally unreasonable demands on decision-makers with regard to the information needed and the time and resources necessary to evaluate the costs and benefits of all possible alternative courses of action. Thus, the model is claimed to be impractical, as the costs of undertaking a search for the most efficient means of implementation may well be greater than the savings realized by deploying it. Third, the rational-comprehensive approach is criticized as a normative or prescriptive model. It does not describe how decisions are actually made; rather, it *prescribes* how some theoreticians think policies and decisions *ought* to be made.

Another model is considered more descriptive of the way decision-makers actually proceed. This *incrementalist* model assumes that most problems facing decision-makers are complex and interrelated, and that decision-makers operate in a climate of uncertainty and limited resources. In contrast to the rational-comprehensive approach, the point of departure for incremental decision-making theory is not some ideal goal to be attained in the most efficient manner. In actuality, only a limited number of policy alternatives are considered, and only a few foreseeable consequences are evaluated for each alternative. Incrementalism, therefore, only results in alterations at the margins of existing policies.

The incrementalist model claims to resolve the problem of inadequate information and uncertainty in policy-making, since marginal adjustments to policies and programs can easily be reversed or altered. Thus, incrementalism may be the more *rational* way to proceed, because it avoids making serious, lasting errors. Moreover, successive limited comparisons consume less time and other resources than the exhaustive search process of the rational-comprehensive model. Finally, an incremental approach to decision-making offers endless opportunities for redefining goals and adjusting both the means (programs, activities) and ends (values, priorities) of public policy-making.

The incrementalist approach, too, is criticized on a number of grounds. Many critics argue that, whether or not the model is empirically valid, it is just not the way that decisions *should* be made. Given the preoccupation of advocates of rationalism with "improving" the decision-making process in the interests of technical efficiency, it is perhaps not surprising that they are appalled by the prospect of decision-makers "muddling through" on most issues. The model has been labelled a "conservative" recipe for maintaining the status quo since it provides an "ideological reinforcement of the pro-inertia and anti-innovation forces prevalent in all human organizations, [both] administrative and policy-making."[4]

---

3. Adapted from James E. Anderson, *Public Policy-Making* (New York: Holt, Rinehart and Winston, 1984), pp. 9–10.

4. Yehezkel Dror, "Muddling Through—'Science' or Inertia?" p. 155; and Lindblom's response, "Contexts for Change and Strategy: A Reply," *PAR*, vol. 24, no. 3 (September 1964), pp. 153–57 and 157–58.

A much more important problem, in our view, is the fact that, although the incrementalist model is supposed to provide a general description of how policy decisions are made by making marginal adjustments to the policies and programs already in place, it quite clearly cannot account for occasional radical departures from existing patterns of activity or inactivity. Thus, it cannot explain the entry of governments into new areas of policy intervention, nor can it account for drastic alterations to, or innovations in, existing policy.

Decision-making is only a part of the overall process of public policy activity. Therefore, to the extent that any model can tell us *how* policy decisions are made, it still would not be able to provide guidance as to *why* governments pursue particular directions in public policy, nor *to what effect*. That requires a broader perspective on the role of the state and its relationship with society than decision-making theories can provide.

Macro-Level Approaches to Public Policy Analysis

Macro-level approaches focus on the wide relationship between state and society and, therefore, on the broad patterns of public policy, rather than on the details of how individual policy decisions are made within the government. We outline five of these approaches: *pluralism*, *public choice theory*, *neo-Marxism*, *state-centred analysis* and *feminism*, together with some of their respective strengths and weaknesses.

Pluralism

The **pluralist** approach emphasizes the role of political actors and organized interests in the policy process, especially parties and interest groups. Pluralists treat economic factors and cultural and ideological differences as sources of political conflict. They see shifting groups all seeking to have their members' preferences translated into public policy. These groups may be based on ethnicity, language, religion, gender, region, province, ideology or other interests. For pluralists, politics is the process by which individuals and groups seek to promote their interests through organization, political mobilization and alliance-building in order to influence the policy outputs of government. Political parties are seen as broad coalitions of interests, seeking legislative majorities in the electoral arena. Government is viewed as a neutral arbiter that referees group struggle, adjudicates among competing group demands, and implements and enforces public policies in the national interest or, at least, according to the wishes of the majority on each issue.

Thus, pluralists regard public policies as the outcomes of competition between groups and parties. The essence of the pluralist approach is the assumption that power is widely dispersed in society. Since, in its *extreme* forms, pluralism does not admit the existence of structural inequalities within society, all individuals and groups are seen as having approximately equal access to the policy-making process. Therefore, all groups have potentially equal influence on public policy outputs as long as they organize themselves and play by the "rules of the game"—that is, as long as they abide by the underlying consensus on political values and procedures. The tendency for coalitions and alliances of groups to change composition from one issue to another means that there are no permanent winners and losers in the group struggle. Power, defined in simple terms as "the ability to get things done," therefore shifts from coalition to coalition according to the issue at stake and is never the exclusive preserve of any one group or elite.[5]

The more advanced schools of pluralism assert the importance of competition between elites within an overall consensus from the mass public. In his famous volume, *Capitalism, Socialism and*

---

5. The classic pluralist statement of the diffusion of political power is found in Robert A. Dahl's *Who Governs?* (New Haven, CT: Yale University Press, 1961).

Democracy, Joseph Schumpeter showed how elitist decision-making could be reconciled with democracy. He compared the competition between elites for democratic votes with the operation of an economic market.[6] Later, Robert Dahl invented the term *polyarchy* to depict how minority rule could take place within a consensus on democratic values.[7]

Critics argue that some advocacy groups never get a fair hearing because obstacles prevent them from placing their issues on the agenda of political debate. For example, it may be argued that the federalist organization of Canadian political life is more conducive to the expression of linguistic and regional issues than to the expression of issues based on economic class. Since many class-based issues, such as labour legislation and welfare policies, fall under provincial jurisdiction, it is more difficult to mobilize these interests across provincial boundaries. Thus, they are partially "organized out" of federal politics, while cultural and regional issues are "organized in."[8]

In any case, it is harder for the poor and the working class to become politically organized than it is for the rich or business interests. The latter groups have more political and economic resources, and their relatively small numbers facilitate greater mobilization. The idea that some issues are "organized out" of politics by the "mobilization of bias" inherent in all political systems is taken a step further in the concept of *non-decision-making*. Peter Bachrach and Morton Baratz condemned the pluralists for emphasizing one aspect of power ("the ability to get things done") to the exclusion of "the ability to stop things getting done"—the power of non-decision.[9] They argued that elite groups within or outside government take advantage of the "mobilization of bias," a set of predominant values, beliefs, rituals and institutional procedures that operate systematically and consistently to the benefit of certain persons and groups at the expense of others in order to prevent some issues from ever reaching the agenda of political debate.

This critical approach serves to sensitize one to the fact that some interests and issues are more easily organized than others; that various groups do not have equal political resources or enjoy equal access to the policy-making process. To be sure, interest groups do organize to attempt to influence policy-makers, and it is necessary to examine their effects when studying public policy, especially in a liberal democracy such as Canada's where governments must maintain a degree of responsiveness to pressures from society. But, for a variety of reasons, some groups have *greater* influence on policy-making than others. The next three macro-level approaches attempt to explain *why* this is the case.

Public Choice Theory

The basic premise of public choice theory is borrowed directly from classical liberal economics. It contends that each individual is essentially a self-interested, rational, utility-maximizing actor. Individual wants are constrained in a world characterized by scarcity and populated by other individuals who want the same things. Thus, when people engage in collective non-market decision-making in the political arena (making "public" choices), they behave in exactly the same way that many economists believe they do when making market-oriented choices in the economic sphere—that is, they act in a rational and calculating fashion to maximize their own interests. Voters, for example, will support the party that offers programs most likely to maximize their individual well-being. Interest groups will lobby for their particular concerns. And, when politicians and bureaucrats formulate policies, they do so *not* according to some vague notion of "the public interest" but largely to satisfy their own narrow individual interests.

6. Joseph A. Schumpeter, *Capitalism, Socialism and Democracy* (New York: Harper, 1943).
7. Robert Dahl, *A Preface to Democratic Theory* (Chicago: University of Chicago Press, 1956).
8. See Stephen Brooks, *Public Policy in Canada*, ch. 2.
9. Peter Bachrach and Morton S. Baratz, *Power and Poverty: Theory and Practice* (New York: Oxford University Press, 1970), p. 43ff.

Individuals do not have equal opportunities to realize their respective interests in the public choice model, however. The average voter, for example, is fairly peripheral in the public choice view of the policy process. Voters are important only when they have the periodic opportunity to choose, through elections, which politicians will have most influence in government. Otherwise, except when they participate in an effective interest group, ordinary citizens are little more than consumers of public policies.

According to public choice theorists, the central actors in the policy-making process are powerful interest groups, bureaucrats and politicians (especially the leaders of governing parties). But this is not just pluralism in disguise. First, in the public choice approach, the primary unit of political action is the individual, not the group. Although individuals may join forces in pursuit of their interests, they do so only when collective action promises greater rewards than acting alone, and when the benefits of collective action outweigh the costs of group participation. When the benefits of group action are uncertain, or when they might possibly be derived without paying the costs of group membership, it is often more rational for the individual not to participate in collective action.

Second, some groups have more difficulty organizing and mobilizing support than others. Small, relatively homogeneous groups with much to win or lose from public policy changes, such as specific business interests, are more easily mobilized and enjoy proportionately greater resources than larger, disparate groups such as consumers or environmentalists. Thus, unlike extreme pluralists, who consider that all groups have equal access to, and potentially equal influence on, the policy-making process, public choice analysts argue that "there is no reason to believe that the pressure exerted on decision-makers by special interest groups . . . is in any sense balanced or fair or offsetting."[10]

The third major departure from pluralism is that public choice views government not as a neutral arbiter refereeing the group struggle in the public interest, but rather as a complex process of interaction and bargaining among bureaucrats and politicians seeking to maximize their own individual self-interests. Thus, for example, it is assumed that politicians will support policies that benefit marginal voters in order to maximize the likelihood of their election or re-election to office. Bureaucrats, on the other hand, push for policies that will expand their departmental budgets, increase the number of programs or staff under their responsibility or enhance their opportunities for promotion and influence.

Many students of politics have savagely attacked the assumptions about *rationality in public choice theory*. While its application has produced some interesting insights into the policy-making process—especially in its recognition that politicians and bureaucrats are not mere servants of external pressures, but rather have their own interests and objectives—its focus remains restrictive. Despite its ambitions of formulating a more general theory of the political process, public choice theory is, at best, only a partial aid to understanding how and why public policies are developed. It has had only marginal influence in Canadian political science.

Neo-Marxist Analysis

An alternative political economy approach to public policy is **neo-Marxist analysis**. Neo-Marxism is a generic label for various theories and propositions that seek to develop a systematic conceptualization of politics and the role of the state based upon assumptions originally formulated by Karl Marx concerning the relationships among economic and political structures. There are a number of strands of neo-Marxist theory; the following overview attempts to present only some of the complex concepts and arguments.

10. Michael J. Trebilcock et al., *The Choice of Governing Instrument: A Study Prepared for the Economic Council of Canada* (Ottawa: Supply and Services, 1982), p. 10.

The essence of Marxist theory is that, at all stages of historical development, social and political relations are determined largely by the economic basis of society. The relations between classes are necessarily antagonistic and are based on the mode of production that exists at any given time. In the present era (the capitalist mode of production), two main social classes are differentiated by their respective economic roles: the capitalist class, or bourgeoisie, which owns and controls the means of production (factories, financial capital and so on), and the working class, or proletariat, which sells its labour to the capitalists. According to Marx's economic theory, the dynamics of capitalism require that capitalists extract "surplus value" from labour—that they effectively exploit the working class—because this is the chief mechanism whereby capitalists make profits for further investment and accumulation of capital. This exploitative economic relationship between capital and labour forms the basis for unequal, conflictual class relations in social and political life.

According to Marxists, the primary function of the state in capitalist society is to serve the interests of capitalism by creating and maintaining conditions favourable to profitable capital accumulation. However, in order to reduce conflict between classes and forestall the possibility of revolution by the exploited working class, the liberal democratic state must also create and maintain conditions of social harmony by providing policies that legitimize the capitalist society. Marxists believe that one of the factors in state survival is the dominant ideology of capitalist countries. This includes beliefs about private property, the possibility of upward socio-economic mobility and the economic market, all of which buttress the role of the state and make it difficult for the vast majority of individuals to understand that they are being exploited.

Most public policies, in the neo-Marxist view, may be categorized roughly according to their intentions or effects as serving either the *accumulation* or *legitimation* functions of the capitalist state. Examples of accumulation-oriented policies in the Canadian context include the provision of industrial infrastructure (e.g., transportation networks, public utilities such as hydro), subsidies or tax expenditures for private sector businesses, and fiscal and monetary policies aimed at creating a healthy climate for investment. Legitimation policies include most social welfare programs, occupational health and safety regulations, environmental pollution controls and language and cultural policies. Some programs or policies, however, may serve both accumulation and legitimation roles; hence, these two functions are not necessarily mutually exclusive. For example, the introduction of free, mass education may enhance the legitimacy of the state in the short term but, by providing a better-trained, more skilled labour force, it may also aid capital accumulation.

The key question in neo-Marxist analysis is why the state pursues particular public policies and courses of action. The *instrumentalist* view of the state suggests that it serves the interests of the capitalist class because of the strong links (common class backgrounds, family ties and old school networks) that exist among political and bureaucratic elites and the business community.[11] The *structuralist* view argues that the capitalist class is itself internally divided into a number of competing elements or *factions* (finance capital, manufacturing capital, resource capital, etc.). Hence, the state must be *relatively autonomous* or independent so that it can serve the long-term interests of capitalism rather than the short-term, profit-maximizing interests of individual capitalists. Therefore, the state often pursues policies that respond to working-class demands, such as social welfare programs, even if these policies are opposed by much of the capitalist class.

If one accepts the premises on which their arguments are based, neo-Marxist analyses can be seen to account for broad patterns in public policy in different societies and for the expanding economic and social activities of the state over time. For example, since Marxist economics predicts that the rate

---

11. For the classic formulation see, for example, Ralph Miliband, *The State in Capitalist Society* (London: Weidenfeld and Nicolson, 1969).

of return on capital investment tends to fall as capitalism progresses, it becomes increasingly necessary for governments to underwrite some of the costs of production (e.g., by subsidizing research and development expenditures). Neo-Marxist analysis is also explicitly oriented toward matters of inequality and distribution of power in Canadian society. In addition, more than any other approach considered here, it addresses issues of external constraints on Canadian policy-making, especially in an era of extensive foreign ownership, multinational corporations and the interdependence of capitalist economies. But, despite numerous attempts to get inside the policy process and to develop a neo-Marxist approach to public policy analysis, neo-Marxism remains unclear on exactly how the state makes specific policy choices or decisions at particular moments in time.

State-Centred Analysis

The advocates of a **state-centred** approach object to the notion that social forces determine what state authorities do. Instead, they view the state as able to act *independently* of the demands of society.[12] The state is visualized as "autonomous," independent of the public's interests, as expressed in the pluralist or public choice models, and certainly not derivative of class interests, as asserted in neo-Marxist thought.

According to the rawest form of this type of explanation of public policy, government officials can act in any way they determine is best for the country—irrespective of demands from society. In other words, the argument is state-centred and not society-centred. Although some attention is paid to the role of elected politicians, much of the research based on this approach focuses on bureaucratic politics: how unelected officials (public servants, judges, police and military) initiate and implement public policy.

This state-centred approach is based on the assumption that those individuals with the greatest knowledge determine to a great extent the policy outputs of a society. Apparently, the modern world requires legislation and policy that is based on expertise not possessed by the mass public, interest groups or transient politicians. Since the bureaucracy is the only permanent repository of the knowledge required to carry out modern government, it is able to use this information to manipulate societal forces. Bureaucrats derive their power from the institutions that empower them, and the institutions that they serve in turn shape the perceptions and actions of these officials.

This approach has been attacked as being based on untenable assumptions. First, the knowledge required to govern the country is not "scientific." Those who determine the direction of public policy possess and convince others to accept a guiding philosophy for the direction of governmental action. After politicians determine priorities—more a question of philosophy or personal choice than scientific knowledge—public servants are left with the administration of this choice, which is less significant than the choice of policy orientation. Second, many members of the senior bureaucracy in Canada are as transient as some leading politicians. Deputy ministers may be dismissed, and often are, while some cabinet members remain in government for long periods at a time.

Third, despite the state-centred assumption that political parties do not present clear policy alternatives, this is not always the case. The 1988 election provided a clear-cut choice between those parties that favoured a particular free trade deal with the United States (the Tories) and those that did not (the Liberals and NDP). Moreover, referendums, such as the one on the Charlottetown Accord, allow the public direct decision-making power. In that particular vote, the people chose a course of action diametrically opposed to that put forward by almost every political leader and bureaucrat

---

12. The classic literature includes James G. March and Johan P. Olsen, "The New Institutionalism: Organizational Factors in Political Life," *APSR*, vol. 78, no. 3 (September 1984), pp. 734–49. For a critique, see Gabriel A. Almond, *A Discipline Divided: Schools and Sects in Political Science* (Newbury Park: Sage, 1990).

in the country. Fourth, the bureaucracy cannot act in isolation. Even if the politician's role is discounted, bureaucrats need the help of interest groups. Specific sectors of the public service ally themselves with societal interests to forge "policy communities."[13] This effort to save the hypothesis that the state drives public policy by adding pluralist assumptions to the model merely highlights the weaknesses in the theory.

POLITICAL PLOY # 3726

DO IT DURING THE PLAYOFFS!...

Practical policy-making: The best time to pass unpopular legislation is when voters are otherwise occupied!

Reproduced with the permission of Dennis Pritchard.

Feminism

Major criticisms of mainstream political science have come from feminists. **Feminism** endorses the removal of all societal barriers to achieving the equality of men and women. Feminism is also regarded as a partial theory of the polity in that it is used to explain large segments of political institutions and behaviour.

Feminism is a system of beliefs that has vision, perspective and a program. It emerged first with the suffragettes, who sought and won voting rights for women. Their initial goals were intensified and expanded to include increasing opportunities for women within the existing social structure, and opposition to discrimination and active oppression of women. Proponents seek a greater representation of women in all aspects of life, including politics, and have forced a range of policies onto the public agenda, especially in Western democracies. These policies stress gender equality with equal pay for work of equal value, wider employment opportunities, child-care facilities and the like. A more radical "second wave" of feminists in the past quarter century argues that orthodox theories about politics tend to ignore gender and harbour unconscious assumptions about the role of women.

Radical second-wave feminists argue that social revolution is needed to restructure society. They maintain that gender is a more important social cleavage than class or race. Women, they say, are subjugated because of their biological function (i.e., having babies). Some radical feminists go so far as to advocate test-tube babies and child-rearing by social institutions to break the patriarchal social pattern.

Feminism as a concept and partial theory has challenged, and to a large extent reformed, political science. Its most enduring contribution has been to show that orthodox political science ignored gender issues. Feminists have shown that gender does matter in both domestic and international relations. They have uncovered assumptions and biases about gender in the discipline. They have found and examined the gross inequalities between men and women in both freedom and income. Arguments about what topics should be in the "public" sphere and what in the "private" have been articulated; as well, simple facts, such as housework and daily chores (primarily carried out by women in most countries) not being registered in the gross domestic product (GDP) of a country,

13. William Coleman and Grace Skogstad, eds., *Policy Communities and Public Policy in Canada* (Mississauga: Copp Clark Pitman, 1991).

are now part of public discourse. On the whole, moderate feminist theory has been concerned with attempting to find co-operative solutions to political problems at the local, national and global levels.

The Approaches Compared

It has been argued that a comprehensive approach to the study of public policy should involve different levels of analysis. This broad framework consists of two sets of factors. Furthest removed from the policy process are the resources and constraints that flow from social and economic environments. But the effects of these influences are profoundly shaped by a number of important intervening factors, including the system of power relations, the dominant values and ideas of society and the structure of political institutions. The combination of these three levels of analysis suggests a sort of "funnel of causality." In this model of policy analysis, all three groups of factors are considered relevant, but the relative importance of factors in determining actual policy outputs increases as the funnel narrows from left to right (see Figure 14.1).

We have noted that no single approach to policy analysis has gained overall acceptance. One reason is that the various approaches tend to focus on particular aspects of the policy process—on different parts of the funnel. For example, micro-level models such as incrementalism and rationalism and, to a lesser extent, the public choice macro-level approach are more concerned with the process of policy-making *inside* government than with the wider relationship *between* government and its socio-economic environment, or broader questions of the distribution of power, ideas and institutions.

The neo-Marxist and pluralist approaches bring together more elements from the funnel. Neo-Marxists explicitly address the influence of economic and social environments, linking the role of the state to changes in the social structure and the economy. In addition, inequalities in power, income and resources between social classes and the role of ideology and values are central themes in neo-Marxist analysis. However, as we have already noted, this approach has not yet come to terms with the influence of independent actors within the policy-making process in determining public policy outcomes such as those found in the state-centred approaches.

The pluralist approach implicitly takes into account the socio-economic environment, since the growing complexity of industrial society gives rise to more and more issues and interests for

FIGURE 14.1 **Public Policy "Funnel of Causality"**

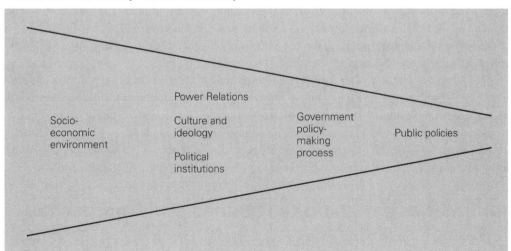

which groups may be mobilized. Pluralists emphasize the interaction of interest groups with the policy-making process; they also stress the mediating effects of institutions such as the electoral process. The traditional pluralist view has often been criticized for its failure to recognize inequalities of power and influence and for its emphasis on government as a reactive agent—that is, as a neutral arbiter that responds only to the balance of group pressures. However, many authors in the pluralist tradition allow that the modern state possesses its own dynamic in the policy process. But, while granting "autonomy" to the state or government frees it from being a mere cipher of group demands, the argument fails to develop a comprehensive analysis of how, why and to what effect the state takes advantage of its newly discovered freedom.

A further problem that has inhibited the emergence of a generally accepted approach to public policy analysis lies in the ideological and political rhetoric associated with some of the theories sketched out above. Too often, theoretical models of public policy are used for support rather than illumination. This problem is particularly acute in the case of the two so-called political economy approaches: public choice and neo-Marxism.

The public choice argument that politicians and bureaucrats pursue their own interests in formulating public policies, rather than some vague notion of the public interest, is attractive to those who think that government has grown too large and that public expenditures have risen out of control. By providing a theoretical rationale for allegations of bureaucratic empire-building and for the supposed self-serving actions of politicians, public choice lends additional weight to the arguments of neo-conservatives who wish to lower tax rates, reduce the size of the bureaucracy and social programs and generally get government "off the backs" of the private sector.

While public choice theory may reinforce the negative views that many people hold toward bureaucrats and politicians, the assumptions of neo-Marxism tend to challenge the way most North American citizens think about politics. Indeed, neo-Marxism provides a critical, alternative way of looking at the role of the state in Canada and causes one to question assumptions about the way government operates. However, neo-Marxist analysis often is difficult to disentangle from ideological rhetoric. Many critics believe that it is impossible to use neo-Marxist concepts as an approach to analysis without also adhering to the ideology of Marxism, with its prescription for the revolutionary overthrow of capitalist society. Others simply refuse to accept the premises of class division and conflict on which neo-Marxist theories of the state are based. In either case, the determinist and hyper-theoretical nature of much neo-Marxist writing further reinforces strong opposition.

Rather than promoting research that will enhance understanding of the policy process and the role of the state or government in formulating and implementing public policies, both public choice and neo-Marxist analysis may be reduced to facile sloganeering. By attributing every perceived evil of the modern state to the self-interest of bureaucrats or to the inequities of capitalism, political economy is sometimes reduced to *polemical* economy.

For a variety of reasons, therefore, it is extremely unlikely that any of the approaches outlined in this section will emerge as a universally accepted theory of public policy-making. But these ideas do represent the dominant frameworks of analysis found in the current literature in political science. Each approach has its strengths and weaknesses in explaining how, why and to what effect governments choose to act on certain issues. Students of Canadian politics should be well-versed in these approaches and be able to apply them to policy decisions and policy frameworks.

International Relations Theories and Approaches

An examination of international politics needs to take into consideration factors other than the individual and state levels of analysis. Such an approach is known as the **levels of analysis issue**.

The traditional approach is to break the investigation into three parts: the *individual level*, the *state level* and the *international level*. In the first instance, scholars examine the role of individuals and their personalities in foreign politics. At the second or state level, they study the role of single or comparative states in the making of foreign policies. The third or global level of analysis refers to examinations of the interactions among states and the effect they have on each other, and also the impact of purely global factors.

While the study of political science and comparative politics in particular follows essentially the various research paths suggested in the list of approaches above—pluralism, public-choice theory, neo-Marxist analysis, state-centred analysis and feminism—the field of international relations tends to add and highlight arguments based on *realism* and *liberalism/idealism*.[14]

Realism

Perhaps the dominant historical force in modern international relations studies has been realism. Essentially the **realist approach** is based on five principles:

1. Individuals and states seek power, particularly military power, in order to ensure their security.
2. International politics is about states and their relationships.
3. In their search for power and security, states are guided by amoral calculations about "national interests."
4. Global politics is essentially a struggle among self-interested states for power and security, and its study concerns the shifting distribution of power among states. Military strength plays a central role in this calculation.
5. The global arena is basically *anarchical* with each state fending for itself. The result poses a **security dilemma**. As each state searches for security in the international, anarchical system, the dilemma is clear: as one state becomes more secure, it automatically diminishes the security of others.

The foremost exponents historically of realism were Niccolo Machiavelli (1469–1527) and Thomas Hobbes (1588–1679). But its intellectual roots go back to the Peloponnesian War and the writings of the Greek historian Thucydides. For hardcore realists, the state is the most important actor in global politics and conflicts among them are inevitable. For this reason, leaders must strive to increase their state's power in a hostile and anarchical environment. The possibility of co-operation replacing conflict is low and states must not be tempted by other philosophical or moral arguments. The realist's argument seems most persuasive during times of conflict, terrorism and war, as it focuses the debate on pragmatism and the military.

Realism is sometimes updated as *neorealism*. In such cases, the focus is on how the anarchy and structure of global politics shapes or determines the behaviour of the states within the system. The absence of a world government compels states to think in terms of their own security and relative power as related to others as the primary factor in global politics.

Liberalism/Idealism

Liberalism is an approach that comes in many forms but, essentially, it also has five core principles that contrast it to realism:

1. Individuals, transnational networks, international institutions and commercial actors play important roles in global politics.
2. International politics is shaped by ideas, values, culture and social identities.

---

14. Robert J. Jackson and Doreen Jackson, *An Introduction to Political Science: Comparative and World Politics* (Don Mills, ON: Pearson Prentice Hall, 2007), ch. 19.

3. Co-operative behaviour, not power relations, explains how states act together, carrying out peaceful conduct in diplomacy, trade, commerce, and financial transactions.

4. The goal of liberal thought is to institutionalize peace and obtain collaborative security by the actions of supranational organizations, international law, democratization, arms control and so on.

5. Liberals believe that the global system is an ordered or organized anarchy, as co-operation best describes the pattern of most global interaction.

The foremost exponents of Liberalism historically were John Locke (1632–1704) and Immanuel Kant (1724–1804). Liberalism/idealism focuses the scholar on the impact that ideas may have on political behaviour. Thus, it tends to define politics not in terms of a power relationship but in terms of a struggle for consensus. In the search for agreements to make the world more orderly, just and co-operative, liberalism highlights issues such as human rights and international justice.

Policy Instruments and Processes

There are several academic approaches to explain how and why governments choose particular policy instruments. One is based on a continuum of governing instruments. Some scholars hypothesize that "politicians have a strong tendency to respond to policy issues by moving successively from the *least coercive* governing instrument to the *most coercive*."[15] Applied to the continuum (as shown in Figure 14.2), this idea suggests that governments tend to respond first with symbolic outputs such as the establishment of a royal commission and with attempts to secure voluntary compliance through exhortation. Later, however, they may shift to expenditure instruments and, if these incentives are insufficient to ensure compliance with policy objectives, they may subsequently deploy more coercive measures such as regulation or even public ownership. Thus, Allan Tupper and G. Bruce Doern suggest that in the majority of cases they studied, "the direct ownership instrument was selected *after* extensive use of other instruments including regulation, spending and taxation."[16]

However, when adopting new instruments as they move along the continuum, policy-makers rarely discontinue the use of less coercive means. Instruments differentiated from each other by the degrees of coercion attributed to them are therefore additive or complementary in nature, rather than constituting alternatives. Thus, when public enterprises are established, rather than replacing other measures, "public ownership is more frequently *added* to an array of existing instruments that have been tried and found wanting, or at least are *believed* to be found wanting."[17]

At first glance, this hypothesis of instrument choice appears plausible, although both it and the continuum from which it is derived are based on some assumptions that may not be acceptable to all public policy analysts. It does have the advantage that it can be tested empirically. However, applications of the hypothesis to different fields of public policy have yielded mixed results. While the study of some policy areas, such as energy policy, supports the contention that governments progress along the continuum in developing policy responses (leaving regulation and especially public ownership as a last resort), examination of sectors such as broadcasting policy indicates that public ownership was among the first instruments deployed by the federal government.

A full explanation for the selection of policy instruments by governments has to take into account a multiplicity of economic, legal, political and external constraints on governmental freedom

15. G. Bruce Doern and V. Seymour Wilson, eds., Issues in Canadian Public Policy (Toronto: Macmillan, 1974), p. 339 (emphasis in original).

16. Tupper and Doern, "Public Corporations and Public Policy in Canada," p. 19 (emphasis in original).

17. Ibid.

FIGURE 14.2 Instruments of Governing

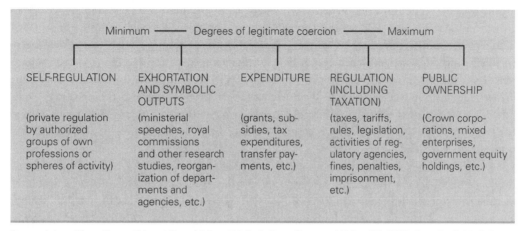

Source: Adapted from Figures 5.1, p. 111, and 5.3, p. 134, in G. Bruce Doern and Richard W. Phidd, *Canadian Public Policy: Ideas, Structure, Process* (Toronto: Methuen, 1983).

of choice. For example, within the Canadian federal system, governments are precluded from using the full range of instruments in some policy areas by the constitutional division of powers among jurisdictions. Thus, the federal government is effectively limited to exhortation and spending in many fields of Canadian social policy. Economic constraints in a period of growing criticism of the expansion of public expenditures and budgetary deficits make both regulation and relatively hidden tax incentives more attractive than large, visible spending programs. International agreements such as the General Agreement on Tariffs and Trade (GATT) militate against raising tariffs (a form of taxation or regulation) and force governments to resort to alternative methods (non-tariff barriers) to control the volume of imports flowing into the country.

Even the nature of the policy-making process itself may have an effect. While routine, day-to-day or year-to-year policy-making may tend toward the kind of incrementalist instrument selection hypothesized above, one study of policy-making in crisis management situations shows that, after initial symbolic responses, governments are most likely to resort to highly coercive instruments, including emergency regulations and the deployment of armed forces. Only after the crisis is over will they return to legislation and public spending in order to pre-empt the occurrence of further crises.[18]

Clearly, we need to learn more about the dynamics of public policy-making in order to reach a more complete explanation of the choice of policy instruments by governments. But while the concept of a continuum of governing instruments has weaknesses, it has proven to be a useful heuristic device in promoting research and in sensitizing policy analysts to the multiplicity of means of policy implementation that governments have at their disposal.

Theories About the Growth and Size of the Canadian State

Theorists about government policies and expenditures need to bear in mind the simple fact that, regardless of dominant ideologies or which parties form the government, the size of the Canadian state continues to grow.

18. Robert J. Jackson, "Crisis Management and Policy-Making," in Richard Rose, ed., *The Dynamics of Public Policy* (Beverly Hills, CA: Sage Publications, 1976), p. 214.

The proportion of total national income spent by the various levels of government has increased greatly over the years. However, the rate has not been constant; there have been distinct periods of growth and decline. Moreover, the overall growth disguises substantial shifts in the relative importance of different levels of government. Eighty years ago, local and municipal governments were the biggest spenders, since they were primarily responsible for financing education and limited social welfare functions. During the Great Depression, local and provincial governments were unable to cope with demands on their budgets, so the federal government began to spend more; it continued to do so to meet the costs of the war effort. Since the mid-1960s, the largest percentage of government expenditure has been at the provincial level. However, it is also true that federal spending in dollar terms has continued to rise substantially.

In 2007–08, the federal government was projected to spend about $200 billion for programs, compared to only $13 billion in 1971. Like expenditures, the revenues of all levels of government have increased over the last half century. In 2007–08, the federal government was to raise roughly $237 billion, leaving no federal deficit and a small surplus. However, the national debt was projected to be roughly $469 billion by the end of 2008, so the surplus was used to pay the interest and some of the principle on the national debt. It is also important to relate the size of the Canadian debt to the size and strength of the economy—in 2007–08, the debt equalled about 31.4 percent of the GDP. The country's financial burdens are not limited to the federal government; the total provincial deficits and debts also escalated during these years (see Figure 14.3 and also Figure 14.5 on page 518).

Not all state activity is measurable in terms of public expenditure. While many public policies do require the outlay of money, others need very little—particularly those that seek to regulate or control the behaviour of individual or corporate members of society. Thus, as the state has become more involved in its citizens' lives, the volume of legislation, statutes and regulations has increased. This aspect of the growth of the Canadian state was aptly summarized by Jacques Flynn, a former Tory justice minister and senator, in a speech to the Canadian Bar Association:

> *We recently published a consolidation of federal regulations—15 563 pages of them. Add to that 10 000 pages of Revised Statutes (Canada's Statutes were last revised and consolidated in 1970) and 8000 to 10 000 pages of Statutes since the revision, plus hundreds of thousands of pages of provincial laws and regulations to say nothing of municipal by-laws, orders and regulations. Now you begin to realize that we've come a long way from 10 clauses on a slab of stone.*[19]

Finally, as the state has increasingly intervened in social and economic life, so the actual machinery of government has become more complex. The number of federal government departments and branches quadrupled over the last hundred years. There are approximately four hundred federal government Crown corporations and agencies, of which almost half were created after 1970. Similarly, the number of people employed by the federal government has also grown to roughly 400 000. As in the case of public expenditure, however, real growth in terms of the percentage of total employment in the public sector has been relatively smaller.

Whichever indicators we choose, it is beyond argument that the state in Canada has grown immensely over the last century—especially in the last 35 years. When measured in real terms, however, this expansion is by no means as large as some critics of government intervention would suggest. Still, the question remains, How do we account for the growth of the state?

19. Quoted by Donald John Purich, "Too Many Laws? There May Not Be Enough!" *The Chronicle-Herald,* Halifax, February 2, 1980.

FIGURE 14.3 Federal and Provincial-Territorial Debt (Public Accounts Basis)

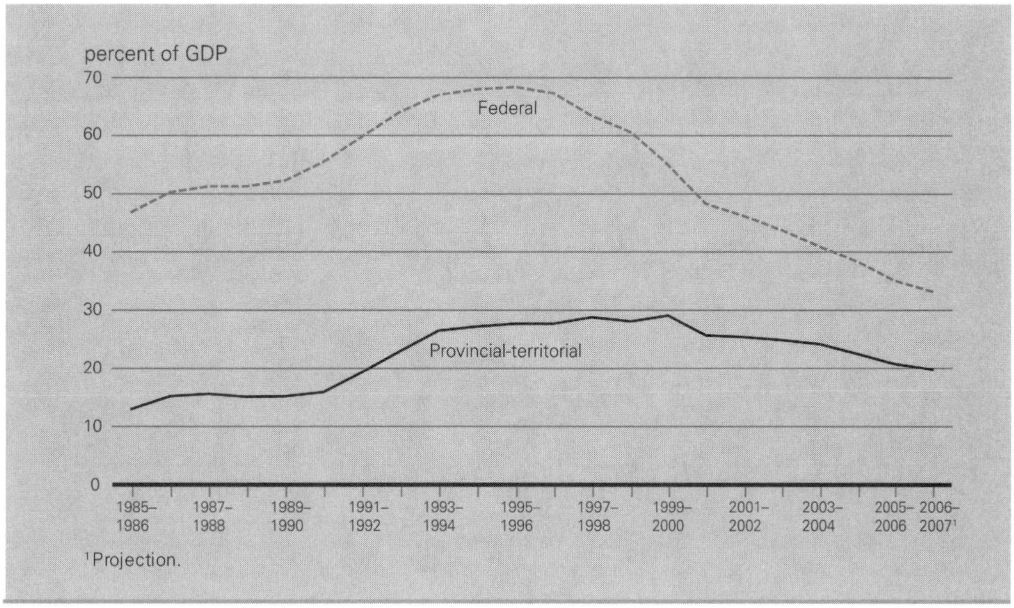

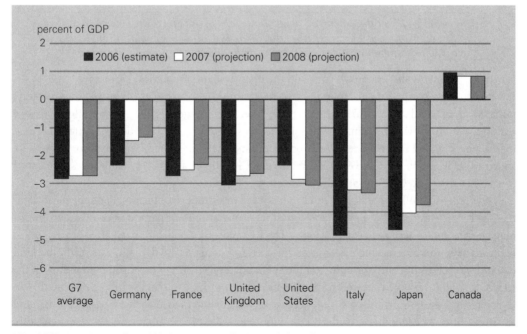

Source: Federal and provincial-territorial Public Accounts and budgets, Finance Canada, Budget 2007. Accessed July 13, 2007, at www.budget.gc.ca/2007/bp/bpa1e.html.

FIGURE 14.4 Total Government Financial Balances, 2006–2007 (National Accounts Basis)*

* The OECD uses the term financial balance to mean "budgetary balance."

Source: *OECD Economic Outlook*, No. 6D (December 2006), Finance Canada, Budget Plan 2007. Accessed July 13, 2007, at www.budget.gc.ca/2007/bp/bpa2e.html.

FIGURE 14.5 **Provincial–Territorial Budgetary Balances, 2006–2007 (Public Accounts Basis)**

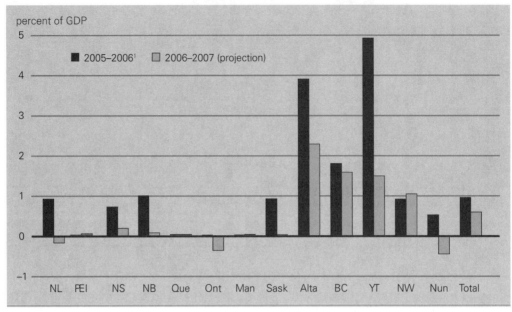

Source: Provincial-territorial Public Accounts and budgets, Finance Canada, Budget 2007. Accessed July 13, 2007, at www.budget.gc.ca/2007/bp/bpa1e.html.

Theoretical Explanations for the Growth and Size of the State

Why did the government, or the public sector, grow in Canada? So many authors have attempted to explain the growth of the state in Canada that, according to Richard Bird,

> *the problem is not that there are no explanations of the growth of government in Canada since the war: it is rather that there are too many explanations, each one of which probably contains both some truth and some misleading elements.*[20]

In the following discussion, we focus on the historical and theoretical arguments.

Most of the major federal programs that make up the modern Canadian welfare state were initiated or consolidated in the quarter-century after the Second World War, including hospital and medical insurance, the Canada and Québec pension plans, the Canada Assistance Plan and federal participation in other shared-cost programs such as post-secondary education. These were added to such wartime initiatives as unemployment insurance and family allowances to create a comprehensive package of social and welfare programs.

The expansion of state activities can be attributed to a number of factors. First, the period was marked by the emergence of Keynesian economics as the dominant paradigm of macroeconomic management in Western industrial societies. The Keynesian model legitimized large-scale government intervention as a means of manipulating the level of aggregate demand to control the kind of extreme cyclical fluctuations in the economy that had given rise to the Great Depression of the 1930s. It should be noted, however, that Keynesian economics was never fully implemented in Canada, since, even though successive federal governments intervened to boost aggregate demand as an incentive to economic growth, they rarely followed Keynes's prescriptions of expenditure cutbacks and tax hikes to deflate the economy in times of expansion and inflation.

20. Richard M. Bird, *Financing Canadian Government: A Quantitative Overview* (Toronto: Canadian Tax Foundation, 1979), p. 82.

Second, the period from 1945 to 1970 was, by and large, an era of rapid and sustained economic growth fuelled by post-war reconstruction, the injection of foreign investment and the spread of mass affluence. This economic growth led to an expansion of government revenues through increasing tax returns and enhanced the fiscal capacity of the state to intervene. It also enabled the government to involve itself in major redistributive programs, since there were sufficient resources to distribute to the less privileged without depriving more affluent and politically influential groups of a share of the ever-expanding national pie.

From a pluralist perspective, therefore, the government as neutral arbiter was able to satisfy the demands of more societal groups, including an increasingly influential labour movement that had organized behind the trade unions and the growing electoral force of the CCF/NDP. In the public choice and state-centred views, however, the growth of the state could be attributed to the competitive bidding practices of party politicians anxious to gain governmental power and to the expansionist tendencies of bureaucrats seeking to enlarge their spheres of influence in the policy process.

The neo-Marxist approach would interpret the growth of the state in different terms again. The need to promote accumulation of private capital after the war required the state to intervene on behalf of capital through incentives to investment, by boosting aggregate demand (e.g., universal child allowances) and by helping to underwrite the costs of reproducing the labour force (e.g., health and education policies). At the same time, the growing power of organized labour led the state to introduce programs that helped to legitimate its capital accumulation role and disguise the exploitative nature of capitalism. As capitalism becomes increasingly monopolistic and as the rate of profit falls (a central tenet of Marxist economics), the state will intervene more and more to maintain both capital accumulation and legitimation until it reaches *fiscal crisis*, a situation in which government revenues can no longer satisfy the simultaneous demands of the dual role of the state.[21] Thus, for some left-wing analysts, the language of restraint and the social policy cutbacks undertaken by governments in Canada are natural consequences of fiscal crisis and the fundamental contradiction between the state's accumulation and legitimation functions.

There are many other less theoretical approaches for explaining the growth of the state. Some are essentially apolitical in that they view the expansion of the role of government as a product of *exogenous* (externally determined) forces. For example, the growth and changing age structure of the population may call for increased state activity. More expenditure and more government personnel are needed to provide services to a larger number of people, and the fact that more people are living longer necessitates more pensions and health care for the aged. Alternatively, the vast technological development undergone by Canadian society in the last century may have increased the scope for government intervention. For example, the advent of the motor vehicle alone gave rise to a great variety of government activity: road building and maintenance, traffic laws, seat-belt legislation, driver and vehicle licensing, exhaust-emission controls, vehicle safety regulations and much more.

But the growth of the state was not the *direct* consequence of demographic change or technological innovation; these are background factors that create increased potential for state intervention. The current extent of state activity *is* the result of an extensive series of political decisions—to increase public expenditure on a particular item, to move into a new functional area, to create another regulatory agency—each one taken by politicians acting in the context of the political process. Thus, although the number of people over 65 already exceeded 5 percent of the population in 1901, it was another quarter of a century before government pensions were introduced for some people over the age of 70, and half a century before pensions were granted to those over 65.

---

21. James O'Connor, *The Fiscal Crisis of the State* (New York: St. Martin's Press, 1973), passim.

Many attempts to explain the growth of the state focus on the bureaucratic forces that underlie its activities. It is sometimes argued that bureaucrats judge their personal success by the growth rate of the budgets, number of employees and volume of programs administered by their departments. A kinder view might ascribe the growth to genuine concern for the target population or to a response to political pressures. The dominant modes and structures of policy-making in state bureaucracies may also play a part, especially with respect to the growth of public spending. Incremental decision-making has predominated in the budgetary process over much of the past century. While attempts have been made to reform the budgetary process in the last fifteen years, it has proven difficult to counterbalance the tendency toward continued expansion of public expenditure. Although the federal deficit was eliminated before the turn of the millennium, the national debt level will continue at high levels for much of the twenty-first century.

The role of political ideas or ideologies is sometimes overlooked in explorations of the decisions underlying the growth of the state. However, it may be argued that an interventionist role for the state has traditionally been considered legitimate in Canadian political culture. Canadians do not share the anti-statist liberalism and free enterprise ethic to the same extent as the general public in the United States. In the nineteenth century, the Canadian versions of Toryism and nationalism motivated state intervention in the interests of private enterprise and national economic development through the National Policy. From the Second World War to the mid-1970s, the acceptance of Keynesian economics and the embracing of a "welfare state ideology" served to legitimate an interventionist role for the state. Despite efforts to reduce state functions by eliminating many bureaucratic institutions in the late twentieth and early twenty-first centuries, the size of the state has not diminished—in fact, it has continued to grow.

With so many alternatives to choose from, it is perhaps not surprising that no universally accepted explanation of the growth of the Canadian state has emerged. One point upon which most analysts agree is that while demographic, technological and economic factors provide the contextual background to the growth of the state, the key to a comprehensive and satisfactory explanation lies more in the political field than in other processes.

Government Restraint and Surplus Renewal

In the past few decades, there has been a concerted attack on the size and complexity of modern government in most liberal democracies. Bureaucrats are portrayed as being motivated mainly by their desire to increase their budgets, staffs and importance. Conservatives, in particular, think that the problems of bureaucracy can be solved by reducing its power. They demand that government administration be made smaller, more decentralized, less expensive and more flexible in responding to public demands. On occasion, the election platforms of the Conservative, Liberal and even New Democratic parties have included proposals to weaken the federal bureaucracy.

Such political demands have often been accompanied by ever-grander schemes for reform. The *new public management* or *managerialism* schools in social science call for the introduction of business management practices into government.[22] One example would be the claim that "pay for performance" or *merit pay* should be more common in the public sector. This idea is often accompanied by the philosophy that "customer orientation" should be the reigning principle for public servants. This approach has become so shrill that it is more like an ideology than a theory of public administration.

---

22. See A. Massey, *Managing the Public Sector* (Aldershot: Edward Elgar, 1993); C. Campbell, *Political Leadership in an Age of Constraint* (Pittsburgh: University of Pittsburgh Press, 1992); and J. Dilulio, *Deregulating the Public Service: Can Government be Improved?* (Washington, DC: The Brookings Institute, 1994).

Another approach has been to call for the "privatization" of government, either by selling off government enterprises or by "contracting out" services to the private sector. The idea is based on the premise that self-interested decisions in the marketplace will be made more efficiently than those made by tenured civil servants in the bureaucracy. Probably the clearest example of this philosophy in recent years has been the decision to privatize many Crown corporations such as Air Canada, Petro-Canada and so on (see "Government for Sale: Public Ownership?" below).

Lastly, a case has been made against the centralization of bureaucracies in capital cities. The claim is that decisions would be better (read "more efficient") if they were made closer to the people that they affect. In other words, decentralization is supposed to enhance decision-making and prevent the waste that is prevalent in large, centralized administrations.

The philosophy inherent in such policies is clear. When the marketplace is used to enforce efficiency, it is to the advantage of the more conservative forces in society. "New public management" is essentially a belief that the more politicians can be kept out of public administration, the better off the country will be. However, when governments do privatize their functions a substantial measure of democratic control is lost. How, then, can democratic responsiveness be enhanced by these new managerial techniques of government? No answer has come to solve this challenge. Optimists continue to endorse the ideas put forth by David Osborne and Ted Gaebler in their best-selling book, *Reinventing Government*, in which they argue that "the entrepreneurial spirit" can transform public administration.[23]

One major consequence of modern economics has been the advent of what US economist Lester Thurow has labelled "the zero-sum society."[24] In some times, governments can redistribute resources to the underprivileged without eroding at least the money income, if not the relative position, of more affluent groups. The growing national pie permits "positive-sum" politics. However, if the pie stops growing, redistribution to some groups can be undertaken only at the expense of others. In zero-sum situations, then, distributional conflicts become more polarized, since somebody must "lose" for someone else to "win." Thus, new or expanded social programs must be financed from savings obtained from reducing other programs. Such a situation gives rise to greater conflict and intense ideological rhetoric in politics. However, in recent years, governments at both the federal and provincial levels have had the luxury of having surpluses and have not had to face the challenges of the "zero-sum" logic.

Government for Sale: Public Ownership?

The direct provision of goods and services by corporations owned partly or wholly by the government has had a long history in Canada. Indeed, some observers have even labelled Canada a "public enterprise culture." Among major federal enterprises, the most enduring has been Canadian National Railways, which was finally privatized in 1995. It was established soon after the First World War, but it was predated by provincially owned enterprises such as Ontario Hydro and publicly owned telephone systems in the Prairies. From these early beginnings, public ownership has expanded to other transportation, energy and communications facilities, as well as resource development, manufacturing, finance and a number of other sectors of the economy. Today, several federal public corporations, such as the Canada Post Corporation and the Canadian Wheat Board, can be found among Canada's largest business enterprises.

23. David Osborne and Ted Gaebler, *Reinventing Government* (New York: Plume, 1993). Their ideas were foreshadowed by Tom Peters and Robert Waterman in their best-seller about management in business, *In Search of Excellence* (New York: Harper and Row, 1982).

24. Lester C. Thurow, The Zero-Sum Society: Distribution and the Possibilities for Economic Change (New York: Basic Books, 1980).

The realm of public ownership partly overlaps with that of public corporations (discussed in detail in Chapter 10), but the two are not identical. Federal agencies classified as corporations or other agencies may be mechanisms for policy implementation or advisory bodies that contribute to the formation of public policy. On the other side of the coin, public ownership need not entail 100 percent government ownership and control. Apart from wholly owned Crown corporations and their subsidiaries, governments may turn to mixed (public–private) enterprises or to equity-holding (share-holding) in a private company in their attempts to realize certain policy goals.

The objectives of public ownership as a policy instrument are many and varied. Some early public enterprises, such as state-owned railways and Trans-Canada Airlines (later Air Canada), were established to develop essential economic infrastructure in situations where "the private sector was unwilling or unable to take the initiative."[25] These transportation facilities also played a part in national integration; a similar motive lay behind the creation of the Canadian Radio Broadcasting Commission (now the Canadian Broadcasting Corporation—a.k.a. the CBC) in 1932. Other public enterprises were founded to provide financial infrastructure for the Canadian economy. Thus, the Business Development Bank of Canada and the Export Development Corporation were designed to "fill gaps in the financial system and to assist interests whose financial needs were only partially met by established (private) leaders."[26] As well, public ownership was used to develop enterprises involving high cost or commercial risks that were deemed to be in the long-term public interest. For example, federal government involvement in Atomic Energy of Canada was intended to foster new technologies.[27]

In many of these cases, public enterprises complemented, rather than competed with, the interests of the private sector. In recent years, however, more controversial examples of government ownership have brought the public sector into conflict with private enterprise over market shares and investment resources. Opposition to public ownership crystallized around two major issues: first, growing concern about a perceived lack of accountability of Crown corporations; second, the losses suffered in recent years by some corporations. These issues lent extra ammunition to arguments that resources devoted to public enterprise might be more profitably and efficiently allocated in the private sector. Critics of public ownership adopted as a solution to both problems the privatization of a number of Crown corporations.

Between 1984 and 2006, the federal Progressive Conservative and then the Liberal governments privatized many Crown corporations, in particular those that could operate in a competitive business environment. Arguing that the private sector operates more efficiently than the public sector, and that the government had to reduce the deficit, the Tories and Liberals sold off such illustrious Crown corporations as Air Canada, Development Corporation of Canada, Canada Ports Corporation, Canadian Arsenals, Canadian Communications Group, CN Hotels, CN Railways, Canadair, Cape Breton Development Corporation, de Havilland Aircraft, Eldorado Nuclear, Fisheries Products International, Northern Canada Power Commission, Northern Transportation Commission, Petro-Canada, Polymer Corporation, St. Lawrence Seaway Authority, Teleglobe Canada and Telesat. As well, Canada Post Corporation was changed from a government department to a Crown corporation so that it could function like a private enterprise. The Canada Wheat Board had its statutes amended so that now the government has only five members on the board and farmers appoint ten members.

25. John W. Langford, "Crown Corporations as Instruments of Policy" in G. Bruce Doern and Peter Aucoin, eds., *Public Policy in Canada* (Toronto: Macmillan, 1971), p. 248.

26. Allan Tupper and G. Bruce Doern, "Understanding Public Corporations in Canada," *Canadian Business Review*, vol. 9, no. 3 (Autumn 1982), p. 34.

27. Marsha Gordon, *Government in Business* (Montréal: C.D. Howe Institute, 1981), ch. 6

Public ownership continues to be under fire from neo-conservatives, who view any government intervention as an infringement upon the supremacy of the free-market economy. Thus, while it is improbable that privatization will be carried as far as it has been in some countries, it seems certain that public ownership will be much less prominent in the federal government's arsenal of public policy instruments during the twenty-first century and that the privatization of public agencies and Crown corporations will continue.

Public Policy and Expenditure: The Mulroney, Chrétien/Martin and Harper Governments

In the last two decades of the twentieth century, *restraint* was a watchword of federal policy-making as successive governments attempted to cope with inflation, recession, declining tax revenues, growing deficits and the task of reviving a faltering Canadian economy. Government restraint became the policy of choice during the 1984 and 1988 PC governments and also for the Liberals in 1993 and the early years of the 1997 government. As the government finally got out of deficit in the late 1990s, all parties began to speak of balanced budgets, surpluses and choice in public policy once again.

One consequence of the restraint philosophy was the efforts of the Mulroney and Chrétien governments to reform public policy and the public service along the lines of managerialism or new public management theory. This business-oriented philosophy can be summarized as an effort to *privatize* public policy services whenever possible and to *deregulate* the economy to the maximum possible. At the bureaucratic level, this philosophy resulted in cutbacks and layoffs in the public service in an effort to reduce the overall costs of government. The 1984 Nielsen Task Force (a ministerial task force on program review) may be cited as the first of the studies and programs intended to make the federal government more like a business. But it was not the last.

The result of the Nielsen Task Force was essentially negative. The bureaucracy fought the changes at every stage, and the actual effects on public administration were minimal. Therefore, the 1988–1993 Mulroney government attempted another strategy. In line with managerialism ideas, an effort was made to change the basic attitudes or culture of the bureaucracy. It instituted *Public Service 2000*, a comprehensive philosophy to make the bureaucracy more service-oriented (i.e., to provide better services to the clients of government), more flexible (to respond to the public's wishes) and more decentralized (i.e., to make the managers manage rather than follow orders or rely on the central agencies of government for direction). The concrete results of Public Service 2000 were quite different from the rhetoric. Public service morale plummeted and many senior bureaucrats retired or were fired.

After the disastrous effect of Kim Campbell's short-lived government on the public service, the 1993–1997 Chrétien government undertook another comprehensive review of all government programs. The prime minister appointed Marcel Massé, the minister responsible for *Public Service Renewal*, to begin "reinventing" government. Despite the rhetoric about the "tests" of good government that enveloped these reports, the ultimate objective was to reduce government expenditures by eliminating programs and laying off 45 000 public servants. To alleviate other public pressures about government expenditure, Chrétien also reduced the size of ministerial staffs. For example, under Mulroney the number of political staffers in the Department of International Trade was 78. Chrétien reduced this to 20.

The impact of Public Service 2000 and Public Service Renewal was in line with managerialism and the new philosophy of neo-conservative governments. A smaller bureaucracy, carrying out fewer tasks, has been created by program cutbacks, public service reductions, privatization and deregulation. The Canadian government under both Progressive Conservatives and Liberals adopted almost without question the philosophy of "the less government the better."

Paul Martin's tenures as finance minister and prime minister were blessed with seven years total of balanced budgets and a growing surplus. Unfortunately, from the Liberal point of view, it was also afflicted with financial scandals, especially AdScam. This did not dampen enthusiasm to reform public expenditures and the public service, but it shifted the orientation from restraint to financial control mechanisms. As Reg Alcock, president of the Treasury Board, put it so proudly, "We are at a truly transformative moment in modern public sector management. The public sector needs to restructure, to speed up decision-making, respond to change, and focus on citizen-driven service delivery." The administration then set about strengthening the role of controllers in departments, introducing new human resources institutions and procedures, bolstering the comprehensive audit function and introducing new financial rules for public corporations.

Stephen Harper's Conservative government came into its mandate in 2006 with surpluses and consequently began a new strategy for financial control. In its budgets, the government used part of the surplus to pay down the principal on the national debt—in 2006, it paid off $13.2 billion; in 2007, $9.2 billion. But the novel idea was to link these decisions to a policy called the *Tax Back Guarantee*, which allocated all interest saved on the federal debt—$2.4 billion—to be returned directly to Canadians in the form of tax cuts. Thus, the Tories managed to link their financial and political strategy. Canadians are likely to appreciate the tax refunds and Canada is now the only G7 country in surplus and possibly is on its way to eliminating its debt by 2021.

Critical Debate
Public Policy: Comprehensive and Rational?

Is public policy in Canada made in a comprehensive and rational manner?

Point

No, public policy is not made in a comprehensive and rational way. The dominating philosophy of Canadian government is one of ad hoc, incremental and essentially irrational decision-making. There are reasons for this.

Whichever perspective one takes on the role of the state in Canadian society, it is clear that certain fundamental realities of Canadian political life have a continuing influence on federal policy-making. Their net effect is to militate against comprehensive decision-making in favour of a general tendency to allow the growth of the state based on incremental policy-making or the art of "muddling through." The federal government has continued to grow in terms of expenditure and staffing since 1867, and nothing it does seems to be able to stop this.

Consider some of the fundamental realities that influence federal policy-makers.

First, Canada is a liberal democracy in which political parties must compete for electoral support. Governments must be responsive to the policy concerns of key interest groups and to their potential as organizers of public opinion and votes. Governments need to win, and especially maintain, electoral support from societal groups. This usually requires them to refrain from making major policy changes that might alienate significant portions of the electorate.

Second, Canada has a federal system of government in which the constitutional division of powers imposes both legal and political constraints on federal policy-makers. The legal constraints limit the instruments available to the federal government in pursuit of its objectives in many policy areas, while the values and goals of provincial governments and their policies often contradict and reduce the effectiveness of federal policy outputs. The need to secure federal–provincial co-operation in many policy areas dictates that policy-making must move in small, incrementalist steps rather than in giant strides.

Third, Canada is not a political system in isolation. Changes in world economic and political environments create a climate of uncertainty for policy-makers of all states. But the political and economic influence of the United States, and of US-based multinational corporations in particular, imposes extra demands and constraints on policy-makers in Canada; federal policy-makers must constantly adjust their priorities and instruments of policy implementation in response to events south of the 49th parallel.

This is not to say that policy-makers do not attempt to make good policy decisions. All Canadians would like to think that their federal government makes the most rational policy choices available to it, subject to the constraints under which it is working. However, the requirements of a democratic political process, a federal institutional structure and the constraints imposed by domestic and international economies usually combine with short-term political expediency to ensure that policy-makers follow the path of least resistance by muddling through.

Canadians should, perhaps, demand of their governments that, if they are going to muddle through, they at least do so in a more "rational" way. Perhaps the *public choice* model offers some clues to this process. It explains public policy in terms of selfish actors, and once we understand the principles of political action, perhaps we will realize what types of control mechanisms are necessary. Some form of business experience and perhaps more *managerialism* in government would help.

Counterpoint

Of course, Canadian public policy is comprehensive and rational. This debate is nonsense. The federal state has not grown as much as a cursory examination would suggest, and the various theories of government only partially explain the manner of making public policy.

The most important principle in our system of government is that it is democratic. Democracy may cause inefficiencies, but it is still the reigning principle of Canadian governments and this should not be forgotten. Efficiency—meaning working toward only one goal—may be more effective in authoritarian than democratic regimes. In the short run, authoritarian regimes may be able to pull their people together to run a "command" or communist economy. But in the long run, such regimes fail their citizens. In a democracy, the people should get what they want.

Actually, the *federal* government does not spend the major proportion of government expenditures in Canada. The provinces and municipalities spend most funds. Of course, that is reasonable given that they are assigned the most expensive items under the Constitution, such as education and health care.

The assumptions of pluralism may be mistaken in terms of the relative weight assigned to the participants in the process, but at least people and institutions are assumed to have some impact on public policy. Canadian governments have always tried to use the state to improve the lives of their citizens. For example, in order to militate against north–south economic pulls, governments of both major parties have continually implemented protective policies, from the tariffs policies of the nineteenth century to the development of government enterprises such as the railways (CNR), aircraft (Air Canada) and regulatory agencies (CRTC). The eventual sell-off of dozens of Crown corporations is evidence of just how much the US capitalist economy has affected Canadian politics.

Marxism, feminism, public choice and state-centred theories all contribute explanations for how parts of the political system work, but only pluralism gives a comprehensive view of why Canada has the public policies it does. Efforts to sell off some of the federal government's institutions and lessen Ottawa's policy interventions because of the financial difficulties of the 1980s and '90s will not work in the long run. When there are surpluses, Canadian governments at all levels increase their commitments to spend the taxpayers' money in order to produce the services the people want. The Conservatives have even found a way to link reductions in the size of the national debt to direct reductions in citizen's taxes. Democrats would not have it any other way.

Discussion Questions

1. Which side of the Critical Debate do you feel better fits the facts and your explanations of Canadian policy? Can you add to the debate? For example, should "moral conflicts" be added to the discussion?
2. Why are broad concepts such as *public policy* used in the analysis of Canadian government?
3. Which macro-level approaches to public policy analysis do you favour? Why?
4. Are different theories of public policy necessary in the study of Canada's role in the world? Do the international relations theories of realism and liberalism/idealism help in the analysis?
5. Explain the growth and size of the Canadian state. Does it matter which political party controls the government?

 Visit our new Companion Website at **www.pearsoned.ca/jackson**, where you can use the interactive Study Guide and link to additional resources on topics discussed in the text.

Selected Bibliography

Brodie, M. Janine. *Women and Canadian Public Policy*. Toronto: Harcourt Brace, 1996.

Brooks, Steven. *Public Policy in Canada: An Introduction,* 3rd ed. Don Mills, ON: Oxford University Press, 1998.

————— and Andrew Strich. *Business and Government in Canada*. Scarborough, ON: Prentice Hall, 1991.

Carleton University, School of Public Administration. *How Ottawa Spends*. Ottawa: Carleton University Press, annual. Edited by various scholars in different years.

Clark, J.D. *Getting the Incentives Right: Toward a Productivity-Oriented Management Framework for the Public Service*. Ottawa: Treasury Board, 1993.

Coleman, William, and Grace Skogstad. *Policy Communities and Public Policy in Canada*. Mississauga: Copp Clark Pitman, 1990.

Dobuzinski, Laurent, Michael Howlett and David Laycock, eds. *Policy Studies in Canada: The State of the Art*. Toronto: University of Toronto Press, 1996.

Gillespie, W. Irwin. *Tax, Borrow and Spend: Financing Federal Spending in Canada, 1867–1990*. Ottawa: Carleton University Press, 1991.

Johnson, Andrew F., and Andrew Stritch, eds. *Canadian Public Policy: Globalization and Political Parties*. Toronto: Copp Clark, 1997.

Kuttner, Robert. *Everything for Sale: The Virtues and Limits of Markets*. New York: Alfred A. Knopf, 1997.

Massey, Andrew. *Managing the Public Sector*. Aldershot: Edward Algar, 1993.

McQuaig, Linda. *Shooting the Hippo: Death by Deficit and Other Canadian Myths*. Toronto: Viking, 1995.

Osborne, David, and Ted Gaebler. *Reinventing Government*. New York: Addison Wesley, 1992.

Parsons, Wayne. *Public Policy: An Introduction to the Theory and Practice of Policy Analysis*. Aldershot: Edward Elgar, 1995.

Sproule-Jones, Mark. *Governments at Work: Canadian Parliamentary Federalism and Its Public Policy Effects*. Toronto: University of Toronto Press, 1993.

Strick, John C. *The Public Sector in Canada: Programs, Finance and Policy*. Scarborough, ON: Thompson, 1999.

Tatavolich, Raymond, and T. Alexander Smith. *Cultures at War: Moral Conflicts in Western Democracies*. Peterborough, ON: Broadview Press, 2003.

Tuohy, Carolyn J. *Policy and Politics in Canada: Institutionalized Ambivalence*. Philadelphia: Temple University Press, 1992.

Weaver, R. Kent and Bert A. Rockman, eds. *Do Institutions Matter?* Washington, DC: The Brookings Institution, 1993.

Chapter 15

Canada in the World

Foreign, Trade, Defence and Security Policy

anada is far from self-sufficient in the areas of national security and economic prosperity. Increasingly, the security and well-being of Canadian citizens depend on how they collectively respond to the dangers, constraints and opportunities that flow from the international environment. The world has entered an era of violent turmoil, terrorism, rapid technological change and increasing economic interdependence. The study of Canadian government can no longer legitimately be undertaken without an understanding of global affairs.

Canadian students of international relations have always had considerable difficulty depicting Canada's place in the international power hierarchy. Some scholars simply accept the self-description of Canada as an influential *middle power*. The Canadian government endorsed this notion after the end of the Second World War, when it rallied with like-minded states to contest the domination of the United Nations by the "great powers." After that period, officials and scholars alike began to use the phrase somewhat indiscriminately. Andrew Cooper boldly states that the middle power framework "remains the consensual champion among the competing conceptual frameworks."[1]

However, those on the intellectual left in Canada have never accepted the term *middle power*. Believing that Canada is dominated by US economic interests, they argue that Canada overwhelmingly depends on its southern neighbour for security as well as prosperity. For some, Canada has gone from being a colony of Britain to being a colony of the United States. While this argument has some merit, it is nevertheless true that Canada has frequently opposed US policies and has not always acted as a satellite—Canada's continued opposition to the US embargo of Cuba or the second Iraq war are obvious cases in point.

A third group of academics asserts that Canada is more significant than either a satellite of the United States or a middle power. They claim that Canada is a "foremost" or "major" or "principal" power. Many justifications have been advanced for this high ranking: public opinion surveys show this is how Canadians regard their country; Canada is a member of the prestigious economic club, the G8; and the end of the Cold War reduced the bipolarity of the world and allowed countries such as Canada to ascend to new power positions.

In the final analysis, whether Canadians consider their country to be a major, middle or dependent power may be irrelevant. What matters most is what *other countries* think about Canada's importance and political resources in the global competition. But here, too, the record is mixed.

Determining Canada's relative economic performance in terms of its gross domestic product (GDP) is, of course, much easier than measuring overall international power and significant influence. By this narrow economic measure, Canada certainly hovers in the top group. In 2007, for example, Canada had one of the largest economies in the world, and its per capita income was measured at $31 263 (US). This means that in a global perspective, Canadians are economically very well off. They have a high standard of living that furnishes them with goods, from MP3 players to SUVs,

---

1. Andrew Cooper, *Canadian Foreign Policy: Old Habits and New Directions* (Scarborough, ON: Prentice Hall, 1997), p. 25.

that citizens of other countries consider extreme luxuries. As the former diplomat John Holmes put it, Canada is regarded as "filthy rich."[2]

In this chapter, we first examine the concept of foreign policy. Then we turn to a study of the sources of foreign policy in Canada and a discussion of the three main components of Canadian foreign policy: trade policy, foreign affairs, security and defence policy. In examining Canadian defence, we focus on our role in defence organizations and peacekeeping. We conclude with a section on Canada's security policy since the September 11, 2001, terrorist airplane bombings of the World Trade Center and the Pentagon. Major changes in Canada's intelligence organizations, anti-terrorist laws and decisions to ban certain groups from the country are discussed. The Critical Debate, therefore, invites readers to consider a vital issue—can Canada maintain an "independent" foreign policy in an age of international terrorism?

What Is Foreign Policy?

The study of **international relations** refers to the broad network of relations among states, including the activities of their citizens and non-state institutions. The **global system** is the result of the behaviour of states and also non-governmental actors. The **foreign policy** of countries, on the other hand, is much narrower. It concerns the behaviour of states or governments that has external ramifications.[3] It includes diplomatic and military relations among states, as well as their cultural, economic, technological and, increasingly, ecological and security interests.

There are basic similarities and dissimilarities between domestic and international affairs. Both consist of the struggle for advantage among organized groups with different interests and values. In neither situation can all the interests and values at stake be satisfied; therefore, disputes and conflicts often erupt. In domestic politics, the result of such conflict may extend to violence or revolution. In international politics, the result may be warfare among states or international terrorism.

The main distinction between the two types of politics is that the international system has no world government to mitigate disputes and determine "who gets what, when and how." The world's states exist in a kind of anarchy without a higher form of government to guide them. They compete in a world of insecurity and danger. Of course, states sometimes co-operate for their own interests, and in that sense they develop "law-like" customs and practices that shape their behaviour. On the whole, then, the external behaviour of states is characterized by legal and political anarchy as well as by customs and proper behaviour.

Politics among states takes many forms, ranging from diplomacy to war. Routine relations are carried out by negotiations between diplomats and other officials who assert the claims of their states in "bilateral" (between two of them) and "multilateral" (among several of them) frameworks.[4] Diplomacy may result in agreement or conflict among states. Treaties and protocols may be negotiated and signed. If agreement cannot be reached among states, other approaches to the disputes may be sought, ranging from public complaints to propaganda, subversion and even outright war.

---

2. John Holmes cited in Peyton V. Lyon and Brian Tomlin, *Canada as an International Actor* (Toronto: Macmillan, 1979), p. 70.

3. Robert J. Jackson and Doreen Jackson, *An Introduction to Political Science: Comparative and World Politics*, 4th ed. (Don Mills, ON: Pearson Prentice Hall, 2007), ch. 19–22.

4. For an overview on this subject, see Sir Harold Nicholson, *Diplomacy*, 4th ed. (New York: Oxford University Press, 1988). On diplomacy, see Christer Jonsson and Martin Hall, *Essence of Diplomacy* (London: Palgrave, 2005): on law, see Christopher C. Joyner, *International Law in the 21st Century* (Lanham, MD: Rowman and Littlefield, 2005).

Official relationships outside Canadian borders are conducted in two ways. One involves active multilateral relations, particularly through international institutions. The other is through selective bilateral relations: Canada has missions and satellite offices in most countries of the world. Canada's foreign policy generally aims to build strong relationships with countries that are most important to our economic development and that offer long-term markets for Canadian exports. The parameters of these relationships are determined to a significant degree by defence and security arrangements with the United States and Europe.

Unlike domestic politics, which takes place within a set of more or less developed laws and which is related ultimately to the authority of government and sovereignty of the territory, international politics possesses no international government that can impose its laws on people everywhere. States may join international organizations for mutual benefit, but few accept the authority of a set of decision-makers or laws other than those provided by their own domestic authorities. But, to be realistic, powerful countries often dominate their weaker neighbours and even on occasion colonized them.

Making foreign policy is considerably different from making domestic policy. The state is able to achieve domestic objectives because it has authority over its internal environment. A government has no legal authority outside its borders; as a result, foreign policy decisions must be set within the context of the opportunities and constraints of the international system. In concrete terms, foreign policy–making in Canada differs from domestic policy–making because the former sometimes amounts to little more than striking an image. Only rarely is legislation necessary; often, Parliament and even the bureaucratic elite have little more than spectator status, because the prime minister and the ministers of foreign affairs, international trade and national defence determine initiatives.

Sources of Canadian Foreign Policy

The traditional and somewhat simplistic view of the relationship between politicians and civil servants depicts elected politicians as responsible for determining the policy that bureaucrats administer. Politicians make decisions; bureaucrats merely implement them. However, as we have shown in Chapters 10 and 14, governmental bureaucracy has always been involved in policy-making. This situation is especially evident in the formulation of foreign, security and defence policy areas. where Canada's political leadership depends heavily on bureaucratic expertise and advice concerning the conduct of its international affairs. Nonetheless, the prime minister and the ministers of foreign affairs, international trade and national defence remain at the apex of decision-making.

Prime Minister and Cabinet

Responsibility for foreign policy falls primarily to the prime minister and his ministers. In fact, until 1946 the prime minister personally retained the foreign affairs portfolio. It is only recently that foreign policy has begun to involve the participation of other cabinet members. Recent insistence that the bureaucracy and ministers provide cabinet with alternatives, rather than simply allowing single-option recommendations and attempting to establish national priorities at the cabinet level, has helped to open the foreign-policy process to other departments and ministers. Still, the prime minister remains the central political actor, able to provide leadership and place his or her concerns high on the political agenda. The Mulroney government's implementation of a free trade arrangement with the United States in 1988 and the signing of the North American Free Trade Agreement with Mexico and the United States in 1992 are dramatic examples of the strong role the prime minister plays in foreign affairs. Another example would be Prime Minister Jean Chrétien's decision in 2003 not to join the US war in Iraq, but to send troops to Afghanistan.

When he became prime minister, Jean Chrétien did not bother setting up a specific cabinet committee to look after foreign affairs; responsibility for high policy went directly to cabinet. Chrétien also attempted to distinguish himself from Mulroney in specific policy fields. He cancelled the refit of an Airbus 310 for ministerial travels, talked about making the foreign policy-making process more democratic and began the "Team Canada" trade trips around the world. On first assuming office, Paul Martin continued the tradition of firm prime ministerial control of foreign affairs by initially appointing himself chair of the cabinet committees on global affairs and Canada–US relations. He also immediately went to Washington to meet President George W. Bush and try to smooth damaged relations with the United States.

Stephen Harper has gone even further than Martin. For a minority government prime minister, Harper has been very active internationally. He has made good relations with the United States and the Bush Administration central to his government by starting initiatives in trade and foreign affairs. Harper has also increased expenditures on security and defence policy, supported the United States on climate and missile shield issues at the 2007 meeting of the G8 and extended Canada's military commitmment in Afghanistan to 2011.

The role of the minister of foreign affairs is also extremely important. This minister is not only the chief spokesman on international affairs and the top administrator for the Department of Foreign Affairs and International Trade, but often also the second most powerful person in the cabinet. Louis St. Laurent and Lester Pearson both became prime minister after being secretary of state (now the minister of foreign affairs); Allan MacEachen held the dual position of secretary of state and deputy prime minister for several years. Joe Clark became minister of external affairs after being ousted as leader of the Progressive Conservatives. Peter MacKay's rise to the foreign minister job also illustrates the importance of politics in the selection of ministers. As the leader of the former Progressive Conservative Party, MacKay helped to negotiate its 2004 merger with the Canadian Alliance and then did not stand for the leadership of the newly formed Conservative Party. After throwing his political support to the winner, Stephen Harper, MacKay was rewarded with the position of deputy leader of the party and eventually with the foreign affairs portfolio. When the sitting defence minister encountered numerous difficulties, MacKay was moved to the DND as minister.

The Department of Foreign Affairs and International Trade

The Department of Foreign Affairs and International Trade (DFAIT) is at the centre of the bureau-cratic complex responsible for Canada's external relations. The term *external* was originally used rather than *foreign* because many of the relationships Canada had with other countries involved other members of the British Empire, who were not regarded as foreign in the strict sense. A 1909 act of Parliament established the department and charged it with the conduct of all official communications between the Government of Canada and the governments of other countries in connection with the external affairs of Canada. These responsibilities have grown substantially over time. Today, DFAIT performs two interrelated functions: the coordination and integration of Canada's foreign relations and the implementation of foreign operations.

As the repository of policy advice, the department conducts research and analysis, contributes to domestic policy formulation and provides leadership in establishing policies in the international sphere. The coordination and integration of foreign policy involves providing a framework for the full range of governmental activities overseas, monitoring and influencing other departments' and the provincial governments' international activities, and bringing coherence to a patchwork of priorities and programs. Foreign operations include representation of Canada's interests to other countries, analysis of information regarding developments abroad, negotiation, management and supervision of programs overseas.

While DFAIT retains primary responsibility for the conduct of Canada's foreign policy, other governmental and non-governmental bodies have become increasingly salient to the foreign policy-making process. What were once considered purely domestic matters have increasingly taken on an international dimension. The foreign policy process has become more diffuse within government and also more open, in that non-governmental groups increasingly are involved. Domestically, interest groups, private citizens, business people, and regional interests and their provincial government representatives seek to influence foreign policy decisions. Internationally, a new layer of non-governmental organizations is active, including multinational firms pursuing commercial relations and private groups advocating protection of human rights.

Changes in federal intragovernmental structures have also eroded the dominance of DFAIT in foreign relations. The prime minister's support agencies—the Prime Minister's Office and the Privy Council Office—have become much more influential in foreign policy decisions. New or revamped departments have also eroded the former predominance of the department, to the point of duplicating some of the department's functions. Many contemporary issues require departmental expertise that Foreign Affairs does not possess: environmental policy, energy policy and nuclear and grain exports, for example.

Provincial governments and their agencies, as well as federal departments and Crown corporations, have become important actors in the foreign policy process. While Québec's international activities tend to receive the most publicity, nearly all the provinces are active on the international scene. Western provinces concern themselves with matters such as resource exports and tariffs, while Atlantic Canada has interests in fisheries and offshore resources—all issues with important foreign and trade policy implications.

As a response to the diffusion of the contemporary foreign policy–making process, attempts have been made to coordinate the various departments, groups and policies involved. In 1962, the Glassco Commission, in its review of the Department of External Affairs, recommended structural changes and suggested periodic reviews and reforms of the department's internal structure. Further studies resulted in a 1970 federal White Paper, *Foreign Policy for Canadians*, which led to the establishment of the Interdepartmental Committee on External Relations. In March 1980, the federal government announced further consolidation of responsibilities. Foreign Service officers from the Department of Industry, Trade and Commerce and the Canadian Employment and Immigration Commission were integrated into the Department of External Affairs, along with Foreign Service officers from employment and immigration at the operational level and the field staff from the Canadian International Development Agency (CIDA). The stated purposes of the consolidation were to improve the economy and efficiency of foreign operations without affecting the policy and program development roles of the departments involved; to create a more cohesive and coherent foreign service; to strengthen the role of heads of posts; and to improve the career prospects and experiences of foreign service personnel.

External Affairs was restructured further in January 1982. Its aims were expanded "to give greater weight to economic factors in the design of foreign policy, to ensure the conduct of foreign relations serves Canadian trade objectives, to improve the service offered exporters in an increasingly competitive international marketplace and to ensure policy and program coherence in the conduct of Canada's range of relations with the outside world."[5] The functions of trade policy and promotion of the Department of Industry, Trade and Commerce were therefore transferred to external affairs, completing the consolidation on economic matters. Then, in 1992, another shuffle took place and the primary responsibility for immigration was returned to the Department of Employment and Immigration.

5. Marcel Massé, "Department of External Affairs: Changes to Organizational Structure," memo no. USS-241 (Department of External Affairs, July 8, 1983), p. 1.

From 1994 to 2003, the prominence of economic objectives was reflected in a two-minister team. The minister of foreign affairs was responsible for the management of the department, but was supported by the minister for international trade. They, in turn, were backed up by two secretaries of state—one for the Asia-Pacific region and one for Africa and Latin America. These ministers were to provide a link between the concerns of government outside and within Canada. Concern for coordination was also evident at the senior bureaucratic level of the department.

After a short period with another new system during Paul Martin's tenure as PM, Stephen Harper once again imposed a two-minister team on Foreign Affairs and International Trade (DFAIT): Peter MacKay and David Emerson. A minister of international co-operation and a secretary of state were added to help as were four parliamentary secretaries. At the head of the department were two deputy ministers—one for foreign affairs and one for international trade.

After the Conservative victory in 2006, DFAIT was mandated to

- ensure Canada's foreign policy reflects true Canadian values and advances Canada's national interests;
- strengthen rules-based trading arrangements and expand free and fair market access at bilateral, regional and global levels;
- work with a range of partners inside and outside government to achieve increased economic opportunity and enhanced security for Canadians at home and abroad.

Parliament and Political Parties

In liberal democracies, legislatures and political parties provide an important link between citizens and their government. In Canada, Parliament provides a forum for public debate, while parties mobilize public opinion, coordinate political activity and function as intermediate instruments of political activity for those not elected to office. Therefore, in the realm of foreign policy formulation, Parliament and political parties provide channels through which diverse pressures from the domestic community are brought to bear on the policy process.

For example, Question Period in the House of Commons provides MPs with the opportunity to raise foreign policy issues. The four House of Commons Standing Committees on Foreign Affairs, International Trade, Defence, and Veterans Affairs and the relevant Senate committees have conducted major reviews of various aspects of Canadian foreign and defence policy in addition to performing their routine function of examining the budgetary estimates of the foreign policy establishment. Special parliamentary task forces and subcommittees have been formed to report on important issues such as Canadian–US relations and peacekeeping.

In 2006, Parliament renewed the Standing Committee on Public Safety and National Security. While talk continued that its members should be sworn in as privy councillors so they could have groundbreaking access to government-classified intelligence information, this had not taken place at the time of writing. The issue provides members with

Canadian Forces in Afghanistan.

a dilemma because if they did have access to information, they probably would not be allowed to divulge any wrongdoings or illegal spying that they might learn about.

Parliament's oversight function requires that committees overlook the functions of the intelligence community. However, the role of Parliament and political parties in making foreign policy is constrained by the powers of the government. Control over foreign policy is firmly in the hands of the executive. While cabinet takes into consideration the anticipated reaction of Parliament to cabinet's policy deliberations, formal parliamentary debate rarely has a decisive impact on government behaviour in the foreign policy field.[6] Because of the nature of diplomacy, governments have almost exclusive control over information in this area. Requirements for discretion over matters involving national security and relations with foreign countries therefore limit the impact outside groups and individuals can have on the foreign policy process; the government's ability to assume policy and make treaties with foreign countries without ratification by Parliament constrains the impact of government backbenchers, opposition parties and societal groups. The fact that the government can take the country to war without Parliament's approval is the capstone of this argument.

Non-Governmental Actors: Interest Groups, the Media and Public Opinion

Other means of expressing international policy interests and viewpoints include representations from interest groups, the media and popular opinion as measured by polling. How much influence each has varies from issue to issue.[7] Some interest groups possess sufficient expertise or political clout to be asked by government to participate in the process. For example, representatives of domestic interest groups are included among the advisors to Canadian delegations attending international conferences. Most groups, however, must gain access to politicians and bureaucrats through meetings, presentation of position briefs, the media and/or mobilization of their constituents. The number of interest groups concerned with foreign policy has grown substantially over the years. New issues such as terrorism, nuclear waste, acid rain, survival of whales and seals, the over-fishing of cod and turbot and the disruption of Arctic communities by resource development have joined traditional foreign policy issues, including the wars in Afghanistan and Iraq, global security and nuclear proliferation.

The media's impact on the foreign policy process is indirect. Overall, the press has little effect on the substance of foreign policy, but has a very significant impact on the day-to-day activities of the individuals who make it. By providing coverage of external events and taking editorial positions, the media disseminate information and opinion and, at times, prescribe solutions, thereby articulating public and elite foreign policy concerns.

Professional diplomats are critical or ambivalent about the role of public opinion in foreign policy–making. Many believe that it is not an appropriate guide for the conduct of foreign policy. Because of the constraints diplomats face in the international arena, as well as the complexity of the issues, the impact of public opinion may at times be detrimental:

6. Important exceptions include the Suez Crisis of October 1956, in which the Liberal government supported US-sponsored efforts to force British, French and Israeli troops to withdraw from captured Egyptian territory; the issue of equipping Canadian fighter planes and its missile system with nuclear warheads during Diefenbaker's prime ministership; and the TransCanada Pipeline debate. See Dewitt and Kirton, *Canada as a Principal Power*, pp. 171–77; and Lawrence Martin, *The Presidents and the Prime Ministers* (Toronto: Doubleday, 1982), ch. 12.

7. On the impact of interest groups and the media on policy, see Lisa Young and Joanna Everitt, *Advocacy Groups* (Vancouver: UBC Press, 2004). More specifically, on foreign policy, see "Domestic Causes of Canada's Foreign Policy," *International Journal*, vol. 39, no. 1 (Winter 1983–84); and Elizabeth Riddell-Dixon, *The Domestic Mosaic: Domestic Groups and Canadian Foreign Policy* (Toronto: Canadian Institute of International Affairs, 1985).

> *From the professional's traditional perspective the international working
> environment is . . . a world of nuance and subtlety and craft, and certainly no
> place for the amateur. But nuance, subtlety, and craft are not the most obvious
> characteristics of the constituent public, or of their opinions. Public reactions to
> foreign policy issues, especially but not solely in political-security contexts, are
> often one sided, ill informed, transient, fickle, and given, at their worst, to
> emotional excess.*[8]

While public opinion may not have an immediate impact on the specifics of policy, it has the capacity to set limits on what policy-makers can do "politically." Policy-makers must take into account opinions and anticipate the public's reactions to various policy alternatives. Thus, decision-makers follow election campaigns and public opinion polls not as a source of policy ideas but rather as an indicator of the public's potential response to various policy options. Some elections convey a sense of what the public wants: in 1988, the free trade issue was crucial, whereas in 1993, 1997, 2000, 2004 and 2006, there was very little debate on foreign policy.

Provinces and Foreign Policy

Foreign and defence policy is essentially a task for central government. The United States' Senate and the German Bundesrat (both of which embody a federal element) have a role in the ratification of treaties, Germany and Switzerland allow sub-units treaty-making powers, and Belgium even allows the language communities to sign treaties in their areas of competence. But this is not the case in Canada, where the federal government is the primary actor in international relations.

Despite federal control of foreign affairs, provincial governments have a keen interest in the conduct of Canadian foreign policy and over the years have attempted to increase their international visibility, often by opening foreign offices. Such offices are important to provinces that depend heavily on external trade. Provincial governments sponsor trade and cultural missions, receive visiting foreign dignitaries, participate in ongoing multilateral conferences and become involved in joint federal–provincial programs.

Fields over which provinces have concurrent or exclusive jurisdiction have become increasingly important in the international arena, and this necessitates the inclusion of provincial concerns in the formation of Canada's foreign policy. Provincial interests are important to the extent that "the range and frequency of provincial international activity is now sufficient to complicate the design and conduct of Canadian foreign policy, indeed, to frustrate central control over foreign policy in some areas."[9]

Federal–provincial conflict in this field is exacerbated by the absence of a clear delineation of constitutional authority regarding treaties and international relations. Section 132 of the *Constitution Act*, for example, refers only to the implementation of treaties affecting the British Empire. Moreover, the range of powers vested in the provinces necessitates at least some measure of involvement in foreign policy. Consequently, there has been, and to some extent continues to be, both legal and political debate over the proper role of the provinces in foreign affairs.

Advocates of *exclusive* federal competence in all international matters argue that the prerogative of treaty-making power for Canada was vested exclusively in the Queen in 1867, as stated in section 9 of the *BNA Act*. Through a process of evolution from 1871 to 1939, direct power over foreign affairs devolved to Canada to be exercised by the government in the name of the governor general. At no

8. Denis Stairs, "The Press and Foreign Policy in Canada," *International Journal*, vol. XXXI, no. 2 (Spring 1976), p. 142.
9. P.R. Johannson, "Provincial International Activities," *International Journal*, vol. 33, no. 2 (Spring 1978), pp. 357–78. See also Douglas M. Brown, "Provinces have a Role in Canadian Foreign Policy," *Federations*, Special Issue, 2002, pp. 11–12.

time during this period did the provinces acquire treaty-making power. Rather, as evidenced by the new Letters Patent issued to the governor general by the Crown in 1947 and the *Seals Act* of 1939, the federal government was given all powers previously exercised by the British Crown.

The complex situation has necessitated a functional approach that recognizes the concerns of both levels of government. While federal government might like to prevent provincial government initiatives when possible, jurisdictional realities necessitate a framework that accommodates them. The federal government has even issued what it perceives to be the proper international role for the provinces:

- The provinces have no treaty-making powers, but they do have the right to enter into private commercial contracts with foreign governments, as well as to make bureaucratic agreements of a non-binding nature with foreign governments.
- The provinces may open offices in foreign countries in pursuit of their legitimate needs and interests in that country, so long as the offices only engage in arrangements of a non-binding nature.
- The provinces claim the right to be involved in the formulation stages of treaty-making activities when the subject matter of the treaty falls within provincial legislative competence.
- The provinces may be included in Canadian delegations attending international gatherings and play a role in formulating and enunciating the Canadian position, when the subject matter falls within provincial legislative competence.[10]

Québec Foreign Policy   The province of Québec shares many of the same international interests and objectives as the other provinces. However, because of the sovereignist aspirations of some of its governments, it also has its own unique agenda. Québec nationalism is discussed in Chapter 7, but it is important to note here the impact of the nationalist agenda on Québec's relations with foreign countries and the consequent strain often placed on Ottawa–Québec relations.

With the advent of the Quiet Revolution in 1960, the Québec government assumed the role of protector of Québécois culture, language and ethnicity. Initially, the emphasis was on developing special relations with the international francophone community in order to bolster Québec's new interest in science, commerce and management. This generally manifested itself in the form of delegations to international conferences on francophone education, culture and training. As Kim Nossal notes, however, once the Parti Québécois came to power in Québec in 1976, what had begun as "an external expression of functional provincial interests" became "an issue of symbolic national interest for the Québec government."[11] Québec began to challenge the federal government's monopoly over the conduct of Canada's foreign relations. At the same time, the nationalist goal began to shift from seeking special provisions within Canada to bringing about the separation of Québec from Canada and international recognition of Québec's sovereign status. France provided international support and encouragement for this project.

In 1980, when the Québec government held the first referendum on sovereignty-association, its political leaders sought to impress on the world that it would be a responsible member of the international community. The White Paper released by the Lévesque government before the 1980 referendum included a full foreign policy program for an independent Québec. Again, in 1995, the PQ government released a pre-referendum plan stressing that an independent Québec would continue traditions of peacekeeping and multilateral involvement. To win international acceptance, the government stressed that it would work jointly with Canada in these endeavours.

10. Johannson, "Provincial International Activities," pp. 361–62.
11. Kim Richard Nossal, *The Politics of Canadian Foreign Policy*, 3rd edition (Scarborough, ON: Prentice Hall), p. 317.

Québec separatists' goal of forming a sovereign state has created conflict within Canada and has perplexed foreign governments. The primacy of the Canadian government in external relations is universally recognized. However, protocol, particularly in France and the United States, has often been awkward as Québec has sought, and sometimes received, treatment that created implications for domestic politics in Québec and also for Canada–France and Canada–US relations.

During the 1995 referendum, French president Jacques Chirac promised that France would recognize Québec as a sovereign country after a Yes vote. This was a break from the more qualified approach of "non-interference but non-indifference" that had held since the 1980 referendum. On the other hand, the United States increased the volume of its standard line—that the United States prefers a united Canada, but it is up to Canadians to make their own decisions. Two weeks before the 1995 referendum, then US secretary of state Warren Christopher noted that no one should assume that agreements such as the North American Free Trade Agreement (NAFTA) would remain unchanged if Québec became independent. A few days later, President Bill Clinton said that "a strong and united Canada has been a wonderful partner for the United States, and an incredibly important and constructive citizen throughout the entire world"—a "great model for the rest of the world and I hope that can continue."[12]

Over the past few decades, the federal government has made several changes in the content and process of foreign policy to meet Québec's challenges. For example, the countries of la Francophonie have been singled out for increased development assistance, Québec's participation at summits of la Francophonie has been highlighted, and French-language services in Canadian missions abroad have increased.[13]

In the meantime, Québec continues to assert itself abroad. Between 1964 and 2008, it made over 550 international agreements and undertakings. Although these are not binding in international law, they do indicate Québec's proactive approach to foreign policy. As of 2008, Québec has major offices in Tokyo, Mexico, Brussels, London, Munich, Paris, Rome and Washington. It also staffs 5 smaller missions in the United States and trade branches and bureaus in 12 other countries. As Louise Beaudoin, Québec's former separatist minister of intergovernmental relations said, "We all believe we have to project ourselves as a nation outside Québec."[14] Recent federalist governments in Québec have toned down the rhetoric, but even Liberal premier Jean Charest took part in a France-inspired trade mission to Mexico and emphasized the need for an international convention on cultural diversity. His government continues the PQ's initiatives—appointing a minister of foreign affairs, employing 400 quasi-diplomats and spending over $100 million on international activities.

Canadian Trade Policy

Canada's prosperity depends greatly on exports of goods and services and foreign investment in its currency, stocks and bonds. Foreign trade is vital to Canadian economic interests. Canada has a low ratio of population to land and resources and is by necessity one of the largest trading states in the world. The domestic market of over 33 million people is too small to sustain all of the flourishing industries, so well over one-third of the gross domestic product (GDP) depends on exports. Most of these exports are from primary industries based on natural resources, of which Canada has an abundance.

12. Ibid., p. 325.

13. Robert J. Jackson and A. Dann, "Quebec Foreign Policy?" in *New Nationalism* (New York: Praeger, 1979). For a US view, see Charles Doran, *Why Canadian Unity Matters and Why American Care* (Toronto: University of Toronto, 2001).

14. *The Globe and Mail*, May 20, 2002.

Canada has three main kinds of natural resources. The first is agricultural land, which climatic and soil conditions make amenable to cultivating crops and raising livestock. It is limited to the southernmost part of the country and is steadily encroached upon by industrial development and urban sprawl. Canada is one of the largest exporters of agri-food products. The second category is non-renewable resources, such as mineral deposits. Canada is a leading exporter of minerals—crude petroleum, natural gas, iron ore, nickel and copper. The third type of natural resource consists of renewable resources, of which wood, fish, fur and grains are, or have been, particularly important to Canada's economic growth.

This present-day pattern of the Canadian economy was laid out in the colonial period. Basically, Canada exports primary resources and imports secondary or manufactured products. Most Canadians live and work in urban, industrialized areas, but agricultural products, lumber and mineral resources provide the bulk of our exports and pay for imported manufactured goods. In 2006, Canada exported $440 billion worth of merchandise and imported $397 billion. In particular, manufactured goods, motor vehicles and parts, metals, minerals, pulp and paper, lumber and sawmill products, natural gas and wheat sell extremely well. However, Canada consumes more *services* (such as tourism, freight and government procurement) from other countries than it sells, and pays more interest to investors abroad than it earns on foreign investments.

Canadian trade is conducted on a bilateral basis, and requires careful day-to-day management of issues that arise between Canada and its main trading partners. However, the fact that the contractual framework for most of Canada's bilateral trade is provided by international treaties illustrates the important multilateral dimension of economic relations. As an export-oriented economy, Canada's prosperity is vitally linked to maintaining a multilateral, transparent and rules-based world trading system.

Canada and Global Economics

At the end of the Second World War, the leading economic countries met at Bretton Woods in the United States to reorganize the wartorn economies of the trading world. They decided to fix (peg) the exchange rate of the US dollar to the gold standard and other currencies to the dollar. The currencies could be "unpegged" only within stipulated regulations. Eventually, however, the rules unravelled due to pressures on the US dollar, and the entire exchange system became unregulated. Since then, currencies have floated freely.

As for international trade, the US, Britain and Canada were the principal proponents of a new order that resulted in 1947 in the **General Agreement on Tariffs and Trade (GATT)**, an agreement that sought to establish a trading order based on reciprocity, non-discrimination and multilateralism. It covered over 80 percent of world trade and included most major industrialized countries. The GATT treaty set out a code of rules for the conduct of trade; as an institution, it oversaw the application of the trade rules and provided a forum in which countries could discuss trade problems and negotiate reductions in trade barriers.

The main benefit of the GATT for Canada was that it provided a contractual basis for Canada–US trade relations while facilitating the expansion of trade relations with other countries. As a signatory of the GATT, Canada could negotiate basic resource needs with its powerful southern neighbour more easily. In its efforts to improve the world economy and reduce protectionism, the GATT held several rounds of negotiations to amend the trading rules. Discussions, named the *Uruguay Round*, lasted seven years and were completed in 1994. Major breakthroughs were made in solving difficulties concerning international trade. The participants agreed to transform the GATT secretariat into a somewhat more powerful **World Trade Organization (WTO)** and to reduce tariffs on a long list of goods. Tariffs on industrial goods, for example, were reduced, and technical agreements were concluded on issues in the service sector, including banking, insurance, telecommunications, broadcasting and so forth, and on intellectual copyright for subjects such as patents and licences. As of 2008, there are 151 members in the WTO.

In November 2001, trade ministers met in Doha, Qatar, and launched a new round of multilateral trade negotiations. This round continues to chug along. Its mandate is further liberalization in the fields of agriculture and services, clearer rules on subsidies and trade remedies, and improvements to dispute-settlement mechanisms. Canada maintains a permanent mission at the WTO in Geneva, Switzerland, where it stresses three priorities: reforming trade in agriculture, opening markets for Canadian goods and services and strengthening the international rules of trade.

As the global economy grows, so, too, does the importance of international economic organizations such as the **International Monetary Fund (IMF)** and the **World Bank**. Both organizations were set up at the end of the Second World War.[15] The purposes of the IMF are to foster stability in money markets, to encourage co-operation among states on monetary matters, to aid in the establishment of a payment system and to promote international trade. Currently, 185 states are members of the IMF, which lends funds to member states and provides technical assistance to their economies. The importance of each state in the IMF is based on its voting strength as determined by its financial contributions to the fund. The World Bank also lends money. It focuses on countries or states that commercial banks or other lenders will not support, and generally tries to reduce poverty among its members. A total of 185 countries belong to the World Bank. It makes decisions in a manner similar to that of the IMF. It tends to support problem projects and has large holdings with several developing countries. By tradition, its president is nominated by the US and has always been an American.

Canada also belongs to many other multilateral organizations concerned with the global economy and development. The best known is the **G7**, which includes the world's seven largest industrialized democracies—United States, Japan, Germany, Britain, France, Italy and Canada—and the Commission of the European Community. (It becomes the G8 when Russia is included.) This prestigious group holds annual economic summits, keeping up a tradition that began in 1975 at Rambouillet in France. The summits have taken on a semi-permanent character, although there is no permanent secretariat. They have become huge media events, but, primarily, they provide the opportunity for leaders to discuss trade issues and international economic topics.

The meetings are particularly important to Canada for several reasons. First of all, the economic summits provide recognition of status; political leaders want to be part of this elite group. Canada joined largely due to US and Japanese sponsorship. But more important, Canada has a major stake in the economic relationships among the "Big Seven." Of the seven, Canada is the most affected by the economic policies of the United States. Prime ministers usually express strong satisfaction with how the G8 serves Canadian interests and foreign policy; however, many observers believe that the summits are meaningless exercises. A more balanced view might attest that the meetings are significant, but that their importance is easy to exaggerate.

Canada has also been affected by world trends. The rise of multinational corporations has combined with more open trade rules to develop what many observers call *globalization*. Its impact on the Canadian economy has been dramatic. For example, recently almost every province's economy has depended more on exports to foreign countries than on trade with other Canadian provinces. Goods and services are not the only things that flow more easily around the world—so, too, does money. There has been an emergence of a *global economy* in terms not just of trade but also of all the

15. On capitalism, globalization and international institutions, see Robert J. Jackson and Doreen Jackson, *Introduction to Political Science: Comparative and World Politics* (Toronto: Pearson Prentice Hall, 2007), ch. 21.

CLOSE-UP ON
International Economics

GLOBALIZATION, GLOBALONEY OR GLOBALPHOBIA

The term **globalization** has become very popular. It is defined as the integration of states through trade, communications and contact. It is widely used to explain various major international events, from world economic relations to world terrorism. In fact, it has become so widespread and controversial that its critics have termed it nothing more than capitalism or even "globaloney." In response, its proponents say that we now have "globalphobia."

Globalization is a reorientation of cultural, economic, political and technological activities and processes in such a way that they transcend state or country borders. It is a cluster of interconnected factors making states more economically interdependent and transforming world politics, including the integration of goods, services, capital and markets. But that is not all. The speed of the flow of capital around the world—calculated at almost $2 trillion per day—and the growing importance of non-state actors have also undermined the state's ability to regulate its own economies.

The state retains its primary responsibilities in the military security fields but increasingly shares powers with broader forces in other aspects of international life. To some extent the forces of globalization are determining which countries and individuals win or lose in the world market.

Do you think the term *globalization* helps or hinders your understanding of Canada's place in the world?

---

elements of wealth creation—finance, investment, production, distribution and marketing—which are increasingly being organized regionally and globally. The changing structure of the world economy has seriously affected the Canadian economy and trade patterns in other ways as well. New technologies are developing rapidly and forcing industries in developed countries, such as Canada, to adapt to increasingly competitive conditions or be left behind as standard technologies are taken over by developing countries with lower labour costs.

International and Multilateral Organizations

For historical and political reasons, Canadian foreign policy has always been directed predominantly toward Europe (especially Britain) and the United States. Political relations, defence and economic policies, therefore, have all developed certain basic continuities. Long-standing defence ties, considered in detail later in this chapter, are with the US and Western Europe through the North Atlantic Treaty Organization (NATO) and North American Aerospace Defence Command (NORAD). Multilateral relations are primarily conducted through the United Nations and its related agencies. Bilateral political and economic relations are strongest with the US, the Commonwealth, Western Europe and French-language communities. But Asia, especially China and Japan, has recently become even more important to Canada than Europe in purely economic relations.

Canada and the United Nations

Canada played a central role in creating the United Nations and in directing its evolution as an international organization. Sponsorship of the United Nations by the Canadian government demonstrated the radical change from the pre-war policy of isolationism to postwar internationalism as a means of avoiding war. Both Louis St. Laurent, who became secretary of state for external affairs in 1946, and Lester Pearson, who followed in that position, were avowed internationalists. Pearson wrote in his memoirs, "Everything I learned during the war confirmed and strengthened my view as a Canadian that our foreign policy must not be timid or fearful of commitments but activist in accepting international responsibility."[16] The United Nations seemed the natural medium for bringing states together to promote peace.

Initially, the UN had 57 charter members and Canada was a major participant in the 1950s. But the club was too restrictive. In 1955, Paul Martin, Sr., chair of the Canadian UN delegation, persuaded the UN Security Council to agree to a package deal for accepting new members. New members flooded in, and today Canada is no longer a principal player, but merely one of 192 countries.

As president of the UN General Assembly, Lester Pearson was responsible for introducing one of its most important innovations: the *peacekeeping force*. The UN Charter provided for a standing army, but one was never created. However, no other organization has arisen to replace the UN as a forum for the discussion of world problems. Canada has been involved at the UN in several significant areas, including the law of the sea, the north–south dialogue between rich and poor nations, human rights, chemical warfare, abolition of land mines, halting the traffic in small arms and putting an end to the conscription of children. Canada is also a strong supporter of the UN's many specialized multilateral agencies—the World Health Organization, the International Labour Organization and the International Monetary Fund, among others—which have earned considerable respect throughout the world. Another agency, the International Civil Aviation Organization, has its headquarters in Montréal. These agencies are all working to improve the quality of life, particularly in the large number of new states represented at the UN.

The rather tarnished contemporary image of the UN may be a result of exaggerated expectations of what it can accomplish. John Holmes summarized the situation this way: "When people worry whether the UN has lived up to the ideals of the Charter, in some ways it's the wrong question. Rather than see whether it has been able to carry out a mandate carved in stone it may be better to ask whether it has been able to grow and fit in with changing circumstances. . . . To a great extent it has."[17] Holmes was correct. (See the discussion of Canadian peacekeeping starting on page 554.)

Canada is the seventh-largest contributor to the UN regular budget—in 2006, it paid 2.8 percent of the budget, or about $201 million, for regular and peacekeeping costs. It has been elected six times to membership in the Security Council. Canada also shares in leadership roles at the UN. In 1998, Canadian Louise Fréchette was appointed as the deputy secretary general of the UN, and in 2004, Louise Arbour became the first Canadian commissioner for human rights. In 2006, Canada appointed career diplomat John McNee as ambassador to the United Nations.

CLOSE-UP ON Public Policy

ETHICAL FOREIGN POLICY?

Soon after his appointment as minister of foreign affairs in 1996, Lloyd Axworthy began to speak of the need for a more ethical dimension in Canada's foreign policy. While not denying the need for realistic self-interest in making foreign policy, he stressed the role of morality in this process. To involve the public more in the foreign policy process, Axworthy set up a series of national forums on Canada's international relations and an advisory committee to the minister. The government sought new policies concerning child soldiers, land mines and the International Criminal Court (ICC). Denying that only states should determine foreign policy, Axworthy declared that the UN Commission on Human Rights should "develop standards that apply globally, and... monitor their implementation without the bias inherent in any purely national review." *

Do you share this concern about "human security" or do you think Canadian foreign policy should be based mostly on Canada's national interests? Are the two objectives compatible?

---

* Lloyd Axworthy, Speech to the 54th Session of the UN Commission on Human Rights, 1998.

---

16. Lester B. Pearson, *Mike: The Memoirs of Lester Pearson, vol. I: 1897–1948* (Toronto: University of Toronto Press, 1972), p. 283.

17. John Holmes quoted in the *Toronto Star*, November 20, 1982.

The Commonwealth

At Confederation, Canada was part of the British Empire, exercising autonomy in domestic policy but dependent on Britain in foreign affairs. The First World War was the catalyst for Canada attaining complete autonomy, and for the transformation of the Empire into the Commonwealth. The transition was achieved at a succession of imperial conferences that culminated with the Balfour Declaration in 1926, by which the dominions within the British Empire were equal, autonomous communities united by a common allegiance to the Crown, and freely associated as members of the **Commonwealth of Nations**.[18]

This sentiment was enshrined in the 1931 *Statute of Westminster*, which formally laid the old Empire to rest. The Commonwealth at that time consisted of Britain, Australia, Canada, Newfoundland, the Irish Free State, the Union of South Africa and New Zealand. Now, almost 8 decades later, it numbers 53 member states and embraces more than a third of the world's population and about a quarter of the Earth's surface. Louis St. Laurent and Lester Pearson played important roles in the evolution of this new Commonwealth. Pearson particularly was a key figure in negotiating an acceptable formula for admission of new republics—a development that changed the essentially Anglocentric focus of the Commonwealth association. Canada has consistently encouraged the strengthening of the association as a vehicle for practical co-operation among member states.

Commonwealth heads of government meet regularly every two years and sponsor various fields of technical co-operation, scholarships and the Commonwealth Games. There are no binding rules of membership, and decisions are made by consensus rather than by vote. Canada contributes about $25 million a year to Commonwealth activities and is the second-largest contributor.

Perhaps the most valuable feature of Commonwealth meetings, however, is simply the opportunity for heads of state and governments to meet relatively informally and discuss vital common issues such as human rights and intra-Commonwealth aid. Canada played an important role in Commonwealth activities over apartheid in South Africa. Canadian leaders worked assiduously to keep racial cleavages from dividing the organization over the quarrels that led to South Africa's departure until its eventual return in June 1995 with Nelson Mandela as the newly elected president. The 1991 meeting in Harare, Zimbabwe, was used by Canada mainly to highlight issues of human rights, democratic development and equality for women. Perhaps the most important work since then has been Canada's participation in the Commonwealth Action Group, which helped to encourage democracy in Nigeria, Pakistan and Sierra Leone. Recent summits, such as Malta's in 2005, have concentrated on trade issues. In December 2006, Fiji's membership was temporarily suspended after a military *coup d'état*.

La Francophonie

In 1970, the French-language community formed its own organization similar to the British Commonwealth. Under Lester Pearson's leadership, and especially under Pierre Trudeau, the Canadian government encouraged strengthening Canada's ties with francophone countries, mainly through multilateral programs and organizations such as the Agency for Cultural and Technical Cooperation. The agency's programs centre on three main areas: development, education and scientific and technical co-operation. The issue of Québec's participation as distinct from Canada's has occasionally caused overt hostility between the respective governments when the federal government interpreted Québec's actions as a challenge to its primacy in foreign policy. However, since 1971, Québec has had

18. In 1947, the term *British* was dropped from the name to reflect the changing nature of the Commonwealth.

"participating government" status in the agency, a privilege that was also extended to New Brunswick in 1977. In 1986, **la Francophonie** was born in Paris. Canadian representation was fleshed out with members from Québec and New Brunswick using a controversial formula that implied an enhanced role for the provinces in foreign affairs. Today, there are 53 members of the organization. There is a summit of heads of government every two years while the ministers of foreign affairs meet annually.

The organization has had limited success. In 1995 at Cotonou, Benin, Prime Minister Chrétien tried to encourage la Francophonie to become "more active in political debate."[19] However, the members could not commit themselves because they were split over what policy to adopt on a number of issues. The 1999 meeting in Moncton, New Brunswick, was particularly contentious. Opponents of the conference complained that the leaders of Burundi, Burkina Faso, Congo and Rwanda should not have been invited because of their poor records on human rights. Chrétien worked around the criticism by allowing the leaders into the country but proclaiming, "Let us work to ensure that the legacy we leave to future generations is a Francophonie made up of countries where democratic values are embraced." Journalists in English and French Canada used the occasion for making unusually vitriolic comments about the leaders from the four countries in question. *The Globe and Mail* ran a cartoon showing a uniformed African dictator seated on a pile of skulls. A well-dressed Frenchman was shown sipping champagne and saying, "Still, his accent is flawless!" The franco–New Brunswick paper *L'Acadie Nouvelle*, on the other hand, proclaimed Moncton to be the "centre of the Francophone universe."

The effort to strengthen Canada's two languages internationally is shared by both Liberals and Conservatives. At the 2006 meeting in Bucharest, Romania, Stephen Harper said, "I plan to make sure that Canada's bilingual and multicultural personality is reflected on the international scene."

Canada and the OAS

Canada was late to join the **Organization of American States** (**OAS**), the main institution that unites the 35 states of the western hemisphere. It was formed in 1948 from the Pan-American Union at a time when Canada was primarily concerned with seeking security through NATO and the UN, and hence did not seriously consider joining the organization. The issue of Canadian membership first became significant in the early 1960s. Proponents argued that Canada should become a member of the hemisphere group and thereby establish prestige in the region and increase trade opportunities. Opponents warned that if Canada did join the OAS, the country would become embroiled in disputes between the United States and Latin America. The government accepted the latter view and the issue was not seriously raised again as a foreign policy option until the 1980s.[20] During this period, Canada maintained a limited "permanent observer" status at the OAS.

Over time, arguments for joining the OAS became stronger. Advocates believed that membership would give Canada a stronger voice in planning development strategies for Latin America and would allow Canada to make a contribution in the field of human rights. As countries such as Mexico and Venezuela became stronger, the fear that Canada would be caught in disputes between the United States and Latin America diminished. Canada finally ratified its full membership in the OAS in January 1990. One of the most important results has been increased co-operation between Canada and other OAS members to stabilize democracy throughout the region. Canada also found that issues such as trade, drug enforcement, terrorism and the environment were aided by membership in the OAS.

19. *The Globe and Mail*, December 24, 1995.

20. Robert J. Jackson, "Canadian Foreign Policy in the Western Hemisphere," in Viron P. Vaky, ed., *Governance in the Western Hemisphere* (New York: Praeger, 1984), pp. 119–34.

Prime Minister Harper's July 2007 trip to Colombia, Chile, Barbados and Haiti was intended to revive interest in the region. He called for a re-engagement in the area, referring to it as "our neighbourhood." Two-way trade between Canada and Latin America has grown to about $39 billion (CDN) and Canada has long-standing free trade arrangements with Chile (1997) and Costa Rica (2002). During his 2007 trip, Harper called on the 15 states of the Caribbean Community (Caricom) to begin discussing a new free-trade deal with Canada.

Canada's Relations with the United States

United States president John F. Kennedy said that "geography made us neighbours, history made us friends and economics made us partners." He was correct. There is no more important external relationship for Canada than that with the United States. But the long history of co-operation in NATO and NORAD belies the fact that much of Canada's history, including Confederation itself, was inspired by efforts to be independent of the United States and protected from US domination.

The United States is Canada's largest trading partner. Approximately $710 billion in trade crossed the border in 2005 (and roughly $2 billion of goods and services each day)—by a large margin, Canada–US business is the world's leading two-way trade relationship. The United States accounted for about four-fifths of Canadian exports and two-thirds of imports. On the other hand, Canada took only a small percentage of total US exports and provided even less of its imports. Even at these significantly lower percentages of total trade, Canada is the most important trading partner of the United States. Leading Canadian exports to the States include passenger autos and chassis, communications and electronic equipment, aerospace components, natural gas, forest products, and crude petroleum and petrochemicals. In turn, Canada imports motor vehicles and parts, electronics (e.g., computers), crude petroleum and aircraft. Both import and export trade with the United States have grown dramatically in recent years. (See the next section on free trade.)

Relations with the United States clearly are critical to Canada's overall well-being. The high degree of dependence is not, however, mutual. Although both geography and history provided the backdrop for an early special relationship, that tie has inevitably been one-sided. This fact was perhaps best illustrated in symbolic terms by the relative urgency assigned to initial political visits at the highest level. The first Canadian prime ministerial trip to Washington was in 1871; the first official US presidential visit to Ottawa did not occur until over seven decades later, in 1943. The relationship between these unequal neighbours over the years has been friendly, but, on the part of Canadians, necessarily guarded, as the attitudes of US leaders have fluctuated from extremes of "annexation fixation" to complete indifference. Ulysses S. Grant, for example, aspired to absorb Canada into the US in time for his 1872 election bid—in fact, he wanted Britain to cede Canada in exchange for damage caused by a British ship![21]

There are significant differences between the two states that affect every aspect of the relationship. The governments differ in structures and functions, and subtle differences deriving from these variations are not always understood or appreciated. In the early 1980s, for example, a bilateral fishing agreement achieved after long negotiations was scuppered when the US Senate refused to give its assent. This ratification procedure, which is foreign to the Canadian political system, brought howls of outrage on the Canadian side of the border. In Canada, ratification is part of the powers of the executive and there is no constitutional requirement for the government to seek parliamentary approval. This incident was not unusual. In fact, according to Christian Wiktor, there have been more than two hundred treaties negotiated by US administrators with various

21. Martin, *The Presidents and the Prime Ministers*, p. 12.

countries over the past two hundred years that were never ratified by the Senate, eighteen of which concerned Canada directly.[22]

There are other important differences. The two governments have disparate approaches to the roles of government in the economy. In Canada, both federal and provincial governments take active roles in the marketplace to a degree unknown and unacceptable in the United States. Perhaps the most obvious difference, however, is that Canada's population is only approximately one-tenth that of the US. We have earlier discussed some of the inevitable repercussions of such a disparity; basically, it makes Canada vulnerable to pressures from the United States in the fields of culture, economy and defence.

The underlying economic and cultural differences between the two countries surface periodically as policy conflicts. This was particularly evident in the late 1970s and early '80s, a time of tensions between the two countries, which were deep in an economic recession. The poor economic climate exacerbated cleavages when each country acted to protect and strengthen its home industries. Disputes arose in such areas as fisheries, trucking regulations and advertising rights.[23] Most conflict, however, centred on the Liberal government's Foreign Investment Review Agency (FIRA), set up to monitor and restrict foreign investment, and the National Energy Program (NEP), designed to increase Canadian ownership of natural resources. Both impinged on foreign interests, especially those of the United States. The conflict continued until the 1984 Progressive Conservative government got rid of the NEP and drastically changed FIRA, eventually turning it into Investment Canada.

Measures such as the NEP and FIRA were adopted by the Canadian government to regulate escalating foreign ownership, which was seen as depriving Canadians of the ability to control and benefit from the country's industries, particularly resource-rich ones. Canada's prosperity is linked to the rest of the world not only through trade, but also via the importation of foreign capital. We have seen that the level of foreign investment has been particularly high. As one expert put it,

> *Canada cannot be compared with capital-rich economies such as the American and British. The combination of a small population and huge natural resources necessitates, even in the best of economic times, reliance on external financing to satisfy our economic expansions.*[24]

Individual Canadians save at a higher rate than Americans, but the country does not come close to satisfying its own capital requirements. In recent years, however, much foreign investment has not been "new" US capital but has come from within Canada itself. Foreign subsidiaries simply retain earnings and depreciation reserves and put them back into the Canadian economy as investments.

Most foreign capital enters the country in the form of direct investment, not interest or portfolio investment. This means that rather than involving bank loans or bonds, which can be paid off, investment in the Canadian economy brings a high degree of control and ownership by foreigners, especially in the manufacturing and resource sectors. Branch plants allow Canadian importation of technology and US market access, but they also make Canada subject to US values. They are subject not only to market forces and Canadian government regulation, but also to US interests.

22. *The Globe and Mail*, May 7, 1981.

23. For an interesting view of Canada–US tensions, see Stephen Clarkson, *Canada and the Reagan Challenge* (Toronto: Lorimer, 1982). For a clear-cut anti–free trade position, see Mel Hurtig, *The Betrayal of Canada*, 2nd ed. (Toronto: Stoddart, 1992).

24. James R. Niniger, president, The Conference Board of Canada, quoted in the *Ottawa Citizen*, May 14, 1984.

There can be little doubt that foreign investment improves Canada's standard of living and has helped to transform Canada into an industrialized country. However, there is equally little doubt that it has greatly increased the dependence of Canada's economy on the United States.

Irritants in Canada–US relations are ongoing. The US ban on Canadian cattle following the BSE (or mad cow disease) incident, limitations on Canada's participation in the reconstruction of Iraq, and levies on softwood lumber are among the most public issues that concern our bilateral relations. Sometimes, the tensions infect political discussions, as when an aid to Prime Minister Jean Chrétien referred to President George W. Bush as a "moron" at a NATO summit.[25]

Free Trade: FTA and NAFTA

One of the most controversial ongoing trade issues concerns free trade, a recurring theme in Canada's relationship with the United States. The issue originated—and caused heated debate—as far back as the 1870s. In the early years of statehood, Conservative prime minister Sir John A. Macdonald won the hearts of Canadians with his National Policy of high tariffs to protect fledgling Canadian industries. Much later, in 1911, Sir Wilfrid Laurier failed to win re-election partly because he wanted to eliminate tariffs on less than one-quarter of cross-border trade. He could not compete with the Conservative opposition slogan, "No truck or trade with the Yankees."

Much later, in the early 1980s, controversy developed over whether to move toward full free trade across the border or, as the Liberal government recommended in 1983, to build *sectoral free trade* in selected items, among them steel, agricultural equipment, urban mass transit equipment and "informatics." This type of policy had been implemented in the 1965 Auto Pact and had proven extremely successful in increasing the flow of Canadian automobiles and parts across the US border. Advocates of further sectoral free trade argued that it would raise productivity, lower inflation and create jobs, unlike protectionism, which, it was argued, hinders increased trade.

However, the sectoral free trade policy was abandoned when Brian Mulroney brought the Progressive Conservatives to office in 1984. The new government's position was buttressed by the 1985 report of the Royal Commission on the Economic Union and Development Prospects for Canada (the Macdonald Commission), which argued strongly in favour of *general free trade*.[26] Opponents of this new policy argued that free trade would destroy many Canadian companies (especially in textiles and footwear) and inevitably lead to the formation of common institutions that would be dominated by the US, thereby eroding Canada's political sovereignty.

In the course of his first mandate, Mulroney reversed the PCs' earlier position *against* free trade and entered into negotiations for a comprehensive, general trade agreement with the United States. The reasons for this shift are not completely known, but he received strong political support from Québec and the Western provinces for doing so. At the time, many Canadian business people were worried about a growing demand for protectionism in Washington due to the massive US trade deficit. Two major trade disputes came to the fore while Canada–US free trade negotiations were taking place. In 1986, the United States introduced a countervailing duty against softwood lumber imported from Canada, a source of trade worth about $4 billion annually to Canadian companies. Canada negotiated with the US to apply its own 15 percent export tax rather than

---

25. For details on these issues since September 11, 2001, see the excellent collection, Thomas O. Enders, "Issue on the State of the Canada–United States Relationship" in *The American Review of Canadian Studies*, vol.33, no.1 (Spring 2003). For a left-wing Canadian perspective on these issues, see Daniel Drache, *Borders Matter: Homeland Security and the Search for North America* (Halifax: Fernwood, 2004).

26. *Report of the Royal Commission on the Economic Union and Development Prospects for Canada*, vol. 1 (Ottawa: Minister of Supply and Services, 1985).

submit to the countervailing duty. Later the same year, the United States imposed a five-year tariff on Canadian red cedar shakes and shingles, and Canada was forced to retaliate.[27]

On September 26, 1985, Canada formally requested that the United States enter negotiations for a comprehensive free trade agreement. Two years later, the deal was concluded; the legal text was released and signed by President Reagan and Prime Minister Mulroney on January 2, 1988. In the meantime, federal Liberal leader John Turner called on the Liberal-controlled Senate to block the deal. The 1988 election ensued with the free trade deal as the primary election issue. When the Tories won the election, they allowed the agreement to come into being on January 1, 1989.

The *Canada–United States Free Trade Agreement* (FTA) was intended to enhance market access and reduce trade conflicts between the two countries. The agreement provided a set of *dispute resolution mechanisms* and the goal of gradual elimination of all tariffs between the two countries. Special and technical agreements were made in the fields of services, investment, finances, energy, agriculture, automobiles, cultural industries and even alcoholic beverages. However, free trade as such was never completed. Each country reserved the right to continue to impose trade retaliation in the form of countervailing duties, anti-dumping or other trade remedies. Each country also reserved the right to change its trade legislation after the agreement came into force.

Canadian opposition to this deal was widespread and centred on three issues. First, it was argued that the deal did not obtain *secure* access to the US market for Canadian products since US trade remedies continued to apply. Second, the agreement was attacked as giving away too much in investment, financial services, agriculture, energy and service sectors and getting too little in return. An important issue also centred on the definition of what constituted a trade "subsidy"; opponents of the deal argued that Canadian social programs—such as unemployment insurance and provincial health insurance—could fall into such a category and therefore be subject to retaliation. And, last, the deal was attacked by some provincial leaders for eroding provincial powers and by some federal politicians for reducing the ability of Canadian governments to act freely in the economy and hence for reducing Canadian sovereignty.

Although the 1988 election results authorized the free trade deal,[28] questions about the impact of the trade agreement on Canadian interests and, indeed, on Canadian sovereignty, remained.[29] Almost before the ink was dry on the agreement, the Canadian government began negotiations with Mexico and the United States for a *North American Free Trade Agreement* (NAFTA).[30] This agreement called for a three-country deal that incorporated the FTA and expanded it to include clauses on intellectual property, medical services and more explicit rules about national treatment. In May 1993, Parliament approved the legislation, allowing the government the right to implement the agreement if side deals on labour and the environment were worked out among Canada, Mexico and the United States. In the November 1993 general election, the Liberals under Jean Chrétien promised to reopen some of the most controversial parts of the agreement for renegotiation. However,

---

27. For a summary of these disputes, see Leyton-Brown, "Canada–U.S. Trade Disputes and the Free Trade Deal," in Maureen Molot and Brian W. Tomlin, eds., *Canada among Nations 1987: A World of Conflict* (Toronto: Lorimer, 1988).

28. It should be noted, however, that more Canadians voted *against* the PCs, who espoused free trade, than voted for them. See the election figures in Chapter 10.

29. The arguments in favour of the free trade deal have been carefully summarized in John Crispo, ed., *Free Trade: The Real Story* (Toronto: Gage, 1988). An informative summary of the opposition arguments is found in Marjorie M. Bowker, *On Guard for Thee* (Hull: Voyageur, 1988). For a longer view, see Robert Bothwell's *Canada and the United States* (Toronto: University of Toronto Press, 1992).

30. Much more opposition came from outsiders than from political parties. See Maude Barlow and Bruce Campbell, *Take Back the Nation* (Toronto: Key Porter, 1991) and Mel Hurtig, *The Betrayal of Canada*, 2nd ed. (Toronto: Stoddart, 1992).

TABLE 15.1 **The NAFTA Equation**

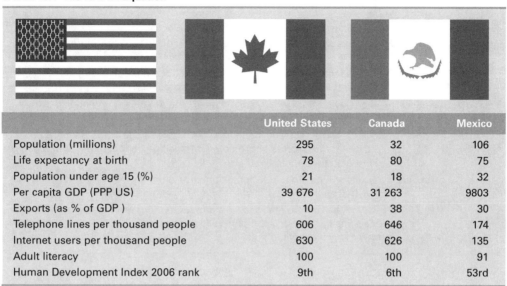

	United States	Canada	Mexico
Population (millions)	295	32	106
Life expectancy at birth	78	80	75
Population under age 15 (%)	21	18	32
Per capita GDP (PPP US)	39 676	31 263	9803
Exports (as % of GDP)	10	38	30
Telephone lines per thousand people	606	646	174
Internet users per thousand people	630	626	135
Adult literacy	100	100	91
Human Development Index 2006 rank	9th	6th	53rd

*Figures in US dollars.

Source: Adapted from the *Human Development Report, 2006* (New York: United Nations, 2006).

despite the Liberal victory, the agreement was made law on January 1, 1994, without the resolution of any of the issues Chrétien had promised to reopen. The agreement linked Canada to a market at that time of 383 million people and a combined economy of $7 trillion.[31] (For basic information on the three countries and NAFTA, see Table 15.1 and also Table 15.2 on the next page.)

The free trade debate has continued, but all four major parties seemed to agree that, as captive neighbours on this continent, the only reasonable policy for the three states to adopt is one that fosters a mutually satisfactory relationship. In 1994 at the Summit of the Americas, negotiations were announced to extend NAFTA and create a hemispheric free trade zone, but negotiations have broken down on this controversial proposal and progress in unlikely for some time. (Canada already has free trade with Costa Rica and Chile.) The same year, Canada signed the Asia-Pacific Economic Cooperation (APEC) agreement, which periodically proposes the establishment of a Pacific free trade and investment zone.

In 2005, Canada, Mexico and the United States signed an ambitious Security and Prosperity Partnership (SPP), an initiative aimed at deepening the integration of the three countries. The agreement calls for government actions to increase competitiveness in three hundred fields, from specific trade irritants to common standards in products to border controls. Some critics have called the SPP a "grand conspiracy" toward a North American Union such as the European Union. Others say such arguments are nothing but fear-mongering, but that much still needs to be done in building a security perimeter, building a customs union to eliminate rules-of-origin difficulties and reducing the unnecessary discrepancies in regulations. So far, progress has been slow. The 2007 Summit at Montebello Québec continued the efforts to increase security and prosperity across the region. Topics such as how to handle pandemic influenza were added to the agenda on security and trade.[32]

31. Robert J. Jackson, et al., *North American Politics: Canada, USA and Mexico in Comparative Perspective* (Don Mills, ON: Prentice Hall, 2004).

32. See the Council on Foreign Relations' *Building a North American Community, Task Force Report 53, Washington, 2005.* To keep abreast of new details on this topic, visit www.spp.gov.

TABLE 15.2 NAFTA Framework: Facts About the North American Free Trade Agreement

Tariffs:	Eliminated over a 15-year period. Levies on half of the more than 9000 products phased out immediately, 65 percent of them within five years
Agriculture:	Some tariffs on all farm products phased out but producers given 15 years to adjust to duty-free status on sensitive products
Automobiles:	To qualify for duty-free treatment, the North American content of cars (then 50 percent) must reach 62.5 percent within eight years
Financial services:	Mexico allows US and Canadian banks, brokerage firms and insurance companies free access after a six-year transition period, during which bans on foreign ownership are phased out
Textiles:	Mexico avoids high duties on shipments to the US and Canada as long as the clothing is made from yarns and fabrics from North America
Trucking:	Mexico allows foreigners to invest in its trucking firms, and US, Mexican and Canadian trucking companies allowed to do business on cross-border routes previously prohibited

Since September 11, 2001, Canada has been joining the United States and to some extent Mexico in forging an enhanced North American or continental security network. The issue is how to make North America's borders remain as free and efficient as possible while providing a security framework for all three countries. New structures and procedures sprout almost daily. A 30-point plan (later increased to 32) between Canada and the United States calls for Canadians to be integrated into the US foreign terrorist tracking task force; issue new visitor visa policies; combine joint units to assess information on travellers; send more immigration control officers overseas; implement new biometric identifiers for documents; pass a safe third-country agreement; expand border enforcement teams; and enhance Project North Star. All these things are meant to improve communication and co-operation between Canadian and US law enforcement personnel.

Canada's Relations with Other Areas
Canada and Western Europe

Canada's historical and cultural ties with Western Europe have always been close, and Canadian governments have counted on this region of the world to counterbalance US influence. In the 1970s in particular, fears were rife that Canada was too dependent on US markets. It was at this time that Prime Minister Pierre Trudeau initiated his so-called *Third Option*, whose purpose was to increase trade with Western Europe and Japan in order to diminish reliance on the United States. As an extension of that philosophy, Trudeau achieved a weak contractual link with the European Community, known as the Framework Agreement. However, the document contained little but platitudes, and trade with the United States continued to increase while business with Western Europe stagnated.

The Canadian–British link, Canada's strongest tie in Western Europe, weakened after Britain entered the European Common Market in 1973. The Canadian share of the British market decreased, and the trade balance eventually tilted in Britain's favour, largely because of North Sea oil exports to Canada. Despite this, Britain was Canada's second-largest single buyer of Canadian goods in 2006 and educational and travel links continue to be very strong today.

The countries that make up the European Union (EU) constitute the world's largest trading entity. The EU is one of Canada's largest markets for agricultural products and several resource-based products, including forest products and fish. In 2006, the EU received only about $34 billion of Canadian exports. Since this figure represents only a small percentage of total EU imports, the relationship is much more important to Canada than to the EU.

European Union members generally want access to Canada's pulp, oil, uranium and other mineral resources, and in return would like to offer Canadians manufactured goods. The Canadian government is justifiably reluctant to accept these nineteenth-century conditions of trade. On the other hand, access to European Union markets is also difficult for Canadians to achieve, and despite traditional political ties, the trade relationship is unlikely to improve much.

In 1990, Canada and the EU signed the Transatlantic Declaration, which brought the two together on good terms but did very little for economic interests. In 1996, the two signed a Joint Action Plan (JAP), which is very broad in scope but does not include a free trade agreement as envisaged at the beginning of the negotiations. In 2007, the EU-25 and Canada had a two-way trade of $78 billion (see Figure 15.1 for a breakdown of Canada's exports).

Canada and the Pacific Rim

While Canadian trade with Western Europe stagnated in recent years, it increased rapidly in the Pacific Rim. In 1983, for the first time, Canada traded more with Asia than with Western Europe. It is increasingly evident that trans-Pacific trade is another opportunity for a counterbalance in the US-dominated Canadian economy; it may eventually be Canada's new "third option."

Countries of the Pacific Rim—Japan, Korea, Taiwan and Singapore—in particular are challenging world markets with outstanding management, technological and production techniques. While Japan's economy has slowed, those of the "Asian tigers" continue to grow strongly. From 1973 to 2005, Japan was Canada's second-largest national trading partner. In 2006, two-way trade between the countries reached only $23 billion—a low total compared to previous years. Despite its recent sluggish economy, Japan remains one of Canada's fastest growing export markets among its major trading partners. Canadian–Japanese trade relations are those of a resource-rich supplier and a

FIGURE 15.1 **Canada's Major Merchandise Export Markets, 2006**

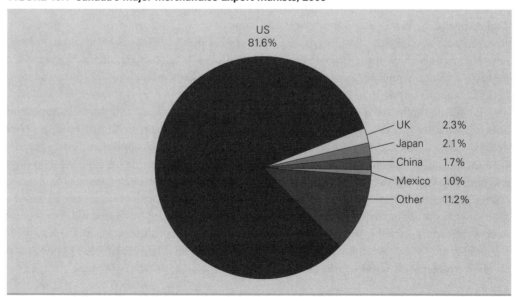

US 81.6%

UK 2.3%
Japan 2.1%
China 1.7%
Mexico 1.0%
Other 11.2%

Source: Adapted from DFAIT, *Canada's State of Trade*, at www.international.gc.ca/eet/pdf/07-1989-DFAIT-enpdf. Accessed September 12, 2007.

resource-poor industrial nation: almost all of Japan's exports to Canada are fully manufactured, while most of Canada's exports are either raw materials or semi-processed products. China, too, is looming as an important trading partner for Canada, as it now has one of the largest economies in the world and is likely to become an even more significant major international player. In 2006, China was Canada's fourth-largest recipient of exports and, in turn, sells Canada a whopping $35 billion of merchandise.

Canada, Developing Countries and the Rest of the World

Under the World Trade Organization (WTO), the developing countries of the world enjoy various types of differential and preferential treatment in an effort to nurture their nascent agricultural and manufacturing industries. Some developing countries have economic situations similar to Canada's and thus compete in many of the same areas. Many export competitive raw materials. On the whole, therefore, developing countries continue to be more important trade partners for Japan, the US and the EU than for Canada, because Canada competes with some developing countries to sell raw materials. Another serious problem inhibiting trade with developing countries is their enormous debt burden.

Since Canada has no coherent foreign policy that embraces the entire hemisphere in all facets of foreign policy (perhaps because, in some senses, they are not a coherent single economic entity), Canadian relations with countries in South and Central America and the Caribbean consist mainly of bilateral trade and political, economic and humanitarian interests.[33] A high percentage of Canada's exports to the area are processed or manufactured goods. Canadian imports from the area are about twice the volume of the exports. They consist primarily of petroleum products, particularly from Venezuela and Mexico, and tropical food products, as well as some manufactured products from Brazil and Mexico. Although trade is paramount, Canada is also an active investor in the region. Canadian banks have been active in Latin America and the Caribbean since the nineteenth century.

Economic and commercial matters are the most concrete evidence of Canadian relations south of the United States. Despite protests from the United States, Canada maintained political relations with Cuba after the 1959 revolution led by Fidel Castro. Today, Canada continues trade and maintains political relations with Cuba, even in the face of a US embargo. The Canadian government has disagreed with the ideological commitment and some of the policies and activities of the Cuban government, but, unlike US administrations, it does not condemn Cuba and communism. In 1996, Jesse Helms, then chair of the United States Senate Foreign Relations Committee, likened Lloyd Axworthy, Canada's minister of foreign affairs, to Neville Chamberlain and his appeasement of Hitler for Canada's opposition to the US embargo against Cuba.

Canada naturally has links with many other countries and areas, which, although important in other ways, are not very significant in an economic sense. Relations with Australia and New Zealand are long-standing and close because of the early Commonwealth connection. These countries are a small but important part of Canada's global trade relationship. Canada has important political and humanitarian interests in Africa and the Middle East, but little trade has developed from these links. Canada's relations with Turkey were not improved when, in 2006, Canada recognized the 1915 deaths of an estimated 1.5 million Armenians as genocide. Mention should also be made of Russia, the former republics of the old USSR and other Eastern European countries. These states account for only a tiny percentage of Canada's total trade, but Russia is a major grain importer and therefore economically important to Canada.

33. These are considered in Robert J. Jackson, "Canadian Foreign Policy and the Western Hemisphere." For a historical summary, see D.R. Murray, "The Bilateral Road: Canada and Latin America in the 1980s," *International Journal*, vol. 37, no. 1 (Winter 1981–82), pp. 108–31.

Canadian Defence Policy

The objectives of defence and security policy are intertwined with foreign policy objectives and, more specifically, with deterring war. Over time, Canadian objectives in this field have varied according to changes in the international strategic environment and the political configuration of the country. But at all times, there have been commitments to preserving the independence of Canada, its borders, institutions and values, to pursuing the peaceful settlement of disputes and to preventing hostilities and warfare.

Almost all Canadians accept such aspirations. However, the policies and programs required to fulfill these goals are constantly in dispute. Should Canada continue to be a part of a collective security arrangement such as NATO or, like Sweden, be completely independent? Should Canada be part of the nuclear bomb club or continue to keep nuclear devices off native soil? Even if there were agreement on such general policies, an analyst would still need to know what programs would be required to execute them. For example, should government funds be spent on arms rather than on social programs? Should Canadians be deployed overseas in potential combat zones? Should Canadians participate in international peacekeeping missions? What should be Canada's policies toward international terrorism? How should the military be used in Bosnia, Haiti, Somalia, Kosovo and Afghanistan? Is Iraq another possibility? Darfur?

These are deep and difficult questions that touch on the basic values of the country. Given that Canadians like to think of themselves as essentially a non-militaristic people, what visible security policies have been developed? Furthermore, what set of policies could be designed to protect Canadian citizens and to defend the second-largest land mass and the longest coastline in the world?

Since the end of the Second World War, Canada has sought security in collective agreements— it has not been neutral. The mission of the Department of National Defence and the Canadian Forces is to defend Canada and Canadian interests while contributing to international peace and security. As stated on the Department of Defence's website in 2007, the DND's mission is

- to protect Canada;
- to defend North America; and
- to contribute to international peace and security.

The Context of Canadian Military Policy

The basic pattern of the international environment today is one of sharply decreased East–West differences and a large increase in local, religious and regional conflicts throughout the world, particularly in the Middle East and the developing world. Explanations for the continuation of hostile acts throughout the globe are beyond the scope of this book, but they include economic, cultural, religious and ideological frustrations and aggression.[34]

In the face of issues such as international terrorism, wars in Iraq and Afghanistan, and large peacekeeping requirements, coupled with the fact that the annual number of conflicts and wars around the world has been relatively stable for a decade, it could be said that Canada's defence forces are insignificant. However, given the size of Canada's population and the few direct conflicts in which Canada is engaged, its military commitment is reasonable. Still, the expenditure on defence does not represent a high or very serious commitment and the government faces many critics inside and outside the country.

---

34. See Jackson and Jackson, *Introduction to Political Sciences: Comparative and World Politics*, chs. 20 and 21. On international conflict, see Robert J. Jackson and Philip Towle, *Temptations of Power: The United States in Global Politics Since 9/11* (London: Palgrave, 2006).

In 2006, approximately $15 billion was included in the budget for the defence envelope. This placed Canada seventh among NATO budgets, but still near the bottom of NATO contributors in terms of military spending as a percentage of GDP. Canada spent only 1.1 percent of GDP on defence. One author put it plainly: "Canada has disarmed itself, unilaterally, unashamedly, and dangerously."[35] After taking office, Stephen Harper's Conservatives began to repair this problem by delivering an increase of approximately $3 billion over the following three years.

North Atlantic Treaty Organization   Canada is a member of the **North Atlantic Treaty Organization(NATO)**. Until the fragmentation of the Soviet Union in late 1991, the competition between East and West or, as it was often phrased, between democracy and communism, was best understood in the context of the division of Europe by an Iron Curtain, giving rise to two powerful military alliances—NATO and the Warsaw Pact. Since the disintegration of the USSR, however, in purely military terms, the basic global pattern can be characterized as one of sharply decreased East–West hostility in the developed world and continuing competition and conflict in many developing countries.

At NATO's 1991 meeting in Rome, member countries agreed on a new strategic concept to replace the Cold War strategy. The alliance members concluded that a full-scale, surprise attack from the East had effectively been removed and that the new threats were more multi-faceted and multi-directional. Risks, they calculated, were more likely to emerge from economic, social and political difficulties, including ethnic rivalries and territorial disputes, than from the East. This thinking led to a reduction in the overall size of allies' forces, a reduced forward presence in central Europe and a lessened reliance on nuclear weapons.

NATO's membership has also shifted eastward. In April 1999, Hungary, Poland and the Czech Republic joined the alliance, making it an organization of 19 members. In November 2002, seven new members were admitted—Bulgaria, Estonia, Latvia, Lithuania, Romania, Slovakia and Slovenia. The body of 26 members has expanded NATO's responsibility for Eastern European territory and made the organization more cumbersome to administer. The April 2008 NATO summit is expected to admit three more countries to the organization: Albania, Croatia and Macedonia.

In 1995, NATO deployed 60 000 troops and took charge of the peacekeeping mission in Bosnia-Herzegovina. Later, in 1999, it took the lead role in Kosovo. After 9/11, NATO invoked for the first time Article 5 (the mutual defence principle, which called on member states to support the US in its fight against terrorism. Despite its non-involvement in the Iraq war, NATO began training Iraqis in 2004, and in 2006, it took command of the stabilization force in Afghanistan (ISAF), providing muscle for Karzai's government, and becoming the first and only NATO mission outside the Euro-Atlantic region.

The focus of Canadian defence policy has changed dramatically over the years. At the end of the Second World War, Canada punched far above its weight in international affairs.[36] Canadian soldiers fought valiantly in the First and Second World wars and in the Korean War. By the time the armistice was signed ending the First World War, in 1918, 56 634 Canadian soldiers had been killed and 150 000 wounded. In the Second World War, over a million Canadians served in the Armed Forces and 42 004 died in the fighting. In Korea, there were 1557 casualties and 312 deaths. In other words, Canada made outstanding contributions to all three of those war efforts.

When the Cold War began, Canada entered perhaps its most significant period in international affairs. Fear of Russia pushed the number of "peacetime" Canadian troops to over 120 000. Fourteen thousand Canadian troops were kept in Europe, and Canada spent roughly 7 percent of its GDP on defence. It ranked fourth among NATO partners on defence spending per capita.

35. Andrew Cohen, *While Canada Slept: How We Lost Our Place in the World* (Toronto: McClelland & Stewart, 2003), p. 37.
36. Ibid., p. 47.

However, the Cold War, which had defined world politics after 1949, ended suddenly and with astonishing speed when the Berlin Wall fell in 1989. The two superpowers no longer threatened to collide in warfare: the United States and Canada no longer had a reason to combat Soviet expansionism overseas. Canada did not pull out of NATO, but it removed all of its bases from Europe, and government budgets earmarked for NATO were reduced. The numbers of men and women in the service and the amount of funds spent on defence have continually fallen since then and Canada's strategic importance has declined accordingly. Recent budgetary increases for the military by the Harper government are working their way into the process and improving Canada's defence posture to some extent.

Canada's geographical location between Russia and the United States is no longer as important as it used to be. For example, while North American Aerospace Defence Command (NORAD) remains operative, the North Warning System has been downsized and many CF-18 interceptors have been mothballed. NORAD's tasks have also shifted to new emerging issues—in 1991, NORAD was given responsibility for counter-narcotic monitoring and surveillance and, as of 2001, initiatives against terrorism have dramatically increased.

The September 11, 2001, terrorist attacks in the United States shook Canadians' faith that North America is immune to overseas attack. Canada has participated in the hunt for terrorists in the Arabian Gulf and joined other NATO countries in supplying troops and advisors for Afghanistan. Anti-terrorism activities have increased the budgets of the DND and focused attention on a new series of responsibilities and priorities.

Canada and the United States have also announced an expanded role for NORAD as a possible beginning to Canada's participation in the US ballistic missile-defence (BMD) program. As of 2004, NORAD added radar and satellite monitoring responsibilities to the US command in charge of developing a future missile-defence system. As Canada holds the deputy commander position in NORAD, any enhancement of the role of this institution draws Canada further into its policy development. Domestic controversy over this topic ranges from the viewpoint that if Canada joins it will have "lost its soul," to the belief that it would be "irresponsible" not to join with the Americas in this new defence system. Former prime minister Paul Martin turned down any direct Canadian participation in the program. However, unlike his Liberal, NDP and Bloc Québécois opponents, Stephen Harper has implied on occasion that he favours some positive moves in this direction, and his comments at the June 2007 G8—that Russia should agree to negotiations with the US on putting missile interceptors in Poland and the Czech Republic—appeared to strengthen this position. Harper has promised a vote in Parliament, but since he has only a minority government, this will most certainly not take place soon.

Organization of National Defence

The Department of National Defence (DND) was created by the *National Defence Act* in 1922. Led by the minister of national defence, the DND is involved in the formulation and implementation of Canadian defence policy. Foreign affairs and defence policies are inextricably interrelated, and therefore they concern both the minister of foreign affairs and the minister of defence. The defence minister specifically, and the cabinet generally, are accountable to Parliament for national defence matters.

The responsibilities of the defence minister include the control and management of the department itself, the Canadian Armed Forces and all matters relating to works and establishments concerned with Canada's defence. The minister is also responsible for Defence Construction Canada, a Crown corporation that functions as a contracting and construction supervisory agency for major construction and maintenance projects of the DND.

The senior *civilian* advisor to the minister is the deputy minister of the DND. It is the deputy minister's duty to ensure that governmental policy direction is reflected in the administration of the DND and in military plans and operations. The senior *military* advisor to the minister is the chief of the defence staff (CDS), who is responsible for the conduct of military operations and for the preparedness of the Canadian Forces to meet commitments assigned by the government.

The Canadian Forces

The Canadian Forces are the military element of the government and are part of the Department of National Defence.[37] In 2007, the total military personnel in the Canadian Forces was 77 000—including 62 000 regulars and 21 000 primary reservists and 4000 Canadian Rangers.

Since 1968, the Canadian Forces have had a unified structure. They perform a number of roles, including the surveillance of Canadian territory and coastlines to protect Canadian sovereignty, the defence of North America in co-operation with US forces, the fulfillment of NATO commitments and the performance of international peacekeeping roles. The military engages in combat operations, mine-clearance and protection of displaced persons. It also provides assistance to other federal government departments, civil authorities and civilian organizations—for example, air and ground transportation for royal visits, meetings of foreign government officials, sporting events, emergency and disaster relief, and a search and rescue program. Finally, the forces train allied military personnel in Canada and also provide military training for developing countries.

Expenditure on defence is not, however, without critics. Moderate opposition is expressed particularly in the writing of centre-left scholars.[38] Further left-leaning opponents claim that there is a military-industrial complex that controls governments, especially in the United States. Their basic argument is that powerful industrialists and military planners collude to keep international tension high in order to sell expensive weapons to the government. This assertion is usually coupled with a belief that such expenditures would be better used in other fields such as health-care, education and social welfare. Its exponents believe that the costs of Canadian defence could be reduced by a radical shift toward neutralism in international affairs. The issue is raised here not to resolve it, but to point to a fundamental debate over whether government funds should be spent on the military or on other policy areas. This issue has been compounded because of scandals in the department (see the "Close-Up on Public Policy: The Shame of Somalia").

Where do these expenditures on defence go? About three-quarters of the funds are for the combined maritime, land and air forces. They basically cover costs related to the defence of Canada's territory, including a special partnership with the US in NORAD and membership in NATO. Although Canada is involved in strategic nuclear planning, it has no nuclear weapons of its own. The country's chief role in NATO has until recently involved stationing Canadian land and air forces in Europe as part of the forward defence strategy. In 1994, Canada closed these bases and brought all troops home from Europe. Canada's commitment to NATO is now lower than its allies would prefer.

Peacekeeping, Peace Enforcement and Terrorism

In keeping with the fundamentally "non-militaristic" nature of Canadian security policy, the government's most visible activity has been in the field of international peacekeeping and peace enforcement. Since 1947, Canada has sent troops to almost all UN and NATO peacekeeping missions and has sometimes served in other coalitions with like-minded countries. Over 100 000 members of

37. Formally, the governor general of Canada, as the sovereign's representative, is commander-in-chief of the Canadian Forces.
38. Desmond Morton, *Understanding Canadian Defence* (Toronto: Penguin/McGill Institute, 2003).

CLOSE-UP ON
Public Policy

THE SHAME OF SOMALIA

The Department of National Defence has been under severe organizational stress over the past decade. Since the end of the Cold War, budgets have been slashed and the number of troops cut. But none of these cuts has affected activities and morale as much as the Somalia tragedy.

Canada's glowing image as a peacekeeping nation was severely tarnished after an incident that occurred in Somalia in 1993. Members of the Canadian Airborne Regiment in Belet Huen tortured and killed a young Somali, Shidane Arone, whom they had caught entering the Canadian compound. Several members of the Canadian Forces were charged, and in 1995 the regiment was disbanded. The minister of national defence initiated a civilian-led public inquiry. Following revelations that documents relating to the scandal had been destroyed, several officers resigned, including, eventually, General Jean Boyle, chief of the defence staff.

Before the affair was over, David Collenette also resigned as minister of defence (although for other reasons). He was replaced by Doug Young, who immediately declared there would be another "shake-up" in the defence establishment. Young forced the commission of inquiry to terminate its investigation by the spring of 1997, well before it had intended to do so. Later, he announced that in order to prevent cover-ups there would be somewhat more independence for military police in future investigations and less reliance on the standard chain of command.

the Canadian Forces have served in hostile areas all over the world. Often, the military has been joined in these tasks by police forces, Elections Canada, the Canadian Red Cross and other agencies. In 1994, Canada established the Lester B. Pearson Canadian International Peacekeeping Training Centre in Cornwallis, Nova Scotia, to honour that former prime minister and to train students in the theoretical and practical aspects of peacekeeping.

Most recently, however, there are signs of a continuing weakened commitment to peacekeeping. Until 1989, Canada had served in every UN peacekeeping mission—it was the world's leading peacekeeper. Since then it has become more selective and has refused to help in many of them. As the nature of peacekeeping changed, with many peacekeeping missions shifting from the traditional task of supervising ceasefires and separating combatants to actually *enforcing* the peace, Canada has begun to lose its will to participate in the dangerous task. Canada's significance as a peacekeeping nation relative to other countries has thus declined significantly. Many countries, especially from the developing world, now contribute far greater numbers of troops than Canada does.

In the twenty-first century, the number of missions has accelerated dramatically, and although Canada has opted out of many, it has been involved in the largest of them, including the Balkans, East Timor, Haiti, Africa and Afghanistan. At its peak, there were 3000 Canadian soldiers, sailors and air force personnel in the Arabian Gulf region and Afghanistan. In the summer of 2007, by far the largest numbers of Canadian troops abroad on overseas missions were in Afghanistan (2545 of 2675 in total)—a peace-enforcement engagement.

Aislin, *The Gazette* (Montreal). Reproduced with permission.

Over the years, then, Canada's military commitment has changed because of world requirements and government priorities. In 1993, Canada withdrew its battalion from Nicosia, where it was part of the UN contingent to prevent hostilities between Greek and Turkish Cypriots. As of 2008, however, Canada continues to retain smaller numbers of troops in scattered places such as the Golan Heights, Jerusalem, Sinai, Democratic Republic of the Congo, Sierra Leone and the Sudan (see Table 15.3). On the whole, Canadian participation in UN peacekeeping represents an important contribution to global and Canadian security, and enhances Canada's international reputation, but recently most of the activity has been in one state: Afghanistan.

Canada in Afghanistan

The Canadian military is playing a vital role in Afghanistan. It is not a peacekeeping mission. Canadian efforts are determined by the Afghanistan Compact, a five-year agreement of the Afghanistan and foreign governments for the stabilization of the country in the face of continued violent threats from the Taliban and al Qaeda.[39]

The Afghanistan contribution consists of about 2500 Canadian personnel divided into three missions. The first, Operation Athena, is the commitment to the NATO-led International Security Assistance Force (ISAF) sanctioned by the United Nations in December 2001. General Rick Hillier, chief of the defence staff, was the first commander of ISAF. It consists of five regional military commands and, since 2005, of the Provincial Reconstruction Team (PRT), which consists of both military and civilians carrying out various types of reconstruction in the Kandahar region. The second, Operation Archer, is the work of the Canadian military personnel who contribute to the US-led Operation Enduring Freedom while working in Kabul, at the Bagram air base, and with Afghan military operations and training. The third, Operation Argus, involves the Strategic Advisory Team working directly for the Afghan government.

The invasion and occupation of Afghanistan, unlike the attack on Iraq, was sanctioned by the United Nations. But the job remains largely unfinished and the threat of global terrorism from bases in that country is growing. The West is largely failing to prevent the Taliban resurgence and their renewed

CLOSE-UP ON
Bureaucrats with Guns

CANADA'S STRATEGIC ADVISORY TEAM IN KABUL

Canada's armed bureaucrats punch above their weight in Afghanistan. They are only 16 in number, but their influence in Kabul is impressive. They are not as noticeable as the 2500 Canadian soldiers fighting the Taliban in southern Afghanistan or the members of the provincial reconstruction teams doing modernization and humanitarian work. But their presence *inside* the Karzai government is immense.

The idea that Canada would contribute soldiers to work alongside the government was initiated by General Rick Hillier in 2004 when he was commander of the International Security Assistance Force (ISAF) in Kabul. An agreement between President Karzai and the Canadian government and military led to the setting up of the Strategic Advisory Team (SAT), which does not report to ISAF or the US-led coalition.

Today, the SAT consists of 15 senior military officers and one CIDA employee who advise and support the work of the Afghanistan government. As armed bureaucrats (they do bear arms unobtrusively but do not wear uniforms) they go to work each day just like civil servants in Ottawa to serve their political masters.

The 16 Canadians work for senior public servants, ministers and advisors to President Karzai. Like bureaucrats in Ottawa, they maintain that their job is "not to manipulate ministers but to put their ministers' ideas and policies into practice." At the present time they are *embedded* in Afghanistan's departments of education, justice, public service reform, transportation and aviation, and rural rehabilitation and development, and in the Office of the Special Economic Advisor to the President. They obviously are not included in Kabul's Department of Defence, as their work is not in the security field. There is a staggering amount to accomplish. Some officials disagree that military personnel should be involved in the policy work of a foreign government, and argue that civilians should be performing these tasks. But the problem with their objection is that the work is extremely important if Afghanistan is to stabilize, and it is also dangerous. Very few Canadians would be willing to work in a war zone. Perhaps SAT could be augmented by more civilian personnel but that would take a major new commitment by the Canadian government.

39. Robert J. Jackson and Philip Towle, *Temptations of Power: The United States in Global Politics since 9/11* (London: Praeger, 2006).

TABLE 15.3 Canadian Forces International Operations, January 2008

Arabian Gulf Region and Southwest Asia Mission	Approx. Number of Persons
The Canadian contribution to the NATO-led International Security Assistance Force (ISAF). OP ATHENA Afghanistan	2500
Canadian Support to the National Training Centre, Combined Joint Task Force 76 (CJTF-76) and Combined Security Transition Command—Afghanistan (CSTC-A, formerly the Office of Security Cooperation—Afghanistan). OP ARCHER Afghanistan	15
Canadian Strategic Advisory Team providing support to the Afghan Government. OP ARGUS Afghanistan	22
OP FOUNDATION Tampa, Florida/Bahrain	7

Balkans Mission	Approx. Number of Persons
North Atlantic Treaty Organization (NATO) Headquarters Sarajevo (NHQSa) OP BRONZE Bosnia-Herzegovina	8

Caribbean Mission	Approx. Number of Persons
CF Contribution to the United Nations Stabilization Mission in Haiti Headquarters (MINUSTAH HQ) OP HAMLET Haiti	4

Middle East Mission	Approx. Number of Persons
Canada's maritime contribution to the continuing US-led campaign against terrorism known as Operation Enduring Freedom OP ALTAIR	250
United Nations Disengagement Observer Force (UNDOF) OP GLADIUS Golan Heights	2
Multinational Force and Observers (MFO) OP CALUMET Sinai	28
UN Truce Supervision Organization (UNTSO) OP JADE Jerusalem	8
OP PROTEUS Jerusalem	1
UN Forces in Cyprus (UNFICYP) OP SNOWGOOSE Cyprus	5

Africa Mission	Approx. Number of Persons
UN Organization Mission in the Democratic Republic of the Congo (MONUC) OP CROCODILE Democratic Republic of the Congo	10
OP SAFARI (CF Operation in Sudan) United Nations Mission in Sudan (UNMIS)	34
OP AUGURAL (CF Operation in Sudan) Darfur: Western Sudan (African Union)	11
International Military Advisory Training Team (IMATT) OP SCULPTURE Sierra Leone	11

Source: Available at www.forces.gc.ca/site/operations/current_ops_e.asp. Accessed January 31, 2008. Courtesy of the Canadian Forces.

threat to provide a home for al Qaeda. The defeat of the forces of Mullah Omar and Osama bin Laden in 2001 was swift and decisive. But, while the United States continued to fight the terrorists along the Pakistan border, US troops were quickly pulled out to prepare for war with Iraq, and insufficient new troops were moved in. A NATO-led coalition of 37 countries eventually took over much of the fighting in the south and southeast of Afghanistan.

Despite some successes in the country since the Hamid Karzai government was set up in 2005, there have been many significant and dangerous developments. American and NATO military have killed thousands of insurgents but also far too many civilian bystanders. Suicide bombings and improvised explosive devises are becoming more common. The Canadians are there fighting as part of the 37 000 soldiers under ISAF and the separate 11 000 US-led Operation Enduring Freedom troops. On the military front, more troops are needed. Political leaders appear to be repeating the same error there that they made in Iraq. At the time of writing in March 2008, 77 Canadian soldiers and 1 diplomat have been killed on duty in Afghanistan. Two political issues continue to be important in discussions of Canada's role in Afghanistan: extending the date for final withdrawal and the rendition of Canadian-held prisoners to Afghanistan authorities.

In June 2007, the government announced that it would not renew the mission in Afghanistan past February 2009 unless there was a consensus in Parliament and the country to do so. But a majority of Canadians say that they are against the war. Pollsters have shown that support for the mission dropped from well over half the population at the beginning of the deployment to Afghanistan to about a third by July 2007, with Québec support much lower. The consistent casualties caused by roadside bombs and suicide bombers have made it nearly impossible to continue the combat mission of Canadian soldiers.

The insurgents come in three varieties. First, there are the hardcore members of the Taliban movement with links to al Qaeda. Second, there are the "rent a Taliban"—mercenaries who can be bought for wages higher than those paid by the government or the criminals in the opium trade. And third, there are religious fundamentalists, ardent followers of their faith, willing to die for their beliefs and their country, which they perceive to be threatened by foreign occupation. The two million Afghan refugees inside Pakistan constitute an inexhaustible pool from which such recruits can be drawn.

> *I'm not interested in just being a cheerleader or parroting government policy.*
>
> **General Tim Grant, Canadian Commander in Afghanistan, quoted in** The Globe and Mail, *July 28, 2007*

The political imbroglio over Canada's military commitment to Afghanistan continues. In 2007, Prime Minister Stephen Harper appointed former Liberal foreign affairs minister John Manley and other notables to produce a report on the future of the Afghan mission. The Manley Report concluded that Canada should maintain its commitment as long as NATO produces an additional thousand soldiers to fight alongside Canadians in Kandahar and more transport helicopters and unmanned surveillance aircraft are provided. The prime minister announced that a career diplomat would be placed in the Privy Council Office to coordinate all of Canada's activities in Afghanistan.

The opposition parties continued to attack the government's policy. The NDP maintained that the troops should be withdrawn immediately, and the Bloc Québécois concluded that the mission should end completely in 2009. The Liberals proposed various ideas about the mission, but essentially argued that Canada's specific combat role should be ended in 2009. In March 2008, the Conservatives and Liberals worked toward an agreement about the continuation of the deployment. While an election was threatened on the issue, both the Conservatives and Liberals compromised on the details of the mission—including extending the Afghan mission until 2011 if NATO committed one thousand more troops and equipment.

HEROISM TO SOME....

Aislin, *The Gazette* (Montreal). Reproduced with permission.

CLOSE-UP ON Foreign Policy

CANADA'S RECENT MILITARY ENGAGEMENT

After the tragedies of September 11, 2001, Canada committed itself to supporting efforts to end "global terrorism." However, there was considerable controversy and anguish about whether Canada should join the US and the so-called coalition of the willing in attacking Iraq to depose Saddam Hussein (who allegedly possessed weapons of mass destruction). The Liberal government declined the invitation, but did send 2500 troops to Afghanistan. The operation helped reduce US criticism of Canada's refusal to participate in the Iraq war.

Should Canada have sent troops to Iraq? What is your position on continuing the deployment of troops in Afghanistan?

Security Policy

After the terrorist events of 9/11, the federal government took steps to strengthen national security. It announced a formal policy, introduced two anti-terrorism bills, reorganized several departments and increased budgets for security for the defence department and other organizations.

The national security policy was outlined in an April 2004 document entitled *Securing an Open Society*. It set out the government's strategy for addressing emergencies and terrorism. Its stated purpose is to protect Canada, ensure Canada is not a base for threats to its allies and contribute to international security. Declaring that the safety and security of Canadian citizens is its highest priority, it called for the set-up of an integrated threat-assessment centre, an intergovernmental forum on emergencies, a round table on security for ethno-cultural and religious communities and the National Security Advisory Council. The document addressed questions concerning intelligence, emergency management, public health, transportation, border issues and international security.[40]

Earlier, the government announced that a new organization—the Department of Public Safety—would be set up to monitor national security, crisis management, emergency preparedness, border functions, corrections, policing and crime prevention. A single minister and deputy minister were put in charge of the department, which subsumes the old department of the solicitor general and five agencies—the RCMP, CSIS (the Canadian Security Intelligence Service), Border Services, Corrections and the Parole Board. As mentioned above, a new position of national security advisor to the prime minister was established in the Privy Council Office. The new advisor also acts as deputy minister for policy for the Communications Security Establishment (CSE).

Opposition groups and civil libertarians vehemently attacked the government's anti-terrorism bills. However, Bill C36 was passed in December 2001, increasing the powers of the police and law enforcement to fight terrorism by amending the *Criminal Code* and other statutes. It gives new powers of investigation and detention to law enforcement officers, and makes it a criminal offence to knowingly aid a banned organization. The groups that are banned in Canada include al Qaeda;

40. For details, see http://pco-bcp.gc.ca/docs/Publications/NatSecurnat/natsecurnat_e.pdf.

Hamas (which has been the governing party in Palestine); the Islamic Army of Aden; Lebanon's Hezbollah; Abu Sayyaf (viewed as an al Qaeda affiliate and based in the Philippines); the Palestinian radical group Abu Nidal; and the Sendero Luminoso, or Shining Path, a Maoist organization from Peru. (See a complete list of all banned groups in Table 15.4.)

The *Public Safety Act* (as Bill C42) was delayed and did not pass before prorogation in September 2002. Many believed that Bill C42 went too far in allowing the government to create new regulations without parliamentary oversight because it gave broad declaratory powers to cabinet. It was eventually passed as Bill C55 in February 2004. This Act permits ministers and officials to make emergency decisions on aviation security and other emergency issues for up to 72 hours.

Despite controversies about the two new laws, then deputy prime minister John Manley declared that

> *Canada is in a better shape now to counter a terrorist threat than it was a year ago, as the result of a new antiterrorist law, greater security measures at the border and other entry points, and measures to identify security risks in the immigration system.*[41]

However, Ward Elcock, former director of Canada's top spy organization, CSIS, warned that Canada might have become a greater target for al Qaeda because of its troops in Afghanistan: "Canadians should not feel that we are insulated from terrorism and we need to remain vigilant if we are to deal with the risks."[42]

TABLE 15.4 Groups Listed as Terrorist Organizations as of June 2007

1. Armed Islamic Group	17. Abu Nidal Organization	29. International Sikh Youth Federation
2. Salafist Group for Call and Combat	18. Abu Sayyaf Group	30. Lashkar-e-Tayyiba
3. Al-Jihad	19. Sendero Luminoso	31. Lashkar-e-Jhangvi
4. Vanguards of Conquest	20. Jemaah Islamiyyah	32. Palestine Liberation Front
5. Al Qaeda	21. Islamic Movement of Uzbekistan	33. Popular Front for the Liberation of Palestine
6. Al-Gama'a al-Islamiyya	22. Euskadi Ta Askatasuna	34. Popular Front for the Liberation of Palestine— General Command
7. Al-Ittahad Al-Islam	23. Al-Aqsa Martyrs' Brigade	
8. Islamic Army of Aden	24. Fuerzas Armada Revolucionarias de Colombia	35. Ansar al-Islam
9. Harakat ul-Mudjahidin		36. Gulbuddin Hekmatyar
10. Asbat Al-Ansar	25. Autodefensas Unidas de Colombia	37. Hezb-e Islami Gulbuddin
11. Palestinian Islamic Jihad		38. Kahane Chai
12. Jaish-e-Mohammed	26. Ejercito de Liberacion Nacional	39. Liberation Tigers of Tamil Eelam
13. Hamas	27. Babbar Khalsa	
14. Kurdistan Workers Party	28. Babbar Khalsa International	40. Mujadedin e Kahlq
15. Aum Shinrikyo		
16. Hizballah		

(For details on each proscribed group, see Listed Entities, posted on the web by the Department of Public Safety.)

Source: Available at http://www.psepc-sppcc.gc.ca/national_security/counter-terrorism/entities_e.asp, Public Safety and Emergency Preparedness Canada. Accessed June 16, 2007.

41. *The Globe and Mail*, November 14, 2002.
42. Ibid.

Police and Security Forces

The organization of police and security forces in Canada is extensive and complex. Policing in the security field is governed by a maze of laws and regulations, making generalization difficult if not perilous. Federalism, provincial police legislation and financing agreements between different governments and the new terrorism laws all complicate the situation.

For general policing in Canada, there are three standard organizational levels: federal (the RCMP); provincial (the Ontario Provincial Police [OPP], Sûreté du Québec [SQ] and Royal Newfoundland Constabulary); and municipal. The *Royal Canadian Mounted Police (RCMP)* was created in 1920 out of the North-West Mounted Police, which had been established in 1873 to enforce Canadian law in the Prairie Provinces. The RCMP is responsible to a commissioner who reports to the minister for public safety. After a 2007 report on corruption and poor leadership in the RCMP, Giuliano Zaccardelli was fired and replaced by the first civilian head of the Mounties, William Elliott. As of March 2008, the parliamentary Standing Committee on Public Safety and National Security remained without the ability to do the job it should be doing in scrutinizing issues of national security. The security functions of the RCMP are still not properly overseen by a parliamentary committee.

Today, the RCMP is responsible for enforcing all federal statutes, including the anti-terrorism legislation. It has liaisons with the FBI in the United States and Interpol internationally for sharing information. As well, it is under contract to every province except Ontario and Québec, and to over one hundred municipalities, to enforce criminal and provincial law. It also polices the territories. The RCMP also maintains forensic labs, identification services, the Canadian Police Information Centre and the Canadian Police College in Ottawa for the advanced education of all police in Canada.

The Ontario Provincial Police and the Sûreté du Québec are the only two provincial police forces in Canada. In Newfoundland and Labrador, the Royal Newfoundland Constabulary shares responsibilities on the island with the RCMP. Besides these special provincial arrangements, specific policing powers throughout the country are also provided in aid of Canadian National Railways, Canadian Pacific Railways and Ports Canada. Every city and sizeable town is required to have police to maintain law and order. They contract police from the RCMP or OPP, receive them automatically (as in Québec) or set up their own forces.

Native policing follows several models. Some communities contract with the RCMP or provincial forces to police their territories. Others have their own police forces with their own codes of conduct, answerable to their own police commissions. Still others are in transition, policed by a mixture of RCMP, provincial police and their own officers.

The security community also includes organizations devoted specifically to anti-terrorism activities. These include CSIS, the Communications Security Establishment (the CSE, a top-secret organization that monitors telephone, wireless and radio communications), Foreign Affairs, the Department of National Defence, Citizenship and Immigration Canada and the Canada Border Services Agency.

The 1984 *Canadian Security Intelligence Act* governs the operations of the **Canadian Security Intelligence Service (CSIS)**, an intelligence-gathering institution (headed by a director). That Act removed the security function from the RCMP (where it had been lodged since 1920), and established CSIS as a separate unit. The *Canadian Security Intelligence Act* defines the functions of CSIS and the threats to Canadian security such as espionage, sabotage, terrorism and foreign-inspired activities for which CSIS is responsible. CSIS also provides security screening for appointments to the federal public service.

The end of the Cold War diminished the role of CSIS. Its budget was slashed by almost 35 percent between 1993 and 1998, and more than one-quarter of the agency staff lost their jobs. After 9/11, the government reconsidered and provided a 30 percent increase over five years. Paul Kennedy, then senior assistant deputy solicitor general, noted, "It was only after September 11, 2001, [that] the resourcing of intelligence work was significantly increased to levels commensurate with the nature of the threat."[43]

Many Canadians, in the belief that such activities interfere with individual liberties, have never accepted the idea that a government agency should maintain a constant watch on the daily lives of citizens. No democracy handles secretive organizations easily. To ensure that Canada's "snooping" institutions are controlled, the *Canadian Security Intelligence Act* called for an accountability framework to be put in place. An external review committee, the Security Intelligence Review Committee, monitors the activities of CSIS. This approach is a double-edged sword, however, as the more scrutiny there is, the less secret, and thus less effective, CSIS may become. CSIS continues to have its detractors. Many members of the police community believe it should have been left inside the RCMP and not "civilianized." The RCMP and CSIS have clashed over even such mundane subjects as data handling.

Aside from these arguments, CSIS manages only a domestic security force. It relies on roughly 50 mostly "liaison" officers to collect foreign intelligence in about thirty countries, but relies mostly on friendly services from the CIA and the UK's MI-6 for most of its external information. The policy issue confronting the government and Parliament today is whether the CSIS mandate should be broadened to include espionage abroad or whether a new foreign spy service should be created. The Harper Conservative government seems to favour enhancing the role of CSIS.

The Communications Security Establishment

The Communications Security Establishment (CSE) was established in 1949 as part of the National Research Council. Its function was to intercept the communications of clandestine organizations. It was transferred to the Department of National Defence in 1975 and put under the authority of the minister. During the Cold War, it was the CSE's task to provide information on the Soviet Union and its allies. Since the disintegration of the USSR, it continues to provide secret information on security, especially terrorism, to the government.

The organization collects foreign intelligence for the day-to-day assessment of foreign intentions and capabilities. It shares information with the US, UK, Australia and New Zealand. Since the December 2001 anti-terrorism law came into effect (Bill C36), the CSE intercepts not only the usual clandestine materials, but also the communications of "legitimate" governments, if those communications enter or depart Canada.

A commissioner of the CSE, currently Charles Gonthier, reviews the legality of CSE actions. He submits an annual report to Parliament via the minister and also provides confidential, classified reviews of the establishment. Members of the newly established House of Commons committee set up to monitor security cannot see these classified documents because they are not sworn members of the Privy Council. This deficiency needs to be corrected, as the watchdog function is vital. Parliament needs to ensure that the CSE acts within the law and does not infringe upon human rights, privacy or other items in the *Charter of Rights and Freedoms*.

43. *The Globe and Mail*, Nov 14, 2004.

Critical Debate
Does Canada Have an Independent Foreign Policy?

Given the general interdependence of the world today, Canada's level of power and significance and the so-called global war on terrorism, can Canada maintain an independent foreign policy?

Point

Yes, Canada can maintain an independent foreign policy. There is a unique role for Canada to play in the world. It does not need to slavishly follow the United States or any other country.

Canada is one of the world's most powerful countries, both economically and politically. It is not a superpower, but its middle rank status enables Canada to participate fully and meaningfully in international organizations such as the United Nations and its specialized agencies.

As Canada evolved into a full-fledged state, it gradually adopted an internationalist posture and dropped its former style of isolationism. Issues of peace, world trade and humanitarian concerns actively interest many Canadians, and the world's political leaders and outside events have forced the government toward a foreign policy that is in tune with Canada's domestic concerns and issues.

The importance of international relations to Canada is illustrated by its defence policy. Canada contributes to the security of the West through membership in NATO and NORAD. Its history of involvement in twentieth-century wars has been notable—successful missions were carried out in the First and Second World Wars, Korea, the Balkans and today in Afghanistan. While our overall military budget is small compared to that of many countries we continue to do our share. Because of our essentially non-militaristic policies, Canadian diplomacy is sought in many troubled areas where intervention might otherwise not be acceptable. A concrete example is Canada's contribution to peacekeeping. Canada has contributed to a great many UN missions.

Canadian foreign policy has been changing due to widespread threats to peace internationally, changing definitions of security and a growing awareness of the importance of globalization and trade to the Canadian economy. Canada's role in international trade organizations such as the WTO and NAFTA are crucial.

After 9/11, Canada was forced to confront the United States over issues of security and trade. While US leaders insisted that security "trumps" trade, Canada was successfully able to argue that both were vital. The framework agreement, called the *Security and Prosperity Partnership of North America*, showed Canada's ability to influence the States. It was important for Canada that new "smart border" initiatives and other trade agreements be put forward and accepted. Canada did not cower in front of its much larger neighbour, but negotiated successfully in its national interests.

As evidence of Canadian independence in foreign affairs, one need only point out that Canada joined Britain in the Second World War long before the United States did, and Canada also recognized the People's Republic of China before the United States. Today, despite constant US pressure, Canada maintains recognition of communist Cuba and refused to send troops to support the United States in the war in Iraq. Canada has demonstrated both the rhetoric and the actions of an independent state. Let's keep it that way.

Counterpoint

No. Canada does not have an independent foreign policy and it would be foolish to try to establish one. In an era of global terrorism it must follow the lead of the United States.

Today, everyone realizes that no country can be an island unto itself. Globalization is prevalent and the idea that no country can be totally self-sufficient is an accepted maxim of international and Canadian politics. Canada's prosperity depends overwhelmingly on the United States, which buys almost 80 percent of all our goods and services. Economic difficulties caused by US blockage of imports of cattle from Canada and our irritation over their efforts to close the border to Canadian lumber and softwood illustrate just how vital this market is to us.

Canada–US economic integration continues to grow. The FTA and NAFTA have imposed conditions on Canadian independence in terms of energy, water and other social areas. It will not be long before top business leaders will demand that Canada join in a customs union with the United States and adopt the US dollar as our currency. In short, the benefits of the FTA and NAFTA have been substantial, but they have made it more difficult for Canada to chart a separate course in international trade, defence and foreign policy. The plan to have a free trade zone of the Americas will further enhance US control over the economies of the 32 states of that part of the world, including Canada. The Security and Prosperity Partnership signed in 2005 by Canada, the United States and Mexico, and enhanced by the 2007 Harper–Bush summit at Montebello, Québec, are good recent illustrations of how much Canada is dominated by US interests.

The reality is that Canada's defence and security depend totally on the United States. Canada was fairly independent in military policy some years ago, but it no longer is today. In 2006, approximately $15 billion was forecast for the defence envelope. This paltry amount put Canada seventh in terms of overall NATO budgets, but even then, Canada spent only 1.1 percent of its GDP on the military. As members of NORAD, we are roped into supporting the ballistic missile shield despite our misgivings, and although we did not send troops to Iraq, we are, as a NATO partner, participating in the war on terror in the Arabian Gulf and supporting independent US actions in Afghanistan as well as those of NATO. We are co-operating, and reasonably so, in the development of a continental security system from policing to border guards.

The international strategic environment is changing. Most conflicts take place outside the Western European theatre and, except as peacekeepers, Canada has a very small role to play in the ethnic and religious conflicts of the Middle East and the Balkans. In the rest of the world, essentially south of the Tropic of Cancer, Canada plays a modest, usually rhetorical, role. Canadian efforts to help end apartheid in South Africa and bring a political solution to other troubled areas have sometimes landed on fertile ground, but in sum, the Canadian contribution to world politics outside North America, Europe and a few countries with old Commonwealth ties is marginal and largely symbolic, except at the important humanitarian and peacekeeping levels. We are not an independent actor in international affairs, but this is not necessarily a bad thing.

Discussion Questions

1. Which side of the Critical Debate do you find most compelling? What can you add to the discussion?
2. Do you agree with the contention that, in Canada, foreign policy is domestic policy? Is the government's military policy in Afghanistan in Canada's national interest?

3. Do you agree with the idea that Canadian foreign policy should be a projection of its national interests?

4. Does Canada spend too much money on defence? On security and intelligence? On the war on terror?

5. Does Canada's domestic security policy reduce the chance of terrorism? Reduce civil liberties? Should Canada increase its co-operation with the United States in creating more integration of security functions? Should the mandate of CSIS be broadened to include foreign espionage?

Visit our new Companion Website at **www.pearsoned.ca/jackson**, where you can use the interactive Study Guide and link to additional resources on topics discussed in the text.

Selected Bibliography

Banting, Keith G., George Hoberg, and Richard Simeon, eds. *Degrees of Freedom: Canada and the United States in a Changing World.* Montréal: McGill-Queen's University Press, 1997.

Blanchard, James. *Behind the Embassy Door: Canada, Clinton and Quebec.* Toronto: McClelland & Stewart, 1998.

Bratt, Duane, and Christopher J. Kukucha, eds. *Readings in Canadian Foreign Policy: Classic Debates and New Ideas.* Don Mills, ON: Oxford University Press, 2007.

Carment, David, Fen Osler Hampson, and Norman Hillmer. *Canada Among Nations 2003: Coping with the American Colossus.* Don Mills, ON: Oxford University Press, 2003.

Clarke, Tony, and Maude Barlow. *MAI and the Threat to Canadian Sovereignty.* Toronto: Stoddart, 1997.

Canada Among Nations. Don Mills, ON: Oxford University Press, annual.

Canadian Council of Chief Executives. *Security and Prosperity: The Dynamics of a New Canada–United States Partnership in North America.* Ottawa: Canadian Council of Chief Executives, January 2003.

Cohen, Andrew. *While Canada Slept: How We Lost Our Place in the World.* Toronto: McClelland & Stewart, 2003.

Cooper, Andrew F. *Canadian Foreign Policy: Old Habits and New Directions.* Scarborough, ON: Prentice Hall, 1997.

Cutler, Clare A., and Mark Zacker, eds. *Canadian Foreign Policy and International Economic Regimes.* Vancouver: UBC Press, 1992.

Dewitt, David B., and David Leyton-Brown, eds. *Canada's International Security Policy.* Scarborough, ON: Prentice Hall, 1995.

Doran, Charles F.F. *Why Canadian Unity Matters and Why Americans Care.* Toronto: University of Toronto Press, 2001.

Drache, Daniel. *Borders Matter: Homeland Security and the Search for North America.* Halifax, NS: Fernwood, 2004.

English, John, and Norman Hillmer, eds. *Making a Difference? Canada's Foreign Policy in a Changing World Order.* Toronto: Lester, 1992.

Granatstein, J.L., and Robert Bothwell. *Pirouette: Pierre Trudeau and Canadian Foreign Policy.* Toronto: University of Toronto Press, 1990.

Head, Ivan L. *On a Hinge of History: The Mutual Vulnerability of South and North.* Toronto: University of Toronto Press, 1991.

Head, Ivan, and Pierre Trudeau. *The Canadian Way: Shaping Canada's Foreign Policy, 1968–84.* Toronto: McClelland & Stewart, 1995.

Himes, Mel. *Canadian Foreign Policy Handbook.* Montréal: Jewel Publications, 1996.

Holloway, Steven. *Canadian Foreign Policy: Defining the National Interest.* Peterborough, ON: Broadview Press, 2006.

Jackson, Robert J., ed. *Europe in Transition.* New York: Praeger, 1993.

————— and Philip Towle. *Temptations of Power: The United States in Global Politics after 9/11.* London: Palgrave, 2006.

Jockel, Joseph T. *Canada in Norad, 1957–2007: A History.* Montréal: McGill-Queen's University Press, 2007.

Morton, Desmond. *Understanding Canadian Defence.* Toronto: Penguin Books/McGill Institute, 2003.

Nossal, Kim Richard. *The Politics of Canadian Foreign Policy*, 3rd ed. Scarborough, ON: Prentice Hall, 1997.

Rothgeb, John. *Defining Power: Influence and Force in the Contemporary International System.* New York: St. Martin's Press, 1993.

Sloan, Elinor. *Security and Defence in the Terrorist Era: Canada and North America.* Montréal: McGill-Queen's University Press, 2005.

Stein, Janice Gross, and Eugene Lang. *The Unexpected War: Canada in Kandahar.* Toronto: Viking, 2007.

Thomas, David, ed. *Canada and the United States: Differences that Count.* Peterborough, ON: Broadview Press, 1993.

Welsh, Jennifer. *At Home in the World: Canada's Global Vision for the 21st Century.* Toronto: HarperCollins, 2004.

Appendix 1

A Consolidation of the Constitution Acts, 1867 to 1982

EXCERPTS FROM THE CONSTITUTION

*   *   *

VI. DISTRIBUTION OF LEGISLATIVE POWERS

Powers of the Parliament

91. It shall be lawful for the Queen, by and with the Advice and Consent of the Senate and House of Commons, to make Laws for the Peace, Order, and good Government of Canada, in relation to all Matters not coming within the Classes of Subjects by this Act assigned exclusively to the Legislatures of the Provinces; and for greater Certainty, but not so as to restrict the Generality of the foregoing Terms of this Section, it is hereby declared that (notwithstanding anything in this Act) the exclusive Legislative Authority of the Parliament of Canada extends to all Matters coming within the Classes of Subjects next hereinafter enumerated; that is to say,—

1. *The amendment from time to time of the Constitution of Canada, except as regards matters coming within the classes of subjects by this Act assigned exclusively to the Legislatures of the provinces, or as regards rights or privileges by this or any other Constitutional Act granted or secured to the Legislature or the Government of a province, or to any class of persons with respect to schools or as regards the use of the English or the French language or as regards the requirements that there shall be a session of the Parliament of Canada at least once each year, and that no House of Commons shall continue for more than five years from the day of the return of the Writs for choosing the House: Provided, however, that a House of Commons may in time of real or apprehended war, invasion or insurrection be continued by the Parliament of Canada if such continuation is not opposed by the votes of more than one-third of the members of such House.*

[Note: Class 1 was added by the *British North America Act (No. 2), 1949* (No. 33 *infra*) and repealed by the *Constitution Act, 1982* (No. 44 *infra*).]

1A.   The Public Debt and Property.
[Note: Re-numbered 1A by the *British North America Act (No. 2), 1949* No. 33 *infra*).]
2. The Regulation of Trade and Commerce.
2A.   Unemployment insurance.
[Note: Added by the *Constitution Act, 1940* (No. 28 *infra*).]
3. The raising of Money by any Mode or System of Taxation.
4. The borrowing of Money on the Public Credit.
5. Postal Service.
6. The Census and Statistics.
7. Militia, Military and Naval Service, and Defence.
8. The fixing of and providing for the Salaries and Allowances of Civil and other Officers of the Government of Canada.
9. Beacons, Buoys, Lighthouses, and Sable Island.
10. Navigation and Shipping.
11. Quarantine and the Establishment and Maintenance of Marine Hospitals.
12. Sea Coast and Inland Fisheries.
13. Ferries between a Province and any British or Foreign Country or between Two Provinces.
14. Currency and Coinage.
15. Banking, Incorporation of Banks, and the Issue of Paper Money.
16. Savings Banks.
17. Weights and Measures.
18. Bills of Exchange and Promissory Notes.
19. Interest.
20. Legal Tender.
21. Bankruptcy and Insolvency.
22. Patents of Invention and Discovery.

23. Copyrights.

24. Indians, and Lands reserved for the Indians.

25. Naturalization and Aliens.

26. Marriage and Divorce.

27. The Criminal Law, except the Constitution of Courts of Criminal Jurisdiction, but including the Procedure in Criminal Matters.

28. The Establishment, Maintenance, and Management of Penitentiaries.

29. Such Classes of Subjects as are expressly excepted in the Enumeration of the Classes of Subjects by this Act assigned exclusively to the Legislatures of the Provinces.

And any Matter coming within any of the Classes of Subjects enumerated in this Section shall not be deemed to come within the Class of Matters of a local or private Nature comprised in the Enumeration of the Classes of Subjects by this Act assigned exclusively to the Legislatures of the Provinces.

[Note: Legislative authority has also been conferred by the *Rupert's Land Act, 1868* (No. 6 *infra*), *Constitution Act, 1871* (No. 11 *infra*), *Constitution Act, 1886* (No. 15 *infra*), *Statute of Westminster, 1931* (No. 27 *infra*) and section 44 of the *Constitution Act, 1982* (No. 44 *infra*), and see also sections 38 and 41 to 43 of the latter Act.]

Exclusive Powers of Provincial Legislatures

92. In each Province the Legislature may exclusively make Laws in relation to Matters coming within the Classes of Subjects next hereinafter enumerated; that is to say,—

1. The Amendment from Time to Time, notwithstanding anything in this Act, of the Constitution of the Province, except as regards the Office of Lieutenant Governor.

[Note: Class 1 was repealed by the *Constitution Act, 1982* (No. 44 *infra*). The subject is now provided for in section 45 of that Act, and see also sections 38 and 41 to 43 of the same Act.]

2. Direct Taxation with-in the Province in order to the raising of a Revenue for Provincial Purposes.

3. The borrowing of Money on the sole Credit of the Province.

4. The Establishment and Tenure of Provincial Offices and the Appointment and Payment of Provincial Officers.

5. The Management and Sale of the Public Lands belonging to the Province and of the Timber and Wood thereon.

6. The Establishment, Maintenance, and Management of Public and Reformatory Prisons in and for the Province.

7. The Establishment, Maintenance, and Management of Hospitals, Asylums, Charities, and Eleemosynary Institutions in and for the Province, other than Marine Hospitals.

8. Municipal Institutions in the Province.

9. Shop, Saloon, Tavern, Auctioneer, and other Licences in order to the raising of a Revenue for Provincial, Local, or Municipal Purposes.

10. Local Works and Undertakings other than such as are of the following Classes:—

a. Lines of Steam or other Ships, Railways, Canals, Telegraphs, and other Works and Undertakings connecting the Province with any other or others of the Provinces, or extending beyond the Limits of the Province:

b. Lines of Steam Ships between the Province and any British or Foreign Country:

c. Such Works as, although wholly situate within the Province, are before or after their Execution declared by the Parliament of Canada to be for the general Advantage of Canada or for the Advantage of Two or more of the Provinces.

11. The Incorporation of Companies with Provincial Objects.

12. The Solemnization of Marriage in the Province.

13. Property and Civil Rights in the Province.

14. The Administration of Justice in the Province, including the Constitution, Maintenance, and Organization of Provincial Courts, both of Civil and of Criminal Jurisdiction, and including Procedure in Civil Matters in those Courts.

15. The Imposition of Punishment by Fine, Penalty, or Imprisonment for enforcing any Law of the Province made in relation to any Matter coming within any of the Classes of Subjects enumerated in this Section.

16. Generally all Matters of a merely local or private Nature in the Province.

Non-Renewable Natural Resources, Forestry Resources and
Electrical Energy

92A. (1) In each province, the legislature may exclusively make laws in relation to
(a) exploration for non-renewable natural resources in the province;

(b) development, conservation and management of non-renewable natural resources and forestry resources in the province, including laws in relation to the rate of primary production therefrom; and
(c) development, conservation and management of sites and facilities in the province for the generation and production of electrical energy.

(2) In each province, the legislature may make laws in relation to the export from the province to another part of Canada of the primary production from non-renewable natural resources and forestry resources in the province and the production from facilities in the province for the generation of electrical energy, but such laws may not authorize or provide for discrimination in prices or in supplies exported to another part of Canada.

(3) Nothing in subsection (2) derogates from the authority of Parliament to enact laws in relation to the matters referred to in that subsection and, where such a law of Parliament and a law of a province conflict, the law of Parliament prevails to the extent of the conflict.

(4) In each province, the legislature may make laws in relation to the raising of money by any mode or system of taxation in respect of
(a) Non-renewable natural resources and forestry resources in the province and the primary production therefrom, and
(b) sites and facilities in the province for the generation of electrical energy and the production therefrom, whether or not such production is exported in whole or in part from the province, but such laws may not authorize or provide for taxation that differentiates between production exported to another part of Canada and production not exported from the province.

(5) The expression "primary production" has the meaning assigned by the Sixth Schedule.

(6) Nothing in subsections (1) to (5) derogates from any powers or rights that a legislature or government of a province had immediately before the coming into force of this section.
[Note: Added by section 50 of the *Constitution Act, 1982* (No. 44 *infra*).]

Education

93. In and for each Province the Legislature may exclusively make Laws in relation to Education, subject and according to the following Provisions:—

(1) Nothing in any such Law shall prejudicially affect any Right or Privilege with respect to Denominational Schools which any Class of Persons have by Law in the Province at the Union:

(2) All the Powers, Privileges, and Duties at the Union by Law conferred and imposed in Upper Canada on the Separate Schools and School Trustees of the Queen's Roman Catholic Subjects shall be and the same are hereby extended to the Dissentient Schools of the Queen's Protestant and Roman Catholic Subjects in Quebec:

(3) Where in any Province a System of Separate or Dissentient Schools exists by Law at the Union or is thereafter established by the Legislature of the Province, an Appeal shall lie to the Governor General in Council from any Act or Decision of any Provincial Authority affecting any Right or Privilege of the Protestant or Roman Catholic Minority of the Queen's Subjects in relation to Education:

(4) In case any such Provincial Law as from Time to Time seems to the Governor General in Council requisite for the due Execution of the Provisions of this Section is not made, or in case any Decision of the Governor General in Council on any Appeal under this Section is not duly executed by the proper Provincial Authority in that Behalf, then and in every such Case, and as far only as the Circumstances of each Case require, the Parliament of Canada may make remedial Laws for the due Execution of the Provisions of this Section and of any Decision of the Governor General in Council under this Section.

[Note: Altered for Manitoba by section 22 of the *Manitoba Act, 1870* (No. 8 *infra*) confirmed by the *Constitution Act, 1871* (No. 11 *infra*); for Alberta, by section 17 of the *Alberta Act* (No. 20 *infra*); for Saskatchewan, by section 17 of the *Saskatchewan Act* (No. 21 *infra*); and for Newfoundland, by Term 17 of the Terms of Union of Newfoundland with Canada, confirmed by the *Newfoundland Act* (No. 32 *infra*). See also sections 23, 29 and 59 of the *Constitution Act, 1982* (No. 44 *infra*).]

Uniformity of Laws in Ontario, Nova Scotia, and New Brunswick

94. Notwithstanding anything in this Act, the Parliament of Canada may make Provision for the Uniformity of all or any of the Laws relative to Property and Civil Rights in Ontario, Nova Scotia, and New Brunswick, and of the Procedure of all or any of the Courts in those Three Provinces, and from and after the passing of any Act in that Behalf the Power of the Parliament of Canada to make Laws in relation to any Matter comprised in any such Act shall, notwithstanding anything in this Act, be unrestricted; but any Act of the Parliament of Canada making Provision for such Uniformity shall not have effect in any Province unless and until it is adopted and enacted as Law by the Legislature thereof.

94A. The Parliament of Canada may make laws in relation to old age pensions and supplementary benefits, including survivors' and disability benefits irrespective of age, but no such law shall affect the operation of any law present or future of a provincial legislature in relation to any such matter.

[Note: Substituted by the *Constitution Act, 1964* (No. 38 *infra*) for the section 94A that was originally added by the *British North America Act, 1951* (No. 35 *infra*).]

Agriculture and Immigration

95. In each Province the Legislature may make Laws in relation to Agriculture in the Province, and to Immigration into the Province; and it is hereby declared that the Parliament of Canada may from Time to Time make Laws in relation to Agriculture in all or any of the Provinces, and to Immigration into all or any of the Provinces; and any Law of the Legislature of a Province relative to Agriculture or to Immigration shall have effect in and for the Province as long and as far only as it is not repugnant to any Act of the Parliament of Canada.

VII. JUDICATURE

96. The Governor General shall appoint the Judges of the Superior, District, and County Courts in each Province, except those of the Courts of Probate in Nova Scotia and New Brunswick.

97. Until the Laws relative to Property and Civil Rights in Ontario, Nova Scotia, and New Brunswick, and the Procedure of the Courts in those Provinces, are made uniform, the Judges of the Courts of those Provinces appointed by the Governor General shall be selected from the respective Bars of those Provinces.

98. The Judges of the Courts of Quebec shall be selected from the Bar of that Province.

99. (1) Subject to subsection (2) of this section, the judges of the superior courts shall hold office during good behaviour, but shall be removable by the Governor General on address of the Senate and House of Commons.

(2) A judge of a superior court, whether appointed before or after the coming into force of this section, shall cease to hold office upon attaining the age of seventy-five years, or upon the coming into force of this section if at that time he has already attained that age.

*   *   *

CANADIAN CHARTER OF RIGHTS AND FREEDOMS

Whereas Canada is founded upon principles that recognize the supremacy of God and the rule of law:

Guarantee of Rights and Freedoms

1. The *Canadian Charter of Rights and Freedoms* guarantees the rights and freedoms set out in it subject only to such reasonable limits prescribed by law as can be demonstrably justified in a free and democratic society.

Fundamental Freedoms

2. Everyone has the following fundamental freedoms:

(a) freedom of conscience and religion;

(b) freedom of thought, belief, opinion and expression, including freedom of the press and other media of communication;

(c) freedom of peaceful assembly; and

(d) freedom of association.

Democratic Rights

3. Every citizen of Canada has the right to vote in an election of members of the House of Commons or of a legislative assembly and to be qualified for membership therein.

4. (1) No House of Commons and no legislative assembly shall continue for longer than five years from the date fixed for the return of the writs at a general election of its members.

(2) In time of real or apprehended war, invasion or insurrection, a House of Commons may be continued by Parliament and a legislative assembly may be continued by the legislature beyond five years if such continuation is not opposed by the votes of more than one-third of the members of the House of Commons or the legislative assembly, as the case may be.

5. There shall be a sitting of Parliament and of each legislature at least once every twelve months.

Mobility Rights

6. (1) Every citizen of Canada has the right to enter, remain in and leave Canada.

(2) Every citizen of Canada and every person who has the status of a permanent resident of Canada has the right

(a) to move to and take up residence in any province; and

(b) to pursue the gaining of a livelihood in any province.

(3) The rights specified in subsection (2) are subject to

(a) any laws or practices of general application in force in a province other than those that discriminate among persons primarily on the basis of province of present or previous residence; and

(b) any laws providing for reasonable residency requirements as a qualification for the receipt of publicly provided social services.

(4) Subsections (2) and (3) do not preclude any law, program or activity that has as its object the amelioration in a province of conditions of individuals in that province who are socially or economically disadvantaged if the rate of employment in that provide is below the rate of employment in Canada.

Legal Rights

7. Everyone has the right to life, liberty and security of the person and the right not to be deprived thereof except in accordance with the principles of fundamental justice.

8. Everyone has the right to be secure against unreasonable search or seizure.

9. Everyone has the right not to be arbitrarily detained or imprisoned.

10. Everyone has the right on arrest or detention

(a) to be informed promptly of the reasons therefor;

(b) to retain and instruct counsel without delay and to be informed of that right; and

(c) to have the validity of the detention determined by way of *habeas corpus* and to be released if the detention is not lawful.

11. Any person charged with an offence has the right

(a) to be informed without unreasonable delay of the specific offence;

(b) to be tried within a reasonable time;

(c) not to be compelled to be a witness in proceedings against that person in respect of the offence;

(d) to be presumed innocent until proven guilty according to law in a fair and public hearing by an independent and impartial tribunal;

(e) not to be denied reasonable bail without just cause;

(f) except in the case of an offence under military law tried before a military tribunal, to the benefit of trial by jury where the maximum punishment for the offence is imprisonment for five years or a more severe punishment;

(g) not to be found guilty on account of any act or omission unless, at the time of the act or omission, it constituted an offence under Canadian or international law or was criminal according to the general principles of law recognized by the community of nations;

(h) if finally acquitted of the offence, not to be tried for it again and, if finally found guilty and punished for the offence, not to be tried or punished for it again; and

(i) if found guilty of the offence and if the punishment for the offence has been varied between the time of commission and the time of sentencing, to the benefit of the lesser punishment.

12. Everyone has the right not to be subjected to any cruel and unusual treatment or punishment.

13. A witness who testifies in any proceedings has the right not to have any incriminating evidence so given used to incriminate that witness in any other proceedings, except in a prosecution for perjury or for the giving of contradictory evidence.

14. A party or witness in any proceedings who does not understand or speak the language in which the proceedings are conducted or who is deaf has the right to the assistance of an interpreter.

Equality Rights

15. (1) Every individual is equal before and under the law and has the right to the equal protection and equal benefit of the law without discrimination and, in particular, without discrimination based on race, national or ethnic origin, colour, religion, sex, age or mental or physical disability.

(2) Subsection (1) does not preclude any law, program or activity that has as its object the amelioration of conditions of disadvantaged individuals or groups including those that are disadvantaged because of race, national or ethnic origin, colour, religion, sex, age or mental or physical disability.

[Note: This section became effective on April 17, 1985. See subsection 32(2) and the note thereto.]

Official Languages of Canada

16. (1) English and French are the official languages of Canada and have equality of status and equal rights and privileges as to their use in all institutions of the Parliament and government of Canada.

(2) English and French are the official languages of New Brunswick and have equality of status and equal rights and privileges as to their use in all institutions of the legislature and government of New Brunswick.

(3) Nothing in this Charter limits the authority of Parliament or a legislature to advance the equality of status or use of English and French.

17. (1) Everyone has the right to use English or French in any debates and other proceedings of Parliament.

(2) Everyone has the right to use English or French in any debates and other proceedings of the legislature of New Brunswick.

18. (1) The statutes, records and journals of Parliament shall be printed and published in English and French and both language versions are equally authoritative.

(2) The statutes, records and journals of the legislature of New Brunswick shall be printed and published in English and French and both language versions are equally authoritative.

19. (1) Either English or French may be used by any person in, or in any pleading in or process issuing from, any court established by Parliament.

(2) Either English or French may be used by any person in, or in any pleading in or process issuing from, any court of New Brunswick.

20. (1) Any member of the public in Canada has the right to communicate with, and to receive available services from, any head or central office of an institution of the Parliament or government of Canada in English or French, and has the same right with respect to any other office of any such institution where

(a) there is a significant demand for communications with and services from that office in such language; or

(b) due to the nature of the office, it is reasonable that communications with and services from that office be available in both English and French.

(2) Any member of the public in New Brunswick has the right to communicate with, and to receive available services from, any office of an institution of the legislature or government of New Brunswick in English or French.

21. Nothing in sections 16 to 20 abrogates or derogates from any right, privilege or obligation with respect to the English and French languages, or either of them, that exists or is continued by virtue of any other provision of the Constitution of Canada.

22. Nothing in sections 16 to 20 abrogates or derogates from any legal or customary right or privilege acquired or enjoyed either before or after the coming into force of this Charter with respect to any language that is not English or French.

Minority Language Educational Rights

23. (1) Citizens of Canada

(a) whose first language learned and still understood is that of the English or French linguistic minority population of the province in which they reside, or

(b) who have received their primary school instruction in Canada in English or French and reside in a province where the language in which they received that instruction is the language of the English or French linguistic minority population of the province,

have the right to have their children receive primary and secondary school instruction in that language in that province.

[Note: See also section 59 and the note thereto.]

(2) Citizens of Canada of whom any child has received or is receiving primary or secondary school instruction in English or French in Canada, have the right to have all their children receive primary and secondary school instruction in the same language.

(3) The right of citizens of Canada under subsections (1) and (2) to have their children receive primary and secondary school instruction in the language of the English or French linguistic minority population of a province.

(a) applies wherever in the province the number of children of citizens who have such a right is sufficient to warrant the provision to them out of public funds of minority language instruction; and

(b) includes, where the number of those children so warrants, the right to have them receive that instruction in minority language educational facilities provided out of public funds.

Enforcement

24. (1) Anyone whose rights or freedoms, as guaranteed by this Charter, have been infringed or denied may apply to a court of competent jurisdiction to obtain such remedy as the court considers appropriate and just in the circumstances.

(2) Where, in proceedings under subsection (1), a court concludes that evidence was obtained in a manner that infringed or denied any rights or freedoms guaranteed by this Charter, the evidence shall be excluded if it is established that, having regard to all the circumstances, the admission of it in the proceedings would bring the administration of justice into disrepute.

General

25. The guarantee in this Charter of certain rights and freedoms shall not be construed so as to abrogate or derogate from any aboriginal, treaty or other rights or freedoms that pertain to the aboriginal peoples of Canada including

(a) any rights or freedoms that have been recognized by the Royal Proclamation of October 7, 1763; and

(b) any rights or freedoms that may be acquired by the aboriginal peoples of Canada by way of land claims settlement.

(b) any rights or freedoms that now exist by way of land claims agreements or may be so acquired.

[Note: Paragraph 25(b) (in italics) was repealed and the new paragraph substituted by the *Constitution Amendment Proclamation, 1983* (No. 46 *infra*).]

26. The guarantee in this Charter of certain rights and freedoms shall not be construed as denying the existence of any other rights or freedoms that exist in Canada.

27. This Charter shall be interpreted in a manner consistent with the preservation and enhancement of the multicultural heritage of Canadians.

28. Notwithstanding anything in this Charter, the rights and freedoms referred to in it are guaranteed equally to male and female persons.

29. Nothing in this Charter abrogates or derogates from any rights or privileges guaranteed by or under the Constitution of Canada in respect of denominational, separate or dissentient schools.

30. A reference in this Charter to a province or to the legislative assembly or legislature of a province shall be deemed to include a reference to the Yukon Territory and the Northwest Territories, or to the appropriate legislative authority thereof, as the case may be.

31. Nothing in this Charter extends the legislative powers of any body or authority.

Application of Charter

32. (1) This Charter applies

(a) to the Parliament and government of Canada in respect of all matters within the authority of Parliament including all matters relating to the Yukon Territory and Northwest Territories; and

(b) to the legislature and government of each province in respect of all matters within the authority of the legislature of each province.

(2) Notwithstanding subsection (1), section 15 shall not have effect until three years after this section comes into force.

[Note: This section came into force on April 17, 1982. See the proclamation of that date (No. 45 *infra*).]

33. (1) Parliament or the legislature of a province may expressly declare in an Act of Parliament or of the legislature, as the case may be, that the Act or a provision thereof shall operate notwithstanding a provision included in section 2 or sections 7 to 15 of this Charter.

(2) An Act or a provision of an Act in respect of which a declaration made under this section is in effect shall have such operation as it would have but for the provision of this Charter referred to in the declaration.

(3) A declaration made under subsection (1) shall cease to have effect five years after it comes into force or on such earlier date as may be specified in the declaration.

(4) Parliament or the legislature of a province may re-enact a declaration made under subsection (1).

(5) Subsection (3) applies in respect of a re-enactment made under subsection (4).

Citation

34. This Part may be cited as the *Canadian Charter of Rights and Freedoms*.

PART II

RIGHTS OF THE ABORIGINAL PEOPLES OF CANADA

35. (1) The existing aboriginal and treaty rights of the aboriginal peoples of Canada are hereby recognized and affirmed.

(2) In this Act, "aboriginal peoples of Canada" includes the Indian, Inuit and Métis peoples of Canada.

(3) For greater certainty, in subsection (1) "treaty rights" includes rights that now exist by way of land claims agreement or may be so acquired.

(4) Notwithstanding any other provision of this Act, the aboriginal and treaty rights referred to in subsection (1) are guaranteed equally to male and female persons.

[Note: Subsections 35(3) and (4) were added by the *Constitution Amendment Proclamation, 1983* (No. 46 *infra*).]

35.1 The government of Canada and the provincial governments are committed to the principle that, before any amendment is made to Class 24 of section 91 of the *"Constitution Act, 1867"*, to section 25 of this Act or to this Part,

(a) a constitutional conference that includes in its agenda an item relating to the proposed amendment, composed of the Prime Minister of Canada and the first ministers of the provinces, will be convened by the Prime Minister of Canada; and

(b) the Prime Minister of Canada will invite representative of the aboriginal peoples of Canada to participate in the discussions on that item.

[Note: Added by the *Constitution Amendment Proclamation, 1983* (No. 46 *infra*).]

PART III

EQUALIZATION AND REGIONAL DISPARITIES

36. (1) Without altering the legislative authority of Parliament or of the provincial legislatures, or the rights of any of them with respect to the exercise of their legislative authority, Parliament and the legislatures, together with the government of Canada and the provincial governments, are committed to

(a) promoting equal opportunities for the well-being of Canadians;

(b) furthering economic development to reduce disparity in opportunities; and

(c) providing essential public services of reasonable quality to all Canadians.

(2) Parliament and the government of Canada are committed to the principle of making equalization payments to ensure that provincial governments have sufficient revenues to provide reasonably comparable levels of public services at reasonably comparable levels of taxation.

PART IV

CONSTITUTIONAL CONFERENCE

37. *(1) A constitutional conference composed of the Prime Minister of Canada and the first ministers of the provinces shall be convened by the Prime Minister of Canada within one year after this Part comes into force.*

(2) The conference convened under subsection (1) shall have included in its agenda an item respecting constitutional matters that directly affect the aboriginal peoples of Canada, including the identification and definition of the rights of those peoples to be included in the Constitution of Canada, and the Prime Minister of Canada shall invite representatives of those peoples to participate in the discussions on that item.

(3) The Prime Minister of Canada shall invite elected representatives of the governments of the Yukon Territory and the Northwest Territories to participate in the discussions on any item on the agenda of the conference convened under subsection (1) that, in the opinion of the Prime Minister, directly affects the Yukon Territory and the Northwest Territories.

[Note: Part IV was repealed effective April 17, 1983 by section 54 of this Act.]

PART IV.1

CONSTITUTIONAL CONFERENCES

37.1 *(1) In addition to the conference convened in March 1983, at least two constitutional conferences composed of the Prime Minister of Canada and the first ministers of the provinces shall be convened by the Prime Minister of Canada, the first within three years after April 17, 1982 and the second within five years after that date.*

(2) Each conference convened under subsection (1) shall have included in its agenda constitutional matters that directly affect the aboriginal peoples of Canada, and the Prime Minister of Canada shall invite representatives of those peoples to participate in the discussion on those matters.

(3) The Prime Minister of Canada shall invite elected representatives of the governments of the Yukon Territory and the Northwest Territories to participate in the discussions on any item on the agenda of a conference convened under subsection (1) that, in the opinion of the Prime Minister, directly affects the Yukon Territory and the Northwest Territories.

(4) Nothing in this section shall be construed so as to derogate from subsection 35(1).

[Note: Part IV.1 was added by the *Constitution Amendment Proclamation, 1983* (No. 46 *infra*). By the same proclamation, it was repealed effective April 18, 1987. See section 54.1 of this Act.]

PART V

PROCEDURE FOR AMENDING CONSTITUTION OF CANADA

38. (1) An amendment to the Constitution of Canada may be made by proclamation issued by the Governor General under the Great Seal of Canada where so authorized by

(a) resolutions of the Senate and House of Commons; and

(b) resolutions of the legislative assemblies of at least two-thirds of the provinces that have, in the aggregate, according to the then latest general census, at least fifty per cent of the population of all the provinces.

(2) An amendment made under subsection (1) that derogates from the legislative power, the proprietary rights or any other rights or privileges of the legislature or government of a province shall require a resolution supported by a majority of the members of each of the Senate, the House of Commons and the legislative assemblies required under subsection (1).

(3) An amendment referred to in subsection (2) shall not have effect in a province the legislative assembly of which has expressed its dissent thereto by resolution supported by a majority of its members prior to the issue of the proclamation to which the amendment relates unless that legislative assembly, subsequently, by resolution supported by a majority of its members, revokes its dissent and authorizes the amendment.

(4) A resolution of dissent made for the purposes of subsection (3) may be revoked at any time before or after the issue of the proclamation to which it relates.

39. (1) A proclamation shall not be issued under subsection 38(1) before the expiration of one year from the adoption of the resolution initiating the amendment procedure thereunder, unless the legislative assembly of each province has previously adopted a resolution of assent or dissent.

(2) A proclamation shall not be issued under subsection 38(1) after the expiration of three years from the adoption of the resolution initiating the amendment procedure thereunder.

40. Where an amendment is made under subsection 38(1) that transfers provincial legislative powers relating to education or other cultural matters from provincial legislatures to Parliament, Canada shall provide reasonable compensation to any province to which the amendment does not apply.

41. An amendment to the Constitution of Canada in relation to the following matters may be made by proclamation issued by the Governor General under the Great Seal of Canada only where authorized by resolutions of the Senate and House of Commons and of the legislative assembly of each province:

(a) the office of the Queen, the Governor General and the Lieutenant Governor of a province;

(b) the right of a province to a number of members in the House of Commons not less than the number of Senators by which the province is entitled to be represented at the time this Part comes into force;

(c) subject to section 43, the use of the English or the French language;

(d) the composition of the Supreme Court of Canada; and

(e) an amendment to this Part.

42. (1) An amendment to the Constitution of Canada in relation to the following matters may be made only in accordance with subsection 38(1):

(a) the principle of proportionate representation of the provinces in the House of Commons prescribed by the Constitution of Canada;

(b) the powers of the Senate and the method of selecting Senators;

(c) the number of members by which a province is entitled to be represented in the Senate and the residence qualifications of Senators;

(d) subject to paragraph 41*(d)*, the Supreme Court of Canada;

(e) the extension of existing provinces into the territories; and

(f) notwithstanding any other law or practice, the establishment of new provinces.

(2) Subsections 38(2) to (4) do not apply in respect of amendments in relation to matters referred to in subsection (1).

43. An amendment to the Constitution of Canada in relation to any provision that applies to one or more, but not all, provinces, including

(a) any alteration to boundaries between provinces, and

(b) any amendment to any provision that relates to the use of the English or the French language within a province,

may be made by proclamation issued by the Governor General under the Great Seal of Canada only where so authorized by resolutions of the Senate and House of Commons and of the legislative assembly of each province to which the amendment applies.

44. Subject to sections 41 and 42, Parliament may exclusively make laws amending the Constitution of Canada in relation to the executive government of Canada or the Senate and House of Commons.

45. Subject to section 41, the legislature of each province may exclusively make laws amending the constitution of the province.

46. (1) The procedures for amendment under sections 38, 41, 42 and 43 may be initiated either by the Senate or the House of Commons or by the legislative assembly of a province.

(2) A resolution of assent made for the purposes of this Part may be revoked at any time before the issue of a proclamation authorized by it.

47. (1) An amendment to the Constitution of Canada made by proclamation under section 38, 41, 42 or 43 may be made without a resolution of the Senate authorizing the issue of the proclamation if, within one hundred and eighty days after the adoption by the House of Commons of a resolution authorizing its issue, the Senate has not adopted such a resolution and if, at any time after the expiration of that period, the House of Commons again adopts the resolution.

(2) Any period when Parliament is prorogued or dissolved shall not be counted in computing the one hundred and eighty day period referred to in subsection (1).

48. The Queen's Privy Council for Canada shall advise the Governor General to issue a proclamation under this Part forthwith on the adoption of the resolutions required for an amendment made by proclamation under this Part.

49. A constitutional conference composed of the Prime Minister of Canada and the first ministers of the provinces shall be convened by the Prime Minister of Canada within fifteen years after this Part comes into force to review the provisions of this Part.

PART VI

AMENDMENT TO THE CONSTITUTION ACT, 1867

50. The *Constitution Act, 1867* (formerly named the *British North America Act, 1867*) is amended by adding thereto, immediately after section 92 thereof, the following heading and section:

"Non-Renewable Natural Resources, Forestry Resources and
Electrical Energy

92A. (1) In each province, the legislature may exclusively make laws in relation to

(a) exploration for non-renewable natural resources in the province;

(b) development, conservation and management of non-renewable natural resources and forestry resources in the province, including laws in relation to the rate of primary production therefrom; and

(c) development, conservation and management of sites and facilities in the province for the generation and production of electrical energy.

(2) In each province, the legislature may make laws in relation to the export from the province to another part of Canada of the primary production from non-renewable natural resources and forestry resources in the province and the production from facilities in the province for the generation of electrical energy, but such laws may not authorize or provide for discrimination in prices or in supplies exported to another part of Canada.

(3) Nothing in subsection (2) derogates from the authority of Parliament to enact laws in relation to the matters referred to in that subsection and, where such a law of Parliament and a law of a province conflict, the law of Parliament prevails to the extent of the conflict.

(4) In each province, the legislature may make laws in relation to the raising of money by any mode or system of taxation in respect of

(a) non-renewable natural resources and forestry resources in the province and the primary production therefrom, and

(b) sites and facilities in the province for the generation of electrical energy and the production therefrom, whether or not such production is exported in whole or in part from the province, but such laws may not authorize or provide for taxation that differentiates between production exported to another part of Canada and production not exported from the province.

(5) The expression "primary production" has the meaning assigned by the Sixth Schedule.

(6) Nothing in subsections (1) to (5) derogates from any powers or rights that a legislature or government of a province had immediately before the coming into force of this section."

51. The said Act is further amended by adding thereto the following Schedule:

"THE SIXTH SCHEDULE

Primary Production from Non-Renewable Natural Resources and Forestry Resources

1. For the purposes of Section 92A of this Act,

(a) production from a non-renewable natural resource is primary production therefrom if

(i) it is in the form in which it exists upon its recovery or severance from its natural state, or

(ii) it is a product resulting from processing or refining the resource, and is not a manufactured product or a product resulting from refining crude oil, refining upgraded heavy crude oil, refining gases or liquids derived from coal or refining a synthetic equivalent of crude oil; and

(b) production from a forestry resource is primary production therefrom if it consists of sawlogs, poles, lumber, wood chips, sawdust or any other primary wood product, or wood pulp, and is not a product manufactured from wood."

PART VII

GENERAL

52. (1) The Constitution of Canada is the supreme law of Canada, and any law that is inconsistent with the provisions of the Constitution is, to the extent of the inconsistency, of no force or effect.

(2) The Constitution of Canada includes

(a) the *Canada Act 1982*, including this Act;

(b) the Acts and orders referred to in the schedule; and

(c) any amendment to any Act or order referred to in paragraph *(a)* or *(b)*.

(3) Amendments to the Constitution of Canada shall be made only in accordance with the authority contained in the Constitution of Canada.

53. (1) The enactments referred to in Column I of the schedule are hereby repealed or amended to the extent indicated in Column II thereof and, unless repealed, shall continue as law in Canada under the names set out in Column III thereof.

(2) Every enactment, except the *Canada Act 1982*, that refers to an enactment referred to in the schedule by the name in Column I thereof is hereby amended by substituting for that name the corresponding name in Column III thereof, and any British North America Act not referred to in the schedule may be cited as the *Constitution Act* followed by the year and number, if any, of its enactment.

54. Part IV is repealed on the day that is one year after this Part comes into force and this section may be repealed and this Act renumbered, consequentially upon the repeal of Part IV and this section, by proclamation issued by the Governor General under the Great Seal of Canada.

[Note: On October 31, 1987, no proclamation had been issued under this section.]

54.1 *Part iv.1 and this section are repealed on April 18, 1987.*

[Note: Added by the *Constitution Amendment Proclamation, 1983* (No. 46 *infra*).]

55. A French version of the portions of the Constitution of Canada referred to in the schedule shall be prepared by the Minister of Justice of Canada as expeditiously as possible and, when any portion thereof sufficient to warrant action being taken has been so prepared, it shall be put forward for enactment by proclamation issued by the Governor General under the Great Seal of Canada pursuant to the procedure then applicable to an amendment of the same provisions of the Constitution of Canada.

[Note: On October 31, 1987, no proclamation had been issued under this section.]

56. Where any portion of the Constitution of Canada has been or is enacted in English and French or where a French version of any portion of the Constitution is enacted pursuant to section 55, the English and French versions of that portion of the Constitution are equally authoritative.

57. The English and French versions of this Act are equally authoritative.

58. Subject to section 59, this Act shall come into force on a day to be fixed by proclamation issued by the Queen or the Governor General under the Great Seal of Canada.

[Note: The *Constitution Act, 1982* was, subject to section 59 thereof, proclaimed in force on April 17, 1982 (No. 45 infra).]

59. (1) Paragraph 23(1) (a) shall come into force in respect of Quebec on a day to be fixed by proclamation issued by the Queen or the Governor General under the Great Seal of Canada.

(2) A proclamation under subsection (1) shall be issued only where authorized by the legislative assembly or government of Quebec.

(3) This section may be repealed on the day paragraph 23(1)(a) comes into force in respect of Quebec and this Act amended and renumbered, consequentially upon the repeal of this section, by proclamation issued by the Queen or the Governor General under the Great Seal of Canada.

[Note: On October 31, 1987, no proclamation had been issued under this section.]

60. This Act may be cited as the *Constitution Act, 1982*, and the Constitution Acts 1867 to 1975 (No. 2) and this Act may be cited together as the *Constitution Acts, 1867 to 1982*.

61. A reference to the *"Constitution Acts, 1867 to 1982"* shall be deemed to include a reference to the *"Constitution Amendment Proclamation, 1983."*

[Note: Added by the *Constitution Amendment Proclamation, 1983* (No. 46 *infra*). See also section 3 of the *Constitution Act, 1985 (Representation)* (No. 47 *infra*).]asss

Appendix 2

Reference Re
Secession of Québec

IN THE MATTER OF Section 53 of the Supreme Court Act, R.S.C., 1985, c. S-26;

AND IN THE MATTER OF a Reference by the Governor in Council concerning certain questions relating to the secession of Québec from Canada, as set out in Order in Council P.C. 1996-1497, dated the 30th day of September, 1996

Indexed as: Reference re Secession of Québec

File No.: 25506.

1998: February 16, 17, 18, 19; 1998: August 20.

Present: Lamer C.J. and L'Heureux-Dubé, Gonthier, Cory, McLachlin, Iacobucci, Major, Bastarache and Binnee JJ.

* * * * *

Pursuant to s. 53 of the *Supreme Court Act*, the Governor in Council referred the following questions to this Court:

1. Under the Constitution of Canada, can the National Assembly, legislature or government of Québec effect the secession of Québec from Canada unilaterally?

2. Does international law give the National Assembly, legislature or government of Québec the right to effect the secession of Québec from Canada unilaterally? In this regard, is there a right to self-determination under international law that would give the National Assembly, legislature or government of Québec the right to effect the secession of Québec from Canada unilaterally?

3. In the event of a conflict between domestic and international law on the right of the National Assembly, legislature or government of Québec to effect the secession of Québec from Canada unilaterally, which would take precedence in Canada?

Issues regarding the Court's reference jurisdiction were raised by the amicus curiae. He argued that s. 53 of the Supreme Court Act was unconstitutional; that, even if the Court's reference jurisdiction was constitutionally valid, the questions submitted were outside the scope of s. 53; and, finally, that these questions were not justiciable.

Held: Section 53 of the *Supreme Court Act* is constitutional and the Court should answer the reference questions.

(1) *Supreme Court's Reference Jurisdiction*

Section 101 of the *Constitution Act, 1867* gives Parliament the authority to grant this Court the reference jurisdiction provided for in s. 53 of the *Supreme Court Act*. The words "general court of appeal" in s. 101 denote the status of the Court within the national court structure and should not be taken as a restrictive definition of the Court's functions. While, in most instances, this Court acts as the exclusive ultimate appellate court in the country, an appellate court can receive, on an exceptional basis, original jurisdiction not incompatible with its appellate jurisdiction. Even if there were any conflict between this Court's reference jurisdiction and the original jurisdiction of the provincial superior courts, any such conflict must be resolved in favour of Parliament's exercise of its plenary power to establish a "general court of appeal". A "general court of appeal" may also properly undertake other legal functions, such as the rendering of advisory opinions. There is no constitutional bar to this Court's receipt of jurisdiction to undertake an advisory role.

The reference questions are within the scope of s. 53 of the *Supreme Court Act*. Question 1 is directed, at least in part, to the interpretation of the *Constitution Acts*, which are referred to in s. 53(1)(a). Both Questions 1 and 2 fall within s. 53(1)(d), since they relate to the powers of the legislature or government of a Canadian province. Finally, all three questions are "important questions of law or fact concerning any matter" and thus come within s. 53(2). In answering Question 2, the Court is not exceeding its jurisdiction by purporting to act as an international tribunal. The Court is providing an advisory opinion to the Governor in Council in its capacity as a national court on legal questions touching and concerning the future of the Canadian federation. Further, Question 2 is not beyond the competence of this Court, as a domestic court, because it requires the Court to look at international law rather than domestic law. More importantly, Question 2 does not ask an abstract question of "pure" international law but seeks to determine the legal rights and obligations of the legislature or government of Québec, institutions that exist as part of the Canadian legal order. International law must be addressed since it has been invoked as a consideration in the context of this Reference.

The reference questions are justiciable and should be answered. They do not ask the Court to usurp any democratic decision that the people of Québec may be called upon to make. The questions, as interpreted by the Court, are strictly limited to aspects of the legal framework in which that democratic decision is to be taken. Since the reference questions may clearly be interpreted as directed to legal issues, the Court is in a position to answer them. The Court cannot exercise its discretion to refuse to answer the questions on a pragmatic basis. The questions raise issues of fundamental public importance and they are not too imprecise or ambiguous to permit a proper legal answer. Nor has the Court been provided with insufficient information regarding the present context in which the questions arise. Finally, the Court may deal on a reference with issues that might otherwise be considered not yet "ripe" for decision.

(2) *Question 1*

The Constitution is more than a written text. It embraces the entire global system of rules and principles which govern the exercise of constitutional authority. A superficial reading of selected provisions of the written constitutional enactment, without more, may be misleading. It is necessary to make a more profound investigation of the underlying principles animating the whole of the Constitution, including the principles of federalism, democracy, constitutionalism and the rule of law, and respect for minorities. Those principles must inform our overall appreciation of the constitutional rights and obligations that would come into play in the event that a clear majority of Québecers votes on a clear question in favour of secession.

The Court in this Reference is required to consider whether Québec has a right to unilateral secession. Arguments in support of the existence of such a right were primarily based on the principle of democracy. Democracy, however, means more than simple majority rule. Constitutional jurisprudence shows that democracy exists in the larger context of other constitutional values. Since Confederation, the people of the provinces and territories have created close ties of interdependence (economic, social, political and cultural) based on shared values that include federalism, democracy, constitutionalism and the rule of law, and respect for minorities. A democratic decision of Québecers in favour of secession would put those relationships at risk. The Constitution vouchsafes order and stability, and accordingly secession of a province "under the Constitution" could not be achieved unilaterally, that is, without principled negotiation with other participants in Confederation within the existing constitutional framework.

Our democratic institutions necessarily accommodate a continuous process of discussion and evolution, which is reflected in the constitutional right of each participant in the federation to initiate constitutional change. This right implies a reciprocal duty on the other participants to engage in discussions to address any legitimate initiative to change the constitutional order. A clear majority vote in Québec on a clear question in favour of secession would confer democratic legitimacy on the secession initiative which all of the other participants in Confederation would have to recognize.

Québec could not, despite a clear referendum result, purport to invoke a right of self-determination to dictate the terms of a proposed secession to the other parties to the federation. The democratic vote, by however strong a majority, would have no legal effect on its own and could not push aside the principles of federalism and the rule of law, the rights of individuals and minorities, or the operation of democracy in the other provinces or in Canada as a whole. Democratic rights under the Constitution cannot be divorced from constitutional obligations. Nor, however, can the reverse proposition be accepted: the continued existence and operation of the Canadian constitutional order could not be indifferent to a clear expression of a clear majority of Québecers that they no longer wish to remain in Canada. The other provinces and the federal government would have no basis to deny the right of the government of Québec to pursue secession should a clear majority of the people of

Québec choose that goal, so long as in doing so, Québec respects the rights of others. The negotiations that followed such a vote would address the potential act of secession as well as its possible terms should in fact secession proceed. There would be no conclusions predetermined by law on any issue. Negotiations would need to address the interests of the other provinces, the federal government and Québec and indeed the rights of all Canadians both within and outside Québec, and specifically the rights of minorities.

The negotiation process would require the reconciliation of various rights and obligations by negotiation between two legitimate majorities, namely, the majority of the population of Québec, and that of Canada as a whole. A political majority at either level that does not act in accordance with the underlying constitutional principles puts at risk the legitimacy of its exercise of its rights, and the ultimate acceptance of the result by the international community.

The task of the Court has been to clarify the legal framework within which political decisions are to be taken "under the Constitution" and not to usurp the prerogatives of the political forces that operate within that framework. The obligations identified by the Court are binding obligations under the Constitution. However, it will be for the political actors to determine what constitutes "a clear majority on a clear question" in the circumstances under which a future referendum vote may be taken. Equally, in the event of demonstrated majority support for Québec secession, the content and process of the negotiations will be for the political actors to settle. The reconciliation of the various legitimate constitutional interests is necessarily committed to the political rather than the judicial realm precisely because that reconciliation can only be achieved through the give and take of political negotiations. To the extent issues addressed in the course of negotiation are political, the courts, appreciating their proper role in the constitutional scheme, would have no supervisory role.

(3) *Question 2*

The Court was also required to consider whether a right to unilateral secession exists under international law. Some supporting an affirmative answer did so on the basis of the recognized right to self-determination that belongs to all "peoples". Although much of the Québec population certainly shares many of the characteristics of a people, it is not necessary to decide the "people" issue because, whatever may be the correct determination of this issue in the context of Québec, a right to secession only arises under the principle of self-determination of people at international law where "a people" is governed as part of a colonial empire; where "a people" is subject to alien subjugation, domination or exploitation; and possibly where "a people" is denied any meaningful exercise of its right to self-determination within the state of which it forms a part. In other circumstances, peoples are expected to achieve self-determination within the framework of their existing state. A state whose government represents the whole of the people or peoples resident within its territory, on a basis of equality and without discrimination, and respects the principles of self-determination in its internal arrangements, is entitled to maintain its territorial integrity under international law and to have that territorial integrity recognized by other states. Québec does not meet the threshold of a colonial people or an oppressed people, nor can it be suggested that Québecers have been denied meaningful access to government to pursue their political, economic, cultural and social development. In the circumstances, the "National Assembly, the legislature or the government of Québec" do not enjoy a right at international law to effect the secession of Québec from Canada unilaterally.

Although there is no right, under the Constitution or at international law, to unilateral secession, the possibility of an unconstitutional declaration of secession leading to a de facto secession is not ruled out. The ultimate success of such a secession would be dependent on recognition by the international community, which is likely to consider the legality and legitimacy of secession having regard to, amongst other facts, the conduct of Québec and Canada, in determining whether to grant or withhold recognition. Even if granted, such recognition would not, however, provide any retroactive justification for the act of secession, either under the Constitution of Canada or at international law.

(4) *Question 3*

In view of the answers to Questions 1 and 2, there is no conflict between domestic and international law to be addressed in the context of this Reference.

* * * * *

IV. <u>Summary of Conclusions</u>

148   As stated at the outset, this Reference has required us to consider momentous questions that go to the heart of our system of constitutional government. We have emphasized that the Constitution is more than a written text. It embraces the entire global system of rules and principles which govern the exercise of constitutional authority. A superficial reading of selected provisions of the written constitutional enactment, without more, may be misleading. It is necessary to make a more profound investigation of the underlying principles that animate the whole of our Constitution, including the principles of federalism, democracy, constitutionalism and the rule of law, and respect for minorities. Those principles must inform our overall appreciation of the constitutional rights and obligations that would come into play in the event a clear majority of Québecers votes on a clear question in favour of secession.

149   The Reference requires us to consider whether Québec has a right to <u>unilateral</u> secession. Those who support the existence of such a right found their case primarily on the principle of democracy. Democracy, however, means more than simple majority rule. As reflected in our constitutional jurisprudence, democracy exists in the larger context of other constitutional values such as those already mentioned. In the 131 years since Confederation, the people of the provinces and territories have created close ties of interdependence (economically, socially, politically and culturally) based on shared values that include federalism, democracy, constitutionalism and the rule of law, and respect for minorities. A democratic decision of Québecers in favour of secession would put those relationships at risk. The Constitution vouchsafes order and stability, and accordingly secession of a province "under the Constitution" could not be achieved unilaterally, that is, without principled negotiation with other participants in Confederation within the existing constitutional framework.

150   The Constitution is not a straitjacket. Even a brief review of our constitutional history demonstrates periods of momentous and dramatic change. Our democratic institutions necessarily accommodate a continuous process of discussion and evolution, which is reflected in the constitutional right of each participant in the federation to initiate constitutional change. This right implies a reciprocal duty on the other participants to engage in discussions to address any legitimate initiative to change the constitutional order. While it is true that some attempts at constitutional amendment in recent years have faltered, a clear majority vote in Québec on a clear question in favour of secession would confer democratic legitimacy on the secession initiative which all of the other participants in Confederation would have to recognize.

151   Québec could not, despite a clear referendum result, purport to invoke a right of self-determination to dictate the terms of a proposed secession to the other parties to the federation. The democratic vote, by however strong a majority, would have no legal effect on its own and could not push aside the principles of federalism and the rule of law, the rights of individuals and minorities, or the operation of democracy in the other provinces or in Canada as a whole. Democratic rights under the Constitution cannot be divorced from constitutional obligations. Nor, however, can the reverse proposition be accepted. The continued existence and operation of the Canadian constitutional order could not be indifferent to a clear expression of a clear majority of Québecers that they no longer wish to remain in Canada. The other provinces and the federal government would have no basis to deny the right of the government of Québec to pursue secession, should a clear majority of the people of Québec choose that goal, so long as in doing so, Québec respects the rights of others. The negotiations that followed such a vote would address the potential act of secession as well as its possible terms should in fact secession proceed. There would be no conclusions predetermined by law on any issue. Negotiations would need to address the interests of the other provinces, the federal government, Québec and indeed the rights of all Canadians both within and outside Québec, and specifically the rights of minorities. No one suggests that it would be an easy set of negotiations.

152   The negotiation process would require the reconciliation of various rights and obligations by negotiation between two legitimate majorities, namely, the majority of the population of Québec, and that of Canada as a whole. A political majority at either level that does not act in accordance with the underlying constitutional principles we have mentioned puts at risk the legitimacy of its exercise of its rights, and the ultimate acceptance of the result by the international community.

153   The task of the Court has been to clarify the legal framework within which political decisions are to be taken "under the Constitution", not to usurp the prerogatives of the political forces that operate within that framework. The obligations we have identified are binding obligations under the Constitution of Canada. However, it will be for the political actors to determine what constitutes "a clear majority on a clear question" in the circumstances under which a future referendum vote may be taken. Equally, in the event of demonstrated majority support for Québec secession, the content and process of the negotiations will be for the political actors to settle. The reconciliation of the various legitimate constitutional interests is necessarily committed to the political rather than the judicial realm precisely because that reconciliation can only be achieved through the give and take of political negotiations. To the extent issues addressed in the course of negotiation are political, the courts, appreciating their proper role in the constitutional scheme, would have no supervisory role.

154   We have also considered whether a positive legal entitlement to secession exists under international law in the factual circumstances contemplated by Question 1, i.e., a clear democratic expression of support on a clear question for Québec secession. Some of those who supported an affirmative answer to this question did so on the basis of the recognized right to self-determination that belongs to all "peoples". Although much of the Québec population certainly shares many of the characteristics of a people, it is not necessary to decide the "people" issue because, whatever may be the correct determination of this issue in the context of Québec, a right to secession only arises under the principle of self-determination of peoples at international law where "a people" is governed as part of a colonial empire; where "a people" is subject to alien subjugation, domination or exploitation; and possible where "a people" is denied any meaningful exercise of its right to self-determination within the state of which it forms a part. In other circumstances, peoples are expected to achieve self-determination within the framework of their existing state. A state whose government represents the whole of the people or peoples resident within its territory, on a basis of equality and without discrimination, and respects the principles of self-determination in its internal arrangements, is entitled to maintain its territorial integrity under international law and to have that territorial integrity recognized by other states. Québec does not meet the threshold of a colonial people or an oppressed people, nor can it be suggested that Québecers have been denied meaningful access to government to pursue their political, economic, cultural and social development. In the circumstances, the National Assembly, the legislature or the government of Québec do not enjoy a right at international law to effect the secession of Québec from Canada unilaterally.

155   Although there is no right, under the Constitution or at international law, to unilateral secession, that is secession without negotiation on the basis just discussed, this does not rule out the possibility of an unconstitutional declaration of secession leading to a de facto secession. The ultimate success of such a secession would be dependent on recognition by the international community, which is likely to consider the legality and legitimacy of secession having regard to, amongst other facts, the conduct of Québec and Canada, in determining whether to grant or withhold recognition. Such recognition, even if granted, would not, however, provide any retroactive justification for the act of secession, either under the Constitution of Canada or at international law.

Glossary

A

Aboriginal Affairs Committee — a cabinet committee formed by former prime minister Paul Martin.

additional member system (AMS) — see **mixed systems**.

adjournment (recess) — a break period taken by the House of Commons within a session.

advisory bodies — federal organizations whose activities are closely related to the formulation of public policies. They include royal commissions, government and departmental task forces and advisory councils.

advocacy advertising — advertising that advocates a political point of view rather than trying to sell a good or service.

alternative vote system — a majoritarian electoral system in which voters rank candidates in order of preference.

approach — a particular orientation or conceptual framework adopted when addressing a political issue.

appropriation bills — see **supply bills**.

assistant deputy minister (ADM) — one of two or more individuals who head a branch or bureau and reports directly to the deputy minister.

attitudes — orientations toward political objects that are more differentiated and fleeting than basic values, but which may be more immediate determinants of political behaviour.

auditor general — the official who appraises the effectiveness of public spending and accounting practices and reports directly to Parliament and the Public Accounts Committee.

authoritarian political system — a system of government that imposes one dominant interest, that of the political elite, on all others.

authority — the government's power to make binding decisions and issue obligatory commands. **Traditional authority** arises from custom and history and is most frequently gained through inheritance, such as that enjoyed by royal dynasties. **Charismatic authority** derives from popular admiration of the personal "heroic" qualities of the individual in whom authority is vested, such as a prophet or warlord. **Rational–legal** or **bureaucratic** authority is vested in the offices held by those in power and in the mechanism that placed them there.

autocratic political system — a system that imposes one dominating interest on all others.

B

bilingualism — the right of Canadians to communicate with the federal government in the official language of their choice, and to have their children educated in that language, wherever numbers warrant, as outlined in the *Official Languages Act.*

Bill 101 — the 1977 Québec language law that sought to make French the official language of Québec and put restrictions on the use of English in the courts, schools and private sector.

block grant — a grant of one large sum of money from the federal government to the provinces to be spent in certain policy fields.

British Commonwealth of Nations — an organization that evolved from the dominions within the British Empire. Today it numbers fifty-four states and provides the opportunity for heads of state and governments to meet relatively informally and discuss vital common issues.

bureaucracy — a form of hierarchical organization intended to facilitate arbitrary decision-making.

C

cabinet — the body of advisors (selected from the ministry and appointed by the prime minister) which acts in the name of the Privy Council.

Canada Assistance Program (CAP) — a program of the federal government that helps finance welfare and other provincial social services.

Canada Health and Social Transfer (CHST) — a new system of block grants formed by adding together the funds for the Established Program Financing and the Canada Assistance Programs.

Canada–US Relations Committee — a cabinet committee formed by former prime minister Paul Martin.

Canadian Security Intelligence Service (CSIS) — an intelligence gathering institution; its functions are defined in the *Canadian Security Intelligence Act.*

central agencies — a type of government bureaucratic organization formally headed by a cabinet minister. Includes the PMO, PCO, Treasury Board, and Department of Finance.

chief whip — see whips.

citizen — an individual who is a formal member of a state, and therefore eligible to enjoy specified rights and privileges.

civil law — the rules that regulate relations between or among private individuals and corporations, mainly concerned with property and civil rights and based on provincial authority.

Clarity Act — from a government bill of 1999 that sets out the rules by which the government and Parliament of Canada would react to any future separatist referendum. It concludes that the government will not enter into any negotiations over separation with a province unless the House of Commons determines that 1) the referendum question is "clear" and 2) a "clear" expression of will has been obtained by a "clear" majority of the population.

class — a rank or order in society determined by such characteristics as education, occupation and income.

cleavages — major and persistent differences among groups that are politically relevant.

clerk of the House — the official responsible for ensuring that relevant documents are printed and circulated and advising the speaker of the House of Commons on the parliamentary business of the day.

clerk of the Privy Council — the head of the Privy Council Office and head of the federal public service; the chief non-partisan adviser to the prime minister and cabinet. Also the secretary to the cabinet.

closure — a measure to terminate debate in the House of Commons.

coalition government — a government formed from more than one party.

collective ministerial responsibility — the duty that holds ministers as a group accountable to Parliament for their government's actions.

collective or **group rights** — privileges or duties owed to certain groups by the state.

commissioner of lobbying — a position created in 2006 with investigative authority into lobbying infractions.

Committee of the Whole — a committee made up of all members of Parliament chaired by the deputy speaker or the deputy chair of committees.

common law — the rules developed by the courts and based on the principle of **stare decisis**. Sometimes referred to as **case law**.

Commonwealth of Nations — countries that were formerly part of the British Empire, currently 53 member states..

competitive party system — a party system with two or more parties that compete for legislative power. In the **dominant one-party** system, a single party wins most elections and opposition parties function freely. In the **two-party** system, two parties dominate; others have minor political strength. In a **multi-party system**, popular support is divided among several parties and the largest party forms a coalition to form a government. If there are three or more parties, it is a **multi-party dominant** system if one party receives 40 percent of the vote; if none regularly receives 40 percent of the vote, it is a **multi-party loose** system. A **mixed and low competitive** system includes elements of both competitive and non-competitive types.

comprehensive claims — Native land claims based on aboriginal title (traditional use and occupancy) rather than on treaties or other legal documents.

comprehensive settlements — see **comprehensive claims**.

comptroller general — part of the Treasury Board staff. Responsible for developing financial control measures and enforcing them.

concurrent jurisdiction — see **concurrent power.**

concurrent power — power shared between the Parliament of Canada and the provincial legislatures.

conditional grant — funds given by the federal government to provincial governments on the condition that they be spent in a certain way. Sometimes called **grant-in-aid** or **shared-cost grant.**

confederation — a form of political organization that loosely unites strong provincial units under a weak central government.

conflict of interest — a situation in which a prime minister, minister or public servant has sufficient knowledge of a private economic interest to influence or appear to influence his or her exercise of public duties and responsibilities.

constitution — the body of supreme law that defines and limits political power and states the governing principles of a society.

constitutional democracy — a democracy in which the constitution outlines and limits political power.

constitutionalism — the principle that everyone, including government, is subject to the rules of the constitution.

convention — a custom or practice that, while not necessarily a legal necessity, is nevertheless based on accepted reasons and practices.

criminal law — the rules that regulate offences against the state, which come under federal authority in Canada.

Crown — the composite symbol of the institutions of the state. The Crown assumes a variety of duties and responsibilities; for example, it may be involved in court proceedings.

Crown agencies — a wide variety of non-departmental organizations including Crown corporations, regulatory agencies, administrative tribunals and some advisory bodies.

Crown corporation — a semi-autonomous agency of government organized under the corporate form to perform a task or group of related tasks in the national interest.

D

debt — the accumulation of deficits over years.

declaratory power — the power that allows the federal government to assume jurisdiction over any "work" considered to be for the benefit of Canada as a whole (e.g., uranium exploration).

deficit — the amount by which government spending exceeds revenues in one year.

delegated (subordinate) legislation — legislative power to make decisions that have the force of law, delegated by Parliament under various statutes to the governor-in-council to members of individual government departments, agencies and boards.

democratic political system — a system of government that reconciles competing interests by competitive elections.

departmentalization — the chief organizing principle of the bureaucracy, whereby at least in theory, every administrative function in the federal government is allocated to a single department.

deputy minister (DM) — a senior public servant who is the administrative and managerial head of a department or ministry.

diachronic approach — an approach in which political facts are examined in one or more countries over time.

direct taxation — taxes collected directly by the government, such as individual income tax, corporate income tax and succession duties.

disallowance — the power of the federal government to void provincial legislation, even in areas of legislation assigned to the provinces.

dissolution — the end of a particular Parliament, which occurs at the request of a prime minister who seeks a new mandate or whose government has been defeated in the House of Commons.

division of powers — the distribution of legislative powers between the federal and provincial governments, largely contained in sections 91 and 92 of the *Constitution Act, 1867.*

divisions — formal role-call votes in the House of Commons in which members' names are recorded in *Hansard.*

Domestic Affairs Committee — a cabinet committee that integrates policy development in social, economic and environmental affairs.

domestic public policy — focuses on the internal economic, social and political environment.

E

economic policy — refers to the overall management and stabilization of a country's economic environment. Also a generic term for a number of sectoral policy frameworks concerning economic development.

electoral system — the means by which votes cast for candidates are translated into legislative seats.

elite theories — theories based on the contention that all states, even democracies, have a maldistribution of power within them.

entrenchment — the embodiment of provisions in a constitution so that they are protected and can be changed only by formal amendment procedures.

equalization payments — unconditional transfer payments to the provinces from the federal government calculated according to the ability of each province to raise revenue.

Established Program Financing (EPF) — a block grant program of the federal government that is essentially conditional in nature.

estimates — the annual spending plans of government departments and agencies for the following fiscal year.

ethics commissioner — replaced the former ethics counsellor who had reported directly to the prime minister only. The new commissioner, appointed for the first time in 2004, reports to the House of Commons and is responsible for the new ethics rules passed by Parliament as well as for enforcing the *Lobbyists Registration Act.*

ethnic origin — the ethnic or cultural group(s) to which an individual's ancestors belonged; it pertains to the ancestral roots or origins of the population, and not to place of birth, citizenship or nationality.

ethnicity — primarily a subjective term used to describe groups of people who share customs, language, dialect and/or cultural heritage, and sometimes distinct physical or racial characteristics.

executive — a broad term that refers to the institutions, personnel and behaviour of governmental power. In modern times, executives are the organizational centre of political systems.

expenditure budget process — the process of determining the estimated spending requirements of all government departments and agencies for the next fiscal year.

Expenditure Management System (EMS) — a process of budgeting set up by Jean Chrétien's government to monitor new expenditure goals.

Expenditure Review — a subcommittee of the Treasury Board mandated to see that government expenditures are related to government priorities.

F

Federal Court of Canada — the court established by Parliament in 1971 to settle claims by or against the federal government on matters relating to maritime law, copyright, patent and trademark law, and federal taxation statutes, and to supervise the decisions of tribunals and inferior bodies established by federal law.

federalism — a form of political organization in which the activities of government are divided between regional governments and a central government so that each level of government has activities on which it makes final decisions.

Federal–Provincial Relations Office (FPRO) — A central agency established within the Privy Council Office in 1975. Now called the Intergovernmental Affairs Secretariat.

feminism — a system of beliefs that endorses the removal of all societal barriers to achieving the equality of men and women. Feminism is also regarded as a partial theory of the polity that can be used to explain large segments of political institutions and behaviour.

financial bills — money bills that authorize taxation and expenditures that must first be introduced into the House of Commons by a minister of the Crown, using a Royal Recommendation.

First Nations — in Canada, the term preferred by Aboriginals to describe themselves, especially status Indians and those on reserves.

flexible constitution — a constitution that can be amended easily and adapted to changing circumstances.

foreign policy — concerns the behaviour of states or governments that has external ramifications. It includes diplomatic and military relations as well as cultural, economic, technological and ecological interests.

franchise — the right to vote.

G

General Agreement on Tariffs and Trade (GATT) — an agreement that sought to establish a trading order based on reciprocity, non-discrimination and multilateralism. The treaty sets out a code of rules for the conduct of trade; as an institution, it oversees the application of the trade rules.

gerrymandering — deliberate manipulation of electoral boundaries by a governing party for its own benefit.

Global Affairs Committee — the cabinet committee that handles foreign issues, defence, and trade and development.

Gomery Commission — formally the Commission of Inquiry into the Sponsorship Program and Advertsing Activities, established to research allegations of corruption related to AdScam. The report was issued in February 2006.

government bills — bills introduced by the cabinet as government policy.

government department — an administrative unit of government that is headed by a cabinet minister and largely responsible for the administration of a range of programs serving the public.

governor general — the representative of the monarch in Canada, appointed by the monarch on the recommendation of the Canadian prime minister and cabinet.

governor-in-council — the formal executive authority of the governor general applied upon the advice of the cabinet.

gross domestic product (GDP) — the market value of all final goods and services produced in a specific period.

granting supply — see **supply bills**.

H

Hansard — a verbatim record of House of Commons debates.

House leader — a member of Parliament who is designated by the leader of a party to manage party conduct in the House of Commons.

I

ideology — an explicit doctrinal structure that provides a particular diagnosis of the ills of society, plus an accompanying "action program" for implementing prescribed solutions for them.

indirect taxation — taxes that are collected by persons or institutions and passed along to the government, such as sales taxes.

individual ministerial responsibility — the duty that holds ministers as individuals accountable to Parliament and the public for their decisions.

individual rights — privileges or duties owed to individuals by the state.

influence-peddling — when money is exchanged for political favours.

institution — a social structure organized to achieve goals for society, such as constitutions, parliaments, bureaucracies and executives.

interest group — an organized association that engages in activities related to governmental decisions.

Intergovernmental Affairs Secretariat — see **Federal–Provincial Relations Office (FPRO)**.

International Monetary Fund (IMF) — established to foster stability in money markets, encourage co-operation among states on money matters, aid in the establishment of a payment system and promote international trade. Currently has 185 states as members.

international relations — refers to the broad network of relations among states, including the activities of citizens and non-state institutions.

iron law of oligarchy — Robert Michels's theory that all large organizations, despite intentions to do otherwise, largely end up in the control of a relatively small group of people at the top.

J

joint standing committees — committees composed of members of both the House of Commons and the Senate.

Judicial Committee of the Privy Council (JCPC) — the superior court of the United Kingdom, which was the court of final appeal in Canada until 1949 when Canada's Supreme Court was established.

L

la Francophonie — a French-language community similar to the British Commonwealth, formed in 1986.

leadership review — in some political parties, a clause in the constitution that allows party members to review the leader's performance and to vote on whether they want a leadership convention.

legality — the constitutional or legal propriety of undertaking certain activities.

legislative committees — committees set up to receive bills for examination after passing second reading.

legislature — the branch of government that makes or amends laws.

legitimacy — the principle that citizens accept that a government should, or has the right to, make decisions for them.

Letters Patent — the prerogative instruments defining the office of the governor general bestowed by the monarch.

lieutenant-governor — the monarch's representative in each province, appointed by the governor-in-council on the advice of the prime minister.

lobbying — activity aimed at influencing policy decisions or appointments. **Lobbyists** are individuals paid to lobby on behalf of an interest group.

M

macro-level approaches — are concerned with accounting for broad patterns of public policy as part of the relationship between state and society.

main estimates — government spending proposals for the upcoming fiscal year.

majority government — a government based on the support of only one party in the House of Commons.

Memorandum to cabinet — formal document used by a minister to put his or her views to cabinet.

merit principle — all appointments to, and promotions within, the public service must be based on the ability to do the job; in other words, on merit.

micro-level approaches — focus mainly on the making of individual policy decisions.

ministerial responsibility — ministers are constitutionally responsible for all of the operations of their departments.

ministry — the group of elected officials appointed by the prime minister to serve as ministers of the Crown or ministers of state.

minority government — a government in which the governing party has less than a majority of the members of Parliament.

mixed systems — electoral systems that represent a combination of plurality and proportional representation formulas. Some seats are filled by plurality voting in single-member constituencies, while the remainder go to parties according to their popular support in order to achieve an approximately proportional representation in the legislature.

money bills — government bills for raising or spending money.

movements — see **social and political movements**.

multiculturalism — the concept that ethnic customs and cultures should be valued, preserved and shared within the context of citizenship and economic and political integration.

multi-member proportional representation systems — provide an opportunity to elect two or more members from each constituency.

N

nation — a politically conscious and mobilized ethnic group (usually with a clear sense of territory) that may possess, or aspire to, more autonomy, self-government or independent statehood.

nation-state — the conceptual marriage between the cultural principle of **nation** and the territorial and governmental principles inherent in the idea of **state**.

national identity — a sense of belonging to a particular community, often (but not necessarily) reinforced by a common language, culture, customs, heritage or the shared experience of living under the same government.

National Policy — a policy of the Conservative Party under John A. Macdonald intended to develop a comprehensive railway system, open up western Canada by means of immigration, settlement and agriculture on the prairies, and encourage national economic development by protecting Canadian industries by means of an external tariff.

nationalism — the collective action of a politically conscious ethnic group (or nation) in pursuit of increased territorial autonomy or sovereignty.

neo-Marxist analysis — a systematic conceptualization of politics, economics and the state, based on a theory originally formulated by Karl Marx.

non-competitive party system — a party system with two or more parties that is dominated by one party that forms a repressive government.

notwithstanding clause — a clause in the Constitution that allows Parliament or a provincial legislature to override most Charter provisions by a simple declaration to that effect when passing legislation.

O

ombudsman — an independent officer responsible to Parliament for the investigation of citizens' complaints against the bureaucracy.

one-party dominant system — a multi-party system of government dominated by one party.

Operations Committee — the cabinet committee that controls the day-to-day coordination of government priorities for the cabinet.

Opposition Days (Supply Days) — days on which opposition motions can be debated in the House of Commons (there are twenty opposition days per session).

Oral Question Period — see **Question Period**.

Order Paper — the schedule of pending parliamentary business.

Orders — see **Orders of the Day**.

orders-in-council — decisions rendered by cabinet under the auspices of the Privy Council that carry legal force.

Orders of the Day — the prime means by which the House of Commons formulates instructions in response to motions and deals with the public business placed before it.

Organization of American States (OAS) — the main institution that unites the thirty-five states of the western hemisphere. Canada joined in 1990.

P

parliamentary democracy — a system of government in which the political executive receives its power to govern from the legislature and requires approval of Parliament to legitimate its policies and activities; in return, the prime minister and cabinet are held accountable to Parliament.

parliamentary government — see **parliamentary democracy**.

parliamentary secretaries — civil servants who aid ministers in their duties but have no statutory authority.

parliamentary supremacy — the basic premise of parliamentary democracy that states that all legislatures have the theoretical authority subject to the Constitution to repeal or modify any principle set out in common law.

party caucus — a group comprising all members of the House of Commons (and any senators who wish to attend) of a particular party in Parliament that meets every Wednesday when Parliament is in session.

party identification — refers to the degree to which citizens identify with a particular political party.

party list system — a proportional representation system which allows electors in a multi-member constituency to vote for a party or a slate of candidates rather than for one or more individuals.

party system — the series of relationships among parties in a political system.

patronage — the awarding of contracts, employment and other benefits to individuals or groups on the basis of partisan support rather than merit.

Planning, Programming and Budget Systems (PPBS) — a budget system, used from 1963–1981, that intended to provide a "planned" approach to government.

plebiscite — see **referendum**.

pluralism — the idea that power is widely dispersed and many groups compete for it.

pluralist theory — a theory that contends that power in democracies is not held by a single ruling class but is reasonably diffused in society, so that public policy reflects the conflict, cooperation and compromise of mainly independent interest groups.

Policy and Expenditure Management System (PEMS) — a budgeting process that integrates fiscal, expenditure and policy-making planning within the cabinet committee system.

policy community — see **policy network**.

policy network — (or policy community) includes all actors or potential actors, whether inside or outside government, who share a common policy focus and help shape policy outcomes over time.

political culture — the broad patterns of values, beliefs and attitudes in a society toward political objects.

political elite — a relatively small number of people who dominate the political process.

political parties — organizations designed to secure the power of the state for their leaders.

political socialization — the process whereby individuals acquire their political values, attitudes, beliefs and orientations.

politics — all activity that involves binding decisions about who gets what, when and how, and that brings together contending interests and differences for the supposed advantage of society.

pork-barrelling — the extension of favours by a political party or politician to whole regions or communities as an inducement for support.

power — the ability to influence and/or coerce others to accept certain objectives or behave in a particular manner.

prerogative authority — the powers of a monarch (or his or her representatives) that have not been bypassed by constitutional or state law.

private bills — bills that seek to change the law concerning specific individuals, groups or corporations.

private members' bills — bills sponsored by individual members of Parliament.

Privy Council — a largely ceremonial body composed of current and former ministers of the Crown and other individuals nominated by the prime minister and appointed for life to advise the governor general. The **Privy Council Office (PCO)** is the main public service organization responsible for developing and coordinating government policy.

proclamation — the act of proclaiming, publishing or declaring a statute that thereby becomes law.

proportional representation (PR) — an electoral system in which parties receive representation in Parliament relative to their respective shares of the popular vote.

prorogation — the closing of a session of Parliament, formally done by the governor general upon the advice of the prime minister.

public bills — bills that seek to change the law concerning the public as a whole, which can be classified as **government bills** and **private members' bills**.

public choice analysis — a theory of politics based on classical economics that assumes that individuals act in a rational and calculating fashion to maximize their own interests.

public policy — the broad framework within which decisions are taken by governments in relation to some issue or problem.

public servants (bureaucrats) — tenured state officials involved in advising government ministers and implementing policies.

public service — the collective term in Canada for the personnel employed in the administrative arm of government.

Q

Québec Padlock Law — a law passed by Premier Maurice Duplessis in Québec in 1937 that allowed him to place a padlock on any building that was being used for the purpose of opposing the government.

Questions on the Order Paper — written questions presented in the House of Commons that are usually answered in print.

Question Period — daily sessions in the House of Commons when, technically, questions are supposed to be asked for the purpose of eliciting information, but in reality provides a forum for the opposition parties to embarrass the government, criticize its policies and force discussion on issues of the day (which are frequently based on media stories, leaks by disaffected public servants, and complaints from the public).

R

referendum — a means by which a policy question can be submitted directly to the electorate rather than being decided exclusively by elected representatives.

regionalism — territorial tensions caused by groups that demand a change in the political, economic and cultural relations between regions and central powers within the existing state.

representative democracy — a political system in which elected officials make decisions with the force of law because they have achieved legitimacy as a result of free elections.

reserve powers — obsolete power of the federally appointed lieutenant-governor of each province to withhold royal assent to provincial legislation and to send it instead to the federal cabinet for its consideration.

residual clause — a clause in the Constitution that allows the federal government to intervene in any matter not specifically assigned to the provinces.

responsible government — the concept that the prime minister and cabinet are accountable to Parliament and may govern only so long as they retain the "confidence" of the majority of the House of Commons.

revenue process — the means by which funds are raised.

rights — legal entitlements owed to individuals or groups, as duties by others, or by the government.

rigid constitution — a constitution that is difficult to amend.

royal assent — the final seal of approval granted by the monarch or the monarch's representative that a bill must obtain before it becomes law.

royal commission — a group or individual appointed by the Crown on behalf of the government to investigate an area of public concern and recommend a suitable course of action.

rule of law — a guarantee that the state's actions will be governed by law, fairly and without malice, and that no individual is above the law or exempt from it.

S

second-ballot system — a majoritarian electoral system in which electors initially opt for a single candidate, but if no one obtains an absolute majority in the first vote, a run-off election is held, usually a week or two later.

secretary to the cabinet — the chief non-partisan adviser to the prime minister and cabinet. The clerk of the Privy Council holds this position.

section 91 — a section of the Constitution that specifies the areas belonging exclusively to the federal government.

section 92 — a section of the Constitution that specifies sixteen areas of provincial jurisdiction, including direct taxation, hospitals, prisons, property and civil rights.

Security Intelligence Review Committee — an external review committee that monitors the activities of the Canadian Security Intelligence Service (CSIS).

Security, Public Health and Emergencies Committee — a cabinet committee that, in addition to its traditional mandate, now includes terrorism and other issues of homeland security.

single-member plurality system (first-past-the-post system) — a political system by which the candidate who receives the most votes (a plurality) wins that constituency.

single transferable vote system (STV) — a PR system in which representatives are elected from multi-member constituencies, but electors vote for individual candidates rather than a party list.

social and political movements — expressions of interests or collective identities with a broad, utopian appeal that often flows across state borders.

social policy — encompasses activities oriented toward the education, health and welfare of a population.

sovereign state — a state that wields power and maintains order within its territorial boundaries and is usually recognizable by its internal and external powers (e.g., to tax its citizens, conduct external relations).

sovereignty — see **sovereign state**.

sovereignty-association — the policy of Québec's political independence while maintaining an economic association with the federal government of Canada.

speaker — see **speaker of the House of Commons/Senate**.

speaker of the House of Commons — the official who acts as impartial arbiter in the House and is elected by secret ballot.

speaker of the Senate — the official who acts as impartial arbiter in the Senate and is appointed by the governor general on the recommendation of the prime minister.

specific claims — Native land claims arising from the alleged non-fulfillment of Indian treaties and other lawful obligations, as opposed to those based on traditional occupancy and use.

Speech from the Throne — the speech that outlines the government's proposed legislative program for the forthcoming session and is delivered by the governor general.

spending power — the federal government's blanket authority to spend money for any purpose in any field, even where it has no legal jurisdiction.

standing committees — committees that are relatively permanent for the life of a Parliament.

Standing Orders — the permanent rules of the House of Commons.

stare decisis — the principle of following precedents set down in earlier court cases.

state — a form of political organization in which governmental institutions are capable of maintaining order and implementing rules or laws (through coercion if necessary) over a given population and within a given territory.

state-centred analysis — a theory based on the idea that the state is often able to act independently of the demands of society.

Statute of Westminster — the 1931 British law that declared Canada and the other dominions to be fully independent.

subcultures — clusters of people within a state who share basic political values and attitudes based on common regional, class, economic or other characteristics.

subordinate legislation — see **delegated legislation**.

sunset clause — a clause in the Constitution that requires renewal of the notwithstanding clause every five years when it is employed. See **notwithstanding clause**.

supply bills (appropriation bills) — bills that authorize the spending of money by the government.

Supreme Court of Canada — Canada's highest court for civil, criminal and constitutional cases.

synchronic approach — an approach in which a comparison is made between one state and another or between several states at the same period in time.

T

theory — a means to make sense of the facts of a situation by explaining how they are interconnected, elucidating the most convincing explanation about the facts. Theories involve generalizations, new observations and testability.

traditional authority — see **authority**.

Treasury Board — a cabinet committee whose primary responsibility is to authorize government expenditures and allocate resources within the government; headed by the secretary to the Treasury Board.

Treasury Board Secretariat (TBS) — an administrative unit of government with a highly qualified staff which assists the six cabinet members of the Treasury Board.

U

ultra vires — an act that is beyond a legislature's jurisdiction on the basis of Canada's federal division of powers.

unconditional grants — funds granted to the provinces by the federal government to be spent as determined by the provinces and not designated for any specific policy field.

unitary government — a form of government characterized by one level of political authority that grants and amends the powers of local or provincial authorities.

unwritten constitution — a constitution that consists mainly of custom, convention, or statutes and is not written down in one comprehensive document.

V

values — shared beliefs that provide standards of judgment about what is right, important and desirable in society.

veto — the power to block legislation or to block a constitutional amendment.

W

War Measures Act — a law invoked during both world wars and during the 1970 FLQ crisis under which the federal cabinet was given powers to deal with a crisis. Replaced by the *Emergencies Act*.

ways-and-means bills — taxation measures introduced as bills in the House of Commons.

whips — members of Parliament assigned by their respective party leaders to help maintain party cohesion.

World Bank — set up after the Second World War to lend money, focusing on countries or states that commercial banks or other lenders will not support. Generally tries to reduce poverty among its 185 members.

Word Trade Organization (WTO) — successor organization to the GATT. The treaty remains in place as the GATT but the WTO performs the organizational functions.

Index